Library of
Davidson College

A History of Finland's Literature

Histories of Scandinavian Literature

Sven H. Rossel, General Editor

VOLUME 4

A History of Finland's Literature

Edited by George C. Schoolfield

Published by
the University of
Nebraska Press,
Lincoln & London,
in cooperation
with The American-
Scandinavian Foundation

Publication of this book was assisted by grants from the National Endowment for the Humanities and from the Finlandia Foundation
© 1998 by the University of Nebraska Press
All rights reserved
Manufactured in the United States of America
⊚ The paper in this book meets the minimum requirements of American National Standard for Information Sciences— Permanence of Paper for Printed Library Materials, ANSI Z 39.48-1984.
Library of Congress Cataloging-in-Publication Data
A history of Finland's literature / edited by George C. Schoolfield.
p cm. – (A History of Scandinavian literatures : v. 4)
Includes bibliographical references and index.
ISBN 0-8032-4189-5 (alk. paper)
1. Finnish literature – History and criticism.
I. Schoolfield, George C.
II. Series.
PH301.H57 1998
894'.54109 – dc21
98-12831 CIP

Contents

Acknowledgments /xv
Introduction /xvii
Maps /xxxi

FINNISH-LANGUAGE LITERATURE

1. Finnish Oral Poetry, *Kalevala,* and *Kanteletar*
Michael Branch

The Romantic Background /4
The Little Tradition /5
The Corpus /7
Performance /8
How the Tradition Might Have Been /9
Cultural and Social Determinants /10
Fixity and Ritual /13
Renewal and Change: Myth Poetry /14
The Spirit World /15
Vikings /16
Christianity /17

Historical Songs /19
The Herderian Idea in Finland /19
An Epic in the Making /21
The *Kalevala* World /22
Compilation /24
Structure /25
Authenticity /27
Reception /27
Kanteletar /28
Structure /29
From Cultural to Political Nationalism /30
The New *Kalevala* /31
After *Kalevala* /32

2. New Beginnings, Latin and Finnish
Kai Laitinen and George C. Schoolfield

The Reformation and Agricola /34
Agricola's Successors /36
The Hegemony of Swedish /38
Learned Works in Latin /40
Devotional Works in Finnish /41
A Finnish Baroque Poetry? /42
Juslenius /45
The Age of Porthan /46
Turku Romanticism and Nationalism /50
Juteini, Kallio, and Finnish Verse /54
Peasant Poets /56
The University at Helsinki and Fennophilia /57
The Finnish-Language Press /59
The Start of Finnish Drama /62
The Dream of a Full-Fledged Literature /62

3. The Rise of Finnish-Language Literature, 1860–1916
Kai Laitinen

The 1860s: Breaking the Ice /64
Academic Poets /66
Kivi, Pioneer and Classic /70
A Quiet Decade /78
Miniature Humorists /80
Poets of the Transition Period /81
The Era of Realism /83
Domestic Roots of Realism /83
Foreign Influences /85
Canth /87
Aho in the Era of Realism /92
Pakkala /95
Other Realists /98
Turning Point of Realism /99
Symbolism and Karelianism: The 1890s /99
Aho's Later Work /102
Järnefelt, the Odd Man Out /104
From the Frost Years to the Threshold of Independence /107
Literature Divided /109
Leino /111
Manninen /117
Minor Poets /119
Prose of the Frost Years: Beginnings of Change /121
Two Woman Writers and a Young Utopian /123
Three Neoromantics: Linnankoski, the Young Kilpi, and Lehtonen /129
Descriptions of the People: Jotuni and Lassila /135
Poets of the 1910s /142
1916: A Turning Point /144

4. The Period of Independence 1, 1917–1960
Markku Envall

Earlier Authors Continue: Koskenniemi and Sillanpää /148

Kianto, Kilpi, Lehtonen /151

New Lyricists: Hellaakoski and Vuorela /154

Poetry of the Torch Bearers /156

Kailas, Vala, Mustapää /159

Jylhä and Viljanen /161

Prose of the New Generation: Waltari, Haanpää, Pekkanen /163

Poets of the 1930s /167

Novelists of the Senses and Sensibility: Uurto and Hämäläinen /171

A Dramatist and Three Journalists: Wuolijoki, Olli, Paavolainen, Kurjensaari /172

Coda: A Problematic Figure /175

Years of War and Peace /176

Poets of the 1940s /180

The Breakthrough of Modern Poetry /184

Haavikko /185

Anhava, Rekola, Manner, Nieminen /187

Mannerkorpi and Holappa /190

Feminine Voices /192

Masters of the Small: Heikkilä and Schreck /195

A Double Gift: Kunnas /196

Postwar Prose /197

Pennanen /198

Linna /199

Korpela /200

Huovinen and Joenpelto /201

Tapio and Vartio /202

Rintala and Meri /204
Laconicism and Naivism: Hyry /206

5. The Period of Independence 2, 1960–1990
Markku Envall

Literary Trends /210
Saarikoski and the Poetry of the Radical Period /215
Prose of the 1960s /223
Salama, the Proletarian Epic, and Beyond /224
Women Novelists /228
Rural and Urban Lives /232
Theater /239
Journalism and Essay /241
Best Sellers /243
Poetry of the 1970s /244
Prose of the 1970s /252
Two Irreverent Outsiders /259
The 1980s: Subtlety and Shock in Novels, Novellas, and Theater /262
Intellectuality: Poets and Narrators of the 1980s /268
Aphorism and Environmental Essay /269

FINLAND-SWEDISH LITERATURE

6. A Part of Sweden
George C. Schoolfield

Jöns Budde's Book /275
Forsius /275
Åbo Academy: Playwrights and Poets /278
Exile Literature /287
Frese and Löfving /289

Åbo Reconstituted /291
Franzén and Choraeus /293

7. National Romanticism — A Golden Age?
George C. Schoolfield

Åbo Romanticism /298
Runeberg /301
Runeberg's Contemporaries /317
Fredrika Runeberg /322
Runeberg's Disciples /326
Pioneers in Fiction /329
Topelius /334
Wecksell /346
Estlander: A Summing Up /351

8. A Sense of Minority
George C. Schoolfield

Finland-Swedish Awareness /354
Tavaststjerna /358
Ahrenberg /369
Memoirists and Critics /375
A Wave of Realists /378
Helsingfors Discovered /386
Theater /389
Realism and Regionalism /391
The New Century's Beginning /398
Ateneum, Euterpe, (Nya) Argus /400
Lybeck /402
Mörne /407
Celebratory Poets: Procopé, Tegengren, Emil Zilliacus /412

Finland-Swedish Decadence: Bertel Gripenberg /416
Reason and Wit: Hirn and Mattsson /421
Autumn Days and Alm /423
Local Patriots /426
Dagdrivare /432
Runar Schildt /435
Idealists, Realists, and the Civil War /440
An Eyewitness: Ruin /451

9. The Age of Modernism, 1916–1960
George C. Schoolfield

How New Was Modernism? /453
Södergran /455
Diktonius /458
Olsson /464
Björling /469
Rabbe Enckell /474
Henry Parland /480
Eklund /484
Ultra, Quosego, 1929 /489
A Second Modernist Wave /491
Skeleton in the Closet: Örnulf Tigerstedt and Fascism /496
Three Women, Three Answers to Life: von Schoultz,
    Wichman, Tuominen /500
Colliander and Russian Orthodoxy /515
Varieties of Karelianism: Stenius,
    Olof Enckell, Oscar Parland /519
A Brilliant Eclecticism: Ralf Parland /527
A Special Lutheranism: Nyman /530
Historical Narrative /532
Sally Salminen and Little Åland /534

Ostrobothnians /542

Poetae Minores /549

Prose of the 1940s and 1950s /560

A Nasty World and a Nicer One: Chorell and Jansson /567

Two Lyricists: Peter Sandelin and Carpelan /575

10. A Startling Growth, 1960–1990
George C. Schoolfield

The Revolt: Kihlman, Donner, and the Serial Novel /590

New Narrators: Bargum, Cleve, Fors /599

Varied Talents: Järner, Valtiala,
Ralf Nordgren, and Others /607

Andersson and the Poets of FBT /614

Huldén and Companion Blithe Spirits /621

The Essay and Other Nonfiction /631

Popularizers of Complaint /636

Flight, Sublimity, and Aggression /638

Confessor Literature and the Tikkanens /651

Women Writers: Ostrobothnia and Elsewhere /658

Regionalism's Boom and Blomqvist /671

Lyric Outburst of the 1970s: Romanticism's Return? /676

The Rock Generation /687

Prose of the 1980s: An Embarrassment of Riches /700

Lyric of the 1980s: A Similar Abundance /715

CHILDREN'S LITERATURE IN FINLAND

11. Children's Literature
Maija Lehtonen

Early Didactic and Moralizing Literature /729

Topelius and the Fennomane Movement /730

Differentiation and New Genres, 1900–1945 /734
The Modern Fairy Tale, 1945–1990 /740
The Illustrated Book /748
The Young Adult Novel /749

Finnish/Swedish Glossary of Place-Names /753
Bibliography /755
The Contributors and Translators /829
Index /833

Acknowledgments

The assembly of material for the writing of a literary history is a tedious task: I have been fortunate in having had the enduring support of the interlibrary loan office at the Sterling Memorial Library of Yale University throughout the several years of work on the project—Maureen Malone Jones, Elizabeth Johnson, Vinita Lovette, and Mae Robertson. In turn, they were aided in cases of need by the librarians of the Åbo Academy, of the University of Turku, and of the University of Helsinki. The circulation department of the SML was constantly helpful and interested, allowing me to have some four hundred books simultaneously on my charge; here, among many friendly faces, Evelyn McLellan, Barbara Gajewski, and Clifford Johnson should be named. The reference department of the SML was forever willing to provide answers to the countless tormenting questions of detail (film actresses, vital statistics) that turned up; the informational virtuosity of Alan Solomon, head of the department; Sue Lorimer; Marianna McKim; Margaret Powell; Sarah Prown; and Mr. and Mrs. Paul Constantine (now at Cornell) was beyond compare. A figure of particular heroism in the SML was Marie Kozak, who photocopied some one hundred and fifty books to supplement the SML's holdings. Åke Koel, former acquisitions librarian for German and Scandinavian, was generous with aid, as were Fred Musto and Margit Kaye of the Yale Map Collection. Russell Shaddox, managing editor of Yale's Auxiliary Services, did yeoman service in preparing the book's maps for publication. Farther afield, Charles Fineman of the Widener Library at Harvard; Richard Impola, professor emeritus at the State University of New York, New Paltz; Leif Sjöberg, professor emeritus at the State University of New York, Stony Brook; and Mariann E.

Tiblin of the University of Minnesota Library (Minneapolis) were unfailingly encouraging and helpful; translator Ritva Poom of New York City was singularly responsible. Virpi Zuck, professor at the University of Oregon, deserves special thanks for her painstaking reading of the manuscript word by word — and words cannot express my gratitude.

In Finland, Marja-Leena Rautalin, director of the Information Center for Finland's Literature, and its former members, Marianne Bargum, now director of Söderström & Co., and Bettina Wulff, were ever forthcoming and interested; I have benefited much from the intellectual and personal stimulus of conversation and correspondence with Seija Tiisala of the University of Helsinki (as well as from her boundless hospitality); Professor Emeritus Lars Huldén, best of friends; Professor Merete Mazzarella; Professor Clas Zilliacus, and Docent Roger Holmström of Åbo Academy; Professor Johan Wrede, recently retired from Helsinki, and — as the following pages often show — the essayist Johannes Salminen. In Finland, too, I have been fortunate in finding such contributors as Kai Laitinen, Markku Envall, and Maija Lehtonen and translator Philip Binham. In Britain the learning and promptitude of Michael Branch have been a spur and an inspiration, as have the wit, style, and enthusiasm of Laurie Thompson at Saint David's University College, Lampeter.

The manuscript could not have been completed without the preternatural computer skills and organizational ability of Lisa Landow and the technical gifts and rich research acumen of Laura Gray, a Sibelius scholar in her own right. Both have been not just instrumental but vital in pushing the project along. Other invaluable if more occasional helpers were David Blocher, Jale Okay, and Michael Schmelzle, all of the Yale Graduate School. Their patience in struggling with names and titles in languages unfamiliar to them was more than admirable — as was the forbearance of my erstwhile German colleagues and of Gloria D. Schoolfield, exposed to a litany of complaint about the albatross, or millstone, hung about my neck by the task I had so blithely assumed.

Finally, thanks must go to Sven Rossel, general editor of the series of Scandinavian literary histories, and to the staff at the University of Nebraska Press. Agnes Risko of the Ohio State University has prepared the index with great care.

Introduction

The literary history of Finland immediately presents a problem to its chronicler. Depending on one's point of view, there are either two distinct bodies of literature in the country, Finnish-language and Swedish-language, or the country's letters are actually unified but bilingual. During the almost seven hundred years (ca. 1150–1809) when Finland belonged to Sweden, Swedish was the instrument of administration, commerce, and formal culture, and Finnish was a largely neglected tongue of the countryside. But then a rush of awareness of the importance of Finnish language and tradition, encouraged by early-nineteenth-century romanticism, created a split between a linguistic minority suddenly put on the defensive and an ambitious majority, which recruited many of its most ardent and effective supporters from the Swedish-speaking middle and upper classes. In the full flush of nationalistic enthusiasm Finnish literary histories were written largely without reference to what had happened and was happening in the other tongue, save for the work of such giants as Johan Ludvig Runeberg and Zachris Topelius: because of their role in national life, and thanks to early and excellent translation, they were regarded as essential parts of Finnish-language literature, albeit they wrote entirely in Swedish. An exclusively Finnish literary historiography was provided by Julius Krohn's *Suomalaisen kirjallisuuden vaiheet* (1897; Changing fates of Finnish literature); Eino Leino's popular *Suomalaisen kirjallisuuden historia* (1910; History of Finnish literature); A. O. Kallio's *Uudempi suomalainen kirjallisuus 1–2* (1911–12, 1928–29; Recent Finnish literature), and — classically and magisterially — Viljo Tarkiainen's *Suomalaisen kirjallisuuden historia* (1934; History of Finnish literature; 4th ed., 1967, revised and extended by Eino Kauppinen). Tarkiainen was followed by the stylistically elegant *Elävä kansalliskirjallisuus 1-3* (1944-49; Living national literature) of Rafael Koskimies. To this Fennocentric list, one might add a widely distributed and long-lived manual for schools, by V. A. Haila and Kauko Heikkilä, later supplemented by Kauppinen, first printed in 1947 and repeatedly amended and reissued.

Modest histories of Swedish-language literature in Finland also appeared: the eerily valedictory *Den finsk-svenska litteraturens utveckling 1-2* (1866-67; The development of Finnish-Swedish literature) of Gabriel Lagus, which came out only three years after Czar Alexander II had given equal rights to the Finnish language over against Swedish, and Ruth Hedvall's *Finlands svenska litteratur* (1917; Finland's Swedish literature). General histories of Swedish literature, published in Sweden, also gave varying amounts of attention to Swedish authors from Finland, usually in sections written by scholars who were their compatriots, such as Gunnar Castrén in Bonnier's *Sveriges nationallitteratur* (1911-12) and in Geber's *Illustrerad svensk litteraturhistoria* (1932). Partly to fill the gap left by "pure Finnish" literary histories, and mindful of the interest aroused in the rest of Scandinavia by the bloom of modernism in "Swedish Finland" during the 1920s, two chroniclers — separately and simultaneously — presented the Swedish-language production of the twentieth century, Bengt Holmqvist in *Modern finlandssvensk litteratur* (1951; Modern Finland-Swedish literature) and Thomas Warburton in *Finlandssvensk litteratur, 1898-1948* (1951; Finland-Swedish literature, 1898-1948). Earlier times were described in *Finlands svenska litteratur 1-2* (1968-69; Finland's Swedish literature), the first volume, subtitled *Från medeltiden till Åboromantiken* (From the Middle Ages to Åbo romanticism), by Lars Huldén, Jarl Gallén, Olof Enckell, and Erik Ekelund, and the second, *Från Åbo brand till sekelskiftet* (From the Åbo fire to the turn of the century), by Ekelund alone. In 1984 Warburton brought his book of 1951 up-to-date as *Åttio år finlandssvensk litteratur* (Eighty years of Finland-Swedish literature); it can be regarded as the third volume of the series.

The Winter War of 1939-40 with the Soviet Union had the salutary effect of leading the language groups together, and a more inclusive attitude prevailed in the eight volumes of the monumental *Suomen kirjallisuus* (1963-70; Finland's literature), under the general editorship of Matti Kuusi, in which discrete portions, translated from Swedish, were devoted to the minority's literature, amid the mass of Finnish material; an accompanying anthology in eight volumes (1963-75), edited by Kai Laitinen and Matti Suurpää, likewise gave space to Swedish-language writers, presented—from volume 3 on—wholly in Finnish translation. Laitinen followed an even more generous course in his book on the literature written between 1917, the year of Finland's independence, and the present (1967; Swed. tr. 1968), where the two streams were regarded as a unity, responding to the same social and political events and frequently interacting; this approach was also followed in Laitinen's *Suomen kirjallisuuden historia* (1981; History of Finland's literature; Swed. tr. 1988). For foreign publics, the two streams had already been presented side by side, without much emphasis on their interrelatedness, in the brilliant and succinct Finland sections, by Johannes Salminen, of the Danish-Norwegian-Swedish combined effort, *Nordens litteratur 1–2*, edited by Mogens Brønsted (1972), and by Jaakko Ahokas in his *Finnish Literature* (1973); in the latter, however, the treatment of Swedish-language literature was occasionally dismissive. Although I find the Laitinen approach illuminating and stimulating, I am convinced that Finland in fact has two literatures, in some periods more closely connected than in others. This volume's structure has been set up accordingly.

Another problem in the treatment of Finland's literature (a literature constantly and closely intertwined with history) is the unusual nature, among the northern nations, of its development. Until fairly recently, Finland's membership in "Scandinavia" was open to debate, since its main language was not Scandinavian but Finno-Ugrian, albeit many of its social patterns were Swedish, leftovers from past centuries. When President Kyösti Kallio made his historic visit to Stockholm in October 1939, he did so to participate in a summit meeting of *Nordic* heads of state. The American-Scandinavian Foundation expressly included Finland among its areas of interest and activity only after the Second World War. Even today "the North" and "Nordic" are the more diplomatic words, automatically used inside the huge area they designate, as in such organizations as the Nordic Council. Finland's history ran differently from that of its neighbors to the west: not its own master in the long Swedish time (while providing valuable manpower for the Swedish crown); a precariously autonomous grand duchy under the czars for somewhat more than a century (and for the first eight decades better off than it had been under Sweden); a democracy that, from 1941 to 1944, was a cobelligerent of Nazi Germany; and then, paying reparations and considerably reduced by the loss of large parts of Karelia (and Finland's second city, Viipuri), a country that lived under the Soviet shadow, essaying a prudent policy not always understood by less exposed nations. At length, Finland became a prosperous partner in the postwar North (making the traditional Finnish admiration for honest poverty sound a little hollow), a prosperity reduced after the Soviet Union's collapse but now regained.

Because of its proximity to Russia, Finland has had more than its Nordic share of upset and bloodshed. The Civil War of 1918 may be seen as a briefer sideshow, ending differently, of Russian events after the Bolshevik Revolution; in the heroic Winter War of 1939–40 and the more suspect Continuation War, Finland was often called a bastion or outpost against the East in patriotic rhetoric; the Lapland War of 1944–45, when the Finnish army had the task of driving German forces out of the country's northern reaches, may be regarded as an act of exculpation, undertaken at Russian behest, for the grandiose dream of a "Great Finland," on the model of Hitler's "Groß-Deutschland," stretching to the shores of Lake Onega. In a more distant past Finland itself had experienced three major invasions from Russia, the cruel occupation during the Great Northern War, from 1710 to 1721 (the "Great Wrath"), the less terrible incursion concluding the Swedo-Russian war of 1741–43 (the "Little Wrath"), and the Russian sweep of 1808–9, against dogged Finnish resistance, made glorious by Runeberg.

In reality as in literature the defeat turned out well for Finland — it got a generous monarch in Alexander I and a wholly rebuilt Helsinki, the new seat of government and of the university. As well, czarist Russia gave Finland's cultural life a leavening absent elsewhere in the North: see Runeberg's epic on Russian themes, *Nadeschda,* the Tolstoyanism of Arvid Järnefelt and Ilmari Kianto, the long Russian residence of "Maiju Lassila," the so-called Byzantinism of Edith Södergran, and eventually, the Greek Orthodox faith persistently displayed by Tito Colliander and the arguments of Paavo Haavikko and Johannes Salminen for a Finland "between East and West." These currents became thinner after 1917. But the value of the quondam Russian presence cannot be ignored and amounts to more than the eastern air sometimes detected by imaginative visitors to Helsinki. The late Annamari Sarajas pursued the Russian strain in Finland's literature with vigor and imagination; the historian Max Engman has laid out the manifold connections of prerevolutionary St. Petersburg with Finland, not least as a receptacle for Finnish migrants of both language persuasions.

Another exceptional element in Finland's literary history is the speed with which the country produced a full-fledged body of writing in the majority language after Alexander II's decree of 1863. The swift bloom had been prepared by the antiquarian efforts of Henrik Gabriel Porthan (1739–1804), by his heirs in the "Turku romanticism" of the teens and twenties of the new century, by the establishment of the Finnish Literary Society at

Helsinki in 1831, and by the achievement of Elias Lönnrot in constructing a national epic on the basis of oral tradition. Nevertheless, the appearance of a bonafide genius, Aleksis Kivi, almost at the beginning of the literature's modern history, was a kind of miracle; in *Seitsemän veljestä* (1870; Seven brothers) Kivi fathered the line of novels — particularly comic or sadly comic novels — that is one of the special glories of Finnish letters. In respect to its abrupt entry onto the Northern Parnassus, Finnish literature can be compared with Norway's sudden emergence with Wergeland and Welhaven and then with Ibsen, Bjørnson, Lie, Kielland, Garborg; yet all these writers — save the obstinate Garborg with his *landsmål* — employed ready-made Dano-Norwegian (and drew on the distinguished culture of Denmark's Golden Age), whereas in Finnish Finland a literary instrument had to be forged. Admittedly, every author of the new Finnish literature had a command of Swedish and had easy access to Scandinavian resources: Kivi's hard-won fluency in Swedish opened the world of Holberg, read in Danish, and Shakespeare, read in Hagberg's Swedish translation, for him. In turn, the most perceptive early presentation of Kivi's dramatic work was written in Swedish by Fredrik Cygnaeus.

A sad but incontrovertible fact about belles lettres in Finnish is the obvious one: that they were and are not accessible to the nearby Scandinavian community without the benefit of translation. Transmission could hardly be as direct, for example, as in the case of the great Norwegians; any reader of Swedish, in Sweden or Finland, could understand their Dano-Norwegian texts without difficulty. To be sure, in the great age of Nordic realism, the works of Juhani Aho were quickly turned into Swedish — the translations were numerous and printed almost simultaneously with the originals; yet, appearing at publishing houses in Finland (often small ones, such as Hagelstam's), their distribution in the rest of the North was spotty — Hagelstam was small potatoes next to Gyldendal of Copenhagen and Christiania, or Bonnier of Stockholm. Wondrous to say, the bitter erotic masterpiece of the young Maria Jotuni, *Rakkautta* (1907; Love) — translated into Swedish by Bertel Gripenberg in 1908 and published at Helios, a tiny Helsinki house — fell into the hands of the great Danish critic Georg Brandes and impressed him. But good luck raised her horizon of expectations too high; the only other books of hers to appear in Swedish translation were *Arkielämää* (1909; Everyday life), in a series of "ten-mark books" in 1920, and then a collection of her stories in 1971, twenty-eight years after her death.

A handful of writers were fortunate in the amount of Swedish translation they received: Aho, Arvid Järnefelt, Johannes Linnankoski, Maila Talvio.

Nevertheless, such a gifted author as Joel Lehtonen had to wait until 1935, the year after his suicide at fifty-three, for a first translation of his masterpiece, *Putkinotko* (1920), by the indefatigable Gripenberg (whose reputation for dislike of Finnish Finland was certainly not borne out by his translation activity), and *Putkinotko* has remained the only one of Lehtonen's works ever to be translated into Swedish. (A new rendering by N.-B. Stormbom appeared in 1973.) Ilmari Kianto's *Punainen viiva* (1909; The red line) was not translated until 1946, and his *Ryysyrannan Jooseppi* (1924; Joseph of Ryysyranta) waited until 1955; Eino Leino's verse chef d'oeuvre, *Helkavirsiä* (1903, 1912; Whitsongs), came out in Swedish only in 1963, preceded by an unsuccessful selection from this greatest of Finnish poets by Elmer Diktonius in 1931. The fountainhead, Kivi's *Seitsemän veljestä*, had first appeared in Swedish in 1919, translated by Per Åke Laurén (to be followed, a sign of its genuine importance, by Elmer Diktonius's idiosyncratic rendering of 1948 and Thomas Warburton's more accurate one of 1987). The point is this: although such major novels as J. P. Jacobsen's *Fru Marie Grubbe* (1876) and *Niels Lyhne* (1884) or Strindberg's *Röda rummet* (1879) were immediately read and reviewed outside their home country — the Dane Jacobsen in Sweden, the Swede Strindberg in Denmark (and both, of course, in Norway and Finland) — Kivi remained unknown, save by hearsay.

Johan Vilhelm Snellman, the fanatic advocate of a monolingual Finnish Finland, never mastered the beloved language and was compelled to write his polemics in his native, brilliantly commanded, and detested Swedish. Late in life he made a remarkable statement: "If Sweden in its time had Swedicized the whole Finnish people, the path of culture would have stood open for [this] people as well, and the generation of the present time would have escaped much strife and hardship. It would have been a relationship resembling that of the United States to England." If the transmission of literature had been on Snellman's mind (as it was not), he might more aptly have said that the situation would have resembled that of Ireland, where the replacement of Irish by English had given Ireland a large role in the literature of England and the world. In Finland the zeal with which the Fennomanes of the nineteenth century struggled to turn Finnish into the nation's prime language, ready for every task, is admirable, as is the speed of their success. Equally admirable is the self-and-language sacrifice of the Swedish speakers who hearkened to Snellman's battle cry of 1845, addressed to the "young men" of Finland: "From this moment on, every Swedish word [you employ] is thrown away for Finnish literature, for the honor of the Finnish name and your own honor." The triumph was achieved at the cost of considerable cultural isolation. Finnish literary scholars, fascinated as they were by the development of their own literature, did too little — before the ecumenical days of Laitinen — to spread knowledge of their literary corpus in Scandinavia at large. Swedish-speaking scholars and critics from Finland did more: Arvid Mörne with his study of Kivi and Kivi's novel from 1911, Werner Söderhjelm with his book on Johannes Linnankoski of 1918, Gunnar Castrén with his book on Juhani Aho of 1922.

Meanwhile, Swedish-language writing from Finland had found its way into Scandinavia proper with ease. A good knowledge of Runeberg and of Topelius was a cherished part of the literary baggage of educated Swedes (and a part of school curriculum) at least until the middle of the twentieth century, a popularity that also spread to Denmark and Norway. Over the years other writers from Swedish Finland, for longer or shorter periods, had a sizable Swedish following — for example, Bertel Gripenberg, Arvid Mörne, Runar Schildt, Jarl Hemmer; subsequently, the modernists — Edith Södergran, Gunnar Björling, Rabbe Enckell — became a permanent factor in the Scandinavian frame of reference. Today most Swedish-language authors of note have contractual arrangements with Swedish publishers and are reviewed in the Swedish press. Of course, authors from the Finnish side have attracted attention in Sweden as well, and beyond — one thinks of the late Väinö Linna, the late Pentti Saarikoski, Paavo Haavikko, and others; but the chanciness of translation, and competition with the flood of translated literature from other larger or more exotic literatures, make the neighbor country's interest in recent Finnish-language literature sporadic at best.

The relative isolation of Finnish-language literature has been still more crucial in its distribution to the extra-Scandinavian world; it has never had the popularity in English enjoyed, or once enjoyed, by such great figures as Andersen and Kierkegaard, Ibsen and Strindberg, Hamsun and Lagerlöf. The number of translators from Finnish into English has stayed small; it has to be suspected that the English versions of such one-time best sellers as Johannes Linnankoski and Mika Waltari were made at second hand, from Swedish. But translators have not been the only rare commodity; of all the major literatures of the North, that written in Finnish has found the smallest number of active scholars abroad, and Finnish language and literature are taught at few institutions of higher learning. (*Kalevala* scholarship, as represented in the present volume by Michael Branch, is an exception proving the rule.) Just as many essential works from the past and the present remain untranslated into English, so there are no monographs in English on such infinitely complex and fascinating figures as Kivi, Eino Leino, Joel Lehtonen, or Haanpää, Haavikko, Meri. Since these authors have been translated insufficiently or not at all, the users of such monographs might be few. (And a question remains: Which comes first, chicken or egg? Does translation always stimulate scholarship? Germany's record in the translation of Finnish-language literature is far better than that of the anglophone world, but in German too, serious critical or biographical studies do not exist.) It is to be hoped that the present volume will encourage both translation and scholarly research and that it may inspire literary and intellectual curiosity, rather different from a laudable but uncritical devotion to "Finnish roots."

Those persons accustomed to large monolingual and monolithic literatures may think it strange that—after the great release of Finnish-language creative forces—the Swedish-speaking minority has played such a disproportionately large role in Finland's literary production. Even today one is confronted by an activity that increases as the proportional representation in the nation's populace falls. In 1890 Swedish-speakers constituted 13.6 percent of Finland's population, and in Helsinki-Helsingfors they were equal in number to Finnish-speakers. (Compare the percentage of German-speakers in Prague at the same time, a dwindling 9 percent.) In 1992 the number for the country at large stood at 5.9 percent and in the capital at 7.4 percent. The causes usually given for the decline are a low birthrate; a large emigration (particularly from Ostrobothnia) to the United States and Canada and, after the Second World War, to Sweden itself; and a process of Fennicization, formerly for ideal reasons and more recently for practical ones (employment, inaccessibility of Swedish schools and social organizations, and—a source of the disappearance of the Swedish-speaking working class in Helsinki—pressures of the workplace or neighborhood). In addition, there was, and is, the common phenomenon of mixed marriages, in which more Swedish-speaking men than women choose partners across the language line; children of such unions normally take the mother's language. The mixed marriage has been facilitated by a common religious background and the absence of distinguishing ethnic or ethnic-social traits, obliterated, over the centuries, by changes from Finnish to Swedish and then from Swedish to Finnish. Today it is inaccurate (and politically incorrect) to speak of a "Finnish" as opposed to a "Swedish" physical type; the Swedish-speakers of Finland have been aptly characterized by the historian Jason Lavery as the world's most invisible minority.

The areas of Swedish concentration in Finland are the coastal strip east and west of Helsinki-Helsingfors, the coastal strip of southern and middle Ostrobothnia, the skerries off Turku-Åbo, and the Åland Islands, whose inhabitants have remained almost entirely Swedish-speaking (and have kept a separate identity from that of Swedish-speakers on the mainland). A conservative historical view is that the Swedish littoral settlement was formed by migration from Sweden proper (the name Helsingfors indicates people from Helsingland in central Sweden) before and during the thirteenth century. (The migration is thus roughly contemporaneous to the movement of German speakers eastward, over a broad front reaching from the Baltic lands to Silesia, Bohemia, and Transylvania.) Some historians, however, want to place the time of settlement from four to eight hundred years earlier, a proposition much bandied about when the language strife was at its height; it seemed necessary to claim that Swedish-speakers had arrived in Finland well ahead of Finnish-speakers! These pioneers were followed by waves of later comers, some given land and position in Finland for military services rendered the Swedish crown — for example, the Ramsays and von Wrights from Scotland; the Wredes from Westphalia, detouring through the Baltic provinces; the Schaumans from Courland by way of Sweden; the Aminoffs from Russia, becoming officers of Gustav II Adolf on the eve of the Thirty Years' War; and so forth; the list is a long one, containing many names distinguished in Finland's history. (Some beginnings were not so splendid: the Nordenskjölds were once upon a time a peasant family, the Norbergs, from Swedish Uppland; the von Willebrands were descended from a German captain in the Swedish army; the Gripenbergs were once the Wittes from Swedish Östergötland; the Donners sprang from a Lübeck amber carver.) Classic and successful examples among the many Finnish families that became Swedicized were the Carpelans (once named Karpelain) and the Alopaeuses, supposedly descended from a peasant named Kettunen: in a display of humanistic learning, Finnish *kettu*, "fox," became Greek *alopex*. To such celebrated clans should be added numerous others whose nineteenth-century forebears sought a better lot in the grand duchy: Georg Stockmann, the founder of the great department store, moved from Lübeck to be a clerk in the Nuutajärvi glassworks; Ferdinand Tilgmann, the founder of the great lithography firm, arrived by way of Sweden from a print shop in Kassel.

It has to be remembered that an enormous chasm divided the powerful and prosperous, with their impressive names and accomplishments, from the fishing and farming population of the southern and western coasts, often regarded (if regarded at all) with vast disdain by their fellow Swedish-speakers higher up on the socioeconomic ladder — until the advance of Finnish showed the necessity of somehow bringing all the speakers of Swedish together. (Other kinds of disdain could surface too: the Finnish zealot Agaton Meurman is supposed to have mocked the "Swedes" as a kind of dumping ground, taking everyone willing to join, even Jews.) Symptomatically, the pioneer of the Swedish movement in Finland, Axel Olof Freudenthal (see chapter 8), had a German grandfather from Riga. Who can deny that the variety of backgrounds among Swedish speakers made international connections easier and more natural? And, making a rough and ready distinction: if the minority was heterogeneous and directed outward, the Finnish majority was (relatively) homogeneous and directed inward — a notion already proposed by Runeberg in his famous distinction (see chapter 7) between a lively and somewhat frivolous coastal folk and a slower but spiritually deeper population inland. In Runeberg's old-fashioned, unified vocabulary they were both readily called "Finns," without reference to language.

The nomenclature applied to minority groups or national fractions is scarcely exact or logical. The once-popular term "Sudeten-German" geographically excluded a good part of the people it was intended to cover. A request for a definition of the term "Anglo-Irish" will bring forth several mutually contradictory answers. The present book uses the terms "Finland-Swede" and "Finland-Swedish" ("finlandssvensk") for members of the Swedish-speaking minority, since — evidently a coinage of Freudenthal — it is the term applied by members of the group to themselves, in contradistinction to "finne" (a native speaker of Finnish) and "finländare" (anyone who is a citizen of Finland). At one time "Swedo-Finn" had some currency in English, as in Alrik Gustafsson's passing reference to Edith Södergran in his *History of Swedish Literature* (1961); Jaakko Ahokas took refuge in the circumlocution "Swedish writers of Finland (hereafter referred to as Swedish writers)." But "Finland-Swede" and "Finland-Swedish" are now generally employed, for example, by Virpi Zuck in her *Dictionary of Scandinavian Literature* (1990) and by Lars S. Vikør in his handbook *The Nordic Languages* (1993). The accompanying term, "Swedish Finland" ("Det svenska Finland," "Svenskfinland," "Svensk-Finland"), has both a geographical meaning (i.e., those parts of Finland where Swedish has historically been spoken) and an institutional one, covering "Swedish" infrastructures, schools, social and artistic institutions, other organizations, and newspapers and magazines. Swedish Finland's Popular Assembly (Svenska Finlands folkting), consisting of seventy-five members, chosen in connection with regular community elections every four years, is an official representative of Finland's Swedish-speakers, supported by funds from the Finnish state (as is, indeed, the publication of Swedish-language literature); its purpose is the maintenance and furtherance of the minority's well-being. The protection of the minority by Finland's law is exemplary, although any reader of letters to the editor in the Finland-Swedish press will quickly become aware of perceived instances of unfair treatment, contrasting sharply with what seems to be the minority's contentment, or at least its acceptance of a historical situation.

No prominent Finland-Swedish writer would dare make a statement like that of William Butler Yeats (not yet under the aegis of a Nobel Prize) in the Senate of the recently founded Republic of Ireland, on 11 June 1925, during a heated debate on the prohibition of divorce, "a measure which a minority of this nation considers to be grossly oppressive. I am proud to consider myself a typical man of this minority. We against whom you have done this thing are no petty people.... We have created most of the modern literature of this country." (Yeats meant the Protestant, Anglo-Irish minority.) Yet the Finland-Swedish minority has contributed to Finland's literary renown in a way out of all proportion to its size. Perhaps Runeberg and Topelius would have written in Finnish, had they been able; at least this claim has been made. But their path to Sweden (and Swedish royalties) would have been an infinitely more difficult one. Save for the *Kalevala* (much aided by Sibelius and Gallén-Kallela), the presence of Finland in the twentieth century's general cultural consciousness is maintained, before all else, by Finland-Swedish modernism: the one "Finnish" name adduced in the *Penguin Guide to European Literature* — the volume on modernism, edited by Malcolm Bradbury and James McFarlane (1976) — is a paragraph on Edith Södergran; the only representatives from Finland in Mikael Benedikt's anthology *The Prose Poem* (1972) are Gunnar Björling and Elmer Diktonius; the latter is also the single Finnish entry in the historical anthology of music criticism edited by Harry Haskell (*The Attentive Listener*, 1995). Södergran is far and away the most frequently and completely translated poet from Finland, and Tove Jansson holds a similar championship among writers of prose. The situation does not lack resemblance to the role played by "Prague German literature," by the young Rilke, Kafka, Werfel, Max Brod, and Gustav Meyrink, in the foreign perception of literature from Bohemia and Moravia; unfairly enough, these names (from a now dead culture) may well loom larger than Jan Neruda and Němcová, Hašek and Čapek, Kundera and Havel. While offering a full account of the riches of Finnish Finland, so many of which deserve a greater currency outside Finland, the present volume is also meant to indicate that the literature of the Finland-Swedish minority has a long, continuous, distinct, and vital history, not to be disguised as the desultory work of "Finnish authors writing in Swedish." More than thirty years ago, defending the claim of

Finland-Swedish literature to be regarded as a separate and equal voice in the North, the late Leo Ågren remarked that there were only half as many Icelanders as there were Finland-Swedes. The literature has a right to its own history, as presented in the second half of this volume.

Both original and translated titles of poems and stories have been given in the chapters dealing with earlier phases of the literatures (2, 3, 4, 6, 7, 8); a user with linguistic skills may want to look them up in anthologies or collected works. The chapters dealing with more recent periods (5, 9, 10) give the titles of poems (which may often be the first line) and stories in translation alone. All translations are by the chapter authors or chapter translators unless otherwise noted. Contrary to the practice of previous volumes in the series, this one does not set a chapter aside for women writers. The establishment of a female reserve in Finland's case would entail extensive dislocation or repetition; ever since Minna Canth's days, women who write have played absolutely central roles in their respective periods. Literature for children and young people, however, deserves a separate chapter, in order to put its richness and variety on display. Some overlap occurs between earlier chapters and the eleventh: Topelius, Tove Jansson, and Kirsi Kunnas belong to both adults and the young.

In the bibliography, because of the above-mentioned paucity of scholarly or critical work in English, recourse has been taken to standard works in the original languages, as an initial indication of what secondary literature exists. As the volume may be used by Scandinavianists who do not control Finnish, pertinent comment in Swedish on Finnish-language authors has also been included. When reference is made in the main text to secondary opinions, indicated by author (and short title if necessary) and page number, the source will be found in the appropriate section of each chapter's bibliography.

The start of the present decade has been taken as the point of closure for all discussions in the main text, save where a book has appeared (for example, a sequel) that rounds off a development. This tying of contemporary letters to a bed of Procrustes leaves me uncomfortably aware that many important new works and new figures have been ignored. Yet such incompleteness is a necessary fault of every literary history that describes recent authorship. Final chapters bear their own death within them; the youngest part of the book ages the most rapidly.

The composition of a literary history, especially of a foreign literature, is a perilous task, sometimes all too lightly shouldered. I would like to repeat what I wrote about these perils, or torments, in a review of the Danish history in the present series, where the problems noted were handsomely overcome:

> The editors and authors of volumes intended to present a "foreign" literature to a new audience are faced with daunting or even unnerving problems, some psychological. Unless the account wants to face charges of superficiality or amateurishness, it must be inclusive, not just a survey of "Great Moments"; but it cannot take in so much that its readers will drown in a torrent of strange names and titles and movements. It has to be sufficiently scholarly that it can be used as a reference source for researchers in other literatures (or, often, in cultural history) who want to orient themselves generally or specifically; but it must also be lively, in order to lure its audience into looking up and reading the available translations. It has to be informative not only about the corpus of letters but about history, sociology, and even politics; but it must also take care not to stray too far away from the literary matter at hand. Its contributors must wrestle with dreadful problems of brief description; in the instance of novels and dramas, this entails a constant and guilt-inducing neglect of details and nuances, and the characterization of poetry is sheer torment—if too many examples are given (losing their bouquet in translation, of course), the result may be a pastiche; yet lacking examples, the description of lyrics may turn out to be like most efforts to conjure up music or painting in words: vague, empty, silly. And how, then, to strike a proper balance between work and life, particularly in the case of major authors? Biography has a role here, lest the presentation be tame and lifeless; but personal vicissitudes—however sensational—should not divert the audience from the literary production. Further, the makers of a literary history are pestered by other niggling but necessary concerns: the tracking down of translations, the effective rendering of lyric extracts and of punning or allusive titles (a much nastier crux than it might seem), the search for helpful comparisons in other, more familiar bodies of literature. (*Danish Literary Magazine* 4 [1993], 31)

In order to make the chapters by Finnish contributors still more accessible to an American public, I have—apart from the additions made in chapter 2—somewhat extended the section on Aleksis Kivi as well as the portions on Kaatra, Lehtimäki, Maiju Lassila, Kyösti Wilkuna, and "Poets of the 1910s" in chapter 3; in chapter 4 I have added or expanded sections on

Vaaskivi, Selja, Saastamoinen, Pylkkönen, Vammelvuo, Heikkilä, Schreck, and Kunnas; in chapter 5, the sections on Salo, Oksanen, Sinkkonen, Parras, Tiainen, Tabermann, Melleri, Aronpuro, Arto Paasilinna, Katz, Liksom, Jouko Turkka, Suhonen, Simonsuuri, Kaila, Kemppinen, and Envall, the last in tribute to the creative work of the chapter's author. In the chapter on children's literature about one quarter has been added, again with the intent of calling up useful comparisons for an American (or anglophone) audience; further, the section on Irmelin Sandman Lilius has been augmented. In all these instances I alone am responsible for the facts listed and opinions expressed.

Following the practice of the Danish volume in this series, which did not discuss Inuit (Greenlandic) writing, and the volumes on Norway and Sweden, which did not include Sami literature by authors living in those countries, the present volume has not tried to portray the miniature world of Sami belles lettres from Finland. However, it is fitting to note that the Finnish-Sami poet Nils-Aslak Valkeapää (1943–), whose work has been translated into English, Finnish, and Swedish, won the Nordic Council Prize for Literature in 1991.

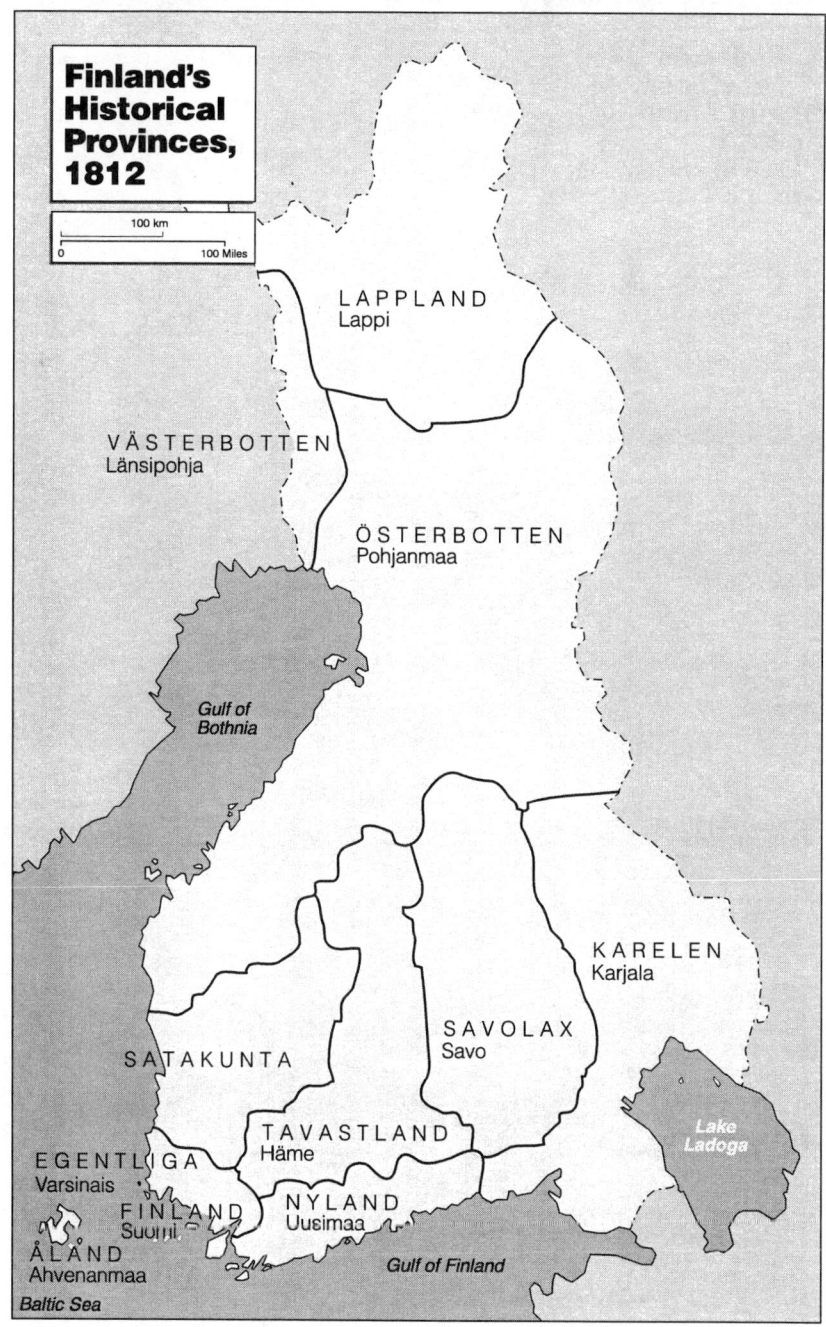

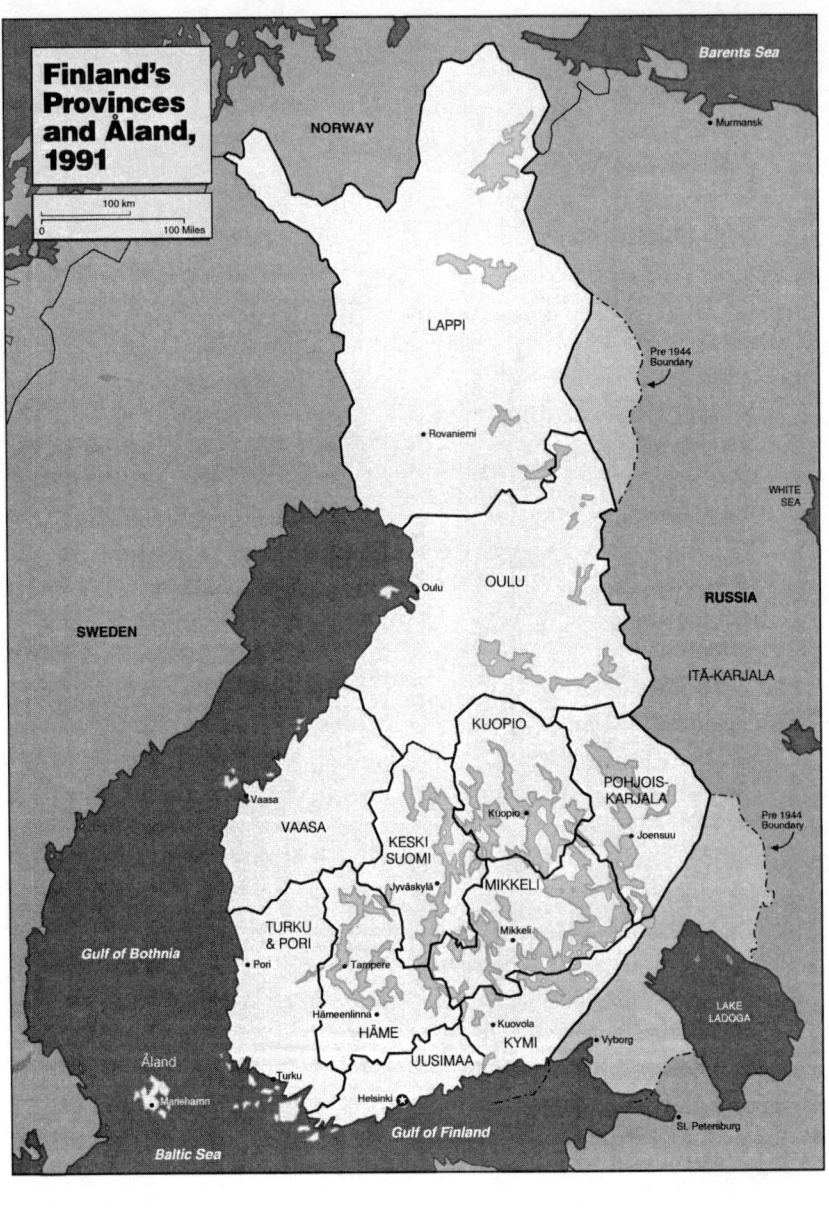

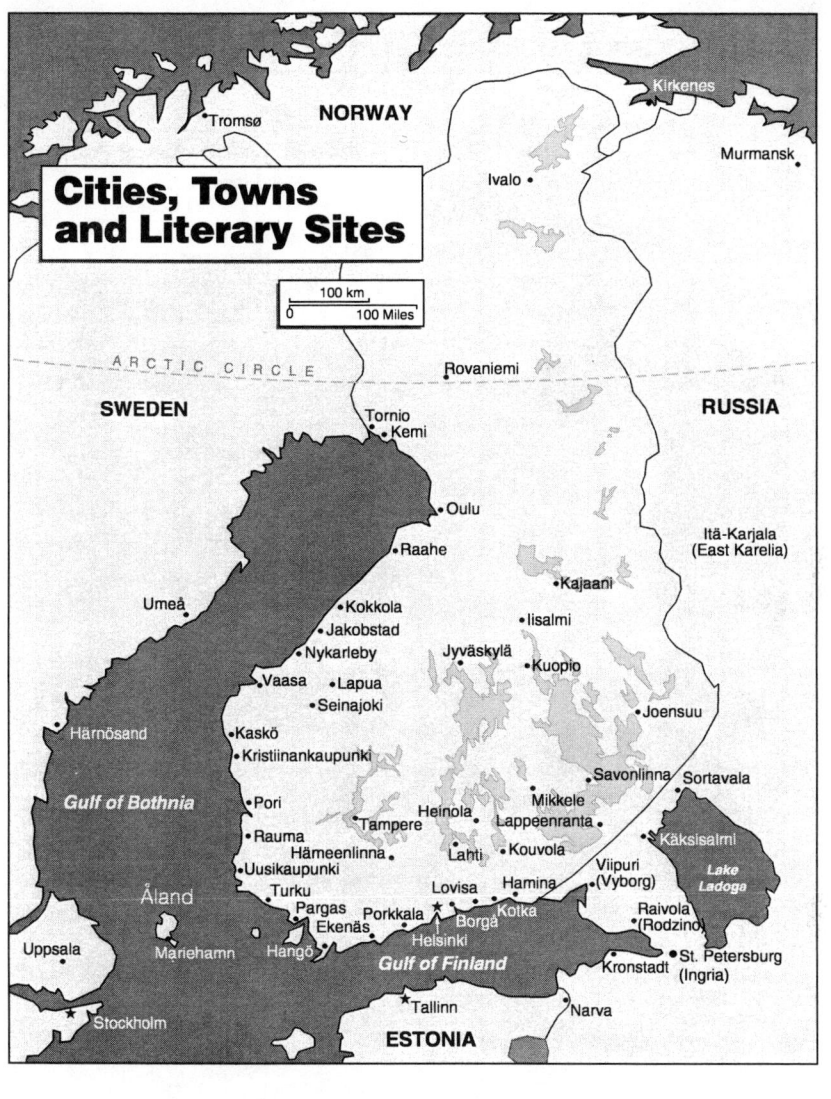

Finnish-Language Literature

Finnish Oral Poetry, *Kalevala*, and *Kanteletar*

Michael Branch

1

This chapter examines the relationship between traditional Finnish oral poetry and two literary works compiled by the Finnish scholar Elias Lönnrot (1802–84; doctor of medicine, professor of Finnish language, author, and editor) and the relevance of these works to the shaping of a Finnish national identity. Lönnrot's two major works, *Kalevala, taikka Wanhoja Karjalan Runoja Suomen Kansan Muinosista Ajoista* (1835–36; Kalevala, or old Karelian poems of the ancient past of the Finnish people; Eng. tr. *The Old Kalevala*, 1969), better known in its second and definitive edition, *Kalevala* (1849; Eng. tr. 1889, 1907, 1963, 1988, 1989), and the *Kanteletar taikka Suomen Kansan Wanhoja Lauluja ja Wirsiä* (1840–41; Kanteletar or old songs and ballads of the Finnish people; Eng. tr. *The Kanteletar: Lyrics and Ballads after Oral Tradition*, 1992 [selection]) have acquired a reputation that transcends their standing as works of literature. In Finland Lönnrot's 1849 *Kalevala* and the *Kanteletar* have a special place among the phenomena that define and give a distinctive tone to the Finns' cultural identity. Almost as soon as the 1835 edition of the *Kalevala* appeared, it was acclaimed "Finland's national epic," and it retains this reputation today. These two works have inspired successive generations of scholars and artists. The important Finnish contribution to the development of oral tradition studies as an international discipline owes its origin to ideas set in train by Lönnrot's works of collection and compilation. Writers, artists, musicians, and architects have drawn on motifs and themes from the *Kalevala* and *Kanteletar* as starting points for the development of individual vernaculars. What Lönnrot's two works were thought to have stood for has also been used by educators, cultural propagandists, politicians, and businessmen for more than a century.

Of Lönnrot's two main works, it is the reputation of the 1849 edition of the epic *Kalevala* which is also dominant outside Finland. Although this can be partly explained by the lack of a translation of the complete *Kanteletar* (the 1992 English translation represents about one-quarter of the Finnish text), the principal reason for the attraction of the *Kalevala* lies in the grandeur and universality of its themes, the coherence of its plots, and the splendor of its poetry. An 1852 translation into German influenced H. W. Longfellow in his choice of the poetic structure of *The Song of Hiawatha*. Since then, translations of the *Kalevala* have been made into forty-five languages with five separate translations published in English (three in the United States, two in Great Britain) together with several adaptations and retellings of selected themes, making the *Kalevala* the most widely known work of Finnish literature in translation.

The 1835 edition of the *Kalevala* comprised 12,078 unrhymed trochaic tetrameters arranged in thirty-two poems; the 1849 definitive edition was revised and enlarged to 22,795 lines in fifty poems. The *Kanteletar* comprises 22,201 lines, for the most part unrhymed trochaic tetrameters, divided into three parts. By his own criteria Lönnrot understood the *Kalevala* as epic poetry and the *Kanteletar* as lyric and ballads. By present-day criteria the *Kalevala* is seen to include lyric materials used for epic purposes, whereas the *Kanteletar* includes material that almost certainly springs from an originally epic tradition. The titles of both works were coined by Lönnrot. *Kalevala* is made up of two elements: *Kaleva,* an uncommon male name, possibly associated by Lönnrot with "giant," "leader," "hero," + *-la,* a suffix indicating locality, hence "land of Kaleva." *Kanteletar* is also made up of two elements: *kantele,* a zitherlike, originally five-stringed instrument, + *-tar,* a suffix indicating female spirit, hence 'female spirit, muse of the kantele.'

The Romantic Background
In their international context the *Kalevala* and *Kanteletar* share much with other compilations of the romantic period that drew their inspiration, themes, and form from what was believed to be traditional oral literature or from surviving medieval or premedieval literary sources — real or imagined — that were reinterpreted in pursuit of particular artistic, philosophical, or political aims. Within the romantic period the works with which the *Kalevala* and *Kanteletar* have most in common in terms of source materials, content, and purpose are those produced in the parts of Europe where

intellectuals were striving to shape a new cultural identity. Their inspiration was the thought of the German philosopher Johann Gottfried Herder (1744–1803), who argued that a nation could exist only if it had a distinctive cultural identity founded in the language and oral literature of the ordinary, nonliterate people. The most useful comparison (and one of Lönnrot's sources of inspiration) is the work of the Serbian patriot Vuk Stefanović Karadžić (1787–1864).

Although the *Kalevala* and *Kanteletar* owe their origin as compilations of traditional oral poetry to cultural and political ideas widespread in Europe in the early nineteenth century, their distinctiveness springs from specific local features. One such feature is cultural: the survival into modern times of an unusually rich oral tradition. Another is political: the process of change — with far-reaching cultural effects — that started in 1809 as the Finns ceased to owe allegiance to the king of Sweden and began to seek a new cultural and political identity within an autonomous grand duchy of the Russian empire.

The Little Tradition

All peoples have folklore. In nonliterate cultures most if not all peoples developed various types of oral literature — from the sacred to the profane — expressed through various genres, in prose and verse, and judged by locally accepted and demanding criteria of composition and taste. Within Europe most "little tradition" of this kind was lost as a literate "great cultural tradition" was disseminated through social institutions — the courts of monarchs and local rulers, the church, schools and universities — and became dependent on the written and printed word. The spread of great tradition did not destroy oral literature as such but weakened the creative generation and renewal of that literary tradition by the elevation of talented poets and storytellers from the ranks of the ordinary people and, even more important, by changing the character and expectations of the audience. Today only tiny glimpses of little tradition at its best can be gleaned from fragments noted down or incorporated into works in the great tradition. Finnish oral tradition is a rare European survival from a region where great-tradition culture spread only relatively recently to areas where the little tradition was the principal form of literary art. Indeed, the little tradition was still active there in the nineteenth century and has not entirely died out even today. Of added importance in respect to Finnish oral tradition as a cultural phenomenon is the fact that numerous scholars, of whom Lönnrot was but one, established reliable ways of collecting and analyzing oral materials (and thereby laid the foundations of international folklore studies).

Thus Finnish little tradition may offer insights into not only the nature of oral tradition in general but also the aesthetic experience shared by performer and audience.

The use of "Finnish" requires some definition. In discussion of the *Kalevala* and *Kanteletar,* "Finnish oral tradition" refers to the themes, motifs, and form of a poetry cast in unrhymed, nonstrophic trochaic tetrameters. Large quantities of this poetry have been recorded throughout most of the northeast Baltic region in five of the seven closely related Baltic-Finnic languages: Finnish, Karelian, Estonian, Ingrian, and Vote. The consistency of the prosody and style of this poetic tradition — anachronistically called "Kalevala-meter poetry" — among peoples spread over a large area and separated rather than united by the vicissitudes of history suggests a poetic form that took shape before Finnish, Karelian, Estonian, Ingrian, and Vote had evolved from a common language known as Proto-Finnic into separate languages. There is no clear agreement as to when and where this could have happened. The consensus of opinion points to an area on the southern side of the Gulf of Finland at least twenty-five hundred years ago (Kuusi et al., 21–27).

At some stage during that common linguistic period, Kalevala-meter poetry took shape. The line was either normal or broken. In a normal line the tetrameter consists of four strong stresses alternating with four weak stresses. The stress of speech and the foot-stress in the poetry coincide, and a caesura is placed between the second and third feet:

Nousi / siitä / / Väinä / möinen At that Väinämöinen rose
(*Kalevala,* poem 2:1)

In the broken tetrameter a syllable not normally stressed in speech occurs in the stressed part of the foot; no caesura occurs in such lines:

saare / hen se / läilli / sehen on the island on the main[land]
(*Kalevala,* poem 2:3)

The quantitative nature of the Baltic-Finnic languages gives the Kalevala meter a flexibility and liveliness that is further heightened by a skilled performer's dexterity in handling various patterns of consonant-vowel or vowel-consonant alliteration, a device that does not seem contrived in languages with relatively few consonant sounds (thirteen in the case of Finnish).

This much is probably of common origin to all five languages in which Kalevala-meter poetry has been recorded. There are also numerous other shared features in the Kalevala-meter poetry performed in these languages, in both structure and theme, although it is not possible to state with any certainty what is material from a common stock and what has been borrowed by one region from another. In addition to a distinctive mode of alliteration, the most common stylistic features in Kalevala-meter poetry are the use of a reprise technique to elaborate in one or successive lines the idea in the preceding line and repetition. As Robert Austerlitz notes, other compositional and functional devices characteristic of oral poetry traditions in many parts of the world are also common in Kalevala-meter poetry, including numerous common topoi, epithets, stock material, and formulaic structures.

The Corpus
No documentary record exists to show how Kalevala-meter poetry might have developed between its conception and the late Middle Ages. We can make certain deductions, however, about the nature of this poetry, its changing functions, and the reasons for its survival by examining the themes, motifs, and distribution of the materials collected over the past 150 years and the scant postmedieval documentary evidence (the latter almost wholly from Finland) in the light of such disciplines as history, language, anthropology, and archaeology. The physical legacy of the Kalevala-meter poetry tradition is preserved in archives in Finland, Estonia, and Karelia and consists of more than 2.5 million lines. Of the Finnish, Karelian, and Ingrian materials deposited in the Folklore Archive of the Finnish Literary Society in Helsinki, 1,270,000 lines have been published in the thirty-three-volume *Suomen kansan vanhat runot* (1908–48; Old poems of the Finnish people); as much again remains unpublished in the society's archive alone. Four main genres are represented: epic, lyric, spells, and festive and ceremonial poetry (accompaniment to bear and calendar ceremonies, various rites of passage, games and dances); Kalevala-meter poetry was also used for cradle songs, nonsense and occasional poetry, proverbs, and riddles.

There appear to have been certain regional genre preferences. It is difficult, however, to be specific about how powerful and how exclusive such preferences were, since collectors — particularly in the nineteenth century — were primarily interested in epic to the extent that the occurrence and context of other genres were likely underrecorded. Epic poetry performed by male singers had a special place in nineteenth-century Archangel Karelia but was less strongly represented in southern parts of Karelia, Ingria, and Estonia. In these areas lyric poetry, performed by women, was far more prominent. In Ingria women also performed a type of Kalevala-meter poetry known as "lyric-epic," which conveyed lyric sentiments by the use of fragments of epic. Although preferences of this kind can be identified, it may well be that in their surviving form they represent an aesthetically developed aspect of the tradition popular in that particular area.

Performance

Whatever the local preference for performances to mark special occasions, it seems likely that in commonplace performance all genres continued in use and that many members of the population as a whole regularly performed Kalevala-meter poems in connection with daily work, the numerous calendar rites marking the annual cycle, and ceremonies associated with rites of passage and other life crises. It is also probable that there was a hierarchy of performers. Though the performance of lyric appears mostly to have been commonplace and often even individual, other genres or special ritual occasions demanded special performers recognized for their skills and temperament. Semiprofessional singers were commonly brought in to sing laments at funeral and wedding ceremonies. The performance of spells required special knowledge. In nineteenth-century Archangel Karelia the competitive performance of epic narratives, which could continue for many hours or even days, had become a popular form of art attracting audiences from long distances.

With the exception of spells, which were chanted, Kalevala-meter poetry was in its surviving form predominantly a sung tradition. The melodies, which were not fixed to particular songs, were relatively few in number and varied from region to region. To what extent the *kantele* was used as the accompaniment is uncertain. By the nineteenth century use of the *kantele* had almost died out, and it owes its more recent popularity to the Finnish national movement of the second half of the nineteenth century. Throughout the Finnish, Karelian, Ingrian, and Vote areas the mode of social performance (as opposed to a person alone and without audience) was common and involved at least two people, the fore-singer and the after-singer. Their roles could also be performed by a group of performers. The fore-singer would start the first line and would be joined by the after-singer in the third or fourth foot (the reprise); the after-singer would continue either by repeating the first line or by singing a parallel line while the fore-singer was silent. In turn the fore-singer would join the after-singer at the reprise in the third or fourth foot of the repeated or parallel line and continue to sing a new line while the after-singer was silent.

In descriptions of the performance of epic poetry attention has frequently been drawn to the style of male singing in Archangel Karelia whereby a fore-singer and an after-singer sat side by side, hands clasped, swaying to and fro with the rhythm of the song. In reality, however, there were numerous modes of social performance. In certain rites, such as celebrating the killing of a bear or at weddings, performances could acquire a sense of drama; singing could also take place as the accompaniment to ring or long dance or to the motion of the village swing; songs could be exchanged by groups standing or sitting, groups in confrontation as in male-female courtship songs, or between groups engaged in various communal tasks (Kuusi et al., 72–77).

How the Tradition Might Have Been

The archival records present us with a paradox. Although the largest archives are in Helsinki and the Kalevala-meter poetry tradition is universally associated with Finland, the archival holdings illustrate a poetry tradition that flourished more powerfully in Karelia and Ingria at the time of collection than in nineteenth- and twentieth-century Finland. Comparable traditions are assumed to have existed in Finland because of the nature of the materials that did survive there and of the scant documentary materials from before the nineteenth century. References in early Finnish printed books to non-Christian gods, spirits, and practices date from the middle of the sixteenth century and represent efforts by the Lutheran clergy to stamp out unseemly heathen ways. The first Finnish prayer book, Bishop Mikael Agricola's (ca. 1510–57) *Rucouskiria* of 1544, contains the earliest known Finnish proverb; an entry in a sixteenth-century crown accounts book contains the earliest record of a Finnish spell (against the plague). A manuscript copy of the widespread thirteenth-century legend poem of Bishop Henry (*Pyhä Henrik*, Saint Henry) survives from the late seventeenth century; the first Finnish grammar, the *Linguae Finnicae brevis institutio* (1649) of Eskil Petraeus (1593–1657), draws on common Finnish riddles to illustrate points of language usage. The texts of two poems used in bear rites were published in 1679 by Petrus Bång (1633–96); the earliest surviving manuscript of the late-sixteenth-century historical poem *Kaarle-herttua* (Duke Charles) dates from 1699. A collection of Kalevala-meter lyric poetry, compiled in the 1660s by Henrik Florinus (1633–1705), appeared in 1702, only two years after the first publication of a Kalevala-meter ballad, *Morsiamen kuolema* (Death of the bride), by Daniel Juslenius (1676–1752) in his history of Turku (*Aboa vetus et nova*, 1700).

In the following century an antiquarian interest drove Finnish scholars to collect traditional poetry following King Gustav II Adolf's exhortation of 1630 to collect stories and legends about the past as a means of constructing the ancient history of Sweden-Finland. This particular interest accounts in part for the increasing attention paid by Finnish scholars to epic poetry about Väinämöinen and the *kantele,* to which reference is increasingly made in both poetry and scholarly works. Concurrently, in seventeenth- and eighteenth-century Finland the form, if not the content, of the Kalevala-meter tradition was adopted by a number of poets brought up in the great tradition and was also widely used for the composition of occasional verse. The awareness in Finland at the end of the eighteenth century of a lost oral poetry tradition is emphasized by the publication of two works that brought together the existing knowledge of the form, content, and context of the Kalevala-meter poetry tradition in Finland. Henrik Gabriel Porthan (1739–1804) provided a guide to the prosody and aesthetics of the tradition in his *De poësi fennica* (1766–78), and the encyclopaedic *Mythologia Fennica* (1789) of Christfrid Ganander (1741–90) listed and described alphabetically the divine, spirit, and heroic personages of traditional poetry and the milieu in which their acts were performed. As Annamari Sarajas observes, both authors illustrated their works with numerous citations from oral poetry collected in Finland (see also Kuusi et al., 33–34).

Cultural and Social Determinants
Thus there seems no doubt that the genres and themes of the Kalevala-meter poetry tradition represented in the archival corpus apply, in general terms, equally to Finland. Insofar as there are regional differences in the poetry, they can be explained in a general sense by variations in cultural and political circumstances. We know relatively little, however, about the detail of those circumstances in the early centuries of the tradition or about the actual process whereby the tradition spread. Archaeologists and historians have shown that the region where the Kalevala-meter poetry tradition flourished has known continuous human habitation for at least ten thousand years. Linguistic evidence indicates that at a relatively early period and lasting many centuries or even millennia, dialects related to the Lapp, Baltic-Finnic, Balt, and East Germanic languages were spoken in that region. During the first millennium after Christ the influence of East Scandinavian dialects spread into the western parts of the northeast Baltic region, while Slav dialects began to penetrate the eastern areas. Language contacts reflect cultural influences. Loans in the Baltic-Finnic languages from Old Balt and Germanic dialects indicate some change from a Stone Age food-gathering way of life to a more mixed culture with some knowledge of agriculture and basic social institutions. It is widely assumed that the religious world view of speakers of the Baltic-Finnic languages was animistic and that contacts with more powerful forces in the otherworld (the place where human souls existed before birth and after death) were

made through the mediation of a shaman. Forms of this way of life—with varying combinations of food-gathering and pastoralism—appear to have continued until the establishment of Christianity in the Middle Ages. The influence of the Eastern Vikings was powerful in Finland with a counterinfluence in the areas farther east from Novgorod.

Although Christianity became formally established in the twelfth and thirteenth centuries, features of Christian belief and legend had begun to penetrate the northeast Baltic region and to blend with local beliefs many centuries before the official conversion to Christianity, a phenomenon termed "barbarian Christianity" by the Finnish scholar Matti Kuusi. During the course of the Middle Ages a permanent cultural division was established between the various performers of Kalevala-meter poetry as the result of a confluence of factors, including formal conversion to the Christianity of either the Eastern or Western Church, the development of trade in the Baltic by the merchants of the Hanseatic League, the spread of German power along the southern shores of the Baltic with some penetration farther north, the spread of Russian influence from Novgorod and later Moscow, and the enforcement of political boundaries between Sweden-Finland and Russia. This division set in train the forces that led the traditional poetry to develop in different directions and that determined the nature of its eventual decline.

One of the most powerful factors in this process of differentiation and decline was the church. For more than three centuries, the missionaries and pastors of the Roman Catholic Church sought with some measure of success to guide the Finns away from the old beliefs and practices. After the Reformation the Lutheran clergy went about the task of stamping out non-Christian practices with renewed vigor. Although the pastors of the Roman Catholic and Lutheran churches succeeded in eradicating many of the non-Christian ritual activities that were accompanied by Kalevala-meter poetry, the form of the poetry itself proved remarkably resilient, particularly when adapted to convey Christian stories and ideas. Surviving versions of the fifteenth- or sixteenth-century melodramatic *Elinan surma* (Death of Elina) indicate the beginnings of adaptation for theatrical performance, and *Pyhä Henrik* and *Kaarle-herttua* almost certainly owe their composition to propaganda: the former to attract pilgrims to a particular church, and the latter to incite Finns to resist the perpetrators of rebellion against the king of Sweden. In contrast, the doctrine, liturgical practices, and organization of the Russian Church were able to be accommodating of indigenous cultural traditions. Compared with their counterparts in the Roman Catholic and Lutheran churches, the local Orthodox priests had had little education and thus lacked the theological understanding necessary to effect any profound changes in the old beliefs. Since many of the major Orthodox rites, particularly those associated with the rites of passage of marriage and death, were much closer to the pre-Christian practices, the adaptation of the old to the new took place with far less conflict and far more gradually than in areas to the west.

On both sides of the frontier between Sweden-Finland and Russia the speakers of the Baltic-Finnic languages inhabited geographical and cultural peripheries. Travel in either region was physically difficult at any time of the year. The principal isolating factor, however, was the lack of the education and social institutions necessary for the development of great-tradition culture. A medieval courtly tradition scarcely existed. Towns and cities were few and widely separated. The scant education that was available in the Middle Ages and for some time afterward was conducted in Latin and later in Swedish. The languages of administration were Swedish, German, Russian, or French; the language of commerce was one of various varieties of German. Thus for centuries, the vast majority of the population in the northeast Baltic region was not exposed to the influence of either the great tradition or Western popular culture.

During the early modern period, however, the effects of the rise and fall of Sweden as a great power followed by the rise of Russian power under Peter the Great gradually effected social and economic changes in Finland that were without comparison in Russia. The very different social traditions of Sweden-Finland brought about an increase in educational opportunities and more frequent contacts with other peoples, leading to the decline of the old traditions and the gradual adoption of Western popular culture, while the areas under Russian rule remained almost totally separated from the outside world. In Archangel Karelia the dominance of the old believers distanced the people from almost all change, while in the southern parts of Karelia and Ingria the Karelian-, Vote-, and Ingrian-speaking populations were bound to the land as serfs of Russian-speaking masters. If possible, the cultural isolation of the Ingrians and Votes was even greater, because they lived in an area that was a patchwork of peoples speaking different languages. The Estonians were also bound to the land as serfs but in a feudal system handed down from the period of German rule and harsher than that of the Russians. Educational opportunities and the right to travel were for most speakers of these languages almost nonexistent until the nineteenth century and then only in restricted circumstances. The effect of these conditions on Kalevala-meter poetry, however, was to maintain it as a functional, socially integrative, and artistically creative force until very recent times.

One example is the lament as the oral accompaniment to various separation rites. In the eighteenth century, with the introduction of lifelong conscription into the Russian army, the traditional funeral lament was developed into a new subgenre performed as the young conscripts were taken away to the army.

Fixity and Ritual
Although it is not difficult to identify the cultural and political features outlined above in the surviving corpus of redactions and variants, care must be taken in drawing historical conclusions: an oral poem can have many ages. At its simplest the age of a particular variant dates from its most recent performance. Yet that variant, or parts of it, may occur regionally in such a way that composition and a phase of popularity can be assumed at a much earlier date. In some cases comparative analysis of textual features and distribution patterns may point to a poem that was once very different in function but that has been transformed in successive cultural periods in response to changing functions and taste. The varying and sometimes apparently conflicting roles of Väinämöinen — creator hero, culture hero, shaman, chieftain, viking, despised pagan leader — can be understood in the light of this process of transformation. Cultural transformation, however, was far from total. Some variants of a poem could be transformed, whereas other variants of the same poem remained unchanged. This phenomenon of fixity and change could repeat itself in each cultural phase, affecting in turn new poems as they were composed and absorbed into the common stock of materials.

The fixity of Kalevala-meter poems is particularly striking when compared with the techniques of composition in performance practiced by Serbian singers. Although formulaic structures and stock epithets played their part and could be handled deftly by skilled performers of Kalevala-meter poetry, the performers' determination to maintain a song unchanged from one performance to the next was powerful. A possible explanation for the fixity/change phenomenon is the continuing association of the poetry tradition with ritual behavior, a level of performance that survived into modern times alongside the aesthetic and entertainment levels. The most obvious surviving forms of ritual behavior concern healing, the prevention or cure of illness in people and their livestock. Less obvious types, though socially very important, deal with courtship and marriage; in these poems the role of erotic themes and the tormenting of the bride and groom can be seen primarily as educational and only secondarily as titillating. Any change in oral poems bound to ritual activity was viewed as a distancing from the mythical events on which the rite was based and therefore likely to reduce the effect desired of the rite. Such was the devotion to perceived continuity that singers would sometimes even perform words or phrases that they themselves no longer understood (especially in connection with lamentation). Yet the singers were not always successful, and change crept in. As Paul Kiparsky points out, singers made mistakes, or when their memories failed they resorted to substitution or composition.

Renewal and Change: Myth Poetry
Matti Kuusi has thrown some light on this pattern of change and diversification by constructing on the basis of theme and style a theory of the periodization of the development of the types of epic poetry that are dominant in Finnish, Karelian, Ingrian, Vote, and Estonian tradition (and that are also central to Lönnrot's *Kalevala*). The epic poetry recorded by Lönnrot and his successors can be divided into five main types: myth, shaman, adventure, church, and historical. Myth poetry describes acts of creation at the beginning of time, the creation of the world and of human, animal, and plant life (cf. *Kalevala*, poems 1, 2, 6). This is probably the oldest stratum of Kalevala-meter poetry and occupied an especially important role in ritual behavior. Knowledge of how a particular phenomenon was created or ordered at the beginning of time was essential to ensure the repetition of that act in the present.

Myth poetry is also the stratum of Kalevala-meter poetry in which universal features are most common. Poems about the origin of the celestial bodies and the earth from an egg are part of a tradition known from the eastern Mediterranean to the Pacific; another belief, attributing the forging of the heavens to a smith, Ilmarinen, also has its counterparts in many parts of the world. The shaping of the primeval seabed by the drifting, newborn god Väinämöinen recalls the performance of the same tasks by a boar in Indian myth. Similarly, the myth of how fire was brought to man by animals can be compared with myths recorded in Bengal and in northwestern America. The "world tree" myth of Kalevala-meter is also known over the same area as myths about the egg-origin of the world. Tales of the primeval bear who comes down from the sky, its life on earth, and its return to its father in the sky are known in most parts of the far North (cf. *Kalevala*, poem 46). The two predominant characters in this early myth poetry are Väinämöinen and the smith Ilmarinen. Their origins are obscure; they may have been gods of water and land, respectively. In the surviving material from this early period their roles are variously those of gods and culture heroes. The milieu in which they perform their deeds is an obscure North

Land inhabited by featureless godlike beings who exist through their acts rather than as personalities.

The Spirit World

The second phase in Kuusi's periodization theory comprises in large measure poetry describing superhuman acts, reflecting the animistic world view and the central role of the shaman. Dated by some scholars to the centuries immediately before the birth of Christ until about A.D. 500–600, this was a time of contacts with ancient East Germanic and Scandinavian peoples from whom the Baltic-Finns borrowed numerous technical concepts (e.g., plow, spear, sword, gold, iron, trade) and certain features of organized society (e.g., power, king, governance, judging). Evidence of early Scandinavian contacts is also present in themes about journeys and conflict. In the poetry from this phase the milieu becomes unmistakably that of northern Europe: forested, close to water, inhabited by small communities whose heroes struggle for brides and other possessions. The universe becomes more ordered. The god-heroes Väinämöinen and Ilmarinen are reduced in scale to shamans and tribal leaders; they are joined by other characters—Lemminkäinen, a young, reckless, impertinent shaman (cf. *Kalevala,* poems 11–15, 26–27), and Joukahainen, a feeble aspiring shaman whose hubris brings about his downfall (cf. *Kalevala,* poem 3).

Women also acquire a more prominent role, as mothers, wives, lovers, and servants, not infrequently outsmarting their rambunctious menfolk. Outstanding among the women is Louhi, Mistress of Pohjola (cf. *Kalevala,* poem 7), the land to the north of the homes of Väinämöinen, Ilmarinen, and Lemminkäinen. When Louhi's daughter is sought in marriage by the heroes from the south, Louhi demands as the bride-price the construction of the *sampo,* an object that brings its owner everlasting wealth. Although Ilmarinen succeeds in forging the *sampo* and later marries Louhi's daughter, she is soon lost to him (cf. *Kalevala,* poems 10, 16–20, 26–28). When Väinämöinen, Ilmarinen, and Lemminkäinen try to recover the *sampo,* a bitter struggle ensues between Louhi, transformed into an avenging flying monster, and the fleeing men from the south. As they fight, the *sampo* is smashed to pieces and lost at sea (cf. *Kalevala,* poems 39–43).

The poems that took shape during the second phase of development provide some insight into how the ancient Finns and their neighbors perceived the world around them. A division of the universe into three parts can be discerned. There are hints of a more clearly understood upper world, or heaven, indicated by references to two supreme deities, Ukko and Jumala, the former a typical thunder god. Although the character of the latter is less clearly defined in surviving poems, his importance is implicit in the adoption of his name by early Christian missionaries for the new god. Natural phenomena in the world of the living were governed by animistic powers. Human beings shared their world with a host of unseen nature and ancestral spirits to which were attributed the functioning of all natural phenomena for which people lacked an empirical understanding. Nature spirits, perceived in hierarchies, had to be propitiated through appropriate rites. The most important spirits were personified (e.g., Ahti, master of the waters; Tapio, master of the forests); the lesser spirits were denoted by the name of the object or phenomenon they were thought to govern.

Also close at hand was the third part of the universe, Tuonela—the Otherworld—where Tuoni ruled over the spirits of the dead. The spirits, especially those of one's own ancestors, had to be treated with special reverence and remembered on appropriate anniversaries. As possessors of the knowledge essential for the effective accomplishment of superhuman tasks, the ancestral spirits were able to influence the lives of mortals, even intervening in the acts of nature spirits. Communication between the living and spirit forces was the task of the shaman. Contact with Otherworld forces was believed to occur after the shaman had fallen into an ecstatic trance, often induced by dance and rhythmic chanting, enabling his soul to leave his body and cross the Otherworld River to Tuonela (cf. *Kalevala*, poems 16, 17, 25).

Vikings
The characteristic feature of the third phase in the evolution of Kalevalameter poetry—adventure—dates from approximately A.D. 600–1000, when the speakers of the Baltic-Finnish languages began to have contacts with the East Vikings, whose expeditions into Russia and down to Constantinople they may have joined. Motifs and themes familiar from the early Scandinavian sagas, and closely connected with the stories of the wooing of the daughter of the Mistress of Pohjola and the *sampo*, increase in number in adventure poetry. Further localization occurs in the imagery and language of the poems. Shamans take on the role of viking warriors; Otherworld journeys transform into daring adventures on land and sea. The warriors' deeds are cast against a background of intricate ethnographic detail, from the description of dueling etiquette and the ornamentation of a spearhead to boat design and sailing techniques. The boisterous poetry of the viking phase also brings into greater prominence the male-female relationship. One of the outstanding poems of this period, the stormy courtship and marriage of Ahti and Kyllikki, depicts the conflict arising from the irrecon-

cilability of Kyllikki's desire for a quiet family life and her husband's irrepressible longing for adventure at sea (cf. *Kalevala,* poem 11).

As the common stock of poetry was augmented through the composition of new poems and the re-creation of older material, syncretism came increasingly into play in the generation of new themes. This can be seen by comparing the Lemminkäinen shaman poems of Kuusi's second phase (probably once part of an initiation rite) with the Kaukamoinen viking poems of his third phase. The story of how Lemminkäinen, a precocious shaman, is punished by death for going uninvited to the revels of the gods became confused with the thematically similar tale of the viking Kaukamoinen. The latter attends a feast uninvited, insults the host, and kills him in a duel; Kaukamoinen seeks safety from his enemy's folk by fleeing across the sea to the "Island." Ribald poems about sexual abandon from other poems became associated with Kaukamoinen's adventures and in successive re-creations came to form an integral part of the Kaukamoinen cycle. The syncretic effect is seen in later re-creations of the Lemminkäinen cycle, in which a duel of spells fought by Lemminkäinen and another shaman acquired a new ending: Lemminkäinen defeats his opponent and flees to the Island, where it is he who engages in sexual adventures of Herculean magnitude. In other syncretic versions of the poem Kaukamoinen plays the shaman's role. Lönnrot, following the example of his informants, took the syncretic process one stage further, merging the Lemminkäinen and Kaukamoinen poems and incorporating fragments of several others to create the wholly new composite Lemminkäinen of the *Kalevala* (cf. Kuusi et al., poems 34–38; *Kalevala,* poems 12, 14–16, 26–29).

Christianity
The period of adventure poetry overlaps a period from approximately A.D. 900 to 1450, the fourth development phase: the arrival and establishment of the Christian Church, with its profound effect on the subject matter and function of Kalevala-meter poetry. Although the Church of Rome was officially established in Finland by the crusade of King Erik Jedvardsson of Sweden in 1155, features of Christian belief—"barbarian" Christianity— had been current in Finland for several centuries. Missionaries of the Eastern Church had also been active in Finland long before King Erik's crusade, as the Old Slav origins of the Finnish words for "priest," "cross," and "pagan" indicate.

During both the "barbarian" Christian period and long after the official establishment of the church in Finland the missionaries and priests did not hesitate to use the form and content of Kalevala-meter poetry to communicate the new Christian legends and doctrines. Väinämöinen continues to visit the Otherworld in search of knowledge to work his magic, although on his safe return, having overcome great and vividly described dangers, he advises the abandonment of non-Christian practices (cf. *Kalevala,* poem 16).

Russian Orthodox and Roman Catholic legends come together in the priests' long accounts of the life of the Messiah. Local northern features are introduced to make the unfamiliar landscape of the Holy Land comprehensible: a cherry tree becomes a giant whortleberry, and Mary skis over the winter snow to the stable at Bethlehem. Even the impregnation of Mary assumes a new form linked to the belief that women could become pregnant from eating a small object, in this case a berry (cf. *Kalevala,* poem 50). This early phase of established Christianity saw the translation into Kalevala-meter poetry of the most popular legends of both the Eastern and Western churches. In Finland, Kalevala-meter poetry was also used to propagate a local legend about the life and martyrdom of the patron saint of Finland.

The strength of the old beliefs was not easily overcome, as shown by the need to employ the old poetry, despite all its pagan associations, as a vehicle for conveying the new beliefs. The old pagan characters recur in the Christian priests' poems either in an exemplary reformed role or, later, to denote wicked or unenviable characters. In some poems Väinämöinen becomes a parallel figure with Herod as the symbol of evil; in a Finnish poem Herod and Väinämöinen replace the Emperor Maxentius as the tormentors of Saint Catherine. As the Christian priests grew more confident, they began to use the traditional poetry to denigrate ancient practices and popular heroes. A Karelian poem attacks the practice of fertility rites by suggesting that they make the "forests wither" and that only Christian rites can restore the trees to growth. A ritual healing poem of magnificent imagery, describing the slaughter of a giant ox by a dwarf, was parodied by a Christian priest in a new poem about a giant but thoroughly unheroic pig that frightened the life out of Ukko and his lesser gods when they attempted to sacrifice it (cf. *Kalevala,* poem 20).

It was Väinämöinen who became the object of the Christian priests' sharpest attacks. They mocked him in the eyes of the people for his senility: a man who could not tell the difference between a fish and a miraculous young woman come to care for him in his old age (cf. poem 5). More bitterly, borrowing the French legend of Saint Goar, they accused him of hypocrisy and of concealing an evil past. When Väinämöinen condemns a two-week-old fatherless boy to death, the child accuses Väinämöinen of incest with his mother. The priest thereon christened the child "King of the Forest Land," while Väinämöinen sailed away in a "copper-bottomed boat," to be swallowed up by the Maelstrom (cf. *Kalevala,* poem 50).

Historical Songs

In Finland, Kalevala-meter poetry began to lose its vigor as a creative form at the end of the Middle Ages, although it continued to flourish in Karelia and Ingria. The last creative phase was marked by historical songs composed for the most part during the sixteenth and seventeenth centuries. Many of these were propaganda accounts of wars between Russia and Sweden composed by Karelian and Finnish poets on opposing sides without the slightest regard for historical fact. To some extent they lack the poetic quality and sensitivity of poems of the earlier periods and frequently come close in tone and form to the seventeenth-century Finnish literary fashion of composing Kalevala-meter occasional poetry. On the Russian side of the border a certain amount of poetry was also inspired by the invasion of Napoleon. The final creative flowering of epic poetry was the Ingrian conscript song, which combined the pathos and sensitivity of lament with the detail and action of historical poems.

The Herderian Idea in Finland

Although he knew nothing of the extent or historical depth of the Kalevala-meter poetry tradition on his arrival as a student at Åbo Academy in 1822, Lönnrot found himself among intellectuals who were fully persuaded that a poetic tradition of outstanding grandeur had once flourished in Finland. The early romantic interest in local cultures, particularly in their oral poetry, which had manifested itself in works such as Thomas Percy's *Reliques of Ancient English Poetry* (1765–94), James Macpherson's Ossianic poetry of the 1760s, and the writings of Rousseau, had many decades earlier found a ready and informed response in Finland, as shown by the works of Porthan and Ganander. The need to develop a national culture in the Herderian sense, which had already rooted in Finnish intellectual circles at the end of the eighteenth century, had gained powerful stimulus from the creation of the autonomous grand duchy of Finland in 1809 and the attachment to Finland in 1812 of territory to the west and southwest of Lake Ladoga. Finland had become effectively a state within a state, in which, as the British scholar Anthony D. Smith argues, "the Finns formed a subordinate vertical ethnic community differentiated from the Swedish cultural élite and later from their Russian political masters that was a ready-made ethnic base for the national reconstructions of educator-intellectuals like Lönnrot, Runeberg and Snellman. . . . The past and its heroes was put to striking nationalist use" (*National Identity*, 67).

During the 1820s three national cultural imperatives began to place on a firm footing the collection, study, and publication of Finnish traditional poetry; the writing of national history; and the creation of a literature that was Finnish in spirit and eventually in language. These aims were largely achieved in the 1830s and 1840s. The *Kalevala* and *Kanteletar* are the most prominent achievements of these aims, but their compilation and reception also illuminate an essential part of the philosophical and political process in which history and oral culture shape and legitimize the collective sense of national affinity essential to the ensuing construction of a nation-state. Finnish scholar Lauri Honko has argued (in "The *Kalevala* and the World's Epics") that in shaping a "national epic" from oral poetry, the Finns came closer than any other people in Europe to implementing Herder's ideas. A unique coincidence of three elements contributed toward the development of a national culture: a rich oral poetry tradition (richer than the Finns themselves ever imagined at the beginning of the nineteenth century); an intellectual legacy from Porthan which had already set in train the study of Finnish language, history, and oral poetry; and political innovation that placed the Finns under rulers who for more than three decades looked benignly on the shaping of a Finnish identity.

Thus the change in Finland's political status in 1809 was followed by an upsurge of patriotic activity. The twenty-one years from 1810 to 1831 — the year of the foundation of the Finnish Literary Society to promote the publication of oral poetry and literature — typified the process, as Smith puts it, "of intellectuals in search of their roots" (*Ethnic Origins*, 178). These two decades saw the appearance in Finnish or Swedish of various patriotic journals (in which Finnish history and oral tradition were major subjects of debate), descriptions of the Finnish language and grammars, a major Finnish-Latin dictionary, articles and debate on local and national history, and various collections of oral poetry. A substantial part of this work was the outcome of fieldwork, including a five-year expedition (1824–29) by the Finnish scholar Anders Johan Sjögren (1794–1855) through eastern Finland, Lapland, Karelia, and other parts of northern Russia to study the origins, language, and culture of the "ancient Finns."

During the 1820s specific examples of the compilation of a "national epic" as part of a patriotic movement reached Finnish intellectuals from abroad, offering ways in which Finns might organize their own growing corpus of myths, legends, and fairy tales. Among the most important models reaching Finland were *Frithiofs saga* (1825), by the Swedish poet Esaias Tegnér (1782–1846), and selections from Vuk Stefanović Karadžić's Serbian folk poems translated into Swedish (*Serviska folksånger,* 1830) by Johan Ludvig Runeberg (1804–77). Tegnér's poem cycle provided an example of the use of Homeric models to recall an ancient viking era as a source of renewed moral values in the present and a restored confidence in the future. The Serbian poems offered evidence of the artistic quality and literary merit of "naive" poetry in the little tradition, exemplifying Herder's views of the importance of such poetry in establishing an awareness of one's local culture and thus of one's national identity. Tegnér's and Karadžić's work, particularly the arrangement of the latter's into the two distinct categories of "lyric" and "epic," point to the framework within which Runeberg and Lönnrot were to cast their own work in the 1830s and 1840s. Their cultivation of "lyric" and "epic" corresponds to what Smith calls the "poetic space" and "the golden age," concepts that he sees as characteristic of the early phases in the shaping of a national culture (*Ethnic Origins,* 181–83).

An Epic in the Making

Throughout this same period the corpus of Kalevala-meter poetry materials grew in size and variety. Increasingly, scholars began to attempt reconstructions of characters and events from the surviving materials. As early as 1818 the recurrence of similar fragments about the same characters and events collected in different parts of Finland and Värmland prompted some patriots — above all C. A. Gottlund — to ask whether these poems might be arranged in an epic comparable to the *Iliad, Odyssey,* or *Nibelungenlied.* The mythical character on whom Finnish scholars began to focus their attention was Väinämöinen, whose numerous and various roles were already well known. During the 1810s he had been the subject of art and drama; in the following decade historians began to reconstruct his "historical character" on the basis of Kalevala-meter poetry. Lönnrot himself studied under the most important of these historians, Reinhold von Becker (1788–1858), and in 1827 incorporated his teacher's ideas in a dissertation entitled *De Väinämöine priscorum fennorum numine* (Concerning Väinämöinen, divinity of ancient Finns). Moreover, there was a growing awareness of the existence of traditional Kalevala-meter poetry outside Finland. Gottlund (1796–1875) and other young Finns who had studied at the University of Uppsala in the 1810s had discovered a Finnish poetry tradition among the descendants of Finns who had migrated to Värmland more than two centuries before. Sjögren, while still a student at Åbo Academy, brought back from a visit to Ingria in 1816 firsthand information about the tradition there. Above all, an awareness began to grow of an epic tradition of great richness among the Russian Orthodox Karelians across the frontier in Archangel Karelia. Zachris Topelius (1781–1831) wrote of this in his five-part collection *Suomen Kansan Wanhoja Runoja ynnä myös Nykyisempiä Lauluja* (1822–31; Old poems of the Finnish people together with more modern songs). Sjögren, traveling in Archangel Karelia in 1825, located the villages where some of the best singers lived, noted down their poems, and sent this information back to Åbo Academy. The excitement aroused among Finnish intellectuals by reports of the poetry tradition flourishing just across the frontier can be seen from Runeberg's inclusion of Archangel Karelia and its singers as a theme in his Homeric fantasy of contemporary rural Finnish life, *Elgskyttarne* (1832; The elk hunters).

This recognition of the need for systematic collection of Kalevala-meter poems, wherever they were to be found, and their publication was one of the main reasons for the foundation of the Finnish Literary Society in 1831. The same year, the society decided to support Lönnrot as the man best suited to undertake this work: a man trained in classical studies, about to qualify in medicine (the subject of his thesis was the magic medicine of the Finns), and a vigorous exponent of the need to compile an epic. After completing his study of Väinämöinen, Lönnrot had already set about preparing a more comprehensive collection of Kalevala-meter poetry based on published materials and poems he intended to collect himself. To this end he had traveled to Finnish Karelia and the provinces of Savo and Häme in 1828, and between 1829 and 1831 he had published four parts of what was to be a five-part collection, *Kantele*. With the support of the Literary Society, Lönnrot was able to travel farther afield and between 1831 and 1835 undertook three collection journeys to Archangel Karelia. At the same time — supporting himself partly by grants from the society and partly by working as a physician — he began to arrange his materials into an epic whole.

The Kalevala *World*

The *Kantele* shows clear signs of the development of Lönnrot's collection and compilation methods. Lönnrot used his materials freely, concatenating and patching where he felt it necessary. On his later collection journeys he assembled 25,700 lines of Kalevala-meter poetry, comprising epic, lyric, and spell poetry. His preparatory drafts indicate that he brought together materials, often disparate in provenance, about specific characters and events (e.g., Väinämöinen, Lemminkäinen, weddings). There is considerable debate about his approach to compilation. Although it exhibits certain characteristics of the theory of F. A. Wolf (1759–1824) about the composition of the *Iliad* and *Odyssey*, the extent to which Lönnrot was conscious of Wolf's work and the subsequent debates among German scholars is uncertain. What is clear is the influence of Lönnrot's thorough education in the classics (Honko, "*Kalevala:* The Processual View"). Indeed, Lönnrot himself draws a comparison in the preface of the 1835 *Kalevala* to ancient Greek epic and the Icelandic sagas, concluding his preface on a somewhat apologetic note: I would not want the songs to be disparaged, he said, or, on the other hand, to be biasedly regarded as very great. These are not by any means on a par with those of the Greeks and Romans, but it is quite right if they at least show that our forebears were not unenlightened in their intellectual efforts, and the songs at least demonstrate that (cited by Francis Peabody Magoun Jr. in his prose translation of the *Kalevala*, 373).

The same preface also elaborates in some detail Lönnrot's perception of the relationship of the events in the *Kalevala* to possible historical happenings: that the subjects sung about in the songs were not all without some foundation in fact is easily understood, but what the real truth is — what things may be described in some other way in a song, what ones may be completely invented — is now quite difficult to distinguish. Certain matters, even odd things or somewhat incredible ones, should on careful investigation somehow clear up. None of us should view Väinämöinen's and Ilmarinen's troubles as deriving from the disappearance of the sun and moon, and how should the dame of North Farm (*Pohja*) have hidden them in the hill? But when one remembers what is said of our forefathers' coming here, that they got to the far North from very southerly lands, and in view of what we know about the disappearance of the sun in winter in high latitudes, we will realize that this phenomenon could, as something strange to them, even arouse a great fear that the sun had gone forever (cited by Magoun, 367).

In the same vein Lönnrot comments on the mythologization of the historical characters around whom the main action of the epic revolves. His explanation of his work's title, "Land of Kaleva," illuminates further his own understanding of the epic's role as mythical history, for he presents Kaleva as the ancient leader of the more frequently mentioned heroes: Väinämöinen, Ilmarinen, and Lemminkäinen.

Although the preface to the 1835 *Kalevala* is silent on the time and space in which Lönnrot believed the mythical history of the Finns to have taken place, he discussed this question in an article published a year later and returned to it in some detail in the preface to the 1849 edition. In a section entitled "The Time of the Genesis of the Songs and the Original Home"

Lönnrot dates the events as beginning in the first millennium of the Christian era and ending with the arrival of Christianity in Finland in the twelfth century. The theater of action is located in the area bordered in the east by a line running south from the southwest shore of the White Sea through Lakes Onega and Ladoga, and by the Gulf of Finland in the west.

That segment of the Finns living in Russian Karelia, among whom these songs have been preserved through the centuries, seems to have been a tribe directly descended from the old, rich, powerful, and famous Permian people (Bjarmians of the Norse sagas). More than other Finns, they have a certain external culture inherited from olden times, curious traces of communal life, an extraordinary zeal for trade that throws off all rebuffs and obstacles, speed both in bodily movement and in presence of mind in their enterprises, all of which, including at the same time their remembrance of songs, the Swedish loanwords encountered in their language, and the unique ornaments of the womenfolk, is best explained by the consideration of old Permian times. In physical agility, quick-wittedness, and a desire to trade, the Finnish Ostrobothnians and the Karelians are nearest akin to them, the latter together with the Ingrians also in remembering songs (Magoun 377–98).

Lönnrot elaborated the ancient history of the Finns with an account of how for much of the millennium the people of the land of Kaleva had had to pay tribute to a people farther north, in Pohjola; it was only the heroic efforts of Väinämöinen, Ilmarinen, and Lemminkäinen that had ended this domination and allowed the land of Kaleva to grow in prosperity. The ideas from which Lönnrot shaped his mythical context were not fanciful by the scholarly criteria of his day. Quite the contrary, they represented the very latest thinking on the ancient history of the Finns and Karelians, distilled from the research published by Sjögren in the annals of the Imperial Academy of Sciences in St. Petersburg between 1830 and 1834 following the completion of his five-year journey of investigation of the peoples of the Russian North (see Branch, *A. J. Sjögren*).

Compilation
Against this background of what was perceived as historical fact, inspired by an ambition to show some comparability with classical Greek epic, and with the concatenation methods of the best Karelian singers of epic fresh in his mind, Lönnrot prepared his mythical history of the Finns. The editing and compilation techniques he had already demonstrated were applied to his corpus of freshly collected materials. His sources were very raw: the

motifs were obscure to anyone from outside the singer's district; many themes were allusive, since the singers assumed their listeners were familiar with the narrative; observance of the prosodic conventions of the Kalevala meter was often only partial. Above all, the language of the poems required substantial revision, for many of them were recorded in dialects that were incomprehensible to Lönnrot's readers.

In addition to basic editing tasks, Lönnrot had to shape his materials into a series of self-contained entities complete with an internal coherence and an external logic that would hold together the thirty-two poems of his *Kalevala*. Lönnrot stated that he had been guided in his approach by the example of his most gifted informants. He saw in the concatenation by these singers of runs of poetry on related themes — often producing narratives of up to one thousand lines — a mode of performance handed down by the bards of the "golden age." This assumption persuaded him that he could legitimately imitate the most versatile of his informants and arrange his materials to convey the specific motifs and themes he thought appropriate to meet the needs and aspirations of his own day (see Kaukonen, *Lönnrot ja Kalevala*, 56–86). Honko (*The Great Bear*) points to an outstanding version of the *sampo* poem recorded by Lönnrot from the renowned Archangel Karelian singer Ontrei Malinen as the specific inspiration of the general structure of the *Kalevala*. In Honko's view Malinen's variant of the *sampo* cycle gave Lönnrot the idea of dividing it into its three main parts. He used the first and second parts — creation and courtship, including the construction of the *sampo* — for the opening of the *Kalevala* and to point the direction for its continuation; the last part of the cycle — the theft of the *sampo* — sets in train the series of events that brings the epic to its conclusion.

Structure
Apart from some changes in the sequence of events, the two editions of the *Kalevala* have a common thematic structure. The differences between the 1835 and 1849 editions lie principally in the quantity of material used for each episode. *Kalevala* can be divided into twelve episodes:

— Prologue. Birth of the hero Väinämöinen, his creation of the cosmos and after that the earth. (1835, poem 1; 1849, poems 1–2)
— Väinämöinen's various efforts to acquire a wife, focusing on the wooing of the daughter of the Mistress of Pohjola and the need to construct in settlement of the bride price a magic device (the *sampo*) that ensures its possessor everlasting wealth. The smith Ilmarinen

forges the *sampo;* the people of Pohjola keep the bride price but refuse to hand over the bride to Väinämöinen. (1835, poems 2–5, 31–32; 1849, poems 3–10)
— Though already married, Lemminkäinen woos the daughter of the Mistress of Pohjola and is refused (1835, poems 6–8; 1849, poems 11–15)
— Väinämöinen and Ilmarinen compete for the hand of the daughter of the Mistress of Pohjola by the accomplishment through supernatural means of various impossible tasks. Ilmarinen is finally chosen as the successful suitor. (1835, poems 9–12; 1849, poems 16–19)
— Wedding of Ilmarinen and the daughter of the Mistress of Pohjola. (1835, poems 13–16; 1849, poems 20–25)
— The wedding celebrations are interrupted by the resurrected Lemminkäinen, who provokes a duel with his host. Lemminkäinen's subsequent flight and erotic adventures form a miniature epic within the main structure. (1835, poems 17–18; 1849, poems 26–30)
— The Kullervo story. The son of a great family, cursed at birth and brought up as a serf in Ilmarinen's family, Kullervo brings about the death of his malicious mistress, fails to reconcile himself with his fate, and commits suicide. (1835, poem 19; 1849, poems 31–36)
— Ilmarinen forges himself a new wife, is dissatisfied, travels to Pohjola to woo his wife's younger sister, but is refused. (1835, poem 20; 1849, poems 37–38)
— The heroes of the land of Kaleva sail to the north in order to steal the *sampo* from Pohjola. On the way they create the primordial *kantele* from the jawbone of a giant pike. The music of the *kantele* allows them to put their enemies to sleep and take the *sampo*. When the party is overtaken at sea by Louhi and her warriors, both the *kantele* and *sampo* are destroyed in battle, although small fragments of the *sampo* saved by the heroes of the land of Kaleva bring fertility to their land and waters. (1835, poems 21–23; 1849, poems 39–43)
— The land of Kaleva flourishes. A new *kantele,* carved from birchwood, gives the bard Väinämöinen the power to create harmony among humankind, the spirit world, animals, and the whole of nature. (1835, poems 24, 29; 1849, poem 44)
— The people of Pohjola seek revenge on the land of Kaleva by sending diseases and a great bear to ravage it and by stealing the sun and moon. All three attempts are defeated by the skills of the shaman-leader Väinämöinen, leaving the people of Kaleva secure in their prosperity under his leadership. (1835, poems 25–28; 1849, poems 45–49)

— A child born to the virgin Marjatta brings new songs to the people of the land of Kaleva. Väinämöinen is displaced as leader and departs, promising to return when his people need him again and leaving them his *kantele* and his songs. Epilogue. (1835, poem 32; 1849, poem 50)

Authenticity

As Honko has pointed out in "The *Kalevala:* The Processual View," the *Kalevala* can be approached from three different angles: as folk epic, as Lönnrot's epic, and as a national epic. Honko's consideration supersedes in many ways the generations of dispute, starting almost as soon as the *Kalevala* had appeared, about whether it was authentic oral epic. The extent to which *Kalevala* can be said to represent Finnish, Karelian, or Ingrian Kalevala-meter oral tradition is small. The *Kalevala* itself is based principally on carefully selected poems from a narrow Finnish-Karelian border zone and represents what Lönnrot chose it to represent rather than any mental picture his singers may have had of their tradition. When Lönnrot's *Kanteletar* is taken into account, however, it can be argued that the contents of the two compilations are — though only in the broadest sense — representative of many of the main themes and motifs of Kalevala-meter poetry as a whole.

Lönnrot appears to have perceived authenticity as fidelity to the lines actually sung by his informants. By these criteria he was scrupulous in his use as far as possible of lines recorded in the field; according to one calculation, no more than six hundred lines of the 1849 edition of the *Kalevala* were composed by Lönnrot himself (Kaukonen, *Lönnrot ja Kalevala*, 72). Thus no single episode in the *Kalevala* is represented by a poem as actually performed by Lönnrot's or, with respect to the 1849 edition, his assistants' informants. Instead, each episode is based on a series of poems, often quite disparate, from which Lönnrot selected the required passage, phrase, or single line. Where he had one or more variants of the same poem, he extracted the version of a particular theme which he judged best-suited for his own mental narrative, often regardless of the distinctive stylistic features, much less the function, inherent in the individual variants.

Reception

The 1835 *Kalevala* appeared in an edition of five hundred copies that finally sold out twelve years later. Something is known of the readership from reviews and the documented response of Lönnrot's contemporaries. Although reliable statistical evidence is lacking, an examination of the membership of the Finnish Literary Society and subscribers to the principal Finnish patriotic periodicals prepared by the Czech scholar Miroslav Hroch—two of his benchmarks for gauging the volume and development of nationalist activity—indicates that despite its small circulation, Lönnrot's epic was central to the circles most active in promoting patriotic ideas. Those who had not or could not read the epic would certainly have read about it, for articles of an increasingly polemical nature about Lönnrot's work appeared in the patriotic press in the years following its publication.

The documented response to the 1835 edition of the *Kalevala* reflects the changing nature of the Finnish national movement in the late 1830s and the 1840s as, on the one hand, cultural nationalism gathered strength and transformed into political nationalism and, on the other hand, the once benign attitude of the Russian authorities changed to one of suspicion and fear as the political power of nationalism asserted itself in various parts of Europe. The immediate response in Finland to the publication of the *Kalevala* was to welcome the epic for both its historical and literary value. In 1836 the president of the Finnish Literary Society wrote: The treasure of ancient Finnish songs that has recently been published at the society's expense is important not only because the native literature has been immeasurably enriched but because it has also acquired a European importance. Indeed, one can say without exaggeration that our literature has for the first time emerged from its cradle. In possession of its epic poems, Finland shall learn with growing self-confidence how to understand its future spiritual development. It will be able to say to itself, "I too have a history! My earliest monuments tell not of the bloody deeds of heroes but of the gentle pursuits of the bard who, unnoticed in the valleys, gave expression to the brief joys of life and its many pains."

More detailed responses later in the 1830s and at the beginning of the 1840s treat the *Kalevala* as a true representation of a lost epic, concentrating on and debating the historical accuracy with which the various characters and events have been represented. By the mid-1840s, however, discussion of the *Kalevala* began to question whether it was an epic at all and what should be the function of a "national literature." This shift in interest and attitude was symptomatic of the changing nature of nationalism and the nationalists' aims.

Kanteletar

For his part, Lönnrot turned his attention from epic to what he regarded as lyric and set about the compilation of the *Kanteletar*. The work appeared in its first edition in three parts in 1840–41, comprising 652 Kalevala-meter poems numbering 22,201 lines together with twenty-four examples of more recent songs mostly of west European origin. A posthumous revised edition in 1887 was enlarged by some 77 poems, most of which were removed from the third and final edition of 1901. The *Kanteletar* represents in many ways a continuation of Lönnrot's *Kantele* in that his new compilation combined poems that had already been published with poems he collected himself while traveling in eastern Finland and Karelia between 1836 and 1839. His compilation approach to the poems was very much the same as in his *Kalevala*. Although the nature of his materials did not lend itself so readily to composite line-by-line compilation, he continued to exercise a strong hand in the editing of language.

As in the *Kalevala*, the Preface is illuminating, throwing further light on Lönnrot's perception of oral poetry. His explanation of how oral lyric poems have no authors but are the collective product of the people as a whole ("the folk poem makes itself") reveals yet again the influence of Herder, as does his hope that "the new Finnish poetry will be founded on the cornerstone of the old poetry." Taken as a whole, the Preface with its wide-ranging and often comparative discussion of oral poetry in both a Finnish and a European context represents a major didactic document in the shaping of a literature in Finnish. Keith Bosley has succinctly captured the nature and quality of the *Kanteletar* in the introduction to his own translation: "The *Kanteletar* is about everyday life, so it gives a more comprehensive picture [than the *Kalevala*] of the society which produced it, including its religious beliefs: Christian elements are common, reaching their fullest expression in 'The Ballad of the Virgin Mary.' . . . Such comprehensiveness makes the *Kanteletar* not only a more useful tool than the *Kalevela* for students of Finnish culture, but above all a work of universal appeal, since few other nations have sung of ordinary things in poetry of such intensity" (p. xix). In this respect the *Kanteletar* signals the new ideas that are beginning to preoccupy Finnish intellectuals as the shaping of a national identity adopts a more prominent political stance.

Structure

The first two books of the *Kanteletar* contain lyric poetry, which Lönnrot divides into eight categories, four in each book. The first of his categories comprises "general" poems performed by men and women. For the most part introspective, these poems dwell poignantly, movingly, sometimes melodramatically on the hardships and deprivations of backwoods life. The second category, devoted to wedding poetry, provides a sense of the ritual sung dialogue that accompanied first the courtship and settlement of the marriage terms at the bride's home and then the actual wedding rites. Many of the poems in the third and fourth categories — herdsmen's and children's songs — are in the same tone as the general songs, though spiced with an occasional flash of earthy humor. The four categories of the second book, characterized as "special songs," are "Girls' Songs," "Women's Songs," "Boys' Songs," and "Men's Songs." The songs for female performance dwell partly on the search for a husband, courtship, loss or lack of a husband, and partly on life after marriage, particularly on children and the character of husbands. The search for a wife and courtship are also among the themes for male performance. More specifically for male performance, Lönnrot includes various songs about the act of singing, war, and hunting. Characteristic of all the songs is the awareness of poverty and the frailty of the individual in the face of forces over which he or she has no control. As in the first book, the dominant tone is one of poignant melancholy in which the singers frequently regret the fact that they had ever been born or long for death. In their lullabies mothers even wish the mercy of death on their babies.

The third book of the *Kanteletar* reproduces what Lönnrot called *virsilaulut* (an approximate translation might be "ritual songs"). He ordered them in three loose thematic categories: old religious poems, historical poems, and tales (often supernatural in theme). By present-day criteria most of the materials in the third book would be categorized as epic from the later phases in Kuusi's periodization scheme. They include legend poems and popular poems about supposedly historical events, and the mixed genre of lyric-epic. Curiously, the poem with which Lönnrot introduced his third book, *Suomettaren kosiat* (Suitors of Suometar [Finland personified as a female spirit]), was not a Finnish poem but a translation from an Estonian redaction of a widespread poem warning girls to beware of strangers and to choose their husbands from their own area and background. Lönnrot gave the poem a cosmic dimension by making the suitors the sun and moon, who were rejected, and the pole star, whom the poor orphan Suometar accepted. Later part of the canon of the Finnish national movement, *Suomettaren kosiat* came to symbolize the need for a Finnish culture to preserve its own distinct identity in the face of powerful influences from both east and west (Kuusi et al., 569).

From Cultural to Political Nationalism
It is possible that Lönnrot included *Suomettaren kosiat,* a poem obviously different from anything else in the collection, because of its cultural-political allusions. In the late 1830s some members of his generation had already begun to see their strengthening sense of national identity as leading of

necessity to the creation of a nation-state. The most prominent and influential of those who advanced this idea, Johan Vilhelm Snellman (1806–81), a Hegelian philosopher-politician, believed that a national culture was meaningless without a conscious national spirit and that the basis of a national spirit was the national language and a literature in that language. In the 1840s Snellman established himself as the unchallenged leader of those working for these aims.

Snellman had been one of those who wrote critically about the 1835 *Kalevala* on the grounds that it did not adequately take account of the Hegelian concept of the development of nations. This criticism was taken up and expounded in 1845 and 1846 when the function of epic became once again the subject of debate led by a young philosophy docent at the Alexander University in Helsinki, Robert Tengström (1823–47). Tengström, a powerful exponent of Hegelian thinking, criticized Lönnrot's *Kalevala* for not offering a satisfactory depiction of the life of the ancient heroes at the time of their primeval, unalienated existence. In Tengström's view Lönnrot had not made explicit the development of the Finns through the various stages of family and society toward national unity, nor had he in the latter part of the epic portrayed adequately the essence of the national spirit that should form the basis of the new national identity (see *Lönnrot ja Kalevala,* Kaukonen, 87–112; Karkama).

The New Kalevala

In 1847 Lönnrot decided to rework his *Kalevala*. The debate of the previous years and the cultural-political conditions of the time had worked their influence on his concept of epic and the function of his *Kalevala*. It is clear that he had taken Tengström's criticisms to heart. The hardening attitude of the authorities toward the national movement forced Lönnrot to adopt a political position. In a letter about his decision to rework the *Kalevala* he explained that apart from the practical reason that the old edition had sold out, he needed to undertake the revision without delay before the authorities put a stop to activities of this kind. Although the structure of the much-enlarged *Kalevala* was based on that of its predecessor, each episode was elaborated with the new material that Lönnrot and other collectors, traveling farther afield, had amassed since 1835. The treatment of the material also changed. In the 1849 edition Lönnrot is much more than a chronicler. The role of a politically conscious poet is obvious as he weaves into his mythical history the features that critics and admirers alike considered essential for a national mythology. It is striking to see how the revised *Kalevala* provides the fabric for the communication of the eight motifs Smith identifies as central to the typology of "any national mythology or myth of ethnic origins and descent": origins in time, origins in space, ancestry, migration, liberation, golden age, decline, rebirth (*Ethnic Origins,* 192).

In revising the *Kalevala,* as Pertti Karkama observes, Lönnrot moved away from the Wolfian concept of the epic to one closer to Hegel's: away from the romantic toward neohumanism. The influence of Hegel is especially apparent in the revised structure of the new edition. The first five episodes—the early phases of the people of Kaleva—retain the chronicle approach, though each is amplified with much new material. The remaining six episodes, however, have become far more dramatic in content. Not only are the characters more fully developed artistically but their behavior and actions raise ethical questions of right and wrong. A pertinent example is the seventh episode, the story of Kullervo, which grows from one poem to a miniature epic of six poems, introducing themes of fratricide, incest, suicide, freedom of individual will, and even thoughts on raising children. The *sampo* and *kantele* episodes are similarly developed with added detail, heightening of inner tension, and mythologization in the Epilogue of the *kantele* and Finnish oral poetry as the explicit symbols of a Finnish national culture.

In each episode Lönnrot's new material elaborates a picture of Finnish life in ancient times compatible with the criterion of a golden age. Milieu, dwellings, household duties, modes of travel all draw on contemporary ethnographical research in the depiction of an idealized society. That society itself is also defined more clearly with particular emphasis on women in their social roles—as daughters, wives, mothers—drawing freely and frequently on the materials Lönnrot had already published in his *Kanteletar.* The position of man in a world inhabited by gods and spirits becomes a recurrent theme, developed at length by the inclusion of many thousands of lines of spell poetry. Lönnrot uses these materials to reconstruct in much greater detail communal activities such as ancient hunting and agricultural rites, healing rites, and various *rites de passage* to produce a *Kalevala* that presents a picture appropriate to the requirements of the new times: an ancient society conscious of its identity and living in a well-ordered way according to a coherent and refined system of beliefs (Branch, "Invention of a National Epic").

After Kalevala
With the publication of the 1849 *Kalevala* Lönnrot virtually ended his interest in further development (he produced an abridged version of 9,732 lines in 1862). The impact of his *Kalevala* and *Kanteletar* on scholarship, the

arts, and politics, however, has been enormous and still awaits systematic analysis and assessment. Following the publication of the 1849 *Kalevala*, debate about the authenticity of Lönnrot's materials and the possibility of such an epic's having ever existed in ancient times revived and new expeditions were undertaken to collect Kalevala-meter poetry. The approach of successive generations of scholars to these questions—particularly the attempt to establish prime forms of poems and to trace their dissemination and change—led to the emergence of the discipline of folklore studies in Finland, with its emphasis on oral literature in the widest sense, and influenced the development of comparable studies elsewhere in the world.

In the arts *Kalevala, Kanteletar,* and Kalevala-meter poetry have provided inspiration for writers, dramatists, painters, sculptors, composers, and architects. In particular, Lönnrot's two works and the traditions on which they were based provided a distinctiveness of form and subject for the Finnish expression of the European fin de siècle. In recent years, especially since the sesquicentenary of the *Kalevala* in 1985, academic interest has renewed in the relationship between *Kalevala* and *Kanteletar* on the one hand and Kalevala-meter poetry on the other. In turn, this interest has begun to raise questions about the nature and working of national consciousness in the modern world. Just as the study of *Kalevala* in the past led to a wider knowledge and a more profound understanding of oral tradition, some scholars are now beginning to ask whether closer examination of the "*Kalevala* process" may offer comparable insights into the function of myth and epic in present-day cultural identity.

New Beginnings, Latin and Finnish

Kai Laitinen and George C. Schoolfield
Translated by Philip Binham

2

The Reformation and Agricola
Does God understand Finnish? In the preface to his prayer book of 1544 Bishop Mikael Agricola gave an affirmative answer to his own rhetorical query: "Yes, He hears the Finnish language call / Who understands the hearts and minds of all." Agricola's couplet is connected with two questions evidently much debated in his time: Is Finnish possible as a religious language, that is, a cultural language? and, Is it possible to write Finnish?

Finland was a part of the kingdom of Sweden from some time in the twelfth century (a possible date of "Saint" Erik's crusade to Finland is 1157) until the first decade of the nineteenth century, when, in the Russian-Swedish war of 1808-9, it became a grand duchy of Russia. What was valid in Sweden was also in force in Finland for some six hundred years: a common religion, a common legal code, the same social order and form of government. When the language of the church in Sweden was Latin, Latin was also used in Finland's churches; when the Lutheran Reformation, emanating from Germany, extended to Sweden, it also reached Finland. One of the main theses of the Reformation was that the Bible must be available to everyone in the language of the people. The work of Mikael Agricola (ca. 1510-57) was part of this campaign; his Finnish translation of the New Testament appeared in 1548.

There had, of course, been literary work done within the church before. The first writer known by name was the Swedish-speaking monk Jöns Budde (see chapter 6), from the fifteenth century, who had translated both religious tracts and some books of the Bible into his native tongue. Even earlier Finland had got its own texts in Latin — for example, the legend of Saint Henry, *De sancto Henrico, episcopo et martyre,* from the end of the thirteenth century, about the deeds and martyrdom of the English-born priest and, briefly, bishop of Uppsala, who is supposed to have accompanied Erik on the latter's Finnish crusade and then stayed on to carry out missionary work. In time, Henry became the patron saint of the cathedral at Turku (Åbo), consecrated in 1300, and of the whole of Finland. The first "Finnish" book—that is, a book printed expressly for use in Finland—was the missal of the Turku bishopric, the *Missale Aboense* (1488), from which the beginning of Finnish literature is reckoned today, although the work itself was in Latin, composed according to the Dominican liturgy, and printed in Lübeck. A later guide to funeral ritual, the *Manuale seu exequiale Aboense* (1522; Turku manual or exequial), was commissioned by Arvid Kurck (1464–1522), Finland's last Roman Catholic bishop, and printed at Halberstadt, but never actually came into use.

Latin was still cultivated within the church and among the learned for a long time thereafter. The *Piae cantiones* (1582; Pious songs) was a collection of about one hundred medieval Latin songs, both spiritual and secular, put together by the student and humanist Theodoricus Petri Ruuth (or Ruuta) from Porvoo (Borgå) and printed at Greifswald. Of these songs, research has shown that nearly fifty do not have equivalents elsewhere in Europe, and some clearly point to a Finnish origin. (Five years later, in Stockholm, Ruuth published an epithalamium, making him Finland's first neo-Latin poet.) The collection represents a culmination of Latin literature in Finland; it continued its influence in the Finnish-language sphere when the pastor Hemmingius Henrici (see below) translated it into Finnish in 1616 with the title *Vanhain Suomen maan pijspain ja kircon esimiesten latinan kielised laulud* (Latin songs of the old bishops of Finland and leading men of the church).

It is known that, even before the age of Agricola, Finnish was cultivated within the church in sermons and prayers, but such texts have not been preserved: thus Agricola has received the honorific title of "the father of Finnish literature." A peasant's son from Pernaja (Pernå) in eastern Uusimaa (Nyland), Agricola was bilingual in Finnish and Swedish; he received his preparatory education at Viipuri's (Viborg's) Latin school, went on to Turku, where he served as Bishop Martin Skytte's secretary, and continued his studies under Melanchthon and Luther at Wittenberg. (On his return home in 1539 he became the rector of Turku's Latin school and, in 1554, succeeded the gentle and pliable Skytte [d. 1550], a former Dominican appointed bishop in 1528; Agricola, much more unambiguously devoted to the Reformation than Skytte, had become his coadjutor in 1548.) The exact publication date of Agricola's earliest work, the *ABC kiria* (ABC book), is uncertain; apparently, it lay between 1537 and 1543, and the last of probably three editions came out in 1559. Its existence was not known until 1851, when its first page was found in the library of the University of Uppsala; still more came to light in the Swedish state archives in 1904, and sixty years later, eight final pages were discovered in the Västerås diocesan library, likewise in Sweden. The ABC *kiria* is not a primer in the modern sense but rather a selection of basic Christian texts, such as the confession of faith and the Lord's Prayer. Agricola's subsequent works were a biblical prayer book, *Rucous Bibliasta* (1544; Prayerbook from the Bible), and, most important, the translation into Finnish (from the Greek but with the aid of Luther's new German Bible) of the entire New Testament, a task begun in Wittenberg under Melanchthon's tutelage and finished in 1543 but not published until 1548 and, like the prayer book, printed in Stockholm. Agricola's *Dauidin Psalttari* (1551; David's psalter), a translation of the psalms, was followed by texts from the Old Testament in 1551 and 1552. In his prefaces Agricola also inserted rhymed poetry, modeled on the *Knittelvers* (rough three- or four-foot iambic verse, in rhyme pairs) much used in Germany at the time.

With his preface to the psalter Agricola gave some information about the old Finnish gods and Finnish mythology — thus aptly unveiling the two principal sources of Finnish literature, the biblical and the pagan. And by means of his entire oeuvre Agricola provided an answer to the two questions asked at the outset. Like Luther, he believed that the language of the people is the most important language of church and state. Further, he demonstrated by his example that Finnish could be used for literature and that serious, even sacred matters could be expressed in it. His orthography is still uncertain; he writes a Finnish that sometimes follows Latin, sometimes German, and sometimes Swedish models, but his vocabulary is excellent and extensive, and his sense of prose rhythm keen. Many grammatical solutions that he had to make independently are still valid today. The father of Finnish-language literature was not only a learned man but also a skillful user of his linguistic instrument.

Agricola's Successors
The continuers of Agricola's work were all churchmen, some of them, like him, reaching episcopal rank. Paul Juusten (ca. 1516–75), another product of the Viipuri (Viborg) Latin school (which was of special importance in the sixteenth century), bishop (1554–63) of the newly established diocese of Viipuri, and then Agricola's successor at Turku, not only wrote the first Finnish-language mass; he also compiled and expanded the *Chronicon epis-*

coporum Finlandensium, an account of the bishops of Turku from 1160 until his own day. Further, he told of his not altogether pleasant experiences in Russia—where, having been sent on a peace mission by Sweden's King Johan III, he had been imprisoned—in his *Narratio de legatione sua Russica* (ca. 1575); two hundred years later the tale of misfortune was published by Henrik Gabriel Porthan, Turku's central intellectual figure of the eighteenth century, a preamble to Porthan's scholarly edition of the *Chronicon.* Another follower in Agricola's footsteps, Jacobus Finno or Jaakko Suomalainen (ca. 1540-88), functioned from 1568 to 1578 and again from 1583 until his death as rector of the Turku cathedral school; at the behest of Johan III he put together not only a Finnish catechism (ca. 1580) but a prayer book, *Yxi Wähä Rucous Kirja* (1583; A small prayer book), and the first Finnish-language hymnal, *Yxi Wähä Suomenkielinen Wirsikiria* (ca. 1583; A small Finnish-language hymnal). The hymnal contained 101 hymns, of which about half had been translated by Finno from Swedish, some 10 from German texts (mostly Luther's); still others were from Latin, and 10 are by Finno himself.

The most important of Finno's emulators was the poetically more gifted Hemmingius Henrici (ca. 1550-1619), also called Maskun Hemminki, from Masku, the parish near Turku where he was pastor, already mentioned as the translator of *Piae cantiones,* in which he continued the development of Finnish rhymed verse. Earlier, however, he had compiled a new Finnish hymnal (1605), with the same name as Finno's, where he augmented Finno's work with 141 hymns, again translations from Swedish, German, and Latin, as well as 10 hymns of his own. (His version served as the basis of the Finnish hymnal until 1886.) Hemmingius's ecclesiastical superior, the bishop of Turku from 1583 until his death, Ericus Erici Sorolainen (ca. 1545-1625), brought out a translation of the Swedish church handbook and a larger and smaller version of the catechism (1615), but his major contribution to cultural history is his *Postilla* (1621-25) of twenty-three hundred pages, a sermon collection without a rival anywhere else in the North and a demonstration of the breadth of his learning and interests. (Sorolainen had scarcely led a sheltered life; during the Club War—the civil war in Finland in 1599 between the supporters of King Sigismund and Duke Charles of Södermanland—he had been imprisoned by the latter; eventually released, he regained the favor of Charles, now King Charles IX of Sweden. In the historical drama by J. J. Wecksell, *Daniel Hjort* [1862], about the capture of Turku Castle from the supporters of Sigismund, the bishop, able to see the tragic events *sub specie aeternitatis,* makes the curtain speech, asking if "love and faith / And duty and honor must bend like very reeds / And a thousand hearts be broken, that the world / Shall be shoved along an inch upon its way!") It was under the autocratic Sorolainen, in 1602, that a committee for the translation of the entire Bible into Finnish was formed, but the work dragged on, and by 1638, under Sorolainen's successor, the Swedish-born Isak Rothovius (1572–1652), a new committee — in fact, the third — had to be put together. It worked with surprising speed, completing its job by 1642, a tempo that may be explained by the possibility that Sorolainen and others had already finished a good part of the task. Credit must also go to this committee's chairman, Eskil Petraeus (1593–1657), the first professor of theology at the newly established Turku Academy (i.e., university, from 1640), also its first rector, and the author of the first Finnish grammar, *Linguae Finnicae brevis institutio* (1649), followed in 1689 by the grammar of Mathias Martinius.

The Hegemony of Swedish
The founding of the academy not only brought Finland its first printing press (1642, although the handsome *Biblia* was printed in Stockholm) but also encouraged the flow of learned men and of students to Turku from Sweden proper. The extensive Swedish-language literature that emerged from the academy during the next century and a half is discussed in chapter 6; Finnish-language literature, however, remained undeveloped, once the work of providing necessary devotional literature was completed. Many factors were at work here. In this period, when the Swedish empire was at its zenith, Swedish had to be the connecting link between the empire's several parts, Sweden itself, Finland, and the Baltic lands, and quite naturally it became the language of upward mobility, the language of administration and commerce. Just as Swedish officials and military men were stationed in Finland to a much greater extent than before (and officers who had served in the Swedish army on the Continent during the Thirty Years' War were rewarded with property in Finland's vast hinterland), so gifted young men of Finnish birth could and did make their careers in Sweden proper. The currents went both ways: notably, none of the seven bishops of Turku between Sorolainen (d. 1625) and Jacob Tengström — from Kokkola in Ostrobothnia and installed in 1803 — was born in Finland. (To be sure, one of them, Johannes Gezelius the Younger [1647–1718], first saw the light of day at Tartu [Dorpat] in Estonia, where his father — from Västmanland in Sweden and destined to be Turku's bishop from 1664 to 1690 — was professor of Greek, Hebrew, and Aramaic at the university the Swedes had founded in 1632, one more sign of Swedish expansion.) On the other hand, the noble Finnish family of the Horns provided Sweden with some of

its most effective military men during its Continental adventures, and Arvid Horn (1664–1742), after the death of his great and good friend Charles XII, oversaw the recovery of a much reduced Sweden; Adolf Fredrik Munck (1749–1831), from a much poorer Finnish family, became a favorite of Gustav III and, gossips maintained, fathered his son, the unhappy Gustav IV Adolf.

In Finland, Finnish had no prestige value whatsoever; for example, the citizenry of Turku and Finland's other towns, like the nobility, had become wholly Swedish-speaking, a process of linguistic change that continued and grew stronger throughout the eighteenth century. (Also, it should not be forgotten that considerable sections of the country, notably Uusimaa and Pohjanmaa [Ostrobothnia], had been home since the Middle Ages to an indigenous Swedish-speaking population.) The progress of English and the diminution of Gaelic in Ireland during the same centuries is a somewhat comparable phenomenon, although, under Cromwell's rule and after, it took place amid much crueler circumstances and was exacerbated by religious differences that did not exist in Finland.

Nonetheless, there are monuments of literature, of a kind, in the period from Sorolainen's death to the first sparks of a Finnish revival in Turku during the time of Porthan. It goes almost without saying that the Bible of 1642, printed in only twelve hundred copies and in a large and splendid format, could find its way to the chancels of Finland's churches but not to the Finnish-speaking public at large. At the order of the practical-minded Charles XI, it was reprinted in a much smaller format (and linguistically somewhat revised) so that it could be used, among others, by military chaplains, hence its sobriquet, "Charles XI's War Bible." The director of the project was Henrik Florinus (1633–1705), a pastor serving at the time in his birthplace, Paimio (Pemar), near Turku. The linguistic and organizational gifts of Florinus had already been put to good use in 1678, when he published a rudimentary Latin-Swedish-Finnish dictionary. Earlier, when he was rector of the school in Hämeenlinna, he may have participated in another multilingual project, the Latin-Swedish-German-Finnish version of Erasmus's pamphlet, *Libellus aureus de civilitate morum puerilium* (1530; The little golden book concerning the polishing of boyish manners), commissioned by the elder Bishop Gezelius and printed at Turku's new press in 1670. (The other candidate for the making of the Finnish text was the Turku rector Gabriel Tammelinus [1641–95], who also translated the Lutheran theologian Johann Gerhard's much-reprinted *Meditationes sacrae* [1606] into Finnish in 1680, thus providing a work of religious edification that reached fifteen Finnish editions by 1909.)

Florinus's often reprinted and useful dictionary was not, however, the first of its kind, predecessors having already appeared in 1637 — Ericus Schoderus's little *Lexicon Latino-Scondicum* — and 1644, the latter a project of the enormously wealthy Jöns Knutsson Kurck the Younger (1590–1652), the powerful head of the Turku supreme court. This Maecenas also commissioned a collection of Finnish proverbs by Laurentius Petri Aboicus (ca. 1605–71), which was then augmented and published by Laurentius's son-in-law Florinus as *Wanhain Suomalaisten Tawaliset ja Suloiset Sananlaskut* (1702; The common and pleasing proverbs of the ancient Finns), a work that was a forerunner of the burgeoning interest in Finland's popular poetry later on. Still another project originating with Kurck was the translation of Sweden's law code into Finnish, a task completed, but never published, by the official Abraham Kollanius (d. 1667). Here too, however, the idea at last bore fruit in the next century, when Samuel Forseen (ca. 1686–1744), like Kollanius a district secretary, was commissioned to translate the Swedish code of 1734. Forseen finished his altogether necessary job by 1738, but his work was subjected to such a long process of examination that it did not see the light of day until 1759.

Learned Works in Latin
Obviously, prose literature in Finnish, such as it was, consisted of works of an edifying, practical, or informative nature. Parallel to these efforts, there ran a much larger stream of Latin works, for example, "Finland's first encyclopedia," the *Encyclopedia synoptica* (1672) of the elder Bishop Gezelius, intended by the sternly orthodox Gezelius — who also favored the burning of witches — to keep the ideas of Descartes from penetrating the Turku Academy. This ponderous handbook was followed by his Bible commentary, completed and issued by his son — and then his grandson — in six volumes from 1711 to 1728, the earlier volumes published in Turku on the very eve of the Russian invasion of 1714, the later ones in Stockholm; the commentary was made on the basis of the Swedish Bible. More interesting by far than Gezelius's "encyclopedia" was the work of Petrus Bång (1633–96), from Hälsingland in Sweden and professor of theology at Turku from 1664 to 1678. Bång produced a series of twenty-one dissertations between 1672 and 1675 and had them printed as a book in the latter year under the collective title *Priscorum Sveogothorum ecclesia, seu historia ecclesiastica de priscis Sveogothicae terrae colonis* (The church of the ancient Sveogoths, or the ecclesiastical history of the ancient settlers in the land of Sveogothica), a fantastic account of Sweden's antiquity, whose first inhabitants were sprung from one of Abel's sons (and visited by Bishop Adam, his son Seth, and Cain's

son Enoch). After the Flood, Magog, at the command of his grandfather Noah, went north: Svecia was named after Sveno, Magog's eldest son, and Gothia after Getharus, his second male offspring. The book is close, in spirit, time, and wild imagination, to the notorious *Atland eller Manheim* (1679 ff.; Atlantica or Sweden) of the Swedish superpatriot Olaus Rudbeck (1630–1702), in which the Uppsala polyhistor constructed an extravagant, primeval "Gothic" or Swedish world, to be identified with Plato's Atlantis; but it is also an important step along the way to the world of Porthan and Lönnrot: in book 6, which describes Nordic religion and geography, Bång quotes, with Swedish translations, Agricola's verse list of the Finnish deities and, more striking still, a Finnish folk song about the bear. Thanks to the neo-Latin community of the times, the bear song was the first specimen of Finnish folk poetry to be known abroad. Kiel professor Daniel Georg Morhof (1639–91) quoted the "Bärenlied" in its entirety, with a German translation, in the chapter "Von der Nordischen Poeterey" in his poetics cum literary history, *Unterricht von der Teutschen Sprache und Poesie* (1682, 1700), where it forms the chapter's grand finale. Subsequently, Bång left Turku to become church superintendent at a still more distant outpost of the Swedish empire, Narva in Estonia, and then, in 1681, was appointed bishop in Viipuri. There he distinguished himself by setting up a printing press, in competition with Turku's, and by his exercise of tolerance, rare in the Lutheran clergy, toward the Greek Orthodox faithful of his diocese.

Devotional Works in Finnish

In Finnish two other large religious works of importance subsequently appeared. One was the sermon collection of Johan Wegelius the Younger (1693–1764), which came out in 1747–49 under the name *Se pyhä ewangeliumillinen walkeus* (The holy evangelistic light). With the pietism Wegelius had inherited from his like-named father (d. 1725), he created one of the most popular works of private devotion in Finnish, reprinted well into the nineteenth century and translated into Swedish as late as 1856. Still another work that rather belatedly followed the intellectual-spiritual developments of Germany was the *Hyödyllinen huwitus luomisen töistä* (1791; A useful diversion concerning the works of creation) of Johan Frosterus (1720–1809), called the first Finnish language exposition of natural history but, at the same time, a praise of the works of God as evidenced in nature (Frosterus was a pastor). In spirit it resembles the work of the Hamburg poet Barthold Hinrik Brockes, *Irdisches Vergnügen in Gott* (1721–48; Earthly pleasure in God), and *Die Alpen* (1732) of the poetic Swiss scientist Albrecht von Haller. (This "scientific" manner of devotional thought was often to be encountered in the eighteenth century; almost simultaneously with Frosterus's book, it found much more detailed and personal expression in an English classic, the curate Gilbert White's *The Natural History and Antiquities of Selborne* [1789].)

A Finnish Baroque Poetry?

Frosterus also wrote a poem, "Jumalan pyhästä laista" (1787; On God's holy law), which, composed as it was in so-called runometer (see chapter 1), the "native" Finnish verse form of popular poetry, stands at the end of a tradition cultivated desultorily throughout the seventeenth and eighteenth centuries. Certainly, Johan Cajanus the Younger (1655–81) — son of a pastor at Paltamo (Paldamo) (in Kajaani [Kajana], i.e., eastern Ostrobothnia), who had a reputation for combating the pagan remnants still plentiful there — had heard the runometer in his childhood; what is remarkable, though, is the way Cajanus incorporated suggestions of the strongly alliterative, three- or four-foot trochaic line of folk poetry into the extremely artful web of his great poem, beginning "Etcös ole Ihmis parca, aiwan arca" (printed in 1683; "Are you not, oh human, frail, forever assailed"). The poem's twenty-three strophes have four lines each, the first and third with six feet, the second and fourth with four, the first and third with internal rhyme, the second and fourth with end rhyme. The poem imitates contemporary models to some extent (for example, the funeral hymn of the Swedish poet Lasse Lucidor [1638–74]) but modifies and augments them with a good deal of independence. The result is the most impressive baroque poem in Finnish: a reflection on the evanescence of human life, the impermanence of worldly things, and the omnipotence of death, it is also a *consolatio* for the poet himself, in that the transitoriness of life is perceived as an inevitable law of nature, and security is sought in the Christian faith. In a somewhat altered or censored form the poem received a broad currency when the poet's relative, Erik Cajanus (1675–1737), included it in his new Finnish hymnal of 1701.

Cajanus's brief life was spent mainly in the academic ambience of the Turku Academy, where he served as a specially appointed professor of philosophy but could not be granted the chair in that field because of opposition — by Bishop Gezelius, among others — to the Cartesian philosophy he represented. His contemporary, Matthias Salamnius (ca. 1650–91), lived in a far less intellectual atmosphere; he spent some six years of his pastoral career in Ingria (where St. Petersburg would someday be built), a region where, later still, a large number of pieces of oral poetry would be discovered by Lönnrot and others. Salamnius's Swedish-language funeral sermons (1681) and his memorial for Gezelius the Elder (1690) show him at work in traditional forms of the European baroque; like all poets in Finnish of the time, he was bilingual. (A somewhat older poet in both languages, the Lapland pastor Gabriel Tuderus, is treated in chapter 6, since his poetry in Finnish is essentially a translation of his Swedish verse.) Nevertheless, Salamnius chose Finnish runometer for his major work, a singular treatment of a popular religious-poetic topic of the time, the "Messiad," or life of Christ. The *Ilo-Laulu Jesuxesta* (1690; Song of joy concerning Jesus) is composed of twenty-nine cantos, a total of more than two thousand lines of runometer, in which Salamnius richly demonstrated that folk poetry not only had preserved its vitality but also had extended its influence into Christian poetry.

In Agricola's list of gods Finnish mythology had already made an appearance, but presented critically, paganism as seen from the standpoint of Christian morality. A similar attitude continued to exist within the church for a long time, although small signs from the content of various poems suggest, on stylistic and metrical grounds, that the objectionable "pagan" mythology, and the folk poems that preserved it, was familiar enough to the clergy. (Many pastors collected and recorded the poems, encouraged by the Swedish College of Antiquities, established in 1667.) But from Agricola onward the aim of acceptable literary expression was to follow the models of the West and of classical antiquity. Folk poetry and Finnish mythology remained, as it were, underground, stamped as superstition; it was a kind of belittled or even forbidden undergrowth, over which rhymed poetry, in the Continental European tradition, formed its own, respectable stratum. In Salamnius's poem, however, there appears a phenomenon of blending — of what Michael Branch has called, in terms of cultural sociology, the "little" and the "great" traditions (see chapter 1). The former is home-grown and connected with folk poetry, its metrics, style, and mythology. The latter takes its model from the Bible, classical antiquity, and western European poetry (i.e., at the time of Cajanus and Salamnius, the poetry of the Renaissance and the baroque) and uses their metrics, rhymes, and mythologies. The little and the great tradition walk hand in hand in Finnish literature from this time on; evidence of the popularity of the *Ilo-Laulu Jesuxesta*, and its mixture of the traditions, lies in the fact that sixteen printings of the work appeared during the two centuries after its original publication; country people could "sing" long portions of it by heart, precisely as if it were folk poetry.

In 1700 the mysterious IGHS (initials that may refer to an assistant pastor in Haapajärvi, Joseph Gabriel Calamnius — i.e., "Iosephus Gabrielis

Haapajärviensis Sacellanus") saluted the victory of Charles XII at Narva with a song of joy, in runometer, praising "the great lord of the Swedish army," Charles, and thanking God on high. As the resurgent Russians invaded Finland a few years later in the Great Wrath, the brave Calamnius stayed at his post of duty. Many others fled, however, and what we today would call exile literature came into being. It was written largely in Swedish, both because of the language provenience of its authors and because it was intended as a kind of war propaganda to arouse the populace of Sweden proper (see chapter 6). Of its few representatives in Finnish, perhaps the most interesting—as much because of his checkered fate as by virtue of his writings—is Bartholdus Vhaël (1667–1723), the author of *Waikia walitus-runo* (1714; Melancholy poem of lament), in runometer, in which he implores Charles XII, interned by the Turks at Bender after his terrible defeat at Poltava, to return—"a beloved king" bringing peace to his homeland. Born in Oulu (Uleåborg), a military chaplain in Riga with the Ostrobothnian regiment and then pastor at Ilmola, Vhaël fled to Sweden during the Great Wrath but was taken prisoner by the Russians in Ylitornio in 1717 and was assigned by them as chaplain for the Germans in Russian service; the Peace of Uusikaupunki (Nystad) allowed him to return to his pastoral duties in Finland. His Finnish grammar, *Grammatica fennica* (1733), was a third handbook, after the efforts of Petraeus and Martinius, for those who wished to master the declining Swedish empire's most inaccessible language.

The other Finnish-language poet to write a lengthy verse account of the sufferings of Finland's populace at Russian hands was Gabriel Calamnius (1695–1754), the son of Joseph Calamnius, who looked back to the events of the worst years, 1714 and 1715, in his *Suru-runot suomalaiset* (finished 1720, printed 1734; Finnish poems of lament), a descriptive poem of atrocity in eleven cantos of runometer. But Calamnius, who became a country pastor at Kalajoki, far up the Ostrobothnian coast, also is responsible for a work of a different sort, the first collection of Finnish secular poetry, *Wähäinen cocous suomalaisista runoista* (1755; A little collection of Finnish poems), in runometer (occasional poems, epithalamia, funeral poems, congratulations on birthdays and name days). It also included a personal lament, a subgenre popular in the French Renaissance (with Ronsard's "Derniers vers") and the German baroque (with Andreas Gryphius and Simon Dach), at his own illness, in which he calls on the "Lord, my sole and single helper," for aid. One value of such poetry is that it gives a glance, however small, into the domestic life of the times; the same can be said about the often anthologized "Kehto-runo" (1728; Cradle song) of Henrik Lilius

(1683–1745), with which a Christian mother may sing her little child to sleep, promising it the honey-sweet milk of heaven. The short poem is a worthy predecessor to Anna's cradle song, sung near the end of Aleksis Kivi's *Seitsemän veljestä* (1870; Eng. tr. *Seven Brothers,* 1929, rev. 1973; 1991).

Juslenius

Once the trauma of the Great Northern War was past, the eighteenth century brought much more prose (of an informative nature) than poetry to Finnish-language literature, a statement that holds true for Swedish-language literature as well. As a matter of fact, at the century's very beginning Daniel Juslenius (1676–1752), one of Turku's most learned men despite his tender years, had published three dissertations, of which two, at any rate, were intended to increase the Finns' knowledge of themselves. Writing, of course, in Latin, in *Aboa vetus et nova* (1700; Turku old and new), Juslenius seemed to emulate both Rudbeck and Bång: for him, Turku was founded by Magog, Noah's grandson and Japeth's son, not long after the Flood; the Finnish language itself emerged from the linguistic hubbub occasioned by the Tower of Babel. (In his fantasmagoria Juslenius also included much information about the little governmental and academic city invaluable for cultural historians to this very day.) The second of the young Juslenius's dissertations, *Vindiciae fennorum* (1703; In defense of Finns), continues in the same patriotic vein but more generally. In an often quoted claim, he wrote that "poetry in Finland is cultivated by both learned men and peasants, in the latter of whom it is just as inherent as in the peasants of Arcadia, writing the fairest songs whenever they please and about whatever topic they please," both a curious prophecy of the peasant poetry of the nineteenth century and a reference, evidently, to the surviving folk poetry on which Lönnrot would draw for the *Kalevala* and the *Kanteletar.* Juslenius is thus qualified to be regarded both as a direct academic descendant of an earlier Turku student, the Johan Paulinus who wrote the famous Greek encomium of Finland in 1679, *Magnus principatus Finlandia* (see chapter 6), and as the forefather of Porthan and the myriad of nationalist enthusiasts the latter fostered.

Juslenius's third youthful dissertation, as the historian Matti Klinge (*Professoreita*, 47) remarks with some irony, was "on a theological topic which led to an assistant professorship in theology, and then to a professorship" of languages in 1712, where his inaugural lecture concerned itself, not surprisingly, with resemblances between Finnish and Hebrew. Fleeing to Sweden in 1714, like most of the Turku faculty, he was directly appointed lector of "eloquence and poetry" in the venerable gymnasium at Västerås, contributing to exile literature with a Latin lecture on the miseries of the Finns, "De miseriis Fennorum." Back home after peace was concluded, he advanced to professor of theology (then still the most prestigious discipline at the academy); in 1734, a defender of orthodox Lutheranism as stern as old Gezelius (who had engaged his services for the great Bible commentary), he was appointed bishop in the newly created diocese of Porvoo. (It was formed in 1723 to substitute for Viipuri, which had become Russian under the terms of the Peace of Uusikaupunki.) During the so-called Little Wrath in 1741–43, the swift Russian invasion ensuing on an inept attack launched by the Swedes against the Empress Elizabeth, Juslenius fled to Sweden once more, this time for good, becoming bishop at Skara. His service to his homeland was not yet finished, however: his trilingual dictionary, *Suomalaisen Sana-Lugun Coetus* (1745; Toward a Finnish dictionary), expanded Florinus's vocabularium, the *Nomenclatura* of 1678.

The Age of Porthan

As the century moved along and Finland recovered from the catastrophe of the Great Wrath, the interest in Finnish antiquities grew apace. (During the Little Wrath Turku and Finland suffered little under the mild governorship of the Russian-Scottish general James Keith.) The bishop of Turku from 1756 to 1775 (and previously professor of physics from 1742 until his episcopal installment), the polyhistor Carl Fredrik Mennander (1712–86), was sufficiently interested in folk poetry to arrange for the collection of a large number of songs — a treasure that has regrettably been lost; under his aegis his younger colleague in the academy, Henrik Gabriel Porthan (1739–1804), quickly emerged as the key figure in the now flourishing interest in the Finnish past. Born at Viitasaari in central Finland (his father was a pastor, his mother, née Juslenius, a niece of Daniel Juslenius himself), he spent his childhood — because of his father's mental illness — at Kruunupyy (Kronoby) in central Ostrobothnia, with another maternal uncle, likewise a pastor, and was enrolled in the Turku Academy at age fifteen. By 1763 Porthan was docent in "oratory," that is, classical languages; a year later he was appointed to the academy's library; and from 1772 on he was its extremely energetic director, a post to which was joined the professorship in oratory. The academy's most admired teacher as well as its most active mind, he gave his name to the period in which he lived.

Among Porthan's many deeds was the establishment in 1770 of the Aurora Society, together with the son of Bishop Mennander, recently ennobled as Carl Frederik Fredenheim (1748–1803) for his services to the Swedish crown, and Per Juslén (1739–94), Porthan's cousin, who became the society's first chairman, while Porthan was its secretary. The society's purpose was the furtherance of Finland's culture and literature; a "secret club," it was quite in keeping with the time's enthusiasm for mystifications, as in the case of the Freemasons or the Swedish Utile Dulci (1766–95), of which Fredenheim and Juslén were members. Nevertheless, its main accomplishment was an altogether public one, the foundation of Finland's first newspaper, *Tidningar utgifne af et sällskap i Åbo* (1771–78 and 1782–85; News published by a society in Turku), an undertaking that in its turn inspired the old churchman Anders (Antti) Lizelius (1708–95) to found a Finnish-language equivalent, *Suomenkieliset Tieto-Sanomat* (Finnish-language information paper), of which twenty-four numbers appeared during 1775–76. (Lizelius made another important contribution to Finnish cultural life when he was appointed to lead a committee with the job of reviewing the biblical translations of the past; the Lizelius versions came out in 1758 and 1776, and the second of them was to remain a standard, with some revisions, until 1938: the belletristic prose of Aleksis Kivi was patterned to a good extent on the language of Lizelius's second Bible.)

It is telling for the centrality of Porthan in Turku's intellectual life that, when he went off to Germany on his study trip of 1779, the *Tidningar* ceased publication. More than anyone else in the Finland of his time, Porthan kept up with major European intellectual currents (including the empirical philosophy of John Locke and the protoromanticism of Herder); his own research, however, was devoted entirely to Finnish matters and, save for excursions to Stockholm and the trip to Germany, he did not travel abroad — in this respect much like Runeberg. From the standpoint of Finland's literary history his most important work was *De poesi fennica* (published in separate disputations — i.e., academic theses — from 1766 to 1778 and never completed), in which he offered the first general survey of Finland's folk poetry, its possible genesis, its contents, and its metrics. By comparing different versions of the same poem, and thus attempting to establish the poem's original form, he laid a foundation for modern folk-poetry research and folklore studies. He was also deeply interested in philology and began another project, again unfinished, on Finnish dialects, *De praecipuis dialectis linguae fennicae,* as late as 1801. Some of his work was done in conjunction with other scholars, based on materials they had collected; thus in 1782 he aided Erik Lencquist, the son of a country pastor, in publishing the materials on Finnish paganism collected by the senior Lencquist (1719–1808), a work called *De superstitione et veterum Fennorum theoretica et practica;* he turned over the material he had collected for a great Finnish dictionary to his sometime student, Christfrid Ganander; further, he served as protector, inspiratory force, and fatherly friend to the young poet Frans Michael Franzén (see chapter 6): Porthan himself wrote undistinguished verse in Latin and Swedish.

A Finnish patriot who walked (much more soberly) in the footsteps of Juslenius, Porthan regarded his edition of Paul Juusten's chronicle of Finland's bishops (1784–1800) as his scholarly magnum opus, to which he may have been inspired by his meeting with the great German historian (and friend of Scandinavia) August Ludwig Schlözer (1735–1809) in Göttingen in 1779. Yet he very likely would not have been happy at the separation of Finland from Sweden, which ensued some five years after his death; in his letters he condemns the separatist efforts of such Finnish noblemen (in Russian service) as Göran Magnus Sprengtporten. A humanist who wrote his major works in Latin and corresponded in Swedish; a major author whose works, if read at all by anyone save scholars, are usually read in Finnish translation; a man who in fact completed little in his lifetime but served as spiritual parent not just to Franzén but, at a remove, to Runeberg and to Lönnrot, Porthan somehow defies definition, as can be seen in the question rhetorically posed by Johan Vilhelm Snellman in his Swedish-language but Finnish-spirited *Litteraturblad:* "Who was Porthan?" The question was used by the cultural historian Matti Klinge as the title for his brilliant summary of Porthan's life and work (1989).

Among Porthan's contemporaries and, in a way, co-workers, Christfrid Ganander (1741–90) was the most productive although, as a country pastor, he could not have Porthan's influence. His dictionary, based on materials sent him by Porthan, *Nytt Finskt Lexikon* (New Finnish lexicon), was finished by 1787, but having been returned to Turku for Porthan's correction and approval, it did not receive his nihil obstat and remained unpublished until 1937–40; nevertheless, it became the basis for Gustaf Renvall's *Suomalainen Sana-Kirja; Lexicon Linguae Fennicae 1–2* (1826). A project with a happier ending was Ganander's *Mythologia Fennica* (1789), written in Swedish and originally intended as an appendix to the stillborn dictionary; it was an alphabetical directory (with commentary) of Finnish and Lappish mythical names. A collection of Finnish proverbs made by Ganander also remained unpublished in his lifetime (it likewise seems to have failed to get Porthan's approval), but his collection of Finnish riddles, *Aenigmata fennica,* was printed in 1783.

The poetry of the "Age of Porthan" was unimportant; the time was one of collection and of preparation for a literature as yet unwritten. Ganander had his own small moment as a poet, writing a congratulatory poem to Porthan, in runometer, for the publication of the first part of *De poesi fen-*

nica; poetry—or versifying—ran in the family: a relative of Christfrid, Henrik Ganander (ca. 1700–1743), had composed a strange poem in 1743 called "Haudan mercki" (The grave marker), in which he essays the so-called lapidary style, putting a period after each word to simulate a Roman inscription. The verse of the several Achreniuses might also be mentioned, dotting an otherwise fairly barren poetic landscape. Abraham Achrenius (1706–69) was a productive maker of hymns (his pietistic urges temporarily caused his exclusion from the Lutheran clergy), which became very popular in their time and afterward; a title epitomizing his work is that of the collection from the year of his death, *Zionin juhlavirret, halullisten sieluin ylöskehoituxexi* (Solemn hymns of Zion, for the uplift of yearning souls). Printed in chapbooks, his hymns were spread far and wide through the Finnish backwoods, encouraging the more personal Christianity that lay at the heart of pietism. His son Anders or Antti (1745–1810), writing in the same spirit, put together the popular *Halullisten sieluin hengelliset laulut* (1790: Spiritual songs of yearning souls); a nephew of Abraham, Simon or Simo (1729–82), described in detail the torments of hell, using the two thousand runometer lines of *Uudet hengelliset runot läsnä olewaisista ja tulewaisista tiloista* (1766; New spiritual poems concerning past and future conditions), an ominous title if ever there was one. (Helpfully, Achrenius provided footnotes to illustrate the fires of hell with geographical comparisons; next to them, "Hekla, Aetna, Vesuvius" are as nothing.)

Simon's brother, Henrik Achrenius (1730–98), also had his share in the family's spiritual concerns, as illustrated by his poem "Katoowaisuus" (Transitoriness), written in emulation of Johan Cajanus's great poem of a century before on the same theme, about the fragility of man's existence, and, indeed, using the same complex strophic form, with internal rhyme: "Great creator, give us aid and grace and solace." But he took a much more worldly tack with his songs inspired by the Swedish poet of wine, women, and song, Carl Michael Bellman (1740–95); his imitative contact with the rococo world of Gustav III is further demonstrated by his fables in La Fontaine's manner. And beyond question, his "Tawallinen morsian tanssi" (A customary bridal dance) and his "Laulu papin-frouwille. 1. päiwänä touko kuusa 1792" (Song to the pastors' wives, on 1 May 1792) show a lightening of the spiritual gloom that had characterized much Finnish-language poetry thus far.

None of these Finnish-language poets could remotely compare, in talent or in receptivity of new currents, with Frans Michael Franzén, who left Finland for Sweden in 1811, once his homeland had come under Russian control in the war of 1808–9. The conflict was a sideshow of the Napoleonic Wars but an event of enormous import for Finland. With Porthan's death and Franzén's departure, it because clear that the "Swedish Age" (not just politically) had come to an end, but as yet there was nothing overwhelmingly and distinctly Finnish, in spirit or in language, to replace it.

Turku Romanticism and Nationalism
Finland's new situation was eased by the circumstance that Russian rule was remarkably benign; the country kept its Swedish legal code and its social and political system and enjoyed its special privileges inside the Russian empire almost to the end of the century. The favorable attitude held by Alexander I toward his new grand duchy was extended even to appropriations for the academy, which he doubled. Had he lived on, he would not have had reason to regret his openhandedness, for Finland was well behaved and loyal, remaining faithful to the czar (or emperor, as he was called in Finland, muting his Russianness) as long as those special privileges and laws were respected. Quite in contrast to 1714, almost all the faculty at Turku stayed put, save the luminous Franzén. At their head was Jacob Tengström (1755–1832), a native of Ostrobothnia who had been a member of the Aurora Society, an active amateur poet and musician, professor of theology (from 1790), author of primers for children and of biographies of two of Turku's bishops, editor of *Åbo Tidningar* (1791–93), and, from 1803, bishop—surely the most many-sided man to have held that post. (Elected to the Swedish Academy of Learning, History, and Antiquities in 1793, Tengström made an important contribution to the burgeoning interest in the pre-Christian Finnish past with his inaugural lecture, later expanded as an academic treatise, *Om de fordna Finnars sällskaps-nöjen och tidsfördrif* [1795–1802; On the social pleasures and amusements of the Finns of yore].) Called a traitor in some circles for the readiness with which he accepted Russian rule (his great-great-grandson wrote about him that "fearless stupidity created heroes who were revered, but wisdom that saved the country could not be forgiven"), he played an active part in the Diet at Porvoo in 1809, during which Alexander I assured Finland of its autonomous status.

Not everyone, to be sure, was as positive—or constructive—in the acceptance of the new constellation of power as Tengström. A docent in history at the academy, Adolf Ivar Arwidsson (see chapter 7), the most radical and "romantic" of the faculty's members, earned a permanent place in Finland's history with the winged words attributed to him: "Swedes we are not, Russians we do not wish to become, therefore let us be Finns." Another version has "Swedes we cannot be" in the first part of the tricolon, indicating a stronger emotional tie to the old motherland, to which Arwidsson eventually emigrated, having made himself persona non grata in Turku. The major point of Arwidsson's perhaps apocryphal remark was that Finland no longer shared Sweden's fate but must find its own way; certainly, it could not identify with Russia, which was linguistically and religiously alien, and backward compared to Sweden in social-political conditions and in legislation.

Other members of the Turku faculty and student body chose a more cautious or conciliatory policy and concentrated on continuing the cultural-patriotic line of the Age of Porthan in the Swedish-language albums *Aura* and *Mnemosyne*, the newspaper *Åbo Underrättelser* (Åbo intelligences), and the Finnish-language *Turun Wiikko-Sanomat* (1820–27 and 1829–31; Turku weekly paper), established and edited by Reinhold von Becker (1788–1858). (Despite his German name, von Becker came from an old Swedish-Baltic-Finnish military family.) In the columns of *Aura* the philosopher Johan Jacob Tengström (1787–1858), the bishop's nephew, presented an extensive article about the development of the Finnish language and the necessity for compiling and studying folkloric material. (Later Tengström became a leading figure in the Saturday Society of Runeberg's Helsinki, which continued the enthusiasms of the Turku cultural patriots on new ground, once the academy had been removed to the new capital and renamed.) Von Becker had already traveled through Ostrobothnia, Lapland, and northern Savo (Savolax) in the summer of 1811, collecting songs and other linguistic and ethnographic material about Väinämöinen; the same summer, Arwidsson had also journeyed through Savo, setting down more than a hundred pieces of folk poetry. This wish to dig out the treasures of a pristine and ancient Finnish people had received an impetus from the work of Porthan, Ganander, and their predecessors, but it had been urged on, more recently, by the example of the Heidelberg romantics (who, in their turn, had been inspired by Herder): Arnim and Brentano's anthology *Des Knaben Wunderhorn: Alte deutsche Lieder* (1806–8); (The boy's wondrous horn: Old German songs) had just come out, shortly to be followed by the first volumes of the Grimms' *Kinder- und Hausmärchen*. But more specifically, Elias Lönnrot (1802–84) later said that von Becker's article on the Väinämöinen poems in the *Turun Wiikko-Sanomat* had inspired him to forge Finland's folk poetry into the epic of the *Kalevala*. (Lönnrot, the Finnish-speaking son of a village tailor at Sammatti in western Uusimaa, wrote a doctoral dissertation entitled *Disputatio de Väinämöine priscorum Fennorum numine* [1827; Disputation concerning Väinämöinen, god of the ancient Finns]; his medical dissertation—he had begun to study medicine

New Beginnings, Latin and Finnish 51

in 1830 — was *Om Finnarnes magiska medicin* [1832; On the magic medicine of the Finns].)

In the groves of academe on the banks of the Aura, thoughts similar to von Becker's and Arwidsson's and Tengström's were developed by Johan Gabriel Linsén (1785–1848), an instructor in Roman literature at the academy, who, writing in Swedish, demanded that the position of the Finnish language be strengthened; subsequently, in Helsinki (as a professor of "eloquence and poetry" at the university), he would function for a long time (1833–41) as the chairman of the new Finnish Literary Society. Meanwhile, young Finlanders also studied at Uppsala and imbibed ideas from Swedish romanticism: Arwidsson himself; the linguist and folklorist Anders Johan Sjögren (1794–1855), who eventually would become one of the most widely traveled of all the pioneer Finno-Ugrists; the poet Abraham Poppius (1793–1866); and the author and indefatigable amateur researcher Carl Axel Gottlund (1796–1872). In 1817, with a review article (on Friedrich Rühs's *Finnland und seine Bewohner* [1809; Finland and its inhabitants], a much-read introductory study by Germany's leading expert on the North) for the Swedish periodical *Svensk Litteratur-Tidning*, Gottlund proposed that a poetic entirety resembling the Homeric epics, the *Songs of Ossian*, or the *Nibelungenlied* could be formed from Finland's own folk poems, thus projecting the premise on which the *Kalevala* was built.

Subsequently, Gottlund's zeal for the Finnish cause took various and, initially, useful forms. In 1818 he published what may be the first actual collection of Finnish songs from the oral tradition, *Pieniä runoja, Suomen pojillen ratoxi* (Some small songs for the delectation of Finland's sons, second fascicle 1821), and in 1819, together with another foreign student at Uppsala, Hans Rudolph von Schröter, he brought out German translations of thirty-four songs, accompanied by the original text. This collection, reprinted in 1834 by von Schröter's brother, did much to arouse the interest of later German romantics, such as Ludwig Uhland, in Finnish folk poetry. During his long residence in Sweden, where he also became the advocate of the Finnish-speakers whose forebears had migrated to the forests of Värmland and Dalarna in the sixteenth and seventeenth centuries, Gottlund partly wrote, and partly assembled from other sources, the huge *Otava eli Suomalaisia huvituksia* (1–3, 1828–32; 1929; Otava [i.e., Big Dipper] or Finnish diversions). This work is a hodgepodge of essays on Finnish archaeology, history, folklore, and language, together with poems of Gottlund's own (including an ode in rhymed Sapphic strophes on the great Turku fire, "Churches, homesteads, towers, and walls of stonework / All is assaulted"), poems by others, translations from the Greek and Latin lyric, and so forth — an attempt to appeal to a cultured public that wanted to read Finnish, a public well-nigh nonexistent at the time. Returning to Finland, Gottlund was appointed the university's lector in Finnish in 1839 but fell into bizarre behavior, revealed not least in his insistence on his own Savo dialect and other linguistic idiosyncrasies, which came to be known as Gottlundisms. His isolation from other enthusiasts for the Finnish movement was increased by his unsuccessful runs (1851–52) for the professorship in Finnish at Helsinki, which went first to the great Finno-Ugrist Mathias Alexander Castrén (1813–52), then to Lönnrot (1853–62), then to the critic and poet August Ahlqvist (1863–88). Gottlund consoled himself for his lack of academic recognition by a frantic productivity in both Finland's languages, writing, among other things, on Finnish etymology (1853), genealogy (1862, the Kurck family), *Gud, verlden och menniskan* (1870; God, world, and man), onomastics in Savo and Karelia (1872), and the Sampo myth (1872), and finding time to translate Bellman into Finnish (1863).

At various times Gottlund — nothing if not self-confident — tried his hand at poetry without notable success (e.g., in *Otava* itself, *Runola* [1840], and *Sampo* [1847]); but the only gifted poet writing in Finnish to come out of Turku romanticism was the above-mentioned Poppius, who was most active poetically in his early Turku days: he contributed poems to *Mnemosyne* and to the pamphlet Arwidsson — forbidden to continue the publication of his *Åbo Morgonblad* (1821), "Finland's first political newspaper" — conceived to pay off his subscribers. (The tart-tongued Arwidsson gave the pamphlet the title *Oskyldigt ingenting* [Innocent nothing].) Poppius's verse is neither obviously patriotic nor patently uplifting, but there is a muted love of country in his best-known poem, "Varpunen" (The sparrow), in which that little bird tells, at considerable length, why it remains in Finland during the winter while other birds fly away. Actually, "Varpunen" was written decades after his student days: Poppius had gladly returned to his home parish, serving as pastor there for the rest of his life. His biography and collected works were published together in 1899, a modest tribute to a modest life.

Sharing the ideals of the Turku romantics, other figures proved themselves to have more clear-cut goals, which they pursued tenaciously. The lexicographer Gustaf Renvall (1781–1841) was named docent in Finnish at Turku Academy in 1811, and his great dictionary (see p. 48) took shape during his time on the faculty; but he left the academy in 1819 to accept a countryside pastorate. Given the title of professor just before the academy's move to Helsinki in 1828, Renvall continued to live and to practice pastoral care in the coastal town of Pori (Björneborg), and from there he championed the cause of a standard Finnish, based on western Finnish dialects.

Another man of learning still farther from the academy was Zacharias (Zachris) Topelius the Elder (1781–1831), who had studied briefly at Turku before going on to Sweden and Denmark for medical training; even before Arwidsson, von Becker, and Gottlund undertook their collections, Topelius began to pick up examples of folk poetry. As a young physician in 1803, sent out to vaccinate Ostrobothnian peasants, he had become closely acquainted with the country population, and one wonders if Lönnrot's decision to study medicine (as a way to win the confidence of simple people) was not encouraged by Topelius's example. After his paralysis, probably caused by an accident during an inspection tour in 1820, Topelius continued his avocation, getting specimens of songs from the Karelian peddlers who came to his home; his remark that he had obtained his best songs from the eastern reaches of Finland is supposed to have inspired Lönnrot to visit the same parts. From 1822 until his death Topelius published *Suomen kansan wanhoja runoja ynnä myös nykyisempiä lauluja* (Old poems of the Finnish people, together with more modern songs), five sets of old songs and of more modern folk poetry, real and imitation, such as the "Neion valitus" (The maiden's lament) of Eerikki Ticklén (1794–1827).

Juteini, Kallio, and Finnish Verse
For whatever reason, the most vital Finnish-language poetry of the time came not from the Turku romantics but from writers who, although sometime students at the academy, led their lives elsewhere and in nonacademic callings. (To be sure, the youngest elements in the student body at Turku during the academy's last years there, inhaling the spirit of Porthan and, of course, the Turku romantics themselves, would turn out to be the giants of the coming golden age of Finland's culture: Runeberg, Lönnrot, and Snellman were enrolled at Turku in 1822, and the critic-to-be Fredrik Cygnaeus, a year later.) Not the customary son of the manse but a gifted youth who took his name from the estate where he had been a herd-boy, the poet Jaakko Juteini (Jacob Judén, 1781–1855) had studied at Turku during Porthan's lifetime (he first won attention with a poem in the great man's memory); but his career as a public notary took him far eastward, first to Hamina and then to Viipuri, where he served the municipal administration until his retirement. (Viipuri and the rest of extreme southeastern Finland, "Old Finland," as it was called, partly lost in the peace negotiations of 1721

and then, still more, in 1743, had been returned to Finland in 1812.) The traditions of the Enlightenment were continued in the homely and simple verse of Juteini, a didactic rationalist who advocated admirable causes — the prevention of cruelty to animals, equality and tolerance among mankind, and even freedom of religion; August Ahlqvist wrote, "His goal is not beauty but rather goodness, and he seldom lets his imagination rise above the province of everyday life." In an embarrassing episode from the history of freedom of thought in Finland, Juteini's Swedish tractate *Anteckningar af tankar uti varianta ämnen* (1827; Notes of thoughts in various themes), charged by the Lutheran clergy with spreading anti-Christian sentiments, was condemned and publicly burned on Viipuri's market square, an instance of clerical obscurantism prefiguring the penalties for blasphemy meted out to Hannu Salama and his publisher in the *Juhannustanssit* affair of the 1960s (see chapter 5). (Subsequently, Finland's Senate rescinded the judgment on the burned book, but not until after Juteini had sworn to write no more, a promise, however, that he did not keep.) At his best, Juteini — a diligent reviser of his poems, albeit not always to their advantage — shows a perceptive use of language. Some of his poems have even reached the status of folk songs, as in the case of his sentimental plea of a child to its widowed mother ("Weep not so, my mother"), while others, because of their patriotic content, have become national property of a different sort: a case in point is his "Laulu Suomessa" (Song in Finland), sometimes called the "first national anthem," with its grand and challenging opening, "Arvon mekin ansaitsemme / Suomen maassa suuressa" (We too should be vouchsafed honor / In Suomi's wide-stretched land). Juteini was a skillful user of runometer but by no means a slave to it, employing "European" meters and forms as well, so that he qualifies as a pioneer in bringing the Finnish-language lyric into the mainstream of European versification. Furthermore, wanting to give Finnish letters all the genres of more developed literatures, he tried his hand at plays, with *Perhe-kunda* (1817; The family) and *Pila pahoista hengistä* (1817; Jest with evil spirits), and prose narrative, *Nimipäivä* (1824; The name day), efforts at cultural rather than artistic enrichment. He always hoped for a broader public: in 1833, with Poppius, he founded the Finnish-spirited paper *Sanan Saattaja Viipurista* (Messenger from Viipuri), but like so many other ventures of the same sort, it came too early and soon failed. (It existed from 1833 to 1836 and again in 1840–41.) On the point of language, Juteini, a man of practicality and reason, was a champion of a standard national language, free from foreign elements and dialect oddities. In this connection he wrote a Finnish grammar, in Swedish, whose introduction contains a moving encomium of the native tongue, which "in respect to its outer form and inner harmony, fostered more in its own way, could scarcely be surpassed by any other language."

Samuel Gustaf Bergh (1803-52), who wrote under the pseudonym Kallio, was infinitely less prolific than Juteini (he left only a handful of poems, some of them first printed in Gottlund's *Otava*) but far more the born lyricist; blindness put an end to his promising career. He has remained in the annals of Finnish-language poetry because of the flexibility and expressiveness of his language and his keen metrical awareness. Not only did he use the traditional runometer, as in "Runo" (Poem), "To the sea the day did wander, / Shining like a golden threadball / Down into the western waters," with an innate melancholy like that in some of Runeberg's short poems; but also, a classicist like Runeberg, he wrote in antique meters, including the first poem in distichs in Finnish, "Oma maa" (My own country). Kallio's refinement, his "purity of form, plainly influenced by Goethe" (as Eino Leino wrote), may have limited his appeal; for a larger public, Johan Fredrik Granlund (1809-74) attained a kind of semiclassic stature. His earlier poems are supposed to have inspired the young Aleksis Kivi: in the wake of Henrik Achrenius, he was a successful imitator of Bellman and made fun of still another famous Swede, Esaias Tegnér, and the viking romanticism of the latter's vastly popular *Frithiofs saga* (1825), in his "Punssipullon kuolemasta" (Concerning the death of the punch bottle). The first line of Granlund's song for schoolchildren, "Koto-mamme" (Our homeland) — "Täällä Pohjantähden alla" (Here beneath the North Star) — provided the title for a major prose work of the middle twentieth century, Väinö Linna's cottager trilogy (see chapter 4).

Peasant Poets
This small harvest of poetry in Finnish stretches over more than half a century: Juteini's "Laulu Suomessa" is from 1810, Kallio's "Oma maa" from 1832, Granlund's "Koto-maamme" from 1863, the year Alexander II was persuaded by Snellman to grant Finnish full rights in the legal (and so the cultural) life of the country where it was the majority language. Parallel with this (relatively) more sophisticated poetic development, there was another, the fascinating phenomenon of the *talonpoikaisrunoilijat* ("peasant poets"), self-taught men (and some women) who used rhymed folksong style or rhymeless runometer to comment on events and figures of the time or gave their readers moral precepts. Their motifs were taken not only from their immediate vicinity but from more distant horizons: they might pillory unpopular local officials or pastors or offer praise to the emperor

(pictures, particularly of the first two Alexanders, were often hung in Finnish cottages). A sign of cultural awareness lies in the pleas for an expansion of the use (and power) of the Finnish language. More homely subjects were the pleasures, or dangers, of coffee, tobacco, and liquor. The practice had existed since the seventeenth century, but—simultaneously with the popular-literary enthusiasms of first the Turku romantics and then the national-romantic movement stemming from Helsinki—these poets had their heyday in the first half of the nineteenth century. Lönnrot himself collected some of their verse, publishing it in his monthly, *Mehiläinen* (1836–37 and 1839–40; The bee); early in his career the historian Kustavi Grotenfelt (1861–1928) put together an anthology of their work, *Kahdeksantoista runoniekkaa* (1889; Eighteen bards). Actually, there seem to have been more than a hundred "bards" active at one time or another in this homespun art, which flourished especially in the northern reaches of Savo and, more precisely, in the Rautalampi district.

The best-known of the peasant poets was Paavo Korhonen (1775–1840), some of whose verses were published by Lönnrot as *Paavo Korhosen viisikymmentä runoa ja kuusi laulua* (1848; Paavo Korhonen's fifty poems and six songs), a volume including a lampoon on the detestable constable Kokki, a song in praise of the Finnish language, a report on the burning of the Turku Academy, and Korhonen's reflections on "song, beer, and wine," on his own life, and on death. Whatever may be said about the technical qualities of the peasant poets' "labor" (which they took seriously, calling it "plowing with the pen"), it is a remarkable example of a demotic and democratic literary tradition, representing an element of Finland's population that would find its voice again in the Finnish novel, from Kivi onward to the twentieth century. (It may be meaningful that Rautalampi also had a particularly strong tradition of peasant independence: Jaakko Ilkka's Ostrobothnian peasant revolt inspired a companion uprising here in 1595, which resulted in a migration to the so-called Finn forests of central Sweden; from there, grandchildren of the Rautalampi peasants went on to the Delaware colony of Queen Christina, and a further descendant of one of them, John Morton [ca. 1724–77] of Chester County, was a signer of the Declaration of Independence.)

The University at Helsinki and Fennophilia
The great Turku fire of 1827 caused the removal of the center of Finland's learning to Helsinki, which had become the seat of government in 1812. Here the traditions of Porthan were continued and built on, at first particularly in the circle of academic friends, mostly Swedish-speaking, called the

Saturday Society, from which so much literary activity of the 1830s (and, by extension, the following decade) emanated; it is described in greater detail in chapter 7. Its member with the most significance for Finnish-language literature was, of course, Elias Lönnrot; and "Helsinki romanticism" may well be said to have fostered Lönnrot's publication of the *Kalevala* (first in 1835 and then, completely revised and expanded, in 1849) and his collection of lyric poetry, the *Kanteletar* of 1840, which were both crucial for the development of Finnish-language poetry and the entirety of literature in Finnish. Few members of the Saturday Society, though, would subscribe to the demand for a monolingual Finland subsequently to be made by their sometime comrade Johan Vilhelm Snellman, for all the importance of his thesis that Finland must have its own national spirit and central form of expression. The establishment of the Finnish Literary Society, the Suomalaisen Kirjallisuuden Seura (1831), can likewise be counted a result of the intellectual and patriotic ferment of the Saturday Society.

Although the group itself, whose membership was constantly shifting, broke up after Runeberg's move to Porvoo in 1837, its goals were obviously inspiring for the young men who came to maturity during the next decade—for example, Herman Kellgren (1822–56) from Kuopio (which town became a center of Finnish enthusiasm during Snellman's sojourn there as school rector from 1842 to 1849). Docent of Sanskrit at the university from 1849 to 1854 and then briefly professor of Oriental languages before his untimely death, Kellgren published a Finnish grammar in German (1847), thinking in this way to spread the Finnish gospel to the land whose passion for its own folk poetry had helped inspire a similar movement in Finland. In Swedish, Kellgren also issued a *Fosterländskt album* (Patriotic album), where he included translations of Finnish and Estonian folk songs; one of his collaborators, Robert Tengström (1823–47), made a popular presentation of the *Kalevala,* and still a third, Karl Konstantin Tigerstedt (1822–1902), offered a compilation of views of medieval Finns and Finland taken from the Norse sagas — an essay predictive of Tigerstedt's future career as a historian. (Robert Tengström, whose promising career was ended by typhus in Paris, was the son of the aforementioned Johan Jacob Tengström; the elder Tengström, named professor of philosophy on the eve of the removal from Turku, had taken up his chair in Helsinki — he was the man who introduced Hegel to Finland and thus to Snellman.) The two Tengströms were both contributors to one of several patriotic publications, popular at the time, that bore Finnish titles but were composed mostly in Swedish; *Joukahainen* was named after Väinämöinen's rival singer in the *Kalevala* and issued irregularly by the Ostrobothnian "nation" (provincial fraternity) of the university. The younger Tengström wrote "The Finnish People as Presented in the *Kalevala,"* and his father contributed articles on Ostrobothnia's past and recent history; another youthful author in the same important issue was Zachris Topelius the Younger, with his essay on the question, Do the Finnish people possess a history? (see chapter 7).

Simultaneously (1845), the younger Tengström also produced a *Finsk antologi* (Finnish anthology), an effort to present Finnish poetry in Swedish translation. The Swedish speaker who wanted to buckle down to the hard task of learning correct Finnish could be aided by the Finnish grammar of Fabian Collan (1817–51), sometime secretary of the Finnish Literary Society (1841–44: his successor was Kellgren) and "curator" (director) of the Savo "nation"; at the same time, Collan was a successor to Runeberg as editor of *Helsingfors Morgonblad* (1841–44), where he had already published articles on *Kalevala* mythology. Moving to Kuopio as rector of the gymnasium there, he returned to Helsinki as associate professor of philosophy, only to die shortly thereafter.

As editor of *Helsingfors Morgonblad,* Collan had earned the praise of the persnickety Snellman himself, who asserted that, while others talked about the Finnish cause, Collan did something about it. Snellman, to be sure, did even more, with his papers issuing from Kuopio, the Swedish-language *Saima* (1844–46, canceled by the Senate under pressure from the Russian governor-general) and the Finnish *Maamiehen Ystävä* (1844–55; The countryman's friend), the former directed to the cultured Swedish speakers whom he wished to persuade to abandon their mother tongue, the latter to Finnish farmers as a purveyor of useful information. (Lönnrot's monthly, *Mehiläinen,* is in many respects its predecessor.) After *Saima'*s sudden demise — Governor-General Menshikov is supposed to have called Snellman a "Communist" because he apparently encouraged social equality by his demand for the abandonment of Swedish, the prestige language — Snellman, nothing loath, directly founded his *Litteraturblad för allmän medborgerlig bildning* (1847–49, 1855–63; Literary paper for general civic cultivation). (In the semibiographical *Vanhempieniromaani* [1927–29; My parents' novel], Arvid Järnefelt tells how his father, a young officer in Russian service at St. Petersburg during the 1850s, had his room stacked full of copies of the paper; Alexander Järnefelt [1833–96] was one of those aristocratic Swedish-speakers who fanatically followed Snellman's dicta.)

The Finnish-Language Press

A prime aim of Fennophilia, in this growing newspaper-and-journal world, was the foundation of a Finnish-language paper in the capital. In 1846 the eccentric Gottlund had tried a weekly, *Suomalainen* (The Finn), aimed at that beau ideal, the cultured reader, but the censors quickly killed it; obstinate as Snellman, he tried again, with *Suomi* (Finland). Also meant to come out every week, its publication grew ever more sporadic, and in 1849 it perished, too, without the censors' aid. The reasons are readily discovered: willing readers of Finnish in Helsinki were still few and far between, and Gottlund put his idiosyncratic stamp on both the paper's materials and its language, the quasi-Savo dialect of his own concoction. *Suomi*'s death was hastened by the foundation in 1847 of *Suometar* (Finland's daughter); it began as a feeble weekly, with only 258 subscribers in its first year, but was able to boast of 4,600 subscribers by 1856. After another decade it too had passed away, but it can be regarded as the parent of a major paper, *Uusi Suometar,* the "new" *Suometar,* founded in 1869, which (from 1919 as *Uusi Suomi*) would survive almost until the end of the present century. The moving spirit in *Suometar* was Paul (or Paavo) Tikkanen (1823–73), the son of a well-to-do peasant; as a member of the intensely active Savo-Karelian "nation," he made a name for himself by, among other things, translating Runeberg and the Danish romantic Adam Oehlenschläger. At *Suometar* Tikkanen surrounded himself with associates who had likewise come from the Finnish-speaking hinterland: the young August Ahlqvist, who translated Franzén, Runeberg, and the Swedish romantics; D.E.D. Europaeus (1820–84), a disciple and aide of Lönnrot (contributing much of the Kullervo episode in the expanded version of the *Kalevala*); and the many-sided Anders (Antero) Warelius (1821–1904), ethnologist, philologist, and lexicographer, who knew the Finnish people and their needs: he went on to become a country pastor. Upwardly mobile, and staying in Helsinki, Tikkanen married one of Johan Jacob Tengström's daughters; Kellgren wed another, and the pioneer of Finno-Ugric studies, Mathias Alexander Castrén (1813–52) a third. From the union of Paavo Tikkanen and Helena Maria Tengström a new Finnish cultural family sprang: they were the parents of the art historian Johan Jacob Tikkanen (1857–1930), who in his turn was the paternal grandfather of the author and artist Henrik Tikkanen (1924–84): Henrik Tikkanen's tribute to his great-grandfather runs: "He founded a progressive newspaper which in time was transformed into a reactionary one."

Still another Finnish speaker who appeared briefly in Helsinki, possessed of educational intentions, was Antti Räty (1825–52) from Sortavala on the shores of Lake Ladoga; his 1849 translation of the William Tell episode from the elder Dumas's *Impressions de voyage* (1847–48) is supposed to have been the occasion for the infamous "Finnish-language rescript" of 1850: "In the Finnish language, only such [publications] may be issued which . . . possess, both in their spirit of composition and in their manner of presentation, religious edification or economic application as their aim; on the other hand, it is absolutely forbidden to make public in print, in the Finnish language, political news or crimes which have been committed abroad." "The publication of novels in Finnish" was also forbidden, "whether they be original works or translations, not even excepting those works whose publication the censors might allow in other languages." The intent of this proclamation was to shield the Finnish-speaking masses from contamination by the revolutionary spirit prevailing on the Continent in 1848–49; it was so patently silly that it could not be strictly applied for long, but while it was sternly in effect, even *Suometar* could not appear, leaving Snellman's harmless farmers' paper in Kuopio as Finland's only Finnish-language sheet. (As a matter of fact, administrative delay caused a strange constellation of events. A proposed professorship in Finnish at the university had won the warm support of old General Alexander Thesleff, the institution's vice-chancellor, and he did what he could to see its realization before his retirement and death in 1847; on 22 March 1850 the plan was given to the Senate with Emperor Nicholas's stamp of approval — only two weeks before the appearance of the censorship decree. A year later Castrén received his appointment to the chair from none other than Alexander, the heir to the Russian throne.)

The Finnish-language press, despite adversities, did not grow in Helsinki (and distant Kuopio) alone. In Oulu the printer C. E. Barck had established Finland's first Finnish-language provincial paper, *Oulun Wiikko-Sanomat* (Oulu's weekly newspaper), in 1829. It lasted, albeit with many interruptions, until 1879. Its first editor, the pedagogue Pietari Ticklén (1792–1838), published the homely verses "Lapsellisen Lapsen Laulu" (Childish child's song) for which he is still remembered today, and Kallio's poems also appeared in its pages, as well as some posthumous poems by Ticklén's younger brother, Eerikki. In Viipuri, following in the wake of Juteini's *Sanan Saattaja Viipurista,* Pietari Hannikainen (1813–99), a surveyor by profession but also an author, established a cultural journal, *Kanava* (1845–47; The channel), which shortly was put to sleep by Casimir von Kothen, the provincial governor. Von Kothen (1807–80), passing from the Russian military into Finland's civil administration, persistently did all he could to stifle the Finnish movement; he was rumored to have been behind the suppression of *Saima* and the language rescript, and in the 1870s, as chairman of the supervisory board of Finland's schools, he made a last stand, trying to check the progress of education in Finnish. After his paper's closing, Hannikainen followed it with other efforts in the same spirit, such as a set of "readings for country people" (1849-50).

The Start of Finnish Drama

In his newspaper Hannikainen had published his farce, *Silmän-kääntäjä* (1846; The conjurer), about a trickster who pulls the wool over the eyes of gullible peasant folk. Performed at Lappeenranta (Villmanstrand) in Karelia in 1848, the work is the first original Finnish-language play to have reached the boards. Hannikainen learned a great deal from the comedies of Ludvig Holberg (1684–1754), as Aleksis Kivi did a couple of decades later, and his *Anttonius Putronius eli Antti Puuronen* (1846), a reworking of Holberg's *Erasmus Montanus* (1731; Eng. tr. 1915), became a favorite of Helsinki university students. Its performance in 1858 was the first use of Finnish on a stage in the capital, and the next year, revised and given local allusions instead of the original version's Karelian ones, it was performed again, with the young Finland-Swedish poet J. J. Wecksell in one of the roles and Aleksis Kivi in the audience. The revision was made by the energetic Ahlqvist and Oscar Toppelius (1828–1904), who would become an active reviewer of Finnish-language theater during its rapid growth in the century's second half. Juteini's theatrical efforts had never reached the boards, any more than the strange dramas of Jacob Fredrik Lagervall (1787–1865), a sometime military man and acquaintance of Hannikainen, who made a Karelian version, in runometer, of *Macbeth,* called *Ruunulinna* (1834; Crown castle), followed, in 1847, by original plays on Joseph, Judith, Cain, and Cinderella.

The Dream of a Full-Fledged Literature

However much we may smile at Hannikainen's stageworthy imitations and Lagervall's failures, we must remember that they were intended to flesh out a Finnish-language belletristic corpus that, thus far, had consisted almost entirely of poetry. The Finnish Literary Society was determined to create a full-fledged literature: Lagervall's *Ruunulinna* was written as an entry for a prize announced by the new organization, as were other more important works to come, such as Kivi's *Kullervo*. The absence of prose narrative was likewise keenly felt, and in 1834 the society published a translation of the "Swiss tale" of Heinrich Zschokke (1771–1848), *Das Goldmacher-Dorf* (1817; The goldmaker village), as *Kultala,* a "useful and entertaining story," done by Carl Niklas Keckman (1793–1838). Keckman was the first lector in Finnish at the university in Helsinki, the first chairman of the Finnish Literary Society, and after Lönnrot had set out again on his research trips, its secretary; the popular little volume came out again in 1851, 1880, and 1898, winning a place as a Finnish classic by adoption. It was followed in 1835 by the translation of one Otto Tarvanen (Otto Tandefelt, 1811–62), *Ensimmäinen purjehtia*, of a prose idyll, *Der erste Schiffer* (1756; The first boatman), by the Zurich author Salomon Geßner (1730–88). (Evidently, some affinity was sensed between Switzerland's independent peasants and Finland's.)

Still another tale by Zschokke, *Die Brannteweinpest: Eine Trauergeschichte* (1837; The brandy plague: A tragic story), came out in 1844, translated "as warning and counsel for rich and poor, old and young" by the sometime Turku romantic Poppius, and was number six in the society's publications, hot on the heels of Lönnrot's first *Kalevala*, his *Kanteletar*, and his collection of riddles of the Finnish people, *Suomen kansan arvoituksia*. Hannikainen himself made modest efforts at original narrative in his papers, as did Nils (Niilo) Aejmelaeus (1812–54) with his *Haaksirikko, suomalainen perustuskielinen taru* (1838; The shipwreck, a Finnish basic-language tale). The censorship decree of 1850 put a stop for a while to such undertakings, however, and it was not until the end of the decade that new stabs at creative prose were made, for example by Yrjö Koskinen (1830–1903) in his historical tale *Pohjan-piltti* (1859; The son of the North), probably written in emulation of Zachris Topelius's *Fältskärns berättelser* (see chapter 7). But Yrjö Koskinen's energies went subsequently into his professional historical studies and his political career as a leader of the conservative and stubbornly anti-Swedish Old Finnish Party.

Without question, the focus of Finland's letters in the first half of the nineteenth century was on literature in Swedish; Finnish-language literature, save for the shining exceptions of Lönnrot's *Kalevala* and *Kanteletar*, grew slowly and tentatively; the lack of sophistication of the target audience, and the lack of authors experienced in using the language, especially in prose, set clear limits to its progress. Yet it provides dozens of examples of heroic efforts, on the part of both Finnish and Swedish speakers; such cooperation would not be seen again, at least for a very long time. A new phase in its evolution began after the Finnish-language rescript was finally repealed in 1859, the year in which Kivi received the prize of the Finnish Literary Society for *Kullervo*.

The Rise of Finnish-Language Literature, 1860–1916

Kai Laitinen
Translated by Philip Binham

3

The 1860s: Breaking the Ice
Zacharias (Zachris) Topelius (see chapter 7) wrote a poem in 1856 called "Islossningen i Uleå elf" (The breakup of the ice in Oulu River). The poem describes how in spring the river breaks the ice cover that shackles it and begins to foam freely and irresistibly. In the cries of the poem, written in the first person, is the voice of desire for life and of defiance: "I will have air! I will have light! My destiny / That I wish to create my own course." Topelius's powerful spring poem was at once understood as a political and patriotic allegory. At the time of writing it was indeed a clear picture of Finland's political and cultural situation. On the one hand, it was as if the country was covered with a layer of ice; on the other, the longing for freedom surged deeply, the desire to get more air, light, to find its own way.

The czar of the Russian empire, Nicholas I, was frightened by the events in Europe of 1848 and up to his death in 1855 tried to control his subjects more strictly. Though Finland enjoyed many privileges and was the freest part of the broad empire, it too had to submit to the new restrictions. Hence the governor-general, Aleksander Sergeyevich Menshikov (1787–1869), issued a censorship decree in 1850 prohibiting publications in Finnish except those on religious or economic subjects; the decree did not apply to Swedish-language literature, so that Topelius, for example, who wrote in Swedish, could publish his historical novels.

Swedish was the dominant language in Finland in the 1850s: it was the instrument not only of officialdom but also of culture, teaching, and legal matters. Although only 15 percent of the population spoke Swedish, the first Finnish-language high school leading to the university did not start at

Jyväskylä until 1858, and the first Finnish-language teachers' school was established in the same city in 1863. In Helsinki, at the same time, there were only three or four cultured families whose language at home was Finnish. The university was entirely Swedish-speaking, but gradually the use of Finnish in academic teaching advanced: Elias Lönnrot gave his first lectures in Finnish in 1856, and the earliest Finnish-language doctoral dissertations appeared in 1858. The censorship decree did not entirely extinguish Finnish-language literature; the first parts of the folktale collection of "Eero Salmelainen" (Erik Rudbeck, 1830–67), for example, were allowed to be published in 1852 and 1854.

A new, more liberal ruler, Alexander II, came to the throne and brought distinct improvements in Finnish conditions. In Finland—unlike in Poland—he was a beloved ruler, and his statue in the center of Helsinki later became a symbol of liberty. The Diet was summoned in 1863 (for the first time since 1809) and was put on a permanent footing. Finland obtained its own coinage (1865), its value tied not to the Russian ruble but to the French franc. The first railroad was completed, a new church law came into force, and the Board of Education was established. From the standpoint of literary development the language manifesto of 1863 was of primary importance, putting the Finnish language on a par with Swedish. This accomplishment was largely attributable to the efforts of the philosopher and senator Johan Vilhelm Snellman (1806–81).

The 1860s saw the ice break up on an equally large scale for Finnish-language literature. It had started to develop in the 1840s, thanks in particular to the works of Elias Lönnrot, but was halted by the censorship decree. When the gates were opened once more, the result was a flood of new books, societies, and institutions.

In 1862 Julius Krohn published the first detailed presentation of older Finnish-language literature, *Suomenkielinen runollisuus Ruotsinvallan aikana* (Finnish-language poetry during the era of Swedish rule), which later evolved into a broader history of Finnish literature published after his death. In 1866 Eero Salmelainen completed his extensive collection, *Suomen kansan satuja ja tarinoita* (Fairy tales and stories of the Finnish people), a classic that still lives and that helped establish a Finnish-language prose style. In the same year, Krohn's *Helmivyö* (Pearl belt) appeared, the first carefully edited anthology of Finnish-language poetry; it too was a pioneer work in its field. In addition, the first part of Yrjö Koskinen's *Suomen kansan historia* (History of the Finnish people) came out in 1869; the first important literary periodical, *Kirjallinen kuukauslehti* (Literary monthly), appeared in 1866; and the newspaper *Suometar*, which had closed down because of a lack of subscribers, began anew under the name *Uusi Suometar*. The foundation for the development of Finnish-language literature was laid with these works.

At the same time, there was a thinning in the ranks of Swedish-language literature. Runeberg published his last work and became paralyzed in 1863; the career of the talented poet J. J. Wecksell was cut short. Only Topelius continued as before, and his historical novels and fairy tales had a powerful influence on Finnish-language literature. The shift of focus from Swedish-language literature to Finnish was visible quantitatively, for Finnish-language publications caught up with Swedish-language literature in numbers at the start of the 1870s and grew larger from then on. On the one hand, the new situation led to the exacerbation of relations between the two language groups and a long-lasting language conflict; on the other, it set new demands and challenges for the development of the Finnish language and for the rise of Finnish-language literature. The language of Finnish poetry at the end of the 1850s was stiff and the metrics fumbling; almost the only living traditions came from folk poetry, hymns, and folk songs. With the coming of the 1860s, Finnish-language novels did not exist either; there were a few attempts at plays and some prose narratives.

Academic Poets
The great Swedish-language poets were a model for the first Finnish-language poets of the 1860s. It was typical that Finnish was the mother tongue of only one of them, August Ahlqvist (1826–89), the illegitimate son of a young officer in Russian service, Johan Mauritz Nordenstam (destined to become a general, governor of Uusimaaa Province, and vice-chancellor of the university in Helsinki), and a Finnish servant girl, Maria Augusta Ahlqvist. The other, Julius Krohn (1835–88), was originally from a German-speaking family that had moved from St. Petersburg to the largest city in eastern Finland, Viipuri.

Both worked in academic research and became professors; poetry for both of them was only one area alongside research and teaching. In order to separate one sector of their life work from the others, they used pen names as poets: the title page of August Ahlqvist's books of poetry bore the name of A. Oksanen; the literary works of Julius Krohn, the pen name of Suonio.

One source for Ahlqvist was the poetry of Runeberg, particularly his patriotic poems. Among his first works was a selection of Runeberg's poetry (1845) translated into Finnish, and he also translated into Swedish — very well — some samples of the *Kalevala*. He held Finland's Swedish-language culture in high esteem, and in many of his poems he emphasized the importance of the former mother country, Sweden, as a supporter and the closest friend of Finnish culture.

"A. Oksanen" published only one collection of poems, *Säkeniä* (1860; Sparks), but he enlarged and supplemented it with a second volume in 1868; six different versions appeared, the final edition in 1898, after the poet's death. The collection contains a large number of translations from various languages, especially from Latin and German; a major achievement of 1859, the centennial of Schiller's birth, is the German poet's "Das Lied von der Glocke" (The song of the bell), whose varying meters and types of rhyme set the translator a difficult task. Oksanen also wrote the first Finnish-language sonnet (in 1854) and the first Finnish-language poetic ballad (i.e., in the Western manner, not designed according to the ballad of folk poetry), "Koskenlaskijan morsiamet" (The rapids-shooter's brides), set by Jean Sibelius for baritone or mezzo soprano and orchestra in 1897 (opus 33).

Oksanen used an abundance of poetic meters. He cultivated the Finnish so-called Kalevala line with great success but also used antique meters and blank verse and experimented with their suitability for the Finnish-language poem. In the introduction to the 1874 edition of *Säkeniä* he emphasized that these were "experiments" he had made "to adapt the Finnish language to the forms of modern poetry." As in many of his studies concerning grammar and linguistic usage, Oksanen saw his task in poetry as a kind of normalizing and stabilizing one. Poems with different themes and in different meters were also technical specimens, examples, one purpose of which was to show where the road of the Finnish poem was leading.

At first, Oksanen constructed his meter according to the duration of syllables, creating effects — in his sonnets, for example — that violated accent and were actually comic in their scansion. Gradually, he achieved a compromise: both word stress and length had to be taken into account. Oksanen emphasized this in his handbook on Finnish prosody, *Suomalainen runousoppi* (1863; Finnish poetics), where he puts forward the concept that syllables where the word stress and length correspond are metrically strongest; hence they must make their effect together. Thus Oksanen established European, chiefly Germanic, metric systems in the Finnish language. For more than a hundred years, Finnish-language poetry, especially translated poetry, has followed the paths he opened up.

The title poem of Oksanen's collection describes a smith's forge, from whose chimney a cluster of sparks flies out into the autumn sky. They are soon extinguished, but they tell of the work in the smithy and remain in the minds of their young spectators. In the same way, the end of the poem emphasizes, these lines aim to arouse new interest and new fire in Finnish hearts. In other words, Oksanen sees his task as that of a pioneer, pointing onward. Thus it is no accident that much of his poetry is patriotic and idealistic. He wrote the first so-called song of a province, in which — following the meter of Runeberg's "Vårt land" (Our land), sometimes with an almost identical turn of phrase — he describes the beauty of his home province of Savo (a lake district in the Finnish interior) and the tenacity of its inhabitants under severe conditions. In some of his poems he dealt with the status of the Finnish language and emphasized the importance of cultivating and developing it. His interest extended beyond the border of Finland, too, to small nations and tribes related to the Finns, among whom he made numerous expeditions and whose languages and folk traditions he presented in many of his works. The prose piece "Satu" (Fairy tale), whose subtitle is "a folkloric dream," describes in visionary style the reuniting of these dispersed peoples. The poem "Suomen valta" (The Finnish dominion) catalogs, a little overdramatically, those external landmarks of Finland (such as the White Sea and Lake Onega in Russian Karelia) to which the might of the Finnish language and the Finnish ethos in general extend. After Ahlqvist's death this poem gained significance in two ways: it inspired the vision held by writers and artists at the end of the nineteenth century, of Karelia, on the far side of the Russian border, as a stronghold of the nature and people of Finland; and its words were quoted in the young republic between the world wars, where radical patriots dreamed of a Greater Finland and of joining the Karelian lands beyond the border to Finland.

In a few poems personal themes are handled, too: love, grief, feelings of melancholy, childhood memories. "Sydämeni asukkaat" (The dwellers of my heart) can be considered a kind of confessional poem. It describes two creatures that live in the heart of the poem's speaker, "one devil" and "one angel"; they are engaged in eternal conflict. There are real reasons for the idea, for in his private life — as August Ahlqvist — the poet was known for his sharp reactions and scathing criticism, directed at, among others, the most gifted writer of the time, Aleksis Kivi.

Ahlqvist's life work extended far beyond his poetry. It includes his long career as a professor at the university and finally its rector, his diligent and painstaking research concerning peoples related to the Finns, his basic grammars of several languages related to Finnish, and the first broad presentation of Estonian literature (1855). Ahlqvist was also an energetic collector of poetry and gathered part of the material Lönnrot used in his final version of the *Kalevala*.

Ahlqvist-Oksanen is remembered as one of the pioneers in the history of

Finnish-language poetry, the establisher of poetic meters and forms, but also an acerbic critic and dictator of rules, to whom a student of his works, Ilmari Kohtamäki, has applied a fitting epithet: "the severe gardener." The extent and variety of his life's work have gradually become clear, and his best poems have not lost their vigor and pertinence after almost a century and a half.

Julius Krohn, who wrote under the pen name Suonio, is a more gentle and lyrical type of poet than Oksanen. If Oksanen's model was Runeberg, Suonio can be linked to Topelius. Common to both poets was their versatility. Krohn spent much of his time in academic teaching and research; he wrote and translated into Finnish a great deal in various fields and for several years published the first Finnish-language illustrated magazine. Adroitness of this kind was characteristic of all the members of the Fennomane movement in the era of national awakening. The field of Finnish-language culture was almost uncultivated, and much work was needed on every side. One early example was Elias Lönnrot, the most hardworking and many-sided of them all.

Suonio's mother tongue was German, but he mastered Finnish with amazing speed and used it with perfect ease. In his metrics he followed the lines Oksanen had laid out, taking his stimuli from Scandinavian and German poetry. To a large extent he can be considered a representative of the Biedermeier style in Finland; the middle-class idyll flourished in his poetry, with its glorification of family life and domestic happiness. Love is seen, indeed, as a tremendous force, but it is channeled, in accordance with Christian morality, into the sphere of the home. It is not surprising that some of Suonio's writing is for children, including children's poems and illustrated books.

Like Oksanen, Suonio concentrated his poetry into a single collection; *Runoelmia* (Poems) appeared for the first time in 1865 but was published in several supplemented editions, the last not appearing until 1897, after the writer's death. In addition to his patriotic poems, which are typical of the time, his love poems and nature poems are noteworthy; he wrote more of both than Oksanen. Suonio also differs from Oksanen because of his humor. His best poems follow the style of folk songs; like Oksanen, in this respect Suonio is linked to a Finnish tradition that thus far had been little cultivated. He also wrote prose and published a collection of stories called *Kuun tarinoita* (Tales of the moon), inspired by *Billedbog uden Billeder* (Picturebook without pictures) of Hans Christian Andersen. The work also had a pedagogical function, for the tales were partly connected with geography and history.

Krohn was not a collector of folk poetry, nor did he go on scholarly expeditions; but the study of folk poetry and the *Kalevala* was his life's work. He became the first Finnish scholar of folklore and achieved international recognition for his geographical-historical method. He drew attention to the preliminary work done on the collection of *Kalevala* materials before Lönnrot and devoted part 1 of his *Suomen kirjallisuuden historia* (1883–85; History of Finnish literature) to the great epic and folk poetry. The second part was not completed during his lifetime but was published in 1897, revised by his son, Kaarle Krohn. It was basic in its field and was used as a university textbook for more than fifty years.

Julius Krohn's family was later to have a broad influence in Finnish cultural life. His eldest son, Kaarle Krohn (1863–1933), became the first professor of folklore at Helsinki University; Ilmari Krohn (1867–1960) was a composer and musicologist. Three of his daughters became writers: Helmi Krohn (1871–1967) was a productive author, translator, and editor; Aino Kallas (1876–1956) became famous for her works on Estonian themes; and Aune Krohn (1881–1967) was a religious writer and translator. Many of their descendants have continued as writers or achieved conspicuous positions in other cultural fields. The Krohn family has added significantly to the breadth and depth of Finnish-language culture, an accomplishment with which only the Järnefelt family's contribution can bear comparison.

Oksanen and Suonio were not professional writers in the proper sense of the word; writing poetry was only one of their wide-ranging activities. The first professional Finnish-language writer arrived on the scene at the same time as they—Aleksis Kivi—and Ahlqvist became his enemy and nemesis, Krohn his supporter. The ranks of the rising Finnish-language educated class were also split by conflicts, linguistic and political as well as personal.

Kivi, Pioneer and Classic
Aleksis Kivi, born Alexis Stenvall (1834–72), followed different roads from Ahlqvist or Krohn both in his life and in his work. He laid the foundation stone of Finnish-language drama, which had hardly existed before. He wrote the first Finnish-language novel, which—contrary to the expectations of his contemporaries—has remained the leading classic of its kind. He composed a great deal of poetry, so exceptional in both metrics and style that it was ignored for decades. He created his entire production within a span of ten years, fell ill after completing his great novel, and died at the age of thirty-eight, gaining the reputation of a tragic genius in the eyes of posterity.

Kivi was born at Nurmijärvi, about twenty-five miles north of Helsinki, the son of a village tailor. His home language was Finnish, but he went to a Swedish-speaking school, passing his matriculation examinations privately in 1857 only after great difficulty. His university studies were desultory, but from Fredrik Cygnaeus's lectures Kivi became familiar with the classics of drama and from Lönnrot's lectures with the *Kalevala*. His basic education is sometimes belittled, but his catalog of favorite writers speaks against this — it forms a genuine course in the world classics: Homer, Dante, Shakespeare, Cervantes, Ludvig Holberg. At an early stage he announced his aim of becoming a writer "like Runeberg" and published his first poems in a collection edited by Julius Krohn in 1860; the same year, he won a drama competition held by the Finnish Literary Society with his manuscript of *Kullervo*, first printed in a revised version in 1864.

In 1864 Kivi also published his first comedy, *Nummisuutarit* (Eng. tr. *The Heath Cobblers*, 1993), which won a large state prize the following year and made its author a well-known but also an envied figure. Both Runeberg himself and Oksanen were defeated in the competition and are known to have entertained hard feelings about the result. But Kivi was encouraged and continued his career as a writer with new enthusiasm. The young writer found a place to live in Siuntio (Sjundeå), some twenty-five miles west of Helsinki, in the idyllic farm cottage of Fanjunkars, owned by an energetic woman older than he, Charlotta Lönnqvist, famous as the cook for neighborhood festivities. In the shelter of her house Kivi lived with few interruptions until the spring of 1871. There has been much dispute about the nature of Charlotta Lönnqvist's feelings for Kivi — were they maternal or erotic? No certain answer exists: it is only clear that the best achievements of Finnish-language literature were produced during that period under the wing of a patroness of scant means who, a Swedish-speaker, could not even read her protégé's works.

Kivi's creative tempo in the 1860s was furious. He wrote twelve plays (of which seven were published), a large novel, and a collection of poetry, together with an amount of poetry not published in book form. Constantly haunted by worries about money and increasing debt, and subsequently by disappointment at the reception his chief work received, he suffered the beginnings of an illness that upset the balance of his mind and forced him to enter a mental hospital in the spring of 1871. When he was discharged, he was no longer his former self, and he spent the last months of his life at his brother's cottage in Tuusula, where he died on the last day of 1872.

Kivi's dramatic work included both tragedies and comedies. His first play, *Kullervo* (1864; Eng. tr. 1993), is a tragedy, the plot of which follows the cantos (31–36) of the *Kalevala* describing the unfortunate Kullervo. Brought up in an atmosphere of fraternal enmity, Kullervo loses (it is thought) his parents, becomes the foster child and slave of his hated uncle, but proves impossible for practical work: he destroys everything he touches. He has the mark of a slave on his brow, and the least reference to it arouses his wrath. After committing murder, Kullervo finds that his parents are alive after all, but he becomes involved in a new crime: he meets his sister, whom he does not know, seduces her, and drives her to suicide. After destroying the house of his foster father in terrible revenge, Kullervo finally throws himself on his sword, like his prototype in the *Kalevala*. The Kullervo in Kivi's play differs from the hero of the *Kalevala* in that his behavior has two motivations: his unfortunate circumstances and his own nature, which he is unable to control. His fate is in his own hands, but he does not listen to warnings or adapt himself to life with other people. His fate is reminiscent, even to the incest theme, of that of the heroes of antique tragedy: by his own deeds he draws down punishment and a curse on himself.

Kullervo is the best known of Kivi's tragedies, but *Karkurit* (1866; The runaways) and *Canzio* (finished in 1869 but not published during the author's lifetime) merit attention. The theme of both is the conflict of family vendettas and love. In the former the sons of two barons who hate each other — they are the "runaways" of the title, returning from wartime imprisonment as friends — have fallen in love with each other's sisters, but because of treacherous subsidiary characters and mischances, the play ends with the death of many central characters in Shakespearean style. Like Shakespeare, Kivi uses blank verse and prose in turn, also resorting to conventional theatrical tricks such as disguises and sleeping potions.

Canzio is set in a country that Kivi had never visited, Italy. Returning from a military academy, the young Canzio falls passionately in love with Marcia, who proves to be the widow of a robber chief who has slain Canzio's father. As the truth is gradually revealed, the road is opened for bloodshed and the tragic conclusion. The play has its weaknesses, but in two respects it is exceptional in Kivi's work. First, it contains an unusual abundance of serious discussions between the main characters, and second, the main character, Marcia, is the most forceful woman in Kivi's work, throwing herself with utmost passion into her love, unhesitatingly putting her whole life at stake.

Love and the conflicts it causes are also the key ingredients of Kivi's comedies, but in them there are humorous variations on the theme, even though marriage plans may fail. A typical situation is presented in the little one-act comedy *Kihlaus* (1866; lit. "The engagement"; Eng. tr. *Eva*, 1980).

The hot-tempered Eeva leaves her work as a housekeeper and consents to the proposal of a tailor, an old bachelor, but she realizes her mistake at once, improvises a quarrel, and departs. The comedy stems from the slow, steady, old-fashioned way of thinking of the tailor and his companions. It is also typical of Kivi that Eeva is a newcomer and represents a different world of values from the bachelor tailors, who are rooted in their own sphere of life.

The clash between the outer and inner world is revealed in different forms in almost all Kivi's works. The collision leads in the tragedies to the gravest conclusions and in the comedies to solutions that happily release tensions but are not always optimal for all the main characters.

Kivi is at his best in his classic comedy *Nummisuutarit*. The childish but honest cobbler's son Esko sets off to the neighboring parish for what he thinks will be his wedding, but he suffers humiliation and disappointment when he finds another groom standing beside Kreeta, his intended. What has happened is that Esko's father, the master cobbler Topias, has made a marriage contract with the well-to-do Karri, Kreeta's guardian, while intoxicated, failing to realize that the whole matter was a joke, not a serious arrangement. Earnest and good-natured, Esko begins to resign himself to the misunderstanding, but when he is provoked, a fight ensues, in which he is beaten up and flees. On his way home a tremendous (and, in Finnish stage annals, famous) drunken scene occurs in which Esko, imbibing hard liquor for the first time, feels, "I'm getting wings on my back and a long tail on my backside, and I'm rising to the heights." A subsidiary plot is introduced by the catastrophic trip to town of Esko's tipsy brother, Iivari, and his equally weak-willed maternal uncle, Sakari, a sometime policeman who has lost his job for being half seas over.

In the end there is a great scene of forgiveness in which all former hurts and grudges are forgotten. An inheritance that was supposed to fall to Esko if he married before Jaana, the master cobbler's foster daughter, or to Jaana, if she wedded first, is divided instead between the cobbler's family and Jaana, who at long last gets the hand of her beloved, the stalwart blacksmith Kristo. The proposal for this generous solution comes simultaneously from Jaana, willing to let bygones be bygones (she has suffered hard discipline at the hands of her virago of a stepmother, Martta), and from Jaana's long-lost father, the seaman Niko; making his way to an uncertain reception after years of absence, Niko has gotten a ride from Iivari and Sakari by tricking them into "arresting" him as a notorious thief. Unmasking, Niko says: "The curly-haired angel of reconciliation truly reigns today.... Another such day I shall never see, and, therefore, would live it joyfully, without foe and with no one to envy my joy. You dwellers of this house, let us today be reconciled" (Douglas Robinson's translation). Within Nordic literature this speech has an equivalent, in its witty and yet noble generosity of spirit, only in General Löwenhielm's toast near the end of Karen Blixen's *Babettes gaestebud* (1958; Eng. tr. *Babette's Feast,* 1958). The cantor Sepeteus, as usual overawing his listeners with his pious truisms, reinforces Niko's words, and the whole company marches happily off to the tones of the clarinet of Antres, a puny tailor—whom Esko, now vastly relieved, had thought he had killed in his drunken rage.

Although Kivi had learned much from Holberg, particularly *Jeppe paa bjerget* (1723; Eng. tr. *Jeppe of the Hill,* 1906, 1990) and *Erasmus Montanus* (1731; Eng. tr. 1915), he reveals an exuberant fantasy and a human compassion all his own. Change of mind and reconciliation are a repeated theme in Kivi's comedies and his other works that end happily. His one-act play of 1867, *Yö ja päivä* (Night and day), has a less complex development than *Nummisuutarit* but a similar message: the peasant girl Liisa, blind since early childhood, is healed by a miraculous cure and brings two hostile families together; a seal is set on the reconciliation by her marriage to Tapani, from the other clan. Another one-act play written in Kivi's frantic outburst of dramatic activity during the later 1860s (but not printed during his lifetime, perhaps because it would have seemed a commentary on his relationship to Charlotta Lönnqvist) is *Leo ja Liina* (Leo and Liina). The farm owner, Liina, is somehow drawn to this stern surrogate mother who is almost a decade his elder, but in his emotional confusion he plans migration to America. (Finland's new railroad passes near the farm.) The two are persuaded to realize the true nature of their feelings for one another by Liina's clear-sighted curmudgeon of an uncle, and their marriage brings reconciliation, as usual.

Nummisuutarit is one of Finland's best-known and most acted plays. Less well known is Kivi's other long comedy, *Olviretki Schleusingenissä* (Pub crawl in Schleusingen), written in the productive year of 1866 but not printed until his collected works appeared in 1916. The subject is taken from an item in a newspaper describing an amusing episode in the war of 1866 between Bavaria and Prussia, in which some beer obtained as booty and imbibed to excess plays the main part. In Kivi's comedy, warfare as a whole is exposed in the light of parody, and the actions and reactions of the drunken soldiers turn out to be central; there is also a humorous love story. The drunken scenes in this and other works are unfortunately based on expert knowledge; alcohol was an ever greater temptation for Kivi himself, and some of his own reactions bordered on delirium.

Kivi's play *Lea* (1868) lies in the terrain between comedy and tragedy. Its opening night on 10 May 1869 is considered the beginning of the activities of the Suomalainen (Finnish) Theater, later the National Theater. (The production is also legendary in that the main role was played by the Swedish actress Charlotta Forsman-Raa, who, though she did not know the language at all, learned her part in Finnish by heart.) The subject of *Lea* is from the Bible (Luke 19) and deals with the conversion of the miser Zacchaeus to the teachings of Jesus and with the love story of his daughter Lea and the Christian Aram. The change of mind, Kivi's favorite theme, has perhaps been expressed most beautifully in this play. The emphasis on the altruism and luminosity of the compassionate doctrine of Jesus, who does not appear in the play, also tells a great deal about Kivi's own religious predilections. Kivi is supposed to have been so impressed by Charlotta Raa's performance that he undertook to write two other plays with her in mind, the serious *Alma* and the farce *Selman juonet* (Selma's deception), but only fragments survive. His farewell to the theater came with the one-act play *Margareta*, written with the aid of the man-of-letters Emil Nervander and Kaarlo Bergbom. The work's patriotic pathos, Runeberg-inspired, would be praised decades later by the superpatriot V. A. Koskenniemi (see below); when it was printed in 1871, the generous introduction by Fredrik Cygnaeus let readers know that the playwright had fallen prey to madness.

Kivi's only novel, *Seitsemän veljestä* (1870; Eng. tr. *Seven Brothers*, 1929, rev. 1973; 1991), has become established as his principal work. In many respects it is exceptional both for its time and in its genre. To begin with, the plot is unusual: seven brothers who have been left as orphans flee to the forest from the pressure of the community and spend ten years on their remote farm, hunting at first, later tilling the land. There are two external reasons for the move: the brothers are obliged to learn to read under the strict parish clerk (a task they hate from their very souls), and their clashes with the young men of the neighboring village have turned violent. At the novel's end the brothers have matured in the hard school of the backwoods and return to their former home as literate citizens; then all but one go their separate ways to establish families.

The isolated forest environment gives the book the flavor of an adventure novel. From one angle it is a sort of Robinson Crusoe tale, in which the brothers' survival skills and inventiveness are severely tested. But at the same time, mythical dimensions open up in their life, in the form of stories and fairy tales told by one of the brothers, Aapo. When they move to the forest, the brothers are naive children of nature who believe in goblins and ghosts and experience life as a mythical reality. Gradually, as they accumulate knowledge and skill — and with their increasing literacy — the fearful, unknown powers retreat ever further, while a rational relation to life becomes stronger. (One sign of this change is the shift from a hunting economy to deliberate cultivation.) Thus the novel becomes an *Entwicklungsroman,* the story of the change in the brothers and of their becoming civilized.

The author's skill is revealed in the fact that he does not moralize or turn the story into a pedagogical, exemplary tale. During the course of the novel the brothers find themselves in various critical situations demanding a choice, situations that threaten their whole existence and force them to make their own decisions about their future. Kivi has carefully developed the brothers as individuals, each with his own character, his own strong and weak sides, his own intelligence, and his own way of speaking and reacting. A great part of the novel is in dialogue form: as in a play, the speaker's name is given along with his lines, and conclusions are left to the reader. Thus the characterization of the brothers emerges from their speeches and their reactions, without pointed comments or explanations by the narrator. In the Scandinavian novels of the later nineteenth century this technique was quite exceptional, although it had been employed by the Swede C. J. L. Almqvist in his *Drottningens juvelsmycke* (1834; Eng. tr. *The Queen's Diadem,* 1993); in the matter of telling versus showing, Kivi clearly comes down on the side of the latter.

The male preponderance in the novel may seem strange to many readers. Women appear only in the early pages, in a comic courting scene that comes to nothing, and in the review of the brothers' later lives that brings the novel together in the last chapter. There are few novels in world literature — apart from *Robinson Crusoe,* some sea stories, war novels, and tales of the wilds — in which the gallery of characters is so accentuated toward the male. But this one-sidedness has its own significance in the novel as a whole: on the one hand, it emphasizes a certain primitivity and helplessness in the brothers, and on the other hand, their heroic struggle against the forces of nature is revealed in all its harshness. The lyrical and mythical tones of the intermediate tales are a softening, enriching feature, as is the humor coloring the relations between the brothers throughout. The narrator does not make them ideal figures by any means, nor does he exaggerate the hardness of their life, but he points out the amusing features in their speech and behavior. The combination of realism and humor is indeed typical, from Kivi onward, of the Finnish tradition of the novel as a whole; the roots of many of its other features can also be traced to Kivi and to some extent through him to Runeberg and the *Kalevala.*

Linguistically, the novel enters territory that had been very little charted. Kivi was forced to a large extent to trust his ear and his instinct and to build partly on the basis of his local dialect. In one of his letters he rebels against the stiff and sterile use of language by his contemporaries and cries that reading them "is like chewing chips of wood and stones." His pioneer work in language has in two respects proved an obstacle to the impact of *Seitsemän veljestä:* because August Ahlqvist, who started from the foundation of another dialect and adopted the role of the purist guardian of the language, attacked the novel, and because the translation of the novel into other languages has proved extremely difficult. The most successful renderings have been made into "neighboring" languages — Swedish and Estonian — whereas translation into English has proved difficult. Several translations have appeared in German, and two in French, but it still seems that the foreign reader's road into Kivi's novel is stony and tortuous. The Finnish reader, on the contrary, can fully enjoy Kivi's language, its full-bodied rhythm, the rare verbal richness, and its archaic features, to which time has given its own charming patina.

The power of *Seitsemän veljestä* is its diversity. One can read it as an exciting adventure story, a tale of survival growing to almost mythical dimension, a study of the relations between man and nature, a description of the actions and conflicts of a small group under difficult conditions, a character study of seven diverse young men, a description of the move from a natural economy to organized farming, an incomparably humorous novel, or a serious *Entwicklungsroman* in which the characters grow from a state of nature to civilization — and from many other points of view as well. It is surprising and paradoxical that the first Finnish-language novel has become the most beloved in Finland, the most read for almost a century, a work known to all.

Kivi was equally original as a poet. He constructed his meter to a great extent on spoken language, abandoned rhyme almost completely, and took advantage of the opportunities offered by Finnish for vowel harmony and "sound painting." The poems of Oksanen and Krohn are much more mechanical and stiff than Kivi's verse. Kivi had to pay for his solutions: the development of Finnish poetic language followed the Germanic usage cultivated by Oksanen and Krohn, whereas Kivi's style won no followers. His range of subjects also proved a barrier; Kivi wrote little of the patriotic poetry expected by the times, though he created his own version of Runeberg's "Vårt land" (Our land) as "Suomenmaa" (Land of Suomi). His love poetry seldom has the romanticized personal tone employed by contemporaries; he favored broad descriptive panoramas and wrote long narrative poems focused on human fate epically described. He published only one collection of his poems, *Kanervala* (1866; Where the heath grows), and a broad selection in the monthly literary magazine *Kirjallinen kuukauslehti*. His contemporaries fought shy of the form of his poems and called them, in Kaarlo Bergbom's words, gold "that is not minted as money at all." It was not until far into the twentieth century that the value of Kivi's poetry was recognized and readers learned to perceive the original features of his poetic style.

Kivi's principal work met adverse winds because of Ahlqvist's murderous reviews. They affected Kivi's precarious health and evidently contributed to his breakdown. Ahlqvist's harsh, scathing opinions also influenced the judgments rendered by other contemporaries — with the exception of Fredrik Cygnaeus and, to some extent, Kaarlo Bergbom — and acted for a long time as a damper. Scholars and critics who were sincerely enthusiastic about Kivi labeled him a kind of a natural genius, creating spontaneously without strict intellectual control. The history of the genesis of Kivi's works, however, reveals quite the contrary: we know he wrote *Seitsemän veljestä* at least three times, and the manuscripts of his poems that have been preserved show how he polished, changed, and revised, writing his drafts again and again. His correspondence — which, it is true, consists of only a little over seventy letters, some of them brief settlements of money matters — reveals undoubted intellectual awareness and interest in a variety of general questions. Knowledge of the books Kivi owned or read show that his taste was discerning and that he was especially interested in those classics whose example encouraged him to adopt unconventional stylistic or structural approaches. His pen was constantly guided by a critical and judicious attitude, an uncompromising awareness of his own special quality, and a deep conviction of the worth of his best works. When the decision of his publishers, the Finnish Literary Society, to print *Seitsemän veljestä* was delayed, he wrote sharply to the readers of the manuscript: "Do as you think best; I myself will never reject the brothers, even if you consider it totally insignificant. I will not take away a single page from it, even if it means that in time I should publish it myself" (letter to Kaarlo Bergbom, 19 May 1869). Surely, only a writer who knows what he is doing can speak thus. The estimation of later readers has proved Kivi's self-assurance justified and has crowned his novel as the first classic of Finnish-language fiction.

A Quiet Decade

The vigorous expansion of the 1860s did not continue as intensively (in Finnish-language literature) during the subsequent decade. Aleksis Kivi was gone; the academic poets Oksanen and Suonio did not continue their literary work on any considerable scale — they were content to supplement their earlier collections with new poems and applied themselves more thoroughly to academic research and teaching. The 1870s were a sort of intermediate phase in Finnish-language literature (unlike the situation in Denmark, Norway, and Sweden), a quiet decade that did not produce new accomplishments but prepared the ground for the future. The nature of cultural life changed in particular because, alongside Swedish-language mass media and institutions, Finnish-language equivalents began to appear at a brisk rate. Language associations were established (such as the Philosophical Society, which became an important academic forum for debate, in 1873). Finnish-language publishing expanded. Previously, there had been little more than the Finnish Literary Society and a few booksellers who did some publishing. There now appeared two new publishing houses, Weilin & Göös and K. J. Gummerus, both established in Jyväskylä, the most important school-and-seminary city in the interior. Their vitality was shown by the fact that both are still in operation. In 1878 Werner Söderström (WSOY) was established in Porvoo; today it is the largest publishing house in Finland and one of the biggest in the whole of Scandinavia.

The Finnish Theater, which had begun with the production of Kivi's *Lea* in 1869, became a permanent establishment in 1872 and was managed from the first by the energetic brother and sister Kaarlo and Emilie Bergbom. Their directorship lasted into the new century, until 1905. Kaarlo Bergbom (1843–1906), the friend of Kivi, was himself a writer but did his most significant work as a literary critic and especially as a theater manager. During his time the Finnish Theater repertoire included classics of world literature — Shakespeare, Molière, Holberg, Schiller, and the new Norwegian playwrights, led by Ibsen. Bergbom also played a key role by bringing a new dramatist, Minna Canth, into the theater in the next decade.

The advent of a Finnish-language theater had been prepared by a series called *Näytelmistö* (starting 1861; Plays), containing both translations and original dramas, including Kivi's *Karkurit*. Since the Finnish Theater, especially in its early years, toured the country, it created a foundation both for future drama and for expanding interest in the theater.

The decade also saw the growth of the press. The papers contained much literature — serials, short stories, causeries. As Finnish came to be used in a great variety of functions, it developed rapidly in both vocabulary and sentence structure. At the end of the 1870s Finnish was a quite different kind of language, more flexible and richer in expression, than twenty years before.

The press and increasing interest in the theater also created opportunities for writers, starting in the 1870s. Their forum was often a newspaper or a periodical, and the informal short story and short comedy became established as their most typical genres.

Miniature Humorists

The literary scholar Unto Kupiainen has established the general name of the writers of this period as the "miniature humorists" (in a study of the same name, 1939). The title suits the next-named two writers well; the third (Päivärinta) goes his own way, farther from the field of humor.

K.G.S. Suomalainen (1850–1907) was a teacher at the Sortavala Seminary and used the pen name Samuli S. Some of his works can be placed geographically in the idyllic little town of Sortavala on the shores of Lake Ladoga, in an area that was ceded to the Soviet Union after World War II. Tales describing the petit bourgeois and craftsmen appeared in the collection *Novelleja* (1876–85; Short stories). The most interesting of Samuli S.'s works historically are the short stories in *Kevään ajoilta* (1900; Springtime), about the Finnish colony in St. Petersburg. Here he has caught for posterity a milieu and way of life long since past. Suomalainen, born in St. Petersburg, knew Russian well — a rare thing in Finland — and did excellent translations of Russian literature, in particular Gogol's *Dead Souls*.

Robert Kiljander (1848–1924) was a postmaster in Jyväskylä and developed into a clever playwright. His little comedies are without exception located in an environment familiar to the writer: a stagnant small town peopled by civil servants conscious of their worth, and their wives, whose interests hardly extend beyond their homes and town gossip. There are satirical elements in Kiljander's plays, but in general their atmosphere is gentle and conventional, though the characters may be caricatures, as in *Amalia ystävämme* (1881; Amalia, our friend), and comic types, as in *Postikonttorissa* (1887; At the post office). The period of biting social criticism did not arrive until the following decade, to which many of Kiljander's plays belong chronologically but not in terms of their atmosphere.

The third writer of the same period became known in translation both in the Scandinavian countries and in Germany, and his name appeared for a long time in international indexes of writers. He was Pietari Päivärinta (1827–1913), a parish clerk from north Finland. He did not go in for the cheerful lightness of the miniature humorists or their small-town milieu and types. He was a portrayer of the countryside, describing his own life, what he saw and heard, a little monotonously but with effective originality. His works reveal the world of poor people, harsh and gray, and show social contrasts. The laconic and modest names of Päivärinta's chief works are typical: *Elämäni* (1877; My life) and *Elämän havainnoita* (1879–89; Observations of life). A historically significant document is *Pikakuvia 1867 katovuodesta* (Snapshots of the famine year of 1867), describing a catastrophe that affected the whole Finnish countryside; his account of it was published a quarter of a century later, in 1893. There is a direct line from Päivärinta's works to subsequent Finnish descriptions of the common folk, and many attitudes that were to become familiar later on can be distinguished here. Päivärinta even criticizes the clergy, with a harsh irony that is otherwise rare in his writing.

The society Päivärinta describes is still static, almost immobile, though the famine years cast their own gloomy shadow. The other miniature humorists or their contemporaries also note the changes that are beginning. In a novel by Wilho Soini (1854–1934) called *Kirjavia kuvia pölkkyjen historiasta* (1877; Colorful scenes from the history of logs), a new and in many ways topical theme opens up: the invention of forest management and matters related to it. Soini describes both the increase in the value of the forests and the speculation and downright swindling of the lumber business. Cracks are beginning to appear in the agrarian, patriarchal Finnish society, to which the writers of the subsequent decade immediately directed their attention.

Poets of the Transition Period
The Finnish-language poetry that found its beginnings during this decade did not proceed along the lines marked out by Kivi. Its points of departure were first Runeberg, second the more recent folk song, and partly also Oksanen and Suonio. Much of the poetry of the period is sentimental and conventional. One of the most personal poets of the time, Paavo Cajander (1846–1913), devoted himself to translating Shakespeare and Runeberg into Finnish. Another, Arvid Genetz (1848–1915; his nom de plume was Arvi Jännes), who succeeded to Ahlqvist's professorship, wrote patriotic poetry, the leading idea of which is the spirit of kinship, the affinity of Finno-Ugric peoples.

Two poets, however, clearly stood out: J. H. Erkko and Kaarlo Kramsu. Juhana Henrik Erkko (1849–1906) was one of the first pupils at the Jyväskylä Seminary and for a long time was a teacher in Viipuri; his poetry reveals ideals of popular education and various beneficial endeavors (teetotalism, the youth association movement, the national ideal, and later the workers' movement as well). Following in Oksanen's footsteps, Erkko wrote songs for the provinces, the style of which is roughly the same as in N.F.S. Grundtvig's poem "Jyllands Priis" (1816; In Jutland's praise). Erkko's poetic soul was also readily kindled by love, as witnessed by his numerous lines praising the charm of girls and the excellence of women. He was equally inspired by nature, that of both Finland and Italy.

Erkko's wide range is explained by the fact that his career as a poet covered three and a half decades, a time of new ideals and diverse political changes. Erkko tried to follow his era closely and also interpreted the social themes favored by realism in his plays, whose subject matter was often from the *Kalevala: Aino* (1893), *Kullervo* (1895), and *Pohjolan häät* (1902; The Pohjola wedding), the last of which inaugurated the new building of the National Theater.

Erkko's plays have been forgotten, but many of his poems still live. Some of his lines are so well known that people have thought them to be from folk songs, and some have been set to music, providing a basic repertoire for school singing lessons and popular concerts. Erkko's flexible diction and meter also capture attention: his poetry forms a bridge in style and poetic technique from Oksanen and Suonio to Eino Leino.

If Erkko is one of the most wide-ranging poets of his time, the strength of his contemporary, Kaarlo Kramsu (1855–95), is in the narrowness of his gamut and the concentration of his style. Kramsu's special field is the Club War, the tragic peasant revolt at the end of the sixteenth century, which had become topical thanks to a study (1857–59) by Yrjö Koskinen (1830–1903), historian, writer, and Finnish nationalist politician. In his collection, *Runoelmia* (1878–87; Poems), Kramsu wrote gloomy ballads about lost battles and the executions of the revolt's defeated leaders. The structural models for the poems were evidently Runeberg's *Fänrik Ståls sägner* (1848–60; see chapter 7), but their tone is darker, inconsolably pessimistic. The whole history and society of Finland seems to be the battleground of the oppressive lords and the exploited people; the work of the peasant, says the ballad "Jaakkima Berens," has always been the building anew of what the lords razed to the ground.

Equally dark is the vision that appears in Kramsu's poems dealing with his own fate. Life is seen as brief and transient; the views of eternity offered by religion, or its consolation in general, do not exist. The logical, almost unbroken pessimism of the poems is emphasized by Kramsu's telling style, compact as a proverb. Bare and avoiding metaphor, his style is a virtue in his poetry, imprinting his muscular lines, which exude historical and social defiance, on the reader's mind. Kramsu's straightforward, concentrated language may seem meager and somber but never insignificant. After Kivi, his is the most individual and angular poetic profile of the period. Together with Kivi and Wecksell he also established the legendary concept of the poet as a short-lived, sick, tragic figure — a concept that was unfortunately confirmed until the 1930s by the fates of many later poets of the same kind.

The Era of Realism

A new generation of authors stepped forth at the beginning of the 1880s to bring a new current to Finnish literature: programmatic realism. For the first time, a group of writers was formed that can be considered comparatively close-knit (the literary societies of the eighteenth century and the Turku romantics at the beginning of the nineteenth century were not very uniform). Also for the first time, the debut of the new trend occurred at almost the same time as its breakthrough in other Scandinavian countries.

In 1885 Juhani Aho defined the nature of Finnish realism in *Kaiku* (Echo), an Oulu newspaper, as follows: "Realistic literature, as indeed its name reveals, is based on real circumstances. In its descriptions it aims at making its stand on the foundation of natural life, taking from it elements from both its good and its bad sides."

Aho continues the article by rejecting the idea that realism is "literature presenting only the dark side of life." It does indeed describe this, but another of its aims is, on the contrary, to "remove the dark side." Aho believes realism actually has an idealistic purpose: "The banishing of all that is ugly, wrong, and bad, and its replacement by all that is beautiful, right, and good."

Aho's definition is perhaps too idealistic, but it contains much that is characteristic of Finnish realism of the 1880s. The writers did their work according to high moral aims and attacked what they thought were obsolete, petrified institutions and ways of thought. Their motive for destroying the old was that "they wanted something new in its place," and their objective was "to aim at the truth and to reach the truth." Earlier writers had done their work without manifestoes, whose appearance was a novelty. What was new besides the forming of the literary group was its polemical nature and the way it used the press and sought and found support for its ideas in contemporary foreign literature.

Domestic Roots of Realism

The roots of Finnish realism of the 1880s lead in three main directions: a reflection of a general change in living conditions, a new kind of emphasis on some special features of Finnish literature, and the influence of the trends and theories of foreign art. A tangible change, plain for all to see, was the broad structural process of social transformation. The change in old-fashioned agriculture had been hastened by the years of crop failure in the 1860s. Alongside farming, forest management began to establish itself; its importance had previously been chiefly restricted to the obtaining of firewood and tar-burning. Industry began to appear, attracting to the cities the excess rural population, whose increase was already a problem. As the cities began to grow, especially the capital, Helsinki, industrial centers also began to form, such as Tampere and Kotka. The system of government based on a Diet with four estates started to disintegrate, and the working class began to stir. New means of transport shortened distances: it was no chance that the name of Juhani Aho's first novel was *Rautatie* (1884; The railroad). The newspapers brought fresh news from the world at large; they were now edited in a different way, and they appeared more frequently.

All these factors created a favorable soil for the germination and growth of realism. The proportion of Finnish-speakers, as opposed to speakers of Swedish, also began to change. The language decree of 1863, which placed Finnish on an equal footing with Swedish, had entailed a transitional period of twenty years, which ended in 1883. The new writers had already received part of their school education in Finnish. The press was at their disposal to a greater extent than before; Juhani Aho worked as a journalist in a couple of rural towns, and when the group's own newspaper, *Päivälehti* (later *Helsingin Sanomat*), was founded in 1889, he became a contributor to it. Along with the newspaper, an important literary album began to appear, *Nuori Suomi,* whose name refers to the new liberal-radical "Young Finns" party. An important cultural periodical was *Valvoja* (The watchman), started in 1880.

For a long time, there had been a tradition or partial tradition in Finland's literature that may be called "pre-realism." It had already appeared in the epics of Runeberg and in the poems of the *Kalevala.* Kaarlo Bergbom considered Kivi to be one of the "exuberant, original realists." The conflict of society and the individual is one of the main themes of *Seitsemän veljestä,* and this conflict is not alien to Runeberg's heroes either. In the works of both writers the everyday life of common people makes a strong appearance.

The writers of the 1870s who followed Kivi based their works on personal, precise, and to some extent critical observations, but they did not yet attempt to generalize them. In the 1880s the younger generation began to ask the significance of these observations, to combine them into a coherent chain, and to draw their own conclusions from them. Some older writers had opened up the trail: in Päivärinta's works there is even biting social criticism, and Kiljander is clearly a predecessor of Minna Canth's early plays. The critical consideration of defects and the vigilant registering of changes is a key principle of the realists of the 1880s. Juhani Aho's early short story "Siihen aikaan kun isä lampun osti" (Eng. tr. "When Father Brought Home the Lamp," *Squire Hellman and Other Stories*, 1893) shows how the old times are inexorably giving way to the new: the story describes how a new oil lamp brings bright light to a cottage formerly illuminated by shingle or candle and transforms people's living conditions.

The realists regarded the changes and reforms, and the coming of new technical inventions as well, as progress. A decade later they were no longer so sure.

Foreign Influences
Other great underlying factors were the strengthening of scientific thinking, especially with the coming of Darwinism, and the increased influence of Scandinavian literature.

The Norwegians achieved a special status among Scandinavian writers. Ibsen's *Et dukkehjem* (1879; Eng. tr. *A Doll's House,* 1880) was played in Helsinki, in Finnish, as early as February 1880. A year earlier a Helsinki man, Valfrid Vasenius (see chapter 8), had been the first in the world to publish an academic dissertation about Ibsen, following it in 1882 with a biography of the playwright. Ibsen's tremendous popularity is also witnessed by the little-known fact that his *John Gabriel Borkman* (1896; Eng. tr. 1897) was given its world premiere in Helsinki—a few days before the Norwegian first night—simultaneously in two theaters in two languages, Swedish and Finnish.

Bjørnstjerne Bjørnson visited Finland several times, and many of his works were translated; Jonas Lie became a real best seller; some of his works were even turned into Finnish three times. Before 1890 some thirty translations of Norwegian literature had appeared, not including those published in newspapers or plays in manuscript. In addition, it must be remembered that educated Finnish-speakers knew Swedish well enough to read other Scandinavian languages and even learned, like Juhani Aho, to read Arne Garborg's difficult *landsmål*, radically different from the then standard Dano-Norwegian. When the literary historian Viljo Tarkiainen laconically states that around 1880 Finland became a literary colony of Norway for a decade, the assertion is not greatly exaggerated (*Suomalaisen kirjallisuuden historia,* 203).

The most important Danish influence was Georg Brandes. Minna Canth began to translate and publish Brandes's series, *Hovedstrømninger i det nittende aarhundredes litteratur* (1872–90; Eng. tr. *Main Currents in Nine-*

teenth-Century Literature, 1901–5), but the enterprise dried up after the first volume appeared in 1887. Nonetheless, Brandes became the theoretical leader of Finnish realism. When he claimed in the introduction to his series that the vitality of literature was revealed in its ability to set problems under debate, this idea became a preceptlike slogan in Finland. Other of his ideas were carefully followed as well, including his turning away from realism toward an aristocratic individualism. Among Swedish writers, August Strindberg early became well known in Finland; his works were read in their original language before they were translated.

For a long time, the underlying influences on Finnish realism were considered to come from Scandinavia and to some extent from France and England (Darwin's theory of evolution, Herbert Spencer's sociology, John Stuart Mill's ideas about women's rights, Henry Thomas Buckle's historical Darwinism, Hippolyte Taine's theories on milieu). But there was one more important factor: the Russian influence. The intermediary was the family of General Alexander Järnefelt (1833–96), and especially his wife Elisabet (1839–1929), whose maiden name was Clodt von Jürgensburg, a daughter of the liberal St. Petersburg intelligentsia. She learned Finnish and gave her children and their friends fresh information about the new Russian literature, especially Dostoyevsky and Tolstoy. Her literary salon, which began in 1881, was a veritable "school of the Järnefelts," as it has been called in correspondence and later studies.

The essential feature of Finnish realism, the use of types to represent whole groups of people — yet without losing individual features — was partly based on the theories of the Russian critic Vissarion Belinsky (1811–48). As Annamari Sarajas pointed out in her 1968 study, this theory reached Finnish writers before similar French ideas arrived via Scandinavia. The Järnefelt circle certainly was a kind of authors' workshop; for example, Aho's *Rautatie* (1884; The railroad) was gone through sentence by sentence. The core of the Järnefelt circle was made up of the children of the family, who soon became important cultural figures: Arvid Järnefelt, a writer; Erik (Eero), a painter; Armas, a conductor; Kasper, a translator; the daughter of the family, Aino, later married the composer Jean Sibelius. The circle was joined by Juhani Aho and his brother, and when the Järnefelts moved to Kuopio in the Finnish interior in 1884, by Minna Canth and Kauppis-Heikki as well. The essence of Elisabet Järnefelt's concept of art was sincerity and naturalness and the avoidance of artificial effects; art was "the worship of truth in the world of feeling." This concept, alongside the type theory, became the guiding principle of the circle's members. At the same time, the importance of social criticism and free thinking was emphasized according to Russian and Scandinavian models (Sarajas, *Tunnuskuvia;* Kopponen, "Arvid Järnefelt"). The influence of the Järnefelt school continued through its members far into later times — indeed, through Eero Järnefelt's family all the way to the young Sillanpää.

The change of generations also facilitated and hastened the coming to the fore of the realist generation. Runeberg had been silent since 1863 and died in 1877; Snellman died in 1881; Lönnrot in 1884; Topelius, it is true, continued his work and influence, but as an idealist he remained alien to the new currents. The field was open to the attack of the new and rebellious generation.

Canth

The earliest and oldest representative of the realists was Minna Canth (née Johnsson, 1844–97). She had been a student at the Jyväskylä Teachers' Seminary but had been forced to cut short her studies when she married her instructor, J. Fr. Canth, in 1865. After her husband died in 1879, Minna Canth moved to Kuopio (in 1880) and maintained her family of seven children with a dry-goods shop inherited from her father. The most militant representative of Finnish realism was thus in many ways an exceptional phenomenon: a woman, the mother of a large family, an independent entrepreneur.

Minna Canth began with little tales and achieved popularity with a folk play, *Murtovarkaus* (1882; The burglary); here and in *Roinilan talossa* (1883; In the house of Roinila) she continued Kiljander's comedy line; the language is seasoned with proverbs, and a happy end is achieved after many complications and misunderstandings. Then the tone suddenly changes: the play *Työmiehen vaimo* (1885; A worker's wife) became the first explosive charge of realism. Canth's "realism of indignation" begins with it, raising one topical problem after another for critical examination.

The principal character of the play, Johanna, is a woman who, after getting married, loses her independence and is subjugated to and exploited by her husband. The existing law decrees that the property and funds of the family, including the wife's former savings, are controlled by the man. The husband, Risto, spends the family's money on drink and steals the cloth his wife has woven. When those who have ordered the cloth put pressure on Johanna and threaten her with imprisonment, she breaks down, becomes ill, and dies. The frivolous Risto seems to have been finally brought to account when Homsantuu, the gypsy girl he has seduced and betrayed, intends to shoot him. The bullet misses, however; Homsantuu is imprisoned, and at the end of the play the man is off again to the tavern with his drinking companion. But the words of Homsantuu in the last act continue to resound: "Your law and your justice . . . it's them I ought to have shot."

For the first time, *Työmiehen vaimo* gives the theater and audience—educated and middle class—a realistic picture of workers' life. Simultaneously, the picture is critical: the barb of indignation is aimed at the existing law, which unjustly sets up the husband as the autocrat of his family, even when he irresponsibly wastes the family's money, destroys his wife, and finally gives his child to foster parents so that he can be "quite carefree of the boy." Conventional Christian morality, which promises redemption after death and does not interfere in obvious evils, is also censured. Finally, the contrast between the middle and working class is shown when the well-to-do folk who have ordered the cloth, Mr. and Mrs. Vörsky and Mrs. Hanhinen, arrive to look for it and threaten Johanna. (These may very well be comic names: "Vörsky" suggests the Russian *vor*, "thief, robber," and Hanhinen the Finnish *hanhi*, "goose.") Thus, all at once, the play brings up women's rights, criticism of the law and religion, social contrasts, and, through drunkenness and the worthless man, temperance as well. Injustice against women is further emphasized by being presented in two different forms, in the destruction of both Johanna and Homsantuu.

The novel *Hanna* (1886), a story about the development of a young girl, also stresses the disparity in the status of women and men. Where the object of comparison in the play was the husband, alongside Hanna are set her father and brother, whose life seems to be regulated by quite different moral concepts from those governing Hanna and her mother. The education of women, or rather its lack, is a theme to which Canth returns in various connections; it is dealt with in the works of other idealists too, especially Juhani Aho and Teuvo Pakkala.

In the long story *Köyhää kansaa* (1886; Poor folk) and the play *Kovan onnen lapsia* (1888; Children of misfortune) Canth continues her portrayal of the workers. Now the most wretched members of the proletariat are considered; the criticism in the story is directed at poorly organized social care and especially at the cruel treatment of the mentally ill, but more broadly it is about the position and living conditions of the poor as a whole. The same issues are the essence of *Kovan onnen lapsia*, which contains the most powerful social accusations of Canth's combative period. In it there appears the contumacious Topra-Heikki, who has been called the first communist in Finnish literature. "The law protects the rich, but it persecutes us," he says, and later asks, "Isn't there a war between the rich and the poor?" The social contrast is thus exacerbated to the point of armed conflict.

Kovan onnen lapsia was received with shocked bewilderment. People felt Canth had put matters too aggressively and one-sidedly, exceeding the bounds of decency. The play was removed from the Finnish Theater after only one performance, although Bergbom did not want to submit to the censorship of the board of directors. Canth presented the most radical ideological line of the workers' movement in her play, socialism in its anarchistic form; but the fact that at the same time she condemned its violent expression received less attention.

Although Canth was aware of what sort of reactions realism had aroused in Norway, she was nevertheless disappointed by the fate of her play. Her next work was again an extended novella, *Kauppa-Lopo* (1889; Peddler Lopo), the best known of her pieces of fiction. The main character is a rather simple but goodhearted market vendor who comes up against the law because of her misdemeanors. Actually, she is exploited in many ways, and in particular the hardness and selfishness of "decent people" comes under a revealing light. The shabby, clumsy Peddler Lopo proves to be a warmer and more genuine human being than they; the scale of social values is turned upside-down in the story as the good and the bad change places, although the respectable middle-class wives do not realize it.

Kovan onnen lapsia and *Kauppa-Lopo* marked the end of Canth's period of social criticism. In the latter, as in some of her other short stories, the focus had already begun to shift from accusations against the law, the church, and social evils to individual characterization. *Kauppa-Lopo* is a psychological study of how different traits of character can exist in the same person and how Kauppa-Lopo's reactions can be wrongly interpreted.

There was still one problem that Canth had not dealt with: the clash between the generations, the question of the liberation of young people from the toils of authority and old-fashioned family ties. She handles these matters in a play called *Papin perhe* (1891; The parson's family). It is notable that criticism of the clergy and a new interpretation of their position were favorite themes of the realists. In the same years, Juhani Aho wrote his *Papin tytär* (1885; The parson's daughter) and *Papin rouva* (1893; The parson's wife), and the position of the clergy and the church was debated in many newspaper articles and polemical controversies. During 1889–90 Canth edited a little periodical called *Vapaita aatteita* (Liberal thoughts), the first article of which dealt with Darwinism and which otherwise spread realistic theoretical concepts through its popular natural-scientific writings.

In *Papin perhe* the old-fashioned father, Valtari, and his full-grown children are in opposite camps. The daughter, Maiju, wants to go on the stage, which the father of course believes is sinful, and the son, Jussi, writes radical articles for a newspaper of the Young Finns, articles that infuriate the father. After relations have been broken off—the daughter has run away from home and the son has begun to live his own life—the father realizes that he has brought his children up too strictly and begins to apply the Christian doctrine of love to his own family life. The result is a reconciliation in which both parties begin to understand each other's motives. "Life cannot stop," says Jussi, the son, in the final scene, "it must be allowed to go ahead freely. The old truths must make way for the new." *Papin perhe* is Canth's first play in which the lights and shadows are no longer divided with irrevocable rigor. But Jussi's remark shows that Canth has certainly not abandoned her former battle station. "Old truths must make way for the new" remains a motto for her work to the very end.

Canth wrote her next play, *Sylvi* (1893), in Swedish and offered it to the Swedish Theater after she had a difference of opinion with Kaarlo Bergbom. Here the focus has shifted to a psychological portrayal of the individual: Sylvi, the principal character, has received a typical upbringing for the period and lives in her own fantasy world. After getting married, she becomes a doll, the child-wife of her older husband, not understanding much of the demands of everyday life. When a former love of her youth comes into her life, she gives herself entirely to the new affair and sees the poisoning of her husband as her only possibility. In prison she still thinks that her new lover approves of her deed, but she breaks down when she realizes that he too has rejected her.

Sylvi's character is one of great intensity: she throws herself utterly into her new love, unable to distinguish right from wrong and not realizing that her deed is criminal. She lives detached from the moral rules of society and acts quite sincerely, according to her own way of thinking. By setting Sylvi's uncompromising attitude and the rules of the society around her against each other, Canth again criticizes familiar objects: the upbringing of women, which produces women like Sylvi who are unaware of the real nature of things; the institution of marriage, which permits the union of an old man and an immature young woman; and legislation that condemns Sylvi without understanding the deeper reasons for her deed. But the criticism is less direct than previously: it arises from the conclusions to be drawn about the patterns of the play, and the theses are no longer presented in such a pointed way and as openly expressed in the dialogue as before.

The change in Canth's dramas reflects not only her personal development but also her time. A similar turning point occurred in the works of other authors, especially Juhani Aho. Individual questions superseded general problems as Finnish literature turned in the direction indicated by Brandes and perceptible in the development of Ibsen and Strindberg. With regard to Finland we must again bear in mind the contribution of Russian literature, which was felt, in the Järnefelt circle, in the strengthening of the influence not only of Tolstoy but of Dostoyevsky. (None of the members of the circle was attracted by Nietzsche's ideas of the superman; Tolstoy's undogmatic approach and the doubting of old truths seemed much more human and close at hand.) The influence of Tolstoy has been detected in Minna Canth's last play, *Anna Liisa* (1895; Eng. tr. 1997), but this work can be seen equally well as the reverse of *Sylvi*. Anna Liisa is a farmer's daughter who has been seduced when young and, to hide her shame and in her ignorance, has killed her child. When she is about to get married, her former seducer starts to blackmail her and demands that she marry him instead; his object is to inherit a large house and its property. But Anna Liisa does not give way to this proposition. She chooses a harder road: to confess her crime publicly and go to prison to atone for it. Contrary to the situation in *Sylvi,* her fiancé does not turn away in fear but understands Anna Liisa's honesty and declares that he will stand by her.

The theme is thus, as in Dostoyevsky's novel, crime and punishment. The main emphasis is on the process of Anna Liisa's inner maturing and on her choice: the truth is worth more to her than an externally blameless but inwardly false life with the wrong man. By choosing the more difficult alternative, she cleanses herself and atones for her former crime. Let the truth come forth! — the old war cry of the realists is thus the essence of Canth's last play, this time in an individual application but nonetheless impressive. *Anna Liisa* is one of the best of Canth's plays.

Minna Canth was the most pure-blooded realist in Finnish literature. She began as a fighter of social battles and directed her criticism fearlessly at the same targets as Ibsen in Norway and Strindberg in Sweden. She was also the most idealistic of the idealists, presenting requirements to men like those of Bjørnson concerning the obligations of marriage; her uncompromising demands for male purity drove her at times to break with Juhani Aho. Her relation with the Järnefelt family also suffered, for example, because of the harsh disclosures of her long story *Köyhää kansaa*. Canth was the most inflexible and courageous of the realists; she did not give way to compromise but put her whole personality in the balance. She financed her work as a writer with her shop, and her plays only gradually became remunerative.

Minna Canth showed the way for future women writers. She was the most important playwright after Kivi; among the dramatists to follow her, two of the most significant have been women: Maria Jotuni and Hella Wuolijoki. This is a typical phenomenon in Finnish literature: since Kivi, the best drama in the country has been produced by strong women.

Aho in the Era of Realism

Along with Minna Canth, the most conspicuous representative of the realists was Juhani Aho (born Brofeldt; 1861–1921), a clergyman's son, journalist, and in the last years of his life a kind of "national" writer. But there is a difference between the realism of Canth and that of Aho: whereas Canth's accusations could often be abstracted as clear theses, aimed at changing social conditions and remedying evils, Aho was content first and foremost to describe people in their own environment and as products of that environment. Some of Canth's works, such as *Köyhää kansaa,* even led to real improvements. Aho, however, presented his social criticism and demands for reform in newspaper articles and dealt with people's fates in his literary work; their problems might point in several directions. Canth was uncompromising and severe in her demands; Aho was a relativist — the conclusions often grew indirectly from his works. Aho also changed so much as a writer during his long career that the young realist and the later lyrical and more melancholy Aho should be dealt with separately, as is done here.

In two respects the young Aho was closely connected with the realists' endeavors: he wished to describe the reality he saw and felt faithfully and without embellishment, and he was alert to notice the changes brought by the new times. His first masterful short story described the coming of the oil lamp to a small, remote village; his first novel, *Rautatie* (1884; The railroad), described the fancies of an old country couple concerning the railroad and their unsuccessful train journey. The new means of transport interested Aho in other works, too. In a long short story, *Helsinkiin* (1889; To Helsinki), a young student travels by steamship and train to the capital to study, and when he arrives at the station changes to horse-drawn transport. The principal character in a novella called *Yksin* (1890; Alone) goes to Paris by ship and train. In both works the travel impressions of the main characters are carefully described, and for the first time in Finnish literature things are seen from a moving vehicle. The new times thrust aside the old, bringing with them a new world of values.

But at an early stage there is also doubt whether the new is always better after all; in *Rautatie* the disappointment of the old couple leaves a melancholy aftertaste, and in the novella *Maailman murjoma* (1894; Ill-used by life) the railroad and the train destroy the life of a simple countryman. The contrast of the old and new times, of the remote, stagnant village idyll and the fast-paced city, are key themes in Aho's work, and it becomes clear at the same time that technical progress may be a threat to peace of mind.

The areas that are most Aho's own are thus from the start the remote countryside on the one hand, whose dwellers he describes knowledgeably and humorously, and on the other hand the city, where one moves in the circles of students, artists, and office workers. The two milieus may appear side by side: the main character in the novella *Yksin* thinks of the landscapes of his native district while he is in Paris, and in the novels *Papin tytär* (1885; The parson's daughter) and *Papin rouva* (1893; The parson's wife) a traveler coming from Helsinki and later from Paris adds color to the story. Nor was it any accident that while he was in Paris, Aho wrote perhaps his most lyrical short story describing Finnish summer scenery, "Kosteikko, kukkula, saari . . ." (Wetland, hilltop, island . . .).

Aho reformed Finnish prose style. The school of the Järnefelts and of French literature proved fruitful. His writing is expressive and at the same time precise; his dialogue follows the speech of the common people in both its rhythm and its vocabulary, and descriptive passages draw a detailed picture of people and environment. Aho skillfully adopted the impressionistic style popular in Scandinavian literature: changes of illumination, changing perspectives, and, in particular, movement interested him, but the nuances of the human mind and relations of characters only hinted at also receive attention. In his later work and especially in the short stories, which Aho called *Lastuja* (Chips from the block), the lyrical element might penetrate to the foreground so powerfully that the result resembled a prose poem more than a clear-cut short story. *Lastuja* appeared in eight series (1891–1921) and formed a kind of hallmark of Aho's which tended to overshadow his more significant achievements in the public eye.

Most of the works of the young Aho were certainly achievements; within ten years he created a series of books that have remained permanently in Finnish literature. The early work *Rautatie*, both as a description of the common people and as a humorous-melancholy novel, is a classic of its kind, the most significant novel since Kivi. *Helsinkiin* and *Yksin*, which in their time gave offense because of their description of drunkenness and erotic scenes, have remained unusually fresh and alive in spite of being written a century ago. To end his realist period, Aho wrote the novels *Papin tytär* and *Papin rouva*, both of which are among his best works.

Papin tytär describes the childhood and youth of Elli. She is an exuberant girl, a bit wild, who wants to climb up to high places and to look far out over the wide world. Both at home and at school an attempt is made to prune these boyish tendencies and to demonstrate that they are unsuitable for a young girl. Her time in school is nevertheless a liberating and happy period, but she is not allowed to continue her studies, since they are considered unnecessary for a girl. She falls for a student visiting her home, Olavi Kalm; momentarily feels a strong affinity with him; and is disappointed when he goes away. It is decided that she is to marry a curate, a decent, petit bourgeois, rather clumsy man. Elli's mother intimates that she herself was married against her will and had to deny herself many a budding desire. The mother's fate is repeated now in her daughter's life.

In *Papin rouva* Elli is married and lives in a remote parsonage; five years have passed since the events of the earlier novel. Elli has submitted to her fate but still awaits something more from life. From her lookout space she gazes at the lake:

> From here she had for many a summer looked out at the world without anyone's knowledge. And she called, looking at ships going by far away there, looking at the world; in calm weather she heard the throbbing of their engines and glimpsed them moving from the shelter of one promontory to behind another. It was the only connection she had with the outside world, that great and secret world dreamed of since she was a little girl, that she had read of in books and in which she believed that people lived a rich, full, and happy life.

Then the admired young man of her youth, Olavi Kalm, comes to the parsonage, straight from Paris, his suitcase full of French novels, about which he plans to write a doctoral dissertation. The old feeling is aroused again, and Olavi too enjoys being in the young wife's company, though he does not dare enter into an intimate relationship with her. The end of the novel is a repetition of the earlier one: Olavi Kalm goes away, and Elli remains in her house more lonely and disappointed than ever. In the final pages she looks out from her old spot "still, for the last time at her world, which was lost, closed, all the hopes vanished." Only the long winter awaits her, a desolate future with a husband she feels is a stranger.

Papin rouva is one of Aho's most lyrical works: nature in summer, the timid contacts of the lovers, and awakening hopes color the early part; deep depression and the closing of perspectives color the end. It can be read like the earlier books as a criticism of women's upbringing and position in the manner of Canth's work, but above all it is a study of a woman's life under the pressures of prejudice and moral concepts. At the same time, the sensitive description of Elli's inner life points to a new phase in Aho's work. The theses of realism have been gone through, and writers' eyes turn in a new direction. In spirit, *Papin rouva* belongs to a large degree to the 1890s.

Pakkala

Teuvo Pakkala (1862–1925) was a year younger than Aho and was not a member of Canth's salon or of the Järnefelts' school. He came from farther north, from Oulu, where he was employed for a time as a journalist. His university studies did not lead to a degree, but his employment as a teacher of French and Finnish and as a translator fitted in well with literary endeavors. During the last years of his life Pakkala became interested in the movies, too, and even tried his hand as a film director.

Pakkala's work is clearly divided into four main parts. The products of his younger days, *Lapsuuteni muistoja* (1895; Memories of my childhood) and *Oulua soutamassa* (1886; Rowing the Oulu River), are autobiographical descriptions of a poor childhood and working trips on the long waterways. The second phase began with *Vaaralla* (1891; On the hill), which was followed by a novel, *Elsa* (1894). The subtitle of the former is "pictures of the city outskirts"; the name refers to the part of Oulu where the poor folk lived. A small community is described by following the lives of a few people—widows, sailors' wives, children growing up in modest circumstances. Living in the same place and in shared conditions have united people, so that they are helpful, support each other, and feel solidarity. Research has shown that the picture Pakkala paints is historically and socially accurate.

Pakkala is connected with realism in the way he shows the contrast between the decent people of humble means and the uncomprehending bourgeois wives who reside in the town's center. One may also note criticism of religion: the moral teachings of the Christian faith are less in evidence than middle-class selfishness and utilitarian morality; the most truly religious woman in the book wonders why God punishes the poor by denying them worldly joy; and the novel's most skeptical character, the invalid Nikkilä, is more sharp-sighted in social and religious questions than other members of the cast.

In *Vaaralla* the children are almost as important as the adults. Their games reveal contrasting propensities and anticipate their future fates but also point to different alternatives. For Pakkala, children are a microcosm whose study reveals a picture of an entire life still at the stage of development. The chief character in *Elsa* is familiar from the earlier work: there she is a well-behaved, obedient girl, praised by parents to their own children for her good nature. Her mother is strongly religious, trusting God's guidance in everything. But things do not work out this way: in her credulity, Elsa is seduced by her former childhood companion, Jori, the son of gentlefolk, and dies unhappy. Almost her only help and her most faithful supporter is the tomboy of the novel, Liisa, who grows up from a wild, bold, overeager child to a balanced, prudent woman. The caliber of the two main characters has thus ironically changed: the unruly Liisa manages quite well in her life, the exemplary Elsa fails. There is also strong irony in the final scene of the novel, in which the clergyman Aappo, who has been feted, and Mari, whom he has seduced and who is on her way to prison, leave town on the same train.

Elsa is a link, in name as otherwise, between Scandinavian and Finnish realism: one thinks immediately of the Norwegian Alexander Kielland's short novel *Else* (1881; Eng. tr. *Elsie: A Christmas Story*, 1895), about a young woman's seduction and decay. The story of a seduced girl is an established part of the Scandinavian realist repertoire, and the hypocritical clergyman is an equally popular figure. In Pakkala's work one might even see something like Ibsen's "livsløgn" — "lie of life" — in Elsa's mother being led astray in her religion.

Pakkala shifted almost directly from his novels about Oulu to his third phase. In his collection of short stories called *Lapsia* (1895; Children) the same characters appear as in the earlier novels, even the same scenes viewed from a different angle. Contemporary and later readers have admired Pakkala both as an acute psychologist of childhood and as a fine humorist. Both viewpoints are justified, for the children's reactions in various situations are described realistically and their humorous side is observed. But the short stories do not have the moralizing, educational attitude that often marks earlier descriptions of children; although they are seen from the standpoint of the adult narrator, he is understanding and sympathetic; he does not set himself above those he describes but perceives, as in the novels, that play can also reveal a serious content.

All these features are present in Pakkala's later collection of short stories, whose title, *Pikku ihmisiä* (1913; Little people), emphasizes that these are character studies, not tales intended for youthful readers. The collection consists of four stories, three of which could have appeared in his previous book, except perhaps "Iikka raukkaa" (Poor Iikka), dealing with the life of a mentally retarded boy; in this story, too, the protagonist is described from a sympathetic angle, from that of his own circumstances, but the heartlessness and hardness of other people is also observed. The masterpiece of the collection is also the longest story, "Veli" (Brother). The principal character is a little girl, Laura, who projects her longing for a brother on a doll and registers the crises in her parents' marriage with events in her doll's house, without consciously realizing what she is doing. As in a puppet show, the doll's house has become a mirror of adult life, and little Laura's games and fantasies also reveal the tightening tension in the sensitive child. The situation is relieved when Laura brings home a beggar boy she has found on the street, who turns out to be a good lad and fills the place of the longed-for brother in just the right way. In the story Pakkala proves himself a master of nuance and small, revealing details: the network of human relations becomes more complex from page to page, the slight details of the environment begin to acquire symbolic meaning, and the final resolution grows inevitably from the events themselves, liberating and combining the different elements of the story.

"Veli" represents Pakkala's fourth phase, which began with the novel *Pieni elämäntarina* (1902; A little life story). It is one of the most impressionistic works in Finnish literature, but impressionistic in a different way from Aho's long novellas. The narration is noncontinuous, with gaps that the reader has to fill, and the main character's reactions are sudden and inexplicable. In accordance with its title, this is a life story, the tale of Ester Kalm, who has been left motherless from birth and whose relation with her father is problematic. Throughout her life Ester seeks her mother and her father's approval, but without success. She strays from one love affair to another, rootless and uncertain both of her own and of others' feelings. As in "Veli," unconscious forces and tensions direct people's actions; if the date of the novel were not so early, one might claim that Pakkala operated on the basis of Freudian or at least depth-psychology theories. But the sources of his characterizations are probably elsewhere, in Russian or Scandinavian literature (especially in the works of Knut Hamsun) and above all in Pakkala's own short stories about children, which show how the roots of adult fates stem from childhood, how completely opposite and conflicting endeavors can, side by side, influence a child's mind, how apparently accidental impulses may push a child in a wholly unexpected direction. "Veli" shows that the parents discovered childlike features in themselves and that the child's games could reflect serious adult problems. The concept of humanity in the novella and *Pieni elämäntarina* is the same, although the works are quite different in their interpretation. In *Pieni elämäntarina* the chaos prevailing in the chief character's mind determines the nature of the narration, whereas the short story—in a controlled manner but with equally little explanation—describes the development of the family crisis and its happy resolution. In both works the main character seeks the member of the family she needs, without whom she feels her life to be incomplete; the persons sought in the novel are the mother and the father, who is felt to be a stranger; in the short story it is the brother who becomes the double of the doll.

Pakkala's plays are very far from the atmosphere and style of *Pieni elä-*

mäntarina. The best known of them is *Tukkijoella* (1896; The loggers' river), which premiered in 1899. It is a harmless "comedy with song," the most popular of its kind in Finland, in good part because of the tunes of Oskar Merikanto (1868–1924); if one did not remember that Pakkala had recounted his own hard experiences as a logger in his early *Oulua soutamassa*, it would be difficult to believe he had written it. To some extent, it resembles the first plays of Minna Canth.

Teuvo Pakkala was not a fighter and accuser like Minna Canth, but his Oulu novels contain sharp social criticism, pointing the finger at the arrogance and heartlessness of the rich as Canth does in *Kauppa-Lopo*. Nor did Pakkala ever achieve the same kind of key position as Aho, though as a portrayer of women and children he attained at least as fine results. He did his life work a little aside from the mainstream and cultivated many literary genres — the distance between the play *Tukkijoella* and the novella "Veli" or *Pieni elämäntarina* is surprisingly great. But unlike most other realist works, his writings seem to contain concealed meanings and symbolic strata that hold the reader's interest and ask for interpretation.

Other Realists

Minna Canth, the young Juhani Aho, Teuvo Pakkala, and on the Swedish-language side Karl August Tavaststjerna (see chapter 8) were the key names in realism in Finland. In fact, the number of realists was much larger: Aho's brothers and numerous Young Finland writers can be included among them. Of these, Santeri Ivalo (1866–1937) in particular won many readers with his realistically handled historical novels, such as *Juho Vesainen* (1894), about a peasant leader and guerrilla fighter against the Russians during the so-called Long Feud (1570–95). Ivalo's novel describing and commenting on events of his own period, *Aikansa lapsipuoli* (1895; Stepchild of his time), is a document of national enthusiasm and its subsidence. Santeri Alkio (1862–1930) has remained alive in the annals of literature mainly for a single novel, *Puukkojunkkarit* (1894; The ruffians with the knives), describing a wave of violence in Ostrobothnia. One of the outwardly most modest but still vital writers of the time was Kauppis-Heikki (Heikki Kauppinen, 1862–1920). At first a servant at the parsonage where Aho grew up, he rose through his talents and stories to become a well-known author. For him, the influence of the Järnefelt school was significant, but in his best works he reveals himself as an independent writer whose novels describing rural lives, especially of women, have lasted beyond their own time.

The realist period did not favor poetry; the only significant poet was J. H. Erkko. In his company Kasimir Leino (1866–1919) should be mentioned; he was perhaps more important as an aesthetician and critic than a poet. His articles played a large part in the establishment of the theories of the realist period and later of symbolism in Finland. As a poet, his younger brother, Eino Leino, soon outstripped him to become the greatest Finnish-language poet of the turn of the century and the decades just beyond.

Turning Point of Realism
In the spring of 1887 Georg Brandes made his first lecture tour in Finland. Speaking of Emile Zola, he did not, as was expected, treat him as a naturalist but emphasized symbolist features in his work. Another guest lecturer from Sweden, the author Gustaf af Geijerstam, had stressed somewhat similar matters in his lectures held the same year.

The lectures did not arouse more than slightly bewildered reactions at the time, but their message was clear: the literary trend was changing. Juhani Aho gained fresh impulses from his trip to Paris in 1889 and arrived at a new concept of art and style. There are already new features in the novella *Yksin,* especially in the part where the Moulin Rouge is seen as a kind of outer court of Hell and the people dancing as bewitched by it. *Papin rouva* is at a still greater remove from programmatic realism.

The turning point in Finland occurred around 1890. When Aho saw Pedro Calderón de la Barca's *La vida es sueño* (1636; Life is a dream) at the Finnish Theater, he halted to consider the characteristic features of different art trends. In his "chip from the block" "Teatterista tullessa" (Coming from the theater) he described realism by comparing it with a fresh morning when the streets are full of bustle, fascinating to look at. But when evening comes, "the earlier mood is forgotten and another replaces it. We desire rest, our thoughts break away from the details of daily chores and activities, the grand, simple features of life begin to shine through and to form into an idea." According to their inherent quality, writers can describe the one or the other.

Symbolism and Karelianism: The 1890s
Aho's trip to Paris was not exceptional for the times. Artists had also hastened there; their former place of study and pilgrimage, Düsseldorf, now had to give way to the French capital. The painters, including a noteworthy number of women, did not yet move directly into impressionism but adopted the principles of pleinairism and a new kind of palette. But with them came knowledge of something else, the new art trend of symbolism, of which the letters of the painter Albert Edelfelt speak in particular. Kasimir Leino's articles about the new French literature complete the picture. In

articles written from Paris and Vienna he understood the rising trend as neoromanticism and established this term in the Finnish art vocabulary.

Budding Finnish symbolism received stimuli from Scandinavia as well as France. The aristocratic individualism and Nietzscheanism of Brandes, the symbolism of Ibsen's and Strindberg's plays, the decadent features of the Norwegian writers of the 1890s, and the works and essays of the Dane Herman Bang all began to have their own effects. Annamari Sarajas pointed out in 1968 that one source of influence was the short-lived but brilliant Danish periodical *Taarnet* (1893–94; The tower), through which the mystical symbolism of Johannes Jørgensen became known: Jørgensen's essay on that topic in the journal's second number was an open attack on naturalism.

Personal and national impulses in Finland joined with these stimuli. In the spring of 1890 the Young Finns' newspaper, *Päivälehti*, had recommended to artists the scenery of their own country and particularly of Karelia, the eastern part of Finland, as an inspiration. In 1891 an art exhibit with *Kalevala* themes was held — and it was the *Kalevala* that most clearly united Finnish Karelia with Russian Karelia, beyond the eastern frontier in the public awareness. Sibelius's "Kullervo: Symphonic Poem" (opus 7), on a *Kalevala* theme, was completed in 1892. Artists and writers took up the challenge and enthusiastically began to make pilgrimages to Karelia. In its untouched nature and its people living under primitive conditions, they believed that they had found something originally and authentically Finnish — that they had reached the source of the *Kalevala*. Journeys to Karelia became first a fashion and then a kind of idealistic trend, given the general name of "Karelianism" by Yrjö Hirn in 1939.

The effects of Karelianism can be seen most strikingly in pictorial art: backwoods scenes were painted by Akseli Gallen-Kallela and others, and Karelian ornaments were sought and found as decorative motifs for buildings, arts and crafts, and book covers. The motifs familiar from the French art nouveau or the German *Jugend* style became naturalized in Finnish art as national variations. The swan, a favorite motif of symbolism, swam in Finnish poetry, music, and art as the sacred bird of the Karelians or as the Swan of Tuonela of the *Kalevala*. Thus a great variety of background factors became attached to Finnish symbolism, or national neoromanticism (as it is generally called in literary and art research). Parisian symbolism, Neoplatonism, the individualism of Nietzsche or Brandes, the decorative *Jugend* style all gave elements to the depiction of Finnish backwoods scenes or *Kalevala* events. It should be remembered too that the Tolstoyanism sowed by the Järnefelt circle yielded a good harvest in the minds of many writers and artists.

The circle of *Päivälehti* and *Nuori Suomi* became established as the crucial force of national symbolism or neoromanticism. Its liberalism allowed connections with Finland-Swedish writers and artists as well. Indeed, the close cooperation of different arts was essential to the whole era. The representatives of different arts knew one another and gathered together in symposia around restaurant tables. Present were writers (Aho, the young Eino Leino), composers and musicians (Jean Sibelius, Robert Kajanus), artists (Akseli Gallen-Kallela, Albert Edelfelt, Pekka Halonen, Eero Järnefelt) and architects (starting with Eliel Saarinen), actors, critics, scientists, and journalists. Scandinavian visitors were frequent; at the end of the century Knut Hamsun lived in Helsinki for several months and published his articles about the new internalized art in its papers, describing and touching the depths of the human mind.

Eino Leino later characterized the period as the Finnish renaissance. The contacts between different arts had never before produced such fruitful results as in the 1890s and the early years of the 1900s, nor would they ever again. The same motifs might move from one form of art to another: for example, the Swan of Tuonela was given musical voice in the famous English horn solo of Sibelius's *Lemminkäinen Suite* (1893–95), in Gallen-Kallela's paintings, and in Eino Leino's verse play (1893). International and national themes did not compete with each other but proved to be parallel sources of strength; the result was a rich synthesis, full of nuances.

National symbolism portrayed the spiritual climate of the era but, unlike realism, did not deal with the social changes. These were great: industrialization continued, towns grew, workers started to organize themselves into their own party, whose ideas became extreme forms of socialism and Marxism. Above all, the country began to be affected by a new external threat: increasing pressure from Russia. Czar Alexander III had already proclaimed a postal manifesto in 1890, whereby the Finnish postal system was merged into the system in Russia, resulting, among other things, in the disappearance of Finland's own postage stamps. Alexander III's attitude toward Finland was, however, sympathetic; he may have been influenced by the Danish-born czarina, Dagmar. The situation changed when his son, Nicholas II, came to the throne in 1894 and the vehemently Russian-minded general, Nikolai Ivanovich Bobrikov, was appointed governor-general of Finland in 1898. The February Manifesto of 1899 was aimed at discontinuing the special rights of Finland and joining it more closely to the parent country, which in language and culture had always been more foreign than Finland's Scandinavian neighbors.

The pressures of the time began to be seen in literature and art as well.

Juhani Aho wrote a "chip from the block" series called *Katajainen kansani* (1899–1900; My juniper people), where, in allegories, Finland is compared with the tough juniper: "Bends but does not break." Patriotic themes and slogans were expressed in the poems of Eino Leino and other contemporaries. Sibelius composed "Finlandia" for the finale of a series of six patriotic "Tableaus from the Past," given at Helsinki's Swedish Theater on 4 November 1899. (The accompanying texts, in Finnish and Swedish, were by Eino Leino and the many-sided Jalmari Finne [1874–1938], then a director at Kaarlo Bergbom's Finnish Theater.) Heroic features in paintings symbolized national defiance and protest. But at the same time as art manifested a spirit of national resistance, there was increasing division between the political parties. The workers asked, Capitalism or socialism? The educated class asked, Finnish or Swedish, and on what terms? And everyone asked, as the pressure of the Russian empire increased, Should Finland choose active or passive resistance? All these questions were soon reflected in literature.

Aho's Later Work
The turn in Juhani Aho's work occurred with his novel *Panu* (1897). It had been preceded by a trip to Karelia in 1892 and a number of "chips from the block" in which decorative, prose poem–type elements had increased. *Panu* is a historical novel about the seventeenth century and thus leaves the main highway of realism. Panu is a seer and a shaman, the last representative of a vanishing paganism. His antagonist is the local parson, who represents triumph and Christianity. The struggle corrupts both of them, but Panu loses the game by resorting to impure means. Only his uncle Jorma preserves his gentle pantheism and withdraws from the new era ever farther into the forest.

For his novel, Aho had studied folklore and knew both the practice of magic by the old shamans and the artifacts connected with a hunting culture. But the best part of the novel is the description of nature, the broad views from high hills, the gleam of water and the glint of snow. As a whole, the novel does not come up to the level of Aho's shorter works. A vital change is also reflected in the theme, the yielding of the old times to the new, which is now weighted differently: the new is no longer necessarily better than the old but destroys a way of life that is close to and respects nature.

Aho's second extensive novel, *Kevät ja takatalvi* (1906; Spring and the cold spell), is located geographically in the same parts but describes more recent history. "Spring" is a brief period of national awakening in the 1840s;

"the cold spell" is the political regression that follows it. The seasons, like the points of the compass and temperatures, were often given political-allegorical secondary meaning in Aho's "chips" of this period. In this novel Aho follows two great idealistic currents of the time from the viewpoint of their different representatives. At the beginning of the novel young, eager students come to a farmhouse where the people are religious and are met with suspicion and coldness when they ask about folk poetry. Thus the young intelligentsia inspired by the national awakening and the pietist countryfolk are set down as opposites. Pietism had originated in Ostrobothnia and Savo as a kind of spontaneous folk movement, criticizing the clergy for superficiality and worldliness. One of its leaders was a small farmer, the lay preacher Paavo Ruotsalainen (1777–1852), who meets Lönnrot and Snellman in the novel — as far as is known, this actually happened — and lectures Snellman, setting the word of God as a counterweight to his philosophy. The young students also come into contact with the pietist clergy and make an effort to achieve a synthesis between national ideology and pietism.

Aho had already been interested in pietists at an earlier date; he had met them in his own home parsonage and in his family circle and had published a collection of "chips" about them, *Heränneitä* (1894; The pietists, lit. "the awakened ones"). Aho himself had never been religious but remained a liberal skeptic: pietism interested him as a psychological and moral phenomenon. In *Heränneitä*, on the basis of historical documents, he impressively describes the conversion of young clergymen, and in *Kevät ja takatalvi* the intense battle in the soul of a clergyman is presented through extracts in a journal. Elements of this depiction were taken from the work of the fanatic Lars Stenbäck, who had engaged in polemics about pietism with Runeberg for the latter's attack on the movement's spiritual stringency in *Den gamle trädgårdsmästarens brev* (1837; The old master gardener's letters; see chapter 7).

In spite of its unevenness, *Kevät ja takatalvi* is a more vital and interesting novel than *Panu*. It prepared the way for Aho's next novel, *Juha* (1911), set in a similar landscape but not connected so clearly with any particular period. Juha is an honest, hardworking settler with a beautiful young wife, Marja, but burdened by an ugly appearance and a lame leg. A Russian Karelian peddler, Shemeikka, finds his way to Juha's remote cottage; he induces Marja to come away with him and puts her in the harem at his home, where there are already several girls. Marja is disappointed with her new circumstances and goes back with Juha when he comes to fetch her;

but when it becomes clear that she was not kidnapped but went willingly with Shemeikka, Juha breaks down and lets his boat drift into the rapids, to suicide.

Juha is stylistically one of the more close-knit of Aho's novels; both the dialogue and the descriptive parts are concentrated and compact, departing — to the novel's advantage — from the loose style of some of the "chips." In its layout it resembles *Papin rouva,* but the point of view is now the husband's. The solution is also reversed: unlike Elli, Marja goes off with the object of her fancy but encounters circumstances different from what she has imagined. In a way *Juha* is also a farewell to Karelianism; its splendidly described Karelian landscapes are now the framework for tragedy: nature does not relieve man's misfortune. In its apt characterization and accurate observation *Juha* is one of the best works of Aho's later period. (*Juha* inspired two operas, by Aarre Merikanto [1893–1958], written in 1919–22 but not performed, on radio, until 1958; and by Leevi Madetoja [1887–1947], from 1935, both using a libretto by Aino Ackté, the great Finnish soprano. The first staging of Merikanto's work by the Finnish National Opera in 1967, for the fiftieth anniversary of Finland's independence, made it an essential part of the Finnish musical repertoire.)

Aho continued to write for another ten years or so, but he never again achieved the intensity of *Juha. Rauhan erakko* (1916; Hermit of peace), set in the years of World War I and the mountain scenery of central Europe, is a novel about the wrongfulness of violence and war. It is exceptional in Aho's work for its milieu and its pacifist message. In his journals (1918–19) from the time of Finland's Civil War, problems of the same kind occur; now they have become a terrible reality for him. As a humanist, Aho tried to find the middle way between the extremists on both sides, the victorious Whites and the defeated Reds, while attempting to understand those who had lost and their motives.

Aho's last work was a lyrical, impressionistic novel, *Muistatko — ?* (1920; Do you remember — ?). The main character tries to overcome the feeling of depression and loss from the death of one close to him by returning to childhood memories and the bright moments of his life. It is a turning away from oppressive reality and a deliberate transference to a fantasy level. The former realist has traveled far away from realism.

Järnefelt, the Odd Man Out

Arvid Järnefelt (1861–1932) was the same age as Aho and his companion at the university, but his starting point was quite different. He came from an aristocratic family famous for its literary salon; from the start, he was a master of several languages (beside Finnish and Swedish, he knew Russian, German, and French). He studied psychology in Leipzig in the laboratory of Wilhelm Wundt, and law in Helsinki and Moscow, and became qualified for a career as a judge. But while he was serving at a district court, he suddenly felt that judging others was not for him; he determinedly took his own road and kept to it.

Järnefelt's first work, *Isänmaa* (1893; The fatherland), immediately aroused great attention. It was a novel about student life, the general idealistic currents of the time, the problems of the rising Finnish-language educated classes — and much more. The Norwegian Arne Garborg had described students who came from a farming background and the problems of the educated first generation (*Bondestudentar;* 1883, Peasant students). The chief character of Järnefelt's novel, Heikki Vuorela, is this kind of rural student, who falls between the countryside and the city in seeking his own way. His home farm draws him in one direction with its obligations, but the attraction of a career and the city are greater. Finally, Heikki chooses his course by relinquishing his share in the farm. The choice is not only existential but social: one must do what one can best do to benefit the fatherland.

In the following year Järnefelt published a book that indicated his own choice: *Heräämiseni* (1894; My awakening). The name reminds one of Aho's pietist short stories, but this work is not about a Christian "conversion," though it does resemble a religious one. Järnefelt internalizes Tolstoyanism and takes it literally as his guide in life. People must earn their living by manual labor; they must reject unnecessary luxury and live simply, close to the fundamental values of life. The teaching of the Sermon on the Mount and the commandment to love one's neighbor must be adopted from Christian morality. One must uncompromisingly oppose both secular and church authority when one's conscience so bids. Järnefelt started to learn various crafts, including that of a cobbler, and began to farm a small holding. The promise of a fine career was exchanged for everyday, modest toil. Tolstoy's requirement of the rejection of art was fortunately not put into practice by Järnefelt (nor was it ultimately by Tolstoy himself); his career as a writer continued, but in a different way.

Questions of ideology and personal choices between alternatives appeared in Järnefelt's next works, as in the stories of *Ihmiskohtaloja* (1895; Human fates) and the novel *Veljekset* (1900; The brothers). A play, *Orjan oppi* (1902; A slave's doctrine), later called *Titus,* deals with the destructiveness of power. *Kuolema* (1903; Death) is one of the few symbolist dramas in Finnish literature; Sibelius composed his "Valse Triste" as part of the incidental music for it. The collection of short stories *Elämän meri* (1904; The sea of life) is also symbolist and presents Järnefelt's philosophy of life. Man, the individual, is a drop on the way to freedom, the great sea of life, where antitheses expire. But existence "as a drop" also demands that one knows one's part and perceives one's affinity with other human beings. On the one hand Tolstoyanism, on the other hand symbolism led Järnefelt to an uncompromising doctrine of the brotherhood of man. When Sillanpää speaks of "basic man" in his later works, there are traces of Järnefelt's philosophy and ethics in the concept.

The concept of the equality of man took Järnefelt close to socialism. Evidence of the socialist theories of Henry George is to be found in the novel *Maaemon lapsia* (1905; Children of Mother Earth), and Järnefelt explains his standpoint concerning the question of land more polemically in a pamphlet, *Maa kuuluu kaikille!* (1907; The land belongs to all!). The pamphlet is also concerned with topical political problems, such as the tenant-farmer question — that is, the efforts of the poor tenants of holdings leased from big estates to become independent and their chances of getting land of their own.

Järnefelt's next work is topical, too. The novel *Veneh'ojalaiset* (1909; The people of Veneh'oja) describes events of 1906: in connection with attempts at revolution in Russia, there was a mutiny at Sveaborg, the fortress off Helsinki, led by a schoolmate of Järnefelt's. The novel had a broader social background, for it also dealt with the position of people who had come to the city from rural conditions; it considered the sense of uprootedness caused by the move to be one reason for the unrest. This theme is repeated in novels by Eino Leino describing the same period.

During World War I Järnefelt went more and more deeply into Tolstoyanism, as shown by the consideration of the significance of sexual purity in his novels and his diminishing interest in literature. It was not until the next decade that his career as a writer took a new turn in the novel *Greeta ja hänen Herransa* (1925; Greeta and her lord). The chief character is an aging Swedish-speaking woman whose son has married a Finnish-speaker. The novel is Greeta's reckoning after her son's suicide and an account of her relation with his wife. Gradually, she arrives at a serene, tolerant attitude and achieves peace of mind. The novel is one of Järnefelt's most integrated works and marked his victorious return to literature.

The next book was to be Järnefelt's principal work. The first part of *Vanhempieni romaani* (1928–30; The novel of my parents) directly stems from the memories of his mother, Elisabet Järnefelt. Although the title speaks of a "novel," the work is based throughout on recollections. The rigidity of the young and fanatically Fennomanic officer of engineers, Alexander Järnefelt, is described, along with his marriage in St. Petersburg to the vivacious daughter of a prominent and artistic German-Russian family; then follows a section, lively and interesting from the standpoint of cultural history, about Elisabet's arrival in an "unknown" Finland and its little towns. The work goes on to deal with the "Old Fennomane" circles—the Järnefelts were in fact one of the few families that adopted Finnish as their home language—ending with the birth and activities of Elisabet's literary salon.

It was *Vanhempieni romaani* that first made known the Järnefelts' school and its central ideas, long before the correspondence of various writers became public. It reveals Juhani Aho's fascination with Elisabet, who was much older than himself, and his later love for the daughter of the family, Aino (who married Sibelius), who inspired Aho's novella *Yksin*. In addition, the initial stages of the young writers' careers can be seen: they write exercises on given themes and go through them together, sometimes to the accompaniment of severe criticism. The most exacting critic proves to be Kasper, the eldest Järnefelt son, who did not himself publish a single work. His guidance of a work by Kauppis-Heikki is so detailed that Elisabet decides it is interfering too much with the writer's special quality.

Vanhempieni romaani is above all a book about Elisabet Järnefelt, her powerful personality and ideals. But at the same time, it is a presentation of a whole era and the rise of a young generation of writers with a common endeavor and, to a large degree, common aims. The work also contains a letter written by Juhani Aho in his later years, in which he gives heartfelt thanks to Elisabet and recalls the importance of the Järnefelt circle for his own development.

Arvid Järnefelt is one of the characters in the novel, but he is mostly a bystander, commentator, and provider of additional information. It is difficult to assign the work to any literary genre, because its focus always seems to be shifting, but this is typical of Järnefelt. The focus of his oeuvre as a whole likewise changes restlessly: after his classic first book he describes his conversion to Tolstoyanism, writes symbolist short stories and plays, tackles topical political and national issues, does not return to literature until the 1920s, and leaves as his testament the rich, unconventional *Vanhempieni romaani*. In this mobility can be found the strength of his work: he never seems to be ready to stop, he never wants "to lie in art," he always reminds his readers of the ethical imperative that he believes man must fulfill. Järnefelt is the incorruptible voice of conscience in Finnish literature.

From the Frost Years to the Threshold of Independence

The twentieth century began ominously in Finland. The February Manifesto in 1899 had set in motion pressure from imperial Russia which increased during the next few years. The period has been given a descriptive name in history: *routavuodet,* the Frost Years. (More precisely, *routa* means the freezing of the ground in the fall before the snow comes; it numbs all nature, freezes the lakes, and prepares the coming of winter.) Still another name is *sortovuodet,* the Years of Oppression.

The process of Russification experienced two severe setbacks, however. The first was a political assassination, rare in Finland: a junior official of the Senate, Eugen Schauman, shot Governor-General Bobrikov on 16 June 1904 and then immediately turned the pistol on himself. (The day is the same as that on which James Joyce's *Ulysses* takes place; the assassination is mentioned in the book.) A second breathing space was afforded by the outbreak of the Russo-Japanese War (1904–5) and the widespread unrest that extended to Finland in the fall of 1905 in the form of a general strike. As a result of political unrest, the parliamentary system of the country was reformed (1906–7); instead of the former Diet with its four estates, a new unicameral Parliament came into being, elected by equal and secret voting; the vote was also given to women — the first case in Europe and second in the entire world.

The activities of the new Parliament at first were limited, it is true, by a serious obstacle: the Russian czar had to ratify the laws it enacted. This did not always occur, by any means; the conflict between the czar and the Finnish Parliament was constant. In 1909 the grip of the czarist regime tightened again, and at first Finns who had served in Russia and then only Russians were placed in the Senate (the governmental apparatus of Finland). The outbreak of World War I suspended the work of the parliament so that it did not meet a single time between August 1914 and the spring of 1917. The privileges enjoyed by Finland were thus disappearing, and its special status was a thing of the past. From the perspective of the Frost Years, nineteenth-century Finland seemed idyllic.

The new parliamentary establishment marked a reshaping of the party system as well. New parties were formed on the basis of the old ones, and the Social Democratic Party, founded in 1905, was a rising force, soon developing into the mouthpiece of the radical opposition. Party disputes increasingly divided the nation — as described, for instance, in Juhani Aho's play *Tuomio* (1907; Judgment) and Eino Leino's Frost Years novels. The attitude toward Russian oppression was a watershed. The Conservatives supported a flexible opposition; the Young Finns, who had begun to be known as the "Constitutionalists," were in favor of a more uncompromising though passive resistance. The most radical element among them and the Swedish Party formed a group of activists and began to prepare for armed revolt. In 1905, in connection with the general strike, two Civil

Guards were formed; one developed into the "Whites" and the other became the Red Guard of the 1918 Civil War. The first confrontation between them took place in 1906. The seeds of the Civil War had been sown.

Literature Divided

The 1890s had marked a boom in literature. Finnish-language publishing was strengthened at that time (the second biggest publishing house in the country, Otava, was founded in 1890), the press grew, and libraries were established. The Finnish Pavilion at the Paris World's Fair in 1900 assembled all the forces of the arts into a joint manifestation of Finland's cultural identity, and the intelligentsia of western Europe protested against Russian oppression in a petition signed by such well-known figures as Thomas Hardy, George Meredith, Anatole France, Emile Zola, Herbert Spencer, and the aged Florence Nightingale. Many Scandinavian intellectuals, with Brandes in the forefront, also made pronouncements in Finland's defense. For a short time, national symbolism was given heroic and patriotic features, but soon signs of skepticism and weariness, isolation and depression could be seen in literature. Karelianism was no longer connected with the symbolism of the younger generation of writers; in its stead appeared individualism and Nietzscheanism, which had been alien to, for example, Aho and Järnefelt. The picture of the Finnish people in literature also began to change. Realism had already eroded Runebergian idealism, but the literature of the first two decades of the twentieth century moved still further away from it.

Besides the estrangement of writers from one another, leading to increasingly individual achievements, division in language and politics began to appear more clearly than before. Finland-Swedish literature felt that its territory was being narrowed as the country became more Finnish-minded, and it began to withdraw into a defensive position. A. O. Freudenthal's doctrine of a separate Finland-Swedish nationality, an ideology that arose partly as a reaction to Snellman's philosophy of Finnishness, began to gain ground. The metaphors favored by Finland-Swedish poetry, a shrinking ice floe or a lone cornered fighter, clearly testified to the minority's increasing unease. Among Finnish speakers, Runeberg and Topelius had always been considered writers for the whole nation, but with Tavaststjerna, the language barrier became more apparent (see chapter 8). Topelius died in March 1898, and Tavaststjerna, who still had close ties with the Finnish realists (including Aho), eight days after him. Connections between Finnish- and Swedish-language writers were certainly not broken completely; Eino Leino, Otto Manninen, and many others had contact with the *Euterpe* circle (see chapter 8), and cultured people generally knew Swedish and read in it. But the roads of the two literatures started inevitably to diverge, traffic through the language barrier thinned out, and literature in Swedish grew more and more alien to Finnish-speakers.

Another division was revealed when literature began to appear among the workers, who dissociated themselves from prevailing national ideals and labeled them bourgeois. The boom in militant proletarian literature took place from the end of the 1890s until the end of the Civil War in 1918. The leaders of both the old and the new, more radical, workers' movement were interested in literature and themselves wrote, particularly poetry. (One of them was Otto Ville Kuusinen [1881–1964], who moved to the Soviet Union in 1918. If political activity had not swept Kuusinen along with it so completely, he could have developed into a Marxist aesthetician of international importance, a kind of Finnish Georg Lukács.) The authors of the proletarian movement followed prevailing stylistic norms and conventions, however. No reformer of the caliber of Mayakovsky or Diktonius (see chapter 9) rose from among them. Their leading star was most often Eino Leino, and sometimes Runeberg, too — in a quite different sense, it is true, that is, in parody.

One of the most talented of the proletarian poets was Kössi Kaatra (1882–1928). He aimed his poems at both Finland's upper class and the tyranny of the czarist era. After the Civil War he fled to Sweden and spent his last years there. Other poets worthy of mention are Kössi Ahmala (1889–1918) and Kasper Tanttu (1886–1918), executed within a few days of each other by White firing squads. Kaarlo Uskela (1878–1922) was at his best a verse satirist, making cruel fun — in *Villiomenoita* (1912; Wild apples) and *Pillastunut runohepo* (1921; Runaway Pegasus) — variously of Russian aggrandizement and the righteousness of the Finnish clergy. Before and during the Civil War his antiestablishment verse was brutally direct and inflammatory; after the Red defeat he was imprisoned until 1920. The playwright Elvira Willman (1875–1927) achieved success at the National Theater with her play *Lyyli* (1903), dealing with the fate of a working girl. After moving to the Soviet Union in 1918, she was liquidated in one of Stalin's purges. Another emigrant to the USSR, Hilda Tihlä (1870–1944), managed to adapt to the new conditions, and some of her works were published in Soviet Karelia.

The best-known proletarian writer was Konrad Lehtimäki (1883–1937), journalist, official of the Social Democratic Party, and member of Parliament from 1911 to 1917, who later achieved a recognized position in the Republic of Finland. Out of his political convictions, he wrote the play

Spartacus (1913), which was translated into Swedish by the young radical Allan Wallenius (see chapter 8); in his stories, *Kuolema* (1915; Death), he cultivated a romantic horror tale akin to the work of Edgar Allan Poe. During World War I he wrote a pacifist novel, *Ylös helvetistä* (1917; Up from Hell), a fantasy about the uniting of the human race into a realm of peace, the birth of which is promoted by fantastic technical inventions typical of science fiction. Many-sided in his ambitions and talents, after the Civil War Lehtimäki published two parts of the autobiographical proletarian novel *Taistelija* (1922, 1924; The fighter), perhaps inspired by the multivolume *Pelle Erobreren* (1906–10; Eng. tr. *Pelle the Conqueror*, 1913–16) of the Danish writer Martin Andersen Nexø; it remained incomplete.

The flourishing of the radical side of proletarian literature was broken off by the Civil War of 1918 and the victory of the Whites. Though it did not bring major writers to light, its effect was indirectly felt later. Interest in literature and the amateur theater persisted within the workers' movement, and with the stabilizing of conditions, self-taught writers appeared, some of whom became important figures in Finnish-language literature.

Russian censorship, directed most strongly at newspapers and periodicals, did not manage to slow down the development of literature perceptibly in the first years of the twentieth century. (During World War I control naturally grew tighter.) Generally speaking, Finnish cultural life at the beginning of the century was lively: long trips were taken to France, Italy, and Germany; Scandinavian literature was followed by Finns as well as Finland-Swedes; new literature was amply available in translation. Russian influence, on the other hand, diminished for political reasons. Indeed, Finland could receive political refugees with surprising ease: for example, Maxim Gorky and many Estonian writers found refuge there. It is one of the whims of history that Lenin and Stalin met for the first time in Finland, at Tampere in 1905, and Lenin is supposed to have visited Finland a grand total of twenty-six times!

Leino

If one had to name a single classic Finnish-language prose writer, the choice would inevitably be Aleksis Kivi. If one had to mention a single poet, the choice could hardly be other than Eino Leino (at first Lönnbohm, 1878–1926). Many lines of development in Finnish literature are concentrated in his work in a kind of focal point, considered from the standpoint of both poetic expression and ideas.

Eino Leino grew up in northeastern Finland (in Paltamo), near the "singing lands" of Karelia, in a big family. His father had attended school for a few years — a classmate was August Ahlqvist — and was employed as a surveyor. The family was interested in literature and produced two well-known poets, Eino Leino and his brother, Kasimir Leino, eight years his elder, who was to gain a doctorate and become an aesthetician. Eino Leino went to school in Oulu at first, then in Hämeenlinna farther south; there, in a respected lyceum attended by Sibelius a decade earlier, he learned Latin, German, and French and also taught himself Estonian, while Swedish went without saying. While still at school he published his first poems and translated Runeberg, among others. Matriculating in 1895, in the following year he published his first collection of poems, *Maaliskuun lauluja* (Songs of March), at the age of eighteen.

Unlike his brother Kasimir, Eino Leino did not get an advanced degree, though he did study at Helsinki University. He became a journalist and was soon the youngest contributor to the liberal newspaper *Päivälehti*. Together with Kasimir, from 1898 to 1899 he edited the periodical *Nykyaika* (New time), which closely followed the trends of European and Scandinavian literature, with both original articles and translations. He soon developed into an acute critic, a lively author of causeries, and above all a fine poet. After his first marriage broke up, he spent several months abroad (1908–9), traveling via Stockholm and Copenhagen to Berlin, Dresden, Munich, and Rome. There he started to translate Dante's *Divine Comedy* (a project not published until 1912–14) and stayed in Berlin once more on his return journey.

Back in Finland, Leino continued his literary work with feverish haste. He soon became "Finland's greatest bohemian," the habitué of restaurants and a boon companion, yet at the same time he grew increasingly lonely and isolated. In his final years he went rapidly downhill, a process hastened by excessive drink; nonetheless, there were still high points in his ample production. When he died at the beginning of January 1926, less than forty-eight years old, he was burned out, "a bookless, cowless man," as he described himself in one of his last great poems, "Löysäläisen laulu" (Song of a vagabond).

Presenting Leino's poetry to foreign readers is a thankless task. His poetry is closely bound to the Finnish language in rhythm and idiom, morphology and syntax; he is a master of vowel harmony and uses it as expressively as Paul Verlaine in his famous "Art poétique." Translating Leino's poems into any language is problematic and difficult, and understandably, not many good English translations exist.

Leino tuned Finnish poetic language anew. His closest predecessor is J. H. Erkko, but Leino exceeds Erkko's achievements in almost every respect. Leino's university of poetry contains many elements: he has learned equally from the *Kalevala* and the newer, rhymed folk song, from Runeberg and Heinrich Heine, and has taken as much from the poetry of classical antiquity and German and Scandinavian verse as from French symbolism. When there are so many influences, none of them becomes completely dominating, but the result is a synthesis with Leino's own stamp on every line. The Finnish poem was transformed in his hands, becoming flexible, alive, and expressive and, in technique, rising for the first time to the level of Swedish-language poetry. Naturally enough, Kivi's poetry was in its own class, but it was based on individual and exceptional rhythmic and technical solutions. Eino Leino was the first to open up the complete range of the Finnish language in his poetry.

Like all his work, Leino's poetry contains so many themes and genres that any brief presentation of them must remain incomplete. His work as a journalist is continued and extended, in a certain sense, by his topical poetry: in a poem written on the day of the February Manifesto, "Helsinki sumussa" (Helsinki in the mist), he describes the statue of the beloved Czar Alexander II hidden by an impenetrable mist, through which only an order from a Russian army unit marching past can be heard. In a few rapidly improvised lines a picture crystallizes of the common distress of the whole country. Leino wrote several similar patriotic poems connected with the times. Their names and key lines become slogans, and their symbolism can be directly perceived: in the poem "Kansa kalliolla" (A people on the rock) an immovable boulder becomes an image of Finland's essence and strength. "Carmen saeculare," a tremendous future vision of the new century, describes in freely undulating lines the time when "the right of the individual is trampled, the right / of nations is tyrannized, freedom of speech is persecuted," when "country is joined with country" and "the worker rises, earth shakes, thrones / quake," and when — perhaps — still "humanity rises, the nations' best rebel, gods or slaves are no more." "Sekasorto" (Chaos), inspired by the general strike of 1905, tells how "crashing fall the great trees, / the old convictions," and how "time's hinges turn." As a topical poet, Leino is penetrating, swift, and sharp-sighted.

But the spearhead of criticism was not directed solely against Russian oppression; Leino's own country and people receive their share. Especially in the poems written during his long stay abroad, Leino lashes the "excellent country," satirically portraying the land "where all is upside-down"; he strikes out, too, at small-minded critics, even the popular Juhani Aho, in "Lammas ja vuohipukki" (The sheep and the billy-goat). But most of Leino's satires were linked with his journalistic work and found their best channel in his causeries, which contain hilariously sharp attacks on bureaucracy, conservatism, and all narrow cliquishness. Leino is a splendid liberal critic, the unwearying mocker of evils and stupidity.

In Leino's poetry, as in all Finnish verse, two eternal themes are conspicuous: nature and love. They are interwoven in one of Leino's perhaps best-known lyrical poems, "Nocturne." In it the poet first paints a summer night landscape — the light summer nights are a motif running through all Finnish literature — and finally combines the peace of nature with love or waiting for love. The poem begins:

> The corncrake's song rings in my ears,
> above the rye a full moon sails;
> this summer night all sorrow clears
> and woodsmoke drifts along the dales.

It continues with a list, at once ecstatic and detailed, of the elements — the darkness of the forest, the red clouds of sunset, "the blue of windy hills asleep, / the twinflower's scent, the water's shade" — of which "my heart's own song is made." The second of the poem's two ten-line strophes then addresses a "girl as sweet as summer hay, / my heart's great peace," who has wrought a mysterious change in the speaker:

> around me life tightens its ring,
> time stops, the vane has ceased to swing;
> the road before me through the gloom
> is leading to the unknown room.
> *(Tr. Keith Bosley, 1981)*

Leino's summer poems are often linked to happy moments; they are still waters in the wild stream of life. But summer too may have melancholy features: in the poem "Lapin kesä" (Lapland summer) Leino reminds us of the brevity of the northern summer, the swift evanescence of floral splendor, and he sees in this a metaphor for all Finnish culture, which struggles under severe conditions and in which so many promises fail to materialize, whereas "elsewhere the gray-headed still burn with fire, / the sun of the spirit glows in the old." "But long and hard is the rule of winter," the poem ends.

Winter is a tragic, destructive symbol in Leino's middle phase. "Nocturne" is included in a collection called *Talvi-yö* (1905; Winter night). Its successor has the equally characteristic title *Halla* (1908; Frost). "Now I stand weaponless / before you, Winter of life," the poet says in a piece from the earlier collection, "Niin olekin maani matka — " (Let my journey be my country). In this poem the narrator knows his fate to be "without faith, without dreams," "to walk the field of winter / to talk with the frost" (the Finnish word translated "talk with" also means "challenge"). Pictures of winter appear in Leino's poetry during his marriage crisis, but they reflect a more general disillusionment with life, the feeling of a turning point. At the same time, they contain national symbolism, the fears of the time of oppression in the increasingly strained political atmosphere. Summer and winter belong together inseparably, like joy and grief, life and death.

Leino's winter poems also express defiance, an almost Nietzschean rising against the powers of fate. The speaker of the poems knows destruction lies ahead but does not surrender—he falls with head held high. This attitude has been called "tragic optimism." Later, too, in the collection *Elämän koreus* (1915; Life's splendor), when signs of decline are already visible— the previous collection has the apt name *Painuva päivä* (1914; The dying day) — the poet still praises life. He knows he is sinking, but "perhaps that is why / I live high Sunday, / I feel all is beautiful."

One area of Leino's poetry has not yet been touched on: the mythical poems in Kalevala meter in the *Helkavirsiä* collections (1: 1903; 2: 1916; Eng. tr. *Whitsongs* [1], 1978). They are long epic ballads that seem in style and stage properties to be connected with Finnish mythology. But the similarity is only apparent; no characters or events of the *Kalevala* or folk poetry are present; the coloring suggesting ancient times comes from the meter and vocabulary. Leino does not use ready-made patterns; he creates his own personal mythology, reflecting the same problems as his lyrical poetry. In some places he may use elements from Christian legend, but even then the interpretation is quite his own. Also, Leino modifies the old meter, the Kalevala line (which is much more nuanced than most translations suggest). He avoids the parallelism favored by folk poetry; he compresses his writing in many ways and cultivates enjambment, which is scarcely ever encountered in folk poetry.

The poems of *Helkavirsiä 1* often tell about a single person and his fate. Tuuri, in a poem of the same name, begs for a deferment of death, obtains it, and awakes in his cold, empty house after sleeping for a hundred years. He realizes the situation and understands that the gods have a different way of measuring time from humans, accepts his fate, and mounts the sleigh of death. Ylermi drives his horse to church, abuses God, and is destroyed, but at the end he still longs for a time "which does not bow to death, / does not go crawling to the Underworld." "Räikkö räähkä" (Räikkö the wretch) is a poem about a traitor who guides the enemy to his village and, when he sees the consequence of his deed, goes off to the forest to hang himself: his last look at his native village summarizes in a few lines both the beauty of the world and the poignancy of bidding it farewell. Kouta is a seer who has solved all problems except the riddle of death; head held high, he strides toward it at the end of the poem. All these heroes struggle against the might of death and meet their fates on equal terms with it, proud and unbending. The problem is solved differently in the final poem of the collection, "Tumma." The main character is a young boy, "strange from birth," who "saw horrors everywhere" and failed in everything he did; in this respect he resembles Kullervo in the *Kalevala,* but in character he is Kullervo's opposite. Unhappily seeking death, he hears his father's voice from the grave and receives advice from him; then he returns, wild no longer, to the land of the living and finds a balance,

> not rejoicing, not grieving,
> putting the days one on another,
> both the coming and the going,
> both the better and the worse,
> uppermost the better.

The poems of *Helkavirsiä 2* differ from those of the first series in that they are now more cosmic visions, in which the sun, the earth, and the stars, light and darkness, play a central part. The Sun, disappointed with the Earth, announces in the last poem: "Now I go to return no more." One of the most lyrical legend poems is "Herramme Vapahtajamme" (Our Lord and Savior), telling how Jesus wanders on earth, is given rough treatment on his journeying and in seeking accommodation for the night; but finally, when he asks to enter a sauna, receives the answer: "Whoever you may be, come in!" The sauna steam becomes strangely perfumed, the water for washing heals the sick, and the whole sauna becomes a magnificent temple. The miracle legend ends with Jesus' forgiveness, but it has also become a poem in praise of the Finnish sauna.

Lyrical poetry and the *Helkavirsiä* ballads are only a part of Leino's extensive production. He wrote a number of plays, some of them historical, some colored with symbolism, and some based on the *Kalevala.* In the plays with *Kalevala* themes Leino aimed at creating a new kind of decorative "sacred drama," which at its best would be a combination of national romanticism, symbolism, and expressionism. His most important plays appeared in a six-part series, *Naamioita* (1905–11; Masks).

Leino was also productive in the field of prose, though his novels do not come up to the level of his poetry. Among them, however, is the excellent picture of the times *Päivä Helsingissä* (1905; A day in Helsinki), which in spite of its subtitle, "a caricature," gives a lively idea of contemporary party controversies and some of his theories about art. Leino described the general strike and the beginning of the second era of oppression in the series of novels *Tuomas Vitikka, Jaana Rönty,* and *Olli Suurpää* (1906–8). The novels, dealing with various types of character, are journalistic in their execution, but in presenting the controversies of the times, they are observant and interesting from the standpoint of cultural history.

Leino was also an excellent critic; his *Suomalaisia kirjailijoita* (1909; Finnish writers) contains the best Finnish-language essay writing of the period and gives a good cross-section of the literature that had appeared until then. As a writer of causeries, he is a classic in the genre. As a translator into Finnish, he also had a long and fruitful career. He translated works by Runeberg, Topelius, and newer Finland-Swedish poets; plays by Goethe and Schiller, Racine and Corneille; works by Anatole France and Rabindranath Tagore; and, of course, the whole of Dante's *Divine Comedy.*

Eino Leino was the jack-of-all-trades of Finnish poetry. On the one hand, he wasted and diffused his abundant talents; on the other hand, he wrote poems that are a crucial and important part of the literature of his times and whose vitality has proved constant. At his best he is, like the title of one of his poems, "Päivän poika" (The lad of the sun), the most fascinating, wide-ranging, versatile, and impressive representative of Finnish poetry. He came to literature as a wunderkind, performed his life work frenziedly and unsparingly, and with his renewing and sensitizing of expression left ineffaceable traces on Finnish poetry.

Manninen

When Eino Leino wrote his *Helkavirsiä I* in the spring of 1903, he was the guest of his friend Otto Manninen at the latter's farm home in the lake district of the Finnish interior. Leino composed in his attic room, and then the two poets went through the text together critically. The result of this cooperation was splendid, one of Leino's chief works.

Otto Manninen (1872–1950) was in many respects the opposite of Leino. He led a quiet, withdrawn bourgeois existence, held an appointment as lector in Finnish language at Helsinki University, and issued only four volumes of poetry during his lifetime, with a fifth published posthumously. His wife, Anni Swan (1875–1958), was also a well-known writer of fairy tales and children's stories. In her own field she was one of the most important Finnish writers and also did considerable work as the editor of children's periodicals (see chapter 11).

In the eyes of his contemporaries, Otto Manninen's own poetry generally remained in the shadow of his translations. For Manninen was a truly great translator into Finnish. His range extended from the classics of antiquity (Homer, Sophocles, Euripides) to French and German poets (Molière, Goethe, Heine), to Scandinavian dramatists (Bjørnson, Ibsen) and Finland-Swedish poets (Runeberg, Topelius). Manninen was Leino's equal in his mastery of languages, but his translations have suffered to some extent with the passage of time; sometimes they are too "Manninen-ish," seeming too tightly packed and very personal in language.

The same things that may be disturbing in the translations are turned to advantage in Manninen's original poetry. His typical features are tautness of expression, conciseness, and the active use of the whole scale of the language, down to rare words and grammatical forms. If Leino is a master of musical expression and spontaneously flowing rhyme, Manninen does not fall behind him in either of these respects but works in a highly controlled manner in the field of vowel harmony and rhyme. He speaks, like the Spartan in one of his poems, "in laconic phrases." His typical stylistic means are ambiguity and understatement. Like the French symbolists, he is often content merely to suggest, to speak between the lines.

Though the stylistic devices of Manninen's poetry are linked with European poetry of the time, his poetic landscape is extremely Finnish. As in the case of many Finnish poets, his time of happiness is summer, or the anticipation or memory of summer, connected with the nearness of the loved one. The swan, the symbol favored by national neoromanticism, has a dual function for him: it is connected with summer and its passing, and it stands for poetry in general, in the intense flashing of its eyes and its vanishing. Swans are also a point of contact with tradition — the poetry of Runeberg, which Manninen knew so well from the task of translation.

Manninen is very definitely a cultured poet. His comparisons and imagery often refer to antiquity, and the properties of his satirical poetry in particular may be, both openly and latently, classical. Latin names sometimes appear in his poems, and he constantly turns to the mythology both of antiquity and of the *Kalevala*. Manninen was a popular writer of festival poems, and it is in them that his learnedness comes into its own, sometimes even too copiously.

Manninen's poems range from sensitive, clear, harmonious verse to aphoristic, reflective poetry. He is a wise observer of life, understanding that the best moments are soon past and that it is the evanescence of harmony that gives it value. In the poem "Ääret" (The limits) art is like a bubble on the water's surface, reflecting "the earth's power, the air's perfection"; but its task is here, and man must realize "the harshness of life's extremes." "Seize the day!" might be Manninen's motto in the work of his middle and old age.

Manninen's laconic epigrams are most abundant in the collections of his younger days. The difficulty of human contact, the disappointments brought by love and friendship, the superficiality of intercourse between people, and the conventional, even false and treacherous features that accompany it earn his condemnation.

> Buy a dozen friends,
> sell your words for words,
> do not raise your mask—
> you'll find it pays,

he says in a little poem called "Modus vivendi." Sometimes Manninen's poetry is ironic or satirical, sometimes ambiguously humorous, as in "Rauhanmies" (Man of peace), where the poet plays with multiple rhyme.

Manninen did not write much. His first two collections, *Säkeitä* (Verses), appeared fairly close to each other (1:1905, 2: 1910), but the third, *Virrantyven* (Still waters) did not appear until 1925, and the last, *Matkamies* (The traveler), in 1938. The collection *Muistojen tie* (Road of memories) was assembled from the poet's literary estate in 1951. Some of the collections contain artistic but rather superficial commissioned poems, the number of which increased with the years. Here and there the writer admitted a few translations of lyrical poems not otherwise collected in a unified volume. New printings have appeared of some translations, but a few have never been republished; they include Heinrich Heine's *Deutschland: Ein Wintermärchen* (Germany: A winter's tale) from 1904, splendidly translated.

The rich vocabulary and personal syntax of Manninen's poems and the poet's fondness for indirect, associative expression have meant that his readership has been relatively small. One might say that he wrote for the happy few; but even if his readership has been limited, over the years it has proved to be enduring. Though the vocabulary of poetry has changed, and many of the stylistic means that Manninen favored have become outdated, the sinewy structure of his poems, the passionate study and exploitation of language material, the unceasing self-control, and above all his exacting poet's ethos are features that do not readily age.

Minor Poets
The term "minor poets" is not used pejoratively here but in T. S. Eliot's sense to mean poets who have important individual achievements but whose production as a whole has not stood up to the wear and tear of time.

The primus inter pares at the beginning of this century was Eino Leino;

he left his colleagues overwhelmingly in his shadow. Nietzscheanism and tragic optimism mark the attitudes of many a poet of the same period, and Leino's sovereign harmony becomes superficial warbling with several of his imitators. As regards expression and idiom, most of the lesser poets follow in Leino's footsteps. The one who most clearly differed from him was V. A. Koskenniemi, perhaps the best of whose work belongs to his early years but whose influence grew to be so great during the era of independence that he must be dealt with later (see chapter 4).

L. Onerva (Onerva Lehtinen, 1882–1972) did not become Leino's epigone, though she was personally very close to him indeed. In her work the woman's voice begins to be heard in a new way—no longer the prosecutor like Minna Canth, indicting the social status of women, but the interpreter of woman's personal freedom and independence. In particular her novel *Mirdja* (1908) has retained its interest not only as a picture of the times but also as a manifesto of a new, individual morality; for this reason, it has provided rewarding material for feminist literary research. Onerva's work includes other prose, such as a collection of short stories, *Murtoviivoja* (1909; Broken lines), where in addition to women's problems there are clear points of contact with international symbolism. Onerva was the most clearly oriented toward French literature among the writers of her time and did important work as a translator (of Voltaire, Baudelaire, Anatole France, Benjamin Constant, Paul Bourget, and Hippolyte Taine, among others).

The best-known element of Onerva's work is, however, her poetry. It began with a collection called *Sekasointuja* (1904; Jangled harmonies). The title alone reveals that she did not see her task as the composition of smooth chords or folk song–like jingling. She became a proclaimer of life's ecstasy, of sensuality, announcing that when "once in a lifetime the fire-rose opens," that moment must be taken advantage of and its enjoyment accepted, lived fully, without fear of the consequences. In some poems she opens the way to a new concept of man, which has points in common with the depth psychology of the time and with Freud.

Onerva's production continued until after World War II; but her later lines, tinged with quiet melancholy, no longer achieved the same intensity as the defiant, flaming poems of her early period. In spite of its unevenness, Onerva's work has repeatedly found readers and researchers; the colorful and bold, eccentric personality of the writer has increased its attraction.

If Onerva's points in common with Eino Leino lay in her defiant, positive attitude to life and her desire to put all into the game at a single throw, the same attitudes cannot be found in Larin-Kyösti (Kyösti Larson, 1873–1948), at least in any Nietzschean sense. His points of contact with Leino were in his light, effortless-seeming expression and folk song–like accents.

One godfather of Larin-Kyösti's poetry was the Swede Gustaf Fröding, especially the Fröding who cultivated dance rhythms, not the later melancholiac. *Tän pojan kevätrallatuksia* (1897; This lad's spring-lilts) was Larin-Kyösti's first collection; the title points forward to the collections that follow. Poetry connected with the more recent folk song, along with events and characters from a rural village, remained close to Larin-Kyösti's heart, though there were deviations from this line. *Ad astra* (1906) was a symbolist drama, and in the series *Korpinäkyjä* (1-2, 1915-17; Visions of the wilds) the poet wrote long ballads, perhaps developing inspirations gained from Leino's *Helkavirsiä* in his own fashion.

The most clearly Nietzschean of the poets at the beginning of the century was Aarni Kouta (1884-1924), the name of whose first collection, *Tulijoutsen* (1905; Swan of fire), combines the swan of national symbolism and the fire of the portrayer of the new feeling for life. Kouta, like many of his colleagues, was a diligent translator — of Nietzsche, Strindberg's verse and narrative prose, Selma Lagerlöf and Viktor Rydberg, and, in 1915, Ibsen's *Kjærlighedens komedie* (1862; Eng. tr. *Love's Comedy*, 1900).

Prose of the Frost Years: Beginnings of Change

The general strike of 1905 and subsequent events — the first democratic parliamentary elections, the first clashes between the Reds and the Whites — left deep traces in literature. They are already visible in Leino's topical poems and novels touching on events of the period. The change in attitudes is revealed still more clearly in prose, starting from 1905. Annamari Sarajas has shown in *Viimeiset romantikot* that there was a change in the description of the common people: the concept of the lower social classes, "the people," became critical.

The criticism of the era of realism was generally directed toward the governing institutions — the church, the school system, legislation — and so primarily at the upper classes, although in Minna Canth's works people belonging to the working class are also criticized. A possible continued development along these lines had been broken off, however, for a few years by the February Manifesto and the increasing burden of the czar's Russification policy. National symbolism established connections with the period of Helsinki romanticism, of Lönnrot's *Kalevala* and Runeberg. With continuing economic pressure and the change in circumstances in and after 1905, however, the working class became restless and splits began to be noticeable in national attitudes: the situation had been transformed. The era of heroic patriotism was over; it was realized that the idyllic picture given by Runeberg and Topelius of a persevering, honest people was an idealized one.

Where Finland-Swedish narrative described the educated classes and their growing sense of isolation, Finnish-language prose turned in another direction. To be sure, some of it was colored at first by the same sort of decorative neoromanticism as the poetry of the time (Kilpi, Lehtonen, Linnankoski), but elsewhere it took up once again the description of the common folk favored by realism, the lower strata of society or the indigent rural population. The new realism, however, was different from that of the 1880s. It lacked the former's biological background; it indeed tackled social evils, but indirectly, through individual cases. It scrutinized the world and human nature skeptically and critically. The earlier realism made indictments and went on the attack, in order to disclose evils and to build something better to replace what it tore down. The new realism was a literature of observation, demonstrating what life is like and what the living conditions of people may be. Its critical current later gained added force from the events of 1918, which proved that many of the matters dealt with earlier were anticipatory warnings. For this reason, the tradition of critical description of the people continued vigorously in the literature of the era of independence.

The writers at the beginning of the century had generally been born in the 1870s and 1880s. For them, the realists of the 1880s were a background already passed by, although Aho, for example, continued writing at the same time as they did. They had strongly experienced the political crisis at the turn of the century and the colorfulness and joy of life brought by national symbolism. The new divergent lines, too, the alienation of Finland-Swedish literature and proletarian literature, were familiar to them. But it was typical that all reacted individually to the artistic and ideological challenges of the period.

One element of literature was formed by the island of neoromanticism, from which a few writers later detached themselves to continue their work under a quite different aegis. Johannes Linnankoski did most of his work within this field, as well as Maila Talvio, whose production went on for a very long time. The early work of Volter Kilpi and Joel Lehtonen belongs to this sphere, and to some extent that of Ilmari Kianto, all of whom later turned off sharply to follow their own roads. Maiju Lassila had almost no contact with neoromanticism, and the same is true of Maria Jotuni; in the early, rather unoriginal production of Aino Kallas its traces can be seen, but not for long. The grouping of writers at the beginning of the century is thus extremely problematical; only one thing is certain: literature changed, and many writers continued changing far into the period between the world wars.

The writers that follow are presented more or less in the order of the years they were first published. Except for Linnankoski, Lassila, and Kyösti Wilkuna, they continued their work until the 1930s and 1940s. The final work of Kianto, Kilpi, and Lehtonen thus differs so distinctly from that of their early period that their later production is treated in connection with the literature of the era of independence (see chapter 4).

Two Women Writers and a Young Utopian

Maila Talvio (1871–1951) began in 1895 with novels revealing from the start a moralist's attitude and more than a touch of pathos. She often sets the patriarchal countryside and the corrupt city life in opposition. The juxtaposition of these values is the central theme of a novel called *Pimeänpirtin hävitys* (1901; Destruction of the dark cottage); at the same time, the work is a comment on the then topical tenant farmer question, which Arvid Järnefelt also dealt with in his novels and pamphlets. *Niniven lapset* (1915; Children of Nineveh) reveals in its title the writer's attitude to the new urban lifestyle. *Elämän kasvot* (1916; The face of life) and *Silmä yössä* (1917; An eye in the night) are the peak achievements of Talvio's early period, impressive in their characterizations and intense in style in spite of the melodramatic features. In *Silmä yössä* there are also signs of two sources of inspiration remote from each other: the basic plot of this tale of two generations shows the power of heredity, but the fairy tale–like style of narration resembles the handiwork of Selma Lagerlöf.

In her later trilogy *Itämeren tytär* (1929–36; Daughter of the Baltic) Talvio turned to the historical novel. The title refers to Helsinki; its history is dealt with colorfully but nevertheless on the basis of documentary material. Her last novel, *Linnoituksen iloiset rouvat* (1941; The merry wives of the fortress), has the same theme. It considers the riddle of the surrender of the Sveaborg fortress off Helsinki in 1809, and the title of the novel indicates one of the factors that the writer feels lay behind the event.

Maila Talvio was active in many cultural and social fields. She was an ardent fighter for the Finnish cause in a capital then dominated by Swedish-speakers; she took part in a campaign against tuberculosis by writing a didactic novel about the matter; she participated in theater life; and she was a popular and inspiring speaker at patriotic occasions and temperance gatherings. She was an effective leader of cultural opinion over a long period by means of her literary salon, the star of which was the young poet V. A. Koskenniemi. Through her husband, J. J. Mikkola (1866–1946), a distinguished professor of Slavonic studies, she became interested in Poland and Lithuania and worked to make their culture known, until—on the eve of World War II and during it—her German sympathies came to the fore and colored her activities. (In 1918–19 she had been vastly disappointed when the plan to import Friedrich Karl of Hessia — Kaiser Wilhelm's brother-in-law — as the "king" of the newly independent Finland collapsed.) Yet her description of the events of her time and her polemical participation in them should be remembered, as well as her work as a historical novelist.

Aino Kallas (1878–1956) was born in the same decade as Talvio and lived about the same number of years, but she followed entirely different lines in her work and cultural orientation. She was a Fennomane by birth, the daughter of Julius Krohn (the poet Suonio), and published her first two works under the name of Aino Suonio. But her marriage with the Estonian folklorist, teacher, and journalist Oskar Kallas (1868–1946) turned her toward a new career. In Estonia and its center of cultural life, the university town of Tartu (Dorpat), she found herself in a neighboring country with a language closely related to Finnish but an altogether different history, where conditions under the pressure of the German aristocracy and Russian bureaucracy suddenly opened her eyes to social evils and national controversies. For the young wife who had grown up in the free conditions of Finland, the new environment was a shock, transforming the writer who had begun in a sensitive salon style into a critical observer ready for action. Her attitudes began to resemble those of the radical realists of the 1880s.

In two collections of short stories, *Meren takaa* (1–2, 1904–5; Beyond the sea), Aino Kallas described the era of serfdom that had still prevailed in Estonia a couple of generations before she arrived there. She restricted her themes effectively and crystallized her style. In the short story "Ingel" a nursemaid at a manor dresses up in the fine clothes of the gentry's children when her master and mistress are away, wishing at least for a moment defiantly to change the roles of dominators and dominated. In "Häät" (The wedding) the young bride prepares to kill the lord of the manor, who, following the traditional custom of the *jus primae noctis*, has summoned her to him on the night of her wedding. In Kallas's early stories an atmosphere of a time only recently past lives on, when the peasants' rights were kept at a minimum, when their burden of labor was inhuman, and when punishment by whipping was still in force. (Flogging was reintroduced as a penalty for those who took part in the attempted revolt of 1905–6.)

The novel *Ants Raudjalg* (1907) described how the efforts of a young Estonian to develop a national culture were ground to nothing in the mill of the Russian bureaucracy. His resignation is seen as a micropicture of the disillusionment and exhaustion of the nation as a whole. The central symbol of the novel is a marshy landscape where the birch trees wither because the earth is too wet. At the end of the novel Ants Raudjalg submits, going off to earn his bread somewhere in Russia, since no other possibility exists for him: "What will become of us? Manure for Russia's boundless fields."

After her realistic phase Kallas added new features to her work. She joined a group of Estonian writers called Noor-Eesti and met the best young writers of the period: Gustav Suits, Friedebert Tuglas, Villem Ridala. With them she adopted impulses from symbolism in her next collection of short stories, *Lähtevien laivojen kaupunki* (1913; City of departing ships), in her poems, and to some extent in an impressionistic autobiographical novel, *Katinka Rabe* (1920).

When Estonia became independent in 1918–19, Oskar Kallas was appointed Estonian ambassador, first in Helsinki (1918–22), then in London (1922–34). Aino Kallas's career as a writer also entered a new phase. In her handling of Estonian themes she moved further from recent history, more and more seeking her material in the chronicles of the sixteenth and seventeenth centuries, in ecclesiastical registers, folklore studies, and Estonian mythology. Stylistically, too, she adopted an archaic, chronicle-like expression, with archaic word forms and syntax, in her works of the 1920s. The approach aroused astonishment at first in critics and readers but later proved its worth; in these works Kallas is at her best.

The short stories in the collection *Vieras veri* (1921; Strange blood) are still written in normal language, but they already approach the sentence rhythm of the chronicles. The central theme of the collection is love—fateful, forbidden love that breaks all boundaries. In the short story "Gerdruta Carponai" a clergyman's daughter realizes that she is the only survivor in a village laid waste by the plague. She wanders off and meets a stranger, a fisherman on the shore; in a desolate world love suddenly draws the young people irresistibly together, and they become the progenitors of a new family. Lauri Viljanen has aptly called the story Aino Kallas's myth of paradise. From now on her works follow the basic pattern of myth or mythlike historical events.

Kallas's works of the 1920s were—exceptionally—translated into English soon after they appeared. The way was opened with a collection of short stories, *The White Ship: Estonian Tales* (1920), with an appreciative introduction by John Galsworthy. It was followed by *Eros the Slayer* (1927), containing *Barbara von Tisenhusen* (1923) and *Reigin pappi* (1926; The rector of Reigi); the English version of *Sudenmorsian* (1928), *The Wolf's Bride*, appeared in 1930. Aino Kallas was one of very few Finnish writers to succeed in breaking into the English-language world and to be well received by critics in the insular Britain of that time. (She was fortunate in having the bilingual and literarily acute Alex Matson [1888–1972] as her translator.) Otherwise, only F. E. Sillanpää, who won the Nobel Prize, and Mika Waltari, who achieved the reputation of a best seller, have attained similar results.

The title *Eros the Slayer*, which Kallas also used for translations into Estonian and German, aptly describes the main theme of her work in the twenties. The theme of *Barbara von Tisenhusen* is from Russow's chronicle (1578): the noble maiden Barbara falls in love with a clerk of lower degree, elopes with him, is tried by a family court when she is caught, and is drowned. She does not regret what she has done, and at the end of the novel the narrator, Barbara's father confessor, writes, "But I, Mattheus Jeremias Friesner, do here write down that nothing more marvellous have I seen on earth than the love of this man and woman."

The first-person narrator of *Reigin pappi*, the vicar Paavali Lempelius, has been dismissed from his high office and banished to the remote parish of Reigi (on the island of Hiiumaa/Dagö), where his young wife, Catharina, is not happy. She and the curate Jonas Kempe fall in love, an affair that develops in the same way as in Barbara's tale: elopement, capture, execution. Since the narrator is the deceived husband, the birth of forbidden love is seen through his bitter eyes, and this gives the work its own special double perspective: it is both a presentation of past events and a self-scrutiny of the narrator.

The basis of *Sudenmorsian* is a myth about a werewolf, widespread in the Baltic countries, which the writer studied through archival research and folkloristic monographs. Aalo, the young wife of a forester, hears the call of wolves from a swamp on midsummer eve, is lured away by it, and experiences a supernatural ecstasy in her new wolf's shape when she meets the demon of the forest, the "Diabolus sylvarum." The result is again punishment, at first the destruction of the human Aalo, then the killing of her form as a wolf by means of a silver bullet fired by her husband. The theme of forbidden love has expanded to mythical dimensions, transgressing the limits permitted to man. *Pyhän Joen kosto* (1930; The revenge of the sacred river) also crosses the confines of nature's different elements, when the builder of mills, Adam Dörffer, falls in love with a water sprite and is killed in her embrace. As a portrayer of the irresistible power of love and as a revealer of human duality and the vital forces that rise from the depths of personality, Kallas links up with one of the main streams of European literature, entering the zone where the works of David Garnett (*Lady into Fox*) and Herman Hesse (*Steppenwolf*) moved.

Kallas later adapted several of her stories as plays, but their linguistic charm or structural muscularity was not retained. Nonetheless, these stage versions have been successful in adaptation for opera, where their highly dramatic features have been turned to advantage: the first opera of Tauno Pylkkänen (1918–80) was based on Kallas's one-act play *Bathseba Saarenmaalla* (1932; Bathsheba on Saarenmaa), and in 1950 his opera *The Wolf's Bride* won the coveted Prix Italia. A new peak in Kallas's work was marked by her authentic journals, published in her old age (1952–56). They cover a period from 1897 to 1931 and bring to light the grand passion of her life, her love for Eino Leino; as well, they contain entries concerning her time in the diplomatic circles of London, interesting from the standpoint of cultural history. Still another personal document of great interest is her correspondence, published as *Kolme naista, kolme kohtaloa* (1988–89; Three women, three fates), with her older sister, the author and editor Helmi Krohn (1871–1967), and textile designer Ilona Jalava.

Aino Kallas's life was divided among many countries: from Finland first to St. Petersburg (1900–1903) and Estonia, from there back to Finland, then to London, her years of retirement in Tallinn, as a refugee in Sweden from 1944 to 1953, and finally a return to Helsinki. (In this respect Kallas shared the experience of many European intellectuals in the troubled earlier decades of this century.) Her literary career was equally exceptional among her Finnish contemporaries. She does not resemble any other writer in Finnish literature, was not connected with any group of writers, and did not have any followers. Her closest links were with Estonian literature, but she became increasingly estranged from it during her London years, and in her chronicle novels, which she herself called prose ballads, she created her own lonely path.

Ilmari Kianto (earlier Calamnius, 1874–1970) made his literary debut a year before Kallas. He too was "different" as a writer and as a person. There was a good deal of the Strindbergian self-scrutinizer and aggressive saboteur in him, though as an artist he does not reach the level of the great Swedish master of abuse. Later study has revealed an unexpected abundance of Tolstoyan features in the work of his youth; Maria-Liisa Nevala sees him "as an anarchist and defender of humanity," "the hater of authority and lies, the critic of double standards, the overthrower of taboos" (*Ilmari Kianto*, 299). The streak of Tolstoyanism was strengthened by Kianto's period of study in Moscow (1901–3); in the trend of his studies he also had a different orientation from his contemporaries.

Kianto's first work, *Väärällä uralla* (1896; In the wrong career), brings out a principle of design that was typical of him, later as well: the use of autobiographical material but with pronounced modification, which distances the final result from the possible sources in the author's own experience. The narrator of the first novel is like Kianto himself—a young man planning a military career who perceives that it is wrong. Then Kianto published several collections of poetry: subjective poems resembling folk songs, in which the lakes and deep forests of his native district appear, arousing melancholy. There are patriotic themes too, but in those days that was only natural.

A new phase began in 1907. The themes and attitudes of several novels are expressed in their subtitles: *Pyhä viha* (1908; Sacred wrath) is "a novel of love in the Finland of the era of storm and struggle"; *Kärsimys* (1909; Suffering) is "a sexual inner picture of young people's lives"; *Pyhä rakkaus* (1910; Sacred love) is subtitled "or the life and death of a little child." These and the works written between them deal mostly with the relation between woman and man, colored at first by consideration of Tolstoyan purity, then by an eroticism that bursts forth with greater and greater strength, becoming ever more liberated. *Pyhä viha* criticizes the upper classes and especially the clergy; in *Metsäherran herjaaja* (1912; The reviler of the forest lord) state bureaucracy and a lone socialist idealist who desires contact with genuine nature are in opposition; the latter loses the struggle.

The best-known work of Kianto's early period was *Punainen viiva* (1909; The red line), which has become a classic description of Finnish life in the poor backwoods; the landscapes suggest his native district of Suomussalmi, in north-central Finland near the Russian border. The title alludes to Finland's first democratic parliamentary elections of 1906, when people voted by making a slanting line in red in the top corner of the appropriate election ticket. A poor cottager, Topi of Korpiloukko, grows excited about the coming elections and listens responsively to the speech, reeking of brimstone, of a political agitator with a hypnotic red necktie. (Before speaking, the agitator leads his audience in singing *The Internationale,* albeit many of the cottagers do not know the words. For Riika, Topi's bossy wife, "it was a remarkable song indeed, altogether different from the ones she had heard in church or cottage get-togethers.") But the elections do not bring a change in his life: his wretched hovel, full of children and vermin, does not change in any way, his thin and exhausted wife does not get the cloth for a skirt she needs, and finally Topi himself is killed in a fight with a bear; blood flows from his throat and forms a red line.

At the beginning of the third chapter the narrator directs his words to the more prosperous reader: "The inner sufferings of poor backwoods dwellers cannot be imagined by many people in the great world. If an omniscient being exists, he it is who alone knows them, but perhaps tells nobody. The mockery of those more fortunate may sometimes be justified, but raw reality does not change its coat like the squirrel in the woods." The quotation is typical of Kianto's novel. It shows the life of the poor man but also his "inner sufferings." There is as well a place for "the mockery of those more fortunate," humor that is at times so predominant that the work could be considered a comic novel. In reality, though, the humor is always counterbalanced and darkened by the tragedy of man struggling in harsh conditions. *Punainen viiva* is a novel about the events of its time, the breakthrough of a new era, or the premonition of it, in the backwoods (as in Aho's *Rautatie*); at the same time, it is a classic example of the great tradition of the Finnish novel, the description of the common people.

This tradition was established in Kivi's *Seitsemän veljestä*. In it, as in later novels, man's relation to nature is described; nature is seen sometimes as a friend, sometimes as an enemy. The characters are ordinary folk, often poor dwellers in the backwoods, antiheroes. But they are not portrayed condescendingly, as clowns or subhumans: they have their own human value. Against the "little man" is the bureaucratic machinery of society, which sometimes discourages or destroys him; the writers demand social justice and put themselves on the side of the weaker part. The chief characters are individualists, often unsympathetic, and though their point of view predominates, they are described critically. The realism and criticism of the books is softened by humor, which from Kivi onward is an important element in the traditional Finnish novel.

These main points are generalizations that are not all put into practice, as such, in any single writer. Yet, speaking roughly, there exists a tradition that begins with Kivi—to some extent, with Runeberg—and continues through Aho, Kianto, Lehtonen, Jotuni, Lassila, and many other writers until Haanpää, Pekkanen, and Väinö Linna, with individual variations, of course, and weighted in various ways. It is also continued in Kianto's later work, especially in the novel *Ryysyrannan Jooseppi* (1924; Jooseppi of Ryysyranta), which belongs to another era (see chapter 4).

Three Neoromantics: Linnankoski, the Young Kilpi, and Lehtonen

As early as the work of Maila Talvio, the young Kianto, and the young Kallas, there are features that point toward neoromanticism, almost without symbolism, it is true, and, in Talvio and Kallas, without the elements of Karelianism. The same features appear still more strongly in the youthful work of three other writers, where they are given colorfully decorative and stylized additional nuances. The young Johannes Linnankoski, the young

Volter Kilpi, and the young Joel Lehtonen can with justification be called neoromantics. They have also another quality in common: each of them changes his direction and style in his later work.

The real name of Johannes Linnankoski (1869–1913) was Vihtori Peltonen, and he had already achieved a conspicuous position as the editor-in-chief of a provincial newspaper, a propagator of popular education, a powerful speaker, and a leading figure of the Finnish cause when his drama *Ikuinen taistelu* (1903; Eternal struggle) appeared. The identity of "Linnankoski" long remained a secret, for the drama with its biblical themes about Cain and Abel was difficult to connect with the image of the practical Peltonen. The following work, a novel called *Laulu tulipunaisesta kukasta* (1905; Eng. tr. *The Song of the Blood-Red Flower*, 1920), seemed still further removed from Peltonen. It became the first genuine best seller in Finnish literature: fifteen editions appeared in ten years, with translations into many languages. The book has been, surprisingly enough, a success in France since it appeared as *Chant de la fleur rouge* in 1934, with many new printings since then.

Laulu tulipunaisesta kukasta is neoromantic in theme and style, or perhaps rather a romanticizing novel, the Don Juan story adapted to Finnish circumstances. The principal character is the young charmer Olavi; along with a gang of loggers he goes down the river from farm to farm and from girl to girl. Though it follows the pattern of an entertainment novel, the book has, nevertheless, a serious ending, when Olavi finally meets the "right" woman, Kyllikki, starts a family, and settles down as a farmer. Olavi and Kyllikki became fashionable names when the book was published and acquired numerous namesakes in various parts of Finland. The style of the novel, which follows Juhani Aho's weaker mannerisms with its inversions, purple passages, and pathetic fallacy, infected many amateur authors, and sentimental variations spread in newspaper stories and school essays.

But Linnankoski did not continue in the same vein; in a novella appearing in the same year, "Taistelu Heikkilän talosta" (The struggle for Heikkilä's farm), he showed that he could do other things. The plot of the story—a murder and its solution—is still calculated to attract readers, but the focus is on the problems of human relationships. The conclusion of *Laulu tulipunaisesta kukasta* was in a moralizing vein, though most readers hardly remembered this fact. In style, too, Linnankoski underwent reorientation and began to aim at "simple greatness," as a precept in his journal said. A trip to Italy, and especially the contact with Renaissance art, had opened his eyes to classical ideals and monumental architecture.

The novel *Pakolaiset* (1908; The refugees) is the most significant achievement of this new phase and of all Linnankoski's work. The principal character is the old farmer Juha Uutela, a widower who has married a farmer's daughter much younger than himself. She becomes pregnant by another man but tries to hide the situation from Uutela. The couple has moved to another part of Finland; the name of the novel thus gains additional meaning, different for the husband and for the young wife. When Uutela realizes what has happened, he collapses; lying on his deathbed, he overcomes his desire for revenge after a difficult spiritual struggle and destroys his will, in which he would have left his wife without inheritance. Although he has been wronged, he no longer wishes to compound that wrong, and he achieves inner peace through his decision. *Pakolaiset* is a dramatic, classically concentrated novel. The writer has pruned away all that is unnecessary from both plot and style; instead of his former flowery style, he writes precise, clear prose, with short sentences and carefully considered epithets. His laconic style is close to that of Maria Jotuni, who, it is true, used more dialogue and especially humor.

After *Pakolaiset* Linnankoski published two plays on biblical themes, *Jeftan tytär* (1911; Jephta's daughter) and *Simson ja Delila* (1911; Samson and Delilah); in essence, they reflect conditions in Finland at the time. But his most enduring achievements, mutual antitheses, have proved to be the two novels, the romanticizing *Laulu tulipunaisesta kukasta,* which approaches a prose poem, and the sinewy psychological study and morality, *Pakolaiset.* The extraordinary popularity of Linnankoski is demonstrated by the fact that both the erotic novel and the moral tale were translated twice into Swedish (respectively, 1906 and 1928, and 1913 and 1955), and the young Hagar Olsson (see chapter 9) turned both plays into Finland's other official language in 1919.

In taking his subjects from the Bible, Linnankoski was by no means alone; Volter Kilpi (1874–1939) found his inspiration for his first book in the same quarter. His work at the beginning of the century forms its own chapter both chronologically and in its artistic attitudes. It differs from other contemporary writings because of its extreme aestheticism and is separated from the writer's final production by three decades. A difference between the early and late works can also be noted in Kianto and Lehtonen, but in neither case is the division so clear and striking as in Kilpi's.

Kilpi's first work was *Bathseba* (1900), with the subtitle "David talks with himself." The novel consists of first-person fragments in prose-poem style, colored with a strong biblical tone but also with Nietzschean echoes. The moods of the speaker go from one extreme the another, in accordance with different situations. "Now I have thought on life, and I have observed that it is naught other than love. And all else is a dreaming and an empty raving, and love alone is unique and ever-present and love is life," says David in the days of his good fortune. When his beloved dies, he sees life as a mere void: "Now I am alone, and now the world has become the garden of death in mine eyes. And when I look ahead of me, there is only bare withering before me, and gray and stiff goes my way out into the distance before me." *Bathseba* is a book about love, its ecstasy and pain, and both are experienced and expressed fully, without fear of exaggeration, plunging totally into emotion.

A student of Volter Kilpi's youthful work, Vilho Suomi, has demonstrated that the background to *Bathseba* was the writer's own experience and that its panting, "hypnotic" tone, swinging from one mood to another, mirrored the writer's own subjective feelings ("Nuori Volter Kilpi"). "Love the capacity to love, was one of the young Volter Kilpi's hypnoses," Vilho Suomi states in his introduction to Kilpi's selected works, and continues: "There were two more: art and thinking." Where love was dealt with in *Bathseba*, other elements were dominant in *Parsifal* (1902) and *Antinous* (1903). The former considered the artist's vocation and is partly constructed on musical principles. The latter is a book about contemplation, the experiencing and enjoying of the beauty of life and art. (With these books, both devoted to cultural icons of the fin de siècle, Kilpi quite clearly intended to bring Finnish-language letters into the world of Wagner and Wilde—Walter Pater would have admired Kilpi's cool and measured prose. Yet only thirty-odd years separate the backwoods cabin of Kivi's seven brothers from the Athenian temples and Roman and Egyptian monuments contemplated by Kilpi's Bithynian aesthete.) As in his first work, Kilpi now shows a special ability to write about nonoccurrence: how man's inner life seems more significant than the external world and actually pushes it aside. This feature, exceptional in Finnish literature of the period, reappears as one of the basic principles of Kilpi's later work—very differently, it is true, and using quite different material.

Kilpi delved into aesthetic speculations in a collection of essays, *Ihmisestä ja elämästä* (1902; Of man and life), which throws considerable light on his other works. In the essay "On Art and Morality" he begins by presenting his thesis, "Art is always immoral," and demonstrates it with reference to Shakespeare's *Macbeth* and *Hamlet,* Fröding's poems, the works of Maeterlinck and Milton, and Byron's *Don Juan*. In the second part of the essay the thesis is reversed: "Art is always moral." Man is in the world to feel; his purpose is "to be the world's eternal mirror." "What makes man so deep-reaching? Art. Art awakens man's deep moments." Schopenhauer, Nietzsche, Kierkegaard, and Shakespeare, Byron, Fröding, Ibsen—the same poets as in the first part—now bear contrary evidence. "Art is only the awakening of the inner man." The same themes are dealt with in a broad survey published in the periodical *Valvoja*, called "Nykyaikaisista taidepyrinnöistä" (Attempts toward a modern art), which was an influential manifesto of symbolism and neoromanticism.

Kilpi's youthful work was the time's boldest proclamation of an aesthetic attitude toward life, yet simultaneously it claimed that art has a direct connection with life and that only through and with the help of art can life be experienced to the full and valued. Having said this, Kilpi fell silent and gave himself over to his library career, in which he rose to a prominent position, in 1921 becoming head librarian of the new Finnish university in Turku. He broke his silence with two pamphlets dealing with topical problems, *Kansallista itsetutkistelua* (1917; National self-scrutiny) and *Tulevaisuuden edessä* (1918; Faced with the future). The publication of his chief works had to wait for another decade and a half (see chapter 4).

Kilpi's extreme neoromanticism was the result partly of his own burgeoning creative powers and partly of conscious aesthetic deliberation, even research. Joel Lehtonen (1881–1934) started much less deliberately, searching spontaneously for his own form of expression, trying out various possibilities, and also pouring out his own contradictions. His origin surely provided a problematic starting point: the son of a woman of doubtful reputation and behavior, he did not know who his father was. He grew up as the foster child of a clergyman's widow but returned in his works to the riddle of his origins. If Kilpi's early works are colored with aesthetic seeking and rebellion, Lehtonen's revolt was existentialist and philosophical. The most suitable channel for its escape was a wild and free neoromanticism with Nietzschean emphases.

One of the four books Lehtonen wrote and published at high speed within a couple of years was actually a collection of stories called *Villi* (1905; Wild). The earliest was a long poem in the Kalevala meter called *Perm* (1904); the next was a novel, *Paholaisen viulu* (1904; The devil's fiddle); and the best was the tale *Mataleena* (1905), with the subtitle "Laulu synnyinseudulle" (Song to my native district). The characters of the novels are artistic souls rebelling against fate, often decadent defiers, according to the Scandinavian model, of conventional Christian and bourgeois values, sometimes also romantic and carefree wanderers as well. In addition to the Finnish neoromantics and the inevitable Nietzsche, the godparents of Lehtonen's early works were Hamsun, Strindberg, and Gorky—especially the young, rebellious Gorky who hid in Finland from the Russian military police, not the later model of socialist realism. The writer's search for his own identity also provided the background of these works, most clearly in *Mataleena,* where he writes about meeting his mother and sees her as "a kind of Madonna of sin and decay," as Pekka Tarkka writes in his introduction to Lehtonen's collected works (p. 6). His native landscape is described as a fertile and flowering summer idyll, though the people in it may live in extreme poverty and destitution.

After brief university studies Lehtonen became a newspaperman and began his long career as a translator. The general strike and the changed political situation had shown that the time for romantic rebellion had gone by. Returning to his native district, Lehtonen acquired a property near Savonlinna as his summer home; its name became Putkinotko—later the title of his chief work—and he put his half-brother there to farm it. He worked up a couple of collections of folktales for publication, *Tarulinna* (1906; Castle of legend) and *Ilvolan juttuja* (1910; Tales of Ilvola), but it grew increasingly clear that a certain phase in his work and life was over. Like Eino Leino, he traveled to Italy via Switzerland in 1908 and stayed there almost a year, particularly in Rome and Florence. Contact with the culture of the Mediterranean countries proved important for Lehtonen. He translated a good deal of Italian and, especially, French literature into Finnish (the *Decameron,* Stendhal, the brothers Goncourt, Anatole France, Romain Rolland) and collected his impressions of his Italian travels in a work called *Myrtti ja alppiruusu* (1911; The myrtle and the rhododendron), which opened up a new line in Finnish travel literature and was a turning point in Lehtonen's course as a writer.

In 1911–12 Lehtonen went south to the Continent again, this time to Paris, where the impressionist work *Punainen mylly* (1913; Le moulin rouge) was produced. It was a cross-section of big-city life, where splendor and poverty, history and the present mingle in many ways. Two years later he traveled still farther south, to Tunisia, seeking relief from worsening rheumatism. This trip also produced a book, this time of poetry, *Puolikuun alla* (Under the crescent moon), not published until 1919.

During his years of travel Lehtonen brought out, in addition to translations, four collections of poetry: *Nuoruus* (1911; Youth), *Rakkaita muistoja* (1911; Beloved memories), *Markkinoilta* (1912; From the market), and *Munkki-kammio* (1914; The monk's cell). If one may speak of realistic poetry, this paradoxical name fits some of Lehtonen's verse. He often took his subjects from the life of the common people, as in the narrative poem *Markkinoilta,* used Runeberg's variant of the trochaic pentameter line (employed by the master, among other places, in his *Idyll och epigram,* both for erotic vignettes and for the portrait of the Job-like peasant, Pavo [see chapter 7]), assembled robust folk characters and grotesque events, and extended his vocabulary to uninhibited everyday language and his meter toward the rhythms of everyday speech. Pekka Tarkka has seen the poem as a mischievous travesty of Runeberg's *Elgskyttarne* (The elk hunters) epic, in which "appeals to antique muses live side by side with Finnish sleigh songs and ring dances" ("Lehtonen 27.11.1881–20.11.1934," 37). Lehtonen said farewell to the second phase of his youthful work through the comic folk epic and lines of poetry that break the accustomed rules of meter. The journey toward *Putkinotko* and the works around it could begin.

Descriptions of the People: Jotuni and Lassila
"Life after all is quite ridiculous if you take it seriously," says a character in Maria Jotuni's play *Tohvelisankarin rouva* (1924; Wife of a henpecked husband). The paradox is typical of all the work of Jotuni (1880–1943). In her eyes the ridiculous and the serious go together in life, as inseparable as the two sides of a coin. Circumstances, human nature, fate turn one side into view, but knowledge of the existence of the other side always remains.

Maria Jotuni published *Suhteita* (1905; Relationships) as her first work and showed her fundamental quality in it. From the outset she was a short-story writer, the master of concise form, a user of dialogue. Her works do not contain narrator's comments and extensive explanations; her characters express their reactions through their asides, and one can read between the lines what is not said directly. Slight nuances in the speech of common folk, apparently empty asides, little Swedish expressions in the phrases of gentlefolk and of parvenus trying to be gentlefolk reveal how things really are and expose people's attitudes. Jotuni is a master of understatement.

Early on, Jotuni developed two of her own types of short story: the dialogue story and the monologue, which may equally well be reminiscence, one side of a telephone conversation, or a letter. The names of the speakers are not always mentioned, nor even their sex, which gradually becomes clear as the conversation progresses, as does the central problem of the story. The main characters are usually a woman and a man, as the titles of her collections suggest: *Rakkautta* (1907; Love) and *Kun on tunteet* (1913; When there are feelings). Both titles are ironic, because the stories are usually about the lack of real love or about pretended emotions. Marriage is a deal between two people, in which the woman is bought on financial or other terms connected with prosperity. Nevertheless, a woman accepting the bargain against her fundamental desire is by no means passive merchandise; she entrenches herself in her own sphere by intrigue and little deceits, by concealing money and acting otherwise than the man thinks she does. The stakes are equal when both offer false coin.

Resignation, compromise, and loneliness are the lot of Jotuni's characters. In the title story of *Rakkautta* an aging woman working in an office accepts the courtship of a wealthy shopkeeper, after weighing the advantages and disadvantages in her mind:

> Happen what may, I thought to myself, this can't go too badly. You can get used to a man in the course of time. It's always best to do what must be done when the time comes. After all, he's wealthy and steady. There's nothing to worry about there, and I'll manage all right otherwise. Not that I couldn't have been a poor man's wife. I was made for a poor man. I would have made a good wife for a poor man. I would have understood a poor one better, and worked hard without complaining, and soon put things right. But it didn't happen that way. The one I fancied didn't look at me. Probably didn't know what thoughts had been moving in my mind and haunting me for years. . . . But if it's not to be, it's not to be. And after all, there are lots of men. And one of them's no different from another.

The longest continuous work in Jotuni's early production is a short novel or long short story, *Arkielämää* (1909; Everyday life), a description of a remote rural village within the scope of a single day. The central character is the "Reverend" Nyman, who has gained this title from having studied theology once upon a time — or perhaps something else: nobody quite knows. He is a rootless wanderer with no permanent dwelling place, a drinker, skilled in practical jobs, but above all an intimate and forgiving father confessor. He can listen to people without judging and console them by his mere presence: "it was as if he weren't a stranger whom you had to avoid and you always had to beware of, as with all strangers."

Going around the village, Nyman meets people belonging to its various social groups, from those in domestic service to the wealthy farmers and their proud daughters. He sees how unevenly the gifts of happiness are divided: the happiest are a couple consisting of a poor servant girl and a farmhand, the loneliest the old master of a farm whose daughter is entering a loveless marriage. The gallery of characters in the story is not only a representative cross-section of the villagers but also a kind of scale of different attitudes to life. Directly or indirectly, their religious or primitive beliefs are also revealed: the work both quotes the hymn book and refers to folk beliefs and mythology. Within the period of a day and night, in the frame of everyday life, the different sides of human life are revealed. The range of the characters' remarks extends from high-flown expressions to the rough language of common speech. The description of the summer environment is given more space than is usual in Jotuni's works, so that different human fates are set lyrically in nature, seen in different lights.

Jotuni did not write many later short stories, just those in the collection *Tyttö ruusutarhassa* (1927; The girl in the rose garden). On the other hand, she wrote several plays, as might be expected from one so skilled in dialogue. More frequently than in the short stories, they deal with the middle or cultured classes. The problems of love come to the fore in the comedy *Miehen kylkiluu* (1914; Adam's rib); the title not only is a biblical reference to woman's creation but also points to her subordinate position in marriage. *Kultainen vasikka* (1918; Eng. tr. *The Golden Calf*, 1997) deals satirically with phenomena of World War I, speculators and parvenus who exploit the exceptional circumstances, indifferent to moral standards. *Tohvelisankarin rouva* (1924; Wife of a henpecked husband) is again a comedy of love and its complications.

Jotuni also wrote two volumes of reflections, which in abstract form reveal the same ideas as her short stories or her plays about human relationships, on a concrete level. Her final work differed from that of her early period in two respects: tragic elements rose to the surface, and the novelist evolved from the short-story writer. Written during World War II, the tragic drama *Klaus, Louhikon herra* (not published until 1946; Klaus, master of Louhikko) is based on the theme of a well-known folk ballad, "Elinan surma" (The murder of Elina). More surprising than the shift of the writer of comedies to tragedy — tragicomic elements had been apparent throughout Jotuni's work — was the sudden publication in 1963 of her late novel, *Huojuva talo* (Tottering house). The manuscript had been submitted to a novel competition but had not won first place and had remained unpublished at the author's request.

Huojuva talo is both a family tragedy and a picture of the political ideologies of its time, the 1930s. One of the main characters, a tyrannical husband, shows what brutality can be concealed under the surface of a person considered cultured. At the same time, he is a study of someone carried away by totalitarian political movements — a Finnish fascist. The novel contains elements of Jotuni's own marriage to the literary historian Viljo Tarkiainen (1879–1951), her alienation from her husband and from the increasingly tense political situation of the years on the eve of World War II and the rise of Hitler's Germany, which Jotuni was capable of examining critically (as were her contemporaries Joel Lehtonen and Aino Kallas and, among slightly younger writers, F. E. Sillanpää). The road from the short stories of the first collection to the last posthumously published novel is a long one, but the same forces of selfishness and the battle of the sexes are present in Jotuni's world in both remote, cramped cottages and the neat drawing rooms of cultured circles. Jotuni examines these two spheres of life with a sharp and mercilessly critical eye, showing a little more understanding and warmth for the former, however.

In one of the short stories in *Rakkautta* the girl Erikka, having broken her engagement and striving to recover her balance, stands at the door of the dance hall and whispers to her cousin: "Don't you pity these people? Don't you think that each one of them has his little sorrows, that life isn't anything like what it seems?" In Jotuni's works the latter observation is confirmed time after time: life is different from what it seems. But the question in the first part of the quotation also remains valid: at her most revealing, at her most cynical, as the portrayer of resignation and defeat, Jotuni, like the old Strindberg, is always able to feel pity for people.

Maiju Lassila (1868–1918) is a nom de plume behind whose feminine form hides a man, originally baptized Algoth Tietäväinen. Later (in 1901) he changed his last name to Untola. As a writer he used, besides Maiju Lassila, the other pseudonyms Irmari Rantamala and J. I. Vatanen. There is no equivalent role-play in Finnish literature. Equally great contrasts are to be seen in the writer's private life.

The author was born in North Karelia and became a folk-school teacher. He worked in this capacity in Viipuri for some ten years and then was a timber merchant in St. Petersburg (1900–1904), marrying a Russian woman there. After the general strike he was a traveling speaker for the Old Finnish (Conservative) Party and a journalist, even the editor-in-chief of a Pori newspaper, *Satakunta* (1908). He started his career proper as a writer in 1909 and gradually shifted more and more to the Left in his politics, beginning to write for the socialist newspaper *Työmies* in 1916–17; he became the last journalist working—in a hopeless situation—on this most important paper of Red Finland. After the capture of Helsinki by the Whites in the spring of 1918 he was imprisoned and shot when attempting to escape from a boat carrying prisoners to a place of execution near Helsinki. The most important of the writers on the Red side during the Civil War, politically he became a lonely and enigmatic martyr to his ideals.

The extent to which writers' personal lives belong to the history of literature can be discussed and disputed. Sometimes their lives, like their dwelling places, can be significant, at least for the analysis of their works, as in the case of Ibsen and Strindberg, or to demonstrate their foreign cultural connections, as with Järnefelt, Kallas, and Lehtonen in Finland. In the case of

Lassila, his time in St. Petersburg may be a kind of key; generally speaking, little is known of this period. His first novels, *Harhama* and its sequel, *Martva* (1909), contain descriptions of Russia or of working people and social conflicts at the beginning of the century; there are also parts that suggest the writer's possible contacts with revolutionary elements of the period.

Harhama and *Martva* are mammoth novels; their joint length approaches three thousand pages. They are also learned works, bearing witness to their author's rare mastery of languages and wide reading. Above all, they are chaotic. The former is a description of the struggle between the forces of good and evil in the world through which the chief character, Harhama, roams — his name comes from the Finnish word *harha,* "astray." The title figure of the latter is a woman whose life goes off the rails. *Harhama* "represents the last, over-ripe blooming of neo-romanticism at the turn of the century, its decay and withering," according to Liisi Huhtala. "Its chief character is a sensitive, exceptional person like his predecessors a wild hater of authority and defier of the gods, and in it life is idolized as mystic, personified" ("Maiju Lassila," 20). There are clear points of connection with the literary fashions followed by the young Lehtonen and Linnankoski.

Harhama and *Martva* appeared as works of "Irmari Rantamala," which subsequently disappeared from the writer's nomenclature. "Maiju Lassila" now came to the fore, the best known and most used of Untola's catalog of roles. The first novel under this name, *Tulitikkuja lainaamassa* (1910; Borrowing matches), has become established as the writer's main work; his numerous later novels and plays do not come up to its level. The title aptly describes the theme of the novel. In Finnish there is a proverb, "to make a matter out of matches," meaning to start doing something for a fictitious reason or to exaggerate a slight detail for little reason. The subtitle of the novel could well have been "much ado about nothing." Vatanen, a small-time farmer, notices that matches have run out at home and goes over to his neighbor's to borrow some. On the way he meets another neighbor, Ihalainen, and goes into town with him. The liquor they imbibe causes many complications; it takes the two friends to the police cell and gives rise to the notion in their families that they have gone off to America. In the end, when he returns home, Vatanen notices that he has got a box of matches containing only one match from his neighbor, and that a used one. Lassila denied that he had written the novel with artistic aims; he claimed he wanted only to entertain his readers. The characters of the novel are common folk, mainly interested in material values, who in fact seem to be at a great remove from the cast of an "artistic" novel. But in two respects Lassila proves himself a first-class writer: as a describer of his characters' roundabout way of speech and of rural behavior and as a spinner of a surprisingly complicated plot. In his aim of attaining a great philosophical synthesis in *Harhama* and *Martva,* he failed; in setting out in *Tulitikkuja lainaamassa* to describe people whose lives are narrow and who know precious little about anything other than the everyday matters closest to them, he achieved excellent results.

Lassila's production is extensive — twenty-six works all told — and includes many descriptions of the common people, humorous pictures of children, and plays. In the novel *Pirttipohjalaiset* (1911; Cottage Ostrobothnians) the dispute of two farmers is a political allegory: their attitude toward a bear reflects the attitudes of political parties of the time toward Russia. A later peak in Lassila's work is marked by the novels *Liika viisas* (1915; Too wise) and *Kuolleista herännyt* (1916; Wakened from the dead). Both touch on religion ironically and farcically and could be taken as criticisms of religion if one did not know from the writer's unpublished manuscripts that he was concerned with religious problems, and especially the person of Jesus, all his life.

Liika viisas is a novel about a man, Sakari Kolistaja, who has been stirred by the sermons of a stupid clergyman to realize that, according to the Bible, worldly wisdom and knowledge are evil. "After hearing the pastor declaring the horror of wisdom, he had begun to examine himself, realized he was too wise, been horrified by the situation, become distressed, and begun to seek help and salvation." From this realization his new life begins. Preaching against wisdom to others, he confuses the affairs of the whole congregation, gathers a religious sect around him, becomes the director of a lunatic asylum, and frees his patients, leading them off in a wild procession. The speeches he makes are as topsy-turvy as his thoughts; they are excellent parodies of sermons with their pious phrases and halting comparisons. *Kuolleista herännyt* reveals the same kind of exaggerating imagination. Its chief character is a wharf rat called Jönni Lumperi, who makes a small winning in a lottery, starts to boast, and ends up as a high-level speculator, setting the business world on end with his maneuvers. The farcical side of the plot is enhanced by the fact that several times he is thought to be dead but is always returned to the land of the living, "wakened from the dead." Thus the novel hits out at both capitalism and religion, with equally extravagant and exaggerated emphases.

Surprising situations, rapid turns of plot, and type-drawn common folk are also characteristic features of Lassila's plays, all comedies: *Kun lesket lempivät* (1911; When widows fall in love), *Kun ruusut kukkivat* (1912; When the roses bloom), *Luonnon lapsia* (1912; Children of nature), *Nuori mylläri* (1912; The young miller), and *Mimmi Paavaliina* (1916). In them he is more conventional than in his novels, though the basic elements are similar. But in his plays Lassila does not develop his situations sufficiently for them to achieve the same level of absurdity as in his best narratives.

The neoromantic early phase and the struggle with great problems makes Lassila resemble the young Lehtonen, Linnankoski, and to some extent Kilpi; the illusion-free concept of "the people" and the gray ordinariness of their everyday life joins him to Jotuni and, to some degree, Kianto. Lassila also has points of contact with Aho, especially the Aho of *Rautatie*, but superficially, perhaps the Aho of *Heränneitä* as well. He took a caustic attitude toward his contemporaries in his works, however, and employed figures who, behind their transparent names, obviously conceal critically portrayed and recognizable models. But he was capable also of parodying himself, by referring mischievously to his own pen names and works; in this respect, through conscious intertextual connections, he went very much his own way. He was an independent exceptional phenomenon in his time. In his considerable, rapidly written oeuvre many features of necessity became repetitive mannerisms, but in his best books he moves freely, breaking the bounds of convention and genre. The pace and flight of imagination in these works are without comparison in Finnish literature.

Many other prose writers of the same period have vanished into oblivion or revealed the limitations of their significance. One who deserves mention, however, is Kyösti Wilkuna (1879–1922). In his first collections of stories (1907, 1908) he described the life of the common folk, and then he turned to the difficulties of the farmer's son who studies at the university in the autobiographical novel *Vaikea tie* (1915; The difficult road), a descendant of the Norwegian Arne Garborg's *Bondestudentar* (1883; Peasant students). Long interested in history and historical fiction, Wilkuna then became a writer of numerous novels and short stories about Finnish intelligence and prowess. In them he projects the Finnish idea of independence far into the past and presents classic representatives, starting with Mikael Agricola himself and including, among many other admirable Finns, the famous partisan of the Great Northern War, Stefan Löfving (see chapter 6). The tone of these narratives can be deduced from the title of a two-volume set of stories written with Santeri Ivalo, *Suomalaisia sankareita* (1915–21; Finnish heroes).

Wilkuna was not afraid to put his patriotic zeal into practice. Arrested by the Russian authorities for his efforts to recruit young men for the light infantry battalion of anti-Russian Finlanders being formed in Germany, he was imprisoned in St. Petersburg from 1916 until the outbreak of the Russian Revolution, an experience he described in *Kahdeksan kuukautta Shpalernajassa* (1917; Eight months in Shpalneraya Prison). He then participated in the Finnish Civil War (see *Kun kansa nousee* [1918; When the nation awakes]) and, finally, in the spring of 1919, was a member of the so-called Aunus expedition, a group of Finnish volunteers, veterans of the Civil War (or War of Liberation, as the Whites called it), which set out to aid anti-Bolsheviks in eastern Karelia. It briefly captured the town of Olonetz (Aunus) before being forced to retire.

Poets of the 1910s

Eino Leino, Otto Manninen, and V. A. Koskenniemi, along with L. Onerva, dominated poetry so clearly that only a few new poets appeared beside them. In addition, the focus of literature was on prose for some time around the year 1910, as the works of Ilmari Kianto, Maria Jotuni, and Maiju Lassila show.

One of the few important new poets was Juhani Siljo (1888–1918). He started with a collection called *Runoja* (1910; Poems), followed by *Maan puoleen* (1914; Toward the earth) and the posthumous *Selvään veteen* (1919; To clear waters). Siljo did not fling himself into a decorative-symbolist eulogy of life's pleasures like Onerva, or virtuoso verbal harmony like Leino, but followed another road. "Ethicality is the breath of poetry," he wrote in his journal, which had the characteristic working name of "Tilikirja" (Book of reckoning). Siljo was a seeker after truth as a poet, an examiner and critic of himself; he also wrote for newspapers and periodicals, such as *Helsingin Sanomat* and *Valvoja*, making lofty demands on literary art in his reviews. His natural form of expression was the aphorism; he is one of the best aphorists of his time and in Finnish literature. Many of his aphorisms have become proverbial sayings, sometimes quoted or referred to without a knowledge of their origin.

Among the key forces in his poetry is the will. Siljo sets his aim high and desires to create his personality consciously, avoiding compromises — "Vastavirtaan" (Against the stream), as one of his best-known poems is entitled. In the poem "Kalkki" (The chalice) he speaks of a promise "to be oneself" and wishes to fulfill it uncompromisingly. "Like a strung bow is this will of mine," the poem "Excelsior" characteristically begins. The poet should be "the builder of his own self," an honest self-scrutinizer, an ethical contender and striver.

Siljo's poetry has had many followers; a "Siljo line" has even been spoken of, in connection with his strict poetry of conviction and self-examination. But there is another side to Siljo's poetry: gradually, the strictness and self-control are loosened. As the title of the second collection says, the poet understands he must turn "toward the earth," admit the power of life and love. Siljo is an ascetic at first, but he is not a narrow dogmatist and denier of life. In his masculine program, which stresses purity, warm sensual tones appear. All the same, poetry is for him often a battle against the trolls in the caves of his own mind, as Ibsen says in his little poem "Et vers" (A verse), extremely well known in Finland. Along this road, preserving strict intellectual control but at the same time accepting and admitting emotional factors, Siljo might have developed into an important poet and cultural influence in the new, independent Finland.

Going to the front as a correspondent on the White side in 1918, he soon took up arms himself but was wounded in the fighting at Orivesi in March, captured by Reds, and died in a military hospital in Tampere in May, a month after that key city had been conquered by his comrades. In him the Whites lost their most important writer, as the Reds did in Maiju Lassila. The posthumous reputation of Siljo lived on and influenced later generations; he became a sort of legend, still turned to even after World War II.

Along with Siljo, one of the foremost poets of the time was his friend Lauri Pohjanpää (1889–1962), whose first book was published in 1910. Pohjanpää won fame with his beast fables; the animal figures of his poems reflect human weaknesses (a tradition in such poems since the days of La Fontaine and the Russian Krylov) and give gentle moral lessons to their readers, as was altogether appropriate: Pohjanpää was a Lutheran clergyman and for almost forty years an instructor in religion at Helsinki's Suomalainen yhteiskoulu (Finnish coeducational high school). In the collection *Metsän satuja* (1924; Tales of the forest) Pohjanpää is at his best as a fabulist. But at the same time, he is a full-blooded lyrical poet; in his long career he published some ten volumes of poetry, containing sensitive nature poems, meditative lines, and religious poetry. He was labeled too precisely, as is often the case, for representing only one kind of poetry, and it has been the task of later readers to find other elements in his verse behind the accepted facade.

In the 1910s several poets came to the fore; their work has not lived on except in one respect: their renewal of meter and rhythm. The earliest of them was Huugo Jalkanen (1888–1969), later a journalist and theater critic. In his first work, *Kevät* (1912; Spring), he started to use free rhythm, with which Eino Leino had already experimented at the turn of the century. His lyric production was actually quite small, and his poetic vein dried up after *Rakkausuhri* (1914; Love sacrifice) and *Elämän helle* (1919; Life's heat); his models were chiefly such users of the French *vers libre* as Henri de

Régnier and Francis Vielé-Griffin, and the result is often an exclamatory, dithyrambic style. Viljo Kojo (1891–1966) employed free rhythmic patterns more naturally than Jalkanen; the main part of his work belongs to a later period. These early users of free meter did not form a school, but their rhythmic experiments and reforms were to be of importance to the next generation of young poets.

1916: A Turning Point
Many of the writers of the beginning of the century went on long into the era of independence (Jotuni, Kilpi, Lehtonen, Manninen) and in some cases even until the years following World War II (Kallas, Kianto, Koskenniemi). After them a new generation began to appear with new artistic aims and beliefs.

The turning point was the year 1916, in the middle of World War I. The older generation was still very active then: the second part of Leino's *Helkavirsiä,* Aho's *Rauhan erakko,* and Lassila's *Kuolleista herännyt* appeared. But the new writers who were first published in the following decade were to show the path of the future — on the Finnish-language side, F. E. Sillanpää and the poet Aaro Hellaakoski, and on the Swedish-language side, Edith Södergran and the prose writer Hagar Olsson. When the Civil War radically changed the political and cultural situation in 1918, it was obvious that a page of literary history had also been turned. The older generation continued its work in diverse ways, conscious of its European ties, skeptical of new phenomena; the new generation, studying its own time, continued in the new direction: forward.

The Period of Independence 1, 1917–1960

Markku Envall
Translated by Ritva Poom

4

The autonomy that had existed in Finland as part of the Russian czarist empire determined the social and cultural conditions of Finnish independence. This gradual evolution was dramatized at the turn of the century when Russia began to adopt a policy of restricting its peripheral areas and Finland initiated a legal struggle against these measures. The general strike of 1905 resulted in the unicameral Parliament of 1906, which was elected by universal and equal suffrage. This sequence of events reached its highest intensity in 1917: the czarist regime was toppled in Russia, the Parliament assumed power in Finland, and the Senate proclaimed Finland an independent republic.

The evolution of Finland as an independent state began with a national tragedy, however. Finnish society had split into two factions, the Whites (bourgeoisie) and the Reds (socialists), both of which were armed. A considerable Russian military presence also continued to exist in Finland. In 1918 fighting erupted between the White and Red factions, and the acts of terror that followed continued to divide the Finnish nation until the Winter War (1939–40), which somewhat abated this enmity. The Civil War had the effect of causing Finnish culture in the decade of the 1920s to deny the past, to negate history, and to adopt a superficial internationalism. There existed in the nation no desire to confront the trauma of the civil war; it was evaded. Instead, metaphors for the past were sought in deeper layers of history, even from antiquity: the analogy between Finland and ancient Greece was a favorite. The claim of internationality was ironic because the young generation that proclaimed it was clearly less able in its contacts with Continental Europe than preceding generations had been. This national trauma also had an effect on Finnish literature. In Finnish-language prose its influence became most quickly and deeply felt in F. E. Sillanpää's novel *Hurskas kurjuus* (1919; Eng. tr. *Meek Heritage,* 1938, 1971).

During the decade of the 1920s the Finnish republic, with the energy of new beginnings, embarked on a campaign of reform in the spheres of both material and spiritual culture. The circumstances of those on the losing side were alleviated through social legislation. The Social Democratic wing of the workers' movement began to be integrated into society as a whole, while its Communist wing was declared illegal — it continued its activities in exile in the Soviet Union and underground in Finland. Working-class literature became a separate entity, distinct from the rest of Finnish literature, and was only gradually integrated into the cultural mainstream.

During the late 1920s and early 1930s Finland experienced a depression and right-wing extremist activity (the Lapua Movement, the Mäntsälä Revolt). The depression was followed by a boom that continued until the outbreak of the Winter War in 1939. The threat posed by the rightist movement was overcome by the victory of the Finnish parliamentary democracy. Tension in Finnish society was also heightened by conflicts over language and issues involving alcohol. The Finnish-speaking populace struggled against the traditional prerogatives of Swedish speakers. This conflict was resolved legally by the Language of Law of 1922, which has been internationally acclaimed for its impartiality. Nevertheless, the language issue was not truly settled until the 1930s. The Prohibition Act encouraged the smuggling of alcohol and worked against its intended goals in other ways as well; this law was repealed in 1932, a state alcohol monopoly was established which has remained in force ever since. A law requiring universal compulsory education was enacted in 1921, and another that guaranteed freedom of religion was passed in 1922. Finland began to change from a nation whose primary sources of livelihood were agriculture and forestry to one whose economy was based mainly on industry. As a result, there was a large migration from the countryside to the cities.

For Finland, World War II actually meant three separate wars. The Winter War was a defense against an attack by the Soviet Union. The Continuation War (1941–44) was also fought against the Soviet Union. This time, however, Finland was allied with Germany and the war was initially one of aggression. After the armistice of September 1944 Finland immediately went to war once more. In this conflict, the Lapland War (1944–45), Finland drove the German forces out of its northernmost territory. Although Finland was defeated in the Continuation War, it retained jurisdiction over its own territory. Nevertheless, the influence of the war on Finland's political, social, and cultural life was profound. The isolated role of the extreme Left was "inherited" by the extreme Right. The Communists participated in affairs of state, although they remained a minority. Relations with the Soviet Union were now based on the Treaty of Friendship, Cooperation, and Mutual Assistance. It became customary to speak of the First and Second Republics, actually metaphorical terms, since Finland has retained the same constitution throughout, although there have been changes in points of emphasis; the status of and regard for workers were restored; distrust of the Soviet Union decreased; Finland became open toward both the East and the West; and new ideological winds began to blow throughout the country. In 1955 Finland joined the United Nations, and in 1956 the Soviet Union returned the Porkkala area to Finland before the actual termination date of the lease. Both these events strengthened Finland's position as an independent, neutral nation.

The end of World War II also brought about considerable changes in Finnish cultural life. Although V. A. Koskenniemi, who represented the values of the First Republic, became the first writer appointed to the Finnish Academy, for the most part the end of the decade of the 1940s heralded a period of cultural democratization and internationalization in Finland. Translation activity grew more lively and broad-ranging. It was only at this time that the modern classics of English and American culture (by D. H. Lawrence, Aldous Huxley, William Faulkner, Ernest Hemingway, and others) were translated into Finnish. Finnish prose and poetry, which had remained isolated from international literary developments during the 1930s, began to close this gap. Of these two genres, the most salient revolution was in poetry, which received its primary impulses from Finland-Swedish and Continental European modernism. The Finnish novel also underwent a process of literary reform during the 1950s.

Ideologically, the Finnish literary generation of the late 1940s and the 1950s sought to distance itself from the war and its values. This generation was not particularly leftist in its views but rather was of bourgeois liberal and radical persuasion: values of skepticism, relativity, and a sense of reality characterized its quest. It aimed to cleanse the Finnish language of the remnants of national idealism; using techniques that had proved enduring, it sought political freedom through simplicity, objectivity, and purity of expression. Thus the "poetic radicalism" of this generation led, in part, to the political radicalism found in Finnish literature of the 1960s and thereafter.

Literary developments do not always coincide with periods of political history. The most recent history of Finnish literature, Kai Laitinen's *Suomen kirjallisuuden historia* (1981), considers the period from the general strike to the Winter War (1905-39) as a single unit; the next period is defined as the war and the years that followed. It is true that the year 1917 does not mark a specific break in the development of Finnish literature; the work of the most significant authors of the earlier generation continued after this watershed year, and the new generation of writers did not produce any noteworthy works during the beginning of the 1920s. In general, it can be stated that the literary reform that occurred at the end of the 1940s and the beginning of the 1950s was deeper and more enduring than the one that followed Finland's independence. From an international perspective Finnish-language literary development lagged decades behind events abroad. Such literary reforms as freedom from regular metrics in poetry and from traditional conventions in prose, which had already been initiated in the literature of Continental Europe after World War I, came to Finnish-language literature only after World War II.

Earlier Authors Continue: Koskenniemi and Sillanpää
Although the upheavals of 1917 and 1918 had a significant effect on Finnish-language literature, a number of writers who had gained renown during the era of Finnish autonomy under the czarist regime continued to write long into the era of independence. Some, such as Otto Manninen, remained true to their early period, and the political changes of the times were not reflected in their writing; others, such as Joel Lehtonen, who changed his style to realism, and Volter Kilpi, whose work was influenced by the new period in the extreme, reflected these developments in their writing.

Almost symbolically, each of the factions lost one important author to the Civil War: the Whites lost Juhani Siljo, and the Reds, Maiju Lassila. The lives of both men came to a tragic end: Siljo succumbed to a battle wound; Lassila was slain during the reprisals that followed the war. As a result, these two authors also symbolize two phases of the destruction wrought by the war: the war itself, and the ensuing deaths of prisoners in prison camps and by execution.

Authors typical of the older generation who yielded to these events were Juhani Aho and Eino Leino, whose quality of writing declined after the war. Their main contributions had been made during the era of autonomy, and both men can be viewed as having stepped aside to make room for the new generation of writers. The most visible group to represent the new generation was the Torch Bearer circle, although the most enduring period for these authors actually came after they had left the group. The most vital of those older authors who went on writing (Aino Kallas, Arvid Järnefelt, Joel Lehtonen) achieved a higher artistic level than the new writers who were just beginning at that time.

There also exists a kind of author who perseveres through all upheavals, either by accommodation or through obstinancy. V. A. (Veikko Antero) Koskenniemi (1885–1962), a poet, critic, essayist, and scholar, was typical of this literary species. Koskenniemi's first collection, *Runoja* (1906; Poems), introduced urban themes into Finnish poetry, as an example not of human communality but of loneliness. This work heralded Koskenniemi's long and celebrated career in poetry, which continued until 1950. In his poetry solitude and urban metaphysics gave way more and more to feelings of communality, historical themes, and commemorative poetry. Read today, Koskenniemi's *Kootut runot* (Collected poems), which had its sixteenth printing in 1977, gives the effect of artistic decline as its grandiloquence and hollow solemnity steadily increase. Koskenniemi had a stellar public and professional career: he was professor at Turku University, rector of that university, and, as said, the first literary member of the Finnish Academy (established after World War II). His adherence to the values of the First Republic, however, as well as the old-fashioned nature of his poetics, caused his stature to plummet during the breakthrough of modernism in Finnish literature. Koskenniemi's affiliation with the Nazi-led European Literary Alliance during the war was as difficult to accept as his commitment to the poetry of antiquity and the old poetic conventions of Continental Europe (elegiac meter, the sonnet). From a current perspective individual examples of masterful achievement exist in his poetry although it is no longer greatly esteemed as a whole. Koskenniemi was influenced by the material nature philosophy of both antiquity and his own era. Although the pious tone of his poetry won him the support of the church, he remained an uncompromising agnostic. It is possible that the themes of life and man's place in the universe, which continued to interest him throughout his life, will help revive his stature once again. Nevertheless, his centenary in 1985 inspired no more than a dutiful commemoration.

Koskenniemi was an industrious critic, essayist, and scholar. His series of essay collections entitled *Kirjoja ja kirjailijoita 1–5* (1916–31; Books and authors), two biographical studies of Goethe (collected edition, 1948), and his lesser biographies of Talvio and Kivi are the fundamental achievements of this aspect of his work. Koskenniemi's essays on literature are biographical and genetic, a methodology now dated. But his literary insights were so masterful that they can be considered the most enduring aspect of his work. Koskenniemi also wrote a novel, two books of memoirs, and three collections of aphorisms. Of these genres, he was most successful with the aphorisms.

A world view that includes an interest in natural science unites Koskenniemi's work with that of F. E. (Frans Eemil) Sillanpää (1888–1964), although Sillanpää focused on the biological sciences whereas Koskenniemi's interests lay in the physical sciences. Sillanpää was overjoyed to find "matters of substance" rather than poetic clichés in Koskenniemi's first poems. Sillanpää's first novel was *Elämä ja aurinko* (1916; Life and sun): depictions of summer by a stylistically self-assured young man and a work in which nature, as a stage for human life, was represented with a new intensity. Sillanpää's primary genre was the novel, enhanced by a long series of brief prose collections alternating between the objective short story and reminiscences. Sillanpää's second novel, the aforementioned *Hurskas kurjuus*, made a significant impact at its publication because of its bold, probing attempt to comprehend the Finnish Civil War and the developments leading to it. Sillanpää's sympathies lay with the losing side. In his five other novels, *Nuorena nukkunut* (1931; Eng. tr. *The Maid Silja*, 1933), *Miehen tie* (1932; A man's road), *Ihmiset suviyössä* (1934; Eng. tr. *People in the Summer Night*, 1966), *Elokuu* (1941; August), and *Ihmiselon ihanuus ja kurjuus* (1945; The beauty and wretchedness of human life), Sillanpää went on, in contrast to his contemporaries, to depict the emotional lives of his characters and their existence as part of nature with singular depth and sensitivity. In Kaarlo Marjanen's judgment, other authors described "nature through man" whereas Sillanpää described "man through nature" (p. 77). The most recent study of Sillanpää tends to discount completely the biological aspect of his work; this is an overreaction to the previous overemphasis placed on it. In Sillanpää's world view the concept of man as an integral part of nature is complemented and enriched by other, no less significant components: first, an interest in sociohistorical structure and in the possibilities for the "little person" to realize his or her fate within this framework; and second, a talent for fine-tuned psychological analysis in which depth psychology, including a focus on the importance of the subconscious, plays an important role. In order to achieve this latter goal, Sillanpää required an author-centered narrative style that has, at times, been considered too commentative. Another aspect of Sillanpää's world view is a general metaphysical belief in a better future for humankind, based on an evolutionistic perspective. Sillanpää's viewpoint is a unique synthesis derived from so many diverse sources that scholarship has had great difficulty reconstructing it.

Sillanpää is one of the most read and studied of Finnish authors. Recently, a third literary biography, significantly more exhaustive than the previous two, was completed in three parts (by Panu Rajala, 1983, 1988, 1993). Sillanpää is the only Finnish author to have received the Nobel Prize in literature, a fact that continues to keep him in the limelight in Finland, although this is not necessarily the case in other countries. With time, his narrative art has begun to seem dated, but it has continued to draw advocates and ongoing analysis that has led to discoveries of previously unnoticed levels. In the final phase of his career, after World War II, Sillanpää produced sentimental reminiscences that served, unfortunately, to diminish the achievement of those years when he was at the height of his powers.

Kianto, Kilpi, Lehtonen
Other authors who began to write during the era of autonomy but who achieved new dimensions in their work during the era of independence were (in order of their literary debuts) Ilmari Kianto, Volter Kilpi, and Joel Lehtonen. These writers focused primarily on prose, although, except for Kilpi, they all wrote poetry as well.

The primary literary achievements of Kianto (1874–1970) are generally considered to be two depictions of the lives of country people, *Punainen viiva* (1909; The red line) and *Ryysyrannan Jooseppi* (1924; Joseph of Ryysyranta); the latter has been compared to Lehtonen's *Putkinotko* (1919–20). Kianto's and Lehtonen's epic novels of poverty analyze the reasons for and the nature of poverty in Finland. Both Kianto's Jooseppi (Joseph) and Lehtonen's Juutas (Judas), the main characters in their novels, are heads of families that include many children. They hold temporary jobs and earn their livings either as liquor distillers or as bootleggers. The primary focus of these novels is a substantiation of the fundamental worth of their protagonists. Hagar Olsson was the first to characterize them as the "Finnish Oblomovs," in actuality a rather weak metaphor: although these characters are similar to Oblomov in their lassitude, the factors that generate it are completely opposite. In the case of Oblomov, it is the purposelessness of the upper class that made Goncharov's hero passive, whereas Juutas and Jooseppi are prevented from achieving their objectives because of their flocks of children and their wretched poverty.

Ilmari Kianto authored more than fifty works; the last were published during the 1950s. Like Strindberg, although not at his level of achievement, Kianto openly chronicled his own life. The confessional roman à clef was his primary genre. In these novels Kianto's main characters, the various aspects of his persona, are structured in a pathetic ideological struggle. This aspect of his work has traditionally been understated in Finnish literary criticism. The most recent study of Kianto's work (Nevala, *Ilmari Kianto*, 1986) attempts to raise its stature, stressing that previous analyses of his writing made no distinction between confession and the use of autobiographical material.

After three decades of silence Volter Kilpi (1874–1939) forged his so-called archipelago series. In these novels he used powerfully individualized, unconventional language to express his affection for the peasants and seafaring people of southwestern Finland. To date, Kilpi's role as the Joyce or Proust of Finnish literature has not been greatly challenged. He was a leading neoromantic at the turn of the century whose reemergence in the literary landscape during the 1930s was a great surprise. Kilpi's archipelago series includes *Alastalon salissa 1–2* (1933; In the parlor of Alastalo), *Pitäjän pienempiä* (1934; The lesser in the parish), and *Kirkolle* (1937; To church). *Alastalon salissa* sets a record for slow tempo in Finnish literature: a novel consisting of almost one thousand pages describes a meeting approximately six hours long which focuses on the construction of a sailing vessel. In the force of its description this novel is without peer in Finnish literature; it is a testament to Kilpi's unique creative powers and the culmination of his years of artistic silence. Kilpi explained that he wished to abandon silhouette narrative for a "malleable narrative" in which "each sentence has been honed to cast light in almost innumerable directions." The text is unique in both its vocabulary and its syntax. Kilpi paid a price for his literary philosophy, however: the indifference of the reading public. A second edition of the novel was not published until 1965 and a third only in 1988.

Everyday language is merely a point of departure for Kilpi, furnishing the raw material used to create something further: a richer, more complex individual style that embodies dialect, newly coined words, grammatical innovations, and complex sentence structures. In describing his characters, Kilpi is lavish with external details and he aims, as much as possible, at psychological transillumination — the primary technique used in his narrative style is internal monologue. An observation made by Aaro Hellaakoski in 1937 remains valid today: "In the luminosity of its style and the purity of its composition, this work attains a high international standard" (*Kuuntelua*, 66). Kilpi's linguistic innovations were so radical, however, that the first full translation of *Alastalon salissa* did not appear until 1997.

Kilpi's *Pitäjän pienempiä* is a series of novellas with a more accessible narrative than that of *Alastalon salissa*. In this work the topic has changed from that of proprietors to indigents. In *Kirkolle*, however, Kilpi's innovation in language and imagery achieves even greater virtuosity than in *Alastalon salissa*. As innovative as Kilpi's archipelago series may be in Finnish literature, its style is Kilpi's own creation and not based on foreign models. The series contains no introspective artistry; rather, its descriptive technique evolves organically as a result of the artist's thematic requirements: Kilpi's attempt to describe the lives of the island people uses a broad span of emotions, leaving room for both humor and tragedy. His elimination of plot makes it possible for him to illuminate fully and in detail both the internal and external truths of society and the individual.

The work of Joel Lehtonen (1881–1934) evolved from neoromanticism to realism and naturalism. After considerable searching, Lehtonen's definitive turn toward realism was heralded by the novel *Kerran kesällä* (1917; Once in summer), the first in a series of novels united by the same subject matter, which became known as the Putkinotko series. The next work in this series was a collection of short stories entitled *Kuolleet omenapuut* (1918; Dead apple trees), followed by *Putkinotko* (1919–20), the main work, and *Korpi ja puutarha* (1923; Wilderness and garden).

Lehtonen was, above all, a portraitist of character with a singular ability to construct various types of human beings. *Kerran kesällä* describes, critically, the Finnish quasi-intelligentsia of the time. Through his depictions of these "dandies" and "boorish gentlemen," Lehtonen criticizes the alienation of the intelligentsia and its flight into romanticism and Karelianism. Lehtonen's portrayals relate to a favorite theme of this period: analysis of the social climber. In his study *Putkinotkon tausta* (1977; Background to Putkinotko), the Finnish literary critic Pekka Tarkka has clearly and systematically analyzed the Putkinotko series from the viewpoint of character. Using the bookseller Aapeli Muttinen and his tenant farmer Juutas Käkriäinen as the central characters, Lehtonen analyzes the relationship of the bourgeoisie to the folk. Of less significance is the fact that Lehtonen's depiction is based largely on his own relationship with his stepbrother. Lehtonen is critical of both the bourgeoisie and the folk; his evaluation of the bourgeoisie is harsher, however, for he considered it reasonable to expect more of them.

The action of *Putkinotko* takes place in a single day. The novel is at once a praise of summer, an analysis of Finland's sociocultural circumstances, and a statement of the author's philosophy of life. The somberness of human existence is balanced by the warmth and light of a summer day. *Putkinotko* has been described as a study of the burden of life: its pessimism derives from the failure of all the plans initiated by the characters in it. Appreciation of Lehtonen's verbal virtuosity in this novel has increased decade by decade. Among other enduring traits of the series are the power of its observations and the balance and maturity of its vision.

Lehtonen's literary style has been described as "disenchanted romanticism." Although his work progressed toward a vision of ever-growing pessimism in his late period, this vein of romanticism never disappeared from his work. In *Onnen poika* (1925; Son of fortune) Lehtonen cheerfully recalled his childhood and, in *Lintukoto* (1929; Birdhouse), his summers. But in his most important works, the series of novels from *Rakastunut rampa* (1922; A cripple in love) to *Henkien taistelu* (1933; Struggle of the spirits), Lehtonen painted vitriolic, gloomy portraits of the society of his time. The latter novel, which uses as its vehicle the story of a well-meaning person who is handed over to the devil's realm, is often compared to Maria Jotuni's *Huojuva talo* (1963; The quaking house), another misanthropic, epic novel written during the 1930s (see chapter 3). Lehtonen was also a poet: his final collection, *Hyvästijättö Lintukodolle* (1934; Farewell to the Birdhouse), is considered his most successful, praised for both its simple beauty and its appalling harshness; in it the poet bids farewell to life. Lehtonen's tenacity in his endeavors and the power of his depictions have kept alive Eino Leino's characterization of him as "the August Strindberg of our literature."

New Lyricists: Hellaakoski and Vuorela

Among the poets, Leino, Larin-Kyösti, Manninen, and Pohjanpää belonged primarily to the era of autonomy, although they continued to write into the First and, in Pohjanpää's case, even into the Second Republic. On the other hand, Aaro Hellaakoski and Einari Vuorela belong to the era of independence. Hellaakoski began writing in 1916, thus during autonomy, and Vuorela began in 1919, at the beginning of the new and independent Finland. The careers of both writers continued beyond World War II. Hellaakoski published poetry for almost four decades, Vuorela for more than six; Hellaakoski wrote a total of twelve collections, Vuorela nineteen. (Hellaakoski ceased writing poetry for twelve years, time he devoted to his profession, geology, both as a teacher and in research.) Hellaakoski was a poet, a scholar, a pedagogue, a critic, and an essayist; Vuorela concentrated solely on poetry. Both also published prose works, although not with any particular success. They are distinguished from Koskenniemi by their talent for innovation, forming a bridge between traditional and modern Finnish verse. In this regard they can be viewed as related to P. Mustapää and Viljo Kajava.

Aaro Hellaakoski (1893–1952) is one of the most independent and visionary Finnish poets of this century. The goal of "Conceptio artis," the poem that sets the tone of his first collection, was to attain an art

> naked,
> stripped, unpainted,
> without clutter
> the bestowal of others.

Although Hellaakoski's period of artistic silence, followed by his literary innovations, emphasized the division of his work into two periods, the driving force of the poem cited above, which strives toward a personal, antiliterary, powerful, vernacular poetry, while also seeking spiritual expression, permeates his entire body of work. Hellaakoski's first period is characterized by an individual's defiance and maladjustment, individualism, and an assault on the bourgeoisie; his latter period is a pantheistic acceptance of the unity of man and the world. In the subtitle of her 1972 study Kaisa Kantola summarizes these periods with the phrase "the ego and existence." An anxious, ethical-individualistic struggle binds Hellaakoski's poetry to the dominant interwar trend, from which it is distinguished by a victory in this struggle and achievement of an affirmative stance toward the world. Subsequently, Hellaakoski won acceptance, whereas Vuorela began with a struggle and persevered in it throughout his work.

In addition to the daring and independence of thought in Hellaakoski's poetry, the genius of its rhythmic auditory forms gives it enduring value. Hellaakoski was well aware of the newest artistic trends and demanded perfection of himself, although he never became conventional. In his use of a seemingly limitless vocabulary and meters that differed from the norm, he was a leader in pioneering new directions for poetry. The highest point of his youthful period was the collection *Jääpeili* (1928; Ice mirror). The experimental pictorial typography of this collection, recalling Apollinaire's *Calligrames* (1918), was so innovative that there was no one to continue its initiative until the poetry of the 1960s. The culmination of Hellaakoski's achievement is the collection *Sarjoja* (1952; Series), a cycle of alternating long and short verses about nature and travelers there. In this collection the boundaries between the ego and the other, between the spirit, man, and nature, are transcended, and a vision of the world as a unity, with man as an integral part of it, is achieved. The style of this poetry is, at times, similar to speech, with even greater divergence from metrical verse. Hellaakoski's vision bespeaks a sense of harmony achieved through hard work.

Also worthy of mention are Hellaakoski's essay collections, *Kuuntelua* (1950; Listening), *Runon historiaa* (1964; A history of poetry), and *Niinkuin minä näin* (1959; As I saw); a biography of the artist Tyko Sallinen (1921); and a posthumous collection of aphorisms entitled *Lumipalloja* (1955; Snowballs).

Einari Vuorela (1889–1972) is among the most archetypal of Finnish poets, a timeless singer from the landscape of Finland's interior. Vuorela began his writing with folk songs, and in this respect he continued the poetic tradition of J. H. Erkko, the young Eino Leino, and especially Larin-

Kyösti; but he soon distinguished himself from Larin-Kyösti by his greater sensitivity and the emotionalism of his poetry, as well as the originality of his images. Vuorela's poetry is impervious to the influence of time and history; his landscape remains the same from one decade to the next: wilderness, swamp, village — Vuorela studies these features from a roadside or through a window. Keuruu, a parish west of Jyväskylä, is generally considered the prototype for his landscape. Vuorela was most successful with the folk song and the ballad forms, but poetic ambition led him to attempt more literary poetic forms as well, including an entire collection of sonnets (1934). His greatest achievement lies in poems that describe the landscape in very brief verses, mentioning a person, spectator, or singer as an aside. Because there exists no literary term to describe these poems, they have been called "watercolors."

The span of a year and a day is Vuorela's unfailing subject matter. He describes this in verses that are characteristically straightforward yet inventive in their images and songlike harmony. A poet of both eye and ear, he has a narrow emotional range, focused on love and loneliness, and the intellectual content of his poems is not particularly striking. As an archetypal, at times even archaic singer, however, Vuorela is among the most sensitive of Finnish poets. He is also one of the classic Finnish poets whom the generation of the 1950s adopted as its own, something that has added considerably to his stature. In almost every decade following the war a volume containing a broad selection of his works has been published. At a time when the dominant trend in poetry was to probe the depths of the soul, Vuorela remained independent enough to depict nature and to include people in the landscape ever so faintly. In his poetry one listens to the spirit of the forest; it has been characterized as *"Kanteletar*-like," after the famous collection of folk songs published by Elias Lönnrot. Indicative of a certain naiveté in Vuorela's poetry is the fact that, when the subtitle "poems for young people" was omitted from one of his collections, the book could not be distinguished from his other collection, *Runot* (1966; 1979; Poems).

Poetry of the Torch Bearers

Numerous new dimensions emerged in the literary life of the young republic in the 1920s. Although the most enduring literary works written during both the 1920s and the 1930s came from the generation that had begun writing during the era of autonomy, a group of young poets known as the "Torch Bearers" was the center of literary attention at this time. Evidently, the trauma of the Civil War had cut these young writers off from the past, resulting in numerous manifestations of escapism in their writing, including a longing for faroff places and the exotic, a preference for fairy tale and horror in their subject matter, contemporary romanticism, and an adulation of technology and the urban.

For the new generation, the Torch Bearer movement became a cult. The parameters of this movement were undefined and its intellectual program was both contradictory and filled with slogans, but it managed to keep itself in the mainstream. The influence of the Torch Bearers on literary developments in Finland has long been underrated. Kaarlo Marjanen wrote that it was not a modernist movement but rather an "assault of youth." The Torch Bearer circle has been characterized as a phenomenon created, then destroyed, by Olavi Paavolainen, a talented manipulator of publicity (by means of his pamphlet *Suursiivous* [1932; The great housecleaning]). There is beginning to emerge a concept of "the Torch Bearer generation," meaning those writers whose literary debuts were in the 1920s. In its time this movement and the group were highly visible, and the feeling inspired by the forward march of "the young poets" (with an anthology, 1926) and the "new generation" was powerful. (See Hagar Olsson's essay collection, *Ny generation* [1925; New generation].)

A third slogan was coined by Paavolainen in his collection of essays entitled *Nykyaikaa etsimässä* (1929; In search of the present). From a historical point of view the Torch Bearer movement channeled new European artistic trends into Finland (expressionism, futurism, dadaism, surrealism). From the present perspective, however, this movement was overly involved with self-promotion and the clash between the generations. It was also lacking in literary achievement. Viewed historically, there is an ironic aspect to the Torch Bearer movement: the literature created by writers external to the group ultimately proved to be superior: Hellaakoski's *Jääpeili,* the most skillful collection of verse written in the 1920s and the one that furthest extended the parameters of Finnish modernism at the time, came from outside the Torch Bearer movement. In their actions the Torch Bearers were characterized not only by youthfulness but also by immaturity. Their achievement remained far below that of Finland-Swedish modernism, which was then developing simultaneously. Contacts between the Torch Bearers and these Finland-Swedish writers were sparse. When this superficial modernism in Finnish-language literature was followed, in the 1930s, by a period of restrictive, nationalistic rigidity, Finnish literature was left far behind international literary developments. Only with a great deal of effort by the generation that began writing after World War II would this chasm be bridged.

Compared with the generation preceding them, the interwar poets were much more troubled. Five leading poets of this generation died of tuberculosis in their youth or during middle age: Södergran, Kailas, Vala, Sarkia, and Harmaja. As a consequence, a myth developed that illness and death were the source of great poetry and a poet's inevitable fate. It went largely unnoticed that, like Koskenniemi and Vuorela, Viljanen and Mustapää, most poets had a long career. The myth of the poet's tragic fate was strengthened by the world view and subject matter of the new poetry: inward turning, morbidly self-involved subject matter that tasted of death and ethical conflict was the norm. This myth has since been criticized as fundamentally misguided, for the poets had sufficient individual causes for their neuroses. The Torch Bearer movement was filled with the fires of life, heralding a new optimism; it is as if Nemesis repaid their optimistic superficiality by enticing these poets into deeper, darker maelstroms of the soul than the generation preceding them. Of the older poets, Vuorela, and of the younger ones, Mustapää, "went along." Hellaakoski, however, is an example of a poet who transcended this poetic turmoil. Each in his own fashion, Kailas and Sarkia led both the flowering and the demise of the old poetic mode: Kailas with his points of view and his classicism, Sarkia with his achievement of so great a degree of rhythmic-melodic virtuosity that the only recourse for the poets who followed was to begin anew. But no matter how greatly Sarkia's highest achievements were admired, from the point of view of literary history his poetry ended in a cul-de-sac. The road forward was paved by other poets: among the oldest were Hellaakoski and Vuorela, and among the youngest, initially Mustapää and then Kajava. The interim generation that, with the return of peace in the 1940s, began to liberate Finnish poetry, would draw on these achievements.

The Torch Bearers introduced new themes into Finnish-language poetry (reverence for life, the brotherhood of mankind) and also a new world of subject matter (the city, technology, distant lands). Their more literary innovations signified an attempt to shed regular meter. Although free verse had already existed in Finnish poetry during the previous century (Eino Leino, 1898), and at the beginning of the twentieth (Huugo Jalkanen, Viljo Kojo, Einari Vuorela), the poetry of this new generation marked the first time an entire movement attempted to liberate itself from meter. The most passionate champion of this reform, as well as its most skilled practitioner, was Katri Vala. Vala was also the only poet of the group to remain true to vers libre throughout her literary career; among the Finnish poets of this period, she is the only one who can be compared with Edith Södergran. The others acquiesced to the classical trends of the 1930s. Most typical of this latter group was Kailas, who adopted the ideal of concise, pure form.

Of the renowned prosaists among the Torch Bearers, a number remained prisoners of the movement; the greatest independent creative growth was in the writing of Mika Waltari. It is the poets, however, who were preeminent in the movement. Among those who made the greatest impact were Uuno Kailas, Katri Vala, P. Mustapää, Yrjö Jylhä, and, somewhat more controversially, Lauri Viljanen and Elina Vaara. The ranking in order of influence assigned to them by Unto Kupiainen in 1948 remains valid today: the four best are Kailas, Vala, Jylhä, and Mustapää, followed by Viljanen, and then the "rear guard," which includes, for example, Vaara, Arvi Kivimaa, Olavi Paavolainen, and Waltari (p. 282). Kailas and Vaara made their literary debuts in 1922, Vala and Viljanen in 1924, Mustapää in 1925, and Jylhä in 1926. The most recent study of this period, Pertti Lassila's, chronicles the intellectual history of Finnish-language poetry, discussing only Kailas and Vala individually. They appear to be the preeminent poets of the 1920s, whereas Jylhä's and Mustapää's strongest period comes later.

Kailas, Vala, Mustapää
In a single decade Uuno Kailas (1901–33) published five volumes of poetry (1922–31), which he honed and adapted for inclusion in *Runoja* (1932; Poems); this became his poetic legacy. Kailas was also a prominent translator of verse into Finnish; his novellas have received less acclaim. Kailas has been interpreted in numerous ways. His artistic style is based on alternating between free and metrical verse toward a fully classical, Parnassian, ideal form. It was Kailas's intention to overcome his human deficiencies through poetry that would outlast himself and preserve the essence of the poet's personality: "The pyramid endures and is seen. / But the Pharoah is forgotten" ("Pyramiidilaulu" [Pyramid song]). Kailas may have derived this idea from a return to Juhani Siljo's teachings "on constructing the self" and also, perhaps, from the work of Horace, who, with his odes, wished to create for himself "a monument outlasting bronze."

Kailas's subject matter and world view are centered on the individual. The dominant tension in his poetry is derived from feelings of guilt and a search for liberation from these feelings. His poems contain images of terror, illness, and madness; their power is unsurpassed in Finnish poetry ("Partaalla" [At the brink]). Misfortunes in adolescence serve as the source of his feelings, but those who find reflections of Finnish society in the 1920s in them are also correct: guilt and a need for reconciliation generated by the Civil War, psychological images of divisions within society, the violent demands placed on the individual by a rising tide of idealistic nationalism. Kailas's intellectual world is complex. It contains expressionism, depth psychology, sensual and ethical tension, darker aspects of the Christian religion, a blending together of ethical-aesthetic individualism, and sensations of illness, madness, and death. Kailas was a caustic and talented satirist who targeted unthinking contemporaries as well as vacuous figureheads in cultural life. He has been characterized as the Finnish author who best depicted the internal truth of the First Republic, and as such, he was an opponent of Koskenniemi, the preeminent representative figure in the literature of the time. The enduring worth of the artistic and philosophical achievement Kailas attained in his poetic struggle is indisputable. Although his poetry tended toward a laconic maturity of form, the fact that it always approximated living speech kept it alive. Kailas's poetry was never subject to affectations. His art provides a caustic documentation of a period during which superficial optimism concealed the repressed truth of both individual and societal pain in Finland. In the poetry of struggle Kailas is the most archetypal of Finnish poets. The universality of his feelings is confirmed by the breadth of the response they evoked: by 1945 thirty thousand copies of *Runoja* had been published.

Like Kailas, Katri Vala (1901–44) succumbed to tuberculosis, although she lived a decade longer than he did. These poets were born the same year, and both published five collections of poetry. Free verse, one of the techniques used by Kailas in his first collections, dominated Vala's poetry throughout her career. Vala apparently adopted this technique independently, without the aid of any models. It simply expressed the pattern structure of her poetic imagination. Initially, her use of free verse was considered stylish, but toward the end of her career quite the opposite was true. Nevertheless, that did not deter her. In addition to her poetic radicalism, Vala became a radical in her social views. This chronicler of life's ecstasy and exoticism gradually began to depict suffering and to reveal its social causes. Her poetic language is eidetic and replete with images. Its powerful empathetic qualities are well suited to Vala's free verse, which is similar to discourse. When the clash of opposing political forces in Finland reached its climax during the 1930s, Vala found her place with the Left. The illness she depicted in her poetry was coupled with her descriptions of the suffering of society's underprivileged.

Vala lived to see the wars break out, making her declare her pacifism. Not even her fate could metamorphose this poet of ecstasy or one who worshiped life into a songstress of death: Vala's ecstasy was refracted through pain and evolved no further. Within the context of literary history the evolution of the ethics of a poet can be judged by the courage with which he or she has realized the impulse to go against the mainstream. This adds stature to a poet such as Vala, whereas it clouds the achievements of poets such as Koskenniemi, who have too great a tendency toward the expedient. History has vindicated the stand taken by Vala. After World War II free verse came to dominate the poetry of at least four decades, and following Viljo Kajava and Arvo Turtiainen, the inclusion of social issues in poetry was no longer considered out of place.

Like Koskenniemi and Hellaakoski, P. Mustapää (1899–1973) was a prominent and complex cultural figure: P. Mustapää is a pseudonym for Martti Haavio, a leading folklorist who rose to become a professor and a member of the Finnish Academy. His poetry emerged gradually over a long period. He wrote a total of seven collections, and twice there was more than a decade of silence between them. In his poetry Haavio's approach to culture and tradition is playful. He had the courage to contrast superficiality with depth, playfulness with gravity, life with death, and love with suffering. Haavio's ear, artistically sensitive to word and verse, made a poet of him. He and Hellaakoski are considered the most important poets of the transitional period between traditional and modern verse in Finnish. In contrast to Hellaakoski, Mustapää had strength and a life long enough even to realize his late colleagues' tenets in his verse.

As a poet, Mustapää is neither confessional nor revealing of himself; rather, he is a more old-fashioned type of lyricist: a troubadour, a forger of song. Because a paradigm of self-revelation reigned in Finnish poetry at the time, Mustapää's poetry was labeled a concealed self-revelation, and it was considered necessary to interpret his charming, comical hero, the tinsmith Lindblad, as a portrait of himself. This interpretation hardly does justice to a poet such as Mustapää. His poetry can be divided into three periods: the Torch Bearer period, his poetry of the 1940s and 1950s, and the poetry of his old age, represented by a single volume. Even in its erudition, his poetry is simple and mellow; perhaps Mustapää was freed from writing ponderous verse because he had no need to use poetry as an enhancement to his career, as it was a supplementary activity for him. Unlike Kailas, he did not feel necessary to erect a refined monument to himself with his poetry. Having begun as a Torch Bearer, Mustapää continued to write poetry until 1969 and, contrary to the trends of the times, maintained a candid style that was both independent and spiritually vigilant, the artistic path of a singer of traditional and cultural knowledge.

Jylhä and Viljanen
Yrjö Jylhä (1903–56) was a Torch Bearer who was not drawn to free verse. In addition to being classical, his concept of poetry included honing verse

to laconic precision. Jylhä remained faithful to these tenets and also practiced them in his outstanding translations, which included such great writings as Milton's *Paradise Lost* and Shakespeare's main works as well as numerous collections and anthologies. The spiritual landscape of Jylhä's early verse is reminiscent of Kailas in its tone of gloom, masochism, and horror: the difference between the two poets lies in Jylhä's stern, aggressive response. The decisive event in his life as a poet became the Winter War, in which he served as a company commander. The experience of the war channeled his emotional life and style of expression into a unique synthesis in his art. The Winter War itself, which was the most morally justified war in Finnish history, played a role in this — the Finns successfully defended themselves against the aggression of the Soviet Union, a great power ruled by a dictator — as well as concepts of will and honor, straightforwardly expressed by Jylhä. *Kiirastuli* (1941; Purgatory) is the finest account of the Winter War, superior to Hellaakoski's *Vartiossa* (1941; On patrol) and Koskenniemi's *Latuja lumessa* (1940; Ski tracks in the snow), and the highest achievement in Finnish war poetry; its humanistic portrayal of the battlefield is largely unsurpassed, even in world poetry. *Kiirastuli* contains neither pacifism nor heroic pathos; rather, it is characterized by acceptance of the tasks inherent in a defensive war, including the losses and sacrifices. The obligations of a soldier in wartime are depicted without any illusions. The poet's voice became so powerfully merged with the message of this collection that, after peace came, Jylhä wrote no more poetry and concentrated instead on translating.

Lauri Viljanen (1900–1984) is typical of the professor-poet often found in Finland: others in this group are Suonio (Julius Krohn), A. Oksanen (August Ahlqvist), V. A. Koskenniemi, Unto Kupiainen, and P. Mustapää (Martti Haavio), with whom the tradition apparently ended. Poetry forms only one aspect of Viljanen's literary career. He was also a leading literary critic of his generation, and this work eventually led to his achievements as a literary scholar. Viljanen published a long series of scholarly works and essay collections, of which *Taisteleva humanismi* (1936; Struggling humanism) had the most impact on the development of Finnish literature. During the polemics of the 1930s this collection advocated vitality and humanism. In his role as a poet Viljanen was a member of the Torch Bearer circle, and as a critic, he was also a leading champion of this movement. His work was deeper than that of Paavolainen, whose contribution was more salient. The sum of Viljanen's life work is exceptional: scholarship, criticism, and poetry would suffice for any literary career. Both as a poet and as a scholar, Viljanen began as a student of Koskenniemi and was to remain more a traditionalist than a revolutionary. Viljanen's poetry is traditional in form, restrained in tone, and grounded in humanistic values.

Viljanen's wife from 1926 to 1930, Elina Vaara (1903–80), can be included among those Torch Bearer poets whose translation work made an outstanding contribution to Finnish literature. For example, Vaara turned Tasso's *Jerusalem Delivered* and Dante's *Divine Comedy* into Finnish. The roots of her own verse are in folksong; her poetry is in part classical and in part romantic. Vaara's poetry is songlike; its subject matter is often drawn from fairy tales and dreams, and her world view bears a similarity to pantheism.

Prose of the New Generation: Waltari, Haanpää, Pekkanen
Of the prose writers whose first works were published during the 1920s, three made significant, lasting contributions: Mika Waltari (1908–79), Pentti Haanpää (1905–55), and Toivo Pekkanen (1902–57). These three authors are strikingly representative of Finnish society itself: Waltari was a member of the educated middle class, Haanpää came from an agricultural family, and Pekkanen was from the working class. Waltari's milieu was Helsinki, Haanpää's the parish of Piippola in northeastern Finland, and Pekkanen's the industrial port city of Kotka. Waltari received a master of philosophy degree; Pekkanen and Haanpää were self-educated. Through the work of these writers each of the three major constituencies in Finland was given a voice in literature, and the healing that had taken place in Finnish society became apparent in the fact that their readership gradually overlapped.

Of the three, only Waltari belonged to the Torch Bearer movement. The way he began his career foretold the immense literary productivity he would achieve. By the age of twenty he had published a collection of poetry and another of fairy tales as well as a book for young adults. In 1928 *Suuri illusioni* (The great illusion) became Waltari's literary breakthrough. A portrayal of the angst of Helsinki youth and of their quest, it struck a responsive chord. Waltari's literary output was so broad and spanned so many genres and subjects that a comprehensive bibliography was compiled only in 1992. Although his primary genres were the novel and the short story, he also wrote plays, fairy tales, poems, detective novels, travel books, and film scripts as well as literary criticism and drama reviews.

Waltari's writing progressed from the romanticism of his own time to mastery of the historical novel. After numerous contemporary novels his use of subject matter based on his own family evolved into a historical Helsinki trilogy (1933–35; collected edition *Isästä poikaan* [From father to son], 1942). Gradually, Waltari's literary ambitions were channeled into the two genres that would become the source of his most enduring literary contribution: the short novel and the historical novel. Waltari's short novels garnered critical acclaim in Finland, while the historical novel gained him popularity with readers both at home and throughout the world. In his short novels, which can be called novellas in the German sense of the term *Novelle,* Waltari analyzes the psychology and moral dilemmas of contemporary life, using a compact, experimental form. A collected volume of thirteen of these shorter works, entitled *Pienoisromaanit* (1966; Miniature novels), subsumed—along with several additions—two earlier collections, *Kuun maisema* (1953; Moonscape) and *Koiranheisipuu ja neljä muuta pienoisromaania* (1961; The tree of dreams and four other miniature novels); it also included works from as early as 1942, the intense psychological-erotic studies *Ei koskaan huomispäivää!* (Eng. tr. *Never a Tomorrow,* 1965) and *Fine van Brooklyn* (Eng. tr. 1965). (Five of Waltari's miniature novels appeared in English as *Moonscape and Other Stories* [1953], five more in *The Tree of Dreams and Other Stories* [1965]; their contents are not altogether identical with those of their Finnish namesakes.) Waltari's short novels did not attract the critical attention accorded his historical novels in the American and British press.

Waltari's series of historical novels began with *Sinuhe, egyptiläinen* (1945; Eng. tr. *Sinuhe the Egyptian,* 1949), which depicts Egyptian history in the fourteenth century B.C. during the reign of Akhenaton (i.e., Ikhnaton, or Amenhotep IV). (It was made into a film by American director Michael Curtiz in 1954.) This major work, compared in its day with Thomas Mann's *Joseph* novels, had been immediately preceded by the historical romances *Kaarina Maununtytär* (1942; Karin Månsdotter), about the low-born mistress and wife (1550–1612), much beloved in Finland, of Sweden's Erik XIV, and *Tanssi yli hautojen* (1944; Dance over graves), a novel from the time of the Diet of Porvoo (1809), as well as the ambitious five-act historical drama *Paracelsus Baselissa* (1945; Paracelsus in Basel). *Sinuhe* was followed by six further historical novels concerned with critical periods of world history in which the liveliness of the descriptions is combined with an excellent knowledge of the historical period itself. The hero in the pair of novels *Mikael Karvajalka* (1948; Eng. tr. *Michael the Finn,* 1950) and *Mikael Hakim* (1949; Eng. tr. *The Sultan's Renegade,* 1951) has adventures during the sixteenth century in both Christian and Islamic lands. *Johannes Angelos* (1952; Eng. tr. *The Dark Angel,* 1953) is a diary kept by the main character of the novel in 1453, the year Constantinople was finally captured by the Turks. *Turms, kuolematon* (1955; lit. Turms the immortal; Eng. tr. *The Etrus-*

can, 1956, 1957) depicts the Etruscans and, through its adventurous main character, other empires in antiquity as well. In his last two historical novels, *Valtakunnan salaisuus* (1959; Eng. tr. *The Secret of the Kingdom*, 1960) and *Ihmiskunnan viholliset* (1–2, 1964; Eng. tr. *The Roman*, 1966), Waltari focused on the beginnings of Christianity; in these novels, however, he no longer achieved his former intensity. Religious issues distinguished the contemporary novel *Feliks onnellinen* (1958; Eng. tr. *The Tongue of Fire*, 1959) from the others; it is, perhaps, the foremost religious novel in Finnish literature. Waltari's historical novels have been interpreted as analogues for his own time and as projections of this on the past; in actuality, however, Waltari's interest in history for its own sake is at least as important.

The action in Waltari's contemporary novels takes place in Helsinki, but Haanpää's writing was more closely related to Piippola and Pekkanen's to Kotka than Waltari's was to the capital. Haanpää and Pekkanen derived a greater part of their subject matter from their own life experiences than did Waltari, who based a great deal of his writing on literary sources. Haanpää and Pekkanen were also erudite authors; they were bound more closely to their social origins, however, and their work naturally yielded a more critical analysis of Finnish society than did Waltari's writing. Although Pekkanen was the oldest of the three, his work was the last to be published, a circumstance that is indicative of his contemplative, thorough, painstaking nature. He did not possess Waltari's and Haanpää's early genius in writing. Nevertheless, history has justified Pekkanen's diligence: in 1955 he became the first writer of working-class origins to be inducted into the Finnish Academy. Waltari was accorded this honor in 1957.

Haanpää has been characterized as ironic and Pekkanen as contemplative (Laitinen, *Suomen kirjallisuuden historia,* 421). In his point of view Haanpää was a social critic of Marxist leanings; added to this, and contrasted to it, was his anarchistic inquiry into the foundations of individual liberty. Without a great deal of oversimplification, Pekkanen can be characterized as a social democrat: he was not a proponent of revolution, and he advocated workers' rights without threatening the principles of bourgeois society. Waltari was at times a liberal and at times a radical bourgeois humanist.

Both Haanpää and Pekkanen made their literary debuts with collections of short stories. It was Haanpää's natural proclivity to continue writing in the short-story form, and this preference also became evident in the structure of his novels. Pekkanen's short stories grew to include seven volumes; they are compiled in the first part of *Teokset* (Works). Pekkanen became a master of the social epic and, as such, was among the most ambitious authors in Finnish literature. Like Väinö Linna after him, Pekkanen also wished to depict the bourgeoisie accurately and without bias by transcending the limitations inherent in describing only his own class; he strove also for spiritual transcendence. Pekkanen wanted to portray the social origins and life experiences of his opponents in their own terms, from a point of view opposite his own circumstances. Both authors succeeded in doing so.

Haanpää's literary stature has risen steadily after the war. This is all the more paradoxical when one considers that, after receiving praise at the time of publication, his writing was banned in the 1930s and became subject to legal action. Haanpää angered the establishment with his caustic critique of the army in a collection of short stories entitled *Kenttä ja kasarmi* (1928; The drillfield and the barracks). Some of the novels he completed at the beginning of the 1930s, such as *Noitaympyrä* (Witch's circle) and *Vääpeli Sadon tapaus* (The case of Sergeant-Major Sato) were only published posthumously. Haanpää waged the most tenacious struggle in Finnish literature for an author's right to freedom of expression. He did not change his views to suit the times but rather waited for the times to become more tolerant. As a result of Haanpää's critical stance, which was Marxist in tone, the Communist wing of the workers came to consider him their author. This characterization was quite as simplistic as the bourgeoisie's appreciation of his skill as a portrayer of the people. Only after Haanpää's time has it become possible to appreciate the complexity of his views, including their irony and relativism, impartially. Although Haanpää sought social justice and opportunity for humanity through socialism, he recognized its tendency to enslave. Freedom was at the heart of his system of values.

In addition to the depth of his thought, Haanpää's prestige and his reputation for literary virtuosity are based on the power of his portrayals: he draws on the richness of the language of the folk, composing sentences that are veritable minefields with their many allusions. Haanpää had a natural talent that continued to develop throughout his life; he persisted as a professional writer despite the lack of understanding he experienced in his rural surroundings. A 1982 study by Aarne Kinnunen revealed the richly complex world of image, motif, and structure in Haanpää's work.

Pekkanen did not achieve Haanpää's level of complexity or his suppleness of language; his style remained rather dry. But this is also his strength: with the intensity inherent in his seriousness of purpose, Pekkanen sought to delineate the fundamental values and truths of Finnish society. His literary breakthrough was *Tehtaan varjossa* (1932; In the shadow of the factory), a novel of inner development that describes the spiritual evolution of a working-class youth. In its use of subject matter from Pekkanen's own childhood the work is reminiscent of *Lapsuuteni* (1953; Eng. tr. *My Child-*

hood, 1966), a masterpiece of Pekkanen's late years which eschews the fictive. Pekkanen's ambition to write social epics initially led him to undertake his pair of novels (1937, 1940), in which class structure, conflicts, and world view are portrayed through characters representative of social types, appeared in a combined edition, *Jumalan myllyt* (1946; God's mills). Even more ambitious was his Kotka series (1948–52), which Pekkanen left as a trilogy when he suffered a stroke. It is indicative of his tenacity that he struggled back to health and also to creative achievement. *Lapsuuteni* is the best evidence of this.

Although Pekkanen used the novel form as the genre for his social epics, he required the short story as a vehicle for his more experimental and symbolic writing. *Musta hurmio* (1939; Black ecstasy), which evolved into a novella, is a skillful, moving depiction of island people who, in the manner of an allegory, symbolize aspects and powers of the human mind. Pekkanen's experimentalism is also apparent in his final collection of short stories, *Mies ja punapartaiset herrat* (1950; A man and the red-bearded gentlemen). The impact of this work is diminished, however, by the influence of Kafka, an influence that is all too apparent.

Poets of the 1930s
The generation of poets younger than the Torch Bearers arose from a double source: the intellectual background of that group and the circle of leftist authors and artists called Kiila. Most prominent among the former are Kaarlo Sarkia and Saima Harmaja; among the latter the greatest impact was made by Viljo Kajava and Arvo Turtiainen, whose literary debuts were in the mid-1930s. Sarkia and Harmaja published four collections each, and both died of tuberculosis, Sarkia in middle age and Harmaja in her youth. From their class origins Kajava and Turtiainen became advocates for broad human rights, Kajava because of sudden crises, Turtiainen as a result of a gradual evolution.

Kaarlo Sarkia (1902–45) is comparable in many respects to Kailas: because of illness, the poetic worlds of both these poets were inward looking; both sought salvation through somewhat divergent kinds of idealism. Sarkia turned toward France, Kailas toward Germany. Sarkia surpassed Kailas as an aesthete and as a servant of beauty. The ethics underscored in Sarkia's final collections of poetry are of a meditative nature and lack the intense striving inherent in Kailas's writing. The music of Sarkia's poetry is unsurpassed in Finnish verse: he is a virtuoso in both melody and rhythm, whereas Kailas delights in laconic plasticity. Sarkia managed to edit his collections into a single volume entitled *Runot* (1944; Poems). Its breadth, nearly seven hundred pages, is indicative of the prolific nature of his writing—at its worst, chatter. Individual examples of poetic virtuosity must be sought out in Sarkia's abundant writings.

The position Sarkia holds in Finnish literature and the critical response to his poetry have remained almost constant since the war: he refined rhymed, metrical verse in Finnish to such a degree that the abundant style of his poetry threatens to make the entire period seem one of lush imagery. Sarkia's stellar achievement in traditional verse can be described as the splendor of this form's "Indian summer," an unawareness that, in this glorious achievement, lay a cul-de-sac that would force Finnish poetry to seek new points of departure. Sarkia's dreamy softness seems feminine. It is telling that Kailas's stern nationalism corresponds to the pacifism of Sarkia's late period. Sarkia's collected poems may not endure as living poetry. Their aestheticism, even their vocabulary, seem too limited for future generations. Sarkia lacked the independence and the power of a Hellaakoski to seek beauty beyond its conventional spheres. It is clear, however, that his best poems will always be remembered for their exceptional musicality.

During her brief life, which was plagued by illness, Saima Harmaja (1913–37) managed to write four collections of poetry. There has never been any doubt about the naturally expressive, lyrical talent evident in these verses. Harmaja did not modernize poetry; she made skillful use of existing poetic techniques. Along with her posthumously published journals, her poetry has always been categorized as confessional and has become the archetype of "girl's poetry." It was Harmaja's custom to date her poems, and this further underscored the poetic-diary aspect of her writing. Free verse held no interest for her or for most of the other Finnish poets of the 1930s, although her metrical phrases occasionally evolved into freely moving rhythm (as in "Öinen vieras" [Night visitor], "On maa" ['Tis a land]), which gives her work a more personal flavor.

The almost apolitical attitudes of the 1920s were followed by a rapidly growing tension between political opposites in the 1930s. The Torch Bearers and their followers were thrust to the right or to the center by the growing leftist movement. In Finland the turn of the 1930s was marked initially by an economic depression and then by extreme rightist movements. In reaction to these developments there evolved a literary group of Marxist persuasion, and in 1935 it was organized into a group called Kiila (Wedge). More than ten events that preceded the group's formation are recounted by Raoul Palmgren (*Kapinalliset kynät,* 2:235–36), a historian who has chronicled the literary history of Finnish workers in great detail. Events noted in the press overshadowed the development of these groups and organizations. In its later period *Tulenkantajat* (1932–39; Torch bearers) was leftist, and *Kirjallisuuslehti* (1932–38; The literary journal) was, in fact, Marxist. From the perspective of literary history the bridge between the poetry of the Torch Bearers and that of Kiila was created by Katri Vala. In looking after proletarian concerns, Kiila proceeded under a Marxist banner; in their poetics its members favored radical free verse; their Finnish model was Vala, and their most significant influences from abroad were the Americans Walt Whitman, Edgar Lee Masters, and Carl Sandburg. From Kiila there emerged two poets whose significance has transcended boundaries of class and epoch: Viljo Kajava and Arvo Turtiainen. Kajava's literary debut was in 1935, Turtiainen's in 1936.

Viljo Kajava (1909–) began his exceptionally long career as a proletarian poet. He has displayed a continuous talent for regeneration. As early as 1938 his third collection of poetry contained perceptive and sensitive portrayals of nature and the countryside, as well as images based on proletarian topics. Kajava is one of the most visual of Finnish poets and, for the benefit of his visual observations, can completely forego the visible subject (imagism). Kajava supported the official, patriotic point of view during the war, including the rejection of class divisions. Although he accepted poetic meter during this time, for the most part his poetry is in free verse, even approaching prose discourse.

Kajava spent the years from 1945 to 1948 in Sweden, where he sought to escape the wartime reality of Finland and the role he had played in it. There, influenced by the Swedish poetry of the forties, he published two Swedish-language collections. In his collections published in 1949 and 1950 Kajava returned to Finnish-language poetry. These works were characterized by a continuous process of refinement, and during the 1950s they defined Kajava as the most vital of the Finnish-language poets from the previous era. The Eino Leino Society, a literary organization founded by the modernists, awarded him its first prize in 1956: this award symbolized a gesture of friendship between the two literary generations.

In both subject matter and themes Kajava is a poet who remains true to himself. His milieu includes the city, particularly its working-class sections, as well as the countryside and the archipelago. These settings are further enriched in his writing by inspiration from his travels abroad. Kajava has not always remained apolitical. From time to time he has taken stands on political and social issues, including international matters (the Africa poems in his 1961 collection) as well as Finnish topics. The collections *Tampereen runot* (1966; Tampere poems) and *Vallilan rapsodia* (1972; The Vallila rhapsody) are a related series of images derived from the same milieu. Childhood memories of the battle of Tampere during the Civil War of 1918 and the fates and views of the people of Vallila (a working-class section of Helsinki) are depicted within the framework of the socially conscious poetry of the 1960s in Kajava's synthesis, which unites the young proletarian poet and the mature, humanistic wisdom he achieved later in life.

Basically, Kajava is an optimistic, positive poet who praises life, daily existence, work, the family, and the common man. His career is the longest and most prolific of any poet in Finnish literature. Kajava's most recent collection, his thirty-fourth, was published in 1989. This poetry, which spans more than half a century, is primarily bound to the landscape and its elements: water, land, and air. Within this context people live, and constant, family relationships exist between them. During the 1950s religious themes enriched Kajava's poetry, as in the collection *Tuliteema* (1957; Fire theme). When the theme of departure and farewell appeared in the collections Kajava wrote during the 1980s, life on earth still had a powerful role in his poetry. As one who praises life, he includes death as a part of it.

The background of Arvo Turtiainen (1904–80) is similar to Kajava's: Kiila, immediate acclaim as a poet genius, and proletarian subject matter. In contrast to the refined Kajava, however, Turtiainen's voice and manner are coarse. In addition to his proletarian sympathies, and distinct from Kajava, Turtiainen characteristically satirized the injustices of capitalism and its proponents, as well as the religious world and its functionaries. Turtiainen translated Elmer Diktonius, Vladimir Mayakovski, Edgar Lee Masters, and Walt Whitman — choices that reflect his own qualities and predilections. In his second collection he used a technique of epitaph similar to that of *Spoon River Anthology* to depict the fates of workers.

The Continuation War subdued Kajava but not Turtiainen. He had fought in the Winter War as an officer but refused, like many radicals on the Left, to participate alongside Nazi Germany in the war against the Soviet Union. As a result, he spent the war years in prison, where he wrote the prison diary *Ihminen n:o 503/42* (1946; Human being no. 503/42). It was natural, therefore, that he turned out to be a leading figure in cultural Marxism during the later 1940s. The manner in which Turtiainen transcended class boundaries differed from that of Kajava. Although he maintained his vernacular coarseness and his critical attitude toward society, developments in society gradually turned in his favor. During the 1960s in Finland there was need of a father figure like Turtiainen: talkative, folksy, a veteran poet critical of society. He portrayed Helsinki, present and past, particularly his own neighborhood, Punavuori, making use of traditional Helsinki slang. During his career as a poet Turtiainen changed less than Kajava; it was not he who changed with time, but rather time that evolved to benefit him. Turtiainen's voice began to contain fewer class distinctions, and proletarian literature became an integral part of Finnish literature.

Novelists of the Senses and Sensibility: Uurto and Hämäläinen

The 1930s did not give rise to Finnish-language prose writers as noteworthy as those of the 1920s. Nevertheless, two names stand out: Iris Uurto (1905–94) and Helvi Hämäläinen (1907–98). Both began writing in 1930, but Hämäläinen continued to work for decades longer than Uurto. Uurto's vision crystallized in her novel *Ruumiin viisaus* (1942; The body's wisdom): by freeing instincts and feelings, Uurto sought a new, total human being who would be liberated from the shackles imposed by intellect and consciousness. Her novels analyze middle-class relationships, marriages, and family dynamics. They examine, in particular, the role of consciousness and of the unconscious in actions and decision making. Uurto has remained an author bound to her own time. The publication of her selected works in 1965–66 did not arouse a great deal of interest. Uurto also wrote many tragic dramas that, from the beginning, had difficulty reaching the stage.

In Helvi Hämäläinen's prose, aesthetics and ethics form a unified whole. Her origins were in the working class, and this world is, in part, reflected in her novels, most effectively in *Katuojan vettä* (1935; Gutter water). Her greatest literary achievement turned out to be *Säädyllinen murhenäytelmä* (1–2, 1941; A proper tragedy), in which Hämäläinen, as the portraitist, succeeded in capturing the milieu of the cultured upper class. She depicted it aesthetically, in a detailed, embellished description of objects and customs, and satirically, as a moral dead end, an evasion of problems, and a paralysis in matters of tact characteristic of people who lived in such circumstances. This work also became famous for reasons other than its literary qualities: it was interpreted as a roman à clef, a satire considered to be a cruel attack on individuals who could be identified. The wartime censor deleted parts of the novel thought to be offensive to Nazi Germany, and an uncensored version was not published until 1981. The tension inherent in family life and marriage among the intelligentsia derives from the narrator's admiration for a cultivated way of life and, simultaneously, her pity or contempt for this life as an overly refined facade that serves as an exaggerated protective mechanism.

If the full range of her achievement is taken into account, Hämäläinen is one of the greatest and most versatile of Finnish authors. In addition to her novels of manners, a genre rare in Finnish literature, she has concentrated primarily on short novels and poetry (including poetic plays). Although her novels contain historical subject matter (ancient Rome and Palestine), for the most part her works depict village society and its reaction to various intimidations and pressures for change. Since 1936 Hämäläinen has published twenty collections of poetry. Its objectives have remained admirably independent of the literary trends of her time: she paints richly colored scenes and spins verbal magic. The critics noted the influence of Marc Chagall on her poetic world. Fairy tale and fantasy reign in her poems; some also have evidence of shamanism and the folk tradition of the woman's lament. Hämäläinen's poetry was in danger of being overshadowed by her prose; only later did it come to be appreciated. In 1987, after twenty years of silence, Hämäläinen unexpectedly published a collection of poetry entitled *Sukupolveni unta* (My generation's dream). In her introductory comments to this collection she condemns "poetic mystification"; matters are spoken of directly and their proper names are used. The frankness of this collection with regard to world affairs is unusual not only in Hämäläinen's work but in Finnish poetry generally. Her topics here range from Finnish wars to the "death" of the Rhine. This wise old woman broke her silence with searing descriptions of poignant sights as well as proclamations against war and destruction of the environment. Through Hämäläinen's voice in this collection the Winter War generation wakes to defend its honor and, loudly, to lament. *Sukupolveni unta* was awarded the Finlandia Literary Prize in 1988, a tribute that created interest in Hämäläinen's earlier work as well.

A Dramatist and Three Journalists: Wuolijoki, Olli, Paavolainen, Kurjensaari
In addition to the main literary forms, poetry and prose, some mention must be made of other forms, particularly the strongest among them. Among the Finnish dramatists of this period, the most successful and enduring has been the Estonian-born Hella Wuolijoki (1886–1954). Hers was an innate dramatic genius transformed by her excellent and very stageable plays into what amounts to a Finnish national mythology. The foremost among the columnists was "Olli" (Väinö Nuorteva) (1889–1967): in the newspaper *Uusi Suomi* (New Finland) and in many essay collections, Olli doubtless published more than ten thousand humorous essays and became a classic Finnish practitioner of this art—in Finland the best of the cultural journalists and critics are considered a part of literature. During the First Republic the leading proponent of this art of the essay was Olavi Paavolainen (1903–64). During the Second Republic Paavolainen's mantle was inherited by Matti Kurjensaari (1907–88), his colleague and biographer.

Hella Wuolijoki first wrote novels and plays in her native Estonian and only during the 1930s began to work in Finnish. Although she continued to compose fiction and memoirs in her adopted tongue, her name is forever linked to Finland's drama, her production consisting of approximately twenty full-length and ten short plays. Her first play written directly in Finnish, *Laki ja järjestys 1918* (1933; Eng. tr. *Law and Order,* 1997), set in Helsinki during the Civil War and ending with the city's liberation from the Reds by German forces on 12 April 1918, was the occasion of a veritable theater war between conservatives, who abhorred its leftist message, and moderates, who believed in freedom of speech. Wuolijoki's collaboration with Bertolt Brecht, who in 1940 was a guest at her estate in Finland, resulted in the twin dramas *Herr Puntila und sein Knecht Matti* (1948; Mr. Puntila and his servant Matti, by Brecht) and *Iso-heikkilän isäntä ja hänen renkinsä Matti* (1946; The master of Iso-Heikkilä and his servant Matti, by Wuolijoki). In addition to her fame as the author of *Juurakon Hulda* (1937; Eng. tr. *Hulda Juurakko,* 1996), which achieved international recognition, becoming the basis of the Hollywood film *The Farmer's Daughter* (1947), for which Loretta Young received an Oscar, Wuolijoki is primarily known in Finland as the creator of the Niskavuori series. The five plays in this cycle came into being between 1933 and 1953. Through depiction of one household's relationships and its extended family, Wuolijoki describes the development of Finnish society from the 1880s to the end of World War II. The Niskavuori plays have been favorites of Finnish theater, and some of the finest Finnish films have also been based on them; in addition, they have been published as books (collected edition *Niskavuoren tarina* [1979; Niskavuori tale]). The main strengths of her dramas are a clear depiction of conflicts of will, portrayal of conflicts between the interests of the household and the interests of individuals (with the interests of the household as victorious), period description, character types with which the audience can identify, and, above all, dialogue born of Wuolijoki's natural flair for the dramtic. It is paradoxical that Wuolijoki, from Estonia, was the author to depict the Finns in the light in which they prefer to see themselves. A striking feature of the relationships in Wuolijoki's plays is the weakness of the men and the power of the women; as a result, these plays have been viewed as portrayals of Finnish matriarchy.

Olli's first work was published in 1921, beginning the career of Finland's most brilliant humorous essayist, whose last original work appeared in 1963. Numerous posthumous collections, the most recent of them published in 1989, have continued to keep Olli in the public eye. His subject matter consists not of mundane, everyday topics but rather of recurring, fundamental situations of existence within the context of family and public life. Olli gently pokes fun at the middle class; he is more a humorist than a satirist. The strongest aspect of his art is his linguistic adaptability: he is able to create and mock many different types of speech — from quasi-cultivated pomposity to bureaucratic hair-splitting. Olli also created his own dialects and languages, modifications of standard Finnish. In his adaptations and distortions of normal expression he was a genius of the first order. He had his own gallery of characters whom he portrayed from one book to the next. The most memorable is the Black-Bearded Man, who threatens bureaucrats by using their own techniques.

Olavi Paavolainen made his literary debut with the publication of his collection of essays *Nykyaikaa etsimässä* (1929; In search of the present). These essays introduced new European trends in the arts and in lifestyle, not deeply perhaps, but with a great deal of spirit. Then in the pamphlet *Suursiivous* (1932; The great housecleaning) Paavolainen berated the young Finnish writers of his day for their lack of culture and style. In *Kolmannen valtakunnan vieraana* (1936; Guest of the Third Reich) he described and analyzed his travel impressions of Nazi Germany; his depiction of Nazism was conflicted, a mixture of enthusiasm and apprehension about the future. Only one other volume, on South America (1937), of Paavolainen's intended travel trilogy was completed; his plans were interrupted by World War II, in which he served as an information officer. The journal Paavolainen kept of this time, entitled *Synkkä yksinpuhelu* (1946; Gloomy soliloquy), marked the climax of his career. It has become the most enduring Finnish nonfiction description of war. At its publication this book caused considerable controversy because of its evaluation of the self-serving nature of wartime politics, including a lack of communication with the outside world, and of the atmosphere that reigned during that time. A myth long endured that it was the reaction to this book which truncated Paavolainen's literary career. Only the most recent scholarship has begun to question this assumption. Although reaction to the book was mixed, it received a great deal of praise. There were, apparently, other reasons why Paavolainen became a bureaucrat and an alcoholic.

Matti Kurjensaari continued Paavolainen's work. He also published three novels that are significant as depictions of the times, but they are of secondary importance in his oeuvre as a whole. Kurjensaari was a chronicler of his time, a travel writer, essayist, and cultural critic, the genres that are the foci of his literary passion. He began as a columnist at the liberal paper *Nykypäivä*. The best of his writing has been compiled as part 1 of his *Valitut teokset* (1–4, 1962–67; Selected works). With the essay collection *Taistelu huomispäivästä* (1948; Battle over tomorrow) Kurjensaari discovered the genre for which he was best suited. This book was widely read in its time and influenced perceptions of the path taken by Finland into the war it lost and, subsequently, into the unknown future. It is this same book that produced the labels the "First Republic" and the "Second Republic" (the periods of independence before and after World War II); although there was no factual basis for these terms, they had a psychological impact.

The basic dichotomy portrayed in Kurjensaari's work is nation versus society. Initially, Kurjensaari combated nationalism for the good of society. Later, however, he came to view "the history of Finnish feeling" as his primary subject matter. His literary output includes travel books about Paris, China, and the Silk Road; journals in which contemporary times are examined in great detail for public reckoning; and collections of humorous essays and aphorisms. During the years 1966–71 Kurjensaari published three collections of character portraits that are considered among the best of that genre in Finnish literature. In these collections he maintains an excellent balance between the general and the particular with characterizations of Gallic precision and economy. The subtitle for them as a whole is "portraits from memory," borrowed from Bertrand Russell. This subtitle is better suited to portraits of friendships from Kurjensaari's youth than to his depictions of celebrities of his own time, which are, at times, not critical enough. In Kurjensaari's final work, the biography *Loistava Olavi Paavolainen* (1975; Magnificent Olavi Paavolainen), which honored his spiritual father, and the last two volumes of his journals (1973, 1978), he grew more private in his concerns.

Coda: A Problematic Figure

T(atu) Vaaskivi (1912–42) was, like Paavolainen, a figure of great complexity, not least in his political attitudes; the sudden cutting off of his career may have meant a considerable loss for Finland's literature. Beginning as an interpreter of Frans Eemil Sillanpää (1937), he attracted attention by his pioneering introduction — quite unusual in Finnish Finland at the time — of psychological knowledge and method into literary analysis. Then he abruptly changed course with his historical novel *Loistava Armfelt* (1938; Magnificent Armfelt), on the remarkable Gustaf Mauritz Armfelt (1757–1814), the favorite of Gustav III who eventually played a major if ambiguous role during the early years of Russian rule in Finland after the war of 1808–9. After a trip to fascist Italy in 1939, on the very eve of World War II, Vaaskivi wrote his masterly novel about the Emperor Tiberius, *Yksinvaltias* (1941–42; The absolute ruler), in which a commentary — likewise ambiguous—on the several dictatorships then flourishing in Europe may be sensed. A still more ambitious venture, a novel on the life of Christ, *Pyhä kevät* (1943; Holy springtime), remained a fragment, published by his widow, the poet and translator Elina Vaara, discussed earlier.

Years of War and Peace

Although poetry was more quick to react to the war than prose, Jylhä's *Kiirastuli* (Purgatory) remained the only collection to achieve a level comparable to Runeberg's *Fänrik Ståls sägner* (1848, 1860; Eng. tr. *The Tales of Ensign Stål*), and it became the standard against which the success of other poets was measured. Hellaakoski's achievement remained a bit below this mark, and Koskenniemi's by a considerable amount.

The nature of the Winter War differed from that of the Continuation War, and the two can, in fact, be viewed as opposites: whereas the Winter War was brief, full of idealistic pathos, and nationalistically unifying, a spiritually pure, defensive struggle, the Continuation War divided the nation once again. Finland's allies in the Continuation War caused moral conflict in the nation, and the length of the war was demoralizing. This may be one reason why no great work of prose emerged in Finnish literature from the Winter War and why no great work of poetry emerged from the Continuation War. The disparate nature of these conflicts is reflected, for example, in Haanpää's works *Korpisota* (1940; Wilderness war) and *Yhdeksän miehen saappaat* (1945; Nine men's boots). The former describes the Winter War, and within this context an anarchist's revolt is slight or directed against the aggressive great power. In the latter work Haanpää's caustic irony blooms anew with its former force.

The novels that best describe the wars were published about ten years after peace was declared. By any measure the best depiction of the Continuation War is Väinö Linna's *Tuntematon sotilas* (1954; Eng. tr. *The Unknown Soldier*, 1957). This novel overshadowed Jussi Talvi's *Ystäviä ja vihollisia* (1954; Eng. tr. *Friends and Enemies*, 1957) and Unto Seppänen's *Evakko* (1954; The evacuee); notably, all three were published in the same year. The first of them became the opus magnum of the Continuation War, as did *Kiirastuli* for the Winter War. In this case, the judgment of history is logical, for the Winter War was "lyrical" and the Continuation War was "prosaic." The two other novels further complemented Linna's point of view. Above all, Talvi depicted the twists and turns of the relationship between the Finns and the Germans; Seppänen described the fate of people in the areas of Finland that were ceded after the war.

Speculations about how the childhood and youth of various literary generations was influenced before, during, and after the war are problematical, and in this case, individual exceptions have more weight than generalizations. It can be stated, however, that it was more difficult for the authors who began writing during wartime to find their orientation. This was true not only in poetry but also in prose. The end of the 1940s and the beginning of the 1950s entailed so great a turning point for both genres that it became necessary for writers either to join in or to experience themselves as outsiders. For example, the career of Olavi Siippainen (1915–63) was interrupted by illness, which may be seen as a metaphor for an artistic blind alley. Siippainen began writing in 1940 and, in 1959, finished an autobiographical novel of inner development, an *Entwicklungsroman*, entitled *Nuoruuden trilogia* (A trilogy of youth); its first two parts had appeared long before, *Suuntana läntinen* (1943; Course westward) and *Maata näkyvissä* (1946; Land in sight). This novel is reminiscent of the works of such Swedish proletarian authors as Jan Fridegård. Siipainen also published short stories, whose success varied between average and brilliant, but the rest of his novels had no solid foundation or program.

Hellaakoski, Mustapää, and Kajava are fine examples of regeneration among the older Finnish-language poets, as are Pekkanen, Haanpää, and Waltari in prose. Of those who began writing during the war, some remained traditional while others were more bold in their literary innovations. Typical of the more traditional poets are Aale Tynni and the prosaist Eila Pennanen. Lauri Viita, Jorma Korpela, and Juha Mannerkorpi can be included among the "extremely individualistic" writers, as Laitinen classifies them (*Suomen kirjallisuuden historia*, 473). Among the prosaists, the work of Oiva Paloheimo, Jussi Talvi, and Matti Hälli did not transcend their own period, although they were important writers in their time.

The Finnish-language literature that followed the wars was dominated by two conflicting trends: leftist workers' literature, which gained momentum in consequence of the war, and modernism (the modernism of the fifties, modernism in poetry), which realized aesthetic, apolitical reforms, including language purification as well as an increased emphasis on perception. The modernist movement was more enduring than that of the leftist workers, which subsided in the 1950s. Modernism may be viewed as the most recent great directional change in Finnish literature; most of its principles have enjoyed broad acceptance throughout the decades following World War II. The influence of the authors of the 1950s was apparent in numerous ways: they dominated both the leading literary journal, *Parnasso*, which had been founded in 1951 by uniting two older journals, and the Eino Leino Society, founded in 1947. As a result of its annual literary award (initiated in 1956), the society came to be highly esteemed and was regarded as innovative. It also initiated the Lahti International Writers Conference, established in 1963.

Finnish literature revived and became unified in three important spheres: first, progress was made in bridging the chasm between Swedish- and Finnish-language literatures, and linguistic competitiveness between the two groups lost much of its former tension. Second, leftist and workers' literature grew more lively and gradually became integrated into Finnish mainstream literature. Third, translation activity increased and there was a shift to modern classics. During the 1950s the primary texts of most of these works became available in Finnish.

Whereas radical authors and others critical of society during the 1930s were sued for libel, the hallmarks of the period following the wars were the so-called book wars, extensive public polemics precipitated by specific literary works. During the 1940s one such controversy was prompted by Paavolainen's *Synkkä yksinpuhelu;* during the 1950s even greater controversy surrounded Linna's *Tuntematon sotilas* and, during the 1960s, Salama's *Juhannustanssit* (1964; Midsummer dance). In addition to public controversy, publication of the latter novel led to a trial in which Salama and his publisher were sentenced. This was the last instance in which legal proceedings were initiated against a literary work because of its content. As a result of these struggles, literature in Finland achieved freedom of expression, and with the exception of some translations having to do with relations with the Soviet Union (Solzhenitsyn), this freedom of expression endured.

Postwar proletarian literature included several ideological directions. The Marxism of Kiila was represented by Elvi Sinervo, who had already begun writing before the war, although her most outstanding work, *Viljami Vaihdokas* (Viljami the changeling), was published in 1946. This novel combined fairy tales, fantasy, and social realism. But the most enduring literary achievements were made by writers who were not part of Kiila, among them Väinö Linna and Lauri Viita from Tampere, who were first published in 1947. Linna was a prosaist and the author of epic novels, an extremely ambitious student of the historical structures of truth. Through his literary works he was able to break down established concepts in historical writing. Viita was by nature a poet, although he also published a well-crafted novel entitled *Moreeni* (see below).

Literary reform started with poetry. In metrics the poetry of the 1940s began to shift from regular to free verse. It has been stated that the ten-year period between 1943 and 1952 was "the last great flowering of traditional poetry" (Polkunen, in Kivikkaho, *Kootut runot,* 387) in Finland, but this evolution can also be viewed differently. It is true that Hellaakoski and Mustapää made impressive literary comebacks and that the verse of even the most visible of the new poets, Aila Meriluoto, was founded on tradition, but there were also many indications of the change to come. The struggle over which direction poetry was to take was kept alive because both the traditional and the new poetry had powerful writers as proponents. Helvi Hämäläinen continued to write brilliant and original poetry that evolved into modernism. Anja Vammelvuo's free verse developed from the Kiila tradition, particularly the influence of Katri Vala. The work of such laconic, polished practitioners as Eila Kivikkaho and Helvi Juvonen indicated that reform could also be based on the tenets of Manninen and Kailas. Juha Mannerkorpi and Lauri Viita were other literary reformers who worked within the framework of tradition; Viita's was a natural and virtuoso expertise in poetry.

Another indication of the new direction in poetry was the fact that, in their third collections, several women poets shifted toward modernism: Sirkka Selja in *Taman lauluja* (1945; Tama's songs), Eila Kivikkaho in *Niityltä pois* (1951; Out of the meadow), and Eeva-Liisa Manner, who, with *Tämä matka* (1956; This journey), produced one of the most powerful modernist collections. It was not until 1958, with the publication of *Pahat unet* (Bad dreams), that Meriluoto began to liberate her poetic style. Because it was characteristic of the new spirit in the Finnish lyric, the sole poetry volume by Impi Kauppila (1909–95), *Paratiisin valloitus* (1947; Conquest of paradise), is also worth mentioning, an inherently modernist collection in the spirit of Södergran. Influenced by the Swedish poets of the 1940s from the beginning, Lasse Heikkilä was a modernist (his first collection was published in 1949). This was true, too, of the French-oriented Pentti Holappa, whose first collection was published in 1950. But there were also powerful proponents of the new movement who began their poetic reform primarily from within the tradition rather than from outside it: they included Juha Mannerkorpi and Lauri Viita.

The decades of the 1930s and 1940s saw the last stand of regular metrical patterns, actually a final attempt to remain insulated from literary developments in Continental Europe. Although there had been many previous tries at vers libre, only in the decade of the 1950s did it achieve a conclusive victory. At the forefront of this struggle to achieve new poetic form in Finnish-language literature during the 1950s were Paavo Haavikko, Tuomas Anhava, and Eeva-Liisa Manner. Haavikko became the leading Finnish writer of the postwar period. Tuomas Anhava wrote no more poetry after 1966, but his work came to be considered classic all the more quickly on this account. Of the three, Manner has remained truest to poetry. In her infrequently published collections she has sustained a masterful level of achievement. Other notable poets who joined with the modernists immediately or within a short time include Mirkka Rekola, a very individualistic poet known for her "difficulty"; Lassi Nummi, who wrote rhetorical poetry; and Pertti Nieminen, better known for his Finnish translations of ancient Chinese poetry. Although he is generally considered a poet of the 1960s, the most gifted and outstanding of the poets who began writing at the end of this decade was Pentti Saarikoski.

Poets of the 1940s
Of the Finnish-language poets who began writing in the 1940s, the most noteworthy are Eila Kivikkaho, Aila Meriluoto, Lauri Viita, and Helvi Juvonen. Aale Tynni, who had begun writing in the 1930s, can also be included in this group. Lassi Nummi made his literary debut in 1949, the same year as Juvonen, but it is more natural to include him in the modernism of the 1950s.

Aale Tynni (1913–97) ended her essay in *Miten kirjani ovat syntyneet* (How my books were born) with the statement, "My primary aim in poetry — has not been to tell of myself, nor to confess or promulgate," but "simply to create poetry" (Ritva Rainio, 32). This is the most salient characteristic of Tynni's poems, which use traditional forms and cultural subject matter. Koskenniemi, Kailas, Manninen, Sarkia, and Siljo are usually mentioned in conjunction with Tynni. Initially, Tynni's themes centered on nature and woman's life. Gradually, however, the role of poetry concerned with culture grew more powerful and became central to her image as a poet. In lieu of confession and proclamation, Tynni focuses on history, mythology, and ancient strata of literature. She also favors dramatic monologue. Because of the prevailing opinion of poetry as self-expression, it has been thought that she assumed a confessional role in her poems (a similar assumption has been made regarding P. Mustapää). This is not necessarily true, however, and in both cases the poet's own testimony contradicts this assumption. In the poetry collections Tynni wrote during the 1940s, a polarity is set up between the destruction wrought by war and the cumulative life force embodied in motherhood. During the 1950s her use of historical and fairy-tale material became dominant. Tynni's poetic objectives are embodied in the titles of many of her collections: *Maailmanteatteri* (1961; Theater of the world), *Balladeja ja romansseja* (1967; Ballads and romances), and *Tarinain lähde* (1974; The source of tales).

It is not a great transition from Tynni's objective of "creating a poem" to creating Finnish poems out of foreign ones: Tynni has made an important contribution to Finnish literature with her translations of world poetry. She has edited and translated into Finnish a comprehensive anthology of European poetry ranging from the Middle Ages to the present day entitled *Tuhat laulujen vuotta* (1957; 2d ed. 1974; A thousand years of song). She has also translated French modernists (1962), a collection of Yeats (1966), and, in an anthology (1976), twenty-one lyricist winners of the Nobel Prize (1976), and she has completed the translation of Shakespeare's sonnets begun by Paavo Cajander (1965).

The primary influence on the style of Eila Kivikkaho (1921–) as well as her point of view is indisputably Otto Manninen. Kivikkaho's poetry focuses on the fate of Karelian evacuees, homesickness for Karelia, and an acceptance of the inevitable: a Finland reduced in size. Her two first collections (1942, 1945) revealed a talented versifier, an expert in constructing lyrical, metrical poetry. As with Manninen, Kivikkaho's style is concentrated, but her poetry draws closer to natural, standard language. In *Niityltä pois* (1951) Kivikkaho adopted free verse and a style similar to spoken language. Critics have characterized her as alternating between two modes of expression: song and speech — which can be seen as her way of interpreting the difference between traditional and modern poetry. Kivikkaho's concept of modernism is not centered on the independent poetic image; rather, hers is an original way of uniting image and concept. In this sense Kivikkaho has been compared with Lasse Heikkilä, for both wished to take a stand and to delve into public matters. Mirjam Polkunen has called Kivikkaho "a lyric rationalist" (p. 391). Although she does not make direct use of political language, she employs techniques of veiled political statement, concerning herself, in broader terms, with the experience of her generation, including that of the Karelian immigrants: sorrow at this loss never leaves her bitter. Even within the narrow focus of these poems Kivikkaho's spiritual outlook and opinions remain open, realistic, and without illusion.

Although Kivikkaho's collections also include poems that are intellectually and technically demanding, the most popular of her poems are heavily represented in Finnish anthologies. Another memorable aspect of her verse is the fact that she mastered the Japanese tanka and haiku forms. The tanka, in particular, is suited to her poetry, with its epigrammatical, biting subject matter, motivated at least as much by the intellect as by the emotions. In her mysteriousness and her concealed themes, as well as the long pauses between her collections, Kivikkaho is again reminiscent of Manninen. Five collections of her poetry have been published, together with *Kootut runot* (1975; Collected poems). The main body of her work was written during that uncertain artistic period when two differing poetic paradigms were competing in Finnish literature.

The debut of Aila Meriluoto (1924–) has become part of Finnish literary legend. At its publication in 1946 twenty-five thousand copies of *Lasimaalaus* (Stained glass), her first collection, were printed. Although she used traditional poetic techniques in this book, albeit loosely and freely, it served to express the voice and sensibility of postwar Finnish youth and was received enthusiastically. In these poems Meriluoto sought an escape from an epoch and culture marked by war. The style of her poetry bears an affinity to that of Saima Harmaja, although the influence on her work of Rilke, whose *Duineser Elegien* (1923; *Duino Elegies*) Meriluoto translated into Finnish in 1974, was more significant and long lasting. Meriluoto's first collections were dominated by a romantic individualism, channeled by the model roles of woman and artist. Only in her third collection, *Pahat unet* (1958; Bad dreams), did her poetry become liberated from the strictures of traditional verse. In the collections she wrote during the 1960s Meriluoto strove "to objectify her feelings with the help of cosmic, physiological, or biological images" (Tarkka, *Suomalaisia nykykirjailijoita,* 1989, 114); in her collections of the 1970s Meriluoto's style became diffuse and even mundane. In addition to her poetry, Meriluoto is remembered for her children's books and young adult novels. She is particularly notable for those of her works similar to memoirs—her depiction of her husband and her marriage, *Lauri Viita* (1974), and her diary, *Lasimaalauksen läpi* (1986; Through stained glass), written in the 1940s, which sheds light on the genesis of her first collection.

In her use of cultural history as subject matter Meriluoto resembles Aale Tynni, just as she is like Lauri Viita (1916–65) in that her poetic genius sought independent expression within the framework of traditional poetry. Viita's first collection, *Betonimyllāri* (1947; Cement mixer), was a literary event in Finland: this proletarian writer immediately proved himself a master of rhymed verse, yet his voice and perspective were fresh. Viita had a first-class talent for language; he was a creative spirit who was eventually institutionalized in a mental hospital. His subject matter, which is bound to everyday reality, hints at his proletarian origins, yet he is also a forceful spokesman for the aristocratic creative spirit. Viita's perspective is a mixture of satire and idealism. His poetic work was limited to four collections (a selection appeared in BFF [1988], 212–18, translated by Herbert Lomas). Of these, the second, *Kukunor* (1949), is a poetic fairy tale; it was followed by *Käppyräinen* (1955; Withered) and *Suutarikin suuri viisas* (1961; The cobbler is a great wise man indeed). The stature of Viita's poetic oeuvre has consistently remained high, and the reasons are obvious: he was able, with his poetic genius, to unite a biting intellectuality, the creative aspect of speech, and the power of feeling. Viita believes in the power of the creative spirit, and this idealism is not estranged from reality but rather pierces it.

Viita's talent and versatility are further confirmed by his masterful novel about his environs and experiences, *Moreeni* (1950; Moraine). This novel gives voice and image to the country people, who were attracted to the growing city of Tampere and built new lives there. Pispala, a working-class section of Tampere built on a ridge, becomes the symbol for these hardy, tenacious folk. Erkki, the main character, is a self-portrait of Viita and also his vehicle for studying the nature of a creative person. Although Viita died prematurely in an automobile accident, his last work, the novel *Entäs sitten, Leevi* (1965; And then, Leevi), demonstrates that his creative powers were waning. The series of poems *Onni* (1965; Joy), in which themes of praising life and relinquishing it are prophetically united, became his last will and testament. The final lines of this cycle, "When I have died, when I have died. / Summer will continue. Summer," have become a well-known saying in Finnish.

The themes of the poetry of Helvi Juvonen (1919–59) are illness and suffering, struggle and faith. Between 1949 and 1959 Juvonen was able to complete six collections of poetry. Along with Kivikkaho's collections, they represent a skillful search for a style of expression both traditional and new. Manninen and Kailas, a lapidary poet and a laconic one, are considered Juvonen's spiritual fathers. Her poetry is also related to that of Kailas on a thematic level—illness, struggle, and a Christian intellectual world, adhering, however, to no single confession. Emily Dickinson, whom Juvonen translated, was a primary influence from abroad. The conflict between the two poetic schools in Finland simultaneously stimulated Juvonen in her artistic expression and provided tension in her perspective. She was bound to the past by feelings of isolation, loneliness, and deformity of the self. But the experience of joy and love, as well as a pantheistic feeling for the unity of all things, was also part of her world view and finds natural expression in poems constructed on a single image in nature. The most famous of these is "Pikarijäkälä" (Cup lichen), in which a tiny object with discernible parameters, a droplet on a lichen, initially becomes an image of heaven and then a paradoxical symbol of the richness of human life. In Juvonen's poetry imagism is tinged with mysticism. Her standpoint is unconventionally Christian, transcending boundaries, seeking various types of spirituality and love. Although her poetry became freer in form from one collection to the next, it is suffused throughout by a uniform point of view: the search for a lasting ethos in the midst of anguish. *Kootut runot* (1960; Collected poems) also includes the poet's translations.

The Breakthrough of Modern Poetry

During the 1950s the modernist school replaced the traditional poetry. Initially, the leading names of this school were Paavo Haavikko and Tuomas Anhava. Toward the end of the decade they were joined by Eeva-Liisa Manner and Mirkka Rekola. Lassi Nummi, who had begun writing poetry during the 1940s, belonged to the modernist school from its inception, although he was not one of its leaders. Anhava and Rekola continued to write poetry exclusively, while Haavikko and Manner broadened their repertoires to include other genres as well. It is also important to remember two poet-novelists who were on the periphery of this movement, Juha Mannerkorpi and Pentti Holappa.

Lassi Nummi (1928–) was involved with modernism from the beginning and proved to be one of the most vital poets of his generation. He began in 1949 with two collections that hinted at the prolific nature of his writing to come. Nummi is an aesthetician: for him, the closest points of comparison to poetry are found in other art forms, music and the visual arts. From the very start Chinese landscape painting has had a place in his poetry. A sensitive individual of ageless youth, Nummi deals mainly with love; initially romantic love, it gradually became more ironic, at his own expense, and more oriented toward the family.

Nummi is not given to conciseness, and imagism elicited no response from him. The basic model for his poetry is speech; his rhetorical concept of poetry favors repetition, development, conversation. There is a danger of sentimental ornamentation in his poetry at times, but it is indicative of his skill as a poet that, for the most part, he manages to avoid this pitfall. On one hand, his poetry plumbs the depths, asks questions, and is a metaphysical quest in the religious sphere; on the other hand, it is a celebration rooted in the mundane, an appreciation of art, and a depiction of the joys of family life. The poems include a sympathetic acknowledgment of his own limitations, the ability to see himself and those like him from within and without, which generates both humor and self-irony.

Nummi's actual or apparent ease in writing has led him to put together collections dealing with specific subject matter. The first of them was *Keskipäivä, delta* (1967; Midday, delta), a depiction of a family vacation. Happiness and loss, joy and pain are balanced, although the poems turn toward the light more often than not. Within the context of schools of Finnish poetry Nummi can be included among those with the most positive outlook, such as Viljo Kajava. During the 1980s Nummi's collections expanded to nearly two hundred pages. The theme of *Kaksoiskuva* (1982; Double image) is division: various experiences are unified by a dual form that can be interpreted as a return to the dualities inherent in romanticism. Although Nummi draws on the mundane, for him it is filled with cultural history. *Matkalla niityn yli* (1986; On a journey across a meadow) takes place in several stages (China, Greece, Italy); *Karu laidunrinne* (1989; Barren pasture slope) is the fruit of Nummi's experiences as a member of the Bible Translation Committee.

Haavikko

Paavo Haavikko (1931–) spent the decade of the fifties pioneering the new poetry. In the decades that followed, he went on to have a profound influence on many other genres as well. His literary achievement is particularly rich and varied, and as a result, Haavikko has become the leading writer of his generation and of the entire postwar period in Finland. During the 1950s he was both the most lauded and the most controversial figure in the new poetry movement, the literary personification of modernism in Finnish poetry. His collections (1951, 1953, 1955, 1958, 1959) contained extremely innovative verse, and yet these collections differed greatly from one another. His first, which dealt with historical topics, was followed by one of brief, romantic poems. This phase of his writing culminated in 1959 with the publication of *Talvipalatsi* (The winter palace), in which the new poetry discusses itself, takes this technique to its zenith, and celebrates its own dense ambiguity and rhetorical boldness. Haavikko's only collection of poetry during the 1960s was *Puut, kaikki heidän vihreytensä* (1966; The trees, in all their verdancy). This collection added a new dimension to Haavikko's poetry: a sarcastic refutation of interpretations of Finland's recent history. English-language selections from his poetry, done by the gifted Anselm Hollo, have appeared in 1968, 1974 (in a Penguin volume shared with the major Swedish poet Tomas Tranströmer), and 1991, the last including the whole range of his lyric production from 1949 to 1988.

At the beginning of the 1960s Haavikko published three novels and a collection of short stories. His drive to innovate had shifted from poetry to prose. Among the trio of novels *Yksityisiä asioita* (1960; Private matters), *Toinen taivas ja maa* (1961; Another heaven and earth), and *Vuodet* (1962; Years), the first was judged to be the best. It took some time before this seemingly dry narrative about commercial activities in Helsinki in 1918 came to be read correctly—as reproducing the point of view of an archetypical businessman with no interest in ideas. Of his short stories, "Lumeton aika" (Snowless time), in the collection *Lasi Claudius Civiliksen salaliittolaisten pöydällä* (1964; A glass on the table of Claudius Civilis's secret allies), became the most famous. Here Finland is imagined as a people's republic within the sphere of Soviet influence.

Haavikko's verbal art was born of an abrupt rupture with Finnish literary tradition. Its power is derived from a first-class creative mind that produces images and scenes at its own volition. Haavikko's tie to the past is based on forceful topics, for history is a constant source of material in his writing. Initially considered strange, his poetry came to be accepted and is now included among the most enduring classics of Finnish modernism. It has also become obvious that Haavikko is not merely sketching in a new manner; as an important writer in the traditional sense, he is building on a solid vision and has his own philosophy about the world. Haavikko has been characterized as an extreme skeptic and realist. His vision of the world and of history, which he examines in large units, is pessimistic and without illusion. Beneath its penetrating, captivating, and absurd surface it is also more rational than it appears at first glance. Above this all hovers a chilling sarcasm, black laughter at humanity's madness.

The third genre Haavikko conquered was drama, and here his writing flourished beyond all expectation. The first of his plays to be published were contained in a single volume, *Münchhausen/Nuket* (Münchhausen/The dolls), of 1960; it was followed by more than thirty different dramatic works, including plays, radio plays, film scripts, and opera librettos. The subjects of these dramas are historical, their vision one of gallows humor and without illusion. Haavikko seeks joy in the macabre aspects of the world, and it is not always possible to distinguish joy from despair. Aarne Kinnunen's study of Haavikko's dramas is entitled *Syvä nauru* (1977; Deep laughter).

During the 1980s Haavikko cultivated numerous genres side by side: poetry (*Toukokuu, ikuinen* [1988; May, eternal]), aphorisms (collected as *Näkyväistä maailmaa* [1985; The visible world]), and works that are syntheses of these genres and also shatter the boundaries between them (*Kansalaisvapaudesta* [1989; On civil liberties]); new interpretations of the *Kalevala* (*Rauta-aika* [1982; The iron age], accompanied by *Kullervon tarina*, [1982; Eng. tr. *Kullervo's Story*, 1989]); polemical history that diverges from academic interpretations (*Kansakunnan synty* [1988; The birth of the nation]); and corporation histories, plays, and other works that simply cannot be categorized, such as *Erään opportunistin iltapäivä* (1988; An opportunist's afternoon).

Haavikko's extraordinary position in postwar Finnish literature is apparent in many ways. No matter whom Haavikko is compared with, his productivity, the multiplicity of his genres, his unprecedented originality, and the diversity of his subject matter are remarkable: he is the only Finnish author to have received the Neustadt Award in literature, and he has long been Finland's primary candidate for a Nobel Prize in literature. Haavikko's output, written both under his own name and employing noms de plume, is equivalent to that of several authors. He has had various publishers, has set up his own publishing house, and has written privately circulated works that cannot be cited, commented on, or evaluated.

As a newspaper columnist, Haavikko scrutinizes Finland's leading politicians and civil servants with a harshness that is atypical. And by writing his books and columns while serving as a director of a publishing house, he indirectly ridicules the growing state support of artists' salaries and so-called free-lance writers. Haavikko is a bourgeois dissident and an economic guru who is critical of the burgeoning government bureaucracy. He embodies the paradox of being a leading author without having an actual social role as a writer in any real sense of the word.

Anhava, Rekola, Manner, Nieminen
Tuomas Anhava (1927–), who made his literary debut two years after Haavikko, was initially viewed as a similar literary reformer, although there were differences between the two. Although he was the leading Finnish theoretician of modernism, Anhava was a humanist, knowledgeable about tradition. Initially, his poems were considered sample exercises by a theoretician. Anhava's separate volumes of verse were published between 1953 and 1966; *Runot 1951–1966* (1967; Eng. tr. selection, *In the Dark Move Slowly*, 1969) in his last appearance to date. Anhava wrote his best literary essays during the 1950s. At first he was viewed as a harsh critic; later he became known as a discoverer of new talents and as a creative advisor. Since the publication of *Runot,* Anhava's literary output has been limited to translations, including masterful renditions of some of the most difficult and demanding poetry to be translated into Finnish (Japanese tanka, Ezra Pound, and the Finland-Swedes Gunnar Björling and Bo Carpelan).

Anhava's poetry is melancholy in feeling. Its style is that of scholarly rhetoric, and despite its experimental nature, it is extremely polished. The role of the speaker in these poems is reminiscent of an Asian aristocrat who has withdrawn from the world. The dryness of Anhava's titles for his collections is telling: the 1953 title *Runoja* (Poems) is not very different from that of his final collection, *Kuudes kirja* (1966; The sixth book). The questionability of speech, in comparison to silence, is a theme that steadily grows in Anhava's poetry. His verse seemed to talk itself out and evolve into translation—the final poem in his collected works is a rendering of Petronius. Anhava views the events of his time from a distance and sees them as insignificant. In his poetry the fundamental issues of life are observed within the private, internal context of close relationships, nature, dreams, and the silence of a wise man.

Mirkka Rekola (1931–) began writing traditional verse in 1954. She was skilled at expressing herself concisely, somewhat like Juvonen and Kivikkaho, but soon developed a poetic style unique in Finnish literature. Her original, enigmatic, elliptical, poetic style can be compared only with that of Gunnar Björling. Rekola is reminiscent of Manner in that although they are erudite and anything but pastoral poets, they are both opposed to rationalism. Rekola has always been drawn to Eastern philosophies; she gives expression to actual experiences, mystical unity, the experience of boundlessness. The elliptical nature of her poetry and its openness, complexity of meaning, and configuration have made a "poet's poet" of Rekola and have estranged the larger public from her work, but its difficulty is also what guarantees that it will endure. One does not tire of Rekola's poetry; it reveals itself with time, gradually instructing the reader in its distinctive grammar. Rekola is a poet of the eye and of the landscape. During the course of her development modern poetry evolved from traditional forms and eventually also came to include prose poetry and aphorisms, never making a clear distinction between these genres. Rekola's collected poems were first published in 1979, her aphoristic works in 1987. A poet whose objective is the dissolution of language that depicts reality in unambiguous terms and the mapping and development of a multiplicity of new roles for language, Rekola can be characterized as working toward a monism created by the obliteration of all boundaries and the mysticism of a spirit that pierces the truth. Both these aspects of Rekola's poetry strive for the victory of light over darkness, for many interpretations rather than noninterpretation, and for perception of the whole rather than limitation to logically imposed categories.

Compared with Haavikko and Anhava, Eeva-Liisa Manner (1921–95) has had a less startling literary evolution. Of the three, her poetry collections have appeared with the most regularity. Each has been a literary event. Manner has also cultivated other genres, which are of secondary interest in her oeuvre (a parody of a detective novel in 1963, a radio play in 1970). In addition to her poetry, only the novel *Varokaa, voittajat* (1972; Victors, beware), a political analysis of conflicts within Spanish society, and three plays, whose main themes focus on the self-delusions of the intelligentsia, belong to Manner's highest achievement.

Although Manner began writing poetry in 1944, her first two collections have remained in the oblivion to which she herself consigned them: her collected poems, *Runoja 1956–1977* (1980; Eng. tr. selection, *Fog Horses*, 1986), does not contain a line from these first two collections. Manner found her true poetic voice with the drastic change of style in her third collection, *Tämä matka* (1956; This journey), which has come to be considered her real beginning as a poet. In this collection she not only governed but also mastered, with sovereign brilliance, the techniques of modern poetry. It is the most celebrated collection of Finnish-language poetry written in the 1950s. In his review, which became one of the poetic manifestos of the time, Tuomas Anhava summarized the significance of this collection, citing the following three factors: the arrangement of rhythm into "free meter," liberation from "the conventional subject matter of poetry," and "the independence of the image."

Manner is not partial to short or laconic poems; instead she prefers long series of poems. There are two excellent examples of this in *Tämä matka*: "Kambri" (Cambrium) lists, in inventory fashion, images of the history of the earth and the evolution of life, as the voice of the speaker melts into these images, and "Lapsuuden hämärästä" (From the dimness of childhood) is a series of remembered objects and a tapestrylike interweaving of childhood memories with no conceptual boundaries. Manner is, paradoxically, a learned, cultured poet who opposes Western rationalism. For her ammunition, she draws on existentialism, psychoanalysis, and mysticism as well as Eastern philosophy and religions. The swiftness of her thought, her unpredictability, cursory logic, sequencing of objects according to their internal value, and her images make her poetry "difficult," or "demanding." For the most part, Manner has published her forceful collections, which are equal in weight, with regularity: 1960, 1963, 1964, 1966, 1968 (the same year, she also published a quickly written volume of political poetry expressing her views on the occupation of Czechoslovakia), 1971, 1977. In addition to *Tämä matka*, the collection *Fahrenheit 121* (1968) and *Kuolleet veilet* (1977, Dead waters) are considered her most important works.

In the year of Manner's breakthrough, 1956, Pertti Nieminen (1929–) issued his first collection, *Kivikausi* (The stone age); a sizable volume containing his poems from 1956 to 1972, *Luen muutosten kirjaa* (I read the *I ching*), was published in 1979. This volume by no means marked the end of

Nieminen's publications, however. From the beginning Nieminen has been better known as a sinologist and translator of Chinese literature than as a poet; his translation of *Tao-te-king,* the basic text of Taoism, was published in the "selection of Chinese wisdom" *Keskitie* (The middle course), the same year as he made his lyric debut, but there is no Chinese allusion in the titles of any of his verse collections, except in that of the collected works themselves. For Nieminen and his generation, modernism was already a natural point of departure and well integrated with their love of traditional literature. The metrical poems in Nieminen's first collection are, in fact, more an indication that the dispute over modernism had been resolved than a stand taken on behalf of traditional poetry.

Nieminen can be characterized as a conservative in his values; in him there coexist an everyday romantic and a devotee of solitude who despises the technical barbarism of his own time. Along with Mirkka Rekola, he is the most important prose poet of the generation that had its debut in the 1950s, for example, in *Rautaportista tulevat etelätuuli ja pohjoistuuli ja vihassa kaikki tuulet* (1968; From the iron gate come the south wind and the north wind and in anger all winds), and then in *Vaikka aamuun on vielä aikaa* (1989; Even if morningtime still lingers). In Nieminen's poetry the comparison between new and the old, like the comparison of Western and Eastern civilizations, is to the benefit of the latter. Nieminen is unpredictable and surprising in his choice of subject matter, critical to the point of sarcasm in his examination of events. He has his own rather startling obsessions, ranging from Vivaldi to cigars, and he does not conceal them in his poetry.

The several translations Nieminen has made of classical Chinese literature have been unanimously praised: he has done this work with care. It is erudite, well edited, and always effective in Finnish. Here his main emphasis has been on poetry. His primary achievement is the series *Kiinan runoutta 1–4* (1987; Poetry of China). Other translations include selections of poetry, folk poetry, short stories, and philosophy. Further, the translator's point of view is shown in his independent, polemical, and erudite essays about classical Chinese literature; a collected volume, entitled *Mandariini kainalossa* (A mandarin under your arm), was published in 1989. Nieminen's renderings of Chinese poetry, together with Anhava's of Japanese tanka, have brought an Asian influence to modernism in Finnish poetry.

Mannerkorpi and Holappa
There were two noteworthy authors in the postwar literary generation who wrote poetry and prose side by side from the beginning: Juha Mannerkorpi

and Pentti Holappa. Both were oriented to French literature, an interest also apparent in their translation activity. Although other prosaists, including Eila Pennanen, Marja-Liisa Vartio, and Veijo Meri, likewise experimented with poetry, this remained a minor aspect of their literary work. Mannerkorpi and Holappa are discussed here, between the sections about poets and prosaists.

Juha Mannerkorpi (1915–80) published his first works, collections of poetry, in 1946 and 1947. These collections dealt with problems of the period preceding the wars. The dominance of traditional poetry is apparent in their poetic technique: Mannerkorpi's main influences at this time appear to have been Sarkia and Hellaakoski. In addition to these works, *Runot 1945–1954* (1962; Poems 1945–1954) contained the collection *Kylväjä lähti kylvämään* (1954; The sower went off to sow), in which psychological analysis and a moral quest are associated with a freer poetics. In the beginning of the 1950s, drama became Mannerkorpi's second genre. "Pirunnyrkki" (The devil's fist) and "Kirje" (Letter) (printed in *Pirunnyrkki*, 1952) were studies of the disintegration of a seemingly stable personality. The monologue *Avain* (1955; The key) is an analysis of the pain inherent in loneliness: the speaker is a translator whom no one has come to greet on his fiftieth birthday. Mannerkorpi continued his work in drama by writing several radio plays.

Mannerkorpi's most ambitious literary undertakings were his novels. His collections of short stories (1950, 1956) were uneven, although, at their best, they were exceptional achievements. They may have served as trial runs for his full-length novels. Having succeeded at the short story, Mannerkorpi abandoned the genre. The theme of his first novel, *Jyrsijät* (1958; The rodents), is self-destruction. In his next novel, *Vene lähdössä* (1961; A boat departing), a minor, external event becomes a basis for mirroring symbols; here Mannerkorpi achieved mastery of the form. Thematic interrelationships form a trilogy of the novels *Jälkikuva* (1965; Afterimage), *Matkalippuja kaikkiin juniin* (1967; Tickets for all the trains), and *Sudenkorento* (1970; Dragonfly). The last-named, which is the climax of the trilogy, parodies such formalistic genres as autobiography and intermingles sequences of essays into the narrative. *Päivänsinet* (1979; Morning glories) depicts the final stages of an ill man's life, uniting anticipation of death, the frenzy of life, and the beauty of nature — the last is symbolized by flowering houseplants. As an author, Mannerkorpi set himself only the most difficult tasks and bore into them mercilessly, joining the commonplace with the symbolism that derives from it.

Pentti Holappa (1927–) lived in Paris during the 1960s and served as a transmitter of new developments in French culture to Finland (in an essay collection *Tuntosarvilla* [1963; With antennae]). The French influence on his work is apparent in numerous ways. In the Finnish context it is most salient in his concept of literature, which does not hark back to Snellman's idea that literature has a role in building national identity. Holappa began with a collection of poetry in 1950, but his second work, presaging what was to come, was prose: a collection of short stories entitled *Peikkokuninkaat* (1952; The troll kings). The first stage of Holappa's poetry ended with his fourth collection, *Katsokaa silmiänne* (1959; Look at your eyes), and is characterized by a concentrated, discourselike style. The poetry questions certainties, points out threats and perils, unites "aspects of tenderness and violence" (Laitinen, *Suomen kirjallisuuden historia,* 558).

Holappa's breakthrough as a prose writer was the collection of short stories *Muodonmuutoksia* (1959; Transformations), in which the author liberates his unique fantasy for the first time. His second novel, *Tinaa* (1962; Tin), begins with the deceptively secure image of a conventional world that is, in fact, very different beneath the surface, where violence and anarchy are revealed but authentic truth is also found. *Perillisen ominaisuudet* (1963; The heir's qualities) brought the style of the *nouveau roman* to the Finnish novel. Its topic, the choosing of a new director for a company, would also have provided politically rewarding subject matter, but Holappa did not incorporate politics into his writing until the novel *Pitkän tien kulkijat* (1976; Travelers on a long road), an attempt to enrich the realism of proletarian literature.

Eventually, Holappa returned to poetry. From 1979 on, he has published several extensive collections—most recently, *Älä pelkää!* (1997; Don't be afraid!)—reminiscent, to some extent, of his first period, although the style of these collections is less polished and more similar to spoken language. In Holappa's mostly long narrative poems the action takes place in many different countries and continents. They are further enriched by free-flowing fantasy and a personal mythology that culminates in Tamao, a youth who is a combination of "animal, human, and deity" (Tarkka, *Suomalaisia nykykirjailijoita,* 1989, 44). The highest of values is love, which Holappa does not hesitate to call a wonder and which is contrasted with a world of violence and destruction. Nevertheless, "flute playing subdues prisons" in this utopia, which does not deny the existence of reality.

Feminine Voices
Sirkka Selja (1920–) captured some attention immediately after the war with *Taman lauluja* (1945; Tama's songs), in which the feminine subject of

the poems went through experiences that had been the province of Edith Södergran almost three decades before; now they were expressed in an apparently rhythmless and rhymeless language still novel in the Finnish lyric sector:

> Tama's soul was in bloom.
> But the Stranger came and awakened it.
> Tama's soul had the aroma of the hyacinth.
> But the Stranger went away.

Selja has never given up her feminine — but not feminist — voice in her fairly sparse production; the collected *Runot* (1970; Poems), edited and provided with an afterword by Lassi Nummi, who admired her luminous identification with a beloved world of nature, offered many more poems with the tone of wistfulness she had found long ago: "Their love is a homeless wanderer" and "What the day took the night brings back, / in its giant bird's long beak." Her skill at discovering the mild but unexpected image for her verse (as in *Pisaroita iholla* [1978; Drops on the skin] — "The late winter's white day / a white cow that flies / in the tempest through the clouds" — has also been a central element in her prose poems, as in *Vierailulla ketun talossa* (1966; Visiting in the fox's house), *Kissansilmät: Unia, ufoja, kissoja* (1971; Cat eyes: Dreams, aromas, cats), and *Talo nimeltä villiruusu* (1975; A house called wild rose); gentle sensations, wisps of memories, and a sense of loss more implied than stated predominate. Quiet as she is, Selja has never received all the attention she deserves; yet the American Anne Fried entertained so high an opinion of Selja's art that she included her as one of five major representatives of women's writing in the anthology *Thank You for the Illusions* (1981), together with Helvi Juvonen, Eila Kivikkaho, Eila Pennanen, and Mirkka Rekola.

The name of Anja Vammelvuo (1921–) is sometimes loosely coupled with Selja's because of chronological propinquity and protomodernist prosody, but Vammelvuo, starting with *Auringontytär* (1943; The daughter of the sun), was far less discreet in her poems of love. Also, in her admiration of Katri Vala, she quickly developed a passion for the political Left, to which she often gave vent, as in the threnody for Alexandra Kollantay (1872–1952), the Soviet envoy to Sweden who helped prepare the armistices of 1940 and 1944: "I tell women: our mother has died." (Kollantay was a worthier object for sadness than Josef Stalin, for whom Vammelvuo's Finland-Swedish opposite number, Eva Wichman, lamented less than a year later.) Straightforwardness was a trait on which Vammelvuo much depended, as in *Kuinka voitte?* (1978; How are you?):

> I am a tradesman's daughter
> I cannot trade,
> not with ideas,
> not with love
> not with poetry.

This quality, together with her political and social biases, allowed her a comeback in the 1960s, when she appeared as an older sister to the radical decade's writers of proclamation poetry. Not by accident, her selected poems were brought out by Otava in 1968, just before the death of her husband, Jarno Pennanen (1906–69), with whom she shared political convictions. Her autobiographical novel, *Viimeinen Kleopatra* (1950; The last Cleopatra), described the path to a meeting of like minds—which eventually allowed her to reside in the Soviet Union from 1957 to 1960 while Pennanen was the Moscow correspondent of the leading Finnish Communist daily, *Kansan Uutiset* (The people's news).

Tyyne Saastamoinen (1924–) underwent a transformation of sorts in mid-career, writing stories in traditional patterns during the 1950s and then changing to a tempered modernist lyric with *Yön sarvet* (1960; The horns of night). Further—as in the case of Ulla Olin, who left Finland for Sweden and underwent the pangs of estrangement—she moved to France, a displacement at which the titles of two of her collections hint: *Olen lähtenyt kauas* (1965; I have gone afar) and *Vieras maa* (1969; Foreign land). Kai Laitinen's remark is accurate: her titles tell a good deal about the nature of her verse: *Perhosen siivissä keltainen tuuli* (1975; Yellow wind in the butterfly's wings) and *Hiljaa, hyvin hiljaa teen päivistäni kirjaa* (1976; Slowly, very slowly I make a book of my days) have the air of delicate journals. Thanks to this atmosphere, she has kept a faithful following of readers, for whom Otava published a selection of her oeuvre in 1975 in its series of modern classics. Like Olin, too, Saastamoinen is perhaps at her most skillful in the prose poem, in which her tangential observations have a suggestive succinctness comparable to that in the prose poems of Selja: "On the table was a hearse, it was like a silvered apple of a bishop's mitre in a foreign land, small and of metal, it could perhaps make off with my son's soldiers. I took the hearse and put it in the clothes' cupboard, at the very top. The cupboard's doors were open and all the clothes dead, they belonged to no one, but the women's clothes—there I could just recognize the colors not the years and not a single dress was black. And as always in a dream I awoke: I didn't have time to shut the cupboard's doors."

Maila Pylkkönen (1931–86) marked herself off from the many new lyricists of her day by employing the monologue poem, a variant of the nineteenth century's dramatic monologue or role poem, in which the poetic voice speaks, at some length, words that characterize its role in life or in some emotional crisis. Her early poems, in *Klassilliset tunteet* (1957; Classical feelings) and *Jeesuksen kylä* (1958; Jesus' village), spoke of what seem to have been, quite literally, the classical sensations of a young and sensitive poet, a sense of outsiderness and abandonment and indecision ("I seek the company of the old, / listen to fates where everything has happened" and "I am unable to show myself, / am afraid to attach myself to anything" and "I am no one, / I can easily be taken by the hand"). But Pylkkönen found her specialty in *Arvo: Vanhaäiti puhuu runonsa* (1959; Worth: Grandmother speaks her poems), *Ilmaa: Kaikuu* (1960; Air: It echoes), which contains a child's monologue in its special speech, and *Valta* (1962; Power), in which the wife of a history teacher, an actress, and a piece of bronze sculpture speak. The same talent for entering a single personality or thing was also evident in the lyrics and prose poems of later collections, such as *Muistista* (1972; From the memory) and *Marjamiesnaisen muistiinpanoja* (1975; Notes of the woman berry picker), but her essential poetry has remained the monologues, published together in *Monologit* (1976).

Masters of the Small: Heikkilä and Schreck
The initial stages of the small production of Lasse Heikkilä (1925–61) proved that he had read Sweden's "difficult poets" of the 1940s (Lindegren, Vennberg, and others); his early poems are harbingers of the belated modernism that would bloom in the Finnish lyric of the 1950s, *Miekkalintu* (1949; Sword bird) and *Paatos ja lyyra* (1950; Pathos and lyre). In the former, Heikkilä bids an oddly dispirited farewell to the angst-ridden decade just past:

> our sail Terror flutters tiredly
> and falls in a meaningless heap
> on the dirty, decaying deck,
> then we perhaps understand
> that being saved is not a new life
> but a new death.

Despite the vaunted obscurity of his models, Heikkilä's own verse was full of cogent formulations, significant for an understanding of his time; the debates on loyalty and faithlessness waged in Sweden during the 1960s by Lars Gyllensten and others may be predicted in his lines from *Unet ja Medeia* (1953; The dreams and Medea):

> like others
> I am given to lying do not love truth . . .
> I betray sea betray land
> and the clouds betray me.

Heikkilä's production is uneven, but his poetic seismograph seems always at work — the remarkable and lengthy elegy (or verse reflection) "Finland," in his last collection, *Terra Mariana* (1959), looks forward with irony to the statements or squabbles about Finland's recent history and role in the world which were shortly to come: "Finlanders are the quickest / to march off to battle as to return from it. / Of a surety they have swift feet in both directions."

The small and precise production of Jyri Schreck (1927–82) consists almost entirely of short descriptive or reflective lyrics, using a language of exemplary clarity: *Lumi* (1959; Snow), *Päiviä, sateita* (1962; Days, rainy), *Leijan ilma vihreää* (1966; The kite's sky is greening), *Mustan perhosen aika* (1970; Time of the black butterfly), *Muuttopäivät* (1973; Moving days), *Kaupunki ja villivaahtera* (1975; City and wild maple), *Että olisit läsnä* (1977; That you might be present). After his death all his poems were put together by Otava, where he had long been employed, as *Myöhäinen kevät, varhainen syksy* (1982; Late spring, early autumn), a telling title. Schreck had waited until rather late for his poetic debut: his first book (1956) had been a history of the Renqvist-Reenpää family, Otava's owners. The small and careful views of the city in which Schreck spent his life have a permanent and somewhat bittersweet appeal, for example, his "pathetic reed-yellow café" on Humallahti Bay, a place that "bears the name Mississippi," a choice understandable when spring comes to its pinched, stony location.

A Double Gift: Kunnas

The oeuvre of Kirsi Kunnas (1924–) falls into two distinct categories, albeit with connections. She began as an exponent of a moderate Finnish-language modernist lyric, and the poetry from *Villiomenapuu* (1947; Crab-apple tree), *Uivat saaret* (1950; Floating islands), *Tuuli nousee* (1953; The wind awakes), and *Vaeltanut* (1956; Wandered), put together in *Valikoima runoja* (1958; Chosen poems), was full of pleasant landscapes and some pastoral humor amid obligatory melancholy. A switch into verse ostensibly for children (although the animals turning up in her modernist poetry had hinted at the change) came as a great sensation (see chapter 11). In *Tiitiäisen satupuu* (1956; Tumpkin's fairy-tale tree) animals and things act and speak in zany parables, rhymed and rhythmed. Some of them have been handsomely translated into English by Herbert Lomas, such as the poem about "Old Mattie, / Water Rattie," who "freezes and wheezes: / A-snee, a-snee, a-sneezzery, / Oh what Misery!" (see BFF [1979], 45–47, and Lomas's *Contemporary Finnish Poetry,* 70–75). Lomas has noted how these innocent verses, widely read, have supplied "wisdom, often erotically nuanced, taking the masks off recognizable neurosis."

Continuing in this vein with other books, *Tiitiäisen tarinoita* (1957; Tumpkin's tales), *Puupuu ja Käpypoika* (1972; Treetree and Coneboy), and *Kani Kaniinin kuperkeikat* (Benjamin Bunny's somersaults), Kunnas also took up other tasks for which she had the right equipment, translations (with Eeva-Liisa Manner; 1972, 1974) of Lewis Carroll (Charles Dodgson, 1832–98), the fables (1974, 1979) of the great Russian fabulist Ivan Krylov (1769–1844), and the nonsense verse (1980) of Edward Lear (1812–88). (She also translated some Tove Jansson—a kindred spirit in Finland-Swedish children's literature—into Finnish.) In 1980 she returned to "adult" lyrics with *Kuun kuva meissä* (1980; The image of the moon in us); now she was much less lighthearted: on a summer day the wind blows and "thus memory calls me by name / a departed being wishes / to remind me to see." This other Kunnas, aware of aging and death, has persisted in *Kaunis hallayö* (1984; Fair frost night) and *Valoa kaikki kätketty* (1986; Everything hidden in light). Lomas sees a "half-ethereal, mystical side" of the once jolly Kunnas, but one may sense some small traces of an older jokiness here as well:

Such insubstantial stuff:
the stars soar through me —
so chiffon-gauzy
I'm gone in myself and from myself.

Postwar Prose

Among the authors who began writing after World War II and whose most important genres have been the novel or the short story, ten merit literary portraits here. In order of the year of their literary debuts, they are Eila Pennanen, Väinö Linna, Jorma Korpela, Veikko Huovinen, Eeva Joenpelto, Marko Tapio, Marja-Liisa Vartio, Paavo Rintala, Veijo Meri, and Antti Hyry.

The Nestor of this group is the late bloomer Korpela, and the youngest of them is Hyry. Although Hyry's primary literary achievement actually took place in the following period, this author, who began writing in 1958 and whose works are among the purest examples of the literary tenets of the

1950s, is more appropriately included here. Three of these ten authors are women, and three began their literary careers in the middle of the 1940s. On the average, the contribution of these prosaists to the structure of the Finnish novel is related to how late they began to write. Among them, Korpela is the author with the fewest works published, although he is not the least influential; those with the greatest number of works published are Pennanen, Joenpelto, and Rintala. The careers of Vartio and Tapio were cut short by premature deaths. Both these authors made their literary debuts in 1952; Vartio died in 1966 and Tapio in 1973. In this group Linna, Korpela, and Joenpelto have published only novels; Huovinen, Tapio, and Hyry have published short stories as well. Pennanen, Vartio, and Meri have written poetry, although it has had little impact on their image as authors. Pennanen, Rintala, and Meri have also worked with drama.

Pennanen

Eila Pennanen (1916–94) began writing during the war. Her first novel, *Ennen sotaa oli nuoruus* (Before the war there was youth), was published in 1942. This title became a symbol for her generation. Pennanen grew to be a multifaceted, productive, and innovative author: in addition to novels, her primary genre, she has written short stories, dramas, criticism, and essays, and she is also a translator. At times the repetitive features in her novels have been irritating, but her work has also included considerable innovation. During the 1950s Pennanen wrote two wide-ranging, expertly crafted historical novels. Both had religious themes: *Pyhä Birgitta* (1954; Saint Birgitta) depicted the medieval Swedish mystic; *Valon lapset* (1958; Children of light), the birth of the Quaker movement. The novels that followed each dealt with some special problem. *Mutta* (1963; But) depicts a woman who is a social misfit, *Tilapää* (1968; Circumstance) focused on life in a commune, *Naisen kunnia* (1975; A woman's honor) satirized literary social life, and *Kapakoiden maa* (1977; Land of taverns) was concerned with the problem of alcoholism. Pennanen's primary achievement is a trilogy, the novels *Himmun rakkaudet* (1971; Himmu's loves), *Koreuden tähden* (1972; For the sake of finery), and *Ruusuköynnös* (1973; Garland of roses). Set in turn-of-the-century Tampere, this trilogy is a splendid depiction of that epoch and includes, among its characters, actual historical figures as well as a number of the author's relatives.

Pennanen has received more praise for the artistic achievement of her short stories than of her novels. In her five expertly written collections (1952–80) she has made literary innovations based on the example of such English-language authors as D. H. Lawrence and Katherine Mansfield.

Although Pennanen's subject matter varies, it primarily deals with difficulties between couples, sometimes described with empathy, at other times with irony or humor. Her extensive translation work as well as her literary essays have also focused on English-language literature. The latter have been collected into three volumes: *Tunnustelua* (1965; Probing), *Kirjailijatar ja hänen miehensä* (1982; The author and her husband), and *Luettua, läheistä* (1990; Read, near). Her essays include E. M. Forster and Virginia Woolf, Finnish classics, and Finnish authors of popular fiction, about whom Pennanen has written the most perceptive analyses in Finland.

Linna

Somewhat like Volter Kilpi, Väinö Linna (1920–92) is an author who has two phases. He began with two novels, *Päämäärä* (1947; The goal) and *Musta rakkaus* (1948; new ed. 1957; Black love). It is indicative that the author did not permit new editions of the former, and of the latter only with revisions. Delving into ethical and religious problems led Linna into a cul-de-sac from which a crisis in his literary perspective freed him: his world view changed from that of Dostoyevsky to that of Tolstoy. He ceased depicting the internal life of the individual and turned instead to the group, examining its members within the context of social and historical determinants. This new approach yielded two works that sufficed, for a long time, to make Linna the most widely read and discussed author in Finland. The first of these novels grew out of his own war experiences: *Tuntematon sotilas* (1954; Eng. tr. *The Unknown Soldier,* 1957); the second, the trilogy *Täällä Pohjantähden alla* (1959–62; Here beneath the North Star), was based on historical research. More than thirty editions (approximately half a million copies) of *Tuntematon sotilas* have been printed. The breadth of this response indicates that Linna's depiction of the war corresponded to the understanding of the generation that had lived through it. The novel depicts the Continuation War through a collective of men whose members are drawn from various parts of Finland. The basic technique used for characterization is conversation in dialect. Aleksis Kivi's *Seitsemän veljestä* is the obvious source of this technique. *Tuntematon sotilas* is the unsurpassed model for the Finnish war novel, and it has gained recognition abroad through numerous translations. Its relationship to the war is not easy to define. Often cited is Linna's statement that he wanted to dispel the concept of a war of honor but to retain honor for the Finnish soldier, who had done his job well. In the novel the soldiers at the front rebel against the purposelessness of the military but are skilled at their task and willing to make sacrifices in battle.

In a manner unique in Finnish literature Linna has managed to unite artistic aspiration and popular appeal in his writing. He is a social realist, an expert in documenting speech, a dramatist, and an author sensitive to conflicts. Even in creating models the reader can identify with or dislike, Linna aimed for fairness or impartiality. The trilogy, whose title is taken from a popular school song by Johan Fredrik Granlund (see chapter 2), depicts the fundamental social groups and forces in Finnish society from the 1880s to the 1950s, focusing on the life of sharecroppers in a rural area. The objective of Linna's novel is to explain the conflicts within Finnish society, above all in 1918. There is a tendency to recall the sense of honor of the Red side and of the disadvantaged in general. Linna's power as an author, coupled with his continuing polemics against professional historians, made a social epic out of the author himself, which has greatly influenced overall perceptions of Finnish history and society. The relatively swift completion of this trilogy, more than fifteen hundred pages long, exhausted Linna's powers. Subsequently, his role became that of national oracle, a wise deliberator. Linna compiled his most important observations in a collection of essays entitled *Oheisia* (1967; Peripherals), and he continued to follow and guide the course of his novels after their publication. They were adapted into film and radio versions and numerous theatrical pieces. The main characters of Linna's novels have become part of a national "mythology" in Finland, their names suitable for use as slogans in public debate. An officer rigidly wedded to rules is called "Lammio," and an insubordinate but brilliant soldier is referred to as "Rokka."

Korpela
Jorma Korpela (1910–64) began writing a year after Linna although he was a decade older. Both analyzed ethical questions and described the war, each in a discrete period of his career. Korpela's first novel, *Martinmaa, mieshenkilö* (1948; Martinmaa, a male being), was exceptionally mature in its analysis of the problems faced in life by an idealist: self-deception and dead ends. His second, *Tohtori Finckelman* (1952; Doctor Finckelman), has maintained its stature as a Finnish classic, an experimental novel that shattered plot and explored inner worlds. At its publication even the critics considered it a difficult work, and a second edition was not published until 1969; the general public never discovered it. In the spirit of Dostoyevsky, using a first-person narrator, the novel describes a doctor who, in his isolation and ambition, is going astray. He metamorphoses into a superhuman predator and later returns to love, compassion, and human unity. Scholars have analyzed and praised this novel, which might have created a funda-

mental literary breakthrough, offering an alternative to realism in the modern Finnish school. There have been conjectures that the public reception of the novel's style prevented Korpela from continuing in this direction; his two later novels are less difficult and by the 1960s were already in their fourth and fifth editions. *Tunnustus* (1960; The confession) is concerned with wartime morality; in its clarity it threatens to become simplistic. The posthumous *Kenttävartio* (1964; Field guard) describes the destruction of a simple, pacifist soldier in the gears of the military machine. The primary influence of Korpela's brief literary output derives from his first two novels. The lack of comprehension met by the earlier works, which were out of the mainstream, is dramatized by the decline in the two latter novels.

Huovinen and Joenpelto

Among the authors of this age group, Veikko Huovinen (1927–) is a humorist and satirist, and Eeva Joenpelto (1921–) is a master of the popular novel. Their first works were published in 1950, and they continue to write. Huovinen is the only author of the postwar generation to persist, innovatively, in the tradition of describing people of the countryside. Warmly portrayed in the light of folk humor, the character Konsta Pylkkänen in Huovinen's novel *Havukka-ahon ajattelija* (1952; The ponderer of Havukka-Aho) has become a national myth. A backwoods philosopher who views the scholarly world from his unschooled point of view, Konsta Pylkkänen also appears in the works Huovinen wrote in 1950 and 1961. Beginning with *Ihmisten puheet* (1955; People's conversations), satire appeared as a parallel to humor in Huovinen's work and then supplanted it. *Rauhanpiippu* (1956; Peace pipe), in which a professional soldier and a philosopher who espouses peace compare their views, was considered pacifist in its viewpoint. Except for his student years, Huovinen has lived at Sotkamo in northeast Finland, and it is from there that his mockery of our media-dominated civilization derives. Huovinen is a satirist of modern life, a conservative in his values, an author who ridicules the shortcomings of civilization. More successful than Huovinen's novels are his six collections of brief sketches, varying among the causerie, the humorous reflection, and the satirical novelette, from *Kuikka* (1963; The grebe) to *Matikanopettaja* (1986; The math teacher). In *Veitikka* (1971; Little rascal) and *Joe-setä* (1988; Uncle Joe), which diverge from the main body of his work, Huovinen attempts to apply his skill as a humorist to the two icons of terror in our century, Hitler and Stalin.

Eeva Joenpelto is a productive novelist of monomaniacal intensity. Her career and stature flourished quickly from the start, and the artistry of her second and third novels (1951, 1952) immediately drew attention. The masterful *Neito kulkee vetten päällä* (1955; Eng. tr. *The Maiden Walks upon the Water,* 1991) analyzes the relationship between a weak man and a powerful woman, a standard constellation of characters subsequently developed by Joenpelto. The same theme reappears in her most important novel of the following decade, *Halusit tai et* (1969; Whether or not you wanted). Her crowning achievement was a tetralogy, the so-called Lohja or Uusimaa series: *Vetää kaikista ovista* (1974; A draft at all the doors), *Kuin kekäle kädessä* (1976; As with a firebrand in hand), *Sataa suolaista vettä* (1978; It is raining salty water), and *Eteisiin ja kynnykselle* (1980; Into the hallways and onto the thresholds). The focus of the action in this series is Lohja, a south Finnish market town, during the period after 1918, and its characters represent its main political and social movements. Joenpelto depicts her people in crises of will; she favors those who are strong and driven to new endeavors by their defeats. The narrative is sequential at times, and it is here that the influence of television series has been noticed. In her depiction of human nature Joenpelto gives equal weight to psychological and sociological determinants. The accessibility of the narrative, characters who can easily be identified with, and the old-fashioned pivotal role of intrigue have kept the public faithful to the tetralogy: Joenpelto is the most widely read of those Finnish epicists who cannot be simply categorized as popular writers. The Lohja series did not sap Joenpelto of her vigor: she has continued to publish a substantial new novel almost every other year: among the most brilliant was *Elämän rouva, rouva Glad* (1982; Eng. tr. *The Bride of Life,* 1995), the story of an extraordinarily successful businesswoman. The artistic level of these novels has not decreased, although a certain repetition in content has been unavoidable.

Tapio and Vartio
Both Marko Tapio and Marja-Liisa Vartio were born in 1924, made their literary debuts in 1952, and died during their most creative periods. Tapio wrote ten novels and one collection of short stories, whereas Vartio wrote five novels, two collections of poetry, and one collection of short stories. Tapio's main influences are Dostoyevsky and Sillanpää, the clash between life in the countryside and modern culture, and the effect of existential dilemmas on a traditional set of values. In his first novel, *Lasinen pyykkilauta* (1952; The glass washboard), the influence of Sillanpää cast a shadow over the obvious talent of his debut. His second novel, *Aapo Heiskasen viikatetanssi* (1956; Aapo Heiskanen's scythe dance), turned out to be one of

Tapio's major works and, together with Korpela's *Tohtori Finckelman,* the best example of the psychologically refined novel in Finnish of the 1950s.

With his scythe dances the protagonist of Tapio's novel gives expression to war traumas, his wounds, his feelings about women and suicide, the doubleness of his being, the world of nature, and the limits inherent in the future. The primary technique used in the narrative is an internal monologue. The search for and experimentation with various types of narrative solutions was also a characteristic of Tapio's later novels. During the 1960s Tapio became interested in the detective novel, a genre to which he added psychological probing in the spirit of Dostoyevsky. The result was another important work, the unfinished *Arktinen hysteria* (1–2, 1967–68; Arctic hysteria). In the ambitious nature of its goals this novel has been interpreted as the antithesis of Linna's *Pohjantähti:* common to them both is an attempt to give a full description of Finnish society in recent history; the difference between them is that Tapio is something of a "psychological historian" for whom sociohistorical factors do not suffice as explanations. He considers the primary impetus of society to be "crime, sorrow, and suffering" (Tarkka, *Suomalaisia nykykirjailijoita,* 1980, 239). The unfinished series also reveals the extent of Tapio's narrative ambition. The first part describes seventy years in an act of awareness lasting twenty minutes. Tapio's description of the war in the second novel of the series does not achieve the depth of the first, but the author may have designated a role for this novel in his overall plan, which must remain unknown. Given the relative frequency of suicide among Finland's authors, it may be best not to include such details in descriptions of literary production, but perhaps Tapio's case presents an exception. Tapio's Aapo Heiskanen escaped suicide after a severe struggle, but his creator was able to delay his own voluntary death only until 1973.

Whereas Tapio altered and further developed the traditional novel, Vartio was able to create a radically new kind of narrative and depiction of life. Her first novel, *Se on sitten kevät* (1957; This then is spring), was her fourth book; it immediately put its author at the forefront of the new prose. The novel's subject matter is conventional: a man and woman draw closer and fall in love, followed by the woman's death and the man's sorrow. The ascetism, temperance, and sparencss of narration in this tale are new, however. What a novelist of the First Republic (and even his disciples in the Second) would have explained, analyzed, and qualified, Vartio depicts merely as events: spoken words and completed actions. Interpretation is left to the reader; the author provides only the starting point. This style appears easier but is, in fact, more difficult than the old psychological realism. Vartio's five novels, including *Hänen olivat linnut* (1967; His were the birds), published posthumously, revealed new and original solutions for character portrayal as the author's career progressed. *Hänen olivat linnut* indicated exceptional growth: humor, symbolism, tragedy, madness, and the grotesque sought a balance here. In the novel a mistress and her servant, an upper-class widow and a peasant woman, recount their life histories to each other, a situation reminiscent of Maria Jotuni's works.

Vartio's first and last novels are her greatest achievements, something that is rare in literature. Her poetry and short stories are skillfully written but have not found favor with the reading public. Vartio's prose was ahead of its time in numerous ways and provided inspiration for younger novelists, particularly those developing a behaviorist narrative. She is one of the most important role models in Finland for the school of novelists that seeks precision in observation and depiction rather than the correctness of explanation and interpretation.

Rintala and Meri

Paavo Rintala (1930–) and Veijo Meri (1928–) were first published in 1954. Initially, they were the leading novelists of their generation, but the parallels in their respective literary developments largely ceased during the subsequent decades. Meri's work in the epic novel waned, and his writing began to diverge, becoming channeled into a number of different genres: drama, essays, poetry. Rintala, however, proceeded to penetrate deeper into ossified levels of reality by means of the epic novel. As Kai Laitinen puts it, where Meri stylizes reality, Rintala moralizes. Meri is one of the leading modernists of Finnish literature, superb at depicting a random, chance, mechanical view of life. Rintala's roots are in the past: in the Laestadian religious movement, and in Augustine, Pascal, and Jung; these are his weapons against the lack of values in modern civilization. (Laestadianism, named after its founder, Lars Levi Laestadius [1800–61], a missionary active in Swedish Lapland, is a fundamentalist belief emphasizing simplicity of manner and intellect, alcoholic abstinence, public confession, and a rejection of any ecclesiastical hierarchy.)

Rintala began with a novel about Jesus entitled *Kuolleiden evankeliumi* (1954; Gospel of the dead). His second novel, *Rikas ja köyhä* (1955; Rich and poor), has been interpreted as the inverse of his first: the stage is Finland, the point of reference Palestine at the time of Jesus. Of the novels published in the 1950s, *Pojat* (1958; The boys), a depiction of boys' overwrought upbringing in an Oulu filled with German troops, and *Jumala on kauneus* (1959; God is beauty), a biographical novel about Vilho Lampi (1898–1936), a painter of flat, open lands, have become classics. In a trilogy published between 1960 and 1962 Rintala alternately examined the fates of Marshal Mannerheim and a wise old woman of the folk. In 1980 these novels were published in a single edition entitled *Mummoni ja Mannerheim* (My grandma and Mannerheim). Like his *Sissiluutnantti* (1963; Eng. tr. *The Long Distance Patrol*, 1967), this trilogy caused a violent debate in which a solid conservative was mistakenly taken for a subversive. This was "an ethical and religious problem formulated in terms of contemporary history" (Tarkka, *Suomalaisia nykykirjailijoita*, 1989, 153) which was not initially understood.

Rintala's next period entailed a mapping of the potentials of the documentary novel. The first and also the best book in his series about the Continuation War was *Sotilaiden äänet* (1966; Soldiers' voices), which was followed by three others, *Sodan ja rauhan äänet* (1967; Voices of war and peace), *Leningradin kohtalonsinfonia* (1968; Leningrad's symphony of fate), and *Napapiirin äänet* (1969; Voices of the Arctic Circle). Rintala used oral archives, soldiers' letters, and diaries that he put in order himself. His editorial work was based on the Jungian concept of a national soul, a collective psyche, the endurance or dissolution of which would decide the war. The Finnish identity did not collapse with the collapse of the eastern front, and according to the novel's point of view, this was the reason Finland was saved. Rintala's participation in the leadership of the Marxist-leaning peace movement (1969–84) yielded pacifist literature dealing with international topics as well as more satirical after-accounts. His most recent major work is the quasi-trilogy consisting of *Nahkapeitturien linjalla 1–2* (1976; 1979; The tanner's way) and *Valehtelijan muistelmat* (1982; Memoirs of a liar), a social history running from the Winter War (1939–40) to the end of the Kekkonen period (1982).

Veijo Meri is among the postwar Finnish modernists most widely recognized abroad. He began with a collection of short stories on war themes entitled *Ettei maa viheriöisi* (1954; Lest the land grow green), and the short story has remained one of his strongest genres; a collected edition of them was published in 1985. His second work, the novel *Manillaköysi* (1957; Eng. tr. *The Manila Rope*, 1967), was his breakthrough. In its structure this work vacillates between a novel and a collection of oral tales. The main plot is trivial; pivotal to the book are the tales and discussions that take place within its framework. This structure is repeated in Meri's collection of erotic stories, *Yhden yön tarinat* (1967; Tales of a single night), a title alluding to the Arabian Nights. Other novels followed, set in both civilian and wartime milieus; the former includes the historical novel *Irralliset* (1959; The separate ones) and a depiction of contemporary life entitled *Peiliin piirretty nainen* (1963; A woman sketched in a mirror), followed by

The Period of Independence I

Vuoden 1918 tapahtumat (1960; The events of 1918) and *Sujut* (1961; Quits). Meri depicts life during peace and war as essentially alike: both are warped by distortion in relationships, the rule of chance, mechanical events, and difficulties in communication. Meri's world view is permeated with threat and uncertainty: anything whatsoever can happen at any time.

A restless searching, a quest for the new, and an effort to destroy the boundaries between genres characterize Meri's later work. This includes poetry that seems extremely unpoetic, the shifting writing of a restless mind (four collections, 1976–87), and a poetic play called *Runoilijan kuolema* (1985; A poet's death). More sensational and more discussed were his biographies, in which the facts are based on scholarship while the whole is the artist's synthesis. The first of them was *Aleksis Stenvallin elämä* (1973; 2d ed. 1975; The life of Aleksis Stenvall), Meri's biography of the great author who wrote under the name Aleksis Kivi; it was followed by *Suomen marsalkka C. G. Mannerheim* (1988; The marshal of Finland C. G. Mannerheim), which, Pekka Tarkka says, bears the stamp of a classic. Meri's fast-paced, capricious, startling essays, which are structured like discourse, have also garnered a great deal of praise. During the years 1967–78 three such volumes were published, followed by his collected essays, *Julma prinsessa ja kosijat* (1986; The cruel princess and her suitors). The same genre is represented by *Tätä mieltä* (1989; Of this opinion), which, according to its subtitle, is a collection of "essays and monologues."

Following *Everstin autonkuljettaja* (1966; The colonel's chauffeur), a brilliant novel composed as a stream of consciousness (a section from this book and a chapter from the Mannerheim biography are included in *Dimension* [1994]), Meri's writing in narrative form either waned or became lyrical. Surprisingly, however, Meri returned to this genre in 1980 with renewed strength: *Jääkiekkoilijan kesä* (The ice hockey player's summer) is an erotic novel about people searching for their identities in a small postwar town. During the course of the action a stereotypical officer and a war-weary drunkard destroy themselves; the idleness of a young athlete's summer thrusts him into the arms and schemes of a beauty he desires, and their subsequent anguish proves almost unbearable. Meri has also been prolific in writing dramatic works for the theater, radio, and television.

Laconicism and Naivism: Hyry

In the prose of Antti Hyry (1931–), which sought mastery by setting limits, the decade of the 1950s took a more independent or willful turn. Hyry's first published works were a collection of philosophical tales called *Maantieltä hän lähti* (1958; He started from the highway) and a novel about an orphan boy who becomes a member of a village community, *Kevättä ja syksyä* (1958; Spring and autumn), which presages, in its simplicity of tone, his more successful works to come. He found a form suitable to him in the Pauli series: this tetralogy includes the novels *Kotona* (1960; At home), *Alakoulu* (1965; Primary school), *Isä ja poika* (1971; Father and son), and *Silta liikkuu* (1975; The bridge moves). His subject matter is autobiographical, although it is a minor aspect of the novels. The milieu is a northern village dominated by the Laestadian religious movement: Hyry examines, within the context of family, the life of a boy growing up there. The novel lacks the clichés typical of depictions of childhood; the boy is a person in his own right. His tradition, permeated by Christianity, is portrayed as a self-evident source of obligation and security. The naive approach used by Hyry in his descriptions — the terseness and simplicity of his sentences, his lack of a psychological or any other explanation — is initially strange and gradually captivates. His narrative has been characterized as "stating facts"; although behaviorist, it has more than one level. Nature and man, as a wanderer therein, become metaphors for the metaphysical.

The city and technical civilization (Hyry is an engineer by training), subject matter that entered his writing in the collection of short stories *Junamatkan kuvaus* (1962; Description of a train journey), symbolize alienation. Hyry grew attached to his small childhood community, with its closeness to nature and the earth and its conventional way of life. Those of his works that are situated elsewhere, such as "Leveitä lautoja" (1968; Broad boards), the title tale in a collection of short stories, seek to retain this atmosphere even in other circumstances. Material reality and its relationship to human endeavor, family and kin, land and nature, and the unproblematical, all-permeating force of Christianity are the foci of his philosophy. Hyry has consistently rejected the vision of reality imposed by the media, which, to a growing extent, regulate even literary life. Hyry has expressed himself solely through his books.

The Period of Independence 2, 1960–1990

Markku Envall
Translated by Tuula Starck

5

In the development of Finnish society and culture the year 1960 does not denote a border, except, of course, through a mirror. It has become a custom to characterize decades, to search for simplifying labels with which to stamp them. In general, it can be stated that social development after 1960 has been steady but rapid. The country's position in regard to foreign policy has remained unchanged. The relationships to the East were kept stable through the friendship and cooperation agreement, to the North through cooperation that increased under the auspices of the Nordic Council, and to the wider world within the membership of the United Nations. Finland joined the European economic integration as a member of the European Free Trade Association.

The standard of living rose steadily, foreign trade increased, urbanization and industrialization advanced. Emigration and the move from the country to the city were experienced as social disturbances; Finland was unable fully to employ its population, of which a considerable proportion moved to Sweden. The shift from rural to urban areas caused extensive problems both in the countryside and in the cities; the development of the former stopped, and the latter attracted a rootless population. These problems were also widely reflected in literature.

Urho Kekkonen served an exceedingly long time as the country's president (1956–82); his successor was Mauno Koivisto. The latter was the first Social Democrat in the country's history to be elected president, but this fact did not mean any practical change. A representative of the Agrarian Party, Kekkonen was clearly a more radical leader of the country during the 1960s and 1970s than Koivisto turned out to be in the 1980s.

Changes in the power structure of the various political parties were not great; nevertheless, in a country of multiple parties, they caused alterations in the government coalitions. After a long pause the political left wing entered the government in 1966; the People's Democratic Party left it in 1982. The basic political power rested with Social Democrats; they were mockingly called "the party of the state's caretakers." They changed their coalition partners from the agrarian Center Party to the Conservative Party in 1987. As we approach the present, the influences of these changes are perceived as less and less significant. The 1980s witnessed the narrowing of differences between the political parties and a unanimity on important issues (the period of consensus).

In the ideological and cultural sphere the changes were more distinct, but correspondingly less profound, from the point of view of social unity. It has become customary to say about the 1960s that during this decade the aesthetic radicalism of the 1950s changed into political radicalism. There was more knowledge and awareness of the ills that existed in society and in the world, but optimism and the spirit of reform also increased. The exchange of ideas became freer; attacks against political, moral, religious, and national taboos escalated.

The decade belonged to cultural radicalism, which in turn became channeled and solidified under political symbols during the 1970s. Politically defined cultural associations were formed, and most artists joined the various groups. The field was opened up by the Union of Cultural Workers (KTL), led by Marxists who were loyal to the Soviet Union. This determined the themes of debate; the other groups were forced into defensive positions. The 1970s politicized and party-politicized culture, so that the counterreaction in the 1980s was logical, or "dialectic." A new subjectivity was born, and the problems of an individual's subconscious again came to the foreground. The belief in political ideologies and in their ability to explain everything disintegrated. They were replaced by neoromantic, escapist, depth-psychological conceptual models.

The following kinds of generalizations have often been espoused, and they are not totally lacking in truth. The individualism of the 1950s became transformed, through the spirit of cooperation in the 1960s, into collectivism in the 1970s; and the 1980s brought individualism back again. The glad decade of the 1960s was followed by the rigid and ritualized 1970s. The 1950s scrapped the spiritual collectivism of the First Republic, not through protests but through ignoring it. The 1960s continued the work with the weapons of radical protest. The 1970s supported ideologies and group power, the belief in which died out in the 1980s. The fashionable person of this last decade thought only of himself, his career, his economic situation, his consumerism, and the private sphere of his life. All these features can be seen as reactions to the emphases of the 1960s and 1970s.

Naturally, the above-mentioned features are generalizations that bury beneath them many individual cases and nuances. A decade is stamped by the trends that begin during its course; if the literature and culture produced in that period are examined in toto, the picture is always different, because older generations continue their work on different ideological and artistic grounds. Waltari and Kurjensaari still belong to the 1960s; Kajava and Pennanen still belong to the 1980s, to mention but a few.

Literary Trends
At the turn of the 1950s and 1960s the battle of literary ideologies was presented as a series of novels that depicted the Civil War. The second volume of Linna's *Täällä Pohjantähden alla* (Here beneath the North Star) was published in 1960, as were Haavikko's *Yksityisiä asioita* (Private matters) and Meri's *Vuoden 1918 tapahtumat* (The events of 1918). The ideological generational conflict was at its sharpest. Linna, in the vein of historical science, aimed at explaining and understanding, whereas Haavikko and Meri used historical projection to present their own perceptions.

In the light of its audience reception, Haavikko's novel was exceptionally interesting. The novel's main character takes care of his "private matters" in the Helsinki of 1918. The book's second printing (1973) includes Tuomas Anhava's essay, which repeats and corrects the misconceptions of the criticism aimed at the novel. The critics generally perceived the novel's hero as pitiful and self-centered, a man without ideals, blind and callous to history's great movements, and believed that the author, in his unemotional way, had satirized this petty materialist. Anhava, Haavikko's fellow modernist, sees the matter differently; the main character is a mouthpiece for Haavikko's (and his generation's) anti-ideological thought, a projection of the criticism of ideologies toward an era in which ideologies caused destruction. Thus the work presents not an example of a narrow-minded speculation but a defense of the basic pragmatic man, the man who is capable of assessing the various social sectors with cold practical eyes, from the point of view of getting things done. The main character sees that the Reds will not remain in power, but his viewpoint has a solely pragmatic, not ideological, basis. For him, the conflict between the Reds and the Whites is only a question of which of them can make practical life run smoothly and can satisfy the needs of the majority, thereby being able to stay in power. The novelty of Haavikko's thought, and even more of his narrating, which is indirect and, minimizing the author's role, demands more from the reader, led the critics astray.

Veijo Meri, on the other hand, drew a picture of war as a phenomenon that is impossible to conceptualize. It is governed by the chaos encountered by the individual soldier. This projection into history of modernist nearsightedness, the idea of the unforeseeability and uncontrollability of events, was a strong counterargument to Linna's fiction of history.

This was a part of a literary historical drama, in which a rationalist of the 1940s and the modernists of the 1950s waged battle. But the prose writers of the 1950s mocked ideologies at the same time that the poetry, reacting quickly, had already started to tell of their return. Haavikko's collection of poems *Lehdet lehtiä* (1958; Leaves are leaves) has been viewed as the first symptom; in it Finnish politics are the focus of satire and polemics. The change can be seen particularly in Pentti Saarikoski's and Väinö Kirstinä's development as poets and as representatives of that decade. Both began as skilled practitioners of the imagistic poetry of the 1950s, the former in 1958 and the latter in 1961. Saarikoski's fourth poem collection, *Maailmasta* (1961; From the world), gave hints of freer nuances, but the breakthrough in all its strength did not take place until the following year, in the collection *Mitä tapahtuu todella?* (1962; What is really happening?), usually called the most "important" collection of the decade — not the "best." The critics emphasized the symptomatic value of the work, and also its effect as an ideological groundbreaker, without daring to speak in the language of aesthetic values. The poetic revolution was based, above all, on collage technique; the material consisted of political slogans, quotations from the classics, phraseology from everyday language. In poetry the collection accomplished the biblical mixing of languages at Babel. The "lyrical limitations" in subject matter and vocabulary were toppled; poetry was being created which speaks of the real world in a "more democratic" manner. Kirstinä's development was similar to that of Saarikoski. After *Lakeus* (1961; The plain) and its nature lyric, and the "classic surrealism" of *Hitaat auringot* (1963; Slow suns), Kirstinä brought out an "intermezzo," the counterpart of Saarikoski's *Maailmasta,* entitled *Puhetta* (1963; Talk), in which he lit the bomb that exploded in *Luonnollinen tanssi* (1965; Natural dance). Nature and observation are replaced by the urban environment, seen in the mirror of mass media. The collection contains capriciously associative prose poems that aim at chartering the restless movements of the mind. The present is given its own myths, such as "anonymph Mrs. Gadillac" [*sic*], an attempt at a complete leveling of the walls of topics and vocabularies that might or might not be suitable for poetry. Together with Saarikoski's *Mitä tapahtuu todella?* Kirstinä's *Luonnollinen tanssi* was the strongest poetic expression of the spirit of the 1960s.

Poetry searches for parallels to its own aims in international poetic expressions. Without too much of a simplification, it can be said that whereas the 1950s drew inspiration from the ancient poetry of China and Japan, which was also manifested in the liveliness of translations (i.e., by Pertti Nieminen and Tuomas Anhava), the 1960s looked toward the West, above all toward Latin America. Two poets who began in 1965, Pentti Saaritsa and Matti Rossi, introduced and translated works of poets from that part of the world (Saaritsa, for instance, Pablo Neruda's work, and Rossi, the poems of Cesar Vallejo). With his first Neruda translation Saaritsa also included Neruda's essay "In Defense of the Unclean" (1964), which demands in poetry "food stains and indecent positions" and "cold shivers, idylls, political tenets," that is, the entire kaleidoscope of human life. The program burst against the Finnish poetry of the 1950s, which was becoming classical "pure poetry."

A seminar on poetry, held in Turku two years earlier, expressed the beginning of the new spirit. Arvo Salo (1932–), the central ideologist of the 1960s, gave the introductory speech, in which he demanded poems that were different: long, sonorous, and suitable for songs, and that dealt with battles and love; he also spoke for more proper nouns in poems. (Salo put these ideas into practice in his dramas, discussed below.) He wanted to take apart the pure poem of the 1950s, and his program, which was published in a book in 1963, was widely followed.

In the sphere of prose writing the arguments concerned the relationship between the novel and recent history. Paavo Rintala's *Sissiluutnantti* (1963; Eng. tr. *The Long Distance Patrol*, 1967) caused widespread polemics, in which the image of the war was fought over by the generation that had experienced the war and the younger generation, which freely used the war as a topic for religious-metaphysical visions. A more dramatic battle was waged about Hannu Salama's novel *Juhannustanssit* (1964; The midsummer dance). With the influence and power of the archbishop and the minister of justice, the author and his publisher were taken to court for blasphemy, the ostensible reason being a drunk's single utterance, in which Jesus is referred to in an irreverent manner. The author was sentenced to prison, but the president used his power to reverse the sentence. Pekka Tarkka has presented the best analysis of the "literary wars" of the 1960s in his studies *Paavo Rintalan saarna ja seurakunta* (1966; Paavo Rintala's sermon and the congregation) and *Hannu Salama* (1973). Religion and the fatherland were untouchable basic values for those who held onto the spirit of the First Republic; the new generation fought for the right to interpret the concepts with artistic freedom. It won the fight, at least for the time being.

The reformist, idealistic-practical spirit of the 1960s did not feel that the novel was efficient and quick enough to remedy the world's ills. It wanted to replace the novel with reports and pamphlets. Toward the end of the decade nearly every publisher established its own series of pamphlets; the most visible and ambitious one was Tammi's *Huutomerkki* (Exclamation point) series, which began in 1968. The argument between the novel and the pamphlet, seen from the vantage point of today, is superficial and misleading. The novel has its own tasks, which are slower but above all deeper than those of the reports that uncovered the ills and injustices of the world. Belief in the novel was finally reestablished by Salama's *Siinä näkijä missä tekijä* (1972; Where there's a crime there's a witness). The work describes a Communist resistance movement in Tampere during the Continuation War. Some of the characters are relatives of Harri Salminen, the author's alter ego. Both an external narrator and the novel's characters tell the story; the novel encompasses both the time during the war and the present. The work proved that an ambitious novel has its own language format and thus that the purposes of the novel cannot be served and replaced by other genres.

During the entire postwar period one of the most fruitful tensions in Finnish literature has been provided by the conflict between realism and modernism. In the 1950s and 1960s the tension became localized as an opposition between Tampere and Helsinki. The stars of the former were Viita and Linna; of the latter, Haavikko and Meri. The third power in the 1950s was so-called Kainuism (after the province of Kainuu), which consisted of rural prose and depictions of the country people; its leading figure, Veikko Huovinen, soon disassociated himself from it. Prose depiction of the countryside remained, and it received new impetus from the changes in the societal structure, from the "great move" of the 1970s, the escape from the countryside. Provincial literary power centers appeared, above all in North Karelia, a movement led by Heikki Turunen.

The serial novel, social epic and family-focused, which for brevity's sake came to be called a trilogy, was already a longtime favorite literary format; it was revived and grew stronger still after the success of Linna's *Pohjantähti*. Rintala, Tapio, Pennanen, Eino Säisä, Joenpelto, Jorma Ojaharju and Turunen, among others, each wrote a series. One of the last struggles over trends in Finnish literature was waged at the end of the 1970s, when a regional, social epic, centered on a single family, found challengers and critics in the ranks of leading modernists, especially Erno Paasilinna and Veijo Meri—a final battle in the war between the realists and the modernists. The modernists felt that the tasks given literature by the writers of the epics were wrong in their charting of vanishing lifestyles, occupations, and regions and in their depiction of attempts at solving social problems in various periods of Finland's history. Instead, the critics wanted "cold and hard modernism," literature that dealt entirely with the human condition in the present-day world.

The argument soon seemed not to be so very important after all, and the battle lines disintegrated. The wave of the trilogies waned in part, too, because other authors realized that it was impossible to reach Linna's level of popularity. At its best, the epic prose of the realists was not as trivial as its critics claimed, and even the modernists could not avoid a vast national charting: Antti Tuuri changed sides, Paasilinna wrote his Petsamo epic, Haavikko wrote two idiosyncratic national histories, and Meri wrote biographies of the national heroes Kivi and Mannerheim.

If, as a reaction, the pamphlet wave fed trilogies, they in turn fanned the flames of the authors' self-assessments and confessions, a trend that began in Finland's Swedish-language literature, above all with Christer Kihlman and Henrik Tikkanen. The starting point was Kihlman's book of confessions *Människan som skalv* (see chapter 10). Two of the largest Finnish publishers had series of popular autobiographies and self-presentations: Otava's *Vuosi elämästäni* (A year from my life) and WSOY's *Ihmisen ääni* (The human voice). Instead of social issues, interest was strong in individuals, their lives, and their idiosyncrasies. Again, it can be observed that Hannu Salama had the strength and courage to combine the demands of the spirit of the times with an artistically ambitious mammoth project. He started the *Finlandia* series, which contains hidden autobiography and analysis of sociological situations but also a search for new expressive dimensions in the novel. The confession literature of the Finland-Swedish authors may have exerted an influence on the autobiographical elements in some of the Finnish-language novel series, such as in *Kukkivat roudan maat 1–6* (1971–80; The Lands of frost are flowering), by Eino Säisä (1935–88); but among Finnish-language authors, only Teuvo Saavalainen can be correlated with Tikkanen and Kihlman as a confessor (see p. 255). However, the untranslated series of Saavalainen's outpourings (1980–91) has not achieved the general Nordic notoriety of its Swedish-language counterparts.

As we approach the present day, a lack of clarity in trends and groupings becomes apparent. This may derive from a faulty vision caused by the lack of distance but also by genuine diversity in values. In the sphere of prose the share of short stories and other short prose writing has been growing; the writing of essays and aphorisms has also increased its foothold. The short story in particular has gained independent strength, having ceased to be merely a training field for novelists. Martti Joenpolvi grew from a writer of mediocre novels to a master of the short story. Antti Tuuri started as a skilled writer of behavioral short stories; in the 1980s the sturdy novel became his principal genre. The short prose of Erno Paasilinna's early period moved skillfully in the quadrangle of short story, satire, humoresque, and essay.

Literary critics and researchers no longer compile their newspaper articles into books. For decades, such volumes were the basic event in Finnish essay publication, but now the concept of the essay is perceived as being more demanding. Aphorism writing has been on the ascent since the late 1960s and early 1970s; when first Mirkka Rekola (1969) and then Paavo Haavikko (1972) published collections of aphorisms, the genre had again been taken up, after a long pause, by the most notable writers. Samuli Paronen and Erno Paasilinna joined the group of aphorists in course of the 1970s.

Saarikoski and the Poetry of the Radical Period
Pentti Saarikoski (1937–83), a versatile writer capable of renewal, precocious and self-destructive, modernly restless and moving in international spheres, became the leading figure of the poetry of the 1960s. Hidden behind a bohemian public image, Saarikoski was an industrious and ambitious translator of both classical Greek and modern European literature. His principal work in the first realm was Homer's *Odyssey* and in the second, Joyce's *Ulysses,* and thus it is not surprising that Odysseus was a central focus of correlation for Saarikoski, who liked to play various roles.

When Saarikoski made his debut with two collections of poems in 1958, he showed his ability to adopt and master the technique of the poetry of the 1950s; his observations were precise, his images clearly defined. His own mischievous voice could already be heard as well; disrespect toward authorities and in their stead a wunderkind's belief in himself, expressed impudently and self-importantly. His third collection, *Runot ja Hipponaksin runot* (1959; Poems and the poems of Hipponax) introduced the Greek satirist Hipponax of Ephesus (fl. 546–520 B.C.) as a soulmate; according to Saarikoski, his fourth collection, *Maailmasta* (1961; From the world), was influenced by Italo Calvino's comic writing.

Saarikoski's breakthrough, *Mitä tapahtuu todella?* (1962; What is really happening?), was the most effective and visible manifesto of the poetic aspirations of the era. Compared with the poet's earlier work, the collection carried out the radical mixing of languages; the method was "democratic," or (as Saarikoski himself wanted to express it) "dialectic." Quotations from the classics, advertising slogans, newspaper headlines, phrases from everyday speech, and poems reminiscent of those from earlier collections were in harmony or in conflict. A political revolution took place together with the poetic one: the mocking of the bourgeoisie, the leaning toward the Left, the taking of a stand on the side of the Soviet Union and Marxism.

But Saarikoski's own development is also dialectic: beside the long, conversationlike, apparently or truly aleatoric poem, the polished, laconic, private small poem lived in his production; it was epigrammatic here and directly lyrical there in its nuances. The series of contrasts began when the political poem had flowered and withered in the collections *Kuljen missä kuljen* (1965; I wander where I wander) and *Ääneen* (1966; Out loud). The very titles express the nature of the collections: *Laulu laululta pois* (1966; Song after song), *En soisi sen päättyvän* (1968; I wouldn't wish it to end), *Onnen aika* (1971; A time of happiness), *Alue* (1973; Territory), and the bilingual *Meille jäi kiireetön ilta / Kvällen gör sig ingen brådska* (1975; And for us the evening lingered leisurely/The evening does not hurry), written with Mia Berner. The focus is on an individual's inner feelings; love replaces politics. A third stage is manifested in a trilogy called the Tiarnia series (1977, 1980, 1983), which Saarikoski wrote after his move to Sweden; here the polarities are the brilliant beginnings of our civilization in the cultures of antiquity, and civilization's going astray. (Compilations of Saarikoski's poems were translated into English by Anselm Hollo in 1967 and 1983, with further selections from his late poetry in *Dimension* [1994]; after Saarikoski's death *Hämärän tanssit* [1983] came out as *Dancers of the Obscure* [1987], rendered by Michael Cole and Karen Kimball. It seems sure that Saarikoski will continue to fascinate translators.)

Saarikoski was a poet above all, but he was also active in other areas. He translated a number of classical Greek authors (Xenophon, Euripides, Homer, Theophrastus, Heraclitus, Aristotle) and modern authors (Joyce, Bellow, Calvino) into lively modern Finnish. Saarikoski's translations influenced the written Finnish language by expanding the borders of propriety into the areas of slang (J. D. Salinger's *The Catcher in the Rye*) and sexual depiction (Henry Miller's *Tropic of Cancer*), among others. He also wrote prose in which confession shattered privacy and political defiance shattered taboos in general thought. In Saarikoski's radio plays (compiled as *Köyhyyden trilogia* [1986; Poverty's trilogy]) the topics were taken from history, and the treatment was unemotional and universally human. Prose entered

Saarikoski's writing in his youthful newspaper columns (*Nenän pakinoita* [1960; The nose's columns]); the writer's ridiculing of reactionary and frozen modes of thinking has given the collection better staying power than that of other, average assemblies of newspaper columns in book form. The posthumous work *Nuoruuden päiväkirjat* (1984, 2d, longer ed. 1995; Youthful diaries) revealed the path of a precocious and overly gifted young man from a religious to an aesthetic milieu.

The poetry of Väinä Kirstinä (1936–) began with a reversal reminiscent of Saarikoski; at first Kirstinä was tied to the classicism of the nature poem of the 1950s, from which he broke free to admit the linguistic richness and even the chaos of the surrounding world. His third collection, *Puhetta* (1963; Talk), implemented a quick poetic revolution, acknowledging modern language usage explored for the use of poetry. As noted above, Kirstinä's development reached its zenith in the collection *Luonnollinen tanssi* (1965; Natural dance), which corresponds to Saarikoski's collection *Mitä tapahtuu todella?* It contains a long series of prose poems with the title "Atomipompotusta" (Atompompom) and is dedicated to a "Committee of One Hundred Associations." The poems are capriciously quick, depicting the subject's confusion in the modern world. The rich collection allows space for traditional nature and love poetry, prose poems praising sexuality, praises of inebriation, and concrete image poems and sound poems in which words have no symbolic functions. "Frolicking pairs of words" is a list of words, like a poet's bag of tools. The present is mythologized; the Abominable Snowman as well as "a giant doll run by atomic energy" appear in the poems.

Like Saarikoski's, Kirstinä's voice developed from a noisy to a more subdued tone. *Pitkän tähtäyksen LSD-suunnitelma* (1967; The long-range LSD plan) rehashed the previous collection; a change came in 1969 in the collection *Talo maalla* (A house in the country), in which the countryside returns as Kirstinä's landscape. Oriented toward French culture, Kirstinä has always been susceptible to surrealistic influences, having translated André Breton's *Manifeste du surréalisme* into Finnish in 1970. Pessimistic visions about the dead end at which technical civilization has arrived are counteracted by the withdrawal into the inner self. The use of materials from dreams can be seen, for instance, in the collections of 1973 (*Säännöstelty eutanasia* [Rationed euthanasia]) and 1986 (*Yötä, päivää* [Night, day]). Kirstinä's collected poems, *Runoja 1958–1977* (Poems 1958–1977) were published in 1979. Since then the pace has been slow; Kirstinä published further poem collections in 1984, 1986, and 1994.

Among other poets who made their debuts in the 1960s are the very individualistic Jyrki Pellinen (first published in 1962), the above-mentioned Matti Rossi and Pentti Saaritsa, and four poets of similar strength, Risto Ahti, Jarkko Laine, Niilo Rauhala, and Caj Westerberg, who made their debuts in 1967.

Jyrki Pellinen (1940–) is a confusingly independent poet, the great loner of the 1960s generation. It is not easy to get a grasp of his poetry; at times it feels too difficult, at times too easy. Pellinen documents his private thoughts, mixing the esoteric and the banal. He studied music and has exhibited paintings; the arts form the central background reference to his poetry. In Pellinen's early work Paavo Haavikko's influence has been detected; both show the aim of studying and dispersing the structure of language. But Pellinen soon found his own way and began to cultivate a capriciously unexpected poem that often seems to point at poetry in general or at the poem itself, so that it has been possible to speak of metapoetry, a line continued as late as his *Huulilla kylmä tuuli* (1990; A cold wind on the lips).

To literary critics, Pellinen has offered the same kind of problem as Eric Satie has to musicologists. Pellinen fascinates some as much as he irritates others. A subjective perception is his governing aim, "let everyone live his own world," but ample publications together with a technique that repeats itself have not convinced everybody; there is too much "finger exercising and surface embroidery" (Tarkka, *Suomalaisia nykykirjailijoita*, 1980, 174). By 1992, twenty-six collections had been published and, in addition to these, a series of prose works, in which the program of remaining in the microcosm of the self is defended, at its best in a manner that speaks to others.

Matti Rossi (1934–) began as an international poet but gradually developed in a national direction. Even before his own literary work, he was a visible introducer and translator of Latin American literature. His debut work, *Näytelmän henkilöt* (1965; The characters of a play), moves about the world and history with the aid of proper names. Of the poems, the most notable one is a protest against the Vietnam War; disseminated as a song, it attacked American actions in the Left manner of the period. Rossi's second work, *Leikkejä kahdelle* (1966; Games for two), depicts in four acts the development of a love relationship; in its sensuality the expression was new in Finnish poetry. Political poems had their turn in the collection *Tilaisuus* (1967; The opportunity); its view of the world is governed by the deep chasm between the rich and the poor nations. His next work was a swift reaction against the occupation of Czechoslovakia (*Käännekohta* [1968; Turning point]), but Rossi's development rapidly made the poems seem ironic: in the collections of the 1970s Rossi was a dogmatic Communist who watched the multihued world through the simplifications of Soviet Marxism. "I am now a Party soldier," he wrote in the opening poem of his collection *Agitprop* (1972). Slowly, Rossi perceived clashes of class struggle in Finland and in its recent history rather than on the world stage. At the same time, his range of genres expanded: he published a collection of short stories (1977), a collection of essays (1981), and four novels, which received a mixed reception. In his poetry of the 1980s Rossi cultivated the Kalevala meter in a manner that has been compared with the work of the nineteenth-century folk poets (Tarkka, *Suomalaisia nykykirjailijoita,* 1989, 157).

In the literary development of Pentti Saaritsa (1941–) the concentration on poetry and politics has had a stronger lyric bias than in Rossi's case. Saaritsa is a poet who is persistent and faithful to his genre; the series of his collections from 1965 to 1988 consists of fourteen books. His career has shown an ability for renewal, so that it can be divided into distinct periods. Although Saaritsa's perception is intense, it is ambiguous, with tendencies toward amusement, irony, and a sense of everything's relativity. Throughout his work Saaritsa has opposed the ready-made and stiff structure of the "bourgeois" world. He has reached for and documented his own inner experiences, peeled them out from under preexisting models. At the same time, he has listened to the people of the world, showing sensitivity toward suffering and its social causes in a more influential way than purely political agitprop poetry. Another literary field for Saaritsa has been translation, mainly of Spanish-language literature.

Saaritsa is among the most typical builders of a poetic output in his generation. The surrealistic influence evident in his early work was followed by a move toward social activism; and this again was followed by a turn toward a hearkening to inner experiences. Nevertheless, the discussion of general matters continues, although individual and inner experiences become more frequent as the poet's observation platform. In the 1980s Saaritsa's poetry gained new melodiousness as it began to include rhymes and incantations influenced by folk poetry. Where Rossi repeats, with poetical means, that which already has been said and that which is known, Saaritsa's poems have lately begun to search for the saying of the unsaid, the expressing of the unexpressed—one of the classical tasks of poetry. Saaritsa's work will probably remain among the most notable achievements of his generation.

The quirks of history contain hidden logic, although it is not always easily understood. All the poets who began their careers in the 1960s and who now appear to be important are men, whereas in the 1940s and 1970s the feminine share was substantial. In the 1940s the losses caused by the war played a part, and in the 1970s the poetry of individualism, nature, and everyday life was born as a reaction to the social poem; both instances gave poetic space to many women. Another historical oddity is the fact that all the notable poets who made their debuts toward the end of the 1960s began their careers in 1967. Each of them clearly had a different view of the world, however, as if manifesting one of the slogans of the 1960s about "pluralism." Risto Ahti is somewhat conceptual-didactic, a poet for a small audience, who observes the world through the eyes of Eastern and Western mystics. In contrast, Jarkko Laine is the voice of his generation, contemporary, using popular culture and material from the media. Niilo Rauhala, who draws inspiration from the world of the northern Finnish Laestadian religious revival movement, became the best exponent of Christian values and experiences in the poetry of the 1960s. To Caj Westerberg, a poet is a seer and a prophet, the principal reason for characterizing him as a romantic.

Risto Ahti (1943–) has published numerous collections but has remained rather little known to readers, an obscurity explicable by the very nature of his poetry. He cultivates ironic and satiric interpretations of the individual or universal experience, not much worrying whether his texts speak to or are understood by the general public. Ahti's poems do not have stanzaic, rhythmic, or melodic values; instead, they contain a rather superficial or mockingly learned weightiness, explanations, even didacticism. A poem sometimes changes into a prose poem, and poetic narrating, sometimes into an aphorism. Pekka Tarkka characterizes Ahti as a "pyromaniac of the imagination" (*Suomalaisia nykykirjailijoita,* 1989, 13). The strong features in Ahti's poetry are the seeing in alternative ways, the introduction of new combinations, the limitlessness of storytelling. The opposite side of the same strength is a tendency to present a private theology and to lecture the reader. Mysticism is the unifying tradition in his perception: Ahti believes in the immediate experience and through its power attempts to scatter the structures of ready-made worlds; at its best, Ahti's criticism produces "wild chains of events, surrealistic visions, erotic dramas, quick fables" (Tarkka, *Suomalaisia nykykirjailijoita,* 1989, 15).

In contrast to Ahti's elevated frame of references, Jarkko Laine (1947–) makes use of popular culture. He is the first Finnish poet to whom entertainment and popular media gave essential materials. The titles of Laine's collections often combine the sublime and the banal, as in *Viiden pennin Hamlet* (1976; Five-penny Hamlet) and *Muovinen Buddha* (1967; The plastic buddha). Laine was the poet of his generation, of the "children of Marx and Coca-Cola," a contemporary romantic. The nonpolitical front of the youth revolution of the 1960s received its voice in his poetry. The banality of his material is only a starting point; from the very outset Laine was linguistically nimble and a sure user of diverse nuances. The anarchy of attitude levels and the consumption of entertainment were the springboards for his early work; the West and its mass culture, and especially the poetry of the beat generation, were his inspirations. It was clearly impossible to continue indefinitely with this method of composing poems, and a turn in a more classical direction appeared in the collections of the 1970s; "the street wanderer" changes into "a learned expert in the work of words" (Tarkka, *Suomalaisia nykykirjailijoita*, 1989, 96). Laine remained a poet dependent on subject matter, but he discovered literary traditions beneath the popular culture. A middle-aged man, susceptible to fatigue, threatened by alienation and lack of purpose, speaks in the collections of the 1980s. The barbarism of the new youth cloaks the generational difference with irony. The poem's allusions have become richer and classical; its expression displays a new ambition for the possibility of ambiguous interpretation.

Along with numerous poem collections, Laine's work includes novels and short-story collections. His first novels depicted the youth revolution against attitudes and customs; then Laine experimented with the variation of the formulas of popular literature: the world of the Gothic novel is the topic in *Vampyyri* (1971; The vampire), and the spy story in the novel *Nick Naantali itäisillä mailla* (1974; Nick Naantali in the East). A strong tie to surface feelings prevalent at the time of publication or to preexisting patterns threatens the future life of the author's prose work. Laine's center of gravity is in producing poetry, and an expansion of this area seems to have been his leading ambition.

Niilo Rauhala (1936–) is a clergyman by education and a critic who looks at modern civilization through the values of Laestadian Christianity. Among the values of the 1960s, religion was very much in the background: Rauhala was the only poet of that decade able to combine Christian perception with the contemporary development of poetic expression. His poetry is not true religious poetry; he simply observes nature and life with Christian points of attachment and value markers: the seasonal cycle and the ecclesiastic calendar year are almost identical for him. The subject matter is the everyday and the shared experience: nature, family, work, children. Central values in the images are observations of light; the contrast of seasonal changes in the north of Finland partly explains this feature of his works. Children above all shed light on the apparent sadness of human life: "I know that autumn kills all / but you [children] not even death." In an individual's experience, ecclesiastic life and the church as an institution constitute value strata supported by the community and tradition. Rauhala succeeds in one of the most difficult tasks in an already secularized culture — in the writing of good, religion-based poetry. In poetry he is an example of what Antti Hyry and, to an extent, Paavo Rintala are in prose; the Laestadian revival movement perceived in the south as narrow-minded and stern is able to produce writers who cross not only the borders of the religious movement itself but also borders of varying viewpoints, and they break into the most esteemed layers of literature. The church's other factions do not have much to show in regard to the same ability.

Rauhala's expression is sensitive to a point of sentimentality; his basic techniques include the personification of nature and the bestowal on it of a soul. All artistry is alien to Rauhala; the poem remains open both in its expression and in its ethos. The Laestadian dogma rarely surfaces in Rauhala's poems, although the attachment to children can be correlated with the movement's negative attitude toward birth control. Rauhala's recipe has partly proved its ability to function; the total number of his collections is large, the latest from 1995. The settings and constructions of the poems are, however, repeated in too similar a fashion. Rauhala knows the technique of creating poems based on observation and image, but he does not seem to have any desire to renew his expression or to vary his technique. The danger of repeating himself lies close at hand.

Caj Westerberg (1946–) is not, like Rauhala, a "poet with another profession." In his case, to be a "mere" poet is connected with the totality of the poetic task. Poetry is everything, or at least transcends everything. This starting point brings richness to Westerberg's poetry, but the program of the saying of the unsaid, the search for and the defense of the way to mystic experience produce a counteraction; not much is always said about anything, but instead scant observations are presented. Westerberg is a romantic and, as such, a critic of modern lifestyles and civilization. The key poem, which is also the title poem of his collection of 1975, defines the alienation:

> We buy and sell
> sell and buy
> our life.
> Oh, oh.
> It's expensive to buy
> and is sold cheap.

Westerberg's demanding poetic perception did not immediately produce results. After a promising start his work in the early 1970s froze into a documentation of nature observations in the form of small poems. The fashion for lyrical nature idylls attracted him, too.

Among Westerberg's nine collections, the three latest ones are the best; they have a strong, independent expression that varies the construction technique. *Reviirilaulu* (1978; Territorial song), *Elämän puu* (1981; Tree of life), and *Kirkas nimetön yö* (1985; Clear, nameless night) form an ascending series that reaches its zenith in the third collection. Its best poems search for the saying of the unsaid and a mystic unity in the midst of life's conflicts. Now Westerberg's poem chants or repeats, now it chats or reminisces; and then it becomes crystallized in the manner of Japanese haiku or an epigram. "Dim sun / from a branch / drops snow" is an observation-centered haiku; "Wherever I look / is as if I saw something / which already was given up" is an epigram cloaked as a haiku. The varied ways of writing poems, the ambition inherent in expression and reception, and the high value given lyrical poetry and its task have taken Westerberg to mastery. During the second half of the 1980s a continuation of his work was awaited in vain. Instead, he published translations from Finland's and Sweden's Swedish-language poetry, for which his bilingual background was an excellent prerequisite.

Prose of the 1960s
In the prose of the 1960s a visible place was held both by Linna, who began in the 1940s, and by the modernists of the 1950s. The 1960s produced some fifteen prose writers who have created an outstanding and valued body of work. Certain other writers, whose principal genre has been felt to belong to the periphery of the literary field, must be added to the group.

While Olavi Siippainen was tied to his proletarian background and Pekkanen and Linna conquered the analytical total picture of society from the standpoint of their working-class beginnings, the 1960s turned notably to the integration of working-class literature and to new tasks. Some writers were overtaken by dogmatic Marxism more than by their own experiences (Marja-Leena Mikkola). The viewpoint of working people has been most tenaciously adhered to by Alpo Ruuth. Picaresque and adventure traditions, in the manner of Jack London, have also appeared (Jorma Ojaharju). Two writers who have gone the furthest from their proletarian starting points are Hannu Salama and Samuli Paronen. In regard to both its structure and its perceptions, Salama's epic prose is unsurpassed. From the point of view of the lowest and poorest societal strata the very individualistic Paronen created a body of work that has proved to be remarkable, even as a criticism of civilization.

Women, in particular, concentrated on epic prose that focuses on the middle class, among them Kerttu-Kaarina Suosalmi, Anu Kaipainen, and Eeva Kilpi. Suosalmi's powerful prose plumbs the depths of ethics and analyzes society. Kaipainen created her own layered type of novel, using folk traditions and mythology; her work includes some successes and some books that will remain formalized prisoners of their time. Kilpi did not so much renew structure or expression as rework values and perceptions: she is the only writer of her generation, and the first woman in Finnish literature, who can be called a feminist in the contemporary meaning of the word.

Regionalism stamps the image and the work of some writers (Timo K. Mukka from Lapland, Eino Säisä from the province of Savo). Writers from Helsinki have been more eager for experiments (Markku Lahtela). Leo Kalervo made a lifelong career charting rural culture change and the development of the Finnish lifestyle. Further, space must be given to practitioners of the more peripheral genres: drama, children's literature, newspaper columns, satire, and popular writing.

Salama, the Proletarian Epic, and Beyond
Hannu Salama (1936–) has found creative and lasting solutions to many of the challenges of his time. Although his books deal with major social and behavioral problems, he has continually shown a spirit of innovation aimed at the novel's structure. His reply to confessional literature was that, in the majority of his work, the main character is the author Harri Salminen; Salama's Salminen, however, is no mere alter ego in a roman à clef.

Salama's first novel, *Se tavallinen tarina* (1961; That common story), has remained a modern classic. It describes the use and abuse of a country girl in the city and her escape into mental illness; the image is simultaneously cruel and nonaccusatory. Although Salama has been thought of as a "naturalist" from the beginning, the painting of sporadic evil, the presenting of wrongs or horrors, is alien to him. His glance seeks the dark basic structures of the community, the family, and the individual, but his approach is analytical. It is possible to see in Salama a writer who is thoroughly able to illuminate the society of his time, comparable, for instance, to Balzac. Salama's second novel, *Juhannustanssit* (1964; The midsummer dance), brought him a prison sentence for blasphemy, yet the novel itself would not have merited a trial. It is a collective depiction of Finnish people who, in a rootless limbo between the countryside and the city, fail to perform the customary rituals of celebrating midsummer: ties to others as well as to the self and to a lifestyle are severed. Pekka Tarkka's interpretation of the novel as a tragedy (*Hannu Salama*), whose pattern is placed among common people, has been the best in-depth analysis of the reasons that underlay the court case.

Minä, Olli ja Orvokki (1967; Me, Olli, and Orvokki) and *Siinä näkijä missä tekijä* (1972; Where there's a crime there's a witness) are the great novels of Salama's middle period. In the former the protagonist, Harri Salminen, is writing a novel that very much resembles the latter. The work is a depiction of a game of betrayal and revenge, a portrayal of human baseness. Its subject matter and group of characters are held together by the grip of a writer of epic prose. The novel is Salama's strongest description of a human hell before the *Finlandia* series.

Siinä näkijä missä tekijä introduces different layers of time. Salminen represents the present, but the wartime Communist resistance movement and terrorist activities in Pispala (a working-class district in Tampere) are depicted through his relatives. The work is a chronicle of the Salminen family as well as a political novel. Harri, his mother, and his father, a self-confessed Communist turncoat, are the tellers of the story, but in addition there is an outside narrator. The power of the perceptions, the intensity of the descriptions, the masterfully varied structure are all in balance. The novel has been called the best in Finnish literature of the 1970s; soon after its publication it received the status of a national classic. In 1991 Salama, through the medium of the long-awaited *Ottopoika* (Otto the adopted), gave a view of Otto Ville Kuusinen, the great and good friend of Diktonius (see chapter 11) and Stalin, among others, by having an alter ego, a journalist named Risto Mikkola, another product of radical Pispala, plan to write Kuusinen's biography.

But Salama's striving for great, complex composition brought forth yet another experiment, the *Finlandia* series (six novels, 1976–83, published together in 1984), whose world is governed by crime, violence, and the collapsing structures of human relationships. The novels present a perception that Finnish society is in a state of psychosocial illness for which political parties, the church, and other institutions cannot provide a medicine.

Salama's other genres have been the short story and lyric poetry, the former used as a laboratory for epic prose writing. His five collections (1962–88; a compilation of the four first appeared in *Novellit* [1984; Short stories]) show him to be a master of the genre. "Catarrh," from *Lomapäivä* (1962; Vacation), a tale of physical disease and the narrator-observer's emotional dissolution, was translated in *Dimension* (1994). As a poet, Salama has a debatable position, somewhat like Veijo Meri's. The vocabulary in his poetry sometimes functions as a slap in the face; his language is private, his feelings varieties of aggression.

Samuli Paronen (1917–74) is in many ways an odd apparition in Finland's literature. After he worked in several blue-collar occupations, he came into the public eye as if from nowhere, publishing a notable body of work during a decade: eight novels, a collection of short stories, and a collection of aphorisms. His approach, which was individualistically critical of society and looked at its floundering from a marginal perspective, was already evident in his second work, a novel with the war as its theme, *Kuolismaantie* (1967; Road to Kuolismaa). The life of a communications patrol, from trench warfare to retreat to discharge from the army, is described in the experiences and thoughts of soldiers who think and who discard force-fed values.

Paronen's proletarian descriptions break with Finnish tradition in that society's underdogs are not objects but subjects; they not only see the injustice in their lives but grow spiritually and intellectually to a point where they examine the destructiveness of society's leading values and practices, their shortsightedness and absurdity. When the subject matter is closely delineated, as in *Kaivos* (1970; The mine), *Huone puutalossa* (1971; A room in an old house), *Laiva* (1972; The ship), *Kortteeri* (1974; The rental pad), a broader sociocritical analysis, striving for universalities, develops from a narrow basis.

Paronen's collection of aphorisms, *Maailma on sana* (1974; The world is a word), is a brilliant summary of the author's thought and themes. Through simple, incontestable paradoxes the work maligns the values and ways of thought of that majority of the population which moves forward, becoming ever more prosperous. The book is divided into ten chapters, whose themes — competition, "decent citizens," Finland, war, law, democracy, religion, values, knowledge, and language — make up the sum total of Paronen's perception. Samples are: "Most sense is consumed by great sillinesses," and "We don't know. We sell it as God."

The epic writing of Alpo Ruuth (1943–) is light, unlike Salama's demonic and Paronen's apocalyptic prose; its characters are ordinary Finnish workers with their ordinary human problems. Politically, the perspective can be localized within the People's Democratic Party, which is the extreme left within Finland's divided left wing. The opposing powers are employers and the administrative machinery but also party and trade union officials. In his novels Ruuth has described his contemporary society as it is experienced by a thinking, although not intellectual, worker. The polarities in his description consist of humor and morality, joie de vivre and solidarity. After his debut with *Naimisiin* (1967; Getting married) he published the breakthrough novel *Kämppä* (1969; The den), which soon achieved the status of a classic. The novel describes boys from a working-class section of Helsinki, Sörnäinen, and their unsure, anarchistic, but still innocent journey toward an adult world.

Among Ruuth's books the novel *Korpraali Julin* (1971; Corporal Julin) is the only one with a historical theme; the events take place during the Continuation War, and the mockery directed at the military has been compared with Jaroslav Hašek's *Osudy dobtého vojáka Švejka za světové války* (1921–23; Eng. tr. *The Good Soldier Švejk*, 1930; unabridged, 1974). Ruuth's social epics include *Kotimaa* (1974; Native land) and *Nousukausi* (1977; Upward trend); both titles are ironic. In the first a young man sincerely tries to succeed but ends by having to migrate to Sweden when the harshness of his native land becomes intolerable. During a time of large-scale emigration the novel was notable for its representation of a social reality. *Nousukausi* takes the main character to a divorce, to a new relationship, and to the intensive care unit of a hospital. The two novels from the 1980s have been followed by a motley, less focused output. Ruuth's description leans toward dialogue that is lively and smooth; sometimes it has been suspected of being too facile because of its abundance. The merit of his socialistic popular novels is that the reality, which is avoided in middle-class narration, is presented through a basic human, multifaceted, and thoughtful conceptualization. Ruuth has been Finland's leading novelist to espouse the views of the People's Democrats.

The work of Marja-Leena Mikkola (1939–) and Jorma Ojaharju (1938–) moves within the same ideological camp. The former made her debut in 1962 with a collection of short stories, *Naisia* (Women); the latter in 1966 with a novel dealing with prison life, *Kakku* (The cake). If the left-wing ideology of Mikkola is thinned out by a certain learnedness, Ojaharju is distinguished by narration that feels at home with exceptions rather than stereotypes.

In the Finnish literary world Mikkola is among the women who wear many hats. She wrote scripts for cabarets and musicals on order; she experimented with entertainment formats applied to leftist depictions as well as with the documentary novel based on interviews. The projects were tied to fads and grew dated as soon as the period in which they were written had passed. More high-reaching literary novels are Mikkola's *Tyttö kuin kitara* (1964; Girl like a guitar) and *Maailman virrassa* (1981; In the world's stream). The former is a love story about pop musicians; the latter exhibits an ambitious attempt to combine the 1920s and 1960s, transmitting ideological ponderings about the general and individual on the making of art and the explanation of illness. Mikkola has received more unanimous praise for her work in short-story writing. She has shown the diversity of her talents by publishing fairy-tale novels and poems, children's books (see chapter 11), a collection of newspaper columns, and translations into Finnish of English-language poets (Sylvia Plath, Dylan Thomas).

Jorma Ojaharju is relaxed and adventurous, basing his work on speech, whereas Mikkola is contemplative and literary and searches for the typical. Ojaharju has depicted male milieus, such as the prison, the harbor, boxing, seaman's life, the shipyard, and the saloon. His program is notable for remaining unaffected by the prescriptions offered by the politics of either the Left or the Right. He started as a social cartographer, making use of his experiences in various occupations. Oral tradition is the basis of his method; he tells stories that have been told before, perceiving life in the manner in which oral narrating colors it. His major work is a regional historical trilogy; despite succumbing to the trilogy fad of the 1970s, Ojaharju was able to make his work into an individualistic variation. The parts of his Vaasa trilogy have ironic titles: *Valkoinen kaupunki* (1976; White city), *Paremmassa maailmassa* (1978; In a better world), and *Maa kallis isien* (1982; Dear land of our fathers). Vaasa was the port of debarkation for the Jäger during the Civil War, the men who had received military training in Germany and whose role was decisive in the country's gaining of its independence. In 1918 Vaasa was also the seat of the White government, but the novel series describes the history of the century by skirting this official level and mocking it. Nonetheless, Ojaharju also keeps his distance from the Reds; his most important characters are proletarians with a greater love for adventurous freedom than for a common ideology. The series makes use of the tradition of the picaresque novel; it has also been compared with Latin American "magical realism." Ojaharju's socialism leans in the direction of Jack London: bold, loose storytelling.

Women Novelists
Women, above all—writers such as Kerttu-Kaarina Suosalmi, Anu Kaipainen, and Eeva Kilpi—renewed the novel with a middle-class basis and subject matter. They have the common denominator of a university education; Kaipainen and Kilpi earned master's degrees. All are experts at prose writing. Suosalmi's early poems were forgotten; in Kilpi's work, poetry has its own independent niche.

Pekka Tarkka has defined the style of Kerttu-Kaarina Suosalmi (1921–) as baroque: "ample, grand, multilayered, with the dynamics of rich details" (*Suomalaisia nykykirjailijoita,* 1989, 197–98). Suosalmi began her career in 1950 and 1952 with books of poems, but she was first noticed as a prose writer; together with the novel, the expansive short story is her favorite format. *Synti* (1957; The sin) contained two short stories that, under the influence of Kierkegaard, analyzed the existential states of women: sin and guilt. Her first novel, *Neitsyt* (1964; The virgin), pummels a group from an educational setting, a school; these people have become rigid, and the novel sets the searching individual free. Suosalmi's breakthrough came with the novel *Hyvin toimeentulevat ihmiset* (1969; Well-heeled people), which, at the time of its publication, was celebrated as the definitive critical description of the middle class. The main characters are a high school teacher, a writer, and a pastor's wife. Underneath their well-being lie malaise, impracticality, and the fear of losing out in economic matters to new groups better able to cope with contemporary life. The struggle is more materialistic than in works of the 1950s. Here middle-class cultural idealism is trampled by a rising materialism.

As a personality, Suosalmi is a powerful woman, an illuminator of passions and an analyzer of angst. She is also baroque in that feminism is alien in her world; it is a fashionable trend in which she appears to have no interest. Among her works, which consist of plays, books for children and youth, and short stories, three novels from the 1970s and 1980s stand out: *Jeesuksen pieni soturi* (1976; The little soldier of Jesus), *Onnen metsämies* (1982; Hunter for happiness), and *Ihana on Altyn-Köl* (1988; Beautiful is Altyn-Köl). The primary characters of the first are a junk dealer who directs and makes use of the flow of refuse from the material world; a strong businesswoman and a wife who reaches for Christian values are the important women in his life. *Onnen metsämies* is Suosalmi's principal work; the main character and narrator is a male writer, but his viewpoint is presented ironically and relativistically in this novel of many voices; its narration is Suosalmi's most inapproachable. The description of a nocturnal trip through evil and crime is headed by mottoes from Hamlet, but it has an intensity that also brings to mind Dostoyevsky, Tolstoy, and Chekhov, the writers who, according to Suosalmi, have influenced her the most (Haavikko, 180). *Ihana on Altyn-Köl* competes with *Onnen metsämies* as Suosalmi's most important achievement. The novel, whose setting is the Helsinki of the 1940s, rolls along passionately, painting a picture of the despair of the era and using a student girl as the narrator; in the reviews the girl was compared to Louhi, the Mistress of the North in the *Kalevala*.

Anu Kaipainen (1933–) invented a method for the novel which became her trademark: the crossing of mythology and contemporary problems. In the manner of the 1960s she was interested in society's ills and how to correct them, but she realized that this interest was not sufficient for the creation of a novel that would last. Counterpoint demands a countervoice; problems have to be made relative, correlated to or combined with tradition, legend, and myth. Success was dependent on the functioning at this dual level: after hits, there also came some misses.

Kaipainen's first novel described the family of a county medical officer (1960); it was followed by two novels about school. Her fourth book, *Arkkienkeli Oulussa* (1967; Archangel in Oulu), provided the breakthrough; in it Kaipainen found her method. The novel projects social dialogue of the 1960s, especially dialogue concerned with war and peace, to the time of the Russo-Finnish War of 1808-9; the tendency is pacifistic, in the spirit of the decade. For material, she uses the Ostrobothnian reminiscences of Sara Wacklin, Runeberg's *Fänrik Ståls sägner* (see chapter 7), and a fairy tale about a child who grew up in a barrel. The grotesque story line, in which a crazed girl takes as her husband the corpse of a soldier who has fallen in the war, is skillfully contrasted with the ideological polemics of the 1960s, for which the girl speaks — even in her madness she is a healthy cell in the world's body. Through naive and awkward language, the girl proclaims the author's values, peace, friendship, and love. *Magdaleena ja maailman lapset* (1969; Magdalene and the children of the world) reversed the arrangement of settings so that the basic time is the present accompanied by the past. The family of a pharmacist (the mythological counterpart is the family of Lazarus) and a radical county medical officer (Jesus) conduct an ideological conversation that, when read now, is no more convincing than a document of the superficial reformist optimism of the 1960s. Still, the counterpoint of the mythological and the current eras is skillfully carried out and in a manner opening new ways of expression for the novel.

In her next novel, *Surupukuinen nainen* (1971; The woman in mourning dress), Kaipainen made use of Shakespeare's *Midsummer Night's Dream* and urban legend, a modern story about a hitchhiker, dressed in black, who speaks of the otherworld and disappears. *On neidolla punapaula* (1973; The maiden with the red ribbon) attempts to combine three layers: the main plot, in which a Finnish woman and a young German hitchhiker find each other; a medieval ballad about the love between a merchant of the Hanseatic League and a burgher maiden; and concern about Finland's threatened position in a Europe uniting as an economic community. The combining of the layers and the reflections they cast on one another do not, however, function as well as in the previous novels. After producing a novel placed in a contemporary setting, *Naistentanssit* (1975; Ladies' dance), Kaipainen published *Kellomorsian* (1977; The bell bride), an attempt at the format of the miracle story. The main character is a girl who, through bell-shaped stigmata, receives a call to heal the world by singing. Kaipainen's next novel dealt with a historical figure: *Poimisin heliät hiekat* (1979; I'd gather the bright sands) tells about a woman rune singer, Larin Paraske (1833-1904).

In the 1980s Kaipainen published a series of three books of personal recollections, camouflaged as romans à clef.

Eeva Kilpi (1928–) has not renewed literary forms but, with the aid of her individualistic perception, has developed visions essentially arising from ingenuousness; they have had a resounding reception. Like Kaipainen, Kilpi is susceptible to ideological infection, but she is more centered and internalized. The feminist perspective became more defined in her examinations of the problems of an independent and single woman who lives in a family-oriented society; during the 1980s this changed into heated talk on behalf of nature, forests, and animals.

Twice Kilpi has described the journey of Karelian evacuees in novels. *Elämä edestakaisin* (1964; Life back and forth) was the principal work of her early period; *Elämän evakkona* (1983; Life's refugee) examines the subject matter from the distance of many years. Kilpi's prose in particular is autobiographical, varying between the formats of the novel, the short-story collection, and the confession. Her first book was an assembly of short stories focused on children, *Noidanlukko* (1959; Witchlock); it was followed by further collections in 1967, 1970, 1971, 1979, and 1986. The relationship of a single woman to her family and to men is a constant, varying theme, in which independence slowly grows into a liberation supported by strength. Among her novels, *Tamara* (1972; Eng. tr. 1978) drew international attention; its situation, reminiscent of *Lady Chatterley's Lover*, is a relationship between a paraplegic man and a woman who exercises her individual freedom. Tamara is the dispenser of love, a merciful granter of release from sexual hunger. A disadvantage of the situation described is its theoretical basis.

The poem collections *Laulu rakkaudesta* (1972; A song about love), *Terveisin* (1976; Greetings), *Ennen kuolemaa* (1982; Before death comes), and *Animalia* (1987) present Kilpi's ideologies and their development in a simple and easy form. The two first books, which give consolation to women oppressed by life, are effective popular poetry and were well received. Kilpi also uses laconic polemics. "Go ahead and believe that all is politics / I believe that each day is a story" was a sharp quip against overpoliticizing. To Paavo Haavikko's dictum, which has become crystallized into a popular saying, "Life belongs to institutions," Kilpi answered just as sharply, "Be your own institution." Her new attitude is manifested in the last two collections: love for the forest, animals, and nature, and hatred toward the civilization that is destroying them. The thin veil of fiction in the novels and short stories is removed in Kilpi's suite of essays, *Ihmisen ääni* (1976; The human voice), in her journals, *Naisen päiväkirja* (1978; A woman's diary), and in her recollections, *Talvisodan aika* (1989; Time of the Winter War), and *Välirauha, ikävöinnin aika* (1990; Interim peace, time of longing).

Rural and Urban Lives
It would be easy to make the mistake of taking Leo Kalervo (1924–) for a mere rural conservative; his skillful, albeit traditional, narrating emphasizes the values of country life and steadfast optimistic diligence. Human relationships are harmonious and warm, their conflicts can be resolved, the goals of life are clear, the action sensible and motivated. But Kalervo's central topic, the coming into conflict of this nonalienated lifestyle with the modern urban world, has increased in its contemporary meaning, especially if considered in conjunction with the ideological "green" movement of the 1980s and its search for alternatives.

Kalervo's principal work consists of eleven novels. *Malttamaton nuoruus* (1957; Impatient youth) described tuberculosis patients and their struggle toward health in a sanatorium. *Pyörille rakennettu* (1958; Built on wheels) compares a determined businessman and complacent bureaucrats; the author's sympathies lie with the entrepreneur, who meets his defeat in the challenges of the new era and afterward gains peace of mind. The main character in *Pelivara* (1961; Alternate action) has changed his occupation because of a war injury; the fact of being left behind gives the man a better view of the changes in society. The opponent is an unscrupulous businessman; their conflict is a variation of Kalervo's main theme, the collision of the old and the new. After the novel *Tyttö, poika ja voileivät* (1963; Girl, boy, and sandwiches) Kalervo published *Kiinnitys menneesyyteen* (1967; Adherence to the past), which approaches the collision of different eras in the light of a generational conflict between a father and a son. *Tuppisuu suomalainen* (1969; The taciturn Finn) is a monologue in colloquial language; a man who has moved from the countryside to the city speaks his mind.

The comparison of agrarian and urban lives continued, by means of collective description, in *Pihlamäkeläiset* (1974; The Pihlamäki people) and in *Maa kuuntelee sinua* (1977; Earth listens to you) from the perspective of an individual who recalls the postwar period of culture change. *Vuonna 1932* (1978; In 1932) analyzes, in the form of the family novel, a year of change when economic recession and right-wing political movements threatened the stability of the rural lifestyle. *Syömäköyhä* (1983; The poor glutton) is a lighter, humorous depiction of a large-scale lumber dealer. *Hyötysuhde* (1989; Efficiency) is a resigned description of an aging writer's creative crisis, of memories and of closing life's accounts. In addition to novels with sociohistorical emphasis, Kalervo has published a collection of short stories, an autobiography, and, as a skillful writer of dialogue, a series of radio plays as well.

Kalervo's ancestral roots and descriptive nuances allude to the province of Häme, but the province of Savo is a more visible focal point in the oeuvre of Eino Säisä (1935–88). His principal work is the above-mentioned six-volume novel series *Kukkivat roudan maat* (1971–80; Lands of frost are flowering), in which rural cultural change is the general theme and the private theme is the development of an exceptional individual, an artist, within this framework.

Säisä started with a romantic description of Gypsies, *Tummat* (1963; Brunettes). His second book, *Yöstä tullut* (1964; From the night), began a body of work that grew into six short-story collections. Of his six novels, *Afrikan tähti* (1987; Star of Africa) was his last. In the 1980s Säisä's work was characterized by his abandonment of fiction. *Aika saaressa* (1980; On the island) is a personal journal about the author's life in nature. *Kuvat kertovat* (1983; The pictures tell) is a collection of autobiographical reminiscences. In *Kevättä kohti* (1988; Toward spring) Säisä compiled some of his essays.

Säisä's body of short stories is uneven, despite its high points. At his best, Säisä continues the tradition of the childhood short stories. The novel series stands out as the undisputed zenith of his production. In the series he carries the description of a village community in Savo from the end of the war to 1963, simultaneously telling the story of the development of the autobiographical figure of Epi. The collective description of the beginning gradually gives way, and at the end the narration shifts the focus to Epi, who is growing up to be a writer. The focal points of narration about the village are the railroad station, the grade school, and the workers' hall. A fight for votes between the Agrarian Party and the People's Democrats is the main general conflict. Through his fictional representative, Epi, Säisä shows his sensitivity toward the nuances inherent in the events. The novel series has been compared with Joenpelto's Lohja series (Laitinen, 607–8); whereas the former describes the post–World War II era, the latter narrates the social history of the time after the First World War.

Timo K. Mukka (1944–73) gave a powerful description of Lapland, which was (and still is) like an exotic far-off land to southern Finns. Mukka combines naturalism and myth. His level of success varied, dividing the critics. His early death has been connected with uncomprehending treatment and with the destructiveness of the tabloid press of the 1970s. In 1974

Erno Paasilinna wrote a nonemotional and cutting biography of Mukka; it grew into an implicit accusation against the intolerance that exists in literary life toward what is different.

During a creative period that lasted six years Mukka was able to publish nine books. His first work was a novel, *Maa on syntinen laulu* (1964; The earth is a sinful song); the description combines Laestadian religiosity, the heat of love, and the fire of violence of northern people who are tied to harsh living conditions. *Tabu* (1965) described a young girl's sexual and religious awakening. *Täältä jostakin* (1965; From here somewhere) was a collage of the author's year as a draftee in military service. Ultimately, the pacifistic novel gets its power from a mythical wolf, the animal that parallels the main character. *Punaista* (1966; Red) contains Mukka's songs and confessional poems. The best of his novels is *Laulu Sipirjan lapsista* (1966; Song of Sipirja's children), a balanced and objective description of a village community; the novel compares two eras, the postwar and the present. Mukka's principal work in the short story is *Koiran kuolema* (1967; Dog's death), a collection of classically clear descriptions of human fate; in the stories death becomes a merciful power in the midst of life's overwhelming difficulties. A second collection of short stories in the following year did not achieve the same strength. The prose ballad *Kyyhky ja unikko* (1970; The dove and the poppy) was Mukka's last book, in which the main themes, love and death, once more reach their paradoxical union.

The career of Markku Lahtela (1936–80) was also cut off in its prime. Whereas Mukka was a writer of the periphery, Lahtela was an author of the center (Helsinki), a restless experimenter, a seeker of both ideologies and expressive forms. Symptomatically, Lahtela's first book was a fashionable experiment in form, the collage novel *Jumala pullossa* (1964; God in the bottle). At its publication his second book, *Se* (1966; It), became a famous non-novel, a combination of noncontinuous texts that shattered the forms of the genre. The subject matter consisted of the questions of the 1960s, and the disintegration of the form was a manifestation of the disintegration of a world view and the breaking of established patterns. Lahtela's work toward the end of the 1960s closely followed the ideological themes and arguments of the times; his middle period led to a synthesis, his so-called human trilogy (1971–73). The trilogy's first two volumes examine, in the form of a proclamation, the new human being made possible by the findings of research in biology and psychology and by the educational and emotional revolution of the time. The third volume, *Matias Tallgrenin yksityiselämä* (The private life of Matias Tallgren), pointed to the destructiveness of standardized practices through a telling counterexample and a medical report.

The period of ascendance in Lahtela's career began with the novel *Yksinäinen mies* (1976; Lonesome man), a book that parallels *Se;* it showed the maturing of thought and the victory of artistic conceptualization over dogmatic declaration. The adult is explained through his childhood, in the manner of psychoanalysis; the failure of the principal character is correlated with the injustices he experienced during his formative years. The rise in Lahtela's career was also evident in the novel *Sirkus* (1978; The circus), in which the author moved even further from realism and from the mixing of philosophy with fiction. Imagination, capricious combinations, and free correlations create an image of the modern world. The same goal was given to the posthumously published, unfinished *Hallitsija* (1980; The ruler), in which a former dictator teaches about the essence of power. The work pointed toward new possibilities of irony and satire for Lahtela. A collection of philosophical lyric was also published posthumously; like an earlier poem collection, *Rakastan sinua, musta tuuli* (1975; I love you, black wind), it demonstrated that poetry was not Lahtela's strong suit.

Another author struck down in what may have been his prime was Lassi Sinkkonen (1937–76), from a Viipuri refugee family and "the child of a Red"; Sinkkonen knew the worker's world of Helsinki from his own experience in various jobs and from his membership in the Communist Party—toward which, however, he maintained some critical distance. His literary career began in the lyric—he was often described as an offspring of Arvo Turtiainen—and his collections of verse, written in a language colored with Helsinki slang, bear this description out; they were *Harhaileva aamupäivä* (1965; Meandering forenoon), *Väljät vaattet* (1966; Loose clothes), *Sinusta huomiseen* (1967; From you to tomorrow), *Meitä kohti* (1968; Toward us), and *Minä, maani, maailmassa* (1969; Me, my country, in the world). Near the end of this intense lyric phase he turned to the novel, in which form he received much critical attention and (in a record four out of five cases) quick translation into Swedish, so that he became, for a short time, one of Finnish-language literature's most accessible figures in Scandinavia at large. *Sumuruisku* (1968; Spray gun) was the grimy story of a young man who finds work as a painter at an automobile assembly plant; its notable element was not so much the depiction of wretched conditions (and a lack of solidarity among the employees) but the fact that the business is owned by a Soviet parent firm and that the exploitative managers are members of the Communist Party. Instead of protesting, the sometime operator of the spray gun is promoted and, in the favorite term of the 1960s, "co-opted," becoming a comfortable link in the hypocritical apparatus.

Sinkkonen's *Solveigin laulu* (1970; Solveig's song) was a best seller: the representatives of three female generations captured the public's interest — a strong paternal grandmother, a heartless and brutal mother, and a spunky daughter, Solveig, who has the narrative voice. Readers were also excited by Sinkkonen's frank reproduction of insulting family discourse and, in the grandmother's case, were particularly prepared to love her as a counterpart, from the city, of Paavo Rintala's peasant grandmother in the latter's much-read tetralogy; Saara, the daughter-in-law, was an equally worthy object of audience mass hatred. Trapped by his own successful formula, Sinkkonen tried to break out with the semiautobiographical artist's novel *Mutta minulla ei olisi rakkautta* (1972; But if I had not love), but he returned to Solveig, the detestable Saara, and Solveig's boyfriend in *Solveig ja Jussi* (1973; Solveig and Jussi). Sinkkonen's last book was *Sirkkelisirkus: Balladi* (1975; The circular-saw circus: Ballad), in which his first-person narrator was as put-upon and resilient as Solveig, but with a difference. Born in Viipuri in 1929 of mixed Finnish-Russian parentage, and growing up in Helsinki, Mitya is tormented by neighborhood children, abused by an alcoholic father and an uncle, protected by a mother who, however, loses her mobility and her wits as a result of her husband's brutality (and dies horribly in Nikkilä Asylum), and sheltered by a kindly blacksmith. The victim of a brain fever as a child, Mitya is slightly simple-minded. A kind of Finnish Forrest Gump, he often flees to an imaginary world inhabited by such figures from history as the martyred founder of Finland's Christianity, Saint Henry, the peasant Lalli (the missionary's murderer, who is remarkably pleasant), Marshal Mannerheim, and General Lothar Rendulic, commander of the German forces during the Lapland War of 1944–45. Yet unlike Forrest, Mitya — thanks to the generosity of the blacksmith, who shares his "housekeeper" with the youth — is sexually active, and the orgiastic eroticism, burlesque violence, and scatology of this attempt to flee from programmatic social realism laid Sinkkonen open once more to the charge of literary pandering, or providing, in Pekka Tarkka's unkind phrase, entertainment for the proletariat.

Two writers whose careers began in the late 1960s may also deserve attention here, since each in her own way contributed to the social criticism growing out of that decade. Aulikki Oksanen (1944–) began by assailing the establishment from a somewhat unusual angle, in her capacity as actress, singer, and writer of her own leftist texts. (In 1973, celebrating the fiftieth anniversary of the official naming of the Soviet Union and the twenty-fifth of the signing of the Pact of Friendship and Aid between the Soviet Union and Finland, she wrote "Avaruuslintu" [The space bird] with the devout Communist Matti Rossi.) For political and personal reasons, she could not resist the temptation of having a go at the novel, which she did with the autobiographical *Tykkimiehen syli* (1968; The cannoneer's embrace). Oksanen's father was an elementary school teacher, a calling Oksanen also briefly followed; in the novel a young woman leaves the pious atmosphere and boredom of her village for the big city and its bohemian circles, including, of course, the fiery embraces of the would-be artist of the title. The didactic element in Oksanen's production could be easily spotted in *Isosisko ja pikkuveli* (1973; Big sister and little brother). Having lost her own beloved little brother, the singer Aino feels sympathy for the bullied or abused children she meets; to one of her charges she tells the story of two little Vietnamese boys blown up by a land mine. A speck appears in the sky; "perhaps it was the cry from a child, the seed of a song which flew as far as the world reached." As in Sinkkonen's case, these early novels earned Oksanen a Swedish public in translation.

As Oksanen grew older, her programmatic optimism — her conviction that a better world would come, as soon as political systems were changed — decreased. A grim reality took its place, as in the short stories of *Entiset vyötäröt* (1986; Former waistlines), in which the boredom of industrial suburbs is broken only by drunken squabbles or crimes of violence. In the novel *Henkivartija* (1990; The bodyguard) former radicals are variously intoxicated or overweight, and the supernatural makes a surprising appearance: the hapless hero is repeatedly saved from death by a crow, which bears the soul of his sometime girlfriend, a suicide. But in fact, this swerve in Oksanen's career is not so surprising after all; just as her sometime affection for an exemplary eastern neighbor had strong aspects of the wish-dream, so she has had a weakness (which has produced some of her most interesting writing) for a magical Finnish past: see her fantastic novel *Alumiinipaita* (1984; The aluminum shirt).

Sprung from a social ambience altogether unlike Oksanen's, Tytti Parras (1943–) lambasted the well-to-do middle class, but with a certain lightheartedness: the heroine tries hard to break out of a stagnant home milieu in the short novel *Jojo* (1968), which, with its thoughtless sexual pairings and painful abortions, was quickly translated (1970), as in the case of Sinkkonen and Oksanen. Parras pursued the same line with *Rakkaat* (1970; Dear ones), in which the youth collective, flourishing at the time as an alternative to the nuclear family, makes its literary appearance; another possibility for escape of the dissatisfied young, the journey, already used in *Jojo*, reappears in *Turkkilainen satula* (1975; The Turkish saddle), which takes place in the growing Turkish sections of a north German city (i.e., Bremen). *Pieni hyvinkasvatettu tyttö* (1978; A little, well-brought-up girl) returns to the background of the first novel and its sterilely refined and bilingual world. In 1993 Parras made a comeback as a special kind of social critic in *Vieras* (The stranger), directed at the self-imposed hardships of summertime Baltic sailors, registered by a pleasure boat's sensitive and skeptical woman skipper.

Finally, some prose writers' central ambition was channeled away from the novel's form. Hannu Mäkelä (1934–) writes rapidly and publishes in abundance. Symptomatically, he made his debut with two novels, *Matkoilla kaiken aikaa* (1965; Constantly traveling) and *Kylliksi: tai Liikaa* (1965; Enough: Or too much). A young man's initiation rites, his travel abroad, and his time as a military conscript join the works as a pair. In the series of Mäkelä's novels the most memorable is *Vetsikko* (1988), which shows the author's ability to employ stream of consciousness and to use allusion and written language in the manner of thoughts and the spoken word. The topic is the struggle of a man who jumps off the wheel of the business world, with its concomitant confinement and dependence. Mäkelä began a series of poem collections in 1966 with *Sinisen taivaan, harmaan jään* (Blue sky, gray ice). An alternating movement of joy and pain, with both universal and private backgrounds, is the trademark of his poetry. Mäkelä's expression has become more precise and the nuances more sure from one collection to the next, the most notable high points being *Synkkyys, pohjaton, niin myös iloni, onneni* (1976; Bottomless darkness, so also my joy, my happiness) and *Unelma onnesta numero 5* (1985; A dream of happiness number 5). Attaining various levels of success, his poetry reached the twelfth collection in 1989. In his plays Mäkelä favors historical subject matter and major national personalities (K. A. Gottlund and Eino Leino, among others). Three plays were published as a compilation with the title *Tähtirinta* (1988; Starbreast); many radio plays have appeared in anthologies. The principal part of Mäkelä's work in children's literature (see chapter 11) is a series of three books (1973–75, combined into one volume in 1976 and 1986) that tell about the individualist "Herra Huu" (Mr. Boo). Mäkelä is also the author of many commissioned works, from poems to short stories to aphorisms.

Martti Joenpolvi (1936–) can be compared with Pentti Haanpää; both wrote novels that confirm that their natural genre is the short story. Joenpolvi was late in finding mastery. He started with novels; the first one was *Kevään kuusi päivää* (1959; Six days of spring), the story of a young man's development. Its "intense grayness" brings Toivo Pekkanen to Pekka Tarkka's mind (*Suomalaisia nykykirjailijoita*, 1989, 67). Joenpolvi's narratives were expansive at first but became more concise in the 1970s. The basic stage for his novels of the 1960s is the single-family home, the people who live in it and are tied down by it. The subject matter becomes freer in his 1970s novels. *Yö jona jäät vahvistuivat* (1971; The night in which the ice thickened) follows a family confirmation party as it is experienced by an intellectual with a blue-collar background; instead of external subject matter, the focus is on the personality of the main character. *Kaikki alennuksella* (1973; Everything at a discount) defends, in a Dostoyevskian manner, the advantages of being an outsider and the ability, enhanced by distance, to observe the world. *Marmoriuni* (1977; Marble dream) compares the solutions to life's problems of a Social Democratic pastor, who leads an orderly life, with those of a restless writer.

Joenpolvi's two novels of the 1980s are different from each other. *Valkoinen huvimaja* (1980; White pleasure house) suffers from both the lack of focus and the formalized search for symbols. The main character in *Tupakkakauppiaan moraali* (1986; Tobacco merchant's morals) has a dual personality; the sensitive and vulnerable self has developed a hard shell for its protection. Through two time layers the novel is connected with the life of the writer's father: Joenpolvi is able to make the conciseness of the short story work in the novel's form.

Joenpolvi's shift toward the short story began in 1967 with the collection of two mininovels, *Johanneksen leipäpuu* (Johannes's livelihood). The theme of the title story is the denial of truth in one's life. Joenpolvi has published five subsequent collections of genuine short stories: *Kuparirahaa* (1969; Copper coins), *Yksinäisyys* (1975; Loneliness), *Kauan kukkineet omenapuut* (1982; Apple trees in bloom), *Haastemies* (1984; Process server), *Pronssikausi* (1988; Bronze age), and *Terveessä ruumiissa* (1990; In sound body). They make up his most lasting work; the style of the writing has been connected to both Chekhov and Maupassant. The expression is laconic, with multiple layers of meaning; surprises and turns of events guarantee the reader's pleasure. The targets of universal experience are anxiety and joy; the typical development has the latter break through in the midst of the former, to result in a synthesis, which always contains new inventions. A danger for Joenpolvi lies in his becoming mired in angst, depression, and an exaggeration of the burdens of the past. But when he succeeds in breaking this basic atmosphere into joy, zaniness, or fantasy, his work is sovereign.

Theater

Arvo Salo was the author of far and away the most discussed theatrical text of the 1960s, *Lapualaisooppera* (1966; The Lapua opera), with music by Kaj Chydenius (1939–). This work is a Brechtian portrayal of the homegrown semifascistic movement of the early 1930s, with special attention to Vihtori Kosola (1884–1936), "the Ostrobothnian Mussolini," and complete with a chorus of Blackshirts. (In the congenial translation of Lars Huldén and N.-B. Stormbom, the "opera" also had considerable success on the Swedish-language stage.) Juhani Niemi has investigated the pronounced "documentary" element in the text, calculating that about 15 percent of the dialogue consists of quotations from memoirs and the like, and the Chydenius score likewise makes use of familiar tunes (workers' songs, songs of the "White" Ostrobothnians in Mannerheim's army from the Civil War of 1918, songs of the Reds in the same conflict, Ostrobothnian folk songs, hymns). Drama historian Irmeli Niemi, not uncritical toward the play in its capacity of propaganda drama, noted, "The traits of the conservatives are often parodied and grotesque, those of the Reds are sentimental or idealized" (p. 181). Others, however, thought the play (or operetta?) lacked close political analysis, and the author himself hinted in hindsight that it may have been too gentle, especially in its concluding plea for reconciliation. But in its day it was a theatrical event of the first magnitude.

Salo's subsequent stage works have been similarly oriented toward an argumentative use of the Finnish past. *Yks perkele, yks enkeli* (1985; A devil, an angel) lines up many great names of the Golden Age and its aftermath — Snellman, Runeberg, Fredrik Cygnaeus, August Ahlqvist, Yrjö Koskinen, Kaarlo Bergbom, jurist Jakob Oskar Forsman (1839–99), man of letters Emil Nervander (1840–1914), and nobleman, soldier, and official Johan Mauritz Nordenstam (1802–82), Ahlqvist's biological father — around Aleksis Kivi and the woman in his life, Charlotta Lönnqvist. (The title is the first line of a well-known confessional poem by "A. Oksanen," the nom de plume of the scholar and critic Ahlqvist, whose savage attacks on *Seitsemän veljestä* helped destroy Kivi's delicate mental equilibrium [see chapter 3].) A year later Salo turned to very recent events in his giant revue (again with music) of the political players in the era of the late Urho Kekkonen (some seventy of them, not least the president himself), *Vallan miehet* (1986; The men of power). Such politically conditioned spectacles can, of course, age rapidly; witness the fate of the once highly praised musical on Lyndon B. Johnson and the Kennedy assassination, Barbara Garson's *McBird* (1965), or Robert Brustein's *Watergate Classics* (1973). Salo's works on earlier periods may have a greater chance of revival. Particularly in the Ahlqvist-Kivi play Salo joined what had become something of a major strain in Finnish theatrical writing, the biographical or biographical-historical drama. For example, *Viimeiset kiusaukset* (1960; The last temptations), on the evangelist Paavo Ruotsalainen (1777–1852), by Lauri Kokkonen (1921–85), turned into an opera by Jonas Kokkonen (1921–96), became an international success. Recently, the dramatization of Bo Carpelan's *Axel* (see chapter 9), on Axel Carpelan and Sibelius, has continued the tradition, not a surprising one in a country as aware of its history and its great figures as Finland has been.

Jussi Kylätasku (1943–) started as a poet; his three collections (1966, 1967, 1969) have become dated. His romans à clef have not fared much better with their satire of leftist intellectuals, *Revari* (1975; The revisionist), *Mona-Lisa, rakkaudella* (1978; Mona Lisa, with love), and *Jalmarin kirja* (1983; Jalmari's book), the last of which has the subtitle "video." Kylätasku found himself as an author in the dramatic forms: the stage, the film, and the radio play. His strength lies in his ability to make an adaptation between the selected topic and the medium and to replace the task of self-expression with general demands. In 1970 and 1971 he wrote two farces for the stage, which dealt with the traffic and military worlds, as well as screenplays for the films of director Risto Jarva (1934–77). Among Kylätasku's best dramatic texts, many have been composed for the radio theater; the radio-play version has often surpassed the one for the stage. *Matti Väkevä* (1972; Strong Matti) is a verse drama about a topic of national interest, the fate of a Finnish immigrant in Sweden. The radio plays *Hentomielinen Hilarius* (1974; Tenderhearted Hilarius) and *Uuni* (1979; The stove) are also memorable; the subject matter in each is crime. The stage play *Haapoja* (1989) describes a stereotypical Finnish murderer, a primitive being who confronts the great reformer of Finnish prisons, Mathilda Wrede (1864–1928). *Runar ja Kyllikki* (1974; Runar and Kyllikki) took its topic from Finland's most notorious sexual murder; *Maaria Blomma* (1980; Eng. tr. *Mary Bloom*, 1989) was based on the figure of Maria Åkerblom (1898–1981), an evangelist and the founder of a religious revival movement. In these, his principal works, the author most clearly presents the trinity of sexuality, violence, and religion, which becomes crystallized as his perception of the moving forces of the Finnish soul. Kylätasku's scripts are difficult to come by; they have been published in anthologies and magazines, not as books. Although the Finns love the theater, they do not read plays, at least according to publishers' surveys.

Journalism and Essay
Jouni Lompolo (1936–), writing under the pen name Origo, rose in the course of the 1960s to become Finland's leading newspaper columnist; his position has been threatened only by Bisquit (Seppo Ahti). Although Origo has been called a successor to Olli (see chapter 4), his quality as a

columnist is different; not until Bisquit does the verbal anarchy favored by Olli return to column writing, and then it is wilder than before. Origo writes ordinary, even somewhat dry prose, hiding his explosions beneath a smooth surface. His method is to lead current topics of conversation beyond that fine border where their ultimate senselessness and grotesque nature come into view.

In his collections of the 1960s, which number more than half a dozen, Origo was the young generation's voice, mocking established values and attitudes. The pace of his publications slowed down in the 1970s, and parody became his technique; the basic patterns — news presentations and interviews — came naturally to a newspaper columnist. As in Olli's case, one of Origo's strong subgenres has been causerie aphorisms. The spitting of social ills on the column writer's lance has diminished with time; the inconveniences of everyday life have taken more space. The frank, rather leftist political slant has sometimes made his statements seem single-minded. At his best, Origo is a master of the minefield of language; he balances on the edge between the principal literary genres and the mocking of them.

Erno Paasilinna (1935–) is one of the figures of genuine power in Finnish literature, a merciless critic of social inertia, of hierarchies and standardized practices. He is himself an example of the "nonwriter," a type created by him, who aims at making a quick impact and, for the most part, discards fiction. Paasilinna has written only one book that can be characterized as a novel; a more correct definition might rather be a satire in the spirit of the eighteenth century. *Kadonnut armeija* (1977; The lost army) describes a troop of soldiers who have become lost, from both their own positions and the enemy: this develops into a metaphor for lost civilization. Two hefty volumes that make up the history of Petsamo, *Kaukana maailmasta* (1980; Far away from the world) and *Maailman kourissa* (1983; Mishandled by the world), deviate in their length from Paasilinna's main line. The Petsamo region, on the Arctic Ocean, belonged to Finland during the years between the two world wars. Personal experiences, exhaustive interviews, and research guarantee the factual subject matter in the book; Paasilinna's vision, however, is far from calm. By letting the facts speak for themselves, Paasilinna constructs an image of the fate of a people and culture anchored in nature as victims of the "colonial policies" of technologically superior areas of Finland.

Paasilinna is adept at expansive narrating, without losing his sharpness and irony; but in a total consideration of his work, he is above all a master of short prose. His basic texts consist of diverse genres: the short story, the humoresque, the newspaper column, the essay, and the satire. These exist in both pure form and mixed. Since the first collection, *Kylmät hypyt*

(1967; Cold jumps), nine others have been published. Paasilinna has been called "the reviler of the republic" and "the official dissident." Most visible is his critical attitude; his own perception is not clear-cut or simple. It contains anarchy, albeit more in the nuances than in theory, and socialism, although more in spirit than in dogma. Perhaps the strongest fixed idea is individualism, the uncompromising defense of an individual's freedom. Paasilinna's techniques include slander as well as an irony in which the attack is similarly heated but hidden in an inverted form. His prose can be characterized as staccato and aphoristic; indeed, he has published two collections of aphorisms (1977, 1986), as well as aphorisms with additions culled from his prose writings: *Lausui alustaja, joka korosti* (1989; Stated the speaker, who emphasized). Paasilinna's aphorism makes a direct, aggressive claim: it runs the danger of dullness, but for the most part, the message of the thought and the clarity of the polished expression come together as one.

Best Sellers
A correct picture of the literary arena (and of reading as a leisure-time activity) cannot be seen if the focus is only on authors of high quality. Kalle Päätalo (1919–) and Kaari Utrio (1942–) are literary phenomena, despite the circumstance that the rites of people of so-called refined tastes include a wrinkling of noses when these two names are mentioned. Päätalo's genre is the autobiographical novel, Utrio's the historical romance. The first one maps the masculine experience, the second the female, but both authors' readership is largely composed of women. Päätalo is a building construction supervisor by training; Utrio holds a master's degree. Päätalo made his debut in 1958 and from 1960 to 1969 published his first major work, the Koillismaa series, nearly three thousand pages long; two volumes of the series have been turned into English by the distinguished Finnish-American translator Richard Impola—the first, *Koillismaa* (1960; Eng. tr. *Our Daily Bread*, 1990), and the third, *Myrsky Koillismaassa* (1963; Eng. tr. *Storm over the Land*, 1993). It used the novel form, but Päätalo changed to straight autobiography in the Iijoki series, which began in 1971 and was completed in 1995, when the twenty-fifth volume was published. Most likely the series is the world's longest autobiography. It depicts a Finnish man's journey in enormous detail, a feature that has alienated the more literary audience; but other readers have vicariously experienced his suffering, his persistence, and his successes with such enthusiasm that there are sufficient buyers for the one hundred thousand volumes of each first printing. A great number of Finnish families make the reading of a new Päätalo book one of their Christmas rituals.

Kaari Utrio started publishing historical romances in 1968; *Vendela* in 1989 was the seventeenth. The past lives in the books as a colorful and violent drama of passions; the perspective is that of the female characters. The depictions of specific historical areas, especially in the books whose events take place in Finland's Middle Ages, are full of facts and aim at objectivity. Both Päätalo and Utrio have received unfair criticism; in the former case, for the slow pace of the narration; in the latter, for stereotypical entertainment, the so-called housewives' soft pornography. But both have been accorded notable accolades, Päätalo from Eila Pennanen and Utrio from Erkki Mäkinen, the historical dramatist for television; literary officialdom has also acknowledged the value of these writers: Päätalo received the state's literary award in 1971 and Utrio in 1972. Nor should the historical novels — concentrated on that richest of poetic landscapes, Karelia — of Laila Hietamies (1938–), well known as the breadwinner of a distinguished publishing house, Otava, be forgotten; they began in 1972 with *Lehmusten kaupunki* (The lindens' city) and now number in the thirties. Like their Finland-Swedish opposite numbers by Barbara Winckelmann, they are based on solid research and do not fall into that infamous subcategory of the historical novel, the bodice ripper. In 1988, justly, Hietamies won the Karelia Prize "for the advancement of Karelian culture" as a reward for *Valamon yksinäinen* (1987; The hermit of Valamo). As in the case of Viipuri, Karelia's capital, a bilingual anthology could easily be put together from the creative literature about that Karelian monastery, a religious *locus magicus*.

Poetry of the 1970s
At the turn between the 1960s and the 1970s a change took place in poetic ideology and expression; the focus began to shift from the universal to the individual, from politics to close human relationships, from the city to nature, from the public square to the home. The first sign was Pentti Saarikoski's small-form poetry toward the end of the 1960s; the second, Väinö Kirstinä's collection *Talo maalla* (1969; A house in the country). The change moved in two directions: toward the everyday life of the private individual and toward an idyllic nature. The first trend was most visible in books written by women. Eila Pennanen's only poem collection (1970) and Eeva Kilpi's first one (1972) gave signs of the change; Helena Anhava, too, who takes a stand on general issues, retains her roots in this trend. The other branch was that of the nature idyll: a small, playful, lovable poem that gives nature a soul: Risto Rasa (1954–) served as a forerunner who drew others along in his naivistic wake. The title of his debut collection, *Metsän seinä on vain vihreä ovi* (1971; The wall of the forest is only a green door), tells much

about the drift of his lyric work. This trend did not have much lasting value, although ideologically it shows that attention was directed to what was most endangered.

The poets of outstanding stature and permanent worth who began in the 1970s do not quite partake of the aims that have been seen as typical of the era. In addition to Helena Anhava, they are Kai Nieminen, Sirkka Turkka, Rakel Liehu, and Ilpo Tiihonen. Nieminen, an independent and even mischievous poet, was first excited by China, then by Japan. Turkka has developed a capricious style of poetry with powerful and dense images. Liehu's independent poetic expression is built on the basis of Christian perception. Tiihonen brings his poems from free form closer to poetic meter. Several other names, providing proof of the diversity of poetical form and even about the debates of that decade, could be added, but only the abundant, romantic work of Tommy Tabermann, often accused of banality; the poetry of Arja Tiainen, which mocks the conventional, male-centered lifestyle; and Arto Melleri's individualistic-romantic poetry, in opposition both to the political activist and to nature-centered idyllic poetry, are mentioned here. It is possible to suspect the work of this trio of being ideological *Gebrauchslyrik,* or "utility poetry," in which the ideas of some group or some manner of experience are given voice; such pieces have their place in the transformation of literary ideologies, but their lasting artistic power is still unsure at the present time.

The poetry of Helena Anhava (1925–) speaks for the family, the sensitive human being, and private life from a mother's perspective. She has published six poem collections. The titles of the first and third one define the message, *Murheellisen kuullen on puhuttava hiljaa* (1971; Speak softly in the presence of grief) and *Kysy hiljaisuudelta itseäsi* (1974; Ask silence about yourself). Anhava defends nuances and emotions. She mocks the dogmatic, the ideological, the assumption of responsibility for the world on the level of words, seeing in this a blindness to the needs that exist in the immediate environment. The background of her thought is a childhood in a middle-class family during the First Republic, whose values were destroyed by World War II during the writer's youthful years. Anhava attacked the leftist cultural front of the 1970s, which was noisy and at least seemingly influential; she defended the middle-class values, perhaps displaying some exaggeration in the need for self-protection.

Anhava's poems often come close to a spoken opinion, a contemplation, or a lyric of ideas. Indeed, the title of her second collection was *Vuorosanoja* (1973; Dialogue). She has included maxims in her collections and has also published an ample collection of aphorisms, *Sivusta* (1976; From the sidelines). The aphorisms progress serially, apparently stimulated by Paavo Haavikko's *Puhua, vastata, opettaa* (1972; Speak, answer, teach); proverbs and the Bible may also be among their influences. The aphorisms are usually laconic and straightforward, sometimes more verbose in their explications. *Sivusta* wages an ideological war against the left wing of the 1970s, often keenly but sometimes angrily and with intentional misunderstanding. On one hand, Anhava defends the individual against formulized models of reasoning; on the other hand, these models are perceived to pertain specifically to left-wing, rarely to right-wing, thought. In the 1980s the group that irritated Anhava the most had grown quieter and had taken defensive positions; correspondingly, Anhava's poetry developed in a more universal direction. "I am a Christian. I am a Socialist. I am a humanist. What is that? Bestowing knighthood on oneself." Anhava's stature in the Finnish lyric is indicated by the fact that Otava has brought out her collected poems to date, *Runot 1971–1990*.

Kai Nieminen began in 1971, the same year as Anhava, but since he was born in 1950, he belongs to a different generation. The family names of both writers are well known in literary circles: Kai Nieminen is Pertti Nieminen's son; Helena Anhava is Tuomas Anhava's wife. The son seems to have inherited from his father both a similarity of attitude and an interest in ancient Asiatic cultures. After his China period Kai Nieminen fixed his interest on Japan, whose classical literature he has translated. The father and the son are somewhat epicurean, worshipers of the private life; a detached and mocking attitude toward the demands of the everyday world stamps their work. Nieminen has published ten poem collections; his individualistic voice is distinguishable from the very beginning. He is not infected by the customary Finnish ideological arguments; he examines life from too great a distance in time and space for that. The frame of reference in ancient Asia provides a perspective for his own experiences from which the arguments in his tiny Nordic country seem unimportant.

From this starting point Nieminen succeeds in writing poetry that is intellectually clever, clear in thought, and rich in experience. The standard poetic vocabulary and attitudes are absent. He employs the arrogance of an Eastern hermit against those who would explain the world:

Everyone knows
what is right and what is wrong;
but who explains
what this what is.

His relationship to the supreme authorities of the East and the West is relaxed and inquiring, consciously irreverent: "I understood buddha, I understood jesus / I understood other people as well." Nieminen's period of study in Japan during 1979-80 produced two translations of the classical haiku poet Basho into Finnish and brought themes of the trip and the return home into his own work. The collections of the late 1980s "develop the vegetative wisdom of the lighthearted family hermit toward delicious irony and self-irony" (Tarkka, *Suomalaisia nykykirjailijoita*, 1989, 120). His latest collection, *Keinuva maa* (1989; Rocking earth), contains, as a new feature, an extensive section called "Explanations and Complaints," which contains parodistic adaptations of Eastern learning.

The voice of Sirkka Turkka (1939–) is more powerful than Nieminen's and her expression more dense. In her nine collections (1973–89) Turkka has created a poetic world that, from the beginning, received critical praise but was discovered by the public only slowly. Turkka's poetry advances with quick surprise shifts, aiming at the expression in words not only of a stream of consciousness but also of creatively mad mental associations. Her second book, *Valaan vatsassa* (1975; In the belly of the whale), turned to prose as a means of expression and has been labeled a prose fantasy; it could be called a series of prose poems but is actually designated a "narrative." In a score of short fragments the book describes the reality of the principal character, who is also the narrator; the connection of reality to the myth of Jonah has been interpreted as a submergence into the world's body. Turkka's next two collections consisted of prose poems, *Minä se olen* (1976; It is I) and *Yö aukeaa kuin vilja* (1978; The night opens like a wheatfield). In her poems Turkka's own world is conceptualized and defined; it consists of a mythology filled by biblical deities, marginal humans, and animals. The first-named are understood in a childlike and richly concrete manner, whereas the description of people is almost misanthropic; tenderness and love "shift" from humans to animals. Turkka's basic perceptions include the unity of nature, in which the human is a deviate who "forgot the animals' golden eyes, the green humility of the plants" and "totally lost himself."

The collections from the 1980s increase the volume of Turkka's idiosyncratically powerful voice. Her penultimate collection, *Tule takaisin, pikku Sheba* (1986; Come back, little Sheba), was the first poetry collection to receive the Finlandia Literary Prize, established in 1985. The prize committee praised the collection as "dense, intensive, and touching poetry, in which some basic feelings of what it is to be human receive a wild, individualistic expression." *Voiman ääni* (1989; The voice of power) secures

Turkka's position as a poet; zoomorphic religion, the perception of life intensified by sorrow and death, and the mad gallop of fantasy create an expression that does not bring to mind anyone else in Finnish literature.

Rakel Liehu (1936–) starts from a Christian standpoint, although she is not a true religious poet, any more than Niilo Rauhala. European-Christian philosophy as Liehu's frame of reference corresponds to Rauhala's Laestadianism. Liehu's poetry contains few direct allusions to Christian thought, whose structure and posing of problems, however, are to be felt throughout her work. Her first collections emerged during a time that was overly political and dominated by Marxism. Nevertheless, her audience increased quickly; her poems of the 1970s were published as a collection in 1978, and the volume had a second printing in 1981. In 1986 Liehu received the Finnish Lutheran Church's literary award. The committee saw as the poet's themes "human suffering, the reality of evil, the dialectics of despair and hope, but also grace and love in all their dimensions." Dogma and ritual are the most distant religious spheres for Liehu; the closest are mysticism, ethics, and religious philosophy. The reality of the spiritual is present in everyday life for those who have the ability to receive it, and life is life only in connection with other humans, in the consideration and the helping of others. Liehu's ponderings about the human role are organized by theology and philosophy, although their share has become more subdued as her work has advanced, giving way to more observable reality. Her seventh collection, *Joki sepittää minulle* (1987; The river explains to me), expresses by its very title the change of focus from the self to the world, as does *Sininen Lasarus* (1990; Blue Lazarus).

Liehu cultivates several types of poems. The shortest are close to epigrams or aphoristic flashes about the paradoxes of religion; proselike stories or episodes and dogmatic explorations serve as their opposites. The northern Finnish world of nature, its ruggedness and its light, provides the central imagery. Thematically, her poetry stretches between the joy and the transitoriness of all phenomena: "This world is only on loan to my eyes." Liehu has also tested her strength with the novel. Her first, *Seth Mattsonin tarina* (1976; The story of Seth Matson), describes a man who has his roots in a rural childhood, whose present is formed by an alienated life in the city, and whose possibility for freedom lies in religious experience. In its form the book consists of the man's monologue; critics have correlated its perception with existentialism. Liehu's second novel, *Punainen ruukku* (1980; The red crock), is a story of love and is carried out more experimentally.

Ilpo Tiihonen (1950–) started in 1975 with *Sarkunmäen palo* (The Sarkunmäki fire); by 1994 he had published ten collections. Tiihonen has cautiously returned to the poem the meter and rhyming that modernism scrapped. He even approaches the song but deforms it, breaking the meter and melody into a confusion without rules. With Tiihonen, the tradition of classical mastery of form changes into "a street urchin's bawling" (Tarkka, *Suomalaisia nykykirjailijoita*, 1989, 200). Mayakovsky and Fröding, the classical writers of Russia and Sweden, are thought to be his starting points: Tiihonen published Fröding adaptations in Finnish translation in 1986. Among his domestic models, P. Mustapää is most clearly recognizable; the coming together of emotion and comedy often brings Mustapää to mind, and the union of roughness and tenderness reminds one of Arvo Turtiainen. Tiihonen is the farthest away from the nature poetry of imagery, but he does not cultivate materials from mass media either. Railroads and communities near them, towns big and small, and their cafes and taverns are his theaters. Through the synthesis of the romantic and the naturalistic, he expresses his sympathy toward the common person. He uses slang, phrases from foreign languages, and allusions to the classics. He is aware of tradition but does not act reverently toward it. References to tradition make the starting points comical and ironic, showing the changes that have taken place in urban Finnish colloquial expression. Tiihonen takes his wordsmith's skill to its extreme and beyond in *Ei-Kaj Plumps: Hyppyjä Helsinkiin* (1989; *Ei-Kaj Plumps:* Hops to Helsinki), a collection of themes from the capital. The poems are melodically and rhythmically pounding, but they also provide superb nonsense rhymes. Without having much meaning, they play with and tease the possibilities of language and poem.

Arja Tiainen (1947–), misleadingly or aptly, has been compared with America's Anne Sexton. In Finnish literature she bears some resemblance in her tough bluntness to her contemporary, Aulikki Oksanen, although she is less burdened by a political agenda. Her blend of social, cultural, and basic feminist resentment quickly gave her a position of considerable notoriety in the 1970s: a line from a poem in her first collection, *Nukun silmät auki* (1971; I sleep with open eyes), "sain roolin, johon en mahdu" (I got a role into which I do not fit), was chosen by Maria-Liisa Nevala, literary scholar and subsequently director of Finland's National Theater, as the title for a volume by various hands about women writers in Finland (1989). In one collection after another Tiainen has given men and the male establishment their comeuppance, although she claims to be a proponent of ardent love between the sexes; actually, she can submit considerable textual evidence in support of her claim — she uses words that would have been forbidden in an earlier time. A poem that has often been anthologized, from *Vallan Casanovat* (1979; Casanovas of power), an easily decipherable title about the male concept of love, begins: "Adolescent men / always propping themselves up on woman, / groping for her sleeve," and ends: "You don't have any pleasure from them, even in bed." Although she has railed against the intellectual elite (and boasted of her own lack of education), she has not hesitated to use the great myths and legends of Western culture (in this respect resembling the Finland-Swedes Märta Tikkanen, Inga-Britt Wik, and Gurli Lindén), as such titles as *Isolde, pakolainen* (1981; Isolde the refugee) and *Kalastaja Merlin* (1982; Merlin the fisherman) indicate. Like the late Henrik Tikkanen (or like Rosa Liksom), Tiainen succeeded in making herself a much gossiped-about public personality, using the confessional mode in the prose book *Tukhimo ja Mefisto* (1982; Cinderella and Mephisto), a sensation in its day.

It may be necessary—or may seem necessary—in a literary world as fecund as the Finnish for poets to create a distinct public image into which they subsequently find themselves locked. That has been the case with Tommy Tabermann (1947–), who concocted a personal blend of romantic aestheticism and revolutionary pathos from the start, in the poem collection *Ruusuja Rosa Luxemburgille* (1970; Roses for Rosa Luxemburg). Coupling his "own pain" to events in Vietnam and Chile, he produced a book with the particularly alliterative title *Kun kaikki kellot sydämessä soivat* (1972; When all the bells in the heart resound), followed by *Aivan kuin joku itkisi* (1973; Just as if someone were weeping), *Kaipaus* (1976; Yearning), *Anna minä kumoan vielä tämän maljan* (1977; Grant that I may still drink up this cup), and so forth—the emotional fountain never ceases to gush.

A reputation that has held up better belongs to Arto Melleri (1956–), who, like Tabermann, started as a "romantic subjectivist" but, all the same, seemed to mock his own banalities in *Schlaageriseppeli* (1977; Wreath of hits), *Zoo* (1979), *Ilmalaiva "Italia"* (1980; The airship *Italia*), *Mau-Mau* (1982), *Sopimus Mr. Evergreenin kanssa* (1983; Arrangement with Mr. Evergreen), and *Johnny B. Goethe* (1988). The last of these contains a counterpart to Tua Forsström's Marilyn Monroe poem, here called "Sleep in Peace, Norma Jean." His almost boyish sense of adventure fantasy and his preference for portraits of explorers, discoverers, men of daring was fun while it lasted but darkened into explorations of crime in *Tuomiopäivän sävärit* (1987; Vibrations of Judgment Day) in prose and then apocalyptic visions in the poetry for which he was awarded the Finlandia Prize in 1992, *Elävien kirjoissa* (1991; In the books of the living). A sometime actor, Melleri made a splash in the theater of the later 1970s with the play, or revue, *Pete Q* (1979), in which the dictatorship of neither terror nor artiness is found to be adequate for dealing with the needs of human beings, one of the several signs of a countermovement, in that decade, against the 1960s dogmatism of political and social awareness. Another play, *Siriuksen vieraat* (1984; Guests of Sirius), combined drug experimentation, about which Melleri knows a great deal, with the longing for an Ostrobothnian childhood, a nostalgia that crops up repeatedly in the midst of Melleri's dark thoughts of "a time of the crumbling of letters, the confusion of tongues at the Tower of Babel, literally." A constant interjection of modish or vulgar Americanisms in his own poetic language illustrates his point.

In the great variety of Finnish-language lyric that has sprung up over the past thirty years, Kari Aronpuro (1940–) has remained a largely inaccessible entity, because of the intellectual rigor (or rigidity) and schematization of his work. The fascination exerted on Aronpuro by the texts of others (he is a librarian by training and profession) has turned him, in the winged phrase of Ritva Poom, into a "lord of intertextuality," where the manifold references serve not as stuff for parody, as they so often do in the freewheeling Melleri, but as an inspiration for Aronpuro's own difficult glosses. During the 1960s he produced collages (*Aperitiff — avoin kaupunki* [1965; Aperitif — Open city]), tried a kind of dadaism (1964; *Peltiset enkelit* [Sheetmetal angels]), began his librarian's fascination with other people's texts (*Terveydeksi* [1966; Cheers] and *Minä viihtyy* [1967; The ego burgeons]); in the 1970s he became politicized (yearning for a workers' paradise in *Lokomonyliopisto* [1970; The Lokomo university], *Kiinan ja Rääkkylän runot* [1972; Poems of China and Rääkkylä], and *Moskovan ikävä* [1973; Longing for Moscow]). Then, much more fruitfully, he discovered structuralism in *Kalpea aavistus verenkierrosta* (1977; A pale notion of the circulating system) and essayed the "structuralist prose poems" of *Galleria* (1979; The gallery), a work celebrating (with extensive documents) the economic history of his home city of Tampere. A search for unsung cultural heroes led him to *Vähäfysiikka* (1981; Little physics), glossing the *Physica* of Sigfridus Aronus Forsius (see chapter 6); a far better known provider of materials in the same volume is Hans Magnus Enzensberger (1927–), the German poet of the "ballads on the history of progress," which include such a mixed bag as Gutenberg, Joseph Ignace Guillotin, Isambard Kingdom Brunel (the great Victorian engineer), Darwin, and Vyacheslav Molotov. The characterization of Aronpuro as a brilliant bookworm is not unfair: he is obsessed by a display of learning and of the material world (as in *Merkillistä menoa* [1983; Remarkable progress]) and by the very letters of which the written word is composed, in *Kirjaimet tulevat* (1986; The letters are coming). He is not a poet likely to win a large following, although he has enjoyed a succès d'estime; in 1988 his collected poems from 1964 to 1987 appeared, *Selvää jälkeä: Runoja* (Finally: Poems).

Although the literary production of Pekka Suhonen (1938–) has been many-sided — from a history of modern Finnish architecture and a chronicle of Artek, an art industry firm, to stories — his place in Finland's literature is owed particularly to his essays and poetry. The essayistic writing, collected in *Delfiini* (1973; The dolphin) and *Pikku paratiisi* (1988; Little paradise), shows his strong interests in art and architecture, his literary insights, and his ability to make surprising connections, as in his comparison between Debussy's piano music and Sillanpää's prose, or between the pit into which Topelius's "Star Eye" falls (in the fairy tale of the same name) with the attic hiding place of Anne Frank; by his playful technique he sometimes recalls the great Finnish-Swedish essayist Yrjö Hirn. His essay on Topelius's tale was translated for *Books from Finland* in 1984. In the lyric, too, he is similarly adept at surprising confrontations, as in the surrealist poems of *Kootut runot* (1965; Collected poems), where his favorite animal, the dolphin, becomes a lovely Polish woman, Delphine Potocka. In *Palava omaisuus* (1968; Burning possession) the same technique is applied, with a more melancholy tone (as in the handsome "Pushkinesque": "The sweet-gale bloomed, drooping in the bog, / she an hour farther away"). Suhonen's fascination with the small perceptions, losses, and memories of life is the principal (and extraordinarily attractive) characteristic of *Moskovalainen huivi* (1976; The Moscow shawl) — no wonder he has found an empathetic translator in Bo Carpelan. The mood of his poetry darkens still more in *Tulia yön puutarhassa* (1979; Fires in the garden of night):

> The blackbird flew anxiously
> back and forth outside the window,
> the blackness on the snowdrift awaits the night,
> awaits the color with which it paints fate;
> the final prey: emptiness.

Prose of the 1970s

In prose writing the 1970s are synonymous with diversity, the healthy disintegration of the ruling literary groupings. The decade produced perhaps eight writers whose value now is undisputed. They are, in the order of their debuts, Leena Krohn, Veronica Pimenoff, Teuvo Saavalainen, Antti Tuuri, Heikki Turunen, Pirkko Saisio, Matti Pulkkinen, and Olli Jalonen. It is easiest to characterize these writers by region. The strongest provincial ties are between Turunen and North Karelia and Tuuri and Ostrobothnia. The change in societal structure, the depopulation of the countryside, and the centralization of the population in urban areas, "the big move," is apparent in the work of many writers, most strongly in Turunen's. Those whose locality is Helsinki, such as Krohn and Saisio, are perceived as national authors. The most cosmopolitan in the group is Pimenoff. Saavalainen adopted the confession as his genre. Pulkkinen, with his three novels, has been a provocateur, shaking and surprising his readers. Jalonen has obvious inclinations toward the ethical; he is a critical describer of the academic world or of those who move in its vicinity. Krohn has been labeled a writer of "fantasy" literature, which, in the main, is misleading, for she uses surprising materials skillfully in developing her own perceptions. Saisio's economical prose has dealt with, among other things, the themes of religion and homosexuality.

Leena Krohn (1947–) is a multitalented writer who moves in the area of short prose. She began with fairy tales; it took a while to notice that, as conduits, they provided a philosophy of life and metaphysical feelings for the searching writer. Two books of such tales (1970, 1973) were followed by a collection of other stories, *Viimeinen kesävieras* (1974; The last summer guest) and a fairy-tale novel, *Ihmisen vaatteissa* (1976; In human garb), whose themes are taken from the conflict between the city and the countryside, between civilization and nature, in which values lie on the side of the latter. (Two of her stories presenting this argument, "Ranatra" and "The Most Beautiful Day of Summer," were translated by Richard Impola in *Dimension* [1994].)

The form of Krohn's best work is that of the miniature novella, which at times is reminiscent of a prose poem or a fairy tale. Both Baudelaire and H. C. Andersen can be assumed to be her models. The city is her stage, no longer the other side of a contrastive pair but a sounding board for human experiences of alienation. A certain didactic tone has slowly disappeared from Krohn's text. The rise in her career began with a collection of brief short stories that were held together by the same main character, an urban eccentric, *Donna Quijote ja muita kaupunkilaisia* (1983; lit. Donna Quixote and other urbanites; Eng. tr. *Donna Quixote and The Gold of Ophir,* 1995). The superb *Tainaron* (1985) followed; it is a novel without people, whose material, however, is drawn not from fantasy but from the world of insects. The work consists of a series of letters that are sent from a faraway insect city. The book does not create anthropomorphized creatures, allegories, or satires at the expense of the insects; rather, the aim is to show the unity of and relationships among all living things, something that is basically strange and incomprehensible to the human mind. Animals, mushrooms, the Old Testament, and alchemy are the points of reference in the next novel, *Oofirin kultaa* (1987; *Donna Quixote and The Gold of Ophir,* 1995), which at times is brilliant but less well centered than its predecessor. The eponymous doctor of *Umbra* (1990) has but one passion left to him, the collection of paradoxes for his great archive: "logical, mathematical, philosophical, visual, auditory, physical, geographical, cosmological." But as Soila Lehtonen asks, "Does an evildoer will evil because he must? Or must he do evil because he wills it?"

The world of insects returns in Krohn's book of essays, *Rapina* (1989; Rustle); it includes pieces on literature, portraits of individuals, reminiscences, and short stories. The tension between the known and the unknown, and their paradoxical unity, brings together the colorful materials and creates the collection's inimitable atmosphere. Krohn has also published poems, at times as her own independent production (1977), at times combined with the work of pictorial artists (1982, 1984), at times in a fairy tale–like story that makes use of folk traditions and alternates between poetry and prose (*Näkki* [1979; The water spirit]). Krohn is one of the very few members of her generation to cultivate meter and melodiousness in her poems. She has also demonstrated her models and her skills in the song poem by translating into Finnish a selection of Swedish poetry from the beginning of the twentieth century (*Runon portilla* [1985; At the gates of poetry]).

In 1970, the same year Krohn made her debut, Veronica Pimenoff (1949–) published her own first work, although her writing had already appeared in an anthology of the 1960s. Pimenoff has issued four novels in two decades; the small number is explained by the fact that literature is not her profession. She earned two academic degrees in West Germany, one a medical doctorate and the other in social anthropology. At its publication her novel *Pohjoiset pelit* (1970; Northern games) startled audiences as a political conversation and as a roman à clef in which the new, radical youth spoke about the world's problems, about exploitation and power, about the political Right and Left, about Finland and Europe. The events in Pimenoff's next novel, *Maailman myötä ja vastaan* (1978; With and against the world), take place in a Finnish country village that forces a bookish young man to reevaluate his own values. Berlin is the site of the novel *Pimeän pihan piilot* (1982; The hiding places in a dark courtyard); it is described with expertise and as an amalgamation of confusing contrasts that are in conflict with old structures and activities. Pimenoff's principal work is the novel *Loistava Helena* (1984; Magnificent Helena), which makes use of both the writer's medical education and the genre of the *Entwicklungsroman*. It describes a cycle in the main character's life, from birth to giving birth. One of its themes is an examination of the career possibilities of an intellectual woman in the male-dominated scientific community. In accordance with the conventions of the developmental novel, crises and travels bring about the principal character's maturation into responsible adulthood.

Teuvo Saavalainen (1927–) is also a writer with a second profession; he has earned his living as a teacher. Saavalainen wrote his major books at an advanced age; those from his middle years did not foreshadow his later success. His first book, *Yksilön ylösnousemus* (1971; The resurrection of the individual), was a series of philosophical essays that ardently defended an individual's freedom against ideologies and institutions, with signs of anarchism and, above all, existentialism. It was followed by an early experiment with the writing of a novel (1972), his only attempt in the genre. In 1980 Saavalainen started his principal work, which to date consists of six volumes of autobiographical prose writings, confessions, stamped by an unholy desire to reveal one's most painful affairs as well as those of one's nearest and dearest relatives. *Minä huudan* (1980; I shout), *Velipoika löi kerran* (1982; My brother hit me once), *Ja poika vaikenee* (1984; The boy is silent), *Sitten tulivat laivat* (1986; Then the ships came), *Satama lyö leiman* (1988; The harbor leaves its mark), and *Ja korjaa meri* (1991; And the sea reaps) constitute a series, making Saavalainen a writer who corresponds to Henrik Tikkanen and Christer Kihlman as a master of confessional writing. The series is at its strongest in its first volumes; toward the end it begins to fall apart and the quality becomes more uneven. A gift for lively narration, the absoluteness of perceptions even when documenting deviant experiences, and distribution of feelings of guilt and of understanding to oneself and others guarantee the power of the series. Saavalainen's narration draws backgrounds and analogues from diverse sources: from the memories of his proletarian family, from his own idiosyncratic mythology of females and animals, from the Old Testament and Christianity, from anarchism and existentialism, from psychology and psychiatry. The milieus of a "wilderness settlement," the writer's native land, and the world are all analyzed as communities of madness.

Antti Tuuri (1944–) and Heikki Turunen are the leading epic prose writers of their generation. Tuuri began as a modernist of sparse expression and did not develop into an author of expansive novels containing humor, character portrayal, and adventurous plots until the 1980s. His productivity and principal genres were foreshadowed by his debut with two books in 1971, one a collection of short stories, the other a novel. By now, six collections of Tuuri's short stories have been published; his concise and skillful narrating, his awareness of modern tradition, and his behavioristic approach have gradually given way to more generous and looser narration.

Tuuri is the leading author of his generation to cultivate the behavioristic short story; his cool, detached approach to narrative has irritated many; its task in creating irony about the characters' mechanical attitude toward life has not always been understood. Tuuri's perception is most clearly evident in his short stories; it presents an assessment of the world from foundations that are formed by a reasoning akin to that of a mechanical engineer but that also leave room for metaphysical premonitions. During the period of his novellas and short stories one work betrayed Tuuri's ability and desire to undertake a larger form, the novel *Joki virtaa läpi kaupungin* (1977; The river flows through town). It was a magnificent charting of three personality types whose lives touch one another; one is a rational work supervisor, the second a decayed artist, and the third, and the most interesting, an old scientist who discards normal academic reasoning.

Tuuri's work of the 1980s is stamped by Ostrobothnian topics. *Pohjanmaa* (1982; Ostrobothnia) introduced the Hakala family, whose life has been followed in five subsequent novels. The book, which does not contain any dialogue, is a family saga that searches for dry humor by means of indirect discourse as it describes the southern Ostrobothnian lifestyle, the foolishness of the men, and the wisdom of the women. *Talvisota* (1984; The Winter War) described the men of the region in the war, which is recalled decades later by the narrator. The soldier is seen as a worker employed in defensive killing, a worker convinced of the necessity of his activity. The invader threatens the home district and its lifestyle and thus must be repelled at any cost. The four other novels of the Ostrobothnia series, *Ameriikan raitti* (1986; The American road), *Uusi Jerusalem* (1988; New Jerusalem), *Maan avaruus* (1989; Vast earth), and *Lakeuden kutsu* (1997; The call of the plain) move the scene to the United States and Canada and back; large-scale emigration from Ostrobothnia has taken place to both those countries. The first deals with Finnish tax evaders in Florida; the second and the third form a historical pair about Ostrobothnians battered by the Great Depression and disillusioned by a utopian commune. Guilt and innocence, class conflicts, the collision of the Old and the New Worlds, and the relationship between dreams and reality are the novels' themes. The narration, always built on indirect discourse, is sometimes in danger of becoming formalized. The last novel depicts the return home and provides a final triumph. Tuuri, who started as a modernist writing for a small audience, conquered a vast readership. He is a prolific writer whose work also includes satire, trickster novels, fishing stories, documentary books, and radio and theater plays. His main genres, however, undeniably remain short stories and epic narration with Ostrobothnian topics.

The province of Heikki Turunen (1945–) is North Karelia. His first novel, *Simpauttaja* (1973), was a critical and commercial success. It gave evidence of the writer's strengths: thorough knowledge of the countryside, the village community, and cultural change as well as humor and descriptive power that drew from colloquial expression. The eponymous protagonist of the novel is the village dullwit who grows to mythical portions; he is a hired hand and an *Übermensch,* a relic of the past who, as such, reveals the destruction of the countryside. His opposite is a newspaper reporter who observes the changes through sociological reasoning. Between these two is a character straight out of the developmental novel, a young man who seeks his own solutions. The main figure in *Joensuun Elli* (1974; Elli of Joensuu) has been taken as Simpauttaja's sister and as the beauty and fascination of primeval nature. Turunen's third novel, *Kivenpyörittäjän kylä* (1976; Stoneroller's village), carried the themes of the first two books to a higher level. It is peopled both by small farmers and lumber men from a North Karelian village that is losing its population and by figures who support traditional Finnish culture. An emigrant family, returning from Sweden, tries to settle down into its childhood idyll but ends by finding that the idyll no longer exists. Instead, there is mass movement away from the village, cultural change, and decline. Stoneroller, the original Finn from the forests, is analogous to both Atlas and Sisyphus, the world's supporter and the doer of useless work. *Hupeli* (1978) was the start of a novel series that grew to five volumes and that charts the rise and fall of a population of small farmers. The main character is a wounded veteran who, after his return from the war, starts to clear the land on his farmstead. *Kolmen hevosen mies* (1981; Three-horse man) continues the story from the time when marital problems become central; the man wants to stay on the farm, but the wife longs for the conveniences of the city. The third volume, *Punahongan hehku* (1982; The glowing of the red pines), introduces the artistic son, whose relationship with his father is observed with psychological insight and sensitive humor. *Mustarinnan lapset* (1985; Children of Mustarinta) shifts to the next generation, which is becoming urbanized. The conclusion, *Maan veri* (1987; Blood of the earth), describes the time after the "great change," with the city as the setting, when the mind and health of the forest Finn finally and inescapably are thrown out of balance.

Pirkko Saisio (1949–) is an actress in her other profession, something that is evident in the prevalence of speech in her work and in the drama versions of her novels. Her first literary appearance was in 1975, with the novel *Elämänmeno* (Life's course), an intuitive description of a working-class family in Helsinki during the decades after the war. The relationship between the mother and the daughter, who — painfully — is becoming independent, creates the principal tension. Saisio's two next novels can be counted as intermediate efforts: *Sisarukset* (1976; Siblings) is diluted in its world view; *Kadonnut aurinko* (1979; Lost sun) experiments with the renewal of prose writing but shows an unsure grasp. An impressive and expressive depiction of the city was the novel *Betoniyö* (1981; Cement night). Its dialogue is precise, and tension is provided by the relationship of two brothers; the atmosphere is gloomy, permeated with a sense of impending disaster. In *Kainin tytär* (1984; Cain's daughter) two women are the narrators; one of them is also the principal character. The women are united by lesbian love and divided by their religious backgrounds; one was brought up in the Greek Orthodox church and the other is a Lutheran. Saisio has also written original plays and adapted her novels into plays.

Matti Pulkkinen (1944–) has published three novels at great intervals, but they have drawn more attention to him than many a mediocre writer's dozens of books. Pulkkinen caused a stir in the literary world with his opening novel, *Ja pesäpuu itki* (1977; The nesting tree cried), which discards realism and aims deeper, to the analysis of the Finnish collective soul. The novel describes three periods and three generations, but the chronology is fragmented and the periods become intertwined. The description centers on mental and physical health within the framework of societal development. Pulkkinen's second novel, *Elämän herrat* (1980; Masters of life), is more focused in its aims. Its tension comes from the duel of two writers, in which the conflict between religion and reason is resolved by means of antipsychiatric thought and theories on birth trauma. In 1985 Pulkkinen published a work that was the most discussed book of that year, the novel, or non-novel, *Romaanihenkilön kuolema* (The death of a fictional character). It is a great monolith that contains photographs, applies the literary postmodern tenets that break the conventions of fiction writing, and furiously opposes the representational and democratic standardized thought of the times. In the subsequent debate the writer was accused of reactionaryism, anti-Soviet attitudes, and racism. The work was partly set in international locations, something that in Finnish literature generally has meant a tourist-level superficiality. In addition to Finland, Pulkkinen moves about Sweden, Poland, Germany, and Africa. He compares the developmental problems in nineteenth-century Finland to those in present-day Africa, seeing no solution for the latter. Pulkkinen subscribes to theories according to which the idealization of primitive developmental stages and of communities adhering to strict dogma derives from the same self-deluding escapism. He analyzes ideological and political doctrines with the aid of psychology in a manner that infuriates their supporters. The polemics that the novel caused almost entirely ignored the book's structure, which made the ideas presented in it ironic and relative. The book was read as a collection of the writer's opinions, although, with its structure, it aims at much more, at a kind of allegory for the conflicts of the modern world, for the impossibility of total rule, for fallacies, and for the unpredictability of everything.

Olli Jalonen (1954–) came into the public eye through a contest in short-story writing, but he soon won his present position as a writer of novels that are morally challenging and deal with the great questions of the world. He represents a rather rare combination in Finland, an academic sociologist and an author in one and the same person. On one hand, his ethics draw strength from ideas of critical sociology, and on the other, he finds material in the commercialism that presents itself as research, in its cynicism, and in the diverse organized planning of human destruction. After his initial short stories (1978) and a novel (1979) depicting student life, Jalonen published his breakthrough novel, *Ilo ja häpeä* (1981; Joy and shame). The main character is a sociologist who works in international communications and as a researcher; he concludes that these roles exist only to camouflage with respectability the world's actual despair and cruelty. *Hotelli eläville* (1983; A hotel for the living) is a modern antiutopia that exists not in the future but in the present. It describes how research is coupled to the service of the cynicism that exists within commercial interests; the novel's strong woman moves from critical study of the market economy to unabashed participation in it. The protagonist is a researcher who plans the social dynamics of bomb shelters. Jalonen's fourth novel, *Johan ja Johan* (1989; Johan and Johan), is, like Faulkner's *Wild Palms,* a twin novel, which tells a father's story as a deserter in the Soviet Union and the son's story in Finland. The combination of two life stories is perhaps not totally convincing, but Jalonen's ability to depict the common person's limited alternatives in the world's machinery is related to many classics in Finland's literature. Jalonen's *Isäksi ja tyttäreksi* (1990; Father and daughter) won the Finlandia Prize in 1991.

Two Irreverent Outsiders
The late sixties and early seventies also produced prose writers who did not quite fit, by reason of their very exuberance, into the normal flow of the Finnish novel and who, perhaps on that account, achieved a large readership in Finland and some reputation abroad. The younger brother of Erno Paasilinna, Arto (1942–), had a far lighter heart, which he revealed in his

novel-length yarns, beginning with *Operaatio Finlandia* (1972; Operation Finlandia), about Sweden's fictitious "summer attack" on its eastern neighbor in the year 1977. It is an amusing commentary not only on a North so peaceful that it had lost the attention of the world press, and on holier-than-thou Sweden, always ready to deal out moral instructions to other, less perfect nations, but on the Finnish fondness for war novels. Striking while the iron of his popularity was hot, Paasilinna then produced *Paratiisisaaren vangit* (1974; The prisoners of Paradise Island), in which a group of Finnish lumberjacks is cast up, quite by accident, on a desert island with a detachment of Swedish nurses. Having used one traditional pattern of the novel (the sexual utopia, here placed on a Nordic version of the Isle of Pines or the Tahiti of myth), he went on to another, the picaresque, in *Isoisää etsimässä* (1977; In search of grandfather) and to a variation of the war motif in *Sotahevonen* (1979; The war horse), about adventures behind the lines in the Continuation War. But Paasilinna had already touched another deep yearning in the public's heart, achieving his greatest popularity with *Jäniksen vuosi* (1975; Eng. tr. *The Year of the Hare,* 1994), subsequently turned into one of the few Finnish films — directed by Risto Jarva (1977) — to have received a place in the international repertoire. It is the story of a businessman who hits a hare with his car, flees into the wilderness with the injured animal, and nurses it back to health, all the while pursued by a society that will not let him go his own, apparently aberrant way; its sequel was *Onnellinen mies* (1976; A happy man). Paasilinna's careless style and his apparent wish to curry a broad public's favor have not made him the critics' darling; but his works, singly or in collection, adorn a great many Finnish homes and, seen in the larger context of Finnish-language literature, continue the great tradition of the comic novel begun by Aleksis Kivi, whose seven brothers, as every Finnish schoolchild knows, also flee civilization.

Another kind of humor — with numerous counterparts in American literature and popular culture — has been promulgated by Daniel Katz (1938–), who has a special place as a Jewish writer in a society where the Jewish community is minuscule. His first novel, *Kun isoisä Suomeen hiihti* (1969; When Grandfather skied to Finland), already showed him at full strength; a Jewish cavalryman (and cornetist) in the czarist army (like Katz's forebears in reality) finds life in the autonomous grand duchy at least more tolerable than in anti-Semitic Russia itself: marrying and settling down in Helsinki, he is recalled to service in the First World War but survives. The burlesque or slapstick episodes in Katz's narrative may distract the reader's attention from the text's many subtleties — for example, the chapter title "The Cornet Sets Forth to War" is an allusion to the painting by Akseli Gallen-Kallela, "Kullervo's Setting Forth to War," in which the *Kalevala*'s tragic hero, blowing a birchbark horn, goes forth against his enemies. (Music lovers will recall Sibelius's symphonic poem.) Mixing eastern European Jewish lore with Finland's history, Katz also mixes the Yiddish tradition of the episodic comic novel (see Sholem Alechem's *Marienbad* [1917]) with its Finnish equivalent, the line stretching from Maiju Lassila's *Tulitikkuja lainaamassa* to Veijo Meri. The protagonists of Katz's next novels, *Mikko Papirossin taivaallinen niskalenkki* (1972; Mikko Papirossi's heavenly excursion) and *Orvar Kleinin kuolema* (1976; The death of Orvar Klein), would seem familiar to an American public that knows its Malamud and Bellow—and its Woody Allen—ironic and clumsy self-deprecators who repeatedly fall victim to painful situations not of their own making. Mikko Papirossi is a student of aesthetics who becomes an interpreter at an oil refinery; Orvar Klein is a secondhand book dealer who, swept into political intrigue, has to change identity in order to survive.

In *Laturi* (1979; The explosives expert) Katz moves into a somewhat different realm: his hero, whose mother has died in a Nazi camp, is brought up by a Turk in northern Finland; eventually, he is released from his obsession with explosives by discovering the identity of his biological father, a member of the Romanian guild of popular minstrels. Katz's knowledge of eastern Europe gives his novels a larger and more exotic range of cultural reference than is customary among Finnish novelists; in this respect, he resembles the Swede Jacques Werup (1945–) in the latter's *Shimonoffs längtan* (1983; Shimonoff's longing). *Peltisepän päivällinen* (1981; The tinsmith's daily bread) returns to a milder and gentler central figure, Härri Roome, a novelist at work on a book about the absurdities of world politics; he wants to change a world that constantly outsmarts him, as does the eponymous intellectual of *Antti Keplerin lait* (1987; Antti Kepler's law). Both Roome and Kepler are storytellers, and their anecdotal proclivities serve to swell Katz's texts, or, more kindly put, to turn his novels into kaleidoscopes; the same urge in Katz has led as well to books of stories, *Satavuotias muna* (1983; The hundred-year-old egg) and *Naisen torso* (1989; Woman's torso).

In 1993 he returned to the novel, and his main Jewish thematology, in *Saksalainen sikakoira* (German *Schweinehund*), in which a Finnish Jew, suffering from an incurable illness, sets out to take revenge on the aged sometime tormenter of his father in a little East German town; into the novel's absurd happenings Katz injects his thoughts about the Holocaust and, more uniquely, his insights into Finnish xenophobia, a topic not often addressed in Finland's creative literature. Although his main figures are almost entirely males, Jewish or Jewish-like men, he is not an autobiographical writer; Tuva Korsström concluded that "he is one of the few male Finnish authors who does not write from a wounded, introverted ego" (p. 122). Instead, in the midst of his abundant jokes, he is a keen observer.

The 1980s: Subtlety and Shock in Novels, Novellas, and Theater
It is a given that the shorter the distance in time, the more difficult it is to present lasting assessments. The psychiatrist and writer Claes Andersson analyzed the world of values and perceptions of the young writers of the 1980s in his essay "Disillusions," which gave rise to talk about the "School of Evil." Its representatives are Esa Sariola, Annika Idström, Eira Stenberg, and the Finland-Swede Paul von Martens (see chapter 10). This literature describes a new urban type of human being who concentrates on either his career or his internal problems, tossing aside the tradition in which responsibility for others, for nature, and for the future still had some meaning.

Not all writers of the 1980s analyze these problems, however, which sometimes are called postmodern. Alongside those who deal with the new human who has no history, traditional confessors and reformers exist; their successes have been no less celebrated. The diversity of solutions may be exemplified by comparing three notable debut novels. *Sonja O. kävi täällä* (1981; Sonja O. was here), by Anja Kauranen (1954–), was a critical and commercial success, a description of student bohemians of the 1970s; an innovative feature was that the writer and the principal character were women who had appropriated the old freedoms of men. The novel, brilliant in its language, was not the starting shot of an illustrious career: in her subsequent work Kauranen has never again reached quite the same level. When not yet twenty years of age, Anne-Leena Härkönen (1965–) published the novel *Häräntappoase* (1984; Bull-killing weapon), which, even with the palpable influences from J. D. Salinger's *Catcher in the Rye*, was an exceptionally clever and multihued description of youth. Yet, since her debut, Härkönen has published only one book, clearly inferior to the first. *Amorfiaana* (1986), by Mariaana Jäntti, has not as yet received a successor. The novel, in the Finnish context, is all too "French": difficult to conceptualize, fragmenting the normal conventions of description. Its intelligence and independence are of such high quality that literary circles still await Jäntti's next book.

Not coincidentally, all three above-mentioned writers are women. The 1980s were a women's decade to a much larger extent than any previous period. Of the new writers who have achieved notice, a larger number have been women than men; the lift of feminism has also been felt in literature.

The list of examples could possibly also include the pseudonymous "Jukka Larsson's" three miniature novels, *Kiusaaja* (1986; Tormentor), *Viettelijä* (1987; Tempter), and *Kantaja* (1991; Bearer) taut depictions of crime, violence, and suffering. In 1993 it was revealed that behind the pseudonym was a woman writer who earlier published under her own name — Pirkko Saisio.

Among the work of those who have been reckoned as members of the School of Evil, the work of Annika Idström (1947–) has attracted the most interest — outside Finland as well. To some extent, her fame may derive from her sensational subject matter. Idström's four novels have brought new ideas and perceptions to the literature of the decade; above all, she is a suggestive analyst of family dynamics and dysfunction. Her first work, *Sinitaivas* (1980; Blue sky), still represents her apprenticeship; it is a description of the everyday life and dreams of four women. Only the wild chaos at the end of the novel, where the Gordian knots of the relationships become unraveled, gives a hint of the writer's future development. *Isäni rakkaani* (1981; My father my lover) decisively shifted to the treatment of mental reality; dreams, memories, and fantasies are the equals of external reality. The novel's coloring is hellish; the places, the people, and their actions ooze sickness, despair, and aggression, within the web of which a struggle toward light nevertheless takes place. As the title implies, the novel's subject matter is that of a relationship between a father and a daughter, with its love and hate; the Electra complex can also be mentioned in this connection. There is no differentiation between a child and an adult; in the inferno of the nuclear family the battle of wills is desperate and unending.

The best of Idström's novels is the third, *Veljeni Sebastian* (1985; Eng. tr. *My Brother Sebastian*, 1992); it lacks the exaggeration of negative elements that are disturbing in its predecessor. The book is a description of a precocious boy, actually of a mythical child-adult's oedipal power struggle with his mother. The technique of terrorism in a human relationship is depicted both suggestively and analytically. The boy succeeds in enslaving his mother; he becomes a "domestic despot, a cruel messiah, and at the same time a victim" (Tarkka, *Suomalaisia nykykirjailijoita*, 1989, 58). Sebastian's name was taken from a poem by Katri Vala; the connection is rather that of changing tasks than of paying homage; social material as an explanation for life has been minimized in the novel, and the individual psyche and close relationships are the frameworks for its descriptions. Idström's fourth novel, *Kirjeitä Trinidadiin* (1989; Letters to Trinidad), describes the ailing psychodynamics of a family of three in Finland and during a vacation in Israel.

The daughter in the family continues the development of one of Idström's basic figures, the ageless mythical child. The father is the principal character; his initially safe and rational world falls, under strange circumstances, into masochistic humiliation, hallucinations about werewolves, and the final loss of his distant daughter.

The name of Eira Stenberg (1943–) is often mentioned with Idström's. Stenberg began as a poet as early as 1966 and has intermittently published poem collections over the years, which reached their peak in three books published in 1979–83. Sharply, and making use of myths, these poems treat problems within the family unit and in the relationship between man and woman, as well as problems of women. Stenberg's three novels, *Paratiisin vangit* (1984; Prisoners in paradise), *Häikäisy* (1987; Blinded), and *Kuun puutarhat* (1990; Gardens of the moon), have made her Idström's equal as a depicter of family hell. The subject matter in the first novel is a struggle between two sisters for attention and power in the family; the positions of the victor and the victim change hands many times, and at the end the battle gets more and more surrealistic. The protagonist of the second novel is a teenage girl whose awakening to sexuality and to the power play in human relationships is depicted both analytically and poetically.

Raija Siekkinen (1953–), dealing as she does with quiet isolation and exquisite emotional pain, might seem to be a late-come Finnish equivalent of Mirjam Tuominen (see chapter 11); by virtue of her close attention to apparently unimportant details of behavior and milieu, however, she has reminded some commentators of Chekhov himself. Marianne Bargum has noticed how Siekkinen deals in "soul-scapes"; this predilection for the probing of human interiors has led her to cultivate the short story, first in *Talven tulo* (1978; Winter's coming) and *Tuomitut* (1982; The condemned). *Elämän keskipiste* (1983; The midpoint of life) provides one of her classic tales, "The Ice Shifts" (translated by Ritva Poom in *Dimensions*, 1994), about a subtle change in a relationship; *Pieni valhe* (1986; A little lie) contains the title story (opening with the disturbing sentence, "The white cat had started to hate her") and "Lüneburg," which begins and ends on a train passing through the north German heath, a succinct summary of the random and hopeless encounters of life. Conscious of her mastery of the small, suggestive form (into which, nonetheless, she presses a multitude of times and scenes), Siekkinen has ventured only once thus far into the novel, *Saari* (1988; The island): disappointed in love, a woman enters actual and emotional seclusion; as so often in Siekkinen, conversation is at a minimum or does not exist at all. Bargum acutely notes how one of the few spoken lines in "The Ice Shifts" is the husband's "Sorry," and how footprints in the sand — but not the actual makers of them — are a recurrent image in Siekkinen's short stories. In 1993 Siekkinen received the Finlandia Prize for the short stories of *Metallin maku* (The taste of metal).

The work of Esa Sariola (1951–) has been more disputed than that of the above-mentioned writers, and it is clearly inferior in its linguistic and descriptive merits. Sariola is a psychologist by education; he came into the public eye with a collection of short stories in 1984 and published four novels in the following years (1985–88). The thematic novelty in them can be crystallized into the term "civilized crime." The novels describe a type of a person who is able to isolate the values in his own life and in the circle of those closest to him from a wide sphere of activities to which different morals — or pure cynicism — are applied. Sariola's people have lost their sense of wholeness; they live their lives in separate compartments. Their essential belief in an individual's sense of honor is not disturbed by their grasp for money, power, and the satisfaction of their lust for pleasure or their failure to acknowledge the value of other humans. The new human being is depicted in Sariola's novels without accusation and without analysis, revealingly but without moralizing.

Among the writers of the 1980s who focus on the renewal of tradition rather than the break with the past, Joni Skiftesvik (1948–) is the most notable. He attracted interest with his short stories, *Puhalluskukkapoika ja taivaankorjaaja* (1983; The dandelion boy and the sky saver), which provided possibilities for the development of literary tradition, especially that of Pentti Haanpää. From the very beginning the writer's grasp was stylistically sure and the compositions faultless. Since his debut Skiftesvik has alternated between novels and collections of short stories. The latter are *Tuulen poika* (1985; Wind's son) and *Suolamänty* (1988; Salty pine). The skillfully constructed short stories describe northern Finnish life, regulated by stern natural conditions and the demanding patterns of human relationships.

Skiftesvik began writing novels with *Pystyyn haudattu* (1984; Buried standing up), which was praised by the critics, who compared it to Hemingway, among other authors. The alternating layers in time, the relationship of the father and the son, the balladlike arrival of the son in the northern community as a messenger of justice, and the giving way of both time and space to timeless morality characterize this exceptionally mature first novel. *Isäni, sankari* (1987; My father, the hero) is placed around 1915, when patriotic young Finlanders went to Germany for training in a light infantry (Jäger) battalion and service on the Russian front, in the thought that they would then lead an uprising in Finland against czarist rule. Instead, they formed much of the officers' corps in Mannerheim's White army during Finland's Civil War, fighting the Red Guard. In its plot the novel is an adventure tale but at the same time becomes a morality. Stylistic experimentation and the renewing of tradition are the starting points in *Likinäköinen adjutantti* (1989; Myopic military aide), which continues the tradition of Finnish satire on war (Veikko Huovinen, Henrik Tikkanen, and Erno and Arto Paasilinna, among others). The novel tells of an imaginary war between Finland and Sweden. The Finns invite a Portuguese general to be their leader; he gets a nearsighted corporal as his aide. The values, practices, and clichés of war are spun around by the means of satire, humor, and fantasy. In 1990 Skiftesvik returned to actual events with *Tuulenpesä* (Witches' broom), about a Finnish deserter in the Second World War.

By dint of her construction of an abrasive public personality, Rosa Liksom (1958–), born Anni Ylävaara in Lapland, stands in shrill contrast to the shy Siekkinen; like Siekkinen, she is a specialist in the short story, but the effect of her little narratives is anything but muted. The nom de plume contains a reference both to a favorite martyr of the Left, Rosa Luxemburg (1870–1919), and to the Swedish conjunction/adverb *liksom,* meaning both "like" and "as if"; Liksom's photographic poses with dark glasses and in military uniform are likewise meant to attract attention. She has also been in the public eye with her art exhibitions and her well-advertised travels, such as that to the dying Soviet Union, *Go Moskova Go* (1988, with photographs by Jukka Uotila). These activities, however, are subsidiary to the genuine literary value of her stories and sketches. Drawing on her close knowledge of an international dropout "culture" (she lived for a while in Copenhagen's scruffy Christiania) and her uninviting home region, she made her debut in *Yhden yön pysäkki* (1985; One-night stands), the title then used by Anselm Hollo for his translations (1990) of a selection from both that volume and two subsequent collections.

Liksom's descriptions of the varieties of sexual experience in *Unohdettu vartti* (1988; Frozen quarter of an hour) have been compared to Maria Jotuni's in *Rakkautta* at the century's beginning, although Liksom uses language and situations that would have been quite unthinkable in Jotuni's more sedate day. *Tyhjän tien paratiisit* (1989; Paradise of the empty road) continues in the same vein but with still more attention to savage or deviant behavior. (Liksom has at her disposal a huge range of narrative voices and specimens, female and male.) It is vital to note that Liksom has academic studies in ethnology behind her, at Helsinki and Copenhagen; a collector's impulse is obvious in her album of short stories from the Soviet Union, *Väliasema Gagarin* (1987; Gagarin way station). The aimlessness and often grisly humor of Liksom's characters has been compared with that found in the films of the brothers Aki and Mika Kaurismäki, for example, the former's *Tulitikkutehtaantyttö;* (1990; The match-factory girl) and the latter's *Zombie ja kummitusjuna* (1991; Zombie and the ghost train); her exploration of a lost generation also bears some resemblance to the rock music world of Thomas Wulff, Henrik Jansson, and Joakim Groth in Finland-Swedish literature, and the liberated woman's scruffy world of Monika Fagerholm (see chapter 10). Her unruffled (and often seemingly flat) retelling of disgusting, horrifying, or bizarre events shows, however, a peculiar and impressive artistic discipline; if she has forebears in Finnish literature, they are Pentti Haanpää and Veijo Meri.

Like Arvo Salo before him, Jouko Turkka (1942–) belongs more to the world of theater than to literature. After a sensational if bumpy career as director of municipal theaters in Seinäjoki, Joensuu (where he was dismissed for "political reasons"), and Kotka, from 1967 to 1975, he was assistant director of the Helsinki City Theater until 1982. Professor at the capital's School of Drama from 1981 to 1988, he was its rector, and storm center, from 1982 to 1985; his pedagogical methods led to an investigation by the Finnish Parliament and charges brought by the minister of justice. A result of this hullabaloo was Turkka's highly personal *Selvitys oikeuskanslerille* (1984; Statement to the minister of justice), a book compared with Strindberg's *Plaidoyer d'un fou* (1887; Eng. tr. *A Madman's Defense,* 1967). Turkka's actual literary debut had come earlier, in *Aiheita* (1982; Notions), sketches, thoughts, and short-short stories (which could be regarded as predecessors of Rosa Liksom's more carefully crafted works in the same minigenre). Theater critic Soila Lehtonen summarized them thus: "Things happen continually, as in a silent movie: the destinies of people and things are unbelievable" (p. 167). Many of the tales read like scenarios for movies without an ending: "You can finish this story any way you like." The climax of *Aiheita* comes with Turkka's plans to write a book intended to end with varied (and extremely bloody) modes of his own suicide.

In 1987 Turkka—whose disregard for the theatrical texts he ostensibly employs has been notorious—allowed two of his own plays to be printed, *Hypnoosi* (Hypnosis) and *Lihaa ja rakkautta* (Meat and love); the cast of the first includes a madwoman, from the floor of whose apartment eight pairs of hands (with specific functions) emerge, "an endless succession of theatrical trick and treat"; the performance of the second at the Gothenburg City Theater upset theatergoers by its central twist of plot: a sausage factory owner includes diced vagrants, impregnated with alcohol, in his products. Again, as offshoots of the synopses in *Aiheita,* Turkka's plays have little dialogue and much in the way of summaries, that is, suggestions for the all-powerful director. As might have been expected, Turkka's television redoing of Kivi's *Seitsemän veljestä* was an occasion for some outcry during the 1986–87 season. It was not the first Finnish classic to fall victim to his method: Minna Canth's *Murtovarkaus* (1882; The burglary) had simply been deprived of its dialogue when he directed it at the Helsinki City Theater in 1981. Lately, Turkka has tried to outdo Strindberg again, with the novel *Häpeä* (1993; Shame), about the battle between the sexes.

Intellectuality: Poets and Narrators of the 1980s
In the same line of intellectualism as Kari Aronpuro, but more accessible, Tiina Kaila (1951–) — daughter of the aesthetician Eino Leopold Krohn — began with poems in *Keskustelu hämärässä* (1975; Dialogue in the twilight), a self-styled "discussion with Kafka about the absurdity of the world," and *Talven talossa* (1978; In winter's house). She went over to larger cosmological poems in *Kala on meren kuva* (1983; The fish is the image of the sea); in *Valon nälkä* (1986; Light hunger) she condensed her "basic thought that small and large, detail and universe, all are the same." She then found another way of expounding her principle of pantheistic infinity, the novel *Bruno* (1990), about the late Renaissance philosopher and scientist Giordano Bruno, burned by the Inquisition in 1600 — in Kaila's opinion "the first thinker in our European history of ideas to argue that the infinity of the world is a concrete fact." As a writer of books for the imaginatively gifted young, Kaila presented a lighter side of her thought of cosmic unity, suggesting that another world is present in all matter yet seldom perceived; among these works, evidently inspired by C. S. Lewis, were *Auringonlaskun torni* (1976; The sunset's tower), *Simon matkat peilikaupunkiin* (1978; Simo's trips to the looking-glass city), and *Saari joka nousi merestä* (1984; The island that arose from the sea).

Kirsti Simonsuuri (1945–) is again from a learned background (her father was the director of the Archive for Finnish Folk Poetry) and has herself had a considerable career in the scholarly world, with a Cambridge doctoral dissertation on Homer. Her own high standards are reflected, *ex negativo*, in the thrashing she gave the new Finnish university at sub-Arctic Oulu in *Pohjoinen yökirja* (1981; Northern night book), calling it a place where "the capacity for platitudes exceeds even the ugliness of the milieu." A second and much different prose book from Simonsuuri's hand is also an offshoot of her intellectual pursuits, a plan to write a monograph about the French philosopher and convert from Judaism to Catholicism Simone Weil (1909–43). The monograph turned into the novel *Paholaispoika* (1986;

Eng. tr. *Boy Devil*, 1992), a description of Weil, a "thinker who linked the Roman Empire and the Third Reich with a common bond, and who built daring bridges from the Greece of antiquity to early Christianity and from Catharism and Druidism to our own time," by a young and sometimes bewildered Englishman. Simonsuuri's poetry—*Murattikaide* (1980; The ivy balustrade), *Tuntematon tekijä* (1982; Maker unknown), *Euroopan ryöstö* (1984; The rape of Europe), *Meri, ei mikään maa* (1987; Sea, no land), and *Enkelten pysäkki* (1990; Angels' bus stop) — show her to be a cosmopolitan poet, supported by unobtrusive confidence in herself and her knowledge, but neither strident nor self-pitying, and evidently uninterested in the shibboleths of feminism. Nevertheless, with her perfect English, she has selected and translated an anthology of "modern women poets in Finland," *Enchanting Beasts* (1990).

Jukka Kemppinen (1944–) is — once again — a learned poet; with a long training and experience in jurisprudence, publishing, and teaching behind him, he turned to poetry after a religious awakening, in the poems of *Ylistys* (1984; Song of praise). A favorite Finnish theme from the Runebergian tradition (see Runeberg's "Kyrkan" [The church]), the praise of God's work in nature, came back in *Linnusta länteen* (1985; West of the bird), which also used a tried-and-true structural device of Christian poetry, the church calendar — witness Gryphius's *Sonn-und-Feiertags-Sonnette* (1639), Herbert's *The Temple* (1633), and Droste-Hülshoff's *Das geistliche Jahr* (1851). These thoughts are continued in *Kiertävä kivi on kuollut* (1986; A rolling stone is dead), poems and prose poems, between which, like many of his contemporaries, he does not make an absolute distinction. Like so many other authors, too, he memorialized the fiftieth anniversary of the Winter War in the central section, "Karelia," of *Riitamaa* (1989; Disputed land), portraits of soldiers (surely not members of the heroic progeny of *Fänrik Stål*) in that conflict, with side glances to the ghastly battlefields of World War I. The extent of Kemppinen's learning and verbal inventiveness came to the fore in a different way in his rendering of Catullus's poems (1991), a rewriting into his own poetic language, an explosion of boldness unexpected from an author of Kemppinen's piety. But it may have been as much Catullus's awareness of death as his notorious eroticism that attracted Kemppinen.

Aphorism and Environmental Essay

In general, it has been argued that the poetry of the 1980s has been anemic, repeating standard solutions of the past. Older generations have been in the lead of the poetic front; the 1980s do not seem to have produced a single poet whose position at this time would seem indisputable. The literary field has shown growth in the variety of genres. In prose the position of short forms has received more emphasis, and writers have emerged whose only or most important genre is the essay or the aphorism.

The Finnish aphorism received new blood in the 1980s with the appearance of Markku Envall (1944–) as a creative writer. A literary historian by training, Envall gave an objective demonstration of his scholarly concern for the genre with his doctoral dissertation *Suomalainen aforismi* (1987; The Finnish aphorism). He had already shown that he belonged to the aphorists' guild with the collections *Rakeita* (1983; Hailstones) and *Pahojen henkien historia* (1986; The history of evil spirits), in which he followed a central theme, the impotence of the individual confronted by the "world body," the institutions and forces that control human life. As Envall has said, his interest in the aphorism stems from his school days, but the boom in aphoristic writing of the 1980s on the part of established Finnish-language authors, Haavikko foremost among them, led both to his entrance into the field as a participant and to his academic studies. A longtime reviewer for *Helsingin Sanomat,* Envall has emphasized the vital importance of literature as a humanizing instrument or defense against the "evil spirits" of the title: "Censorship is a tribute to the importance of literature. If the threat were a small one, no government would bother." A profoundly and constructively conservative spirit, however, Envall recognizes (more than many of his contemporaries) that "to rejoice in complete freedom of speech is shortsighted. The more one is allowed to say, the fewer the people who will listen." This conservative strain in Envall's thought is also evident in his thematic approach to literary studies: on treatments of military life in Finland's literature, *Kirjailijoiden kentät ja kasarmit* (1984; The fields and barracks of authors); on the figure of Jesus in literature, *Nasaretin miehen pitkä marssi* (1985; The long march of the man of Nazareth); and on the doppelgänger, *Toinen minä* (1988; The other ego); as well as his life-and-works study of Mika Waltari (1994).

The importance of Envall's accomplishment as a figure of literature (and not a commentator on it) was recognized in 1990, when he was awarded the Finlandia Prize for his *Samurai nukkuu* (1989; The samurai is sleeping), in which he expanded the aphoristic form in the direction of both the prose poem and the essay. ("A literary genre is a prison, I have tried to burst the boundaries of the aphorism, I should like to reach an open field, even as Paavo Haavikko has.") The aphorisms are arranged in sections resembling poem cycles, in which — often with quiet wit — Envall illuminates problems from different sides or creates succinct national portraits: "The Finn does not express his love, his yearning, his faith himself. The tango singer and the pastor do that for him. And why does the Finn love the theater? In the substitute experience he can liberate himself. He cries laughs shouts through his substitutes. Just the way he also applies his smidgen of power. In love the Finn is divided. His desire for possession concerns the body; he purchases his spiritual needs from the entertainment industry." Since the award of the Finlandia Prize, Envall's collections have come thick and fast; *Uni palaa rikospaikalle* (1991; The dream burns in the place of crime) is still in the aphoristic form, but in *Marmorilaiva* (1993; The marble ship), for which his interest in Chinese culture provides the basis, he again approaches the lyric.

In the area of nonfiction Pentti Linkola (1932–) continues to become more prominent. A fisherman by occupation, he publishes essays at a slow pace. His first book, *Ihmisen ja isänmaan puolesta* (1960; In defense of humanity and fatherland), defended individual radical pacifism; afterward he developed into a merciless critic of environmental destruction and the destructive spiral of industrial-commercial civilization. His books, which have appeared at intervals of a decade, are *Unelmat paremmasta maailmasta* (1971; Dreams of a better world), *Toisinajattelijan päiväkirjasta* (1979; From a dissenter's diary), and *Johdatus 1990-luvun ajatteluun* (1989; Introduction to thought of the 1990s). The greatest unanimity exists regarding Linkola's merits as a master of nonfictional prose, as a stylist comparable to the best traditions. He is able to describe the values of nature, and of the human being as their destroyer, with a suggestive clarity that impresses both those who agree with him and those who do not. It has been said that if Linkola were, for instance, an American, he would be a world-famous author. Instead, his views about the direction of our civilization and the corrective measures necessary because of them have continuously caused arguments. On one hand, he is seen as a mythical prophet of Judgment Day, on the other as a rational thinker with a gift of clairvoyance; but all have had to agree on the scrupulous independence of his thought from authorities and ideologies. It is a lucky coincidence for nature conservation that it has on its side a first-class literary talent, despite the fact that Linkola's perceptions have increasingly departed from the program of organized conservation. His demands for a rapid decrease in population, for the dismantling of industrial-consuming structures, and above all, for the ascetic lifestyle required of each individual in order to save the human species aroused opposition for a long time; but the assessment of Linkola has started to move away from that of a power-hungry man to the image of a seer without illusions. In his three collections of writings Linkola has tirelessly taken apart the fallacies of present-day human beings and of civilization in its entirety; even those who do not agree with his demands for action concede his merits as a critic.

Linkola is the best example of the vitality and influential power of nonfictional literature, a healthy reminder that literature does not consist only of poems and stories. It is also proper to end with Linkola because the questions he has raised regarding the environment and lifestyles are challenges and issues about which the rest of the literary field has been forced, and will be forced, to form an opinion.

Finland-Swedish Literature

A Part of Sweden

George C. Schoolfield

6

Jöns Budde's Book
Finland's Swedish literature had a false dawn with the translations made by the monk Jöns Budde at the cloister of Saint Birgitta in Nådendal (Naantali); the place-name is taken from the institution itself, "Monasterium vallis gratiae," the "Monastery of the Vale of Grace." On the basis of Budde's language, philologists have deduced that Budde came from Vörå (Vöyri) in Ostrobothnia; his activity at the cloister stretched some thirty years (ca. 1461–91), and his work was a part of an effort to make Latin devotional literature accessible to unlettered members of the religious community. The manuscript that came to be known as "Jöns Budde's Book" contains a rendering of the *Lucidarius* (Light spreader), a treatise in dialogue form for the teaching of Christian precepts, and a number of holy legends and meditations; its concluding entry, which breaks off in midsentence, is an account of Katarina of Vadstena, Birgitta's daughter and the first prioress of the mother cloister of the Birgittine order at Vadstena in Sweden.

Budde can also properly be called the first Swedish-language translator of biblical texts; in 1484 he turned the books of Judith, Esther, Ruth, and the Maccabees into his mother tongue. The poet Frans Österblom (1870–1907) was inspired to treat Budde (in a poem of eighteen strophes from 1895) as the father of Finland-Swedish creative literature, his mind flying from his cloister cell to "heroic men and fair women in the Orient"; Österblom's exaggerated claim arose in an atmosphere of a growing Finland-Swedish self-awareness and, indeed, separatism.

Forsius
After Budde, a vacuum ensued; the Nådendal cloister succumbed to the Reformation, and in Åbo (Turku), the capital of the duchy of Finland, a

brilliant court maintained at Åbo Castle in 1556–63 by Gustav Vasa's son, Duke Johan (to be Johan III of Sweden, 1568–92), and his Polish bride, Katarina Jagellonica, bore no literary fruit. The events of the "Club War" between followers of Sigismund, the son of Johan and Katarina, and his uncle Charles of Södermanland (later Charles IX of Sweden) devastated large parts of the country and left Åbo a shambles after two sieges by Charles's troops — the second of them would be the background of Josef Julius Wecksell's great historical drama *Daniel Hjort* (1862). It was not until the age of Gustav II Adolf and his daughter, Kristina, that the town assumed its proper place as the modest fountainhead of Finland's culture.

Meanwhile, a striking figure came from an unprepossessing port to the east, Helsingfors (Helsinki), founded in 1550 to lure trade away from Tallinn (Reval) on the other side of the Gulf of Finland. Little enough is known of the early life of Sigfrid Aronus Forsius (ca. 1550–1624): after study at German universities and at Uppsala, he was consecrated a pastor at Åbo in 1597 and became court preacher to Duke Charles, the future king of Sweden. In 1601 he was sent on a sort of scientific expedition to Lapland in the company of Daniel Hjort, who had been instrumental in surrendering Åbo Castle to Charles; following another sojourn in Germany and, in Sweden, a brief imprisonment on suspicion of supporting Sigismund (the Catholic king of Poland still laying claim to Sweden's crown), he was named professor of astronomy at Uppsala (1608–10) and styled himself "Royal Astronomer." For two years (1613–15), he was pastor at the Riddarholm Church in Stockholm, the home of the city's "Finnish congregation"; in this spiritual capacity he put together *Andelige psalmer och wijsor* (1614; Spiritual hymns and songs), which made him the first known writer of hymns in Swedish in Finland and the beginner of a long line that would include Johan Ludvig Runeberg (1804–77), Zachris Topelius (1818–98), and Lars Huldén (1926–). He was suspended from the post ostensibly because he used astrology for prophecy and was insubordinate; the archbishop of Uppsala also scored him for his drunkenness and for squabbles with his wife and fellow pastors. (More sensationally still, Daniel Hjort, Forsius's old friend, had been stabbed to death in a fight outside Forsius's pastoral dwelling on Pentecost Sunday in 1615; Forsius was not accused of the deed, but nasty words had fallen between him and his "sworn brother," who was drunk, shortly before.)

Then he seems to have tried to live by his pen. Two important translations from these hard years have been attributed to him, both of satirical beast epics. The one is of the anti-Catholic (and anti-imperial) *Gans-König* (1607) by Wolfhart Spangenberg-Lykosthenes (ca. 1570–ca. 1636), rendered into Swedish as *Gåås Kong: En lustig och kortwilig dicht om Mårtens*

Gåås (1619; Goose King: A merry and entertaining poem about Saint Martin's goose), purportedly done by one "Johannes Sigfridi from Viborg" (Viipuri) in Karelia; the other, done anonymously by "a well-learned man" at the behest of a Stockholm printer, is *Reyncke Fosz. Thet är: En skön och nyttigh Dicht full medh Wijsshet, godh Läro, och lustige Exempel* (1621; Reynard the Fox: that is: A fair and useful poem full of wisdom, good teaching, and merry examples). If these translations, respectively from High and Low German, are probably by Forsius, a third bears his name, the *Speculum vitae humanae: Om menniskionnes Leffuerne* (1620; Mirror of human life: Concerning the lives of men), based closely on a Danish work with a Latin title, *De vita hominis* (1514; Concerning the life of man), by a Roman Catholic priest, Michael Nicolai of Odense, a depiction of the various ages of man in monologue form. Carl Fehrman, in his 1952 study of the image of death in literature (pp. 279–80), has called attention to the extraordinary popularity of this work of Forsius during the seventeenth century, not only through the several reprintings of the original but because it was included, from 1662 on, in the Swedish *Bondepraktiken* (Farmers' almanac) and thus reached the simplest homes — albeit not attributed to Forsius: it "continued to influence the imagination and the plastic arts through the centuries." After its appearance Forsius returned to the little Finnish coastal town of Ekenäs (Tammisaari), serving as pastor there until his death.

Much in Forsius's turbulent life appealed to creative writers: Topelius used him in both stories and verse as "Master Sigrid," the irascible but kindly and patriotic old man who gladly returned to Finland to read "my stars, my dear stars." Later still, Anders Cleve (1937–85) had the protagonist of his novel *Vit eld* (1962; White fire) become intrigued by Forsius's poetry, of which a main display is to be found in *Physica Eller Naturlighe Things Qualiteters och Egendomars beskrijfuelse* (1611, first published 1952; Physics or description of qualities and properties of natural things), and more recently, the poet Kari Aronpuro (1940–) has been inspired by the same book for his *Vähäfysiikka* (1981; Little physics). Each of the original's nine books addresses, in vivid prose, elements of the creation — for example, book 4 is "Heaven and Its Parts and Their Courses," and book 8 is "Living Creatures on the Earth That Feel and Move" (including human beings). Several of the books are concluded by "Hymns of Praise" in unrhymed psalmic lines; the entire work ends with a summary in twenty-three seven-line strophes — the finale that fascinated Cleve's student, a grandiose description of a creation even containing "the sirens who so merrily / Play out their game within the sea." Forsius evidently planned to expand this magnum opus of his, but he was perhaps diverted by his subsequent tribulations.

The single extant work of a younger contemporary of Forsius, "En annan ny visa" (1651; Another new song) by Christina Regina von Birchenbaum (?–?), was long attributed, after its publication by the antiquarian Per Hanselli in the mid-nineteenth century, to the Swedish poet Lars Wivallius (1605–69). The author (who names herself in an acrostic composed of the opening letters of each of the poem's twenty-nine eight-line strophes) offers an autobiography: from Karelia, she married an officer for love and followed him to Germany during the Thirty Years' War, only to learn that he had died on the battlefield. For seventeen years, she goes on, she drove "all worldly joy and pleasure" from her mind, but then ("I am flesh and blood") became enamored of a "young nobleman." Gossip and "false friends" separated them; now she finds solace in her "heavenly bridegroom." (Other evidence indicates that she also found a second husband, a major who died in 1662.) Birchenbaum is thus the first woman author in Finland and is likewise singular by virtue of her glimpses of the Thirty Years' War, in which troops from Finland, under the Swedish flag, were the terror of Continental battlefields. No other contemporary belletristic record exists of the Finnish participation in the great European conflict.

Åbo Academy: Playwrights and Poets
The establishment of Åbo Academy in 1640 (expanded from a gymnasium founded ten years earlier) was a turning point in Finland's intellectual history. Although the intention was to attach Finland even more closely to the Swedish crown, a purpose similar to that of the creation eight years before of the university at Dorpat (Tartu) in Estonia, the academy gave Finland a sense of cultural identity that in fact would mark its difference from Sweden. The foundation took place during the first governorship (1637–40) of the talented Per Brahe the Younger (1602–80), and the little university became the apple of his eye. Striving to emulate its older brothers in the outside world, the infant institution immediately began the practice of producing plays for solemn academic occasions. Michael Wexionius (1609–70), professor of politics and history and the first dean of faculty, managed to enliven the grand opening with the Latin play *Studentes* (1545; The students) by the Brandenburger Christoph Stymmelius (1525–88), a comedy first performed at Wittenberg and meant to show the rewards of scholarly virtues and, by means of copious examples, the wages of scholarly (and other) sins, a transposition of the story of the prodigal son to the groves of academe.

The performance (of 17 July 1640), by the academy's recently arrived students, is the first recorded staging of a play in Finland. In 1643 the academy got a member with some talent for original dramatic writing, Jacobus Chronander (?–1694), from Västergötland in Sweden. (Of the academy's original forty-nine enrollees, only eight were from Finland.) On 6 May 1647, to celebrate the graduation of a class of masters of art, Chronander's *Surge eller Flijt-och oflijtighetz Skode Spegel* (Arise, or the mirror of industry and sloth) was performed; the exhortatory Latin opening of the title was taken from God's command to Abraham (Genesis 13:17) to arise and "walk the length and breadth of the earth." By means of a disingenuous introduction Chronander tried to assuage faculty and ecclesiastical opponents of play-acting by means of the familiar argument, lifted from Cicero, that comedy is "a mirror of human life, teaching us to ransack ourselves and not seldom awakening us to the approach of evil"; besides, acting will refresh students' "spirit and mind, sometimes brought to wrack and ruin by lengthy pursuit of studies." In the seven-act play the virtuous Palladius hearkens to his good spirit Diligentia, while the lazy Circeius (played by Chronander) obeys Negligentia and is also assisted down the primrose path by the wastrels Tubbe and Nimmergodt ("No-Good"). Like contemporary comedies in Germany, *Surge* has entr'actes, called "Facetiae intercalares" ("Inserted drolleries"), in which characters from the action proper — two honest peasants, Dragwaal and Styrbiörn, and the drinking companions of Circeius — are juxtaposed. These pairs parallel, of course, the two lead figures but are used also for drastic social criticism. In the important entr'acte between the second and third act Dragwaal and Styrbiörn are informed by a "praetor" or overseer (whom they have to bribe as well) of the heavy taxes they must pay; they implore him to keep away "troopers," who rape wife and servant girls, leaving the husband to bring up the children sprung of violence. As he speaks, Dragwaal applies a half-Swedish, half-Finnish phrase to himself "arme mies" ("poor man"), an indication that Chronander was aware of the plight of Finnish-speaking country folk.

In the summer of 1649 Chronander wrote a second play, to be performed in celebration of a marriage between members of two of Finland's great families, Jöns Kurck the Younger (1590–1652), reputedly Finland's richest man, and Kristina Horn (1604–73), from the Horns of Kankas, the widow of the admired cavalry general, Torsten Stålhandske. Despite its frivolous-sounding title, *Bele Snack* (Wooing talk) was an ambitious undertaking, meant to illustrate the making of a happy marriage in accordance with Luther's prescription. The first act offers some crass anti-Catholic propaganda; the loose-living nun, Virginea, and the lustful monk, Franciscanus, are caught by Philippius (a name doubtless taken from Luther's great associate, Philipp Melanchthon), and she claims that she has been raped by her fellow religious. When he is threatened with castration, however, she pleads for him, offering her shirt or shift as a ransom. Again, Chronander inserts a Finnish word, "paita": did it have some social-ethnic significance? Other textual evidence is absent; the entr'actes of the play were not printed, in order to save money. The statement at the end of the dramatis personae was correct; even in its printed form the play was "somewhat extensive." Throughout its later acts the audience could follow the life of the admirable Apollonius, stubbornly Lutheran, a contrast to the prodigal Acolastus ("Improvident," a typical name from Continental prodigal son plays); Anabaptistus, the representative of free love; and the womanhater Diogenius. In good time Apollonius wins the hand of Pulcheria, while Acolastus (Anabaptistus's disciple and also called the "village goat") is forced to marry the whore Thais, whose seven little bastards surround their new father, crying out — in Finnish — for "bread, food, and aid." Chronander attempted to keep his audience awake not only by his scandalous material but also by the employment of a variety of poetic meters (in which he likely followed the example of a major German marriage play, Paul Rebhun's famous *Susanna* [1536]) and several sorts of prose, and by his not inconsiderable wit (not always on the side of the angels): receiving Pulcheria's agreement to wed him, Apollonius delivers a speech in extremely sober and businesslike language.

The promising dramatic start at Åbo petered out; a play by Ericus Kolmodin (ca.1630–ca.1665), *Genesis aetherea eller Jesu Christi födelse* (1657; Heavenly genesis, or the Birth of Jesus Christ), was a simple retelling of the familiar story mainly in the rough four-beat verse (*Knittelvers*) that had been standard in German during the previous century. Kolmodin was sufficiently up-to-date, however, to experiment briefly with the alexandrine (six-foot iambic verse with a strongly marked caesura and usually in rhyme pairs), which had now become standard in French classicism and the German baroque; he employed it for Herod's command that the innocents be slaughtered and again in the solemn epilogue. Thraso, one of the king's executioners, gets the following instruction: "All small male children that have reached two years or less / You shall with shield and sword straight into dying press," and Thraso obediently repeats the order, later on, in an abrupt and cruel three-foot line:

Where'er I make my way
I am prepared to slay
So that the entire land
Will tremble at my hand.

The alexandrine would become a favorite prosodic form for Finland's Swedish poets during the next half-century.

Michael Wexionius, under whose aegis drama had been fostered in Åbo, left his professorship in 1650 to go back to Stockholm, ennobled as Baron Gyldenstolpe; his (relatively) cosmopolitan spirit was replaced by the rigorism of Enevald Svenonius (1617–88), a sometime member of the academy's first class who, after studies at Wittenberg, had returned to his alma mater in 1655 as professor of rhetoric, then swiftly advancing from "third" to "first" professor of theology. The Swedish-born Svenonius was so strictly orthodox that, in a sensational struggle, he had the bishop himself, Johannes Terserus (1605–78), deposed for the latter's presumably ecumenical utterances; plainly, the Åbo climate was not favorable to academic dramatists. During more than twenty years Svenonius's hand lay heavy on the academy, until he was recalled to his native Sweden as bishop of Lund in 1687, although he did not live to assume the post.

Poets fared only a little better. A brother of Michael Wexionius, Olof, had gone to Finland in 1644 and played the role of the virtuous Palladius in Chronander's *Surge;* he then proceeded to a professorship at Dorpat, where he fathered Olof Wexionius the Younger (1656–89/90). When the family, fleeing Dorpat before the invading Russians, returned to Åbo, Olof junior was enrolled in the academy at the age of eleven. Faculty children, as is well known, sometimes do not turn out well; the younger Wexionius left Finland in 1683 for an administrative post in Gothenburg but was almost immediately fired for employing his time "with his peculiar affairs and his own pleasure." He landed in debtors' prison and attempted in vain to get further positions in Finland and Sweden, until an early death freed him from further humiliation and his family from further embarrassment.

Wexionius is remembered for his sole collection of verse, *Sinne-afvel* (1684; Sense progeny). A main display is the long funeral poem for a maternal uncle, "Melancholia," which expatiates on the theme of the vanity of human life so common in seventeenth-century verse. The preamble to the poem is a statement about his poetic masters—Wexionius intends to show that he knows the literary giants of the time: the Silesians Martin Opitz and Andreas Gryphius, the Dutchman Jacob Cats, the Italian Battista Guarini. Like Opitz in Germany, some sixty years before, he wants "Sweden, the mother of heroes, the queen of all the North," to have a poetic voice equal to its political power; addressing his unspecified fellow poets, he says: "Our poetry's late come / But, trust in what I say, will be the fairest stone, / The brightest of all jewels set in your honor's crown." (In his catalog of models he mentions only one Swede, the mysterious "Mr. L. S.," no doubt a misprint for G. S., Georg Stiernhielm [1598–1672], whom, later on in the body of his book, he salutes, "the father of Swedish poetry" and "the Swedish Opitz." Later, too, he mentions Lars Johansson, or "Lasse Lucidor" [1638–74], "a man deserving more than fortune meted him" and a *poète maudit* with whom Wexionius probably identified.) Wexionius can be forgiven a certain amount of bragging; he displayed his poetic gift not only in the traditional epithalamium and epicedium but in such formal experiments as an upside-down sonnet on the final Judgment Day (sestet first, octet second). Further, he expanded traditional thematics, writing "En Siö-mans olägenheet" (A seaman's predicament), about the perils of nautical life, a poem later described as the first example of sea poetry in Finland-Swedish letters. And in a self-analysis delivered by the biblical Dinah (Genesis 34) after her assault by Shechem (a deed in which she participated with a willingness she now regrets), Wexionius composed a passionate dramatic monologue strongly reminiscent of a contemporary piece of German baroque verse, Daniel Casper von Lohenstein's tirade of the Spanish lady Maria Coronelia, who kills herself with a firebrand, thus consuming her own burning lust. The collection is dedicated to the infant crown prince, Charles (XII); unfortunately, Wexionius did not live to describe the career of that turbulent and often wrongheaded warrior king, to whom he might have applied the undeniable energy and inventiveness displayed in *Sinne-afvel*. In some poems intended for a second edition Wexionius predicted that the little boy would be "in peace a Solomon, in war an Alexander." He was right, more or less, on the second count.

Johan Paulinus (1655–1732) offers an instructive contrast to the ne'er-do-well Wexionius; the son of a poor pastor at Björneborg (Pori), he enrolled in the academy five years after Wexionius. He quickly established himself as a coming man with his hexameter epyllion composed in Greek but bearing a Latin title, *Magnus principatus Finlandia* (1678; The great principality of Finland), in which he depicted the virtues of its inhabitants (like Runeberg and Topelius later on, he made Finland's poverty into its main strength) and its abundant wildlife: a peaceable kingdom, its streams harbored no crocodiles, its forests no tigers. Ambitious as he was, Paulinus quickly found his way into government and was ennobled as Count Lillienstedt in 1690; with the accession of Charles XII to the Swedish throne, his responsibilities increased. After Charles's death he was the chief Swedish negotiator with the Russians during the peace conference of 1721 at Nystad (Uusikaupunki) in his old homeland, bringing the disastrous Great Northern War to a close: albeit mutilated, Finland was saved, while the Baltic provinces went aglimmering. Instead of choosing Finland as a retirement home, however, Paulinus-Lillienstedt lived out his days on his estate in

Swedish Pomerania. He had accrued such a considerable fortune that rumor claimed the Russians had paid him, at Nystad, to abandon eastern Finland; further, both his marriages had allied him with powerful Swedish families — in the second he was brother-in-law to Arvid Horn, his fellow Finlander, who was Sweden's leading statesman after Charles XII's death.

Paulinus-Lillienstedt had known how to do the advantageous thing in poetry as well; his Swedish verse, mostly from the beginning of his career, always chooses appropriate themes. He demonstrated his piety, and his ability to reel off thundering alexandrines, in his three-part epic, or messiad, called *Christus nascens, patiens et triumphans, eller Den Nyfödde, Korszfeste, och Opståndne Christus* (Christ aborning, suffering, and triumphing, or the newborn, crucified, and resurrected Christ). In his little introduction of 1694 he claimed that he had worked on it for fourteen years and had now decided to publish it "at the urging of friends" (in fact, the crucifixion section had come out separately in 1686). The poems are quite similar to undertakings from other literatures of the age, such as Giles Fletcher's *Christ's Victorie and Triumph,* the Dutchman Daniel Heinsius's *Lof-sanck van Jesus Christus* (Panegyric of Jesus Christ), Opitz's *Klage bei dem Creutz unseres Erlösers* (Lament at the cross of our Redeemer), and Gryphius's Latin epics, *Herodes* and *Olivetum.* They contain much rhetorical display (in the use of antithesis, apostrophe, climax) and have the advantage of a certain compelling vividness and relative brevity.

Otherwise, Paulinus (before he became Lillienstedt) proved he was a competent enough sonneteer, a skillful spinner of glosses (on poems of Opitz, Guarini, and the French religious poet Georges de Brébeuf); he even made a stab at erotic poetry with his "Klagan öfver Iris afresa" (Lament at Iris's departure), assuming the voice of the Propertian-Petrarchan lover who wants nature to join him in lamenting his loss. Disseminated in manuscript, the poem was not published until 1820, by the Swedish romantic Lorenzo Hammarsköld. In his pioneering history of Finland-Swedish literature (1866–67) Gabriel Lagus called the poem "a poetic confession, of which the statesman was perhaps ashamed, but which possibly, in its small way, led his career to the heights"; Runeberg's friend, the philosopher and cultural historian Johan Jacob Tengström (1787–1858), had likewise been an admirer of the "Iris." Writing at a time when "baroque" was not a positive cultural concept, Lagus does not mention Paulinus-Lillienstedt's epics on Christ and his partial rendering of Guarini's *Pastor fido* (1590) into Swedish, where his work was quickly overshadowed by the full translation by the Swede Gunno Eurelius Dahlstierna (1661–1709), a much greater poetic talent. Probably, Paulinus-Lillienstedt understood his limitations very well; in his autobiography, written in his old age, he does not dwell on his poetic work.

Other poets—for whom poetry was also an amusement or means of advancement—stayed in Finland, unlike Wexionius and Paulinus-Lillienstedt. Gabriel Tuderus (1638–1703) was expelled from Åbo Academy for bad behavior but reformed and became a missionary to the Sami, where his methods of conversion are said to have sometimes been brutal. He was bilingual; his contribution to Finnish-language literature is the comic poem *Yxi caunis suomen-kielinen weisu, talonpoille cunniaxi ja ylistöxexi* (1703), which had already appeared in Swedish as *Een skön och lustigh wijsa om bondeståndet och thes embete* (1685; A beautiful and jolly song about the peasant class and its task); both versions may have been written in Tuderus's Åbo days. At his post in faraway Torneå, in 1697, he wrote a lament on the death of Charles XI, paying much attention to the late monarch's simplicity of lifestyle (which the king had also forced on his sometimes unwilling subjects): indeed, Tuderus suggests that Charles, who died of cancer, may have been prematurely carried away "for our egregious sins."

The hardhanded joviality and simplistic moralizing of Tuderus should be seen alongside the biliousness of his sometime contemporary at Åbo, Daniel Achrelius (1644–92), the son of a professor of medicine. As a boy of fifteen, Daniel had played the angel Raphael in Kolmodin's *Genesis aetherea;* as an adult, his temperament was scarcely angelic. Himself professor of eloquence at Åbo but a dabbler in many fields (physics, the natural sciences, political theory, history), he has been called (by Matti Klinge 1989, 34) a last representative of the Renaissance ideal of a universal man. Unhappily, "his satirical and violent nature" made him unpopular with colleagues and church officials alike, all the more since, as university orator, he could weave his criticisms of the legal system and the pastorate, among other things, into his funeral and memorial speeches. In his poetry, to the publication of which he turned late in his overactive life, he is dry, and his verse, like his prose, has a largely didactic purpose. Yet his *Laus manus* (1690; The praise of the hand; in Swedish despite its Latin title) possesses an odd charm as an encomium of human inventiveness and industry. Just before his death he produced, again in verse, *Moralia eller Några Korta Regler* (Moral teachings, or some brief precepts): each of the twelve sections has an "argument," in which a general rule of conduct is promulgated, followed (usually) by a Latin *sententia* summarizing the precept and by an "interpretation" that, through examples, makes the lesson clearer still. The interest of the manual lies in its target audience, young noblemen; under Svenonius the academy had gone more and more in the direction of training the clergy, and

Achrelius wished to stem this tide. A section of the *Moralia* concerns the "virtues," of which there are seventeen—the last is "Urbanitas," or "Jestfulness": one must learn to joke "with politeness" and at the right time, whereas "a crude peasant oaf has no regard for jest." In a modest way Achrelius encouraged not only the refinement but the intelligence of the nobility (which probably needed some urging on both points): one of the seventeen virtues is "Scientia," or "Knowledge of all things."

Michael Renner was among those numerous theological candidates with whom Achrelius was little concerned; a pastor's son from Raumo (Rauma), born in 1662, Renner got a position as chaplain of the Björneborg Regiment and passed away unhonored and unsung, at thirty, in the same year as Achrelius. The three "Songs of Lament and Consolation" opening his *Vijsor* (1690; Songs) are taken from a larger project that has been lost, *Tårar wedh Frelsarmansens Jesu Kristi korss* (Tears at the cross of the Savior Jesus Christ), an example of a popular subgenre of seventeenth-century neo-Latin and vernacular verse, "Lacrimae," "Tears," in which the theme of lament is constantly embroidered. (The subject may be spiritual, personal, or even patriotic.) Renner's "tears" are strictly religious and have struck a commentator (Olof Enckell in Huldén et al., 101) as being very close to the simple, emotional faith of pietism. In the second part of *Vijsor* Renner, using a stock name from pastoral poetry, Myrtilo, sings of his almost erotic love for Jesus:

> Sweet Jesus, when I have you
> Within my heart's confine,
> When You are mine, and I am Thine,
> I do not ask for more.

This saccharine eroticism (reminiscent of what Philipp Spener was doing in Germany) gives way to a search for spiritual peace in "Nöjder äger nogh" (The content man has enough), an extension of 1 Timothy 6:6–8: "But godliness with contentment is great gain." Renner's most impressive work, a so-called New Year's poem, was printed separately, as "Ett Andeligt Siökort och Seglations Konst" (A spiritual sea chart and art of navigation); in it he employs the traditional image of the trip through life as a dangerous voyage, with the soul as the seafarer, the Christian faith as the trusty ship, and Christ as helmsman. In a surprising twist of the imagination, however, Renner turns the dubious journey into a struggle between two almost equal contestants; evil becomes "the world's seagod, base Neptune, / Satan and a very nix" ("rätta näcken"), a brilliant transfer of the threatening and seductive (fresh)water sprite to the realm of the ocean, thus combining, in the two lines, classical, Christian, and Nordic mythology. Among the agents of this evil deity are "whales," "worldly sirens' songs," "treacherous reefs," "illness's dark fogs," and "death's cold north wind," tempting the spirit to despair. Yet Christ himself is "the mighty seagod" who will best them all. Near the end of his twenty-two strophes Renner turns from the ship of the soul to the ship of state, placing the vessel and its "royal skipper," Sweden's king, under Christ's command. As matters turned out, the Swedish ship would sorely need His aid.

In the last years of the reign of Charles XI all looked rosy enough, and Finland itself seemed a land of opportunity, not at all endangered from the East. In 1692, the death year of Achrelius and Renner, a brilliant young man came to Åbo from Uppsala, Torsten Rudeen, born to "simple but honest parents" in Värmland in 1661. As "poeseos professor" (professor of Latin verse and poetics), Rudeen shortly undertook a defense of classical learning for its own sake against the forces of Lutheran orthodoxy; in *Humanism in a Christian Society* Iiro Kajanto has demonstrated the effectiveness of Rudeen's championing of humanistic values at the academy — he was far more adroit than the choleric Achrelius. Bringing the academy into a (relatively) more modern world, he dared, in November 1696, to deliver an academic poem in Swedish instead of Latin, speaking ex cathedra on the occasion of Charles XI's birthday. The poem was then subsumed into his *Finska Helicons underdånige Fägne-Sånger* (1704; The Finnish Helicon's subservient songs of praise), which contained what may be called Rudeen's public poetry. In it, naturally enough, he took note of the just-begun military career of Charles XII, with a birthday poem of 1702, containing an extremely vivid picture of the boy-king's victories, particularly over the Russians at Narva.

Today Rudeen's literary fame rests less on his excellent verse for the royal house (he was a worthy rival to Gunno Eurelius Dahlstierna) than on his personal poetry of love, not printed during his lifetime but distributed in manuscript. It grew out of his devotion to Anna Brunell, also called "Caliste": he married her a few weeks after getting his professorship in 1692 and lost her to childbirth in 1695. These poems are about the lover who "builds castles in the air"; he gives a sonnet to the hardhearted "Caliste" on her birthday and in time receives a tulip from her "which does the name of queen of flowers bear." At last he celebrates his engagement to "Caliste," now called "my Anette," who has saved his thoughts from "a beachless sea" of doubts. The cycle has a double climax, first with the famous "Gavotte de l'amour": "The winter now has gone and left us, / The darkness now has lost its force," and then the lament on her death, which has a sincerity putting it in a class with the Dutch poet Constantijn Huygens's sonnet on the death of his beloved Sterre earlier in the century: "My sighs go upward, earthward go my tears." That Rudeen could often strike an individual note is also witnessed by his mock threnody for one Hartvich von Geldern, an Åbo original: talking to himself on the street, driving a crooked course in his cart, the old man proved that a lovable "foolishness dwells in us all."

Thirteen months after Anna's death Rudeen married again. The quick remarriage was altogether acceptable in the age: the Altenburg official Johann Thomas (1624–79) — who directly prefigures Rudeen in the personal quality of his pastoral novel, with verse inlays, about his early-dead wife, *Damon und Lisille* (1663/1672) — had likewise quickly found a second helpmeet; besides, since Rudeen intended to become ordained (and he did, in 1699), he was expected, as a Lutheran pastor, to have a wife. From 1706 to 1709 he was professor of theology at Åbo and then was called back to Sweden, as bishop of Karlstad in his native Värmland. His personal poetic vein had dried up, although he continued to write verse on royal patriotic themes. In 1716 he became bishop of Linköping, and in 1719 his children were ennobled under the name Rudenschiöld. Rudeen himself was left out only because of his ecclesiastical calling; instead, he was twice spokesman of the ecclesiastical estate in the Swedish Parliament before his death in 1729.

Exile Literature

Rudeen's decision to leave Finland was prudent. On 27–28 June 1709 the Swedish army of Charles XII was destroyed at Poltava by Peter the Great, and within a year, Viborg (Viipuri) and Kexholm (Käksisalmi), the bulwarks of eastern Finland, had fallen to the invading Russians. The "Great Wrath" (Stora ofreden, Isoviha) had begun, in the course of which Finland would be wholly occupied and ravaged. By 1714 Åbo itself surrendered and Prince Galitzin made it his Finnish headquarters. The academy was closed, and at least one faculty member who had not fled in time, the professor of moral philosophy and history, Johan Munster, was taken captive with his children and died in a prison transport, while another, Petrus Hielm, made it to the Åland Islands, only to be apprehended and sent to Narva as a military physician, dying there in 1716. The academy did not reopen until 1722 and held its first graduation in 1726; it did not fully recover until the age of Henrik Gabriel Porthan, in the late 1770s.

An exile literature came into being in Sweden, in which the Russians' atrocities and the sufferings of their victims were described at length, most graphically perhaps by Karl Serlachius (ca. 1690–ca. 1755) from eastern

Nyland. An Åbo student, he had left the city before the enemy arrived, and it is not certain that he had himself observed the horrors chronicled in the "festive song," *Dråtte-Skald* (Royal bard), which he composed for the accession of the late Charles's sister, Ulrika Eleonora, to the Swedish throne in 1719. His description, in alexandrines, of gang rapes "by shameful animals, by Kalmucks flat of nose" seems an unpromising topic for celebratory verse, as does the theme of another poem he wrote for the occasion, *Det kvidande och muntrade Sverige* (Sweden whimpering and enlivened), in which the country is described as "misfortune's mustering place, the stall of poverty." Serlachius's propaganda poetry was meant specifically to arouse the charity of the citizens of Gothenburg, where he now resided, playing his role of the poor refugee to the hilt. A perhaps more authentic sufferer was Zacharias Lithovius (1672–1743), sometime pastor at Nyen (Nevanlinna), a fortress town on the Neva, established by Charles XI not far from the place where St. Petersburg would shortly be built. During his long exile (the fortress was captured in 1703) Lithovius wrote both a lament on the death of Charles XII and the obligatory poem of congratulations to Ulrika Eleonora. These opuscula are bilingual (in Swedish alexandrines and Finnish runometers) or even trilingual (with Latin inlays); they emphasize the poet's Finnishness in their very titles: *Bedröfvade Finnars under-dåniga Sorge-Quäde och sörjande Norrlänningars bedröfveliga Klage-Wijsa* (Saddened Finns' devoted lament and lamenting Norrlanders' saddened dirge) — the complex name also takes care to include an adjacent Swedish province with a large Finnish population — and *Finska Nationens Underdånige Lyck-Önskan och Glädie-Sång, efter mycken Sorg och Tvång* (The Finnish nation's devoted good wishes and joyful air, after much constraint and care). Eventually, Lithovius got back to Finland, as pastor in his hometown of Uleåborg (Oulu), and stayed there until his death in 1743, near the end of a second disastrous Russian war, the "Little Wrath" (Lilla ofreden, Pikkuviha).

Ernst Gestrinius (1663–1739), who went from his birthplace, Helsingfors, to the academy and then to school posts in Viborg and a pastorate in that unfortunate city's vicinity, had also reached Sweden after "a lengthy and miserable flight." By 1718 he succeeded in getting a pastorate in Roslagen, a coastal section near Stockholm; he had called attention to himself by his New Year's poem *Nödlijdande flychtingars klagan öfver sitt långsamma kårss och elände* (Destitute refugees at their slow suffering and misery), a chapbook followed in 1722 by another outcry in the same vein, *Klagelig röst i en tro-innerlig bön om hielp uti nöden till frelsaren Jesum* (Lamenting voice in a sincere prayer for help in need to the Savior Jesus). The message is clear enough; barely escaped "from danger's clutch," the pastor sees a threat to the Swedish heartland itself and beseeches Jesus for aid, since the whole Swedish empire "is now afire in war." Gestrinius's mastery of elementary baroque rhetoric, especially the repetitive figure of epizeuxis ("Our fatherland, our fatherland," "Our cloud of tears, our cloud of tears," "But Jesus help, help, Jesus, help"), has a hypnotic effect. A hint of criticism may lie beneath the customary refusal to look deeper than "our sins" for the cause of the disaster. Arvid Hultin, a pioneer investigator of Finland's Swedish letters of the seventeenth and eighteenth centuries, noticed that at the end of the New Year's poem of 1718 (the year in which Charles XII would be killed at Fredikshald in Norway), Gestrinius wishes good luck and prosperity to "all the [parliamentary] estates of the kingdom" but does not mention the monarch whose infatuation with his own military prowess surely contributed to Sweden's and Finland's ruin (*Finlands svenska vitterhet 4*, cclxvii).

Frese and Löfving

The most distinguished of the refugee poets is Jacob Frese, born in 1690 as the frail youngest son of a powerful mercantile family (with German forebears) in Viborg and enrolled in Åbo Academy at twelve. In 1711 he went over to Stockholm and worked as a copyist in government offices until the onset of tuberculosis and his death in 1729. More than any other author mentioned thus far, Frese made poetry his main concern—not that his production was large: the "spiritual and worldly poems" of 1726, prose aphorisms and moral teachings from the same year, and then *Passions-Tankar* (1728; Thoughts on the Passion), about the Savior's "bloody struggle in torment and death," and *Några Poetiske Samblingar* (Some poetic collections) — these last from his sickbed. At the start of his Swedish career Frese had become known for his epithalamia; but he first achieved a kind of fame with his *Frögde-Qwäde* (Paean), delivered as a poetic oration in 1715 to celebrate the return of Charles XII from his Turkish internment after Poltava, in which poem (following the unfulfilled prediction of his Åbo teacher, Rudeen) Frese speaks hopefully of a future reign of peace. Encased within the paean is Frese's great apostrophe to the city of his birth, Viborg, "the fair maiden" threatened and then taken, a dove seized by a hawk. In his vision of a lost home city, as in so much else, Frese resembles his fellow victim of tuberculosis, the Baltic German Simon Dach (1605-59), a native of Memel but bound by duty and illness to Königsberg.

Of all Frese's verse, what has rightly attracted the most attention is his desultory series "Verser i siukdom wid åtskillige wåhr-tider" (Verses in illness at various springtides), seventeen short poems in quatrains, set down from 1712 until 1728. In them Frese writes, as the modernist poet Rabbe Enckell put it in an appreciative essay, "not about a landscape but surely about nature," which, for him, "lives an independent life without an observer" (p. 20). Yet it should not be forgotten that the observer *is* there, slowly dying and aware that all the world's beauty will soon be taken from him. At the same time, though, he is profoundly grateful that the Almighty has vouchsafed him the gift of earthly life and has promised him something better still: "The lovely earth is now released from winter's chains," and just so, he will be released into an eternal spring, "Oh blessed joyfulness, that does all joys exceed." From year to year Frese maintains a mixture of happiness and anxiety, neither emotion excessive in its expression. The last poem of the cycle (addressed to the "lovely nightingale, which still beholds my woes") ends in a blending of the two currents: "I have no fear of death, and have no hate of living." Joy in nature, fear at its loss, and ultimate serenity would reappear, two centuries later, in the last poems of another consumptive from Karelia, Edith Södergran.

The Swedish scholar Carl Fehrman ("Karolinska tiden," p. 69) has also called attention to a quite different note in Frese's poetry, a fascination with apocalyptic thoughts of the world's end and his own; the gentle poet had a weakness for blood and thunder, as shown in the *Passions-Tankar*, the dirge for Charles XII, and the short but tremendous, "Yttersta dagens tecken" (Signs of the Judgment Day), when the elements themselves are dissolved in fire, "and the day grows harshly dark": "A giant storm blew towers and turrets away, / The very air tore loose to whip the ocean's madness, / The very heavens stood in fire and flaming's sway." (The comparison with Södergran can be carried still further, by a reference to her apocalyptic poetry written during and after the Civil War of 1918.) Nonetheless, the essential Frese is serene and wistful, the quiet voice who rounds off his last collection with "Auktorens saliga förtröstan och slutsång" (The author's blessed consolation and final song), in which, he says, his death will put an end to his insubstantial existence: "what I've been in this world, / A dream, a stream, a shadow, and no more."

Literary history has ignored the circumstance that a youth named Stefan Löfving, born in Narva in 1689 as the son of a cannoneer, was employed by an elder brother of Jacob Frese at Viborg from 1702 to 1708 and, boxed on the ear by his master, gave the latter such a beating in return that, afraid of legal action, he had to leave town for good. Literary history has likewise not paid heed to the *Dagbok* (Diary) of Löfving, who became the most feared and praised partisan fighter for the Swedes during the Great Wrath, although creative writers have given him his due — Fredrika Runeberg in her novel *Fru Catharina Boije och hennes döttrar* (1858; Lady Catharina Boije and her daughters) and Zachris Topelius in *Fältskärns berättelser* (1853-67; Tales of a field surgeon). Löfving finished his diary, based on "journals" kept during the war years, in 1734 and submitted it in an unsuccessful attempt to resell his military skills to the Swedish crown; on his death in 1777 the diary was passed to a teacher at the gymnasium in Borgå (Porvoo), where Löfving spent his sunset years, and then became a part of the school's library. It was not published until the next century; excerpts appeared in a Borgå newspaper in 1843, and the complete text was printed in 1865.

Long an object of interest to historians, the diary, with its high literary qualities, deserves a place in Finland-Swedish letters: it can be proposed that Löfving, who lived for a time in Holstein, had some notion of the German picaresque novel of Grimmelshausen and others. Löfving stylized the events he had jotted down in his "journals," organized them into annual sections, each with a central theme (which, in modern reprintings, handily serve as chapters), and constructed a skillful narrative that begins with his capture and bloodily clever escape from the Cossacks, tells of his swift advancement from an insignificant soldier to a legendary scout, and then, the "novel's" climax, moves him from Finland to south Sweden, where he meets and manages to charm Charles XII. The rest is anticlimactic; Löfving returns to Finland, to ever more perilous adventures on land and sea, and, while the hopeless war runs down, loses interest in the métier for which — strong, steel-nerved, quick-witted, linguistically gifted — he was born. Löfving's diary is the age's most vivid document from Finland, and the one most read; a small but worthy counterpart to Esteban Gonzáles's *Estebanillo* (1646), Grimmelshausen's *Simplicius Simplicissimus* (1669), and Defoe's *Memoirs of a Cavalier,* the last-named almost contemporaneous (1724) with Löfving's manuscript.

Åbo Reconstituted
When the cruel war was over, literary activity in Finland had almost come to a standstill. To be sure, Åbo Academy briefly found a new and curious poetic voice: Alexander Hacks (?-1740) was one of forty-seven students who registered at its reopening in 1722. In 1725, when a seventeen-year-old Swedish nobleman, Claes Ekeblad, was named "rector illustris" of the dilapidated institution (Ekeblad was destined for a long career as a statesman, dying on the very eve of the coup that brought Gustav III to the throne), the highhearted Hacks greeted the charming boy with an elegant epibaterion, a poem of welcome; then, for the first graduation after the long

lacuna, he provided "Dygdenes lön, i Lager-Krantz grön, Wunnen och funnen" (Virtue's reward, in green laurel snared, desired, and acquired), a parade piece with interior rhymes, lengthy anaphoras, and a basically dactylic six-foot line, in loose imitation of the meter of Stiernhielm's *Hercules* (1658), a form rapidly losing ground to the alexandrine but still employed by, among others, the amateur poets who described the Swedish catastrophe at Poltava. Mars, the god of war, is defeated, and Apollo's "sons and men," Pallas Athene's "fairest host," triumph. The occasion was solemn, to be sure, but near the end of the poem the impudent Hacks got away with calling the goddess the "nursemaid of virtue" (in Swedish "dygdenas amma") and "wisdom's sole-only defense and wonderful, lovable mamma" ("härliga kiärliga Mamma"). Nor was this Hacks's last word; other celebratory poems show not only the bold metrical experimenter but a foe, so he claimed, of classical languages, striking a blow (in the graduation poem of 1732) for "simple Swedish" and "Finnish, which ought not to be despised." This unusual interest in language and its nuances then became the moving force in the comic poems for which Hacks was still remembered by a nonacademic public as late as the 1880s, *Eskola gubbens visor* (Songs of the old man of Eskola), affectionate reports on the marriage (1732) and the much lamented death (1735) of one Joseph Petrei, an Åbo merchant who owned the "Eskola property" in the "very middle of city." The wit of these poems lies largely in their verbal dress, Swedish as it was spoken by the Finnish middle class of the town. The spirit, it must be added, is not condescending, as it sometimes can be in the depiction of Irish characters on the eighteenth-century Dublin stage (for example, Thomas Sheridan's *The Brave Irishman or Captain O'Blunder*, 1743), but warmhearted.

The major figures of the new age were infinitely more serious than Hacks, who, like other college wits, slipped into obscurity, earning his bread as an Åbo lawyer and dying in 1740. The respectable names to remember in the age of Finland's rebuilding after the great disaster, the "Economic Age," belong to authors of practical or scientific treatises: the adept of Carl von Linné, Pehr Kalm (1716–79), whose *En Resa till Norra Amerika* (1752–56; Eng. tr. *Travels into North America*, 1770–72, 1937) became an international success; the many-sided and progressive Ostrobothnian pastor Anders Chydenius (1729–1803), the author of a treatise on economics, *Den nationella vinsten* (1765; Eng. tr. *The National Gain*, 1931); Pehr Adrian Gadd (1727–97), like Kalm on the Åbo faculty, and the author of a standard work on agronomy; the Orientalist and natural scientist—and Linné disciple—Petter Forsskål (1732–63), who got into hot water with his treatise *Tankar om den medborgerliga friheten* (1759; Thoughts on civil freedom), before participating in the Danish expedition to Arabia Deserta (1758–1809) during which he died of disease.

A little later there is the *Anteckningar under en resa till Ostindien 1782–1786* (Notes during a journey to the East Indies in the years 1782–86) by the Swedish-born physician Klas Fredrik Hornstedt (1758–1809), a pendant to such works from Sweden as Karl Gustaf Ekeberg's *Ostindisk resa, 1770–1771* (East Indian journey, 1770–1771) and, of course, to Jacob Wallenberg's classic and subjective travel book *Min son på galejan, eller En Ostindisk resa* (1781; Eng. tr. *My Son on the Galley*, 1994). Further, in this Finnish annex to the boom in Swedish travel books, there is the *Anteckningar under en ekonomisk resa från Finland öfver nordvestra Tyskland samt Nederländerna till Paris 1799–1800* (Notes during an economic journey from Finland across northwestern Germany and the Netherlands to Paris in 1799–1800), by another Ostrobothnian and the great Chydenius's disciple, Peter Johan Bladh (1746–1816), a remarkable figure who had lived for many years in Canton as a representative of the Swedish East India Company; on Finland proper, Bladh wrote *Om finska landthushållningen och medlen till dess upphjelpande* (Concerning the Finnish agricultural economy and the means of its improvement). All these are valuable factual works but not by any stretch belletristic or even of particular stylistic excellence. Creative literature, indeed, seemed to have moved to Sweden in the person of the Finnish-born nobleman Gustaf Philip Creutz (1731–85), who, after brief studies at Åbo, went to Stockholm and became an ornament of its court life, its diplomatic corps, and pastoral literature; later Johan Henrik Kellgren (1751–95), born in Sweden, spent some eight years in Åbo as student and faculty member, but his literary work, like Creutz's, belongs to Sweden's literary history, not Finland's (see volume 3 in this series, *A History of Swedish Literature*).

Franzén and Choraeus

The last and greatest poet to come from Finland while it was still a part of the Swedish empire was Frans Michael Franzén (1772–1847), the eldest son of a prosperous merchant of Uleåborg (Oulu) and grandson of a man who, "when the whole of Finland had been taken by Russian arms" (as Franzén put it in his autobiographical sketches written in his old age), had left Kexholm in Karelia and gone from Finland's southeastern to its northwestern corner, not far from the Arctic Circle. It has been remarked that the attachment to light in Franzén's poetry may have come from the place he spent his boyhood: after winter darkness the return of the sun has an overwhelming significance. (In the autobiography Franzén proudly proclaimed that Uleåborg lay farther north than any other European town save

Torneå and Tromsø!) Another factor in Franzén's childhood was his extremely close relationship to his mother, who was only sixteen when he was born: the poem "Morgonrodnaden" (The sunrise), later subjected to one of Franzén's many revisions of his work as "Moderen och sonen" (The mother and the son), couples the almost mystical experience of sunlight with the picture of the lovely and devoted girl. The tendency of Franzén to seek idealized love objects, presented in his verse as "Selma," "Lilly," "Fanny," may well have come from this maternal source; but the practice was also a part of the sentimental literary times, as in the work of Franzén's much-admired model, Klopstock.

At thirteen, "fragile and weak," Franzén was sent off to Åbo; luckily, he was taken under the wing of the great Porthan (among whose many good deeds for the academy was the elimination of hazing). Franzén became a prize disciple and was appointed docent in 1792. Meanwhile, he had already attracted literary attention in Sweden: Kellgren, a friend of Finland, printed a number of Franzén's poems in his newspaper, *Stockholms Posten,* among them "Människans anlete" (The human countenance), in which Franzén—who knew his Milton—salutes "the human face divine" as the special signature of humanity. The poem was an "ode to Selma," the sister of a comrade from Åbo; to her, Franzén also addressed such examples of his chaste erotic poetry as "Skilsmässan" (The separation) and "Den enda kyssen" (The only kiss). In these years Franzén was determined to absorb all he could of authors opposed to the ideals of French classicism still admired in some quarters of Swedish letters (and assailed by the volatile Kellgren and the hyperemotional Bengt Lidner, among others); thus he plunged into Danish (Baggesen), English (not only Milton but Shakespeare, Gray, and Thompson), and German literature (the all-important Klopstock, the sentimental Ludwig Hölty and Friedrich Matthisson). Nevertheless, he retained his devotion to Finland and Finnish simplicity in such poems as "Den gamle knekten" (The old soldier) and "Den fattiga flickan" (The poor girl), which presage Runeberg's admiration for seeing the unpretentious strength, amid vicissitudes, of Finnish country people. (In the summer of 1794 he made a journey through Finland with his mentor, Porthan, which he then described in the newspaper *Åbo Tidning,* Finland's only one of the time, which Franzén edited.)

During 1795–96 Franzén undertook a long journey to Germany (where he looked up Baggesen and Klopstock and was not disappointed: Baggesen's face was "the best one could imagine"), France (where, like many other idealists of the time, he was shocked by the excesses of the Revolution), and England (where he admired much and detested much: "to be poor in England is the most contemptible of all conditions"). A wonderfully vivid travel writer, like Baggesen and the German Georg Forster, whose *Ansichten vom Niederrhein* (1791–94; Views of the lower Rhine) the literary excursionist had in his pocket, he nonetheless kept his account of his journey from publication, and it did not appear in full until 1977. Back in Finland he responded to a contest announced by the Swedish Academy for a commemorative poem on the late Creutz: Franzén's entry won the prize but was printed only after it was much revised and expanded at the insistence of the rationalist critic Carl Gustaf Leopold (1756–1829). The two-part work (respectively, seventeen and twenty-eight strophes) deals with a major concern of proto-romanticism: how the "northern" cultural and mythological past can be brought into harmony with the classical heritage. In essence, Franzén was doubtful that such an agreement could be achieved; only Creutz might have succeeded, the argument went, since he had an ideal concept of absolute beauty. At a simple level Franzén solved the problem by means of his versions of Finnish folk songs such as "Komme han, komme han igen" (Would he but come again, come again) and "Spring, min snälla ren" (Run, my good reindeer), a favorite of composers: he was able to treat these uncomplicated northern themes with agile grace. His popularity with a broad public lay in such verse and in his numerous cheerful but certainly not orgiastic drinking songs. To a much smaller and more discerning readership he was known, of course, for the splendid vistas of the poem on Creutz or the sublimities of "Det nya Eden" (The new Eden), a vision of a humanity united in perfect happiness, a poem inspired by Matthisson's "Elysium" and suggestive of Schiller's "An die Freude" (To joy). (It may be worth noting that Franzén was an almost direct contemporary of such German idealists as Beethoven and Hölderlin.)

In 1798 Franzén was named professor of the history of learning at Åbo, later holding the chair in history and "practical philosophy"; he has been called Finland's first Kantian. He was also the last of Åbo's poetic professors, becoming ever more beloved for his verses about children and the happy home. In 1798 he had married the young woman who appears as "Lilly" in his poetry (presumably a less overwhelming experience than that with "Selma" — "in [Lilly's] mouth a trifle has it charms"). But poor Lilly died of tuberculosis in 1806, and Franzén, a widower with four small offspring, straightaway wed again, this time the widow of his friend and fellow poet Michael Choraeus, addressed in unimpassioned verse by her real name of Sophie. (Choraeus had praised her as "the great prize" to Franzén, but Franzén appears to have taken a more prosaic view of his new union.) Later still Franzén conjured up the ideal figure of "Fanny," a name taken, like

Selma, from Klopstock: "Fanny, yes, is Selma's daughter." The "Fanny" cycle, of twenty-one poems, appeared in 1821 and was a special display of the collected *Skaldestycken* (Poetic works) that Franzén's son-in-law published in 1824. In the poem that provided the vignette for the edition's title page, Fanny is a birdlike or angelic creature, sitting on a cloud.

Franzén had richly saluted Finland's natural beauty (with a "thousand lakes") and its sometimes unhappy but heroic history in the speech in verse he gave before the Finnish Economic Society in Åbo on 2 January 1800; but in the same poem he had emphasized Finland's tie to the mother country: "Finland, lifted up to Sweden's side," will be admired by a world that long has ignored its existence. In 1811 he left his homeland, now a part of Russia, for Sweden, serving as the pastor of various congregations (he had been ordained in 1803) before becoming bishop at Härnösand. The literary products of these many Swedish years (he passed away in 1847) are extensive but seem pale beside the Åbo poetry; even while Franzén was still in Finland there had been a flattening out of what Runeberg would call "the sublime poet's primal originality." His historical plays and epics are simply dull, and the verse, as might be expected, grows variously more ethereal or domestic. In 1840 Bishop Franzén was invited to the bicentennial of Åbo Academy—moved to Helsingfors in 1828 and now called the Imperial Alexander University—and received accolade upon accolade; Runeberg had dedicated his first collection of poems to him a decade earlier expressing the wish that the old gentleman would return: "Did you forget, in Sweden's flowered valleys, / The forests of your fatherland?" But the gentle, dreamy bishop was comfortable where he was; Sophie, appropriately lamented, had died in 1829, and Franzén had chosen his housekeeper as his third wife.

Exceptionally, Michael Choraeus (1774–1806), whose widow Franzén would take to wife, had not attended Åbo Academy; from Vörå in Ostrobothnia, early orphaned, he had been brought up by relatives in Sweden and had studied at Uppsala, returning to Finland in 1797. In Jakobstad (Pietarsaari) he served as a private tutor for two years before getting a docentship in rhetoric at Åbo; Franzén had already published some of Choraeus's verse in the newspaper he edited. Troubled by ill health and in constant hot water because of his sharp tongue, Choraeus flitted back to Sweden in 1802, to become chaplain in the royal military school, Karlberg; he had already been given a prize by the Swedish Academy for a poem about Augustin Ehrensvärd (1710–72), the builder of the great fortress of Sveaborg in Helsingfors harbor. Choraeus was popular in Stockholm because of his sermons, his wit, and his mildly scandalous rococo verse, such as "Förvandlingen" (The transformation), on the process by which "the lover's goddess fair becomes / The husband's granny and the children's drone." Freshly married (to the much-desired Sofia Kristina Wester-Robsahm, already once widowed) and hoping to get a professorship in Åbo, he went back to defend his doctoral dissertation in the autumn of 1805, but on the return trip to Sweden his ship was held up by unfavorable winds and his tubercular condition worsened; he died in June of the next year, having had time to write, like Frese before him, some deathbed poems, attempts to reconcile himself with his fate. The poems in which his small but genuine talent can best be seen are those about an estate where he had been a tutor, for example, "En helsning från Jockis till min vän" (A greeting from Jockis to my friend) and about the parkland near Åbo, "Afsked från Runsala" (Departure from Runsala), to which Runeberg alluded in his own poem "Färd från Åbo" (Journey from Åbo). (The former poem depicts the healthy simplicity of life in the country's interior, represented especially by a hut that served as a gazebo for the estate's master, General von Willebrand; Choraeus's letters, however, reveal that the lot of von Willebrand's "people" was not a wholly happy one, although the "patron" was an energetic and enlightened man: "I have often had the chance to see their unbearable toils and their almost invisible reward.") Choraeus's early death gave a special pathos to his well-known poem "En tanke på min egen graf" (A thought about my own grave), one of his several verses popularized during this sentimental age, by the musical settings of the composer Olof Åhlström (1756–1835). In an essay from 1895 the Swedish poet Carl Snoilsky (1841–1903) wrote, "It is no small thing once to have lived, like Choraeus, on the lips of the people." And the aged Topelius told Gabriel Lagus, the historian of Finland's Swedish literature, how Choraeus's songs were often sung when he was a youth—until musical settings of Franzén's texts slowly put Choraeus in the shade.

With the removal of Franzén to Sweden and the early death of Choraeus (who had had such close Stockholm ties), a literary age came to an end. From now on, with Sweden and Finland separate, Swedish-language authors in Finland would have to acquire a new identity, and Åbo Academy, so near Sweden, would shortly be closed and moved eastward. Runeberg did not visit Sweden until he was in his fifties, and then only once; and Topelius, making a trip to Sweden in 1843, directly announced, in his *Svenska vyer* (Swedish views), that he loved his land, Finland, above all other places on earth.

National Romanticism — A Golden Age?

George C. Schoolfield

7

Åbo Romanticism
The Aurora Society, founded by Porthan, Carl Fredrik Mennander, and Per Juslén in 1770, had as its goal the cultivation of the Swedish language and Finnish culture. Its most important product was the newspaper *Tidningar utgivne af et sällskap i Åbo* (News published by a society in Åbo), which lasted until 1778 and resumed, after Porthan's momentous German excursion, from 1783 to 1785; in 1789 it started up again as *Åbo Nya Tidningar* (Åbo new news) and, after another brief hiatus, lived on under simpler names, *Åbo Tidningar* (1791–99) and *Åbo Tidning* (1800–1809); its importance for letters was that it provided a showcase for the aims mentioned above and contained contributions from a Kellgren and a Franzén. Especially, it served as a repository for items dealing with Finland's past and present; among its contents were the long obituary of Stefan Löfving (to which so much of our knowledge about that guerrilla is owed), Paulinus-Lillienstedt's autobiography, and the account by Franzén of his journey through Finland with Porthan. After the initial shock of 1808–9 was past, the paper became an official government organ, and its original cause was continued in other, shorter-lived publications: the annual *Aura* (1817–18), which was named after the river at Åbo, but its title also alluded to Porthan's old society, whose name, in turn, had alluded to the Roman goddess of the dawn; *Mnemosyne* (1819–23, entitled after Memory, mother of the muses); *Åbo Morgonblad* (1821), which had the distinction of being the first paper to be shut down by Russian censorship in Finland; and a novelty of a different kind, *Turun Wiikko-Sanomat* (Turku weekly), which lasted from 1820 to 1827 and again, following its interruption by the great Åbo fire, from 1829 to 1831.

The directly literary quality of the works emanating from this so-called Åbo romanticism is small, and its most striking personality, Adolf Ivar Arwidsson (1791–1858), finds his way into literary history largely on the strength of that frequently quoted aperçu about not being able to be Swedes, not wanting to be Russians, "thus we shall be Finns." Arwidsson had spent his boyhood in a Finnish-speaking milieu and as an adolescent had tagged along with the Finnish-Swedish army during the war of 1808–9. Filled with the spirit of German romanticism, he became docent in history at Åbo in 1818 but, because of his Finnish-national activities, was dismissed in 1822 and went to Sweden; his departure is seen as the end of the short-lived romantic movement at the little university, itself soon to be removed. As for Arwidsson's accomplishments as a writer, the later pope of Finland's Swedish literary criticism, Carl Gustaf Estlander (1834–1910), had to admit that Arwidsson possessed "lively imagination, a good ear, great desire, but the genuine poetic sense was missing. It did not take long for him to notice this lack, which became one of the great disappointments of his life" (1921 [1893], 29). A poem such as "Vid en smälthytta" (At a smelter's furnace) leaves no doubt about his energy and his wooden diction:

> In eternal streams
> The fires go running,
> Burning and melting
> The frozen element's
> Ancient inertia.

His viking poems may look forward to Runeberg's *Kung Fjalar* ("Happy the hero / Who dies amidst flames"); his poem about Väinämöinen's harp feeds on the Finnish folk poetry just then being collected at Åbo:

> Even ancient Väinämöinen,
> Even he took up the smith's task,
> Made his harp out of a pike bone,
> Made his *kantele* of fish bone.

In Sweden the industrious Arwidsson became a publicist, and his long service at Stockholm's Royal Library was rewarded when he became its chief, some fifteen years before his death — romantically enough — at Viborg during a visit to Finland.

The talent of the men around him was not markedly greater. Anders Johan Sjögren (1794–1855), Abraham Poppius (1793–1866), and Carl Axel Gottlund (1796–1875) properly belong to the cultural history of the Finnish language (see chapters 1–2); others have a subsidiary role in the history of Finland's Swedish literature. Johan Gabriel Linsén (1785–1848), whose idea it was that *Aura* be founded, had briefly been Franzén's student and, in turn, was Runeberg's Latin teacher at Åbo (becoming professor of poetry and eloquence when the academy was transferred in 1828). The nature of Linsén's poetic talent can be seen from his poem "Den finska fosterbygden" (The Finnish fatherland) in *Mnemosyne,* written in (of all things) ottava rima: in it Linsén thanked Sweden for nurturing Finland in its "childhood," and Russia, which would give it "similar care" in its "youth," but it must recognize its own value. Yet in his *Mnemosyne* essay "Om finsk nationalitet" (On Finnish nationality) he went further, arguing for the advancement of the Finnish language and "its incomparably rich poetic content and alluring fullness of sounds." He predicted, too, a Finnish poetic art with a "romantic spirit." Like Runeberg a decade later, he saw Finland's Finnish speakers as dreamers of a special purity: "The Finnish nation has never played a political role, and therefore it has uninterruptedly led a quiet, contemplative life."

Linsén's *Aura* was filled with translations from Goethe and the German romantics done by, among others, Axel Gabriel Sjöström (1794–1846), some few of whose original poems got him a short-lived reputation as the white hope of poetry in Finland—for example, "Den första kyssen" (The first kiss), bestowed by Adam in the Garden of Eden, when "Nature in its prayer / Did trust itself unto the Cherubs' care." This fame did not last long; by the time Sjöström had become professor of Greek at Helsingfors, spending much time translating Homer, Euripides, Anacreon, and Theocritus, he had to defend the artificial language of his renderings against malicious critics in the faculty—that is what the journalist and memoirist August Schauman (1826–96) remembered of the "self-satisfied, ill-tempered old man." But his translation (1844) of Paulinus-Lillienstedt's *Magnus principatus Finlandia* (see chapter 6) came at an opportune time, when national romanticism was in full flower.

If high hopes had been placed in Sjöström, they had also been given to Gustaf Idestam (1802–51, born Idman), who made his debut as a sixteen-year-old in *Mnemosyne;* but his literary career was stopped in its tracks. His uncle and guardian (Carl Johan Idman, ennobled in 1814 as Idestam) put pressure on the boy to break away from the radical and anti-Russian Arwidsson, and he did, becoming a mining engineer, mint director, and estate owner. His sometimes mentor Arwidsson mentioned, in his memoirs, Idestam's "young, bright, active mind with promising poetic talents," and perhaps such a poem as "Vinternatten" (The winter night) shows that he was somehow exceptional in his sensitivity to natural atmosphere and to his own moods, a forerunner of Josef Julius Wecksell:

> Mute as fate the night is resting,
> In their shrouds the trees stand dressed.
> Laid waste is the lindens' greening,
> Waves of blue in bonds are pressed.

Or, again, his Åbo contemporaries may have overestimated him, anxious as they were to find some striking new talent. Whatever may be thought of Idestam's lyric gifts, his political poetry offers some odd insights about attitudes among Åbo students, freshly become subjects of the czar. A manuscript "National March" of 1820 claimed: "We shall stand and we can fall— / For freedom, prince, and fatherland"; the second line was then changed to, "For emperor and fatherland."

Runeberg

Runeberg was born on 5 February 1804—a date faithfully observed in Finland to this day—at Jakobstad (Pietarsaari). His mother's family appears to have been in Swedish-speaking Ostrobothnia for several generations; his paternal grandfather had come from Sweden. His father, who had briefly studied theology at Åbo, was a sea captain and not much at home; his mother, a distant relative of Franzén and an admirer of Choraeus's verse, had some small literary interests. Rather as in the case of Ibsen's father and his bankruptcy, the Runeberg family's fortunes took an abrupt turn for the worse when the handsome Lorens Runeberg was lamed by a stroke in 1821, at the age of forty-nine. The boy had already been sent off to a relative in Franzén's old town, Uleåborg, and then went on to the gymnasium in Vasa (Vaasa); Runeberg's subsequent lack of interest in, and closed-mouthedness about, his parents has often been noted. The overwhelming experience of the Vasa years was his long attachment to a pastor's daughter, Fredrika or "Frigga" Juvelius, the first of the love affairs that would inspire his erotic poetry (and his biographers) and make his apparently conventional life turbulent. In 1822 Runeberg went down to Åbo to continue his studies but was in such straitened circumstances that, within the year, he took positions as a tutor on estates in the interior of Finland, first at Saarijärvi in the wilds of northern Tavastland (Häme), then with the same family at Ruovesi, north of Tammerfors (Tampere), in a more settled agricultural district.

The two years spent "up country" were of vital importance for Runeberg's development: he made comparisons between the lively temperament of the Swedish-speaking coastal dwellers he knew so well and the slower, patient, and simple peasants and hunters of the interior, who lived against the grandiose background of the forest. There is something of the Rousseauesque admiration of the noble savage here and of Herder's entrancement with unspoiled "Homeric" peoples; it is the time, as well, of the European fascination with James Fenimore Cooper's novels and with John Filson's account of Daniel Boone. Here, too, Runeberg lived in close contact with veterans of Gustav III's Russian war of 1788–90 and the war of 1808–9. Nor was this all: he fell head over heels in love with a rural official's daughter, Maria Nygrén, to whom he became secretly engaged. Back at Åbo to complete his studies (in classics), he became tutor at the Pargas (Parainen) home of Archbishop Jacob Tengström (see chapters 2 and 6), a central figure in the city's and the country's cultural life and a sometime friend of Porthan and Kellgren; thus he entered a more demanding intellectual milieu than he had known before, becoming attached to Tengström's plain but gifted niece, Fredrika Tengström. He was already fast friends with such future greats in their various fields as Fredrik Cygnaeus, Johan Jakob Nervander, and Johan Vilhelm Snellman, all of whom had literary interests and who, like the widely read Fredrika, encouraged him in his own writing plans—in particular getting him (he was not an enthusiastic reader) to delve into the Swedish romantics Erik Johan Stagnelius and Esaias Tegnér.

When the academy was reconstituted as a university in Helsingfors, he settled down in the capital, marrying Fredrika in 1831 and supporting himself and his bride with a number of jobs, as lector at the newly established Helsingfors Lyceum and, from 1832, as the editor of (and chief contributor to) the newspaper *Helsingfors Morgonblad*, while becoming an unpaid docent in Latin at the university after defending a fairly perfunctory dissertation of the Medea plays of Euripides and Seneca. The story of his academic ambitions is not a very happy one; his efforts—with a monograph on the choruses in antique tragedy—to get an associate professorship in Greek and Roman letters (previously held by A. G. Sjöström) failed, a disappointment that ultimately led to his departure from the city in 1837. In other respects, though, the Helsingfors years were a time of great productivity and much success for him. In 1830 he made his debut with *Dikter* (Poems), a collection whose first part—in addition to the sentimentality and high-flown idealism (echoes from Franzén, Stagnelius, Schiller) of some of its entries—had verse in which Runeberg's special intensity was already quite apparent, "Flyttfåglarne" (Birds of passage) and "Svanen" (The swan) among them. "Färd från Åbo" (Journey from Åbo) is his description—in Alcaic strophes: imitation of Horatian meters had been fashionable in Germany (see Klopstock, Hölty, Hölderlin) and Finland (Franzén, Choraeus) —of the poetic voyage out to Pargas to find his new "Frigga" (Fredrika Tengström) patiently waiting for him. (More daring erotic poetry, such as "Simningen" [Swimming], was held back and did not appear until after his death; in her memoirs about her husband, Fredrika called him a "wild, stormy, passionate lover.")

The second part of *Dikter* was "Idyll och epigram" (Idylls and epigrams), short, objective poems, in trochaic trimeter and tetrameter, describing situations of love or passion; the inspiration was the German translation (1827) by Peter von Goetze of Serbian folk songs. (Runeberg also translated an entire collection of Goetze's renderings.) The suite ended with narrative poems, of which the story of the quietly enduring peasant Pavo, "high 'midst Saarijärvi's heathlands," gave Finland a hero of Job-like patience for its national mythology. Finally, *Dikter* contained the long and turgid "Svartsjukans nätter" (Nights of jealousy), in which critics have seen *longueurs* but also passages of remarkable beauty. All of a sudden, Runeberg had appeared as the creator and master of a new kind of poetry, apparently unadorned but made with consummate skill and singular emotional power. Sibelius would one day capture this quality in his settings of some of the texts, notably the dark "Flickan kom ifrån sin älsklings möte" (The girl came from the meeting with her lover) and the wistful "Våren flyktar hastigt" (Swiftly flees the springtime).

Encouraged by his new fame, Runeberg competed for a prize announced by the Swedish Academy (as Franzén had in the past) with a poem about bloody events and family loyalties in the Russian war of 1741–42, "Graven i Perho" (The grave in Perho), which received only second place—it is assumed because of the academy's timidity about offending the Russians. In Helsingfors university circles some anti-Russian feeling had arisen (at an institution treated generously but sternly by Nicholas I) because of the Polish uprising of 1830–31, and this sentiment may be reflected in the poem—where, for the rest, a line of thought was begun shortly to be developed in the narrative poem "Molnets broder" (The cloud's brother) of 1835, again about guerrilla warfare against the Russians and loyalty and heroic death. In its turn it would be incorporated into Runeberg's most famous work, *Fänrik Ståls sägner* (1848–60; Eng. tr. *The Songs of Ensign Stål*, 1925; *The Tales of Ensign Stål*, 1938).

Runeberg's thoughts went back, during these city years, to his experiences in the Finnish interior, and one result was the essay, published in his newspaper in 1832, *Några ord om nejderne, folklynnet och lefvnadssättet i*

Saarijärvi Socken (Some words concerning the districts, spirit of the people, and the manner of life in Saarijärvi Parish), with its concentration on what Runeberg saw as the Finnish national character, mentioned above. During the same year, he also published the hexameter epic in nine cantos, *Elgskyttarne* (The elk hunters), a story of a winter hunt and a wooing told with great good nature: the poem even hovers at times on the brink of the mock heroic but always maintains respect for its solid and honest Finnish characters — all of whom seem to be a good deal better off, by the way, than the peasants described in the essay, save for the tragic figure of the beggar Aron, once prosperous, who lives on the readily given alms of the landed members of this patriarchal society. The essay had been written as an appeal for charitable aid to those Finnish farmers who had fallen on hard times as the result of bad harvests, whereas the epyllion conjured up a more ideal world.

Runeberg himself proposed that the income from his second lyric collection, *Dikter: Andra häftet* (1833; Poems: Second fascicle), should go to the needy. In the opening sections of his new little book he was fully at home with the objectivity he had striven for previously; the characters of the portrait poems often speak for themselves: the servant girl, the peasant boy who eats bread made of bark to curb his hunger ("My arm was muscled once and strong, / Now it is that no more"), the young huntsman, the girl who loves a seaman sailing afar, the seventeen-year-old girl ("I know not what I hope for, / And yet hope all the same"), the feminine voice who speaks about the sudden coming of love in "Vem styrde hit din väg?" (Who turned your path this way?), someday to be set by Sibelius. The new collection's second series of "Idyll och epigram" had the Greek anthology as its impetus: here the best-remembered poem is the laconic "Den enda stunden" (The only moment), again about the quick, transfigured moment of the recognition of love, the supreme moment (like that of the heroic death) that was central to Runeberg's poetry and his emotional makeup. (The voice of the speaker in "Den enda stunden" is feminine: the admirers of Runeberg who once upon a time liked to gush about his "manly art" and "manly nature" might seem to overlook this other side of his mode of expression. Yet, in his vanity, which was considerable, he may very well have imagined himself in the role of the irresistible lover.)

Runeberg then waited ten years to produce his third and last lyric collection, *Dikter: Tredje häftet,* generally conceded to give proof of a weakening of his lyric vein. Nevertheless, it contains poems of the greatest importance for getting at the secrets of his complex personality: the portrait of the old man who "seems a king," now that his passions have "fled from his silent realm," a reworking of a thought from the school classic, Cicero's *De senec-*

tute (Concerning old age); the melancholy autumn poems; and the curiously desperate "Mitt liv" (My life). Later Runeberg wrote another memorable poem about release from desire, "Fåfäng önskan" (Vain wish), as well as the cycle in trochaic tetrameter (an approximation of runometer) about a girl loved and deserted, "Ett litet öde" (A little fate), evidently with a literary source, a Swedish translation of Lönnrot's *Kanteletar*, but the choice of theme also had something to do with Runeberg's own past. Once again, one of the poems, "Men min fågel märks dock icke" (But my bird is still not sighted), would inspire Sibelius. If Runeberg had written in a major tongue, he would be reckoned among the masters of the European lyric in the nineteenth century: in his simplicity with many meanings, he is, perhaps, most reminiscent of Wordsworth or Eduard Mörike. Such comparisons may mislead; at his best, Runeberg the lyricist is sui generis and defies translation.

In *Hanna* (1836) Runeberg returned to the hexameter epic, or epyllion, now only three cantos in length: a country pastor's daughter falls in love with a friend of her brother's when the students visit the parsonage at midsummer. Despite Runeberg's probably disingenuous denials, the poem strongly suggests the hexameter idylls of the German Johann Heinrich Voss (1751–1826), particularly *Luise* (1795); and its charm, like that of *Luise,* lies in the conjuring up of a gentle atmosphere and in the heroine's quite believable innocence. (Each of the cantos has an epigraph, by the way, taken from the lyric "Vem styrde hit din väg?") Not long afterward Runeberg wrote the best known of his handful of prose narratives, "Den gamle trädgårdsmästarens brev" (The old master gardener's letters), for *Helsingfors Morgonblad:* in nature the gardener sees an expression of God's love, while his daughter Rosa — at the outset quite as lovely and fresh as Hanna — falls prey to a severe pietism. (The pietistic movement then sweeping the Finnish countryside had resulted in part from the efforts of the inspired but illiterate peasant Paavo Ruotsalainen [1777–1852]; Sweden saw a similar phenomenon in the work of Lars Levi Laestadius [1800–1861].) The good and wise old man cannot drive away the "dark phantoms" that spiritual seduction has called forth within her, and she pines away and dies. The tale got a reply from Runeberg's fellow poet Lars Stenbäck (see below), who had embraced pietistic tenets, and Runeberg in his turn answered Stenbäck, saying that his intention had been to "heal the terrible chasm into which one falls upon assuming that the world simply and solely stands as a hostile authority against God." Belief in the unity of nature's phenomena and the divine will was central to Runeberg, just as was his belief in a constant hearkening to an inner voice and his search for the transfigured moment. Later, in the "Legender," narrative poems he attached to his third collection of verse, "Kyrkan" (The church) and "Chrysantos," he would state his case again. (Here he sought to emulate the German pastor Gotthard Ludwig Kosegarten [1758–1818]; Runeberg had a gift for learning from poets considerably less talented than himself.)

In *Helsingfors Morgonblad* Runeberg also printed both his other narrative prose (including a fragment of a novel about the war of 1808–9) and the majority of his literary criticism, in which he declared his independence from the mother literature of Sweden, daring to make fun of Tegnér and Per Daniel Amadeus Atterbom and admitting that the quality of Franzén's work declined once that bard had moved across the Gulf of Bothnia. To be sure, he admired, he said, some Swedish figures: Anna Maria Lenngren and her "realism," Carl Michael Bellman's wit and his swift art of characterization, even "the unevenness of Almqvist, which shifts between beauty and mistakes, not between flatness and mediocrity." (The Swedish reaction was one of rage, and Runeberg was called "that Helsingfors scoundrel," among other things.) But Runeberg had the advantage not only of his self-confidence but of membership in a group of intellectuals who knew they belonged to a new and separate literature *in statu nascendi:* the "Lördagssällskap" (Saturday Society) or "Kronohagsällskap" (Kronohagen Society, so dubbed after the section of the city where most of the members lived). They met once a week to talk about literature, philosophy, and Finland's past, present, and future: from this Swedish-speaking group (Elias Lönnrot was the only non-native speaker among them) the Finnish Literary Society emerged. The members had come largely from the old academy at Åbo, and most of them would make essential contributions to the nation's culture; Cygnaeus, Lönnrot, Nervander, Nordström, and Snellman are all names to conjure with, and Runeberg's decision to leave Helsingfors in 1837 could have meant a significant loss of stimulus for him. He was an unusually self-sufficient personality, however, and as his wife observed, he "needed surprisingly little in the way of external influences . . . his remarkable ability to obtain nourishment for his spirit from everything, even the most insignificant matter, and the ease with which he, merely through a quick glance, could get a whole picture of something, made the loss of a constant contact with a larger, external world of but small import to him."

Runeberg went to the cathedral town of Borgå as senior master of the venerable gymnasium there, a move undertaken primarily to achieve financial security; he remained for the rest of his life, spending the summer at a cabin in the Borgå skerries to fish and hunt, his favorite hobbies — winters were for writing, he said. The Borgå years, before the stroke that laid him low in December 1863 (he was stricken while checking the poisoned bait in his fox traps), were satisfying ones for him, less so for Fredrika, who had several crosses to bear: not least among them, the responsibility for the house (in their first Borgå dwelling she and the boys had a dank and dark ground floor, while Runeberg got the sunny upstairs), so that her husband could give his full attention to the school and, above all, his careful authorship. But she also missed the intellectual comradeship she had enjoyed in Helsingfors, and she had to put up with the new passion of Runeberg's heart: his infatuation with Maria Prytz, Archbishop Tengström's granddaughter (depicted as "Maria," the flirt in *Hanna*), and Emilie Björkstén, with whom Runeberg carried on a long semiaffair under Fredrika's nose. His letters to Emilie were published by Gunnar Castrén in 1940, doing some damage to Runeberg's still carefully preserved monumentality. The entanglements may have caused Runeberg a good deal of anguish (he told a friend he had "wept many a pillow wet" on Maria Prytz's account) but were also literarily fruitful: the brief return of his lyricism in "Fåfäng önskan" of 1848 is but one proof. Otherwise, he remained as measuredly productive as before; he was frequently looked in on by friends from Helsingfors and visitors from abroad (with false or true modesty, he told a Norwegian journalist he was "merely an old peasant fiddle on which God condescends to play now and again"), and his moods and opinions were recorded by Johan Elias Strömborg (1833–1900), the gymnasium's lecturer in natural science who had elected to play the part of Boswell or Eckermann. As for Runeberg's pedagogical career at the school, it had been bumpy at first, because of his laudable efforts to bring order into the institution and his less laudable fondness for corporal punishment. After twenty years of service he was freed from all teaching duties: he had become a national treasure.

Runeberg's stature was immeasurably heightened by the works of the Borgå years. In his first winter there he began a new epyllion in hexameters which, once more, returned to the Finnish interior he had known as a tutor; this time he went not to the farmhouse or the pastor's manse but to the *corps de logis* (the main building of an estate). *Julqvällen* (Christmas Eve, which came out for the Yuletide trade in 1841) describes the unhappiness of the in-laws of a young captain, serving in the Russian army during the Russo-Turkish War of 1828. No news has come from the Caucasus for a long time, and the officer's wife, her sixteen-year-old sister Augusta, and their parents fear the worst; but Augusta — another of Runeberg's highhearted girls — tries to keep the family's spirits up. Likewise, she concerns herself with the old soldier Pistol, whose son has accompanied the young master; a veteran of the war *against* the Russians, like the major (the owner of the estate), Pistol lives alone in a forest hut and now, at Christmas, pays a visit to the manor house (or rather, knowing his place, "goes to the people in the servants' cottage").

In the second canto Augusta consoles her sister by reciting a poem she seems herself to have written, in which a beautiful Turkish sultaness persuades her husband to free their Serbian prisoners. (As inspiratory works, Augusta names Thomas Moore's *Lalla Rookh* and Washington Irving's *Legends of the Alhambra*.) After this lengthy display of Orientalism, written in seven-line strophes, interrupting the flow of hexameters, Augusta tells her sister about Pistol, "with his pipe, satisfied with his lot," before she turns to her little nephew in his cradle, touches his cheek, and disappears "like a summer's sweet mist from the chamber." In the finale, as a part of the irenic spirit that informs the poem, Pistol tells his listeners in the servants' cottage — following some hair-raising tales of Turkish atrocities — about his own battlefield mercy, subsequently repaid in kind, to a Kalmuck serving with the Cossacks during what the reader assumes is the war of 1808–9; from this personal experience Pistol concludes that "the Turk is a human being, too." Unexpectedly, the missing captain returns, and there is a happy reunion; but he brings the news that Pistol's son has fallen. The major has to inform his old comrade, Pistol, and in what must be one of the most famous passages in Finland's literature, Pistol refuses the major's invitation to move to the estate, choosing instead to continue his lonely but independent life. The major "felt that his heart grew deeper":

> Before his soul Finland stood, his fatherland, chilly and poor,
> Hidden and sacred, and the gray cohort from the banks
> Of the Saimen, his life's joy, the pride of his fifty years,
> Before his sight rose once again his comrade-in-arms,
> Artless, laconic and calm, with ironhard honor deep in him.

Not even a second plea, from Augusta, can move the old soldier. Thus the poem juxtaposes at the end its two main characters: hardbitten and proud Pistol, gentle and loving Augusta. In its conservative social views, its sentimentality, its exoticism, and its patriotic pathos, *Julqvällen* was full of material appealing to Runeberg's audience, and it was certainly flattering to the national spirit. Yet Runeberg does not go too far in his glorification of Pistol: he gives him the name of a Shakespearean *miles gloriosus* and sometimes has him talk too much (as Augusta points out); further, Kim Nilsson has noticed how Runeberg hints that sweet Augusta is herself in love with her missing brother-in-law. Such details add to the general humanity of

Julqvällen, as does the fact that the blustering major, a cantankerous oldster, is also the character in the poem who most fully understands Pistol's nobility as an epiphany or transfigured moment of patriotism.

In *Julqvällen* Runeberg's dislike of the Russians has surely been muted: Adolf, the captain, serves voluntarily in the czar's army. The poet had become acquainted, in some small measure, with Russian belles lettres through Jakov Grot (1812–93), a philologist of German extraction who had visited him at Borgå in 1838 and who, two years later, was appointed professor of Russian literature at Helsingfors; Grot's correspondence with Pyotr Pletnov, his academic counterpart in St. Petersburg, is an important source for a contemporary picture of Runeberg, whom Grot vastly admired, as he did Finland itself. But Runeberg's envious friend J. J. Nervander, in a letter, implied that Runeberg's new Russophile stance had another cause: a lifetime pension of one thousand rubles a year, bestowed on him by Nicholas I (who, once upon a time, had threatened to stick Runeberg and other firebrands at the university into the ranks of the Russian army). Perhaps meaning to show his gratitude for the Russian pension, Runeberg put *Julqvällen* aside for a time to work on the epic *Nadeschda: Nio sånger* (1841; Nadeshda: Nine cantos), the tale of the love of two dissimilar noble brothers, the sunny-natured Voldmar and the gloomy Dmitri, for the eponymous heroine, the flowerlike daughter of a serf. Voldmar marries the girl, but the Empress Catherine, egged on by the mother of the "two falcons," gets him banished, thinking thus to wean him away from his wife. Dmitri has evil designs on the forlorn Nadeshda, but moved by a faithful servant's account of her suffering and her loyalty to her husband, he renounces her and vanishes "to a fate unknown." In the grand finale the Empress and Potemkin visit the haughty mother at her estate, which has been spruced up for the visit by the erection, not surprisingly, of bogus and notorious "Potemkin villages." "Russia's mother, the Empress Catherine," not only learns of her adviser's trick but, seeing through her hostess, promotes Nadeshda on the spot to the rank of princess and restores her, and her two sons by Voldmar, to her husband. The poem reads almost like a libretto, and Glinka's *A Life for the Czar* and *Ruslan and Lyudmila* are its direct contemporaries; in 1885 the British composer Arthur Goring Thomas turned it into an opera: superficial characterizations, love duets, passionate outbursts, and pleas for mercy make it an apparently thankful object for musical treatment. Runeberg himself accomplished what he could in verbal instrumentation, using a large variety of meters in his text. As for the picturesque details of Russian estate life, a world he knew only by hearsay, he learned much, the story goes, from Henriette Ahlstubbe, a sometime member of the ladies' auxiliary of the Saturday Society, who had been a governess "in the interior of Russia." The poem is interesting today as a sign of the times—Finland was prospering under Russian rule; it also shows Runeberg's urge to expand not only his subject matter but his language. The relative restraint of his previous poetry gives way to virtuoso display.

The palpable pleasure Runeberg took in working with his mother tongue is one of the hallmarks of *Kung Fjalar: En dikt i fem sånger* (1844; Eng. tr. *King Fjalar: A Poem in Five Songs,* 1904, 1912). This time, retaining the rhymelessness of *Nadeschda,* Runeberg locked himself in each canto into a complex strophic and metrical scheme of his own devising that (like Klopstock in the past) he rigidly maintained, even while he groaned at its difficulties. *Kung Fjalar* has received exceptional praise: in 1934 the essayist Knut Hagberg (p. 173) called it "our literature's greatest poem" (by which he meant the whole of literature written in Swedish, not just Finland-Swedish letters), and Frans G. Bengtsson exaltedly wrote in 1927 that it was "absolutely without flaw from beginning to end . . . the incomparably greatest, most beautiful, and most sterling poetic work ever to have been produced in a Nordic tongue" (p. 570). More soberly, it can be characterized as an example of the viking romanticism that had already flourished in such a work as Tegnér's enormously popular *Frithiofs saga* (1820–25), blended with a somewhat belated Ossianism; also, it shared a theme with Greek tragedy and, in particular, the Oedipus dramas. Fjalar is king of Gauthiod (the land of the Goths, in Sweden) and has determined, after a career of conquest and plunder, to make his kingdom a richly blooming realm of peace. The aged visionary Dargar tells him that his plan will come to naught; his young son Hjalmar will someday marry his infant daughter Gerda, and his family will end in awful shame. Meaning to make the fulfillment of the prophecy impossible, Fjalar has Gerda thrown into the sea:

> Years came and fled once more,
> King Fjalar's honor was known from land to land;
> But of his daughter's fate no one
> Heard in the world's wide breadth a word, a sound.

Gerda has been saved by a pirate and adopted by Morannal of Morven (Scotland), growing up to be the lovely Oihonna, hopelessly loved by Morannal's three sons. Her reputation attracts the attention of the grown Hjalmar, who—defying his father's desire that he study war no more—has set out on a viking's career. All of Morannal's ineffectual offspring fall in duels with him, and he wins Oihonna's hand, since "For Oihonna that song alone is sweet / When with the sounds of clashing swords / The harp resounds." After Oihonna, "the girl from the sea of waves," has told Morven's monarch of his sons' deaths, he too passes away, asking his foster daughter to give him and the "princes of the land of Shelma" a proper "monument in the land of harps." (Runeberg prefigures a major thought of European decadence here: the weaker poetic culture is destroyed by a ruthless man of action.) In the final canto Fjalar is prepared to take his own life, not wishing to submit to the infirmities of age. As he looks out, in his self-sufficiency and pride, over the prosperous land he has created, Hjalmar appears, to tell him that, unwittingly, he has married his sister and, on discovering her identity, has killed her. Then he slays himself. At last Fjalar submits to the will of the gods:

> What is man, that he does storm against you:
> Like the stars, in unreached space,
> You smile through the clouds at the fates of earth,
> Which in play a breath of your will directs.

Then he "cuts runes in his scarred breast."

The debates that have arisen around the poem have to do, mainly, with the apparent divine indifference to what Fjalar has accomplished and to the sacrifice of Oihonna and Hjalmar so that the gods may make their point. But for Runeberg, the overwhelming factor was that the noble human, Fjalar, be taught there were forces greater than himself. Rabbe Enckell, who had grown up in the midst of Runeberg veneration, rebelled against it when, in an essay of 1949, he disagreed with the comparison often made between Fjalar and *Oedipus at Colonnos* (a play of which Runeberg was greatly fond and which his Christian convert, Chrysantos, reads in the "legend" of that name): "Oedipus is a human being, Fjalar on the other hand a monster of self-satisfaction and self-righteousness. His conscious battle with the gods is a construction born of the writing desk." Yet Enckell admitted that the poem was "rhythmically and linguistically a masterpiece, containing natural pictures of unforgettable grandeur" (pp. 143, 147). Whether *Kung Fjalar* is indeed a full-fledged masterwork or an aging cultural artifact, notable (as so often in Runeberg) for the beauty of its verbal music, it has been a text of tantalizing interest for Runeberg biographers, who have seen Fjalar as a monumental self-portrait.

Once *Fjalar* was out of the way, Runeberg began to work in earnest on *Fänrik Ståls sägner*, the project that was to be the crown of his oeuvre, at least in the popular mind. He had long been fascinated by the war of 1808–9, rather as the Civil War of 1918 (and two wars with the Soviet Union) continues to haunt Finland's authors almost until the present. From early childhood he remembered having been dandled on the knee of the Russian general Kulneff; during his tutoring years he knew several veterans of the war; members of the Saturday Society had concerned themselves with the conflict (especially J. J. Nordström, aware of Finland's special legal position in the Russian empire in the war's aftermath); in 1842 Gustaf Adolf Montgomery, a Swedish nobleman whose youthful career in the war had been capped by a battlefield commission at nineteen, published his detailed account of the campaign's events. To all these elements must be added, of course, the very spirit of the times: a growing Finnish nationalism that nonetheless was quite willing to accommodate itself within the Russian empire, and a desire to depict the war as a great display of directly Finnish heroism, although abetted by the valor of some Swedish officers. (The villains are the lazy and ineffectual commander Klingspor, the traitor Cronstedt, and the foolish Swedish king, Gustav IV Adolf; the Russian foe, on the one occasion when he appears full-length in "Kulneff," is gallant.) Whereas in other lands 1848 brought revolution, in Finland it brought a mostly self-congratulatory national poem that could offend few indeed.

The work on the first cycle went rapidly, and it was finished in time for the Christmas trade of 1848. Its first canto, "Vårt land" (Our country), a hymn to Finland (set to music by the German immigrant Fredrik Pacius [1809–91]), was already on its way to becoming a national anthem, having been performed at a university festival the preceding spring; it is the only part of the cycle that is lyric rather than narrative. In the second canto the narrator is introduced, old Ensign Stål, who tells the tales to a young listener, a youth arrogant at the outset but quickly enchanted; the third canto — from the past, "Molnets broder" — strikes the overriding message of the whole: the nobility of death for the fatherland, as stated by the girl who learns that her beloved was not a coward but died bravely: "More than to live, I found, was to love, / More than to love to die as he has done." Then the portraits begin (a germ of the book was the plan of a Borgå publisher to have Runeberg compose the texts for a collection of engravings of the heroes of the late war): the ancient veteran of the war of 1788–90, who wants to be put "on this fair day" in the forefront of the battle; Lieutenant Zidén, who gaily leads his troops to death; the farm girl who discovers that her lover has run away ("He lay not 'midst the corpses there, / And therefore I must die"); Sven Duva, magnificently stupid and brave, who defends a bridge until he falls. (In this eminently quotable epic, Duva was allotted a splendid chiasmus: "A wretched head [Sven Duva] had, / But that heart of his was good"; from his years of teaching Runeberg knew full well the persuasive powers of rhetorical figures.)

The first cycle contains eighteen poems in all; "Sveaborg," however, was held back by Runeberg out of concern for the descendants of the man it shamed, Cronstedt, who, it was assumed, betrayed the great fortress in Helsingfors harbor, "Gibraltar's equal in our North." His name is never uttered in the poem: "Name him alone the treacherous arm they set as Finland's stay." Other figures have achieved a kind of immortality thanks to the colorful simplicity of the portraits given them: the calm and matter-of-fact Finnish officer von Fieandt; the dandified but ultimately valorous Swede Sandels, on his white steed Bijou, who, in his transfigured moment, becomes almost a Napoleon; the rival dragoons; the old soldier who wishes to retreat no more; the genial Kulneff, the worthy foeman; then, in rapid succession, the wretches: the king, the inglorious field marshal, the traitor. The cycle ends with the free-thinker Döbeln, who cries, on seeing his Finnish troops (he is a Swede): "With men like these, one can defy the world," and who does not, like Fjalar, get his comeuppance: "My God, my brother, whatever I shall call you, / Giver of victory, I give you my thanks." No wonder that this extremely skillful poetry ran like wildfire through Finland, and Sweden as well. (The little king—who in canto 15 tried to wear the boots of Charles XII—had long since died in a Swiss backwater.)

Much of Runeberg's poetic energy in the 1850s was taken by his membership in the hymnal committee for Finland's Swedish-speaking congregations; its purpose was to replace the old book of 1695. (Consecrated as a minister in 1838, Runeberg liked to be painted and photographed in his pastoral garb.) In 1857 he published his *Förslag till svensk psalmbok för de evangelisk-lutherska församlingarne i storfurstendömet Finland* (Proposal for a Swedish hymnal for the Evangelical-Lutheran congregations in the Grand Duchy of Finland), commemorating the putative seven hundredth anniversary of Christianity's coming and including sixty new hymns from his own hand, of which the one most often sung is "Bevara, Gud, vårt fosterland" (Preserve, oh God, our fatherland). A new committee then rejected some sixteen of his hymns and made changes in many others; he did not display the most scrupulous conformity to dogma.

At the same time, though, the continuation of the patriotic cycle was not far from his mind. In 1852 he had published his *Smärre berättelser* (Smaller tales), originally printed almost two decades before in *Helsingfors Morgonblad*. Among these efforts at narrative prose—interesting mostly for the light they shed on his boyhood and his view of the coastal population from which he sprang—are the fragments of a novel about the war of 1808–9, in which he had struck a comical tone, a tone not by any means absent from some of Stål's narratives. The second Stål cycle (1860) was much anticipated by the public; as in 1848, some of its numbers immediately attracted composers (in an age when social and ceremonial singing was an important means of transmission of literary texts): such was the case with "Soldatgossen" (The soldier lad), about a boy who wants to die on the battlefield as his father and his forebears have. In the "Björneborgarnas marsch" (March of the men of Björneborg [Pori]) Runeberg set words to a quickstep from the Napoleonic Wars to make his point about "the sons of a folk that bled / On Narva's heath, on Poland's sand, / On Leipzig's field and Lützen's hillocks." Familiar types reappear: the hero early dead, Vilhelm von Schwerin, who falls at fifteen; the traitor in "Bröderna" (The brothers); the laconic trooper, "Munter," who saves his general from a stray grenade at the cost of his life ("He was a Finn"); the man who detests retreat in "Trosskusken" (The teamster); the unflappable officer in "Von Törne." The brutal affection between officer and man, seen in the first collection's "Von Konow och hans korporal" (Von Konow and his corporal), comes back in "Von Essen," about an irascible nobleman who threatens, but does not beat, his coachman, a sometime ordinary soldier. This poem, like "Fänrikens marknadsminne" (The ensign's market memory) and like *Julqvällen,* takes up the question of high and low, separate but joined forever, and with the socially and economically superior partner "transfigured" by the realization that the union exists.

The war — in "N:o femton Stolt" (No. fifteen proud) — is also seen as the means of (limited) social improvement: here the wretched nameless man, called "cur" for most of his life, finds identity (and a uniform) at last in military service. A specific veteran of the war, Gregori Tigerstedt, gets a salute in "Fänrikens hälsning" (The ensign's greeting), which also contains one of the cycle's three great battle paintings, the others being "Den femte juli" (The fifth of July, the date of the battle of Hörnefors, late in the war and on Swedish soil, in which Zachris Duncker, the commander of the retreating forces, fell) and "Adlercreutz." These last also contain eulogies addressed to the Finnish people and their army; in "Den femte juli" the Ensign shows the land and its people ("Their courage still, their calmness hard, / Their loyalty death-defying") to his listener and scribe, the poet — the Ensign's reply to his own rhetorical question: "Say, can one perish for this land?" "Adlercreutz," the finale, is addressed to the general who, like Napoleon's Marshal Ney "the bravest of the brave," was in command at Siikajoki early in the war, one of the few victories of the Finnish-Swedish forces; Adlercreutz apostrophizes the Finnish "spirit which does not break or bend." Runeberg draws very heavily on formulas of the century's battle poetry: Adlercreutz holds his "sword still-shining in a manfully clenched hand," and the arrival of a relief force, in the nick of time, is heralded by the sounds of the Björneborg March, coming over the ice. (British readers, in Tennyson's "The Defense of Lucknow," could likewise thrill to the story of how a garrison, besieged by Sepoy mutineers, took heart when it heard the pibrochs of the Highlanders in the distance.)

Yet amid these tunes of glory there are poems of a less expected sort. Older women have replaced the young girls of the first cycle: in "Främlingens syn" (The stranger's vision) the bereaved mother who forever mourns her sons, "two noble Ramsay brothers"; and "Lotta Svärd," the sutler who gave her name to the woman's auxiliary corps of the Finnish army in the wars of 1939–40 and 1941–44 (and who, in a profitable misreading, seems to have inspired Bertolt Brecht, during his sojourn in Finland between those wars, to the conception of Mother Courage). Yet the poem with the most direct impact on the future was "Landshövdingen" (The provincial governor), whose hero, Wibelius, demonstrates civil courage in his defense of the system of Swedish law, guaranteed by Alexander I; the poem was often recited as the later czars nibbled away at Finland's cherished autonomy. In C. W. Stork's translation the governor says:

> You are the masters, no one can deny.
> Do what you like with me; I'm not afraid.
> The law will outlive me as much as I
> Live since the time 'twas made.

Supremely dramatic (or melodramatic) in his verse, Runeberg tried the drama several times: the comedy *Friaren från landet* (1834; The suitor from the country) had first been used to fill space in *Helsingfors Morgonblad,* and the fragment *Belägringen* (1845; The siege), on an episode in the Russian war of 1741–43, held more promise, containing a stubborn commander (his talking name is Stålman, or Steelman), a pusillanimous mother, a brave daughter, and a Finnish bugler with language difficulties in its dramatis personae. Runeberg could be a keen commentator on drama; he noted the operalike quality of Almqvist's novel, *Drottningens juvelsmycke* (1834; Eng. tr. *The Queen's Diadem,* 1993) — before Verdi's librettist turned the story of Gustav III's assassination into *Un ballo in maschera* — and he argued convincingly that *Macbeth* was in essence a "Christian tragedy" (the king succumbs to temptation, gaining the whole world but losing his soul); *Kung Fjalar* itself has a clearly dramatic concept. Yet Runeberg's serious dramatic efforts of the 1860s (surely encouraged by the opening of the New Theater, later called Swedish Theater, in Helsingfors) are wooden if not stillborn: *Kan ej: Familjemålning i 2 akter* (1862; Family painting in two acts) has a constellation of characters rather like that of Ibsen's directly contemporary *Kjærlighedens komedie* (1862; Eng. tr. *Love's Comedy,* 1900), that is, rich old man, beautiful young girl, artistic young man, but totally lacks the erotic tension and dark implications of Ibsen's verse comedy. The much more ambitious *Kungarne på Salamis* (1863; The kings on Salamis) is a continuation of Sophocles's *Ajax;* Leiokritos has assumed power in the late hero's island kingdom but fears that Ajax's widow, Tekmessa, and her son, Eurysakes, will appear. Appear they do, and Leontes, Leiokritos's son, a devoté of obedience to law (like Governor Wibelius) joins them; eventually, Leiokritos kills his offspring in battle and then, realizing what he has done, kills himself when Eurysakes is about to slay him. Like Fjalar, he realizes that higher powers have determined his fate, and he wishes to fall by their hand, not his political opponent's. *Kan ej* had its premiere at the New Theater in December 1862, but the Greek play was not given in its entirety until 1873, an act of piety toward the stricken author.

During the long years of paralysis Runeberg wrote nothing, although he was intellectually active. Strömborg and Fredrika Runeberg have left detailed accounts of the last years; the poet's death in 1877 was the occasion for national mourning, and he directly became the object of such veneration that a British visitor in the early twentieth century wrote that it was almost impossible to go to any public building in Helsingfors, and "many a private one," without finding his bust. The flood of encomiastic and scholarly writing became enormous and remained so almost until the middle of the present century. His reputation abroad was also large: Xavier Marmier had introduced him to a French public in 1839; Longfellow read the first cycle of the tale of *Fänrik Ståls sägner* in 1849 (in Swedish); by 1878 the young Edmund Gosse had broken a lance for him in England; and in 1904, the centennial of his birth, Rudolf Eucken, the Nobel Prize winner to be, compared him with Goethe. Finland was glad to have not just a patriotic bard but a poet for whom much greater claims could be made. His hand rested heavily on Swedish literature in Finland after him, and a character in Karl August Tavaststjerna's first novel, *Barndomsvänner* (1886; Childhood friends), dared to parody his verse, "with great pathos and drastically cynical force."

Today the reader may have some difficulty appreciating Runeberg's literary greatness, although his cultural-historical importance is beyond question. The narrative poem, to which he gave so much of his efforts, is a literary form long out of style; it flourished in an age when reading aloud in social circumstances was common and when the audience was able to value metrical refinements, rhetorical ornaments, and "word painting": Walter

Scott's *Lady of the Lake* and *Marmion* are not read today, Ibsen is not remembered for his *Terje Vigen,* Longfellow (who once occupied a place in the American literary pantheon like Runeberg's in Finland and Sweden) surely does not have much currency. Nor can it be denied that, in *Fänrik Ståls sägner,* Runeberg—who never heard a shot fired in anger and never served in any army—glorifies war and heroic death, however patriotic, to an almost oppressive degree; like his Lotta Svärd, he comes off at times as a lover of war and, in his concept of the transfigured moment of battlefield bravery and death, may sound a little protofascistic, an Ernst Jünger before the fact. Yet here he worked within the confines of his century's military and patriotic poetry; even Tennyson—in an intelligent poem that pillories the stupidity of military leadership, "The Charge of the Light Brigade"— transfigures the loyalty to command of the "noble six hundred" with a seductive technical skill. And Runeberg, too, is a verbal seducer, of a very high order.

Runeberg's Contemporaries

Among the brilliant men associated with the Saturday Society in the 1830s, none had the creative gifts of a Runeberg, although several made distinguished contributions to Finland's Swedish letters. Fredrik Cygnaeus (1807–81) tried his hand at poetry and ponderous historical drama but made his true mark as a literary critic: he can fairly be called the father of Finland's tradition of literary-critical writing with his essay on the tragic element (the Kullervo episode) in the *Kalevala* and his repeated illuminations of Runeberg's works, almost as soon as they appeared. Much of his criticism was consigned to what he called his "pamphlets," which had such poetic names as the Finnish *Jääkynttilät* (1837; Ice candles) and *Höstispiggarne* (1841; The autumn icicles). Cygnaeus was, to say the least, a colorful personality and a florid orator; his bachelor's villa in Helsingfors's Brunnsparken (Kaivopuisto) still houses his highly eclectic art collection. But he could also assemble his thoughts for entire books, such as his "observations" of 1861 on *Fänrik Stål* and his retrospective exhibit of various studies on the master from 1873.

Cygnaeus, professor of aesthetics and modern literature at the university from 1854 until his retirement in 1867, was more a stylist than a scholar; but he had his equal in brilliance (and certainly his superior in pithiness and consequential thought) in Johan Vilhelm Snellman (1806–81), whose case, as far as Finland's Swedish literature is concerned, could be called proof of divine irony. The fanatic champion not only of Finnish linguistic rights but of a monolingual (Finnish) Finland, Snellman, whose own Finnish was, by all accounts, shaky, wrote entirely in Swedish, which he used at its best like a rapier, "swiftly and mercilessly" (Johannes Salminen, "Är Snellman passé?" 23). Snellman was primarily a polemicist, but some "imaginative" literature from his hand exists — his reply to Almqvist's succès de scandale of 1838, *Det går an* (Eng. tr. *Sara Videbeck*, 1919; *Why Not! A Picture Out of Life*, 1994), in which the independent-minded glazier's daughter consents to live with her adoring sergeant, Albert, but refuses to marry him, having seen too much ruin in matrimony. Snellman was so incensed that he published a reply with the same name but with the subtitle *En tavla ur livet* (1840; A picture from life), in which he imagined the unhappy subsequent fates of Almqvist's characters: in Stockholm, Albert deserts Sara and takes up with one Celestine (who becomes a prostitute and has a schoolteacher, easily recognized as Almqvist, as one of her clients). As for Albert, he takes to drink and drowns himself; meanwhile, Sara develops tuberculosis and wastes away while trying to support the illegitimate offspring of her union with her inconstant lover. A different (and very readable) Snellman can be found in the travel book he issued two years later, *Tyskland, skildringar och omdömen från en resa 1840–41* (Germany: Depictions and judgments from a journey, 1840–41), at once factual, lively, and witty — and even the straitlaced Snellman let himself be charmed by the Viennese, "the most likable people in the world. Frank joy was to be seen everywhere, without becoming unbridled or violent." In an age that, with the sudden proliferation of the steamboat and the train, produced a whole host of gifted travel writers in the North, Hans Christian Andersen most prominent among them, Snellman reveals himself, all too briefly, as a valid competitor.

Snellman was not the only member of the Saturday Society to go abroad; Cygneaus made a long European trip (1843–47), and Johan Jakob Nervander (1805–48) kept his friends abreast of his travels, in his capacity as a physicist, with contributions to Runeberg's paper: these reports, together with portions of his diary, were published posthumously in book form. (His trip had the ancillary advantage of keeping him apart from his wife, whom he had married young and heartily detested; on his journey he sought out not just scientific colleagues but literary men — in Copenhagen, the old Adam Oehlenschläger and the young Hans Christian Andersen, who had "in his body, his legs, his gait, his eyes, and his whole face the most perfect resemblance to — a crane.") Apart from lyrics, more to be praised for the sincerity of their emotions than their skill (he had fallen in love with a literarily interested friend of Fredrika Runeberg, a member of the ladies' auxiliary of the Saturday Society), his literary work consists of *Jephtas bok: En minnes-sång i Israel* (published 1840; The book of Jephta: A Song of remembrance in Israel), based on the song of the victor over the Ammonites who must slay his daughter to fulfill a hasty oath (Judges 11:34–39). Nervander's real concern is not the tragedy that had attracted baroque dramatists but a display of colorful Orientalism, primarily in verse, and with prose *textes de liaison*. The poetic silence into which Nervander fell, after receiving the Swedish Academy's second prize for *Jephta* in 1832, can be ascribed to his growing reputation as a physicist and his love-hate relationship with Runeberg, in whom he recognized a much greater talent. His perhaps apocryphal remark to Cygnaeus after the appearance of *Elgskyttarne* is often quoted: "Finland is too poor to have more than one poet at a time."

Nervander had acquired his not very religious concern with the biblical world while serving as a tutor in the homes of the theologians Jakob and Johan Bonsdorff (1763–1831, 1772–1840), the former of whom had changed sections of the Old Testament into a metric Swedish prose. The orientalist and exegetist Gabriel Geitlin (1804–71) was also a Bonsdorff pupil; his prize student, in turn, was Georg August Wallin (1811–52), today remembered not so much for his considerable scholarly accomplishments as for the fact that he was Finland's Richard Burton (in fact, Wallin beat the Englishman to Mecca by eight years) and its C. M. Doughty: Wallin's letters and diaries from his long series of trips through the Near East (1843–49) are certainly worthy of comparison with Doughty's *Travels in Arabia Deserta*. The travel notes were first published by the librarian Sven Gabriel Elmgren (himself a bilious diarist of note) in 1864–67, the letters and some diary entries in 1905 by Knut Tallqvist. Modern Finland-Swedish authors have admired the excitement of Wallin's prose and the boldness of his journeys, which ended with his appointment as professor of "Oriental" literature in 1851 and his death, shortly thereafter, of syphilis, contracted perhaps in Cairo, perhaps in Paris. Göran Schildt has emphasized the very daring of Wallin's trips among the Arabs; Gustav Widén has noted what must have been (as in the case of T. E. Lawrence) his acting talents; and Johannes Salminen, the element of "free sexuality," which the prudish Elmgren carefully excised from Wallin's texts and which—see Flaubert's notes and correspondence from his Egyptian trip—was so much a part of the fascination the Near East exerted on Europeans of the time.

It would be hard to imagine a figure in starker contrast to Wallin than Lars Stenbäck (1811–70). A pastor's son from Ostrobothnia, Stenbäck was sent as a boy of eight to the cathedral school at Åbo, and it may be that his inclination to become involved in passionate friendships arose early; in 1834 he devoted a lament to his sometime schoolboy friend Gustaf Adlercreutz: "I stood mute in pain / At my friendship's, my gladness's grave." The pattern would shortly be repeated; in another poem from the same year he tells how he wants to press the hand of the youth at his side and "sweetly whisper in his ear / A trembling word: Beloved, take all from me!" The object of his affections now was J. J. Östring, whom he had met while they were studying in Helsingfors. A period at Uppsala, and acquaintance with Sweden's romantic poetry, encouraged him in literary plans, and back in Finland he was caught up in the Finnish-patriotic fervor of the 1830s, writing a salute to the young Snellman for his defiance of the university's authorities and composing a long poem for the centennial of the birth of Porthan, in which he simultaneously addressed the Åbo scholar who "had lifted the veil concealing days long gone," that is, the world of Finnish mythology, and Runeberg, already called "the king of Finnish poetry."

But Stenbäck was not just the poet of private torment and the bard of high-sounding declamatory verse; he was intensely interested (like Uhland, Platen, and Rückert in Germany) in the cultivation of strict and difficult poetic structures: the "romance" or short ballad, the sonnet, and the ghasel, a Persian form with repetitive rhymes. Sent down from the university, with Östring, for an "illegal meeting" to protest a negative decision about the filling of a professorship in theology (they were upset that Axel Adolf Laurell, a member of the Saturday Society and the founder of the progressive Helsingfors Lyceum, had been passed over), Stenbäck came back to the capital transformed, a pietist and a zealous moralist. The short poem "Den väcktes suck" (The sigh of the born-again), with its opening, "My heart is but a pile of smoking ruins," describes the misery ("the storm of sin") that had preceded the change — and was written in still another artfully constructed form, terza rima, the stanza of the *Divine Comedy*. The poetry born of his crisis is often impressive, for example, the cry *de profundis,* "Suckan" (Sighing), with its opening, "How dark all is within this house of death," and still others of the "Nattstycken" (Night pieces) and then the ecstatic "Accorder" (Chords), first published in his personal newspaper, *Evangeliskt Veckoblad.* The first "Chord" begins: "I am God's child, / O blessed peace and gladness." It was obvious where Stenbäck was heading; the debate with Runeberg of 1837–38 (see above) about the old gardener's letters also made the direction clear. Further, Stenbäck had received another personal shock: Östring had died of tuberculosis in March 1836, and the result was "En natt" (A night), which starts with the shattered friend by the grave, at night, and ends with the dawn and the realization that the beloved friend lies not in the tomb's darkness but rather on God's "lovely breast." (In the midst of his sorrow Stenbäck still shows off his verbal artistry with identical and complexly interwoven rhymes: in the "Accorder" he had already written spiritual ghasels, an odd employment of the form the old Goethe and Marianne von Willemer had used not so long ago for quite different purposes in the *West-Östlicher Diwan* [West-eastern divan]).

Stenbäck's collected poems appeared in 1840, a closing off of his poetic activity save for hymn writing; the same year he married and was ordained shortly thereafter. In "Ett fragment om poesien" (1841; A fragment about poetry), in his one-man newspaper, about to be shut down by the Lutheran establishment because of its extremism, he announced point blank: "Poetry has always, in one way or another, lived the life of the natural man but never the life of the spirit and of faith." He became a teacher in Vasa and was such a success that he was called to a professorship of pedagogy in Helsingfors (1856), but he left the worldly capital almost immediately for a pastorate in his native Ostrobothnia. Despite his zealotry, which now included enthusiasm for Snellman's Fennomane cause, his residual reputation as a Swedish-language poet got him a place on the hymnal committee with Runeberg. After Runeberg's illness he continued the task — only to have difficulties again: he found the contributions of his colleagues, Bengt Olof Lille (1807–75), professor of church history and sometime member of the old Saturday Society, and Zachris Topelius too popular and too little concerned with formal questions of poetics, "as if just anything would be good enough for Our Lord." According to Topelius's memoirs, Stenbäck complained that his distinguished colleagues got their hymnal work out of the way as fast as possible, "between attending parties." The gentle and liberal Topelius admitted that Stenbäck and he "never understood one another. . . . [Stenbäck] combined a child's piety with the nervous irritability of a sickly grownup."

Finland's Swedish literature flowered in the Helsingfors of the 1830s and 1840s, its products mostly growing out of the intellectual ferment of the Saturday Society and the patriotic fervor leading, among other things, to the foundation of the Finnish Literary Society in 1831 — which for years carried out its business of necessity in Swedish. In 1844–45, however, one of Finland's minor classics appeared in Stockholm, the work of a maiden lady, Sara Wacklin (1790–1846), the grandniece of the fashionable (and internationally recognized) portrait painter Isak Wacklin (1720–58). She had grown up as a *pauvre honteuse* in Uleåborg, Franzén's town, and then had supported herself first as a tutor and then as headmistress of girls' schools in Uleåborg, Tavastehus (Hämeenlinna), Åbo, and Helsingfors — where she had the young G. A. Wallin on her faculty. A woman of broad linguistic interests (her Helsingfors school offered instruction in French,

German, Russian, and, a rarity at the time, English), she set her sights too high and the school eventually failed, so she moved to Stockholm. Encouraged by Gustaf Henrik Mellin (1803–76), a relative and an earlier émigré from Finland who had made a respectable name for himself with historical novels and novellas in Walter Scott's manner, she tried her own hand at letters, and the result was *Hundrade minnen från Österbotten* (Hundred memories from Ostrothnia), a set of sketches, short tales, and views having to do with her hometown and its environs during its recent past, a work that is spiced throughout by Wacklin's gentle (or, at times, half-malicious) humor, exemplified in "Den välvises dubbla bröllop" (Eng. tr. "The Venerable Mayor Renews His Vows," *Swedo-Finnish Short Stories*, 1974). The work's climax is formed by "various scenes from the great Uleåborg fire on 23 May 1822," which put an end to her school there. Runeberg, whose childhood experiences at his uncle's home in the "town of gold and tar" were described in the latter part of the book (together with similar tributes to Franzén and Mellin), wrote to her that he had especially appreciated the book's glimpses of roguish humor; he found a resemblance between her and Washington Irving, "who has always been one of my favorites." He was probably thinking of Irving's *Sketchbook,* which, like much else in contemporary English-language and French literature, had been translated by the estimable Lars Arnell (1781–1856), a Swedish officer who had migrated to Åbo: Arnell's role as a transmitter of "modern" literary currents to Finland cannot be underestimated.

Fredrika Runeberg
Another enthusiastic Wacklin reader was Fredrika Runeberg (1807–79), the master's patient wife. From childhood on, Fredrika Tengström — like Wacklin — had been keenly interested in modern languages and contemporary literature; during her courtship and afterward she kept Runeberg abreast of literary developments outside Finland and helped her husband with *Helsingfors Morgonblad*. As she wrote with subtle phraseology in her account of her own life as an author, *Min pennas saga* (The tale of my pen, not published until 1946), she and other wives were not precisely excluded from the meetings of the Saturday Society: "The gentlemen did not see themselves obliged to show us the condescending courtesy of sinking to our level of comprehension, and so the conversation continued with the greatest liveliness and interest." In Borgå she found the time, somehow, to follow her literary impulses: "For me, writing was a necessity not to be put aside, a consolation . . . , a safety valve when my spirit was overfull of thought and feelings." To the credit of Runeberg, it must be said that he

encouraged her, as did his friends Snellman — who published her tales and sketches in his paper *Litteraturblad för allmän medborgerlig bildning* (Literary paper for general civil cultivation) — and Topelius, who summed up the gifted couple thus: "Runeberg was a great *man*, but Fredrika was a great human being."

When the sketches from Snellman's paper were assembled in 1861 as *Teckningar och drömmar* (Sketches and dreams), Topelius's favorable review immediately spotted the book's vital part, its attention to "the justified complaint of womanhood," which finds special expression in "Facetter av kvinnans liv" (Aspects of woman's life). This is a double story comprising the oral account of "an insignificant craftsman's wife," whose life has been stunted by the conventions of the layer of society from which she comes, and the subsequent discussion by her listeners, women of an ostensibly more favored class, who realize that their several talents, too, have come to naught. Another of the items in the book, "Tre som flyttade till Sverige" (Three who moved to Sweden), is a salute to a trio of women, all Finnish-born, who did fulfill their promise: Fredrika Bremer, Sara Wacklin (Fredrika Runeberg laments that her work has already been forgotten), and Fika Lindkvist, a learned friend of the Swedish romantics Lorenzo Hammarsköld and Atterbom. Otherwise, much of the collection consists of what Fredrika Runeberg herself termed "fairy-tale parables," still dealing in part with questions of the day but in fanciful or exotic disguise, with backgrounds taken by the housebound Fredrika from a variety of sources — the Old Testament, Captain James Cook's South Sea journals, the Fennologist Mathias Alexander Castrén's account of his expeditions to Siberia, and the *Kalevala*. Her Christian reaction to the national epic is quite apparent in "Manala jungfrun" (The maid of Manala); the maid dwells by Tuoni, the river of death, and is led away, together with the spirit of the youth she loves, not to the *Kalevala*'s underworld, Manala, but to the "higher home" from which "the Mighty One" (Christ) has come in His shimmering garments. These tales (which rightly reminded Snellman of H. C. Andersen in their romantic-idealist tone and their repeated giving of a human voice to animals, flowers, sunbeams, breezes) should be examined in the light not only of Fredrika's mildly feminist interests (as in a tale about the world turned upside-down, where women are in charge) but of her own situation: the illnesses that often beset her, and her sense of guilt at her compulsion to write, led to dreams of travel, of spiritual release, of a (very innocent) eroticism. But such a study would require cutting through a good deal of saccharinity and sentimentality, even as in the case of Andersen himself.

Teckningar och drömmar was not her first published book; in 1843 she had completed a novel, *Fru Catharina Boije och hennes döttrar* (Lady Catharina Boije and her daughters), which she took out of the desk drawer in 1858. Runeberg had praised it, she recalled, but timidity kept her from looking for a publisher. The book, which could be called Finland's first historical novel, was inspired by Scott and, in Sweden, Gustaf Henrik Mellin, and by the publication of Stefan Löfving's diaries (see chapter 6). Fredrika need not have been fearful about her work, which has both tight construction and telling characterizations: the partisan Magnus Malm (based on the historical Stefan Löfving), who saves Lady Catharina's elder daughter from the marauding Russians and eventually weds her; the forthright daughter herself, Margareta; Johan Bruce, who may be a mouthpiece for the ambivalence many Finlanders maintained toward the relatively benevolent rule of the czar-emperors. The novel is certainly not anti-Russian in its drift, although it takes place during the Great Wrath of 1710–21; if anything, it is rather anti-Swedish: Carl Lejonanckar, the intended of Lady Catharina's younger daughter, Cecilia, flees to Sweden and becomes a Stockholm fop. As for the lady herself, she opposes her elder daughter's marriage to Malm because of his humble birth and, at novel's end, retires to Sweden for good, leaving her estate in Carl's hands (now that peace has been made and it is safe for him to come back): he changes its name to Hattanpää in honor of his aristocratic political party, the Hats, while Magnus and Margareta settle down at a simple farm.

The book has some late romantic paraphernalia: for example, Cecilia (who loves Bruce, not Lejonanckar) dies during the preparations for her wedding to the latter when she spots a large gray spider (she suffers from severe arachnophobia), and it is her dying plea, coupled with the wise words of old Vappo, a Finnish sorceress, that persuades the proud mother to countenance Margareta's marriage to Malm. (For the sake of propriety, and the possible audience's sensibilities, they had in fact been wedded long ago, during their precipitous flight from the Russians.) But the novel is at least as convincing as the historical narratives of Topelius, and Fredrika, forever modest, was pleased at the critical reception it got, save that she felt obliged to defend her Bruce, the "turncoat" and the novel's most complex figure, against moralizing criticism of his behavior; her audience expected black and white. "It went with him as it most often goes with someone who is too sensitive to accommodate himself to a difficult position. He accuses himself, and is therefore condemned by the reader." (Bruce is interesting in another respect, too: he has been brought up by a Finnish peasant after his parents' early death and — a prefiguration of Snellman — demands the proper place for Finnish in the nation's life.)

Fredrika Runeberg ended her literary career on a sad note. As long ago as 1830 she had toyed with the notion of writing a tragedy about the Club War of the late sixteenth century, but eventually, she destroyed her sketches, turning the material into another historical novel, *Sigrid Liljeholm,* published at Christmas 1862. It got a bad press from her friend Snellman, who found it episodic (with "themes for several novellas and a rather rich draft of a novel, but only a draft"); Carl Gustaf Estlander, the young lion of Finland's criticism, claimed she had imitated the recent dramas of Cygnaeus on the same period. Fredrika never forgot Estlander's hard words: "*Helsingfors Dagblad* [i.e., Estlander] threw itself upon the book with a review of the sort one imagines can only be given to a woman," she said. Had she wanted to steal, she added, she would have chosen an author more pleasing to her than Cygnaeus (whom she regarded as a windbag). Snellman was right about the book's not hanging together despite its several striking portraits of historical personalities (Klas Fleming, the deputy of Sigismund; his wife and son; Aronus Forsius and Daniel Hjort) and its fictitious ones (the powerful mistress of Tannila Estate and her daughter). The latter, who refuses, finally, to marry the man she has loved, has been seen by Merete Mazzarella as a statement of Fredrika Runeberg's own advanced emancipatory feeling. Taking particular umbrage at the complaint that heroine and hero did not fall into each other's arms at book's end, Fredrika Runeberg decided to write no more, a decision made all the easier by her husband's illness and the doubts she still entertained about herself. "The end is near, I am sixty-two years old, and will leave the earth without knowing whether or not what I have written, thought, dreamed, and loved is simply 'smudges and shame' or not."

Feminist considerations aside, Fredrika Runeberg is a figure of great literary-historical import in that she took the novel seriously as a means of expression, even though she lived in an aesthetically old-fashioned literary world that still did not regard the genre as a fit vehicle for the loftiest literary creation. (Thackeray and Dickens were only a little the junior of Johan Ludvig Runeberg, while Stendhal, Balzac, and Hugo were his seniors — but he persisted in his loyalty to the verse narrative. In this respect as in others, Fredrika was the more modern spirit.) Modestly, though, she designated her first novel as a "Berättelse från stora ofredens tid" (A narrative from the time of the Great Wrath) and was unhappy because the printer added the word "roman" (novel) to the story about the Club War. It would appear she thought what she had wrought was too small to deserve the more ambitious term. But she also thought the novel was a genre where women excelled: "America's, Sweden's, yes, in my opinion France's best novelists [*romanförfattare*] are women: Beecher Stowe, Fredrika Bremer, George Sand."

Fredrika Runeberg did not quite keep her promise of silence. She continued to write for periodicals, both stories ("Ella vid Vastusjaur" [Ella at Vastusjaur], about a "little Lapp woman's little fate") and poems. "Bittrast" (The most bitter thing) and "Den fångslade bardens maka sjunger" (The wife of the imprisoned bard sings) are patently concerned with her husband's paralysis; yet the former must also allude to the pain Runeberg's interests *extra muros* caused her: betrayal by a beloved and a beloved's death are bitter, but the torment of seeing him fail and suffer, "that torment is bitterest of all."

Runeberg's Disciples
In their simplicity Fredrika Runeberg's few poems resemble those of her Borgå neighbor, Vilhelmina Nordström (1815–1902), who founded a girl's school in Finland's Weimar shortly before Finland's Goethe fell ill. Like Wacklin, she had traveled abroad, to Germany and Switzerland, for training in pedagogy, and her Borgå school got state support, so excellent was its reputation. More actively than Fredrika, she was a spokesperson for women's liberation. Runeberg encouraged her to publish her verse, writing flatteringly that "true drops of dew ... can mean more than a hundred cans of water," and she burst into print in 1861; three years later her protector persuaded his Swedish publisher (and Franzén's), Abraham Bolin in Örebro, to bring out an expanded edition, praising her poetry for its "peculiarity of mood" and its "clearness and concentration" of expression. He was right: her poems—extremely terse and filled with a stoic pessimism rather than the weepy or overly tender sentimentality so common in verse of the time—are exceptional; it is disappointing that (perhaps because of the very smallness of her oeuvre) she has never received quite her due in Finland's literary history; a comparison with Emily Dickinson would not be untoward.

Another woman poet, attached to the Runebergs during their Helsingfors days, was the vastly cultured Augusta Lundahl (1811–92), whose verse—occasionally printed in newspapers, including Runeberg's *Helsingfors Morgonblad,* but never collected—gives a less interesting picture of her literary discernment and knowledge than do her letters. Her marriage in 1844, to the clergyman Gabriel Wallenius, effectively put an end to her creative efforts, all couched in a somewhat sentimental and certainly melancholy lyric vein. Runeberg held a flattering opinion of her work; in 1834 Fredrika Runeberg wrote to "Hebe" (the nickname Runeberg had given Augusta) that her husband was "quite cross" because she sent him no more verses for his paper, a topic to which he returned later on, without success. To a much greater degree than her friend Fredrika, she suffered from a lack of self-confidence that made her "throttle her muse," in Fredrika's regretful phrase.

Nordström and Lundahl were by no means the only talents Runeberg nurtured; Fredrika recounted how Jakob Gabriel Leistenius (1821–58) refused to believe "Uncle Runeberg" when the latter told how he "hammered and filed" his verse; Leistenius — the "poet and improviser," as Fredrika called him — wrote too rapidly, and his friends encouraged him to be speedy. He was a born student-poet, and his first collection, *Pojken* (1847; The boy), showed his high spirits to the full; a companion volume from the same year, *Ynglingen* (The youth), gave signs of an effort to find a more earnest persona. A clever employer of classical themes for amusing ends (and a master of equally clever rhyme), he took up the rape of the Sabine women (neglected by their husbands, they enjoy all the Roman attention they are getting), the tyrant Dionysius of Syracuse (driven into exile, he becomes a schoolmaster and dies waiting for a salary increase), and Xanthippe (the extraordinarily unpleasant wife of a professor of philosophy named Socrates). Unfortunately, this kind of humor can be carried only so far; a gloomier side of Leistenius is to be seen in the poem "Döda havet" (The Dead Sea), which still hangs on in anthologies, a catalog of shattered dreams and lost illusions: the fickleness, selfishness, and voracity of the human heart are like the apples of Sodom that grow beside the Dead Sea's bitter waters. Leistenius died of typhus as a poorly paid teacher in Viborg; at his funeral Topelius memorialized him as "the happy poet."

In 1843 Runeberg helped another young man, or rather a boy, Emil von Quanten (born in 1827), to get a poem printed in *Borgå Tidning;* an officer's son, von Quanten had been sent (as Bertel Gripenberg and Gunnar Björling would be, later on) to the Finnish Cadet School in Fredrikshamn (Hamina), a kind of Finnish West Point, where he was miserable; eventually getting his release, he changed to the university and participated in student publications, such as the literary annual *Lärkan* (1845; The lark). A subscription was taken up by his friends and admirers, led by Cygnaeus, to send him on a sea voyage for his health, and he stayed at Cape Town for a while before going on to the East Indies. Back in Scandinavia he settled in Stockholm and had a long career (he died in San Remo in 1903) as a publicist, making propaganda for the return of Finland to Sweden, hopes that were encouraged during the Crimean War. As an anti-Russian voice and quasi-expert on his old homeland, he wrote (or edited) such tractates as *Fennomani och skandinavism* (1855; Fennomania and Scandinavianism) and *Finska förhållanden* (1857–61; Finnish conditions), interesting in that they presage the eventual reaction of many of Finland's Swedish speakers to Snellman's demands — which were still a very long way from being realized. For a while, von Quanten had the ear of Charles XV of Sweden, as that monarch's librarian, encouraging the king in his thoughts of a Scandinavian union; but he is known today mainly for his Fennophile poem from his salad days (first published in *Lärkan*), "Suomis sång" (Suomi's song). Like Runeberg's "Vårt land," it was set to music by Pacius and became a sort of supporting text for Runeberg's anthem — which was written after the master had heard the young student's song: "Hear the lofty fir trees rustling, / Hear the streams, deep-channeled, rushing. / It's Suomi's song!" Otherwise, von Quanten's poetry (to which he added during his Swedish years) is shot through with late romanticism and epigonic medievalizing. He was semioriginal only when he discovered a new *sujet* (in the verse from South Africa) or a fairly new form (the prose poem about the Hebrides, in the wake of Mendelssohn's overture), or, of course, in Fennicizing poems in runometer, imitations (in Swedish) of the *Kanteletar:*

> Greetings come from one's own mother,
> Message from the fair preserver;
> "Do not stray in far lands longer,
> Homeward turn your course, my darling."

Obviously, von Quanten did not listen to this self-concocted plea from Mother Finland; he was too well off as a professional refugee.

Von Quanten went west; born at Falun in Sweden, Fredrik Berndtson (1820–81) went east, arriving in Finland with his father, a mining engineer, when he was twenty; almost immediately, he established himself in the little university world of sentimental literary annuals and a rather bogus Finnishness. Directly, he published a long narrative poem, *Mathilda* (1840), in which the Finlander Gustaf, mortally wounded at Breitenfeld during the Thirty Years' War, is nursed by the devoted eponymous heroine but breathes his last words to Anna, his beloved in the North — a theme lifted from Esaias Tegnér's *Axel* (1822). Next Berndtson imitated Stagnelius in the book-length *Qvinnans skapelse* (1842; The creation of woman), in which the Almighty turns the goddess of beauty into the first woman in the Garden of Eden. (Gustaf Idstam-Idestam had tried the same trick a few years before.) He essayed a clearly Finnish subject with *Den gamles minnen,*

Bilder från finska skogsbygden (1843; The old man's memories: Pictures from the Finnish woods), using an imitation of Finnish runometer (easily acquired) to tell a long story of the poor but virtuous Erik and his love for Anna, the rich peasant's daughter. Berndtson was an opportunist; August Schauman, with some irony, remembered him as "the almost ideally imposing and handsome Berndtson, who . . . with his great literary talent and his pleasant personality, made himself warmly treasured here." He could write about everything and do everything; he was an editor of Runeberg's old paper, *Helsingfors Morgonblad;* he composed novellas on Helsingfors's high society (which he knew well); he got the university's first docentship in aesthetics in 1847. Also, spotting another main chance, he wrote for the stage, the comedy "with song and dance" *Friaren från Åbo* (1845; The suitor from Åbo), retrieved from the archives in 1966 to celebrate the hundredth anniversary of Swedish Theater's (re)opening.

Berndtson had his greatest theatrical success with the blank-verse "historical drama" *Ur lifvets strid* (1851; From life's strife), using material from the war of 1808–9. Liberally sprinkling his play with a traitor, a self-sacrificing young girl who slays him but is herself mortally wounded, and patriotic young lovers who fall into each other's arms, Berndtson ends by having Döbeln, the victor of Juutas, suddenly appear, to repeat the words Runeberg made the general utter in the finale of *Fänrik Stål's* first cycle: "Giver of victory, I give you my thanks!" The success of the play was enormous; but pride goeth before a fall. Having lost his first fiancée, an Aminoff, to death in 1845, Berndtson fell in love with another young lady from the cream of society, a de la Chapelle, and in order to legitimize himself in the eyes of her family and to get a high-paying position, he took a job as editor of the government's reactionary paper, *Finlands Allmänna Tidning,* and then as a director in the office of the Russian governor-general, in which capacity he had to function as official censor. Somewhat hypocritically, Helsingfors society ostracized him, although he continued to write theater reviews until blindness and illness completed his isolation. His life reads like a novel, and two authors treated his fate after his death, the Swede Anne Charlotte Leffler (1849–92) in her story "Dömd" (Condemned), in which Georg, the Berndtson figure, leaves a suicide note with a quotation from Runeberg's "Sveaborg," and Tavaststjerna in his "Sångarlön" (The bard's reward).

Pioneers in Fiction

In her memoirs about Runeberg, Fredrika tells about a visit paid to Borgå by "the musician" Axel Gabriel Ingelius, who became such a burden to the master that he finally arranged to get Ingelius out of town. Poor Ingelius

(1822–68) was his own worst enemy, a failure at academics, an ambitious composer without the proper training to realize his projects, a music critic whose judgment was often distorted by envy, a novelist whose interesting undertakings foundered on a lack of artistic control. If there is a literary high point in Ingelius's extremely checkered but fascinating career, it is the novel *Heinolablomman* (1856; The flower of Heinola), the still readable romantic tale of the lovely Helena (Elin) Wainonen and the musician Lennart Lärka, who loves her from afar. Orphaned at fourteen, Elin is taken in by the "money aristocrats," the Hjerpéns; before his passing, her father had favored a marriage between the not unwilling Elin and Otto Hjerpén, a dandified skirt chaser. She rejects the cad after Otto, jealous at the attention she gives her pet siskin, kills the unfortunate bird. Meanwhile, Lärka has gone to Leipzig for the musical education he cannot get in Finland; at the conservatory the Danish composer Niels Gade (1817–90) takes him under his wing, and his (unfinished) symphony is performed. Escaping the clutches of his German landlady and her daughters, both of whom have set their sights on him, the virtuous young man returns to Scandinavia, after a triumphant concert which ends with cheers for "the new composer, the Beethoven of the North!" On his way to Stockholm, Lärka attends a performance of Hugo's *Angelo Malipieri* and finds his lost love, who has become an actress and singer, in the cast. He cries, "The flower of Heinola!" (her old nickname), and the couple is reunited.

Ingelius tried the musical novel again with *Spelmannen* (1863; The wandering musician), published only as a serial in *Helsingfors Dagblad,* with a central figure who is an unbalanced village fiddler, Abel Fån, who before his madness was the French refugee Abelard Faune; his former career on the Continent (Ingelius's wish-dream again: some of the settings are Nancy, Baden-Baden, Danzig) is told by flashback. Like Berndtson, Ingelius came to a wretched end; he froze to death in a snowstorm in 1868, having left a party at an estate where he fancied he had been insulted — a character out of one of his own novels. Yet he deserves mention as the composer of music to texts from *Fänrik Stål* and as the creator of Finland's first *Künstlerroman*, a subgenre to which Tavaststjerna would return with his debut novel of 1886. Topelius, some of whose poems Ingelius had set to music, called him "an outlawed spirit from the strand of light" that "groped to find his fatherland, / Where all is clarity" in a necrological verse; in his memoirs Topelius told how, as he said good-bye to Ingelius shortly before the latter's icy death, "a sad thought about the lovely songs and the broken violin" passed through his mind.

A novelist with skills still smaller than those of poor Ingelius, Marie Linder (1840–70) represented, like him, currents that would get better formulation later on. The daughter of the Russian courtier, Vladimir Mussin-Pushkin, and the feted beauty Emilie Stjernvall, Marie was brought up, after her mother's death, by her still more beautiful maternal aunt, the legendary Aurora Stjernvall-Demidov-Karamzin; moving in the highest circles of Russian (and Finland-Swedish) aristocracy, she wed Constantin Linder (1836–1908), whose submissiveness to czarist demands would one day make him one of the most hated men in Finland. She pursued ideals that cannot have been appealing to her husband, sometime officer, member of the Russian court, owner of Finland's largest estate, and financier; like other women writers, she was encouraged by Topelius, who, late in his own life, devoted an essay to her memory in which he hinted at the tensions that marred her marriage; baptized in the Russian Orthodox Church but inclined to Lutheranism, she is supposed to have said to Alexander II, when he visited Helsingfors in 1863, "Sire, give Russia freedom of conscience!" (Of her three children, her son, Hjalmar [born 1862], continued his mother's brave tradition by protesting the hideous conditions in the concentration camps set up by the victorious Whites after Finland's Civil War of 1918 and was effectively hounded out of the country, dying a suicide in Marseilles on 4 June 1921.)

Her only larger piece of creative writing, the novel *En qvinna af vår tid: Karaktersteckning* (1867; A woman of our time: A character sketch), was published in Helsingfors under the pseudonym Stella. Lucy Suffridge, the only surviving child of the thrice wed, thrice widowed, and vastly eccentric Lord Robert Suffridge, is urged by her father to marry the baronet Edward Glithingham, to whom she conceives an aversion almost as soon as he appears at the Suffridge estate, "stately Abbey Hall." (The family's loyal retainers also see through the "wolf in the sheep fold"; Lord Suffridge's predilection for Edward stems from a sense of guilt: in the past he murdered Edward's father, who had won the woman Robert loved.) Glad to get away from Edward, Lucy travels to New York, accompanying the energetic Anna Rush, her late mother's cousin, and—in a sketchy chapter—finds her spirit of independence strengthened by contact with "Columbia's noble folk"; she returns to the Old World with a forthright American maid and "renewed strength." Before setting out she has met a frank and manly aristocrat from Finland, Oskar Lejonstjerna and has been attracted to him, as he to her; they meet again in Paris, where she has gone for intellectual improvement, but are kept apart by her desire for freedom and his shock at her liberated manner. Meanwhile, Edward—expecting to capture Lucy—has had his mother's innocent young ward, Alice, kidnapped, in an effort to get her out of the way; he had promised Alice marriage in an effort to seduce her. Back in the "gloomy prison" of Abbey Hall once more, Lucy agrees to accept Edward so that her father will not carry out his threats of suicide; in the nick of time she is saved by Edward's mother, Lady Starling, who has discovered her son's evil plots. Alice is rescued from her confinement but quickly goes to join the angels; Lord Suffridge also dies, having been pardoned by Lady Starling for his crime of long ago; Edward "attempts to stifle his conscience in the hurlyburly of London life." Lucy and Oskar are reunited once more, yet Lucy still hesitates: "Oh, who can tell me if my love for him is strong enough to mute my desire for freedom?" Oskar gets the last word: "United, inspiring one another's courage, we shall try, on the golden wings of freedom, to reach the lofty goal, Life's Truth!"

Praiseworthy as Marie Linder's aims were, her novel represents a deficient imitation of Victorian fiction, in the figure of Robert Suffridge, distantly reminiscent of Sheridan Le Fanu's manipulative *Uncle Silas* (1864), and with an admixture of Fredrika Bremer's well-known admiration for the New World; it is difficult to make out the precise nature either of Lucy's urge to freedom (she spends a pleasant but altogether decorous Christmas Eve with Swedes in Paris) or her social aims (she is kind and trusting with her servants). Who knows what would have become of Marie Linder's writing career, had she lived? The novels of Gerda von Mickwitz and Lilly Londén (see chapter 8), coming less than two decades after hers, are light-years removed in narrative adroitness and knowledge of human nature.

Another member of Finland's high society to embark on a writing career of purposeful idealism was Adelaïde Ehrnrooth (1826–1905), the daughter of a hero of the war of 1808–9, Gustaf Adolf Ehrnrooth (he speaks critically of "the Field Marshal," Klingspor, in *Fänrik Stål*), who made a quick adjustment to Russian rule; her younger brother was Casimir Ehrnrooth (1833–1913), a notoriously loyal servant of the czar-emperors. The homely Adelaïde never married; instead, usually under the letters "A-i-a," she devoted herself to the dawning woman's cause and to the plight of the poor. Encouraged by Topelius, she set out in print rather late, with *Sagor och minnen* (1863; Fairy tales and memories), mostly verse, followed by *Gråsparven* (1868; The gray sparrow), but found her vocation in novels and stories for adults, from *Bilder ur familjkretsarne i Finland: Familjen Wärnsköld* (1866; Pictures from family life in Finland: The Wärnsköld family) to *Bland fattiga och rika* (1887; Among poor and rich); unlike Marie Linder, she took advantage both of her long experience of estate life and of observations made among the well-to-do and the poor of Helsingfors, the latter of whom she knew through her many programs of social help. The energetic eponymous heroine of *Dagmar: En hvardagshistoria* (1870; Dagmar: An everyday story), the daughter and goddaughter of veterans of the war of 1808–9 (the godfather is named Pistol, like the old soldier in Runeberg's *Julqvällen*), has the practical knowledge and the will to take over the management of a rundown property—and she is a lifesaving swimmer besides. (The short novel is full of an interesting modernity, coupled to its Runebergian patriotism; Dagmar Sköldeborg's foster-brother, Berthold Walden—who has just returned from the Great Exhibition of 1851 at the Crystal Palace—tells an enthusiastic Fennomane, with the unlikely name of Alcibiades Lumpenfors, that if Finland wishes to participate in the advances of nineteenth-century industry, transportation, science, and commerce, it would do well not to burden itself with a "clumsy, unknown, and poorly crafted [linguistic] instrument.") The ending of *Dagmar* hints that the strong-minded new mistress of Kruutila Manor, having renounced the affection of Walden to make way for her sister, will wed the provincial physician, Dr. Sommer.

In *Tiden går och vi med den* (1878; Time passes and we with it) Lydia Mansén gives up romantic love to marry a professor who has embraced new ideas of societal responsibility. To be sure, she feels a thrill at the mention of a sometime youthful flame (he was "Bengal fireworks"), but she realizes that her heart now belongs wholly to her husband, "the noblest, most perfect being [she has] met in life." Many of Ehrnrooth's girls and women are concerned with the disadvantages attached to their sex—for example, the lack of useful education, a topic addressed in the novella "Många döttrar" (Many daughters), first published (as was her custom) in a newspaper and then eventually placed in *Hvardagslifvets skuggor och dagrar* (1881; Shadows and lights of everyday life). Likewise, they are unwilling to accept their traditional lot; in "Vid en badort" (At a bathing resort), the story that fills out the same volume, Pauline Hägerflygt, possessed by the impossible dream of becoming a physician, instead finds the helpmeet with whom she can share a meaningful future: once upon a time engaged to the irresponsible Baron Woldemar, she has become an independent woman after the loss of her parental fortune, and he has likewise matured as a volunteer in the American Civil War. United once again by chance, at summertime Nådendal, they establish "the marital firm of Woldemar and Pauline Arnsköld, which lasted until life's evening." (The choice of husbands in Ehrnrooth will make Americans think of Louisa May Alcott's Jo March and Dr. Bhaer.) Sometimes, to be sure, things go badly awry; in the early *Tidens makt* (1868; The power of time) a frivolous husband wastes first his wife's inheritance and then the pittance she earns by newspaper writing, and in the late and bitter story "Hon var ändå försörjd" (After all, she was taken care of), from *Bland fattiga och rika*, a foolish countryside tailor does away with his capable wife's savings and then with her unexpected inheritance from a godfather.

No extravagant claims can be made for Ehrnrooth as a literary artist; apart from the praiseworthy persistence with which she assailed her day's problems, her main attraction lies in her flashes of irony, which also made her an excellent journalist, "Finland's first woman journalist," in Helena Westermarck's phrase. (In 1928 Westermarck included Ehrnrooth in one of her several volumes celebrating the major feminine figures of Finland-Swedish intellectual life from the previous century.) The title of Ehrnrooth's pamphlet on women's suffrage shows her wit, *I dagens intressanta samhällsfrågor, röst från en icke röstberättigad* (1882; On interesting social questions of the day: Vote from someone not entitled to vote — the pun lies in *röst*, "voice" and "vote"). Getting ahead of her much younger sister-battler for women's rights, Alexandra Gripenberg (see chapter 8), in the field of instructive and vivid travel books, she also wrote works that deserve reprinting today, *Två finskors lustvandringar i Europa och Afrika åren 1876–77 och 1884* (1886; Two Finnish women's pleasure trips in Europe and Africa, 1876–77 and 1884) and its sequel, with the subtitle *Resor i Orienten* (1890; Travels in the Orient). In this genre she is no longer fettered by the practices of her technically old-fashioned fiction.

Topelius

In her *Hundrade minnen från Österbotten* Sara Wacklin has several anecdotes about an Uleåborg painter, Mikael Topelius (1734–1821), who occupies a place in the history of Finland's art because of his altarpieces and murals in Ostrobothnian country churches; his son, Zachris (Zacharias) Topelius the Elder (1781–1831, who altered the spelling of the family name), became a physician, settling at Nykarleby (Uusikaarlepyy). His hobby was the collection of Finnish oral poetry; the results of this avocation have been described in chapter 2. His son and namesake (1818–98) was born at Kuddnäs, the family's home just outside Nykarleby, a modest house (now a Topelius museum) to which the poet remained deeply attached throughout his life. After some primary education at the grammar school in Uleåborg (where Franzén, Runeberg, Snellman, Nervander, and M. A. Castrén had been pupils once upon a time) he was sent off to Helsingfors in 1831, boarded for a time with the Runebergs, and witnessed some of the meetings of the Saturday Society ("they were far above my horizon"). As long as Runeberg lived, Topelius's relation to him was that of disciple; in the well-known photograph of the two taken in February 1863, when Topelius had become the second great luminary of the Golden Age of Finland's Swedish letters,

Runeberg looks straight ahead, his hand in his pastor's frockcoat like a Napoleon, and Topelius gazes anxiously at him from the side.

The young Topelius was a voracious reader, and his special idols in the lyric, the genre to which the lively university student first turned, were, not surprisingly, Franzén and Runeberg. His debut collection, *Ljungblommor* (Heath blossoms), appeared in 1845, to be followed by other volumes of the same name in 1850 and 1854. Topelius's popular image would someday become that of the lovable uncle of the nation's young, but the earlier poetry has evidence aplenty of an exceedingly emotional youth who managed to involve himself in passionate love affairs. The most intense of them was with an innkeeper's daughter at Kahra, on the road between the capital and Nykarleby; the "girl from Kahra" appeared to him to be a child of nature (something like Almqvist's Tintomara in *Drottningens juvelsmycke*), and he was devastated when he learned she had married a peasant's son from the neighborhood. Some of this poetry to "Greta" was not published during his lifetime; in 1931 Werner Söderhjelm brought out the long poem "Hangolas dikt," which dealt with the episode in runometers and with spicier detail ("maiden with the softly fleshed waist") than Topelius allowed to enter his printed works. A more presentable kind of eroticism appears in the verses inspired by Emilie Lindquist, whom he married in 1845; she got the nice Biedermeier tribute of "Du är min ro" (You are my rest), a gloss on the German Friedrich Rückert's "Kehr bei mir ein," known to the world at large in Robert Schumann's setting. Throughout his life a naturally pious soul, Topelius apparently suffered pangs of conscience, giving rise to such poems as "Irrskenet på heden" (The will-o'-the-wisp on the heath); a study of the manuscript shows how he tried to erase specifics from the texts he sent to the printer.

The fierier side of Topelius can also be seen in his copious (and still stirring) patriotic poetry, to wit: "Det går ett rop kring Nord, kring Söder" (A cry goes round the North, the South), held back by the censors because of anti-Russian tones in some of its lines; but Helsingfors students sang it all the same. Another specimen of his rhetoric is his verse for the graduation of 1844, with its climactic outcry: "One folk! One land! One tongue! One song and one wise learning! / From sea to sea and breast to breast the words proceeding." The long ode has large section written in the runometer Topelius often favored at the time; in it he apostrophizes the heroes of the *Kalevala* and (as elsewhere) the men who have reconstructed the national epic, Lönnrot and Castrén. A capstone of his Fennicizing national poetry is "Finlands namn" (Finland's name), inspired by the Flora Festival on 13 May 1848, when "Vårt land" was publicly sung for the first time (and

Cygnaeus delivered a long-winded address to Finland); the climax runs, "It is your mother's name, oh youth!"

A more original side of the national verses of Topelius is his hydrography, his use of rivers to describe cultural forces (a practice he shared with such disparate poets as Hölderlin in Germany and Sidney Lanier in the southern United States); the prize has to go to "Islossningen i Uleå elf" (The breakup of the ice in Uleå River), written during the new liberalism of Alexander II's rule and concluding with a statement of hope, or more than hope, for a new freedom: free the river was born, and free it will die — but there is a plenitude of other river images in Topelius's large production. The ease with which Topelius churned out poetry on contemporary topics, and the volatility of his images, could often get him into trouble, first with the authorities and then with their opponents: he greeted the revolutionary year of 1848 with "Våren 1848" (The spring of 1848): "He comes, he comes, the mighty storm," but he extensively lamented the passing of the despotic Nicholas I.

When British marines made a brief sally onto the shore near Ekenäs in the "Oriental War" (as the Crimean conflict was called in Finland), Topelius was quick to laud the bravery of the Finnish sharpshooters who turned back the intruders in "Den första blodsdroppen" (The first drop of blood). Erik Ekelund made the acute observation that, in Topelius, a deep split ran between the journalist with an eye for events of the day and the reclusive idyllist. Alongside the many (and almost always interesting) verses that address topical matters, there are the nature poems of "Sylvias sånger" (Sylvia's songs, a special favorite of composers) and such ethereal poems as "Vintergatan" (The Milky Way); no wonder Topelius was so fascinated by Aronus Forsius. And he never stopped writing poetry or, at any rate, verse: *Nya blad* (New pages) came out in 1870, *Ljung* (Heather) as late as 1889. Admittedly, there is a falling-off in quality after the songs of Sylvia, that "angel from heaven's realm / Who conquers every care" (and who so obviously is the daughter of Franzén's Fanny); but, among much that is routine, unexpected entries can be found: the highly perceptive "Kommunismens vagga" (The cradle of communism) from 1884, whose explosive, staccato opening could have been written by the expressionist Diktonius a half-century later, or the farewell to his wife of 1889, "Noli me tangere": "You who came loving, and forgiving went away." Topelius has much more to offer than the perennial favorites of songbooks, "Under rönn och syrén" (Beneath rowan and lilac), "På Roines strand" (On Roine's bank), based on a Finnish folk song, and the "cradle song" that Karin Månsdotter sings to calm the ever madder Erik XIV, inspired by a painting of the once popular Erik Johan Löfgren (1825–84), one of those touching historical scenes the nineteenth century loved.

If some of Topelius's poems, in Finnish translation or the original, are common Finnish property, so are his tales for children (see chapter 11) and at least some of his stories from Finland's past, where he emerges as a historical painter himself. As early as 1843 Topelius gave a talk at the annual festival of his student "nation" or fraternity, the Ostrobothnian, meant to answer the rhetorical question of its title, "Äger finska folket en historie?" (Do the Finnish people possess a history?); his answer was essentially negative, since, he argued, until 1809 Finland's history had simply been a part of Sweden's. Printed in 1845, the lecture caused a good deal of stir, for and against his thesis, which was primarily an exaggerated formulation of a Fennomane argument, emphasizing the singularity of Finnish strivings to become a nation. For Topelius, it was the start of another split in his own life: that, without much scholarly qualification, he was appointed professor of history at Helsingfors and eventually the university's rector, while becoming one of the North's most assiduous spinners of historical fiction. For the newspaper he edited, *Helsingfors Tidningar*, he had begun providing stories in the 1840s; much of this harmless and mildly sensational material was then collected by him decades later in *Sägner i dimman* (1882; Tales in the mist), tales sentimental and romantic told on a steamer during a foggy Baltic crossing.

This early work was training for his novel *Hertiginnan af Finland* (1850; The duchess of Finland), which, in a remarkably sober and compact style, told of the war of 1741–43 and the energetic Eva Merthen, given the sobriquet of the title because of her power over her lover, the Scots-Russian general Keith, who treated the occupied country with memorable generosity. (Topelius offered his genteel readers a convincing social excuse for the immorality of the relationship.) At about the same time, with his customary industry, Topelius started a series of novellas for his paper, which he again collected in old age as *Vinterqvällar* (1880–97; Winter evenings); many of these likewise have a historical setting, in the eighteenth century and the reign of Gustav III, the splendor of whose court provided the chance to contrast Swedish wealth and Finnish simplicity. (He also tried his hand at modern tales: *Vincent Vågbrytaren* [1860; Vincent the wave breaker] is a picture of Helsingfors student life in the 1840s with a completely sanitized visit to the infamous Green Villa; in *Det gyllene spöket* [1857; The golden ghost] and *Pastorsvalet i Aulango* [1867; The pastoral election in Aulango] he comes close to social criticism of financial shenanigans and clerical corruption.) Yet when Topelius put all these tales together in *Vinterqvällar*, he again gave the entire undertaking a historical cast by prefacing it with *Hertiginnan af Finland* and with a tale he had first published in his paper back in 1856, *Ungdomsdrömmar* (Youthful dreams), and which he now characterized as a prologue to another large and continuing project he had then had under way. In this "prologue," set on the eve of the Thirty Years' War, Aronus Forsius reads in the stars of terrible and heroic events to come.

In 1850, feeding *Helsingfors Tidningar*, Topelius had embarked on a string of tales told by an old military surgeon, Andreas Bäck, born 15 August 1769, the same day as Napoleon. (Although Bäck does not mention it, he also shares a birthday with Walter Scott, born two years later.) A prose equivalent to Runeberg's already popular ensign, Bäck tells his stories to a group of listeners in his attic room in a little Finnish town; among them are another veteran of the war of 1808–9, something of a boaster about his military past; an intellectual and humane schoolmaster; a grandmother; and several young people who, according to gender, like either the blood-and-thunder or the hearts-and-flowers in the old man's repertoire. The stories in *Fältskärns berättelser* (Tales of a field surgeon; the first cycle was translated twice, as *The King's Ring*, 1901, 1912) began to come out in book form in 1853 and were continued until 1867, in five cycles of varying lengths; they go in time from Gustav II Adolf's victory over the imperial general Tilly at Breitenfeld in September 1631 to the beginning of the age of Gustav III, and are the mega-saga of the intertwined fates of two families, the Bertelskölds and the Larssons. Before the epic's beginning the prideful peasant Aron Bertila has sent his daughter to Stockholm for schooling; there (the scandal is hushed up for the listeners in the attic) she has had an affair with the young Gustav Adolf and its fruit is Gustaf Bertel Bertila, eventually to be ennobled for battlefield bravery by his father but cursed by his maternal grandfather, who has hated the aristocracy "ever since the days of the Club War." In the German campaign the right-hand man of Bertila-Bertelsköld is the vigorous Larsson, whose family remains true to the land, albeit parts of his line, for narrative purposes, eventually become honest merchants.

By the time the fourth cycle has come, Ester Larsson, a descendant of the original Larsson to whom Aron Bertila, enraged at his grandson, had once given his farm, marries Carl Victor Bertelsköld, the scion of the noble line. As Sweden goes from war to war, the Finnish actors play a very large part in its fortunes; a main argument is that selflessness and courage are more important than pride of birth. But Topelius's depictions of the colorful Bertelskölds are more engaging than those of the lackluster Larssons; and the historical figures that turn up constantly in the flood of events — Charles XII, for example, or the imperious Arvid Horn or the temptress

Aurora Königsmarck—often outshine the simple men and women who throng the two thousand plus pages. The earlier parts of the series are stronger than the ones that deal with the some fifty years after the Great Northern War (i.e., the fourth and fifth cycles), where the pace slows considerably; their battle scenes, derring-do, and hairbreadth escapes are inherently more exciting than the salon-and-town interiors in which the latter tales abound. But Topelius is scarcely as avid a fan of heroic death as Runeberg; the first and second cycles, dealing with the Thirty Years' War and the Polish wars of the Swedish crown, make no bones about the degradation and senseless slaughter of warfare, and one of the more memorable portraitures is that of the transformation of the idealistic Gustaf Bertel Bertelsköld into a ruthless condottiere.

Unhappily, the psychology of other characters is seldom as complex (and even in Bertelsköld's case the result is presented, rather than the process). The pious Catholic Regina von Emmeritz, entrusted with the task of murdering Gustav Adolf, falls in love with the monarch instead; but Topelius shrinks back from all too clearly imputing sexual motives to her infatuation. He likes to employ black and white: his most notorious villain is the rascally "Jesuit monk" Father Hieronymus, who keeps a stiletto concealed in his crucifix, but other scoundrels appear as well: a brutal overseer of the Bertelsköld lands, a crafty chamberlain who gets a later Bertelsköld into debt so that he can take over the family estate, Mainiemi, evidently planning to seduce the count's spendthrift wife as well. (Almost lynched by the enraged peasants, tired of his tyranny, the overseer at least shows the Finnish virtue of blind courage.) On the other hand, Topelius can betray a certain originality: he has a number of energetic and doughty women, among them the overseer's plucky daughter, who swims like a fish and has a bravery to equal any man's; later in life she participates in the rescue of a presumed witch—another independent woman, by the way—from Åbo Castle. And however often Topelius burdens the reader with his piety, he is also ready to pillory the narrow dogmatist or the clergyman too respectful of authority; a justly famous episode in the fourth cycle is the speech of the Vasa pastor, Claudius Hedman, to welcome King Adolf Fredrik. He can usually be depended on, too, for genre painting that likewise entails criticism of excessive pride; an example is the Stockholm section at the end of the Great Northern War, depicting the sublime arrogance of Arvid Horn, and the efforts of a degenerate Bertelsköld to navigate around him, while outside the Horn palace a mob of refugees from Finland demands food. As in Scott, the readership is constantly reminded of human rights and of the author's humane spirit.

Much, to be sure, conforms to the wishes of the nineteenth-century audience: not just the stock characterizations and situations but also the careful details of clothing, furniture, and architecture, and then the burdensome supernatural element, incorporated in the ever-returning magic ring of the Bertelskölds. (But Wagner's audiences were also quite willing to follow the fate of the Ring of the Nibelung.) *Fältskärns berättelser* cannot be accurately ranked among the historical epics of the century to which it so clearly belongs: it lacks the depth of *War and Peace* (to which it is directly contemporary), but it has a sweep that, say, Charles Kingsley (in *Hypatia, Westward Ho, Hereward the Wake*) never quite achieved, although Topelius and Kingsley are alike in much — their attention to factual minutiae, their persistent moralizing. At what audience did Topelius in fact aim? Was he writing for adults, or for adolescents, or both? Reading the tales, one may sometimes suspect that he provided a Finnish equivalent to G. A. Henty (1832–1902) and his once enormously popular novels of empire (*With Clive in India, With Wolfe in Canada*); but Henty was quite aware that he wrote for boys alone whereas Topelius believed he wrote for a young nation that needed a history, just as it needed a national poet and a national epic. Flattering, like *Fänrik Stål*, to national vanity throughout, Topelius's panorama offered no difficulties of comprehension, and so, like *Fänrik Stål*, it could serve as a national inspiration as late as the Continuation War of 1941–44; at least, this is what the historian Eirik Hornborg claimed: he refused to put these products of a childlike and noble spirit "on the Procrustes bed of criticism" (p. 8).

The dramatic production of Topelius was likewise written to fill a gap in the national culture and is largely an outgrowth of his novelistic work. His first play, *Efter femtio år* (1851; After fifty years), dramatizes his story *Gamla baron på Rautakylä* (1849; The old baron of Rautakylä), fitting it out with a long preamble in which the characters of the novella — desiccated oldsters at a tumble-down Finnish estate, living on their memories and variously regretting or attempting to profit from their frivolous past — are seen as gilded youths at the court of Gustav III, in 1788. His opera libretto, *Kung Carls jagt* (1852; King Charles's hunt), has the same material as portions of the second cycle of *Fältskärns berättelser;* the young Charles XI goes to Åland to hunt elk, and the brave fisher-girl Leonora (Charles's "sister," it turns out, baptized with him sixteen years before) saves the life of the young monarch. The plot of the "romantic opera" is less important than its choruses, in which Finland is repeatedly praised; the music of Pacius shows how much he was in debt to C. M. von Weber's *Der Freischütz* (1821) and to Fredrik Kuhlau's music for the Danish patriotic musical, with a text by Johan Ludvig Heiberg, *Elverhøj* (1828; The elves' hill).

Regina von Emmeritz (1853) has the most exciting story of the surgeon's first cycle as its source; in the tale, however, Regina, the Franconian zealot, is shipped off to castle-arrest in Finland after the assassination plot (cooked up by the rascally Father Hieronymus) against Gustav Adolf is revealed, whereas on the stage she dies of a wound delivered by one of the king's enraged soldiers. After the premiere of the play, critics observed that too much of Regina's struggle against her growing love for the intended victim occurs within her, quite unknown to the audience, and Topelius revised his text before it was printed; but at any event he had given Finland an actable vehicle on a theme, loyalty and treachery, much debated in the country early and late. Also, its finale was both rousing and heartrending; the curtain went down to the strains of "The Finnish Cavalry's March in the Thirty Years' War," as Gustav Adolf led his troops away to make "faith free, from the South unto the North," and Regina's body was carried off for burial. It hung on in the repertoire for years, and when Swedish Theater in Helsingfors was reopened on 3 May 1918, after the White triumph in the Civil War, it was the vehicle chosen for the festive occasion.

Another drama by Topelius, *Prinsessan af Cypern: Sagospel efter motiver ur Kalevala* (The princess of Cyprus: Fairy-tale play after themes from the *Kalevala*), was written for the original opening of the same theater, on 28 November 1860, again with music by Pacius. In it the Don Juan of the *Kalevala*, Lemminkäinen, somehow arrives at the island of Venus, Cyprus, falls in love with Chryseis, and returns to Finland with her in the second act, only to learn that his mother, Helka, is unhappy with his choice. By means of song, Lemminkäinen changes his simple hut into a splendid palace, but Chryseis (whom the Finns call Kyllikki, after the hero's wife in the *Kalevala*) seems — in the altogether confusing finale — to return to her homeland. Despite a great deal of pomp and circumstance, including the playing of a proto-Sibelian *Kalevala* overture by Filip von Schantz (1835–65), the play quickly went into the cupboard of theatrical oddities, and Topelius decided to write for the stage no more. In his memoirs he told how an inner voice warned him against making concessions to a "mixed public," and he remembered how he had lost two of his children while he was at work on theatrical texts; further, when he was ill with inflammation of the lungs in May 1863, the New Theater burned down "in the third year of its existence." "From then on I said farewell," but he made an exception with his plays for children.

His resolve faltered only once when, in 1867, he dramatized his "modern" story, *Brita Skrifvars,* about a sailor's wife in Ostrobothnia whose husband, long disappeared, suddenly returns from America, alcoholized and speaking broken Swedish. Its theme of the returnee from the New World was topical enough (Ibsen used it in a much more effective way in *Samfundets støtter* [1877; Eng. tr. *Pillars of Society,* 1888] ten years later); but the play failed miserably when produced in Gothenburg. This was on the eve of 1868, which Topelius himself characterized as the "trouble-filled year" and which his biographer Paul Nyberg has marked as a turning point in his life. He became more concerned than ever with the moral and pedagogical import of his work; as a member of the hymnal committee, he wrote the ever-popular "Giv mig ej glans, ej guld, ej prakt" (Give me not show, nor gold, nor pomp), increased the didactic and religious content of his series *Läsning för barn* (Reading for children), and composed a school classic, *Boken om vårt land* (1875 ff.; The book about our country), a brilliantly executed primer meant to instill not only a knowledge of the geography and history of the homeland but a genuine love of it into its young readers. (It had been preceded by *Naturens bok* [1856; Nature's book], about the homeland's flora and fauna.) Instantly translated into Finnish (1876), it was repeatedly reprinted and revised in both languages; its nearest equivalent in the United States would be the *Eclectic Readers* (1836–57) of William Holmes McGuffey. Another example of Topelius's desire to teach was his *Evangelium för barn* (1893; The Gospel for children), in whose preface, written at his retirement home near Helsingfors, Björkudden (Koivuniemi), he spoke of the responsibility he felt and the need to make use of "children's brief attention." To the last, he put the skills of the experienced newspaperman to edifying use.

As a creative artist in his later years, Topelius continued to provide the historical narratives to which he owed so much of his fame; he returned to the century in which *Fältskärns berättelser* had begun its action. *Planeternas skyddslingar* (1886–88; The protégés of the planets) became better known under the name Topelius gave it before his death, *Stjärnornas kungabarn* (1899; Royal children of the stars). The children are born on 8 December 1626; one is Kristina, the daughter of Gustav Adolf, and the others are Hagar and Ben-Oni, the offspring of a Jewish mother (herself the daughter of a Regensburg banker, Ruben Zevi) and Johann von Götz (1599–1645), the cruelest of the Imperial generals in the Thirty Years' War. Robbed by a treacherous servant and an envious cousin during a trip to Finland, the unhappy woman is abandoned in a snowdrift (she dies almost immediately after the twins' birth) and the children are brought up by Sigfrid Aronus Forsius, who sees to it that they get distinguished godparents. The long novel, three volumes, follows the career of all three children, joined by the stars. Ben-Oni early becomes a soldier and fights for Torstensson in Germany, then dies in Jerusalem leading an army of "eleven thousand men, Jews and Arabs," recruited by his grandfather, the banker, who plans to establish a Jewish homeland in Israel — the opponents are members of a Jewish messianic sect led by still another member of the Zevi family. Hagar becomes Queen Kristina's librarian and one of the most learned women of her time, rivaling the queen in the theological studies that eventually lead to the monarch's notorious abdication and conversion to Roman Catholicism; in time, like her brother, Hagar has been found by her grandfather, the internationally powerful Zevi, and has been sent by him to Istanbul with Ben-Oni, on a mission to the Sublime Porte. There she is chosen by the seven-year-old Mohammed IV to be his wife; clever as she is, and good, she rules over the Turkish realm for six years before fleeing in order to save her juvenile husband's life. Returning to Finland and poverty, she prays at the lonely grave of her mother; then she disappears. It is believed, the book's last paragraph says, that Kristina, visiting Paris, found her former librarian working as a nurse in Vincent de Paul's hospital.

The novel has plenty to interest a reader patient enough to slog through its less-than-believable events. Hagar may be a semiportrait of Emma Irene Åström (1847–1934), the first woman to receive a master's degree in Finland, whose cause Topelius had fostered while rector of the university; the story of Ben-Oni and his grandfather's master plan is a demonstration of Topelius's awareness of the Zionist movement — and of an ambiguous attitude toward Judaism in general. (Topelius liked to boast of the drop of Jewish blood he had discovered in his family's genealogy, but his Ruben Zevi — whose money has financed both sides in the Thirty Years' War and who plans to take over the world once the Christian soldiers have exhausted themselves — offers an unnerving prefiguration of the infamous anti-Semitic forgery, the *Protocol of the Elders of Zion*.) The portrait of the vain Kristina is likewise ambiguous, perhaps because of Topelius's unwillingness to deal directly with her strong admixture of "masculine" traits and her conversion; yet he told his Swedish friend, "Uncle Adam" (Carl Anton Wetterbergh [1804–89]), an author of children's stories like himself, that the novel was "an attempt to solve Queen Kristina's psychological riddle." Of the trio, Hagar has his special sympathy and attention because she learns to chasten her pride and to love in the deepest sense; he informed his sister Sofie that the basis of the novel lay in 1 Corinthians 13, which opens, "Though I speak with the tongues of men and angels, and have not charity, I am become as sounding brass or a tinkling cymbal."

In 1896, urged on by his Swedish publisher Bonnier (who had a gold mine in him), Topelius went once more into the historical breach with

Ljungars saga (The tale of Ljungars), actually an amalgamation of two narratives he had published in his newspaper more than thirty years before, spinoffs of Walter Scott's *The Monastery* and *The Abbey*. The altogether turgid action takes place during the last days of Catholicism in Finland; its main characters are three children who are ill-used by their stepmother, Fru Ursula — for the rest, the novel's most powerful character, a prideful woman said to be the daughter of a Livonian Jew and "versed in the magical arts." Eventually, surrounded by the forces of the Danish king Christian and suspected of betrayal of the king's cause, Ursula blows up her castle and herself with it; of her sometime charges, two — the younger son who intends to become a priest and his sister — are drowned while trying to escape to Sweden with Finland's last Catholic bishop. Their protector, the honest Finn David, who stays behind on that fateful night, then goes to Sweden himself and becomes a faithful servant of its new monarch, Gustav Vasa. A last member of the Ljungars family, marked by illness, is killed by robbers when he returns, under David's protection, to the castle ruin. Because of the author's popularity, the novel was a publishing success, although Topelius had burdened it with all the apparatus of a romanticism long since grown old-fashioned: a family curse, a protective and prophetic castle ghost ("Ljungars's white maiden"), and so forth. By this time he was wholly out of sympathy with literature's new currents (although the hodgepodge of *Ljungars saga,* with its sinister woman and feeble scion, might suggest a pattern that was popular in the decadence); he had warned Bonnier that he would withdraw from the publisher's lists if the firm continued to publish Strindberg's shameful books. But he never did.

As a journalist, Topelius had not always been so easily shocked. The feigned letters written for *Helsingfors Tidningar,* sent to "Lieutenant Leopold in Grusia" (1842–53), a fictive Finnish officer in Russian service, and then to his cousin Leopoldine in Alaska (among the several Finlanders in the Russian-American colony), were a running sardonic comment on conditions in the capital. And as late as 1885 Topelius was persuaded by the journal *Finland* to provide sixteen pieces for *Anteckningar från det Helsingfors som gått* (Sketches from the Helsingfors that has disappeared); Torsten Steinby, who reprinted the *Anteckningar* in 1968, points out that they are in part a résumé of Topelius's journalism from the middle century. Certainly, they offer a picture of literary and university life of the time, but unhappily, Topelius was unwilling to include the pithiest elements of his sometime journalism. The eye for detail that served him so well in the antiquarian details of the surgeon's tales could also be turned on hidden corners of the idyll. In *Helsingfors Tidningar* for 1858 he wrote about the absence of the simplest sanitary provisions even in better homes and remarked on the utter cultural deprivation of the city's growing proletariat, lacking the pleasure of "a balcony, a flowerbed, even a covered stair."

The collected works of Topelius in thirty-four volumes, published in Stockholm by Bonnier and in Helsingfors by G. W. Edlund between 1899 and 1907, do not present the journalistic works, so important for a correction of his fixed public image as the sweet-voiced poet, the celebrator of Finland's past, and the avuncular teller of children's tales. A genuine complete edition of the prodigiously productive Topelius would be an impossibility; it would have to include not only the innumerable contributions to *Helsingfors Tidningar* during the twenty years of his editorship, and his articles and reviews in other papers, but a huge amount of unpublished items, journalistic, creative, and private. When he died, on 12 March 1898, he was mourned in his homeland and throughout the North as an author of the first magnitude. (Elmer Diktonius claimed that his first childhood memory was of the funeral cortège.) The admiration he received in Sweden was particularly great; he had encouraged the young Verner von Heidenstam, and Heidenstam's *Karolinerna* (1897–98; Eng. tr. *The Charles Men*, 1920) was Topelius-inspired. Selma Lagerlöf was so taken with his work that in 1920 she published a popular and richly sentimental biography, taking him up to the end of the 1850s. In Finland his position was beyond question; in the great volume by various hands which Topelius himself edited, *Finland i 19de seklet* (1893; Finland in the nineteenth century), he entrusted the chapter on literature to Carl Gustaf Estlander, who called him, among other things, "a poet by the grace of God" and "an object of his nation's esteem and gratitude." Although he never became quite the same point of national reference as Runeberg, his heritage has certainly been as long-lasting. Could it be suggested that Mika Waltari's best-selling novelistic oeuvre of the middle twentieth century (imparting comments on contemporary matters even as it engaged in a dazzling reconstruction of the past) was a continuation of the Topelian practice? It would be a mistake not to take Topelius, or Waltari for that matter, with sufficient seriousness. In the "gentle poet" many discoveries are to be made.

One surprise lies in the attitude Topelius held toward the literature of which he was a main representative for so many decades: he believed he was the end of the line. In consideration of his generous and liberal attitude in so many matters, it is troubling to learn how, as early as 1848, he called authors in Swedish, himself included, "a doomed line ... losing ourselves as a final glow of the past day in the dawn of a new morrow," or how, apparently without regret, in earlier editions of *Boken om vårt land* he predicted that "Swedish literature in Finland will slowly fall into silence." Albeit no Fennomane, adamantly calling for a monolingual Finland, Topelius came from a Finnish country family and (unlike Runeberg) knew Finnish fairly well. In *Fältskärns berättelser* the Bertilas or Bertelskölds hang on, at least some of them, to their native Finnish tongue for private purposes; in Stockholm, Gustaf Adolf, the brave grandson of the first Count Bertelsköld, throws a silly Swedish nobleman down the stairs because the latter says that Finnish noblemen are lummoxes, "not ashamed to speak their ugly Finnish mother tongue among themselves in the royal palace itself."

Topelius's pessimistic thoughts about the future of his literary instrument were in fact not at all uncommon among Finland's Swedish writers in the 1850s and the 1860s, when the Finnish nationalist movement was just getting up steam. (To be sure, the "Åbo romantics" had advocated the cultivation of Finnish and the disappearance of Swedish as literary language, long before there was any prospect at all of such a shift.) The Finland-Swedish literary history *Den finsk-svenska litteraturens utveckling* (1866–67; The development of Finnish-Swedish literature), by Gabriel Lagus (1837–96), emphasizes the literature's melancholy spirit and claims (at a time when literature in Finnish itself, save for the *Kalevala* and *Kanteletar,* was much more dreamed-of than extant) that it has been "a stepchild neither recaptured in Sweden nor recognized in Finland." The lectures on Finland's Swedish literature given by the university librarian and poetaster C. W. Törnegren (1817–60) in 1859 had flatly predicted an end to Swedish literature in Finland, to the speaker's own regret; as August Schauman recalled, the audience listened in amazement as Törnegren — speaking at a university and in a city where Swedish was easily the predominant and still the only official language — predicted that "after a couple of generations cultured people in Finland would have to have a dictionary and a grammar to work their way through the writings of a Runeberg, a Nordström [the legal scholar], a Castrén [the Fenno-Ugrist]." At first people thought Törnegren, known for his satirical vein, was joking, but he was not: "He spoke in an almost gloomily serious tone." And after Runeberg had fallen ill, Fredrika wrote to Topelius, on New Year's Day 1868, that the younger man must keep going as long as possible, "in order not to leave the place empty before a pretender to the throne appears." She was thinking especially of the thinness of Swedish-language letters, now that Runeberg was stricken and Josef Julius Wecksell had gone mad.

Wecksell
Wecksell was born in Åbo in 1838, the son of a prosperous hatmaker and a mother with literary inclinations but little time to give them expression,

save through her eldest son; his first poems appeared in *Åbo Underrättelser* before he finished the gymnasium. One of them, "Åbo slott" (1857; Åbo Castle), was recalled by Fredrika Runeberg as she wrote to Topelius: "Among the young people who have made their appearance in these years, who awakened such hopes as did [Wecksell] when his 'Åbo slott' appeared?" Even earlier, his farce, *Tre friare* (Three suitors), had been performed in Åbo and Helsingfors; expectations were high when, at twenty, he went on to the university. In 1860 his *Valda ungdomsdikter* (Selected youthful poems) came out, including several lyrics demonstrating his knowledge of German poetry—a tribute to Schiller on the great idealist's centenary (for a festival arranged by Cygnaeus) and, more important, a variant of Klopstock's antiphonal ode, "Die beiden Musen" (The two muses, i.e., English and German), called "Svenskan och Finskan" (Swedish and Finnish). Here Wecksell is fair toward both tongues but lets Swedish say, plainly enough, that if she is thrown away, into a stormy sea, "half of Finland then will follow to my oblivion's open grave," a reference to cultural values. (The little book contains, as well, a sufficiency of Heine imitations.) Some of the poems have achieved a kind of international currency, thanks to Sibelius's settings: the wistful "Demanten på marssnön" (The diamond on the March snow), "Var det en dröm?" (Was it a dream?), and the rambunctious "Har du mod?" (Do you have courage?).

By April 1861 Wecksell had come down with a venereal infection, and although pronounced cured within a year, he became more and more prone to fits of melancholy (it ran in the family: two brothers went insane, one became an alcoholic, and one was "extremely peculiar"). While he was at work on his historical tragedy, *Daniel Hjort,* he began to hallucinate. Recovered enough to attend the premiere at Helsingfors's New Theater on 26 November 1862, he is supposed to have said, "It sounds so familiar, but I don't recall where I read it." The next spring he was shipped off to the Endenich asylum near Cologne where Robert Schumann had died seven years before; the treatments were unsuccessful, and he was brought back to the family's new home in Helsingfors. Some hopes were still held out for his recovery; in 1865 *Daniel Hjort* and Runeberg's *Kungarne på Salamis* were submitted for a prize announced by the Finnish Literary Society for the encouragement of "literary activity" in Finland, but Kivi's comedy, *Nummisuutarit* (*The Heath Cobblers*), won instead—his victory meant little or nothing to the losers. In September of the same year Wecksell was committed to the Lappvik asylum in the capital and remained there, hopelessly insane, until his death in August 1907. For nine months in 1872 his fellow patient was Aleksis Kivi; as luck would have it, Sibelius's brother, the psychiatrist Christian, was head of the institution when Wecksell died.

Quite understandably, Wecksell's ghastly fate got attention from other writers. In the novel *En patriot utan fosterland* (1896; A patriot without a fatherland) Tavaststjerna has a subsidiary figure, "W-ll," who plans to use the book's protagonist as a model for "a great historical play from Finland's past, treating of a traitor against his country," and Tavaststjerna appears also to have thought of Wecksell as he composed his poem cycle about a half-mad poet, *Laureatus* (1897). Hjalmar Procopé memorialized Wecksell's death with a poem, "Dödens fånge" (Death's prisoner), and Diktonius, thirty years later, made a little portrait of him in "Så snabbt du brann" (You burned so quickly). In *Mörkret som ger glädjen djup* (1982; The darkness that gives gladness depth) Märta Tikkanen dedicated a poetic suite to Sofia Wecksell in a long outpouring of sympathy for the mother of a lost genius and a woman herself unfulfilled. The Finland-Swedish author to have made the most important contribution to Wecksell's memory, though, was Arvid Mörne. Going through his own adolescent crisis, Mörne had quoted Wecksell's "Jag midnattens barn" (I, midnight's child) in a letter to a friend — a terrifying poem written in the summer of 1862 and included in the *Samlade dikter* (Collected poems) put together by Wecksell's admirers in 1868. As an adult, Mörne — both poet and literary scholar — wrote a biography (1909) and followed it with *Nya Wecksell-studier* (1920; New Wecksell studies); these volumes contained fragmentary poetry from the early days of madness, as well as other hitherto unknown material.

Much of Wecksell's poetry is imitative, not just of Heine but of Runeberg, and a Topelian sweetness prevails in his pictures of nature. His several love poems to "Helmi" (Pearl) are full of a routine and harmless anacreonticism, or of sentimental idealization, again à la Topelius. But his urge to imitate or emulate can be also artistically productive, as in the Klopstock-like ode and in his Byronic dramatic monologue "Don Juans avsked från lifvet" (Don Juan's departure from life). The Swedish poet Karl Vennberg (in 1947) also saw an influence of Byron in one of the greatest of Wecksell's poems, the "Almqvist monolog," in which Almqvist ponders the attempted poisoning of the loan shark von Scheven that resulted in the Swedish author's flight to America: "To venture it or not — that's what comes first, / And to succeed or not — that's what comes second, / And in between the two there lies the deed." Such poems hold a major promise never fulfilled; the best and most original of Wecksell's poetry was written on the brink of his collapse or immediately thereafter. One of the short poems from his more-or-less lucid months, "Septembers klara himmel" (September's clear sky), published by Mörne in 1920, bears an uncanny resemblance to Hölderlin's "Hälfte des Lebens" (Half of life), also written on the verge of insanity; another poem was scribbled by Wecksell on the last page of his copy of *Valda ungdomsdikter:* "En sorgsen sorgsen sakta musik / Igenom mitt väsen klingar" (A mournful, mournful muted music / Resounds throughout my being). "Tomma händer" (Empty hands) laments Wecksell's perception that words are dead; a painful prose poem, "På moln stod du!" (You stood on clouds!) perhaps written at the Bonn asylum, foreshadows the unexpected and irrational imagery of modernism; the essayist and psychiatrist Mikael Enckell has compared it with the work of Hölderlin: "You stood on clouds: Your feet were earth and your thought reached up to God! . . . And a poplar stood green in the innermost part of your eye and your greatness disappeared." Mörne printed most of the poem in his study of 1909; in 1920 he added two concluding verses he had omitted before: they would indicate that—as in a self-portrait by Egon Schiele—the poem describes a fantasy during masturbation, a far cry from the old-hat quality that Mörne admits is typical of much Wecksell, "images taken from the common property of romanticism . . . [that] make the impression of being epigonic."

Daniel Hjort is part and parcel of the age in which Wecksell lived. The historical drama was tried again and again by Finland's Swedish poets in the 1850s and 1860s (Cygnaeus, Gabriel Lagus, Theodor Lindh, Karl Robert Malmström), and the Club War, with its clashing allegiances, was particularly enticing to minds aware of Friedrich Hebbel's demand for plays whose action fell "at the hinges of history." From Scandinavia proper, Ibsen's *Fru Inger til Østeraad* (1855; Eng. tr. *Lady Inger of Østråt*, 1890), *Hærmændene på Helgeland* (1857; Eng. tr. *The Vikings at Helgeland*, 1890), and *Kongsemnerne* (1863; Eng. tr. *The Pretenders,* 1890), and Strindberg's *Mäster Olof* (1872/73; Eng. tr. 1959) managed to enter the international repertoire. Of all the historical plays from Finland, *Daniel Hjort* alone has remained alive, as an ornament of the repertoire and then in occasional revivals; it is a worthy predecessor to Strindberg's historical dramas. The time is the very end of the Club War. The conflict (which also attracted Cygnaeus, Lagus, and Fredrika Runeberg) had just been the topic of a pioneering piece of Finnish historiography, Yrjö Koskinen's (Georg Forsman's) *Nuijasota* (1857–59; The Club War), translated into Swedish by E. O. Edlund in 1864–65. Åbo Castle, commanded by Arvid Stålarm, loyal to the memory of the late Klas Fleming and to King Sigismund, is besieged by the troops of Charles (IX), duke of Södermanland. The late Fleming's adoptive son Hjort, an adviser to Stålarm, learns that he was in fact fathered by a peasant leader the cruel Fleming had executed and that he has unwittingly signed the order allowing his uncle to be stoned to death; he excites the castle's company to mutiny and betrays the castle to Charles, whereon he is assassinated by a bastard son of Fleming. (Wecksell's Hjort has very little to do with the historical figure, who not only survived the castle's fall but prospered until he was murdered in 1615; see chapter 6.)

The play has its faults; its often torturous blank verse (interrupted, in the best Shakespearean fashion, by prose inlays) and its insistence on a corpse-strewn stage are principal among them. Sigrid Stålarm, who saves Hjort from being blown to smithereens by his rival for her hand, Johan Fleming, Klas's legitimate son, drowns herself, Ophelia-like, offstage, but her body is brought in when Charles takes possession of the castle; offered a new identity by Charles, Hjort falls by the bastard's hand, and his peasant mother weeps over his body; Johan Fleming's execution is described in a teichoscopy delivered by *his* mother, Ebba Fleming. But the characterizations, most of them, are done with remarkable skill: Stålarm, loyal to a lost cause and a distant, uncaring monarch; Åbo's bishop, Ericus Erici, condemnatory of brutal masters but above the battle; Charles, bloody-minded but with a patriotic vision; Johan, who loves his life almost enough to bargain for it; and Hjort, who is a brother to Wecksell's Don Juan and Almqvist in his selfish scheming and yet has good and sufficient reason for his treachery — a treachery that, indeed, will turn out to be to Finland's advantage but that contravenes the Finnish concept of loyalty unto death incorporated in Stålarm. During his brief career Wecksell introduced the element of doubt into a literature that, above all, wanted and got absolutes, blacks-and-whites, from Runeberg and Topelius. In the most unsettling of what Johannes Salminen called "Mephistophelean" poems (p. 58), Wecksell's Almqvist speaks of how good and evil blur: "Thus terribly / Life's sweetly violet-blue shade shifts in the world."

In his introduction to *Hjort* (1863) Cygnaeus — concluding that Wecksell would not get well — wrote that the loss of further dramatic works from him was "one among the hardest blows by which the literature of the fatherland would be struck." With the abrupt ending of the careers of Runeberg and Wecksell, Finland-Swedish literature entered a thin period. Smaller talents likewise vanished. Leistenius, for whom Wecksell held a touching commemorative speech, had died in 1858, the critic Törnegren in 1860; the above-mentioned Lagus, Lindh, Malmström were not striking dramatic talents, nor — for all their efforts — did they have anything new to offer in the lyric. The historical romances and ballads of Lagus are in the style of Ludwig Uhland (*Romanser*, 1865; *Dikter*, 1891), Lindh (1833–1904) follows very much the same late romantic path (*Dikter*, 1862, 1875) but still maintains a shadowy presence through the song he wrote for the annual festival of the Nyland students in 1867, when he chose "the sea, the free sea" as their homeland, a presaging of Finland-Swedish rhetoric to come. (Lindh could be remembered, too, as a gifted translator of verse: Béranger, Byron, Herwegh, Ibsen, Longfellow.) As for Malmström (1830–1900), a devoted son of Åbo, he offered a veritable verse tour through the old town's monuments and lost his literary roots when, in 1886, he accepted a pastorate in Karelia. In Estlander's review of Finland-Swedish literature in *Finland i 19de seklet,* the critic accorded Malmström's poems (1858, 1879) a slap, saying they left only "tired and pale impressions." When Malmström complained to Topelius, the old gentleman sought to console him by describing Estlander's criticism as "intellectually cold."

Estlander: A Summing Up

Born of a pastoral family in Ostrobothnia in 1834, Estlander had made a splash by translating the *Poema de mio Cid* into Swedish (1863) and writing about Provençal literature. During a long trip abroad (1863–65) he became a competent art historian, and his *De bildande konsternas historia från slutet af adertonde århundradet till våra dagar* (1867; The history of the plastic arts from the end of the eighteenth century until our days) became a Nordic manual of "modern" art. (The young Danish novelist J. P. Jacobsen seems to have been fascinated by Estlander's quotations from Gautier about the erotic undercurrent in paintings that depict the scourging of Christ.) Estlander easily succeeded to Cygnaeus's chair as professor of aesthetics and modern literature in 1868 and held the position for thirty years; in this post he wrote his many Runeberg studies, confirming the poet as the patron saint of Finland's letters and the constant strengthener of the nation's moral fiber.

In primary school his rector, Lars Stenbäck, had tried to inculcate him, Estlander recalled, not with pietism but with love for the Finnish language as the "true mother tongue . . . Stenbäck's voice was never warmer than when he read Finnish poetry aloud," and the youthful Estlander was something of a Fennophile; but at the university he was transformed to an ardent spokesman for the Swedish cause in Finland, defending the language as the bearer and defender of culture in the land. This was the spirit behind his foundation of the journal *Finsk Tidskrift* in 1876 (it has lived on to be the oldest cultural magazine in either Finland or Sweden), and he expressed his cultural concept most clearly in "Min ställning i språkfrågan" (My position on the language question) in the journal for 1887 — where he also advocated the finding of a modus vivendi between "the country's two cultured classes, the older Swedish and the newer Finnish one . . . under the proviso that, beforehand, a higher power [i.e., Russia] does not put an end to the matter." Estlander was also instrumental in founding Svenska Litteratursällskapet i Finland (the Swedish Literary Society in Finland) in 1885, in memory of Runeberg, an organization whose mission it was (and is) to further the study of Finland's Swedish literature, language, and cultural history. Estlander's accomplishments were of the greatest importance; they were primarily of a stewardship nature, however — looking backward over an altogether respectable past and guarding its values for the future. By inclination and historical situation Estlander was a conservative; his reception of new literary currents was to be expected: he was uncomfortable about Zola's naturalism, about the "demonism" of Ibsen's later plays, about the French decadent movement, albeit well informed on all three; he did not like Tavaststjerna's "realism" (in which he thought patriotism and "other lofty emotions" were neglected for "moods of the moment, yearning for pleasure"). Yet, on occasion, he could be a perceptive critic; his review of Strindberg's *Röda rummet* (1879; Eng. tr. *The Red Room,* 1913, 1967) immediately grasps the genius of the then little known author.

A handsomely lucid stylist, Estlander could be at once authoritarian and persuasive, as in the famous address given on the bicentennial of Per Brahe's death in 1880, "Ubi patria, ibi bene," in which he reverses the Latin tag (Where the fatherland is, there one is well-off) to say "Ubi bene, ibi patria" (Where one is well-off, there is the fatherland), thus threatening to leave a Finland where Swedish culture was becoming (he implied) an outcast. If "in one way or another, that which you regard as most essential for your soul is denied you by the fatherland, then, rending a thousand tender bonds, you will take your penates, your Runeberg, and your *Kalevala* on board and steer the vessel of your fortune to a distant strand." The adduction of the *Kalevala* in the imaginary flight of the modern-day Aeneas from a burning Finnish Troy is a brilliant feint on Estlander's part; it qualifies him as a possessor and savior, albeit disenfranchised, of the whole of Finland's cultural heritage. He surely did not intend to abandon his professorship and his accumulated power and set out for Sweden; but the threat betrays, again, the pessimism that beset Finland-Swedish intellectuals in those years. The "cold intellectualism" Topelius found in him had its virtues; his "cultural Swedishness" was unemotional in that it emphasized "Swedish" achievements in Finland rather than mere chance ties of language and a vaguely understood "blood," and his intellectualism, too, emphasizing cultural history, may well have had something to do with his advocacy of the emancipation of Jews, not only in Finland but in Russia proper.

In his last years — he died on Goethe's birthday, 28 August 1910 — he grew ever more concerned about the position of Swedish culture in Finland. In 1905, sketching a letter to the great liberal politician Leo Mechelin, he wrote that "Swedish is being shoved off into the private sphere," and in 1906, looking backward to the 1870s, he recalled how "the insane hatred of the Fennomane movement for everything Swedish" had made him decide to protect the language and its values. The same year, in his old journal, *Finsk Tidskrift,* he scolded his minority for foolishly and busily diminishing itself, by means of emigration (the idea he had toyed with a quarter of a century before), voluntary Fennicization for personal advantage, entrance into Russian service (as in the case of C. G. Mannerheim), and sheer indifference. "But let us not despair or neglect or scorn whatever our forefathers have left us that is great and precious, and we shall escape the shame of seeing Runeberg's language and poetic creation put out to pasture in the very fatherland he loved so dearly." Even in an essay Estlander could be wonderfully oratorical.

A Sense of Minority

George C. Schoolfield

8

Finland-Swedish Awareness
The semimoribund decades of Finland's Swedish creative literature between the falling silent of Runeberg and Wecksell in 1863 and Tavaststjerna's lyric debut in 1883 were filled with developments that nonetheless had a large bearing on creation to come. Estlander's "cultural Swedishness" was complemented in the undertakings of Axel Olof Freudenthal (1836–1911), for many years Estlander's colleague at the university. Freudenthal's family background may have had much to do with his life's work as a spokesman of the Finland-Swedish cause: his paternal grandfather was a Baltic German from Riga who had migrated to Sweden, and his father in turn had moved to Finland; his mother was from the old Swedish province of Dalarna. As a member of the university's "Nyland's nation," Freudenthal realized that "many of us are not Finns but rather pure Swedes," and despite imputations that he was disloyal to Finland, he based his subsequent activity on this conviction — which overlooked the very mixed background of many Finland-Swedish families (including his own) but which made an effort to include the hitherto much neglected Swedish-speaking population, peasants and fishermen, of the coasts.

His professional career, at first in saga studies, went hand in glove with his efforts to develop a Finland-Swedish mentality, and after a docentship in Old Norse he was appointed to the newly created extra-ordinary professorship in Swedish language and literature — he now worked on Finland-Swedish (and Estonian-Swedish) onomastics and dialectology. His biographer, Arvid Mörne, admits Freudenthal was a pedant (a favorite examination question was about the number of oars on Olav Tryggvason's ship), but he was also a tireless inspiratory force, the *spiritus movens* of the newspaper with the telltale title *Vikingen* (1870–74; The viking); the last of its editors was his disciple and friend Axel Lille (1848–1921), who continued its work with *Nya Pressen* (The new press) from 1882 on, a much more widely distributed organ of the Swedish cause in Finland. Freudenthal's attention to the Scandinavian roots and nature of Finland's coastal settlements was meant as an obvious counterbalance to the enthusiasm for the *Kalevala* world which had infected so many Swedish speakers, and was directed against the propaganda of those who argued for a total Fennicization of the country; in a larger context it took its support from the "viking romanticism" that, in one form or another, flourished in Scandinavia proper throughout the century and found its way to the world at large. (Longfellow translated parts of Tegnér's *Frithiofs saga* as early as 1835, and every American schoolchild once thrilled to "The Skeleton in Armor" — "I was a Viking old." William Morris published his *Sigurd the Volsung* in 1876, Wagner's appropriation of the Volsung material in the *Ring* put Norse gods and goddesses onto the stage of the Metropolitan by 1889, and on a more scholarly note, the Viking Society was founded in London in 1892.)

In Finland the result was admirable, in that a general Finland-Swedish consciousness was fostered, but its literary expression sometimes bordered on the comic: a name to conjure with is V.K.E. Wichmann (1856–1938), who wrote under the pseudonym of Gånge Rolf, taken from the first duke of viking Normandy, so large that he had to walk (Old Norse *ganga*) because no steed could carry him, and from the exciting Old Icelandic romance of adventure, *Göngu-Hrolfs saga*. Gånge Rolf's verse could be declaimed even under unusual circumstances; Arvid Mörne recalled how, as a student, he had bicycled through Swedish-speaking Ostrobothnia, shouting,

> Scandinavians, Scandinavians,
> Scandinavians are we!
> Let the Nordic song ring out,
> Bold and hearty, proud and free!

Today a perusal of Gånge Rolf's *Dikt och drapa* (1882; Poem and [viking] song) can give rise to some innocent merriment and exhaustion: it opens with almost one hundred seventy pages of "Vikingasägner" (Viking tales) in a variety of stanzaic patterns, followed by a long sweep through history at large but with large dollops of Swedish and Finnish figures and events, from "Arierne" (The aryans — "Beneath Iran's star-studded heaven our forefathers' huts did stand") to the Danish princess Dagmar, who (as Maria Fedorovna) had just become the Russian empress ("Princess and heroic daughter of a free and mighty North"). The emphasis on the connection with the "simple, strong, proud men / Who one passed boldly round the oceans" (in an address to "Finland's Swedes") would have a large and, on the whole, more restrained progeny, most respectably in Mörne himself; but Gånge Rolf's racial pride (and his remarkable technical facility, customarily overlooked) was also carried on by Bertel Gripenberg.

Thanks to Freudenthal, a distinction was made between the words "finne" (a Finnish-speaker), "finländare" (any native of Finland regardless of language), and "finlandssvensk" (a Swedish-speaker from Finland). (Runeberg and Topelius had quite naturally called themselves "finnar"; their linguistic practices were formed in a time before the language struggle had fairly begun.) This new self-awareness — with its inevitable concomitant slide toward isolation — was reflected in the establishment of Svenska klubben (the Swedish Club) in Helsingfors in 1880, to be followed by the opening of similar social gathering points in other towns, and the foundation of the Swedish Party in 1881 (which, in the great democratization of the early twentieth century, when the quadricameral Diet was abolished, became the Swedish People's Party). It was symptomatic of what would happen in literature that Söderström's publishing house, founded in Borgå in 1876 for both languages, was split in 1891 into Werner Söderström Oy. (WSOY; for Finnish) and Söderström & Co. (for Swedish). An organization for the furtherance of Swedish elementary schools was established in 1882 by the physician Wilhelm Grefberg (1842–86), called Svenska folkskolans vänner (Friends of Swedish elementary schools); Grefberg was also the director of the "dramatic division" of the New Theater from 1876 to 1885, the name of which was officially changed in 1887 to Svenska Teatern (Swedish Theater). Thus it was clearly distinguished from the Suomalainen Teatteri, which had been founded in 1872 — to be called Kansallisteatteri (National Theater) after 1902, when it moved into its splendid new building, after years of envying the technical resources of the New/Swedish Theater, now put in the shade.

In the midst of all this organizational activity it was appropriate that the not-yet-quite-beleaguered group should have its special song: this was provided by Johan Fridolf Hagfors (1857–1931) in "Modersmålets sång" (1897; The song of the mother tongue). The song never names the language to which it is addressed — that is self-understood; nor does it list unique beauties the tongue may have; instead, it is called a language of comfort, a clarifier of thoughts, a bearer of "whatever noble things our fathers thought," "our riches," "our best heritage." The appeal of the text is intentionally broad: it could speak to both proponents of Estlander's cultural Swedishness and adherents of Freudenthal's quasi-ethnic line, without making strident viking sounds or offending the speakers of the majority language in any way. Yet the refrain implied a demand for freedom of choice and equality of status: "Sound loud, sound free from shore to shore / In the land of a thousand lakes." Hagfors himself, who had earned his bread for years as the editor of a Finnish-language paper in Åbo, *Turun Lehti*, migrated to Sweden in 1919 and became a citizen there.

There were still plenty of moderates as friction grew between a Swedishness become quite defensive and painfully aware of its minority situation and an every stronger Finnish majority, desirous, as was often said, of being the master in its own house. It was difficult not to take sides; the tolerant Swedish-language newspaper *Helsingfors Dagblad* (Helsingfors daily), founded in 1861, expired in 1889, and the more aggressive *Nya Pressen* took over many of its readers, even as the members of the Liberal Party were absorbed into the Swedish Party. Frequently, the liberals (among them Estlander, August Schauman, and Leo Mechelin) had asked for a clarification of Finland's position inside the Russian empire. Relations had been happy during the reign (1855–81) of Alexander II; after the famine years of 1867–68 the grand duchy had enjoyed an economic boom, which had a symbolic culmination in the Helsingfors Industrial Exposition of 1876, a miniature world's fair attended by the popular czar (or emperor, as he was called in Finland) and his family. After his assassination, an event that caused deep sorrow in Finland (and led to the erection of his statue, by Walter Runeberg, the poet's eldest son, on Senate Square in Helsingfors), the happy relationship slowly went sour, because of the Pan-Slavic policies urged on Alexander III by his advisers and willingly accepted by him, for all the counterarguments of his Danish wife. This foolish casting away of Finland's loyalty was only a preamble to the events of the reign of Nicholas II (from 1894), and with the February Manifesto of 1899, which took away much of Finland's autonomous status, the so-called *ofärdsår* (*sortovuodet*, "years of misfortune") began. The Swedish speaker in Finland found himself more and more (as Estlander had predicted) between the devil and the deep blue sea, between an exaggerated Fennomania and a Russian policy unwilling to respect the autonomy granted long ago by Alexander I. Very slowly, service in the Russian military ceased to be a respectable career for a young Finlander (but Carl Gustav Mannerheim entered the cavalry school in St. Petersburg in 1887), and the Finnish Guard, which not only had surged over the walls of Warsaw in 1831 and participated in the Russian intervention in Hungary in 1849 but had covered itself with glory in the Russo-Turkish War of 1877–78, was eventually disbanded, in 1905.

Nonetheless, the prosperity that had come to Finland under Alexander II continued throughout the century: the industrialization of Finland (welcomed by none other than Topelius, that singer of Finland's nature) grew apace, and it was a good time, economically, for the Finland-Swedish middle and upper classes — as for their Finnish-speaking opposite numbers, ever growing. To be sure, it was less good for the new industrial proletariat and the poorer country population, members of which, from both language groups, began to migrate to North America.

Tavaststjerna

The great Swedish novelist Selma Lagerlöf met Karl August Tavaststjerna (1860–98) on Visby during the last summer of his life, when he was on vacation from his job as editor of the little Swedish paper in a heavily Finnish town, Björneborg. In advance, Lagerlöf knew little about him, save that he was "the most outstanding writer in Finland, who would be the heir of Runeberg and Topelius"; but among the books she had with her was the German anthology of Ernst Brausewetter, *Nordische Meisternovellen* (1896; Nordic master novellas), which included tales by both herself and him. (Brausewetter made considerable effort to introduce Tavaststjerna to a Continental public.) On meeting Tavaststjerna, deaf and with his dissatisfied wife, a not altogether successful actress, in tow, Lagerlöf did not know what to make of him. She and her traveling companion had "the impression of a refined man of the world, . . . as much at home in Paris and Berlin as Stockholm and Helsingfors." But suddenly, "the Finn emerged, defiant and stubborn and [appearing] as though he wrote simply to struggle with and subdue the hard natural world in which he had grown up." She also noted "something wrong with his gifts, a flaw had occurred in the makeup of his brain," and although he had asked the Swedes to criticize his "language," he then refused to listen to their corrections.

Born at the estate of Annila in eastern Finland, near St. Michel (Mikkeli), Tavaststjerna witnessed the famine of 1867–68 that was the background of *Hårda tider* (1891; Hard times) and had the childhood experiences, of defiance and devotion, described in *Lille Karl* (1897; Little Karl). He lost his mother early to typhus, contracted while nursing the famine's victims, but found a surrogate in a maternal aunt, at whose small property he spent a part of his boyhood. His relations with his disciplinarian father, a member of the old military nobility, were difficult (and a father-son conflict is apparent in several of his books); but he forever remained devoted to his mother's memory and to the simple but cultured life he had known with his aunt.

Like Per Hallström in Sweden, Sigbjørn Obstfelder in Norway, and

Henrik Pontoppidan in Denmark (all children of the 1860s), Tavaststjerna was attracted to the technical professions (so often represented by positive figures in the Scandinavian fiction and drama of the second half of the century) and entered the new Polytechnical Institute in Helsingfors; with him the Finland-Swedish author's tie to the university is broken. A trip to Paris, where he met the Norwegian authors Bjørnstjerne Bjørnson and Jonas Lie, confirmed him in his literary plans: he had already brought out *För morgonbris* (1883; Before the morning breeze), the product of vacations in the skerries with another budding poet, Jonatan Reuter. Later on, Lagerlöf would mention how he loved stormy weather and how, in his sea poetry, "the angry wave" was his special muse. Actually, the muses in the first book are several, despite the nautical title: Heinesque love poetry is side by side with addresses to Ibsen and Edvard Grieg, and the scenes are not just watery but urban, from art museums to streets populated by beggars. (Tavaststjerna had learned poetic genre painting from the Swede Carl Snoilsky.) The public was delighted also to get a strong dose of Runebergian patriotism and Topelian sentimentality; but the sea poetry was the genuine novelty, as in "Stormen sjunger" (The storm sings): "Push your hat backward and offer / Free play to the rain and the wind." The edition sold out.

Meanwhile, Tavaststjerna, a strongly autobiographical writer, was chronicling a Parisian love affair with a fellow foreigner, a German lady, in *Nya vers* (1885; New verse), which, particularly in its center section, "Fågelfri därute i världen" (Outlawed out there in the world), titillated stay-at-homes with its erotic frankness. (Tavaststjerna, who had a weakness for literary models and literary comparison, likened the affair to Octave's infatuation with Brigitte in de Musset's *Confession d'un enfant du siècle;* he made the remark in a letter to Hjalmar Neiglick, the coming man — and internationalist — in Finland's literary criticism.) Two other narratives form the outer wings of the triptych of *Nya vers,* a verse cycle about a girl who — very much up-to-date for the 1880s — remains true to herself and marries the man she loves, and "Från pojkåren" (From the boyhood years), about Little Karl, a preparation for the autobiographical novel. In his letters Neiglick lambasted his friend for his haste and slovenliness of language, which were, indeed, his besetting literary sins.

Next Tavaststjerna wrote *Barndomsvänner* (1886; Childhood friends), which has been called Finland-Swedish literature's first artistically valid novel with a contemporary setting. Certainly, topics characteristic of the new Scandinavian novel, and which can loosely be called naturalistic, are present here: frank depiction (by the standards of the time) of physical passion, syphilis, prostitution. Tavaststjerna's story follows the career of Ben Thomén, a promising amateur singer who tries to break out of his narrow Finnish milieu, undertakes studies abroad, loses his voice, lands "in the great mediocrity of society," and ends as a station master in a godforsaken community somewhere in Finland's interior — outshone by his longtime but untrustworthy friend Syberg, a stay-at-home become a big fish in a little pond, while Ben is a figure of fun, sheltered by the constraining love of his mother and sister. (His sometime fiancée, whom he finds again in the same little town, has loved him too, but in the novel's last chapter she succumbs to tuberculosis.) Despite its stabs at objectivity, the novel was a part of Tavaststjerna's ongoing self-analysis; the observation that Ben is the novel's only living character is accurate. But the stock quality of the book's numerous other figures is made up for by the vivid pictures of places and atmospheres. The views range from Finnish nature to Helsingfors itself, the panorama of which was a novelty in Finland's literature: the city had never before received this kind of sweeping treatment. (A "Bird's Eye View," a chapter depicting the author's childhood school in St. Michel, was excluded from *Barndomsvänner* and published separately later on.) Tavaststjerna had learned his arts of description from the Norwegian Alexander Kielland (1849–1906), whose *Garmen & Worse*, with its wonderful opening shot of the sea and the town of Stavanger, had come out in 1880 (Eng. tr. 1885).

Barndomsvänner got sharp criticism, not least from Neiglick, who complained in his review (in *Finsk Tidskrift*) that the book had failed to address the most burning question of the day, the language problem, and paid too much attention to subsidiary matters. Expecting great things of Tavaststjerna, Neiglick was unwilling to see that he had noticed aspects of Finland to which no one had paid much attention before: the disconsolate Finnish springtime, with piles of rotten snow, soaked ground, and dull gray sky, and then the small town to which Ben returns, a nest of hypocrisy in which Lector Syberg, a pillar of the community, can have his way. This was surely not the Finland of Runeberg or Topelius.

Another point on which Neiglick and others found fault was Tavaststjerna's very language, full of Finlandisms. When it was reprinted in 1924, as part of the collected works edited by Erik Kihlman, the nervous view, that Tavaststjerna could not write "correct" Swedish, had become so much an accepted truth that Kihlman, at the behest of Tavaststjerna's (Swedish) widow and the publisher, Holger Schildt, "corrected" Tavaststjerna's text. A new edition, of 1988, has made the original accessible again: as Tavaststjerna told his publisher, in connection with his translation of the novellas of his friend Juhani Aho, his aim was to use an everyday, living Finland-

Swedish, "which looks quite different from the stiff written-or-literary Swedish that all our Swedish books [from Finland] try to approximate." Neiglick's criticism was part of an extremely protracted debate that flourished from the 1880s on, about "correctness" in Finland-Swedish, a debate that came to a kind of climax with the publication of the prescriptive *Finlandssvenska: Handledning till undvikande av provinsialismer i tal och skrift* (1917; Finland-Swedish: Guide to the avoidance of provincialisms in speech and writing), by the philologist Hugo Bergroth (1866–1937). In the 1920s and 1930s the debate popped up again, when Diktonius was accused of writing a Swedish that was "almost Finnish," and it had a coda in the 1950s, when Anders Cleve's Helsingfors classic, *Gatstenar* (1959; Paving stones), came under fire in Sweden for its "incomprehensible" words.

All this hypersensitivity about the "correctness" of the language usages of speakers not resident in the language's birthplace may seem strange indeed to anglophones, long ready to accept and be fascinated by such varieties of English as American or Irish-English; but it would be worthwhile to ponder possible causes, all the more since, paradoxically, the movement flourished at a time when the urge to study Finland-Swedish regional dialects was already strong. An understandable anxiety at a possible bastardization through the omnipresent influence of Finnish was palpable; in the somewhat comparable linguistic situation of Prague the novelist and language philosopher Fritz Mauthner (1849–1923) remarked on the aversion to macaronic *Küchelböhmisch* ("kitchen Bohemian," a German-Czech mixture) and the resultant purity, or "bloodlessness," of Prague literary German. A desire to draw nearer to Sweden, as the minority felt the more isolated in its own country, must have played a role; another factor, for authors wanting a public in Sweden, may have been practical and economic. When, in the 1890s, Tavaststjerna began to publish with Bonnier in Stockholm, a contractual requirement was that his manuscripts be submitted to a strict scrutiny of their language.

In *En inföding* (1887; An aborigine) Tavaststjerna may have had a revenge of sorts on his close friend and severest critic, Neiglick; he again set two friends with different temperaments against each other: Vahlin, the naive and intense editor, the aborigine of the title, and Hård, an elegant and ruthless man of the world. The book's authorial sympathy for Vahlin hinted at a hitherto muffled side of Tavaststjerna, who had done more than his share to bring cosmopolitanism into what he regarded as Finnish backwaters; here he revealed his sometimes bewildering oscillation between Europeanism and Finnishness, which Lagerlöf eventually would note. (The Dane Herman Bang, visiting Finland in 1885, detected in Tavaststjerna a mystical communing with the spirit of Finland.) The friendship with Neiglick did not improve; when Tavaststjerna's stories, *I förbindelser* (1888; In connections), came out, Neiglick paid it the backhanded compliment of saying that Tavaststjerna was better at the short haul. It contains two of his best narratives, the title story (which turns, once more, on the sadder aspects of friendship's obligations) and "Ett missförstånd" (Eng. tr. "A Misunderstanding," *Swedo-Finnish Short Stories*, 1974), Tavaststjerna's first comment on the Russian question. A good-natured Finnish peasant, jailed for debt, tries to borrow tobacco from a bored Russian sentry and is shot to death: neither understands the other's language.

Producing too much, Tavaststjerna brought out two books in 1890, the collection of prose sketches and tales *Marin och genre* (Seascapes and genre paintings), which includes a set of pictures of Hangö (Hanko), Finland's new, ice-free port in the far south, and the "Bird's Eye View" mentioned above; and *Dikter i väntan* (Poems while waiting), a mixed bag of verse. It contains his anecdotal and not particularly moving farewell to Neiglick, who had died suddenly in 1889; some patriotic poetry in which, in peaceful Sweden, "På svensk botten" (On Swedish ground), he yearns for his troubled homeland; the usual effective picture poems in Snoilsky's manner (a tutor, a misanthrope, a patriarch, an old estate — a tribute to his aunt); and the series "Ny fart" (New energy), which seems to be his account of his love for Gabrielle Kindstrand, whom he met when she was appearing in his play, *Affärer* (Affairs), and married shortly thereafter.

The fact that Tavaststjerna moved from these patched-together books and theatrical failures to the work generally regarded as his masterpiece, *Hårda tider,* was attributed, once upon a time, to the invigorating effect his "Nixe," as he called her, had on him; but the passing of the all-too-intelligent Neiglick may have also removed some obscure emotional barrier. The novel with the title suggesting Dickens had a Kielland-like compactness, attention to detail, and, at times, bitter objectivity. The loss of Tavaststjerna's mother is certainly reflected in the death of the noble-spirited Fru von Blume as she tends to the refugees from up-country; otherwise, Tavaststjerna stays at a remove from his cast, especially the sometime officer, Captain Thoreld, who owns a neighboring estate and, by his lights, runs it properly and humanely: he does what he can for the poor, from a practical point of view. Further, Thoreld has the depth of spirit to appreciate Fru von Blume's sacrifice: "We have no cause to lament, as long as our sparse land brings forth characters such as hers." Against this background of great-spirited or morally not wholly obtuse members of the upper class a drama of trickery and eventual murder is played out.

The sensational (and true) story appears to have been the kernel of Tavaststjerna's novel, and later, in *Uramo torp* (1892; Uramo croft), he used it for a play, first performed in Finnish in Juhani Aho's translation. Tavaststjerna himself had tried to write it, he said, in Finnish because the speeches of the crime drama's two main actors came to him in that tongue. They are both Finnish-speaking Ostrobothnians (and, as well, another pair of unlike male acquaintances): the one, Kalle Pihl, is clever and ruthless; the other, Lehtimaa, slow and primitive. Both have fled from the starving north, Pihl leaving a wife and children behind; at Thoreld's estate Pihl enters a bigamous marriage with Anna, the handsome dairymaid whom Thoreld wants to see well provided for, now that he has decided to marry the von Blume daughter, Louise. (This palming off of a sometime lover is not Thoreld's only master stroke; he has gotten Louise's suitor, the honest engineer Halldén, out of the way by giving him a stipend for study abroad.) Needing a certificate to prove he is free to marry, Pihl buys the necessary document from Lehtimaa; things go well for Pihl and his bride until Lehtimaa — in his simplemindedness, something of a ward of Louise — finds Pihl's first wife among the refugees and attempts in vain to press the truth out of Pihl. At last, deprived of his identity and distrusted even by the goodhearted Louise, the despairing Lehtimaa believes himself to be "chosen as one of God's instruments of punishment" and kills Pihl and Anna. Suspected of the deed, he can clear himself by swearing a false oath, but he refuses and is sent to Siberia for life.

In the play, perhaps written under the influence of Tolstoy, the complexities of Lehtimaa are at the center, but in the novel the contrast between haves and have-nots occupies Tavaststjerna's main interest. Behind the estate owners stands an equally self-satisfied government, which, failing to find any easy means to alleviate the suffering, resorts, as usual, to a call to prayer, "the old flight to the Almighty." Yet even the sufferers are included in Tavaststjerna's persistently ironic view. At the banquet celebrating the coming of the railroad, after the brunt of the famine has passed, the beggars left over from the catastrophe hang about Thoreld's estate, listening to the regimental band and the singing of the guests: "Their eyes shone, their feet kept time with the music, they forgot both bitterness and despair for a moment, and the bravest, whose rags did not attract too much attention, finally dared to venture all the way into the garden."

Tavaststjerna had expected to receive enthusiastic reviews, which he did in Denmark and Sweden; at home the reception was much chillier — he had poked a hole in the national myths of misery nobly and patiently borne and of a caring upper class. He left Finland for the Continent and was abroad for three years (in Switzerland, Italy, Berlin, and on Rügen with Strindberg and the Swedish-Finnish-German author Adolf Paul), returning to Berlin for the fateful winter of 1893–94, after which he told the Swede Ola Hansson, who had had his own Strindberg difficulties, that the dramatist was the "most dangerous acquaintance" he had ever made: he had become a member of the circle "At the Sign of the Black Piglet" (*Zum schwarzen Ferkel*), a membership not made happier by Strindberg's passing affection for his wife and his own growing deafness. While Nixe remained in Germany, he found a refuge on an estate in Sweden and spent time translating Gerhart Hauptmann's *Hanneles Himmelfahrt* (*Hannele's Assumption*) as a vehicle for his wife; she was meant to play the role of the little girl taken up into a child's notion of heaven. (Nixe badly wanted to have a career on the German stage; she did get a role in the German version of Strindberg's *Första varningen* [The first warning].)

The problems that arose in the Tavaststjerna marriage were turned directly into literature of a sort, two feigned correspondences, *Korta brev från en lång bröllopsresa* (1893; Short letters from a long honeymoon) and *Korta brev från hemmets lugna härd* (1895; Short letters from the home's quiet hearth), in which the innocent Totus writes to an old friend, and the sophisticated Carlot writes to her sister. Obviously, Totus is Tavaststjerna; in the second series another Tavaststjerna persona looms large, the poet Rosenlund. "Too bad," Carlot muses, "that he doesn't have more manliness in his character," but at least he is not the usual sort of conversation maker in boring Helsingfors, where "it seems as if every gentleman approached me with the express intention of testing me in the history of the fatherland and *Fänrik Stål.*" The object of many of the barbs in the second book—both were initially published as newspaper feuilletons—is C. G. Estlander.

In September 1895 Tavaststjerna returned to Finland for good. The production of the European years was mixed but showed how sensitive he was to Continental currents. With the story "Impressionisten" (The impressionist), in the collection *Unga år* (1892; Young years), he had already experimented with the hypersensitive and tired men who had flourished in European literature since the appearance of Huysmans's *A rebours* in 1884; the sickly student Marck in Tavaststjerna's story has the fashionable "neurasthenia" and heightened perceptions of Huysmans's Des Esseintes and, by instinct, can discover the secret of every new acquaintance—the claim Knut Hamsun's Johan Nilsen Nagel makes for himself in *Mysterier* (Eng. tr. *Mysteries*, 1927, 1971), which came out the same year as Tavaststjerna's tale. Tavaststjerna's Klercken in the short novel *I förbund med döden* (1893; In alliance with death) belongs to the same literary family, the owner of "a sick soul in a sick body," a bundle of nerves, a "tired man"; the Norwegian Arne Garborg's sensation, *Trætte Mænd* (Tired men), had come out in 1891. On vacation, Klercken, who has left his family at home in Finland, sees the figure of Death during a steamer trip on Lake Como. Death is not terrifying; rather, his countenance shines with an expression of infinite compassion on Klercken, who earlier has rejected this "sure and dependable friend" because of his wife and children. In his pension Klercken then meets the delectable Fru d'Ottange (surely a literary sister of Madame Odero in J. P. Jacobsen's *Niels Lyhne* [1880; Eng. tr. 1919, 1967, 1990]), who instantly restores his will to live. But duty calls him back to Finland; on the approach past Åland he rejoices at the "stimulating smell" of his homeland, rising from the waves. Once in his Helsingfors circumstances, however, he longs for Italy again and begins a correspondence with Fru d'Ottange. Falling gravely ill, he is nursed by his faithful wife; instead of slipping into death or trying to return to the South, he survives — to reenter the living tomb of his old bank job.

Familiar Tavaststjerna themes and figures are readily discernible: the tug of war between the stark homeland and the alluring outside, the dreamer who falls, like Ben Thomén, into a gray vacuum; but acutely aware of what was happening in the larger literary world, Tavaststjerna also adds the thanatophilia so prevalent in the decade — as a matter of fact, he precedes more famous examples of it. Gabriele d'Annunzio's *Il trionfo della morte* (Eng. tr. *The Triumph of Death*, 1896) appeared the next year, as did Ibsen's *Lille Eyolf* (Eng. tr. *Little Eyolf*, 1895), in which Alfred Allmers tells of his mysterious meeting with Death in the Norwegian mountains. In addition, the interest of the times in spiritism of various sorts (and in what would be called extrasensory perception) is evinced in the important fact that the bond between Klercken and Fru d'Ottange is by no means entirely erotic; she is aware that "the natural and the supernatural go hand in hand," and only when his wife has forced him to break off the correspondence does Klercken (whose name contains implications both of the medieval church and of the business office) collapse into the meaningless existence from which he will not escape again. He fills "column upon column with figures" and "never says a word too much"; at home he keeps a watercolor of San Salvatore, the mountain near Lugano in whose view he met Death (and the "woman of the world"). For all its motivational confusions, *I förbund med döden* is one of Finland's most valuable contributions to European literature of the 1890s.

Continuing his febrile rate of production, Tavaststjerna now concentrated on Finland. *Kapten Tärnberg och andra berättelser* (1894; Captain

Tärnberg and other tales) comprises four portraits of quite disparate Finlanders, plus a tale, "Pest" (Plague), about another favorite theme of the times, the threat or appearance of an epidemic at a resort. (See Jacobsen's *Niels Lyhne,* Ibsen's *En folkefiende* [1882; Eng. tr. *An Enemy of the People,* 1888], Wilhelm Raabe's *Unruhige Gäste* [1886; Nervous guests], even Thomas Mann's *Der Tod in Venedig* [1912; *Death in Venice*].) The most important is the title story, told by a Finnish captain at anchor in Genoa's harbor; his ship, *Albion,* has British registry, and he despises his "dear Finnish compatriots, nothing but swine from top to bottom," but admires (and represents) their heroic obstinacy nonetheless. (Using the terminology of Runeberg and Topelius, Tärnberg does not distinguish between Finns and Finland-Swedes, but the captain's mother tongue is Swedish; Tavaststjerna proudly pointed out to Bonnier that Tärnberg's language was littered with Finlandisms.) Antti Metsäntausta—the name hints at "backwoods"—in "En julotta i barkbrödets Finland" (A Christmas service in Barkbread's Finland) is unimpeachably Finnish and demonstrates both almost superhuman indolence and superhuman strength; "Käpp-Lena" (Cane Lena), about a woman driven into misery and a witch's reputation by a drunken husband, is the closest Tavaststjerna ever came to full-blown naturalism—a tale written, he claimed, in the style of Juhani Aho. "Sångarlön" (The bard's reward), mentioned above in connection with the ostracizing of Fredrik Berndtson, returns to the middle-class Finland-Swedish milieu Tavaststjerna knew better; in its obvious sympathy for the sometime poet Oscar Fontelius, lured into his apostasy by financial need, Tavaststjerna again betrayed something of his own constant self-pity.

Kapten Tärnberg is Tavaststjerna's most satisfying collection of short prose; its companion novel, *Kvinnoregemente* (1894; Rule of women), falls flat, despite its intended goal of making fun of certain national sacred cows, the process begun in *Hårda tider:* the target is the Finnish peasant idealized by well-meaning Fennomanes from the city. But the satire is oddly halfhearted: both peasant schemers and the university-educated self-deluder emerge only slightly chastened; the people of the Monola estate (including the bossy widow Harvanen, alluded to in the Knox-like title) prosper and grow fat; the idealist, "Dr." Toivo Udde, turns to "practical work for the homeland." Tavaststjerna's own group, the old gentry, has vanished from the scene before the would-be comic novel begins.

The resignation that might be read between the lines of *Kvinnoregemente* turns to desperation in the potboiler Tavaststjerna published under a pseudonym in 1895, *Finska vikens hemlighet* (The secret of the Gulf of Finland), based on an actual event, the disappearance of a Russian ironclad during a storm in 1893; the climax is the farewell letter of a lieutenant trapped in the sunken vessel: "I have rested with my mouth pressed against the ventilator . . . I have spent nineteen hours imprisoned alive beneath the sea." In the extremely uneven *Dikter* (1896; Poems) Tavaststjerna's similarly dark sensations on returning to Finland were described in the declamatory "Hemåt i höstregn" (Homeward in fall rain):

> Homeward in fall rain, homeward in darkness,
> homeward across the black water's starkness,
> homeward against the wind, against the sea's beating
> I steer my vessel, steer as though dreaming,
> The waves do not waken me out of my dream.

Otherwise, verses about Finland's nature and several artificial folk songs (Tavaststjerna tried to rival Sweden's lyricists of the nineties, Fröding and Karlfeldt, not quite successfully) have to take a back seat to the poems about emptiness: "The crop I sowed has been gathered, / And summer turns to fall; / It grows so still around me" ("Det blir så tyst omkring mig," the line that is also the title of the poem); in "Det ringer till begravning i nyårstider" (The bells ring for a burial at New Year's time) a procession of wraiths from the past goes by, "wreaths of poppies in their hair" (as in a painting of Arnold Böcklin's). Tavaststjerna had an almost inexhaustible vocabulary of despair about his "incarceration"; thinking of Dreyfus, he designated himself (in the newspaper office at Björneborg) as "the prisoner on Devil's Island," and in still another of his poems about return to an unhappy fate, "Den förlorade sonen" (The prodigal son), the prodigal son says, "My path leads away from the beaches of life."

The line stands in bitter and telling contrast to another from Sweden's poetry of the time, Verner von Heidenstam's "För mig finns ingen väg från hemmets dörr" (For me no path leads from the door of home) of 1895, a poem about Gunnar of Hlidarendi in *Njáls saga*. Come home to Finland, Tavaststjerna (as he did not tire of saying) had a strong perception of homelessness, one major cause of which he put into his "Finnbacka Finne," in which the speaker's mother, after his "Swedish father's" death, has married the young Finn of the title and given her attention and love to the children of the second marriage, while the eldest son has become "a stranger in [his] own home." Perhaps, like the Estlander of "Ubi bene, ibi patria," he toys with the idea of emigration; certainly, he has inherited his father's bold spirit: "Never will I be a servant in your house," and "I have before me all the world's wide ring." Torsten Pettersson has written that Tavaststjerna was the "first Finland-Swedish author," because "he experienced himself as being restricted to a certain lesser section of the country's cultural life" ("Nio decennier," 37).

The problem of the allegiance of the Swedish speaker in Finland was approached from another angle in Tavaststjerna's next-to-last novel, *En patriot utan fosterland* (1896; A patriot without a homeland), which suffers technically from somewhat the same lack of clear focus as *Kvinnoregemente* while exploring the dangers first of apparent disloyalty and then of cosmopolitanism. The novel's turning point is drawn from the so-called Tölö affair, in which, during the Crimean War, students met at a Helsingfors inn and gave pro-Swedish, pro-Allied, and anti-Russian speeches; the Russian governor-general got wind of what had happened, and several academic punishments were meted out: expelled, the future explorer Adolf Nordenskiöld chose to go into exile in Sweden. A Russian officer studying at Helsingfors was suspected of having been an informer and was ostracized (as in "Sångarlön"); Tavaststjerna told the Danish critic Georg Brandes that the officer's fate was reflected in his Gregor von Steven, who leaves Finland as a result of his bitter experiences. Yet the rest of the book — about Steven's moral decay and selfish opportunism during his long life abroad — seems to have had its source in Tavaststjerna's reading of Paul Bourget's best seller, *Cosmopolis* (1890), on the perils of internationalism, and perhaps, as well, in Arthur de Gobineau's thoughts about racial impurity, which had some currency in Finland at the time (see below): Steven's father was an honest Finlander but his mother had Tartar blood in her veins. Thus the thrust of the book was blurry; when it came out, it was taken principally as a statement about the threat and lure of Russification. Before he settles down in Sorrento with the widow of his best friend, whom he has killed in a duel, Steven has long been in the czar's service.

Werner Söderhjelm, a friend and the first biographer of Tavaststjerna, recalled that the author was upset by unfavorable reviews of the novel, because (so Söderhjelm surmised) he had "put so much of himself into it" (p. 281). He had indeed: he was smitten with, and clumsily attempted to seduce, Aline Borgström, the wife of his Maecenas, the exporter Arthur Borgström. His unrequited love was also the background of his narrative poem *Laureatus* (1897); seventy years later Tavaststjerna's many letters to the "Diana" of the poem, Aline, were published by Greta von Frenckell-Thesleff, filling in the gaps of this ancient item of gossip. For some time, he had wanted to write a verse epic about the fate of a poet from Finland who ends in loneliness and madness; he may have thought he would emulate the highly imaginative poetry-and-prose epic *Hans Alienus* (1892) of Heidenstam. But as so often in Tavaststjerna, the elements are quite mixed: a currently fashionable Nietzscheanism; a fascination with classical antiquity and myth, especially the stories of Endymion (see Heidenstam's *Endymion* of 1889) and Diana; a Christ identification appearing principally in the episodes of Laureatus's madness; and a challenge to Runeberg in the use of complex meters reminiscent of *Kung Fjalar* (even as Laureatus imagines himself to be that proud monarch). The poem is a treasure trove for students of the literary modes of the 1890s (in that respect not unlike Ibsen's last play, *Når vi døde vågner* [1899; Eng. tr. *When We Dead Awaken*, 1900]), just as it has been for Tavaststjerna's biographers. Its directly literary value, though, lies in the lyric sections, given the collective title of "Indiansommar" (Indian summer), made up of a sonnet cycle to "Diana" and the grab bag of other poems that Tavaststjerna (quite undisciplined in judging his own works) inserted before the book's epilogue, where Endymion-Laureatus awakes and, having been tempted by Satan, undergoes an apotheosis — or lands in a madhouse, as he does in a sketch for the epilogue. (The Tavaststjerna specialist Erik Ekelund [*Tavaststjerna*, 301] saw echoes of *Peer Gynt*'s madhouse scene here, as Peer resists the temptation of "being sufficient unto himself.")

Tavaststjerna's last work of prose, the autobiographical *Lille Karl* (1897; Little Karl), may have been still another of his attempts to follow a literary fashion; it appears directly in the wake of Teuvo Pakkala's *Lapsia* (1895; Children) and the Swede Gustaf af Geijerstam's *Mina pojkar* (1896; My boys). But it may also have been a final attempt at self-study on the part of a man whom his friend, the physician Jarl Hagelstam, described as "a psychopath and man of moods (not to mention [a] habitual drunkard)." The world to which Tavaststjerna returns is a paradise in its way: the little boy gets the rifle he has always wanted, his father is a figure of authority tempered by love and is loved by his obstinate offspring in return. Nonetheless, Karl learns about life's sexual secrets too early, loses his mother, and finds out what fear is when he meets a pack of wolves in the forest. *Lille Karl* rounds off the series of Tavaststjerna's autobiographies in disguise; the stubborn boy is really a younger brother to Laureatus, called "Laureatus obstinatus" in the verse epic's Alpine phantasmagoria.

After Tavaststjerna's death in the Björneborg hospital in March 1898, caused not by pneumonia, as long was thought, but by a nurse's mistake, Georg Brandes wrote of his "great promise," and it is true that he never produced an unflawed larger work. Yet in Tavaststjerna, far more than in Runeberg or Topelius, Finland's literature got a Continental European voice, just as he had acquired far more from the Continent than they.

Ahrenberg

Johan Jakob Ahrenberg, who for literary purposes used the French-looking "Jac.," was born in 1847 in Viborg, where his father, from Åbo, was first

Latin teacher and then rector of the city's new Swedish gymnasium. (He had earlier had a position at the quadrilingual city's German gymnasium, closed in the early 1840s because of a shift in the town's demographics.) Ahrenberg's mother, the daughter of a Viborg official with an Ostrobothnian background, was unusually well read but turned slowly into a stern pietist, which brought her into sharp conflict with her liberal-minded son. The economically acute Ahrenberg senior acquired a number of properties in the Karelian countryside, where the children became acquainted with the privileges of estate life, but the mother, who had absorbed Johann Heinrich Pestalozzi's pedagogical theories, insisted that they learn to carry out quite ordinary tasks; a tension between an essentially patrician view and an admiration for the simple life can be noticed throughout Ahrenberg's work, as can, of course, a constant awareness of ethnic and linguistic collision.

At the university in Helsingfors, Ahrenberg devoted more time to art (his teacher was the distinguished painter Magnus von Wright) than to academic pursuits, and by 1870 he persuaded his father to let him study architecture in Stockholm. Here he gave lessons in watercolor to Joseph-Artur Comte de Gobineau (1816–82), the French chargé d'affaires in Stockholm; and Gobineau's racial teachings, not least his preoccupation with the superiority of the Aryan race, made a deep impression on his young instructor. After having passed his architectural examinations, he undertook a Continental journey, which included Gobineau's Normandy, the obligatory visits to Paris and Italy, and Athens and Constantinople, in which cities he was fascinated by the mixture of tongues and nationalities. Appointed to Finland's Department of Public Buildings in 1877, he climbed from rung to rung, finally becoming its director in 1910, four years before his death.

Ahrenberg's literary career began modestly, with travel sketches and stories with foreign settings; in the collection *På främmande botten* (1880; On foreign ground) the story "Ett konstnärsliv" (An artist's life), on the English painter George Morland (1762/63–1804), already shows Ahrenberg's interest in bizarre or raffish characters and his need to use sturdy factual underpinnings for creative work. Subsequently, Ahrenberg discovered the milieu that would be his specialty, his own Karelian homeland; for some years (1882–86), he lived in Viborg as provincial architect and had occasion to make frequent trips through the countryside. *Hemma* (1887; At home) contained twenty vignettes from Karelian life, some historical, in which the arch-conservative Ahrenberg saw the regrettable disappearance of the picturesque (if often unsanitary) features of skerry and farm life; the almost folkloristic presentation of customs (and colorful natives) discovered by the educated narrator on his journeys is an outgrowth of the sketch genre that had flourished in other European literatures, with Turgenev's *Notes of a Hunter* from 1852 or the Galician tales of Leopold von Sacher-Masoch from the 1860s and 1870s.

Hihuliter (1889; Hihulites), the book with which Ahrenberg made his literary reputation, is more concentrated, dealing with a religious sect that engages in speaking-in-tongues, or ecstatic logorrhea; the worshipers' apparent stuttering gave a name to the sect and to the novel. The book is based partly on Ahrenberg's own observations of the sect, in which he saw a potential threat from darkly chaotic forces, partly on his reaction against his mother's own demanding religiosity, and partly on the example of Kielland's novel about evangelicalism in Norway, *Skipper Worse* (1882; Eng. tr. 1882). (As well, he continued the antipietistic tradition established by Runeberg some fifty years before.) In the novel, though, the hysterical sectarians are not the genuine instruments of ill; as a matter of fact, Ahrenberg feels sympathy for these poor souls, their spiritual needs unmet by the pastors of the state church. Moreover, Ahrenberg, whose reportorial fairness prevented him from being a satirist of Kielland's rank, did not condemn the Lutheran clergy without exception: the novel's Pastor Helm — a contrast to the grasping materialist Pastor Brandt — knows that religious feelings must be nurtured, lest they lead to the excesses that cause the death of the sectarians' preacher, Tobias Pullinen — who, for the rest, reacted against not only a sterile official Lutheranism but also against a mother as coldly pietistic as Ahrenberg's own.

The third part of Ahrenberg's "tetralogy" from eastern Finland, *Österut* (1890; Eastward), consists of tales rather than sketches, of which two have become schoolbook examples of his modest but effective short-story art: "Historien om travaren Jalo" (The story of the trotter Jalo), about a peasant's devotion to a horse, and "Utan modersmål" (Eng. tr. "Without a Mothertongue," *Swedo-Finnish Short Stories*, 1974), in which the harmful side of Viborg polyglottism is represented by the pathetic teller of the tale, who lacks genuine control of any language. Beneath Ahrenberg's linguistic reflections, altogether justified in themselves, there runs a less appealing current; the unhappy Fritz Nikolaivitsch von Drewershausen has a fatal mixture of blood in his veins: "German, Polish, Swedish, Finnish, and Russian blood had been mingled." The person of mixed ethnicity — designated by Gobineau as a symptom of cultural decline — turns up here as the tongue-tied lover, at whom both the young woman and the reader smile.

In *Stockjunkarn* (1882; The timber baron) the "tetralogy's" conclusion, Ahrenberg fastened onto not a mixing of languages and cultures and races but the rivalry between them. Like Kielland in *Garman & Worse*—and preceding Thomas Mann's *Buddenbrooks* (1901) — Ahrenberg describes the decline of an old Viborg mercantile house, established by the Blumes, of German extraction but now Swedish speakers, and its replacement by a group of jobbers lacking any ethical scruples. "An epicure by inclination, rearing, and habit," the scion of the Blume family ends in suicide, and Israel Veikkolin, who has learned brutal business practices during a stay in America, triumphs — to end in loneliness, for all the wealth he has acquired. Although Veikkolin and his accomplice, the sometime "peasant-student" Isak Hultila, are of Finnish background, Ahrenberg does not derive their moral obliquity from their blood; instead, they have become estranged from a traditional Finnish steadiness and patient strength, as incorporated in Veikkolin's former associate, the barge captain Matti Kiiskilä, a figure of Runebergian proportions. Ahrenberg's mouthpiece in the novel is the old pastor, Emanuel Högfeldt, a colleague once upon a time of the great men of the Golden Age, and the true opponent (not the weakling Blume) to Veikkolin in the struggle between patriotic idealism and a greed that led to the ruin of Karelia's peasant society — a worse loss, in Ahrenberg's eyes, than the collapse of the old mercantile house.

In the 1890s, as the special status of the grand duchy was nibbled away by the policies of Alexander III and Nicholas II, Ahrenberg turned from the decline of Karelia's city-and-country culture to a special if related concern: the Russification of Finland-Swedes who, in one way or another, had entered Russian service. The first of a brace of tales from 1891, *Anor* (Ancestors), goes at the matter historically, in a text consisting of the correspondence, from 1819 to 1849, between the Baroness Marie Louise Stjernstedt, née Feychting, and members of her family and circle, — especially her beloved grandson, Carl Alexander. Carl Alexander falls as "an honorable soldier and valiant man" while a member of the Russian expeditionary force sent to put down the revolt in Hungary, but he dies not on the field of battle but in a duel with a jealous Hungarian nobleman. The linguistic verisimilitude of the letters is remarkable; Ahrenberg's ability to recreate the elegantly macaronic style of the baroness and her correspondents (whose stoic insistence on social propriety is their religion) makes *Anor* a masterly piece of literary artifice; Runar Schildt must have studied it before writing his tale of Åbo estate life in the 1820s, *Den segrande Eros* (1912; Eros victorious). The semimemoiristic companion tale *Ungdom* (Youth), about an artist's life in Stockholm and Paris of the 1870s, is pale by comparison, however revelatory it may be about Ahrenberg's unrealized dream of greatness in the fine arts.

The Russian siren call grows much stronger in *Familjen på Haapakoski* (1893; The family at Haapakoski). The title readily suggests the Norwegian Jonas Lie's *Familien på Gilje* (1883; Eng. tr. *The Family at Gilje*, 1894), but its setting is altogether different from the impoverished reserve captain's simple home in the Norwegian mountains. The Haapakoski property itself (on the Kymmene River, the western boundary of Karelia), the survival of the ancient family bearing the distinguished name of Horn, and the right of Finland's nobility to direct the nation's fate are the overwhelming concerns of Baron Alexander Horn (who, Ahrenberg told Ernst Brausewetter, was a representative of his own "view of politics and of the world"); his son, Erik Stålsköld Horn, an officer in the Russian army, succumbs to social lures (depicted on the basis of Ahrenberg's several sojourns in St. Petersburg and a reading of *Anna Karenina*), marries a clever and condescending Russian noblewoman, and becomes a stranger to his family and its stern traditions of duty; their son, Jegor, is baptized in the Orthodox faith. The novel ends with Jegor's address to the Finnish Diet; as Erik Ekelund points out, it reproduces a speech given by a Finnish nobleman — and chamberlain at the czar's court — in May 1885. Jegor understands Swedish only with difficulty; his oration, delivered with "a surprising confidence," is a calamity in its linguistic clumsiness and its pompous contempt for Finland's estates-general and is hissed by the other members of the noble parliamentary estate. Nevertheless, the epilogue predicts that Jegor (whose little-used Swedish name is Erik) will go far: "He will not be fettered by traditions, by nationalistic blindness and unnecessary scruples," and at his side he will have "his splendid, clear-minded, and influential mother."

"*Vår landsman*" (1897; "Our fellow countryman": Ahrenberg ironizes the appellation by means of quotation marks) offers a semisequel; Karl Alexander Segerberg is the scion of a Finnish noble family fallen on hard times. Rather by accident, he gets a place in the pages' corps at the imperial court, becomes an officer, and forgets his mother tongue to the extent that he can barely correspond with his paternal aunt back home in Finland, a patriotic old lady of the Runebergian school. In order to keep up with his wealthy comrades, Segerberg forever takes the main chance, seducing his commander's wife for the advantages she can give him through her connections, distinguishing himself through sheer foolhardiness in the Russian-Turkish War of 1877–78. Replacing a fallen comrade, a Caucasian prince, as adjutant to the czar himself and decorated with the cross of St. George for his brainless heroism, Segerberg expects a brilliant career but is shoved aside. He returns to Finland (a love of Finland's nature, dimly remembered from boyhood, is his only redeeming feature), gets the headship of the

Finnish customs service, a post for which he has no qualifications, and is left yearning for the pleasures of St. Petersburg "amidst the customs officials, publicans, and sinners of poverty-stricken Finland."

In his narratives Ahrenberg never found a style and structure all his own, but he had been a fairly skillful borrower from Turgenev and Kielland, and in the Haapakoski novel (and still more in *"Vår landsman"*) he employed a limited impressionism, adducing independent scenes (some of them very effective, such as the boy Karl Alexander's awakening in the strange world of the pages' dormitory, or the visit of the war hero to the St. Petersburg opera and his meeting with a young woman, brighter than he, from Finland's middle class) that are reminiscent of techniques employed by J. P. Jacobsen in *Fru Marie Grubbe* (1876; Eng. tr. *Marie Grubbe: A Lady of the Seventeenth Century*, 1917, 1952, rev. 1975) and *Niels Lyhne*. Unfortunately, though, in the last phase of his career, he returned to his boyhood passion for Walter Scott, with a blend of ideas gleaned from Gobineau; *Med styrkans rätt* (1899; By right of strength) pits Scandinavian Varangians, Novgorodians, and Finnish Karelians against one another sometime in the Middle Ages. The artistic catastrophe is compounded by the bogus saga style (Gånge Rolf's viking romanticism rears its head) Ahrenberg uses as he reflects on the Karelians' inability to govern themselves unless they are strengthened by a Varangian backbone. (A contemporary reader might well have seen the parallels in the submissive policies of the "Old Finnish" party, confronted by Russian demands, and the activism of many Finland-Swedes and "Young Finns.") With *Rojalister och patrioter: En sommarsaga från år 1788* (1901; Royalists and patriots: A summer tale from 1788) Ahrenberg turned to a period and an event he knew better, the age of Gustav III and the "Anjala conspiracy" of Finnish officers against the monarch at the beginning of the Russian war of 1788–90; Gustave François Glansenstjerna wavers between the royalists and the patriots, as the latter dream of Finnish independence under a Russian shield; but ultimately, he cleaves to the king's cause, perceiving that the Swedish tradition is necessary for Finland. (The wise pastor who helps him attain this insight is named Forsius, like Sigfrid Aronus Forsius of old.)

The bad press Ahrenberg got for the book put him off creative literature; in his last years he worked at *Kronofogdens pengar* (The crown administrator's money), a fragment of which was published in 1917, three years after his death. In it Ahrenberg took up a theme that Jörn Donner would discover much later on, the rise of a great industrial house; in his review Arvid Mörne saw much promise in the figure of Tollstadius, the troll-like founder of the fortune, "one of the few figures from the literature of Finland-

Swedish realism who could meet the demands of a later time" (Ekelund, *Jac. Ahrenberg,* 328). The fragment was further evidence of Ahrenberg's gift for amusing and sometimes scurrilous portraiture, a gift that makes his seven volumes of short biographies, *Människor jag känt* (1904–14; People I have known), so thoroughly entertaining. The portraits — of Gobineau and the Russian governor-general Obolenski, among many others — have often been criticized by sobersides for their inaccuracy (and Ahrenberg had the reputation of being one of Helsingfors's most accomplished prevaricators); but they are jewels of their kind, frivolous, malicious, suggestive, sometimes subtle. At last, Ahrenberg's affection for the picturesque and the piquant detail had full play, without his having to worry about character development or plot. Amid constant artistic posing (see Johannes Takanen's bust of him, with devilish goatee and outsize beret), he never took his literary work quite seriously enough. (Apart from his technical flaws, his lack of political correctness and his pervasive ultraconservatism would stand in the way of a revival today.) Nonetheless, in *Hihuliter, Stockjunkarn, Anor,* and *Familjen på Haapakoski* Ahrenberg provided a captivating view of milieus and attitudes long disappeared, and he addressed important questions of his time. He deserves a place of modest honor in the annals of realism in Scandinavian literature, taken large.

Memoirists and Critics
In connection with Ahrenberg's *Människor jag känt,* the whole bloom of Finland-Swedish memoir literature — a genre that has never slackened off, even today — should be mentioned. The cause of the flowering may have been a sense, on the part of its authors, that the Finland-Swedish hegemony was fading fast and that the record of its final glory days, its "farbenvoller Untergang" (colorful decline), in Stefan George's phrase about the moribund Austrian empire, must be preserved. Anders Ramsay (1832–1910) was a member (and, fittingly, a bachelor and childless) of the Scots family that had first come to Finland in the sixteenth century and had given so many more or less distinguished military men to Swedish and Russian service; he was a nephew of the Anders Edvard Ramsay who had commanded the Finnish Guard at Warsaw in 1831, the Finnish contingent at the defense of Vitsand immortalized by Topelius, and the Russian troops in Poland during that country's uprising of 1863. Anders himself was a failed businessman; settling down in Helsingfors after years abroad (and horrified by the creeping Fennicization of the city), he wrote the eight volumes of *Från barnaår till silfverhår* (1904–7; From childhood years to silver hair), despite its sickly-sweet title a work of supreme condescension, self-

justification, and snobbishness and quite as amusing to read as the little biographies by his friend, Ahrenberg. Ramsay also tried the historical novel, but his chronicle of a great family, *Genom sekler* (1908-9; Through centuries), was stillborn, whereas his memoirs are very much alive, even today. Similarly, the historical novels of Petrus Nordmann (1858-1923) are unreadable, but his Wacklinian book about Finland's Weimar, *Borgå barn och borgare* (1906, expanded 1917; Borgå children and citizens), remains vivid and had a new printing as recently as 1976. Intellectually more discerning than Ramsay or Nordmann, August Schauman (1826-96), the founder of the long-lived liberal paper *Hufvudstadsbladet* (1864-), was a member of still another great Finland-Swedish family, whose ancestors had come from Courland in the seventeenth century. His *Nu och förr* (1886; Now and before) and *Från sex årtionden i Finland* (1892-94; From six decades in Finland) are even-tempered accounts of public and literary life and of the language squabbles, in which he was critical of the extremists on both sides.

The urge to look backward extended into scholarship as well. Valfrid Vasenius (1848-1928), following in the footsteps of Gabriel Lagus's lecture of 1867, devoted a detailed monograph to Jacob Frese in 1884 and subsequently turned out the de rigueur books on Runeberg before he produced his ponderous biography of Topelius in six volumes (1912-20). But Vasenius had not always devoted himself to Finland's Swedish greats; in 1879 he issued the first scholarly dissertation on Ibsen and in 1882 a more general work, *Henrik Ibsen: Ett skaldeporträtt* (Henrik Ibsen: A portrait of a poet), a pioneer book of lasting value that helped inspire Swedish Finland's several enthusiasts for Norwegian letters. Similarly, the many-sided Werner Söderhjelm (1859-1931) — a zealous translator of contemporary Finnish literature, a specialist in German and then Romance philology, the biographer of Tavaststjerna and Runeberg, the holder of several chairs at Helsingfors, and eventually (1919-28) the new republic's ambassador to Sweden — had a view at once international and local, his internationalism stemming, perhaps, from his Viborg background and his undeniable self-confidence. He even attempted the novel, under the pseudonym Pekka Malm, *Brytningstider: En historia från Finland* (1901; Times of change: A story from Finland). In *Brytningstider,* published at Stockholm because of its statements against Finland's growing Russification, Daniel Autio — the foster son of a prominent official in an unnamed and linguistically tolerant eastern Finnish city (read Viborg) — goes to the university in Helsingfors and abroad; with Finnish as his mother tongue but a moderate in the language question, Daniel observes the shifts and subterfuges of the language strife first dispassionately, then indignantly. (Seeking personal and political gain, for example, the opportunist Hjalmar Ekroth, Daniel's foster brother, becomes Jalmari.) As an ideal, Daniel sees the union of his Swedish-spirited friend Kuno Ahlfelt, Hjalmar's cousin, and his Finnish-zealot wife, who work together for the well-being of Finland's people: "Out of such a marriage could arise . . . generations which from birth would be able to bear the spirit of tolerance and in their blood unite the best of what our two national elements possess," a standpoint close to Söderhjelm's own. The career of Daniel Autio does not exactly parallel that of his creator, however: he becomes a teacher at a school in his old hometown, refusing offers to join the staff of Helsingfors University while — here like Söderhjelm — he fights the "submissive" policies of the Old Finnish Party (viewed by many Finns as helpful to their language cause). "Pekka Malm" was much less self-effacing.

Even the admirers of the cultural achievements of the Protestant ascendancy in Ireland have noted the arrogance of its members; a like trait cannot be ignored in patricians such as Söderhjelm. He has been compared, for his contributions to Finland's cultural history, with Sweden's Oscar Levertin and Denmark's Georg Brandes (although he was certainly not as creative as the one nor as wide-ranging as the other), and when, in 1928, he left his post in Stockholm, the Gothenburg editor, Torgny Segerstedt, wrote that he was "as much at home in Rome and Paris as in the Nordic capitals, as well acquainted with Europe's salons as with the Finnish backwoods." His range extended from Petrarchism in German literature (1888) and the Italian protobaroque poet Francesco Molza (1911) to Finnish-language theater and literature. Indeed, he bothered some of his fellow Finland-Swedes by his seemingly Fennomane stance, and at the same time, he annoyed the very authors of the Finnish literature he championed by condescending to them and occasionally writing (poorly, according to Juhani Aho's judgment) in Finnish itself. Eino Leino doubted that Söderhjelm knew as much about Finland's Finnish literature as he thought he did, but his essays and reviews presented new Finnish literature to a larger Nordic public, just as his vast knowledge of the European literatures fed the international strain so important for the vitalization of Finland's Swedish letters, before and after the turn of the century. His role in the creation of the journal *Euterpe* is discussed below.

Finally, it can only be wondered what role Tavaststjerna's and Söderhjelm's friend Hjalmar Neiglick (1860–89) would have played in the expansion of Finland-Swedish literature had he not been carried away so young. With his demands for complete freedom of thought (in which many detected a sharp anti-Christian tendency), his requirement of high standards of theatrical repertoire and performance, and his startling interest, shortly before his death, in such phenomena as hypnosis and spiritism (which became the objects of much attention in European neoromanticism but were rather underrepresented in Finland, save by Tavaststjerna), Neiglick was "Finland's eye toward Europe," as another internationalist, the painter Albert Edelfelt, wrote to Tavaststjerna after Neiglick's death. Georg Brandes was struck by his passionate intellectual engagement and mentioned, as if they were symbolic, "his uncommonly shining eyes." The stringent honesty that characterized Neiglick led him, in the midst of the rage for Ibsen, to refuse to venerate *Rosmersholm* because of what he considered its obscurity; he had an independence of view that, whatever its shortcomings, would have added salt to the remarkably large and varied feast offered by Finland-Swedish literary criticism.

A Wave of Realists

Tavaststjerna and Ahrenberg were certainly not the only literary artists passionately concerned with what was happening outside Scandinavia; the much smaller talent of Adolf Paul (1863–1943) was lured away from Finland altogether, and he has since been pretty well ignored by scholarship because of his lack of a clear national provenience. Born in Sweden, Paul was taken to Finland by his parents at the age of nine; a would-be musician, he went to Germany at the end of the 1880s to further his musical studies and eventually fell in with Tavaststjerna and Sibelius, becoming a hanger-on in Berlin's Black Pig coterie. His largest claim to fame has lain in his propensity for attaching himself to greater men; an extensive portrait of the young Sibelius (as the naive genius Sillén, who "loved cigars even more than himself—which meant not a little") is included in his debut novel, *En bok om en människa* (1891; A book about a human being). The book is also dedicated to the composer, although the main topic is, of course, Paul himself, lightly disguised as the emotionally labile Hans, the victim of a despotic father, and a would-be musician. Paul's interest in aberrative sexual conditions, which played some part in his debut book, got further exposure in the bizarre collection *The Ripper* (*Uppskäraren*) (1892; a bilingual title), of which the parade piece is a fragment of the English "vivisectionist's" notebooks. Hans's story was continued in *Med det falska och det ärliga ögat* (1895; With the false and the honest eye), dedicated to the pianist and composer Ferrucio Busoni, whom Paul had got to know at the Helsingfors conservatory. It is a confusing roman à clef that takes place in Berlin artist circles (Zum schwarzen Ferkel is again somewhere in the background) and is a weak representative of the bohemian novel then flourishing in Germany and elsewhere—see Otto Julius Bierbaum's *Stilpe* (1897), which uses some of the same models as Paul. *Ung Hans kärleksbrev* (1897; Young Hans's love letters), a title partly borrowed from the Swede Ola Hansson's prose poems of 1892, *Ung-Ofegs visor* (Eng. tr. *Young Ofeg's Ditties*, 1893), has as its subtitle *En bok om en människa, III* and is intended as the capstone of the trilogy. At last, Hans seems to be on the brink of being saved by the love of his fiancée: "The whole morning, ever since your letter arrived, I haven't been able to do anything but stand before the mirror and give myself enamored glances."

The next year, 1898, Paul achieved his greatest triumph with the production of the play *Kung Kristian den Andre* (1899; King Christian the Second), about the Danish king—almost as unstable a figure as Paul's alter ego in the trilogy, a monarch who briefly and bloodily conquered Sweden before losing his own kingdom—and his love for the low-born Dyveke; it was performed at Helsingfors's Swedish Theater with music by Sibelius, and thus Paul's name still figures occasionally in concert programs. Its successor, *Karin Månsdotter* (1899), on the Finnish-born mistress and queen of still another disturbed sixteenth-century monarch, Sweden's Erik XIV, was less successful. During the remainder of his career Paul wrote principally in German, grinding out historical fiction. In Finland-Swedish letters he has a certain importance for his imitative employment of themes from European decadence in his novels about Hans and for the portraits he offered of his contemporaries. The notorious femme fatale Dagny Juel ("she lured one man after another unto herself, and then let them go after she had borrowed and shone with their light for a brief time"); her husband-to-be, the zany Polish "poet," Stanislaus Przybyszewski; and the painter Edvard Munch turn up, thinly disguised, in *Med det falska och det ärliga ögat;* the identities of other figures in the novel's extremely talkative coterie, "a society of the shipwrecked," in Hans's opinion—such as "the Chinese philosopher" who, in his misogyny, excels in drawing women to him, "the gray shadow," "the old gypsy"—are less readily pinned down.

Strindberg is evidently the source and maybe the model of the nervous main figure in the story "En charlatan" from the collection *En saga från ödemarken* (1895; A tale from the wilderness): "He turned his cowardice into a sort of necessity by calling it a persecution complex." Strindbergians know about Paul as well for his malicious *Strindberg-minnen och brev* (1915; Strindberg memories and letters). In this last instance Paul took revenge for the portrait Strindberg had given of him in *Fagervik och Skamsund* (1902; Eng. tr. *Fair Haven and Foul Strand,* 1914) as the "unimportant, uncultured

Ilmarinen, whom he [the narrator] had pulled up out of nothingness, introduced into his circle, fed, and sheltered," and then as Mister Anjala, "the false martyr" of Finland's lost freedom in Strindberg's dinner of dunces at the opening of *Svarta fanor* (1907; Black banners). In his memoirs of the Berlin days of the nineties, however, Przybyszewski remembered the almost pathetic devotion with which Paul clung to Strindberg.

Another author whose career lay mostly outside Finland was Konni (Konrad) Zilliacus (1855–1924): after an unusual marriage (to a widow with seven children) and some spendthrift years as an estate owner in Karelia, Zilliacus went off to the New World as a journalist, visiting Central America and spending considerable time in the United States, where he observed emigrant life and the last of the Indian Wars (at Wounded Knee), and then continued around the world, to Japan and Paris; he did not return to Finland until 1898, just in time to get involved in the struggle against Russian oppression. Shortly, he went underground (he was engaged in arms smuggling and the editorship of an illegal paper) and fled to Sweden; there, during the Russo-Japanese War of 1904–5, he arranged meetings between the mikado's agents and Russian revolutionaries. Back in Finland again at the end of the "years of misfortune," he was forced once more to flee ("the Russian secret police had not forgotten me") and did not venture home until after the Civil War. The remainder of his life was spent composing memoirs, the finale of a nonbelletristic production that had begun with such useful products as *Amerika: En handbok för menige man* (1891; America: A handbook for everyday people), published in Chicago, and the giant compendium *Amerikas Förenta Stater* (1893; The United States of America) and included books on revolutionary currents in Russia.

As a creative writer, Zilliacus is remembered principally for his tales of the New World (1890, 1892, 1897, 1899), assembled as *Utvandrare* (1922–23; Emigrants), *Indiankriget: Amerikanska gränsmarkshistorier* (1898; The Indian war: American border stories), and tales and sketches from Japan (in which he tried to emulate Lafcadio Hearn). The actors are often tough and unlettered Finns whose backwoods skills are eminently useful in the jungle or on the prairie — or in the American big city; a message running through many of the stories is that the emigrants found opportunities (e.g., as "Judge Uusitalo," alias "Finn Mike," ruling his little realm somewhere in Minnesota) they would never have had at home. Preyed on by crooked immigrant agents and thieving Indians, the Finns can fight their way through thick and thin; their departure for America has meant a loss for their homeland. (To be sure, Zilliacus does not identify with them; sometimes, as the narrator entering the story, he interprets for them and observes them with amused admiration.) A Finn who has abandoned his simple beginnings, however, is the repulsive star of Zilliacus's *I societeten; En Helsingfors-berättelse* (1895; In society: A Helsingfors story), in which the upstart calls himself Henry Kraus but an old friend remembers him as "Rausin Heikki" from Kuopio. After a time as a lieutenant in the Russian army he makes a fortune in timber speculation: "Lieutenant Kraus was not the sort to let grass grow under his feet." The constellation is familiar from Ahrenberg's novels: the Finn who slips his moorings, changes language, and forgets the Runebergian ideals represented, albeit in a coarsened form, by the honest Councillor Walkonen. Kraus's mistress from the countryside, who makes the mistake of pursuing him to Helsingfors, is brutally rejected by him and sinks into prostitution, while the lieutenant, having vainly pursued a baron's clear-sighted daughter, instead marries another and less choosy member of Helsingfors society.

The false glitter of the social world Zilliacus entered in his short novel was scrutinized more closely by women novelists who, perhaps inspired by such examples as Amalie Skram (1846–1905) in Norway and Anne Charlotte Leffler (1849–92) in Sweden, proved that, like their sisters abroad, they could see through the surface respectability of the lives led by the better sort of people. Gerda von Mickwitz (1862–1948) at first followed Alexander Kielland, as did so many other Scandinavian writers of the time, in the skepticism (and anticlericalism) of some of her novellas in *Solglöd och andra skizzer* (1885; Sun glow and other sketches), but she ventured into realms that Kielland avoided with the implication of mother-son incest and its effects in the title story, and the cases of enervation and impotence that turn up elsewhere in the book. (One of her male protagonists is rendered incapable of love, and life, by excessive consumption of "Turgenev, Sacher-Masoch, Jacobsen, [Herman] Bang.") Growing bolder still, she addressed the problem of syphilis — the bachelor's ailment, often carried into matrimony — which had achieved literary currency through Ibsen's *Gengangere* (1880; Eng. tr. *Ghosts*, 1885). (The Ibsen play had had its premiere in Finland at Swedish Theater in 1883, providing a shock to be reinforced on the same boards two years later when the notoriously decadent Bang appeared as Osvald.) In von Mickwitz's *Ett giftermål* (1889; A marriage) a doctor dies of the disease after his marriage, but his death (the reader is left wondering about the possible transmission of the infection to his wife and infant son) is not the only marital tragedy the two-part novel contains; another young bride discovers that, before marriage, her husband — a longtime friend of the unfortunate physician — has not maintained the chastity he has expected of her, and so she leaves home. (She is scarcely alone in her dismay: see, e.g., Svava Riis in Bjørnson's *En handske* [1883; Eng. tr. *A Gauntlet*, 1913] and the heroines of Skram's *Constance Ring* [1885; Eng. tr. 1989] and *Forraadt* [1892; Eng. tr. *Betrayed*, 1987]; the syphilitic physician returns in the tragic Dr. Kvaale of Arne Garborg's *Trætte Mænd* [1891; Tired men].) Persuaded by her mother, she returns and resigns herself to her fate; her social identity lies in her marriage, and a child is on the way. Yet men are not the only erotically experienced beings in von Mickwitz's moneyed world; the cynical curtain lines in the novel belong to a gossipy society dame who, with a devoted husband, maintains a string of young lovers on the side.

The final work in von Mickwitz's small but interesting production is *Kärleken: En utvecklingshistoria i episoder* (1892; Love: A story of development in episodes), in which the dreamer Ulrik Bruhn — obviously a Finland-Swedish offspring of the Dane Niels Lyhne — meets disappointment on disappointment in his relationships with women; it ends thus: "He thought of his life, which had run past him like a dream, where all he had believed he possessed was taken from him, and he was left, alone and freezing, to await old age." The Kielland model had given way to a Jacobsenian one, the critic of society to the hopeless observer. Later, von Mickwitz, very much on the qui vive about social and intellectual interests of her day, gave a series of lectures on Nietzsche (1900–1901) and, in print, debated with another of the German philosopher's Finnish spokespersons, Rolf Lagerborg. As Harald Beyer, the expert on Nietzsche in the North, points out, she was by no means uncritical in her opinion of the great man, maintaining that the glorious skeptic of the middle period succumbed to an "unpleasant self-worship." Thereby, von Mickwitz gave voice to the laudable suspicion of extremists and extremism characteristic of the Finland-Swedish mindset.

Alexandra Gripenberg (1857–1913), the daughter of Baron Sebastian Gripenberg, a distinguished practical agronomist, served in her youth as secretary to Topelius and was urged by him to take her own pen to hand: a collection of her stories from 1877 was written in his spirit. Her belletristic career was short but notable in both its feminism and its obvious devotion to the Fennomane cause. Using the Finnish-sounding nom de plume Aarne, she followed the short stories of *Strån* (1884; Straws) with the novel *I tätnande led* (1886; In closing ranks). As its chief figure — and Gripenberg's mouthpiece — it has Sofie Veyman, who, from prosperous circumstances, decides to serve the nation's linguistic majority by attending a teachers' seminary somewhere in the interior of Finland (easily recognized as Jyväskylä, a fountainhead of Finnish enthusiasm). There she collides with (and eventually falls in love with) her ultraconservative teacher, Saarela. At her first job she is adored, in turn, by the village schoolteacher Ilmari, with whom she discusses burning questions of the 1880s (albeit the novel is set in the 1860s, at the time of the Jyväskylä Seminary's foundation) such as the sexual double standard, the women's movement, the heavy hand of an obscurantist clergy, and so forth; and her zeal for the Finnish language outdoes that of the native speaker. The "modernity" of her Bible lessons brings her into (loving) conflict with Saarela, now a school inspector, once again, but he is already married to an unpretentious soul of the sort Sofie can only pity or scorn. Rejecting the suit of a cousin, an estate owner, she renounces any thought of Saarela and decides to lead a life of devotion to her several ideals.

How close the novel is to a roman à clef has been the object of some discussion; Gripenberg (who had powerful connections) became not a schoolteacher — unlike many another heroine in novels of the time, following in the footsteps of Jonas Lie's Inger Johanna in *Familien på Gilje* (1883) — but an extremely vocal proponent of woman's liberation. In 1888 she traveled to the United States as the representative of the Finnish Women's Union at the International Women's Congress in Washington DC, and the result of her journey was *Ett halvår i Nya världen* (1889; Eng. tr. *A Half Year in the New World*, 1954), one of those serious but thoroughly entertaining travel books that, in the manner of the works of Pehr Kalm, Georg August Wallin, and Konni Zilliacus, reveal the self-assurance and the keen intelligence of the author: Gripenberg's episode about Mormon men, observed in Salt Lake City, is memorably vitriolic. (Her later essays on Elizabeth Cady Stanton and Susan B. Anthony, included in the 1890 volume of the *Biografiskt album* published by the Finnish Women's Union, show how interested she continued to be in the promised land of feminine liberation.) Busy as she was, Gripenberg did not return to creative literature; she continued both her feminist and her Fennomane activity and eventually became a member of the Old Finnish Party, with its anti-Swedish stance. (The little book about the American trip had come out in 1891 in Finnish translation; it was made by Hilda Asp [1862–91], who in her short life did much to turn major writers — Bjørnson, Ibsen, Paul Heyse — into Finnish.)

Gripenberg's direct contemporary, Helena Westermarck (1857–1938), had begun to think of a literary career while studying art in Paris (a field for which she also had a clear talent). Not that she embraced the current gods of French literature, Flaubert and Zola, whom she found morally offensive; her idol was George Eliot, on whom she wrote the first book in Swedish (1894). (The Westermarck family's Anglophilia was increased by the call of her younger brother, the sociologist Edvard [1862–1939], to a chair at the University of London.) As she noted in her autobiography, she had already been encouraged in her literary endeavors by C. G. Estlander, a friend of the family, and had soon become a contributor to his *Finsk Tidskrift*. Her progress toward the novel was relatively slow; she attracted some attention with the more or less autobiographical *Framåt* (1894; Forward), in which a young woman, well situated, reacts against the sharp contrast between rich and poor in Finland's social structures; disappointed in love, she goes abroad to study painting but returns when signs of Russian oppression appear on the Finnish horizon. Reading her memoirs (which end in 1918 but were not published until 1941), one easily gets the impression that her life, after she had prematurely ended her painting, was devoted entirely to the advancement of women, and much of her copious later production consisted of biographies, of Fredrika Runeberg; Elisabeth Blomqvist (1827–1901), a pioneer in the education of girls and women; Mathilda Rotkirch (1813–42), whom Westermarck called "Finland's first woman painter"; Adelaide Ehrnrooth (see chapter 7), the author, social worker, traveler, and "our first woman journalist"; Rosina Heikel (1842–1929), "Finland's first woman doctor"; and, in one volume, three early woman artists, Fanny Churberg (1845–92), Maria Wiik (1853–1928), and Sigrid af Forselles (1860–1935).

Looking backward, Westermarck ignored her own contribution to Finland's Swedish literature, including the trilogy of novels in which, with some tardiness, she followed the practices and concerns of the 1880s: *I Fru Ulrikas hem* (1900; In Mistress Ulrika's home), *Ljud i natten* (1903; Sounds in the night), and *Vandrare* (1911; Wanderers). The series bears the blanket title *Tecken och minnesskrift från 1800-talet* (Signs and memorials from the nineteenth century) and runs in time from 1808–9 to the turn of the century. Of the three books, the first—which has as a subtitle "Interiörer från farmödrarnas tid" (Interiors from the grandmothers' time), a painterly identification similar to that of Jacobsen's *Fru Marie Grubbe,* "Interiors from the Seventeenth Century," and Lie's *Familien på Gilje,* "Interiors from the 1840s"—concentrates on Fru Ulrika Ehrendt and the two men in her life, her husband, the hardworking owner of Lindby Estate, and his gifted but fly-by-night brother. Fru Ulrika, of course, chooses the path of duty but becomes "a woman of few words, and she seldom smiled nowadays, but on her countenance lay once again a hopeful expression, as it were a reflection of the past happiness of youth."

In the much briefer second part the son of the couple that stayed together, the medical professor Carl Fredrik Ehrendt, visits (in the 1870s) an old university friend in the country, thereby allowing Westermarck to deviate from her linear narration and return to the middle of the century. Paying a sick call to a patient of a medical colleague, Professor Ehrendt realizes that the sick man's wife is the great love of his youth, whom he — like several of Ibsen's male characters — abandoned to pursue other goals and, eventually, to make an advantageous marriage. During the century's last decade, in *Vandrare,* one of the daughters of Carl Fredrik, Eva, is brought to an early grave by her husband Herman's "bad business speculations" (her vain and superficial mother had encouraged the match), and the other, Emmy, maintains her independence, turning down suitor after suitor, and has almost the last word in the trilogy. "We must remember that, in the old home at Lindby the ceilings were low, both literally and figuratively, and the air was often heavy and stale . . . very heavy for the women. Now, at any event, we are all modern folk, who must look to the future, . . . yes, even hopefully, despite the present's darkness," a reference to the Russian pressure. Her father, the old physician, retorts: "You women are all alike. You always keep your faith in the miracle that must come." As Emmy directly points out, a miracle has happened: her brother Gustaf, a physician in America, has come home to Finland with his family: in the New World he found again and married a love of his intern days, the therapeutic gymnast Maria Grahn, the foster daughter of the professor's abandoned flame. (Maria's "sister," Rosa, was once upon a time desperately in love with Gustaf but committed suicide when Maria, in a fit of jealousy, told her the truth about her parentage: Rosa was Carl Fredrik's illegitimate daughter and thus Gustaf's half-sister!)

Westermarck made generous use of fateful Victorian coincidences like those of Eliot in *Middlemarch*. While not blind to the palpable weaknesses of the novel's second and third parts, Merete Mazzarella ("Helena Westermarck") praised the trilogy's total concept and the Helsingfors scenes of its conclusion: pictures of the boardinghouse where the "sisters" live and the charity committee meetings attended by Professor Ehrendt's wife (satirical writing on the level of Strindberg's in *Röda rummet*). But only the first part, with its relatively few characters and tauter structure, is artistically satisfying, and it, too, suffers from a rejoicing in the details of estate life that is a reminder of Westermarck's fondness for Selma Lagerlöf's *Gösta Berlings saga* (1891; Eng. tr. *The Story of Gösta Berling,* 1898). Yet the toying with the supernatural that gives Lagerlöf's famous book its special charm was ill-fitted to the sober Westermarck; when she tried this tack, as in the "Choses mystérieuses" of *Dolda makter: Bilder och hägringar* (1905; Hidden forces: Pictures and visions), she fell flat. Like so many of her Finland-Swedish contemporaries an adherent of the rationalist realism that had swept over

Scandinavia in the 1880s, she was constitutionally unable to break out into more imaginative realms.

Helsingfors Discovered

From the first collection by Ina Lange, *Bland ödebygder och skär: Berättelser från Finland* (1884; Among wilderness lands and skerries: Tales from Finland), it was clear that she meant to call attention to the victims of poverty, alcohol, and violence who populated not only the countryside (she carefully gives the location of every story) but, in the sentimental Christian tale "Lyx" (Luxury), the workers' districts of Helsingfors. Lange—born Ina Forstén (1846–1930)—has a life that, in its very variety, deserves a biography: a pianist, she studied with Karl Tausig, Liszt's protégé, in Berlin and with Nikolai Rubenstein and Tchaikovsky himself in Moscow; in 1876 she married Algot Lange, an actor and singer from Kalmar then engaged at Swedish Theater in Helsingfors (and destined to become one of the leading bass baritones in the Scandinavia of his day). Moving to Stockholm and then to Copenhagen with him, she became chamber pianist and piano teacher for the princesses at the Danish court. She figures fairly large in Strindberg's *Le plaidoyer d'un fou* (1895; Eng. tr. *The Confessions of a Fool*, 1912; *A Madman's Defense*, 1967), where he described her as the "fiancée of a friend of mine, an opera singer . . . she was of indeterminate age, between twenty-nine and forty-two, in a daring dress, . . . a flirt, a man-eater, a chaste polyandrist." Victoria Benedictsson, the Swedish novelist and briefly the mistress of Georg Brandes, who got to know her well in Copenhagen, commented in her diary that Lange's "Swedish was bad" and "her process of thought as raw and immature as a green potato. . . . My dear Mrs. Lange, you have too many irons in the fire."

Beyond question, something hasty or unfinished pertains to Lange's production, written under the pseudonym Daniel Sten. In the title of "*Sämre folk*" (1885; The worse sort of people) the quotation marks are meant to indicate that the judgment is not necessarily the author's own. Hardworking, good-looking, and fanatically clean, Kajsa, a poor girl on Drumsö (Lauttasaari), in days long before it became a suburb of Helsingfors, marries first a shiftless cobbler and, after his death, a Russian officer's batman, who vanishes on the ice of Drumsö Sound in a winter storm. Her child from the former union, Weli, wants to be a fiddler like his father but loses an arm in an accident and peddles cigars in Helsingfors's parks (to his mother's pleasure: "He is not dirty and not a musician"). Her daughter, Nadja (on whom Lange heaps far and away the most attention), becomes a prostitute, to the horror of her respectable mother: she cannot bring herself to imagine that Nadja's "bad nature" comes from her late father, a handsome Cossack. Eventually, Nadja is saved from her life of pleasure and degradation by the faithful love of the true-hearted Samuli and thus gets a happier fate than her many colleagues in the same calling elsewhere in the novel of the time. (The title character in Edmond de Goncourt's *La fille Élisa* [1877] murders her special lover and is sent to prison for life, and in *Nana* [1880] is devoured by syphilis; in Kielland's *Else* [1881; Eng. tr. 1894] she dies, frozen to death while drunk, after a bungled burglary; and in Christian Krogh's *Albertine* [1886] she becomes a drunken nymphomaniac.) In *Luba: En studie* (1889; Luba: A study) a step upward is taken on the social ladder; the eponymous heroine is turned by unfulfilled artistic ambitions and erotic needs into a hysterical paralytic but is saved from this predicament by a pastor, Lämmenen, who has already won a large following among the ladies of Helsingfors society (they flock to his vigorous sermons without understanding a word of the Finnish text). In a development reminiscent of events in Skram's *Constance Ring*, Luba dies on discovering that in the past her husband, as he confesses, has fathered a child with a coarse girl from the countryside.

Ina Lange ended her career in imaginative literature with *Berättelser från Finland* (1890; Tales from Finland), seven stories placed variously, again, in the poor quarters of Helsingfors and in the country; with less weakness for the shock effect of her naturalism than before, Lange wrote about small lives with small expectations, modest victories, and intimate defeats: a very old flame flickers in "Vart femtionde år slår en blomma ut" (It blooms every fiftieth year); a peasant wife is briefly reunited with the "young gentleman" of six years before in "Mot afton" (Toward evening), but her husband takes to drink in "Natt" (Night); fatherless children are neglected in "Vid Raiala mo" (At Raiala heath). From the evidence the judgment of Victoria Benedictsson seems unnecessarily harsh; in her novels and city stories (she knew perhaps too little about Finnish country life) Lange gives exceptional pictures of down-at-the-heels Helsingfors, although Arvid Mörne, who rediscovered her work in 1939, questioned the accuracy of her observations, as he did the extent of her knowledge of the city's growing language problem. Like Adolf Paul, she left the country early and used her Finnish settings as a kind of window dressing. (The novel of 1887, *En skæbne: Fortælling fra vore Bedsteforældres Tid* [A fate: A tale from our great-grandparents' time] came out only in Danish translation and was meant to capture a readership by its colorful depiction of Finnish estate life during the reign of Nicholas I.) Nevertheless, she had an eye for aspects of municipal life that had not yet received much attention in fiction: shanties on Drumsö, workers' quarters in Rödbergen (Punavuori); with the sexual content of *"Sämre folk"* and *Luba,* she contributed to the destruction of taboos that still kept a Tavaststjerna from being as frank as he might otherwise have been. Oddly, the world of music had very little part in her serious writing; in later life she ground out popular biographies of great composers, from Handel to Sibelius, and of the dancer Barberina Campanini, "Frederick the Great's mistress," about whom Adolf Paul also published a novel, in German, the same year (1915).

Other writers of Helsingfors fiction are semijournalists, given to moralizing, picturesqueness, or sentimentality. The stories of Victor Pettersson (1846–1919) about the old sailors' section of town, Skatudden (Katajanokka), largely razed in the 1870s, *Bilder ur Skatuddslifvet i forna dagar* (1881; Pictures from life on Skatudden in former days), and his *Den gamle polisgevaldigerns berättelser: Bilder ur Helsingforslifvet* (1884; The old police constable's tales: Pictures from Helsingfors life) were meant to entertain the city's still very substantial lower-middle-class Swedish reading public. Judging by the plots it consumed, this audience was less concerned with language or larger social questions than with nostalgia for simpler days or with the immorality, luxury, and Russian connections of its betters. The tales of F. J. (Frans Johan) Valbäck (1852–1923) — an editor of weekly papers, like Pettersson — were particularly edifying; Valbäck's depiction of Helsingfors life, *En afton i Kajsaniemi* (1892; An evening in Kajsaniemi), has as its muscular hero Albert, an honest Swedish-speaking seaman, and as a villain "the slippery, furtive Javetz," employed at the governor-general's office. Albert loves and is loved by demure Maria, whose father, Colonel Danielsson, becomes convinced in the book's course that Albert, risen to the command of the full-rigger *Gustav Vasa,* is worthy of his daughter's hand.

Under the pseudonym Sphinx, the all-around writer Rafael Hertzberg (1845–96) produced *Helsingfors-Monaco* (1887), in which the heroine is the poor but honest schoolteacher Olga Berggren, and the blackguard the factory owner Frisk, whose "cultured Swedish home" is a den of overstuffed iniquity, the walls adorned with oleographs of Cleopatra as the serpent bites her breast and of a "naked woman partially concealing herself behind a light blue veil." Torn between the lure of Frisk's conspicuous consumption and the virtuous charms of Olga, the weak protagonist shoots himself after final reverses at the gaming tables of Monaco. In *Statsrådet* (1887; The councillor of state), by "Jung Junior" (another of Hertzberg's pseudonyms), the life of the moneyed classes is similarly shallow: the corrupt councillor, returned to Finland after long service in Russia, puts the leading Finnish newspaper, *Uusi Suometar*, on his parlor table to convince Fennomane visitors he is on their side, even though he and his wife seem unable to read it. For the same couple, Swedish Theater is a place for the exchange of gossip rather than a temple of the arts, and the actors on stage, all from Sweden, care more about amorous conquest than about their roles. (Jung Junior enlists Fennomane propaganda to chastise his own group.) The councillor also attends the Finnish Theater in the old Arcadia auditorium; the house is stuffy and smells, but its audience is devoted and proud. The "guests," the councillor and his wife, are carefully observed, and they know it: "The lorgnette of the . . . wife now had nothing critical about it . . . it expressed the most friendly attention."

Theater

As might be expected in the age of Ibsen and Bjørnson, efforts were made to supply works for the Swedish-speaking stage, just as Minna Canth supplied them in Finnish, encouraged by Emilie Bergbom (1834–1905) and her brother Kaarlo (or Karl) Bergbom (1843–1906). (The latter had begun his career with a tragedy in Swedish, *Pombal och jesuiterna* [1863; Pombal and the Jesuits], set in eighteenth-century Portugal, and a dissertation, again in Swedish, on the historical drama in German [1868].) Always looking for new material, Bergbom accepted the historical drama *Erik Puke* (1888) of Gustaf von Numers (1848–1913), translated into Finnish, for his Finnish Theater after the Swedish Theater had turned it down: *Eerikki Puke* dealt with events from the fifteenth century, and *Tuukkalan tappelu/Striden vid Tuukkala* (1889/1892; The battle at Tuukkala) had to do with a still earlier time, before the Christianization of Finland, and with a feud between the people of Tavastland (Häme) and Karelia. But von Numers's breakthrough on the Finnish-language stage came with *Elinan surma* (1891; Elina's death), based on a ballad in the *Kanteletar* about the nobleman Klas Kurck, his young mistress Elin, and her rival Kirsti (or Kerstin) Fleming. Its premiere, in October 1891, with the great Ida Aalberg in the jealous woman's role, was a sensation; but it was not produced in Swedish until 1907, now called by the name of the murderess, *Kirsti Fleming;* the Swedish version was printed in 1928 as *Klas Kurck och liten Elin*. While work still proceeded on the historical projects under Bergbom's aegis, however, Numers had written the first of his comedies on contemporary themes that made him one of the most played dramatists on Finland's stages, *Kuopion takana* (Behind Kuopio), which came out in Finnish translation at Otava in 1891 and in the original Swedish at Söderström & Co. as *Bakom Kuopio* a year later; its stage premiere—the versions printed by leading publishers demonstrated how interested the public was — had taken place in Finnish in February 1890.

Keen observers have noted that, despite the title, which places the action in the province of Savolax (Savo), many of the details are from Ostrobothnia — von Numers was a native of Vasa. No doubt, much of the play's popularity lay in its amusing sugar-coating of figures and problems from contemporary Nordic literature; its main figure, Elias Jussilainen, is a bumptious (but not wholly unlovable) pastor's assistant, an ultraconservative, engaged to the daughter of a rural dean; he is duped, without his quite realizing it, by Lilli, a smart young lady from Helsingfors and an advocate of women's rights. The play was given in its original Swedish by pupils from the Swedish Theater's training school in 1894 (the belatedness a sign, perhaps, of the suspicion with which that institution still regarded von Numers) and had its professional premiere the next year, with the stellar comedian August Arppe in the adjunct's role; he was still performing it in 1919, to celebrate his fortieth year on the stage. Von Numers wrote a sequel, *Pastor Jussilainen,* in 1895, whose premiere took place in Swedish in 1896: von Numers had broken with Bergbom. In it Jussilainen's first fiancée, Naemi, herself become a modern woman, has ended her engagement to the reactionary pastor, and he in turn has married a docile district sheriff's daughter but still carries the torch for Lilli, making extensive modernizations in his home for her planned visit (she does not come). Given his comeuppance verbally and physically by his vigorous mother-in-law, the household tyrant is finally transformed into an advocate of causes he once reviled (for example, adult education), presenting them as his own. In the Jussilainen plays, von Numers humorously argued for a bringing of rural Finnish attitudes, especially among the clergy, up-to-date, yet his emphasis on forceful situation comedy, keeping his plays on the boards for years, reduced whatever literary value they had. In both the country's languages, was he Finland's Arthur Wing Pinero?

Von Numers enjoyed a popularity far greater and more lasting than the military surgeon Ferdinand (von) Wahlberg (1847–1920), who made deeply serious attempts to emulate Ibsen's and Bjørnson's problem plays for the Finland-Swedish stage. In the title and the preface of his *Det omöjliga möjligt* (1881; The impossible possible) Wahlberg called attention to his play's function as a reply to Ibsen's *Et dukkehjem* (1879; Eng. tr. *A Doll's House,* 1880): his Nora figure, Betty, returns to a home in which the impossible — Ibsen's "most miraculous thing" — has taken place: a genuine community of affection and responsibility has been established. *Samhällsuppfostran* (1882; Training of society), like some of Bjørnson's plays, such as

En fallit (1875; Eng. tr. *The Bankrupt,* 1914), deals with financial corruption and business failure; its most striking figure is Karl Björnson, an honest working man. Wahlberg's drama with an ironic, Ibsen-sounding title, *Hörnstenar* (1883; Cornerstones; cf. *Samfundets støtter* [1877; Eng. tr. *Pillars of Society*]), presents what the playwright must have considered a juicy role to the actress who plays Marta Gerens, the wealthy fiancée of Dr. Georg Fredby, a politician (and imitation of Stensgård in Ibsen's *De unges forbund* [1869; Eng. tr. *The League of Youth,* 1890]). Accused by Fredby of a sexual misstep in the past, Marta humiliates him by first pretending to beg for forgiveness and then pulling out a letter that reveals his own long affair with her impoverished predecessor in his affections: "Look here, read your own condemnation — now you can no longer creep behind your lies! Look here at what will prove which of us is the guilty party!"

Such heavily unimaginative speech also pulls down Wahlberg's next play, *Våld* (1884; Violence), a less-than-living text for the stage; it presents a conflict between a conventional father, Chamberlain Örngård, and his religiously radical son, an assistant pastor who has joined the Free Congregation, a revivalist movement. The son rescues his father from arrest for the embezzlements the ostensibly respectable chamberlain has committed: going into exile for his refusal to abandon his new-found beliefs, the son turns the inheritance that would have fallen to him, had he agreed to return to the state church, over to the elder Örngård, who saves himself by making restitution. Followed by his faithful wife and members of his congregation, Albert departs after taking leave of his father (who collapses) and his mother, "sunken," as the stage direction says, "in heartrending grief." His last words are: "Poor mother, in you I kiss not only my mother but my whole native country, you both have given me your love and you both suffer from violence, violence against conscience." A close study of von Wahlberg's Ibsen-and-Bjørnson discipleship would be interesting, as would an investigation of his life; Wahlberg became still another case of ostracism because of his compliant attitude toward the Russian regime (he was ennobled in 1904). After a break in his authorship he began a second writing career with religious tractates and novels in German, his native language: the son of a pastor to the Volga Swabians, he had been sent off as a boy to Helsingfors for schooling. He told about his remarkable career in *Mein Lebenslauf* (1912; My life), at once matter of fact and pious.

Realism and Regionalism
Regionalism, a subform of realism focused on a single section of the country, began to prosper in Finland, as it did in other literatures in the 1880s, for

example, in the Scanian (south Swedish) settings of A. U. Bååth and Ola Hansson, or, in the United States, in the Maine stories of Sarah Orne Jewett and Hamlin Garland's tales of the upper Middle West. Without question, the new self-awareness that the Swedish-speaking countryside had acquired, through the efforts of Freudenthal and his followers, had been essential in this growth. Yet regionalism's roots were pre-Freudenthalian, in the edifying little stories about the western Nyland skerries by the pastor Ernst Odert Reuter (1815–90). With the verse and prose of E. O. Reuter's youngest son, Jonatan Reuter (1859–1947), a friend and sailing companion of Tavaststjerna, the urge to depict the special moods of the coast and its inhabitants got a much more artistic formation. A handful of Reuter's poems — his lyric debut came in 1884 — has found a permanent place in the Palgravian golden treasury of Finland-Swedish verse, expressing a sea mysticism that was summed up, eventually, in Ture Janson's often quoted line of 1913 about the Finland-Swedish predicament: "For us the sea's the only fatherland." Reuter himself is much less desperate in his short poem in distichs: "There is no rest as great and deep as the quieting ocean's, / Never a charm as rich as the ocean's infinite peace"; later the Ostrobothnian publicist and pedagogue J. J. (Johan Jakob) Huldén (1880–1959) would play with the association, expressed by Reuter in metrics, between the coastal waters of ancient Greece and Finland in his essay "Homerisk kust" (Homeric coast). Reuter was also capable of giving a mythic or a quasi-supernatural air to scenes on land, as in the fine poem, in trochaic octameters, "Natt på myren" (Night on the mire), in which an elk like "a prince in exile gazes out toward the lake's white waters."

Reuter's tales about the skerries and small-town life, beginning with *Lovart och lä* (1895; Windward and leeward), depend less on his limited but fairly original powers of imagination; he continued with *Berättelser om levande och döda* (1900; Tales of the living and the dead), in which the comical story "Krukmakare Willberg och hans hustru" (Eng. tr. "Willberg the Potter and His Wife," *Swedo-Finnish Short Stories,* 1974) tells much about his hard and fast belief that old ways were the best ways. In his later collections (and he continued to publish until the 1930s) Reuter's view of life darkened, and his mind went back to tragedies of the past, as in the story "Kapten Sunds död" (Captain Sund's death) from *Kaptener och kaptenskor* (1931; Captains and captains' wives), about a disastrous shipboard fire that had occurred in 1897. Writing for a German public in 1899, Ernst Brausewetter called Jonatan Reuter "the last great representative of a certain 'romanticizing,'" and he was right, in that Reuter seems to lag behind the literary times in the generally romantic atmosphere and the prevalent good nature or natural piety of his best verse and his earlier stories; he found his way only belatedly to the bitter sobriety that characterized much Scandinavian realism.

Reuter was a part-time creative writer, earning his keep as a teacher at the Polytechnical Institute in Helsingfors and producing technical handbooks as well as factual volumes on his hometown, Ekenäs; his cousin, Odo Morannal Reuter (1850–1913), also had literature as an avocation—he was a well-known entomologist and professor of zoology at the university. Brausewetter put him into the class of "painters of reality," perhaps because of the social pathos (or bathos) he injected into his collections of verse. Alongside the skerry poetry required of members of the Reuter clan, there are items in *Dikter* (1881; Poems) that could still deserve entry in a complete, historical anthology of Finland's verse, as representatives of a lyric "naturalism" (in the sense of an illumination of social ills by means of their close description), somewhat in the style then current in Germany, represented by such writers as Karl Henckell or the young Gerhart Hauptmann: see the poem about a mother who is "blind and deaf and dumb," or about a flower seller whose parents drink up her small income, while she is exposed to sexual harassment from her customers, so that she becomes a drunkard and a whore, in the classical naturalistic manner. Subsequently, Reuter became more concerned with the Russian presence and wrote verse — again historically interesting if aesthetically depressing — about Finland's predicament.

As a patriot, though, Reuter made a far greater contribution to Finland's cause (which was attracting more and more attention in the outside world) with the huge factual-descriptive volume *Finland i ord och bild* (1901; Finland in word and picture), almost a thousand pages printed in Stockholm with copious illustrations. In his introduction Reuter regretted that limitations of space prevented him from including further chapters, among them some on "Finland's cultural conditions during the most recent time." All the same, he managed to write at great length about the Swedish-speaking sections of the country, thus returning in spirit to the regionalism from which he had sprung; the province of Nyland is presented (with some distortion) as largely Swedish-speaking, and Åland and Ostrobothnia get extensive treatment. Notably, Reuter says that in Ostrobothnia, "the good qualities of both groups [Swedish and Finnish speakers] appear only where the populace has remained to some extent pure, while in those sections where the one element has begun to decay on account of the other, a perceptible enervation allows the reverse sides of both nationalities to appear, frivolous Swedish presumption or Finnish stubbornness, with its inclination to cause trouble," a reminder that Reuter was a contemporary of Ahrenberg and shared the latter's theories of ethnic impurity.

A belief that the Swedish-speaking sections of Finland were slowly (or rapidly) being decimated informs much regional writing. Anders Allardt (1855–1942), for many years a teacher and then rector of the Borgå lyceum, came from peasant parentage in Lappträsk (Lapinjärvi) in eastern Nyland and was painfully aware of the inroads immigration from the north had made on his home parish, once completely Swedish; he was equally aware of the indifference of many highly placed or economically favored Finland-Swedes to what was happening. Allardt published four collections of tales (*Byberättelser* [1885–1908; Village stories]): a typical figure is the simple, hardworking farm laborer Erlund in "Jordtorparen" (The crofter), "with long, strong arms and large broad hands," who manages to improve his condition ever so slightly after ill-treatment and hardship; or Gubben Malmberg (Old Malmberg), in the story of that name, who speaks "a classic dialect with old-fashioned words and turns of speech, and [has] something solid and true-hearted about his whole being"; the title character of "Halten" (Gimpy), who, despite his wooden leg, labors hard and eventually wins the girl of his heart's desire. The affection of Allardt for his local dialect led him to introduce it in fragments of dialogue or, sometimes, as the total instrument of narration, to be taken as a sign of the pristine honesty of its speakers. In the story "Av olika mening" (Of different opinion) in his first collection, a farmer, rejecting the arguments of Finnish zealots who want him either to change languages or to get out, proclaims, "Born I am of Swedish parents, and Swedish have I been put into the cradle!"

Much less inclined to happy endings, Oscar Behm (1867–1933) forms a contrast to Allardt, whose stories customarily have an edifying or comical bent, intended to inspire or amuse. A case in point is Behm's "Rote-Maja" (District Maja), a description of the last hours of a paralytic, doomed to be shoved from farm to farm in her district, now that "her work and ability to take care of herself were past." The story is from Behm's *Folkliv* (1886; Life of the people): like Allardt, Behm knows the lot of the landless worker on Nyland's large estates, but he demonstrates much more persistently how often such existences ended in degradation or defeat—as in "Fattigdom" (Poverty), in which the parents and the youngest child die; the other children are parceled out, finding a home of sorts, "one here, one there." Some sufferers who attempt to escape have their spirits broken and fall into indifference, as in the case of John, the gifted schoolboy in "Till stan i skola" (To the city to school); others succumb to alcohol or end in prison; girls who bear illegitimate children, or wives who take control from weak husbands and are troubled by their consciences, likewise are victimized by systematic or chance oppression and deprivation. (But Behm occasionally allows a small light to shine in the darkness: the farmer's wife who displaces her feckless mate decides at last that "Our Lord Himself stood beside her that evening and directed her hand.")

When Behm's first volume of stories appeared, they were criticized by *Finsk Tidskrift* for being too "ordinary," and when *Under rasten* (1887; During the pause) followed, the same journal announced that Behm was more pessimistic than the situation warranted. In 1936 the scholar P. O. Barck retorted that, at their time, Behm's tales were distinguished by the painful frankness with which they examined the agricultural proletariat. Behm was little interested in the folkloristic details Allardt piled up; instead, he had been trained as a practical farmer — in Sebastian Gripenberg's institute at Mustiala — and worked as an estate manager, so that he was quite familiar with what he described. Further, he seldom employed dialect in his stories, which were intended to make a large public aware of horrendous conditions, and he seems to have been indifferent to the question of Finnish intrusion that so troubled Allardt. At the time, Sibbo parish, his home, was much less exposed to Finnish immigration than Allardt's Lappträsk; yet the cause for his indifference may lie, too, in his straightforward intention of instigating social reform.

Nyland, Freudenthal's home province, produced the majority of regional literature during these decades, the works of the Reuters, Allardt, and Behm and the description of Nyland skerry life in Petrus Nordmann's *Mot fyren* (1889; Toward the lighthouse). The other Swedish-speaking parts of the country had less representation, save through the sketches of Adèle Weman (1844–1936), who for years was a teacher at Kimito (Kemiö) in the Åbo skerries and wrote under the ornithological nom de plume Parus Ater (black tomtit), and the verse of Frans Österblom (1870–1907), her sometime pupil and likewise an elementary schoolteacher. He leads a modest life after death in literary histories because of his song "Min hembygd" (My home region), which became the secular hymn of his small corner of the world:

> Here my forefathers fought a thousand years ago
> Against the murk and wildness of the soul,
> Here there's a struggle still, today as long before
> For the mother tongue, and for knowledge, culture's goal.

The rather ponderous words are sung to the tune of Sweden's national anthem, "Du gamla, du fria, du fjällhöga Nord" (Thou ancient, thou free-born, thou fell-lofty North), and it may be wondered if the third strophe of Österblom's text, quoted above, and the choice of melody are directed against Fennomane zealots. Österblom plays on the historical fact that the Swedes, recently Christianized themselves, had brought the faith to the heathen Finns. Otherwise, Österblom is remembered for the manner of his death: he was killed by a lightning bolt while watching a summer storm, gathering poetic material.

Farther west, Åland, quite untouched by Finnish encroachment, remained almost silent, as it would for several decades to come: "Alandia non cantat." Nevertheless, its artists' colony, growing up in the wake of Karl Emmanuel Jansson (1846–74) and around Victor Westerholm (1860–1919), gave the islands, at least in the summer, an artistic nimbus. The painter Hanna Rönnberg (1862–1946) also painted Åland in words; in *Från Ålands skär* (1899; From Åland's skerries) she plumbed the islands' history, rather as Allardt did with some of his tales, which he set in the Middle Ages or during the Crimean War. Similarly, Anders John Nygren (1869–1902) made repeated efforts to give Ostrobothnia a clear if not very elevated literary profile, and his collections are heavily larded with rural originals and native good humor, as in his story "Huru Hamaxin fick ny hustru" (How Hamaxin got a new wife); going farther than Allardt, he composed three collections of tales (*Byyrallor* [1889–1902; Village yarns]) entirely in his Kvevlaks (Koivulahti) dialect, to the vast (but probably unshared) delight of his Ostrobothnian readers. Ostrobothnia's skerries were also one of the settings used by Onni Wetterhoff (1835–92)—not a native son but a former army officer from Helsingfors—for some of his hunting sketches in *Från skog och sjö* (1883, 1887; From forest and lake), admired by sportsmen, it would seem, for their intensity and accuracy of detail.

Wetterhoff, like Runeberg, distinguished the good-natured Swedish-speakers of the coast from the solemn Finns of the interior, and others (for example, Ahrenberg himself) also fostered an ethnic regionalism in their stories. Hunting in Ostrobothnia and in Tavastland (Häme), John Hedberg (1840–1916), a forester, a newspaperman, and eventually a member of Finland's new unicameral Parliament, hunted in Karelia and saw other ethnic contrasts there. As in Wetterhoff's case, Hedberg's *Skogsstämning* (1891; Forest moods) and *Från stigar och hult* (1907; From trails and groves) have a sportsman as narrator, in the wake of Turgenev and Sacher-Masoch, and are almost directly contemporaneous with the *Jagtbreve* (1889, 1892; Hunting letters) of Vilhelm Dinesen ("Boganis"), the father of Karen Blixen. Hedberg is far less inclined than the Danish captain to put himself in the middle of what he observes; he lets the exoticism of the landscape he has chosen speak for itself. (He was from the other end of southern Finland, Pemar [Paimio], near Åbo.) In the striking little story of adultery and murder in the backwoods, "Utmarkens hemlighet" (1907; Eng. tr. "The Backwoods' Secret," *Swedo-Finnish Short Stories*, 1974) he makes a distinction between Russians, who demonstrate considerable indifference to marital unfaithfulness, and Finns, who "cause a lot of trouble for their women's sake"; the femme fatale is a gypsy, like Homsantuu in Minna Canth's *Työmiehen vaimo* (1885; The laborer's wife). Authors of the age in Finland (and scarcely there alone) were inclined to think in racial stereotypes and to distribute moral approval or disapproval accordingly.

Hedberg largely leaves it up to his audience to read between the ethnic lines, as does Lilly Londén (1862–1937) in her novel *En misstanke* (1892; A suspicion), which was followed by *Berättelser och bilder* (1893; Tales and pictures), before she made an abrupt end to a promising career. Londén's father had been a country pastor in Karelia; thus she knew (but was not a part of) the Finnish-speaking population she described, and she knew, as well, what went on in the manse. The novel's chief figure, Vilppo, is of gypsy blood (on his father's side) and has "the oddly aristocratic bearing that always distinguishes the gypsy, even though his clothes hang on him in rags." Abandoned by her husband, his mother has been sent from farm to farm, a ward of the parish like Behm's Maja; fortunately adopted by an old peasant, Vilppo works hard and is far more intelligent and dependable than Tuomas, an orphaned cousin of the peasant whom the kindly old man has likewise taken into his home and who will someday, it is assumed, inherit it. In time Vilppo wins the favor of the peasant's daughter, too, and Tuomas, who has become his fast friend, does not object. But luck and his family's past turn against Vilppo; he sees his father in a prison transport, he is introduced by his sly half-brother to a band of moonshiners, he is suspected of theft, although innocent, and when the good-hearted but simpleminded Tuomas drowns on a fishing trip in Vilppo's company, rumor has it that his foster brother caused the death. All goes downhill for Vilppo, and his formerly happy marriage to Anni decays; at last, convicted of the attempted murder of an official, he ends as his father did, in chains on his way to prison.

This sad story is played out against a counterplot, centered on the parsonage, in which the men of the cloth are either lazy or overambitious. The senior pastor, who has encouraged Vilppo in the past, is too timid to point to the web of unfounded suspicions that has pulled the young man into his thoughtless crime. As well, the uxorious old man is distracted by his new wife, his former housekeeper, who has broken off a hole-in-the-corner affair with his son when it becomes plain that the dean means to marry her: station is better than sex. The dean's daughter, Sylvia, who would have preferred to capture a squire from the local estate, has had to make do with Pastor Abel Sopanen, an upstart like Ahrenberg's Israel Huovinen and Zilliacus's Henry Kraus, although infinitely less successful than they. Londén's bitter wit is nicely demonstrated in her description of the procession of the pastor's party to the wedding of Vilppo and Anni, before the final catastrophes take place. The dean, "looking good-hearted and anxious," tries not to step on the hem of his bride's long skirt, while she strides along with "concentrated dignity, like a chicken with the wind at its back." Following them, Sylvia, with her new husband, sulks because she has noticed that her gown, bought by Sopanen in St. Petersburg, is of poorer quality than her stepmother's. Behind the two newlywed couples walks Hannes, the son of the house and the stepmother's summertime lover, now a callow candidate for the university. Nothing in Swedish Finland's realistic literature is closer to the cynical spirit of de Maupassant's novels, for example, *Une vie* (1883), or to the lack of illusion in the masterpiece among Anglo-Irish novels of the nineteenth century, *The Real Charlotte* (1894), by Edith Oenone Somerville and "Martin Ross" (Violet Martin), than Lilly Londén's *En misstanke*. A similar cruel clear-sightedness and a highly effective laconicism characterize some of her handful of stories. Even more than in the case of Gerda von Mickwitz, one must regret that her literary career ended so quickly.

The New Century's Beginning

With some pathos, it has often been remarked that Finland's Swedish literature was itself about to die out when the aged Topelius and Tavaststjerna passed away, almost simultaneously in March 1898. The anecdote of Yrjö Hirn, then assistant at the University Library, has become canonical: riding with a young writer named Mikael Lybeck in the Topelius procession, Hirn felt he was in the company of the whole of Finland-Swedish letters. A Cassandra could have listed, too, the attrition of still living talents through various and sometimes unknown causes—the marked decline of Ahrenberg, the withdrawal of Paul to Germany, the absorption of Ina Lange and Konni Zilliacus by other endeavors, the silence of von Mickwitz and Londén. It shortly became ever plainer, as well, that the days of a Swedish hegemony in the country's political and social life was over. The speech of Viktor Magnus von Born, "the last marshal of the land," to the final assembly of the quadricameral estates-general at Helsingfors's Riddarhus (House of Knights) in September 1906 was a graceful valedictory: "Deeply rooted in the essence of the Finnish constitution and in our history, representation by the [four] estates has seen centuries disappear and fates change. Its work lies in a land built with law, its memory shall rest in the history of its deeds." At a dinner for the "knighthood and nobility" of Finland a few days later von Born said, "I have never been afraid of universal suffrage and the unicameral system . . . and in this area I join the future with an open heart." Universal suffrage meant that the Swedish-speaking middle class lost its power too, such as it was; at the university and in the country's lyceums, as Klaus Törnrudd has noted, "the number of Finnish-speaking students was [now] larger than the Swedish. . . . Thus there was already an important Finnish-speaking cultured class" (p. 11). Furthermore, the threat of a *finis Finlandiae*, put in pointed form in the czar's February Manifesto of 1899, had grown painfully clear.

The very imminence of the loss of Finland's special status in the Russian empire brought about some unity from moderates on both sides in the language question, however, and the well-reported instances of Russian brutality—as presented in Edvard Isto's much-reproduced painting of 1899, "Attack," in which a brave but obviously distressed Finnish maiden, standing by a stormy sea, is about to have Finland's legal code ("Lex") torn from her arms by an extremely unpleasant-looking Russian eagle—led to a new concern in the outside world for the grand duchy's plight. Finland's culture was put on display at the Paris World's Fair of 1900, featuring "Karelian" architecture in the new Finnish pavilion and concerts by the orchestra of the Helsingfors Philharmonia Association, with works by Sibelius, Armas Järnefelt, and Robert Kajanus on the program (and Kajanus, mostly, on the podium). The growing reputation of Finland's architecture (and the firm of Gesellius, Lindgren, and Saarinen) was paralleled by the already established international *renomée* of the painter Albert Edelfelt; Axel Gallén (from 1902, Gallén-Kallela) won a gold medal at the Paris exhibition, his ticket, if he needed one, to his own worldwide fame.

The crisis with the Russians was paradoxically of great value for Finland's self-respect, as distinguished Finlanders went into temporary exile in Sweden and elsewhere: von Born had observed, "For us there can be but one way to go . . . read *Fänrik Stål*, if you have forgotten your Bible, and the answer will be clear." The sense of national self-assertion persisted even when the crisis slackened off, temporarily, after the assassination of the hated Russian governor-general Nikolai Ivanovich Bobrikov in June 1904 (carried out by a member of the Schauman family) and the Great Strike of 1905. The importance of connections with the Western world was more obvious than ever, and the Finland-Swedish intelligentsia, with its network of foreign ties, was in a particularly advantageous position to further such connections and, intellectually and literarily, to profit from them. This is not to say that the authors who came to the foreground in the first decade of the twentieth century had any real prospect (as musicians, artists, and architects did) of a substantial audience abroad, save in Sweden, although some few of them — like Tavaststjerna in the previous decade — may have dreamed of it; the same dream was revived later on by the modernists (who heaped scarcely justified scorn on the narrow outlook of their predecessors). Yet members of the circle around the journal *Euterpe,* and others, had already had their literary sights broadened; in the 1880s and 1890s the producers of serious literature were essentially borrowers from foreign literary currents (particularly from Norway and France). From Lybeck on, while the imitations or emulations continued, there was more of a sense of specialness, Finland-Swedish specialness, at a European level of accomplishment.

Ateneum, Euterpe, (Nya) Argus

The cultural journals that sprang up in Swedish Finland around the turn of the century were scarcely provincial. *Ateneum* (1898–1903) was led by the lively and inventive publisher Wentzel Hagelstam (1863–1932), whose house issued, among other things, the work of Londén, Paul, and Zilliacus. The *viveur* Hagelstam, whom Sibelius, with some irony, called an "innocent lamb," was an author himself, composing confessional novels; exiled from Finland by the Russians in 1903 (he gave a rousing account of his flight in his *Personer och minnen* [1923; Persons and memories]), he lived in Paris until 1919 and, because of his amorous escapades, became the object of admiration in Scandinavian circles there. The contributors to Hagelstam's journal — the first issue of which was dated 14 January 1898, in honor of Topelius's eightieth birthday — included well-known names (Juhani Aho, Edelfelt, Werner Söderhjelm, and Tavaststjerna, represented by his last piece published before his death, on Topelius) as well as figures shortly to make their mark, again from both sides of the language line (Yrjö Hirn, Volter Kilpi, Eino Leino, Arvid Mörne, Jacob Tegengren); from abroad, there was Knut Hamsun, who lived in Helsingfors during 1898–99 and was a friend of Hagelstam, and the Swedish nondoctrinaire feminist Ellen Key. From farther afield, *Ateneum* contained translations of Rudyard Kipling, Tolstoy, Verlaine, and the late Angel Ganivet, who had known Helsingfors well, having lived there as Spanish consul. (Transferred to Riga, Ganivet "yearned to return" to Finland, Hagelstam wrote in his memoirs, and after three months drowned himself in the Dvina.) In his *Cartas finlandeses,* published posthumously in 1905, Ganivet complained that "the exaggeration of the cosmopolitan spirit," together with the "obdurate antagonism between what is Swedish and what is Finnish . . . prevent[ed] the entire culture from producing the fruit it might," a statement as wrong on the first point as it is right on the second.

Among the causes of *Ateneum*'s demise, apart from a chronically weak economic base and Hagelstam's exile, was the appearance of an important rival. At first, *Euterpe: Veckoskrift för musik, teater, och skönlitteratur* (Euterpe: Weekly for music, theater, and belles lettres), founded in 1901 by music critic Karl Flodin, had occupied the musical field neglected by *Ateneum,* but shortly it expanded its range. The enlistment of such young academics as the Söderhjelm brothers, Werner and Torsten (1878–1907), and Gunnar Castrén (1878–1959) made it quickly into Finland's equivalent of Sweden's *Ord och bild*. It followed a more unified line than its Swedish opposite number, fighting — as Castrén put it in a tribute to the Danish critic Georg Brandes on his sixtieth birthday in 1902 — for "new paths of thought, new values in emotional life." Castrén himself was a great champion of recent Danish authors (Holger Drachmann and Johannes V. Jensen, among others) and of the Swede Hjalmar Söderberg; Emil Hasselblatt (1874–1954) took Norway as his special field, looking at such neoromanticists as Arne Dybfest, Hamsun, Hans E. Kinck, and Sigbjørn Obstfelder; Alexis von Kraemer (1871–1927), who had defended a dissertation on Villiers de l'Isle-Adam in 1900, was the all-important authority on French letters. (In 1904 his wife, née Agnes Palmgren, published the Swedish translation of Georges Rodenbach's *Bruges-la-morte,* which inspired one of Oscar Levertin's most evocative essays.)

The journal's impatience with a set of static moral ideals, and the occasional daring nature of some of its material (not just by the latest Norwegians but piquant verse by Bertel Gripenberg and a novella by one Nils Heyman, under the pseudonym of Ibsen's syphilitic Osvald Alving), brought charges of "decadence" against it, despite the careful intelligence of its academically schooled and, by present-day standards, extremely circumspect staff. In turn, Castrén and the cultural philosopher Rolf Lagerborg (1874–1959) protested against this derogatory characterization, observing that *Euterpe*'s emphasis was simply on the development of the individual personality, wherever that personality might choose to go. On one point, all the Euterpists agreed, according to Olof Mustelin, who has written an invaluable monograph on the journal: "The personality was for them the highest thing in life as in teaching. If this was decadence, they were decadents with all their heart and soul" (p. 322). To be sure, they not only brought out homemade "decadent" poems (such as Gripenberg's "Herod to Salome" and his poem on the exotic danseuse Loie Fuller) but made their readers conversant (if they were not already) with Baudelaire and such depicters of odd or fragile emotional states as Rodenbach, Marcel Schwob, Oscar Wilde, and, from Japan, the Irish-Greek-American Lafcadio Hearn. Anatole France was a special favorite, and Emil Zilliacus, whose debut occurred in *Euterpe,* later wrote that all the Euterpists were devoted to France's "skepticism, his cult of beauty, his philosophy of pleasure, and his pure, clear, supple French style" (Mustelin, 184). When the journal passed away, on 30 December 1905, it was mourned not only by its immediate circle but by others who appreciated its openness and polish. Its last issue contained, among other things, a chapter from a novel by Mikael Lybeck that would someday be a chapter in his *Tomas Indal,* a review essay (by Olaf Homén, another critical bright light) on a new book of verse by the Finn Otto Manninen, a poem by Arvid Mörne about "the dark countryside," and presentations of the French literary rage Remy de Gourmont and the Viennese architect Josef Hofmann—plus reviews of a selection of old Estlander's essays by Werner Söderhjelm (who approved Estlander's "cultural Swedishness") and of Andreyev's *The Red Laugh,* and Oscar Levertin's final verse volume, *Salomo och Morolf.* To the end, the mixture was stimulating.

Euterpe's successor was *Argus,* which did not appear until 1908; in 1911 the name was changed to *Nya Argus,* and the journal has existed until the present day. Among the Euterpists who continued with *Argus/Nya Argus* were Emil Zilliacus (its editor from 1911 until 1932), Gunnar Castrén, and the architect-essayist Sigurd Frosterus (1876–1956). Torsten Söderhjelm was interested in the project but set out to Italy on a research trip during which he died of typhus; the ambitious Werner Söderhjelm and the chemist and journalist Gustaf (Guss) Mattsson saw to it that the project was realized, with the support of the Swedish-minded newspaper *Nya Pressen.* Although the former Euterpists were drawn to the new journal, they felt it never quite reached *Euterpe*'s extraordinarily high level: Emil Zilliacus wrote to Bertel Gripenberg that *Argus* (in 1908) "has a certain mission, in my opinion: to be a Swedish cultural organ in Finland, of a lighter, less academic cast than *Finsk Tidskrift.* . . . Of course, it's quite natural that a comparison with *Euterpe* cannot come into question. But times are different now, and we are too" (Mustelin, 359). In its collection of talent and its setting of a standard for times to come, *Euterpe* was an equivalent—in an infinitely smaller literary world—to *The Yellow Book* in Britain.

Lybeck
A connecting link between the ethical rigorism of the 1880s (which, as it were, extended well into the 1890s in belated Finland) and the new century

with its regard for the uniqueness of the individual (and its regard for a polished literary style) is represented by Mikael Lybeck (1864–1925), one of the most deliberate (and sometimes tantalizingly laconic) authors in the Finland-Swedish canon. His life was uneventful; the son of the wealthiest man in Nykarleby (a great and good friend of Topelius), he had been sent off to the gymnasium in Helsingfors and had continued at the city's university and at Munich, perhaps with plans of an academic career; but deafness—growing worse with the years—made him decide for literature, which his family's resources readily allowed him to follow. In 1907 he built the handsome villa Vallmogård (Poppy Manor, the name he had given a dreamed-of sanctuary in a poem of 1901) out in the new and fairly exclusive community of Grankulla (Kauniainen), and evidently happily married, he resided there for the rest of his life, devoting himself to a small but constant production. Grankulla swiftly became a writers' and artists' enclave of note, beautiful in its surroundings and easily reached from the capital by suburban train.

Lybeck had made his debut in the 1890s, with poetry and prose, and had got special attention for the former; but in his slow maturation his short novel, *Den starkare* (1900; The stronger), was his first work clearly to bear his mark. (It shares a title, but not substance, with Strindberg's one-act *Den starkare* [1889; Eng. tr. *The Stronger*, 1906]. For his *Samlade arbeten* [1921; Collected works], Lybeck changed the title to the purist—and illogical—form, *Den starkaste* [The strongest].) In its dramatic concentration (and skillful exposition) one immediately sees how much influenced Lybeck had been by his Ibsen studies. The action takes place in a few dark winter days before and after the death of the mother of Robert Viding, heir to the family estate of Vidingfors. Correct and self-controlled, Viding is accompanied from Helsingfors to the dying woman's bedside by the violin virtuoso Edit Hernmark. At the manor they confront Kurt Hedelius, Viding's childhood friend, who has become an evangelist; Hedelius likes to speak in a biblically prophetic language, but he also depends to a good extent on his sexual magnetism—a type not unfamiliar to readers of Ahrenberg and Ina Lange. Edit, herself come from a home of religious sternness, is drawn to Hedelius and is not even put off by his attempt to rape her; she follows him, "the stronger" of the two men, to an unknown fate. Åke Gulin (p. 169) has observed that it is a variant of Ibsen's *Frun fra havet* (1888; Eng. tr. *The Lady from the Sea*, 1890), in which the past wins out over the present (and not the contrary, as in Ibsen): part of Hedelius's lure is the resemblance of his teachings to those of Edit's parents, killed in a fire—their deaths freed her to pursue an artistic life but left her with a sense of guilt.

The dark force of storm and winter in *Den starkare* (the blizzard in

Helsingfors with which the book opens, Vidingfors in its snowy isolation) returns in Lybeck's *Dikter III* (1903; Poems III), in which his simple but forceful symbolism and his tight-lipped pessimism are displayed, as in "Trötta träd" (Tired trees), with its grandiloquent close: "No morning waits for us, / For us, grown tired of standing in the storm, the storm defying," and in "Klockbojen" (The bell-buoy), whose speaker is lost in a fog at sea: "No living waves, / no living wind! / The bell-buoy rings." Lybeck was devoted to his mother tongue and its speakers, threatened as they were in one way and another; and his biographer, Erik Kihlman, dedicated a chapter (pp. 600–622) to the fanatic pains Lybeck took to achieve precision and brevity. (Lybeck's emphasis on reserve and lack of ostentation, even though put in a highly dramatic form, was characteristic of much Finland-Swedish literature in the years between the February Manifesto and the Civil War; the attitude also has strong symptoms of isolation and withdrawal.) The Belgian Maurice Maeterlinck's employment of that which is unspoken, "les silences," quite naturally made his plays appealing to Lybeck, and Lybeck's first effort for the theater, *Ödlan* (1908; The lizard), remembered largely—like Paul's *Kung Kristian den Andre*—because of the incidental music Sibelius wrote for it, draws heavily on Maeterlinck as it does on Ibsen. The constellation of the man between the passionate, cruel woman and her chaste, soft opponent is distinctly Ibsenian—see, for example, Ejlert Løvborg, Hedda Gabler, and Thea Elvstad. The play has a favorite Lybeck setting, the old estate, and a small cast like that deployed in *Den starkare:* Alban, the sensitive scion of the family; his older cousin, Adla (a name meant to suggest the green lizard of the Eyringe family's scutcheon and of the title), a lissome being who has awakened Alban's shy sexuality; and Alban's innocent cousin, Elisiv, who is killed in a fall, startled by a lizard on the mansion's steps. Alban succumbs briefly to Adla, but when she signals her triumph by putting on a green lizard's costume, he pushes her off a balcony and goes mad. In fairness, it must be remembered that the contemporary neoromantic theater of d'Annunzio, Gerhart Hauptmann, Rilke, and Rodenbach has similar extravagant symbolic action; the play is important for an understanding of Lybeck, who once again betrays his own gnawing concern with and aversion to the sexual urge.

Lybeck's relation to the theater is complex; his succeeding works for the stage are likewise flawed by artificial situations and stilted speech. Of the plays, two—*Dynastien Peterberg* (1913; The Peterberg dynasty) and *Den röde André* (1917; The red André)—are valuable as documents reflecting the time, dealing as they do with high-minded industrialists and their black sheep relatives, Russian-supporting opportunists. In the former, which

Lybeck gave the subtitle "a quiet comedy," the efforts of "His Majesty the Emperor's chamberlain," André Peterberg, and his weakling brother Ladislas ("stepcousins" of the refined Sebastian Peterberg and his lame brother Lorens) to bring the respectable branch of the family to a fall are thwarted; in the latter, "an edifying play," André Peterberg murders the "wonder-worker Akím," a Rasputin figure, and in his turn is shot by his late brother's widow, Lidia Vasilievna Peterberg, a sometime opera singer and femme fatale (her bosom "perhaps overdeveloped," her complexion "ruined by cosmetics") who has become a highly dramatic revolutionary.

Between the Peterberg plays came Lybeck's stage masterpiece, *Bror och syster* (1915; Brother and sister), in which the demanding theater critic Olaf Homén admired the "astonishing richness" of "the psychological course of events" and "the moral process of development." Per Ennius, the good-hearted brother of the title, suffering from weak eyesight like several of Ibsen's characters, has let the conduct of the shipping firm branch he manages fall on the shoulders of his devoted younger sister while he makes imaginary trips around the world in his atlas; meanwhile, she has embezzled some of the firm's funds to aid the artistic career of the egotistical young man with whom she (at age thirty-four) is in love. At the end of the second act she kills herself; full of self-reproach, the brother attempts to take the blame for her theft on himself. The plot might seem banal, but by virtue of its intensity and the skill with which Lybeck suggests the pettiness of the town where the siblings have spent their limited lives, the play has shown staying power and found gifted champions; in the 1948–49 season at Swedish Theater, Axel Slangus, a major figure of the Finland-Swedish stage, gave the brother's role a memorable interpretation. *Bror och syster* is thus not just a closet drama. Subsequently, Lybeck wrote two more plays, *Schopenhauer* (1922), in which the young Schopenhauer has a vision of himself as the misanthrope of seventy, and *Domprosten Bomander* (1923; Dean Bomander), in which a churchman, old but still vigorous, realizes that he has thrown much of his life away as a servant of the organized church. Lybeck never denied the heritage he had received from Kierkegaard and Kielland.

His plays can be read as novellas in dialogue, and Lybeck was unquestionably at his best as a writer of compact narratives. In 1911 he brought out the novel on which he had worked, evidently, since early in the century, *Tomas Indal: En början och ett slut* (Tomas Indal: A beginning and an ending), the story of the last months of a physician, alcoholized and his training never really completed, who has returned to the small town of his birth—another of Lybeck's visits to Nykarleby. An aging cynic, Indal might be saved by the love of the town's book dealer, Rut Bertels, who understands his intelligence—but she fears sexuality, having once almost been subjected to a gang rape by the crew of her father's ship and saved by Romarbacken, a boyhood friend of Indal who has gone to sea. Charming as he is, Indal is offered erotic salvation by a little waitress but refuses to take advantage of her innocence. Perhaps a partial portrait of the self-defeating Paul Werner Lybeck (1861–1911), the author of a collection of Ostrobothnian stories published posthumously by his brother, Indal is tormented by the knowledge that he has never realized his gifts; the book's most often quoted passage is Indal's outcry: "I envy all those who have used their powers to the full. It does not matter for what—I envy all of them, all of them." In an unnecessary errand of mercy to the sailors of an English steamer, caught in the ice offshore, Indal—more and more unstable, resembling the Nagel of Knut Hamsun's *Mysterier*—hears footsteps behind him and shoots his unknown pursuer; then he collapses in the cold to die. The pursuer is Romarbacken, who has gone out over the frozen sea to save him. For all its melodrama, *Tomas Indal* is a little classic of desperation, marked by the laconic hinting at which Lybeck had become ever more skillful: for example, does Indal know it is Romarbacken he has shot? The reader is never told.

Hennerson (1906), "the story of a hired man," is another illustration of Lybeck's belief that religious fanaticism and eroticism are part and parcel of each other (as in the case of the lay preacher Kurt Hedelius of *Den starkare*). But in his way, Hennerson is an honorable and even admirable man who drowns himself when he understands that he has almost forced himself on a "bride of Christ," one of his followers (with a cruciform birthmark on her breast). Hennerson acts not in despair but rather in atonement: singing a hymn, he walks "in a straight line" into the water. In *Breven till Cecilia* (1920; The letters to Cecilia) the author of the correspondence, Sven Ingelet, drowns himself too, throwing himself overboard from a Hamburg-bound steamer after he has discovered that Cecilia has betrayed him with an old schoolfriend of his—or, rather, has taken up that affair again after a happy winter she and Ingelet have spent in Sicily. The plot, as usual in Lybeck, sounds banal in retelling; yet Lybeck's revelation of Ingelet in his letters—naive, vain, learned unto pedantry, suddenly awakened to love in middle age—has nuances Lybeck suggested but did not give full form in his other spiritually virginal males, Robert Viding and Per Ennius. Lybeck's remark to a younger writer-colleague, Runar Schildt, that it was a pleasure at last to be rid of Ingelet, tips his hand about his identification with such figures.

After the death of Ingelet, Lybeck turned to men who had achieved the serenity of spirit the art historian searched for in vain. The protagonist of

Samtal med Lackau (1925; Conversations with Lackau) is not unlike the dean in his final play, an old man unbroken by life and even amused by it, the baron whose daughter, Frida, joined the sectarians of Hennerson's band in the earlier novel. There Lackau found words more of respect than comprehension for the evangelist: "That Hennerson was a personality, Frida, an earnest personality who meant well. To a certain degree exalted, that's true, but devoted to duty and solid!" Here Lackau — to whose role of a miniature Goethe his patient friend Uggelberg plays Eckermann — is deeply humane, sometimes pompous, often obtuse, and incapable of understanding that his old world has been shattered forever while "the new one has run over him," in Uggelberg's formulation.

The air of good-natured resignation emanating from the last book Lybeck wrote should be taken with a grain of salt; perhaps he had given his deepest view of existence in the poem cycle that grew out of his horror at Finland's Civil War, *Dödsfången* (1918; The prisoner of death). The fictive speaker of the eighteen poems is a mortally wounded man in a field hospital, one of the volunteers from Finland who fought in Germany as members of a light infantry battalion. Even as the veterans of the unit were welcomed in Finland by sympathizers with the Whites (they provided an officer cadre for Mannerheim's White army), Lybeck — beyond question a supporter of the White cause — published the little book, which seemed to express a distrust of all human effort. The dying man reflects:

> Dream of Freedom! Fragile as a dragonfly's
> wing you were, bright-blue and shimmering.
> Force is the reality that's left.
> Darkness and force. But the stars are lit on high.

Johannes Salminen called the collection one of Finland-Swedish literature's "great humanistic documents" ("Aspekter på inbördeskriget," 93); it is marred, to be sure, by sentimental tones in its visions of a beloved at home in Finland, just as much of Lybeck's other work betrays a weakness, amid all its subtlety, for overly obvious effects. Nevertheless, Lybeck possessed a disciplined artistry, a sense of the seriousness of the literary undertaking, that Finland's Swedish literature may not have seen since Runeberg, and he created a Finland-Swedish literary type that would appear again and again, the inevitably lonely man.

Mörne

Loneliness is a word that often appeared in the work of Arvid Mörne (1876–1946) as he grew older; his early career, on the contrary, was marked by his repeated attempts to struggle for the greater good of his nation and his linguistic group. Mörne was born in Kuopio in "the heart of Finnish Finland," where his father was a director of customs, but when Mörne was six, the family moved to Nystad (Uusikaupunki), on the Gulf of Bothnia, and "lived literally on the border between Swedish and Finnish," as Hans Ruin put it (*Mörne*, 28). After schooling at Helsingfors, he entered the university, where he would someday be docent in Finland's literature (1913–43), but his studies were desultory at first because of his political and social concerns. His matriculation took place the year Nicholas II came to the throne: he was soon involved in the resistance movement against czarist collaborators and officials (his first biographer, Hans Ruin, tells how he almost assassinated a Helsingfors police commissioner and asked the chemist and journalist Guss Mattsson how to make a bomb for use against Governor-General Bobrikov), and his patriotism remained a constant throughout his life. At the same time, he was keenly aware of social injustice, although he never became a member of the Socialist Party, and often spoke on behalf of the working class, an element in his public activity reflected in his third verse collection, *Ny tid* (1903; New time), with "Den röda fanan" (The red banner), in which he tells "the gray and despised Finns," once the cannon fodder of Sweden's army: "Today the drums are beat no more, and pikes no more are drawn, / The flag of red's unfurled to greet the springtime and the dawn."

In the poem "Vår tid" (Our time) he sounded still more revolutionary, proclaiming: "Our time's the red time of revenge, when the masses will repay / The blows which they, through centuries, have received." Mörne could be a wonderfully exciting poet, writing, though, in a language the vast majority of Finland's workers did not understand. The culmination of his career as a fighter for the masses came during the Great Strike of 1905, when he barged into the chambers of Bobrikov's successor, Obolenski, demanding that he leave the country and Finland's Senate resign. Another, related side of his activism was his contribution, as an heir to the teachings of Freudenthal, to the movement for adult education in the Swedish-speaking countryside; in order to further this program, he was principal of the "people's school" at Finns, in Esbo (Espoo), just west of Helsingfors, for ten years (1899–1909). He was at last forced to resign, although he continued for two more years as a teacher; his political and religious standpoints were too radical for his constituency. The title of *Döda år* (1910; Dead years) shows how deeply disappointed he was at the failure of much he had stood and fought for; he did not realize, he said in "Efter striderna" (After the struggles), that it was only in his own eye "a sky shone blue" and only in his own soul "a longing sang ... / To storm the tyrants' citadels."

Erotic attachments are often enough described in the young Mörne's work, from his debut book, *Rytm och rim* (1899; Rhythm and rhyme), on, and apparently they offered little relief; the "Young Beloved" addressed in *Döda år*, standing unveiled before him "like Aphrodite," does not realize he is "broken in [his] being's root." Mörne was an irritating figure, making enemies on several fronts all at once; to conservative Finland-Swedes, he seemed to be a promulgator of class warfare; he was disliked by many Finns because of his insistence on the preservation of not just Swedish culture but of "the Swedish earth" (i.e., traditionally Swedish-speaking sections) in Finland. (He was anything but blind to Finland's other national literature, however; his monograph on Kivi's *Seitsemän veljestä* [1911] is a milestone in the presentation of that classic both to Finland's Swedish speakers and to a larger Scandinavian audience.) As for his anti-Russian efforts, he felt that they had been in vain, too; the Russian hand had grown heavier again, and the Russian presence in Helsingfors much more obvious, following the apparent success of the Great Strike.

A consolation for Mörne came (as it would for many another Finland-Swedish author) in an almost mystical contemplation of nature, in his case, the Nyland skerries, the piece of Finland he, lacking a clear provincial identification, chose as his own (while living during the academic year in Grankulla). This contemplation was the stuff of *Skärgårdens vår* (1913; The skerries' spring) and *Sommarnatten* (1916; The summer night). The Civil War of 1918 and the declaration of Finland's independence brought about a mixed reaction in Mörne: disgusted shock at the much-reported atrocities committed under the Red banner, muted rejoicing at the prospect of a new nation, and, before all else, an awareness of the responsibility independence entailed, as expressed in "Plöjaren" (The plowman), in *Offer och segrar* (1918; Sacrifices and victories): "But where, bent down, he strides along, the plow must wage its silent fight, / The earth is tamed, and thereby a people raised toward the light." The danger both in *Offer och segrar* (where a plea is made to Åland not to leave Finland for Sweden) and in *Höstlig dikt* (1919; Autumnal poem) is that Mörne might become the victim of his gift for poetic proclamations or, then, for an unceasing celebration of the beauties of the seacoast: "but the morning sun awakes on its bed of roses, / And the wind begins to play and the wave to find its note," or "With flocks of wandering breakers / Lady June wades onto land." Also, as often in Mörne, he put his masochism on display: "My heart's a white-hot iron on the anvil, / To suffer torments is my being's goal."

A lyric silence ensued; when Mörne returned to poetry—in *Vandringen och vägen* (1924; The wandering and the way)—he had undergone, as

Johan Wrede argued in his study of 1968, a "poetic renewal," in which he experimented with the innovations of the modernists (for whose works he showed sympathetic fair-mindedness in his reviews), using free verse and Edith Södergran's effective catalog technique. Turning to larger existential or even metaphysical problems, he expanded the theme of loneliness, to which he had long been drawn, in "Tystnad" (Silence), from *Morgonstjärnan* (1928; The morning star):

> As the salamander's drawn to the flame of fire,
> As the swallow seeks the light bed of the air,
> I long to go back to my element
>   Of never-broken, timeless, holy silence.

But Mörne could not suppress the indignation that had been quiescent during the 1920s; in the 1930s he responded to the growth of dictatorships in Europe (and the threat of the fascist Lappo movement at home) and in *Atlantisk bränning* (1937; Atlantic surf) apostrophized Heine, who "should have lived today — when bards complain / Like swans put out to die in winter ice," while in "Fatum" (Fate), from *Över havet brann Mars* (1939; Above the ocean burned Mars), Hitler was costumed as Napoleon in a poem about the "Conqueror bent over the map of the world." Nineteen collections of Mörne's verse were published during his life, and a twentieth, *Solbärgning* (1946; Saving the sun), came out posthumously. Mörne admired the free-wheeling imagery of the modernists but had little of it himself: the sphinx and the pyramid (from the title poem of the last collection published during his lifetime, *Sfinxen och pyramiden,* 1944) are time-honored symbols of the vanity of human wishes, which "speak to the world come after / In riddles without reply"; in fact, he does not present riddles but elicits respect because of his forthrightness. Some of his vast personal embitterment arose from his perception that he was not sufficiently appreciated in his own time; he stood first in the shadow of Gripenberg and Hemmer, both more musically seductive, and then of the modernists. Yet, by the very force of his personality, which permeates all his collections, he remains a major moral voice in the minority's literature.

The plays of Mörne are negligible as works for the stage, informative in their reflection of his basic fairness of mind — *Fädernearvet* (1918; The fathers' heritage) demonstrates how the sometime singer of the Red flag could appreciate the ideal side of the Finland-Swedish patricianate. His prose narratives are a mixed bag, addressing national (and minority) problems or personal cruxes with his usual energy but hampered by a sometimes wooden style and narrative technique. *Den svenska jorden* (1915; The Swedish earth) pillories the landowners who sell off traditionally Swedish territories in Nyland to Finnish-speaking interests, a topic to which Mörne returned, in *Atlantisk bränning,* with the poem "Tidningsklipp" (Newspaper clipping): "Note: the people [there are] patriotic, like to work, / Low living standard, modest salaries." *Den svenska jorden* was the opening of a trilogy called, collectively, *Strandbyggaröden* (Shore-dweller fates); its two later volumes (both from 1917) likewise show the admiration Mörne gave those who, like himself, wholeheartedly adhered to a cause, however hopeless: in *Lotsarnas kamp* (The pilots' struggle) he approached justifiable propaganda as he described a recent event, the strike of the Finnish pilot service against the Russians in 1912; *Från fjärdarna* (From the bays) was a gallery of four portraits of hard-bitten skerry dwellers. *Inför havets anlete* (1921; Before the sea's countenance) and *Kristina Bjur* (1922) are historical tales, the one taking place in the Åbo skerries after the great fire of 1828, the other set in Ostrobothnia during the Russian invasion of 1713 and dealing with an unhappy marriage, a subject Mörne knew well from his own life. *Klas-Kristians julnatt* (1923; Klas Kristian's Christmas night), with its hymn of praise to isolation, ends with a suicide, like *Kristina Bjur; Ett liv* (1925; A life) was still more plainly personal (but not a roman à clef), the story — to paraphrase W.N.P. Barbellion — of a disappointed man, an account of shattered ambitions and ultimate resignation, an unintentional sequel to Tavaststjerna's *Barndomsvänner.* It concludes with the Great Strike of 1905, which may have been Mörne's moment of greatest fulfillment: "The great struggle was finished, a smaller, more obscure one began."

Ett liv is complemented by Mörne's essays, *På finländsk grund* (1927; On Finnish ground) and the tellingly titled *Det övergivna samvetet* (1943; The deserted conscience), utterances by a stubborn man who demanded much of himself and others: "The human conscience is the only ineluctable reality bearing witness to the existence of a God." *Det förlorade landet* (1945; The lost land), his last prose book, is primarily an assembly of stories or reflections about Porkala, the headland west of Helsingfors, evacuated for Soviet occupation in the armistice of 1944 (and returned in 1956). In it Mörne expressed a doubt that, three hundred years after the end of the Second World War, thought or sympathy would be given to its victims or survivors, any more than his own contemporaries recalled the Thirty Years' War (on which he quotes Schiller's history). Nevertheless, he asked his reader to remember "their loved ones who had fallen." "What you lost with them was a loss for humanity." To the end, Mörne was the sincerest of rhetoricians.

Celebratory Poets: Procopé, Tegengren, Emil Zilliacus

Unlike Mörne, Hjalmar Procopé (1868–1927) did not want to belong to a cause or have a cause belong to him: although (in Sven Willner's words) "the most sought-after writer of festival poetry in Swedish Finland during the first two decades of the twentieth century" (p. 47), he was philosophically rootless. He enjoyed — as he said in a poem from his second collection, *Mot öknen* (1905; Toward the desert) — playing the role of the prodigal: "And were I given once more my youth-time's wine / I'd laugh defiantly," enjoy the cup, "and settle down once more amidst the swine." The son of a general in the Finnish military, Procopé was an apple that fell far from the tree, earning his keep as a not very effectual newspaperman (among other jobs, he held the late Tavaststjerna's post in Björneborg). His *Dikter* (1900; Poems) did not make much of a splash; his collection of 1905 had to be published in Sweden because some of its poems upset the censor in Finland. (No activist, Procopé was still a good patriot.) The critical success of the volume, however, and the premiere of his biblical verse play, *Belsazars gästabud* (1905; Belshazar's feast), at Swedish Theater (one more drama to which Sibelius contributed incidental music) persuaded him that he could live as a professional writer in Helsingfors, his home city. He did so until 1923, when he became the first occupant of Diktarhemmet (the Poet's Home), the Flensborg House in Borgå, a dwelling designated by Finland's Swedish Authors' Union for a writer regarded as a Finland-Swedish *poeta laureatus:* Procopé was qualified, among much else, by his cantata written for the university graduation of 1907, "Vid frågornas port" (At the gate of questions), and included in his collection *Röda skyar* (Red clouds) from the same year. Thereby he had acquired a reputation as an intellectual and reflective poet; in the cantata he saluted skepticism itself. The same skepticism, or relativism, was apparent in his suite about poverty, "Trasparaden" (The ragged parade). Once again, he confessed his inability to give himself wholeheartedly to a pressing cause: "I call the poor man my brother, / Yet I cannot stand his smell," and "I feel very sorry for beggars, / But love them I cannot," and "I sit at the rich man's table / And feel myself safe and free," yet "I feel quite at home 'midst the rich folks / But give them love I cannot." Even in his vision of a fin-de-siècle paradise, Procopé sees himself alone: if he were transported to "Den vita staden" (The white city), where "white souls" walk "on paths between black cypresses and buildings pillar-cool," he would still be as unattached as he had been on earth: "And if some day we shall meet there amidst the cooling mists, / We'll pass each other by silently as all the rest have done."

Much in Procopé's verse is reminiscent of more famous poets of the time: just as Wilde's *Salome* had figured in *Belsazars gästabud,* so the fascination with Old Testament themes of Oscar Levertin and Gustaf Fröding is readily discernible. (Procopé published a tribute to Fröding in *Under stjärnorna* [1913; Beneath the stars].) His knowledge of a third important Swedish poet of the 1890s, Erik Axel Karlfeldt, comes out in his verse techniques: long and heavily rhythmed lines, unusual rhymes, striking and often colloquial turns of phrase; but he may have learned these habits from Rudyard Kipling, too. It should be added that Procopé was distinctly philo-Semitic; in *Vers och visa* (1909; Verse and song) there are translations of three "Songs of the Ghetto" by the Yiddish poet Morris Rosenfeld, and *Oväder* (1910; Tempest) concludes with Procopé's versions of poems by Heine; he had already made a free rendering of *Deutschland: Ein Wintermärchen* (1906), emulating Otto Manninen's Finnish translation of two years before. In his introduction to Heine's epic he hinted that the German poet would also have found an ideal target for his satire in the petty tyranny to which the Russians were now subjecting their once loyal grand duchy.

The admiring reviews given *Oväder* for its defiant picture, in "Finis Finlandiae," of the Russian Duma as a noisy band of evil, stupid men (who believe "Tashkent is Europe") overlooked the epigonic stuffing of much else in the volume; *Under stjärnorna* had patriotic and local-patriotic poems aplenty (including a cantata for the three-hundredth anniversary of the founding of Vasa), but its lyric weight lay in the cycle "Disjecta membra," Procopé's most extended statement about the now classic Finland-Swedish theme of loneliness. It opens with the line, "There is a ring drawn tight around our spirits," to which, it has been suggested, Edith Södergran may have alluded in the opening poem of her debut book, *Dikter* (1916; Poems). The aging bon vivant (a bachelor familiar with Helsingfors's café life) allowed himself some dejection with *I sanden* (1915; In the sand), which contained the hard truths of "I en gammal kyrkogård" (In an old churchyard) and the disappointed dreams of the suite "Vid åmynningen" (At the river's mouth), addressed not to "one of the giant streams" but to "a dwarfish brook, which tried / Its strength against a stone that blocked it"; its playful but tired spirit reflected a mood cultivated by the younger writers of the *dagdrivare* (idlers) group, just then flourishing in Helsingfors. The Swedish poet Birger Sjöberg would shortly (in 1922) immortalize *his* idyllic small town, Vänersborg, as "little Paris"; in the noise and smell (of gasoline) and inevitable fog ("where all is gray in gray") of Helsingfors, Procopé—"a free flaneur"—found a "greeting from Paris." He welcomed the White victory in the Civil War with stereotypical enthusiasm (in *Osamse strängar* [1920]; Quarreling strings) and memorialized his life in Borgå in

Diktarhemmet (1924; The poet's house) without adding to his poetic stature. Long associated with Swedish Theater as a dramaturge, he provided it with a good many texts; back in 1913 Olaf Homén predicted that Procopé's stage version of an entertainment novel by one W. A. Örn (1853–1913), *Inspektorn på Siltala* (1903; The manager of Siltala), might introduce a series "of modern and why not historical comedies and plays" from Procopé's hand which would "further our dramatic art and enrich our dramatic literature." In 1922 Procopé tried the historical side, with *Medaljongen* (The medallion), one more play about the Finland-Russian war of 1808–9. Homén was wrong: none of the stage works of this Finland-Swedish Edwardian has remained alive.

Jacob Tegengren (1875–1956) is another of those who made their debut around 1900 and who succumbed for a while to the lure of the Swedish 1890s, even taking a tentative turn toward the more perverse varieties of literary love in *Dikter* (1900; Poems), addressing "Dolores, child of night and pain," who makes the poet forget God in "His bright and shining mansion." It might strongly be suggested that Tegengren knew not only Levertin but Swinburne's "mystic and somber Dolores, Our Lady of Pain." Princesses of passion turn up elsewhere, too, in the early verse, as "Melancholy, you dark princess," who catches the poet in her net, or "Isa, Iseala," whose "red heart" and "yellow locks" and "love's warm wine" the Fool describes for a heartsick King in one of the short tales from Tegengren's very Levertinian *Miniatyrer* (1904; Miniatures); Bengt Holmqvist's observation about the belated 1890s experienced by Finland-Swedish poets in the early twentieth century is quite applicable here (pp. 21–22).

Very quickly, however, Tegengren changed course and put himself at a distance from Helsingfors's literary circles, although he had contributed to *Euterpe* in the year of its founding. He involved himself in the adult education movement, first on Åland and, from 1901 to 1915, as director of the "people's high school" at Närpes (Närpiö) in his native Ostrobothnia, then going on to a bank directorship in Vörå (Vöyri), near his birthplace of Vasa. Like Mörne and Procopé, Tegengren kept up a steady verse production, becoming a constant (but unostentatious) celebrator of his home province and writing religious lyrics, which eventually got him a place (like Runeberg, Topelius, and Stenbäck before him) on the committee for the Finland-Swedish hymnal. Once upon a time, Levertin had praised Tegengren's natural piety in *Nya dikter* (1903; New poems), writing that "something of the Reformation's loveliest and quietest devotion" lay in one of its poems, and Tegengren remained the singer of such gentle and reverent tones, seldom venturing into political or social realms. In 1925, as he characterized the poets who had emerged at the turn of the century, Gunnar Castrén diplomatically mentioned the monotony of Tegengren: "Time after time the same moods return, [and] only the attentive reader can perceive the nuances and the shifts" (p. 584). Three decades later, doing much the same sort of task for a Swedish literary history (1957), Castrén had not changed his respectful estimate of Tegengren's "contemplative, harmonious" poems, with their "basic tone of melancholy" (pp. 402–3). In his final collection of verse, *Sista milstolpen* (1946; The last milepost), he piously ended the first strophe of one of its poems with "God's smile," the second with "God's goodnight."

Tegengren also tried his hand at prose about his province and managed to ignore the hard facts that had made so many Ostrobothnians migrate to the New World; his son, Helmer Tegengren (1904–74), professor of Nordic cultural history at Åbo Academy, admitted: "No problems existed in my father's peasant society." In *Sånger och hymner* (1919; Songs and hymns) Tegengren had included a long catalog poem, "Österbotten" (Ostrobothnia), beginning, "You are wide-sight and distant-gaze toward the lands of dreams"; such exaltation makes it almost inaccurate to classify Tegengren as a regionalist—he turns Ostrobothnia into a province of his imagination. Yet he feared that his imagination did not reach high enough, a fear expressed in one of his best poems, from *Den svåra vägen* (1929; The difficult way): "I am not of the race of swans—earth clings unto my foot."

Emil Zilliacus (1878–1961) had been an important member of the *Euterpe* circle, but the distraction of academic demands (a doctoral dissertation in 1905 on classical mythology in recent French poetry and then a monograph on Giovanni Pascoli [1855–1923], the Italian and neo-Latin poet) and editorial duties (at *Euterpe* and *Nya Argus*) kept him from making his debut until 1915, with *Offereld* (Sacrificial fire). Thereafter he published nine other books of verse, the last in 1953. Among the poets of his time, Zilliacus had far and away the closest ties to antiquity; he was a noted translator, a Finland-Swedish Gilbert Murray, of Greek tragedy and in his monographs and essays was a popular and highly respected interpreter of Greek and Latin literature: his *Grekisk lyrik* (1911; Greek lyric, often reprinted) made his name as well known in Sweden as it was in Finland, a reputation to which his Mediterranean travel sketches also contributed. In his original verse he was a careful formalist, a fine sonneteer (perhaps because of his study of the French-Hispanic Parnassian, José Maria de Heredia [1842–1905], some of whose *Les trophées* he translated); further, unique in his time, he took up a practice that had fairly well vanished after Runeberg's early verse: he was a master of the Horatian meters. With his reverence for noble serenity, Zilliacus is very much in the Runebergian tradition; in turn, Zilliacus's quietly handsome and sculptured poetry must have made an impression on the classicist among the modernists, Rabbe Enckell, just as Zilliacus's translations of Greek theater informed the plays on Greek themes of the nonacademic Enckell.

Yet Enckell was intuitively aware of something to which Zilliacus wished to close his eyes — the cruel and orgiastic underside of Greek culture. Zilliacus had a "purity of heart," in Johannes Salminen's nice phrase ("Zilliacus," p. 88), which shielded him from the Dionysian element, a naiveté that set him off as well from another disciple of the Greeks, the Swede Vilhelm Ekelund (1880–1949). Also, devoted to the ideal of the golden mean (one of the essays in *Lans och lyra* [1933; Lance and lyre] is an imaginary conversation with Horace), he never let his cult of beauty become too sensual, and much of his poetry can simply be called ethical, dealing especially with loyalty. The poems of lament for his dead wife in *Minnesaltaret* (1936; The altar of memory) and *Vandring* (1938; Excursion) are among his most moving creations. In order to fill out the picture of Zilliacus's aristocratic and heroic Hellenism (which in fact resembles Goethe's and Tegnér's), we must remember that he had spent his youth in Viborg (attending the Finnish classical gymnasium) and remained closely tied to the outpost city; for him, it was easy to see the people of Finland, like the Greeks, beset by hordes from the east. Yet he was too refined an artist to write much patriotic poetry (with the exception of *Finlands festspel* [1940; Finland's festival play]). Zilliacus, like Bertel Gripenberg, may have seemed out-of-date, especially as modernism — with prescriptive contempt for traditional forms and traditional values — became more powerful, but he has had a surprisingly large progeny: if Rabbe Enckell learned from him, so did a still later poet, Bo Carpelan (1926–).

Finland-Swedish Decadence: Bertel Gripenberg

In his backward look of 1925 Castrén finds Bertel Gripenberg (1878–1947) one of the true spots of color in the lyric class of 1900; by 1957, while admitting that Gripenberg did not have "a deep and a large store of ideas, or a strikingly nuanced scale of emotions," Castrén still claimed that he "often possessed the great lyricist's ability to let the moment's emotion ring out full and strong." Castrén was trying to be fair to glories past: for a while, Gripenberg had had such enormous popularity in Sweden that he was a front-runner for the Nobel Prize in literature, once in 1917 and again in 1930 and 1931, when Verner von Heidenstam, a fellow aristocrat and praiser of the military past, appears to have been his strong supporter.

Although Gripenberg kept the relationship quiet in his autobiography, *Det var de tiderna* (1943; Those were the days), he was a nephew of the aggressive Alexandra; his father, Baron Johannes Gripenberg, was an official at the imperial ministry for Finnish affairs in St. Petersburg, where Bertel was born "in the shadow of the imperial throne"; and his mother came from another aristocratic lot, the Aminoffs, who — despite the Russian-sounding name — had been in Sweden and Finland since the seventeenth century. (Gripenberg never lost his royalist leanings; in his early verse he kept well clear of anticzarist outcries, and after Finland had achieved independence, he proclaimed his detestation of its republican government.)

Johannes Gripenberg became governor of St. Michel's province when Bertel was eleven and then moved to Helsingfors as a senator. Desperately unhappy in the Finnish Normal Lyceum, into which his father — an idealizing sympathizer with the Fennomane cause, like Alexandra Gripenberg and Alexander Järnefelt — had put him, Bertel demanded that he be enrolled in the Finnish Cadet School at Fredrikshamn; he had dreams of military prowess. But at the military academy, physically weak and used to "a soft and comfortable life," he was so miserable that, after the father's passing when Bertel was fifteen, he ran away. The death brought somewhat straitened circumstances — like Rilke, and Herman Bang, Gripenberg liked to romanticize himself as the last scion of an illustrious house, fallen on hard times and evil days. Sympathetic relatives put him into the gentler Nya svenska läroverk (New Swedish Lyceum) in Helsingfors, and there he met some of the young men with whom he would be associated in the *Euterpe* circle; his enthusiasm for the poetry of the 1890s, from Sweden, France, and England, and his sense of an elegant style recommended him to his new companions.

The first books of Gripenberg's poetry — he never made any serious sallies into other genres — provide a happy hunting ground for an investigator of the Finland-Swedish outskirts of the European decadence. *Dikter* (1903; Poems) opens with a Salome suite and is further decorated by poems to "Satanella," to Swinburnian "fair women," to "Dalilah," to the erotically poisonous orchid, to "Teodora" (loosely resembling the notorious Byzantine empress), and to "Green Eyes"; the next year, *Vida vägar* (Wide ways) discovered Paris and its manifold temptations, the "deserted splendors" of Versailles (made fashionable in decadent literature by Henri de Régnier with *La cité des eaux* [1902; The city of the waters]), and Spain (where Carmen's dance drives men mad). In the same collection's suite, "Höst-erotik" (Autumn eroticism), the insinuating presence of the actress Elli Tompuri (1880–1962) can again be detected — she had already inspired

"Salome." *Gallergrinden* (1905; The wrought iron gate) was Gripenberg's dream of a realm of beauty, a wondrous garden that tries to exclude the commonplace and the vulgar. "The distant murmur from a distant world" seeping through the "golden gate" of the collection's first sonnet had been heard before, by the artist Basil Hallward and Lord Henry Wotton at the opening of *The Picture of Dorian Gray* (1890) and by the pupils of the great painter in Hugo van Hofmannsthal's *Der Tod des Tizian* (1892; The death of Tizian).

A nobleman and an aesthete, Gripenberg also discovered that he belonged to a besieged minority; the collection's salute to the Swedish tongue becomes an appeal to its speakers to "fall for a hopeless cause . . . / To die in steel and armor," and "Germaniskt blod" (Germanic blood) is a gauntlet thrown in the face of "those who hate Finland's Swedes." (If a tinge of Gobineau's thought can be detected here, so can some simplified Nietzscheanism: "Humility [is] the teaching of thralls.") One wonders if the unspecified "enemies" in the poem on Eugen Schauman, the assassin of Bobrikov, are not the agents of the czar but rather the members of the Old Finnish Party who condemned Schauman's deed as the work of a Swedish-speaking troublemaker: "hatred of foes pursues you in death / But your honor will never die." *Rosenstaden* (1907; The rose city) is apparently directed to the young woman who would become Gripenberg's wife; she is called "Lindagull," a fairy-tale name suggestive of Hamsun's Iselin, the treacherous but passionate beloved of the medieval fantasy in *Pan* (1894; Eng. tr. 1920, 1956). The poetic affair ends badly; Lindagull, once a "daughter of the spring," is condemned to walk "the slippery path of shame." *Svarta sonetter* (1908; Black sonnets) is a series of Parnassian poems in the difficult form of which Gripenberg had not quite made himself the master; following the often dramatic octets, full of images of defiance or defeat, the requisite intellectual content of the sestets is often weak or repetitious. Addressing a dead fir tree, he says: "Oh mountain's fir, instruct me how to fight / Years and the storm, and mute await the night / And die and wither upright, even as you!" And, to the Grim Reaper: "I do not fear—whatever you give to me / Is known and old and tested frequently. / Calmly I press your hand, my darkling lord."

Defeat becomes a magic word for Gripenberg, who, in his next books, wrote from a new milieu: he had withdrawn to the Finnish interior, to Tavastland (Häme), where he lived for the rest of his life (save for an interlude, 1928–33, at Borgå's Diktarhemmet) on isolated estates, first as tutor, then as manager, finally as owner: the baron had found his natural habitat. In *Drivsnö* (1909; Drifting snow) he turns up, in one of his many self-dramatizations, as the man who once owned "rich men's clothes" but now rides along "scarred" and clad in "dark rags"; in a poem once much quoted he salutes "the sons of defeat, / The children of the sun that's set." The book has an epigraph from Rostand's *Cyrano de Bergerac* (1897), and Cyrano and Quixote are among Gripenberg's favorite poetic figures. Yet even the defeated have their pleasures: Gripenberg's were solitary wanderings (he tells his readers) through the stern landscape he had come to love ("Land, where lonely lakes reflect / The bluish splendor of soughing woods") and the hunt. (One of the great events of his prewar life was a trip Gripenberg made to England in 1913 as "second secretary of the bird-dog section of the Finnish Kennel club"; "amidst dogs, horses, and lords," he was considerably strengthened in his view of himself as a variant of the English country gentleman.) *Aftnar i Tavastland* (1911; Evenings in Tavastland) continues amid manors and woodlands, where he is often quite alone, save for the ghost (in the poem "En öde herregård" [A deserted estate]) of the former owner of the place, "a lost castle in a lost land"; similarly, he comes on "a lonely ski track which ends / At a suddenly failing brink."

Skuggspel (1912; Shadow play) and *Spillror* (1917; Remnants) mingle echoes of the earlier aesthetic collections and the Tavastland poems; sometimes tones from Baudelaire turn up, in "Don Juan" and "Don Juan in Paradise" and "Spleen" (Sven Willner cruelly wrote that Gripenberg was an epigone of a Baudelaire epigone ["Gripenberg," 78]), and sometimes the prophecies of Kipling's "Recessional" are imitated in poems on Finland's fate. (Like Johannes V. Jensen in Denmark, Gripenberg admired the virility and activism, if not the linguistic subtleties, of Kipling's verse.) When the Civil War broke out in 1918, he managed to get a commission as supply officer in Nyland's dragoons; feeling himself "a man among men," he underwent a renewal of poetic vigor. *Under fanan* (1918; Beneath the banner), *Efter striden* (1923; After the battle), and *Den stora tiden* (1928; The great time) all have to do with events of the war, its aftermath, and, variously, Gripenberg's exaltation or disappointment. Now he could bring to bear his knightly fantasies, his aestheticism (even as Ernst Jünger, he regarded battle, which he did not experience, as a thing of beauty), and his undeniable class hatred: in the poem "Klyftan" (The chasm), a word that would also become the title of Anna Bondestam's novel of 1946 (see chapter 9) about the defeated side in the war, the split yawns, for Gripenberg, between "the children of men in the land" and "the wild animals' red ranks." Gripenberg loved a parade; in "Den drömda armén" (The dreamed-of army) Finland's new army strides by, its "white banner borne by weaponed arms," and in another poem "murdered friends" are made to pass in review; but in "Dan-sen i Dorpat" (The dance in Dorpat) the Finnish Republic's peace with the Soviet Union is mocked ("Where's the cock gone that once did crow / When Peter betrayed his Master?"), and so forth. Gripenberg was not ready to forgive and forget. Nonetheless, before the last of the volumes of war poetry had appeared, he had begun — with *Skymmande land* (1925; Emerging land) — to write a relatively gentler kind of poetry about the pleasures of music (in a poem on the orchestra, to be sure, a lonely cello plays "manfully") and hunting (again) and simple dreaming. But neither here nor later — for example, in *Vid gränsen* (1930; At the border) or *Sista ronden* (1941; The last round) — could Gripenberg restrain his fantasies of war and daring and death: apostrophes to "a dead knight" and a "hero's death"; a fanciful vision of the soldier of fortune, Ernst von Mansfeld, riding mortally wounded into battle; Raoul Amundsen, "the old eagle," disappearing in his plane over an "icegreen sea"; songs about the honor of being on the losing side ("and bearing a ragged banner, / Covered with dirt / and smoke and dust and blood") and about dreaming a "Germanic dream":

Fathers in the hall of heroes,
Your dream is the best that can be!
Your prideful and manly heaven,
Your Valhalla belongs, too, to me!

With his ultraconservatism and his faithful clinging to poetic modes that seemed outdated, Gripenberg presented an easy target for criticism by the Finland-Swedish modernists. In 1925, however, he took a witty revenge by writing, under the pseudonym Åke Erikson, *Den hemliga glöden* (The secret ardor), unrhymed poems in free rhythms and with unexpected imagery, which — after they had been praised by Hagar Olsson and Elmer Diktonius as the work of a hitherto unknown modernist master — were revealed as hoaxes, intentional parodies of the modernist style. Johan Wrede ("*Den hemliga glöden*," 273) contends that Gripenberg had been drawn, willy-nilly, into the modernist orbit and that his poems may be regarded as involuntary but valid specimens of the modernist spirit. Had Gripenberg, with his undeniable verbal skills, allowed himself a serious shift of styles, he might have become a much greater poet, or at least a more varied one. Despite the hunting-and-shooting impression he gave in his autobiography, he had rather extensive literary interests, was an active translator from Finnish into Swedish, and made the first Swedish translation (1928) of the *Spoon River Anthology* (1915) of Edgar Lee Masters. But he was frozen into attitudes that would not allow a change, either of poetic style or of general outlook: he held Artur Eklund (1880–1927), an outspoken Finland-

Swedish proponent of theories of racial superiority (and the author of the hyperathletic *Idrottens filosofi* [1917; The philosophy of sport]), in high regard; he flirted with the fascistic Lappo movement of the early 1930s; and he was not at all immune to the disease of Nazism. (Eklund contributed the essay "Race, Culture, Politics" to the volume by various hands, sponsored by the "Party Delegation of Swedish Students," *Svenskt i Finland: Ställning och strävanden* [1914; Swedishness in Finland: Position and goals], an argument for a "Germanic spirit" that had been "the most powerful spur of [Finland's] development and the strong backbone in its national elevation.") Beneath his bluster and posing there was elemental fear of obliteration by the Finnish majority. Johannes Salminen proposes that the poem "Ett ensamt skidspår" (A lonely ski track) "affords a glance into the mortal terror which lives deep down in the Finland-Swede — most often avoided and denied and therefore unresolved" ("Varianter av utposttanken," 46). Gripenberg may have spoken for and to his minority in a basic way of which neither poet nor audience was conscious, nor wanted to be: "How light the flakes keep falling / on tracks that are covered with snow."

Reason and Wit: Hirn and Mattsson
Zilliacus ranked his work as poet, translator, and popular essayist far above his academic merits; one of his attractive features is the lightness with which he bears his learning, a trait he shares with other Euterpists (Söderhjelm, Castrén, Homén) and with Yrjö Hirn (1870–1952), who was not directly a member of the circle. Although never producing creative literature in the strict sense, Hirn was constantly creative in his essays and thematic studies. A member, again, of a notable cultural family, Hirn had become docent of aesthetics and modern literature at Helsingfors in 1898 and — beating out Söderhjelm — professor in that amalgam of disciplines from 1910 to 1937. Hirn's wide-ranging interests make it impossible to bring his twenty-odd volumes under a single heading; an Anglophile like his teacher Edvard Westermarck, he saw his first book come out in English — the *Origins of Art: A Psychological Study* (1900) — and *Det heliga skrinet* (1909) was quickly translated as *The Sacred Shrine: A Study of the Poetry and Art of the Catholic Church* (1912). What would the devout Lutheran, Topelius, have thought of this sympathetic study of Roman Catholicism by an agnostic? Other volumes dealt with the English eighteenth century (Boswell, Johnson, Swift) and the French (Beaumarchais, Diderot); fairly late in life Hirn made the inevitable turn to Runeberg and dared to be slightly irreverent in *Runebergskulten* (1935; The Runeberg cult), followed by other Runeberg publications of 1937 and 1942.

Hirn almost always wrote in a graceful and easily accessible style; he was a man of letters in the best sense, to be compared with his contemporaries Irving Babbitt and Paul Elmore Moore in the United States, save that his learning and linguistic resources were far greater and his desire to pontificate less well developed: his hallmark is a certain playfulness, and perhaps the most seminal of his books is *Barnlek* (1916; Child's play), about children's games and the importance of play in art. Hirn had a serenity of spirit that distinguished him from Rolf Lagerborg (1874–1959), another Euterpist and pupil of the relativist Westermarck; a professional philosopher, Lagerborg felt the same confinement as did Hirn within the limits of a single discipline. His enormous production contained works of a sufficiently belletristic nature (for example, the meditative prose of *Invita Minerva*, 1918) for him to be chosen to occupy the Poet's House in Borgå from 1945 to 1959 — but maybe more on the strength of his colorful personality and strongly disputatious intellect than because of any direct contribution made to Finland's Swedish literature. Perhaps the best way for a patient reader to gain some notion of Lagerborg's manifold interests and acquaintanceships is to dip into his autobiographical work, *I egna ögon — och andras: En bok om att känna sig själv* (1942; In one's own eyes — and others: A book about getting to know one's self). Lagerborg's habit of referring to himself in the third person is not necessarily a sign of modesty.

Finland-Swedish intellectual life during the decade and a half between the February Manifesto of 1899 and the outbreak of the First World War had still another figure difficult to fit into a literary-historical category, Gustaf (Guss) Mattsson (1873–1914). Only one book, on the Canaries, *En sommarfärd till de lyckliga öarna* (1907; A summer trip to the Fortunate Isles), came out during his lifetime; his tale of an interrupted trip around Africa, *En herre for till Zanzibar* (1914; A gentleman journeyed to Zanzibar), appeared right after his funeral: riddled with tuberculosis, he had dragged himself back to Finland. Admired by a large circle of readers, his "I dag" (Today) columns (916 of them) as star and editor-in-chief of the newspaper *Dagens Tidning* (1912–14) were collected and published, from 1915 on, as a major part of his *Valda skrifter* (1915–18; Selected writings). These columns, all beginning with the same little phrase, are a matchless source book for prewar life among the then still very numerous Swedish-speakers of Helsingfors; many are inspired by local or foreign events, some are actually prose poems or short stories, almost all are marked by Mattsson's special humor but sometimes give a hint of the pessimism, even nihilism, that lay at the bottom of his wittiness. A chemist by profession, Mattsson taught in that field at the university and the polytechnical institute, at the same time carrying on his hectic editing and writing career, as the columnist "Ung-Hans" for *Helsingfors Posten,* 1902–5, and for *Argus/ Nya Argus* among other organs, before embarking on the venture with *Dagens Tidning,* which probably shortened his life.

A comparable achievement might be found in the career of the Austrian publicist Karl Kraus (1874–1936), who single-handedly produced *Die Fackel*. But Mattsson, keeping his misanthropy well hidden, gave the effect of a much greater kindliness and never engaged in the literary polemics that were the acidulous Kraus's specialty. Instead, ever the curious newspaperman, Mattsson closely observed a city that was growing and, in the process, changing social and linguistic composition. (In a biography his friend and academic colleague Edvard Hjelt solemnly concluded that the breadth of his interests and perceptions presented a temptation he could not withstand [p. 247]. What would Mattsson, had he lived, have made of Hjelt's own maladroit role in the comic-opera effort to import Kaiser Wilhelm's brother-in-law as the monarch of a new Kingdom of Finland?) A spice is added to his columns by the circumstance that, as a native of Åbo and a lover of its medieval mystique, Mattsson regarded Helsingfors as a brash and noisy upstart. Even so, he gave the capital a special nimbus: a city of the (still quite Swedish) university, of restaurants filled with cigar-smoking and lustful Finland-Swedish gentlemen and buxom waitresses from Sweden proper (much sought after), of the concert hall and the opera (Mattsson was a gifted amateur musician), and of street scenes ludicrous (a lady loses her house key and is suspected of harboring immoral intents by male passersby) or sinister (an apparently senseless street murder). In his causeries on the international news Mattsson is aware of the approach of a world conflict: "It would be fine to experience the time after the great war, when the surviving insects would grasp the extent of their wretchedness, and exchange a cannon for a poem, an armored cruiser for a telescope." As for the money the Swedish government was spending on a new torpedo boat, "with it, Sweden could get back thousands of its sons from America." The secret of Mattsson's art was his sense of the absurd.

Autumn Days and Alm
A reader of Mattsson's columns will know the lay of the land in a novel that appeared in Stockholm in 1907, at the house of Bonnier, called *Höstdagar: En Helsingforshistoria* (Autumn days: A Helsingfors story). Its author used a pseudonym, Gustav Alm, understandably enough, for the little book presents a band of unusually unattractive characters: the indolent and somewhat supercilious Finland-Swedish narrator; the pious and fanatic Master

Säynävä, a Fennomane who demands nothing for himself but everything for his people; and Master Lohisaari, "the materialist" for whom the concept of honor does not exist; "I get pains in my stomach when I hear talk about honor," he says — "the concept is so strange to us Finns that we even lack a fully equivalent word for it." To these believable caricatures, "Alm" added others: the pussyfooting socialist Vallmark, whose socialism provides a cover for his own ambitions; Samson, the well-to-do and priapic father of the prim Finnish student and zealot Elli; Elli herself, who wants to see the streets awash with Finland-Swedish gore; and "little Angelica," the object of the narrator's feeble passion, who goes home to Sweden, hurling scornful remarks at the country and city she has visited: "The only impression I'll take with me from Helsingfors is that of a monstrous pig with gold-rimmed glasses on its snout." The narrator lets her go: "I had rather the same feeling I have when I return from a successful party." Meanwhile, Master Säynävä has come to a terrible end; walking with Lohisaari one dark autumn evening, he is brained by "a form in a broad fur cap," perhaps a drunken laborer who has taken the poor Finnish idealist for a "gentleman." (Picking up the murdered man's wallet, Lohisaari uses its contents to carouse all night long.) Miss Samson wants to put the blame for what has happened on "the Swedes": "For our country you are what Roman culture [which she detests as immoral] was for the whole world: infection with the plague, rottenness, misery. You ought to be scoured away with blood."

Höstdagar created a sensation, because of both the mystery surrounding its authorship and the nature of its satire, which, putting a plague on both houses, so confused an early reviewer that he took the book as a blatant anti-Swedish document. Actually, it reflected a creeping anxiety from the Swedish side, especially in the frankness with which it reproduced, in literature, extremist Finnish statements. In some respects, it resembles a notorious novel from Bohemian-German literature, *Die Vaclavbude* (1902), by Karl Hans Strobl (1877–1946), which takes place in a Prague made unsafe for German university students by Czech zealots; there, however, the German speakers are the brave bearers of a superior culture and the Czechs faceless members of a mob. "Alm" was much more evenhanded.

The identity of the author was revealed in 1915, through an anonymous review of "Gustav Alm's" new book, *Herr Agaton Vidbäck och hans vänner* (Mr. Agaton Vidbäck and his friends) in a tiny provincial newspaper. "Alm" was Richard Malmberg (1877–1944), a pastor's son from Ostrobothnia who had attended the university in Helsingfors and then become a primary school teacher; in time he would be appointed a member of the Swedish school board and then inspector of Helsingfors's Swedish schools. *Höst-*

dagar was based on Malmberg's experiences in the capital early in the century and portrays a considerably nastier side of life than the prosperous milieu from which the Euterpists mostly came; much of its action is centered on the student restaurant Osmola (whose Finnish-speaking cashier Malmberg, himself usually out of pocket, married).

In *Herr Agaton Vidbäck* Malmberg turned his jaundiced gaze on another place he knew well from his childhood, from early teaching assignments, and from summer vacations spent in Nykarleby (the putative site of Lybeck's *Tomas Indal* and *Bror och syster*). Vidbäck is a naive idealist who wants to win a place for his democratic notions in a narrow-minded society represented by his "friends" (the title is ironic) and thus is buffeted between the town's self-satisfied bourgeoisie and its socialist agitators, the most dangerous of whom is the unscrupulous Tobias Makkinen. The dream Vidbäck has of "conscious action with healthy conditions as its goal" comes to naught; but he retains his faith as he wanders through the night accompanied by a genuine friend, the history teacher Avellin, shoeless and coatless, thrown out into the weather by his virago of a wife. Avellin is doubtful that the world, "a huge monster, a terrible bubbling chaos, blind and brutal," will ever improve; but Vidbäck (who, among his misadventures, has been bloodied by a mob of quarry workers, incited by Makkinen) leaps onto a stone, waves his hat, and cries, "I greet thee, oh morning, morning of truth, dawning over the land of the future!" A critic, Erik Kihlman, wondered in 1928 (p. 72) which of the two, Vidbäck or Avellin, spoke for Malmberg, and previous reviewers had also found the book difficult to assess; it presents a blend of Anatole France's irony with the rowdier humor to be found in the cartoons, tales, and poems of the Swedish humorist Albert Engström (1869–1940), and it crowds too many characters into a small text, rather as did the Danish satirist of small-town life, Gustav Wied (1858–1914). Still, hovering between a sly analysis of hypocrisy and scenes of burlesque violence (for which the dyspeptic Malmberg clearly had a fondness), it presents what Avellin calls "the innards of this incomprehensible being [in which] our life is lit. It flickers there, bleeds, and is extinguished."

Kihlman further wrote that Alm-Malmberg's last book, *Fångstmän* (1924; Hunters), formed the end of a "kind of trilogy" ("Alm," 75). The place is the south Ostrobothnian skerries, and the characters are mostly fishermen whose way of life is whittled away by the farmers of the shore. In the longest of the stories, "Kungen och hans dotter" (The king and his daughter), an old man fights off these encroachments and, aided by his daughter and her sickly admirer (who dies in the process), saves the life of the island society's renegade. In another, "Zackris Matt," a fisherman attempts to live on land, only to realize that he must return to his old calling, cost what it may: "[Farm life] was a hell of manure and growth and envy and piggishness that men and Satan had created on the old sea bottom." (The Ostrobothnian coastline has moved steadily outward, leaving the ghosts of ships and skippers behind, as Lars Huldén wrote in a poem from the 1970s.) The third of the major tales in the collection is "Patrons juljakt" ("The master's Christmas hunt"): Klas Sebastian — a self-destructive and socially stranded member of the upper class — goes out for a winter hunt in the skerries and, in a grand and drunken gesture, shoots himself. These stories are framed by a prelude about the island people who refuse to understand that the sea has become "simply a profit-bearing financial resource" and a postlude, "Nu säljer Östman fisken" (Now Östman is selling the fish), a comical comment on the independent fisherman who has learned, in his small way, how to outwit modernity. The speaker of the prelude and Östman's paying summer guest are outsiders, but sympathetic ones; and Malmberg is far more friendly than in his other works toward the sliver of culture he describes: "Out here, you take care of yourself" is the opening line of "Kungen och hans dotter." Nevertheless, the "master," Klas Sebastian, has seen through the vanity of human wishes: he knows too much, he says, about "life's sickening hunt, with beaters, for the running hare of the Lord," a prey itself "not even worth a lead cartridge."

The tired wife of Klas Sebastian's good-hearted but dim-witted hunting companion says about Christmas: "Dark. Dark. All shall be dark, all is dark." Much about Malmberg remains a mystery: his view of life is undoubtedly part and parcel of his constitutional melancholy (he suffered bouts of extreme depression); yet it also reflects his sense of artistic unfulfillment (save for Wecksell, no Finland-Swedish writer of note has a smaller oeuvre) and his perception of what he and many of his contemporaries saw as the endangerment of the minority to which they belonged. Regarded in a larger context, he is a modest pendant to such pessimists on the grand scale as Huysmans and Strindberg: in Finland-Swedish literature he is distinctive among other prophets of doom, Lybeck, Mörne, Gripenberg, because of his Swiftian bite.

Local Patriots
Malmberg was not a regionalist, but *Fångstmän* helped even the balance in a regional literature still heavily weighted toward Nyland. Of course, the peculiarities of Ostrobothnia had gotten specific attention before, in the stories of Nygren and Paul Werner Lybeck, but with Alexander Slotte

(1861–1927) it came more fully into its own. Slotte, whose father had been the speaker of the peasant estate in Finland's Parliament, fashioned a Helsingfors career as a theater and book reviewer and the author of ambitious dramatic texts. His *En svag stackare* (A poor wretch, first produced at Swedish Theater in 1892 but not printed until 1914) shows the influence of Ibsen's *Rosmersholm; Halfdan skald* (premiere 1896, printed 1914) looks farther back in Ibsen's production, to the latter's *Hærmændene på Helgeland* (1857; Eng. tr. *The Vikings at Helgeland*, 1890). Getting back to roots, *Den stora islossningen* (premiere 1910, printed 1912; The great breaking of the ice) takes place in the "northern part of Swedish Ostrobothnia" the year after the Great Strike of 1905, combining Slotte's strong regional and folkloristic concern with an effort to demonstrate how "the silent struggle" for social reform (but without excess) has reached even distant corners of the land.

Slotte's place in literary history primarily depends on his songs and his stories of peasant life. Of the former, some — "När sommarns sol går strålande opp" (When the summer's sun all beaming rises), "Plocka vill jag skogsviol" (I will pick the forest's violets), and "Slumrande toner" (Slumbering sounds) — are standards in the Finland-Swedish repertoire, along with "Där björkarna susa" (Where the birches rustle) of his Ostrobothnian fellow, Viktor Sund (1891–1966). Very popular, "Slumrande toner" also gives a taste of the zeal for the Swedish tradition that elsewhere in Slotte's poetry (collected as *Sånger och syner* [1918]; Songs and visions) assumes still more outspoken form; the tones bring "the message of the forefathers to the sons" and urge a lighting of "the fires of the past" in quasi-viking turns of phrase. In his stories Slotte is the ever-faithful (and quite good-natured) son of his native Ostrobothnian soil: *Karlebybor: Historier från allmoge och småstadsliv* (1912; People of Karleby: Stories from country and small-town life) gives a mostly untragic and ebullient picture of local types that Slotte idealized a little; he built his stories principally around hard-working souls with a vigorous sense of humor — but also eccentrics and religious visionaries, of whom Ostrobothnia had a large crop.

Well educated and the son of a well-known father (of whom he gave a not uncritical portrait in "Flytlera" [Liquid clay]), Slotte had rather little empathy for the social misery to which representatives of the 1880s (notably, Oscar Behm) had paid so much attention: he does not ask for reform but rather views his people as the static salt of the earth, Finland's true strength. In *Solskensfolk* (1923; Sunshine people) the Swedish speakers of Ostrobothnia (and by extension, the whole of Swedish Finland) are the blessed folk of the book's name, who live alongside the "people of midnight," "melancholy beings seeming to bear the burden of some mortal sin" and prone "to religious ecstasy on the wings of mass suggestion." But when "the bear was let loose in earnest, and it was necessary to break the violence which oppressed our people," the two neighbors marched together to meet the foe. The characterization of the Finland-Swedes as the happy, reasonable folk, in this transparent post–Civil War parable, is a striking twist on Runeberg's argument about lighthearted coastal dwellers and the spiritually deeper people of the forest. And it is further interesting that, for the optimistic Slotte, his people all had "a bright faith in the future," while Lybeck, Mörne, Gripenberg, and Malmberg, each in his own way, predicted the minority's demise. The Ostrobothnia Slotte knew and loved was a relatively compact linguistic section, proud of its tradition of peasant independence ("free people," as Slotte liked to say, unlike those of the south, with its large estates) and little infiltrated by Finnish-speakers, protected by a clear language boundary.

In his local patriotism (which occasionally gave rise to exaggerated ethnic-linguistic praise) the physician Ernst V. Knape (1873–1929) can be coupled with Slotte. Together, Slotte, Knape, and Jonatan Reuter edited a widely distributed collection, *Toner från stugor och stigar* (1913; Melodies from cottages and pathways). It was sponsored by the Brage organization (named after the Nordic god of poetry), established in 1906, for the preservation and encouragement of Finland-Swedish popular culture, by the folklorist and musicologist Otto Andersson (1879–1969) — a close friend in student days, by the way, of Richard Malmberg. Often using traditional tunes set down by Andersson, Knape wrote songs that once again express loyalty to the home soil and unshakable faith in the virtues of peasant life, as in the little march beginning "Över bygden skiner sol i blånande sky" (Over the countryside shines the sun in the sky of blue), from Knape's *År och öden* (1918; Years and fates). Knape also produced several volumes of verse with greater artistic pretensions, the strongest of them the debut book *Akvareller* (1907; Watercolors), which contained, just the same, a marching song equivalent, in its inspirational quality, to *Men of Harlech:* "Män från slätten och havet" (Men from the plain and the sea), men filled with a "mysterious longing . . . / Passed as a heritage for a thousand years / From generation to generation." (That is: the Swedish-speaking Ostrobothnians had been there since time immemorial and were in no sense intruders.)

Like Slotte too, Knape essayed other genres: his play, *Biskop Thomas* (1917; Bishop Thomas), on an ambitious and criminal thirteenth-century prelate, was later turned into a historical novel, *Bispen* [1925; The bishop]); his tales, *Österbottningar* (1916; Ostrobothnians), less sanguine than Slotte's, take up the question of emigration to the great world outside: in the brief "Fähuset" (The cattle shed) Petter Stenvatten labors in the mines of the Transvaal to get money for his Ostrobothnian farm and contracts the tuberculosis that kills him. *På Vikarsvallen* (1921; At Vikar's dike), dedicated to "the youth of Swedish Finland," is a somewhat stiff (and surely tendentious) tale of viking days in Finland, when the people from "Svea's land," who have lived in peace with the country's aborigines, the Lapps, are confronted by "a new people with new weapons . . . from the East, [who] bear evil in mind," "men of a foreign race, called Finns." A novel, *Erik Falander* (1925), concerns the decline of an old mercantile house, under the pressure of a Finnish lumber magnate, Koski. (To the refined Erik, Koski is someone "who has come up from nothing by means of energy and cleverness, cleverness that nonetheless rests, perhaps, on a sort of unabashed lack of sense of responsibility and lack of a feeling for right and wrong.") If Knape is read today, however, it is for the sake of his poems, some of them clearly Topelian ("Björken" [The birch tree]), others, such as "Dansvisa" (Dance tune), using the traditional themes of folk song, passion given and passion betrayed: neither Ants nor Matts wants the poem's forlorn singer, who has given herself to both of them.

None of these Ostrobothnian regionalists could live by his pen, or wanted to: Slotte was a teacher, Knape a physician (and, from 1912 on, docent in ophthalmology at Helsingfors). Like Tegengren a central figure in adult education and like Malmberg (and Knape) starting his writing career late, with *Ödemark* (1913; Wilderness), Joel Rundt (1879–1971) then continued his extensive production year after year without much varying his Ostrobothnian landscape. In Tegengren's way, too, Rundt became more and more pious: otherwise, there is relatively little change in his language between his debut and his farewell, *Tala, o sång* (1968, Speak, oh song), save that, in a discreet concession to the practices of modernism, he sometimes abandoned rhyme. All is well made, all is muted; not only a constant restraint characterizes Rundt, but his ability to find ever fresh subjects in Ostrobothnian nature. He differs from a Slotte or a Knape in that he never strives for a directly popular mood and shuns the ethnic patriotism that inspired those more aggressive colleagues of his. On the contrary, he made a contribution to a drawing together of Finland's two language groups with his numerous translations, from the 1930s on, of Finnish lyric poetry, including the anthology of 1952, *Fågeln flyger långt* (The bird flies far).

Obviously, regional rhetoricism flourishes, a self-assertion justified if regarded from the standpoint of its time but seeming exaggerated or even offensive to later and forgetful eyes. Hugo Ekhammar (the nom de plume, "oak hammer," of Hugo J. Ekholm [1880–1955]) is an apt illustration. Born in Helsingfors, the son of a cabinetmaker sprung of a Nyland family of tenant farmers, Ekhammar was trained in Nordic philology at his home city's university and engaged in pro-Swedish activism with the paper *Studentbladet* (1913–17); both to support himself and out of idealism, he worked in the adult education movement in Ostrobothnia, and his experiences there gave rise to his novel *Det norrfångna landet* (1920; The northern land), in which the protagonist, Erik Ramm, is plainly Ekhammar himself. Ramm utters panegyrics to "the earth's most noble race, the lofty, bright tribe of the Germanics," and condescends (or worse) to the Finns, "the crude, poor, wild people, who came wandering from the distant Orient's dark lands" and were taught discipline by the Swedes of Finland. "Never, it seemed [to Ramm's disciples in his school], had one people saved and nurtured another so much, as had the Swedes, retrieving the Finns from the jaws of the Orient." Ramm thinks Nordic mythology is better suited to these "East-Swedes" (a then fashionable term preferred by Knape and Ekhammar, among others, to "Finland-Swedes") and gets into trouble with the ecclesiastical establishment because of his anti-Christianity; he is detested by the region's pentecostal preacher because of his arguments "for intellectual clarity," while his teaching of economic self-improvement causes the formation of a "clique of the well-to-do" and the local authorities against him, abetted by supercilious youths from the city who have come not to improve the lot of the country people but merely to study them. "Tricked by the masters of their home parish, not understood and betrayed by those who called themselves the hope of the nation [i.e., the students from Helsingfors]," the peasants "have the melancholy sense that their voice will not reach far, that it will die away without an echo." The book ends abruptly; on a summer hike in the Norwegian mountains Ramm receives a letter from the parish authorities, who ply him with empty compliments and ask him to resign.

Ekhammar's other novel, *Under torparsolen* (1922; Under the tenant farmer's sun), turns to the milieu in which his father had grown up; the "sun" of the title is actually the moon, by which the sharecroppers of Nyland must work to meet their quotas for the owner and to support themselves. The time is the 1870s and 1880s, and as in the first novel, it is unclear what the subsequent fate of the hero, with the talking name of Gustav Jordman ("earth man") will be: after years of "poverty, hunger, exhaustion, humiliation," he wants somehow to become his own master—but he intends neither to emigrate to the New World nor to grasp what he views as the greater opportunities of "the Finnish section," where he would forget his mother tongue. Presumably, like Ekhammar, he will devote himself to furthering the Swedish countryman's cause: "Hereafter the Swedish earth would be his master," a phrase echoing Mörne's title from seven years before. In fact, Ekhammar set out on a career as the "learned vagabond," for whom Swedishness had become a religion. Something pathetic, heroic, and zany attaches to the rest of his life, supported not even by a tight and specific regional bond. His homeland became a dreamed-of "greater Sweden," and his last work was quasi-history, *Det forntida Östersverige och svenskdomen* (1944; East Sweden of the past and Sweden-dom). Hans Ruin, who knew him in his days as a student editor, wrote in 1969 that he became "a relic, like Don Quixote with his ideals of knighthood" (p. 79).

Alongside Ekhammar's fate, that of Josefina Bengts (1875–1925) seems prosaic and as stationary as his was restless (she was an invalid from childhood on); the Nyland she depicts is altogether different from that in Ekhammar's second novel, albeit her best-known work, *Fäderna* (The fathers), came out in 1921, just a year before the saga of Gustav Jordman. She spent her life at the farm in Pernå parish her family had owned for generations (and thus she belonged to a class quite distinct from Ekhammar's landless forebears); thanks to the efforts of Mörne and Ossian Reuter (1849–1908), an older brother of Jonatan and the editor of the newspaper *Östra Nyland*, she broke into print early with sketches of country life, *I nyländska stugor* (1902, 1906; In Nyland cottages), followed by a quasi-ethnographic picture of Nyland life during the age just before her own birth, *Från vargtider och vallpojksår* (1915; From wolf's [i.e., bad] times and shepherd boy's years), about which she had learned every detail (and her details are many) from her father. For *Fäderna*, Bengts set herself a more ambitious task, a chronicle of the fortune and fall of a peasant family from the 1850s until the auction of the Smeds' goods and property sometime in the 1880s—they have been laid low by the greed (and resultant petty dishonesty) that Runar Schildt, in one of his eastern Nyland stories, had seen as a besetting vice of some members of the same peasantry. The book's title is taken from a poem by Erik Axel Karlfeldt ("Their name is not found in grand history's pages, / They lived in small conditions and in peace"), and Bengts again lets very little of the ascertainable facts of the fathers' lives escape her, down to the reproduction *in extenso* of legal documents (and their signatories). Her conversations (as in her earlier books) reproduce her home dialect, and her digressions provide, as before, a wealth of folkloristic detail from times when families were self-sufficient. Her characterizations are predictable: she admires the wise conservatism of the elders of the clan and is critical of later generations who will not cling to the old ways. One of these newfangled folk, the indolent Gustava Beata, "never dreamed of putting her foot farther than the skin-rug reached, or that bread should be eaten in the sweat of one's brow." Inevitably, "God's blessing [is] removed from the Smeds people," once they have sold their forests to a timber jobber—an act symbolic for decline in Nordic literature from the days of Ibsen on. Yet Bengts was anything but a pessimist and despite her awareness of the threats to her peasant society not only by economic forces but by Finnish penetration, she asks her readers to view the fate of the Smeds family as a warning but not a prophecy; the neighbors, returning from the auction "in the mild, sun-shimmering September evening," ask themselves, "Could you see anything finer than your home village on such an evening? . . . God be praised for home and hearth and everything."

Dagdrivare
The name of the *dagdrivare* literary grouping—it was never really a school but rather a community of attitude—is taken from the short novel by Torsten Helsingius (1888–1967), *Dagdrivare* (1914; Idlers), in which a well-to-do young-man-about-Helsingfors, Otto Bergius, leads an aimless existence of desultory studies and rather more persistent attention to the city's cafés and restaurants. Helsingius's little production of his twenties—supplemented by the memoir *Det var* (It was) two decades before his death—is notable less for its mild decadence or the account, in *Utveckling* (1915; Development), of the efforts of Bergius, after the shock of a syphilitic infection, to redeem himself, than for the mood the first book created of indecision and lassitude and for the views of Helsingfors the peripatetic student beheld, especially Brunnsparken and the prospect "out to the Oriental cupolas above Sveaborg's colorful reaches." The apparent cynicism of the *dagdrivare* may seem to be worlds away from the jealous love-of-place of regional writers contemporary with them; but in their way the former are also regionalists, almost parochial in their devotion to their city, or to the slice of its life they knew. In their attachment to the capital, as in many other respects, they are the heirs of Hjalmar Söderberg (1869–1941) in Swedish literature proper; Helsingius's *Dagdrivare* could not have been written without the example of Söderberg's *Förvillelser* (1895; Aberrations), *Martin Bircks ungdom* (1901; Eng. tr. *Martin Birck's Youth*, 1930), and *Doktor Glas* (1905; Eng. tr. *Doctor Glas*, 1963), or, for that matter, the Stockholm novellas of Bo Bergman (1869–1967); in Sweden, too, the name of a very similar literary current was taken from the novel *En flanör* (1914; A flaneur) of still another Stockholmer, Sigfrid Siwertz (1882–1970). (The idle

young Viennese in Arthur Schnitzler's *Anatol* cycle [1893] and his stories also had their part in the creation of the type and attitude.) But Finland's idlers had to confront a violence or at least a threat of violence their Stockholm opposite numbers did not (Malmberg's narrator in *Höstdagar* has been called the first of the *dagdrivare*), and their Helsingfors was distinctly different from the Swedish capital: it had its exotic Russian element, its gray and growing Finnish masses (which may turn up peripherally, while the city's Finnish middle class mostly does not), and what Malmberg's "little Angelica" perceived as its harsher, cruder air. But all this was forgotten in a concern about the missing crease in the boulevardier's trousers, a flirtatious pursuit of "respectable" young ladies, or an affair, brief or not, with the more accessible girls of a lower class and, maybe, another language.

Helsingius's debut book presents the *dagdrivare* in their basic form (if Malmberg had not done that already); in Henrik Hildén (1884–1932) there are elaborations, and even before the term became current, Hildén offered the type grown old, tired, and overrefined (thus showing the considerable connections of the idler with the European decadent of the 1880s and 1890s). Hildén's first and perhaps best book, *Indiansommar* (1910; Indian summer), shares a title with Sigfrid Siwertz's play of two years before (a comedy about a triumph of fresh will over discouragement and misanthropy), but Hildén's diarist, a famous painter, tries in vain to divest himself of artificiality through contact with the healthy, unreflective vigor he finds in the Nyland skerries. Hildén pursues the theme throughout his several books, for example in *Drottning Liv* (1913; Queen Life), in which his Henning Heger, wealthy and sophisticated, becomes a "succès mondain" all over Europe — but loses himself. (One wonders if Heger's name is meant to suggest Henning Berger [1872–1924], whose impressionistic style in his Stockholm novel *Drömlandet* [1909; The dreamland] was much admired by Finland's *dagdrivare*.) At last, in *Storön: En bok om havet och kärleken* (1914; The big island: A book about the sea and love), the narrator seems to be cured of his falseness by the inhabitants of the island of the title, "young and healthy and strong."

The collection of novellas, *Den röda frun* (1916; The red lady), demonstrates the weakness Hildén had for the neoromanticism of the 1890s: the title story offers a widow who once upon a time lived on a lonely estate, "always clad . . . in red, a wine-red silken gown with Venetian lace," and never attained the great love for which she waited — shades of Rilke's *Die weiße Fürstin* (The white princess) of 1898! After her death she appears to lovers, to teach them that "happiness is a *trompe l'oeil*, an illusion, which leads human beings to ruin." The lyrically vague style (not very convincingly imitated from the early novels of Knut Hamsun) is quite unlike the sharpness of detail to be found in the less ambitious (and less well read) Helsingius. Still another tale in *Den röda frun* is called "Författaren och självmördaren" (The author and the suicide); the author — named Hildén — asks if it would not have been better to shoot himself than to have written "a book about the sea and love." The collection ends with a letter to a friend in Finland, addressed as "Old idler" and dictated by a sometime member of a Helsingfors coterie who — in an effort, again, to give his existence meaning ("many were the times I longed to get away from the life [of] sad idleness at home, mine and yours and all the others") — has volunteered for service in the French army and loses his legs in battle. But he still yearns for Helsingfors, "the Esplanade where music plays and taxis and droskies drive happy folk out to the promenades in the park," that is, Brunnsparken. After producing less and less successful publications and taking a stab at scholarship (writing on nature in Swedish-language literature of the seventeenth and eighteenth centuries), Hildén took his own life.

The desire for engagement took a different form in the career of Ture Janson (1886–1954); more than Helsingius or Hildén, Janson, a professional journalist, was aware of the attrition of the Swedish-speaking group (which had become a minority after 1890, when half the population still registered Swedish as the mother tongue) in the city he had adopted as his own (he was from Åbo). In the book of verse *Mitt Helsingfors* (1913; My Helsingfors) he complained about being "a stranger in one's own city," for whom nothing remains "but to be a bold flaneur, / content with this outsiderness." (Two decades before, Juhani Aho's student from up-country, a Finnish speaker, had told about his sense of having come to "a foreign capital" in Helsingfors.) The sense of alienation Janson felt was strengthened by social factors: he was also, he thought, an outsider among the city's still very powerful Swedish establishment ("Behind closed doors all decisions are taken, / Behind closed doors all parties are held") and so interested himself in an altogether different part of the population, the dwindling Swedish working class. His efforts along this line (somewhat resembling those of Arvid Mörne and others in countryside adult education) are the stuff of his novels, *Inga medmänniskor: Fragmentarisk berättelse* (1911; No fellow men: Fragmentary tale) and *De ensamma svenskarna* (1916; The lonely Swedes). A decade later he concluded his factual report, *Boken om Helsingfors* (1926; The book about Helsingfors), with a chapter on Swedish workers: "a repudiated and abandoned group, stationed at an outpost in another linguistic milieu, and given constant opportunities either to deny or to assert its national [i.e., linguistic] character." (Shortly, in 1929, Janson moved to Sweden, leading a troubled journalistic and creative career, shadowed by his growing alcoholism: his dream, like Ekhammar's, of a common Swedish consciousness, existing on both sides of the Gulf of Bothnia, was a hopeless failure.)

The farewell book to Helsingfors, in its love-hate relation to the city, also looks back to another aspect of Janson's creative writing, his stories in *Knock me down: Helsingfors noveller* (1914; Knock me down: Helsingfors novellas) and *Journalisten Bergman* (1915; The journalist Bergman). In these books his protagonists, the student and newspaper artist Birger and the reporter Bergman, are alter egos quite different from the pedagogically inclined reformers Gunnar Holming and Bernt Bjelke, of the two socially engaged novels, and are cast in the idler mold: skirt chasers, café denizens, but always careful observers. Janson was good at taking swift looks at Finland-Swedish peculiarities: "as far as Swedish conversation was concerned, the pauses played an especially large role." But he was genuinely devoted to the bearers of the Helsingfors cultural tradition: his affectionate portrait of a professor of art history (Johannes Tikkanen) proves it.

In 1923 Henning Söderhjelm (1888–1967) — a son of Werner, and still another *dagdrivare*, with his novel *Lärospån* (1915; Apprentice efforts) — had migrated to Sweden, for a career in journalism as smooth as Janson's would be bumpy. Five years later, in the journal *Ord och bild*, he published a survey called "Modern Swedish Literature in Finland," in which he was particularly critical of the many and (by his lights) incorrect "Finlandisms" in the early works of Janson, an argument in which he followed the spirit of Hugo Bergroth's manual for the avoidance of "provincialisms" from 1917 ("Finlands moderna svenska litteratur," 58). But, Söderhjelm continued, Janson had subsequently become supercorrect; a reason for the curiously dead quality of his production in the 1920s and after may lie in linguistic inhibition. (Likewise, Erik Kihlman found that Janson's style suffered from "a certain mannerism" and "was scarcely the most thankful means for expressing what he long had had in his heart" ["Hr. X i genomskärning," 119].) The humanistic and pacifistic aims of his trilogy, *Verkligheten* (1923; Reality), *Maskinmänniskan* (1924; The machine man), and *Vänskapsbyn* (1925; Friendship village), were admirable; the novels gave an international dimension to the reforming instinct that informed the books on Helsingfors's Swedish working class. Yet the trilogy lacked the very seediness that enlivened Janson's accounts of *dagdrivare* days and nights.

Runar Schildt

In his survey Söderhjelm — who, like his famous father, tended to be magisterial — announced that those who debuted around 1910, "the 'idlers' and their comrades," had a set of characteristics in common: almost all of them wrote prose, "their prose [was] surer, more solid, more artistically controlled than had been the practice until now in Finland" (Söderhjelm blithely ignored Lybeck), and they sought to depict "situations where feelings of disappointment and isolation were mingled with a skeptical-ironic guardedness toward the whole of life." And "Runar Schildt [was] foremost among them" ("Finlands moderna svenska litteratur," 60). Schildt (1888–1925) is one of Finland-Swedish literature's major figures, for all the smallness of his oeuvre and the brevity of his career; his production consists of eight novella collections or independent tales, from 1912–20, and three plays written not long before his suicide. He had toyed with the idea of self-destruction for a long time, having discovered the circumstances surrounding his father's mental deterioration and death, and he had come to believe, as well, that he could no longer write. His friend Hans Ruin has also mentioned his "unbelievable desire for perfection" ("Runar Schildt," 22) and his aversion to and fear of those who were tougher and stronger than he: the combat between the dreamer and his bullying cousin in one of his final stories tells much about him.

Schildt's first and second collections are those most closely connected to the world of the *dagdrivare*. The title story of *Den segrande Eros* (1912; Eros victorious) is placed, to be sure, on an estate near Åbo in the 1820s, telling of the ramifications of the stranding of a Swedish theatrical troupe in that "Garden of Eden." (As noted above, in connection with Ahrenberg, Schildt could recreate the language and social practices of the past with remarkable skill.) But the other tales in the book grow out of contemporary Helsingfors or a nearby and financially failing estate or the modest bathing resort life of Lovisa, the little eastern Nyland town from whose vicinity Schildt's mother had come. Schildt's unforgettable types are already present: the shy youth and the exotic charmer in the title story and in "Det gynsamma ögonblickets gud" (The god of the favorable moment); the girl who yearns for a fuller life than her family can or will allow her in "Raketen" (Eng. tr. "The Rocket," BFF, 1988); the variously superficial or sensitive students and the young noblemen, one determined to enjoy himself while he can, the other devoted to the dying cause of the estate, in "Mot skymningen" (Toward the twilight); or, again, the inexperienced youth falling victim to a self-assured young woman in "Ett nytt liv" (A new life). In a kind of pendant, *Asmodeus och de tretton själarna* (1915; Asmodeus and the thirteen souls), Schildt used a legend in Anatole France's manner (a minor devil wagers he can win a baker's dozen of souls during a three-day visit to Helsingfors) to give a tour through the city's boardinghouses, apartments, and offices; an unforgettable coda to the long and episodic story is the wonderful "En sparv i tranedans" (A sparrow in the crane dance, a title borrowed from J. C. Hostrup's Danish comedy of 1845), about a boy's humiliation at a school dance and after.

With *Regnbågen* (1916; The rainbow) and *Rönnbruden och Prövningens dag* (1917; The ash bride and The testing day) Schildt—always conscious of his double heritage, his late father's well-born line and his mother's peasant ancestry—turned to eastern Nyland again and in "Regnbågen" (which is set in Lovisa during the Crimean War, when a British-French naval squadron terrorized the Gulf of Finland) made another bow to the historical tale; the story deals not with war but with the small town itself, the abuse of the weak by the strong, and the blessedness of the biblical poor in spirit. The brace of stories takes place in "Räfsbacka," a little community just outside Lovisa. "Rönnbruden," with a touch of the supernatural, is the balladlike story of a girl wed, by a half-breed gypsy's curse, to a tree; "Prövningens dag" (Eng. tr. "The Testing Day," *Swedo-Finnish Short Stories, 1974*) is an account of the legless beggar who momentarily transforms the inhabitants of Räfsbacka, even making a dent in the niggardliness and self-confidence of the wealthy and heavy-handed Kuggas. (The story is not sentimental; the beggar is discovered by Kuggas, to his relief, to be not Jesus but a clever and hard-drinking trickster—yet his mutilation is real, all the same.) *Perdita* (1918) contains, among other tales, the novella many regard as Schildt's masterpiece, "Den svagare" (The weaker one); Fredrik Blomqvist, a mild and simple hardware clerk, is cuckolded by his bored and (again) vaguely exotic wife Manja: his jealousy is described in a scene of Chaplinesque clumsiness and frustration, and his acceptance of her adultery is heartrendingly naive in its truth: "What did it matter, weighed against the fact that life without her no longer could possess the value of life?" The tale of the *coeur simple* has a worthy companion in the little story in letters of an archivist, "Sinande källor" (Eng. tr. "Failing Sources," *Swedo-Finnish Short Stories, 1974*), letters addressed to a young girl with whom he is distantly and tentatively in love: he renounces her and returns to his solitary life. (His archive is a thinly disguised re-creation of the university library, where Schildt was long employed.)

During the Civil War Schildt was trapped with his young family (he had married in 1914) in the capital city, then held by the Reds; after the liberation he served for a short time as a registrar in the prison camp on Sveaborg. Like many another Finland-Swedish and Finnish author, he reacted literarily to the events of the war and its immediate aftermath, but his reaction is less clear-cut than most. In *Hemkomsten* (1918; The homecoming) the story "Aapo" (Eng. tr. *Scandinavian Studies*, 1977) provides Schildt's single larger picture of a Finnish-speaker, a stableboy who nurses a grudge at an estate manager for a fancied insult and in the Civil War takes his revenge. The more sensitive reviewers were left wondering, not about the manager's quiet heroism in confronting his death (with which Schildt fully met the expectations of his readership) but about the riddle Aapo presented. Is he a dullard urged on by agitators (if this interpretation is correct, Schildt would surely have done what his conservative audience wanted from him) or a representative of the quasi-religious fanaticism that an Ahrenberg and an Alexander Slotte seemed to think was specially Finnish, or has he become, in his crazy role as an angel of death, ultimately a victim of the teasing humiliation visited on him by the other servants and so reveals himself as a brother under the skin to many of Schildt's male characters? In "Köttkvarnen" (The meat grinder) Schildt came closest to empty patriotism and sentimentality: Manja, of "Den svagare," redeems herself running guns for the Whites and dies looking for her high-minded lover, slaughtered by the Reds. "Karamsinska hästen" (The Karamzin horse) offers a much grimmer tale: an old upholsterer, linguistically isolated (like Ture Janson's artisans), is left desperately alone in an icy Helsingfors by the death of his wife — once given the nickname, for her strength and good looks, of the horses of Aurora Karamzin, the legendary Helsingfors beauty and philanthropist. The title story "Hemkomsten" — on a mother's love for a favorite son, a fugitive from the Whites' local defense force in the wake of the war — puts just enough of the erotic into the relationship (they are sensitive, as her husband and her other son are not) to save the narrative from a banality of theme, if not of execution.

All these tales have to do with death; one of Schildt's two books from 1920 was an affirmation of life — the slender *Armas Fager*, a "silhouette," as its subtitle said, and apparently the beginning of the novel Schildt was never able to complete. Fager is an extra in the Helsingfors summer theater, originally a Finnish speaker who is justifiably proud of his mastery of "cultivated Swedish," and an aesthete tied to an ugly (but, unlike him, hardworking) wife. An aging figure of fun, he is an embarrassment to his daughters, also employed at the theater and the willing companions of Russian officers in their off-hours. Fager, though, loves the theater (and has written an impossible play) and is a man of goodwill: as he sits, half drunk, on a park bench, he thinks of the "twenty million people who just then were busily killing one another," and he wishes he could drink with them all and cry (he is a blowhard, to be sure): "Stop that, life's wonderful, after all." Yet in the last collection of novellas, *Häxskogen* (1920; Witchwood), the Russian refugee Zoja, in the tale bearing her name, kills herself because she cannot endure the hopeless emptiness of existence in a small Finnish town (Lovisa again); in the title story the author Jacob Casimir is tormented by his cousin, Fabian, whose guest he is, and learns that his beloved Veronica (an Austrian, another of Schildt's foreign beauties) will leave her husband not for him but for another man. Humiliated, and yet still hoping desperately to complete the eighth chapter of his novel, Jacob Casimir lies on his bed in his guest room and reflects that there is no place for him, either "in the White or the Red Guard of life.... He lay there with closed eyes and stared into the sick point of the soul where the pearl of art hardens," a grand verbal gesture in a story that turned out to be Schildt's narrative farewell.

Schildt had had trouble finding employment that allowed him to pursue his literary career; an engagement as the director of the so-called domestic (i.e., Finland-Swedish) division of Swedish Theater lasted less than two years (just before the predominance of directors and performers from Sweden at the theater was ended); his work as reader and then associate director at his cousin Holger Schildt's new publishing house became so burdensome that he eventually decided to abandon it; an ill-planned stab at running a bookstore in Borgå failed. After a crisis in the winter of 1922, already much preoccupied by thoughts of suicide, he wrote both the short play *Galgmannen: En midvintersaga* (Eng. tr. *The Gallows Man, A Midwinter Tale*, 1944), set in Nyland in the 1840s, its hero an old colonel confronted by loneliness, unexpected love, and death, and the full-sized *Den stora rollen* (1923; The great role), in which the boaster Armas Fager returns and, through his very self-importance, is killed on a Helsingfors street during the Civil War — a play much resembling Sean O'Casey's *Juno and the Paycock* (1924) in theme, atmosphere, and quality. These dramas were distinctly successful, in Helsingfors as in Stockholm, and his prospects brightened; but a third play — *Lyckoriddaren* (1923; The fortune hunter), located in abstract diplomatic circles — lacked the sense of place so essential for him. Two years later Schildt was dead by his own hand, like Zoja and like Irben, the protagonist of his last play, who is brought down by a single misstep in his past.

Schildt's friend Alma Söderhjelm (1870–1941), herself a scholar and a novelist, remembered him as someone quite indifferent to Finland's burning political questions but fascinated by "the analysis of human beings" ("Söderhjelm—Mattsson—Schildt," 96). She noted too that like the late Guss Mattsson — who described much the same Helsingfors — he suffered from the narrowness of Finland-Swedish conditions and complained that his works were not translated and valued in Finnish Finland. But they were so specifically Finland-Swedish in their mood and their frame of reference that, at the time, such a wish was vain; still, because of their limpidity of style (and their depiction of a related but foreign milieu), they were widely read in Sweden for years, and Virpi Zuck has made an important study of the several films based, more or less closely, on Schildt texts, by such distinguished directors as Mauritz Stiller and Alf Sjöberg.

Idealists, Realists, and the Civil War

Contemporary to the authors who represent the *dagdrivare* mentality, there are others who avoid ultimate negativism; Thomas Warburton (in 1984) put them under the heading "ethicists and engaged authors." (Torsten Pettersson has come on a curious kind of idealism among the *dagdrivare* themselves; a common theme is the constantly disappointed search for life's elusive meaning or purpose.) Erik Grotenfelt (1891–1919) started off as an aesthete very much like Gripenberg, proclaiming a love of life and "all the beauty it bestows, / A bowl of fruit where yellow mandarins / Fight boldly with huge pears for primacy," and urging his readers to "seize the second that briefly flames" and "Fill the cup with wine!" Nonetheless, near the end of his debut collection of *Dikter* (1914; Poems), he also seemed to see through the very poses he praised: "We love the dream of strife and deed and danger, / But we love ourselves most of all." Rather confusingly, he took the title of *Det röda vinets barn* (1915; The children of red wine) from the celebratory opening poem of his previous book, a praise of emotion uttered by "the hot blood's children, yearning for a mood." Now the yearned-for mood was even more erotic and smacks of the unintentionally comic decadence of the "Intérieur" poems by the notorious Austrian imitator of Baudelaire, Felix Dörmann (1870–1928): "a panther-skin, a tall and slender vase, / A hanging lamp that gives a muted, dreamlike light, / A Moorish tray that bears two glasses, filled"; he continues, "I know, this very night I shall possess you." Grotenfelt viewed this febrile hedonism more skeptically, though, in the novel *Bengt Walters lycka* (1916; Bengt Walter's luck); the titular hero falls heir to an estate and so gets a mission in life, but he refuses to abandon the existence of a moneyed and indolent semistudent in Helsingfors: "He preferred whiskey to honest toddy, a cutaway with well-pressed trousers to the dutiful Finnish senator's tail-coat and baggy pants, the whirring speed of cars to the snail-paced lumbering of horses."

The sudden deterioration of the czar's power and the March revolution of 1917 gave the hyperactive Grotenfelt the chance to write a political novel, *Det nya fosterlandet* (1917; The new fatherland), in which young Helge Borg's "blood boils with hatred and shame" as he beholds Russian troops preventing the assembly of Finland's Parliament, a sensationally swift turning of contemporary events into reportage fiction. Grotenfelt had already attempted to serve his fatherland: in 1915 he had gone to Germany in the light infantry battalion of Finnish volunteers but had been released because of his fragile health. He spent the "Red months" of 1918 in Helsingfors, writing for the underground newspaper *Fria ord* (Free words): from the first number on, Grotenfelt referred to "the struggle of culture against barbarism" and to "the war of liberation," a coinage implying that the Whites intended to free Finland from the rule of revolutionaries controlled by Russian masters. In the novel about Bengt Walter he had expressed a fear of a Finnish hegemony in Finland, leading to the destruction of time-honored cultural values; after the White victory he grew still more dismayed at what he regarded as the attempts of ungrateful Finnish nationalists to limit Finland-Swedish rights in the new nation. Having written a final newspaper article on "the [Finland-Swedish] demands, which do not spring from an old man concerned for a comfortable old age, but from growing vital power and the will to act," Grotenfelt shot himself on 3 April 1919. In an introduction to a volume of Grotenfelt's poetry published shortly after his death, Jarl Hemmer was tactfully silent about the quality of Grotenfelt's well-lubricated verse (has any other poet in Swedish Finland ever adduced the word "wine" so often?) but praised *Bengt Walters lycka* as "one of the two or three works of sterling quality in our so-called *dagdrivare* literature," adding that it was also "the most deeply negative" (pp. 9–10). The novel has never been reprinted, and considering Grotenfelt's reputation as a forerunner of Finnish Nazism, it perhaps never will be. Hans Ruin, who went to school with Grotenfelt, in 1943 recalled the immature, shortsighted, and megalocephalic boy who, grown up, led a liquidation of suspected Reds in Nyland after the war — he had "the brutality of weakness," in Ruin's formulation (p. 218).

In a way, Grotenfelt was an indirect victim of the Civil War, and there were others. Alfred Fahler (1892–1918) entered literature with the schoolboy verses of *Döda drömmar* (1912; Dead dreams), containing a poem to "Irmelin" perhaps inspired by J. P. Jacobsen's well-known "Irmelin Rose," and another to Siddharta, clearly identified as the result of Fahler's having read Sir Edwin Arnold's unreadable Buddha epic *The Light of Asia* (1879), in German translation. The fin-de-siècle verse of *Bland cypresser* (1914; Among cypresses) had the customary elements, not just the cypresses of the title (the trees of Arnold Bocklin's *Toteninsel*) but dark terebinths, white swans, "a fragile violin," a melancholy lute beside a rose-grown balcony, spleen, absinthe, and "your mouth, as sweet as nard." Like other young

Finlanders, Fahler went secretly to Germany in 1915, for training in the Twenty-seventh Light Infantry Battalion then being formed for service against the Russians (and eventual return to Finland in an uprising, it was thought, against czarist rule); but Fahler—in Hans Ruin's phrase "talkative" and "unbelievably oblivious of how what he said could be interpreted" (p. 227)—was immediately arrested as a Russian spy (just before the war he had spent a vacation in the Crimea) and was interned by the German authorities, who subjected him to fairly brutal treatment. He was released in March 1918 and described his experiences in the soberly written *I fängelse och fångläger* (1918; In prison and prison camp), a book that has much in common with e. e. cummings's *The Enormous Room* about the American's experiences as an internee in France. Worn out by what he had gone through, Fahler died, poetically enough, on Christmas Eve, 1918, in Visby; he never returned to Finland. The same year, his short poem cycle, *Isela*, came out in Sweden; he had refined his turn-of-the-century art sufficiently to produce a few intense erotic poems that stand up well, placed alongside similar expressions of yearning by Gripenberg, Hemmer, or, for that matter, the Edith Södergran of *Dikter*.

Allan Wallenius (1890–1942) had a different fate. From a solid, middle-class, Finland-Swedish home, he was inspired to a passion for socialism by his teacher at the Åbo Swedish Classical Gymnasium, the legendary Georg Boldt. Wallenius went to the United States during the First World War for library training but seems to have suffered considerable deprivation in New York; back home in Åbo he became a columnist and reviewer, under the nom de plume Don Q, for the socialist paper *Arbetet*. On the outbreak of the Civil War Wallenius was appointed postal commissioner in Åbo by the Red regime and fled to Sweden after the White victory. (A number of his associates were executed out of hand, and the admired Boldt died in an Åbo hospital, a broken man, tormented by his knowledge of the excesses committed by both sides. Wallenius's older brother Paul, who had trained with the "Jäger" in Holstein, had also fallen, as a captain in Mannerheim's White Army. Ture Janson, who knew both the Walleniuses, wrote an article with title and topic from Runeberg's *Fänrik Stål*, "The Brothers," contrasting the dead hero with the traitor and runaway.) Expelled from Sweden after a time, Wallenius made his way to Russia, was briefly a secretary to Otto Wille Kuusinen, helped organize the Soviet "proletarian" film industry, and returned to the United States from ca. 1925 to 1930, as editor of the Chicago Swedish paper *Ny tid*. In 1927, under the pseudonym Dr. Per Nelson, he published—in Swedish, in Chicago—*Wall Streets imperialistiska intriger* (Wall Street's imperialist intrigues) and, in 1930, again in Chicago a Swedish tract on the wonders of the Soviet five-year plan; back in Europe, Wallenius brought out *Stalinkanalen: Hur bolsjevikerna skapa mänskor och frihet* (1933; The Stalin channel: How the Bolsheviks create human beings and freedom) at Gothenburg; he was then the head of the Scandinavian section of the Communist University for western minorities in Moscow. Nine years later he died in one of Stalin's labor camps.

Wallenius's contributions to Finland-Swedish literature all appeared outside Finland, at the little leftist publishing house Fram (Forward) in Stockholm, save for the first, *Ord* (1917; Words). There he had already become a poet who addressed both industrial workers and oppressed tillers of the soil: "People, who slave in airless factories, / beings who hack at the field strips' clods"; his inspiration was plainly Arvid Mörne, but as Sven Willner pointed out ("Idealist och revolutionär," 66–67), he turned Mörne's impassioned rhetoric against its creator in "Renegade," a poem that castigates his sometime idol (unnamed) for the latter's rejection of radical socialism: "Words it has been, not acts, not deeds." In Sweden, Wallenius brought out a leftover from his more aesthetic Finnish days, the stories of *Trollfiolen* (1919; The magic violin), but otherwise continued his poetic-political career with *Morgonen* (1919; The morning), the allegorical prose of *Helvetets himmelsfärd* (1922; Hell's trip to heaven), and, finally, *I järnhälens tid: Kampdikter* (1925; In the iron heel's time: battle poems). *Morgonen* was still the voice of the idealist of Finland's Civil War, but the battle poems were the work of the convert to international Communism, a strange mixture haranguing the workers of the world, adoring the party, admiring a new age of Soviet industry and the machine, and mocking both another "renegade," the British labor leader and prime minister Ramsay MacDonald, and Jesus Christ Himself, who comes to Sweden by "autoaeroplane," is shown around by Archbishop Nathan Söderblom, supports the employers in a strike at the Wallenberg factories, and phones the government with a complaint: "I've been insulted by some Bolsheviks." Mörne could have been proud of his pupil's mastery of heavyhanded but effective verbal assault. Finland would not see the like of Wallenius again until the radical 1960s, save in the young Diktonius; Wallenius's verse—which is more than a mere oddity—shines by its absence from standard anthologies of Finland-Swedish lyric.

In 1914, when Grotenfelt had his debut, two other much more gifted (and morally more sensitive) poets also entered the literary scene, Ragnar Ekelund and Jarl Hemmer. The reputation of Ekelund (1892–1960) as a painter is easily greater than that as a poet; after a flurry of verse production during the teens and twenties of the century, he fell silent until 1941, when he brought out *Ljust i mörkt* (Light in darkness) and his collected *Lyrik 1912–1926* (1942; Lyrics 1912–1926), only to fall still once again. But careful critics have admired him, Johannes Salminen ("Poeten Ragnar Ekelund") and Hans Ruin among them, captivated by his careful sense of form and his implicit devotion to classical antiquity, not a learned skill (as sometimes in Zilliacus) but an almost intuitive quality that allowed him to put what his painter's eye observed into hexameters and pentameters that were altogether natural, never studied. In *Disticha* (1918; Distichs) he reached the peak of this nonclassicizing classical poetry: "Lately come up from the waves, and your hair filled with drops all of silver / Buoyant and shiningly young, into my spirit you enter."

Some monotony of theme lies in Ekelund's poetry as in his painting; the praise of earth and forest, water and air turns up again and again. But he can provide surprises, too, as in the city poetry of *Gatans dikter* (1915; Poems of the street) or the verse narrative of *Improvisationer* (1922; Improvisations), in the apparently moribund genre that was now and then revived by Finland-Swedish authors, perhaps mindful of Runeberg. Also, Ekelund's "striving for clarity, for crystalline equilibrium" (in Salminen's phrase) has something distinctly Runebergian about it. "Earth there beneath my foot and the stars rising high overhead! / All my impoverished life rests transfigured in this," from *Vägarna* (1919; The ways), repeated the practical transcendence to which Runeberg so often gave voice. The poem in question, however, also contains the seed of a tendency in Ekelund that may have led to his silence—his inclination to self-pity. Singing about beauty in his muted way, Ekelund believed he was ignored in favor of the splashier Jarl Hemmer, and in the last collection before his silence, *Strofer i grått* (1926; Strophes in gray), he gave vent to envy with lines about poets who "intoxicate, drug, and soothe to sleep / A soulful, sensitive public." When Ekelund came back to poetry, he still pursued the light-loving (and as he saw it) feminine spirit of the Greek world. Once it had been Venus Anadyomene or a dryad ("Like to a vision that flees, too fleeting to catch in the hand"); now it was Nausikaa herself ("when on the beach [she] stood in the morning sunlight") in his last book, directed to the literary historian Karin Allardt, Anders Allardt's daughter, whom he married in 1937. Seeing the beloved transfigured by the morning light, he created love poetry oddly like the homoerotic verse of the modernist Gunnar Björling; even though he obstinately went his own way, cultivating two difficult arts, it was Ekelund's fate always to seem vaguely reminiscent of others who had concentrated more steadily on literature.

Jarl Hemmer, born in 1893, was one of Swedish Finland's best-known authors during his lifetime, with a faithful following both at home and in Sweden. Handsome and well-to-do, he won hearts not only for his much photographed good looks but through the romantic verve of his verse, the musical clarity of his language, and his eloquent melancholy: an English-language equivalent might be one of the Georgians, Rupert Brooke or Walter de la Mare. But Brooke was fortunate enough to die young and in a dramatic setting, and de la Mare sensibly kept his production small. Because of this favored position in orthodox literary life and, to an extent, because of his enthusiastic championing of the Whites in the Civil War (in which he did not differ much from the bellicose Gripenberg or the normally pacific Ekelund), Hemmer eventually became the object of critical and personal attack by some of the modernists: Diktonius—who also savaged Schildt and Gripenberg in his reviews—called Hemmer "the blond lad" and made him a favorite target. Such sniping—coupled, of course, with much more deep-seated problems—led to severe nervous crises; a search for religious salvation failed to bring him the peace he sought, as his creative powers diminished. In 1933 he succeeded Gripenberg as the occupant of Diktarhemmet, but almost immediately an unforgettable tragedy occurred; after a visit to the Hemmers in their new residence his close friend Erik Kihlman, Kihlman's wife, and another couple, setting out by car for Helsingfors, were drowned in the river at Borgå. Neither his involvement with Frank Buchman's evangelical Oxford Group, against which he eventually turned, nor a renewed "confirmation" and a residence at the Swedish-Christian center, Sigtuna, could halt the decline, and Hemmer shot himself in a fireplace at the Poet's Home in November 1944.

The triumphant part of Hemmer's career began with *Rösterna* (1914; The voices), followed by *Pelaren* (1916; The pillar), graceful, lightly melancholy verse about May nights and snowy mornings, hawthorns and drops of dew. His poems from the Civil War, *Ett land i kamp* (1918; A land in battle), were a source of spiritual anguish to him later on, and the romantic poem cycle about Prince Louis Ferdinand (1919)—the gifted nephew of Frederick the Great, composer and lady's man, who fell during Napoleon's invasion of Prussia—appealed mainly to an audience that had dreamed of putting a German king on Finland's imaginary throne. In *Över dunklet* (1919; Above the darkness) and *Väntan* (1922; Waiting) he continued largely in the vein of his earlier collections ("Above the darkness is space, where the golden light torrents go streaming," and "The cotton grass nods on lonely tussocks, / late in the evening the curlew calls"); but *Skärseld: Dikter och dokument* (1925; Purgatory: Poems and documents), dedicated to Hans Ruin and Erik Kihlman, was aptly named. In it Hemmer stopped his romanticizing palliatives, at least to an extent, and instead released poems exposing his private vision of a self that was going to pieces. From the cycle of fifteen confessional poems dated 1921–24, the "documents" of the subtitle, the well-known "På nattgammal is" (On night-old ice) is one more link in the long Finland-Swedish chain of poetry about loneliness (Tavaststjerna's New Year's poem, Lybeck's tired trees and buoys in the fog, Gripenberg's lonely ski track); but here the emphasis lies on self-revelation: "Fragile's the layer that separates abyss and height in my soul, / Simply a glass-thin cover, broken perhaps today." "All världens lidande" (All the world's suffering) has an ugly image at its opening and conclusion: "I am a jug, forever filled / with dirtied blood from the world's thousand wounds.— / How long will the weak clay hold?" (In *Över dunklet* the poem "Uppgörelse" [Reckoning] had already cursed "this flesh, / Which as its sole, mighty striving / Cunningly and in tormentingly low forms / Would plunge me into the pit!"— verses that Hans Ruin omitted from the selection of Hemmer's verse he made after his friend's death.)

The Hemmer of *Skärseld* was certainly a less comforting figure than the one his readers (save for the most attentive) had come to expect, readers who had also been enchanted by a long narrative poem, an agricultural idyll laid in Hemmer's home province of Ostrobothnia, *Rågens rike* (1922; Eng. tr. *The Realm of Rye,* 1938), much beloved in its time. Yet even in *Skärseld* Hemmer likes to linger with the ideal (see the suite to the Pharaoh Achnaton) and to praise what is ultimately good, as in the poem to a tree in bloom, in which

> the darkness-choked blood of the underground
> which your blind roots drink
> is met from above by a supernal power
> forcing all things to smiles and life.

In a similar mode the sun is beseeched: "Teach me, / no matter what my blind underground may grant me, / to transform it all to light and color and sweet smell!" (The verbal formula suggests a familiar Swedish hymn, "Lär mig, du skog, att vissna glad" [Teach me, oh woods, to wither glad].) In *Helg* (1929; Holiday), with its "Bön för ett nytt hjärta" (Prayer for a new heart); in *Nordan* (1936; The north wind), with its "Strömstaren" (The water ouzel), which expresses Hemmer's determination, "searching, darkness-possessed," nonetheless to "sing toward the sun"; and in *Klockan i havet* (1939; The bell in the sea), with its legend of the sinner saved ("And the storm was silenced and the bell's sound strong"), Hemmer continued to struggle; the results are touching but poetically less and less effective.

Parallel to this psychomachia in verse, Hemmer also tried to confront his demons in narrative prose. As early as the "scout book," *Onni Kokko* (1920), in which he described a figure from White legend, a boy who became a fanatic killer of Reds, he was led down a path he may not have intended to take at the outset: three-quarters of the way through the novel Onni grows tired of senseless slaughter, and his death at Tammerfors (the climactic battle of the war, in April 1918) releases both him and his creator from a moral dilemma. Hemmer returned to the theme, which had begun to obsess him, in the story "Ett bud från ödemarken" (Eng. tr. "A Message from the Wilderness," *Swedo-Finnish Short Stories*, 1974), in the collection *Budskap* (1928; Messages), about an episode from the guerrilla fighting in Karelia after the Civil War. Some of his personal torments had already been confronted in the stories of *De skymda ljusen* (1921; The hidden lights), and Ruin, again tactfully, omitted these tales of alcoholism, guilty conscience, and sexual obsession—anything but shocking, by late-twentieth-century standards—from the memorial edition; on the other hand, he included *Fattiggubbens brud* (1926; The bride of the "poor man," a reference to the collection boxes in human shape placed outside Finnish country churches), a novel having the touch of the miraculous that had become a necessity for Hemmer's manic-depressive nature and containing the authorial apostrophe, "Blessed the man who in his hour of affliction gets help from his own good deeds."

As a young man, Hemmer had been a close student of Russian language and literature and was especially drawn to Tolstoy and Dostoyevsky; Ruin called his "Anteckningar om Tolstoy" (Notes on Tolstoy), collected in the volume *Brev till vänner* (1937; Letters to friends), one of the "most outstanding" contributions to Finland's essayistic literature. This literary passion, complementing his psychological patterns, can readily be discovered in the novel *En man och hans samvete* (1931; lit. A man and his conscience; Eng. tr. *A Fool of Faith*, 1935), in which a defrocked pastor (bearing the assumed and transparent name of "Bro," bridge), serves as a chaplain's aide in the ghastly White prison camp on Sveaborg in 1918, changes places with a prisoner condemned to death, and is executed. Bro has never been at ease with himself: in his past (recounted in some detail) he offered shelter to a prostitute, became sexually involved with her, and killed one of her customers when she returned to her former calling, an act of manslaughter that led to his imprisonment and ejection from the clergy. One of the book's best-known passages, however, is from the time after his release and just before he goes out to "Gehenna and the searchlights"; in "Den stora dagen" (The great day) Hemmer describes the victory parade of Mannerheim and his troops — Gripenberg's dreamed-of army — through Helsingfors on 16 May 1918, an impressive and even inspiring piece of patriotic writing but followed by Bro's discovery of a booklet of jingoistic verse whose "hateful words" make him shudder. The lines quoted are from *Ett land i kamp*.

The last novel of Hemmer is disappointing: a story set in Åland, *Morgongåvan* (1934; The dowry) allows his now quite bathetic prose ("Her heart was throbbing within her," "His voice grew jubilant in her ear") to run riot while young love triumphs over old aversions. A playful autobiographical sketch in *Brev till vänner* begins, "In the Ostrobothnian city of Vasa there lived, in the excellent home of his parents, a quite exalted youth," and Hemmer remained that exalted youth, however battered, to the end of his days — never able wholly to master his undeniable literary gifts, any more than he could control himself. In a late, uncollected poem, "Dyning" (Swell), he compared himself to the wave become a backwash, "low and indifferent like me, a tired slave of your fate." Today Hemmer's melodrama, played out *de profundis*, may make sophisticates smile; such a reaction is grossly inappropriate, in consideration of the genuineness of his miseries and the validity of his aims.

In *Författare om författare* (1980; Authors about authors) twenty-four prominent Finland-Swedish people of letters were asked to write about their favorites in the literature; no one chose Hemmer, but his contemporary, Sigrid Backman (1880–1938), got two tributes, — a contrast to the silence she received in 1928, when the Swede John Landquist, in an otherwise well informed panorama of the minority's modern literature, left her out altogether. It is to the credit of the Euterpist Olaf Homén that, in *De nya författarna* (1915; The new authors), he devoted a whole chapter to her first novels, *Vindspel* (1913; literally "Windlass" but also a play on the components "wind" and "game") and *Hälleberget och Kavaljeren* (1914; The rock and the cavalier), books in which he noted "fragile delicacy and unmistakable sensationalism." In the former, Astri gives herself to Sven, only to learn that the artist already has a wife (but plans to get rid of her); in the latter, Britt, "a lonely young woman who has built her own house," prefers "the dark cavalier" (part of his charm is his waiflike quality, "a child wandering in the twilight") to the solid "man-rock" who does not need her. Astri is an almost fairy-tale being, in close contact with nature (Homén called her "a sort of Undine"), Britt works in a paint factory, and Miss Ejder, in Backman's *Guds barn* (1916; God's children), is an amalgam of the two, a sweet but independent organist on vacation, and the man in her life is the old sailor Broström, for whom she cares in his last illness. (One of Backman's talents was for the lightly erotic: there is a slight hint of flirtatious attachment between Miss Ejder and Broström, who turns out to be her father.)

Enda sonen (1917; The only son) was a misstep, in that Backman paid her female lead—Susi Hård, a commercial correspondent who puts her male colleagues to professional shame—less attention than the cozened young medical student whose suit she at first rejects, causing him to exchange his callowness for social responsibility. Finally, she accepts his love, "in a trembling, burning kiss," only to lose him to a snakebite; after his death she decides, together with his mother (previously cowed by his domineering father, Susi's boss), to realize his plan of a great and altruistic "health farm": "It was as if a warrior's blood began to course through her veins." Here, as elsewhere, Backman came perilously close to the entertainment novel; but she retrieved herself with *Ålandsjungfrun* (1919; The Åland maid), placed in the eastern Nyland countryside from which her parents—her father was a Helsingfors streetcar conductor, her mother a sometime servant—had come. A seamstress from Åland, first viewed with some suspicion, wins respect by her industry and neatness and gains the affection of local bachelors by her fragile charm; she drowns herself when her light-o'-love, David, an honest young man who detests injustice, is executed as a Red by the German expeditionary force at the end of the Civil War. As she undresses and slips into the well, "ready and shining white," she fulfills Homén's observation about Astri-Undine; one of the book's special qualities is its intermediacy between a fairy-tale tone (as in Schildt's "Rönnbruden") and a bitter commentary on a national and human tragedy. A half-mad squire from the neighborhood predicts that "the red flower of art will bloom in unforeseen splendor where the battles have been fought," and an old woman says of the fallen Reds, "They were so hopelessly stupid that they thought they could arrange for justice in this world." The latter statement demonstrated, in its irony, Backman's dissenting attitude toward the late conflict.

She returned to this attitude in *Familjen Brinks öden* (1922; The fates of the Brink family). In this case, Backman stuck closely to the milieu in which she had grown up, the Helsingfors of the petite bourgeoisie and the worker, a world that, over the years, Ina Lange and Ture Janson and Runar Schildt had entered or tried to, Schildt with far and away the greatest (but certainly nonanalytic) success. Like "that proper person," the Åland seamstress, Ragna Brink loses her lover in the Civil War, but not to death; rather, she rejects him because all her brothers have died for the Red cause: one in battle, one in a prison camp, one executed in the street; she can no longer bring herself to marry her White fiancé (whom she has helped escape from the Reds): "I hate no one, but I do not love victorious authority. I no longer love the victors. I no longer love you." To herself she confesses that her denial of her love for Eskil is "a bitter lie," but "the silence of the dead" has caused her to make her choice; she and her wise father, Shoemaker Brink, may emigrate to America or stay in their side street "as strangers in our own homeland, and sew gold embroideries and fix heels as before," in Brink's words. (As the surviving relatives of Finland-Swedes who had taken the Red side, father and daughter will be shunned; Elvira Elv, the book's opportunist, says, "It was a joy that so few Swedes went along with the Red trash," and her statement is historically accurate.) Sometimes rightly charged with naiveté by her reviewers, Backman lets her characters condemn or redeem themselves out of their own mouths; for her, the measure was not language allegiance or political coloring but basic humanity.

Goodness and quaintness get the upper hand in Backman's succeeding novels about very modest Helsingfors homes. In *Bostadsbolaget Sjuan i Lergränden* (1926; The Residential Company No. Seven in Mud Street) Carpenter Hölander brings about neighborhood peace and a wedding (between a shy young man and a terrible-tempered young woman, whose father is glad to get her out of the house); at the epithalamic close Hölander makes a speech, telling how he is only a simple man, born and reared in eastern Nyland, a man who "has done nothing special in the world, but who from eternity to eternity has striven for what is good, for the so-called ideal," which last word he mispronounces. The wise old man comes back again in *De fåvitska trollen* (1932; The foolish trolls) as Petrus Bagge, the father of Susanna Bagge; the "trolls" are the lovable members of a family overly gifted with imagination, unable to fit themselves into the requirements of practical life, and imperiled by their own exceptionality. Bo Carpelan has noticed that the initials of Bagge's daughter are the same as Sigrid Backman's (p. 116), and the remainder of the novel, after old Bagge's sudden demise, is an account of Susanna's (or Sigrid's?) experiences as a department store clerk in a modernized Helsingfors; a reviewer, Agnes Langenskjöld, saw the novel as a protest against "machine culture ... the mechanization of human labor" (pp. 63–64). By a very few years it precedes the appearance of plays and narratives about eccentric, lovable families in the United States, Hart and Kaufman's *You Can't Take It with You* and Saroyan's whimsical novels. Such books are protests in their way, as are the Moomintroll books of Tove Jansson (see chapters 10 and 11).

Backman had made a stab at gentle historical fiction with *Den gamla spinnrocken* (1929; The old spinning wheel), a picture of an eastern Nyland peasant family in the nineteenth century, "stories told by [the author's] mother, and, before that, to her by *her* mother and grandmother," but by no means as folkloristic as Josefina Bengts's *Fäderna*. With her last book, *Under Häxböles sol* (1935; Beneath Häxböle's sun), Backman went to the countryside again and to a pleasant fantasy of a happy village and an equally happy estate society. (Does the title indicate a reply to Ekhammar's *Under torparsolen?*) The book afforded Backman the chance to make kindly fun of the beliefs — for example, in Christianity and human progress — to which so much lip service is paid at all levels of little Häxböle. Backman's mouthpiece is Fröken Fågelflykt (Miss Bird-flight), who in one of the book's many farcical scenes tells the young poet Schlager that his ode in praise of gasoline and "cultural motors" is praiseworthy indeed, but he can expect to get only ten marks for it, because the cash box of the local cultural festival (the novel's concluding event) is "quite unbelievably weak." One last time, Backman had provided an odd-voice-out, a strain of frivolity in a literary decade that, because of a variety of factors, discussed in the next chapter, took itself very seriously.

An Eyewitness: Ruin

Hans Ruin (1891–1980), who knew and left portraits of so many of his contemporaries in Finland-Swedish letters, seems not to have known Sigrid Backman; they moved in altogether different circles — if she moved in any circles at all. From an academic family (his father was professor and then rector at the university), Ruin was docent in psychology (1927–36) and in "literature and the psychology of art" from 1936 until 1945, when he moved to Sweden. From 1947 until 1952 he was docent in aesthetics at the University of Lund and then became "research docent," with the title of professor; there, in addition to his teaching and writing, he appeared frequently on the radio. Never a popularizer, Ruin had a gift for the lucid presentation of difficult literary and aesthetic materials, for example, connecting poetic creation with the mystical experience in his major work, *Poesiens mystik* (1935; The mystery of poetry). Also, following the example of his sometime teacher, Yrjö Hirn, he was a gifted cultural essayist on a variety of themes; *Gycklare och apostlar* (1934; Jesters and apostles), the title of one of his earlier efforts in this direction, could have come from Hirn's own hand. In it Ruin, a humanist in the word's broader sense, treated examples of "atavism" in art (with side glances at the new threat of Nazism) and declared — an infinitely more cultured Hölander — that he was naive enough to believe in "the eternal return of ideals." He never ceased to proclaim this straightforward program; in *Det finns ett leende* (1943; There is a smile) he wrote, "A touch of obstinate perseverance distinguishes intellectual values."

He was never haughty or elitist: "There will always be room for the good deed in the everyday living of life — [it is] the only thing before which we bow our heads in humility." Growing up with the idlers, he had nothing of their spleen, despite his deep knowledge of life's ills and of the fragility of truth and art, justice and morality, words he could employ without sounding pompous. He went beyond the essay in two of his more personal volumes, in *Rummet med de fyra fönstren* (1940; The room with the four windows) and *Hem till sommaren* (1960; Home to the summer), approaching the short story as he told about himself and his family (and, on a painful occasion, his family's feuds). His "Övertalning till kärlek" (Eng. tr. "Persuasion to Love," *Swedo-Finnish Short Stories,* 1974) in the latter book recreates his father as a young man, studying in Germany, whose culture had meant much for Finland-Swedish (and Finnish) literary life in his father's time and in his own. But Ruin had been a witness to that culture's distortion and betrayal.

The Age of Modernism, 1916–1960

George C. Schoolfield

9

How New Was Modernism?
The aspect of Finland's Swedish literature best known today is surely the so-called modernism that had its heyday during the 1920s, thus contemporaneous with the first decade of Finland's independence. Its critical champions then and since have made much of the break with the literature of the past: in verse it jettisoned rhyme, regular rhythm, and traditional forms and took recourse to unexpected images from realms (particularly, as Arvid Mörne pointed out, from the subconscious and the dream) that had not been much plumbed before; in prose it excelled more in unconventional (and often polemic) criticism and in such marginal forms as the aphorism, the fragmentary reflection, and, occasionally, the experimental novel than in straightforward, traditional narrative. Nevertheless, in its pronounced individualism and its international interests (it learned from recent developments in Germany, Russia, and the United States and even dreamed of reaching a foreign public), it had aims not unlike those of the *Euterpe* circle at the century's beginning. Its pugnacious critical attitudes, its sometimes haughty or condescending stance, and its determination to shock raised hackles among writers of the old school who were much more widely read (e.g., Gripenberg, Hemmer, Mörne); some return attacks were likewise strong and, in the case of certain professional journalists (who found it easy to make fun of the modernists' extravagances), brutal. As recent scholarship has remarked (for example, Johan Wrede in 1986 and Roger Holmström in 1988), some of the reactions against modernism stemmed from an association made between its revolutionary rhetoric and the Red menace (of which the Finland-Swedish minority had had recent and unpleasant experi-

ence); some opposition came, too, from a sense that the modernists, by and large uninterested in the language question, were traitors to the minority's cause or, at best, indifferent to the preservation of its rights and its great cultural institutions—a perception leading to the hesitancy the Swedish Literary Society in Finland showed for a while about furthering the careers of modernist authors.

Nevertheless, Olof Enckell, writing in *Hufvudstadsbladet,* initially skeptical toward modernist innovations, began to explain them to a larger public—no doubt softened by his younger brother, the least upsetting member of the modernist camp. And by the 1930s Diktonius, the enfant terrible, had settled down in Grankulla, as a neighbor of Mörne and Rabbe Enckell, and wrote poetry asking for tolerance and understanding in the wake of the Civil War. In addition, encouraged by the patently conservative editor of *Nya Argus,* Erik Kihlman, Diktonius had become the journal's brilliant music critic, composing odes in honor of Jean Sibelius, whom he had once detested as a musical spokesman of the political right and of Finnish superpatriotism. As early as 1929 Hemmer, a favorite whipping boy of modernist criticism, wrote the introduction to *Min lyra* (1929; My lyre), a selection from the lyrics of Edith Södergran, and within the Swedish Literary Society, Professor Gunnar Castrén, in the chairman's address at the society's annual public festival, on 5 February 1933, emphasized "the renewal of the forms of expression that [Finland-Swedish] verse had undergone during the most recent decades." On the same occasion, a year before, he had observed that youth must have its day, although he had added, "Life is not only impulses and sensations; it is also an act of will, a striving."

Behind the scenes Castrén did what he could to see that Rabbe Enckell got financial support from the Literary Society, and by 1933 Diktonius— who had already received the Paul Werner Lybeck Prize in 1929 for his prose book with the surprising title *Ingenting* (Nothing)—was awarded the same prize for his difficult *Janne Kubik*. An absorption of the modernists into the Finland-Swedish literary tradition was well under way, although Gunnar Björling, the most startling of them all in his mode of expression, would have to wait for the society or, for that matter, the reading public to give him a nod of acceptance. Hesitant though Castrén may have been about the apparent indiscipline of modernism (Castrén was a great admirer of the disciplined Runeberg), one of its features was surely attractive to him, as a former Euterpist: its cosmopolitanism. Like the modernists, he thought it was necessary to discuss problems going far beyond the limits of the minority's immediate concerns.

Södergran

Certainly, Edith Södergran (1892–1923), the pioneer and then the patron saint of modernism, came from a background that was unusually broad and then, at the end, fearfully constricted. Her father was an Ostrobothnian self-styled engineer who had worked for the firm of Alfred Nobel in Russia, her mother the literarily interested daughter of a Finland-Swede from the Åbo skerries who had made his fortune in St. Petersburg as an iron founder. Born in the Russian capital, Edith Södergran spent much of her girlhood at a handsome villa in the little town of Raivola (now Rodzino) on the Karelian isthmus, where her father, propped up by his wife's money, ran a lumber concern until he succumbed to tuberculosis in 1907. Wanting to give her only child the cultural advantages she herself had enjoyed, Helena Holmroos Södergran enrolled Edith in the excellent German-language "Hauptschule zu Sankt Petri" (which Lou Salomé, the confidante-to-be of Nietzsche, Rilke, and Freud, had attended a generation before), and the girl's first poetry was written in German, bearing traces of Heine and the dreamy melancholy of *Jugendstil* verse. For reasons that have never become altogether clear, she then changed over to Swedish, the principal language in her home. (The "oilcloth notebook" in which her early verse has been preserved also contains some French poetry and a single poem in Russian.) The diagnosis of her tubercular infection led to withdrawal from the school; sent to a sanatorium at Nummela, not far from Helsingfors, she was desperately unhappy, but for the only time in her life, she found herself in a mostly Swedish-speaking milieu. In 1911, accompanied by her mother, to whom she was deeply devoted, she set out for Switzerland, where she spent more than two years as a patient in sanatoria, first at St. Moritz and then at Davos. In an atmosphere like that of Thomas Mann's *Der Zauberberg,* she came to believe that she had almost been cured of her disease, but a relapse occurred when the Södergrans returned to Finland in the spring of 1914. Further, she became involved in an unhappy love affair, which led, evidently, to some of the poetry she published at Holger Schildt's new firm at the end of 1916, as *Dikter* (Poems); other verse in the collection had its origin in her Swiss days and in a journey she and her mother had made to northern Italy in the spring of 1913. All the collections of Södergran's Swedish-language verses and her aphorisms have been repeatedly translated (see the Bibliography).

The critical reception of *Dikter,* although by no means devastating, was sufficiently mixed to cause Södergran to have a fit of depression (and, perhaps, thoughts of suicide); events of the new year—the discovery of what she saw as the "life-affirmative" and "activist" philosophy of Nietzsche (she was especially taken with *Also sprach Zarathustra* and its alpine imagery); her last visit to St. Petersburg, already in the initial throes of the revolution in which her mother would lose her fortune; a trip to Helsingfors, where she met such literary folk as Hemmer, Grotenfelt, and Hans Ruin — wrought radical changes in her life. The upheavals of the time and her own continuing personal crisis (she had felt herself very much an exotic bird during her stay in Finland's capital and had played the role to the hilt) became part and parcel of her next collection, *Septemberlyran* (1918; The September lyre), which veered much further away than *Dikter* had from the norm in Finland-Swedish (and Scandinavian) verse of the day. Aided by the apparent hubris of the little book's introduction ("My self-assurance rests on the fact that I have discovered my dimensions") and an open letter to Helsingfors's *Nya Pressen* ("This book is not intended for the public, scarcely even for the more advanced intellectual circles, only for the few individuals who stand closest to the boundary of the future"), the publication of *Septemberlyran* led to a newspaper campaign in which she was nastily ridiculed (especially by "Jumbo," Gunnar Johansson, a columnist for *Hufvudstadsbladet*) and supported by her poetic colleagues (Hemmer, Grotenfelt, and Ragnar Ekelund, among others). A personal result of the tumult was a friendship with the young reviewer in *Nya Pressen*, Hagar Olsson, to whom she addressed the suite "Fantastique" ("My sister, / you came like a spring wind across our valleys") in *Rosenaltaret* (1919; The rose altar), in which she also gave expression to her belief that "beauty" was a primary source of human salvation. The same year, she brought out a little sheaf of aphorisms called *Brokiga iakttagelser* (Manifold observations), in which she continued her Nietzschean admiration for masterful and daring personalities: "What we need now is the most impudent of human beings, he who once bore the name Napoleon." The surge of rapid production ended with *Framtidens skugga* (1920; The shadow of the future), in which, ever more exalted, she reported on her visions of power, the torments of her sexual drives, and her fear of death.

Thereafter she fell silent; the little family, mother and daughter, lived from hand to mouth in Raivola, which had become a Finnish outpost at the very edge of the new Russian Socialist Republic; the sometime poet attempted to make money by taking photographs — she was a devoted photographer — of the soldiers stationed there and their girlfriends. As her health declined still more, she became an avid reader of the New Testament and a disciple of the then modish anthroposophy of Rudolf Steiner. What little energy she had left was used to prepare an anthology of the new

Finland-Swedish lyrics in German translation; unable to find a publisher, she burned most of the manuscript shortly before her death. (She claimed, still, that German was her "best language," and her Swedish — quite old-fashioned and influenced both by her mother's highly literary usages and, some have argued, by turns of phrase from her father's Ostrobothnian dialect — was full of orthographical and grammatical uncertainties and Germanisms.) In March 1922 the Södergrans received a visit at Raivola from the young poet and musician Elmer Diktonius (Hagar Olsson, herself a little leery of meeting her tubercular friend any longer, had arranged the visit), and thanks to Diktonius, some of the simple and serenely pious verse Södergran now wrote appeared in the little magazine *Ultra*. In *Ultra*'s pages, too, Diktonius described his new friend with fairy-tale terms that formed the beginning of the Södergran legend. When Edith Södergran died, on 24 June 1923, Olsson was out of the country; Diktonius assumed the task of assembling the deceased's final poetry, publishing it as *Landet som icke är* (1925; The land that is not), the title of the most moving of her late poems. In the 1930s, as the reputation of her singular genius spread, Raivola, and Helena Södergran, became the goal of literary pilgrims, and, from Sweden, such young poets as Gunnar Ekelöf and Johannes Edfelt (both of whom then made references to Södergran's works in their own) came to absorb the exotic Karelian atmosphere in which Södergran had lived and died. Swedish critics referred to the "Byzantine colorfulness" of her poetry.

A life such as Södergran's can readily be stylized into a narrative of triumph over suffering, played out in the immediate vicinity of world-shaking events. If Södergran has been transformed into the representative figure of the isolated and gifted woman, a Sappho or Emily Dickinson (evidence exists that she thought of herself as an Ariadne, deserted on Naxos by Theseus but then taken up into the skies by the Dionysus of her inspiration), so both Södergrans, mother and daughter, meeting the Belle Epoque at a sanatorium for the very well-to-do (while residing in a nearby hotel) and then suddenly reduced to poverty in a village cut off from a great European capital (shortly to be redubbed Leningrad), have become a symbol of what befell large parts of eastern European society in and after 1918. As for the reaction of Edith Södergran to these changes, she wrote with ecstatic approval about a vaguely delineated revolution and predicted a better world in which beauty reigned supreme, but the beauty of which she dreamed belonged to the past. (The ease with which myth and symbol could be attached to Södergran was enhanced by the very paucity of material about her: a tiny literary production, a tiny circle of friends, a few letters, mainly to Olsson and Diktonius, and the fact that the very site of her life disappeared, as it were, in the Russo-Finnish wars of 1939–40 and 1941–44.)

Happily, the strength of her poetry (translated into more than a dozen languages) is commensurate with the strength of the myth. Although she is forever self-absorbed and self-referential, her poems never become boring products of routine; every poem is written with the same intensity. And despite the smallness of the corpus, there is variety: the melancholy, self-pity, and sentimentality of *Dikter;* the strange mixture of playfulness and pathos in *Septemberlyran;* the aestheticism, sometimes sacral, sometimes homely, of *Rosenaltaret;* the cosmic-emotional visions of *Framtidens skugga;* the childlike (but artful) simplicity of the last verse. In the constantly growing secondary literature critics favor one collection over another; some feminists become uneasy at the submissiveness and piety of the last verse, recommending the aggressivity of the volumes written under a Nietzschean influence; other commentators are made uncomfortable by what they perceive as almost fascistic elements in her worship of power and her apparent celebration of cruelty and war; still others find the visionary poetry all too declamatory.

The obstinate readiness with which Södergran reacts to experience or reading, her wearing of her poetic heart on her sleeve (or exposing it, as she does in one poem, in the cosmos), may seem almost naive. But her language has an unmistakable quality of its own, in part coming from its alluring strangeness — the result, probably, of the German substratum, her acquaintanceship with Russian poetry of the Silver Age, and the circumstance that her Swedish-speaking world was minuscule and idiosyncratic. Whatever the source, her style is unique; her lines are as recognizable as Runeberg's (with whose poetry she may have had only a fleeting acquaintance) — and as readily parodied, just as the inordinacy of her poetic stance was mocked, once upon a time: see "I am no woman, I am a neuter" or the super-Nietzschean "For me there is naught save circling in the eagle's flight." Yet there are the lines that should forbid parody, in the poem of hopelessness, "Be still, my child, for there is nothing"; or the poem of wondering to what culture she belongs: "Where is my homeland? Is it distant Finland, strewn with stars?"; or the very late "I long for the land that is not, / for all things that are / I am tired of desiring."

Diktonius

When Elmer Diktonius (1896–1961) crossed the horizon of Olsson and Södergran, he impressed them by his youthfulness and vigor, just as he upset others by his brashness and pugnacity, the clear pride he took in not having followed the usual Finland-Swedish path of young men with literary interests, that is, a Swedish-language gymnasium and university studies. The son of a print shop foreman, he came from poor but honest circumstances; his family saw to it that he had violin lessons and—for what they hoped would be the practical advantages accruing to a boy from the Swedish-speaking working class—sent him to Finnish schools. However devoted Diktonius was to his parents (his work contains tributes to them both), he was a lazy pupil and ended by playing hooky; he claimed later in life that he had educated himself by voracious reading. After his father's death and a brief stint as a sheet-music salesman (the only regular job this encomiast of the working man would ever hold), he enrolled in the Helsingfors Music Institute as a student of violin and composition, encouraged by the institute's director, the composer and aphorist Erkki Melartin (1875–1927).

His musical skills got him a small income as occasional tutor in music theory to the radical socialist Otto Ville Kuusinen (1881–1964), but when the Civil War broke out, he did not enlist in the Red Guard, despite the fact that Kuusinen had become minister of education and intellectual leader of the Red government: Diktonius's activities during the months of the revolt are unknown. After the White victory he was drafted into the new Finnish army and served as a medical corpsman on Valamo in Lake Ladoga; returning to civilian life, he began a clandestine correspondence with Kuusinen (who had fled to Russia and Sweden before returning to Finland, briefly and secretly, on his way back to Moscow and a post in the Komintern). To Diktonius, Kuusinen preached the aesthetics of a direct and activist poetry, meant to awaken the masses to revolution; it may have been Kuusinen's emphasis on the persuasive power of the word—or a disastrous public performance of six of Diktonius's songs—that made the latter decide to concentrate on authorship rather than composition. Thanks to his leftist friends, he managed to get abroad, ostensibly to study music in Paris, but the attraction of London (and a love affair) was stronger, and he spent a number of months there in 1921, later claiming that he came close to starvation; this experience and a seven-week stay in Cornwall were much used by him in his subsequent poetry.

The 1920s form a clear-cut period in Diktonius's life as in his production. Back in Helsingfors, he began his long association with Axel Åhlström's socialist newspaper, *Arbetarbladet* (The workers' paper), for which he wrote some of his cruelest and wittiest reviews, assailing, among others, Gripenberg, Runar Schildt, and of course, Jarl Hemmer. He participated with Hagar Olsson in *Ultra* and started to make a name for himself with *Min dikt* (1921; My poem), *Hårda sånger* (1922; Hard songs), the translations of recent American, Danish, Finnish, and German poetry in *Ungt hav* (1923; Young sea), the aphorisms of *Brödet och elden* (1923; The bread and the flame), and the verse of *Taggiga lågor* (1924; Barbed flames) and *Stenkol* (1927; Coal). The last-named appeared not long after his second stay in Paris, from October 1926 to February 1927, during which his marriage to the singer Meri Marttinen came to pieces, and — a repetition of the London experience — he stood on the brink of collapse, applying to friends in Finland, Gunnar Björling among them, to save him. The reputation of Diktonius rests, even today, largely on the activist verse of these years, the famous poem about the jaguar destroying conservative society, the several suites about hunger in London, the "Love Fantasy to the Sea" and other storm poems from Cornwall (often with a soft-focused political import), the summons to the workers, including the "Great Moving Day" from *Stenkol,* which gives the signal for revolution. But beyond this sometimes effective, sometimes noisy verse there are the poems of self-revelation, the short portraits (a technique learned from Edgar Lee Masters, to whom he addresses one of them), and the suite "Orchestra," one of the most cleverly allusive and well-informed poems about music in any Scandinavian language. One may wonder if the determined preaching of violent reform did not slowly become a poetic burden for Diktonius; he often comes off far better in instances where he can put his genuine artistic and human insight to work or employ his undeniable sense of humor and of the absurd, a respect in which he approaches his Russian contemporary, Vladimir Mayakovsky. He also resembles Mayakovsky in the sometimes shocking frankness of his poems about himself — about his sexual feelings for a six-year-old girl, "Rachel," in Cornwall, about his self-image in "The Big and Little Me," about the difficulties of literary creation in "The Tightrope Walker."

Undoubtedly, Diktonius wrote too much and did not have the most successful hand in choosing poems (from among the many that had appeared in magazines and newspapers) for inclusion in his books; some of his most original creations, the poetic representations of works of art in "Images," including the fine poem on a Kandinsky still life, were not collected until 1953, when his disciple, Jörn Donner, assembled them as *Ringar i stubben* (Rings in the stump). One of the anomalies of Diktonius's production of the 1920s, too, is that his appeals to the working man and the revolutionary, all written in Swedish, scarcely can have had a large reading public in Finland, where — as Ture Janson and Sigrid Backman well knew — the Swedish-speaking proletariat grew ever smaller. Yet some few of these poems are remarkably effective and readily make an appeal beyond class limits, for example, "Heroes' Graves," in *Stenkol,* concentrated in a single parallelism, between the well-tended monuments to the fallen Whites and the graves of the Red dead, hidden in the forest — the victims of combat or of summary execution?

The poetic 1920s culminated with *Stark men mörk* (1930; Strong but dark), in which, for better and worse, many of the well-known themes were essayed again: the little suite with the Schubertian title "An die Musik" (which includes the expression of the essentially erotic nature of musical performance, "We Sang"), the tormented fantasies of "Mons veneris" and the hangover of "The Devil in the Mirror" (Diktonius was already well on the way to alcoholism), and the tiresome propaganda poetry of "The Thrall's Back" (scarred, of course, by a master's whip); Diktonius's growing sentimentality is all too obvious in the several sets of verses about children. But an expansion of his range was indicated by the poems about Åland and his attempt to look without prejudice at the events of the Civil War in the melodramatic story in verse "Red Emil: A Ballad from 1918." In the often anthologized ballad (containing clear echoes of the Kullervo episode in the *Kalevala*) Emil is seen as a product of his environment and, at the end of his short and brutal life, confronts a firing squad with dumb heroism — or stubbornness. Diktonius does not make a political statement in his favor.

At the same time, all the while continuing his flood of book reviews in *Arbetarbladet* and elsewhere (he had to live by his pen, or typewriter), Diktonius wrote prose of a nature not much seen in Finland before: employing a Swedish full of colloquialisms and Fennicisms (some argued that he had never learned to write his mother tongue correctly), he produced the rambunctious scenes from country life *Onnela: Finsk idyll* (1925; Onnela: Finnish idyll), a happy place (as the Finnish title indicates) whose forebear may well be Alphonse Daudet's *Lettres de mon moulin* (1868; Letters from my mill), which Diktonius had read in translation, and *Ingenting och andra novellistiska skisser* (1928; Nothing and other storylike sketches), whose eponymous segment, albeit based on the poem by Södergran, devolved into a prose hymn to the art of laziness. Also, as the subtitle indicates, Diktonius ventured into narrative, with the terrifying "Hang Yourself, You Damned Kid!" about a young acrobat hounded almost to death by a gang of drunken lumberjacks, and "The Sun Moment," a story from the winter of 1924–25, spent with his first wife as café musicians in Jyväskylä, the central Finnish town to which he also paid decimating tribute in the prose poem bearing the town's name. As so often, Diktonius chose badly;

the story, a tearjerker about the suicide of a Russian emigré cellist, was included in *Ingenting,* but the prose poem was published in the comic paper *Garm* and then had to wait until the 1950s for Donner to put it between the covers of a book: "The small town's winter night: a dog, a policeman, a dog... another dog. But all so far from one another, without outer connection, without inner sympathy. The street lamps like inflamed eyes."

Diktonius's second marriage, his settling down in Grankulla, the birth of a child, the cooling of his political passions gave the humorous, ruminative, and experimental aspects of his literary personality a chance for development. His art of prose—which today provides more satisfaction to his readers than much of his poetry—continued to evolve: in 1933 an assembly of his musical reviews, *Opus 12: Musik* (Opus 12: Music), proved that, with his ability to change aural impressions into literary-visual ones, his apparently lighthearted but acute judgments, and his often outlandish wit, he is the one Scandinavian music critic worthy of being named with a James Gibbons Huneker or a George Bernard Shaw. High accomplishment as a writer on music was to be expected of him, high accomplishment as a novelist was not; yet the year before *Opus 12,* he published the exceptional short novel *Janne Kubik: Ett träsnitt i ord* (Janne Kubik: A woodcut in words), which—in a series of episodes, each provided with a set of footnotes or glosses on the primary text—pursues the Peer Gynt–like career of the boastful and cowardly Janne from the Red Guard to a White prison camp, from bootlegging in the Finland of Prohibition to his death as a strikebreaker. Horrifying, funny, and humane, written in a prose shot through with the Fennicisms in which Diktonius delighted (he claimed that the book was conceived in Finnish, and in 1946 he published the Finnish version, *Janne Kuutio*), the book is one of the handful of unimpeachable masterpieces of the Finland-Swedish novel. Nor was this enough; in 1935 he came out with the sketches of mostly aberrant personalities, *Medborgare i republiken Finland* (Citizens in the Republic of Finland): an organ builder with fascistic sympathies (he becomes involved in the abortive Mäntsälä putsch by members of the far right Lappo movement) and pedophiliac tendencies, an orphan boy driven to suicide by a degenerate farmhand, a devoted mother (a favorite Diktonian type), a necrophile who identifies with Adolf Hitler, a drunkard, an old farmer dying of cancer—and instead of Finnish *grand Guignol,* Diktonius produces portraits as thorough in their understanding as they often are disturbing or disgusting.

A sequel, *Medborgare II* (Citizens II), from 1940 is not as consistent in quality but contains, all the same, "Josef and Sussan," the story of a love affair between a mildly dishonest Jewish boy and a gullible Finland-Swedish girl, proving (in Josef's morally upright uncle, Moses) that Diktonius, like Arvid Mörne, was aware of events in Nazi Germany. Otherwise, in the 1930s Diktonius pasted together a mixture of poems and prose pieces, *Mull och moln* (1934; Clod and cloud); a melange of older and newer poems, *Gräs och granit* (1936; Grass and granite); and still another lyric collection, *Jordisk ömhet* (Earthly tenderness). A marked falling-off in his vitalism and his bombast and a growing urge toward quietism took place; again, there are excellent musical poems ("Unhappy Bass Tuba," "Salvation Guitar"), the inevitable storm poems, muted now ("The Storm Dies Down"), the appeal for understanding between the veterans of 1918 in "The Heart of the World, 1938," and the occasional piece of wonderfully grotesque imagery, as in the beach poem "Villa Golicke" (set on the "Finnish Riviera," where the Diktoniuses vacationed for a couple of summers): the sea is "the blue-pleasure-opened mouth" of a giantess "with sand power on her / lips" "and, deepest inside, / the gull's silver filling." In his surprises, as in his humor, Diktonius was not unlike his American contemporary, William Carlos Williams.

During the Winter War Diktonius — who had many friends among Swedish writers, the refined and difficult Ekelöf, the politically aware and intellectually keen novelist Eyvind Johnson, the proletarian Josef Kjellgren — toured Sweden as a representative of the Finnish cause and then, after the armistice of 1940, became acquainted with Bertolt Brecht when the latter stopped in Finland as a guest of Hella Wuolijoki (see chapter 4). Symptoms of illness appeared in 1941, and throughout the decade an obvious weakening of his powers took place; in *Varsel* (1942; Portents) he was consumed by a search for small moments of peace and beauty (in Schubert, in Sibelius, in the family farm, Tuomistonoja); a tone of resignation marked his picture of a dictator's grave: "Whatever evil he did — and the air growing still / when the name is named — lies dust and ashes even as here." (The dictator is not named; did Diktonius think of Hitler, Finland's then cobelligerent, or of the Soviet Union's supreme commander?) His last book of prose, *Höstlig bastu* (1943; Autumnal sauna), contains his almost mystical apostrophe to that arch-Finnish institution, the background, for the rest, of the greatest of his love poems, "Unreally True," written in memory of his first wife, long ago dead by her own hand. Much of his energy went into the translation of Kivi's *Seitsemän veljestä*, which finally appeared in 1948, a labor of love severely criticized — once more — for its Fennicisms.

Honors came to the prematurely aging poet, who refurbished his sometime Red allegiances when leftist political sympathies became useful, after

1944, in a Finland in the Soviet shadow. Some of the verse in *Annorlunda* (1948; Otherwise) can be taken as a rather lame recantation of the conservatism (and anti-Sovietism) he had evinced a decade earlier when, in "Villa Golicke," he saw the "bastions' excrement" of the Russian naval base at Kronstadt across from Kuokkala. Diktonius's later books contain gems, perfect and flawed; *Annorlunda* has not only the dream vision of Meri Marttinen but eccentric poems about postwar Finland, "Finnish Winter Dawn" and the gloss on Runeberg's anthem, called "Our Country Number 2," which begins in verse and slips off into nondescript prose, listing cultural icons and personal friends. His artistic discipline, never great, was failing, but his gift for telling and ironic allusion remained — for example, to the Beethoven Pastorale and to Swedish Christmas songs. His final book of poems, *Novembervår* (1952; November spring), came out not long before his admission to a mental hospital and, again, shows embarrassing signs of decay, yet it offers poems of a striking originality and a fantastic quality rare in his prior work.

While Diktonius was still alive, his friend Olof Enckell, who had published a biography of his early years a decade before, edited a three-volume set of his works (1957), which of necessity excluded much of his newspaper and journal writing, a set that was a monument to the most variegated and, in many ways, most original of the modernists, a sometimes disappointing but always fascinating figure in Finland-Swedish literature. In his verbal genius as in his lack of poetic and personal self-control he is reminiscent of Eino Leino, some of whose poems he translated, not very successfully, in 1931. In *Novembervår* he painted an unsparing portrait of his Finnish colleague, sitting hung-over on a bench in Brunnsparken, with his coat open (like Balzac in Rodin's statue),

> so that one could behold
> what you've drunk, eaten, and otherwise fooled around with lately.
> You met the waters' shine with bloodshot eyes
> and muttered: Odysseus, Odysseus,
> There's only one of my sort
> in this shitty, beloved country.

Olsson

In *Jordisk ömhet* Diktonius included a poem, "Piano Key" dedicated to "H.O.," Hagar Olsson (1893–1978). There seems to be no connection with Olsson save in its central image — a key whose "ivory sides and back / are cold as ice — / for they belong to the world," and a "face of unpainted wood" within, "turned to a different direction: / toward the depth of the sounding box / in its eternal night / where hot strings make the light resound." The poem refers, perhaps, to two aspects of Olsson's creative personality, the sharpness of her reviews (from which Diktonius himself often had to suffer) and the mysticism that marked much of her novelistic work. Hagar Olsson's first name was prophetic; it belonged to the bondwoman of Sarah sent away with her son Ishmael, into the wilderness, where she was addressed by the angel of the Lord (and thus the name had an air, for Olsson's pastor father, of the woman wronged but ultimately chosen), but it also belonged to the learned and energetic female protagonist of Topelius's *Stjärnornas kungabarn,* which had appeared not long before she was born. (In Olsson's vaguely autobiographical novel, *Chitambo* [1933], the heroine is named Vega Maria Dyster by her father, the first name in honor of the ship on which Adolf Erik Nordenskiöld completed the navigation of the Northeast Passage.) She spent her early childhood on Åland and in Åbo, but in 1906 her father was transferred to Räisälä in Karelia. Olsson finished her schooling in Viborg, briefly attended a commercial academy and the university of Helsingfors, and in short order decided to strike out as a journalist, writing for *Dagens Press,* later transformed into *Svenska Pressen.* In this capacity, as the new literary critic of Helsingfors's Swedish evening paper, she made her initial contact with Edith Södergran.

Some admirers of Södergran have tended to view Olsson as an appendage of her early-dead friend. Instead, she was, first of all, the most prolific representative of modernist criticism. Though not as colorful as Diktonius, not as careful with distinctions as Rabbe Enckell, certainly not as balanced as his brother Olof (who, in time, would break a lance for Olsson herself), she had a boldness that allowed her to take on the pope of Swedish reviewers, Fredrik Böök (bearding the lion in his den, she assailed him in 1928, in the pages of *Stockholms Dagblad,* as "the infallible Swedish critic"), and an awareness of foreign currents that led her to introduce Joyce and Pirandello, Lagerkvist and Vilhelm Ekelund in her essay collection of 1925, *Ny generation* (New generation), which also included one of her many salutes to Södergran. Making another collection of her reviews and essays in 1935, *Arbetare i natten* (Workers in the night), she dwelled on Eugene O'Neill and a galaxy of other foreign artists: D. H. Lawrence, Sherwood Anderson, Jean Cocteau, Franz Werfel, and the storyteller in woodcuts, Frans Masereel. She also included figures in her own language: Lagerkvist again, the Swedish romantic C.J.L. Almqvist (a passion she shared with Södergran), a contemporary Finland-Swede named Örnulf Tigerstedt (see below) whom she took the trouble to detest, and Arvid Mörne, whose bitter idealism she admired—and, in Finnish, Toivo Pekkanen, whom she introduced to the Swedish-speaking world. The collection ended with a presentation of the Persian classics: her fascination with a large, ill-defined Eastern world, in which she perceived greater spiritual values than in the rational West, would continue her whole life through; a pronounced individualist in her personal behavior, she was fascinated by what she saw as the salubrious collectivism of Eastern cultures.

Olsson's critical activity, in which her polemical urges collided with her mystical inclinations, has a counterpart in her narratives. Her first novel, *Lars Thorman och döden* (1916; Lars Thorman and death), is the account, in highly lyrical prose, of a young man beset by an overwhelming fear of death (another of Olsson's idées fixes); he does not pass away (albeit his beloved does), however, since he has gained new strength from a northern Pan, a forest god bearing the Old Norse name Samr. The debut, which got only a few but not unfriendly reviews, was followed by *Själarnas ansikten* (1917; The souls' countenances), an introductory panegyric to the "noble fanatics" prepared to fight and die for their ideals, illustrated by short, exemplary tales about such beings (who likewise suffer from thanatophobia); perhaps because of a common Nietzschean source, *Själarnas ansikten* anticipates Södergran's adoration of exceptional figures, although Södergran objected violently to the story "Starchild," complaining bitterly about its "mysticism." In the same vein, *Kvinnan och nåden* (1919; The woman and grace), based on the story of the prophet Samuel's birth, was centered on "Elkanah's woman," Samuel's mother Hannah, and the visionary experiences she undergoes. These early works are interesting today because of their reflection of literary currents of the time (such as the influence of the young Pär Lagerkvist and the German expressionists, with their often inchoate plans for a spiritual transformation of the world), but as Jörn Donner— who reprinted them in the 1950s—admits, Olsson was not yet a "finished artist."

Olsson's overriding but nebulous ideas (about death, salvation, the necessity of a life calling) and her habit of weaving self-made fairy tales into her work (a habit shared with Södergran) prevent *Mr. Jeremias söker en illusion* (1926; Mr. Jeremiah looks for an illusion) from becoming a firmly contoured narrative. Jeremiah is unable to interest himself in any cause, or "illusion," until he dies in a traffic accident and is carried away by a magical airplane to the "illusion of illusions," death, as the little novel comes to an end: "Now the adventure begins! Now the prologue is over!" *På Kanaanexpressen* (1929; On the Canaan Express) is closer to normal prose fiction, with its glimpses of newspaper life in Helsingfors, its romantic intrigues, and its gilded youths who suffer from the "degradation of [being] the chosen ones"; *Det blåser upp till storm* (1930; A storm is brewing) has an almost banal plot: a romance between a wealthy boy and a poor girl in a Helsingfors school leads to the boy's suicide and the girl's turn to a brave future: "When I look out to sea, I behold the new worlds born at the gates of the sunrise."

Like Sigrid Backman, but making far greater demands on her audience, Olsson concentrates her attention more and more on the figure of the young girl, something she does most successfully in the above-mentioned *Chitambo*. Set in Helsingfors in the days before and after the Civil War (with a glance into the coming world of the dictators), it describes the development of Vega Maria, who learns, to her horror, that the "tellurian revolution" she has wanted to embrace, a world of collectives, not individuals, will bring disaster on Europe, whereas the individualists of her own life, her tyrannical but devoted father, Carl Johan Dyster, perhaps a portrait of Karl Sixtus Olsson, and her lover, Tancred, have in fact done little damage, and some good, in their small world, a world portrayed with Backmanesque or Dickensian quaintness (in an essay of 1959 Olsson confessed her fondness for *David Copperfield*). The idealist Vega Maria finally decides to be like David Livingstone (the book's title is the name of the African village where Stanley found the Scots missionary), a great individual ready to sacrifice himself or herself for the masses.

Träsnidaren och döden (1940; Eng. tr. *The Woodcarver and Death*, 1965) borrows both from the realm of Edith Södergran—the death-fearing woodcarver, Myyriäinen, flees to a picturesque Karelian village bearing easily detectable traces of Raivola—and from the exotic Karelianism that was nurtured, decades before, by Ahrenberg, Gallen-Kallela, and Sibelius. In the 1930s and 1940s, thanks to Tito Colliander, Olof Enckell, and Göran Stenius, it had once again appeared in the Finland-Swedish novel, expressing a devotion to what Hagar Olsson called "the holy places of Finnish culture." That the novel about the woodcarver came out in the wake of the Winter War, just after a good part of Karelia had been amputated from Finland, increased its popularity; Karelia, too, with its Russian Orthodox believers, provided Olsson a new and thankful setting for two of her besetting questions, the meaning of death and the individual's relation to a community: both are incorporated in little, abused Sanni, whom her father, the carefree but pious Iivana Lampinen, has brought to the great cloister church at Valamo to die. The woodcarver associates himself with both Sanni and another young girl, Sabine, the daughter of an evidently Swedish-speaking family on a nearby estate: the novel's happy end, a vision of a union between the no longer youthful Myyriäinen and the misunderstood and spoiled adolescent, is inspiratory but implausible. Olsson's long opening essay on spiritual renewal in *Jag lever* (1948; I live, reportedly the last words of Aleksis Kivi) may be regarded as a pendant to Sanni's transfiguration; Olsson has still another of her dreams of a wondrous (but indeterminate) future: "There can be no doubt that a new cultural idea, which aims at unity and togetherness in human affairs, is beginning to emerge in the world."

Olsson's remaining narratives are all short; the miniature Märchen novel, *Kinesisk utflykt* (1950; Chinese excursion), and the collections of tales, *Hemkomst: Tre berättelser* (1961; Homecoming: Three tales), *Drömmar* (1966; Dreams), and *Ridturen och andra berättelser* (1968; The riding tour and other stories), continued to concentrate on girls or young women, tart-tongued and vulnerable, and on death, terrible and fascinating: "We had never seen a corpse, but I desired to see the dead body so passionately that I salivated at the thought, as if someone had offered me a molasses sandwich," a character says in the title story of *Ridturen*. Flights into mystical sensations and the fairy tale have remained standard elements of Olsson's fictional world; but the gruesome story just mentioned (touching on childhood experiences, noted by the well-informed Olof Enckell in a study of 1949), and the unsettling sexual fantasies of "Gargantua" (in *Drömmar*, tr. in *Swedo-Finnish Short Stories*, 1974) are fairly isolated in her production. In the latter an enormously fat girl becomes a devourer of men and is killed in a fire as she "triumphantly danced her dance toward death, herself burning like a torch, crying until the last for flame, more flame."

Olsson is the only modernist who did not try lyric poetry; on the other hand, she essayed the drama, with some success. In 1927, under the spell of Strindberg and German expressionism, she wrote *Hjärtats pantomim* (The heart's pantomime), a dream play in which the heroine attempts to escape her loneliness by communing with an image of Buddha (like Sabine, the girl from the Karelian estate in *Träsnidaren och döden*); in 1928 she presented echoes of Georg Kaiser's *Gas* (1918/1920) in *S.O.S.*, in which a manufacturer of poison gas, abetted by a young woman, decides to abandon his work and is subjected to political persecution as a pacifist; in 1931 she wrote *Det blå undret* (The blue wonder), in which a sister and brother represent, respectively, communism and fascism, contrasted to the supposedly out-of-date liberalism of their father. The political upheavals of the 1930s were also the topic of her Finnish-language play, *Lumisota* (The snowball war), rehearsals of which were stopped under government pressure in the tense autumn of 1939; it was not performed until almost twenty years later, by amateurs in Jyväskylä. The play's action takes place at Easter in the home of Finland's foreign minister; he wants his little nation to survive, even though it means compromise with Moscow. His elder son is a member of a fascist organization; his younger son pleads for reconciliation within the family and the nation and at a political rally is badly beaten by the older son's colleagues for his "betrayal." (Olsson gave this mouthpiece of idealism the name Outi, which, as a commentator wrote in a note pasted onto the rehearsal manuscript, could also be a girl's name; the playwright evidently refused to change it, since it emphasized the role's androgynic quality.) The miracle play of 1944, *Rövaren och jungfrun* (The bandit and the maiden), demonstrated at great length, in a countryside setting from the past, that a light shines in the darkness, borne by the young girl Sanna; conversely, *Kärlekens död* (1952; The death of love) showed how the bored and selfish guests at a shabby hotel torment one another, a situation something like that in Sartre's famous *Huit clos* (*No Exit*) of 1944.

Erik Ekelund, a perceptive reader of Olsson, saw in *Kinesisk utflykt* and other later works a resolution of "the conflict between her revolutionary individualism ... and her need of human contact," between her "strong self-assertion" and "her devotion to the idea of collectivism" ("Resa till det förflutna," 175). The resolution was "self-obliteration of the same sort as the Christian mystics' absorption into the god-head, or the annihilation of the ego which the Nirvana of Buddhism represents," a desire whose seeds had been present in her creative work from the very start. This may be the reason her novels and dramas, often so promising in their conception, steal away into tantalizing mysticism; her main accomplishment lies in her criticism, in which she does not struggle so obsessively with the conflicts inside herself. She never married, and an engagement to R. R. Eklund (see below) was broken off in 1920; he may be the Tancred of *Chitambo*. A delicate beauty whose personal behavior shocked the would-be hardboiled Diktonius, Olsson led a life that was turbulent and ambiguous in its affections.

Björling

The oldest of the modernists, Gunnar Björling (1887–1960), was also the last to reach full recognition. After his debut, *Vilande dag* (1922; Resting day), which appeared at the short-lived house Daimon, he had to serve as his own publisher until 1937, when Söderström & Co brought out a selection from his work assembled by Rabbe Enckell, who characterized his poems as "not a lyric of the sounds and the words, but a lyric of the human being, full of struggle, a lyric constantly ready for action ... it is the pathos of the heart which nourishes his lyric more unreservedly and directly than in any other case save Södergran's." Björling did not receive a prize from the Swedish Literary Society in Finland until 1947, when, in Sweden and in serious literary circles of his homeland, he had long since become a legendary figure. To some, upset initially by his lifestyle and the defensive clowning of his dadaist period, he remained a scandal and a hissing. The psychiatrist and literary critic Mikael Enckell has written, "His tragedy was that the traditionalists never understood or could recognize how in Björling they possessed a kindred spirit" ("Poeten som profet," 83); in his Runebergian search for the "transfigured moment," particularly in his nature poetry, he honored their own ideal.

Born to middle-class parents in Helsingfors and briefly a cadet at the military academy in Fredrikshamn (from which Gripenberg had run away), he spent years in desultory philosophical studies at his home city's university (becoming a disciple of the apostle of relativism, Edvard Westermarck) and in efforts to write lyrics in the accepted forms, such as the sonnet; he was also attracted by the irrationalism and the acceptance of the darker forces of life he found in Nietzsche and in Jean-Marie Guyau's *L'irréligion de l'avenir* (1887), as well as by Henri Bergson's efforts to rebuild the bridge between metaphysics and science. His whole lyric work thus came to be marked by an attempt to solve an apparently insolvable problem, as Bengt Holmqvist — one of the earlier critics to lay out clear patterns in his production — said: "To find a point of intersection between naturalism's denial of every transcendental reality and an implicitly faithful experience of existence, between moral relativism and absolute ideality, between rationalism and the celebration of life itself" (p. 109). A stint as a substitute teacher at Helsingfors's venerable boys' school, the Swedish Normal Lyceum, ended unhappily because of the close relationships he formed with his pupils (he was seen providing them with cigarettes!); parents did not like to learn of their sons' hearkening to the eternal bachelor's passionately idealistic words, which took "vulgarity and indolence" as their foe, or so Björling recalled in a backward look. He lived his whole adult life in a basement apartment in Brunnsparken, otherwise one of the capital's most elegant sections, and resisted every effort to make him fit into society's normal patterns; nevertheless, during the Civil War he had bravely maintained a secret White radio sender in his cellar. Until his death he kept up his role as a Socrates for the young, and depictions of him, thinly disguised, appear repeatedly in creative literature.

The adulation that surrounded him in his immediate circle, as well as the rejection by the wielders of literary power, may have led to a contempt for the public. His highly elliptical poetry can seem (in Johan Wrede's words ["Birth of Finland-Swedish Modernism," 94]) to be a kind of stammering, and for a long time he was implicitly and explicitly defiant, in both his verse and the aphorisms that accompanied it (and which were initially minted, one suspects, for his disciples): "My nerves are steel, impudence makes a yarnball of that which no one has the power to understand — words! — soon I'll start smashing, everything whole is dustiness, an irritant and cathedrals and fortifications, everything shall go down into the heart's the stomach's catchall. There dwells the darling child of restlessness," he wrote bafflingly in *Fågel badar snart i vatten* (1934; Soon bird bathes in water). Like Södergran, Diktonius, and Olsson, he was relentless in his prediction of a future when the world would be better and different, and, as Wrede remarks, "dag" (day) is far and away the most common noun in his debut. In his second book, bearing a title that sounds like a summons to a crusade, *Korset och löftet* (1925; The cross and the promise), he compared himself to a rat in a backyard: "I scoot over worn planks, screech, gnaw my way to garbage pails," but in fact he celebrates the task of poetry, art, and life, which is to transfigure and elevate the "day," to give it a meaning, to "see God in a vision" — he preaches "programlessness" and "an openness to what is greatest." This superidealism, the quite romantic yearning for what is unattainable, collided with his irritation at the world in which he found himself (and which, according to his rationalist-relativist background, he was bound to observe and, if possible, accept), and the collision led to the dadaist poetry of his contributions to *Quosego* (1928–29), the second of the important community publications of the modernists. Among much else by Björling, it contained the aphorism "My absurdity — a piece of sugar I lick in the presence of others" and the poem "Charlie Chaplin," with the lines: "you paint crazyeyes / with your feet." The *Quosego* pieces were followed by the nonsensically named *Kiri-ra!* (1930), which also has highly original poems about nature:

> As in the Linnaeusspringtime,
> Dandelion dog-violet stellaria
> springbirchleaves and passion
> Sun
> on woodsorrel and the blossom's down.

In his dissertation on Björling, Carpelan recalls that the collection was attacked from within the modernist camp by Hagar Olsson, causing Cid Erik Tallqvist to remark that she was not "the high priestess of modernism" but of philistinism (p. 173). One is reminded, too, of her repeated attacks on Diktonius. The notion that the modernists presented a united front is much mistaken.

Commentators on Björling have observed that *Solgrönt* (1933; Sun green) is a turning point, in that Björling begins to abandon his hectic and willfully annoying tone for a new serenity.

> How shall I not be glad?
> Summer and westwind
> on singing earth.
> The late autumn evening's moon on bay and islets,
> storm has ceased,
> the day is at an end.
> There is a glimmer in mist from all lanterns
> it is as though on the way to a churchyard.

With such poetry Björling made his voice an essential part of the Finland-Swedish lyric tradition, its sensitivity to nature's moods and its underlying melancholy. Hereafter, his books of poetry (mixed with aphorisms) came thick and fast, from *Fågel badar snart i vatten* (1934) to *Att i sitt öga* (1954; That in his eye) and *Du går de ord* (1955; You walk the words). Many of the poems are about fragile natural impressions, captured by Björling in the old park on whose periphery he lived, as in these lines from *Ohjälpligheten* (1943; Irredeemableness):

> A park, a rose garden
> and hundred-year-old trees
> and butterfly's flight on tended lawn
> midst linden and elm and larch tree.

Many bespeak a light and indefinable eroticism, directed to an unspecified "thou":

> Never saw I
> as when in the morning
> I
> you.
>
> As a before the wakening
> you face
> pure-form.
>
> perhaps flees
> and passes
> such you.
>
> It is you I
> you
> always

The lines are from *Där jag vet att du* (1938; There I know that you), in a poem that carries Björling's ellipticism to the utmost. The difficulty of this poetry lies not in identifying the mood or achieving a general understanding but rather, at an elementary level, in parsing. The reader is confronted by a lack of grammatical and syntactical continuity and strains to find words that have apparently been left out.

Sometimes Björling baffles the reader, too, by his extensive use of homonyms and by his discontinuity, as in the following miniature from *Att i sitt öga:*

White gull and ducks' calm beat
and japanlike
a fisherboat and everything gray and blue
as merely . . .

Here "blue" and "merely" are words that sound alike: "blått" and "blott." Also, "white gull" ("vita mås") is a vocative form; Björling loves the outcry, implicit or fully expressed, usually of joy at the very fact of existence: "oh fly fly white clouds / fly in this / day of heaven." The explicators of Björling's language, especially the linguist Kim Nilsson, have noted that the difficulties are often only apparent: "There does exist [for Björling] a reality of the universe that, albeit in constant flux, can always be sensed." The apparent elisions operate "on a system of contrapuntal opposites that define semantic fields. . . . Once so apprehended, the deviation from natural language is rather slight" ("Björling," 62).

As time went on, Björling made efforts to present his work to a larger readership. He brought out a retrospective selection of his verse from 1937 on, *Och leker med skuggorna i sanden* (And plays with the shadows in the sand) in 1947; this was followed in 1952 by a selection of aphorisms from 1922 to 1951, *Så fjärran skäller* (So distant barks), and a companion volume of lyrics from 1922 to 1936, *Träd står i sina rader* (Trees stand in their rows). A general selection from the some twenty collections he had published since 1930, *Du jord du dag* (You earth you day), appeared in 1957, followed by still another selection of the lyrics from 1930 to 1955, *En mun vid hand* (1958; A mouth at hand), and of lyrics from 1922 to 1955, *Hund skenar glad* (1959; Dog darts happy); evidently, he regarded these three chronologically overlapping volumes as the final and authentic version of his work, containing the cream of his huge production; they were reprinted in 1989 as *Valda dikter* (Chosen poems). Obviously, many of the complications that once kept Björling from publishers and public do not seem so daunting any longer; readers have caught up with him.

Now regarded by some as the greatest poet (and deepest thinker) among the Finland-Swedish modernists, he has inspired scholarship to undertake to make a full edition of all his extant works—a staggering task, since he is said to have kept the bathtub in his apartment full of manuscripts, from which he plucked items to present to the world. Some thirty thousand poems are now preserved in the library of Åbo Academy. Realizing how difficult it was to find a way through Björling's massive poetic material, even aided by the several florilegia put together by the poet himself, Bo Carpelan produced still another selection from the total printed work in 1975, in the belief that Björling was best taken in moderate doses. Yet some have detected a narrative line, elliptical to be sure, in certain collections and have especially warned against excerpting parts from the larger suites he favored (even as Diktonius did) during the 1920s; the Dane Poul Borum has written that it is possible to examine the twenty lyric books of Björling as a "single, streaming diary" ("Björling," 193). Although giving many signs of serenity in his later works, he remained true to the almost forced youthfulness of his modernist beginnings; in *Men blåser violer på havet* (1936; But violets blow on the sea) he wrote, "I wish I'd have a long life . . . I shall wake up one day and learn that life lies before me as when I was twenty, and I am just as unprepared, just as full of zeal and worry."

Rabbe Enckell
As a youth, Rabbe Enckell (1903–74) had for a short time been a disciple of Björling, but—as Enckell's son and biographer, Mikael Enckell, observes—possessed enough steady intelligence to go his own way. After Björling's death Rabbe Enckell wrote of a "nature truly touched with genius," who, however, took it as a given that others would be his "eternal followers" and constantly affirm him in his brilliance ("Björling," 135). Enckell was an extremely keen analyzer of those near and dear to him—for example, his father, a distinguished agronomist, and his first wife, Heidi Runeberg; but his gift of empathy was coupled with a dependence on others and an unusual impracticality that made the great personal crisis of his life all the more severe. He was the youngest brother of four, after Olof, critic, sometime novelist, and scholar; Jarl, engineer and industrialist; and Torger, a painter and etcher of international reputation; Rabbe himself, like Ragnar Ekelund, had a professional career as a painter alongside that as an author.

His first book, *Dikter* (1923; Poems), showed an unusual maturity in its delicate love lyrics, as free of standard turns of phrase as it was of rhyme and discernible meter; he had quickly learned the modernists' lessons ("As lightly as a breath of wind brings grass blade against blade, / thus lightly / I will touch you"). The happy epithalamia of *Flöjtblåsarlycka* (1925; Fluteblower's happiness) followed, in which language made an immediate impression by tiny adjustments of what was expected: "The springtime sits behind a stone / with snow in the shadow" and

> I dreamed
> that in your love's arms I lay
> like a dugout between the reeds
> still,
> hidden on gently rocking waves
> close to the beach,
> where the sand shines red through the water.

Enckell represented an intermediate stage between the comforting familiarity of the images favored by a Jarl Hemmer and the apparent irrationality of extreme modernists. *Vårens cistern* (1931; The springtime's cistern) became a showcase of his apparently serene miniaturist poems, in which he celebrated small but important beauties of Finland's country life:

> The Acropolis's
> sunny mass
> does not frighten me.
> I have seen
> the Finnish hill's
> gray barn,
> its templelike
> proportions
> without weight
> rising up
> toward the spring sky's endless breadth.

He called them "match poems" ("They have been content / violently to light my face when struck— / and go out.") and pretended that the public laughed at them, a bow to the programmatic outsiderness of the modernists. "The Freight Car" is another poem of this type: "I have been switched to the wrong track / and stand a lonely car against the buffer," which has an almost childish simplicity but, simultaneously, a dark tone that was destined to grow: "I stand in the rain— the twilight broadens / but I'll never arrive." If autobiographical, the poem is misleading, since Enckell, not out of his twenties, was already a fully accepted member of the Finland-Swedish Parnassus. *Tonbrädet* (1935; The sounding board) provided more examples — thinking of Enckell's other art, one is tempted to say a vernissage —

of his pleasure in sharpened senses; he also turned to Italian subjects, the result of trips to Italy in 1931 and 1934 ("Sienna—cypresses' row and glittering light-points' tones"). On these trips abroad Heidi functioned as interpreter; both Olof and Mikael Enckell have written about Rabbe Enckell's inhibitions when dealing with other languages than his native Swedish; like J. P. Jacobsen in Denmark, this supreme stylist was too much absorbed by his own tongue to have energy for mastering others. His Finnish is said to have been unusually weak.

Poetry and painting were not the only lines of endeavor Rabbe Enckell followed in these years. Although not a regular reviewer (as Olof Enckell, Diktonius, and Hagar Olsson all were), he quickly emerged as a critic of fine sensibility and a cogent spokesman of modernism; the essential essays from the 1920s and 1930s were collected in the volume *Relation i det personliga* (1950; Relation in the personal), including his article of 1926 from *Hufvudstadsbladet* about what was "old-new and truly new in poetry," an unpolemical but stringently analytical definition of the differences in the use of images in "old poetry" and "modern," that is, before and after Södergran: "In the old poetry the image stood as the sure support of the imagination, while the rhythm with its waves sought to bring our emotional life into oscillation"; in the modernist poem "the image no longer has the character of a solid *point d'appui,* an outer symbol, it has received a much more chancy character... it captures us by its quick movement, encourages us toward suggestive empathy and, again, flees just as quickly." Enckell, whom Diktonius described in a letter to a Swedish friend as "our true theoretician, not Hagar Olsson," was surely the proper editor to present the anthology *Modärn finlandssvensk lyrik* (1934; Modern Finland-Swedish lyric): in its lengthy introduction, while emphasizing the great formal difference between the lyric tradition of the past and modernism, Enckell denied there was an unbridgeable gap between literary generations and predicted, quite correctly, that "we are inclined to believe that the points of resemblance will become still more apparent in the future." Toward his fellow modernists Enckell was scrupulously fair and full of insight (another, less private aspect of his empathy), able to approach a poet as radically different from himself as Diktonius with genuine understanding. A weakness is his indifference to literary history; determinedly unacademic (although he would become a favorite of academics), he treats the baroque poet Jacob Frese in a vacuum.

Enckell's function as a critic continued, in one way and another (in the formal essay and then, more and more frequently, in his diaristic books), throughout his life; his essays on the English-Belgian-Finnish painter, etcher, and ceramicist A. W. Finch and on Edvard Munch make one wish that he had devoted more time to art criticism (where his kind of lucidity is fairly rare); his defense of a writer's "aesthetic view of life," as opposed to the poet as a scourge of society, in "Salvo from the Ivory Tower" (1947), would later be used against him. On the other hand, Enckell's substantial production as a writer of seminarrative prose belongs largely to the early 1930s. His debut in this field came with *Tillblivelse* (1929; Origination), a personal account: "Can I really think that my chance observations and my life over the course of a few years will be able to awaken interest?" Enckell added that he could have disguised his account as a novel but wished to break with "the tradition of the art of masking and made-up stories." The book came as a breath of fresh air in a literature in which the autobiographical novel had been (and would continue to be) a standard and often somewhat tiresome item. The practice continued in *Ljusdunkel* (1930; Chiaroscuro) and *Ett porträtt* (1931; A portrait), about his wife, a loving opusculum she may have found inhibitory because of the care with which it gently dissected the elements of her personality. In all these books Enckell might seem to be a forerunner of the "confessors" of a later time, such as Christer Kihlman and Henrik Tikkanen, but he had a discretion to match the precision and simple elegance of his style.

Landskapet med den dubbla skuggan (1933; The landscape with the double shadow) was a novel in actual fact, but even here with a personal core. The brothers Vidrack, Blasius, and Corpus Stewart correspond, to a considerable degree, to Rabbe, Olof, and Torger Enckell; the choleric father, "pieces of food in his beard," is the professor of agronomy, Karl Enckell; the careworn and devoted mother is Vesta Enckell; the author Gerdt, who "lives in a little cellar room," is Björling; Pernille, who "reads everything she can lay her hands on," is a reflection of Heidi. (Some names have plainly literary origins: Vidrack is a lazy boy in one of Topelius's poems for children; Pernille is from a Holberg comedy.) However, the little book, whose title alludes to a Rubens etching, a "compression of idyll and terror," is not only a *nouvelle à clef* but an expression of Enckell's sense that his idyll was threatened. (Because of the story's brevity, it was given a pendant, in the same volume, about the poet's daughter Birgitta and the heedless cruelty of the young [Eng. tr. "The Japanese Children," *Swedo-Finnish Short Stories*, 1974].) The "youthful prose," as Enckell somewhat defensively called all these works when they were put together in a single volume in 1958, was closed off with *Herrar till natt och dag* (1937; Lords of night and day), a collection of stories best read with an awareness of the biographical background in mind: the idyll was torn apart by the growing affection between

Heidi Enckell and a Grankulla neighbor, Oscar Parland: "The Lonely Man" is about the anxious poet himself ("The world hangs like a soapbubble on the end of a straw"), "Evi Refuge" concerns the wife who runs away to the city after a conflict with her husband, and "To Carry Yourself on a Silver Platter" is set in Kuokkala, the resort on the Karelian isthmus. During a summer storm a husband hears his wife's "sleepy, uninterested voice" ask, "Is it thundering?" ("Åskar det?"). Mikael Enckell points out that "Åskar" and "Oscar" are homonyms.

With the troubled poems of *Valvet* (1937; The vault or The arch), Enckell's poetry enters a new phase; themes from classical antiquity appear, dressed in an approximation of classical verse forms, such as the Horatian ode. *Valvet* has rightly been called the most humanly powerful of all Enckell's works. Its poems — on a vaguely uneasy vacation spot ("Like a great cake in the darkness the lamp on the balcony shines. / The wind rolls around in the garden"; on Odysseus carried home to Ithaca from the Phaeacian land, in a slumber "likest unto death," while overhead the constellation of Hercules, laborer and sufferer, "lifts its lever"; on Eubouleus, the swineherd who beholds the kidnapping of Kore by Hades; and on Peirithous, who attempts to save Demeter's daughter (but "unredeemed in the underworld / his soul found dwelling") — are examples of personal travail become moving art.

Enckell found consolation in Greek literature, which he read in Emil Zilliacus's translations (it is possible that original lyrics on classical themes by Zilliacus also inspired the greater poet): the next year, he began the series of semiverse dramas on Greek themes that would be fitfully augmented over the years, *Orfeus och Eurydike* (1938), *Iokasta* (1939), *Agamemnon* (1947), *Hekuba* (1952), and *Mordet på Kiron* (1954; The murder of Chiron). More inventive and lighthearted is the play on the Greek celebratory poet, *Alkman* (1959; Alcman), written with considerable irony about the self-important bard who wants a drink: "I am the climax that gives the festival meaning, / without me an event is embarrassing." The plays became vehicles for radio performance, and in *Dikt* (1966; Poem) Enckell reprinted the Iocasta play (which he considered perhaps the best of what he had accomplished in the genre), together with two new antique plays, on Laius, Oedipus's father, and Latona, the mother of Artemis and Apollo, conceived in what Enckell termed a more everyday language. The Greek drama, taken as a whole, seems to be the part of Enckell's work least likely to survive; as in the case of Runeberg's *Kungarne på Salamis*, a "marble chill" emanates from them, in Thomas Warburton's diplomatic phrase (*Åttio år finlandssvensk litteratur*, 234), a judgment in which Warburton included some of Enckell's later poetry. They may have their prime interest as, again, semipersonal documents or oblique comments on contemporary events, *Hekuba* on the plight of political refugees, the Chiron play on the Korean conflict.

During the war years and afterward Enckell continued to write lyrics of great strength, fed by his personal tragedy; his feelings of betrayal and loss led him to a deed of violence (which for years figured in Helsingfors's literary gossip), of which his son has given an understanding account. His sense of uncertainty and insufficiency — wrenchingly depicted in a piece of prose, "About a Skiing Trip," first published in 1991 — bore poetic profit in *Lutad över brunnen* (1942; Bent over the well) and *Andedräkt av koppar* (1946; Breath of copper), which continue the imaginative use of Greek themes. It is a temptation to read his second poem about Peirithous in the Underworld ("Now let me go, Eumenides") as a further comment on what he had just been through, but there are also signs of a return to questions of literature. The latter book opens with a salute to both Finland's modernists and the Swedish poets of the 1940s, for whom Enckell had become a household god: "Poets forced to the poem," "patient peasants of the poem's Aran" (the windswept Irish island described in Olof Enckell's reportage, *De klagande vindarnas ö* [1937; The island of the lamenting winds]), "you, poets of the difficult school"; it closes with the long elegy, "Oh bridge of words between," concluding, as its interpreter Louise Ekelund says, "in a song of praise to what is broken, since this, in the very midst of destruction, points past itself, to life's constant renewal" (*Enckell* [1982], 355), a process in which the "words between," standing for an undeclamatory muted vocabulary, a sort of complement to English understatements, have played a main role: they are the true instruments of the poet.

Enckell maintained his career as a lyricist to the end of his life, from *Sett och återbördat* (1950; Seen and restored) to the posthumous *Flyende spegel* (1974; Fleeing mirror), in all of which his old joy in nature and his reliance on classical allusions remain constant but are mixed with an increasing melancholy at the mechanization of modern existence, now and then descending into sheer querulousness. An exception is *Kärnor av ögonblick*, brighter and more open, in which he collected hitherto unpublished poems from the 1930s to the 1950s. The prose works of the latter years run roughly parallel to the lyric collections in their motifs; as early as *Traktat* (1955; Tractate) Enckell had been drawn to meandering prose, often aphoristic, and he followed this sometimes self-indulgent line with the revelatory *Essay om livets framfart* (1961; Essay on life's forward motion); *Och sanning?* (1966; And truth?), a defense against the attacks launched by young poets for Enckell's apparent lack of social awareness; *Tapetdörren* (1968; The secret door), a mixture of diaristic prose and poetry; and *Resonören med fågelfoten* (1971; The raisonneur with the bird foot), a similarly mixed composition. Naturally enough, these books are backward-looking (the dream journal in the final volume about the beloved and feared father, the elegy on "this mother's face / a memory / which presupposes all other memories / and remains in the background") and full of complaints about the contemporary world (Rome and its traffic snarls); yet they maintain the refinement of style, the delicacy of perception, and the intellectual integrity (he was strengthened by his third marriage to the graphic artist Aina Erikson-Enckell) that were hallmarks of his work. His brother Olof, who followed his career with unselfish and protective affection, wrote about his years as the resident of the Poet's House in Borgå (from 1960 until his final illness); Olof remarked on Rabbe Enckell's "deep interest in a classic spirit Goethe represented." In Borgå, for the rest, he neglected the representative duties that the position, as a Finland-Swedish *poeta laureatus,* was supposed to entail. Supremely devoted though he was to his linguistic instrument, his mother tongue, he could and would not be a voice of "cultural Swedishness." But he was a representative — much more obviously than Björling — of that pursuit of serenity to be found in an aesthetic or mystic experience of nature, which had been a constant in the minority literature since the days of Runeberg.

Henry Parland

Rabbe Enckell called Henry Parland (1908–30) the "purest incorporation of what went under the name of a 'modern mentality' in the boom years at the end of the 1920s." But he added — perhaps seeing Parland as a closing off of the pioneer phase of modernism — that, like Södergran, Parland was "without roots in our literary tradition" and "created directly out of the atmosphere of the times." Enckell then went on to mention Södergran's knowledge of the "ego futurist" Igor Severyanin (1887–1941) and Parland's evident enthusiasm for Mayakovsky. What Enckell says is a truth that needs some modification. Södergran and Parland both came from Finland's outermost marchlands and had similar problems of national and linguistic identification; but Parland was more aware of literary fads than Södergran and fully deserves the bon mot of Kim Nilsson that, among the modernists, he was "surely the most modern of them all" ("Henry Parland"). He was born in Viborg into a family with a distant English background (hence the surname) which had been in Russia since the days of Catherine the Great: an ancestor is supposed to have been the English tutor of Alexander I, Catherine's grandson. The author's great-grandfather had been a businessman in St. Petersburg but, attracted by the relatively liberal atmosphere of the grand duchy of Finland, became a Finnish subject; the paternal grandfather continued in this "Finnish" attachment; the father, an engineer in Emperor Nicholas II's service, married a daughter of the Sesemanns, a Baltic-German clan prominent in Viborg's history. The October Revolution stranded Oswald Parland in Russia, and the mother and four sons, Henry, Oscar, Ralf, and Herman, were at the Sesemann family estate at Tikkala near Viborg when the border was closed; the father could not join them until 1920. As the eldest offspring, Henry suffered most from a transplantation to the vicinity of Helsingfors; there, as Oscar Parland described it, "despite the fact that Father had Finnish citizenship, we were most commonly regarded as Russian immigrants." The family's home language had been German, and Russian had been the principal external tongue; for a short time Henry was put into a Finnish school in Helsingfors and was badly bullied, and it was not until he had come to rest in the Swedish school at Grankulla, the extremely literary suburb, that he mastered the language in which he would write his works.

After finishing at the Grankulla gymnasium in 1927, the brilliant boy began law studies at the university, but shortly his interest in letters—and bohemianism—got the upper hand, and encouraged by Gunnar Björling, he published his book of avantgarde poetry, *Idealrealisation* (Sale of ideals), after having made his debut, under Björling's aegis, in *Quosego*. His contributions there, such as "Dikter?" (Poems?), were devoted, among other things, to gasoline ("I am a great god / and I cost 3.40 a liter / and people kill one another / for my sake"), and the prose "Sakernas uppror" (Revolt of the objects), his only half-ironic salute to the objects taking over the modern world. "Here it's not a question of Americanism.... Here it's a question of idealism. The idealism of the objects. Of the automobile tires, stockings, cough drops. *They* love life, their hymn of superficiality leads toward deeper connections. Direct as a necktie—then a saxophone in life's jazz band!"

Dismayed at his son's extravagance in Helsingfors nightclubs (Henry cut a dandyistic figure, and a sketch from 1927 is called "With a New Tuxedo"), Oswald Parland sent him off to Kaunas, provisional capital of the newly founded republic of Lithuania. Taken in charge by his maternal uncle, Wilhelm Sesemann, a professor of philosophy, Henry wrote essays in which he presented new Russian and American films and Russian formalism to the Finland-Swedish public; simultaneously, he wrote in German about Scandinavian literature for the Lithuanian press. An appointment as secretary at the Swedish legation promised to stabilize his hectic life, but his health had always been frail, and he died of scarlet fever in November 1930. The sudden death of her favorite son led his mother to mental collapse, from which she never recovered. (His novel about a Helsingfors love affair, *Sönder* [Apart], on which he had worked during the last year of his life, ends with the sudden death by scarlet fever of Amy, the faithless beloved, an episode that, in its turn, was based on an actual event.) In 1932 Rabbe Enckell edited a volume of Parland's unpublished works, entitled *Återsken* (Reflection), which included further poems, *Sönder*, essays, and causeries; a generation later, in 1961, Oscar Parland issued all his brother's poems as *Hamlet sade det vackrare* (Hamlet said it more prettily), following it with two volumes, with commentary, of his prose, *Den stora dagenefter* (1966; The great hangover) and *Säjinteannat* (1970; roughly, You're telling me).

The abrupt verses of *Idealrealisation* are divided into four sections, "Spots," "Stockings," "Influenza," and "Grimaces," and have a blasé, smart-alecky tone that at first is amusing: the poet kills the flies of his thoughts with a newspaper ("Ha, sentimentality / how does it feel to be a wet spot / on the wallpaper"); at the "Big Hangover,"

> when the stars get the hiccups
> and all the archangels drink soda water
> we shall gather at the café to listen
> to women's-legs-melodies.

It would be unreasonable to expect a development during the relatively short time in which Parland wrote his verse; the same sarcasms appear repeatedly:

> I shave
> before a wall-eyed
> mirror
> and my image
> shows an irresistible desire to stick out its tongue at me.

The value of the poems lies in the way they capture a Baltic jazz age, experienced in Helsingfors and in the multilingual backwater of Lithuania; after a mention of Al Jolson's "Sonny Boy" and the people who stamp their feet when they hear it, Parland — who in his poetic persona, as evidently in life, kept up an air of fragile superiority — continues:

> Every hit song says so infinitely much more to me,
> it tells me
> all the wrinkles in my time's face
> and all the cosmetics that will take care of them.

Similarly, there is the snippy remark (Parland's poems are close to the aphorism in their pointed brevity) in "Jazz": "The dictatorship of jazz—a new form of Catholicism, / I have seen a thousand trouser-creases flutter in rhythmic feeling." (The final words are one of Parland's jokes, since *taktkänsla* can also mean a "sense of tact.") Yet amid Parland's deliberate and mocking chilliness, a strain of horror or despair can be detected, as in the poem about the man run over somewhere outside Helsingfors:

> We walked along the cold trees
> to his blood:
> His boots were fine and the coat
> but the face.

And the snapshot from Kaunas:

> Spring in Kaunas
> dirt
> and the puddles of sunshine
> spilled over the corners.

He was never vouchsafed the flight into the idyll (in whatever form) the other modernists undertook.

The prose of Parland is, once more, part and parcel of his time; popular music informs his little sketch, again called "Jazz," in which he ponders why the saxophone has become the instrument of preference of this new style, whose intention is not to arouse sentimentality or sympathy but to make its listeners "possessed"—"Jazz is a devil." Both Björling and Parland were fascinated—the musically conservative Diktonius less so—by jazz as an expression of revolt against an older culture, but Björling knew relatively little about music, whereas Parland came from a musical home and could ask the composer Ernst Pingoud, his mother's cousin, about musical matters. Parland was fond of F. Scott Fitzgerald's *The Great Gatsby,* which he read in the original, and the world of jazz forms the background of the novel *Sönder.* Yet the novel's epigraph points to another and grander idol: "Motto: this novel is perhaps a plagiarism of Marcel Proust," and it has been argued that *Sönder* is actually, in its way, an exercise in Proustian remembrance, a summoning of the narrator's memories of the dead beloved, Amy; Wolfgang Butt has characterized the book as a "metanovel" (p. 161), a novel about the writing of a novel, the author-protagonist's projected book on the departed. Seen simply, *Sönder* is the lengthiest display of Parland's self-mocking, or, in this case, his mocking of the alter ego, Henry Rapp: "When the author had finished the writing of the novel, and gotten his fee for it, he decided to drink it up." Detecting a resemblance between a barmaid and the late Amy, he willingly goes with the girl to her room, and after they have made love (modestly indicated by dashes, like a fade-out in one of Henry's films), Henry asks for a pen — no doubt to begin writing again.

A naiveté lies at the heart of Parland's work, often hidden by his flaunted sophistication. Butt, his German translator, has noted his fascination with things in motion, the automobile, the motorcycle, the bus, and sees a connection with Germany's *neue Sachlichkeit* (new objectivity) of the 1920s; but Oscar Parland recalls that at one time his brother planned to be an engineer like his father and even as a boy could not leave machines alone, developing a "thing animism" long before he was aware of it in contemporary German or Russian poetic practice. In several senses, he was a boy who never grew up, despite all the appearances of an extremely early maturity, a marvelous boy whose early death has lent the special glamour of unfulfilled promise to his name. Yet in one respect, Parland was very mature: the precision, discipline, and spareness of his style, both in poetry and prose, the trait that, understandably, got Rabbe Enckell's special admiration. In the introduction to *Återsken* Enckell wrote: "Despite the fact that Swedish was not Henry Parland's native tongue, in his treatment of language he achieved a completely perfected personal style . . . one notes with admiration the persistence with which [in *Återsken*] he keeps his intellectual grip on the theme to the very end. . . . Parland's last poems betray the same objective accent." And who else, in a literature so rich in praises of wine (e.g., by Franzén and Grotenfelt), had dared write an apostrophe to seltzer, the cure for a hangover? Composed in Kaunas for a lady's magazine, "Mineral Water" is at once a praise of clarity and a Linnaean classification system in which soda water is the best: "The most enchanting feature of soda water is its light, murmuring laughter. Throughout its whole short life, soda water laughs heartily, teasingly, and, it cannot be denied, a little meaninglessly." But "it still laughs in our mouth, and we feel its small, sharp stings on our tongue."

Eklund

R. R. (Ragnar Robert) Eklund (1895–1946) could very well have joined the modernists; he was engaged to Hagar Olsson from 1917 to 1920, and as Olof Enckell detected, Olsson's *Kvinnan och nåden* finds a reply in Eklund's first book, the assemblage of prose poems *Jordaltaret* (1919; The earth altar), a title perhaps connected with Edith Södergran's *Rosenaltaret* of the same year. From Hagar Olsson's *textes de liaison* to Edith's letters, one learns that Olsson had read to the tubercular poet from Eklund's manuscript, making her flee from the room in tears; Edith must have been moved by the ecstatic and prophetic tone: "The day of creation arises.... We see things that are thousands of years old, and we behold them for the first time." (Reviewing *Rosenaltaret,* Arvid Mörne compared it with Eklund's work.) But Eklund did not become a member of the modernist circle: his dislike of debate got him the sobriquet from Hans Ruin of "the great silent one" ("Den store tigaren," 63); he was determined to go his private way, not as a revolutionary but as an observer. Ruin summed up his formal participation in modernism thus: "He began and ended it with a guest appearance in *Ultra.*" In the aphorisms of *Grått och gyllne* (1926; Gray and golden) Eklund made an ironic statement about what he found hard to swallow in the modernists, their urge to self-glorification: "Oh, you new gods of literature, if I could only understand your loftiness: Rhyme or no rhyme, cothurns or bare footsoles—can that be a matter of concern to gods?" Eklund not only put himself at a remove from the modernists as a group (although he could admire them individually, as he did in Södergran's case) but implicitly condemned what he took to be his own highfalutin false start in *Jordaltaret,* which he actually had written under the aegis of the then popular Rabindranath Tagore.

Ruin had become acquainted with Eklund at the university and had been struck by his "cerebral head" and his enormous reading background: in works to come, Eklund made easy and apposite references to Kierkegaard, Baudelaire, the Swedish poet and thinker Vilhelm Ekelund, the Swiss diarist Henri Amiel (with whose feelings of isolation he sympathized), Sigbjørn Obstfelder (the Norwegian whose dreamy lyrics he appreciated but to whose visionary prose he objected), Friedrich Hebbel's diaries, Hans Christian Andersen, the Gustavian traveler and stylist Carl August Ehrensvärd, Silvio Pellico (the author of *Le mie prigioni,* the classic account of political imprisonment), and so on. Yet Ruin was also aware of Eklund's weakness for alcohol. One of the contrasts in Eklund's personality is the extreme discipline of his sparse production (and his admiration of "demigods, house gods, idols" who are the themselves masters of stylistic or personal restraint) and his frequent self-abandonment to a "Bacchus," in Ruin's words, who was "dark, threatening, destructive." (In a late poem, "R.R.E.," Diktonius describes a late-night meeting with Eklund, like himself a lover of books and drink and like himself out of pocket.)

Eklund had come from poor circumstances; born in the "smallest and most Swedish" city in Finland, Nykarleby, he lost his father early and spent his childhood and youth there and in Vasa, cosseted by a devoted sister and mother. He described his growing up in two transparently autobiographical novels, or memoirs, the unfortunately named *Liten drömmarpilt* (1943; Little dreamer lad) and *Ny dag börjar* (1944; New day begins). His alter ego, Edgar, is not unhappy in his loneliness: "It is best to keep people at a distance." After his studies at the university, he returned to Vasa and its newspaper, but Hagar Olsson claimed that she had caused his move back to the capital—he served on the staff of the newspaper *Dagens Press/Svenska Pressen,* of which she now was the star reviewer. Every summer, however, he traveled up to his native Ostrobothnia, to which, without being a regionalist, he had the closest ties. His novel *Himmelstimran* (1937; Heaven's house, a dialect word for a sectarian chapel) is a portrait of a lay preacher, gently mocking but still respectful.

His fellow journalist J. O. Tallqvist remarked, as others did, on Eklund's own spirituality, a quality he greatly treasured (and endured) in his pious mother, without being altogether able to accept the same quality in himself. In a eulogy for Eklund, when his bust was unveiled in Nykarleby in 1962, Olof Enckell—another admirer of his quiet art—told how the two of them watched the "philosopher of sport," Artur Eklund, no relation, execute a perfect dive from a rock and emerge from the icy water like a Greek god, while R. R. Eklund sat wrapped in a blanket, uttering his characteristic half-embarrassed laugh: "He gave the impression that nothing could be more indifferent to him than the fragile human form to which he was bound (for the time being) during his guest appearance on earth." Five years before *Himmelstimran* Eklund had given voice to this spiritual aspect in the hospital novel *Den gåtfulla gästen* (1932; The mysterious guest), which often becomes a series of reflections on existence (and on death) by the patient-protagonist: "I am a branch in a tree that a storm has torn loose . . . but while the leaves begin to wither, I long to be grafted onto the trunk from which I was torn, and to grow together with its living flesh." The simplicity of such a passage resembles that of his aphorisms, in which Eklund does not have to pay attention to a narrative line or to conversations (the weakest element in his novels); he is most at home in the three books in which (like Amiel or the Hebbel of the diaries) he can put down *disjecta membra* of his thoughts unhindered: the above-mentioned *Grått och gyllne,* whose subtitle is "Fragmentariska betraktelser" (Fragmentary observations), *Rymd och människa* (1938; Space and Human), and the tiny *Loggbok på landbacken* (1945; Logbook on dry land). The word "aphoristic" is not always applicable; instead, "desultory prose" might be more suitable: apostrophes (the address to the Ostrobothnian plain in *Grått och gyllne*), prose poems (the picture of three geese marching in a row that opens the logbook), and genuine pithy statements, often semiconfessional: "True constancy is repellent to me. I cannot wholly confide myself even to a sheet of paper."

In his verse Eklund likewise keeps the reader at a distance, not by dint of obscurity but through diffidence or modesty: in this respect, he is at the greatest remove from his modernist contemporaries, all determined to sway the reader in one way or another. He used a number of devices to prevent his audience from being swept away: the dispassionate descriptions of Ostrobothnian scenes and events in *Det unga ögat* (1927; The young eye), the stilted, poetic conversations of *Värld från veranda* (1934; World from veranda), in which three participants—the summer guest Eberhard, the cheery Florio, the rather morose and stubborn artist Andreas—present, each with a poem in turn, thoughts and experiences from their lives, as they sit on a porch in September. Only near the end of his verse career was Eklund able to compose the small group of lyrics that have his special flavor. In a selection from Eklund's poems and "small prose" published after the writer's death, *Rymd och människa* (1950; not identical with the aphorisms of the same name from 1938), Per Erik Wahlund chose the overwhelming majority of the poems from *Du stallbror med gud* (1940; You stall-sharer with God) and *Gissel och möjor* (1942; Scourges and May wreaths), which was represented by twenty-six lyrics against ten from the earlier collections. When *Gissel och möjor* came out, Eklund told his sister Vivi (who published a discreet memoir about her brother in 1957) that he regarded the lyric as the literary genre most difficult to master, as it was also the noblest, and added that he would never write poetry again, a vow he kept until, "more spirit than human," he died in Ostrobothnia.

The fact that Wahlund, a prominent Swedish critic, published his Eklund selection in the series sponsored by Stockholm's Sällskapet Bokvännerna (the Society of the Friends of Books) is but one of several indications of the great interest in Finland-Swedish modernism prevalent in Sweden at the time. A Gunnar Björling Society had been founded in 1949, the major Södergran biography by the Uppsala professor Gunnar Tideström appeared the same year, and Rabbe Enckell's statements on Finland-Swedish modernism were published in Swedish journals. In 1947 Wahlund had edited an anthology of Finland-Swedish lyrics, and in 1953 the novelist Walter Dickson devoted a volume of essays to the same topic, *Hjärtfäste och hungertorn* (Heart fastness and hunger tower), followed by his pioneering appreciation of Björling in 1956. Hans Ruin, resident in Lund since 1945, and Bengt Holmqvist, from Åbo and the literary critic in *Stockholms-Tidningen* and *Dagens Nyheter,* also contributed to this Swedish interest in the very recent Finland-Swedish past. The Swedish perception of the minority's literature would change radically, though, around 1960, with the novelistic debut of Christer Kihlman (see chapter 10).

Torsten Pettersson has demonstrated how difficult it is to pin Eklund down: his oeuvre can be broadly characterized as modernistic, but "it also contains clearly traditional elements" ("Att vara seende," 190). Free verse is mixed with marked rhythms, "striking modernistic imagery" with "Runebergian hexameter narrative" (in which he resembles his contemporaries Hemmer and Ragnar Ekelund); it is hard to find a "consistent thematology and asking-of-questions." For Pettersson, the only constant is Eklund's lyric attitude, — the watcher who, in Rabbe Enckell's words, "in a meaningful way combines self-observation with a close noting of the world around him." The sights seen and described are sometimes marvelous, sometimes shabby: "White Sacrament," in *Du stallbror med gud,* has a (hexameter) vision of Pan in the midst of a Nordic winter: "You look around and astonished / Come upon living fields where you thought to find smothering snowdrifts"; in "Cafe Interior," from the same collection, there is rain outside and boring nothingness within:

> lamp is lit,
> a single one.
> On an umbilical cord from the void
> its ball, shining tiredly, hangs,
> a barren planet that wishes nothing
> and is impotent.

The hope of transfiguration will not be fulfilled:

> And you flowers, do you perhaps expect
> to burst your cellophane envelopes
> and spread your oilcloth leaves
> in a banquet's wonderful lighting
> to the gramophone's heavenly music?

A bare and probably vain hope also informs "Nocturnal Awakening," in *Gissel och möjor,* in which the gnawing anxiety of the first eight lines is balanced, but not canceled out, by the awareness, in the concluding nine lines, of the mysteries lurking in the "apparently dead things" that surround the speaker lying on the bed. Sleep plays a large part in Eklund's late poems; one of them, written in trochaic tetrameter suggestive of the *Kalevala,* opens with the desire to sleep almost forever: "Slumber, slumber, long and endless, / dwelling being-less in nothing," but, as so often in the protasis-apodosis structure of Eklund's poems, a resolution must come: "Then to wake a billion years hence / look around with new-grown vision."

A desire Eklund expressed in an aphorism, "to become a child anew: people are wont to say that in a derogatory way," lies at the heart of his poetry. He admitted that he thought of himself as a child and was surprised to discover that the "full-grown, heavy-limbed, earnest . . . men" he met were "several years younger than [he was]." Mirjam Tuominen claimed that his deep affection for his home region (and hometown) came from the notion that a visit there gave his childhood back to him. Like a child, too, he could turn a quite ordinary object into a source of wonder (in this respect like Diktonius and his transfiguration, in *Ingenting,* of a potato patch). Near the end of *Gissel och möjor* he included a little hymn of praise, in regular rhyme and rhythm, to the "surrogate rose," the dandelion. Eklund was not afraid of banality: "There are others who fear the banal to such an extent that their fear turns into a panic terror at what is everyday in our lives," a belief that resembles the standpoint of Enckell in his "match poetry" and of Södergran in her final verse. To its detractors, modernism often seemed to be intentionally and arrogantly complex; to many of its admirers (see the Swedish poets of the 1940s), it was cherished precisely for the sake of its perceived obscurities. Nevertheless, a search for basic simplicity is a main factor in many of the modernists' creations.

Ultra, Quosego, 1929
Ultra appeared from September to December 1922, in seven issues, the last a double (7–8). The little journal was almost evenly divided between Finnish and Swedish contributions and, as its subtitle said, was devoted to "new art and literature." The editors were Lauri Haarla (1890–1944), a poet and dramatist; Raoul af Hällström (1899–1975), destined to become an important man of the theater; and Hagar Olsson. The financial manager and publisher was the poetaster L. A. Salava (1894–1955); his house, Daimon, brought out Björling's *Vilande dag* and Diktonius's *Hårda sånger* the same year. The contents were extremely varied: presentations of theater in Tallinn, Paris, Sweden, and Finland; artists—Käthe Kollwitz, Eero Järnefelt, T. K. Sallinen, and Van Gogh; composers—Scriabin, Stravinsky, and Prokoviev (by the composer Ernst Pingoud); currently popular stage and film stars; and writers—Joel Lehtonen and, of course, Södergran from Finland, Emil Bønnelykke from Denmark, Dan Andersson, Harry Blomberg, Anna Lenah Elgström, and Pär Lagerkvist from Sweden, Georg Kaiser, Walter Hasenclever, and Franz Werfel from the German-language realm, Severyanin from Russia (by Södergran), Shakespeare, Henri Murger, and Marcel Proust. Hagar Olsson wrote tributes to W.N.P. Barbellion and Walt Whitman, two lines from whose "Salut au monde" were used as column filler; two other Whitman poems were translated by Diktonius into Swedish, and among Diktonius's Finnish essays, one was devoted to Thomas

DeQuincey. Poetry by Blomberg and Elgström was included, as well as by the Estonian Marie Under and, from Finland, Rabbe Enckell, Uuno Kailas, Viljo Kojo, L. Onerva, and, of course, Södergran and the omnipresent Diktonius. An article in installments by "B. P." discussed Chinese poetry at length. Thomas Warburton's retrospective opinion of *Ultra* was, "by no means tame" but "uneven and half-amateurish."

Quosego, which took its name from Neptune's uncompleted curse to the winds in the *Aeneid,* 1:135 ("Whom I — But it is better to calm the troubled waves"), called itself a "magazine for a new generation." It appeared in four issues during 1928 and 1929 at Söderström & Co., edited by Cid Erik Tallqvist (1899-1967), a man of letters and teacher of English much interested in Yeats and Joyce; later Tallqvist would provide translations of Leino, Uuno Kailas, and Katri Vala for Elli Tompuri's anthology, *Voices from Finland* (1947). The principal contributors to *Quosego* were Björling, Diktonius, Rabbe Enckell, and Henry Parland; Hagar Olsson had four editorializing pieces, including the blast, "I assure you: a new generation exists." Olof Enckell gave a cogent explanation of Björling and a panorama of contemporary letters in Sweden, accompanied here and there by pieces from the Swedish poets themselves, Gunnar Asplund, Harry Blomberg, Josef Kjellgren, Artur Lundkvist (with translations of e. e. cummings), and Harry Martinson. Other Finland-Swedish poets were Nicken Malmström, Barbro Mörne, Kerstin Söderholm, and Atos Wirtanen (see below). Save for a Leino translation by Diktonius, no attention was paid to Finnish-language letters (in contrast to *Ultra*'s bicultural orientation) and relatively little to foreign literatures; *Quosego*'s main purpose was to provide a showcase for Finland-Swedish modernism, and thus it was a forerunner of Rabbe Enckell's lyric anthology (1934) and of *20 år ung dikt* (1936), edited by Diktonius and Rabbe Enckell.

1929 appeared in a single volume at Söderström & Co., the publishers of *Quosego.* The editors were the art historian Nils-Gustaf Hahl (1904-41), the theater and film critic Hans Kutter (1904-), the poet Erik Therman (see below), and the young literary scholar Eugène Napoleon Tigerstedt (1907-79). Hahl presented the work of Ragnar Ekelund, Kutter the novels of Somerset Maugham; Therman produced a long and somewhat turgid essay criticizing Södergran's Nietzscheanism and the verse in *Quosego,* "partly tattered nerve-poetry, partly machine-poetry"; Tigerstedt chose to write about Vilhelm Ekelund (1880-1949), a cogent tribute to the Scanian's refined elitism and extreme cultural conservatism. Poetry and creative prose were contributed by the Mörnes, L. A. Salava, Örnulf Tigerstedt, and Kerstin Söderholm; aphorisms by A(a)tos Wirtanen; "Gaga" (against

Björling's "Dada") by Rolf Lagerborg; and — fair enough — a "Quosego Reply" by Björling. The defense of "Western cultural values," so important in the work of Vilhelm Ekelund and of Örnulf Tigerstedt (see below), was proclaimed in an essay by the historian Jarl Gallén (1908–90): "Lord, we beg you not for peace but a sword." Erik Therman's brother Tor (1903–73) praised Torgny Segerstedt (1876–1945), the editor of *Göteborgs Sjöfarts-och Handelstidning*, whose championship of an intellectual aristocracy, coupled with a belief in democratic values, would lead him to become Sweden's strongest and bravest voice of opposition to National Socialism.

A Second Modernist Wave
The lyrics of Edith Södergran, especially in her *Dikter* of 1916, were especially inspiratory to slightly younger poets who found in them an ideal instrument for expressing their own sense of isolation and yearning. When Arvid Mörne's daughter Barbro (1903–87) made her debut with *Tystnadens spår* (1922; Traces of silence) and wrote such lines as "I sought a word and a sob. / But all was caught in the murmuring of the sea," or addressed an "unwitting brother, all too pale, / with you I dream of heavy flowers," it was plain enough whose lyric school she had recently attended. Soon, she swung more toward her father's example, celebrating nature in a traditional way and, in fact, was made fun of by Hagar Olsson in the latter's review of the conservative literary album *1929:* "The Mörne dynasty is represented by the Bard himself, by the poetess, and by the actress and teller-of-fairy-tales" (by whom Olsson meant, respectively, Arvid, Barbro, and Gudrun Mörne, in those years a member in the troupe at Swedish Theater. Another gifted sibling was Håkan Mörne [1900–1961], the travel writer and novelist-to-be whose debut book about a merchant seaman's life, a theme that became his speciality, had received friendly words from Olsson in 1927). Barbro Mörne's closeness to summer-and-skerry life is readily discerned in the long "Ballad from the Sea" in her third collection, *Dikter* (1933; Poems), or, two decades later, in *Skymningsrummet* (1956; The twilight room): "Our sense of being home — darkenedly red / houses, words' shimmer from the line of road, / from the boathouse on the beach." The poem ends in a tribute to her language, the Finland-Swedish of which her father had been such an aggressive champion:

> All calls up memories of the tongue we speak,
> its harsh and tight-lipped melody,
> which never dies away, but is held back
> like a bog hawk's quick cries.

The much admired poverty of the Swedish-speaking fishermen and farmers was the topic of a poem about a sugar loaf, "the poor man's dream of good days," in *Den du är* (1959; The one you are). Nonetheless, throughout this long and respectable poetic career the heritage from the modernists, or at any rate, Södergran, did not disappear. See "The Night North Wind Sweeps from the Forest," in *Jag bands av årets tider* (1948; I was bound by the times of the year), in which Barbro Mörne uses an image that cannot deny its parentage:

> The sandpiper flies restless
> lamenting audibly in the night
> around the same skerry —
> a circle of compulsion
> that cannot be crossed.

Compare Södergran's famous formulation at the opening of *Dikter:* "A circle was drawn around these things / which none can cross."

Arvid Mörne was an admirer of Södergran's "image-imagination, with its short, meaningful, intensively personal symbols and similes," but in his contribution to a volume on Finland-Swedish modernism by various hands, edited by Diktonius and Rabbe Enckell, *20 år ung dikt* (1936; Twenty years of young poetry), he posed a rhetorical question: "How numerous are the counterparts of extraordinarily high value that we find among the successors?" The botanist Nicken Malmström (1897–1967) began, with *I stoftet* (1927; In the dust), as an imitator of the emotional overtones that gave Södergran's first collection its special value:

> My dear old toys do not amuse me any longer.
> My chipped-edged cares I have tossed into a corner.
> My small joys'
> shiny pictures
> lie torn to pieces on the floor
> and I stamp them heavily
> under my feet.

This tone of disenchantment and disengagement, growing ever stronger over the years, turned into the time-honored Finland-Swedish theme of isolation, as in *Under solen* (1939; Beneath the sun):

> Fortified in my stolen peace.
> Caught in my thoughts' long noose,
> Oh to pull myself loose. But can I? Do I wish to?
> Nothing is as strong as one's own trap.

At the end of his poetic career, in *Jordstjärna* (1962; Earthstar), Malmström found religion—an unconscious repetition of the final chapter in the Södergran biography; having begun with Södergran's *Dikter*, Malmström ended, as it were, with *Landet som icke är*—but not with the same intensity.

The emotional temperature in Malmström's eleven volumes of poems is surely not as high as in the lyrics of Erik Therman (1906–48), who set out on the romantic path of Södergran with *Glidande bilder* (1928; Gliding images). His poems have a self-conscious pictorial splendor that never lets up; his stylistic trademark is the repeated word: "On the heath, over the heath, / in the heath, beyond the heath / goes the whispering whisper goes the forest folk's dance," and so forth. Therman makes a constant demand for an experience beyond words: "Life is a dream and more, / life is a song and more," and

> More hot, more red
> is our heath flower,
> more tormented, more heavy
> is our forest power,
> than human blood, and human power,
> redder, truer red than blood the heather shines on the heath.

Therman's would-be hypnotic and orgiastic verse could have its slightly quieter moments, to be sure, in the collection given a title that sounded Södergranian enough, *Inför Dionysos anlete* (1938; Before Dionysus's countenance): "My heart dances on a flute-tip / opens itself as large and as a flower white / at the flute's melody." Noisy or muted, his neopaganism led, not surprisingly, to a fascination with primitive cultures, and—following a tradition that had produced both the account by the missionary Gabriel Tuderus (1638–1705) of his stay among the Lapps and *Anteckningar under min vistelse i Lappmarken* (1844; Notes taken during my sojourn in Lapland), by Jakob Fellman (1795–1875)—Therman undertook several journeys to the extreme north of Finland, which resulted in novels and, more important, excellent travel books, *Lapplandsresan* (1934; The Lapland journey) and *Bland noider och nomader* (1940; Among Noit-singers and nomads), about "the children of nature who . . . preserve the last remainders of primitivity and heathendom in our part of the world." Therman's attraction to Lapland—and his concomitant passion for the viking past, in the novel *Kettil Rödes saga* (1936; The saga of Kettil the Red) and the essay *Eddan och dess ödestragik* (1938; The Edda and its tragedy of fate)—offer a parallel to the Karelian exoticism of the 1930s and, quite innocently, to the Nazi *Blut und Boden* literature of the same time. (In Norway, it should be remembered, the decade saw the appearance of Trygve Gulbranssen's trilogy that began with *Og bakom synger skogene* [1933; Eng. tr. *Beyond Sing the Woods*, 1936], which, translated into German, became an enormous success in the Third Reich.)

Therman is remembered today for his reportages, not his directly creative writing; the poet Kerstin Söderholm (1897–1943) is better known for her diary, *Endast med mig själv* (published posthumously by Karin Allardt Ekelund in 1947–48; excerpted as "Only with Myself" in *Scandinavian Women Writers*, 1989), than for her six books of verse and her single collection of tales. The diary, kept from 1913 until shortly before her suicide, in Sweden, has exemplary value in the glances it gives into the life of the daughter of a prominent Finland-Swedish jurist, painfully shy, burdened with a sense of otherness, and tormented by sexual urges; she confessed rather primly to her diary that she could "go quite mad for the first man (provided he is not totally unattractive) with whom [she] might come into contact of any sort." In actual fact, she had a more selective view of the men who crossed her path, and her passion, requited or not, went out to love objects of genuine distinction, such as Rolf Lagerborg and Hans Ruin. Frequently a prey of depression, she may have modeled her death on that of the Swedish poet Karin Boye (who killed herself in 1941). The events of Finland's Continuation War served, however, as a retarding factor in her "case of neurasthenia," as she called her condition; observing action on the Hangö front in southwestern Finland at fairly close quarters, she felt somehow a part of the nation's trials. In a late diary entry she gave a pitiable accounting of her flaws, listing her impatience toward her conservative parents, her occasional cruelty in her judgment of others, her superior and self-assured manner, her egocentricity, her cutting irony, "but I cannot recall a single instance when I meant to harm someone or cause pain. (Not even H[agar Olsson], who for some reason has been the only person to call me an enemy.)"

Söderholm's expression of her defenselessness, naiveté, and isolation (and her sense of being an "old maid") has given her diary a status that readily lets it overshadow her belletristic work; "perhaps it ought to be judged by a psychiatrist with a sense of stylistic values," according to Torsten Pettersson ("Den svåra gemenskapen," 68). (Some statements in the diary indicate that, at least during the latter years of her life, she was aware of the possibility of publication.) For Pettersson, the lyric work (and, subsidarily, the novellas) is the proper object of literary analysis, and he has discovered that her central thematology consists of the difficulty of finding a community with nature and humanity. Like Rilke, she sensed "voices in things which longed to be interpreted in words," and she says as much in her first collection, *Röster ur tingen* (1923; Voices from the things); her formulation about the "task" of the human observer of things resembles that which the Austrian poet gave in the fifth and ninth *Duineser Elegien* (*Duino Elegies*), which appeared the same year as Söderholm's book. In *Mot ljuset på bergen* (1926; Toward the light on the mountains) the engagement with nature is both painful and hard to maintain, but it must be striven for all the same, as in the climactic cycle "A Walk through Fire":

> Thus alone I will be
> with you,
> earth
> that not a cloud of dust
> dims the clarity of the fells' expanses
> and not a living straw breaks our community.

(The final word is *gemenskap*, a key word in Söderholm's crises.)

In the stories of *Det var icke verklighet* (1930; It was not reality) young women tentatively find their way toward community with men and so with nature; sitting on a hotel balcony in a foreign land with a handsome "son of the high North"—think of Södergran's "son of the highlands" in *Rosenaltaret*!—the girl of "Beneath the Wild Vine" feels that "it was as if everything had always existed around them and would exist in time to come." This section of the volume, though, bears the title "Dream Tales." The poems of *Rödgula vägar* (1928; Red-yellow roads) were full of Södergran echoes; see the vision of metaphorical athletic daring, "I will rest on a thread-fine line over the sea's surface"; the poem of definition, "Suffering is a burning string, / deepest within us, / Suffering is the holiest nypon blossom in our breast"; and the anaphoric catalog, "I am a weed-hoe in his garden land. / I am a nail in his workshop's chest, / I wish to be a strand of his hair," but they show that Söderholm knows Diktonius's snapshots as well—see the poem about the violin virtuoso Bronislav Huberman. She even imitates Björling's ellipses, to an extent that almost smacks of parody. In *Ord i natten* (1993; Words in the night) she published love lyrics having some connection with events described in the diary (a less than happy relationship ending shortly before the lover's sudden death); the whole collection is marked by autobiographical features, as in the cycle on illness, using Södergran's favorite structures (the definition poem: "Death's nearness is hot, bubbling springs, / it is the most nameless of all fairy-tale lands").

The penultimate *Porten* (1937; The portal) has formal surprises, a move away from the prosodic freedom of modernism, to five-, six-, or seven-foot rhymed couplets, which sound like Procopé or Hemmer: "I hold the portal's key within my hand / — then freeze as though I'm fettered by an iron-hard band," and "Who plumbed the wise words of the oak, the rye's muted hum, / — for me you were pure light's design, a figure of the sun." The book also contains aphorisms under such subtitles as "I go and search"; the search is now for some contact with transcendental values. Finally, *Mörkret och människan* (1941; The darkness and the human being), the poetry—close to the diary of the war year—has narratives in free verse about the conflict (e.g., a widow's tale, "We had been married a year when it happened") and poems on radio news reports and on experiences behind the lines; as wartime poetry full of admirable sentiments, the book cannot be criticized: "To be a human being is to know the boundaries / between which we move back and forth / — near beasts and the divine." (Jussi Piekkala has noted the intrinsically pacifistic tone of wartime verse from woman writers; Söderholm—true to her search for community and, one suspects, her parents' code of national devotion—is more patriotic than her poetic sisters.)

Skeleton in the Closet: Örnulf Tigerstedt and Fascism

Rabbe Enckell's *Modärn finlandssvensk lyrik* devotes some twenty pages to a poet who has not remained a favored figure in the Finland-Swedish canon. Örnulf Tigerstedt (1900–62) was a member of the old military and agricultural aristocracy who—like Bertel Gripenberg—never was willing to renounce pride of birth; like Gripenberg, he spent considerable time lamenting the disappearance of the manorial culture of Finland's interior. One of his forebears was the Gregori Tigerstedt to whom Runeberg dedicated a canto of *Fänrik Stål;* his grandfather had been a major-general in Russian service and military historian, and his father a geologist and dendrologist of international reputation—the family was endowed with intellectual gifts: an older brother, Eric (1886–1925), the "Finnish Edison," was a pioneer in radio, film, and even television technology. Brought up on Mustila Estate where his father maintained an extensive arboretum, Örnulf Tigerstedt himself became an advertising executive, a dispenser of the vulgarized mass culture he detested. In reaction, he studied the philosophy of history, favoring Oswald Spengler, the author of *Der Untergang des Abendlandes* (1918; 1922–23; Eng. tr. *The Decline of the West*, 1926–28), and the American Lothrop Stoddard, whose *Revolt against Civilization: The Menace of Under-Man* (1922) was another voice of doom.

The poetry of Tigerstedt, from *Vid gränsen* (1928; At the border) to *Sista etappen* (1940; The last stretch), is impressive enough in its rhetorical verve, but without many of the innovations of prosody, grammar, or vocabulary that distinguished the modernists. It stands under the sign of his struggle between his close interest in primitive culture and the love he felt for his heritage of discipline and duty. His cultural pessimism, a growing fixation on "Caesarism," his attention to what was happening in Italy and Germany, and his fear of the Soviet Union eventually led to his embracing of tenets of fascism and Nazism in his verse, but always with reservations. (In fairness to Tigerstedt, it should be added that he was relatively free of the racism so prominently featured by Hitler's National Socialism.) The opening of the poem "Il principe" in *Sista etappen* has to be taken as an acceptance of what Tigerstedt saw as a necessary wave of history; in Sweden the critic Fredrik Böök came to a similar decision and announced it, something he came to regret.

> Where advantage is, there is right,
> Where right is, there is truth.
> Bent necks greet the victor's banners,
> and in the victor's tent history's goddess has her bridal bed.

Tigerstedt had begun his poetic career with the immature and technically quite unadventurous *Vågor* (1918; Waves), in which—an imitator of Sweden's Verner von Heidenstam (1859–1940)—he revealed both his schoolboy interest in cultural history (the poem on a dead Goethe, "Is the genius' flame / extinguished with its covering too, a weak and fragile human form?") and his equally jejune aestheticism ("I creep on silent feet / across the silver bridge," in "The Cradle Song of the Evening Wind"). The stories (or legends) of *Noveller* (1923) and *Exercitia* (1924) were likewise under Heidenstam's spell. In *Vid gränsen* a poem about the decadent's icon city, "Bruges," mocked "an American friend" for the latter's inability to understand the treasures of Europe. (His brother Eric, head of the Tiger Manufacturing Company, had recently died in New York.) In *Block och öde* (1931; Block and fate) he saw an admonition in a broken oar found on the beach:

> A piece of wood,
> strangely formed.
> A splinter
> from unknown worlds,
> a warning,
> a witness of great events on the old earth.

He announced that he would form his poems like a block of stone beside "this skerry, / this hyperborean sea"—"a heavy repose, / a throb of pulse / fettered in obedience." In *De heliga vägarna* (1933; The holy ways) Tigerstedt praised Marcus Aurelius not for his meditations but for his victory over the Marcomani: "Be hailed therefore, that you fulfilled your measure as Rome's emperor / and freely sacrificed your heart on your fate's altar." The collection's climax is a lament about his family and its estates: "Alas, thralls chop down my father's maples / and loose folk speak boastfully in the emptied hall," and "My father rests beneath an abandoned tombstone / and in my father's manor strange voices resound," a strong hint—as in Gripenberg—of resentment at the shift of linguistic power in Finland. An amusing irony lies in the resemblance between Tigerstedt's admiration for Caesarism and "cold steel" and that of the Finnish poet and cultural leader of the far right, V. A. Koskenniemi. Koskenniemi, however,—who as late as 1943 was an honored guest of Josef Goebbels—emerged from the collapse of dreams of empire unscathed, continuing as professor of literary history at the Finnish university at Turku and, from 1948 until 1955, elected a member of Finland's Academy; Tigerstedt fled to Sweden, where he was granted political asylum only after a diplomatic tug of war. In 1942 he had published an exposé of Soviet espionage in Finland, *Statspolisen slår till* (The state police strikes) and believed he was in danger of arrest by the Soviet control commission after the armistice of 1944.

The remainder of his career in the lyric, represented by four more volumes (1945–53), consisted partly of self-justification, partly of a search for spiritual peace. In prose Tigerstedt paid heed, still, to the disciplined forces of civilization by completing his large history of the great Swedish-German mercantile house of Hackman, *Ett handelshus i Wiborg 1–2* (1940–52; A firm in Viborg), and posthumously by his survey of the cultural union Sweden and Finland had formed in the past, a tribute to the country that had unwillingly received him. *Källorna sorlar i väster: Färder i Sverige* (1964; The springs run in the west: Journeys in Sweden) took up the quest for the "greater Swedish" unity that, paradoxically, the proletarian Hugo Ekhammar had also sought; it reflects the interest in the Swedish past which Tigerstedt rather woodenly displayed in his novel *Katedralen* (1946; The cathedral), published under the pseudonym Axel Falander, the surname of his family in the seventeenth century, before it was ennobled.

Tigerstedt had proved himself to be a travel writer and essayist of some distinction, with *Vi resa söderut* (1930; We travel southward), the polemical essays of *Skott i överkant* (1934; Shots on the heavy side), whose centerpiece is a defense of "the unnatural . . . the work of creation, perfecting and organizing, whose name is culture," and the feigned letters of *Utan örnar* (1935; Without eagles), a more relaxed arguing of the same theme: "We drown in formlessness and perish like Dr. Jekyll in Mr. Hyde." An inevitable melancholy attaches to the products of true culture: "Every work of art has something of autumn about it," and "the state too is a work of art, and its temporal existence depends on the spirit that created it. . . . When faith ceases, the will to sacrifice also ceases. The temple is emptied." Olof Enckell, who knew Tigerstedt well, composed a rather gingerly introduction for a selection of his poems, *Valv och båge* (1951; Arch and bow), emphasizing his importance in the poetic concert of the 1920s and 1930s; he added that despair lay at the bottom of Tigerstedt's work. If an equivalent of such books as John R. Harrison's *The Reactionaries* and Fritz Stern's *The Politics of Cultural Despair* were written for the North, Tigerstedt would have a major place in it; it is too bad he became a figure of embarrassment, resulting in obscurity, in his own literature. Both Olof and Rabbe Enckell—witnesses of the time and able to perceive the nuances in Tigerstedt's standpoint— were more tolerant than later advocates of political and poetic correctness have been. In the foreword to the anthology of 1934 Rabbe Enckell observed that, for Tigerstedt, "Caesar and the mercenary [who speaks the words of praise for Marcus Aurelius as conqueror] are the true servants of the temple. They are the instruments of fate and, as such, reveal the only ethos Tigerstedt recognizes: submission to fate and a recognition of the mission's natural necessity and correctness."

Although neither author would have been happy at the juxtaposition, a figure of the Left who in some ways may be considered Tigerstedt's counterpart was Atos Wirtanen (1906–79), from Åland, who, trained as a printer, eventually became an editorial writer and then editor of *Arbetarbladet* (until 1941); after his participation in the "Peace Opposition" during the Continuation War, he came into his own as a left-wing member of Finland's Parliament and the editor of the newspaper *Ny Tid*. An intellectual voice of Finland-Swedish Marxism, he was a successor to the intellectually much less stringent Diktonius as an aphorist, plainly influenced by Nietzsche's admiration of the human will. A first book of aphorisms, *Den skapande handen* (1931; The creating hand), was published by Wirtanen himself; by 1935, though, he had attracted the attention of Söderström & Co., where *Kaos och kristall* (Chaos and crystal) and *Stoft och öde* (1941; Dust and fate) appeared. Wirtanen's prophetic visions bear an unsettling resemblance to Tigerstedt's (cf. the latter's title, *Block och öde*); both proclaim a reverence for dark, chthonic powers: "Chaos and crystal: we do not wish to go from clarity to clarity, we assert that every living idea shall grow out of chaos's darkness and blossom into the mystery, we wish to go down into earth and darkness." Unlike Tigerstedt, to be sure, Wirtanen had to express—in keeping with his pro-Soviet standpoint—a certain contempt for Western values: "There is something eastward and nomadic in my freebooter's spirit, a hidden Attila — contempt for everything of the west and south," which he ameliorated, however, by adding, "and a constantly growing yearning, westward, southward." Later Wirtanen published books on revolutionaries of various sorts, seen with his Marxist eye, Nietzsche (1945), Strindberg (1962), and Lenin (1970); and political memoirs (1963, 1973); in post-1944 Finland these were received, of course, with a great deal more sympathy than Tigerstedt's *apologiae* written in Swedish exile. Tigerstedt represented an episode in Finland's history that many wanted to forget.

Three Women, Three Answers to Life: von Schoultz, Wichman, Tuominen
The 1930s were still a productive time for the modernists: Diktonius wrote his most original prose and Olsson her most readable novels, Björling began to look for and to gain critical understanding and respectability, the genius of Enckell broadened and darkened. (The relative strength of poetry and prose in modernism may be demonstrated by comparing Rabbe Enckell's *Modärn finlandssvenk lyrik* [1934] with Olof Enckell's *Modern finlandssvensk prosa* [1937]. The former begins with Edith Södergran's *Dikter* [1916], the latter with Tavaststjerna's *Barndomsvänner* [1886] and continues with Mikael Lybeck, Gustaf Mattsson, "Gustav Alm," Runar Schildt, Paul Werner Lybeck, Josefina Bengts, Arvid Mörne, and Jarl Hemmer. The modernists, or quasi-modernists, are Hagar Olsson, R. R. Eklund, Diktonius, Tigerstedt, Rabbe Enckell, and Henry Parland.) The political events of the 1930s — the rise of right-wing political and racial philosophies, abroad and in Finland, and the Soviet threat (or lure) — were noted in one way or another in Finland-Swedish literature; it could not have been otherwise, in a minority with so many international contacts. Yet the threats to the minority within Finland are rather little mentioned by Finland-Swedish authors (Mörne, Gripenberg, Tigerstedt are exceptions), although the ominous signs could not be overlooked: the establishment of the Akateeminen Karjala-Seura (AKA; Academic Karelia Society) in 1922, which turned its attention from the acquisition of Outer Karelia for the new republic to the attainment of monolingualism; the foundation in 1923 of the Aitosuomalainen kerho (Pure Finnish Circle); and the transformation of the Suomalaisuuden liitto (roughly, Finnishness Foundation), created on Snellman's birthday in 1906, into an ever more aggressive Finnish cultural organization, the tone of which was expressed in the title of its perennial, *Suomalainen Suomi* (1933–68; Finnish Finland). These interrelated Finnish movements had aspects certainly of linguistic and maybe of ethnic cleansing and, particularly in the AKA, betrayed a strong sympathy with the racial philoso-

phy of Nazi Germany, a development with some irony if considered, say, alongside the praise of Artur Eklund (1880–1927) for Finland-Swedish "Germanicness." Their demands were for the limitation of Swedish schools, the reduction of the number of Swedish speakers in the diplomatic and officer corps, and the Fennicization of the University of Helsingfors.

Why these danger signals were so seldom brought up in creative literature (in contrast to the attention paid the language situation in the literature of realism up through the time of Runar Schildt and Ture Janson) is a question that has many tenable answers. Modernism, with its international outlook and its concern with the modes of literary expression, was largely indifferent in the language question, which it regarded as the province of the establishment and of literary traditionalists. Semifascist voices, such as Tigerstedt's, which might have spoken out more clearly in defense of Swedish interests, were to some extent restrained by an identity of political attitude between themselves and the Finnish Right. (Amusingly, Diktonius, bilingual and apparently without any good reason for a commitment to the Swedish side, made exquisite fun at the expense of the Pure Finnish enthusiasts who demanded that song texts and titles — for example, "An der schönen blauen Donau" — be translated into the only language "the country's majority population can hear without getting the fantods.") Finally, modernism (and modern psychiatry) had so thoroughly opened up the exploration of inchoate inner human conditions that it was simpler and, in a way, more pleasant to look at one's own interior sufferings and reactions than at an unpleasant, minatory world at the doorstep: Swedish signs were painted out at the university; Göran Schildt recalled, a generation later, how, on Swedish Day (6 November) during the 1930s, Swedish speakers were knocked down on the streets of Helsingfors by Finns.

Long afterward Johannes Salminen wrote, "Finland-Swedish modernism, in its desperate striving to come closer to life, all too often merely *widened* the chasm between literature and our world of the twentieth century" ("Så har jag åter fot mot jord," 134); he also noted the chasm between the modernists and their immediate milieu. How often the literary mise-en-scène is the contemplative porch (as in Eklund's *Värld från veranda*), the immediate family circle (as in Rabbe Enckell's autobiographical narratives), or a Karelian village that never was. (A U.S. reviewer, confronted by the English translation of *Träsnidaren och döden,* said the setting reminded him of Walt Disney.) The threadbare term, a flight from reality, is not out of place. Further along, the events of the Winter War and the Continuation War — which brought an end to the public language struggle — also found relatively few depictions in Finland-Swedish literature, in contrast to the plethora of war novels and war poetry in Finnish, not because there were no Swedish-speaking soldiers (there were plenty, and they suffered heavy losses) but perhaps because the literary gaze was still turned inward. Despite his terrible wound suffered on the last day of the Winter War, and his year-long convalescence, Göran Schildt (see chapter 10) used these experiences only as a frame for his sophisticated erotic novel *Önskeleken* (1943; The wishing game). Perhaps the most memorable pieces of war literature in Swedish are by women, Kerstin Söderholm's diaries, Solveig von Schoultz's *De sju dagarna* (1942; The seven days), partly an account of a trip to Sweden with her children during the Winter War, and the poems of her *Den bortvända glädjen* (1943; Averted happiness):

> But in the seas' blessed rains the ships drowned one another,
> and beneath blasts of destruction the men sank unnoticed
> and floated silent over the shattered wrecks
> and knew no enemies.

In these superb lines war is given a general, not a specific, face.

Of the writers who grew up in the shadow of the modernists, none learned more profitably from their openness and more innovatively than Solveig von Schoultz (1907–96), whose exceptionally long career—her debut came in 1932, with a girls' book, *Petra och silverapan* (Petra and the silver monkey)—shows a development away from early discursiveness toward ever greater compactness, in form and in tone. She was born in Borgå when the Runebergian tradition was in full sway; her father, Albert Segerstråle, was a teacher of history at Runeberg's old lyceum; her mother, née Frosterus, was a gifted painter, to whom, in 1978, von Schoultz devoted a memoir, *Porträtt av Hanna* (1978; Portrait of Hanna). (As so often in Swedish Finland, cultural families were closely linked: Solveig von Schoultz's maternal great-grandfather, Carl Gustaf Ottelin, was bishop of Borgå and Runeberg's friend; her maternal grandfather was the historian Gustaf Frosterus; her great-aunt the painter Alexandra Frosterus-Såltin; her cousin the architect and essayist Sigurd Frosterus; her elder brothers the fresco painter Lennart Segerstråle and the zoologist Sven Segerstråle.) The product of a cultivated home, Solveig Segerstråle married young, "quite improvisedly," and retained her first married name, von Schoultz, as a nom de plume after a divorce some thirty years later; her second marriage was to the composer Erik Bergman. In her autobiographical sketches, *Längs vattenbrynet* (1992; Along the water's edge), she recalled a remark of Rabbe Enckell to the effect that "everything one writes tends toward a self-portrait," and there is surely an autobiographical element in her early prose:

her "second" debut, *December* (1937), was about Ansa, a young girl in an idyllic small town, who reappeared in *Ansa och samvetet* (1954; Ansa and conscience) and in *Där står du* (1973; There you stand), novella collections held together by the same central figure. But unlike Hagar Olsson, fixated on the free-spirited young girl, von Schoultz sought variety, based on personal experience; *De sju dagarna* (1942; The seven days) is a secular heptameron; the seven days of the title represent the "first seven years" of her daughters' lives.

Quickly, von Schoultz decided that not the novel (represented in her work only by *December*) but the novella would be her prose form. In the introduction to a selection from her stories, *Ingen dag förgäves* (1984; No day in vain), she told of the pride she took in the genre: "The story is not easily digestible. It expects the reader to participate . . . its brevity is only apparent, not real. A genuine story is not finished when a period is set to it, it continues." At first, von Schoultz seemed destined to devote herself solely to women's joys and tribulations: in the three stories of *Ingenting ovanligt* (1947; Nothing unusual) there are a war widow, an ungainly girl whose uncertainty carries over into married life, and a wife who tries to slip away from an unfaithful husband; in *Närmare någon* (1951; Nearer to someone) the stories become somewhat briefer, there are more of them, with a greater variety of moods, and von Schoultz achieves both empathy and objectivity: a maiden aunt's muted selfishness is juxtaposed to the calculation of her niece, an imaginative little girl comes up against school discipline, the other woman of a married man is lonely, a mortally ill husband and his wife circle around the question of marital devotion, a grandmother gives her granddaughter love but not sentimentality. The measured style of the stories keeps even those with the most commonplace themes from falling into banality or from a resort to the unexpected happy (or tear-jerking) ending of tales in women's magazines.

With *Den blomstertid* (1958; That time of flowers), its title taken from a familiar song for church and school by the Swedish hymnist Israel Kolmodin (1643–1709), the contours become sharper, the emotional antitheses more charged; in its masterpiece, "Report," von Schoultz lets the middle-class milieu in which she is most comfortable be invaded, repeatedly, by a panhandler, pathetic, loathsome, insinuating — a story that leaves the reader to debate the reasons for a sense of responsibility toward the underprivileged. As the collections appear, von Schoultz persistently provides unusual sidelights; *Även dina kameler* (1965; Your camels too) has a title from the story of Isaac's wooing of Rebecca in Genesis, but the story itself concerns not the growth of a marital bond but the inability to break older links: a bride on a protracted Mediterranean honeymoon finds herself thinking of her father and her beloved sister. In another story, with a title from a Sibelius tone poem, "Night Ride and Sunrise," sturdy peasant-fishermen, the salt of the earth in many a regionalist skerry story, haze an innocent and well-intentioned pastor who has come to comfort a bereaved father, one of the two drunken tormenters.

No slackening occurred in her narrative power as von Schoultz grew older, although it is possible to date some of her stories by their subjects; for example, the title story of *Rymdbruden* (1970; Eng. tr. "The Space Bride," *Swedo-Finnish Short Stories,* 1974) deals in part with the (then) new phenomenon of television as a surrogate for life; another takes up migration from Finland to Sweden in the postwar decades, and several tales, here and in *Somliga mornar* (1976; Some mornings), face the painful topics of the isolation, anxiety, and bitterness of the old. This is also largely the case with *Kolteckning, ofullbordad* (1983; Charcoal drawing, unfinished), but it further includes the brief "Sea Sauna" (tr. in *SBR*, 1989:1), which von Schoultz has dismissed as "a little tale about foreigners" in Finland (a sexual encounter between a curious woman from Texas and a stalwart Ostrobothnian bachelor), full of the subtle erotic aroma von Schoultz, never really daring in what she depicts, is able to spread in a number of her tales.

Looking back over the more than half a hundred stories of her career, of which von Schoultz made a second selection in *Nästa dag* (1991; Next day), one cannot claim that she put together a Finland-Swedish portrait gallery or that she dealt head on with the concerns of external life; in her inwardness, her concentration on emotional cruxes, she is very much the heir of the modernists. But some of her recurrent patterns seem to be classically Finland-Swedish: the concern with close and sometimes stifling family relationships, the awareness of loneliness and often failed attempts to break out of it, and, of course, the enormous affection for coastal milieus that made Ture Janson claim, back in 1913, "For us the sea's the only fatherland." Otherwise, despite her obvious and manifold ties to (and reflections of) Finland-Swedish life, she has rather little that is explicit to say about it. Her Finland-Swedishness is inferential and found most readily, perhaps, in the undemonstrativeness and emotional skepticism of her characters, practiced sometimes for good, sometimes for ill. The supernatural seldom intrudes into the world of von Schoultz, and physical violence is almost as rare; the religious message that may be read into "Report" (in which the narrator delivers the account of Pulli, the tramp, to an "Uncle" who may be God) is otherwise missing. But she recommends, again and again, a generosity of the heart: "Affection lies precisely in a distance. In not begrudging." Matter-of-factly, von Schoultz has written that her stories "have often originated with ruminations . . . on some problem of living together."

For all her devotion to the novella, von Schoultz apparently ranked the lyric higher still—again, a part of the heritage from the modernists: she proposes that it is her true and best form of literary expression, her "mother tongue." The lyric production, which began with *Min timme* (1940; My hour), likewise never abated; up to and including *Ett sätt att räkna tiden* (1989; A way to reckon time), there were twelve collections, which—as in the case of the novella—progress (according to Thomas Warburton) from a "sometimes overdistinct" use of symbols and characters and a superabundant richness of language to a tightened style and structure that admit a multiplicity of interpretations, "a gentle world of ideas" that have increased in "actuality and urgency" (*Åttio år finlandssvensk litteratur,* 319). The oeuvre contains only one pronounced technical experiment, *Terrassen* (1959; The terrace), a suite of poems in imitation of the Japanese tanka, a poem of thirty-one syllables, arranged in lines of five, seven, five, seven, and seven syllables.

Her poetry is best read in the selection from 1989, *Alla träd väntar fåglar* (All trees await birds), in order to see how she returns to certain subjects (children and old women have been favorites of hers, as well as trees and the sound of the sea); but she never repeated herself as she extracted new values and insights from the same material. Also, a perusal of the selection proves she found her own tone despite the sometimes striking reminiscences from Södergran (the attention to women, the natural piety), the more occasional ones from Diktonius (in the insistent adonic pattern of "Journey by Flight" in *Nätet* [1956; The net]), from Björling (in the elliptic "This That You and I" in *De fyra flöjtspelarna* (1975; The four flautists), and, throughout, from Enckell (the measured pace and care of her language). Like Enckell, and like Bo Carpelan, who provided the afterword to *Alla träd väntar fåglar,* von Schoultz had a regard for linguistic precision and a dignity of poetic stance that never fail. Unlike Diktonius, unlike her contemporary Eva Wichman, unlike Claes Andersson (see below), she did not use her faculty for directness in order to comment on politics or society, although plenty of sympathy with individual cases of life's unfairness can be found in her work. Her lyric tools are actually—and here she outdoes the much more self-centered elder modernists—the observant and engaged heart and the equally observant eye, demonstrated repeatedly beginning with *Nattlig äng* (1949; Nocturnal meadow), by which she established herself in the front rank of Finland-Swedish lyricists: in that book see "Inventory," in which the departing maker of a list of things of the past ("faithful only to her faithlessness") compares herself to a "cat that slides on slick ice with claws outstretched," and "The Fish Cleaner," who in a rage throws away fish parts and, as it were, cleanses her soul:

With my long brown arms
I cast innards into the sea

gale and perch scales fight around my neck
sea grass washes my toes
the carcasses yawn
 — there! my trembling heart with a white clump of fat
made a plunging dive.

The opening recalls Södergran's "The Gypsy Woman," her "brown hands full of secrets," but the physicality (and the extensive vocabulary) are von Schoultz's own, as is the amazing vitality. Never a learned poet (although a highly cultivated one), never cryptic, never trying to further a literary program, von Schoultz has maintained that vitality.

Even her collections written in her eighties had no signs of a falling-off; in "Twilight" (*Ett sätt att räkna tiden*) her favorite old woman appears again; she collects what a scythe has left behind, "her skirt is spacious, her pockets are full." Like Rabbe Enckell, von Schoultz resorted, in her later collections, to travel impressions, but — unlike Enckell — she refused to complain; as a matter of fact, throughout the whole of her poetry, even in a poem with the Södergranian title of "Pain" (in *Nattlig äng*), she took pleasure in the power of the heart as "a house with an open door." A poem in *De fyra flöjtspelarna*, which then lent its title to the retrospective collection *Alla träd väntar fåglar*, says, "When the light opens the eye, the landscape is new-fallen snow / and as fresh as frost." The Swedish critic Olof Lagercrantz's ranking of von Schoultz as one of the great figures of the Swedish lyric, in Finland *and* Sweden, is justified. Her lyrics can be seen as an extension and completion of Södergran's work.

In her memoir of 1992 Solveig von Schoultz recalls her cousin, Eva Wichman (1908–75), as she was in the immediate postwar years. "We were very much unlike and that was just why I admired her. As a child she was full of amusing notions, now . . . she was radical and critically aware, I felt her strength beneath her yarns and her chatter." Wichman had begun as a designer of wooden animal toys, for which she twice won gold medals at international expositions; but in the first of the sudden changes that marked her life, she abandoned this career in applied arts to become a writer. Her reaction against the "Toy Mill," where her alter ego, Mania Grööhn, is employed, provided the moving force in stories of her debut book, *Mania* (1937); the suggestion of the homonym, "mania," is intentional. The book not merely is a factual account of humdrum existence in a dehumanizing concern (as in some of the Helsingfors novels of Sigrid Backman) but depicts the flight of Mania into the fairy tale; despising the robotlike people around her, she gives life instead to objects, "doors, potted plants, chinaware, stairways," and then extends her imagination to the squirrel Lorr and its protector, the Monsoon Bird. Such whimsy got Wichman excellent reviews, and she continued the fantastic line in *Här är allt som förut* (1938; Here everything is as before), in which critics could detect traces of H. C. Andersen and Topelius but not their obvious moralizing. Instead of urging improvement, Wichman's little tales were aimed at encouraging freedom of the spirit. (The volume also contained stories about another whimsical girl, Niska; perhaps feeling that Wichman was poaching in her own preserves, Hagar Olsson gave it a bad review, as "misdirected modernism.")

The pinnacle of Wichman's fanciful achievements came in 1942, in *Molnet såg mig* (The cloud saw me), which contains the suite "The Bog," given a Topelian subtitle: "A Story about Pride"; the bog—a full-blown, egomaniacal genius—praises itself: "Who am I, that I seek a similar being? Similar beings do not exist. I am the bog, the bog for all, for all the small twigs stripped fragilely green, the bog for the dark eels of the bottom, the bog for the bog's sake." (Diktonius, who was Wichman's most influential poetic model, had done something of the same in "The Pride of a Grain of Dust," in *Taggiga lågor*.) Another of these hilarious and unsettling anthropomorphizations (Wichman in fact offers a set of human types, overbearing, sinful, humble) is the "Progenitor's Mishaps," subtitled "Story of an Ordinary Louse": "The louse thinks that the world does not sufficiently appreciate him, temporarily falls victim to an extramarital affair, and then learns to estimate the virtues of his wife." (Did Wichman know Don Marquis's *archy and mehitabel* [1927], verse satires starring a literary cockroach and his friend, the cat?)

Less originally, Wichman took up the long linear narrative in her only novel, *Ohörbart Vattenfall* (1944; Inaudible waterfall), about people who try to follow an artistic calling, even as they maintain a contact with nature and "the stream of life" indicated by the title. As in the fables, the young woman, now called Marina (whom reviewers compared with Alberte in a popular trilogy [1926–39] by the Norwegian novelist Cora Sandel), wishes to break out of established and smothering patterns—in *Här är allt som förut* there was a tale of a reed that does not wish to be like other reeds—

but who just the same wants comfort and protection, represented by the enviably energetic Rita, by the handsome Marco (who makes Marina's "small breasts... become tightly extended tonguetips"), and finally by "the beaches of childhood." The dreamlike finale of the novel, the return into a welcoming nature, is reminiscent, of course, of Edith Södergran's "Homecoming" ("My childhood's trees exulting stand around me") and the conclusion of Hagar Olsson's *Träsnidaren och döden,* just as the gamin Marina is reminiscent of the familiar personae of Södergran's poetry and Olsson's novels. She runs along the corridor of her apartment house in Helsingfors, ringing doorbells and awaiting "the magic moment, when suddenly every door in the long, dark hall would let a head stick out, like birds' heads peeking from a collection of cuckoo clocks."

The determinedly girlish personality, the frantic energy, and the communing with nature that are Mania/Marina's main traits are likewise evident in Wichman's lyric poetry. The desire for a rush into freedom bears up her imperative verse, "High Summer," of *Ormöga* (1946; Snake eye):

Break holes in the roof, knock down the walls, let cleverly
the floor be gnawed beneath your feet.
Close your clear eyes
(blind is the flower's glance!)
Obey the law — leave
human beings' wise pettiness.

Likewise, in "The Pyre," of *Den andra tonen* (1948; The other sound):

Oh, lightning of heaven,
descend.
Hasten here. It is I you shall strike.
I will meet your swiftest flame
and perish. I will fly!

Sven Willner called these collections two of the most important lyric products of the 1940s ("Lyrikern Eva Wichman," 96); at any event, they fully prove that Södergran's influence — from the pioneer's Nietzschean period — was alive and well. Such a wish to be consumed had to find a source of the consuming fires, and in 1948 Wichman began her association with the party of the radical Left, the Democratic Union for Finland's People (Demokratiska Förbundet för Finlands Folk), which led to a string of political verses, from *Dikt i dag* (1951; Poems today) and *De levande* (1954; The living) to *Dikter 1960* (Poems 1960). Here she provided inspiratory texts for Finland's Swedish-speaking Communists and fellow travelers: a satirical salute to a dead comrade: "Work—become a pillar in the arch / which presses *you* toward the earth / (Which is *theirs*)"; a stunned farewell to the late Josef Stalin: "Listen comrades: He is dead. / The mighty one gone? / The user / The builder / The lifter of humanity / The keeper of peace / The revealer of the earth," and so forth. (Berlin, West and East, is a "city of hell—and hope.")

However easy it is to laugh at Wichman's propagandistic verse, it would be unfair to ignore her genuine social pathos and her justified dismay at the overcrowding and general grimness of postwar Helsingfors. Its atmosphere was perfectly captured in her prose book of 1949, *Där vi går* (Where we walk), peripatetic observations about Helsingfors streets and their inhabitants. "Expanses of writhing traffic, and wooden huts, pressed together, squatting, the mastodonlike terraces of factories, soup kitchens, saunas, tracks toward the distance . . . stinging ridges of gravel, poured out around panting trees, rushing down toward collapsing board fences among clotheslines, garbage heaps, lost rabbit hutches, down toward the water's shimmer, behind billowing smoke in the harbor's world of loading and unloading." No one was better able than Wichman to express the summertime emptiness of the capital (whose prosperous inhabitants had gone to their vacation homes); the fact that she remained in town was a sign of her acquired membership in the proletariat: "And there is Union Street hill, with its forgotten little sidestreet beside the Trinity Church, where in summer people's soles echo their clapping more-desolately-lonely than anywhere else."

In his generosity toward Wichman, Willner found much to admire in her Helsingfors poetry, especially as it appears in *Färgernas strand* (1956; The colors' beach). But even here, caught up as she was in her political enthusiasm, the occasional piece of genuine lyricism, "Take a walk in the city, / in the evening light," becomes tangled with her polemics—which also remind the reader of her professional past in advertising:

> The advertisements shine
> like ennobled blood
> from stone
> high above the buildings beaming
> in false nets of veins.

In contrast to the capitalistic ugliness of Helsingfors, "Sofia" is "a city of music, / Bulgaria / blooming—blooming land." And in *Dikter 1960* the speaker is delighted to have gone (she says) "from a world where very seldom / people can afford / to have trust in one another" to a

> world that is strangely humanly near
> ... which creates forward time,
> which again gives people
> healthy earthly time.

The subscript reads, "Moscow region, 1959."

Was it an indication of native contrariness that, in July 1963, as poetry of social complaint became fashionable in Swedish Finland (see chapter 10), Wichman turned in her party membership and renounced political poetry? A year after her abrupt abandonment of the cause to which she had been so devoted, she published *Det sker med ens* (1964; It happens all of a sudden), a talking title if ever there was one. The penultimate poem, "The Bathtub Battle," might seem at first, built as it is around the phrase, "throw the child out with the bathwater," to indicate some regret at a decision hastily taken: "But undiscovered the child arises again / from the death notice." Yet unlike the all too obvious poetry in which Wichman had indulged for years, the poem—based, like a work of her master Diktonius, on a homely image—is ambiguous: perhaps the child is her own gift for nonpropagandistic poetry, abandoned long ago: the child "hops around unseen / and pulls the weeds out / where everything was overgrown." And:

> Irreversible prohibitions
> and stiff facial features
> have very little power (really)
> when wriggling
> the new baby
> marches up—and smiles! (While the fighters go at it and
> pull and tug, worse and worse ...).

The cold war, Wichman appears to say in one of her countless parentheses, may continue without her.

Orientering (1967; Orientation) and *Dikter nu* (1975; Poems now) are full of artistic and literary references: to her favorite painter, Hugo Simberg, who mixed the pastoral and the fantastic, to Edith Södergran and Indra's humane daughter in Strindberg's *Drömspel* (1902; Eng. tr. *A Dream Play*, 1973), to Gunnar Ekelöf and Friedrich Hölderlin. Her lyric work had become altogether different from what it had been in the long middle years (with its obviosities, outcries, exhortations, repetitions); now Wichman's language was laconic, elliptical, sometimes even enigmatic: "The unlocked door-inner side / —discovered, undiscovered—remains." Willner's observation, that the tight diction of the later poetry could not always contain her "temperament and need of intense emotional expression," is accurate, but Wichman deserves admiration for her effort to find new modes of poetic speech, an attempt similar to that of Diktonius in his two last collections. Two years after Wichman's death from lung cancer, the poet Inga-Britt Wik edited her fragmentary autobiography, *Bitar av livet, belysta* (1977; Pieces of life, illuminated); according to Wik, it offered "her real essence, [her] striving for authenticity," which lay beneath what she styled as her "clowning," her tendency to "slip frivolously along her way."

Another friend of Solveig von Schoultz in the postwar years was Mirjam Tuominen (1913–67), whose star had suddenly risen with the warm review Hagar Olsson gave her stories, *Tidig tvekan* (1938; Early hesitation): "It has been a long time since we have experienced such an important debut... her novellas are not literary products but actually, within their form, conceal the living word." (Olsson often resorted to biblical language when she wished to indicate high praise.) Tuominen had already found the relentless emphasis on human suffering that would mark all her narrative work, and as in the case of von Schoultz and Wichman, she put her own self into her protagonists. "Irina," closely resembling Tuominen's middle name, Irene, which she began to use as an authorial signature only near the end of her career, relates a ten-year-old girl's confrontation with her illness and the death of a beloved father (a personal experience leaving a void Tuominen never filled). In another story, "The Lost Bills," a still younger girl than Irina realizes that her father, again "passionately admired," has been cruel to her mother, a discovery leading to her intentional loss of the candy money the father has given her; Tuominen turned the little happening into the child's battle with her conscience.

Tuominen's desire to get inside the spirit of the innocent and defenseless received a second display in *Murar* (1939; Walls), with narrative voices belonging to a dog, wholly dependent on man, to an elderly woman selling newspapers in the Paris Metro, and to the preternaturally ugly Anna Sten, who finds happiness in the thought that, even though God does not hear her prayers, "our prayers draw us nearer to Him. We are expanded by them. When we are in God, we are without boundaries. We pray no longer. We are." The words express the mysticism—already seen in little Magdalena, whose torment about the lost money turns into a psychomachia—that would subsequently become all-consuming for Tuominen. (A curious detail about Anna Sten is that she bears the name of a beautiful Russian-born film star of the 1930s, Anna Sten, "Samuel Goldwyn's answer to Greta Garbo"; movie references had become popular—see Björling and Chaplin, Diktonius and Adolphe Menjou.) Emotional discomfort, and worse, is omnipresent: in *Visshet* (1942; Certainty) the narrator of "For All the Life I Wished for Myself" cuts herself off from life because she is afraid of it; in *Mörka gudar* (1944; Dark gods) the title character of "Crazy Greta" — inspired by a Breughel painting — is horribly aware of her own ugliness; in *Kris* (1946; Crisis), a woman, despairing at her wasted sexuality, is killed in an air raid as she contemplates her naked body, "so closed, so untouched, a flower slowly turning toward the light" ("Body Thrown Away"). Inklings of hope may appear in the double story "New Dawning," in *Mörka gudar*: Chérie Kloster, whose diary constitutes the second part, overcomes her emotional illness (she had imagined she was a plant) and departs for Paris (as Tuominen had done); but in "The End of the Depression," from the same volume, a pastor slips further and further into insanity. In *Bliva ingen* (1948; To become nobody), partly tales, partly small essays, a child is beset by demons; a dancer, prey to depression since childhood, falls during a performance that had meant a release for her (as in Södergran's dancing fantasies), breaks her leg, becomes ill, dies — and experiences grace as she passes into God's arms. Small wonder Hagar Olsson admired Tuominen.

In her introduction to the three-volume selection (1989–91) made from Mirjam Tuominen's works, her daughter, the critic Tuva Korsström, argues that despite the overwhelming emphasis on the defenseless, isolated, and ill, and on "children, animals, women," Tuominen was able to convey a broad picture of the immediate prewar and war years. As a soldier's lonely bride, she knew whereof she spoke; one of the sunnier stories in *Visshet* is "Two," a depiction of the tight relationship between a young mother and her small daughter, a parallel to von Schoultz's book about her children: "In her heart she is just as foolish as the child, she believes that the newness will be able to turn into something at once perfect and perfectly new." Tuominen honestly confronts the grimness of the time — bombings, sudden partings, visits to a military hospital; the revelation of Nazi atrocities (after Finland ceased to be a cobelligerent of Germany in 1944) expanded her vision of horror: a newspaper story about a German soldier's brutality toward a Jewish boy — "the executioner never speaks, he is the most laconic being ever created" — led to her nonfictional examination of cruelty in *Besk brygd* (1947; Bitter brew).

In addition to its long, impassioned outcry about tormenters and the tormented, *Besk brygd* contained intertwined reflections on authors who, to Tuominen, complemented her main theme — Franz Kafka, Edith Södergran, and the Swedish novelist Hjalmar Bergman (on whom she had written as a student) — in that they had been victims of illness, of an uncomprehending milieu, of the demands of art itself. Tuominen is assumed by

Sven Linnér (p. 219) to have been the first writer in Finland to approach Kafka's work (in her contribution to the *festskrift* for Hagar Olsson, *Hård höst* [1943; Hard autumn]), and she continued to introduce or further the cause of major but neglected figures of modern literature. She had little opportunity to travel abroad; her foreign experiences were limited to a trip by freighter to North Africa in 1936, for her health, and a stay in Paris, as an au pair, in 1937–38. Her wartime marriage to the artist and teacher Torsten Korsström narrowed her horizons; until her separation from Korsström in 1948, she lived in Ostrobothnia (reflected in a sentence in "Two": "They live very much alone at a quiet place, unfamiliar with almost all the people in the region") and missed the intellectual excitement of her native Helsingfors. Then she resided with her daughters in Kottby, a garden-and-housing development absorbed into greater Helsingfors as the city underwent expansion during the later 1940s — amid Karelian refugees, war veterans, and others whose only common denominator, Tuva Korsström recalled, was a low income. Tuominen described this world of new buildings and trashpiles with a certain optimism in the occasional prose of *Tema med variationer* (1952; Theme with variations): "One saw the scaffoldings around the house fronts disappear almost with a sense of loss."

Hard times did not keep her from taking trips of the mind; the important essays in *Stadier* (1949; Stages) are those on the novelist Cora Sandel, Proust, Strindberg, and — perhaps most fruitful for Tuominen — Rilke's *Die Aufzeichnungen des Malte Laurids Brigge* (1910; *The Notebooks of Malte Laurids Brigge*). In 1957 Tuominen published a selection from Rilke's letters in Swedish translation and, the same year, a rendering of *Die Sonette an Orpheus* (1923), followed, in 1960, by a large "inner biography" (a subtitle evidently borrowed from Else Buddeberg's Rilke book of 1955) on Friedrich Hölderlin. (Hölderlin had been the subject of a study by the Runeberg scholar Ruth Hedvall in 1921; like Kafka and Rilke, he began to attract larger attention in the North only after the end of the Second World War.)

Tuominen abandoned the story form for the more personal statements (fragments, prose poems) of *Bliva ingen* and *Tema med variationer;* she also began a new career as a lyric poet, publishing *Under jorden sjönk* (1954; Beneath the earth sank). In her first collection the language was clearly modernistic: the plentiful use of anaphora in Södergranian style: "I won't get there, / I am terribly frightened, / I have frightened myself very, very badly," and the Södergranian catalog, "I write what's seen in the dog's eyes / what creeps in cat's claws, / what shimmers in the occasional fly's wingpair / what runs in foalish mane," and so forth — a poem that also has Björling's free and easy way with normal language usage. The portrait poem is present in plenitude (Descartes, Spinoza, the Swedish aphorist Vilhelm Ekelund, the painter Helene Schjerfbeck, Nijinsky, Freud), more detailed and longer than Diktonius's snapshots. Likewise, the repetitive, incantatory style of a Therman appears, but used more sparingly and effectively:

> Burn witches
> witches bewitched burn
> bewitched in witchdom by witchdom
> taken
> witches burn.

In *Monochord* (1954), *Dikter III* (1956; Poems III), *Vid gaitans* (1957; At the sound of the *gaita* [Spanish for "bagpipe"], a quotation from one of Tuominen's poems about Ezra Pound), and *I tunga hängen mognar bären* (1959; In heavy catkins the berries ripen) some of the poems become large and excessively ambitious, a tendency exemplified by "Fragment" in *Dikter III*, in which she tries once more to deal with persecutions in the past and cruelties to come:

> Thus every generation must
> anew go through
> the same heavy experience
> mingled blood shame and tears.

In the final collection (with its title reminiscent of the final lines of Rilke's Tenth Duino Elegy) she continued in this vein with the still longer "Backward Glance," equipped with footnotes, at once a reflection on the contemporary world (it contains references to the Korean War) and an intellectual autobiography.

In 1961 her book of spiritual insights, *Gud är närvarande* (God is present), revealed quite clearly the direction in which she was going: "Christianity's long survival and invincibility needs no other explanation than emphasis on the fact that it is the sole teaching that gives uniquely affirmative answers to the problems of suffering and sympathy. All other religions, like the merely humanistic views of the world, explain away, eliminate, liquidate, arrange, commit hidden or open violence." In 1963 she was converted to Roman Catholicism. Two volumes of religious verse, *Jesus Christus lyra* (The lyre of Jesus Christ) and *Ave Maria* were refused by her publisher, Söderström, on the grounds that there was no market for such piety among the Lutheran (read: religiously indifferent) Finland-Swedish public; in her selection Korsström includes a single sample, with the strange title "Falling-mute and carving-in," whose second noun is elucidated by the poem's final lines:

> Let no one imitate God
> but submit himself to God.
> With a glowing coal
> from an altar
> He writes men's names
> and the carving-in
> not the sound has meaning.

During her last years Tuominen became interested in the graphic arts, but this aspect of her search for expression has remained relatively unknown, save for a section of *Dikter III,* nonfigurative drawings called "Without Words."

Thus far, Tuominen's narrative prose has gotten more attention than her verse; her occasional translations of Hölderlin and of Rilke's *Sonnette an Orpheus* have likewise not received their due — the Swedish author Lars Gustafsson, in the preface to his verse rendering (1989) of Rilke's famous "after-storm" to the *Duineser Elegien,* dismissed Tuominen's version as a "linear translation, somewhat erratic." Yet her verse is capable of great power (Birgitta Boucht has called it simply "frightening"), and some of her poems — the glossolalia on witches, quoted above, the voice of the frightened child ("I want to go home to the dolls at home / home to the stove the fire the hearth"), the puzzling about life's singularity ("Have I not lived for many thousands of years? / Yet this life is this / and a never more") — are bound to lead an existence in anthologies when her overarching poetic structures (written under the aegis of Södergran's "Petersburg Fragment," Hölderlin's Graeco-Christian odes, Rilke's elegies) are forgotten. Just so the novelettes and prose poems of *Tema med variationer,* Tuominen's slightest but also (in her words) "heaviest" work in prose, may well outlast her longer narratives, burdened as the latter are by a hyperemotionalism that borders, at times, on the hysterical. Her strongest admirer — Ghita Barck, the author of a book-length appreciation — claimed that she possessed or was possessed by "an overheated, exalted, explosive inner life . . . , akin to the holy anger of the prophets" (p. 246).

Colliander and Russian Orthodoxy

Although Tuominen never devoted a study to Dostoyevsky, she had been a reader of his works, and Tuva Korsström sees a resemblance between the ugly old pawnbroker in *Crime and Punishment,* murdered by Raskolnikoff, and Tuominen's Anna Sten, whom the mortally ill Sven Kolmar, in that story, resolves to eliminate. Dostoyevsky had other admirers in Finland of the modernist age, Edith Södergran and Jarl Hemmer, and the thematology of Tuominen, suffering, guilt, and redemption, lies close to that of the Russian novelist. But the "Finland-Swedish Dostoyevsky," as reviewers liked to call him, turned out to be Tito Colliander (1904–89), born in St. Petersburg, the son of a colonel in Russian service; his maternal grandfather, a von Schoultz, had been an official of the czar's railroads. The family, like others holding Russian appointments, had maintained close ties with Finland, as well as more distant ones with Britain: little Colliander learned English from his mother's reading Edith Nesbit's *The Railway Children* aloud. (As usual, there were also Baltic-German connections and intertwining with such official and cultural Finland-Swedish clans as the Gripenbergs and the von Willebrands.) In the turbulence of the Revolution the adolescent Colliander witnessed the lynching of a suspected thief, an event that was the mainspring of his creative work. Getting to Finland (an elder brother was killed, fighting for Yudenich's White Army in Estonia), the family settled in Borgå, and young Tito, an air of the exotic about him, was much admired by Solveig Segerstråle, as she recalls in her memoirs.

Deciding to pursue an artist's career, Colliander studied at the Ateneum in Helsingfors (like Eva Wichman) and returned to Borgå as a drawing teacher, but by 1930 — the year of his marriage to another artist, Ina Behrens, from much the same background as his own — he began to write, turning out several books of prose sketches and short stories. *Småstad* (1931; Small town) gives hints aplenty of his not altogether happy life in the Borgå he had come to regard as a nest of provincial gossip. Trying longer forms, he started to look into the tight and troubled familial circumstances that would become one of his special objects of fictional attention; he also made literary capital, understandably enough, from the border culture he knew so well: *Huset där det dracks* (1932; The house where there was drinking) and *Taina* (1935) are located in the sometime vacation land of the Karelian isthmus (once again, in Edith Södergran's neighborhood), flooded by refugees after 1917–18; his wife's family owned a villa on the coast there. Both novels are about young girls who find their way to this backwater of tumbledown manors and beach cottages; in both, Colliander exploits a Dostoyevskian vein of sin and guilt, made colorful by the quaintness of the mixed population around Terijoki — Hagar Olsson, writing *Träsnidaren och döden,* would draw on the same elements. *Taina* — a text that, by the way, brings up Adolf Hitler, whose "opposition to the Jews and the Bolsheviks most [of the refugees] share" — was translated into German, and Colliander began to acquire a reading public abroad. He had betrayed some naive admiration for Nazi Germany in *Glimtar från Tyskland* (1934; Glimpses from Germany), scarcely an isolated reaction in Finland of the time; witness Olavi Paavolainen's *Kolmannen valtakunnan vieraana* (1936; As a guest of the Third Reich); as for the first excesses of anti-Semitism, he had little to say in 1934: "The Jews have left many gaps behind them, and they must be filled." Visiting the training camp of Max Schmeling, he felt respect for the boxer, whose self-discipline, Colliander recalled in 1971, had something religious about it.

While staying in a small Estonian town, Colliander became a convert to Russian Orthodoxy. The immediate result of the conversion was the long novel *Korståget* (1937; The procession of the cross), in which he developed the obsessions of two preceding collections, *Bojorna* (1933; The fetters), a set of three interconnected tales, in the titular one of which Colliander gives an early and not very flattering self-portrait, and the shorter tales of *Ljuset* (1936; The light), on emotional obligations, thoughtless cruelty, spiritual blindness, and redemption. These themes are consolidated in the chronicle — the autobiographical elements are palpable enough — of a refugee of Finland-Swedish extraction, from St. Petersburg, named Tomas after the doubting disciple. Fleeing to Finland, he is tormented by alcoholism, adultery, and the belief that he has caused a friend's death at the hands of a St. Petersburg mob; spiritual peace comes to him when he beholds the features of the murdered man in the image of Christ borne in an Ascension procession by communicants of the old Russian faith, living across the border in Estonia. The finale is grandiose, punctuated by lines from the liturgy: "'Lord have mercy,' the chorus says. A single line, more powerful, mightier than ever before, in a great fortissimo, and the whole church echoed with the closing 'Lord have mercy.'"

This plea became the title of Colliander's next novel, the more compact *Förbarma dig* (1939; Have mercy), whose setting is the back streets of Helsingfors. Its narrator is the boy Magnus, one of the poor in spirit, a wistful creature surrounded by his father, the idle widower Martin; the two women, the goodhearted "Aunt" Agda and the coquettish Sylvi, who both love the bereaved man; and the drunken Russian ragpicker, Robkin, who has a ghastly (and symbolic) war wound in his side. Pregnant with Martin's child, Agda has a miscarriage and almost bleeds to death; Sylvi, who tells Martin that his revered wife once betrayed him, is killed by him in a fit of rage, and the novel ends as Magnus sees Robkin in the snowy courtyard behind Agda's shop, drunk, rocking back and forth, singing to himself (in Russian, but Magnus understands him): "Lord, have mercy . . ." (Before being transported to the hospital, Agda instructs Magnus to make his father go to the police; Magnus, she continues, must visit him in prison.) The novel has been taken as a prime example of Colliander's sympathy with all humankind, and especially those who make few demands on life; the feckless murderer, full of notions that will never work out, is treated charitably by an author who sees hopelessness and forgivable evil all around him. Colliander has been praised as one of Finland-Swedish literature's great prose narrators, on the strength of the spiritual struggle portrayed in *Korståget,* the argument for a universal and ultimate innocence in *Förbarma dig,* and the erotic intensity of *Grottan* (1942; The grotto), in which a woman finds herself caught in the midst of the passion of two men and the love of her daughter; but in the last-named work Colliander left picturesque or dilapidated milieus, at whose depiction he excelled, for a colorless, well-to-do background. Märta conceives a child with her estranged husband, having been sexually excited by her admirer's confession that he loves her; what seemed to be shocking explicitness in the 1940s has paled today, as has Colliander's style, gray and slackly uniform, except for his grand quasi-ecclesiastical effects or reproduction of squalor. The same stylistic flaccidity pulls down his short stories as well, even in instances where the situation makes a genuine emotional impact, as in the story "Hop Like a Crow" (*Swedo-Finnish Short Stories,* 1974), from the collection *I åratal* (1949; For years): a father, intoxicated, abuses and degrades his wife and children.

After another novel about jealousy and redemption in a love triangle, *Bliv till* (1945; Become), and the selection of stories from 1949 (he chose twenty of his tales for the representative *Fönstret* [1955; The window]), it appeared that Colliander had abandoned creative writing altogether, in order to issue explanations, one after another, of his religious belief, efforts accompanied by theological studies and service as teacher of the Orthodox faith in Helsingfors's Swedish schools. The most accessible of these tractates to a layman is the account of his long struggle with lameness, resulting from a boyhood injury, *Samtal med smärtan* (1955; Conversation with pain); his books of poetry, starting with *Dagen är* (1940; The day is), had the same religious aim and were collected as *På en trappa: Dikter 1941–1961* (On a staircase: Poems 1941–1961). A comeback as a novelist, in the religious vein, *Vi som är kvar* (1959; We who remain) and *Med öppna händer* (1960; With open hands), did not add to his stature: "Where do you find the kingdom of heaven. You find it in your own heart . . . Lord have mercy on us. Do you believe that we, here in the cloister, forever stand like lighted candles in the church?"

In fact, Colliander had other strings on his bow. Books about the Russian Ilya Repin (1942) and the Finn Tyko Sallinen (1948), painters with whom he had considerable in common—in the overwhelming emotionalism of the one and the emphasis on brutality of the other—had already shown that he was a good writer of gripping factual and interpretive prose; in 1964, with *Bevarat* (Preserved), he began a chain of seven memoir volumes—*Gripen* (1965; Seized), *Vidare* (1967; Farther), *Givet* (1968; Given), *Vaka* (1969; Waking), *Nära* (1971; Near), and *Måltid* (1973; Meal)—which, together with *Korståget* and *Förbarma dig*, will be his lasting literary monument. They constitute an autobiography not of the deepest self-probing and certainly not of embarrassing intimate revelation but of constant anecdotal interest. Even though somewhat cloying, especially in the later volumes, his religious standpoint, all-embracing, all-forgiving, allows him to note and comprehend a variety of persons and places, and his faith is seldom too much on display; in this respect, he differs from another important Scandinavian convert (to Roman Catholicism), Johannes Jørgensen in *Mit livs legende* (1916–29; Eng. tr. *Jörgensen: An Autobiography*, 1928–29). The suite's concluding volume tells rather swiftly about the war years (omitting Colliander's membership in Josef Goebbels's "European Writers' Guild" and his participation in the "Weimarer Dichtertage" of 1943) and ends with the refoundation of the cloister at New Valamo: "This fire from Russian holiness which had been cast up on Finland's soil—should it now be allowed to die?" (The original cloister in Lake Lagoda had been closed in the Winter War; its monks moved to Heinävesi.)

After this apparent finale Colliander wrote *Motiv* (1977; Motifs), a set of parables or reflections on various topics, including his own authorship ("There is so much from which to free yourself"), doubt ("an entrance . . . not a departure"), and faith ("Life's paradoxicality is also Christianity's: it neither seeks nor needs explanations"); the short stories of *Början* (1979; Beginning) are interesting as a display of the stylistic habits of which he had grown so fond over the years: aposiopesis ("And the memories, our memories . . ."), self-interrogation ("Why did I come to just this spot, to Greece? Why did I stay here . . . in this cloister?"), and ecphonesis, or outcry ("An answer! a mysticism in words, songs, absolutions, lasting forever!"). Colliander requires readers who are romantics: "Romanticism is the foundation of faith, and thus of happiness, its truest source."

Varieties of Karelianism: Stenius, Olof Enckell, Oscar Parland

The fascination Karelia exerted on authors of the 1930s and 1940s had many sources: the circumstances of birth or upbringing; the fact that Karelia, contiguous to the Soviet Union, served as a catch basin for emigrés; and the exoticism that emanated from its complex history, as the birthplace of the *Kalevala* and home to the monks of Valamo. Plainly, elements of Finnish nationalism and national romanticism were also at work, a replay of the

Karelianism of the turn of the century, put into music by Sibelius, into art by Gallen-Kallela, into an architectural style by the young Eliel Saarinen, into literature by Jac. Ahrenberg and others. By the 1930s, too, the Edith Södergran cult was growing apace, and the bathing and artists' resort of Kuokkala had the double charm of proximity to Raivola and — a whiff of danger — the Soviet naval complex at Kronstadt. The fixation reached its disastrous peak in the dream of a "Greater Finland," which led, in the War of 1941–44, to the Finnish army's advance into Russian Karelia and the extension of the nation's boundaries as far as Lake Onega, where Petrozavodsk was redubbed Äänislinna. The dream collapsed; by September 1944 Viborg was retaken by the Russians, and Karelian refugees once more flooded westward, as they had in 1939–40.

In her memoirs, *Min värld* (1929–31; My world), Alma Söderhjelm (1870–1949), the redoubtable younger sister of Werner, tells what the Viborg of her childhood was like: "There lay something historical in the air . . . for us, despite the fact that we grew up there, Viborg remained forever fascinating." (A historian by training and profession, who also made sallies into the novel, the drama, and the causerie, Alma Söderhjelm had gotten a special appointment in general history at the newly reconstituted Åbo Academy in 1927, making her Finland's first female professor.) The lure of Viborg and its hinterland is more than plain in the earlier novels of Göran Stenius (1909–), whose *Hungergropen* (1944; The hunger pit) and its sequel, *Fästningen* (1945; The fortress), are placed in the Karelian past. The first involves a godforsaken and lawless community of the outback, to which the Cinneliuses, a pastoral family, attempt to introduce order, embodied in the Lutheran faith; the efforts are pretty well in vain, but in the book's bloody finale the people of the Hunger Pit rise up against the Russians during the War of 1808–9 and wreak horrible vengeance on them. The book was written while Stenius, a convert to Roman Catholicism, was a part of the Finnish diplomatic mission to Pius XII's Vatican; the tone is clearly anti-Russian. The sequel, however, set mostly in Viborg itself during the first decades of czarist rule (see the references to the Russian victory of 1828 at Varna in "the holy war against the Turks" and to the official opening, the same year, of the Imperial Alexander University at Helsingfors), discreetly reflects Finland's sudden and necessary pro-Russian stance after September 1944. As in a solidly made historical movie, the strength of *Fästningen* lies not in its characterizations, less convincing than in its predecessor, but in the extreme care with which Viborg's remarkable quadrilingual culture is presented.

Brödet och stenarna (1959; The bread and the stones) carries the story of the Cinneliuses and others forward to the time of the Crimean War (and a sad report that Sevastopol has fallen, after a heroic defense); it ends in Assisi, when a visitor from Viborg begs Alexander Corpi of Korpela, Alexander I's sometime emissary to the Vatican (and, perhaps, the czar's illegitimate son), now a pensioner of the Franciscans ("this is my Taganrog"), to return to Finland. He refuses, although he still deeply loves his homeland. The monastery's prior explains to the bewildered traveler: "Alessandro had told me that he often had a strong yearning for his home when he was younger. But, alas, he confused it with an un-Christian devotion to nature, and that is why he lives in Assisi now and not in Finland. For someone who loves the things of creation, you see, St. Francis is a better teacher than Pan — or whatever he's called in your language."

Stenius has been termed a philosophical novelist by both Erik Ekelund ("Karelsk exotism") and W. Glyn Jones ("Stenius's Philosophical Novels"), and the description is fitting enough: a firm intellectual and religious standpoint supports the colorful superstructure of the trilogy. Indeed, Stenius's first novel, *Det okända helgonets kloster* (1934; The cloister of the unknown saint), took place in a Russian Orthodox establishment, located in the middle of a nearly trackless bog somewhere in the Finnish-Russian borderlands. The representative of Western thought, Dr. Forss, meets the retired Russian colonel Barzow, living nearby with his tubercular wife, and from him learns the value of suffering and of denial of self. (Note that the similar experiences of Colliander's doubting Thomas at the Estonian cloister and those of Olsson's woodcarver Myyriäinen at Valamo come later, in 1937 and 1940.) In Stenius's case the search for a satisfactory faith ended elsewhere; presentiments of conversion can be found in the poems of *Fiskens tecken* (1940; The sign of the fish), addressed to Assisi and "Roma aeterna": "A word dwells in your stones . . . / the root of the longing / you awake in a rootless heart." The lyrics closely resemble those of Colliander's *Dagen är*, published the same year, as in Stenius's "Mysterium": "But this was your greatest gift: crucified, to be able to suffer / and die. And to come forth once more."

Next Stenius undertook to explain Italian culture and Italy for a Finnish and Swedish public — for example, in *Vatikanen* (1947; The Vatican) and *Från Rom till Rom* (1963; From Rome to Rome) — and his clearly Catholic novels are set in or near the Eternal City. In *Klockorna i Rom* (1955; Eng. tr. *The Bells in Rome*, 1961), a descendant of the Viborg Cinneliuses, an art historian (once again with the doubting name Thomas), undergoes a conversion experience at the little town of Settevetri and, from an intellectual, turns into a simple parish priest, having accepted St. Augustine's dictum,

"Non intratur in veritatem, nisi per caritatem" (One does not enter truth save by love). Stenius wrote at a time when Catholic novels were much in vogue; Evelyn Waugh's *Brideshead Revisited* appeared in 1945, Graham Greene's *The Power and the Glory* in 1947, François Mauriac won the Nobel Prize in 1952, and such catholicizing German authors as Gertrud von Le Fort, Werner Bergengruen, and Edzard Schaper were at the height of their fame — like Stenius, the English authors and the Germans were converts. In Sweden another convert, Sven Stolpe (1905–96), had introduced the *renouveau catholique* as early as 1934–36 with the essays of *Den kristna falangen* (The Christian phalanx). Unlike Stolpe, however, Stenius was not rigidly or aggressively doctrinaire. As a matter of fact, writing under a pseudonym, Georg Keller, in *Mannen som uppfann vädret: En rötmånadssaga* (1937; The man who discovered the weather: A dogday tale), he had revealed a genuine talent for irony. The work is a Helsingfors novel about one Noak Waterman (the nephew of a Viborg shoemaker, Solomon Wasserman), who is able to control the weather and so is misused by several power factors in Finland's society. In *Bronspojken från Ostia* (1974; The bronze boy from Ostia) another Jew, the antiquarian Gianela, reconstructs the life story of the model of this ancient statuette for the sometime humanist (and ironist) Dr. Gregorio, who comes to believe he has discovered "eternal values" in the boy's face. Before he dies, he tells his school class that the statue may bespeak "a divine poverty." While Gregorio's search for religious faith never finds fulfillment (his last words are an aposiopesis, "to possess a call . . ."), he has spent his existence in condemning the greed of a modern society much like that of ancient Rome. As for Gianela, he has maintained *his* faith, according to W. Glyn Jones, "in the face of apparent hopelessness" ("Stenius' Philosophical Novels," 95).

Born at Kronoborg (Kurkijoki) on Lake Ladoga, Olof Enckell (1900–1989), the elder brother of Rabbe, grew up in Helsingfors. His three patriotic-factual books on Karelia are superior reporting (or editorializing): *Vakt i Öster: Vandringar i Gränskarelen* (1939; Watch in the east: Wanderings in border Karelia), which is not, as the author quickly points out, about the "romantic" southeastern corner and its "exoticism" but about the far less colorful "unknown wilderness" north of Ladoga, from which a "Finnish-Nordic spirit with its clear-minded sense of a goal [had] driven away all Slavic mysticism"; *Krigaren och bonden* (1940; The warrior and the peasant), written in October after the Winter War, about the ruin the conflict had left behind; and *Rapport från ödemarken* (1942; Report from the wilderness), on the renewed fighting in the same territory. Several of Olof Enckell's six novels, written before his shift from journalism to scholarship and his appointment as professor of Swedish literature at the University of Helsingfors, are also connected to Karelia, though a Karelia less mystical than that of Olsson and Colliander. Enckell made his rational standpoint plain at the outset, in *Ett klosteräventyr* (1930; A cloister adventure). A man at the classic crisis age of thirty, meaning to spend a vacation near Helsingfors, arrives by accident in Viborg instead and wanders northward to Kexholm ("where he was born" — the novel has some autobiographical elements in it — "but where he had not been since he was four"). Still led by chance, he makes his way to the cloister at Valamo (thus taking the course later followed by the young men of Stenius and Olsson) and, for a time, is drawn into the holy web, but he finally resists: "The cloister church was solemn and exceedingly spiritual. But at the same time he thought that, with all its blue and green surfaces, it looked like a peacock spreading its feathers." And he has much trouble imagining a life of asceticism.

Another intelligent skeptic sets out on a quest in *Halmstacken* (1931; The haystack): this time the protagonist finds a true contact with the nation's majority population in the province of Tavastland (Häme), foreshadowing the "Tavastland Odyssey," Vega Maria's trip to the Finnish-speaking countryside, in Hagar Olsson's *Chitambo*. Enckell was more willing than most Finland-Swedish writers of his generation to speak directly about the actual problems of his linguistic (and, as he indicates here, cultural) minority. In *Vårt hjärta* (1933; Our heart) he went back to Karelia, depicting the Finnish and Russian inhabitants of a largely Orthodox village on the Karelian isthmus: the simple plot seems almost to be a continuation of Lilly Londén's novel, *En misstanke,* from half a century before, which ended with the departure of the essentially innocent hero for prison. In Enckell's novel a sometime convict returns, trying to find a place in a society reluctant to receive him: his growing affection for the abused wife of his employer leads almost to murder. (Again, as in the narrative of realism — see Juhani Aho's *Juha* — eroticism seems to blossom more readily in Karelia than elsewhere in Finland.) In the sequel, *Guldkedjan* (1934; The golden chain), the love of a good (and unattached) girl helps draw Isia out of himself, and the couple — already linked by the golden chain of the title — is united in a ceremony at Pentecost. Interesting as are the implications of Enckell's portrayal of a much more primitive culture than his own (Erik Ekelund ["Karelsk exotism," 86] suspected that Enckell, on the search for authentic values, was attempting to people his own "psychological landscape"), the two books were an artistic blind alley, dismissable as an imitation of works by Finnish-language authors born to the territory.

With the comical novel about advertising and radio life in Helsingfors *Tre (3) månader à dato: Idyll i funkis* (1935; Three (3) months from this date: A broadcasting idyll), Enckell returned to a world with which he was better acquainted and in which the flickering emotions of his nervous Ambrosius are more believedly presented than those of the strong and simple Isia. Whether Enckell thought he had readers faithful enough to be able to compare his weakling with his natural man is a question not to be answered; in his last novel, *Solnedgång* (1945; Sunset), he places his opposites in the same book: the aged liberal, Thomas Argillander, who has led a life of intellectual exploration, moderate cultivation of beauty, and nonengagement, and his grandson, a zealous People's Democrat (the time is the present, directly after the armistice of 1944 and the establishment of the Democratic Union for Finland's People) who calls his grandfather an aesthete and worse. Yet after Argillander has passed away (and the grandson has inherited his modest fortune), the firebrand begins to wonder if the old man's emphasis on individual cultivation was wholly wrongheaded. The forebear's spirit speaks from the grave: "I do not criticize you for your idea's sake. Why should one criticize such a fine intention and — seen most deeply — such a correct thought? But just the same: When I try to look into the future . . . I must smile." The spirit sees a Don Quixote in his grandson, for whom he wishes a "Sancho Panza, wiser than [he] is." *Solnedgång* is dedicated to Yrjö Hirn, the university's great eclectic humanist; its epigraph refers to Horace's ode (IV:7), no doubt cited because of its defense of selfish refinement: "All things you grant to your own dear soul will escape the greedy clutches of your heir."

Enckell cannot be called an accomplished novelist — the portrait of the grandfather in *Solnedgång* is filled out by having the old man remember quotations (like Mikael Lybeck's humanist, Sven Ingelet) from Hume and Juvenal — but he had the eye of the skillful journalist, sharpened during the years as editor and leading critic of *Hufvudstadsbladet;* he feared that the "sunset" of a cherished Finland-Swedish humanistic tradition would be hastened by political and social fanaticism. Probably it was not just a sudden opportunity, and the desire to write dispassionately about the literary figures and events he knew so well, that drew him into his final career as a researcher and teacher; he must have also been quite aware, experienced reviewer that he was, of his own creative shortcomings, and his laudable open-mindedness kept him from the concentration necessary for belletristic success. Even as a translator, he was drawn in opposite directions, toward both the novelist of peasant life, Ilmari Kianto in *Punainen viiva* (1909;

Swed. tr. *Det röda strecket* [The red line], 1946), and the subtle and ambiguous Olavi Paavolainen, with whom Enckell evidently shared some political sympathies.

Oscar Parland (1912–97), the second eldest of the Parland brothers, made his tardy debut as a novelist with *Förvandlingar* (Transformations) in 1945, the year Olof Enckell stopped writing novels. A bystander in literary circles, his energy had been absorbed by medical studies and military service and, after 1944, his practice as a psychiatrist. His profession no doubt contributed to the smallness of his output; only two more novels appeared, *Den förtrollade vägen* (1953; Eng. tr. *The Enchanted Way*, 1991) and *Tjurens år* (1962; Eng. tr. *The Year of the Bull*, 1991). In his collected papers, *Kunskap och inlevelse: Essäer och minnen* (1991; Knowledge and empathy: Essays and memories), Parland reported on the extremely long gestation of his first work, which he began sometime in the 1930s after having translated the novel of Yury Olesha (1899–1960), *Zavist'* (1927; Envy); the translation itself did not appear until 1961. Originally, *Förvandlingar* was called *Kanon* (Canon); like his brothers, Oscar Parland was a skilled musician. He felt, though, that he had not yet succeeded in creating an "expressive, imaginative prose"—an admirable hesitation about rushing into print that distinguished him from many of his contemporaries. Studies of primitive lyrics (in anthologies by the German Eckart von Sydow and the Finlanders Christer Lind and Jarno Pennanen) opened the gates, he said, to an understanding of his childhood at the family home in Tikkala; Thomas Mann's Joseph novels inspired him with their revelation of the "magical-mystical phase in the history of mankind." Gide's *Les faux-monnayeurs* (1926) strengthened his conviction that his debut should have a clear but polyphonic structure; Mann's *Buddenbrooks* and *Der Zauberberg*—as well as his own psychiatric training—made him plunge into the family history and emotional labyrinths of his characters.

All these preparations and influences led to a corpulent manuscript, subsequently reduced (by three-quarters) and rewritten: the final, simplifying force came from a chance reading of Benjamin Constant's short, pioneering psychological novel *Adolphe* (1816). The result was still a sturdy work, concentrated on the relationships within a highly gifted family, in which the central tragedy of the Parlands—the mental collapse and attempted suicide of the mother after Henry's death—forms the climax; the narrator is the wise Uncle Cid, in whom the philosopher Wilhelm Sesemann, Henry's mentor, is portrayed, and the children are reduced to two, Mario (Henry Parland) and Vincent. (The stern father, for whatever reason, is given the name Henry.) Today *Förvandlingar* has to be taken as an analysis of a delicate situation (speaking through Cid, Oscar Parland dwells on the strong sensual element in the love of Eva, the mother, for Mario), a skillfully executed representative of the inward-looking Finland-Swedish novel of the time, by virtue of its graceful style and structure and the lucidity of its creator's mind.

Even while he was at his often interrupted work on *Förvandlingar* (fifteen years passed between Henry's death and its publication), Parland had been tempted to go back to much earlier stages of family life. In a literature so concentrated on the nuclear family the depiction of childhood — the child's world consists of the family and of the first tentative excursions outside that charmed circle — has had a special place, starting with Topelius's idealizations, becoming far more frank in Tavaststjerna's *Lille Karl,* then blooming in Diktonius's writing about children and his own childhood (in *Medborgare II*), in the first of Eklund's memoir volumes, and in Rabbe Enckell's exceptional tale "The Japanese Children"; further, Colliander's most genuine artistic success came with the boy-narrator of *Förbarma dig* and in the early volumes of his memoir series, *Bevarat* and *Vidare,* and Solveig von Schoultz's Ansa stories are a basic element in her fiction, as are Mirjam Tuominen's pictures of children. Parland wrote his two masterpieces along the same line, accurate portraits of the remarkable family from which he came, seen by Rikki, the small boy who is the narrator of them both. Rikki's tutelary figure in *Den förtrollade vägen* is his maternal grandmother, God's representative; in *Tjurens år* she is overshadowed by the Bull itself, an incorporation of the war that threatens the farm where Rikki lives with or near his many kin. (The epigraph is from Södergran: "The world is bathed in blood.") According to Parland, Yury Olesha's gift for making things come alive revealed to him, in adulthood, some of the secrets of his childhood; he has also referred to an influence from Tolstoy's *Detstvo* (Childhood) in the plethora of relatives, comforting or terrifying, that almost engulf the little boy. But the temptation to succumb to picturesqueness, lying so close at hand because of the multicultural Karelian setting, is largely resisted; in his restraint Parland resembles the author of a classic book on Swedish childhood, Bertil Malmberg's *Åke och hans värld* (1924; Eng. tr. *Åke and His World,* 1940) — to be sure, Åke's milieu is far more mundane to begin with. With the care acquired in his psychiatric schooling, but without an air of professional superiority, Parland explores the infinite complexities of childhood; the epigraph of *Den förtrollade vägen* is from Heraclitus: "Though you walked all the ways of the world, you cannot find the spirit's boundaries; so deep is its abyss."

Even in the wartime book Parland never employs scenes of horror, save in the exhibiting of the dead bull's carcass at the end, and his translucent style has attracted a Finnish translator of Eeva-Liisa Manner's sensibility. In an afterword appended to the second edition of *Den förtrollade vägen* (1974) Parland told about a visit he paid as a soldier to the scenes of his childhood: "The countryside all around me was hostile. All this no longer belonged to me, but lay beyond the limits of my reality." The return, after long absence, contributed to the damping of potential sentimentality: Parland did not try to find a specific spiritual goal or revel in vanished glories. Instead, he hunted for the mythical archetypes of which Rikki was dimly aware: "I am surrounded by supernatural, semidivine, semianimal creatures. The animals speak with human tongues—all is an incarnation of the soul, which shapes the material according to its own laws."

A Brilliant Eclecticism: Ralf Parland
A younger Parland brother, Ralf (1914–95), started off determined to continue the brilliant Henry's worldly-wise and impudent tone, with collections of prose sketches whose very titles smacked of modernity if not modernism: *Dusch* (1934; Showerbath) and *Ebonit* (1937; Ebonite, the black synthetic material from which both Victrola records and imitation ebony clarinets were made), amusing if somewhat supercilious pictures of contemporary life—"My father has taken off his yellow-striped pajamas and turned on the shower. In this moment my father resembles a large-nosed Indian with black, streaky hair and a low forehead. . . . I think he looks comical." From the phonograph record's ebonite come "invertebrates with brown, hungry arms. A lone trombone ruminates in sad syncopes on life's premature death in the womb." As a young man, Parland spent a good deal of time with his Grankulla neighbor, Elmer Diktonius, and a Diktonian air (especially the less declamatory Diktonius of the 1930s) can be spotted in the poetry collections *Avstånd* (1938; Distance), *Abel y Aifars sånger* (1941; Abel y Aifar's songs), and *Mot fullbordan* (1944; Toward completion). Like Diktonius with his renderings of Arthur Waley's English versions of Chinese poetry (in *Varsel*), Parland was not loath to include secondhand translations of Oriental verse in his books (his lyric vein never ran very freely), and in *Avstånd* and *Mot fullbordan* he offered his versions of Hans Bethge's German translations of Indian poetry and Klabund's "Chinese" verse. On his own, Parland came up with unusual war poetry: "In a Bomber to the Sounds of a Rhumba" is the "tired and extremely confused prayer" a flier directs to the possible victims of his load; "Companions" is a vision of a war lurching toward its end:

> Although it's a lie
> that we all fought
> for the barge that sank in this war
> but God knows we slogged
> in the same dirt in the same manner.

Already, again in imitation of Diktonius, Parland had turned compositions of his relative, Ernst Pingoud (1888–1942), "The Face of the Metropolis" and "The Song of Space," into words in the collection of 1938 and had tried transforming a Bach sonata for solo violin into "God's gigantic images" and "God's pirouettes" in 1941, just as he had attempted, by his own admission, to imitate the distinct rhythms of a rhumba in his bombing poem. As Diktonius's successor in the musical columns of *Nya Argus,* he published his reviews, assembled as *Mot morgondag* (Toward tomorrow), in 1942.

Parland's postwar production moved away from Diktonius's tutelage, becoming ever more intellectualized or abstract; in *Relief* (1951) he tried out exotic imagery, a jungle ("Under the lofty trees walked the elephants / like gray arches of scaly stone / and broke loose giant pinecones above") or a paradisiacal forest ("Trees of strange stature / plunging into the sky / here the green is always young / and the water always cool"). His imagination led him to the science-fiction poetry of *Hymner från Santsche-Pi* (1959; Hymns from Santsche-Pi), whose name first appeared in a story in *Hårt ljus* (1952; Hard light). This wondrous land has associations with James Hilton's Shangri-La but is a far more complex place than the lost kingdom (with Tibetan trappings) of the 1930s' best-selling novel and film *Lost Horizon* (1933; 1937). Parland put up a "Central Station of the Dream" and composed a whole nomenclature ("age-old Meandrid," "Derivate," "Dior, the preserver of the ball-seal," "Ao, my dancing wind") for the mythology of "the hovering city." It has been cogently argued that Santsche-Pi is not a dreamer's refuge but an antiutopia, in whose dream station manipulation and indoctrination reign. Parland's hymns came out three years after the Swede Harry Martinson's space epic, *Aniara,* to which they make reference in the half-English, half-Swedish continuation of "Ao's cradle song":

> Sleep darling sleep
> your grandfather has a Jeep
> with which he drives to Dorisburg
> and dances Harry's savage jurg.
> Sleep grandmother sleep.

("Dorisburg" and "jurg" are from *Aniara.*) Parland's science fiction culminated in the enigmatically titled *i: En roman om förhävdelsen* (1973; i: A novel about arrogance), a prose expansion of the Santsche-Pi myths, in a world some four eons hence, concluding with a set of poems in which Södergran, among others, was plundered for a mocking pastiche.

A less baffling side of Parland's prose production lies in the parts of his long line of story volumes, *Himlens stenar* (1947; The heaven's stones), *Hårt ljus* (1952; Hard light), *Eros och elektronerna* (1953; Eros and the electrons), *Hem till sitt hav* (1957; Home to his sea), *En apa for till himmelen* (1961; An ape flew to the sky), *En hundpredikan* (1966; A dog sermon), and *Regnbågens död* (1970; The rainbow's death), which build on memories of a Karelian childhood, on wartime experiences, and on the yarns of the huge Parland-Sesemann clan (see "Twelve Uncles' Journey," *Swedo-Finnish Short Stories*, 1974). His lyric production was similarly eclectic, sometimes, in *Sonat för fallskärm och kalebass* (1964; Sonata for parachute and calabash), indulging his affection for Russian culture (recreating Moussorgski in words, making free translations of Lermontov, and paying tribute to Tolstoy), undertaking vaguely anti-American exercises (having moved to Sweden, Parland was impelled to comment on "the Atlantic Pact's field-gray crabs" from a fashionable Swedish-leftist standpoint), and revisiting the wonderworlds of the imaginary Himalayas ("far away / my mountain rests / closed in its cap's white") and the other side of the moon. Among his volumes of poetry the most satisfying is *Eolita* (1956), in which Parland concentrated—with remarkable success—on the short poem. Here, in the midst of his brittle intellectualism, he had moments of genuine insight into the human predicament, as in "Monument":

> . . . you remain.
> Over our poor decades.
> Over the centuries we do not know.
> Betrayed visions of future!

"Subjective" runs in its entirety:

> Like a bell's hollow blow
> in my temple: About years that have passed.
> About years that are fulfilled
> far from myself.
> In the gardens I never shall enter.

Eolita, by the way, has an unsettling historical importance because of its mention of the French defeat at Dienbenphu (1954); the "giantlike woman [Eolita] / . . . leans / over Vietnam's rustling jungle / and kisses the darkness." In Parland's "dramatic poem in three movements," *Bländverket* (1968; The dazzling illusion), Lyndon B. Johnson appears, along with—among other characters—the "nocturnal visionary" Ghanom, Gunnar Björling, and "der fahrende Geselle," a "runaway song text by Gustav Mahler."

A Special Lutheranism: Nyman
When Eugène Napoleon Tigerstedt defended his doctoral dissertation on the religious element in Finland-Swedish literature (1939), he could not have guessed that matters of faith, remarkably, would play an even greater role in the future literary production of a linguistic group whose intelligentsia could fairly be characterized as payers of lip service to Lutheranism or, more often, spiritually apathetic. The phenomenon was not confined to writers with Karelian connections. These decades' most colorful example of a religious novelist allied to a region outside Karelia was Valdemar Nyman (1904–), born in Ostrobothnia but, from the 1930s on, a pastor and teacher of religion on Åland. His first novel, *Som tusen liljor* (1944; Like a thousand lilies), contained the basic elements of his authorship; passion for Åland's past (the nineteenth century's maritime heyday) and a concomitant passion for his own emotionally presented faith, in which moral considerations took a back seat to repentance and to the strength of belief, a Lutheran counterpart to Colliander's all-forgiving Russian Orthodoxy. He made his only stab at a setting in his own lifetime (and at depicting his own life) in *Sko, sko hästen* (1945; Shoe, shoe the horse); the title and chapter headings come from a popular rhyme about a pastoral visit: "Tomorrow the Pastor's Coming." An ecclesiastical bildungsroman, it is the story of the seminarian's and minister's revolt against dusty teachings and authoritarian superiors; on the party line, one of Halvar Sko's new parishioners says: "He's Catholic, as sure as I'm born. To think that somebody like that can become a pastor. Not a word about Luther. But genuflections and candles. Did you see how he crawled to the altar like a papist?"

Broder Kilian (1947; Brother Kilian) is a novel built in dialogue (and stage scenes) like Flaubert's *La tentation de Saint Antoine* (1874; Eng. tr. *The Temptation of St. Anthony*, 1910, 1980); the main voice belongs to a fourteenth-century monk on the island of Kökar: Kilian, a Nordic Saint Anthony, is surrounded by a host of temptations, and animals and inanimate objects speak. The sensualism that inspires or bothers Nyman's protagonists is altogether evident in *Margareta Jönsdotter till Bastö* (1950; Margareta Jönsdotter at Bastö). Margareta is the literary descendant, maybe, of two earlier and better-known Scandinavian heroines with an appetite for men, the title characters of J. P. Jacobsen's *Fru Marie Grubbe* (1876; Eng. tr. *Marie Grubbe: A Lady of the Seventeenth Century*, 1917, 1952, 1975) and Jørgen-Frantz Jacobsen's *Barbara* (1939; Eng. tr. 1948). The powerful and rebellious Margareta, who lives during the change from Catholicism to Lutheranism, reports in detail on her erotic conquests and disappointments, for example: "Sten had a man's body, a man's body through and through, and covered with hair like sparks, but a child's soul. [But] even though this drew me to him, I desired something more." In *Den stora flykten* (1953; The great flight) Pastor Johannes Liliewahn is confronted by invading Russians during the Swedish collapse in the Great Northern War, and confronted, as well, by the lure of homosexuality; Liliewahn introduces his famulus Gabriel to the secrets of Rosicrucianism and more: "Gabriel's skin exudes warmth and the tincture of young manhood. No force can hold you back. You kiss him and kiss him once again. Gabriel kisses you. And wild roses close above you."

Nyman's characters follow at least the first half of Luther's instruction to Melanchthon, "Pecca fortiter, repente fortius" (Sin strongly, repent more strongly); their ecstatic pleasure in sexual activity reminded N.-B. Stormbom ("Inledning," 8) of the subtexts in Gunnar Björling. What is more interesting (and a tribute to Nyman's awareness of literary innovation, in which he resembles Oscar Parland) is his readiness to undertake technical experiments: *Broder Kilian* put Stormbom and Warburton (*Åttio år finlandssvensk litteratur,* 292) in mind of James Joyce's *Ulysses* (the phantasmagoria of its shifting scenes), and over considerable stretches both Margareta Jönsdotter and Johannes Lilliewahn are harangued by the narrator, or harangue themselves, in the second-person singular. (Using this device, Nyman vied successfully with Peter Sjögren [1905–] in Sweden, who tried it in *Mannen som försökte smita* [1949; The man who tried to run away].)

After a long pause Nyman returned to the novel with *Osmund Kåresunds ungdom* (1972; Osmund Kåresund's youth) and *Osmund och aftonstjärnan* (1976; Osmund and the evening star); in the eleventh century the wandering prelate addresses the canoness of Ely, Hrosvitha: "Open rose and fully sounding silver trumpet in the night—even as your great namesake [Hrosvitha of Gandersheim, the dramatist] wished her name to be interpreted—you shall rule between the moon of my manhood's rising and falling, uniting in you the fullness and death of my life." Does Nyman's abandonment of the Åland setting for the Danelaw and Norway and Byzance constitute a modest bow in the direction of the great popularity of Mika Waltari's novels about the much-traveled Mikael Furryfoot (see chapter 4)? A quick comparison with Waltari immediately shows Nyman's limitations: his substitution of verbal energy for narrative invention, the absence of subtleties, the smaller intellectual horizons. Yet Nyman has a distinct importance in the history of the Finland-Swedish novel: his main works tried to avoid the monotony of the still endemic linear narrative (save for such undertakings as Henry Parland's *Sönder* and Diktonius's *Janne Kubik*); their religiosity was a celebration of happiness rather than suffering; their tentative excursions into hitherto forbidden sexual realms were the harbinger of much bolder doings in the 1960s; and they called attention to the still underdeveloped literary landscape of Åland. Nyman also made sizable contributions to Åland's culture with his discovery and publication of the manuscripts of Joel Pettersson (see below) and with his cultural-historical guides to Åland (1964/1967), reprinted in a single volume as *På åländska vägar till lands och till sjöss* (1980; On Åland ways by land and sea).

Historical Narrative

An appropriate question about the Finland-Swedish canon is, Why has it produced relatively little historical fiction of high quality since the days of *Fältskärns berättelser* and *Stjärnornas kungabarn*? (These works, of course, were partly aimed at a juvenile public.) The answer does not lie in the absence of awareness of the past — on the contrary, tradition is a preservative of the minority's sense of individuality. Max Engman has noted the overwhelming importance of the discipline of history in the reestablishment of Åbo Academy in 1918; a large stream of biographies and other historical studies, by professionals and amateurs alike, has never faltered (nor has the torrent of memoirs). Harald Hornborg (1890–1976), writing his many novels about the fictitious Hakensköld family (from 1932 to 1958) and a trilogy about a pastor in the Karelian wilderness (1938–40), moved easily back and forth between fiction packed with historical facts and popular presentations of actual history. (Finland was not enough to satisfy him: from 1928 to 1955 he also wrote nine volumes on imaginary German duodecimo principalities.) If Hornborg, owing to his rambunctious sense of humor, was Swedish Finland's Kenneth Roberts, Margit von Willebrand-Hollmerus (1894–1982) was its Ellen Glasgow, particularly in her long series (from 1941 on) about the Bjurcrona family and its fate in Nyland from the early nineteenth century into the twentieth. Herself a member of a family that had given Finland statesmen, soldiers, sportsmen, and, last but not least, physicians (the discoverer of von Willebrand's disease), she had plenty of material that she could describe in her careful and exemplary style. Yet no towering work in the historical genre appeared (i.e., there was nothing at the imaginative level, say, of the Norwegian Johan Falkberget's *Den fjerde nattevakt* [1923; Eng. tr. *The Fourth Night Watch*, 1968] or the Dane Martin A. Hansen's *Lykkelige Kristoffer* [1945; Eng. tr. *Lucky Kristoffer*, 1974]).

The closest thing to minor-classic status may be found in the miniatures of Lorenz von Numers (1913–94), included (during the course of a large and variegated production) in the volumes *Månen är en säl* (1952; The moon is a seal) and *Basturesan* (1953; The sauna trip), historiettes (sometimes a blending of the tale and the essay) such as those conjuring up the essence of Baltic coastal towns, "Concerning What's Baltic" and "The Measure of Our Competence." In the latter item's few pages the whole life of a sometime mercenary officer, returning to the poverty of his little Finnish estate in 1739, is retold, together with a modern coda in which an Italian visitor to the simple captain's house in the outdoor museum on Fölisön (in Helsingfors) asks, condescendingly, "Why did they make everything of wood?" (In a selection from the two volumes, published in Sweden as *Oting* [1968; Nuisances], the historiette was redubbed "By Senate Square," *Swedo-Finnish Short Stories,* 1974.) Linguistic elegance, the power to suggest, and the employment of dry-as-dust archival material for amusing or ironic ends were likewise the special strengths of the essays in *De hemliga rummen* (1982; The secret rooms), which ranged in their topics from the Swedish sixteenth century to Spain's Carlist Wars and Finland's Continuation War and included another salute, "Fennica," to the country where von Numers — one of the numerous expatriate Finland-Swedish authors, a Hispanophile and Francophile, the author of a novel on Villon (1946) and a biography of the French-Turkish soldier Bonneval Achmet Pasha (1981) — had not resided for years. A cultural conservative often and justly compared with the Swede Frans G. Bengtsson (1894–1955), fascinated by the stirring past (with a novel and a travel book about Palestine of the Crusades [1948; 1964]), von Numers moved to Sweden after the war and then on to France, translating Froissart, Joinville, Montaigne, and Cardinal de Retz into Swedish.

Like many other Finland-Swedish authors after 1944, von Numers looks back to a world that is gone; in "Fennica" he tells about his youthful reaction to the capital to which he had come from Åbo:

> Swedish Helsingfors was a small milieu . . . but in its limitation differentiated with great care. . . . An almost Japanese supersubtlety is perceptible in its ancient flora of anecdotes, distilled tenderly and long, and malicious sayings. The nicknames could be merciless. One of my friends, doomed to use crutches, was called "Boneless Malmström." As a native, he accepted it with bitter satisfaction; it gave support to his opinion of human beings. . . . The city's society, as is well known, had a marked stratification, the class boundaries were plainly drawn. . . . A detail extremely few observers from Sweden have noticed is the difference between the social strata of spoken Finland-Swedish.

Not until Merete Mazzarella's *Samtal* (1991; Conversations) would a Finland-Swedish writer again make such a piercing analysis of the minority's peculiarities. The capital itself would shortly be transformed:

> The population of Helsingfors had, procentually speaking, more foreign elements in those days, it was not as completely and utterly Finnish as at present. . . . Helsingfors lost its air of a Swedish skerry harbor. During the next generation, the neighboring parishes of Nyland were Fennicized up to 90 percent by immigration from the north and east. An out-of-date bus schedule [for communities in these parishes] can be read as an elegy to what has disappeared. . . . The scenery remains but the play has changed. I admit that it awakens a feeling of homelessness in me.

Has a sense of rootlessness, of no longer belonging, prevented the production of vital and not just nostalgic historical fiction? And what about the concomitant dream, of a "great Finland-Swedish novel" on the minority's manners and mores, the peculiarities of which von Numers gave a little taste in his essay? The trilogy by another expatriate, E. R. Gummerus (1905–91), *Fästningen* (1940; The fortress), *Arvet* (1942; The heritage), *Sönerna* (1943; The sons), about the Salander family and its tribulations in the Finland of the last days of czarist rule, the Civil War, and the young republic, proved only that Gummerus was an equivalent neither of Thomas Mann in *Buddenbrooks* nor of Roger Martin du Gard in *Les Thibault*, nor even of John Galsworthy.

Sally Salminen and Little Åland

Although Sally Salminen (1906–72) would not have considered herself a regionalist, *Katrina* (1936; Eng. tr. 1938) bestowed a literary reputation and recognition value on Åland it had never possessed before, even though the islands had received temporary attention in the world press during the Åland crisis of 1919–20 (instead of joining Sweden, the Ålanders got autonomy within the Republic of Finland). From a large and impoverished sailor's family on Vårdö (her father drowned when she was seven), Salminen wrote her novel while working as a maid in New York City, where she had lived since 1930; it won a prize announced by Wahlström & Widstrand in Stockholm and Schildt in Helsingfors (Gunnar Castrén and Elmer Diktonius were among the judges) and was directly translated into English by Naomi Walford. Its success in the United States — the way may have been paved by the critical acclaim given Hemmer's *A Fool of Faith* three years before — was considerable, and Salminen's strong Katrina was compared with O-lan in *The Good Earth* (1931) of Pearl S. Buck. To the U.S. audience, *Katrina* appealed by its straightforward narration (one reviewer said it read like a "Norse saga"), by the moral triumph of Katrina over the tyrannical (but essentially goodhearted) Captain Nordkvist, and by Katrina's laudable devotion to her weak husband; in short, it had elements like those in uplifting Hollywood films of the time and — like *The Good Earth* (made into a film in 1937) or Richard Llewellyn's *How Green Was My Valley* (1939; film, 1941) — was set in a picturesque foreign land. What might be taken as the leftist revolutionary doings of Katrina in the book's early pages became submerged in an edifying tale of stoicism and devotion; the vigorous activist from Ostrobothnia, lured into marriage on clannish Åland, became the resigned, lonely, but self-reliant old woman of the last chapters; the vaguely titillating novelty of a dysfunctional family — seen in the contempt of the sons for their ineffectual father — was glossed over by the pathos of the father's death. A study of the worldwide critical reception of *Katrina,* translated into more than twenty languages, would be valuable; the accolade it received from an important Danish critic of the time, Jørgen Bukdahl, helped send it on its triumphant way in Scandinavia. He found universality in it: "It is a trait of the courage of great poets to dare to hold fast to basic relationships through and in defiance of local and social conditions" (p. 131).

The novel's actual strength lay in its detailed picture of the islands' social structure and in its knowledge of local customs and local nature. (Salminen was an admirer of the use of similar elements by Selma Lagerlöf and by the Norwegian-American novelist Ole Rølvaag.) *Den långa våren* (1939; lit. The long spring; Eng. tr. *Marianna,* 1940), however, disappointed her public, aware that she had already told a similar story about the same milieu; the U.S reception was particularly negative: "We are puzzled as to how a person who writes so well at one time can fail to realize how badly she writes at another." *På lös sand* (1941; On loose sand) was the first of her many efforts to expand her range; its main figure, the Baptist preacher Edgar Lind, confronts and overcomes difficulties in a sketchily described Ostrobothnia and in Stockholm before returning, patriotically, to a Finland ravaged by war, "the land he now, with God's help, would serve and give his strength." Married to the Danish artist Johannes Dührkop and settled in Denmark, Salminen undertook four hefty novels, from 1943 to 1951, about a male protagonist, of which the first, *Lars Laurila,* deals with Lars's growing up, year by year, and culminates in the Åland problem; *Nya land* (1945; New lands) takes Laurila to America; *Små världar* (1949; Small worlds) is located in New York (and the Berkshires); and *Klyftan och stjärnan* (1951;

The chasm and the star) returns Laurila to his Åland home. Possibly an effort to emulate the Olof series of Eyvind Johnson (begun in 1934) and the Lars Hård books of Jan Fridegård (begun in 1935), the Laurila tetralogy is nevertheless Salminen's most informative contribution to Finland-Swedish literature, because of its depiction of the Åland mentality, split between Finland and Sweden, and of immigrant life in Manhattan during the depression. The Åland material was mined again in *Barndomens land* (1948; Childhood's land), which makes use, in effect, of memories for which *Katrina* and *Den långa våren* had no room.

Schildt, Salminen's publisher from the start, continued to accept the lengthy manuscripts by a homegrown author with an international reputation, and she tried once again to live up to her fame with *Prins Efflam* (1953; Eng. tr. *The Prince from the Sea*, 1954). The Laurila books had been, somehow, part of her own experience—a sympathetic essayist, Anna-Lisa Bäckman, says that there she turned herself into a man (p. 452)—but in *Prins Efflam* she tried to construct a figure outside her cultural limits. *Prins Efflam* tells of a refugee who turns up in a Bretagne village and becomes a savior figure for its inhabitants. "The Prince had conquered the sea and thereby performed a new miracle, giving a renewed proof of his supernatural gifts," by bringing an apparently dead man—named Lazare, in case the reader misses the point—back to life; but the evil of which the so-called prince is capable breaks through when he murders a young girl. (An informant for the Germans in the south of France, Efflam had caused his parents, Jehovah's Witnesses, to be sent to a concentration camp. The knowledge that he has committed this deed, among others, has led to amnesia.) The long-winded psychological study came out first in Danish and got the praise of a major Danish novelist, Martin A. Hansen, who in *Løgneren* (1950; Eng. tr. *The Liar*, 1969) had explored a similar personality type with infinitely more skill and in fewer pages. Neither here nor in *Vid havet* (1963; By the sea), which had a Danish setting and still another guilt-ridden protagonist, was Salminen able to overcome her excessive wordiness. Nevertheless, by dint of their themes of punishment or redemption and their religious trappings (the depictions of Catholic piety in *Prins Efflam;* the discovery by Jes, the sinful schoolteacher in *Vid havet*, of "the man I call the teacher, that is S. Kierkegaard"), these books are further specimens of the Finland-Swedish religious novel that flourished simultaneously with Colliander and Stenius. They are, as well, another sign of Salminen's devotion to Selma Lagerlöf, who had made a specialty of flawed heroes who seek grace: Gaetano Falcone in *Antikrists mirakler* (1897; Eng. tr. *The Miracles of Antichrist*, 1899), Gunnar Hede in *En herrgårdssägen* (1899; Eng. tr. *The Tale of a*

Manor, 1917), David Holm in *Körkarlen* (1912; Eng. tr. *The Soul Shall Bear Witness,* 1921).

It may not be an accident that the first of Salminen's travel books from Israel (1970 and 1971) shares a name (and a goal of pilgrimage) with Lagerlöf's novel *Jerusalem 1–2* (1901–2); the second is called *På färder i Israel* (Under way in Israel). Furthermore, Salminen felt she owed it to her devoted readership to tell them still more about her life, which she did in four books of memoirs: *Upptäcktsresan* (1966; The voyage of discovery), which deals with childhood and youth on Åland; *Min amerikanska saga* (1968; My American fairy tale); *I Danmark* (1971; In Denmark); and *Världen öppnar sig* (1974; The world opens up), which covers love, marriage, the German occupation of Denmark, and the end of the war. Merete Mazzarella proposes that the books lie in a "borderland between memoirs and autobiography": Sally Salminen aims at finding "a meaning, a pattern, in a life that appears to be ruled by chance" (*Att skriva sin värld,* 43). The title of the first volume is taken from Strindberg's *En blå bok* [A blue book], to wit: "The wise believe that the very journey of discovery — in search of one's fate — is instructive." Unhappily, searching for a pattern, Salminen again and again showed her inability to distinguish between important and unimportant. Describing her reactions after she had received the letter (reprinted in toto) from Schildt's Thure Svedlin with the news that *Katrina* has been accepted, she adds: "How does the kitchen help in a distant place hidden in the Berkshires takes such a piece of news? Won't she get a little dizzy from it? Yes, I did, at least."

Salminen's short-lived triumph encouraged other would-be regional authors to try their luck. The career of Helle Hellberg (1884–1980) offers sharp contrasts to Salminen's. From Mariehamn on Åland, she was an elementary school teacher — like other regionalists of the past, for example Adèle Weman (Parus Ater) and Frans Österblom — and taught on Åland, at Nystad (northwest of Åbo), and at Esbo in Nyland. She had good reason in one of her stories, "A Wild Rosebush" in *Spelmännen* (1949; The country musicians), to write that, once upon a time, she longed to go to California or the Crimea, but "I yearn to go there no longer; before I die, I want to stroll once again, hearing what old cottage walls have to say in Nyland, I shall listen to water splashing by boathouses in Åboland, and to the songs of wild roses in Åland's pastures," a quotation that affectionately lists her regional experiences in reverse order and gives the false impression that she is a sentimental author. Hellberg made a start as early as 1913, with stories, *Folk i skären* (People in the skerries), but achieved critical success with the extended novella *Glorias gåva* (1923; Gloria's gift), written in the wake of the mininovels of Runar Schildt (*Rönnbruden*) and Sigrid Backman (*Ålandsjungfrun*); it was also contemporary with Aino Kallas's balladesque *Barbara von Tisenhusen* (1923; Eng. tr. 1925). The purehearted Ottelia Gloria gives herself to Peder (a handsome fellow named, it is made plain, after the faithless Herr Peder of Danish folk ballads), aborts their child in what may be a suicide attempt, and is executed for its murder; she is buried with a little statue of the baby Jesus (her wedding gift to Peder's brother) in her lap. *Glorias gåva* is notable for several reasons: its art of elision and hint (like her later stories, it requires close reading), its use of psychological portraiture rather than the traditional ethnographic detail of regional literature, and, its sometimes fairy-tale air notwithstanding, its refusal to idealize the people with whom it deals. (Ottelia Gloria is almost raped by her own father.) It offers, as well, a sense of a larger Baltic world, stretching from Viborg to Stockholm, and a surprisingly long historical perspective, going back, in one of its subsidiary narrations, to the days of the "Great Flight" from the Russians in 1714. (Its main action takes place sometime in the early or middle nineteenth century.)

Some two decades of silence followed; when Hellberg retired from teaching, she embarked on a prolific if not very focused writing career, with *Livet, det är viktigt* (1943; Life, that is important) and its sequel, *Neckermans* (1944), about the fate of *statare*, hired farmworkers, in Nyland, inspired by Ivar Lo-Johansson's novels about a comparable agricultural proletariat in Sweden's Sörmland (see his *Godnatt, jord* [1933; Good night, earth]). She found—or refound—a literary form more suited to her powers in her several collections of short stories, *Skymningens barn* (1948; Children of the twilight), the above-mentioned *Spelmännen, Amaryllis* (1951), *Nya noveller* (1952; New novellas), and *Spegelmakaren och aftonstjärnan* (1954; The mirrormaker and the evening star), in all of which she polished the laconicism of which *Glorias gåva* had given a taste. "The Raisins," in *Amaryllis*, is a rarity in regional literature, a virtuoso stylistic display in broken-off sentences, outcries, repeated verbs, the reproduction of the thought of one of Hellberg's many (and by no means always likable) older women. The energetic and not very popular Widow Stålblad in another story from *Amaryllis*, "Outside," possesses a verbal precision resembling Hellberg's own; the Widow is given the task of writing a report about country life for a newspaper: "But it turned out to be so very much unlike other descriptions of country districts. People pointed out such oddities as the fact that the words 'very pleasant' were changed to 'pleasant'; words such as 'charming,' 'especially fine,' 'grand' were used by her only rarely, and then only in circumlocutions, and the word 'distinguished' she eliminated altogether."

The behavior of the majority of country people (particularly the bullying of gifted members of the community who deviate from the norm) and the prevalent emotional and intellectual poverty are described by Hellberg with an indignation like that of Swedish-Finland's naturalists of long ago, for example, in works of Oscar Behm. But Hellberg is never deeply interested in social reform; she simply aims to reduce the brutality caused by thoughtlessness and wants her people to achieve small moments of happiness, imaginary or not — Runeberg's transfigured moments.

Helle Hellberg suffered from none of the flaws so common in regionalism — the excessive moralizing and self-righteousness, the heavy use of ethnographic apparatus, the superficial delineation of characters, the gray or, conversely, overladen language. Her production, modest as it was, forced critics to take regional literature more seriously; she contributed by means of her disciplined example (just as Salminen had by means of her early popularity) to the expansion of serious regional letters during the 1940s and after.

If Helle Hellberg's career was unusual because of its long hiatus and second blooming, that of Joel Pettersson (1892–1937) was unique because it had no public literary existence at all during his lifetime. Born on Lemland in Åland, the son of poor peasant parents (and not just in money or goods: the medical journal at Grelsby Asylum, where Pettersson died, described them as "feeble-minded"), he acquired a reputation for his paintings and watercolors. In 1936 some of his work was displayed in an Åland exhibition, and he was called a "born painter," "an almost wholly self-taught genius," comparable to Van Gogh for his cubistic self-portraits and his more traditional paintings of his parents, his henhouses (he had his atelier in one) and Åland landscapes. Luckily, three large cartons of his scribblings were retrieved after his death and deposited in Åland's museum; in the 1960s Valdemar Nyman was entrusted with the task of choosing portions suitable for publication. Nyman went to work with a vengeance, issuing four selections from the *Nachlaß* between 1972 and 1975, followed by his discursive biography, *Pojken och den gråa byn* (1977; The boy and the gray village), which also contained samples of Pettersson's verse, such as a lament for a girl who has gone to America ("The Earth Is Freezing"); samples from the plays or dialogues he wrote for the amateur theater of Lemland's Youth Organization; and newspaper articles, including a startling one for *Ålands Nyheter* in 1927: "Åland needs a metropolis, a great city, bubbling with life . . . to which to send our young men, those who lack the inclination for any sort of agricultural labor."

Pettersson's own city experience had been an unhappy stay at the drawing school in Åbo from 1913 to 1915; its director was Victor Westerholm, the founder of the Önningsby artists' colony on Lemland. Westerholm had no idea how to deal with his bizarre pupil, and "the Boy," as Pettersson liked to refer to himself in his writings, ran amok, crushing the plaster-of-paris figure he had been told to draw: "The boy is happy. At any event he has killed Art, stiff and lifeless art . . . which only blocked his way." (Pettersson so detested the master that, in a feigned obituary of Westerholm, whom he called "Klischéfielt," "the great painter, the cow painter" was condemned by the cows he had painted to return to earth, "but not as a human being, rather as a spot of paint, a decorative spot.") After his parents' death Pettersson supported himself as a beet farmer; his latent mental illness came to the attention of authorities following a gruesome experiment in chicken farming, in whose course he managed to kill all his poultry through a radical treatment for lice.

The material Nyman presented in *Jag har ju sett* (1972; Of course I've seen), *Eldtände* (1973; Kindling), *Frifågel* (1974; Outlaw), and *Hallonskogen* (1975; The raspberry woods) is written mostly in the third person, describing Pettersson's devoted but strained relationship to his parents, his desire to be "the Boy who knew everything," his poetic and painterly dreams, and his intense emotional attachments. Fears of ridicule, of mental exhaustion, and of death are foremost in his sometimes ejaculative, sometimes calmly reflective, sometimes wryly humorous prose. The narrative third person can suddenly turn into a self-addressing "you"; the Boy is afraid to talk, in the belief that it weakens his intellectual powers: "Have you noticed how a conversation drains your strength. . . . The well is empty. . . . All of a sudden, the strength is gone. . . . If I only had the firmness of character to stop. But I cannot." He imagined that he should walk on stilts, so that death's chill could not creep up into him from the ground; he thought of himself as "The Lad with the Glance into the Future," imprisoned in a dungeon, "deep within the earth," where he "wrote and wrote and wrote" and "put all his leaves into a bundle." Another revelatory anecdote is that of the "Liver Tree" (the pun is roughly the same in Swedish as in English), which the Boy loves for its conversations with the sunbeams entering his room, a tale almost worthy of Topelius. But one day his parents remove it: "The liver tree was old and ugly and made the cottage dirty." With the writings — one hesitates to say the works — of Pettersson, regional literature has come a long way from either idealization or ethnography.

Consumed as he was by himself, Pettersson was little aware of larger political or social ills, however nasty a picture he gives of life in "the gray village" and however resentful he was of Åland's summer visitors, on one of whom, a "city girl," he visits a horrible imaginary death. Pettersson, Salminen, and Hellberg had no interest in literarily raising the red banner. (Indeed, in such a story as Hellberg's "Carolus," in *Skymningens barn*, a little boy is first tormented and then shot to death by drunken Red militiamen, his cherished picture of Charles XII ["the boy's king, the boy's treasure, the hero of every dream"] pinned to his breast.) But Aili Nordgren (1908–95), the younger sister of Sally Salminen, made her mark in regional literature by means of her leftist political pathos. After a book of verse, *Rödbränd mark* (1940; Earth burned red), she wrote a novel about the plight of a Karelian refugee woman and her children during the Winter War. (Its title, *Mörk längtan* [1943; Dark longing], was symptomatic of the time: compare Tuominen's *Mörka gudar* [1944; Dark gods], Ulla Olin's *Mörk ligger jorden* [1943; The earth lies dark], Bo Carpelan's *Som en dunkel värme* [1946; Like a dusky warmth] and *Du mörka överlevande* [1947; You dark survivor], and Väinö Linna's first novel, *Musta rakkaus* [1948; Dark love].) For Nordgren, the enemies are not the invading Russians (who are never mentioned) but brutal estate owners.

Next Nordgren turned her attention to the promised land of the United States, where she had gone with her sister to find work in the early 1930s. The result of her experience was *Innan dagen börjar* (1946; Before the day begins), in which she wrote far more harshly than Sally Salminen, about hard times in New York City during the early 1930s; but her interesting views of political activities (for example, an anti-Hitler rally at Union Square on May Day, 1933) are often obscured by the irresistible erotic lure of her heroine, which leads to a *crime passionel*. The novel has literary-historical importance in that it offers a Finland-Swedish equivalent to the story of an immigrant's disillusionment at the United States's capitalist society, long since told, for example, by the Dane Jacob Paludan in *De vestlige Veje* (1922; The western roads). In *Visa en väg* (1948; Show a way) and *Brinn eld* (1951; Burn fire) she wrote about the fates of a small Åland farmer's children, who — with greater obstinacy than Katrina in her short-lived revolt — rebel against the islands' social and economic hierarchy: after efforts at scientific farming (mocked by conservative peasants), the intelligent Wilhelm goes to Canada, is expelled from the United States for illegal entry, and eventually makes his way to South Africa and Australia, never to return. His sister Betty — as sexually attractive as Eva in the American novel — stays at home, to light the fire of revolution, urged on by Manninen, a socialist organizer. (Opposition to a Fennicization of Åland is embodied in Gösta, a young peasant who abandons Betty out of social pressure; his place in her affections is taken by the trusty Manninen, evidently a Finnish speaker.)

Nordgren, who had spent a short time in the Soviet Union before the Finnish-Russian wars, and after 1944 had become an official of the Finland–Soviet Union Society, turned next to the events leading up to Finland's Civil War of 1918 in *Väljer du stormen* (1955; Then you choose the storm), a novel of some artistic power in its many scenes of mob violence and mass meetings (the "butter riots" in Åbo in 1917); otherwise, it is burdened by flat characters: Selma, the reasonable organizer; Red Bess, in her scarlet dress, a Carmen of the barricades; Eskolainen, an agitator on impulse, in whose eyes "humanity was erased, in its place there lurked an animal's treacherous glance" (another of Nordgren's several rapists); and the noble Per Allen Berg, who dies leading the charge of the Åbo Red Guard during Åland's so-called Battle of Godby on 17–19 February 1918, in which revolutionary Russian soldiers and their allies were defeated by a White *Freikorps* from Nystad. At Berg's funeral the Internationale is played, and Yrjö Sirola (1876–1936), in reality a member of Finland's short-lived Red government (and later a director, from the Soviet Union, of the Finnish Communist party), delivers the eulogy, in which he quotes a poem by the Swedish poet Viktor Rydberg (1828–95): "Better than peace is peril's embrace. / If you choose me / Then you choose the storm." *Väljer du stormen* has the quality of a Russian propaganda film but keeps its place in the history of the Finland-Swedish novel by its semidocumentary elements; it raises a voice — now to be heard more and more — demanding a reevaluation of the Civil War and its events. (Linna's great trilogy began to appear in 1959, and Veijo Meri's *Vuoden 1918 tapahtumat* [The events of 1918] came out in 1960.)

Ostrobothnians

Anna Bondestam (1907–95), a contemporary of Sally Salminen and Aili Nordgren, proved to be intellectually more independent than either of them. Her father was a metal worker at Jakobstad in Ostrobothnia, but she had the advantage of a university education and eventually produced several volumes of a factual, scholarly nature: on the radical Åbo newspaper, *Arbetet* (1968; Labor); on the Civil War, *Åland vintern 1918* (1972; Åland in the winter of 1918); and on Jakobstad's recent social and economic changes, *En stad i förvandling* (1978; A town in transformation), all written in an unpretentious style that made them digestible for a general public.

Unpretentiousness was also the trademark of her creative work. Competing for the Swedish Novel Prize that Sally Salminen won, Bondestam submitted *Panik i Rölleby* (1936; Panic in Rölleby), a story from a thinly disguised Jakobstad of 1762, to which a new pastor and eligible bachelor comes. When he chooses a servant girl for his bride, the town's dignitaries and their wives turn against him, but after one of those great fires that so often laid waste Finland's towns in the days of building in wood, the pastor organizes rescue efforts and, aided by his bride, gives shelter to his detractors, the town's prosperous inhabitants. Less whimsical than Sigrid Backman and less discontent then Eva Wichman in their novels of the 1930s about young women in business and office life, Bondestam applied her good nature and understatement in *Fröken Elna Johansson* (1939; Miss Elna Johansson) and, mixed with sadness, in *Bergtagen* (1941; Carried away), a story collection about disappointing love whose title may have been suggested by the Swede Victoria Benedictsson's well-known play *Den bergtagna* (1888), based on Benedictsson's unhappy affair with Georg Brandes.

Bondestam expressed sociological interests in *Lågt i tak* (1943; Low ceiling), on Jakobstad in the grip of Finland's Prohibition and depression; but she achieved full-fledged artistry, and probed a wound in her town's history, with the short novel *Klyftan* (1946; The chasm), one more example of the literature's proclivity for narrative by a child. In the Civil War a sudden rush of cruelty (in a society that had little history of such behavior) grew out of class hatred. Rut's father, a socialist, is suspected of being "Finland's enemy" in a town behind the White lines: "He belonged to the 'bandits,' and they were sprung from a mystical source, they had nothing to do with Finland, on the contrary, they were precisely those who had to be wiped out." After the war her father is released from jail, but Rut still suffers from nightmares about what she has seen and heard. Despite her natural sympathy for the side that lost (and whose representatives appear as nervous human beings, not Nordgren's heroic freedom fighters), Bondestam has a much broader view, expressed in the book's often quoted final sentences: "[Rut] does not know that . . . like her, thousands of other children suffer just now. And that they soon will be millions. They have had bad luck, all these millions. They happened to be born in a century that was called the century of the child when it began, but turned out to be the century of terror." By her allusion to Ellen Key's optimistic *Barnets århundrade* (1900; Eng. tr. *The Century of the Child*, 1909), she summarized, at the century's middle, the awful developments she knew all too well.

The stories of *Enskilt område* (1952; Private property) deal mostly with problems of woman's psychology in a contemporary setting, but the last and longest of them, "Brother Urban," takes place in the late Middle Ages, in a time of plague. The same historical sense applied in her two last novels,

Vägen till staden (1957; The way to the town) and *Stadens bröd* (1960; The town's bread), describing the migration of poor Ostrobothnians from a countryside that cannot support them to the new factories of nearby Jakobstad; the town's industrialization had begun in the 1880s under the leadership of Wilhelm Schauman, a member of the numerous Schauman clan. The leading female figure—like Salminen's Katrina, "tall and powerfully built"—is dauntless in the face of difficulty and deprivation. These books have more value as social history put in digestible narrative form than as works of fictional art; Bondestam never reached the level of *Klyftan* again, founded as it was on personal trauma rather than on experiences related by parents and relatives. (Her language, by the way, is worth a second look: in *Klyftan,* dialogue is reproduced in a normal Swedish, with few local colorings; in the longer novels, characters speak in dialect. In 1946, when Bondestam wrote her masterpiece, regional literature had not yet wholly acquired the self-assurance and, sometimes, self-importance it would soon demonstrate.) Looking back at her career in her only collection of verse, *Jordnära* (1972; Earth-near), Bondestam included an autobiographical poem, telling how she had written prose "with almost heroic stubbornness" at a time, "thirty years ago," when "everyone who believed in the future" wrote lyrics; by the 1960s, prose, "turned toward society, almost ruled the roost." Now Bondestam, who always wanted to follow her own path, composes

> lyrics
> turned toward nature,
> or, at any event
> vertically.

She had always been vertical, upright and honest in everything she wrote, no matter what the genre.

In Bondestam's footsteps, several Ostrobothnian writers wrote much grimmer accounts of economic oppression and social upset—for example, Ingmar Nykvist (1917–84), with his novels (from 1956 on) about Elmer, a small-time farmer, and Levi Sjöstrand (1920–), with his tales about fishermen, presented from both a historical and a contemporary perspective (see chapter 10). The Ostrobothnian prosaist who presented the most distinctive profile in the 1950s, however, was Leo Ågren (1928–84). His career began with a fictionalized retelling of his own youth, *Hunger i skördetid* (1954; Hunger in harvest time): Ågren came from a family of tenant or landless farmers and wrote out of a sense of the enormous injustices his social group had suffered. For Ågren, the oppressors were not estate owners (of which Ostrobothnia had few) but well-to-do peasants; the tubercular, hardworking head of a large family—seen through the eyes of his seven-year-old son—detests the brutal crudity of those better off than he is; in turn, these affluent members of the farming community despise him as a socialist. (Sven Willner ["Det anonyma 50-talet," 44] suggests that the idealistic father was given the name Jan as a tribute to Jan Fridegård [1897–1968], who portrayed the Swedish countryside proletariat in his novels.) In *Motsols* (1955; Counterclockwise), written in the same vein, a peasant, a veteran of Mannerheim's White Army, brags of the Red prisoners he killed after the taking of Tammerfors (Tampere) in April 1918 and urges his companions to lynch two Finnish tramps accused of murdering a merchant.

Encouraged by his critical success, Ågren then undertook, ambitiously enough, a historical trilogy. In *Kungsådern* (1957; The royal vein) a hired hand, Olof Gersson, is repeatedly duped by his peasant master and is punished for farming land to which he can make no legal claim; entering military service during the Great Northern War, in hopes of obtaining a plot of earth to be passed along to his son, he learns before his death in battle at Storkyro (in 1713, a major Swedish defeat) that the boy has in fact been fathered by the peasant. In *När gudarna dör* (1959; When the gods die) the action takes place a generation later: Jöns, Olof Gersson's "grandson," has still worse luck than his forebear; growing up in terrible poverty, he works hard, founds a family—and ends an outlaw, driven into the woods to die: he has been accused of the murder of his wife and children, an atrocity actually committed by the peasant who tricked him out of his rightful holdings. (The outlaw episode bears a strong resemblance to the closing sequence of *Rid i natt* [1941; Ride tonight], a historical novel by the Swedish proletarian author Vilhelm Moberg [1898–1973].) The last book of the trilogy, *Fädrens blod* (1961; The blood of the fathers), moves forward to the Civil War; in a White prison camp the victim-protagonist must endure the homosexual attacks of a sadistic guard. Nonetheless, the book's epilogue has an air of reconciliation about it: the last of the Gersson descendants is buried beside the last representative of the oppressor peasant family.

By 1962 Ågren moved to Sweden and in *Ballad* (1962) abandoned his Ostrobothnian settings for a nameless land in which a refugee hides from his pursuers. He is caught at last, but as he climbs into the police van, he is at peace: "I knew that we have triumphed despite all, that life would always emerge the victor, always. That there was no cause for despair. As long as love exists." The social pugnacity that had marked Ågren's earlier, violent works was replaced, as in the finale of the trilogy, by a pan-irenic vision. For the next six years Ågren published little; then came *Krigshistoria* (1968;

War story), likewise a pacifistic plea. In its prologue the author tells how he met a Russian veteran of the Continuation War in Leningrad in 1958. The rest is the story of the veteran: how he was drafted into the Red army, fell asleep at his post, and was about to be executed when he was captured by Finnish troops; sent to Ostrobothnia to work on a farm, he took the place of a son who had fallen in battle. In the memorial *En man gick genom stormen* (1983; A man went through the storm) Gösta Ågren hinted that the great critical expectations held for his brother in Sweden, where his pictures of Ostrobothnian social injustice had gripped the public imagination for a time, made his situation "both absurd and untenable"; with its mild whimsicality, *Krigshistoria* disappointed his readership and was his last book.

On the eve of the Winter War, Otto Andersson (1879–1969), professor of musicology and folk poetry at Åbo Academy, established a publishing house called "Bro" (Bridge); its intention was to form a link between Finland-Swedish regional and city authors, the latter of whom had long inclined to condescension toward their country cousins. Andersson himself was from Vårdö, the birthplace-to-be of the Salminen sisters; a champion of Finland-Swedish popular culture, in 1906 — the centennial of Snellman's birth and a time of great Fennomane enthusiasm — he had established the Brage Society, named after the Nordic god of poetry and meant to preserve and nurture the Swedish-speaking population's customs, music, dances, and games. Its work continues to this day. The Bro undertaking soon fell victim to the deficient quality of some of its publications, albeit it published a valuable pictorial history of Åbo (1947), assembled by the historian Oskar Nikula and the art historian Lars-Ivar Ringbom, and, mirabile dictu, the Swedish translation — by Åke Leander, with an introduction by the esoteric poet Erik Lindegren — of Rilke's only novel, *Die Aufzeichnungen des Malte Laurids Brigge* (1948). A long public debate arose out of the question of "people's culture" as opposed to a culture of refined taste; it became obvious that a chasm yawned between simple and well-intentioned chronicles of farming or fishing life in the isolated settlements of western Finland and Åland and the literary circles of Helsingfors, dominated by an elite with international connections and ambitions. (The debate had its roots deep in the nineteenth century; the Swedish-speaking patricianate disdained Finland's Swedish countryside culture while it waxed enthusiastic about the *Kalevala* and the *Kanteletar*.)

Nevertheless, Bro's example helped inspire the establishment, in 1950, of Svenska Österbottens litteraturförening (Swedish Ostrobothnia's Literary Society), through the efforts of a sometime Bro author Sven-Olof Högnäs

(1910–61), who became the first editor of the society's excellent literary magazine, *Horisont* (1954–), and of the remarkable Evert Huldén (1895–1967). After his debut at Bro, *Och ryktet går* (1946; And the rumor circulates), a fairly melodramatic account of church and farm life, Högnäs, a journalist and adult education teacher, got praise for the careful prose and ironic humor of his novels of the 1950s. *Paradisplantan* (1950; The paradise plant) deals with a time-honored figure in Ostrobothnian narrative, a born-again evangelist; *Vägen till verkligheten* (1954; The road to reality) is a story based on experience, a country schoolteacher up against obscurantism and abuse from the village hierarchy. The plot is familiar from Hugo Ekhammar's *Det norrfångna landet,* but here it has a troubled protagonist, a sufferer from self-doubt who has to drink to get the courage to enter his classroom. *Borta bra* (1960; Away is good, part of a Swedish proverb that continues "but home is best") returns to the eternal Ostrobothnian problems, intolerable poverty, desertion of the land, migration.

Högnäs had started fairly late, when he was thirty-five, and Evert Huldén did not get around to his debut until he was fifty-six, with lyrics, *Jord och drömmar* (1951; Earth and dreams). Huldén had spent his adult life as the owner and tiller of the family farm, Nörråkers, in Munsala, and had been a champion of the temperance and peace movements, was active in local politics, and even after he was established as a poet, wrote a factual account of the problems and prospects of small farmers, *Utblick mot framtiden* (1958; View toward the future). The Huldén family, whose record in Ostrobothnia — as church books show — goes back to the fourteenth century, had strong educational and literary interests; Evert Huldén's older brother, Johan Jakob (1880–1959), had been a teacher at Åbo's Swedish classical gymnasium, an author, and a newspaperman. How devoted Huldén was to his land can be seen from *Hemgården och byn* (1952; The home farm and the village), in one of whose poems he told of a nightmare, "I sold the forefathers' farm," and *Nörråkers: Berättelsen om en släktgård* (1955; Nörråkers: The story of a family farm), six cantos of free verse, each subdivided into shorter poems about country and village life:

> In those days fighting was the right thing for boys to do,
> He who dropped his opponent was best.
> The girls stood there scared and watched the battle.
> The one who fell had trouble getting a girl.
> The victor chose the best one for himself.

Not an idealizer of manners and mores, Huldén tried prose in the stories *Små bönders* (1958; Small-time farmers) and mixed prose and verse in *Emi-*

grantöden (1961; Emigrant fates), concerning the departure of ambitious, superfluous, or desperate people for the New World, Australia, and South Africa. Yet his forte was the short poem, unrhymed, in irregular strophes; he was slightly in debt to Edith Södergran, dedicating "The Swallow," in *Utåt ljungen* (1953; Across the heather), to her: "Sparks of earth's dust for cataract-blind spectacle-poets, / sparks of shining life / for us who from birth have hungered." Huldén looked at all the rites of country life: he wrote portrait poems about the poor boy, the tramp, the slaughterer, the horse-dealer's wife, the missionary, the nurse, the pike fisherman, the old woman dressing the bride; he reflected on farm work and short visits in town. He also composed seasonal verses, such as the icy little "Ox-Week Winter," in *Ådror av sten* (1954; Veins of stone): "Iron-gray cold. / The days the glimpse of apple gray horses / pulling loads in the unendingness-woods," and in his last collection, *Sävens krona* (1967; The reed's crown), a poem about the end of autumn, "The bog's surface already is stiff. / On the pond's water / small needles of ice run out, farther and farther."

Huldén is mostly unsentimental and certainly thing-directed in his poetry, but in his compressed poetic development he discovered unusual subjects ("Dung-Beetles' Evening" in *Ådror i sten,* and the manure pile of "The Grazing Pasture" in *Sand lyser* [1956; Sand is shining]) and gave unusual meanings to country sights, for example in the brief and wonderfully ominous "Marking Men" in *Hemgården och byn:*

> Before his majesty
> comes with the four-in-hand
> hitched to his trap-wagon
> he sends out marking men
> with scissors and branding irons.

The blackened wagon is the chariot of death: "The branded ones are chained / awaiting terror, / where cold darkness blows." Other allusions are wry: the aging poet, a Hector going into battle, sees his Andromache hemming up his old overcoat, which "is long and hangs down around my ankles, / while knee-length is in fashion." (It is not worth the trouble, he adds; he will get a wooden overcoat soon enough.) Evert Huldén's son, Lars Huldén, published a selection from his poems in 1980 with the appropriate title *Dikter om jorden* (Poems about the earth), and in one of his yarns (see chapter 10) told about his father's imaginary journey to the United States and his sitting at the controls of the great explorer Raoul Amundsen's plane in Henry Ford's Dearborn museum. The ultimate charm of Evert

Huldén's poetry lies, despite his nearness to his earth and to his calling, in his awareness of other worlds beyond. In a strange hotel, as an unknown guest saws wood in the room next door, the insomniac speaker opens his window: "The moon's crescent saber shines / over white cities in the desert sand."

Poetae Minores
Lyric anthologies from Swedish Finland offer a dizzying number of poets, considering the size of the population from which they are drawn. Rabbe Enckell's anthology of 1934 had fourteen poets, from Södergran to Henry Parland; Per Erik Wahlund's *Finlandssvensk lyrik* (1947; Finland-Swedish lyric) contained twenty-six names from Södergran to Wichman. Thomas Warburton's *Facklor över jorden* (1960; Torches over the earth, a Södergran quotation) included twenty-three poets from Södergran to Irmelin Sandman Lilius and Gösta Ågren (both born in 1936), the former of whom made a lyric start before going over to her many books for children and young people (see chapter 11). In 1967, trying to give a whole picture of the corpus, from folk songs and Sigfrid Aronus Forsius to the present, Bo Carpelan had ninety-six poets (plus anonyma) in his table of contents, of whom at least two-thirds had made their debut after Edith Södergran. Almost twenty years later Carpelan and Claes Andersson returned with *Modern finlandssvensk lyrik* (1986; Modern Finland-Swedish lyric), which included only living poets; the oldest representative was Viola Renvall (1905–), and the grand total was sixty-eight.

Renvall had made her first anthology appearance in Enckell's collection of 1934; as yet, she did not bother to heed modernism's relaxation of formal requirements, although she caught up with free rhythms and rhymelessness shortly thereafter. Throughout her career her themes have remained pleasant and unsurprising: devotion to nature ("The day is soft and blue. / Light as a dream / its aroma touches against us / touches against closed eyelids"), her memories of her childhood ("When I was little, I rowed on a lake. / . . . Someone was with me in the boat and sang, / And the song made me laugh. / But I remember no words / nor what the singer's name was"), her love for her husband ("My love touches on your forehead, your thought. / Let us never cease to give one another courage"), and, more and more, the spiritual attitude she called — in a late collection among her many, *Vårfrudag* (1972; Day of Our Lady) — her "everyday Christianity," to which, however, she gave picturesque features: "On the hill beyond the naked trees / she raises up the golden candlesticks / lights them at the sun's torch, sets them down upon the mountains' snow." The echoes of

Södergran are, as usual, audible; Renvall becomes most like her model when she describes her rare moments of erotic unease, in the collection *Livsvilja* (1942; Will to life):

> The round moon looks at me and knows.
> Did you know nothing? You are far from me.
> The red sail on your light vessel never
> has found a mirror in this bay.

In her traditional values and her modest employment of modernist devices she resembles a Norwegian admirer of Södergran, Halldis Moren Vesaas (1907–), the wife of the novelist and poet Tarjei Vesaas; Renvall's own husband, Hjalmar Krokfors (1904–81), was a perfect helpmeet to her, and when she edited his selected poems, *Obelyst kust* (1984; Unlighted coast), it was a sweet labor of compatibility. The emotions and beliefs are much the same as in Renvall: the love of nature, although with greater emphasis on the pleasures of sailing, the Finland-Swedish male hobby par excellence ("raise mast / trim rigging / know wind / know way / know weather / know lee and harbor / greet the sea / — the sailor's / best ally"); the tempered Christianity, which grows stronger with the years; the respect for loyalty and devotion. Krokfors's experience in the conflicts with the Soviet Union gave rise to solid but muted patriotism in *Uppbrott* (1940; Setting out): a dogtag is found in the forest and "we all take off our caps"; at a rest on the march eastward, "the men sleep, broad and tranquil." Krokfors was old-fashioned enough to write the straightforward threnody "At a Mother's Bier," in *Före hanegället* (1945; Before cockcrow); in *Kustland* (1952; Coastland) he revived the idyll as employed by Runeberg, Hemmer, R. R. Eklund, using dactylic pentameter: "Off in the leafless copse a piece from the highway / the schoolhouse you see, white-washed and galvanized standing." The schoolmaster's wife makes sandwiches and speaks "soft voiced of the day's tribulations, of shops and of baking"; the schoolmaster takes out Holy Scripture and loses himself in the story of Abraham's departure out of Haran into the land of Canaan. Krokfors's reconstruction of a traditional setpiece of the idyll, devoted and yet with small hints of parody, shows an unusually subtle side of his art.

The Åland poet Georg Kåhre (1899–1969, writing under the nom de plume Stefan Sylvander) stubbornly refused to abandon the old forms: a brilliant rhymer and a sensitive metrician, he kept the sonnet alive, cultivated the dactylic hexameter, and even ventured successfully into such Browning-like preserves as the dramatic monologue in "Why are we sailing out / into the skerries today, Bromander?" (from *Väderilar* [1932; Gusts of wind]). Kaj Lindgren (1898–1976), a Helsingfors schoolman whose lyric collections swelled the book floods of the 1930s and 1940s, closed his eyes to modernism altogether, faithful as he was to old patterns and old thoughts ("How white your hand against the spread, transparent, / how tired your glance, how pale your sunken cheek"); he resembles the modernists only in his persistent call for brotherhood in troubled times. His contemporary, Karin Mandelstam (1908–81), had the same loyalty to a formal art of poetry, rhyming inventively (she had also been a prolific author of popular songs and cabaret texts) and for the most part clinging to the regular strophic forms of the past, just as she clung to fairly threadbare thoughts, happiness in nature, moments of bliss in the out-of-doors. Still, in the last of her three collections, significantly titled *Denna natt är ett prov* (1948; This night is a test), she partook of the anguished soul-and-body searching carried out in prose by Tuominen and Colliander and by Kerstin Söderholm in verse and in her diary. In a poem that bears the almost embarrassing title "I Am Crucified Tonight," the speaker lies like a dead creature, her arms in an "empty embrace," but "burns with fire" just the same, "for my spirit awakes / to a torment that has no name," maybe an unconscious paraphrase of a famous line from Oscar Wilde. Publishing a sparse selection from her verse, *Dansande bin* (1975; Dancing bees), she omitted it.

In some cases the personal fate of the poet (as it can be read in or between the lines) seems more interesting than the verse itself, regarded as an artistic product. The reputation of Christer Lind (1912–42) has no doubt been shored up by anecdotes told about his bohemian life in Helsingfors and his early death of tuberculosis in a Swedish sanatorium. He published only a single collection of poetry, *Vindarnas bröllop* (1940; The wedding of the winds), and thus acquired the nimbus of hopes unfulfilled, like Gustaf Munch-Petersen (1912–38) and Morten Nielsen (1922–44) in Denmark. His posthumous anthology of translations of primitive poetry, *Stigen och regnbågen* (1943; The path and the rainbow), based on Eckart von Sydow's *Dichtungen der Naturvölker* (1935; Poetry of the primitive peoples) and edited by his teacher, Yrjö Hirn, actually got a larger press, especially in Sweden; a distinguished Swedish poet, Werner Aspenström (1918–), has vouched for its importance as an inspiration of his own work. But *Vindarnas bröllop* also received accolades; Hagar Olsson wrote, "I know of no other poet who could have followed [Edith Södergran] on the lonely dream-paths where she wandered," and Carl-Gustaf Lilius (p. 220) accorded the book "a place among the most remarkable collections of verse in Swedish letters." Lind's visionary poems, written in extraordinarily long lines, match only those of Erik Therman in their ability to maintain ecstasy, almost to the point of tiring the reader out. Still, in their rushing imagery, they are much more enigmatic than Therman's work:

> The moondogs howl from the abyss's chasms,
> they plunge through the forest like a flock of hunted wolves.
> The snow whirls up across the expanses' barrenness.
> The villages burn like lonely fires on the plain.
> In the drafty house there is a ringing as though of tiny bells.

Whether these words about a mythic nature in violent action—thrilling enough at first sight—will bear repeated examination is a question Wahlund, although he took Lind's works into his anthology, answered with doubts, calling Lind this "unsatisfied aesthete and traveler" for whom "the journey's end is the journey."

For a time, Lind was the friend of Lorenz von Numers, to whom he dedicated "Morning Fantasy," in *Vindarnas bröllop:* "With quick wingbeats the bird lifts up from the swinging treetop and disappears in widened rings over the forest's edge. / The gold-yellow flower opens in full flame and the settling shadows are filled ever more by lively, fresh colors," lines of life affirmation (such as Artur Lundkvist [1906–91] was presently fostering in Sweden) that have shimmer and sweep but might also be accused of empty grandiosity. For a time Lind had been one of Björling's disciples, although he surely did not share Björling's gift for minimalism, and he turned to the ever helpful Diktonius for help in pulling together his "colorfully equipped visions of angst"—equal to those, Diktonius thought, of another Swede, Gunnar Ekelöf—in order to ready them for publication.

Von Numers's own memories of Lind were mixed, as was his opinion of Lind's verse: "He was about to die for many years, but meanwhile he took the opportunity to write some good poems." The colorfulness presented by von Numers in his own verse was of a different sort; his *Svart harnesk* (1934; Black armor) and *Porträtt med blomma* (1936; Portrait with flower) were far more disciplined than Lind's work and revive the conservative poetics the modernists had tried to overcome. His rhymed views of Helsingfors are as quotable as those by Ture Janson in *Mitt Helsingfors* some twenty years before, and the exotic eroticism of the suite called "Syrinx" in *Svart harnesk* derives from Bertel Gripenberg:

> your foot
> glided over carpets from Teheran and Bokhara
> and in dance-steps
> quite frivolously
> to the ducal bed.

The second collection turned tentatively away from these quasi–turn-of-the-century patterns, for example, in the "Concerto for Gamba and Large Orchestra, A-major," a rendition of Helsingfors in musical movements, but von Numers was never quite able to overcome his literalness: the transformation of a barber's sign, whipped by the storm, into the salver awaiting John the Baptist's head seems labored. By the time of *Havslyktan* (1942; Sea lantern) he had completely settled into the historical-picturesque tone, in verse, which also became his trademark in his prose; his poetry from the Continuation War turns the campaign on the Aunus into something out of an adventure book: "And the clouds hasten, hasten for very life / away from this land of slavery and shadow."

In much, Ole Torvalds (1916–95) would seem to be a lyricist in the style of Renvall and Krofkors; his loving contact with the sea, islands, and sailing gave birth to so many poems that he eventually made a selection from forty years of them, *Vågmärken: Skärgårdsdikt 1937–1987* (1988; Wave markers: Skerry poems 1937–1987). Like Krokfors, too, he was in the Winter War, but in *Ointagligt land* (1942; Impregnable land) he wrote about it with brutal frankness: "I awakened blind, without a left hand, / and my left ear deaf"; *Hemligt medansvar* (1944; Secret coresponsibility) struck out against cruelty or use of force in any form. A growing allegorical urge — in imitation, it must be guessed, of the Swede Pär Lagerkvist (1891–1974) and the latter's *Bödeln* (1933; Eng. tr. *The Hangman*, 1936) — is also evident in his story collection *Svår glädje* (1946; Difficult happiness); the potentiality of evil in every human being is the subject of the parable "The Mountain": "When the executioners tightened their fists on the levers of the rack, with choking repulsion I felt the cruelty deep within myself . . . but I also felt the tearing pain in the victim's body as, cracking, his limbs were stretched. . . . As a general I sent millions into battle, intoxicated by the very fact that my orders could not be countermanded and by the brilliance of my strategies, but also, alone, I was weighed down by the responsibility I felt for my soldiers' lives — and for the lives of those I was wont to call my enemies." (A newspaper editor, Torvalds had raised a discreet voice against the Continuation War.)

Throughout his career Torvalds speaks as an idealist; the exclusionary title of his very first book is *Vi sjunger inte för dem* (1939; We do not sing for them) — the poems are not intended for the complacent or the materialistic. Still, Torvalds never assumed a sanctimonious stance; in *Ointagligt land* he posits as his alter ego a "figurant," an apathetic supernumerary:

My brother the figurant walked in the park
to cure his soul's foreignness with sun.

But his foot felt no root in the soil
like violet or dandelion.

N.-B. Stormbom saw the weakness of Torvalds's morally unimpeachable lyrics in a split between intention and instrument; with his understated and sometimes self-mocking language, in which Torvalds followed the Swedish master of ironic verse, Nils Ferlin (1898–1961), he strove "to find an expression free of pathos for what is basically a pathos-filled attitude toward life" ("Två årtionden finlandssvensk lyrik," 45). After the collections in the 1950s, *Strängar av aska* (1954; Strings of ashes) and *Mellan is och eld* (1956; Between ice and fire), which gave impressive vignettes of the hard sides of skerry life, Torvalds fell silent until 1986, when he published *Livstecken* (Signs of life), a mixed bag of travel, mythical, uxorious, and, of course, skerry poems; as before, he editorialized.

Thomas Warburton (1918–) did not share the military experience of Krokfors and Torvalds; as a British subject he was registered as an enemy alien after England (as an ally of Russia) declared war on Finland during the Continuation War. This sense of outsiderness was strengthened — as in Torvalds's case — by the conviction that cobelligerency with Nazi Germany was altogether wrong, something expressed obliquely in the poems of his *Du, människa* (1942; You, human being) — "I will not live heroically and worship steel, / nor run in jungle herds" — and then, after the armistice, more openly in *Bröd av lera* (1945; Bread of clay). From the start Warburton, as he freely admitted, was a poet of Brechtian indignation; see the song of the dead coward: "now I am neither afraid / nor brave. / You've taken that from me" in "Fallen Soldiers Speak" of the first collection, and "Peace Banquet" of the second:

> Here we stand with glasses lifted and we see
> flushed with solemnity the necks of one another
> and sweat-warm white fingers around the glasses
> lifted in a toast for the world's well-being
> and for the houses that burned around us.

A horrifying piece in the same book is "Torso with Blind Head," reminiscent of both Dalton Trumbo's *Johnny Got His Gun* (1939) and Torvalds's "Two Fragments Took away My Eyes" — a blind, armless, and legless veteran speaks: "Transform me, transform me into stone."

Growing more contemplative, Warburton commented on life's futilities in *Slagruta* (1953; Divining rod), which — in its suites, the pastoral "Summer Sunday" and "Tivoli" — reveals genuine poetic invention; the inventiveness continued in *Kort parlör* (1966; Short phrase book), containing a short biography in thirteen sections (ending with the execution and burial of the subject), which gave the collection its name, and a second suite, "Sixteen Hours," in haiku form, depicting stages of the day. The clear-cut wit, the use of litotes that replaced Brechtian outspokenness, and the careful intellectuality of Warburton's later works (in a production small and precise) served as reminders of his familiarity with English-language poetry, Sassoon and Wilfred Owen, Eliot and Auden. Warburton could experience memorable and original illuminations, as in "Waking," in *Slagruta:*

> And suddenly a lightning bolt
> is lit and casts its white shine
> crosswise through the room
> showing my image:
> a pale, soft-skinned grub
> which gently bores its way
> through the sweet apple of its good conscience
> lives in a tunnel
> full of pleasant smells, slowly stuffs it up behind
> with self-satisfied droppings.

The prodigious industry and talent Warburton has as a translator — undaunted by Joyce's *Ulysses* (1953), Leino's *Helkavirsiä* (1963), Masters's *Spoon River Anthology* (1967), and the *Kanteletar* (1989) — as well as his busy career as a publisher, editor, and literary historian have kept him from overproduction. After *Leve revisionismerna* (1970; Long live the revisionisms), a long poem in which he gave his dark view of a world destroying itself by brainless technology and national blindness (with swipes at the Americans in Vietnam, the Russians, the Afrikaners), he published only the verse tale *Fällas eller falla* (1975; Be felled or fall), the story of a lumberman in the days of the Civil War. Attempting to revive a classic Finland-Swedish and Finnish form, the epyllion (see Runeberg and Joel Lehtonen), Warburton added one more picture to the ever growing creative literature on the events of 1918. As usual, he wanted to depict the human condition, not make a political statement (although his sympathies, as always, lie to the Left): his lumberman, pursued for crimes allegedly committed during the wartime days, saves the life of the policeman sent to fetch him. (For Sven Willner, this Finnish *coeur simple* bore a resemblance to Runeberg's patient peasant Pavo.) Like an experienced conductor who is also a composer, Warburton can be eclectic or derivative. But he has always made a fruitful and independent use of his readings in other poets.

In the aftermath of the wars with the Soviet Union a small but significant migration of Finland-Swedish talent to Sweden took place: Hans Ruin, Örnulf Tigerstedt, Lorenz von Numers, E. R. Gummerus. Harry Järv (1921–) and Bengt Holmqvist (1925–) went west early enough that they could become constituent parts of Swedish literary criticism, and the miniature novels of the precious stylist Willy Kyrklund (1921–) are rightly considered a part of Swedish literature. Ulla Olin (1920–), resident in Sweden since her marriage in the late 1940s (the many poems in her *Efterwärme* [1990; Afterwarmth] are addressed to her late husband), has nonetheless maintained a Finland-Swedish identity. In *Vintertvätt* (1986; Winter wash) there is a verse picture of the Mörne sisters, Barbro and Gudrun ("Like two conspirators they look into each other's eyes"), and a memorial to the graveyard at the fifteenth-century Esbo church, almost swallowed up by suburbia; in *Inte nu men nu* (1989; Not now but now) she goes back to her memories of the war years by naming battles ("Places I have never been / but they have been in me / from year to year they've sunk / toward the sediment in my soul"). She remembers the Porkala headland west of Helsingfors, devotes a poem to the Finland-Swedish painter Sigrid Schauman ("No one painted green as she could") and a prose poem to "the Collectors," the Swede Linnaeus and (the larger part) the Finn Elias Lönnrot. The books brought out before her departure for Sweden — *Vårbrytning* (1939; Shift to spring), *Verklighetens idyller* (1941; Reality's idylls), *Mörk ligger jorden* (1943; The earth lies dark), *Tillblivelsedag* (1945; Day of becoming) — were artistically and morally valid: her nostalgia for an older Esbo was praised by critics, as was her forthright questioning of her right to exist, and to compose poetry, when so many of her contemporaries were dying. Even then, she had an admirable honesty with which she could address crises, without calling excessive attention to what she did.

For a poet as deeply tied to her home region as Olin (she made a literary-historical study of the dialect words and archaisms in Arvid Mörne's lyrics), the move to Sweden was difficult, as *Havsfärd* (1949; Sea journey) made plain, but it resulted in a greater linguistic discipline and a greater subtlety. Living in a literary atmosphere that encouraged complexity or "incomprehensibility" (a topic much debated in Sweden in the 1940s), she was temporarily impelled to keep up with Erik Lindegren (1910–68) or Karl Vennberg (1910–95), as in the poem "Body in November," from her first "Swedish" collection:

Incomplete under ash-dead cloud
the greatest trembling falls to earth

and is a wizened leaf an icepale disappointment
with sharp edges.

Her previous straightforwardness came back, after a decade's pause, in *Dagövning* (1959; Day exercise), *Mötesplats* (1962; Meeting place), and *De levandes mod* (1972; Courage of the living). It was a question, as she wrote, of "not using words as a dress" but seeing "that which is not repetitive / in what one sees . . . of seeing the single and unique / in the very repetition." Her precise observations of what may seem ordinary puts Olin in the company of Solveig von Schoultz, whose progression toward clarity and compactness her own development resembles; her power of imagination seems also to have grown with the years, and the prose poem "Dream," about her childhood home in *De levandes mod,* puts her in the company of Johannes Edfelt (1904–), Sweden's greatest master of that apparently easy but perilous form.

These "minor poets" all of necessity had other means of support while they practiced literature. Huldén was a farmer, Mandelstam a departmental head for Finland's Swedish radio, von Numers a cultural attaché, Torvalds a journalist, Warburton a publisher; Renvall, Krokfors, Lindgren, and Olin were teachers. The industrialist Åke Gulin (1906–88) fell into febrile literary activity just before he turned fifty, with little poems such as "Bedroom Community Idyll:

Smell of fried potatoes
beefsteakonion
the open balcony doors belch toward the evening cool
God's in his Heaven
mankind in its dwelling.

Gulin developed his miniaturist art to considerable perfection, beginning in 1954 with *Höståker* (Autumn field); as late as *Motlut* (1981; Hinder) he maintained the same generally disappointed tone, even as he viewed a spring evening:

stillness silence
purposelessness
all shall bloom —
the birds
and the field. Silence blooms
all shall fall silent
speech and breathless
caller-voices.

Or, from the same volume:

> There laughs a kite
> there barks a dog
> the dawn
> keeps me awake.
> One day
> and all days,
> there were so many paths
> now I have but one
> a last
> to ponder.

An oddity about Gulin's tired and disillusioned cameos is that they seldom concern the field of artistic endeavor to which he gave his genuine enthusiasm; his essayistic survey of Finnish art in the twentieth century, *Målare* (1978; Painters), is a superior introduction to "a number of artists who have crossed my path."

An unsettling air of anachronism pertains in the work of those who debut late; Gulin's poems have an uncanny resemblance to those of the early-dead Henry Parland:

> In the cemetery of ideals
> — walk carefully
> across the path.
> The mourners are the hateful, unreconcilable
> friends of humanity.

Another late bloomer, Runar Salminen (1912–), a younger brother of Sally Salminen and Aili Nordgren, began to publish only in 1974 with *Rummet fullt med svalor* (The room full of swallows); hovering between diaristic and memoiristic views of life on Åland, it could as well have been written in the 1950s or before. Runar Salminen's verses have a four-square realism and homespun common sense that got them the approval of such a poet-critic as Claes Andersson. Andersson found a weapon to wield against poetic ivory towers in Salminen's lines, "I cannot become one with the birds, although they symbol-teach / so prettily," and "All human hearts have / an inherent socialist yearning."

Lars von Haartman (1919–) had a long and distinguished career as an ornithologist as the holder of a personal professorship in zoology at the University of Helsingfors; his poetic tone harks back to the heyday of Rabbe Enckell's elegiac modernism in *Reseskildring* (1960; Travel description). Von Haartman's verse was different from Enckell's, though, in an essential respect; with its many cultural references (to Giorgione, Poussin, Baudelaire) it called to mind the poetry from the 1940s and 1950s of a Danish contemporary, Thorkild Bjørnvig (1918–); von Haartman's Van Gogh poems treat some of the same paintings as Bjørnvig's. Yet von Haartman possessed a restrained playfulness and elegant fantasy that the Dane lacked, demonstrated in the "Letter to the Royal Society" and the "Prophecy about the Docent and Baron Lars von Haartman's Last Journey," gently mocking verse yarns about himself. In the equally well formulated literary and zoological essays of *Av samma blod* (1964; Of the same blood), inspired by another Dane, Thorkild Hansen and his *Det lykkelige Arabien* (1962; Eng. tr. *Arabia Felix*, 1963), von Haartman wrote about the Finlander Petter Forsskål and his accomplishments on the same expedition (1761–63) that Hansen described.

Next von Haartman returned to poetry with the brief poems of *Svarta segel* (1969; Black sails) — the handful of words of "Felis domestica" (". . . evening in Arcadia. I drink tea / and read about the Middle East / the cat waits for the wagtail, and among the stars / its oriental eyes glow a thousandfold"), the evocative "Winter Evenings in Brooklyn," dedicated to Edward Hopper's memory, and then "Triptych in Baroque Style," whose conclusion alludes to the catafalque of a seventeenth-century Finnish nobleman and his wife at Virmo (not far from von Haartman's family estate at Lemsjöholm): "Whose grave? like an all too heavy / trunk it stayed standing on earth / when the slabs were hurled aside and the souls lifted like dry leaves." This glance into a noble past may suggest Gripenberg's or Tigerstedt's regret for a world quite gone but is less aggressive: "You Who have mercy, preserve . . ." is the way the poem drifts off into nothingness. *Vinterljus* (1977; Winter light) showed deep pessimism — "oubliettes / the black holes in the memory" ("Old"), "it is late / over this sun-path / the first flakes / already have snowed" ("Requiem for C"); in "Premonition" the poet looked vainly for consolation:

> well for us the sense of duty
> or habit daily coming back
> but transience snoops like an officious
> customs man for the contraband of hope.

In memoriam (1990) is a harvest of lyrics and prose poems done over twenty years, and despite a category called "Scherzando" (including a one-sided conversation between Castro and Spiro Agnew), the sense of resignation and leave-taking has grown stronger still.

Prose of the 1940s and 1950s
At a time when the novel and novella in Finnish were in full vigor (the comebacks of Haanpää and Toivo Pekkanen; the debuts of Linna, Joenpelto, Mannerkorpi, Viita, to be followed by Meri, Antti Hyry, Vartio) Finland-Swedish narrative made a much paler effect. Single works of value appeared — Parland's *Förvandlingar*, von Schoultz's early novellas, Bondestam's *Klyftan* are cases in point — but weight lay on the side of poetry. Not surprisingly, the straitened circumstances, confusion, and nervousness of the immediate postwar years was at first captured by authors who had come to maturity before the great watershed of 1939–44. Harald Hornborg, after decades writing his historical romances, turned to what his publishers called the "living present" with *Ensam herre* (1953; A gentleman alone), a hefty novel about an elderly man — one thinks of Olof Enckell's Thomas Argillander in *Solnedgång* — who tries rather comically to understand changed conditions after the war and even to participate in them, not least erotically. As always, Hornborg wrote an entertainment novel, here about the *senex amatorius,* but had a competence in storytelling that allowed him, more deftly and convincingly than his young colleagues, to catch a little of the atmosphere of what von Numers called the frostbitten Finnish-Swedish world. Unannounced visitors, speaking Finnish, turn up at the door of Arvid Aeneus, who is not able to grasp that he is well past his prime and that decorum has crumbled.

The war novel, as already noted, was underrepresented in Swedish, and when it came, it was often abstract, as in *Djungel* (1950; Jungle), by Lars Hjalmarsson Dahl (1920–), in which military episodes, forest interludes with a Finnish girl, and prophetic glances into an unhappy postwar home are mingled. The artist Kurt Sandqvist (1919–) twice approached the war novel, first in the confusing *Taskspelaren* (1957; The conjurer), in which a juggler and the circus to which he belongs are taken into border zones where new conflicts are prepared and former ones remembered. How fascinated Sandqvist was by American literature of the time can be told from the juggler's name, Aram (see William Saroyan's *My Name Is Aram* [1940]); the plot resembles that of Albert J. Guerard's once well known novel about a future war, *Night Journey* (1950) — Sandqvist had described his visit to the United States in *Sommarflanör i Amerika* (1950; Summer stroller in America). Probably having learned from the black humor of the highly successful war novels and stories of Veijo Meri, such as *Manillaköysi* (1957; Eng. tr. *The Manilla Rope,* 1967) and *Sujut* (1961; Even), and Joseph Heller's *Catch-22* (1961), Sandqvist tried the same bitterly joking tack with *Mitt kära krig* (1967; My dear war), as did Henrik Tikkanen (1924–84), whose early books based on wartime and postwar experiences, *Hjältarna är döda* (1961; The heroes are dead) and *Ödlorna* (1965; The lizards), were then subsumed into his far more adroit "address novels" of the 1970s (see chapter 10).

Carl Fredrik Sandelin (1925–) started out with soft-focus pictures of childhood, adolescence, and young manhood in *Rummet och regnbågen* (1947; The room and the rainbow); forty years later he looked back at the eve of the Winter War and the conflict itself, as seen by a thirteen-year-old boy, in *Världens ända* (1987; The end of the world) and *Vintertid* (1989; Winter time). In *Övergång* (1950; Transition) he had made a stab at the difficulties of adjustment in the immediate postwar years, mixed with his impressions of America; the portions from the New World, often approaching a travelogue, are more vivid than those from Finland, despite Sandelin's difficulties with American erotic dialogue ("Joan. Yes? Joan. Yes? Joan! Erik!") and sports (the New York Yankees play the Boston Tigers). The story of a young woman's suicide, and the family stresses lying behind it, narrated by a tyro journalist, *Bland annat om Jeder* (1953; Among other things about Jeder), bore traces of American detective and newspaper fiction (and films) in the interplay between the novice and his hard-boiled senior, Jeder.

The fact that Sandelin was employed in Finland's official news service probably caused a long hiatus in his writing; eventually, he took up where he had left off, describing political and personal intrigue at home (i.e., in Finland's foreign ministry) and abroad (mostly the United States). *En man går över torget* (1969; A man crosses the square), *Tre dagar i augusti* (1973; Three days in August), and *Presidentspelet* (1981; The president game) all reveal complete factual mastery of the milieus they portray and maintain a narrative pokerface, as if a Dashiell Hammett detective were transformed into a middle-aged government functionary. "Henrik-Fabian [Tingman] felt tired in his whole being as he walked home. . . . He was glad that he had his raincoat on. People he met shivered in their summer clothes. . . . The city seemed almost deserted although it was the tourist season." Or, in another summer, the journalist Johan Wichman appreciates the view from his office window, but "it would soon be gray and melancholy again. Soon the summer would be over and the colors would disappear." The melancholy of Sandelin's attachés has some justification; Sandelin was willing to address the sensitive question of covert discrimination against the minority in Finland's official life. Tingman is informed by his chief, a Finn of simple beginnings, that he bears several marks of Cain: "You're Swedish-speaking, from a good family, and well-to-do. You belong to the privileged ones." When

Tingman resigns his post in an imbroglio about Finland's attitude toward the (then) East German state, the superior breathes a sigh of relief, but Louhi, a Communist cabinet minister, is disappointed to have been deprived of a useful whipping boy.

The novels of Marianne Alopaeus (1918–), like several of the stories of Solveig von Schoultz from the 1940s, put the changes in Finland-Swedish life into a familial and emotional context. The title of *Uppbrott* (1945; Departure) tells the whole story: a woman of twenty-five, feeling that her marriage to the ostentatiously virile Klaus has become untenable, is drawn to her stepfather Peter but concludes that neither man is satisfactory: "An oppressive egotism lay behind Klaus's feelings, but a still larger, more ruthless, and chillier egotism behind Peter's." She decides to strike out on her own, the step that Solveig von Schoultz's escapee-wife in *Ingenting ovanligt* could not take. Likewise, in *Dröm utan slut* (1950; Dream without end), Ira is dissatisfied with her husband, Joachim, not because of his shortcomings but simply because she wants a life of her own. (Alopaeus was well ahead of her time: "I'd like to have a child with every man I love, she thought, but I want to sleep alone.") In *Utanför* (1953; Outside) Martina is tormented by the same worries about excessive male control as her predecessors, but Alopaeus had moved to a Parisian setting, also used in *Avsked i augusti* (1959; Farewell in August), the fourth of her novels on marriage. Recently, feminist scholarship has found material for discussion in the quartet, in the concluding volume of which several women's fates are intertwined. The final view of one of her heroines, Urda, thirty-seven years old, pregnant, and unwilling to marry, might represent the courage of them all. A kind gentleman offers to help Urda when she grows ill on the street, but she refuses aid: "He handed her the pocketbook she had dropped, she stuck it under her arm, and went away, slowly and stiffly along the gently declining street."

Alopaeus titled her next novel *Mörkrets kärna* (1965; The core of darkness), a name inevitably suggesting *The Heart of Darkness*. (The Conrad novel had appeared in Swedish in 1960, called *Mörkrets hjärta,* a literal rendering.) The book has much the same erotic constellation as her earlier work, but Alopaeus objected to its being called "a woman's book," as her earlier novels plainly were; rather, she wrote Merete Mazzarella, it was "a human's book." An ambitious tale of love and political ideas, it is set (again) in Paris during the eight-year Algerian war of independence, a conflict that inspired much indignation in Scandinavia. A Finland-Swedish journalist, Mirjam, falls in love with an Algerian terrorist, a member of the National Liberation Front ("I lay softly fitted into the intimate, dry, and coolish-warm body, as if there were no boundary between it and me"), and then with a physicist ("nothing is so revelatory of a man's nature as his way of making love . . . and there was no flaw in his way of surrendering his body to me"), who becomes a priest. Both men are of Jewish extraction; Mirjam has been fascinated by Jews since schooldays in Finland when she had a crush on a Russian-Jewish immigrant boy, Jurek ("he held me in his embrace, closely, quite still, then he lifted up my face and kissed me, lightly and tenderly, and threaded his fingers through my hair and tugged a little"). Her father sent her to a boarding school in Sweden, and Jurek disappeared in the Winter War. At the novel's conclusion she wonders why both her kindly tyrant of a parent and her shadowy husband have been anti-Semites; her philo-Semitism (which is given an ecumenical patina by means of the alliances with the Jewish freedom fighter for an Islamic cause and the Jewish-Catholic physicist-priest) has been a symptom of her urge to break out of the patriarchal world. Laden with triple lovers, Parisian mood scenes, lengthy conversations, and numerous references to yesteryear's headlines, *Mörkrets kärna* has aged since its much-lauded appearance. In its views of the prejudices and limitations of the Finland-Swedish upper class (as Alopaeus, a member of that class, saw them), however, she demonstrated her fine eye for cultural distinctions; Mirjam finds an equivalent in a French noble family, describing its foibles in a letter to her father, still beloved, despite all.

This discriminating power served her well in two nonfictional works, the part of her oeuvre with the best chance for survival: *Betraktelser kring en gräns* (1971; Observations around a boundary) dealt with politics in the world at large and with life as a member of a linguistic minority—like Sandelin, she was ready to rock the boat of good relations with the majority; *Drabbad av Sverige* (1983; Struck by Sweden) criticized the country where Alopaeus has lived for many years, using the keen Finland-Swedish sense for Swedish peculiarities. Also, she continued her trenchant commentary on her own background, on the mixed culture of Karelia, and on "the atmospheric pressure in Finland of the 1930s," in which "aggression [prevailed] toward the country's Swedish past and its Russian one. What remained? A throttling atmosphere of aggressive nationalism, simple-mindedness, primitive hatred of foreigners, dreams of a greater Finland." As distressed as she was at some elements in her own tradition, she also made a good defense of it, "at once more provincial and more international," as she compared it with Sweden's.

Another writer with complex ties to the Finland-Swedish patricianate was Helen af Enehjelm (1909–91); in a literature with a sizable share of immigrants and emigrants, she was a special case: born Helen Margaret

Mary Moller in Bakersfield, California, the recipient of a bachelor's degree from Berkeley, she came to Finland in 1931 with her husband, Erik af Enehjelm, the owner of an estate in Tavastland. Her first novels, *Kajornas kyrka* (1934; The jackdaws' church) and *Cypresstunneln* (1938; The cypress tunnel), were translated from English by Ulla Hornborg; they were raked over the critical coals for their "mystically romantic tone" (scarcely a rarity in Finland-Swedish prose of the 1930s) and their air of being aimed at young, sentimental readers — Diega, the heroine of the first, meets the right man during a summer in Finland. Undismayed, af Enehjelm introduced American women writers in the Finland-Swedish woman's magazine *Astra* (Willa Cather, Edna Ferber, Edith Wharton) and in 1942 struck out on her own in Swedish with the stories of *Vår soliga vardag* (1942; Our sunny everyday life), its illustrations by none other than Rabbe Enckell. Her principal role in Finland-Swedish letters for a long time continued to be her presentation of English-language literature, and *Promenad med favoriter* (1945; Promenade with favorites), containing essays on Katherine Mansfield, Poe, Jane Austen, Emily Bronte, and Emily Dickinson, appeared just when the public wanted to know more about the Anglophone world; it became her most popular book and was followed by *Hemlängtan* (1946; Homesickness), whose orientation was more, but not exclusively, toward French literature.

In *På stranden* (1948; On the beach) she did what so many born Finland-Swedes have been wont to do — she wrote a memoir, shaded off into prose poems, about her childhood and girlhood in a largely preautomotive California and New Mexico and her mature life on the Finnish estate. With *Röster över vattnet* (1953; Voices over the water) and *Den älskades anlete* (1957; The beloved's face) she continued as a particularly cultivated essayist, in the tradition of Yrjö Hirn, throwing her net wide, from Chinese poetry of the T'ang dynasty to Solveig von Schoultz's lyrics, and from Michelangelo's *Pietà* to Lady Ottoline Worrell. A travel book, *Holländsk himmel* (1961; Holland sky), a genteel representative of the genre, is dedicated to a "faithful traveling companion and neighbor," the judge Oskar Möller (1888–1971), and may well have been a preparation for her return to the novel with *Wintermusik* (1971; Winter music), dealing with a well-to-do widow who must choose between independence and a new marriage.

At long last, in *Systrar och vänner* (1979; Sisters and friends), she made a statement on Finland-Swedish life as she saw it from her unique position: it dealt with the isolated, affluent Finland-Swedes of the interior, for whom Helsingfors is a distant lure where "Swedish can still be heard on the streets and in the shops." The family chronicle of the Sölfvereckers begins in 1935; by the time it ends, in 1978, the Swedes of the town of X have dwindled to one, gentle Henni, the book's main character and partial narrator, and some of the Sölfvereckers have moved to Detroit, becoming the Seveckers. *Systrar och vänner*—the title is taken from Carl Michael Bellman's *Fredmans epistlar* (Fredman's epistles), number 17, always sung by the town's Swedish Club on "Swedish Day" (6 November)—is an open-eyed view of a minority that is at once "exotic and provincial," living under "our little Finland-Swedish conditions, so precisely differentiated," as Henni tells a kindly English visitor. (Thus her conclusions are close to those of von Numers and Alopaeus.) Helen af Enehjelm remained a U.S. citizen and a Roman Catholic until the end; among the noms de plume she used in her extensive newspaper writing were "Helena Ensam" (alone or lonely) and Helen California.

Systrar och vänner may have been intended as a witty corrective of the savaging of the Finland-Swedish establishment carried out by some of its members, Jörn Donner, Christer Kihlman, and Henrik Tikkanen, since 1960 (see chapter 10) and in which Alopaeus had played a limited part with *Mörkrets kärna*. No doubt, the self-satisfaction of the Finland-Swedish establishment needed jarring. The range of social views in Finland-Swedish literature during the 1930s and 1940s was much larger than might be surmised (as, e.g., Colliander and Tuominen gave evidence); all the same, the people at the bottom of society's pile were largely assumed to be Finnish speakers, whereas in the literary depiction of the Finland-Swedish world, by and large, economic problems appeared to be far less pressing than emotional ones. When Allan Tallqvist (1909–70) published his novels reporting on life in Sörnäs (the workers' region north and east of the center of Helsingfors, famed at one time for its mixed-language slang, its local pride, and its toughness and sentimentality, a kind of Finnish Brooklyn), he indicated by means of snippets of conversation that his characters spoke Finnish or the argot—if such signals were needed for Tallqvist's audience. The first novel was clearly labeled *Topi från Sörnäs* (1930; Topi from Sörnäs), another was *Jaska och hans tös* (1931; Jaska and his girl), a third was *Stålets sång* (1936; The song of steel). Jaska moves among petty criminals, especially bootleggers, and finds consolation with streetwalkers; Tallqvist's sexual frankness was still unusual enough, but his principal characters are redeemed—Jaska gets religion; Maja, the light of his life, turns to Jesus as she dies of tuberculosis.

The journalist Eric von Schantz (1909–) likewise made a small place for himself in literary history because of his picaresque *Slyngeln Måhrberg*

(1936; The rascal Måhrberg) and its continuation, *Ny dag* (1937; New day); in the latter, Måhrberg, a painter, serves a prison term for forgery, harrowingly described, before setting out for America. Von Schantz is especially remembered for the reportage novel *Irene: "Silke-Saras" minnen* (1947; Irene: "Silk Sara's" Memoirs), which purports to be the recollections of a notorious Helsingfors prostitute, born in 1874, who reached her professional peak around the turn of the century. Now and then the memoirs call for reform (in episodes that depict brutal jail conditions), but factually based or not, they turn into another picaresque chronicle when Irene leaves Finland for Sweden and Argentina: "On October 5th we set out, all told eight girls who walked the broad path of vice." The prostitute's voyage to the New World, in the manner of Defoe's *Moll Flanders*, points to literary models; this was the heyday of Kathleen Winsor's once scandalous *Forever Amber* (1944), the film version of which was distributed the year *Irene* was published.

Less sensational than Tallqvist or von Schantz, the psychologist Margit Törnudd (1905–82), who wrote under her maiden name of Niininen, drew on personal and professional knowledge for her humane and by no means insubstantial creative work. Her experiences first as inmate (convicted of killing a man who had raped her) and then counselor in women's reformatories were used to write the sketches and poems of *Bakom gallret* (1930; Behind the grating); *Sökare och syndare* (1931; Searchers and sinners) portrayed other marginal figures in four stories: a drunken and boastful Russian emigré ("he depicted his vanished triumphs for these fools" and "he reveled in self-contempt"), the semiprostitute who "dreamed of a home and a child and a person to love," the elderly bookkeeper who marries a young woman but realizes that he can never truly possess her the way he does his postage stamps, and the eternal innocent, a self-tormenter who finds grace on his deathbed. More cheerfully, *Tora Markman och hennes syster* (1936; Tora Markman and her sister) was built around the familiar figure of the adolescent girl in combination with the equally familiar story of the tight-knit (and, in this case, whimsical) middle-class family: when the sisters are confirmed, their Uncle Felix gives them brassieres. Niininen continued with tales from the home front in *Ensamma ansikten* (1942; Lonely faces) and *Huset med den gröna gardinen* (1944; The house with the green curtain), the latter a novel about interconnected fates in a "gray, old-fashioned building with the stucco flaking off and the paint gnawed away by sun and rain."

Apart from her close view of society's nooks and crannies, Niininen's characteristics as an author were her Christian standpoint and her lightly ironizing sympathy—like that of the Dane Herman Bang, although less cleverly managed—with the people in her case studies. The title character in "Miss Dorothea Sax," in *Ensamma ansikten,* for example, is a little woman possessing a lively imagination, a strong faith, and a constantly bleeding heart, who grows old in her own emotionally self-serving devotion to the poor. "Her tripping steps falter more and more as the years go by, her brown bag, filled with everyone's troubles, grows heavier to bear, her pretty, doll-like face grows ever more wrinkled with each fruitless effort she makes to understand." *Sin egen verklighet* (1949; One's own reality) opens with a story, "At the Job," about an overburdened caseworker: "I don't have time for coffee just now. A divorce and an instance of child abuse are waiting outside. And I haven't even read through the documents yet." Such authors of obvious moral goodness and sociological competence as Margit Niininen or Ester Ståhlberg (1870–1950), the founder of the society for the protection of children (and the wife of Finland's first president), have become almost unread, but—apart from the messages they sent—they have a value as the depicters of forgotten milieus: Niininen's petit bourgeois Swedish and Finnish speakers, mingled together, and Ståhlberg's tiny Helsingfors Jewish congregation in *Se, drömmaren kommer där* (1933; Behold, the dreamer cometh there).

A Nasty World and a Nicer One: Chorell and Jansson

Walentin Chorell (1912–83) had sufficient forerunners and models in the pursuit of tattered existences when he made his second, prose debut just after the war. His first appearance had been as a lyric poet in *Vinet och lägeln* (1941; The wine and the flask), a collection that could be passed by as more epigonic modernism were it not for his sketching skill—the clumsy man of goodwill in "The Poetic Police Constable," the romantic young soldier from a happy home in "Red Planet"; *Spegling* (1943; Reflection) contains verses about military life ("I'm a clerk / and good for nothing— / for my hands tremble / and so I'm afraid") that seem to be an artless confession of self-contempt. As a prose writer, Chorell from the start had conciseness, cogency of portraiture, and phenomenal industry. He did not allow himself to be overlooked, and his novels and plays fitted perfectly, with their grim sense of crisis and disorientation, into post-1944 Finland, when reparations had to be paid to the victorious power, when refugees from the lost eastern territories had to be sorted out, when the country's fate was quite uncertain. Also, an unostentatious religiosity—sincere or not—added to the problematics of his work, corresponded to foreign literary currents of the time, and, once in a while, contributed a small ray of light.

Chorell's prose debut was double, his contribution to the aborning detective-novel craze, *Lektion för döden* (1947; Lesson for death) and the weightier *Jörgen Hemmelinks stora augusti* (1947; Jörgen Hemmelink's great August). Hemmelink, the son of a Finland-Swedish woman and a Polish-Jewish musician, opens Chorell's extremely large gallery of misfits. After a pleasant enough childhood, interrupted by a severe sexual shock, the adult Hemmelink finds it impossible to lead a normal existence: his father had coddled him with dreams and as an adult he exists in fantasies, unable to accept the women who would like to release him from his magic circle. At the conclusion his "great August" — the month whose events once contributed to his twistedness — appears to lead him into a new life. *Calibans dag* (1948; Caliban's day) opens with an unsuccessful coitus in a café's back room between an aging proprietor and a prostitute on a shaky pile of rugs and ends with the café owner's death, of a stroke, the same day — never having really entered into any relationship; the longed-for son who would have carried on his name (there is a touch of Bloom in Justus) died in infancy. *Blindtrappan* (1949; The blind staircase) has a cast made up of stunted or deformed existences: a man blinded in an accident, who will never escape the half-life into which he has been thrust (unlike the blind musician in Ingmar Bergman's early film, *Musik i mörker* [1947; *Night Is My Future*]); a girl who has been the mistress of a Nazi officer and cannot get sadism out of her blood; her present lover, a student paralyzed by his own talkativeness; a former prostitute who cannot get over the loss of her teeth; and her husband, a morgue worker unhappy in his job. This couple, singularly, may find happiness, once the husband resolves to forgive his wife's last fling. But in the wholly black *Intim journal* (1951; Intimate journal) the reader is made privy to the diary of Martin; his relationship to his older sister renders him incapable of normal love and leads to his plotting her murder. (He is killed, instead, in the apparent accident he has planned.)

After these virtuoso compositions on misery, Chorell began to write novels more hopeful, if less penetrating: Lo Simsal in *Sträv gryning* (1952; Harsh dawn) murders a man in a rage, serves his sentence, and is about to succumb to the loneliness of an exconvict when chance assistance at a baby's birth gives him a symbolic ticket for reentry into community life. A trilogy tells about the progress of an independent girl toward maturity, *Mirjam* (1954), *Främlingen* (1956; The stranger), and *Kvinnan* (1958; The woman), ending with her decision to bear and rear her baby and her refusal to marry its well-intentioned father. Mirjam — who seems, by the way, to be a less sophisticated rival to the several undaunted heroines produced in these years by the prolific Swedish novelist Olle Hedberg (1899–1974) — is from the Åbo skerries, transplanted to Helsingfors. True to his wont, Chorell employs local detail only in moderation, and his characters' language is a simple but colorless normal Swedish. For Chorell, the gripping presentation of emotional constellations is more important than the specifics of milieu.

The 1960s saw a new darkening of the mood in Chorell's novels, an effort to regain the intensity of his narrative beginnings: Stig Sundkvist in *Stölden* (1960; The theft) lifts a wallet and almost cuts the fragile ties he has to a normal life; the seaman Ivar in *De barmhärtiga* (1962; The merciful ones) is an alcoholic who misuses a widow and her crippled daughter; Selim Karle, in *Saltkaret* (1963; The salt shaker), a veteran of the Russian wars, plans, in his growing madness, to play a giant practical joke on the church (the "salt shaker" of the title) being erected opposite his apartment. He abuses the trust of a former comrade in order to set the church on fire and inadvertently murders the semiprostitute who has shown him some affection. In *Grodan* (1966; The frog) a servant girl — the title is the nickname her fellow orphans have given her because of a membrane between her toes — gets the upper hand over her gullible employers, a childless couple. Rags-Viktor, an itinerant junkman in *Agneta och lumpsamlaren* (1968; Agneta and the ragman), kills Harald, a kiln worker, out of pity for the man's wife and affection for the couple's nine-year-old daughter; he gets away with it, only to be tormented by the awareness of what he has done. In the sequel, *Sista leken* (1970; The last game), he drowns himself. Both victim and murderer suffer from grotesque afflictions: Harald's skin is impregnated with lime, to which his wife is allergic; Viktor, full of medical jargon, attributes his flushes of excessive sympathy and fits of weeping to what he calls his "climax," his male climacteric.

Chorell's production oscillates: from the pessimism of the forties to the brighter tone of the fifties, from the lonely and half (or wholly) mad protagonists of the sixties to the ill-matched pairs of the seventies. For years, Chorell and his wife taught in a lyceum on Brändö in Helsingfors and had rich experience in the ways of youth; in *Äggskalet* (1972; The eggshell) the love of a couple from different levels of society seems to conquer. But, as often in Chorell's books that prepare for their own sequels, the seeds of future unhappiness are already sown, Seija's vitality and Jupp's passivity. Their marriage goes on for two more books, *Knappen* (1974; The button), the young people's pet name for their baby, and *Livsstycket* (1976; The bodice, but also "the piece of life" they have created together): predictable difficulties arise and the parents part. (The situation resembles that taken up by Lassi Sinkkonen [see chapter 5] in *Solveig ja Jussi* [1973; Solveig and

Jussi] and Solveig von Schoultz in *Somliga mornar* [1976]; the authors reflect a new social reality: early marriage and early separation.)

In his final trilogy (or trio of connected novels), *Dockorna* (1978; The dolls), *Rävsaxen* (1980; The fox trap), and *Lekhagen* (1981; The playpen), Chorell returned to the Åbo milieu in which he had grown up and to the 1930s. (Long ago the critic Lars Hamberg deduced that Chorell fetched some background material—carefully disguised—from Nummisbacken, a poor section of the city, just as his Finnish contemporary Lauri Viita drew on Tampere's Pispala.) The writer Joel—a chronic liar and alcoholic, married to Sonia, a semi-invalid from polio—is one more of Chorell's apparent weaklings who victimize those around them; in Joel's alcoholism Chorell dealt with an illness he intimately understood. Finally, in *Kvarteret barmhärtighet* (1982; The block named mercy), the narrator reconstructs an episode of his early childhood when he pretended that his aunt was dead, in an imagined mercy killing—a complement to the crime novel of Chorell's early career and to *Pizzamordet* (1977; The pizza murder), in which, perhaps intending to use the figure later on, he had introduced a blind detective, Simon Kataris, from still another circumscribed segment of Finnish society, Greek and Italian immigrants.

Unusually large, Chorell's production of novels was nonetheless outdone by his dramatic work, which for a time gave him something of an international reputation; Chorell was probably Finland's most produced playwright during his heyday of the 1950s, and a bibliography of 1963 contained fifty-three entries. The radio plays and stage plays alike deal with the same airless milieus and stunted lives as the novels. The trapped middle-aged man of *Fabian öppnar portarna* (1949; Fabian opens the gates), the aging actress of *Madame* (1952), the haunted couple of *Vandringsman* (1955; Wanderer), the hateful siblings of *Systrarna* (1955; Eng. tr. *The Sisters*, 1971), the confabulating alcoholic in *Guldkust* (1957; Gold Coast), the lovers who turn out to be brother and sister in *Gräset* (1960; The grass), the factory workers who unite against a forewoman different from themselves in the all-female *Kattorna* (1963; Eng. tr. *The Cats*, 1978) are some of the tormented dramatis personae in plays admired in their time but since fallen into neglect; their symbolism is heavy, their psychology dated. The best of Chorell's dramatic writing was done for radio and television, where his swift outlining of persons and moods was readily brought to bear. Eight of the plays were printed together in 1952: among them, "The Empty" is about a retired prostitute who ekes out a living by collecting bottles; "Dialogue by a Window" concerns envy between bedridden old men; the title character in "Andrea Sölfverne" is a lonely old maid who is destroying herself; the three sisters of "Women's House" destroy a young man who stumbles into their midst.

Later, *Fem spel* (1967; Five plays) was added to what Chorell called the permanent part of his work for the mass media. Two are peculiarly Chorellian; in "The Naked Woman over Vitebsk" an old man and his young housekeeper murder the former's son, who has confessed that he imagines the housekeeper as Chagall's nude giantess; in "Gray Eros" a former schoolteacher, his face contorted and his speech thickened by a stroke, pays a visit to his mistress of fifty years before, now the victim of paralysis. What Chorell's characters want from life is love, but they have been frozen into such odd postures that they cannot find it at all or, if they do, they abuse it. But they have no cathartic effect on the reader; Johannes Salminen remarked that nothing tragically monumental pertains to them ("I strandlinjen," 152).

With his implicit request that the human condition, however wretched, be regarded with mercy (thus continuing the plea of Tito Colliander), Chorell may have hinted at a Christian basis for his work seldom openly displayed. (In 1948 his *Ensam sökan* [Lonely searching] had appeared at the Lutheran Youth Publishing House; in it happiness comes to a troubled marriage, thanks to religion, as husband and wife find "community in faith and love." Chorell excluded it from his entry in the Finland-Swedish *Who's Who.*) He was most effective, probably, in the books of his early career, before routine had set in; there, in his ability to conjure up twisted lives, he resembled such British novelists as F. L. Green, the author of *Odd Man Out*, or the Graham Greene of *Brighton Rock*. His characters never emphasize their membership in the linguistic minority, and his works were popular in Finnish translation. Yet again and again, his oeuvre uses "the narrow room" or crowded space that, according to Merete Mazzarella (*Det trånga rummet*), is the Finland-Swedish novel's prime setting.

Swedish Finland's other prose writer who went from a modest beginning in the immediate postwar years to a sizable international reputation (indeed, becoming Finland's most widely read author abroad) was Tove Jansson (1914–). Her career falls into two parts, the chain of books based on her invention, the Mumin (Moomin) Trolls, from *Småtrollen och den stora översvämningen* (1945; The little trolls and the great flood) to *Sent i November* (1970; Eng. tr. *Moominvalley in November,* 1971), and the stories and novels for an adult audience, from *Bildhuggarens dotter* (1968; Eng. tr. *The Sculptor's Daughter,* 1969) — obliquely factual stories about the author's father, Viktor Jansson (1886–1958) and herself, as well as other family members — to the tales of *Brev från Klara* (1991; Letters from Klara). The

Moomin canon is composed of eight books; as their popularity grew, some titles were changed: *Kometjakten* (1946; Eng. tr. *Comet in Moominland*, 1950) was reissued in 1968 as *Kometen kommer* (The comet is coming), in which the author's anxiety about atomic or hydrogen bombs was displayed, while the quasi-autobiography of the Moomin father, *Muminpappas bravader* (1950; Eng. tr. *The Exploits of Moominpappa*, 1952), was republished as *Muminpappas memoarer* (Moominpappa's memoirs) in 1968. Two little books mainly of pictures — and Jansson's illustrations figure large in all her Moomin books — were spinoffs aimed at the very young; otherwise, as has been noted by the commentators on her work (most carefully by W. Glyn Jones, *Tove Jansson*), the series, as it progressed, was directed more and more at both children and adults, in the Hans Christian Andersen tradition.

The good-natured Jansson trolls have none of the malice attributed to the trolls of Nordic myth; they resemble cheerful miniature hippopotamuses who walk upright; they are inveterate but nervous adventurers, yet prefer not to wander too far from Moominvalley, save to an offshore island (as in *Pappan och havet* [1965; Eng. tr. *Moominpappa at Sea*, 1965]). The books have a wonderful flow of fantasy figures — the asparagus-shaped Hattifatteners, "interested only in traveling onward, as far as possible"; the Hemulen, representatives of grownup authority; the Fillyjonks, kinder if sillier beings; and so forth — but they also have a pedagogical intent, just as do the tales of Topelius, Jansson's great predecessor in children's stories from Finland. But where Topelius inculcated patriotism, duty, industry, and modesty, Jansson works with softer virtues, among them kindness, the ability to laugh at one's self, a love of life's small and innocent pleasures. Comparing the Moomintrolls with the animal beings of A. A. Milne's *Winnie the Pooh* and *The House at Pooh Corner*, Alison Lurie makes the important point that the Pooh world is an ideal society of male friends, in which only Kanga is feminine, whereas Moominvalley is populated by "many strongly individualized female characters" — but the tolerant Jansson is scarcely a doctrinaire feminist. The happy and balanced family from which Tove Jansson came may well be the basis of the domestic constellation in her books. Thomas Warburton, her translator and publisher, recalls that the series began with what was a kind of family joke, and it hints at the presence of human portraits in the books; Too-Ticky, the androgynous being who saves Moominpappa when he confronts a threatening world of cold in *Trollvinter* (1957; Eng. tr. *Moominland Midwinter*, 1958), is Jansson's artist friend Tuulikki Pietilä (1917–); the Pappa bears features of Viktor Jansson; the Moomin mother is Tove Jansson's own mother, the noted postage-stamp designer Signe Hammarsten-Jansson (1882–1970).

What the larger intention of the series may be, or may have become, as Jansson's vision and technical accomplishments grew, has been the object of much academic discussion. *Farlig midsommar* (1954; Eng. tr. *Midsummer Madness*, 1955) may well be the juncture at which she left little folks behind: the inhabitants of the valley, discovering a floating theater, perform the Pappa's play specially written in (more or less) dactylic hexameter, a meter beloved of Finland-Swedish poets, but as Jones says, "few children will understand Pappa's problems" with prosody. The pleasantly middle-class yet sometimes drastically threatened lifestyle of the Moomin characters, heterogeneous in appearance and behavior but ultimately alike, may arguably be a metaphor for the situation of the Finland-Swedish minority; it may also be seen as a commentary on Finland's prosperous but precarious location between East and West (to which Jansson's contemporaries, Paavo Haavikko and Johannes Salminen, have devoted much serious thought); or it may symbolize the predicament of humanity threatened with destruction (as the case seemed to be in the cold war years) — yet, for the nonce, at least in western Europe and North America, a humanity getting along quite nicely. Looking for deeper meanings in the unified yet varied phantasmagoria of the Moomin legend, literary historians should not forget that Jansson brought to perfection a line of Finland-Swedish writing, full of *Märchen* elements, that had attracted her immediate predecessors — Sigrid Backman's *De fåvitska trollen,* whose very title indicated the nature of her fable about the small but happy family, Eva Wichman's *Här är allt som förut,* and Hagar Olsson's *Träsnidaren och döden,* with its fairy-tale ending.

The adult portion of Jansson's work has not won the worldwide reputation of the Moomin classics. (The novels of Hans Christian Andersen, translated during the Victorian period, likewise did not achieve the same attention as his tales.) Her earlier collections of short stories — and Jansson's are just that, in the Anglo-American sense, truly brief accounts of a person, a situation, an emotion, rather than longer tales with several strands — are the above-mentioned *Bildhuggarens dotter* (another of the literature's many albums of childhood impressions); *Lyssnerskan* (1971; The hearkening woman), which contains the uncanny "Gray Duchess," about a dress designer with second sight, and "The Squirrel," an unforgettable account of a woman in self-willed isolation, on an island with an increasingly more aggressive squirrel; and *Dockskåpet* (1978; The doll cupboard), in which a central theme is the selfishness necessary for artistic creation. Her willingness to leave much unsaid put her in a class with Solveig von Schoultz: in "Art in Nature," a gallery watchman, barging into a couple's spat about the meaning of a piece of modern art, thinks, "It is the secret part that's important." Subsequently, the stories of travel, devotion, childhood, old age, feminine friendship—*Resa med lätt bagage* (1987; Journey with light baggage), *Rent spel* (1989; Honest play), *Brev från Klara*—could be regarded as stages in a large semimemoir, were they not so carefully polished. Many depend on the depiction of passing trouble and reconciliation between friends or on a sense of uneasiness and release: in "The Premonition," from the latest volume, a chronically anxious woman, mortally injured in a blasting accident, dies happy: "You know, this is the first time in my life I'm not nervous. It feels wonderful."

Among Jansson's four "adult" novels, *Sommarboken* (1972; Eng. tr. *The Summer Book*, 1977) came closest to matching the popularity of her Moomintroll books, and here, too, the world of childhood is not deserted; it tells (with cozy illustrations by the author) about the summer friendship in the skerries between a sweetly inquisitive little girl ("Are there any ants in heaven?") and her wise grandmother. *Solstaden* (1974; Eng. tr. *Sun City*, 1977) is a distinctly unsentimental report on a residence for the elderly in St. Petersburg, Florida, a novel on the borderline between satire and caricature, a cruel and pathetic "American" complement about geriatric high jinks to Swedish Finland's spate of novels, stories, and dramas about the aged, not surprising in a population whose median age is high. Returning to a milieu she knew better, a coastal village somewhere in Swedish-speaking Finland, with *Den ärliga bedragaren* (1982; The honest swindler), Jansson examined a tight community and its slightly odd inhabitants—the honest confidence-girl herself, her rather dull-witted brother, and an eccentric who has achieved a world fame by her repetitive illustrations of children's books (a deprecatory self-portrait). Unlike Chorell, who would have made such characters try to exert control over one another, Jansson implies that there will be a happy ending. She does the same in *Stenåkern* (1984; The stony field), in which an elderly journalist at last discovers a contact with his daughters—once more, on an island in the skerries.

To what extent the egocentric Jonas is related to Viktor Jansson and the impractical Pappa of the Moomin books is a matter for speculation; but the prevalence of paternal types, lovable or not, in Finland-Swedish fiction—think of Petrus Bagge in Backman's *De fåvitska trollen*, Olsson's Dyster in *Chitambo*, the fathers in Tuominen and Alopaeus—cannot be ignored, nor can the variety of maternal, sibling, grandparental, and other family relationships. Obviously, such interconnections appear in every literature, but their importance seems to be accentuated for a minority population, especially when (as Jörn Donner once prophesied in an article for a Swedish public in *Bonniers Litterära Magasin*) Swedish in Finland has become, for many, a "private home language" pure and simple.

Two Lyricists: Peter Sandelin and Carpelan
When Peter Sandelin (1930–), a younger brother of C. F. Sandelin, started out with *Ur svalens loggbok* (1951; From the swallow's logbook), critics quickly detected a resemblance to the nature poetry of the young Rabbe Enckell and Björling; Sandelin had such a tender feeling for nature that he avoided erotic distractions, writing, "I'll never kiss a woman / for I do not wish to walk in darkness," the opening and closing lines of "Love with Shadow." Then, a frequent practice in his lyrics to come, he filled out what he had just said in the next poem, "Love without Shadow": "I and a birch / I kiss the young birch of the beach." (For the first of his two retrospective selections from his verse [1977], Sandelin ignored his swallow's logbook altogether.) Changing the title of Norman Mailer's brutal Pacific war novel, *The Naked and the Dead* (1946), Sandelin wrote *De lysande och de döda* (1953; The shining and the dead), in quiet resistance to such violence: "and I believe / that I think like a child / in order to get nearer to something, too." *Etyder* (1957; Etudes) elucidated this faith:

> I lay still for a long time in the shadow
> down deep in the damp grass
> and saw how a birch burned up toward the sky
> a motionless sky
> a birch which merely burned and burned
> burned into it. Yes, "burned"!!!

(Like Rabbe Enckell, Sandelin is also a painter; he held his initial exhibition in 1957, followed by others in 1982 and 1986.) Sandelin's poetry has been described as having a pronouncedly vertical nature, going from the depths upward, and Roger Holmström ("Rymdperspektivet") has written on the importance of sky space, clouds, and even the cosmos in Sandelin's works. A salient feature has been his gift for squeezing new values out of time-worn generalities: common as birds and plants are in his poetry, his texts never serve as an ornithological or botanical guide — "nature in Sandelin's poetry is experienced nature, not knowledge in verse" (Hedlund, 161). By means of the very title of *Stunder av ljus* (1960; Moments of light), Sandelin emphasized another factor in his experience on the universe, light itself, and in "Almost Yoga" he went still further in his symbiosis:

> I feel myself the belonging-together
> I feel myself as with the seas
> I feel myself as with the earths and the springs
> I am in the shining tree
> and without pain.

In *Hemma i universum* (1962; At home in the universe) he repeated the message:

> A host of a hundred thousand strong marched past — past me without a trace
> then came the rain,
> the drop
> which still shines on the leaf
> its greenness
> in the heart's home region.

That Sandelin was "one of the purest representatives in his generation of the Finland-Swedish tradition of nature lyrics" (Willner, "Sandelin," 134) made him run afoul of the critics, politically and socially aware, of the 1960s; he was charged in 1968 by the Danish expert on modernist poetry, Poul Borum, with "an unbelievable lack of self-criticism, a clinging to puerile credulity." Sandelin thought such criticism grossly unfair, and in *En vanlig solig dag* (1965; An ordinary sunny day) he wrote — with a vehemence unusual in him — about the catastrophes (airplane crashes, rocket misfirings) that could occur on "an ordinary sunny day when nothing happens." *Minuter på jorden* (1968; Minutes on the earth) made common cause with suffering humankind in the self-ironizing "On Wounds":

> I write prescriptions
> for wounds
>   . . . constantly recommend
> country life's fresh air green leaves
> and timeless time.

It was followed by the "Anti-Poem" (or palinode):

> Forgive me brother
> prescriptions do not help
> when you stand starving
> in the ruins of Hué
> with your shrapnel-pierced
> daughter in your arms.

Like Göran Palm (1931–) in Sweden, and a host of other Scandinavian poets, Sandelin thus made his contribution to the swelling body of verse about the Vietnam War; in *Fågeln i stenmuren: Dagboksblad* (1970; The bird in the stone wall: Leaves from a diary) he claimed he was "the bleeding Vietnamese I write about in a poem," so intense was his sympathy and empathy.

Still, he did not apologize for his nature poetry or abandon it; his statement in the same book, "All my poetry is revolt—not least my nature poetry," led into his ecological phase. (Rachel Carson's *Silent Spring* had appeared in 1962.) *Tyst stiger havet* (1972; Silently rises the sea) increases this devotion and defense; in a poem bringing to perfection the laconism toward which he had long striven, he describes the natural phenomenon he apparently loves best:

> Snow snows past
> and asks not after time
> : to move like snow in space
> : to melt like the snow
> into the earths
> snow snows
> time is not time.

Minimalism is displayed again in *Var det du?* (1973; Was it you?): "From the melt-water-light / echoes / the birdsong." (Solveig von Schoultz in *Terrassen* [1959] and Bo Carpelan in *73 dikter* [1966] were his predecessors in the tiny tanka or haiku form, but Sandelin's intentions may have been more mystical and less formal-aesthetic than theirs.)

The prose fragments of *Barnen står på rymdens strand* (1975; The children stand on the edge of space), like those in *Fågeln i stenmuren,* allow Sandelin to speak about his poetic method more extensively than in his poetry itself: "When we do not really know what we are talking about, and have not the faintest idea of what we're going to say in the next second, in the next line . . . just then our words can approach an exactness which is the only important one." The children of the title are the beings most threatened by pollution of the milieu and by war: "The children in the baby carriages. They lie there like roses in the norther's blast—and while the seas darken, are poisoned." *Dikter med varandra* (1977; Poems with one another) tells the story of his frustrations:

> Earlier I left the problems
> to the snowstorms,
> to the silent trees, the invisible
> seagulls.

Now he interrogates specific persons at a railroad station (fast-food man, ticket seller, train conductor, and so forth) about human survival. Once on board the train

> I ask *myself—*
> I ask *myself*

> [I] attempt to grow from a cry [uttered] toward nothing
> to a conversation
> here.

(Someone pulls the emergency cord, but nothing happens and an ultimate stillness ensues.) Repeatedly, Sandelin is drawn to a discussion of large human concerns, only to withdraw into a sense of the futility of his undertaking. *Dikter mellan vinter och vinter* (1980; Poems between winter and winter) puts the question: "poem / where are you going?" and, by way of a novelty for Sandelin, adduces portrait poems, such as a Finnish Gothic, an equivalent to Grant Wood's painting:

> They sit facing one another
> each on their chair
> in the glittering and black room.
> She with her back to the window
> He looking out without seeing.
> Her face
> is already shadowed by death.

Aging and death become ever more prominent motifs; the poetic prose of *Vägen upphör men jag fortsätter* (1982; The road stops but I continue), divided into three musical movements called "Allegro," "Andante-Adagio," and "Moderato," is filled with anxiety: "It is fetched to me in buckets, as a sort of mildly shining dust in the moonshine . . . I hear myself shriek, I shriek: ATOMIC WASTE (as if that would help)." Nightmares of the present mix with nightmarish memories of childhood: "The fire station isn't burning. / But all the houses around it burn. . . . It must be one of the bomb-nights in 1943." In *Den undermedvetna staden* (1984; The subconscious city) the anxiety is ratcheted up another notch, becoming existential: "born with the mark of death / our life became a question of time," and Sandelin's usually comforting snow turns into a threat:

> it snows and snows in the world
> you see only the muzzle of this dog
>   (which is dead)
> somewhere people cry out hysterically, without stop.

Den vita orten (1986; The white place), though, provides surcease in a dream of a paradise, which Sandelin describes in a postcard to "Dear N." (in 1967 he married Nina Parland, the daughter of Oscar and Heidi Parland):

> I think I'm FLYING all the while
> when I move about (yet I haven't drunk anything)

> — I can only hope that the place and its language
> will spread, or that you will arrive soon
> at it, that all our friends [will come]; all.

Existens (1989; Existence) tries to take refuge from the inevitable in nature: "Age draws near in a racing car. / I throw myself to the side, in the grass by the wayside."

Sandelin's poetry was brought to the attention of a larger, Swedish public by the selection *Klockan 5 och klockan ingenting vid havet* (1977; Five o'clock and nothing o'clock by the sea), with an afterword by his special champion, Tom Hedlund; the title poem, from *Tyst stiger havet,* is a prime example, according to Hedlund, of the "sweep of light-shimmering nature poetry" that goes throughout Finland's Swedish lyric. It describes a lazy, transfigured moment at the seaside:

> the tugboat in space comes chugging
> with the silence
>
> no bird no human being emerges
> from no shadow
>
> all sinks itself into sun.

Sandelin remains the idyllist supreme, for all his efforts to become an engaged poet:

> softly the boat glides into the sand
> it is not day and not night
> and gulls sleep white, stones lift them
> toward space, gentle shine
> which comes from within your face:
> you love, you are loved —
> softly the sand surrounds the boat like a water
> your wrinkles smooth out
> and it is not day and not night.

During his more than four decades of lyric production Sandelin's basic melody has not changed; he has simply made endless variations on the vital importance of the immediate experience. (The third of his artistic endeavors after poetry and painting has been the composition of small piano pieces, theme and variations once more.) In one of his rare appearances as a literary interpreter, Sandelin wrote the essay "Björling's Impudence" (1980), but save for his linguistic experiments mostly represented in *Den undermedvetna staden* (i.e., exploded language, half-words, nonsense words), his poetry has remained surprisingly simple, confronting his audience without pose, asking essential questions. In *Existens* — as always in Sandelin, collections are aptly named — he employs images that unashamedly mix the banal and the sublime:

> Eternity belongs to all: it is the gnat's,
> it is the slowly dying sun's
> It strikes the soldiers who come marching from the west
> It knocks down the soldiers who come from the east
> It belongs to the little gray seamstress
> (long ago buried, beyond memory)
> And it is the movement
> which never ends —
> It is in this snowfall, in this forest of snow
> and here: in the lightning's white rope.

After Solveig von Schoultz's lyric debut of 1940 with *Min timme,* the appearance of Bo Carpelan (1926–) with *Som en dunkel värme* (1946; Like a dusky warmth) was perhaps the most important lyric start of the decade. What attracted reviewers' favor to his early verse — the surefooted first book was followed by *Du mörka överlevande* (1947; You dark survivor, a title particularly suited to the spirit of the times) and *Variationer* (1950; Variations) — was a voice that held the promise of shortly becoming wholly Carpelan's own, even though the heritage from the original modernists was palpable enough. His language had a richness and polish, exceptional in a beginner, revealed in a poem from the first collection, here quoted in its entirety:

> In the evening's wool
> someone wanders past with a lantern —
> Like a dark warmth
> until the dawn
> is the pendulum's secret anticipation.

A fondness for ellipses, omitted punctuation, and ecstatic outcries were habits acquired from Gunnar Björling, as in "Morning":

> Beach sky not a shadow moves
> the hand's distance blossoms here
> grass silverclear —

> Oh quiet silence
>> All is near the dream.

But from the start Carpelan avoided Björling's extravagances of vocabulary and demonstrative non sequiturs. (Long employed at the Helsingfors City Library, Carpelan received a doctorate at the university in 1960 for a dissertation on Björling. Although, like so many others, he had once been a member of the Björling circle, the former disciple was refused any aid in his research by the old master. Later, with characteristic modesty, Carpelan called his scholarly product and its abstractions evidence of "how confusedly inspired [he was] by the New Criticism.") In fact, Rabbe Enckell's chiseled lines and muted elegiac tone set a deeper stamp on the young Carpelan; further, as Carpelan readily admitted, he had learned from Wallace Stevens and his *Man with the Blue Guitar* (1937) and from the "image-laden" verse of the leading Swedish poets of the 1940s, especially Erik Lindegren — poets who themselves, starting out, had been inspired by Finland's modernists.

Carpelan never wanted to rival Lindegren, Karl Vennberg, or Harald Forss in difficulty or obscurity, however; "August," in *Du mörka överlevande,* is succinctly suggestive by the very directness of its questioning: "Who weaves on your darkening loom, oh August, / and with his hand moves the distaff between all shadows / which sink into another to be erased." Likewise, throughout *Variationer* a single attitude can readily be discerned — the poet's affection for a world of beauty, particularly to be found in nature, yet an affection troubled by intimations of pain or loss. Commenting on a poem from *Variationer,* "Confused the switchman spreads / his slumber over an autumn without snow," Carpelan — whose reputation had already reached Sweden — wrote for a Swedish anthology, *Diktaren om dikten* (1952; The poet on the poem): "The basic tone is darker than resignation." Carpelan captured a peculiar postwar sensibility, a combination of thankfulness for survival and a sense of despair, the latter reaction understandable in a Finland that had a victorious Soviet Union as a next-door neighbor, with the Communist coups in Poland, Hungary, and Czechoslovakia not far away. Yet relief, achieved largely by the traditional flight into nature, was dominant in Carpelan's emotional complex. A four-line poem in *Variationer* says:

> What is shadow? What is your longing?
> The silence's rain, the autumn's beauty,
> silvergray mist over flaming trees,
> no pursuit, no death.

Carpelan has criticized his early lyrics for being "weighed down with symbols," a judgment emerging from his professional capacity as a critic. A reviewer for the leading Finland-Swedish paper, *Hufvudstadsbladet,* from 1950 to 1964, he demonstrated great acuity and fairness; in an essay on his reviews, which unfortunately have never been collected, Sven Willner saw that Carpelan's strength lay precisely in his New Critical approach, basing analyses and evaluations closely on the text at hand. But he was eclectic in the best sense, according to Willner, "when needed, using historical, psychological, metaphysical and, indeed, even sociocritical points of view." Willner placed him in a venerable Finland-Swedish critical tradition, "orientating and guiding," indulging in neither savage attack nor unnecessary mystification, and never following a rigid methodology ("Carpelan som kritiker," 85).

One of the salient features of Carpelan's own creative work is his gift for changes and development. Flashes of zany humor and topsy-turvy fantasy appeared in the prose poems of *Minus sju* (1952; Less seven) — for example, in "The Night at the Opera," worthy of (and suggested by?) the Marx Brothers' famous comedy; dreams—burlesque, touching, portentious— now came to play a large part in Carpelan's work. *Objekt för ord* (1954; Objects for words) is an effort to render in precise discourse what the poet beholds; like Rilke in his early Parisian years, Carpelan "learns to see" and, like Rilke, practices on objets d'art. In the suite "Upon Contemplating Some Old Flemish Masters," "Our blood takes its course" as we perceive the paintings and "moves quite quietly, / fulfilling our outer vision in an inner reality." One of the paintings is of a woman:

> She is aware of the sufferings she will meet,
> In her white ruff, nonetheless, she keeps her calm demeanor.
> Her childlike hands rest too, thus touching us
> where we hide ourselves in details,
> reminding us
> of our childhood, of the future, like the master himself, unknown.

In *Landskapets förvandlingar* (1957; The landscape's transformations) the poetic voice, which previously had kept mostly to itself, began to posit a common experience with another being; the verses that provide the title open passionately: "The landscape's transformations, / and the sea's sleep-drunken cries by the bed / where love has already wakened," forming a contrast to the collection's many lyrics about isolation, such as "He wanders alone / by the sea's silence" and

> He who has walked paths, alone,
> heard, received those meeting him,
> is alone, simply alone
> if not a voice, a hand like fire has laid waste
> the silent hours, a life's fortifications.

In 1954 Carpelan married, and the couple's son, Anders, was born three years later; the poet confounded his sophisticated public by writing *Anders på ön* (1959; Anders on the island), followed by *Anders i stan* (1962; Anders in the city), children's books about a little boy's growing awareness of his parents' vacation home and the friendly city where he lives the rest of the year.

By *Den svala dagen* (1960; The cool day) Carpelan had fully achieved the conciseness and precision at which he long had aimed. He had mastered the art of producing unforgettable lines, for example, "for you, the springtimes' murmur is already past," thus putting himself squarely in the tradition of Runeberg. To readers inculcated with Runeberg's rhetorical practices, the title poem of *Den svala dagen* must have a familiar ring, with its parallelisms, its triple examples, its single effective simile: "Fleeting is the dawn, fleeting the day, but the cool evening / comes with its twilight, goes like the bay's water / among the dark trees where they stand, unmoving." (Slyly, Carpelan slips in an old-fashioned plural form of the verb "stand.") The collection contains one of Carpelan's best-known poems, "Evening Walk," encapsulating a human fate:

> A man walks through the forest
> one day with shifting lights,
> meets few people,
> stops, looks at the autumn sky.
> He means to go to the churchyard
> and no one follows him.

And in "The Horses" Carpelan gives an unquestioning, nonanalytical acceptance of events:

> The horses stood with bowed necks.
> When they were stretched,
> he saw the hide's play in the summer light.
> The darkness in their eyes took in June's greenery.
> He stood and saw them. Suddenly
> they sniffed, set out toward the horizon,

the bright space beneath a pale, distant moon,
as if he had frightened them with his sureness.

The intention of *Den svala dagen* was summed up in the often quoted command: "Do not seek in the mute grass, seek the mute grass." But pregnant brevity could be carried too far, and — always his own sternest critic — Carpelan called some of the tiny verses in *73 dikter* (1966; 73 poems) almost incomprehensible, even to their creator. Nevertheless, such a poem as: "All were not cast into the chambers, / the children were small and were thrown away directly," poses no mystery, nor does:

People foregather with people
they are many in the burning cities,
they are rinsed with oil,
arise again
in someone's words, in fire.

Carpelan was all too aware of the twentieth century's past horrors and horrors to come.

As if in reaction against the occasional riddles of the miniatures, Carpelan's *Gården* (1969; Eng. tr. *The Courtyard*, 1982, 1992), an album of poem views of apartment life during the 1930s, became his most widely read lyric collection; the perspective is that of an adult remembering the family world of his childhood ("Saturday was best, father and mother as if they / had been children / and I hear their voice / like a hand on my forehead"). The cycle was Carpelan's response to the socially aware 1960s; the courtyard and the cramped flats have shabby and ugly corners:

The elderly man with a room and kitchen alcove
has blackened his sleeve garters with India ink.
He walks with a silver-headed cane
and tries to keep poverty
within cultured boundaries.
He shelters himself as though he had
a constant observer.

Just the same, in its singular devotion to the speaker's parents, *Gården* implicitly goes against the 1960s demand for hatred of the older generation. Another symptom of Carpelan's discreet brand of social and human concern was his pair of books for young people, *Bågen* (1968; Eng. tr. *Bow Island: The Story of a Summer That Was Not*, 1971) and *Paradiset* (1973; Eng. tr. *Dolphins in the City*, 1976), about a mentally retarded boy. Further, he treated the problems of age in *En gammal mans dag* (1966; An old man's day), the most haunting of his several plays for radio and television.

In the 1970s Carpelan's narrative urge, having appeared tentatively in *Gården* and the juvenile novels, burst out with a vengeance. *Rösterna i den sena timmen* (1971; Eng. tr. *Voices at the Late Hour,* 1988) depicted an atomic disaster from the standpoint of an extended family. The book's atmosphere suggests such films as Stanley Kramer's *On the Beach* (1959), Peter Watkin's *The War Game* (1967), and Ingmar Bergman's *Skammen* (1968; *Shame*); and Carpelan employs a cinematographic technique, now rushing forward, now lingering, now indulging in the movies' favorite device, the flashback. The story's horror is intensified by the contrast between the catastrophe and its location in time and place: shortly before midsummer the family members foregather at an island vacation home, to save themselves or to wait for death. A weakness lies in the somewhat blurred characterizations (often expressed through interior monologues); but suspense and the possibility that the refugees will escape are maintained until the end. Suspense and atmosphere are also part and parcel of Carpelan's psychological thriller, *Din gestalt bakom dörren* (1975; Your figure behind the door); the mild-mannered Ewald, a businessman not averse to moral compromises, is harassed by a doppelgänger, who acts out patterns of behavior Ewald has suppressed. The tale's epigraph is taken, ominously enough, from Robert Louis Stevenson's *A Child's Garden of Verses,* "I have a little shadow that goes in and out with me"; also, this work of Carpelan — the longtime professional librarian, who knows world literature intimately — contains distant echoes of Chamisso's German romantic classic, *Peter Schlemihl,* and of Andersen's frightening *Skyggen* (The shadow). (In a study of the motif of the double, Markku Envall has noticed the frequency with which the theme appears in Carpelan's lyrics.)

Carpelan came even closer to the detective story in *Vandrande skugga* (1977; Wandering shadow), which concerns arson and murder in a sleepy Finnish coastal town at the turn of the century. Although Carpelan is anything but a social polemicist, the novel may be a modest contribution to the attacks made during the 1960s and 1970s on the alleged whited sepulchre of the Finland-Swedish establishment. As in his verse, Carpelan skillfully juxtaposes the idyll's undeniable charm with a sense of rot and doom. Once again, he writes within a clearly defined subgenre, but not imitatively. As he puts the small Scandinavian town under a magnifying glass, he has such distinguished predecessors as Ibsen in *Samfundets støtter* (*Pillars of Society*) and Hamsun in *Mysterier* and, in Finland, Mikael Lybeck in *Tomas Indal* and *Bror och syster,* Richard Malmberg in *Agaton Vidbäck,* and, nearer to Carpelan's own time, Veijo Meri in *Irralliset* (1959; The separate ones). Finland's Civil War lies in the offing: Dr. von Adler, the town's mortally ill physician (surely a descendant of Ibsen's Dr. Rank), tells Frid, the simple, honest, and lower-middle-class police chief, "It looks to me as if the whole thing is a colorful balloon, slowly pumped up to capacity with poison gas, that sooner or later will get too close to a flame." Frid discovers that the town's leading citizen, the perverse Consul, is the perpetrator of the novel's ghastly deeds.

Even in *Jag minns att jag drömde* (1979; I remember that I dreamed), in which Carpelan returns to the prose poems of *Minus sju,* he cannot forget his premonitions of disaster. But his dreams for the most part are realms of bliss. As the dreamer (transformed to waterfowl and fish) gazes down into a submarine valley of the imagination, he/it says: "I know I can find no better sanctuary. Perhaps our vale is the only place our language still can live in purity." The Norwegian scholar Leif Maehle, writing in 1977, had argued that to Carpelan, the poet was the main protector of the linguistic environment, constantly aware of language's precious possibilities and their endangerment. The dreamer's thoughts of a blessed vale—another Moominvalley?—may also be interpreted as a statement by a poet belonging to a linguistic minority; the remark of Rilke, who grew up in the midst of a Czech majority, should be remembered here—he spoke of "the gnawed-away edges of language." Yet Carpelan has scarcely closed his ears to Finland's majority tongue; he has produced a large anthology of contemporary Finnish verse in translation (1984) and selections of book length from such major poets as Paavo Haavikko (1985) and Sirkka Turkka (1987).

The 1970s were a decade of concentration on prose, culminating in the dream book, but Carpelan also continued his lyric production. In *Källan* (1973; The source) he looked once more to the sources of strength (familial love, erotic love, love of nature) for which—much like Sandelin—he was grateful; with "In the North" he praised the unique magic of Scandinavian nature: "What one does not see sharpens the eye and the feeling / and most rowanberries are both bitter and lovely." Still, he was haunted by thoughts of the obliteration of humanity: "The cities stand with open walls / . . . / And the people, / where are the people?" A suite within the collection, "Time Is Short," provides the title word: "Farewell to the simple source, the murmur, / the dreaming voices. / They were, existed, ceased to love." In 1976 he published *I de mörka rummen, i de ljusa* (In the dark rooms, in the light), for which he received the Nordic Council's literary prize. The council's citation praised him for the "lucid and taut lyrics in which [he] was able to express the interplay between outer and inner reality, in an exchange between an awareness of death and the sense of life." In fact, Carpelan was often less affirmative than the formal words imply; a poem from the collection is a portrait of a stunted life:

> He covers his gray floor with glowing carpets,
> He has bought them cheap
> . . . .
> He walks swiftly through the darkness
> as though it pursued him.
> He's right: it is pursuing him.

Another poem describes a stop at a filling station: "If you drive up to the ninety-six octane pump, / there's always another car, dirty, empty, / that simply stands there, God knows where the owner is." The details of sordidness, emptiness, and menace are many; the motorist should leave

> before someone from the gang that hangs around outside
> has time to tug at the door and with a face
> pale as paper, staggering, yell something
> you don't understand but that you're afraid of
> or get angry at later
> when you're alone on the road and the radio plays
> Vivaldi, wonderful, clear.

The selection *Dikter från trettio år* (1980; Poems from thirty years) might well be regarded as the summation of a distinguished lyric career; *Dagen vänder* (1983; The day turns) was made up of new poems but had the air of an envoy, as it paid tribute to some of Carpelan's affinitive spirits: the Runeberg of *Idyll och epigram,* the Finnish artist Hugo Simberg (in "The Wingshot Angel"), the sculptor Alberto Giacometti, and Friedrich Hölderlin in his gentle lunacy, "A countenance shadowed by moonshine." (The East Prussian poet Johannes Bobrowski, whose lyric aims much resembled Carpelan's, had already received a eulogy in *I de mörka rummen, i de ljusa.*) Carpelan's cultural gratitude was also the stuff of his *Marginalia till grekisk och romersk diktning* (1984; Marginalia to Greek and Roman poetry), glosses on the poets of classical antiquity, whose "clarity and balance, but also passion and bold concentration of images" he admired. In *År som löv* (1989; Eng. tr. *Years Like Leaves,* 1993) he turned to Hölderlin again, to Karen Blixen (Isak Dinesen) and the house at Rungsted where she spent her last decades, and most important, to his own parents. As he recollects a childhood excursion to Åbo Castle (triggered by an old photograph), the sun is suddenly obscured by clouds, and his father complains at the way his son slouches beside his mother, while the picture is snapped.

> I remember that we took a taxi into town.
> Everything was so strange, as if I had made a departure,
> the first one, without obvious causes. Now
> the day was open, others followed.

It was inevitable that Carpelan, fascinated by music, would recall that a member of his family, his great-uncle Axel Carpelan (1858–1919), had played a significant role in the career of Sibelius. When the novel *Axel* (1986; Eng. tr. 1988) appeared, Carpelan told an interviewer that the eccentric music lover had never been mentioned in his boyhood home; as an adolescent he came across the name — the composer dedicated his Second Symphony to this great and good friend — in Karl Ekman's *Jean Sibelius* (1935; Eng. tr. *Jean Sibelius and His Work*, 1935, 1938). A feigned diary of the clumsy amateur musician, the novel contained a double portrait, of the shy admirer and the often brutal composer; also, it was a kind of history of Finland itself, jotted down by the penurious nobleman, from the mid-nineteenth century (the notations or memories start with the great famine of 1866–67) to the Civil War of 1918. Beyond all this, *Axel* reflected the supreme devotion of its author to music; some of the diary entries are small musical essays. A stage version, in which Sibelius and his drinking habits loomed larger than in the intricate text, had long runs in Finland and Sweden. Carpelan's book of 1982 for young readers, *Julius Blom: Ett huvud för sig* (Julius Blom: A mind of his own), was, in a modest way, a preparatory study for *Axel;* Julius is also a sensitive outsider, marching to his own hidden melodies.

In December 1993 Carpelan was given the Finlandia Prize for his novel *Urvind* (1993; Primal wind), in which, as in *Axel,* there is a single voice, belonging to the secondhand bookdealer Daniel Urvind, who writes fifty-three quasi-letters to his wife, away in the United States, doing research at Harvard. These letters are seldom weekly reports; rather, they dip into the correspondent's past from childhood on. Naturally enough, there are resemblances to *Gården* and to *Jag minns att jag drömde,* but the bizarre cast that inhabits Urvind's apartment house is much larger than in those cases, and the number of literary and artistic allusions greater. The very title and the letter writer's name suggest Rilke's poem in the *Neue Gedichte,* "Uraltes Wehen vom Meer" (Age-old blowing from the sea) — the ancient, primal wind that both comforts humankind and blows it away into nothingness.

Doubtless, *Urvind* has some elements of a self-portrait; aging Daniel remembers little Daniel, gliding into sleep on his grandmother's couch. "Was it now, when I tried to capture the silences in my memory, that I was seized for the first time by the thought of writing, forming, setting down, seeking the proper words that at least could give fragments of the image of myself for which I looked." Carpelan is an artist of paradox: solipsistic in his poetic imagination but never egotistical, almost serenely in love with life's phenomena but beset by premonitions of ultimate catastrophe, a busy man of letters who has created a life's work of unusual solidity — but a life's work somehow fragmentary when it is at its finest: miniature lyrics, prose poems, dreams, diary entries, feigned letters that are no letters at all. Nevertheless, the whole career has been supported by a single belief in poetry's function: "The poet follows his own line, seeks his own voice, and rejoices, the older he gets, that human beings and things exist; theories and ideologies change, but the questions of existence remain. The good poem is forever topical, by refusing to renounce its innermost vision. It stands against what is evil, and for what is good. It opens our senses and always remains in the center of events: in the human heart."

A Startling Growth, 1960–1990

George C. Schoolfield

10

The Revolt: Kihlman, Donner, and the Serial Novel
In the Stockholm newspaper *Dagens Nyheter*, for 31 August 1959, Christer Kihlman (1930–) published the article "Svenskhetens slagskugga" (Eng. tr. "The Shadow Cast by Swedishness," 1986), in which he wondered why Finland-Swedish authors "do not compose 'broad' pictures of society," "why their books are often limited to internal psychological states," and "why they write a prose that is so remarkably impoverished," preferring to compose lyric poetry instead. An answer to his questions, Kihlman argued, lay in an intentional self-isolation of "cultured Finland-Swedes," who "during the first four decades of the century cut themselves off more and more from Finnish speakers, with an attitude of bitterness and exaggeration of self-worth leaving little room for contact across language lines." They had become "voluntary emigrants within their native country." As exceptions proving the rule, Kihlman pointed out two modernists, Elmer Diktonius of *Janne Kubik* and Hagar Olsson of *Chitambo*, novels in which these authors "took the whole of Finland as their point of departure." In conclusion, Kihlman implied that a vital Finland-Swedish prose narrative could come into being only when "inhibitory grievances" were abandoned.

Kihlman himself was a product of the Finland-Swedish cultural establishment at whose door he placed the blame. His great-grandfather, the schoolman and industrialist Alfred Kihlman (1825–1904), had directed the elite Helsingfors boys' school, the Swedish Normal Lyceum, and had erected the Kihlman House, a mansion that was one of the capital's architectural symbols of economic power. Christer Kihlman's uncle had been the critic, scholar, and editor of *Nya Argus* Erik Kihlman (1895–1933); Christer's father was Bertel Kihlman (1898–1977), a prolific translator, sometime editor of *Nya Argus,* and the author of a novel depicting the pre–Civil war atmosphere of Swedish Finland, *Idyll under åskmoln* (1936; Idyll beneath a thundercloud), a time to which he would return in the aptly named *I väntan på krevaden* (1966; Waiting for the explosion). Young Kihlman had entered on the family's literary path with the usual modernist verse, *Rummen vid havet* (1951; The rooms by the sea), in Rabbe Enckell's style, and *Munkmonolog* (1953; Monk monologue), which took its epigraph from Björling — Kihlman had become an intimate of the aging Socrates of Brunnsparken. With Jörn Donner (1933–), an offspring of an even more prominent Finland-Sweden house, he edited the little magazine *Arena,* which contained — like *Ultra* of old — contributions in both Swedish and Finnish and showed a special interest in belles lettres, not least those influenced by Marxism, from the East.

Neither Kihlman's poetry nor his work was exceptional, save for his always felicitous style; the appearance of the novel *Se upp Salige!* (1960; Pay heed, o blest!) came as a surprise and a shock. It did not attempt to do what the essay on Finland-Swedish isolation had promised; instead, with painful exactness, it looked at some Finland-Swedish cultural icons and, in particular, at the vaunted "idealism" already dealt a glancing blow in *Dagens Nyheter.* The book was set in Lexå, a small town not far from Helsingfors, and readers were quick to take Kihlman's punning onomastic point: Lexå was Borgå, the Finland-Swedish Weimar, the focal point of the Runeberg cult, and "lex" itself (Latin "law") was a reference to the minority's veneration for the Swedish legal code Alexander I had allowed the grand duchy to retain — the bulwark, some ninety years later, of resistance to czarist encroachments. Like England's "angry young men" (John Osborne, Kingsley Amis, and others) who had struck out against the alleged hollowness of British middle-and-upper-class values in the decade just past, Kihlman called attention to the perceived rottenness of the Finland-Swedish bourgeoisie (a term Kihlman much used) and patricianate. (There was no clear line of demarcation.) A newspaper editor, Karl-Henrik Randgren, feels overwhelmed by his father and his forefathers, "a clan that had led Finland and its destinies through a whole century, and had bravely withstood all the evil plots forged by Russian barbarism." Egged on by his friend Kimmo, the product of a lower-class, Finnish-speaking home, Randgren sets out to expose the hypocrisy of beloved Finland-Swedish institutions (for example, the shady election of a Lucia bride during the pre-Christmas season) but manages only to create a tempest in a teapot. In his private life the divorcé Karl-Henrik is equally unlucky or inept; willy-nilly, he helps drive his adolescent son, Gus — shipped off by his mother to his father in Finland, after expulsion from a Stockholm school—into suicide by his inattention and by his clumsy attempt to seduce Kimmo's daughter, of an age with the troubled boy. The novel created a hubbub in Finland proper (where conservative Finland-Swedes felt they had been caricatured) and in Sweden (where Kihlman confirmed Swedish beliefs that Finland-Swedish society was largely decadent). *Se upp Salige!* was made the more memorable, too, by Kihlman's wonderfully evocative writer's gift and by his satire—which, however, vanished from his later work.

In a quasi-sequel, *Den blå modern* (1963; Eng. tr. *The Blue Mother*, 1990), the locale remained the same, Lexå, but now Kihlman was interested—in contradiction of his own demand for a pan-Finnish novel—in the ingrown familial situation long a favorite topic of Finland-Swedish prose writers but never before portrayed in such intimate and upsetting detail. The Lindermanns consist or have consisted of a disciplined and distant father, now deceased; an indulgent but uncomprehending mother (the blue figure of the title); two brothers, Raf and Benno (a third and eldest was killed in the Continuation War); and an energetic first cousin, Fred—the father's favorite, he has taken over the family business. Raf is a heavily alcoholized writer, Benno a suicidal weakling. It is revealed that both the rampantly heterosexual Fred and the homosexual Benno, as well as a pederastic pastor, have had a part in Gus Randgren's emotional confusion and death, Fred by encouraging the boy to undertake an affair with a woman much older than himself, Benno by his "tenderness and admiration" for the boy. The novel did not disappoint Kihlman's many admirers and detractors, dealing as it did with Benno's fantasies of concentration camp sadism and Raf's marital difficulties; but it also betrayed a disturbing urge to editorialize and to let itself go in torrents of words (the latter tendency encouraged by the examples of the Swedish novelist Lars Ahlin [1915–] and the American William Faulkner, then at the height of his European popularity). Sharp-eyed critics also pointed out that the brilliant account of an imaginary sea voyage, delivered by Benno's sometime sanatorium roommate, the half-cracked Finnish intellectual Reino, was borrowed, in part, from Richard Henry Dana's *Two Years Before the Mast*.

Madeleine (1965) was a pendant to *Den blå modern,* an unbroken flow of prose set down without punctuation, a chronologically circular diary novel, beginning and ending on 22 November 1963, the day of John F. Kennedy's assassination, an event that robs the diarist, Raf, of his "belief and trust in a liberal, bourgeois order of society." If *Se upp Salige!* had been, in its best pages, a trenchant societal portrait (a reviewer compared it with Strindberg's *Röda rummet* [1879; Eng. tr. *The Red Room,* 1967), and if *Den blå modern*, in its unforgettable descent into Benno's imaginings, was a nightmare, *Madeleine* was, paradoxically, a kind of idyll: the personal (if not the political) storm passes over, and despite the neglected Madeleine's affair with the priapic Fred, the marriage of Raf and Madeleine is restored. Oddly enough, Kihlman never quite abandons his belief in the nuclear family. After a collection of literary and sociopolitical essays, *Inblandningar, utmaningar* (1969; Interventions, challenges), Kihlman once more rode to the attack on middle-class society with his most troubling book to date, *Människan som skalv: En bok om det oväsentliga* (1971; The man who trembled: A book about the unessential); in it he made capitalism, abetted by a vestigial Christianity, responsible for the sense of competition that had driven him to alcohol; aggressive public morality, also hand in glove with capitalism, was hypocritical in its condemnation of "deviant" sexual practices. The analysis of alcoholism and its causes was not a novelty in Finland's Swedish letters, but the frankness with which Kihlman revealed his bipolarity in the book's finale (sex between Kihlman, his wife, and a male friend: "We were generous toward one another . . . filled with the mutual respect that devotion bestows") opened wide the gates for the confessional literature that threatened to inundate Finland-Swedish (and even Finnish) literature during the 1970s and 1980s.

Having thus established a more or less new subgenre, Kihlman returned to the family novel with *Dyre prins* (1975; Eng. tr. *Sweet Prince*, 1983), in which the world of international business is entered by the upstart financier, Donald Blaadh, one of whose wives is a Lindermann, from the family introduced in *Den blå modern;* Kihlman's intent was to show, again, not only the brutal egotism of the self-made man but the chilly self-absorption of his distant relatives and in-laws, the von Bladhs and the Lindermanns, "wealthy, influential, bourgeois to the marrow." (For all his dislike of his own background, Kihlman has the typical Finland-Swedish fixation on genealogy.) Similarly, the internationalism of Blaadh's (and the von Bladhs') horizons and connections is nothing new—either in reality, since the days of the von Haartmans, the von Kothens, the Mannerheims, or in literature, since Gören Stenius, E. R. Gummerus, and then Marianne Alopaeus. *Mörkrets kärna* came out exactly a decade before *Dyre prins*.

Planning a sequel to the Blaadh-Bladh saga, Kihlman traveled to South America in search of material; instead, he was inspired to return to the personal account of *Människan som skalv*. In *Alla mina söner* (1980; Eng. tr. *All My Sons*, 1984) he told about his experiences with Juan, an Argentine male prostitute and would-be popular singer, revealing at the same time the social aspect of his erotic drive: the objects of his homosexual affections and genuine devotion were — and had to be — the children of poverty, an argument continued in *Livsdrömmen rena: Bok om maktlöshet* (1982; The pure dream of life: Book about powerlessness), in which the beloved is José and the scene for the most part Uruguay, through whose back country the aging admirer and the young man (the former playing Saul to the latter's David) careen in a rattletrap car: the romantic, improvised journey of many American novels, from *Huckleberry Finn* to Kerouac's road novels, is played out here with great vividness. The little poems and prose pieces Kihlman wrote for drawings by his friend Henrik Tikkanen, *De nakna och de saliga* (1983; The naked and the blest), reiterated Kihlman's message that any kind of erotic union provides epiphanic release. Still remaining anchored in the traditional family structure he affected to detest, however, Kihlman brought out another personal document in 1986, *På drift i förlustens landskap* (Adrift in the landscape of loss), about his jealous rage at a wife who has taken a lover in her husband's absence, a cri du coeur that becomes a lament at failing artistic powers — a comparison is drawn with Sibelius's long silence after the Seventh Symphony. The fear was premature, since the next year Kihlman returned to the Bla(a)dh family with *Gerdt Bladhs undergång* (1987; Eng. tr. *The Downfall of Gerdt Bladh*, 1989), in which Donald Blaadh's nephew is the head of a great Helsingfors department store, about to be eased out of his post by an efficient Finn, whose career Gerdt had once furthered. Well-known concerns of Kihlman reappear (Gerdt has a weakness for poor boys and is cuckolded by his wife), but the crumbling Finland-Swedish establishment is now treated more gently than before, and Kihlman resorts, as well, to elements of the supernatural, something new in his oeuvre and rare in Finland-Swedish letters, taken as a whole.

Undeniably important, Kihlman's work offers serious problems of evaluation. Although Kihlman has never produced the "Finland-Swedish *Buddenbrooks*" once expected of him, his novels extend the possibilities of the minority literature's large body of serial family narratives and, like his personal accounts and justifications, are invariably borne up by the sheer grace of his prose. On the other hand, his bisexual thematology has grown threadbare, he has repeatedly used devices that a critic of *Dyre prins* said belonged to the soap opera (secrets suddenly revealed, suicides, extremely complex erotic involvements), and he has included ponderous political and sociological pronouncements in both his fictional and his confessional books. For all his dislike of the United States's overwhelming role in world events and its capitalist example, a dislike in which he was scarcely alone, he belongs to a generation keenly aware of postwar American letters, as his very titles demonstrate (with their misleading allusions to Arthur Miller's famous play and Norman Mailer's equally famous novel of the 1940s). In his sexual obsessions and his basic concern (despite his announcement of 1959) with a privileged and limited social class, he is strongly reminiscent of still another American, John Cheever.

The initial resemblances between Kihlman and Jörn Donner are easily listed: the revolt against a conservative background and the concomitant leftward swerve. But where Kihlman at the outset was satirical and fairly subtle, Donner was brash, impetuous, sincere, and self-absorbed; *Välsignade liv!* (1951; Blessed life!) was a miniature novel or set of three stories about a boy and youth named Gustav, bullied at the countryside pension to which he has been evacuated during the Continuation War, bullied by his parents and siblings when he comes home, bullied by himself (divided into "I" and "I, Myself") in painful, idealistic disputes. *Slå dej inte till ro* (1952; Don't calm down) is once more a composite of four stories, full of social pathos and torment, of which the most unusual were views of homosexual and bisexual life in Helsingfors, partly executed with a kind of film technique. (This was the age of such Swedish films as Alf Sjöberg's and the young Ingmar Bergman's *Hets* [1944; *Frenzy/Torment*] and Bergman's *Fängelse* [1949; *Prison/The Devil's Wanton*] and *Törst* [1949; *Thirst/Three Strange Loves*]; already vitally interested in cinema, Donner published *Våra filmproblem* [1953; Our film problems] with Martti Savo.)

The shorter tales of *Brev* (1954; Letters), entering the world of amateur sport and hard-drinking student life, were a preparation for Donner's first (and never completed) suite of novels, *De förlorade* (The lost ones): in *Jag, Erik Anders* (1955; I, Erik Anders) the eponymous hero, bearing a "fine name" and belonging to "one of the old German families," upsets his family by his radical socialism and his writing for Marxist newspapers before setting out on a tour of the postwar Continent (Rome, Naples, Vienna, Budapest), a somewhat tedious demonstration of his — and Donner's — political concerns and erotic irresistibility; in *Bordet* (1957; The table), moving somewhat away from autobiography, Donner follows the empty and supercilious lives of moneyed Finland-Swedes, some of them related to Erik, in particular the cynical Harriet Granberg, in her twenties but already worn out by love and life. All these youthful works are immature and artistically clumsy but provide keys to the author's development; the journey of Erik Anders leads directly into journalistic skills brought to bear in a number of reportages: a particularly informative book on the former German capital after the airlift and before the wall, *Rapport från Berlin* (1958; Eng. tr. *Report from Berlin*, 1961), *Rapport från Donau* (1962; Report from the Danube), and the ambitiously titled *Världsboken* (1968; The world book), in all of which Donner escaped little Finland with a vengeance, giving evidence of a keen eye and (in contrast to the self-mirroring of his initial books) paying much greater attention to his topic than to himself. In the 1960s, too, he transferred his base to Sweden, becoming a film critic and, under the aegis of Ingmar Bergman, to whom he devoted a book, *Djävulens ansikte* (1962; Eng. tr. *The Films of Ingmar Bergman*, 1972), turning himself into a film director of stature.

With the completion of his political change of heart, Donner recommended a plan for a competitive and capitalistic society to his home country in *Nya boken om vårt land* (1967; The new book about our country), issued on the fiftieth anniversary of Finland's independence, with a title conjuring up Topelius's patriotic primer of almost a century before, *Boken om vårt land*. (Like almost all Donner's production after his salad days, the prescription for Finland's economic health appeared simultaneously in Finnish.) As for his temporary base, he did not hesitate to point out the shortcomings of that social paradise in *Sverigeboken* (1973; The Sweden book) — less wittily, to be sure, than Alopaeus would in *Drabbad av Sverige*. (The question of Sweden was much on Finland-Swedish minds in the 1960s and 1970s, when migration across the Gulf of Bothnia, encouraged by the neighbor's booming economy and welfare benefits, was frequent, especially among the disadvantaged of both minority and majority.) After personal escapades, fascinating to the tabloid press, he eventually transformed himself, thanks to preternatural energy (and his undeniable talent as an administrator of the Swedish Film Industry and Finland's Film Institute), into a preceptorial figure, hearkened to by the general public; a highly visible columnist in both the country's languages (he saw to it that his columns also appeared between book covers), from 1987 on he was a representative of the middle-of-the-road Swedish People's Party in the Finnish Parliament.

Donner had also become a creative artist of some stature, producing two series of books — the one autobiographical, the other fictional — that, again because of the breadth of his views, attracted a large readership in Finnish Finland: he aspired to a role as a genuinely national author. The first series is an ongoing record of his attitudes and shifts of opinion, illustrated by telling anecdotes and meaningful facts (of which Donner always has a large store on hand). The journal he kept of his alternative service (as a pacifist) in *På ett sjukhus* (1960; At a hospital) had been a preparatory step in this direction (and inadvertently revealed how Donner, born with a silver spoon in his mouth, was immediately able to take advantage of any situation); in *Sommar av kärlek och sorg* (1971; Summer of love and grief) he explained, among much else, his rejection of his leftist phase; *Jag, Jörn Johan Donner* (1980; I, Jörn Johan Donner) was a more personal account. Yet Donner, amid the confessional excesses of the 1970s, was actually less willing to perform self-analysis than to give his opinions on what he saw and questioned. In general, he has been a perspicacious detector of the large social and political patterns around him but not a piercing commentator on individual personalities or on himself — a curious reticence on the part of a man so constantly willing to put himself on display.

In the 1970s, enjoying the freedom of expression about sexual matters now possible in the written word (as on film), Donner weighed in as a novelist once again with his *Marina Maria* (1972), with the subtitle "A Newsstand Novel, A Feuilleton, An Entertainment, An Attempt, One Thing or Another," in which, among much else, there is an erotic encounter between mother and daughter. Immediately afterward he turned to more serious fictional pursuits, the chronicle of the decline and fall of a great Finland-Swedish industrial family, members of which had already been met in *De förlorade* of the 1950s, from the eve of the Second World War onward, beginning with *Nu måste du* (1974; Now you must). Its reprint, fifteen years later, as *Den sista sommaren* (The last summer), was a sign of the public's abiding fascination with the dynasty. As in Kihlman's books about the Lindermanns and the von Bla(a)dhs, a connecting system of characters goes from novel to novel: a central figure is Gabriel Berggren, a man from the other side of the tracks (like Donald Blaadh) who, as it were, twice marries into the Anders family, first the younger sister of the family's grand old man, Erik Anders (bearing the same name as Donner's youthful alter ego), and then, after a divorce, her niece Angela. In 1976, with *Angelas krig* (Angela's war), the series took up Angela's past, her wartime affair with a German officer, and the revelation, in *Angela och kärleken* (1981; Angela and love), that the officer was bisexual; Angela's younger brother Jakob, involved with Soviet agents in cold-war Berlin, was introduced in *Jakob och friheten* (1978; Jakob and freedom). In what is regarded as the artistic highpoint of the series thus far, *Far och son* (1985; Father and son), a novel manuscript, left behind by the late Jakob, is read and interpreted by the narrator, who in turn sets out in search of his own father. Yet Gabriel Berggren, who in *Gabriels dag* (1982; Gabriel's day) had made an effort during the 1950s to fight off an attempt by a corrupt member of the board of directors to take over United Metals, returns in *Frihetens fångar* (1988; Prisoners of freedom), bringing events to 1961, the year of his retirement. It revolves around the plan of his successor, the efficient Finn Virtanen, to rationalize and dehumanize the old firm.

Ever the experienced reporter (he published another factual book, *Rapport från Europa* [Report from Europe] in 1990), Donner has a sovereign command of his settings, at home and abroad, and is constantly aware of changes in the Finnish scene, shown, for example, by the appearance of the new, clear-sighted, and hardhearted master, Virtanen, in *Frihetens fångar*, a figure closely resembling the Finnish straight-arrow in Kihlman's *Gerdt Bladhs undergång*. (Neither Kihlman nor Donner is as glad to see the destruction of Finland-Swedish tradition and power as once he believed he would be.) Employing a tried-and-true film structure, Donner is also skillful at introducing figures from political life into his narratives, which occasionally may be read as romans à clef; in *Presidenten* (1986; The president) the republic's long-time leader, Urho Kekkonen (1900–1986), is seen in full-length and unflattering decay through the eyes of one of his mistresses. (A wise and sensitive Kekkonen also made a cameo appearance in Kihlman's *Dyre prins,* in contrast to the radical demotion he gets in *Presidenten* and in a burlesque episode of *Frihetens fångar,* both of which appeared after his death.)

In many respects, the mature Donner would remind Americans of an artistically more ambitious William F. Buckley — self-assured, vastly knowledgeable, conservatively nonconformist; his enormous novelistic output, his attention to financial detail, and the range of his cast have led critics to compare him with Balzac, but a Balzac lacking the ability to create living characters, save in those instances where he deals with what may be a personal crux (as in *Far och son*) or draws straight from life. One wonders if Kekkonen, who in all-around masterfulness resembled Donner himself, will return in subsequent volumes of the United Metals series, should the public demand its continuation.

While the serial novel, portraying the present or a recent past, flourished in the hands of Kihlman and Donner, a similar kind of chronicling had gone its parallel way in historical fiction. The carefully researched and neatly written series of Margit von Willebrand-Hollmerus (see chapter 9) began with *Hedvig och Desirée* (1941; Hedvig and Desirée), about the comfortable estate life of the 1870s, and came forward to the present in *Bunden och fri* (1946; Bound and free). The proper world (of entanglements, marriages, small jealousies, births) portrayed with considerable psychological acuity by von Willebrand-Hollmerus was also entered by Barbara Winckelmann (1920–), with *Farväl Julie* (1961; Farewell, Julie) and the trilogy (drawing on her ancestors' lives) *Käpphelvetet* (1971; The cane hell), *Mer än älska* (1973; More than loving, a tag from *Fänrik Stål*), and *Och dagen kom* (1975; And the day came). The last-named is about the lovely Anna Ekhammar's marriage to a general in czarist service twenty years her senior, her passion for a young lieutenant, her divorce and a second union, her beloved husband's service in the Russo-Turkish War of 1877 (she draws on the military surgeon and dramatist Ferdinand Wahlberg's *Härfärd till Turkiet* [see chapter 8]), the happy years of life together, and the death of the husband from asthma a little before the turn of the century. Turning to portrayals of Helsingfors life in the eighteenth century, Winckelmann did not pretend that all had been roses in the world of the forefathers; in the picture of Helsingfors in *Din vredes dag* (1977; Day of your wrath) and *Bortom gryningen* (1979; Beyond the dawn) she broke with propriety and looked unflinchingly at the brutality of the venerable past: a terrifying episode in the latter book describes the gang rape of a servant girl in the town jail. Winckelmann was clearly aware that the energetic commercial and military class that dominated Helsingfors in the last century of Swedish rule depended on — and was indifferent to — a despoiled proletariat. *Kejsarstaden* (1982; The emperor's city) moved forward a generation, to the city's rebuilding under Johan Albrecht Ehrenström after the establishment of the grand duchy in the war of 1808–9, and continued with *Stenslottet* (1984; The stone castle). *Stad i uppror* (1986; The city in tumult) takes up the chronological thread, but not the characters, of the trilogy about Anna Ekhammar, in the days of czarist oppression, the Great Strike of 1905, and the Sveaborg mutiny of 1906. In all Winckelmann's novels Helsingfors itself is at the core, more alive than many of her human creations. Winckelmann has kept her eye on anniversaries as well; like Carl Fredrik Sandelin and Antti Tuuri, she has had her say about the Winter War of 1939–40 in *Fyrtio vintrars snö* (1989; Forty winters' snow).

New Narrators: Bargum, Cleve, Fors

Of the prosaists who came to center stage in the 1960s, Johan Bargum (1943–), started early, like Donner a decade before, but unlike Donner, immediately had a sure artistic hand. Like Kihlman and Donner, Bargum revolted against a conservative family background; but the revolt was only skin deep — one suspects Bargum learned his economy of style and means from his maternal grandmother, Margit von Willebrand-Hollmerus, with whom he spent a good part of his boyhood. (His mother, Viveca Hollmerus [1920–], likewise made a sally into novella writing during the 1950s.) Bargum's impressive debut was *Svartvitt* (1965; Blackwhite), six stories, of which "The Demand Bid" (*Swedo-Finnish Short Stories*, 1974), about a young man estranged from yet deeply attached to a religious father, gave a taste of a favorite Bargum theme to come, the strains of family affection and family dislocation; the collection also bore another of Bargum's marks, the sudden intrusion of violence into normal or even humdrum circumstances. The line continued in *Femte advent* (1967; Fifth Advent), with portraits, at Christmastime, of lonely and unhappy people: a father snubbed by his son, a suicidal nymphomaniac, a drunken Santa Claus.

Bargum fell into the rhythm of regular and careful production that has been his system ever since; *Tre två ett* (1969; Three two one) expands the exploration of violence, petty and large; a television soundman, the prodigal son of a well-to-do family, meets fascistically inclined members of the middle class and admirable working men, the closest Bargum ever came to the programmatic baiting, or analysis, of prosperous Finland-Swedish society practiced by Kihlman, the young Donner, and Claes Andersson (see below). (Always interested in cabaret, plays for stage, radio, and television, Bargum collaborated with Andersson in a number of short theatrical works.) *Finsk rulett* (1971; Finnish roulette) did not indicate a change of theme — as before, the weak are debased by the (relatively) stronger — but Bargum's narrative technique was further refined by means of a filmlike presentation of action scenes (a waitress's bloody revenge for sexual harassment, a police chase through the skerries) and a selectively detailed construction of milieu and atmosphere. Recently closed summer homes of the affluent are taken over by the fugitives (the waitress and her nastily superior boyfriend) during an unusually warm September.

In *Mörkrum* (1977; Darkroom) Bargum began to cultivate a form that would become especially his own, the quasi–detective novel in which a puzzle is ostensibly solved, albeit the investigator is still baffled. (Bo Carpelan's historical detective novel *Vandrande skugga* came out the same year; this was also the time of the international success of the thrillers by the Finn Mauri Sariola [1924–85] and the Swedish couple Per Wahlöö [1926–75] and Maj Sjöwall [1935–].) A free-lance photographer, come down in the world but devoted to his grandmother and little daughter, investigates the death of a retired farmer, relocated to Helsingfors and neglected by his children, a not uncommon fate in a Finland moving away from an agrarian economy. In *Den privata detektiven* (1980; The private detective) a former police inspector pursues his daughter's sordid secret; in *Pappas flicka* (1982; Daddy's girl) a woman in middle age, with artistic ambitions, half falls in love with the young man who is her model. Shattered by the death of a beloved father and out of touch with a practical-minded husband and daughter, she stumbles onto the father's hidden past: the handsome boy is her half-brother.

In *Sommarpojken* (1984; The summer boy) the narrator decides at his mother's funeral to locate his father, a search that makes him relive the summers he spent as the poor-boy companion of rich children at a vacation cottage; in *Den svarta portföljen* (1991; The black briefcase) a tired reporter — another of Bargum's hesitant Holmeses — tries to solve a dangerous riddle of the international drug trade; in the masterpiece of reduction, *Sensommar* (1993; Late summer), a stay-at-home — his brother has become a success in America — tries to figure out his mother's secrets after her death, including a possible incestuous relationship with the more attractive sibling. The reader has become the detective and, with the narrator, is left unenlightened at the end. Quite apart from the emotional and intellectual puzzlers these novels provide (in their steady, quiet, and quite unmysterious prose), they demonstrate Bargum's effectiveness as a depicter of Helsingfors streets and sections (see the grandiose shabbiness of Skatudden in *Den privata detektiven*) and of the offshore islands, those classic summer places of Finland-Swedish vacationers. Far less the reformer (social, economic, political, sexual) than Kihlman and Donner, Bargum is most interested in character, motif, place, mood, concerns that have also served him well in his plays, from those about the trials of small businessmen, *Tre skådespel* (1974; Three dramas), to the radio play about AIDS, *Finns det tigrar i Congo?* (1990; Are there tigers in the Congo?), done in collaboration with the director, Bengt Ahlfors.

An admirer of the novella art of Runar Schildt (two of whose tales he dramatized in the 1980s), Bargum has recently returned to the story, the form in which he so brilliantly began. In *Husdjur* (1986; Domestic animals) he presented three pet stories (wry accounts of human attachments, voluntary or not, to animals, including a ravenous guinea pig concealed under the narrator's shirt on a flight to Paris) and four others in which animals function as symbols, revealing a new side of Bargum's talent, an ability to slide over into the supernatural (as, more scurrilously, Kihlman did in a main episode of *Gerdt Bladhs undergång* the next year) — signs of the so-called romantic 1980s. This unexpected whiff of inexplicable mystery is essential to "The Architect," the first of three stories in *Resor* (1988; Journeys), in which a daughter suspects that her father, living in retirement at his summer place, has first been visited and then crushed by the giant elk of death. In this story, as in its companions (on a publisher cuckolded by a lazy windbag of a poet, with whom he is forced to share a room at the Lahti Writer's Conference, and a movie director who experiences flashbacks to a nasty childhood that has resulted in a deformation of his personality), Bargum demonstrates the taut control that sets him off from Kihlman and Donner; unlike the former, he never obviously enters the autobiographical realm, and unlike the latter, he maintains a constant interest in the varieties and subtleties of human behavior. Notably, Bargum may have made the most inclusive response to Kihlman's old demand for an inclusion of both segments of Finland in the Finland-Swedish novel, simply because of the absence of distinguishing linguistic-ethnic features in many of his characters and his overriding concern with general human characteristics. But something perceptibly Finland-Swedish clings to the spoiled youths and déclassé technicians of Bargum's earlier novels, and to the class-aware and emotionally frozen characters of the later ones, and this Finland-Swedish gallery is perhaps more clearly perceived (by author and reader alike) than the "others" in Bargum's work, whose names or social position (waitresses, honest working men, displaced farmers) may imply that they belong to the linguistic majority.

The debutant of the fifties who made the most extensive penetration into the Finnish world of Helsingfors would become, late in his truncated and ultimately disappointing career, the spokesman of an aggressive and almost anachronistic Finland-Swedishness. Anders Cleve (1937–85) began with verse born of Elmer Diktonius and Eva Wichman: *Dagen* (1955; The day) had as its most memorable part a suite of nine Helsingfors poems clearly Diktonian in their enthusiasm for children and the city's gull-inhabited harbor districts. *Det bara ansiktet* (1956; The bare countenance) was composed of four extensive suites: about the message of St. Francis of Assisi; "The Spring Comes Staggering," about humanity's fate and the imminence of a third world war; "Woodblocks and Nails," another Diktonian title, with the subtitle "Attempt at a Personal Synthesis Escape Attempt Attempt at a Confession of Faith"; and finally, "Love in Helsingfors," the fable of an affair between "a cur from the great market" and a "snowmelterbird," poems that in their vivid imagery and wordiness looked forward to the strengths and mortal weaknesses of Cleve's prose. With *Gatstenar* (1959; Paving stones) Cleve created a Helsingfors classic; certainly, in its inclusion of the Finnish majority and its sheer vitality it readily met the requirements set up by Kihlman in his essay. The quartet of stories—which quickly went through three editions and was translated into Finnish by Pentti Saarikoski—was widely reviewed in Finland and Sweden; in the latter country some critics were put off by its Helsingfors-Swedish slang, shot through with Finnish (and some Russian) words and turns of phrase, while others, including Åke Runnquist in *Bonniers Litterära Magasin*, defended the unusual linguistic dress—the detractors, Runnquist argued, betrayed a deplorable provincialism. (When N.-B. Stormbom's translation of Väinö Linna's *Tuntematon sotilas* was published by Wahlström & Widstrand in Stockholm in 1963, it came equipped with a vocabulary. Anglophone readers, used to dealing with textual representations of the many variants of English, have learned to be more resilient in confronting riddles of vocabulary and syntax.) Actually, what Cleve did was not a novelty; his idol, Diktonius, had drawn on nonstandard Finland-Swedish in *Janne Kubik* and *Medborgare i republiken Finland,* often in order to indicate a Finnish speaker; Cleve was even bolder than his master. Cleve's deed was never remotely approximated by Kihlman and Donner, both of whom were relatively classic in their language attitudes; its example was followed by a number of writers in the next decades, particularly those from the punk-rock terrain of the late 1970s and 1980s.

Another characteristic of Cleve's book which had a precedent in Diktonius's and Wichman's Helsingfors sketches was the author's deep affection for his characters, an affection that could, to be sure, soften into sentimentality. In "The Janitor" (*Swedo-Finnish Short Stories,* 1974) a strong man is hollowed out by cancer; in "The Embryo," which had the subtitle "Or the Morrow's Humanity: Legend in Eight Chapters," young lovers decide not to have a pregnancy terminated; in "The Licentiate," the only one of the stories dealing with a middle-class, Finland-Swedish milieu, an academician, having worked ten years on his dissertation, is shattered by its rejection but saved by his wife's love; and in "The Crow — An Individualist" a lonely and ugly woman defies death as long as she can. The main entity in all the stories, though, is the capital, detested and beloved: "The Gulf of Finland poured its sour breath in over Helsingfors. From all five harbors, all at once, the heavy masses of air rolled over the poor city. The breath of the Gulf of Finland was heavy and wet. I don't think I'm telling a terrible lie if I say it resembled the slushy fish soup served at all the city's greasy spoons. Or maybe I'm getting closer to the truth if I compare it to Russian cucumber's special spiced sauce." Helsingfors becomes a city that can be tasted.

His critical star was on the ascendant, but Cleve never again equaled the accomplishment of *Gatstenar.* Not that his love for his home city or his ability to conjure up its atmosphere had abated; in his first novel, *Vit eld* (1962; White fire), the Swedish novelist Lars Gustafsson detected Cleve's wonderful sensitivity to the city's moods (and to the "weak but still distinct influence from the east . . . a presentiment of something foreign" [p. 850]); both in the stories and the novel Cleve had demonstrated how aware he was of "Greek Orthodox piety," whose grand ceremonials and forgiving piety appealed to him just as they had to Tito Colliander. Yet the novel, like its successors, suffered from gigantism; its central figure, the writer Georg, sees and records too much. He also has enormous sexual appetites, imitating the satyriasis of Ask Burlefot in the Norwegian Agnar Mykle's *Lasso rundt fru Luna* (1954; Eng. tr. *Lasso Round the Moon,* 1960) and *Sangen om den røde rubin* (1956; Eng. tr. *The Song of the Red Ruby,* 1961), which had led to Mykle's much-publicized trial for pornography in 1957; on a singular occasion when Georg's powers flag, his beloved of the moment feeds him a wonder-working powder formerly used to give energy to members of the German Wehrmacht. All the same, the book, in which the word "intensive(ly)" appears again and again, has impressive passages, in particular on Georg's affection for the spirit of a much older Helsingfors (and for the spirit of universal love, which so constantly informs Cleve's work); here Cleve draws on Sigfrid Aronus Forsius's *Physica,* the attempt of the town's first poet to explain the nature of the universe (see chapter 6).

Påskägget (1966; The Easter egg) came next, dealing with friendships in the Helsingfors Bohème; the literary references have been replaced to a good extent by musical ones; a rush of childhood memories competes with the contemporary city, closely observed, and with imaginary scenes from the Thirty Years' War. (Cleve was an instructor in history at the high school level.) The next stage of the quasi-trilogy about the problems of Finland-Swedish artists and authors at home and abroad was fittingly titled *Labyrint* (1971; Labyrinth), in which the protagonist — this time not Georg or Michael, as in *Påskägget,* but Martin — is a devoted schoolteacher, as well as a painter and sculptor, whose energies and interests are much the same as those of his fictional predecessors. In this third big book Cleve openly admits to his admiration for Thomas Wolfe (a model whose wordy influence had long been suspected): detailed descriptions of the flora and fauna of the old Swedish-speaking region of Porkala stand side by side with Prague, Berlin, Paris, London, Manchester, Stockholm, Bruges, and Lübeck. Further, the novel pays exceptional attention to the decimation of Finland's Swedish-speaking population. The climax comes when Martin is pitted in a television debate against the minister of education, who wants radically to reduce the number of Finland's Swedish schools. (The minister is easily identified as Reino Henrik Oittinen [1912–78], one of whose goals was to make English, not Swedish, the first "foreign" language for Finnish-speaking schoolchildren.) In some circles Cleve was seen as a rocker of the national boat; his novels did not appear in Finnish translation, and he was the only Finland-Swedish author of note to be omitted from a guide to Finland's recent literature issued by Finland's Library Union in 1975. To be sure, the guide, otherwise dependable and useful, appeared during the long hiatus that came between *Labyrint* and *Locknät* (1981; Lure net), a last work defined by Cleve's growing sense of persecution, exacerbated by his belief that a politicized and intolerant cultural climate had sprung up in

Finland-Swedish literary circles (and not just there), a "destructive spirit created largely by the so-called radicals, for example the group [around] *FBT*," a magazine of which more is said below.

In *Locknät* Carl, "a writer in early middle age," is tormented not just by the presence of the radical Left but by his perception that he is a member of a timid and dying minority ("Carl got a helpless, desolate feeling that the Finland-Swede's determination to use his language outside the home was utterly a thing of the past"), by his fear of a coming ecological catastrophe (Willner called the chaotic book "the first and most single-mindedly ecological novel in Finland-Swedish literature" ["Anders Cleve," 69]), and by the personal problems that had beset, in one way or several, his predecessors: a turbulent marriage, extramarital involvements, and a growing alcoholism, as well as the protagonist's conflicts with his parents. An authorial revelation may lie in Carl's question about his father, the "intelligent pastor" Engman: "Had his father ever understood [Carl's] artistic strength, his human intuition, and, above all, that which was special for him, his visionary gift?" As so often in Finland-Swedish fiction, Cleve had repeatedly written the story of his own life; his "intuition" and occasional "visionary gift" gave his four novels their remarkable strength but also, never disciplined, made them increasingly unreadable, save by the patient investigator of his tragic case.

Cleve was not the only narrative talent for whom great hopes were held and then shattered. Hans Fors (1933–92) began with a run-of-the-mill lyric collection, followed by the far more impressive short stories of *Blå infart* (1955; Blue entrance), *Nattens rötter* (1962; Roots of the night), *Ohördas rop* (1971; Cries of [the] unheard); one, "The Journey to Karl Axel," appeared in *Swedo-Finnish Short Stories* in 1974), and *Påminnaren* (1973; The reminder). Although from Vörå in Ostrobothnia, a favorite site for his stories (others were Helsingfors, usually seen through the eyes of an outsider from the purely Swedish-speaking region of Fors's youth, and vacation places abroad, especially a tourist's Spain), Fors did not want to be regarded as a regionalist. In his four collections—in retrospect, his most important contribution to literature—his interest lay with the development of the short narrative's technical possibilities, especially in the deployment of carefully distinguished characters: the disoriented old man in "The Journey to Karl Axel," the overage workman and diarist of "The Bridge," in the same collection of 1971, and the lonely old patient awaiting an operation in "The Fall" in *Påminnaren*. Like Solveig von Schoultz, Fors had a predilection for those whom age or illness had rendered useless.

Fors moved slowly away from the form that had fascinated him; perhaps he felt that he reached a larger public with the brief radio play. A collection of nine works in this small format, where much depends on the quick presentation of character by means of easily comprehensible dialogue, was published in 1984 with the title, telltale for Fors's attitude toward his medium, *Röster, händer utsträckta* (Voices, hands outstretched). Its introduction, called "The Theater that Crept into Your Ear," is a general history of the radio play as a European phenomenon and is based on Fors's long experience, from 1966 to 1981, as assistant director and then director of Finland's Swedish radio theater. Writing for the stage, particularly for Ostrobothnian summer theater, Fors was a success of the moment; but it is doubtful that these works, historical in setting and theme, have any lasting literary value, despite the attention and time he gave them. They stretch from *Korsholm* of 1962, produced in that castle's ruins at Old Vasa, to the ambitious *Makten och härligheten: Skådespel från 1600-talets Österbotten* (1985; The power and the glory: A play from Ostrobothnia of the seventeenth century), with musical plus pageantry stage effects, a large cast, and the black-and-white characterizations typical of such outdoor undertakings.

The scriptural title of this festival drama, however, describes the direction Fors's other creative work took during the last decade of his life. As in Cleve's case, Fors's often proclaimed humanitarianism had a nondenominational Christian underpinning, and his lyric novel *Josef från Arimatea* (1982; Joseph of Arimathea), in which twenty-one "songs" are interlarded in the prose memories of the man who provided a tomb for Christ's body, gave full expression to his religious bent. The attention Fors paid to details (for example, the horrifying descriptions of the several modes of crucifixion) took a different form, though, in the limning of Ostrobothnian country life during the 1930s, which Fors—hitherto more concerned with emotional states than the milieus surrounding them—introduced into the otherwise often lyric or even ecstatic prose of what may have been planned as a serial novel in several volumes. In his stories Fors had avoided the use of dialect and specifically Ostrobothnian things or places; in *Livets bryggor: En berättelse om Österbotten* (1980; Life's bridges: A tale about Ostrobothnia) this hesitance was abandoned. The plainly autobiographical novel begins with the birth of Johannes ("The cry was first. It burst out of warm darkness, slime, vapors, then sudden coldness and hardness") and proceeds slowly to the "little old man's" anxious realization that the prospect of war—the Winter War of 1939–40—hangs over an Ostrobothnia in which memories and hatreds of the Civil War are still quite alive (despite a wise elder's reminder that "we are all human beings, and alike"). *Under höga träd* (1990; Beneath lofty trees) continued the story with a greater wealth of characters (as Johannes's world expands), in a countryside whose self-containment has been penetrated as never before: by the yarns of returned emigrants, by radio broadcasts in which Finland suddenly is at the heart of international attention, in the aftermath of the "cruel and devilish deed" of the Soviet attack on 30 November 1939, and by Hollywood films, about which poor Johannes, for the most part, can only read: "Johannes dreams of Errol Flynn, the incomparable, who with his Olivia de Havilland is shown at the movie houses of Helsingfors." The novel ends with the armistice of March 1940 and the strange mixture of relief, anxiety, and disappointed hopes it brings. "People should sing and dance, shout hurrah and throw garlands of flowers. And airplanes should throw down funny papers, pictures of Snow White, Mickey Mouse, and Donald Duck."

Varied Talents: Järner, Valtiala, Ralf Nordgren, and Others
One of the curiosities of the sometimes desultory history of Finland's Swedish literature is that V. V. (Väinö Vilhelm) Järner (1910–), an author old enough to be the father of Kihlman or Donner, Cleve or Fors, came into the public eye at much the same time they did. Not surprisingly, Järner too took his first literary steps in verse, sentimental, exalted, military-patriotic, based on his experiences during the opening of the Continuation War, *Blått och frontgrått* (1942; Blue and front-gray), in which traces of Gripenberg or Örnulf Tigerstedt can be found ("From Eystrasalt to Trollabotnar / there blows a Nordic wind / — springsong, sweep away and whip, / awake and call, bind / the sons of the North together, / blow life into the beacon's flame"). Other verse collections, less symptomatic of the times, followed, as Järner pursued a career in elementary school teaching in Borgå and participated in the Finland-Swedish Dramatists' Society.

He came into his own with the novel *Torget* (1956; The marketplace), in which his hometown of Borgå — but not the classic "Finnish Weimar" of Runeberg — got a due of a kind it had never received before. The bilingual Järner, whose last name until 1939 had been Viherkoski, set up an array of the quaint and sometimes foul-mouthed denizens of the town's market square, each of them speaking an idiosyncratic Swedish; little reviewed in Sweden, *Torget* escaped the linguistic objections to which Cleve's *Gatstenar* was subjected three years later. Järner's benevolence, full of humor and sometimes bathos, toward his cast and its behavior in the years between the Civil War and the Winter War resembled Sigrid Backman's treatment of the people of Rödbergen, likewise economically pinched, mostly good-natured, and linguistically (if not always politically) indifferent. To be sure, Järner includes pockets of leftover resentment, such as toward the German sausage seller J. P. Müller, who, it is rumored, first came to Finland as a noncommissioned officer in Rüdiger von der Goltz's Ostseedivision, the German expeditionary force that had a major part in putting down the Red revolt of 1918: with considerable irony, he is called a "patriot" by his fellow vendors on the square.

In the 1960s Järner's reputation took an upswing, thanks to his plays, which, as critics did not tire of saying, provided the Finland-Swedish and Swedish stage with equivalents of the works of Samuel Beckett and Eugène Ionesco. Like the dramas of Walentin Chorell, which now seemed a little dated alongside Järner's sparse and sometimes brutal exposures of human frailties, Järner's plays got the unusual honor of coming out in print—*Tre skådespel* (1962; Three plays) and *Tre pjäser* (1973; Three theater pieces); but the procedure was not necessarily to Järner's advantage, since they were meant to be acted, not read. In Järner's dramatic realm the characters are customarily few and are confronted by the ugly fragility of age, the last flickerings of family or erotic life: the ancient bon vivant and the retired seamstress of *Goubitsky och jag* (Goubitsky and I), grotesquely aping burnt-out passions; the double-chinned society lady and her well-paid private chaffeur in *Leve generalkonsuln!* (Long live the consul general!), whose lunatic household ("Alex likes to say I'm daffy, but he's the one who's daffy") is disturbed during a rainstorm by a chance visitor, a swimming teacher accompanied by his rubber dummy Anna, "specially constructed for the illustration of artificial respiration"; a retired movie theater owner, his wife, and his sometime flame, the cinema's pianist, in *Ta fast malen!* (Get the moth!); a rickety couple in *Skyddsrummet* (The bomb shelter), listening to a tape recorder that incessantly plays "Make love, not war." Järner's more ambitious plays are less effective: *Exekutionen* (The execution), about jealousy and betrayal in an unspecified war, harks back to German expressionist drama of at least half a century before—a seedy nightclub, its cynical or hysterical clientele, sudden bursts of machine-gun fire, sudden searchlight beams sweeping the stage. *Fru Blubes hus* (Mrs. Blube's house) offers another group of frightened folk, six travelers, terrorized by an invisible Fru Blube; one of the old ladies asks, with obvious overtones of omnipresent angst, "Hasn't Mrs. Blube always threatened us? . . . as long as we can remember?" Like Chorell and Fors, Järner also wrote extensively for radio and television; one of these plays, *Eva Maria,* on a mother-daughter tug of war, was included, translated from manuscript, in Kai Laitinen's *Modern Nordic Plays: Finland* (1973).

Järner's last published work was *Fackeltåget* (1978; The torchlight procession), the life of a Borgå schoolboy who becomes a schoolteacher, from the czarist twilight to the final term of President Kekkonen, that is, some seventy years: it stands out among its many companions in the autobiographical novel because of its quick tempo and time sweep. Another of the book's novelties, within the traditional form, is the use of a narrator who, cheerfully chattering, tells about the fate of Celsius Winter yet seems to be almost one with him; and its constant dipping (in the fashion of an aged character in one of Järner's plays) into Celsius's memories provides a further perspective. Celsius is an ironically inclined but patient outsider: from a poor working man's bilingual home, he changes his surname from Talvi to its Swedish equivalent in order, he says, to improve his chances of getting a job, during the depression days (1935), in the Swedish-language school system. He has tried to be loyal, he recalls, to Borgå's Runebergian tradition but has never "received an invitation to the annual reception at Runeberg's home on 5 February," since he is still regarded as a Finn. Järner's gently mocking voice was a pleasant contrast to more strident criticisms directed at the frozen gods of the Finland-Swedish tradition.

The implicit forbearance that marked the sometimes fascinating, sometimes inchoate prose of Cleve, Fors, and Järner was shared by other prosaists quite uninterested in the misdeeds, real and fancied, of the establishment. The comical novels of Peter von Martens (1932–83) almost monotonously repeat a message (shared with the infinitely more serious Kihlman) of redemption through sexual satisfaction, cost what it may. Von Martens found his particular tone with the marriage novel *Järnsängen* (1960; The iron bed) — "'Lasse, do you think we'll get to make love in heaven?' Anki asked. 'Of course,' I said. 'What else could you do there?'" — and with the overlong erotic contes, told on a train, of *Gamle vän* (1963; Old friend); then came the burlesque novel *Caroline* (1966), whose eponymous heroine piously uses sex to good ends. In *På Karlssons himmel* (1970; In Karlsson's heaven), a novel that the kindly Claes Andersson called "uniquely harmless," von Martens ventured out into the cosmos with a slovenly wretch who is given spiritual depth by helpful beings on a flying saucer; the world comes to an end as he lies in the arms of a beloved prostitute. *Kråkslottet* (1978; The tumbledown castle) has elements of the detective story (mysteries and revelations surrounding the death of a faithless husband) and of fey situation comedy; the widow and the departed's best friend at last find passion together but in a dream sequence unsupported by any stylistic bravura. For von Martens, a euphoric state must somehow be achieved; the self-doubting and highly potent Mikael of *Nu sjunger fåglarna igen* (1973; Now the birds are singing again) tries hard to persuade himself that the happy end will inevitably come, "that the whole world is full of human beings who can be hugged and that the birds still sing if only one listens."

The spotty career of von Martens was filled out by the travel book *Solen på Mallorca* (1967; The sun on Majorca), the island that he loved; the career of Nalle (Kaarle Juhani Bertel) Valtiala (1938–) has likewise swerved among novels, novellas, and travel and essay books but has had access to a much greater variety of ideas. Among his factual productions are the early ecological volume, *Varning för människan* (1968; Warning for—or against—mankind, an intentionally ambiguous title), and several light-fingered volumes of essays about American culture and letters—*Notvarp i Saragassohavet* (1972; Netcasting in the Saragasso Sea), in which he introduced some twenty American writers (including Henry Miller, whom he interviewed); the more historical *Res västerut, unge man!* (1978; Go west, young man), concentrated on great moments of American literature, art, and thought in the eighteenth and nineteenth century, from Hector St. John de Crèvecoeur to Melville and Twain; and *I Mark Twains hjulspår* (1982; In Mark Twain's wheel tracks), a tour going from an aborted visit to New Haven and Yale (he was frightened away by reports of crime, slums, and drugs) to Kennedy Airport, by way of Hannibal, Missouri, and Big Sur; more exotically and learnedly, he also wrote about a year of anthropological research spent in Tonga (1974).

In his creative work Valtiala has been similarly eclectic. His early stories, in *Landet Marita och andra noveller* (1961; The land of Marita and other novellas), *Åtta noveller* (1963; Eight novellas), and *Äventyret* (1965; The adventure), were best when he stuck to Finnish milieus, as in the story "The Foe" in *Åtta noveller*, about creeping fear and violent homosexuality at a half-deserted military installation, or its companion in the same volume, "The Brother," on adolescent insecurities. Valtiala was bound, in time, to try his hand at the novel, where he showed empathy with the vagaries of sexual behavior while never achieving the awful intensity of Kihlman in *Den blå modern*, a book to whose shattering of taboos Valtiala, like others of his generation, was indebted. In *Lotus: En berättelse om kärlek* (1973; Lotus: A story about love) he presented a lesbian affair (with a sad ending) and, much later, in the far more complex book-length prose poem on mythological themes, *Narkissos* (1988), he dealt with all the shadings of erotic experience in a fashion so dense as to discourage even the most prurient reader. (Michel Ekman, reviewing the year's prose ["Finlandssvensk skönlitteratur 1988," 87], confessed that *Narkissos* utterly surpassed his understanding.) During the intervening years Valtiala—constantly *rerum novarum cupidus*—had tried other, less obscure subjects; in *Nationens hjälte* (1985; The nation's hero) he used some bare facts of the Lindbergh baby's kidnapping to tell an American tale of a great aviator's homoeroticism and his wife's frustrations, of babies exchanged and lives wasted under false identities and amid false dreams. (Valtiala's numerous references to American authors reveal how his earlier essays had fed his fiction.) Elements of the detective story constitute much of the Lindbergh novel; the spy novel provided the core of *En galen tebjudning* (1991; A mad tea party), in which — à la Bargum — the intrigue is never cleared up. During his career (which also included extensive activity in radio theater) Valtiala has been carried along by his willingness, typical of a time when Finland's new prosperity and the jet plane made globetrotting easy, to switch scenes and themes. Nonetheless, an ability to penetrate very deeply into any of his topics seems not have been vouchsafed him; the Lindbergh novel is filled with stock figures, tough detectives, drunken former beauties, besotted officers, sensitive blacks. But he has surely escaped "the Finland-Swedish novel's narrow room," to use Merete Mazzarella's winged phrase.

A debutant of the 1960s who stayed closer to home was a second-generation author, Ralf Nordgren (1936–), the son of the determined leftist Aili Nordgren (not altogether sympathetically portrayed in some of her son's autobiographical novels) and thus the nephew of Sally Salminen. (In a further mingling of literary families Ralf Nordgren married the daughter of Thomas Warburton, who in turn was the granddaughter of Rabbe and Heidi Enckell; just so, Christer Kihlman had married the daughter of Rabbe Enckell's brother, the painter Torger Enckell.) In one of his later novels of self-representation, in all of which he figures as the writer Breng, Nordgren tells how he suddenly began to compose poetry in the midst of his job as an inexperienced substitute teacher at Helsingfors's best boys' schools, where Breng, the offspring of parents notorious for their Red leanings, felt like a fish out of water. Yet his parents' world had begun to pall on him; his father gave him a typewriter on which the capital letters no longer functioned. "It didn't surprise me. The machine had worked for the Communists so long that it was a miracle it could even produce small letters." As a lyricist, Nordgren had a talent for forging catchy names: *Folk klättrar omkring* (1964; People clamber around), *På fri fot* (1966; Set free), and *Vägen till himlen stängd* (1970; The road to heaven's closed), a short poem which indicated that Nordgren could occasionally resist pressures to pillory society's ills:

And [I] yearn for the place
where the day is an opened sky,
I want to see lights as lights from higher space,
and the darkness shall be black.

In the time-honored propagandistic tradition acquired from Diktonius and Wichman, however, he concluded: "This is our only performance. We / give no repetitions. / And the road to heaven's closed."

Idyll och program (1972; Idylls and programs, a variant on Runeberg's *Idyll och epigram*) goes down a similar double path, on the one side portraying almost paradisiacal scenes of country life (with which Nordgren maintained an authentic contact, through Ostrobothnian relatives) and on the other writing verses heavy with social realism:

> I speak with a machinist
> about his machine . . .
> I never think of art. I
> help a bricklayer
> put up a new house.

All these laudable deeds will take place "tomorrow" after "we sweep up capitalism's colorless ashes." (The poem's name is "We Must Believe This.") In *Åttonde dag* (1974; Eighth day) political rhetoric, and the old Diktonian dream of effecting revolution through poetry, completely got the upper hand: "The poem becomes a way to be silent / or changes the country"; *Stensamling* (1979; Stone collection) again lets lucidity become obviosity: emptying a bucket of garbage and water, the poet realizes that "many people he has met / have passed through memory's sewer pipe." By *Jag kan inte säga för mycket* (1983; I cannot say too much) the brevity that had been his most effective lyric weapon vanished, as he weaves the story of the fate of Finland's Communist Party into touching memories of Ostrobothnia:

> In a remarkable fata morgana Närpes emerges
> I see my father.
> In his youth he stands leaning against a fence. He
> has the country musician's third fiddle stuck under his arm
> and the bill of his cap cannot conceal that he mumbles: "Here I am
>   nothing."

The vision is uncomfortably combined with reminiscences of the French anthropologist Jean Duvignaud's book (1968) about social changes in Chebina, a village in the North African Maghreb.

If Nordgren became a persistent verse-voice of the far Left in Finland-Swedish letters in the 1960s and 1970s (he fell silent as a lyricist during the more aesthetic 1980s), as a novelist he was an always interesting and critical chronicler of himself, or the persona very much like him. The Breng series began with *Med* (1968; Along) and continued with *Fjärilsörat* (1971; The butterfly's ear); he returned to it in *Det kluvna äpplet* (1989; The split apple), in which Breng is divided into two beings, Lector Ralf, responsible teacher of Swedish literature at Helsingfors University, who cannot rid himself of the political-emotional burden taken over from his parents ("I can very well *think* that it does not matter what happens to the Communist Party, I'm not a member, but I can never get rid of my feeling for them"), and Jean Breng, the creative alter ego ("I must be where you are"). All three books have a permanent value in the views they give of Finland's less than placid social and political history (for example, the memorable description of the great strike of 1956 in *Med,* the student reception at President Kekkonen's official residence which is the climax of *Fjärilsörat,* the recollections of the gauche student's humiliation at Nyland's fraternity-sorority in *Det kluvna äpplet*), as well as snapshots of such disparate personalities as his stubborn mother (whose poem to her four-year-old son from her verses of 1940, *Rödbränd mark* [Earth burnt red] Nordgren quotes *in extenso,* with self-ironizing intent: "My son, one day you'll be a general / in the little army / which fights for freedom and right!") and the contemporary film maker Aki Kaurismäki, demonstrating the latter's wildly improvisatory mode of work.

In other, less self-descriptive novels Nordgren has not been able to free himself altogether from the orientation absorbed with his mother's milk, although, like Lector Ralf, he manages to bring a modicum of objectivity, if not impartiality, into these parallel performances. *Det har aldrig hänt* (1977; It has never happened) is a fictionalized account of the Åland murder of two Red emissaries from Åbo in the winter of 1918, based on Nordgren's research in the sparse documents that survive; in a melange of impersonal balladesque narration, bawdy café storytelling, and interjections by the omnipresent Breng, the overlong *Stjäl dig ett liv* (1980; Steal yourself a life), the unifying background is Ostrobothnian village life — marital devotion, strains between brothers, concentration camps (one of the brothers recounts his internment in Nazi Germany while the other listens in disbelief), bloody murder, and reconciliation. Then, using his penchant for humor in a more coherent way, Nordgren wrote *Pianobärarna* (1989; The piano movers), concentrated on the thinly disguised capital of Åland (here called Ariehamn) in 1946, about to be visited by Soviet cultural representatives. But as in *Stjäl dig ett liv,* other time-and-place elements are intermingled: inevitable memories of 1918, scenes in the Soviet Union before and during the Second World War, New York of the 1930s (a bow to his mother's past), Åland on the eve of the armistice of 1944, when the German Dr. Fischer abruptly leaves for a fate unknown. Not unexpectedly, after the visiting Russian pianist's Steinway has been lugged into the concert hall, music brings all those present into a human unity even greater than that promised by friendship with the Soviet Union. At the end a simple man who plays the fiddle (and who helped carry the piano) is invited to Moscow and, in his hotel room, writes a letter to his beloved wife, at home in Ariehamn: "He tells several times how he loves his Agnes, and how one day the whole world will sing in peace." Yet, as he falls asleep, he does not notice how the cracks in the ceiling grow ever wider. Nordgren's effects and symbols are transparent enough, as is the central problem of his authorship, bent toward the far Left yet much too sophisticated or too skeptical to accept the heritage his mother bestowed on him in the poem of long ago.

Andersson and the Poets of FBT
The energy of Jörn Donner has its equal in the case of Claes Andersson (1937–), save that Andersson has unfailingly directed himself to unselfish social goals and, turning away early from his middle-class background, has remained faithful to his leftist but always humanitarian principles; since 1987 he has been a member of the Finnish Parliament as a representative of the Democratic Union for Finland's People, the bilingual party formed in 1944 by Finland's Communist Party and the socialists of the far Left. In 1993, in fact, he was his party's candidate for the presidency of the republic and, as minister of culture and sport, is a member of the cabinet. Determined to aid humanity in deed as well as in word, Andersson made medicine his profession and psychiatry his specialty; after an imitative lyric debut with *Ventil* (1962; Ventilator), in which his household gods were the quiet poets Tuomas Anhava and Bo Carpelan and the considerably less quiet Pentti Saarikoski, he struck out on his own with *Som om ingenting hänt* (1964; As if nothing had happened). Clas Zilliacus, a particularly intelligent analyst of Andersson's large lyric production (p. 153), has compared this title with Saarikoski's *Mitä tapahtuu todella?* (1962; What actually happens?), remarking that the title and the book's thematology (the enormous importance of seemingly small events) prefigure Joseph Heller's *Something Has Happened* of 1974. The unsentimental empathy of Andersson with suffering was apparent on just about every page—a woman used up by men, a homeless victim of alcohol, the victims of a plane crash, the inmates of an asylum.

The tight bond of Andersson to his home city, transformed by all too sudden growth and all too heavy traffic, informs *Staden heter Helsingfors* (1965; The city is called Helsingfors): "The old houses . . . simply disappear / while the new houses grow up toward the sooty sky / the higher the greater the crowding becomes," a city in which he meets "people without identity / wandering with glances aimed toward nowhere." In this volume Andersson coined one of his many quotable lines (he has been as generous as Runeberg with specimens of simple, direct, and vivid diction): "My poem is open as a marketplace," but his dreamed-of open city ("I love the city as a poem / populated by people in different colors") is built on a real place full of horrors that can be comprehended only by cool description, by an explosion of hideously insulting words (the catalog of obscenity concluding the poem about the "spiritual landscape" of Alexandersgatan, Helsingfors's Fifth Avenue), or by the irony of flat statements (out in the ever-growing suburbs there is "what a modern person needs / There are waste disposals / An elevator that thinks / while floors are imperceptibly changed"). The sequel was *Samhället vi dör i* (1967; The society we die in), a title that (again a Zilliacus observation) refers to Ragnar Meinander's school textbook on sociology, *Samhället vi lever i* (1952, 1954, 1956; The society we live in). Zilliacus has also noted that much of the book's imagery is about eating or being eaten (p. 157); the overture says, "The cat comes out with a bird in its mouth / USA sinks into the sea with Asia in its mouth," and the long poem "Hamlet-66" tells, with a physician's exactitude, what happens to a body after death, devoured by "various bacteria with various sorts of names."

For Zilliacus, Andersson is a poet who not only writes but reads; in his medical poetry he is clearly a descendant of Gottfried Benn (the author of "Morgue"); in "Political Anecdote" Brecht may be at work—Andersson gives the imperialism of the Nixon and Johnson presidencies the form of a fossilized fish, which choked on another, smaller one, some ninety million years ago and is now preserved in a layer of stone in Kansas ("once covered by seas"). This poetry of international reference is spiced with specific items of Fennica: a poem mocks the championing of "Swedishness" by the newspaper editor Axel Lille (1848–1921), and Andersson tosses him into history's dustbin, together with memories of his own father on leave during the Continuation War ("Swedishness? Axel Lille? My father? / The picture grows yellow and blurred / I leave you and go out into the sun"). Also, he argues that poets are useless:

You can't eat poetry
It's not for people in need
but rather for those whose lack
is of another sort.
Poetry is not a lie detector but the lie itself.

The physician's calling is honest in its hopelessness, confronting a patient long in coma: "He's been lying unconscious for three years / after a motorcycle accident / He's in good general condition."

The grim irony with which Andersson meant to shake his readers out of their unwillingness to think and feel ("Worst of all is indifference, / Worst is that it doesn't concern me") permeates *Det är inte lätt att vara villaägare i dessa tider* (1969; It's not easy to own a summer place these days); Zilliacus calls attention to the somewhat different meaning "villa" has in Finland-Swedish usage from normal Swedish (p. 158). In this flawed masterpiece Andersson demonstrates his full range of poetic techniques, some older (the dizzying catalog of "Disassociations," the definitions of "Capitalism Molecules Us," the repetitive love song "Étude for Summerwind") and some newer and essentially antipoetical (the pseudo-official document "Statue-ology for Elementary Schools," the set of comments in "Detailed Inventory for a Biography of Marshal C. G. Mannerheim," a minibiography of a venerated figure whom Andersson, like many of his generation, detested). (The poem presages Veijo Meri's deadpan Mannerheim biography of 1988, save that Meri was no longer obliged to hate the man who was "Finland's Savior" for the Right and "The Slaughterer" for the Left.) Unhappily, Andersson's propaganda can become point-blank: "We had red banderoles where we had written: / USA — Murderers," and he can vie with Nordgren, that other loud voice of the demonstrating sixties, in tear-jerking effects: "The American deserter was beaten to the ground / the police kicked him across his scrotum / Just when I felt hatred coming I saw that one of the policemen wept."

The title of *Bli, tillsammans* (1970; Become, together) is exhortatory in a gentle way, quite unlike the biting titles (and contents) of the past decade; an almost wistful note ameliorates the expected radicalism carried over from the immediate past; "This is a poem about holding hands / It is warm and soft with a mouth full of laughter," albeit the wistfulness (bordering on the maudlin) is spiced by Andersson's surprising images: in the innocently titled "A Dream," the poem's speaker performs an autopsy on himself as a child and, inside, finds the "good smell of licoriced apples and freshly baked bread" and his "grandmother up on the spleen, knitting," as she reads a tale of Topelius. *Rumskamrater* (1974; Roommates) and *Genom sprickorna i vårt ansikte* (1977; Through the cracks in our countenance) complete the long suite of collections in which social (or political) commentary, though not always predominant, is a major preoccupation. In them Andersson continued to apply all the persuasive devices he had made his own over the years: the attack on official euphemisms ("Rob us and call it political economy, / Make us homeless and call it regional planning"), the fables in Brechtian style (the comparison between a tank and a snail), the *faux naif* recitation on hospital roommates ("The first had been changed to a housecleaning machine / The second had been changed to a little child / The third had cut off his member in loneliness / The fourth's weeping kept the three others awake"), the anecdote ("Stalin and Lenin Meet for the First Time," based on the event at the socialists' congress in Tammerfors in 1905: "Between the lectures they practiced target shooting in the park"), the confession ("Slowly I come to life after a bad depression"), and the specifically Finnish idyllic vision (the poem about the beloved composer Oskar Merikanto [1868–1924], which draws on both Andersson's considerable sentimental side and his musical awareness). Everywhere Andersson determinedly follows his program of disturbing his readers, of not being a "likable person"; "Likable people make me sick! They wish everyone well, / They wish no one well" is a total text from *Rumskamrater*. As he said repeatedly, he wrote not "pure but impure poetry."

Long before, in 1965, Andersson had been a founder, and became the principal editor, of the journal FBT, one of the little magazines in which the history of twentieth-century Finland-Swedish literature has been rich. To this day, the initials remain a mystery — an announcement made on Walpurgis Eve, the Finnish Halloween, offered a list of things the acronym did *not* mean, such as "Finlands bästa tidning" (Finland's best newspaper) and "Fröken borstar tänderna" (The young lady brushes her teeth); but its intent was clear enough: it was "the new dustcloth in our Finland-Swedish anteroom." Continuing publication until 1968, the journal was not limited to literature; it provided a forum for the presentation of such current topics as gender roles, anticolonialism, children's culture, city planning, Marxist aesthetics. Its main contribution to letters was the so-called modernist debate, a violent attack on the alleged unengaged attitudes and "nature mysticism" Andersson and his colleagues detected in the poetry of Södergran, Björling, Rabbe Enckell, and their epigones. (The poetry of the rebellious Diktonius, whom Andersson manifestly admired, required no condemnation; but Diktonius too, in his idyllic poetry and prose of the 1930s, had been co-opted, and Andersson, collaborating with Tua Forsström, wrote a play, given at Little Theater in Helsingfors, about his apostasy.)

As the great surviving representative of the modernists (and, whether he wished it or not, a representative of the Finland-Swedish cultural establishment), Rabbe Enckell — since 1960 resident in the Poet's Home at Borgå — became the whipping boy of FBT and of Andersson himself, who, with an unworthy poem in *Som om ingenting hänt* ("Waking Up, An Ordinary

Morning, Dedicated to Rabbe Enckell"), had made a vulgar attack on the aging master and his ivory tower. The details of the feud — which called to mind the excesses in the debates that had swirled around modernism in the early 1920s, save that now modernism's supporters had the conservative role to play — are too complex to be recorded here; Enckell accused his critics of "ignorance, lack of upbringing and broad aesthetic views, indifference, arrogance and unfairness," in the summary of Bror Rönnholm (p. 278). Seen objectively, Enckell's charge that FBT created an artificial enmity between generations in order to call attention to itself has some justification, just as Andersson's criticism of Enckell's "one-sided overemphasis on the nature lyric in particular and private elegiac cadences" (p. 280) is not without foundation. Whatever the rights and wrongs, the debate aroused interest in the manifold possibilities of lyric composition to an extent that, paradoxically enough, had not been equaled since the golden age of modernism; and, in Andersson, the FBT spirit had a highly capable and effective voice: he could practice what he preached.

By the end of the 1970s Andersson's poetry had turned away, in some measure, from calls for a transformation of society; the very nature mysticism (and elegiac notes) at which he had complained came prominently to the fore in *Trädens sånger* (1979; The trees' songs). Even though the volume contains a takeoff on a famous modernist text, "Take all my longing, says Miss Södergran, / Okay, bring it here, I am still crowded by it / It clings like a leech to all my clothes," the message of the concluding tree suite is one of Södergran-like union with nature: "Leaves in my eyes, earth / in my mouth, I love the trees my cousins." To be sure, Andersson still advanced tried-and-true topics meant to stir up his readership, as in the suite dedicated to the Communist poet Elvi Sinervo (1912–86), imprisoned by Finland's government during the Continuation War, and in "Locked Wards," about degrading conditions at mental hospitals, already described by him in the novel *Bakom bilderna* (1973; Behind the pictures). But after the great demonstration of strength in the 1960s and 1970s he entered a period of some artistic exhaustion, and in the finale, significantly named "Summary," of his *Tillkortakommanden* (1981; Shortcomings), he totted up the manifold agonies and ecstasies of his life. By means of autobiographical fiction, *Den fagraste vår* (1976; The fairest spring), he had already looked back at the youth revolt of the 1960s; in *En mänska börjar likna sin själ* (1983; A human begins to resemble his soul), a title taken from the Norwegian Aksel Sandemose's *Det svundne er en drøm* (1946; The past is a dream), he turned to personal problems. A psychiatrist is tormented by domestic vicissitudes (his live-in lover of long standing and his children leave him, the life-support systems of his home, septic tank and furnace, break down) and by personality disturbances (he hallucinates while watching a peace parade, participates in a teenagers' orgy, and becomes tentatively involved with a male prostitute). The freedom of self-revelation that had become widespread in the 1970s, especially after Kihlman's *Människan som skalv* (where Andersson's sometime wife has a bit part), have made considerable inroads here.

Andersson's further lyric collections of the 1980s go along the same personal path: *Under* (1984, a title that may mean "Miracles" or the preposition "Under") opens with eighteen "Living-Together Elegies" about the pitfalls of cohabitational life and continues with poems that, among other things, are devoted to the musician Thelonius Monk (Andersson himself is a jazz pianist), to the hometown ("When I was young / Helsingfors was a middle-size city with cobblestone streets"), and to a middle-aged Andersson, whose dreams "have forgotten the sea which gave birth to them / my dreams have forgotten that they had love." More and more, the poems have the air of improvisations at an imaginary piano, cadenzas that lead, eventually, back to the original key: family life, group actions such as a soccer match (another of Andersson's manifold fields of enthusiasm), and then, much more darkly, the possibility, still hanging heavy, of world destruction—a fear addressed in *Mina bästa dagar* (1987; My best days) in tones of deepest despair: "you never know where it's going to begin / to burn, that which shall burn, like / the family in the Bronx that didn't get out / of the tenement." This terror is coupled with personal anxiety: "What happens with the madness in / my own cells?" and "Fear of death gives my life its principal content." At length, in *Som lyser mellan gallren* (1989; Which shines between the bars), nostalgia for the clear-cut battle lines of a quarter-century ago sets in: "the boundaries are / torn down in Europe to be raised against the world"; solutions or consolations, such as they are, are increasingly sought in the private or even intimate sphere. Sensitivity provides the title and theme of *Huden där den är som tunnast* (1991; The skin where it is thinnest), in which Andersson dedicates poems of understanding to his father and mother, who have so often appeared in his lyric books over the years. The family remains of essential importance for the sometime revolutionary. Tua Forsström (1946–), to whom a poem in the collection of 1991 is dedicated, wrote an afterword to a selection from Andersson's poetry, *Det som blev ord i mig: Dikter 1962–1987* (1987; That which became words in me: Poems 1962–1987), and, characterizing his verse, called it "the meeting between stinging nettle and butterfly orchid."

Editorial colleagues of Andersson at FBT did not have his staying power;

their experiments in "impure poetry" declined, once the glory days of radicalism were past. Johan Mickwitz (1937–) got critical attention with a miniature novel called *Nattvinge* (1963; Nightwing), in which reviewers detected traces of the bored flaneur mentality of fifty years before; a similar chilliness appeared in the prose poems of *Vassvinter* (1961; Reed winter) and the short poems of *Sandsten* (1962; Sandstone) and *Uppgörelse* (1964; Settling accounts):

> sunhaze and sedatives.
> only a cold breeze that, now and then,
> makes us wrap the blanket
> tighter
> around our
> greased limbs.

But in *Fröken Ur ville inte komma* (1968; The time lady didn't want to answer) Mickwitz found an effective way to apply his cold grasp in political-erotic poems:

> It was a summer
> when bombs fell thick on Viet Nam . . .
> That was the summer we awoke and noticed
> that we were alone
> together.

With the prose poems, sometimes tiny editorials, of *Året ingenting hände* (1973; The year nothing happened, a title indebted to Andersson and Saarikoski), Mickwitz returned to the peripatetic manner of *Nattvinge,* making tour after tour through the restaurants and bars of Helsingfors, constantly disturbed by the news from the outside world: a "renaissance of force" is taking place and the year is 1968. But in *Bättre tider måste komma* (1975; Better times must come) Mickwitz decided that, in fact, nothing *had* happened since the Soviet occupation of Prague in 1968; in a poem dated 8 October 1973 he noted:

> Six years later
> [there are]
> the same tanks, the same pursuit planes
> the burning houses and twisted bodies.

After a silence of five years Mickwitz returned with *Mera du* (1980; More you), a veritable catalog of disappointment. Despite his awareness of ongoing injustice and brutality, he is still caught in emptiness: "All these sirens that are not able to awaken us to something long since lost / These signal fires of tumbledown barricades."

Mickwitz was an elegist of revolution, prepared almost from the start to doubt the efficacy of any verbal gesture; Robert Alftan (1940–) was a more troublesome and innovative figure, turning out little books that first accompanied and then continued the work of FBT. His debut, *Splitter* (1964; Splinters), came out on the eve of the journal's birth and immediately introduced altogether impure poetry, as in the often anthologized "Portion," whose tough stance (and culinary images) seemed to bring Diktonius back from the dead:

> with warm sausage I take strong mustard
> and stare all my eyelashes away
> I have slapped life raw in myself
> and without icecubes.

Vida gavlar (1968; Wide open) was a poetry book with a difference; quite literally pasted together, it was an assembly of objets trouvés, beer labels, pieces of telephone books, old postage stamps and labels, amateur photographs, turn-of-the-century sheet music. *Slagsidor* (1975; another punning title: "Lists," as in a ship's tilting, or, literally, "Striking pages") left no doubt about Alftan's view of Finnish society; the imitation national anthem, "Our Country," perhaps inspired by Diktonius's "Our Country No. 2" and parodying Runeberg's original, proclaimed, "Alcohol runs here / water and hymn tunes / in honor of a double moral standard." Just a year before, in the prose of *Våra gossar på Cypern* (1974; Our boys on Cyprus), Alftan had expressed his skepticism about Finland's participation in the United Nations' peacekeeping force on the half-Greek, half-Turkish island. After that, Alftan went his own way, leaving standard publishers and bringing out pamphlets at his own "House of Revolt." Mickwitz and Alftan should not be forgotten because of their silence once the flush of (very bloodless) revolution was past: Mickwitz's skeptical or cynical reaction to a world he saw in capitalist collapse and Alftan's crazy scrapbook are relics of the radical spirit that deserve preservation.

Huldén and Companion Blithe Spirits

In 1969 the venerable Finnish house Otava published a bilingual anthology, *Lyrik i Finland nu/Suomen lyriikkaa tänään* (Lyric in Finland today), which contained poems by twenty-seven Finnish and Finland-Swedish poets; the editors were Mauritz Nylund and Mirjam Polkunen. The poems were printed in both the original and the other language, and the translations were mostly made by poets who had their own contributions in the volume. Of the twelve Finland-Swedish representatives, seven—Alftan, Claes Andersson, Lars Huldén, Mickwitz, Ralf Nordgren, the editor Nylund, and Solveig von Schoultz's daughter Barbro von Schoultz—were designated by the author of the anthology's introductory essay, Kai Laitinen, as associated with FBT and with its interest in social problems rather than linguistic or stylistic display. The statement needs some modification. In Lars Hulden's case a concern with words is palpable from the very start of his career, as well it might be. The son of Evert Hulden, he grew up under an unusual constellation: his father ran the family farm but had keen intellectual concerns, and his uncles were pedagogues; both strains, country life and learnedness, were in Lars Hulden's blood. As a philologist, Hulden distinguished himself by his studies in dialectology and onomastics, becoming docent in Swedish at the University of Helsingfors in 1958 and professor of Nordic philology in 1964; he retired in 1989, to give himself entirely to his creative work and his numerous public appearances: always an attractive figure, he occupied the Poet's House at Borgå for twenty years, from 1972 to 1992. Also, again because of his love of language, he demonstrated an awareness of the Swedish poetic tradition taken large, in particular the Swedish poets of the seventeenth century, Georg Stiernhielm among them, and the great rococo songwriter, Carl Michael Bellman. Hulden liked the verbal ornamentation, the jokiness, and the teleological implications of the baroque and, in Bellman, not only the mixture of wit and melancholy and the allusive vocabulary of Gustav III's great entertainer but the musical factor: Hulden has himself been a fecund writer of cabarets and musical comedy texts. Nevertheless, in his exceptional career Hulden has not been a learned professor-poet, although envy has occasionally called him that; his popularity—in Swedish Finland, in Sweden itself, and in the Finnish-language realm, through the translations by Väinö Kirstinä—is sufficient contradiction of such charges.

More or less of an age with Bo Carpelan and Peter Sandelin, Hulden made a late debut because of his academic studies; once he was under way, however, with *Dräpa näcken* (1958; Slaying the water sprite), it became apparent that a distinct new voice had entered Finland-Swedish poetry. (Some of Hulden's early titles, taken from childhood games or other Ostrobothnian practices, defy full translation.) This voice depended on an extreme clarity of surface diction, shot through with manifold ironies and allusions and built on a close connection to the country life of Hulden's boyhood and an intense and urgent musicality and sexuality. *Speletuss* (1961; Blithe spirits) and *Spöfågel* (1964; Whipperwit) expanded the same veins; the rhetorician Huldén added poems on linguistic morphology, in which grammar is coupled with nature ("the grass's grammar may well seem simple") and the pleasures of poetry writing ("Poet's a person with built-in bathroom"). There is substantially no obvious reforming message in these poems, an absence of propaganda that makes them, remarkably, all the more forceful reminders of social difference, just as the unobtrusive but surehanded references to an Ostrobothnian locale give them a kind of universal regionalism. *Enrönnen* (1966; Lone rowan) and *Herr Varg!* (1969; Sir Wolf!) had a darkening tone amid the humor ("Oh sense of humor, you're as dear to me / as dear to me as the blanket was / my mother used to swaddle me (and fastened it with safety pins)." Quoting from the Swedish poem of Bengt Lidner (1757–93) on a Sicilian earthquake, Huldén describes an atomic catastrophe or ponders, in a most baroque way, eternity (with an epigraph from Lasse Lucidor [1638–74]):

> Every hundred years
> a librarian comes
> takes down the book from the shelf
> blows off the dust that's gathered
> and reads this poem.
> When the whole poem
> has been thuswise worn away
> a second of eternity
> has passed.

The Wolf of 1969, it may be added, devours the poem's speaker.

As a university professor, Huldén was often called on to provide occasional poems (thus putting him in a great chain of academic-festival performers stretching from Torsten Rudeen past Topelius to Hjalmar Procopé), and he managed to give them his special stamp, as he did in the amusing but disturbing grammatical poems of *Dikter i fosterländska ämnen* (1967; Poems on national themes). With *Herdedikter* (1973; Pastoral poems) he turned both to cyclical poetry and to the erotic eclogue, in a collection whose passionate poetry, at once learned, elegant, direct, and exciting, has no real Finland-Swedish or Swedish equivalent: to be fully appreciated in its mixture of restraint and revelation, it should be read alongside Kihlman's self-justifying confessional books and Andersson's laments about the travails of cohabitation. A Theocritan-Virgilian influence could be spied in the pastoral poems; Huldén provided a related classical exercise in the distichs of *Läsning för vandrare* (1974; Reading for wanderers) and the hodoeoporic verse of *Island i december* (1976; Iceland in

December) — having already transformed Ostrobothnia into a northern Sicily, he was equally sensitive to the atmosphere of the North's locus classicus. Constantly full of new plans springing in like measure from his roots and his word fascination, Huldén published a bilingual volume (Ostrobothnian dialect and normal Swedish on facing pages) in *Heim/Hem* (1977; Home). Then he turned to the greatest Ostrobothnian of them all — with whom he fortuitously shared a birthday — in *J. L. Runeberg och hans vänner* (1978; J. L. Runeberg and his friends), poems that sometimes are glosses on Runeberg's own texts, sometimes are couched in a skillfully reconstructed Runebergian tone, and sometimes mildly mock the bard ("National poets are needed principally / for the sake of the parodies and allusions"). *Dikter vid särskilda tillfällen* (1979; Poems in special occasions) is its pendant, containing still another version of Runeberg's national anthem, now called "Our Land, Our People": "Our land is poor but gets along quite nicely" is a trenchant thrust at the Finnish idealization of poverty, venerated even as the nation was hot on the trail of prosperity.

Perceptions of change (not always for the better) and of aging, as well as of a kinship to a particular part of the Ostrobothnian past (the migration to the United States and Canada), are all present in *Jag blir gammal, kära du* (1981; Darling, I am growing old, a quotation from E. E. Rexford's sentimental song of 1873), a book also including Huldén's recollections and mythologizings of Wisconsin, at whose university he served as guest professor. It seems almost incongruous to write of pessimism in Huldén (where the usual estranged complaints of twentieth-century poets shine by their absence); but the contemplation of autumn, winter darkness, and atomic destruction, in *Mellan jul och ragnarök* (1984; Between Christmas and Ragnarök), and of imminent death in *Judas Iskariot Samfundets Årsbok 1987* (The Judas Iskariot Society's Yearbook 1987) — see the "Farewell to the Mother Tongue" ("Soon I shall join the proud band of the dead") and "Quiet as the lake lost in the forest's reaches" — appear to constitute a last will and testament, as does the disingenuous apology for his apparent and unfashionable simplicity: "I've read much about imagery." The churchless church songs of *Psalmer för trolösa kristna* (1991; Hymns for faithless Christians) are expressions (with music) of his never failing popular urge and a reminder that Huldén has fitted himself into the role of Runeberg as hymn writer and into the inherent Christianity of his Ostrobothnian childhood; as before, there is a chilling perception that life is over, stated in "The Darkness Gathers," quite lacking the consolation of John Keble's hymn, "Abide with Me," to which Huldén's text alludes.

Some of these "hymns" come from surprising places; "Morning with Mist by the Sea," for example, has been lifted from one of Huldén's musicals, *Smugglarkungen* (1977; The smuggler king). A detailed treatment of Huldén's oeuvre would have to take into account his works for the theater, such as the play about Edith Södergran, *Resan till Raivola* (1992; The trip to Raivola), and his Shakespeare translations. His true contribution to Finland-Swedish (and Swedish) letters, however, has been as a lyricist sui generis, of genuinely wide appeal — an apparently unsophisticated quality has kept him from some accolades that Finland's poets of the difficult school have received. Not a beater of his own breast, Huldén has never written a novel, autobiographical or otherwise; just the same, he has moved into prose on three noteworthy occasions, first with *Hus* (1979; Houses), in which the topic is the desuetude of old buildings in the Ostrobothnian countryside and the victory of technology. (As he gave the book its bare title, Huldén may well have thought of Carpelan's *Gården* or the street-address titles of Tikkanen's series.) In 1990 he returned as a prose writer with *Berättelser ur mitt förflutna liv* (Stories from my past life). The stories include childhood recollections, Ostrobothnian pastorals, and, above all else, yarns about himself in a variety of semiacademic situations — his confrontation with a formal and unprepared *Kalevala* lecture (which makes fun of the poet himself, of Swedes, and of *Kalevala* enthusiasts), his meeting with Odin on the Faroe Islands, and the quite believable story of the boisterous visit of Norway's national poet, Bjørnstjerne Bjørnson, to Finland at the age of at least one hundred fifty. (The climax is a collision with Finland's seemingly eternal president, Urho Kekkonen, whom Bjørnson resembles and outdoes.) In still another tale, about the perils of scholarship, the onomastic researcher loses his right rubber boot and almost his life in an Ostrobothnian bog. *Berättelser om mig själv och andra* (1992; Tales about myself and others) is a sequel, closing with a hint, as in the verse, of a falling away, a failure of vitality, in "A Summer Day, A Well." Physical powers, a surprisingly large part of this subtle academician's poetic self-image, diminish.

Despite the extraordinary amount of occasional verse, Huldén's production has been sustained at a high and inventive level, a consistency comparable to that of his major contemporaries in the lyric, Carpelan and Peter Sandelin, who remained truer to the modernist tradition; with his literary historical and philological view, Huldén did not worry especially about the modernist burden as he looked back to Runeberg and farther still. Others shared Huldén's wit, if not his good nature. The titles of the verse collections of Mauritz Nylund (1925–) have a dash of Huldén's witty tone but no

Ostrobothnian coloration: Nylund is from Helsingfors and, like so many other residents of the capital (whose proportion of Swedish speakers was reduced by the resettlement of refugees from the east after 1944 and by other demographic factors), is bilingual. After the customary modernist lyric debut, *Om mörker är allt* (1953; If darkness is all) Nylund returned with the much more original *Rävspel* (1961; Foxy schemes), *Den odöpta hästen: Eskapad i tre akter* (1963; The unbaptized horse: Escapade in three acts), and a book with a title that could stand for conservative Swedish Finland's opinion of much of the 1960s literature, *Ofinlandssvensk verksamhet* (1965; Unfinland-Swedish activity). A specialty of Nylund was his sardonic humor, demonstrated in his anticredo:

> I love myself
> more than my neighbor
> and do not believe in the immortality of the soul
> the heritage from Runeberg, Snellman and Freudenthal
> agricultural and communal singing and ivory towers
> and just between us
> this is called anti-Finland Swedish activity.

Another Nylund device was the documentary prose poem (with members of Finland's academy, evidently transformed into imperial penguins, or gentlemen in tails, sighted on the ferry going to Högholmen, the Helsingfors zoo); a third fillip was his habit of tucking poems in Finnish into his ostensibly Swedish collections (the escapade of 1963 also contains some English texts). *Han sa, hon sa* (1969; He said, she said) has the dry charm of self-denigration:

> My wife thinks your poems are worthless
> She yawned at them for twenty-three minutes
> and then said
> This kind of humor bores me, ugh.
> Then she threw your book
> into the wastebasket.
> Better late than never,
> I thought.

A good part of *Han sa, hon sa* is again in Finnish; something like Huldén's "bilingual" *Heim/Hem* of a year later, Nylund's *Men den skrattade bara/Mutta se nauroi vain* (1975; But it just laughed) has Swedish and Finnish texts of the same poem printed on facing pages. The jokes are quotable and, as in Huldén, often depend on extensions or distortions of pat phrases:

> He has a bone to pick [literally, a chicken to pluck]
> with the Continuation War
> he constantly serves it
> with its feathers on.

Rakastavat ne miehetkin (1978; Those men really love) was entirely in Finnish; *En dag tittade jag på dig genom en förstoringsglas* (1984; One day I looked at you through a magnifying glass), which appeared at Alftan's "Revolt" publishing house, had an antimilitary suite in bits of prose as its climax: "The sergeant lifted his bugle to his lips and blew out an SOS across the lines. Shortly thereafter, they found him struck by the echo."

Per-Hakon Påwals (1928–) has also written in Finnish as well as Swedish; has also published a volume solely of Finnish verse, *Keskiviikko, syyskuu, syksy* (1981; Wednesday, September, autumn); and, again like Nylund, has come to view himself as an outsider. His first book, *Glas emellan* (1956; Glass in between), was less in thrall to the modernists than customary in those days; Påwals had already acquired, he believed, a kind of Anglo-Saxon matter of factness from studying Selden Rodman's anthology, *One Hundred Modern Poems* (1949), but for a while he harnessed this sobriety to a sense of fantastic humor that came to the surface in his stories, *Snuviga gatlyktor* (1966; Streetlights with sniffles), and in such poems in *Minnet är en vinge* (1960; The memory is a wing) as "Happy Memories":

> When I was very young I often walked on my hands
> between Stockholm and Helsingfors
> by sea, of course
> keeping myself alive with glittering pikes.

In the same collection Påwals began his long guerrilla war against a segment of the Finland-Swedish (and Finnish) population of which Runar Schildt had been so uncomfortably aware, the athletic well-to-do:

> I've nothing against them indeed I envy them
> their white sails their carefree game with racket and mallet
> but it would never occur to me to write for them
> they are hopelessly beyond all literary culture.

The disaffected leading man of Påwal's sole novel, *Om vintern och om våren* (1962; In winter and in the spring), Martin Borman — the name is his only point of resemblance to Nazism's organizational genius — takes pleasure in crossing the language boundary and wondering if the "gloomy turn-of-the-century Viking hall" of Nyland's Nation — a traditional hangout of Finland-

Swedish students at Helsingfors — will collapse over their heads "like the last of the Mohicans," or if they will depart, one by one, "leaving it empty, empty as a museum."

Påwals's naughty humor culminated in *Min salladsgröna älskarinna* (1967; My lettuce-green mistress), in which the title poem is addressed to the poet's car, "standing softly as a great cat," but much of the book, and its sequels, is abandoned to a bitterness that does not try to correct the social injustices Påwals, like so many others of the day, perceives everywhere. The poem "To Dwell in Finland" says that indifference and isolation are the rule; in the Finnish forest, still beautiful, with its snow-covered branches, "you hear your own heart / throb throb / like a motor on the lake," and "we are very antiseptic / in our relationship to our fellow human beings." Possessions, especially the automobile, are all-important, an Alfa Romeo is "comparable to some of / Hölderlin's most sublime poetry," but "the car is like the dog. Its life cycle is brief," as *En del av världsrymden* (1972; A part of the cosmos) says. Here Påwals — who has found what little happiness he can in the privacy of his home — also writes an equivalent, tight-lipped but deeply felt, to Rückert's *Kindertotenlieder* (1872; Children's death songs): "When I think of my dead son / the cosmos stands before me like a wall." The poems of Påwals change little during the years of withdrawal; he inhabits a Biedermeier world, in which — after a listing of the marvelous things he has *not* done (a variant on the catalog poem used by Andersson to describe his checkered activities, and Huldén's account of the countless fears to which humankind is prey) — he simply states (*Jag sjunger för Bertrand Russell* [1976; I sing for Bertrand Russell]): "I have led a still life, / loved my wife, my children, / my unprepossessing little home."

What may please the faithful reader of Påwals is the absence of self-demonstration in a period when authors had become more and more willing to display themselves: "It's obvious that no one is interested in us / except ourselves" is what he says in *Ovala rutor* (1979; Oval panes), and if admitted to the poet's intimate thoughts (a voice in a dream says: "Love is the genes' trick for surviving"), one comes on a quiet anguish: "He sits in the kitchen drinking coffee / as if that could help" (*Du vet inte att du ler* [1983; You don't know you're smiling]). The minimal gesture becomes all that is left; in *Många är livets drömmar* (1985; Many are the dreams of life) the poem "Finally" consists only of a handful of words: "Finally she had / only the mallards in the pool / to go to." Again and again, Påwals is reminiscent of Huldén in his use of litotes and his uncomplicated style; but he does not have Huldén's generosity of spirit and he has lost what he once possessed of zaniness. Nevertheless, he merits attention in the lyric chorus of the 1960s, and after, because of his soft but needling voice, which fits nicely into English translation. His directness, when it does not descend into platitudes, is worthy of measured praise. As he strolls, in *Kråkdikter* (1988; Crow poems), beside the Firth of Forth, a safe if barren goal for a traveler, he restates his quietism:

I walk here,
alone but without a sense of loneliness.
A brief moment,
some
happy hours.

A hard-won serenity has also entered the poetic voice of Inga-Britt Wik (1930–), who came to Helsingfors from Ostrobothnia for work and study in the early 1950s. The capital in the summer of the Olympic Games (1952), the university and "the great trip abroad," to Salzburg and Paris, and, above all, the marriage to Jörn Donner make up the lost world to which she looked back in her "novel" (where she figures as "Britt" and Donner as "Jens"), *Ingen lycklig kärlek* (1988; No happy love), the title taken from a poem by Louis Aragon. Sven Willner ("Inga-Britt Wik") has noted the unusual quality of her second book of verse, *Staden* (1954; The city), in which her Parisian experiences and a reading of Garcia Lorca and Pablo Neruda were mixed to create a surreal metropolis ("In this city death is near / On streets you hear it coming / among the howling brakes of the cars, unconcerned / about traffic rules and regulations"). *Fönstret* (1958; The window) took up the problems of the creative woman (before they were a regular part of literary discussion); in this respect she was a successor to Solveig von Schoultz. Also, she began to draw, as she would throughout her career, on her Ostrobothnian childhood and youth, but she cannot be classified as a regionalist; memory is a sensual exercise: "I stand listening and remembering the sunwarm / path to Grandmother's, the dancing knitted sock / and the gentle spot of butter in the grits." Likewise, she is not really a protofeminist when contemplating her divorce; she writes: "Let's remember here at / the body's bridge. / Rest your forehead against mine."

In the next decade Wik's poems came sparsely; *Kvällar* (1964; Evenings) makes simple statements about — mundanely enough — a housewife's lot, as in "Paroles":

A woman in a kitchen
A woman cleaning
in a kitchen

> A woman in a cleaned
> kitchen
> A woman in a
> rundown kitchen
> A woman in an aging kitchen
> A woman.

"The Old Woman and the Load of Wood" describes an old peasant woman: "Her heart still storms" yet "she is tired and ready to drop." In another five years Wik was sufficiently free of domestic concerns to turn, in *Långa längtan* (1969; Long yearning), to the great causes of the decade, before all else the Vietnam War and the Prague summer of 1968. Ostrobothnia is a contrastive idyll:

> In this poem there are only roses
> August and the children
> there are no tanks
> the troops and the wars
> no tears, poems and despair.

The next long pause arose in part from her own academic work; like Lars Huldén's, her language was enriched by her research, on the prose style of Diktonius, and by her collaboration with the dying Eva Wichman, to whom a cycle in *Mänskliga människor* (1977; Human beings) is dedicated. It was followed quickly by *Sånger för sena älskande* (1978; Songs for late lovers) and *Jack's Café* (1980), in the former of which a long suite from a night ferry trip on the Helsingfors-Stockholm route is a central piece (its multitude of "late voices" touches once more on the question of Finland-Swedish migration to the prosperous neighbor in the west). In the latter the reminiscences of the traveler in England are compressed into Wik's tribute to Keats, strikingly combined with a bow to the Swedish idealist, Viktor Rydberg (1828–95); Wik is quite willing to own up to her household gods, however unfashionable they might seem at the moment, and her special realm has become "the smallest of paradises," books, children, nature, simply "waking up, well-slept, a sunny morning."

Her poems of the 1980s — whose more relaxed climate was congenial to the continued unfolding of her talent — were collected in the appropriately titled *Kära gamla värld* (1982; Dear old world) and *Vårarna* (1987; The springtimes). Here she goes back to her childhood, to the fairy tale (the story of the Three Billygoats Gruff), and to myth (Narcissus, Echo) and does not hesitate, in her typically quiet way, to make a connection between her grandmother and the German poet most admired by Finland-Swedish poets of the later twentieth century, Friedrich Hölderlin: he wanders through the hills where her mother played as a child, where her grandmother lived. A bond exists between his sublime visions and their simple landscape, just as in *Färdas* (1990; Journeying) Demeter lives on in a Finnish forest ravaged by loggers or developers. *Färdas* also celebrates other female figures (Kore, Lilith, Ophelia, Edith Södergran, a female shaman, the eternal grandmother) and, on a few occasions, falls into the rhetoric of the women's movement ("we sat with / a new day which was our own / and which sufficed for all"). Happily, though, Inga-Britt Wik has never been wholeheartedly enlisted in any cause, save poetry, and her selected poems, *ett hav, ett vatten* (1993; a sea, a water), carefully omit her tendentious verse.

Still another item in *Färdas* is called "Simple Poems," and the phrase, if it indicates a desire to communicate through cogent and suggestive statement, could be properly applied to the work of all the poets included in the present section. One more should be added, Kurt Högnäs (1931–), whose appearance on the literary scene, in the midst of a long career in Ostrobothnian public schools, came late, with *Glashus* (1972; Glass houses), full of nostalgia but not sentimentality:

> Angels sat on my organ,
> my mother has sung it full of her longing
> she plays it from her glory
> far away.

Högnäs then took up muted prose in *Italiensk svit* (1979; Italian suite), *En handfull ljus* (1981; A handful of light), and *Överskridningar* (1983; Transgressions) — not prose poems, not aphorisms, but reflections that approach the essay. The exactitude of his style often enhances the effect of the fantastic or dreamlike contents, dealing with perceptions — the rhythm of nature, failing physical powers, the presence of death — that have also concerned Lars Huldén, a fellow son of Ostrobothnia's Munsala parish: "A sunny forenoon / autumn / comes with a smiling mailman to my table beneath the lilac: 'Appear for an examination on the 29th of this month.'" And: "No streets run as open as death's stretches, strewn with reddish sand. There are no facades to block the view. Transitoriness is set free and forever unhindered." In its understatement and gravity Högnäs's work has been too little noticed.

The Essay and Other Nonfiction
The tradition of the Finland-Swedish essay was a rich one, although it pointed at opinions of literary and cultural life rather than at suggestion or

contemplative discussion; a partial cause for this ad rem bias was certainly its original function as a review or feuilleton. The essays of Hans Ruin, hinting at possibilities that led away from the main theme, were an indication of change, and in the postwar years, while Ruin was still at the height of his powers (say, in *Hem till sommaren* [1960; Home to the summer]), new talents appeared. Sven Willner (1918–) came from an Ostrobothnian farm and was largely self-taught; bravely deciding to become a critic, despite his distance from the seats of literary power, he served for years with the provincial newspaper *Västra Nyland,* published in Ekenäs. At the start Willner was in some ways an adherent of Atos Wirtanen (see chapter 9), but by no means as rigid (or as vatic) as Wirtanen; his prizewinning essay collection of 1964, *På flykt från världsåskådningar* (In flight from world views), proposed an "open and objectively testing attitude toward all phenomena," and in his discussion of literature he proposed to pursue the same "impurity" as the authors around FBT, but without their extremism. "Openness" has remained the cherished ideal of Willner's writing, evidenced in *Möjligheter* (1970; Possibilities) — which, discussing ideological stances (Marxism, capitalism, received Christianity, and so forth), is the farthest removed from the literary arena of all Willner's books — and in the somewhat helter-skelter "unsystematic notes about high and low," *Öppna dörrar* (1972; Open doors).

Willner had already found what would be his true métier in the tauter essays of *Dikt och politik* (1968; Poetry and politics), on the attraction of fascism for authors of the twentieth century, abroad and in Finland; the same worthwhile blend of literature and politics can be found in *Mellan hammaren och städet* (1974; Between hammer and anvil), where he put the conservatives Mikael Lybeck and Erik Kihlman side by side with the radical young Jörn Donner. In the middle 1970s Willner surveyed his past, with a selection from his enormous reviewing activity, *Tecken och spår* (1977; Signs and traces), and with the memoirlike *Tillbaka* (1976; Back) and *Sten i glashus* (1978; Stones in glass houses), dealing with childhood, military life, of which Willner had had a sizable dose, and, not unimportant, hospital experiences in middle life. Beyond his reviews he provided a running commentary on Finland's Swedish literature of the present century, ranging from the literary-sociological explorations of *Söner av nederlaget* (1979; Sons of the defeat), in which he pays attention to the major role social background has had in the minority's literature, to the literary portrait, in *Vägar till poesin* (1985; Ways to poetry) and *Det anonyma 50-talet* (1988; The anonymous 1950s), invaluable guidebooks, especially when Willner draws on his personal knowledge of the time between the wars and the decade of his apprentice critical activity. Sometimes, to be sure, he knows too much about the milieu in which his chosen figures move, and the result is blurriness; the formal sense necessary for the essay as an art form in its own right is missing.

In contrast, there is the considerably smaller and stylistically brilliant production of Johannes Salminen (1925–), the author of an Åbo doctoral dissertation on Jarl Hemmer (1955) and for many years literary director of the largest Finland-Swedish publisher, Söderström & Co. Like Willner, Salminen came from fairly simple origins (his father was a Finnish-speaking peasant on Åland); in consequence, he was not at all insensitive to the arguments presented by FBT, but he stood at a great remove from that circle's clamor for abrupt social and political change. His essays on the nature mysticism of the modernists, in *Levande och död tradition* (1963; Living and dead tradition) and *Pelare av eld* (1967; Pillar of fire), implicitly support Andersson's thesis that the modernists were aesthetes and idealists whose hand had lain too heavy on Finland-Swedish literature, yet he never indulged in Andersson's ax blows and blows below the belt: instead, Salminen was a master of balance and subtlety. His *Slavar kastar ingen skugga* (1971; Slaves cast no shadow) has—again, in its factual, soft-spoken, and elegant way—plenty of the social pathos of the time but collects the majority of its examples far beyond Finland's boundaries. (His broad knowledge requires a particular deftness for its application, since he has chosen the short essay as his special form.)

Salminen's frame of reference is altogether different from Willner's; a quiet convert to Roman Catholicism, Salminen has an enviable knowledge of the Mediterranean world, classical and Christian (as witnessed in *Middagsdemonerna* [1975; The noon demons]), an interest then expanded to include Byzantium, in *Minnet av Alexandria* (1988; The memory of Alexandria) and *Den blå stenen* (1994; The blue stone). The step eastward was a natural one for him; like Paavo Haavikko, he had long been concerned with Finland's position at the edge of the Slavic world, taking this standpoint as early as 1977, with *Landskap i öster* (1977; Landscape in the East), a representative selection from his first three volumes, and then, somewhat more personally, with *Gränsland* (1984; Borderland). His skill as a biographer, in both a miniature and a longer form, has repeatedly been demonstrated, in his introductions to the selected texts of the tormented Lars Stenbäck (1974) and Johan Vilhelm Snellman (1981), whose snappish style and self-contradictory personality require a Salminen to describe them. Returning to home base, he produced a full-length study, *Ålandskungen* (1979; The king of Åland), of the publicist Julius Sundblom (1865–1945), another border figure placed between larger political and geographical entities, in Sundblom's case Sweden and Finland. Never blind to the awful moral shortcomings of Communism (or those of capitalism), Salminen has been a lucid commentator on both systems, especially as they function, or might function, in Finland: these matters occupy him in the dialogue books *Puhe on Suomesta* (1980; The talk is about Finland), consisting of letters between Salminen and Antti Eskola (1934–), a Marxist professor of sociology at the University of Tampere, and *Sjunger näktergalen än i Dorpat?* (1990; Is the nightingale still singing in Tartu?), a friendlier correspondence between Salminen and the Estonian poet Jaan Kaplinski (1941–), written during the last days of Soviet rule in the Baltic republic. In *Pelare av eld* Salminen devoted an essay to Georg Schauman (1870–1930), reminding Finland of its present responsibilities by portraying the liberal politician and librarian, whom Salminen called "the great outsider" for his attempts to give the Finland-Swedish patricianate, and the nation at large, a keener sense of justice. The sobriquet could also be applied to Salminen for his moral sense and for his devotion to the old-fashioned stylistic ideals of brevity, force, and clarity.

In contrast to Salminen's conciseness and stimulating leaps of thought, the essays of Mikael Enckell (1932–) are weightier, more laborious in argument, and painstaking in the adduction of evidence. A psychiatrist, Enckell does not have Salminen's interest in history and politics; instead, he has made the exploration of the creative personality his specialty and in recent years has been at work on a biography of his father, Rabbe Enckell, of which three volumes have appeared (1986, 1991, 1997). His essays are not limited to literary figures; he quickly established himself as one of Finland's authoritative writers on film in *Det dolda motivet* (1962; The hidden motif), which included studies of Michelangelo Antonioni, Sergei Eisenstein, and Fritz Lang, as well as of Enckell's literary favorite, Proust; *Det omvända anletet* (1969; The countenance turned round) continued the Proust investigation (on elements of parody in Proust's work) but also had essays on Alain Resnais and Alfred Hitchcock, closing with a study of Gunnar Björling, in which — as a psychiatrist — Enckell paid attention to the effect of Björling's homosexuality on his lyrics. But a "Finland-Swedish" essay in the volume should not be overlooked, on humor (using material from Guss Mattsson), "with its partial denial of the tragic side of existence" and its "sensitivity to the human element." *Över stumhetens gräns* (1972; Across the boundary of muteness), on Björling and Wecksell, and *Hölderlin* (1975) studied the aberrant personality of the literary genius. As Enckell was wont, he returned for another say on Hölderlin in "Wisdom and Madness," the opening item of *Eko och återsken* (1979; Echo and reflection), before going back to film (Luchino Visconti) and, in Swedish romanticism, examining the case of Erik Johan Stagnelius (1793–1823), who in some respects is Hölderlin's northern counterpart; the book's finale talks about the literary passions and insights of Sigmund Freud, a model for Enckell himself. *Spegelskrift* (1984; Mirror writing) and *Till saknadens lov* (1988; In praise of loss) are on a variety of topics, literary and not; a fascination with the essayist's own drop of Jewish blood may have given rise to the essays on psychoanalysis and the Jewish tradition and Marcus Ehrenpreis (1869–1951), the much-traveled author who in 1914 became grand rabbi of Stockholm. Merete Mazzarella wrote in *Samtal* (p. 130) that Salminen and Enckell are "the two most important Finland-Swedish essayists of today," each representing, in his own way, "an altogether unusual breadth of view, a freedom from customary evaluations, and, above all, an awareness of tradition in T. S. Eliot's uncomfortable, obligating sense." Both men, she believes, are heirs to Montaigne, surely not the smallest praise.

Although Björn Kurtén (1924–88) obtained professional fame in the academic community for his research—the Harvard biologist Stephen Jay Gould called him "unquestionably Europe's finest evolutionary palaeontologist"—he got a different if related sort of international reputation for his "palaeofiction" about the struggles between primitive people (Neanderthal and Cro-Magnon) and terrifying beasts some thirty-five thousand years ago in the northern reaches of Finland and Sweden in his novels *Den svarta tigern* (1978; Eng. tr. *Dance of the Tiger: Novel of the Ice Age*, 1982) and *Mammutens rådare* (1984; Eng. tr. *Singletusk: A Novel of the Ice Age*, 1986). Kurtén's large production also contains such works of popular science at a high level as *Istiden* (1969; Eng. tr. *The Ice Age*, 1972), *Inte från aporna* (1971; Eng. tr. *Not from the Apes*, 1984), and *Björnen från Drakhålan* (1975; Eng. tr. *The Cave Bear's Story: Life and Death of a Vanished Animal*, 1976). All the same, the true heart of Kurtén's contribution to belles lettres may lie in his learned but humane essay collections, *Hur man fryser en mammut* (1981; Eng. tr. *How to Deep-Freeze a Mammoth*, 1986) and *De skuldlösa mördarna* (1987; Eng. tr. *The Innocent Assassins: Biological Essays on Life in the Present and the Distant Past*, 1991), in which his combination of scientific knowledge and stylistic skill has been compared with that of the great (and less systematic) Guss Mattsson.

The many-sided and prolific Göran Schildt (1917–), the son of Runar Schildt, has been an interpreter and biographer of Gide (1946), from whose works he also translated extensively, of Cézanne (1946, 1947), and especially of the sculptor and architect Alvar Aalto (1968, 1982, 1985); he is known to an even larger public for his many and much-translated volumes about his sailing, from 1949 to 1984, in his ketch *Daphne*. These were given extra substance — infinitely more, say, than that of the romantic voyagings of the once popular Richard Halliburton — by Schildt's knowledge of the Mediterranean littoral (and beyond): for example, *Solbåten* (1956; The sun boat) is the story of a sail from Cyprus up the Nile to the Sudan and back. (A selection from the books appeared in 1987, *Farväl Daphne* [Farewell, Daphne].) Ancillary to the *Daphne* books are such reportages as *Dianas ö* (1976; Diana's island) on modern Greece. Yet it is regrettable that Schildt did not find more time to cultivate the essay pure and simple, as he had done in *Daphne och Apollon* (1952; Daphne and Apollo) and *Kontrakurs* (1963; Countercourse). In the latter, apart from thoughts on literature (Dante, Flaubert, a comparison of Gide's and Rilke's interpretations on the prodigal son) and art (or writers about art, Malraux, Hans Ruin, Rabbe Enckell), he included reminiscences of his father and reflections on the Finland-Swedish predicament, past and present, intended to inform the Swedish newspaper-reading public, emphasizing the cultural damage that would occur if there emerged a "wholly Finnish Finland, cut off from its historical traditions and from membership in Scandinavia." (Although it has a novelistic framework, Schildt's excellent *Ön som förtärdes av havet* [1970; The island that was devoured by the sea] is essayistic in content; *Dianas ö* is not so much a travel book as a series of essays about the island of Leros.) International in his outlook as in his public, Schildt appears not to have concerned himself much, in subsequent decades, with such local questions; yet his *Lånade vingar: Ungdomsminnen* (1995; Borrowed wings: Youthful memories) divulges much about his anchoring in a privileged group (toward which he maintains a skepticism something like his father's) and his long intellectual friendship with the great Finland-Swedish philosopher Georg Henrik von Wright (1916–). (Alongside his massive professional output, von Wright has also been a cultural-philosophical essayist, in *Tanke och förkunnelse* [1955; Thought and proclamation], *Humanismen som livshållning och andra essayer* [1978; Humanism as a life attitude and other essays], and the gloomily prophetic *Vetenskapen och förnuftet: Ett försök till orientering* [1986; Science and reason: An attempt at orientation]; a selection of von Wright's essays appeared in English in 1993 as *The Tree of Knowledge*.)

Popularizers of Complaint
The 1960s, offering the catchword of revolt (against bourgeois traditionalism, against social and economic unfairness, against accepted history, against modernism itself), were bound to encourage authors of secondary

talent, with a special ax to grind; the results could be careers of sudden and single successes, followed by a long dwindling. The journalist Gunnar Mattsson (1937–89) won an international reputation with his story of his wife's triumph over cancer, *Prinsessan* (1965; Eng. tr. *The Princess,* 1966), yet was unable to produce another work of the same appeal, and his *Eden* (1967; Eden), setting out to deal with the monotony of the new suburban apartment complexes, instead dealt in great part — and for the time, sensationally — with efforts to dispel boredom through sexual experimentation. Other books were spun out of his major international success: *Prinsen* (1966; The prince), on his infant son, with illustrations by Henrik Tikkanen, and a fictionalized report on his own decline, *Kungen* (1971; The king), about the harm done by literary fame and a weakness for alcohol. After years of silence Mattsson returned with *Gunnar* (1987), a frank account of his own alcoholism, less analytical but less self-flattering than Kihlman's of years before; its serious nature was underscored by an afterword from a medical specialist in the field.

Much earlier, searching desperately for new themes, Mattsson had put together the intentionally amusing *Jätten* (1969; The giant), a description of the pleasures of amateur sailing; professional life at sea was the stuff on which Rainer Alander (1937–) drew. A sometime junior officer in Finland's merchant fleet, he first attracted attention through the apparently documentary quality of his work; his stories in *Ansiktet* (1963; The face) were mostly about the tedious or sexual sides of maritime life, in a hard-fisted conversational style. The absurdist novels *Sandkornet* (1964; The grain of sand) and *Personerna* (1969; The persons), however, drove away critics and the public by their almost impenetrable jumble of events, and Alander perforce returned to the toilers of the sea in *Lastmärket* (1972; The Plimsoll line) and to a harbor town, Åland's Mariehamn, in *En sorts frihet* (1974; A kind of freedom), which purports to expose the doubtful morality of the often absent husbands and neglected wives of that respectable community. In these books, as in *Barlast* (1979; Cargo) and *Hälsningar från San Francisco* (1986; Greetings from San Francisco), Alander played from his strong suits, dialogue of dependable factuality and obscenity, depiction of life under hard conditions, carefully placed erotic scenes. Mattsson and Alander transferred some of the recently discovered freedoms of Finland-Swedish prose into what they hoped was a more popular and catchier idiom; their air of getting at society's problems was a coverup for entertainment.

The same judgment should not be passed on the four novels, his entire production, of Jarl Sjöblom (1932–82), three of which deal, in a straightforward manner, with simple people from the West Nyland countryside — a boy aware of his mother's adultery in *På tallsriksflatan* (1962; On the platter), set during the Continuation War and its aftermath; a family coming up in the world at a cost to itself in *Kärret* (1964; The bog); and *Vägen till Hangö* (1968; The road to Hangö). In the books of 1964 and 1968 the narrators are, notably, older men, a ditch digger, puzzled by his family's strivings, and a war veteran, an amputee and possibly, according to his own words, a "communist," who attempts to explain his experiences and his present standpoint to a long-lost son, a pacifist. (The title refers to the fighting around the Hangö beachhead in the early stages of the Continuation War.) Sjöblom's *Fabeln om den hårlösa kon* (1973; The fable about the hairless cow) has a narrator of a different sort, a sexually overactive girl who comes to grips with her numerous erotic disappointments by writing fables about animals and human beings: she is the cow of the title.

Flight, Sublimity, and Aggression
In a decade when even poets unwilling to enlist in the radical spirit were still touched by it (Carpelan, Huldén, Sandelin), some writers at first remained impervious to the pressures of the time, only to embrace them with a vengeance later on. Sebastian Lybeck (1929–), a grandson of Mikael Lybeck, did not set himself off from other belated modernists with his *I tornet* (1951; In the tower) and *Fågel över sju floder* (1956; Bird over seven rivers), save that he went back to the romanticism of the early Södergran ("Now your song / on zither and violet-blue twilight / — that we ran together and / the halfmoon silvered your mouth") and was ready to try forms, such as the sonnet, that had fallen into disuse. In *Jorden har alltid sitt ljus* (1958; The earth always has its light) Lybeck even resuscitated the baroque *carmen figuratum* (in which the poem's shape on the page represents what its subject is), unintentionally prefiguring the concrete poetry to be cultivated in the next decade by Alftan. At heart, however, Lybeck was not a formal experimenter but, as he claimed in the turgid prose introduction to his second book, a seeker for simplicity. In the 1950s he left Finland, whose atmosphere he found stifling, for the Lofoten Islands off the subarctic coast of Norway and became, as he announced, "a poet in fisherman's boots." He wrote two books from this milieu, *Dikter från Lofoten* (1961; Poems from Lofoten), which contains the telltale lines "Nobody knows who I am" and "In early mornings I have / walked over the rocks / . . . sung myself free from all tired community," and *Liten stad vid havet* (1963; Little town beside the sea), in which the motif of "my life, my fragile flight" is coupled with the vision of a pleasant, welcoming place, on

> A day only for small towns
> With smoke above the horizon
> And children's laughter ringing
> As if they were all beer-bottles in a basket.

Such homely, mildly witty imagery had provided the charm in the prose causeries Lybeck produced from his Helsingfors years, *Patent 711 Krumelur* (1955; Patent 711 paraph), and became, for a while, his stock in trade; meanwhile, he wrote popular children's books in German.

After a move to Sweden, however, he caught up with the radical 1960s in *Mitt i den nordiska idyllen* (1972; In the midst of the Nordic idyll), full of what he hoped would be a broad appeal: "yes, I'd like to write my poems just / as easily, naturally, and necessarily / as one eats and drinks," poems often based on the newspapers (Kent State, the EEC, Vietnam, murder stories bearing witness to a sick society). The exhortations of *Vi ska slå upp portarna!* (1978; We shall open the gates!) echo, belatedly, Swedish radical chic: "And it's the First of May, we demonstrate," followed by complaints about "the security here in the Land of Welfare / . . . [which] was directed by cold cash," and admonitions to "the people of the future! / Proletarians in all the world's lands." Eventually, Lybeck wrote a tribute to a new seaside home in *Dikter från Bohuslän* (1980; Poems from Bohuslän), a replay of his Lofoten fishing poems; his career could have been written off at this point were it not for his discovery of the confessional mode in *Råttansiktet* (1981; The rat face), a tour through a traumatic childhood in a closely knit and eccentric family. In the attic "there stood strangely smelling chests, never opened," and

> weapons packed in wood shavings.
> And Uncle Torvald with the chandelier around his neck
> And Uncle Bengt with his butterfly poison
> And the mutilated body of Nils Gustav, mother's brother
> And Peter with his head shot to pieces.

Henrik Tikkanen's revelations of *his* family's gruesome secrets had appeared just a short time before (see below).

Sören G. Lindgren (1935–) began with the great aspirations of *Ornament* (1954), *De tolv* (1957; The twelve), *Exil* (1958), and *Abals död* (1958; Abal's death) while he was a cultural editor of the Helsingfors afternoon paper, *Nya Pressen*. Despite a tribute in *Ornament* to Björling, "who gives warmth to the sad grayness of everyday life," Lindgren had tried to break away from modernism, in particular by the extended use of standard myth (Narcissus, Daphne, Cain and Abel, Jesus, Mary Magdalene), supplemented by American westerns (*Shane*) and lore of his own devising. The results were murky. His removal to Sweden in 1964 led to a complete reversal of his poetic practices and gave him the material, drawn from his own disappointing experience, for plainspoken laments about the situation of migrants from Finland in the sister society. (Shortly after his departure Lindgren had contributed an article to FBT in support of the new social realism the journal favored, as well as a hostile interpretation of Rabbe Enckell's famous programmatic poem, "Oh Bridge of Words Between," and its "flight into the private landscape.") In *Politiska dikter* (1969; Political poems), influenced by both his recent FBT past and the poets of the "new simplicity" in Sweden proper (Göran Palm, Lars Gustafsson, Björn Håkansson, Sonja Åkesson), Lindgren devoted an entire section to the immigrant's lot: "I spoke Swedish with a Finnish accent / Staring eyes followed me wherever I went"; much of the rest was reporter's verse: dreamed interviews with Stalin, Churchill, and John F. Kennedy and outbursts against the *pied noirs* of Algeria: "They fled / fled like rats, squeaking like rats, fled from the sinking Übermensch ship / which the last of them tried to blow up, set on fire, lay waste." (In his indignation at the excesses of Algeria's French population, led by General Raoul Salan, Lindgren forgot *their* minority predicament.) In *Moln, som slits sönder* (1977; Clouds, which are torn apart) Lindgren once more played the role of the poor immigrant, then returned to his mythic concerns (Egyptian and Norse this time), wrote frank sexual poems, and finally, like Lybeck, uttered a cry for revolt, an address to the guerrilla soldiers of Latin America. New themes had become hard to find.

Formal religion and myth had been fairly rare birds in Swedish Finland's modernist lyric, but Karl (Carolus) Rein (1935–) made a combination of religious and mythic strains the mainstays of his long career: publishing his first collection, *Färd genom verkligheter* (1954; Journey through realities), even before he had taken his final school examinations, he found a publisher — the ever generous Söderström & Co. — willing to follow him from one often inscrutable book to another. He regarded himself as a special case, without relatives in the Finland-Swedish chorus — the title of his second volume was *Syskon till ingen* (1955; Sibling to no one). But in his proud isolation he appeared to suffer from a sense of emptiness, as he said in the splendid but inexplicable images of *Dansens yta* (1956; The dance's surface): "The prince of Byzance waits in the tower / Around the circular staircase the waves of autumn swell, / white wings of Hades birds," and "we stand like haystacks of blackened silver, / with a heart wandering in impotence." The next years Rein rested, poetically, but was converted to Roman Catholicism, which provided him with both a consoling sense of (exotic) community and a set of images more readily understood. The poems of *Vårsvart* (1958; Springblack), *Seende* (1960; Seeing), and *Världen är endast du* (1963; The world is only you) may turn into incantation ("Eternity's Melody" consists of the word "light" five times, together with eight other words) or into the creation of a baroque Christian pantheon, peopled by such allegorical figures as Concord and Discord. Rein remained quite untouched by the currents of the 1960s; his eyes were fixed so constantly on celestial realms that commentators regarded him as a descendant of the most ethereal of Swedish poets, Erik Johan Stagnelius:

> Suddenly you behold again
> the night's flickering signs, glimmering, vanished . . .
> Far away
> rolls a loftier sea.
> Far away pain sleeps which belongs to you.
> Become a stone in the great city. Become far away.

It is impossible to discern phases in Rein's oeuvre; giant word pairs whirl past: "Chaos and Cosmos" is the title of a poem in *Vågbrytningar* (1971; Wave breakings); *Eros och Logos,* the title of a collection from 1973; *Stigar mellan Elysion och Hades* (Paths between Elysium and Hades) appeared in 1978; *Amor och Apocalypsis* in 1984. Rein loves the rhetorical device of ecphonesis (outcry): the finale of the collection of 1978, "Excelsior," says, typically, "Oh temple-holy mystery / pearl of splendor," and

> Oh foam-redeemed column of miracles
> oh Hellas, which like unto the *sectio aurea,* shall arise once more from
>   the waves of Lethe —
>
> in this sign I beheld, unworthy,
> the winds' victory over time.

Still, the cosmic poet can make occasional political references, as in the bizarre reflections held "before the portraits of Ulbricht and Stoph" — East German leaders of yore — in his "German Symphony": "Oh these homeless ones of the soul," "Oh countenances of fair and indelible, hopeless imprisonment," "Oh refugees of time, / chased from yourselves. . . . " Decipherable personal references are largely missing, save in the many odic travel poems (quite naturally, among others, to Tübingen, Hölderlin's town); nevertheless, in his novel *Erinnyerna* (1976; The Erinyes) Rein wrote about himself, in what he claimed was "not to be regarded in principle as a roman à clef," as the poet Erland Hisinger, all too closely tied to his parents, to his sister Brita ("Brita is terribly attractive — but I control myself"), to his spiritual counselor Pater Meijer, and to Celia (her "glance was full of passion then"). Hisinger himself is pursued and prodded by "the mighty birds, which watch over my departure."

The subtitle of Rein's highly lyrical novel is "A Tale about the Captivity of the Soul and Attempts to Flee"; the protagonist of the *Burgundiska sviten* (1966; The Burgundian suite), by Carl-Gustaf Lilius (1928–), has also set out on a spiritual search. "Novel" would not be quite the right word here; the little book contains lyric inlays as well as sets of aphorisms, and in the reprinting of 1987 seventy-three drawings were added by the author, better known as a graphic designer and sculptor than for his small and alluring, if baffling, literary production. At the conclusion Lilius told what he had intended to create: "The Burgundian Suite is what I have called a world that would encompass all other worlds within itself, and throughout my life everything I had worked on and everything I had dreamed most profoundly always touched upon it at some point." A dream book by a gifted artist in other media, it may appropriately be compared with *Die andere Seite* (1909; Eng. tr. *The Other Side*, 1969), of the Austrian Alfred Kubin (1877–1959). Kubin's vision, however, was of the ghastly destruction of Perle, the "Dream Town" made of remnants of nineteenth-century Austrian cities, somewhere in the steppes of central Asia; Lilius's Burgundy is a much better place, reached when, on a spring morning, cranes or swans appear at the poet's house at Hangö. "I get wings too / and can approach Burgundy and Tibet's mountains where the sunbird / has its dwelling." The realm has discernible inhabitants: a bearded painter and his love, Cordula; a poet and his love, Feline (who has "a body like a turbulent sea"); and a Burgundian thinker who does not need feminine company to get "revelatory insights," presented in aphorisms; he is connected to (or is identical with) Doctor Susano — "the old fool the man people say never existed" — who speaks about ways to obtain happiness. In his euphoric world Lilius has created an isolated counterweight to the socially unhappy and unjust Finland perceived at the same time by Andersson (and how many others); the book is dedicated to the author's wife, Irmelin Sandman Lilius, who simultaneously was writing her own, hugely popular books for children or young adults about the imaginary small town of Tulavall (see chapter 11).

Doctor Susano, whose name suggests that of the German mystic, Heinrich Seuse or Suso (1325–66), the author of the *Horologium eternae sapien-*

tiae (Hour book of eternal wisdom), returned in Lilius's *Metsytiska boken* (1973; The Metsytic book); this "novel about thought" is divided into five "movements," again illustrated by Lilius, made up of the observations (in mellifluous prose, short poems, aphorisms) of Doctor Susano; he (or the reporter of his thoughts) complains about the emptiness of contemporary political and religious beliefs, about any "patriarchal system of oppression" that can prevail in the East (for example, Mao's China) as in the West and that depends for the exercise of its control on "temples, churches, priesthoods, congregations, teachings, holy texts, cult objects, ritual gestures." Lilius's book stems in one way from the oppositional spirit of the 1960s but is dead set against their dogmatism; in his horrifying or beatific visions Susano refuses to submit to any reform or to recommend any change other than a genuine "meeting with the gods"—a splendid thought that led reviewers to see *Metsytiska boken* as one more example of the Hölderlinian idealism so palpable in Rein. Lilius's dream world might also be called a positive version of Ralf Parland's Santsche-Pi: Susano's road leads to Tibet of the days before the Chinese invasion, which caused Lilius to make some direct commentaries on world events. Otherwise, for all its keen discernment of the contemporary abuse of power, belief, and learning (early on, psychiatry is condemned as a destructive and debased form of knowledge), the book floats above its time; Susano himself has decided on his thirtieth birthday that he is three thousand years old. At first glance, the benevolent ruminations of Susano may suggest the gentle withdrawal of the flower children of the 1960s: "I imagine, mumbled Doctor Susano, that a human being must first feel a need of a god or several gods and that this need leads to the divine revelation," and "I have no ideas about the details of the construction of [a depot of the gods], muttered Doctor Susano, and I do not concern myself with making sketches showing how I imagine that it does not look." Lilius is actually a disciplined thinker, however, and a poet capable of genuine sublimity as well, as he has demonstrated in *Det himmelska ljuset* (1994; The heavenly light).

A current quite unlike that of either the social reformers or the makers and seekers of myths was represented by Tom Sandell (1936–); only a year younger than Claes Andersson, he sought no cure for the ills of society but instead simply listed them in sharp detail, at first in verse—*Ägg och nejlika* (1957; Egg and carnation), *Lågor under vattnet* (1958; Flames beneath the water), *Isristning* (1960; Carving in ice), and *Ljuset i rummet* (1964; The light in the room). Every prospect displeases, and men and women are consistently vile: men's muscles "tremble like cancerous growths," women seek "a sex soft as a dog's muzzle," an image in a mirror has

> thighs pricked
> by injections,
> the face contorted
> by a terror like
> lepers, the breast covered
> by sickly redness, the heart
> laid bare, black-edged.

By the fourth collection the horrors belong to things as well as humans; cars in a junkyard lie

> On backs and on sides, crustaceans with sucked-out innards and life-
>   juice, they lie here
> and remind one of H. C. Andersen.
> Children finger in their intestines.
> It's Mercedes but Lohengrin too.

The joke that turns a luxury car into Lohengrin's swan-boat, wrecked, comes as a relief in a world where (in "Something about the Weather") "the sunshine is aerosol, and the wind blows a smell of tincture along." Sandell's disgust reached a climax in *Dikter* (1969; Poems); "Little Quartet for Loving Wind" is a main exhibit:

> Lovers' blushes exist no more.
> Lovers' paleness is mostly diarrhea.
> Lovers' kisses ask for naught
> Other than safety from gonorrhea

and

> Gunnar plays the sybarite.
> Gittan thinks that all is shit.
> Börje gets high on preludin.
> Barbro loves LSD and wine.

(These ingredients would become staples in the literary depiction of youth; Claes Andersson repeated them in his novel, *Den fagraste vår*.)

The discovery that the ugliness of existence can be made bearable only by constant potshots at its absurdity was the impetus of Sandell's first book entirely in prose (although he had inserted prose poems before); *Ur clownens garderob* (1965; From the clown's wardrobe) was composed of short essays, well formed and often learned, many of them on nasty facets of humor: a teller of obscene tales regards his listeners with a contemptuous smile, a joking sergeant makes his charges lie down before him: "our shoulderblades shook with laughter even as our selves, tired and ashamed, pressed to the ground, [were] filled with repugnance." *N.N.* (1967; Nomen nescio, "I do not know the name," or Nomen nominandum, "The name to be named") consists of five pieces of polemic prose, of which the first, "Our Time's Kaleidoscope," adduces Claes Andersson, Margareta Starck, and Mauritz Nylund of FBT (a "brief illustration of the fact that one should choose not just any old brains but stick to qualified material"); the fifth and longest is "Monika A's" catalog of her boyfriends, one of whom, "G., dark, 178 centimeters tall," was "something of a gourmand regarding FBT, which he devoured almost with an 'amen' on his lips." The essays (or reflections) of *Just det, dvs livet* (1970; Precisely that, i.e., life) attack such respected intellectual ingredients as "exact pieces of information, factual knowledge, correct terminology or psychology, logical consequence, honesty and straightforward intention" and defend (ostensibly) the excessive use of narcotics and alcohol — Sandell was out to shock, and did so with great precision.

In the short prose, with some poems, of *Obeväpnad till tänderna* (1971; Unarmed to the teeth) Sandell grew more bitter still, deriding political demonstrators in "Agitare necesse est" (It is necessary to agitate: "After all, what is a long, calm, and safe life against a short one, filled with terror?"), mocking spiritual vacuity ("In the soul's empty, blown-out egg of a pantry the little mouse Why / gnawed the thin remains of dead knowledge"), expressing ironic fears — the women's movement in Finland's Swedish literature was springing into life — about men's future in a poem addressed to Edith Södergran ("You sought a man / and found a worm. / You are ironic"), and despairing of himself in "Enfant mortible" (Sandell's play on "Enfant terrible"): "I behave like a child. I break all my views of life into pieces. . . . What shall I do, now that winter's at the door? Suicide?" *Du* (1973; You) was a series of almost-narrative portraits of people (a reporter, a woman of fifty, an industrialist), times ("Sunday, an Afternoon"), and places ("Sauna," "City," "Building"); the very foolishness of existence presses in from every side. A teacher is addressed in the second person (as are all the other entities in the book): "When you stand and look at these heads that move or do not move in the pale afternoon light, you are seized by a sudden and unexpected feeling of unreality, absurdity." The volume ends with a self-address, "The Thirty-Seventh Year": "Nowhere do you find the aroma of expectation any longer, or of adventure, which once gave life's beginning the taste and color of wet, fresh, green grass." The title of *Dikter för medelålders* (1976; Poems for middle age) was scarcely a surprise; in "Outdoor Excursion" simple pleasures pall:

> The dawn is as splendid as in the children's
> coloring book. They wake up in the midst
> of a marriage.
> Look at one another.
> Two window dummies of papier mâché
> in a camping expo.

The slogans of the time can only lead to despair:

> After having read 123 informed articles about equality
> and having carefully compared the factual content with my own
> life experiences, I've concluded that
> there's only one thing equal for us all ... The Shriek,
> mindless, uttered in the presence of the unbearable.

As for nature: "I thought that [the sea] resembled / a tired scrubwoman on the way home."

Sandell's nihilism sprang, evidently, out of a general "Unbehagen in der Kultur" and other, personal factors; the "novel" *Skuggboxaren* (1979; The shadow boxer) is one more attempt to depict the malaise of the alcoholic, but it does not have the social-corrective tone of Kihlman's book on the topic, the plaintiveness of Mattsson's, or the sensational aspects of Henrik Tikkanen's self-revelations (see below). Sandell simply resorts to sordid detail, without hope: "One is locked in with one's monsters. But false windows [are] everywhere, vanity fairs, bulging with arctic and tropical hysteria." (The last reference is to the never-completed novel suite *Arktinen hysteria* [1967–68] of Marko Tapio [1924–73]. Sandell's work is full of allusions, not always flattering, to his contemporaries; "Hamlet-76," in *Dikter för medelålders,* is an utterly dispirited pendant to Claes Andersson's anatomical but vigorous "Hamlet-66" in *Samhället vi dör i.*)

When *Pavlovs hundar* (1983; Pavlov's dogs) appeared, Göran Schildt called attention to Sandell's Strindbergian blend of frightening pessimism and malicious wit. An author with a state stipend and writer's block, resident with a dull-as-dishwater wife and a beloved child in one of the capital's dismal suburbs, awakens each day with "a sense of intense and penetrating loneliness"; wherever he walks, or rides on his motorcycle, he dully registers the miseries, small or large, spawned by affluence or greed or sheer brutishness (represented by some Finnish Hell's Angels). One Pavlovian dog among many, he has been trained to make automatic responses. *Trädet* (1988; The tree) has an epigraph taken from a poem by the Swede Erik Lindegren (1910–68): "But there are days / when the birdsong falls silent";

it is told by a septuagenarian who, from his fiftieth birthday on, has kept a diary; now he lives in a communal home. The novel's existential message is that life and death must be accepted as they are; despite this hard-won insight, it still retains some standard parts of Sandell's equipment, his misanthropy and his carefully honed talent for portraiture of a sardonic or unpleasant sort. The best pages in *Trädet* are those on the vanities of age, on Jörn Donner's hyperactivity, on Rilke's preening "in the midst of his manic-depressive neurosis."

Whether Sandell's story of having two upper front teeth knocked out in a brawl (told in "Moral Odontology," in *Obeväpnad till tänderna*) is true or an invention, it sums up his literary personality; a similar pugnacity is part of the persona of his contemporary, Gösta Ågren (1936–); but whereas Sandell was an informed if choleric member of the Helsingfors scene, Ågren, an Ostrobothnian, for years was ignored or underestimated in the capital. Like his older brother Leo, Gösta Ågren was born with an awareness of social injustice; his family's lot (and the whole of human suffering) was attacked in the would-be hymnic poems of *Kraft och tanke* (1955; Power and thought), which opened with the outcry "After Hiroshima." The novel *Jordlös bonde* (1956; Landless peasant) and the lyrics of *Folkvargarna* (1958; The wolves of the people) continued to hurl the grievances: "The wolves live / as never before!" An autobiographical poem says: "I knew that the old mare soon would be slaughtered. / That was the night I became a factory worker," and this new drudgery underpinned the pathos of the poems in *Bergsväg* (1959; Hill way). Ågren's early production was also marked by Ostrobothnian local patriotism, in the tribute to the eighteenth-century pastor and economist Anders Chydenius ("[you] wept, when you called / in Stockholm, in the barren / dawn: [for] freedom, salaries, earth"), as well as in his quite delicate vision of Ostrobothnia's barns: "dice / cast on the fields, weightless / as light, climbing / outward toward the rains." These Ostrobothnian items appeared in the substantial volume *Ett brev från Helsingfors* (1961; A letter from Helsingfors); much later, in the prose of *Han kommer, han kommer* (1973; He's coming, he's coming), he recalled the difficulties of his move to the capital and of the problems of survival in a labor market for which he did not have the necessary Finnish competence.

The pages of two verse collections published in Sweden, *Säg farväl åt natten* (1963; Say farewell to the night) and *Kungörelser* (1965; Announcements), are marked by Ågren's efforts to emulate Pablo Neruda, the everlasting poetic idol of the Left, and to catalog the various horrors of concentration camps, New York City ("the hot and dirty eye of the world"), and, of all places, Vancouver. The large volume simply called *Ågren* (1968) put all his affections and dislikes on display: his family ("The Grave in Jakobstad" on his sister's death), Ostrobothnia's nature, politics (the anti-Stalin poem, the ambiguous poem on Kekkonen, the picture of the White House where "Rome is perfectly resurrected"); but the most original element lies in his many laconic poems, a descriptive-aphoristic form that eventually would be his specialty, such as "Eight Years Old":

> To walk to school
> was like going toward iron
> Only the way home
> was similarly tormented.

Cellens dagrar (1970; The cell's illuminations) brought a special Ågrenian resentment to the surface (against "professors") as well as his sentimental view of sex and his interest in film ("Let film be black and white like the world!"); he had studied directing at the Swedish Film Institute from 1964 to 1966. *Massmöte på jorden* (1972; Mass meeting on earth) had more obvious propagandistic elements than before:

> The one who chooses revolt
> is chosen. His dreams
> are storms. From life he demands
> the dignity, which the powerful
> purchase only with their death.

The brief form was abandoned, temporarily, for larger historical poems with a purpose, such as the address "The Summer of 1848," with its paradox:

> Many returned disappointed
> from the future, but still
> the future is found only in the past.
> It was begun in 1848.

In the overture to *Massmöte på jorden* Ågren wrote that he would "like to simplify his poetry," but there was no shortcut, and much of what he had had published (and he published much) showed a lack of critical perspicacity. In 1990, when he made a selection of his lyrics from 1955 to 1985, *En dal i våldet* (Eng. tr. *A Valley in the Midst of Violence*, 1992), he admitted quite frankly that "Only a handful of the texts . . . come from the eleven poetry collections that appeared between 1955 and 1976." He regarded *Var inte rädd* (1976; Don't be afraid) and *Molnsommar* (1978; Cloud summer) as his "genuine poetic debut" and drew most of his material from *Dikter i svartvitt* (1980; Poems in black and white), *Det som alltid är* (1982; That which always is), and *Den andra guden* (1985; The other god). Further, in his effort to unburden himself of his poetic past, Ågren stated that many of the poems in the selection had been subjected to a complete revision and were placed not in a chronological but in a thematic order: "Quite simply, I have composed a new collection." Ågren wanted his readers to regard his previous work as a mere training exercise extended over a quarter-century; the selection of 1990 shows a clear formal unity—the almost exclusive use of very short poems (descriptive, aphoristic, didactic) and the heavy employment, of paradox or, conversely, gnomic statement.

En dal i våldet is divided into ten sections: "Life" (on the stages of existence), "People" (from R. S. Thomas, the Welsh poet whose work Ågren much admires, to his late brother Leo and to Gerd Ågren, "a retarded child"), "Discoveries" (aphoristic ponderings on freedom, capitalism, suffering), "Events" (the execution of a Kurdish prisoner, a lethal traffic accident, the vicissitudes of the workers' movement), "The Light, the Darkness" (seasonal poems, "Spring Night," "Summer Vigil," "Hunting Season"), "History" (an Albigensian heretic burned at the stake, "Europe's beginning" in an archaic statue, a village killed by modern society), "A Valley in the Midst of Violence" (which includes the title poem: "It happens that we get / an afternoon, a valley / in the midst of violence. The clock's / ticking holds the future / at a distance," another of Ågren's innumerable paradoxes), "A Profession" (on the role of poetry in life: "Writing poems / is touching / one's self, to see / if one is alive"), "Consolation" (a dying patient is told: "We / are all forced to conquer / at last"), and "The Village" (a return to roots: "Here every village is a / footnote to the forest's / melancholy mass of text"). The intention is to make the reader reflect; the ornamentation is of the slightest; a stern laconicism is everywhere apparent, often coupled with an intense (and repressed) emotionalism. See "Alone" in the final section:

> The evenings were hardest. She
> sat by the window. The sky's
> burning silk was long
> in going out. Finally, memory
> is the only pain we have left.

Ågren's sudden importance, after decades in the shadow, was signaled by the award of the Finlandia Prize in 1989, for *Jär* (1988; Here), the first part of a trilogy, in which the other volumes were *Städren* (1991; The cities) and *Hid* (1992; Hither); all the titles were in dialect, although the verse itself was not. In the trilogy, still using his compressed form, Ågren once again presented his grave nuggets of wisdom and painful miniatures of life; his unblinking solemnity is not a pose, and everything he writes is marked by a grim honesty, making him, perhaps, Finland-Swedish literature's most persistent and unforgiving stoic. He remembers slights, injustices, suffering, loss, but:

> I do not dare forget. To
> remember is to endure
> even if the most difficult part, the darkness,
> remains a bottomless lake.

The straightforwardness and the moralism, always valiant but sometimes leaden, of his mindset led Ågren, in the 1970s, to speak out on touchy matters in two prose works. In the polemic *Hurrarna* (1974; the title is the Swedish plural of an insulting Finnish term, "hurri," for Finland-Swede) he and other Ostrobothnian writers objected to the slow elimination of Swedish speakers in their home region and, by extension, in the whole of Finland, the kind of thing not mentioned in polite society. Its sequel was entirely by Ågren's hand, *Vår historia: En krönika om det finlandssvenska folkets öden, en analys av vårt lands historia* (1977; Our history: A chronicle about the Finland-Swedish people's destinies, an analysis of our country's history). No doubt inspired by *Min svenska historia 1–2* (1970–71; Eng. tr. *A History of the Swedish People,* 1972–74), the chronicle of Sweden's common people, not its captains and kings, undertaken by Vilhem Moberg (1898–1973), Ågren recounted the long story of the economic oppression of a freedom-loving and simple people, Finland's Swedish-speaking proletariat, agricultural and industrial. The chapters on Finland's recent history were a parallel, albeit coming from a genuine experience of deprivation, to the attack on the Finland-Swedish "bourgeoisie" instigated by Kihlman and expanded during the 1970s by the titillating stories of patrician rottenness offered by Henrik Tikkanen and others. The book's effect was vitiated by its presentation of the Winter War, in which "half-Fascist Finland, oriented toward Germany . . . was an undeniable danger for the Soviet Union," the latter a well-meaning state that "tried to carry out its war as gently as possible."

The complaints raised by Ågren and his colleagues in *Hurrarna* — continuing the line of Freudenthal, Axel Lille, Hugo Ekhammar, Arvid Mörne, and (contemporaneous with Ågren) Anders Cleve — still have some validity today, although Ågren himself seems to have grown less interested in them, now that he is accepted as a luminary of Finland's cultural life. His history of the Finland-Swedish (read: Ostrobothnian-Swedish) people was an oddity, but a significant one. By moving his home province to the center of Finland's historical stage, Ågren contributed wholeheartedly to the Ostrobothnian movement that had begun with *Horisont*. Indeed, he had been instrumental in the foundation of a publishing house for Swedish Ostrobothnia in 1973, Författarnas andelslag (Authors' Cooperative), a rejoinder to the unenthusiasm for fledgling Ostrobothnian authors demonstrated by Helsingfors publishers. *Hurrarna*, in typescript, was one of its earliest publications.

Confessor Literature and the Tikkanens
Surveying twentieth-century Finland-Swedish literature in *Horisont*, Torsten Pettersson observed, "The formal novelty that the 1970s introduced consisted, before all else, of the so-called confessor literature," and he added, rightly enough, that Christer Kihlman's *Människan som skalv* was its herald (pp. 6, 47). Confessor literature—also known as the "literature of the (self-)exposer"—immediately put pitfalls before its readers, who quite naturally tended to believe that its authors were giving factual accounts about themselves and others near and perhaps dear to them, whereas the authors, in statements to the press, insisted, perhaps disingenuously, on the fictional nature of what they had written. Pettersson goes on to say that the epithet "confessor literature" is a singularly unhappy term, implying as it does more frankness and accuracy than its authors intended to give. It should be added that, as has been seen, the "autobiographical novel" has long flourished in Finland and in Sweden, where it had received a classic, and ambiguous, form long ago in Strindberg's *Tjänstekvinnans son* (1886–1909; Eng. tr. *The Son of a Servant*, 1913).

The urge to present one's self (or a version of one's self) took various shapes. After making his way through the usual books of nondescript modernist poetry, *Människans anlete* (1953; Man's countenance) and *Vind av stoft* (1955; Wind of Dust), and a collection of abstract Lagerkvistian legends about the human condition, *Väven* (1953; The web), the technically and mathematically gifted Kurt Sanmark (1927–90) published *Insyn* (1958; Observation, originally a military word implying "insight" into the enemy's fortifications). *Insyn* was the story of a "shy and clumsy" chemistry student's trials and erotic involvements, in which the depiction of postwar university life (Sanmark had attended Åbo Academy between 1948 and 1950) is more gripping than the descriptions of encounters between Mikael and the wife of his best friend. Sanmark's novellas, *Förskjutnungar* (1963; Dislocations), likewise deal with erotic malfunctions: an animal tamer achieves too close an identification with his big cat, a lonely woman has delightfully horrible fantasies of rape. Following the brief and still modernistic lyrics of *Blott du* (1960; Only you) — Södergranian ("She waits for a tree / to green") and Björlingesque ("Oh you who come — a light / that bores through all the eye portals") — Sanmark set out on a new and promising course with the distinctly "impure" poetry, dependent on technology, of *osv* (1964; and so forth): "My brain is a data machine / in which impulses are measured," with interfoliated advertisements in the concretist style that Alftan also pursued, and *Obundna texter* (1973; Unbound or unfettered texts; the adjective may also refer to "obunden stil," i.e., prose as opposed to "bunden stil," poetry). The word experiments of these books — associative words and sound effects in the former ("laburnum, SOLARIS VULGARUM / VULGA / VOLGA / DON"), *technopaignia* in the latter (a map shape of Finland typed out in words, fragments of a multilingual menu) — are set off against intimate sexual revelations, especially in the finale of *Obundna texter.*

These exercises prepared for the two prose books that are Sanmark's contributions to the self-revelations of the 1970s. In *Anteckningar, drömmar* (1970; Sketches, dreams) his personal thoughts are mostly literary, on Tuominen, on the Swedish author Sven Fagerberg (1918–), whose analytical-scientific bent attracted Sanmark, on Gunnar Björling, on Rilke's *Briefe an einen jungen Dichter* (1929; Eng. tr. *Letters to a Young Poet,* 1934) and its dictum that poems are not feelings but experiences, on Sanmark's own method of making concrete poetry. The material, though given a personal tone, was still not self-probing, save in the conclusion, in which Sanmark spoke of his hysterical fear of death (a return to the first tale of *Väven*). Then, in 1976, Sanmark's *Dagbok* (Diary) came out, a day-to-day notation of his double life, between work (and a little apartment) in Helsingfors and a home in Borgå ("At home, a freshly painted, good-smelling weekend awaits me, and a bunch of salmon-red roses on my desk"). The revelations were not especially shocking, not even those of his possible adulteries (the book is dedicated to his wife), but frank enough, in their low-voiced way, to make them a sign of the times; authors now told things about themselves and their families they would not have mentioned straight out before or would have disguised as narratives (see *Väven* and *Insyn*). An example is Sanmark's picture of his father, whose life, split between Borgå and Helsingfors, prefigured his own, and of his mother, German-born, sixteen years the father's junior and lonely in the little town, a mother "who in marriage created dreadful scenes about the household's money, scenes that filled [their child] with horror every time." After *Dagbok* Sanmark ceased to publish, perhaps because he could bring himself to reveal no more than he already had, perhaps because the public confessional booth was now occupied by a figure of far greater egotism and fewer inhibitions.

Henrik Tikkanen (1924–84) came, like Kihlman and Donner, from a well-known cultural family. His great-grandfather, Paavo Tikkanen (1823–73), had been one of the founders of *Suometar,* the first major Finnish-language newspaper, and for many years (until his mental collapse) had served as its editor; his grandfather, Johan Jakob Tikkanen (1857–1930), was professor of art history at the University of Helsingfors; his great-grandmother, Paavo Tikkanen's wife, was the niece of Jacob Tengström (1755–1832), professor of theology at Åbo Academy and archbishop of Finland and, after 1808–9, a leading proponent of getting along with the new Russian masters, and the daughter of Johan Jacob Tengström (1787–1858), the historian. However many his complaints about his complex family line, Henrik Tikkanen was in fact extremely proud of it and liked to be photographed with Jacob Tengström's stern face as a backdrop. (Through Archbishop Tengström, too, whose niece Runeberg had married, Tikkanen was somehow related to the bard himself, who "chose to glorify stupidity and became a national poet.") As a boy, Tikkanen had been a zealous patriot, joining the civilian defense corps at fourteen and going to the freshly recaptured parts of Karelia at the start of the Continuation War, a member of a boys' company of the Patriotic Front. After taking his final school examinations in 1943, he entered the tradition-rich regiment Nyland's Dragoons as a volunteer, only to fall into the hands of a vicious company commander and to witness the Russian breakthrough on the Karelian isthmus in June 1944.

Out of service, the young veteran tried his hand at writing, with *Mr. Gogo kommer till Europa* (1946; Mr. Gogo comes to Europe), something he later described as "an immature and childish story about an ape that, arriving in Europe as an African cultural attaché, discovers that capitalism leads to war and that fascism is insanity, pure and simple"; it displayed the grotesque humor (and often inchoate political thought) that would be present in his later production. For a long time, Tikkanen yoked his writing talent to his other artistic gift, as a sketcher — for example, in *Vi ser på Helsingfors* (1952; We look at Helsingfors), for which his friend Benedikt Zilliacus provided the text; he both wrote and illustrated a series of cynically lighthearted travel books, from Rome, Sweden, Ireland, Texas, Yugoslavia, Etruria, the Soviet Union, culminating in *Mitt Helsingfors* (1972; My Helsingfors) and *Dödens Venedig* (1973; Death's Venice): Tikkanen had a highly developed sense of the macabre, demonstrated to the full in his view of Venice as the symbol of an overrich and dying western culture. In all these popular items and others his own persona — sexually boastful, tough but sentimental — became the main attraction. Simultaneously, he worked as cartoonist and columnist for *Huvudstadsbladet* and then (he was bilingual) for *Helsingin*

Sanomat, and collected his various causeries in book form (such as *Henrik tiger inte* [1962; Henrik is not silent]), proving himself a successor to Guss Mattson in capturing the manifold silliness of life.

But his large-scale literary ambitions had not vanished; Tikkanen became a fecund author of plays for radio, television, and the stage, none of which — a common fate of Finland-Swedish dramatic writing — appeared in print. In 1961 he tried his hand at the novel again, with *Hjältarna är döda* (The heroes are dead), a description of a would-be artist in Helsingfors and Stockholm the first years after the armistice with the Soviet Union; with *Ödlorna* (1965; The lizards) Tikkanen returned to his wartime experiences of senseless cruelty and his louche days on the Continent. Later, in two versions in his two languages, *Unohdettu sotilas* (1974; Forgotten soldier) and *30-åriga kriget* (1977; Eng. tr. *The Thirty Years' War,* 1987), he took up the story of Japanese soldiers, unaware that World War II had ended and left behind on Guam and the Philippines, transferring the scene to the Karelian wilderness. His simpleminded Viktor Käppärä (whose name may be related to "käppänä," a dwarf or withered person) is altogether different from the semisophisticates of *Ödlorna;* during his decades of isolation before his discovery Käppärä has remained convinced that the war will end with the final victory Mannerheim promised — yet he has also learned that the soldier's first duty is to stay alive. Ironies pile up: the man who has spent his life at his post of duty has also wasted it. (In a sequel of 1979, *Efter hjältedöden* [After the hero's death], Käppärä, a Rip Van Winckle, inadvertently becomes a television star, reveals a plan for universal demilitarization, and is assassinated for his pains as he shakes hands with the Swedish prime minister, Olof Palme, an unintentional prediction of Palme's murder in 1986.) Tikkanen could not let the war and its aftermath go; in *TTT* (1979), Tor Torsten Torsson, "sexist pig, drunk, whoremaster, and exhibitionist," remembers his experience as a Finnish veteran in the Stockholm of the later 1940s. (*TTT* has the nickname "Tott," which — one of Tikkanen's many linguistic jokes — suggests both German *Tod* and *tot,* "death" and "dead," as well as the name of a Swedish-Finnish general of the Thirty Years' War, the historical Åke Henriksson Tott [1598–1640], just as "Torsten" calls to mind the names of other commanders from that conflict, Torsten Stålhandske [1594–1644] and Lennart Torstenson [1603–51].)

Nonetheless, Tikkanen's literary fame rests primarily on the short and extremely readable "address novels" of which *TTT,* a lightly masked discussion of a middle-aged artist's marital problems, was a by-blow. At the outset Tikkanen may not have planned to provide sequels, but the initial succès de scandale encouraged him to continue, just as Tito Colliander had with his autobiographical books. The parts of the series are *Brändövägen 8 Brändö Tel. 35* (1975; Eng. tr. *A Winter's Day*/British title: *Snob's Island*, 1980), *Bävervägen 11 Hertonäs Tel. 78035* (1976), *Mariegatan 26, Kronohagen* (1977), *Georgsgatan* (1980), and *Henriksgatan* (1982). The first of the books fixes on the childhood, youth, and military service of the narrator; the disclosures about manifold parental weaknesses — his father's alcoholism, his mother's promiscuity — and the suicide of one brother, the rapid decline of another were read by the public with special avidity and expressions of horror. In the next two volumes Tikkanen — who shied away from calling the suite autobiographical: "I have written twenty-five books dealing with myself in world history, but the five that deal with me in the present are fiction" — tells about his growing dependence on drink, his Continental journeys with the left-wing poet Arvo Turtiainen (1904–80), his efforts to establish himself in the newspaper world, his dull first marriage, and his passionate affair with the woman who became his second wife.

The address of the first book is the elegant upper-middle-class islet of Brändö; that of the second is the monotonous bedroom suburb of Hertonäs (where he and his first wife "worked at marriage the way you do at a business"); and the third is in Helsingfors's Faubourg Saint Germain, the location of the new home with the new and admiring spouse. *Georgsgatan* is where his old gymnasium once stood (the site is now occupied by a statue of a woman astride a dragon — the model was his mother, the sculptor his father's successor), where the theater was located in which his play about his father's shortcomings, *Fjäriln* (The butterfly) had been produced, and where the gallery lies in which an exhibit of Tikkanen's graphic work is presently to be held. It also bears his unused first name, which he dislikes, and it has an ominous air for him; he walks it on his way to the physician who will diagnose his fatal illness. Finally, *Henriksgatan* — the prewar name of Helsingfors's main north-south thoroughfare — is once more self-referential; its form is quasi-diaristic, a private newspaper column written on the fifty days of journalistic abstention required by law from Tikkanen as a potential elector during Finland's presidential election of 1982. (Mauno Koivisto became the successor to the aging Kekkonen.) His thoughts circle around his wife (whose star, he enviously notes, rises as his falls), the idyllic marriage of his Tikkanen grandparents, and his own death, as he yearns for the more discreet world in which his forebears lived; the iconoclast is afflicted with nostalgia. Tikkanen had always been fascinated by automobiles (his grandfather, he pointed out, had been Brändö's first pedestrian fatality), and his last independent book was *Renault mon amour: En autobiografi* (1983; Renault, my love: An auto-biography), in which he remembered his own and his father's cars. In the automobile volume he returned to his old practice of illustrating his own texts; for Christer Kihlman's *De nakna och de saliga* (1983; The naked and the blest), he provided line drawings, creating an emblem book of thanato-erotica. The male lover is often given death's features.

The literary ranking of Tikkanen is difficult. Like Kihlman — whose confessional books certainly prepared the way for Tikkanen's, however different their approaches are, Kihlman's owlishly analytical, Tikkanen's luridly witty — he acquired a substantial reputation abroad; his one-sided picture of a Finland-Swedish decadence won him, as it did Kihlman, a large following in Sweden. His admirers have talked about his savage Swiftian humor and his Voltaire-like punishment of human foibles through extravagant irony and have praised the bite of his language; his detractors have called him almost unbearably self-absorbed, forever clutching at the reader's attention, forever boasting or asking for pity, a tabloid journalist whose style, instead of being brilliant, became repetitious in its puns, its striving to make a joke at any cost, and its haste. Or he may be that unusual phenomenon in Finland-Swedish prose, the author who entertains royally even as he stimulates serious or desperate thought.

The rage Tikkanen, ill and aging, felt toward his second wife, Märta Tikkanen, née Cavonius (1935–), was increased by his awareness of publishers' statistics: her popularity had come to exceed his. The daughter of a prominent member of the Swedish-language school system, and herself trained as a teacher, Märta Cavonius was employed as a summer fill-in at *Hufvudstadsbladet* when she met Tikkanen; her own first marriage ended in divorce, and in 1963 she wed the artist-author who would play a large role in her own creations. Devoted to her gifted and restless husband, she was nonetheless drawn to the women's movement; but throughout her career her work has had a nondoctrinaire quality, giving it much of its broad appeal. Her first two novels, *Nu imorron* (1970; Now tomorrow) and *Ingenmansland* (1972; No man's land), deal with a couple, Fredrika and Anders, easily recognized — with the aid of her own later publications and her husband's semiautobiographical series — as the Tikkanens themselves, somewhat fictionalized. Notably, Fredrika shares a name with Fredrika Runeberg, Johan Ludvig Runeberg's talented but self-sacrificing wife; her life is made miserable by her husband's addiction to drink, extramarital affairs, and pathological jealousy, and by her constant exhaustion as a teacher and conscientious mother.

With her next books, sometimes called "pamphlet novels" in the press, Märta Tikkanen left her personal burdens for the problems of other oppressed or neglected women. A Swedish best seller, Stig Claesson's *Vem älskar Yngve Frey?* (1960; Who loves Yngve Frey?), had dealt in a good-natured way with the efforts of old people in an almost deserted country village to make use of their evident uselessness; in Tikkanen's *Vem bryr sej om Doris Mihailov?* (1974; Who cares about Doris Mihailov?) the main if invisible figure in this mystery with a social component, preceding Johan Bargum's similarly plotted *Mörkrum* by three years, is a lonely and emotionally damaged single parent. The puzzle of Doris Mihailov is put together by a woman television journalist — herself exceptionally liberated — and a self-centered male psychiatrist, as they listen to tapes Doris has made before vanishing with her little daughter. Crime itself, and revenge, were the piquant stuff of the book by which Tikkanen won an international reputation, *Män kan inte våldtas* (1975; Eng. tr. *Manrape,* 1977); assaulted by a man whom she has accompanied to his apartment, a divorcée becomes a stalker, plotting and triumphantly inflicting a counter rape on her assailant. Widely translated, the book got further currency through a film (1978) made by Jörn Donner.

The contribution of Märta Tikkanen to the confessor literature in which her husband had already had made such a splash, even among a public that did not customarily read serious literature, was *Århundradets kärlekssaga* (1978; Eng. tr. *The Love Story of the Century,* 1984). Devising a set of prose poems with a narrative thread, she seemed to wreak vengeance on her husband for his complaints about her coldness and ambition, which he had spread abroad in the third of the street-address volumes from the year before. The accuser's voice revealed not only the (unnamed) husband's binges but his emotional vampirism; the book and a subsequent dramatization appealed to female audiences who found in it a replica of their own marital lots. The narrative in poems or lyrical prose now became Tikkanen's form of preference; in *Mörkret som ger glädjen djup* (1981; The darkness that gives happiness depth) she coupled the tale of the devotion and self-abnegation of the mad Josef Julius Wecksell's mother (see chapter 7) with a report on her own child's emotional illness; a companion work, in topic if not tone, was the more matter-of-fact *Sofias egen bok* (1982; Sofia's own book), the case history of the illness and treatment of her youngest daughter, afflicted with minimal brain dysfunction. As Gunnar Mattsson would do with his book on alcoholism, Tikkanen gave her work greater weight by adding a scientific opinion by a professional hand: Kihlman's claim of 1971, that he intended *Människan som skalv* to help fellow sufferers, had borne fruit.

After the death of Henrik Tikkanen (his widow edited a volume of tributes to him), she undertook a self-analysis in *Rödluvan* (1986; Little Red Riding Hood): brought up by a gently domineering father and a compliant mother, she moved from the shelter of her youthful home into the lair of a shaggy and surprisingly vulnerable wolf. Even though intended to illustrate the acquiescence of a woman to male tyranny as she was passed from father to husband, the book was much more than a feminist *j'accuse*, because of the believable quality Tikkanen gave both the girl and the beast of the modern fable. The romanticizing 1980s had a prime representation in *Rödluvan* as they did in *Storfångaren* (1989; The great hunter), about a trip to Greenland and a new grand passion; its sequel, and superior in quality, was *Arnaía kastad i havet* (1992; Arnaia cast into the sea). Tikkanen dug out an obscure detail of Homeric myth, as recorded in Robert Graves, in order to fashion a Penelope (Arnaia's better-known name) less patient than the original and to celebrate, dissect, and lament the subsequent stages of the romance started so bravely in the Greenland book; she concluded with the proclamation of a renewed desire for freedom: "Twice born I swim toward the horizon. / It never comes closer. Here it is not a question of up or down, green everywhere. The sea bears me."

Tikkanen has become one of Finland's most-read contemporary authors in Scandinavia and Germany, through her skillful clothing of some central messages of feminism in a distinct and nonpolemical dress; her revelations about herself and others are variously wry, passionate, humorous, and occasionally sentimental. Her ejaculatory style is an apt instrument for attracting and holding her readership; extremely conversational at the start of her career, her verbal tone has grown more and more exalted with the years, so that it is well nigh impossible to draw a line between prose and free-verse poetry, still another trait contributing to the lush romanticism of her later work.

Women Writers: Ostrobothnia and Elsewhere
An effort to create a separate history of women writers in Finland is futile; women have long been major voices in both literatures of the country, on an equal footing with men. In Finnish there are such great names as Minna Canth, Maria Jotuni, Maila Talvio (in her day called Finnish culture's Grand Old Lady, as much for her imperious ways as for her literary importance), Aino Kallas, and then Eeva-Liisa Manner, Marja-Liisa Vartio, Eeva Kilpi, Eeva Joenpelto—the list can go on and on; in Swedish, starting with Edith Södergran and Hagar Olsson, the names of standard-bearers are equally numerous, and an attempt to label a Solveig von Schoultz or a Märta Tikkanen as a feminist would reduce her stature. One of the readily noted phenomena of the 1970s, however, was the appearance of a group of

women writers in Ostrobothnia, whose concerns were often an exclusive depiction, sometimes with accompanying battle cries, of women's special problems; they swiftly made Författarnas andelslag, established in 1973 by male and female authors, completely their own.

A forerunner of this concerted movement was Wava Stürmer (1929–), who entered literature with fairly solemn lyrics based on Ostrobothnian settings and using modernist tropes, in *Bevingad vardag* (1955; Winged weekday) and *Därför att ljuset* (1967; Because the light); but her impish humor came to light in her detective story, *Ro, ro till Dödmansskär* (1967; Row, row to Dead Man's Skerry), and in the comic novel *Stadens ofullmäktige* (1972; The city's unempowered authorities). A widowed lady in an Ostrobothnian coastal town (Jakobstad) sets the local male establishment on its ear: she puts hairpins in clocks, sets off a record of a cuckoo during an oration at a benefit, stuffs toilet paper into the mouth of a cannon from the war of 1808–9. Interwoven with this plot (a variant on the time-honored Nordic depiction of small towns as whited sepulchers) is a litany of what women have *not* been allowed to do over the centuries: "Not open your mouth, not utter your opinions, preferably not have an opinion, not scold, not speak out." Stürmer had already given women forceful instructions in the verse of *Det är ett helvete att måla himlar* (1970; It's hell to paint heavens):

> In a marriage
> you're the proletarian
> and your Sir Husband is the middle class . . .
> Stop sighing and giving way
> stop serving the coffee while the old boys decide.
> Fight.

As for Mother's Day, it is a male palliative device:

> When evening comes,
> a collective sigh goes through the country:
> Now we've done our duty,
> Now mother has been honored.
> For the next year.

The same vinegary tone runs through Stürmer's third novel, *Slå tillsamman* (1976; Get together): women whose hobby is weaving neglect or abandon their spouses and further demonstrate their freedom by dancing together; in one of the drastic scenes Stürmer does so well, a widow (who has turned her house over to the weavers) reads the riot act to her nosy brother-in-law:

"What a damned patriarch you are. Don't meddle in my life. I'm better off now than I've ever been. . . . Get out. Get out and never come back."

Stürmer's high spirits are muffled in her verse; *Vår dag* (1977; Our day) says, "How long the night becomes / and how many cannot endure," and the mood darkens to the point of desperation in *Solblåst* (1980; Sun gale): "This last day she let loose the line / and gave back the water its boat." Still, in the same collection, her humor glitters in the epicedium for her Bendix Automatic Home Washer ("What things we have talked about / during our times of conversation"), and in her address to a Swede from Sweden:

> You think
> that we're
> your leftover upper class
> and you're ashamed for us
> when we ourselves
> don't have the sense to be so.

The darkness wins out in imaginary atrocities visited on an imaginary small town in *Fågelvind* (1982; Bird wind): the sudden destruction of the Nordic idyll (and of the world) was her recurrent nightmare just as in the work of Carpelan and Huldén: "young soldiers with corpse worms / in their hair like vultures / tramped our streets." In 1985 Stürmer, who had previously published her books at Söderström & Co. in Helsingfors, joined the catalog of Författarnas andelslag with *Väntansväg* (Waitingsway); the narrator discovers she can leave reality at will: "The time I was away from my own life was brief, measured in our clocktime." At length the visionary goes blind: "But happiness, which also existed, which always existed in the midst of the wind, wrapped its wings around my body, which was so light now." Five years later, returning to her major publisher, Stürmer abandoned the mystical vision, not very well suited to her talent (a friend writes to the narrator of *Väntansväg*: "Your sight grows worse because you can no longer bear to see what you see"), for genuine Ostrobothnian memories in *Så länge vi minns* (1990; As long as we remember). These poems, to be sure, are mostly sad: parents who have passed away, a sister who died in her early teens:

> You let her keep
> her blue dressing gown on
> when you and pappa
> put her in the coffin
> that same fall.

Stürmer's retreat from gadfly to elegist robbed Ostrobothnian women's literature of a sprightly voice. Others around her often used heavier-caliber ammunition. Gunnel Högholm (1926–), who was encouraged by Stürmer herself in the writing program "Skrivarstuga" in Jakobstad, began with a picture of a poor childhood, *Solvarm stig* (1974; Sun-warm path); her interest in the sociology of her home region led to a semidocumentary, *I minnet lyser vägen ljus* (1976; In memory the way shines bright). Attendance at the first Nordic seminar for women writers, at Biskops-Arnö (on Sweden's Lake Mälar) in the summer of 1978, inspired a radical feminization of Högholm and many others in attendance. Among other things, the seminar's program demanded "the formation of women's writing groups in the several Nordic countries, the analysis of discrimination against women writers, professional training, a general Nordic women's seminar at least every five years, annual seminars for women writers in their respective countries, research into women's studies and research concerning women writers and their works at universities and colleges, furtherance of women's literature in schools, in education, and in libraries, as well as the translation of women's literature." The seminar led directly to Högholm's novel *Kvinnomorgon* (1979; Woman's morning), a title that promised fiery propaganda but a text that gave a plodding account of two sisters' efforts to improve their lot; at length the brighter sister departs for Sweden with her young husband, all recounted in third-person (and mostly present-tense) narration. It seemed to call for a direct sequel, but Högholm's next novel, *Rotlösa* (1981; Rootless ones), although taking up the problems of Finland-Swedish emigrants to Sweden in the 1950s, had a protagonist who told her own story.

Lilla Guldmärket (1985; The little gold sign) has some figures left over from *Kvinnomorgon* (Anna-Lena, now called Annalisa, who had gone to Sweden, visits backward Ostrobothnia); but the main narrative has to do with a happy-enough couple that has stayed in Finland, and their children, especially the sixteen-year-old Kajsa, with whom the mother, Magda, takes a tour to Rhodes. Mother-daughter bonding is central for Högholm; in the girls' jolly mother of *Kvinnomorgon*, "Fat Stina," she had already created her most living novelistic figure. Högholm, whose male characters are no less decent than her female ones (albeit less interesting), was not cut out for feminism's sterner campaigns or literature's more vexing problems: after her trip to the Mediterranean, Magda ponders the existence of evil and agrees with her solid and practical-minded husband that evil is like weeds in the potato patch; it has to be kept after, so that "the good in life will not be choked out."

A touching naiveté, taking various expressions, clings to many of the otherwise laudable works of the group that emerged in and around Jakobstad and in the wake of the Biskops-Arnö seminar. (All Högholm's books were published at Författarnas andelslag, and the old debate about "refined taste" and "people's taste" was revived, both in separate reviews and in the diplomatic survey by Merete Mazzarella, "Den Kvinnomedvetna prosan efter 1970.") Solveig Emtö (1927–) came from poverty and familial disruption; shortly after she was born, her father migrated to Canada, leaving her mother to rear her and an older brother. During the war years the girl unloaded railroad cars at the Wärtsilä factory in Jakobstad but, unable to bear the heavy labor, became a shop clerk. After a course in creative writing, Emtö put together *Rönnbär och flanell* (1974; Rowanberries and flannel), following it with *Krokushuset* (1976; The crocus house) and *Det gula slottet* (1978; The yellow castle): all were patently autobiographical, about Elvira, leading her from the straitened circumstances of childhood to early adulthood and to what might have been a happy marriage. Unhappily, the repeated efforts of her brutal stepfather to rape her, behavior to which her otherwise devoted mother closed her eyes, have made a sexual relationship with her pleasant groom impossible, and she leaves him to join her mother in Sweden ("He is so nice and I almost believe that I love him, therefore he must be spared anything that could make him unhappy").

The ambitions of Emtö with her trilogy were considerable (the second and third parts were taken on by Söderström & Co., an indication of their greater subtlety and narrative skill); she meant to analyze the stunted emotional life of a dreamy adolescent (who yearned for a father who could read her fairy tales), and at the same time, as she said, she wanted to fill a gap in Finland's Swedish literature by describing the life of a working woman on the home front during the wars of 1939–44. Perhaps aware that her reach exceeded her grasp, she ended the series as Elvira Enbom meets her mother on a railroad platform with the question, "Do you think [Bertel] Gripenberg's books are in the library here?"; she wishes she could have read her husband Gripenberg's florid and old-fashionedly erotic poem "The Grotto." Emtö next wrote on a germane topic in the Finland of the postwar years, the fate of Ostrobothnians in Sweden: *Krigsbarn 13408* (1986; War child 13408) and *Eldvagnarna* (1988; The chariots of fire). The Elvira trilogy had shown a sensitivity to nuances of speech (in the dialogue of home and factory) and an ability to penetrate emotional substrata (Elvira's thoughts during her sexual experiences); the new pair of novels fastened on the special problems of Pelle in Sweden, caused first by his stutter and his Ostrobothnian dialect and then by his "psychic reality," as Michel Ekman put it ("Finlandssvensk skönlitteratur 1988," 86). Like Högholm, Emtö refused to be constrained by narrow feminism's limits: Elvira's brother and her disappointed husband are as much baffled as she is by life and by an economically oppressive society; and Pelle, after all, is a little boy, suddenly set down in a safe, kind, and yet uncomprehending land.

The personal narrative, with which Högholm and Emtö made their initial mark, was tried by Anna-Lisa Österberg (1926–) but stripped of its fictional dress; she came to it only after a career of sporadic publication of poems, stories, and meditations. In several respects Österberg did not fit the pattern of Ostrobothnian women writers; she was not a native of the region where she spent her adult life teaching at a countryside high school (in 1984 she said she had lived "thirty years in Närpes without having become naturalized") but came from the vanishing social class Sigrid Backman had known so well, Swedish-speaking workers in Helsingfors. Further, she was not a product of writers' workshops and did not attend the seminar at Biskops-Arnö (as Emtö had) but rather was a pedagogue trained in Swedish stylistics. Yet she embraced some of the basic tenets of literary feminism: *Kvinnoträdet* (1980; The woman's tree) illustrates perfectly what Carita Nyström (1940–) and Birgitta Boucht (1940–) had postulated in their feminist literary program, *Denna värld är vår! Handbok i systerskap* (1979; This world is ours! Handbook in sisterhood): "Women represent the soft values [in life] and men the hard."

Kvinnoträdet begins with "Forefathers," a set of narrative blocks in which the progress of a family from the Nyland countryside to Helsingfors during the nineteenth century is described, with quick portraits of its several members; a second chapter is devoted to Österberg's father ("He died so young that we never had a chance to collide") and her mother ("She played her role, but there was a bitterness in her which at times spilled out over us"); the family's ethos is described in subsequent chapters: poverty stricken, they still insisted on their respectability. Its lasting strength lay in mothers and daughters; the men spent their lives outside — in her careful way Österberg adds that they died young, "pulling the heavy [financial] load, . . . while we sat and chatted as we worked in our home." The climax comes in the book's apostrophe to Österberg's social and linguistic group and its exploration of the reasons for its disappearance; the remaining chapters trace the experiences of the narrator in the ever more Finnish Helsingfors of her youth. Just as in the case of Emtö, practical questions of language loyalty and language command are not blithely passed by, as was often the case with writers from higher up on society's ladder. In 1983, with *Flickan* (The girl), Österberg does not forget that she is an exponent of a mild "cultural feminism," in that she sees women, in Finland, as the bearers of idealism. In its last chapter she recounts how she got her Christian name,

Anna-Lisa: her mother had seen Minna Canth's play of that name at Swedish Theater, about the valiant and morally responsible woman. "Perhaps there lay something of primal motherliness [in the play] that appealed to Mama; after all, the play concerned a murderer of her own child who voluntarily went to meet her punishment."

Anita Wikman (1938–) was another participant at Biskops-Arnö; like Högholm and Emtö, she had come from indigence, "the sixth child in a large family living in one room and a kitchen." For years she was employed in old people's homes, writing lyric collections in her spare time: the first was *De blå bergen* (1974; The blue mountains), in which she described her literary blooming as part of a larger movement ("We shall go out / of ourselves, / fly like birds, / swim like fish, / crawl like mites" and "we shall once more find / our forgotten dreams"). In *Därför* (1977; Therefore), instead of hopeful declaratives, there is a narrative and descriptive stream (a patient's "body is / crooked from the rheumatism and the hard labor which the earth / and the land offered people in her youth") that goes on in *Väntrum* (1979; Waiting room): "We who never possessed or knew material security / in our childhood after the war, saw the great adventure / in security's pursuit" so that "during the days we smiled behind business counters as pleasant clerks / as crisp waitresses in the third-class cafés." The desire to tell instructive stories grew stronger still in the folk-song mode of *Balladen om Siimas-Fii och Sjunga-Matt* (1983; The ballad of Siimas-Fii and Sjunga-Matt), a tale of love, betrayal, bad conscience, and loyalty, told mostly in runometer, and *Sången om Taimi och Sonja* (1984; The song of Taimi and Sonja), a double "poem narrative" about Taimi and her brood, Finnish migrants to Sweden, and Sonja, a Swedish speaker who also migrates with her own family; the two become fast friends as they work together at (again) a home for the elderly. Wikman also wrote novels, sometimes with narrative verse inlays, starting with *Kära Alexander* (1980; Dear Alexander). Alexander is one of the inmates at a residence for the aged in the Ostrobothnian countryside; a beneficent woman's solidarity prevails among the nurses and nurse's aides, who deal in a mostly humane way with the many foibles of their charges, while putting up with the poor pay they get for their necessary labor.

A different aspect of women's life, and the adjustment to its limited possibilities, is found in her single story collection, *Du skall icke hava lust* (1981; Thou shalt not covet): some women fall into an acceptance of a safe but limited life in Ostrobothnia, others venture across the Gulf of Bothnia to find, they hope, Swedish prosperity. In "Security" Barbro, despite fits of envy, is content to give her husband a bath in the kitchen tub (Sweden would have indoor plumbing); he cannot summon the courage to tell her he has lost his job. An orderly housewife endures her husband's fantasies, during coitus, that she is the week's centerfold, Louella. The next day, she wants to run past the houses of the development where they live, calling "for all the women behind the well-kept hedges, handsome doors, and neat windows. Calling for their different feelings, thoughts, and hopes." In "Damned Whore, What Are You Doing?" Birgitta, a drunken girl at a dance, "begins to walk in front of the men and examine them, one after the other. From top to bottom. From bottom to top." A dutiful wife and mother, Ulla is told by her reflection in a bookstore window that other women "think of the world in large terms. They care about what happens . . . in other countries, too"; at last, the image spits in her face. Her husband is informed by telephone that she has had a nervous collapse. Wikman's later novels, *Kråkvals* (1987; Crow waltz) and *Kråkögat* (1991; The crow eye), are broader, with a large cast, marching determinedly through blood, thunder, poverty, drunkenness, and male brutality during the Ostrobothnian 1930s and beyond. As in the novels of Hans Fors and Olof Granholm which deal with the province during the same period, the reader is kept oriented about chronology by newspaper or radio reports from the outside world; Wikman's picture of the time, it should be noted, is much more turbulent than those provided by her male counterparts.

Wikman's rough-and-ready ascertainment of things as they are (or were) and things as Nyström and Boucht have taught that they should be is accompanied by a fairly transparent psychological structure of her characters and a certain monotony; but she has discovered a special area for her investigation: her women (save those in her "ballads," who are of the old, patient stock) have reached a level of comfort they do not want to lose, yet of whose limits they are painfully aware. They make no effort, save in the occasional outburst of violence, directed at themselves or others, to change their reality. Her slightly younger colleague, Gurli Lindén (1940–), makes no bones about her intention to turn the world upside-down. One of seven children of a farmer in the Ostrobothnian skerries, Lindén had a chance at some education but, rebellious from the start, left the "gray weight of school" to work in a shop. "I was not alone. We were a whole generation. We married and had children. You were supposed to do that, and the dreams vanished. The sixties, the great decade for Europe's intellectuals, for me was simply giving birth and taking care. In 1968, the year of the student revolts, I had just had my third."

Lindén was among the first authors to appear in the lists of Författarnas andelslag, with *Att resa sig* (1973; To lift yourself), preaching women's liberation ("Slowly the boundaries stream out of me / I go out into the open landscape"), and she has kept up a steady barrage of verse since, strengthened by the belief that even private emotional involvements are essentially political. (She has been a considerable writer of love lyrics, mingling erotic passion with what appears to be a failed revolution: "I loved you / it was a strange time / the moon passed sick with longing into the rooms / Now he is dead / the streets twist in agony under the lamps," she wrote in *Brännmärken* [1977; Branding marks]; "Beside the road I see those trampled down in piles / I see myself there collapsed, tattered.") Her novels give plenty of evidence of her revolutionary awakening: the first, as so often, are about the author. Recycling a title Tito Colliander had used thirty years before, Lindén, in *Bli till* (1976; Become), describes her narrator's and her own process of becoming, from a poor rural girlhood to a hasty marriage with a man desired and detested ("However much we hate and despise one another, my body is always ready to receive you, as soon as any part of me touches you"); her amateur painting and the perusal of Friedrich Engels help her to decide to go her own way. The tale of erotic disappointment is intensified by the introduction of italicized passages, in which still more intimate thoughts are revealed; as well, the novel has a parade piece of feminist resentment in an account of the humiliations of the obstetrics ward, even as the husband, drinking beer, is consoled by his friends.

Första damernas (1979; The first ladies' dance) again chronicles a woman's life, and again she is nameless and tells her story in the first person. Employed at a Vasa dress shop, she marries, suffering through a pregnancy while her husband is doing military service. When he is recalled to the army, during a threat from the Soviet Union (the "Note Crisis" of 1961, in which Finland's neutrality was jeopardized), she and other women refuse to accept the Runebergian patriotism handed down from the past: "We shall say to one another, we the women, that we do not want war and heroes but rather human beings who feel responsibility for what the earth has carried and fostered for so long a time." The earth, of course, is a mother, as women are. Ecological thoughts are developed near the novel's end, when a tree is scheduled to be felled so that a road may go through the village where the narrator lives. The other women, now loyal to their practical-minded husbands, do nothing in reality, but in another, imaginary time (a device shortly to be employed by Wava Stürmer in *Väntansväg*), they occupy the tree, "without giving a thought to the side men have taken." Yet, switching back to the real world, the narrator reveals that her husband, home at last, will work hard and buy a house, while she, quite traditionally, cares for their child: "And I could not think any differently from the way [he] thought, or the parents." Revolution has to wait, and accommodation takes place, at least temporarily: Merete Mazzarella ("Den kvinnomedvetna prosan efter 1970," 331) has noticed that, in both the introduction and conclusion of *Första damernas*, there is another female presence, or perhaps the narrator herself at a later stage, who has attended "the great conference [Biskops-Arnö] and hearkened to the words. Interpretations of theories about a reality we [women] had never known and of which we had never partaken."

The move into the realm of the imagination, in order to make dreams of the triumph of woman's preservative spirit come symbolically true, was repeated at length in the fantasy novel *Maras ö* (1984; Mara's island). In its retelling of the myth of a matriarchal island utopia — the Gerhart Hauptmann of *Die Insel der grossen Mutter* (1924; Eng. tr. *The Island of the Great Mother*, 1925) would have recognized the setting, although he would have been alarmed by Lindén's antimale bias — three figures of primary importance can be discerned: the prophetic priestess-artist Mara (plainly a close relative of the speaker of the prelude and postlude of *Första damernas*); the mysterious Raa, to whom "the waves" and "the runes" whisper: "You were once a daughter of the proud woman. . . . You belonged to a clan that had found its way to the great certainty"; and Silja, a creature of everyday life, apparently happy, "measured by the measures of [her] village." But climbing a tree (like the pastor's daughter in Juhani Aho's *Papin tytär* [1885] and like Edith Södergran's "I" in *Dikter* [1916]), Silja becomes one with it and is told to "live . . . take your life," and so she dreams of climbing higher still: it is Silja's mission, in her dream, to bear a waterbird's egg from a wartorn city to a sanctuary, to be hatched in freedom. At the book's end she tries to pass the egg along to Raa but is instructed that she, Silja, must return to her village, there to build a nest to give the bird shelter. Silja apparently does so; Raa, sailing for Mara's island, from which a flame ascends into the night, tells her to hearken to the laughter of women, and thus, in the midst of her mundane labors, she will find "warm islands" of her sisters, deep within herself. The stilted prose of *Maras ö*, reminiscent of the language in Hagar Olsson's biblical tale *Kvinnan och nåden*, is meant to heighten the impact of her message: women, nature's beings, bear the safety and continuation of humanity solely in their hands. *Maras ö* appeared the same year as the poems of Gun Nygren, *Trädmammans famn* (1984; The tree-mamma's embrace): "Come, let us hear the tree-mammas' [*sic*] all-song. / Come let us light a fire, / an homage to the sun and the moon"; it preceded Wava Stürmer's *Väntansväg* by a year. Ostrobothnian feminism, originally springing out of a lucid recognition of social injustice, was in danger of dissolving into "the visionary and the mystical," as Torsten Pettersson observed (pp. 6,

46), or into a tangle of propaganda and mythopoeia. Lindén persisted in this vein with the poems of *Den splittrade båten* (1986; The splintered boat) and the story of the mysterious and mighty Benjala in *Framtid* (1989; Future): "She came with the women's demands. That the men put down their weapons, renounce their power. . . . She wore clothes woven of stone. But in her eyes there were green stars."

Brita Högnäs-Sahlgren (1938–) kept her feet on the ground; like Österberg, she remained outside the group that had attended the revival at Biskops-Arnö. She thought of herself not as a feminist but as a professional writer, come from a family of some literary interests: she was a relative of the Ostrobothnian teacher, journalist, and novelist Sven-Olof Högnäs (see chapter 9), whose *Paradisplantan* she dramatized in 1977, and the daughter of another teacher with literary ambitions, Uno Högnäs. With her husband, the editor and author Karl Sahlgren, in 1982 she established one of the alternative publishing houses that popped up in those days of febrile activity: by 1993 Sahlgren's had brought out seventy-nine titles. Styling itself the "bold publishing house," it has never followed a gender-oriented or wholly provincial line and has been admirably active in the printing of Finnish classics in Swedish translation.

Högnäs-Sahlgren was primarily attracted to the short story, where she was deft at portraying pathetic corners of life; *Ett hutlöst pris* (1973; An outlandish price) approaches, among other things, sexual attraction between young girls ("A Form of Friendship"), the erotic problems of a male escort-for-hire ("Living Together"), a teacher's passion for one of her pupils ("Elementary School Teacher Lundgren"), and a middle-aged narrator who trudges homeward to a one-room apartment for which an outlandish price is paid. The five novellas of *Spiken* (1975; The nail) depend heavily on Högnas-Sahlgren's ability to reproduce conversation; "The Telephone Call" is composed almost entirely of talk, a device given a classic form in Finnish literature by Maria Jotuni in *Rakkautta* (1907; Love). Advancing a technique that would become much more common during the next decade, Högnäs-Sahlgren also puts portions of her dialogue into Finnish, making the language provenience of her characters clear and canceling out the possibility of publication in Sweden. Plainly, in her modest way, she meets one of the requirements Kihlman had set up back in 1959: a good number of her characters are from the majority language group, although she makes no marked effort to track down emotional or attitudinal differences between the two entities. The mixture of languages is particularly effective in a story about a sick child, "Juhani," whereas "Lill-Anders" employs, instead, Swedish-Ostrobothnian dialect in the story, remembered from childhood, of a man who murdered his fiancée. Casts and themes are those so often found in her work: lovers who have succumbed to indifference, the erotic needs of the middle-aged or the old ("Rafael" could have Yeats's line about "the itch of love in ancient veins" as its epigraph), desire between generations (the title story recalls an encounter between a female counselor and a young boy at a summer camp).

Högnäs-Sahlgren simply and effectively presents human entanglements; she has neither a social-reformist nor an obvious feminist program. In *Rosen* (1980; The rose) the Swedish-Ostrobothnian background becomes more prominent; it contains figures whose forebears can be found in the regional literature of long ago but now are fitted out with complex psyches—the fanatically Christian woman, the madwoman kept tucked away for decades, and, again, the would-be lover across generational lines. Her first novel, *Skruven* (1978; The screw), undertook to combine her undeniable talent for handling (limited) sexual abnormality with the story of Finland-Swedish migration to Sweden; working in Stockholm, the Ostrobothnian Tea has nymphomaniac tendencies, and their description almost leads the book into soft-focused pornography; the girl's attempt at suicide makes Högnäs-Sahlgren's serious purpose clear, however: Tea has come from a world of parental repression leading to both erotic liberation and self-disgust. With her own publishing house at her disposal, Högnäs-Sahlgren gave herself over to the production of documentary or semidocumentary works on Ostrobothnian materials: *Hautaviita* (1982), a reportage about a slaying committed by "Finland's strongest man," William Hautaviita; *Anna-Magdalena* (1985), the development of a text begun by the author's father, about a crime of jealousy in North Ostrobothnia in 1825; and *Herman, min Herman* (1988; Herman, my Herman), again based on factual sources, describing hard life at the turn of the century in the home province and migration to the goldfields of South Africa. A secondary story of lust and murder is woven into the narrative, using court documents.

In her titles, Högnäs-Sahlgren for a time had a preference for sharp objects (nail and screw), and her only book of verse is called *Nubb* (1979; Tack); Åsa Stenwall-Albjerg ("Den otillfredsställda kvinnan," 93) has seen this as a sign of her desire to penetrate into painfully intimate emotional regions. The same critic has also concluded that Högnäs-Sahlgren, apparently indifferent to programmatic feminism, has actually given voice to one of its complaints by presenting a gallery of "unsatisfied women," whose wishes, sexual and otherwise, are unacceptable to conventional men. Perhaps, too, her single-word titles were suggested by Tito Colliander's memoirs; her readily tempted figures are related to the Dostoyevskian sinners who populate Colliander's religious novels, and the faith healer Signe Rask in *Rosen* has a Greek Orthodox mother and a house full of icons. In 1982 Högnäs-Sahlgren was converted to Colliander's Greek Orthodox faith: "In Lutheranism I did not find the stringency I sought in Christianity."

Siw Alander (1940–), the sometime wife of Rainer Alander, has had — like Emtö, Wikman, Lindén — a firsthand experience of tedious and poorly paid labor, reflected extensively in her novels. *Bandet: En kvinnas ofrid* (1979; The band: A woman's war) refers in the first part of its title to the conveyor belt in the baked-goods factory where the narrator is employed ("25,000 pirogs made today"); *Tunneln* (1982; The tunnel), at whose end no light shines, takes the woman from the marriage, children, and spousal abandonment swiftly described at the end of *Bandet* to a hospital as destructive of the patient's dignity as the food factory had been of the worker's humanity; *Blå duvan* (1985; The blue dove) is a restaurant at which the third of Alander's woman narrators is hired as kitchen help. (Alander had been a trainee in such an establishment.) Both the hospital and the restaurant novel insert documents to give the misery of the put-upon women full verisimilitude: a summons to the neurological clinic and directions, both hygienic and motivational, for the restaurant personnel. But Alander also indulges in the mythmaking of Lindén's *Maras ö*, Stürmer's *Väntansväg*, and Tikkanen's *Rödluvan*, all approximately contemporaneous with *Blå duvan*, which is replete with bird symbolism — the narrator thinks of her friend Agnes, who has lost a breast to cancer, as a blue dove, and elsewhere there are birds with wings clipped, birds flying away to freedom. (In the friendship between Mona and Agnes in *Tunneln* one may sense the delicate eroticism Ingmar Bergman wove into the relationship between the servant Anna and the dying Agnes — nota bene — in his film *Rop och viskningar* [1973; *Cries and Whispers*].)

In all Alander's novels, as in the vast majority of the fictions about feminism from this time, a community of women exists, from Stürmer's rambunctious weavers to Lindén's island dwellers; but Merete Mazzarella observes that, for Alander, the Finnish women on the assembly line are stronger and "more free from fear" than their Finland-Swedish counterparts; still more important, Alander's defenseless and pitiable protagonists are hesitant to believe in or even mouth the catchwords of woman's solidarity. Mona can experience a sense of feminine community with her "sisters" only when, on an outing, she sees the "scars on bodies stretched out in the sun." Since the semitrilogy (the names and calling of the women change, but not their essential misery) Alander has turned to poetry, *Ända hit de avlägsna vattnen* (1987; Unto here the distant waters) and *Leendets magma* (1991; The smile's magma); in their cryptic language, altogether different from the clear prose of the novels, outlines of personal crisis appear ("put your hand / over the scars / where they hurt most"), as well as statements of defiance ("Carve too / the border of despair / into your subconscious") and, in what may be love poetry, a bizarre reappearance of the medical vocabulary used in *Tunneln:* "Your breathing against the uterus's mucous membrane / In the arching every ecstasy is inescapable" and

> Behind the granite, in
> the refuge of which we both are aware
> I was born (You played
> midwife, the Caesarian section a
> necessity.)

Regionalism's Boom and Blomqvist

Although all the women writers, save perhaps Alander, have a sense of the local culture from which they come, none of them can be called a regionalist: they are more interested in the actresses on the scene than in the scene itself. A traditional woman writer *and* a regionalist, however, attracted an enormous and loyal readership. Anni Blomqvist (1909–90), a peasant's daughter from Vårdö in Åland, was encouraged to write by Margit von Willebrand-Hollmerus; the drowning of her husband and elder son, in 1961, and an invitation by Stig Jaatinen, professor of geography at Helsingfors, to collaborate on a study of her skerry community led to her books about the lives of fishermen and their families (it started as "planless writing . . . before the true day's work began"). Her autobiographical *I stormens spår* (1966; In the storm's traces) looked back over her life as the wife of a sailor in the Åland merchant fleet; after his purchase of his own boat and his short but risky voyages to Stockholm during the Second World War, a happy time ensued, as father and son pursued their calling. The obvious sincerity and authentic knowledge of Blomqvist immediately won her a public that may have wanted to take refuge in the solid values of unsophisticated folk at a time when other parts of Finland-Swedish society were under severe literary attack.

The book's success led to five novels about a fisherman's wife named Maja, *Vägen till Stormskäret* (1968; The way to Storm Skerry), *Med havet som granne* (1969; With the sea as neighbor), *Maja* (1970), *I kamp med havet* (1971; In struggle with the sea), and *Vägen från Stormskäret* (1973; The way from Storm Skerry); in them Blomqvist depended on her absolute mastery of the skerry culture's details, supplemented by considerable reading in folkloristic studies (in this respect her mode of work resembled that of Josefina Bengts). Also, running parallel with the blossoming of feminist literature in Sweden and Finland, the books presented Åland from the standpoint of a sturdy but devoted woman in a patriarchal society; if it was feminism, it was feminism made palatable for the most hard-bitten male chauvinist. (The descent from Sally Salminen's *Katrina* was obvious but not debilitating: Blomqvist was a more disciplined narrator. The model for Blomqvist's Maja was her maternal grandmother's sister, who had loomed large in stories told by her father.) As popular in Sweden as they were in Swedish-speaking Finland, the Maja books gave rise to a television series, conceived by the actor and director Åke Lindman (1928–) and introduced by the theme song "Stormskärs Maja," composed by the vocal artist Lasse Mårtenson (1934–).

After at last writing the proposed study, *Skimskäla* (1977), on her home, in conjunction with Professor Jaatinen, and an independent novel, *I nöd och lust* (1978; In sickness and health), on her favorite topics of hard work and marital devotion, Blomqvist embarked on a new series of novels about another woman of the skerries, Anna Beata (from 1979 to 1983). Her last book was *Havet finns inte mer* (1989; The sea exists no more), an unostentatiously pious report on the drowning of her younger son, Bengt, whose body was found "after a good two months, by means of a helicopter search, lying on a beach, as if lifted out of the sea by God's invisible hand." Anni Blomqvist — an Åland Grandma Moses in words, at once knowledgeable and innocent — will occupy a sizable place on Åland's Parnassus; in Finland-Swedish literature she has become an encouraging legend for other autodidact authors.

The career of Karl Erik Bergman (1930–) provided a lyric accompaniment to Blomqvist's novels. Depending on the same close knowledge of the milieu and the fisherman's life, he has stuck to Åland quite persistently, from *Mellan två skymningar* (1957; Between two twilights) to *I måsens vingar bor en frihet* (1983; In the seagull's wings there dwells a freedom), with an eye for the hardships of the calling and the ecological decline of the island realm ("When I began to fish / things were badly off, with nets / but not with fish. / Now I have plenty of nets / but few fish") and with a sly humor recalling Lars Huldén's ("In books / I have told about my illegal fishing. / For this / I have been awarded / cultural prizes / of various sorts"). Like Huldén, too, he has also tried prose, in *Berättelser om hav och människor* (1975; Tales of sea and people). A feature of Bergman's poetry is his apparent thriving on loneliness: "There is nothing which in stillness / can compete with / a boathouse a deadstill autumn evening." Siv Storå, another Åland native, observed that Bergman can write about "we" and "us," "our Nordic summer," "our threshold," and so forth, but beneath this posited community there is always a longing for seclusion, a desire to be left alone. Even the December darkness fills him with pleasure:

> The alders
> stand bare in the pasture,
> have nothing more to gossip about.
> The damp December darkness
> closes us all.

He may hover on the brink of mystical withdrawal but always catches himself in time. Not as querulous as Gösta Ågren, whom he matches in poetic taciturnity, he is content to go his own way, unconcerned about what happens outside his own circle of perceptions ("A local philosophy, / you say, / which cannot save the waves? / No, who can save the waves. / Wonderful / if I myself can go on"). His poems about conjugal love seem forced or awkward, as in the would-be witty poem about his wife's weight: "some of us are like hardworking people's bank accounts, they swell with the years," not out of failing affection, but because warmer expression might disturb his nonegotistical egotism.

Despite all the storms at sea, Åland's regional literature has an insular placidity appropriate to the islands' nonengaged history, a sharp contrast to Ostrobothnia's recent regional writing. One of the most productive Ostrobothnian authors of the postwar years—and one who refused to share the almost universal fate of his male generation—is Olof Granholm (1924–), a malingerer and then a deserter from the Finnish army after being drafted early in 1944. Now and then echoing Jaroslav Hašek's *The Good Soldier Švejk*, he wrote about the experience with the good humor that is a saving grace of most of his work, in *Bässpojken* (1971; The ram boy), a title using the nickname Granholm's alter ego Gottfrid Ersbeck got on his boyhood excursions with his father, selling sheep. After the war was over (with "Finland's fascistic army beaten and in moral dissolution"), Gottfrid continues his career in livestock and marries a girl of steadier character than his own, who frequently makes fun of her husband's boundless admiration for the Soviet Union; the sequel, *Oxhollen* (1977; The ox calf), starts with Ada's efforts to open Gottfrid's eyes about Stalin's slave labor camps; "And certainly Ada was right. But it made me uncomfortable that she was the one to criticize." As for Gottfrid, who goes through a number of jobs, "my power of imagination was sometimes so strong that I used my left hand a good deal in my work and believed that it furthered my leftist opinions." Feckless, yarning, and lovable, Gottfrid is a kind of sunshine Communist, "a car owner and a People's Democrat"; his friend Leck represents an idealistic leftist standpoint but is colorless in comparison.

A more earnest side of Granholm's production can be found in the intervening novel, *Spånskottaren* (1973; The shavings tender), whose theme is the fortune and fall of a little Ostrobothnian sawmill before and after the Russian wars, and in the historical novel from the Civil War, *Den vita natten* (1979; The white night), a listing of White brutalities. The latter book found a warm reception in Sweden during that country's years of radical chic; a narrative of atrocity, it is heavily laden with long portions of semi-historical writing, in the spirit and style of Gösta Ågren's *Vår historia:* "Finland had become independent and the White Army was on the march. The overwhelming majority of Finland's people still had nothing to say. If they opened their mouths, it meant prison and death. The people were to be cowed and muzzled by former imperial Russian tools." Meanwhile, Granholm had already begun another series about an Ostrobothnian country boy, Enok, in some respects a juvenile Gottfrid. In four novels, beginning with *Hästhandlarens son* (1978; The horse dealer's son), Enok watches Ostrobothnian life from the 1920s to the end of the 1930s; the other titles are *Kobaggen* (1979; The cow ram), *Påläggskalven* (1980; The breed calf), and *Nedoviggen* (1986; The runt). Enok, or Nocke, maintains his innocence and curiosity throughout, a rapscallion of whom an adult says, "People get in a good humor just looking at such optimism." Entertainment, at which Granholm had been quite good from the start, has clearly gotten the upper hand over propagandistic instruction, as his political passions have been laid to rest.

Other Ostrobothnian pastoralists were not as good-natured as Granholm. Erik Ågren (1924–), the elder brother of Leo and Gösta, was also the last of the three to enter literature (via Författarnas andelslag), describing first his war service and then manual labor in *Sårad: En roman från fortsättningskriget* (1973; Wounded: A novel from the Continuation War), *Arbetslust* (1975; Wish to work), and *Modellfilaren* (1982; The pattern filer), about the tribulations of well-intentioned—and Swedish-speaking—workers in postwar Ostrobothnia. (Ågren's change of publishers for his third novel is telling; Författarnas andelslag having become a feminist concern, he went over to another alternative publisher, Skrivor in Vasa.) Ågren repeated a main complaint of his fiction with "The Last Finland-Swedes," his contribution to his brother's *Hurrarna* of 1974, demanding to know why Swedish-speaking workers, unless they commanded

Finnish, were forced out of Ostrobothnian factories (owned by Finland-Swedes), causing them to emigrate.

Erik Andrén, (1920–89), a conscientious objector and pacifist, made use of his wartime experiences in *Jag såg all möda* (1975; I beheld all tribulations) and *En bland dessa* (1976; One among these); Mats, a born-again Christian (whose father has committed suicide in despair at his poverty), refuses to bear arms and is systematically degraded in several internment camps until he flees to Sweden, where he confronts superficial sympathy barely concealing indifference or contempt. Andrén explored the religious zeal out of which he had sprung, and which he had turned into a humane and tolerant Christianity, in *Byn* (1980; The village) and *Var är din bror?* (1983, expanded 1984; Where is your brother?). In 1986 he excavated a hideous episode in Ostrobothnia's past with a novel, *De besmittade* (The infected ones), about a leper colony in Kronoby parish in the seventeenth century, where the inmates are brutalized by drunken officials, pastors, attendants, and guards hardened by service in Germany during the Thirty Years' War, another example of the influence of Moberg's Swedish history: "authority . . . speaks, while silence prevails on the lips of the oppressed and the exiled."

At the start of his career Levi Sjöstrand (1920–94) was less concerned with modern Ostrobothnia than with its past; his novels *Hård kust* (1965; Hard coast) and *Kustbor* (1971; Coastal dwellers) tell of fishermen's lives early in the nineteenth century; the stories, in five suites, of *Brytningstid* (1968; Time of transition) chronicled the change from fishing or hardscrabble farming to factory life in the province's towns, a theme done before by Anna Bondestam, among others: "The narrow space [of the factory] became a prison for him, which he could not leave; outside . . . forests, lakes, plains seemed to wait for him." In a possible provincial reflection of the confessor literature flourishing in the capital, Sjöstrand then began to speak, in fictional disguise, about his personal prison, that of a man confined to a wheelchair since childhood — the material of some of his stories in *Utlämnad* (1973; Exposed) and the novel *Nyårsafton* (1976; New Year's Eve). Following a path laid out by the Norwegian Finn Carling, a sufferer from cerebral palsy, in *Kilden og muren* (1958; Eng. tr. *And Yet We Are Human*, 1962), and, in Finland, by Eeva Kilpi in *Tamara* (1973), in which a woman tries to aid a handicapped and impotent man by recounting her sexual experiences for him, Sjöstrand wrote, less graphically than Kilpi, about a similar situation.

In all the regional literature of the 1960s and 1970s it becomes apparent that the use of local speech and traditions via dialect, folkloristic detail, and history no longer suffices for its authors; each of them either finds an attractive central figure (Blomqvist's Maja, Granholm's Gottfrid) or marks off a special area of laborer's hardship (Erik Ågren), Christian suffering (Andrén), or physical flaw (Sjöstrand).

Lyric Outburst of the 1970s: Romanticism's Return?
In a literature that has favored a large production — an overproduction? — of lyric poetry, it might seem that a sudden flowering in the genre would pass unnoticed; yet the 1970s had a special richness that rivaled, in energy and quality, the great days of modernism. Already established poets published collections to be reckoned among their most original: Bo Carpelan's *Gården* (1969) on the decade's eve and then *Källan* (1973) and *I de mörka rummen, i de ljusa* (1976), Peter Sandelin's *Tyst stiger havet* (1971), *Var det du?* (1973), and *Dikter med varandra* (1977), and Lars Huldén's *Herdedikter* (1973) and *J. L. Runeberg och hans vänner* (1978). An author otherwise known for his prose, Hans Fors, in *Lysaren* (1975; The illuminator), had prepared a Finnish picturebook, describing a hotdog-stand attendant with a bird in her gray, rainwet hair; Kekkonen, skiing on the ice, "with his elkback mounting the gray morning light"; or a facade painter, who, dressed white,

> lifts space
> on fragile shoulders
> he stretches out his hands
> they flap like wings.

New poets of singular quality appeared, a few still clinging to political shibboleths of the 1960s, others ready and willing to abandon them.

Among the former, Leif Salmén (1952–) was the most stubborn: *Vår korta stund tillsammans* (1976; Our brief time together) salutes Lenin and (of course) the Chilean Communist poet Pablo Neruda, looks at the year of civil war, in "1918" ("The revolution went awry / We can say that now"), and defines the poet's giant task ("to give birth to flaming points in earth-darkness, / to conquer the universe with my broken voice!"). In *Att varje dag* (1978; That every day) Salmén sounded like Diktonius imitating Walt Whitman ("I'm wont to meet my fatherland / in bus stations, railroad squares, harbors, and switching yards"); yet the demands for class struggle slowly but surely fade away in the more personal and elegiac poems of *Begäret* (1980; The desire). Until *Dans och tystnad* (1982; Dance and silence) Salmén did not seem to be vitally interested in generating new poetic forms, but in the suite "Brief History of the World" he attempted—as the title promised—to chart the journey of a Promethean figure (his identity never defined) toward ultimate destruction in a hundred poems of two or three lines: number 88, "He lost interest in theories, / afterward, when he was no longer a part of them," indicates a disenchantment with the political arguments Salmén had made before. In "Archipelago and Construction," the collection's second cycle, a despair at the inefficacy of "helpless politics" finds relief in summer sailing and love: "Blessed the darkness / which can sweep over Kronberg's Channel / with a hand as light as yours." In the midst of grand sound effects ("Suddenly the thunder sings Merikanto and Sibelius") Salmén yearns for a quiet life, rather as in the last collections of another champion of the Left, Pentti Saarikoski's dance trilogy of 1977–83.

Salmén became a well-known public figure, not because of the enigmatic quality of *Dans och tystnad* and the satirical prose poems making up part of *Ikon* (1986; Icon: "After a successful day at the stock exchange he thinks that all the women he meets on the street look like high-class whores") but through his work as a political analyst for Finnish-language television; with this job as a background he wrote *Finländsk bokföring: Dagbok från tredje republiken* (1983; Finnish bookkeeping: Diary from the Third Republic) and *Wintermonolog* (1987; Winter monologue), in the first case factual prose accounts of events during the early months of 1983, shortly after Mauno Koivisto had come to power, and in the second a record of Salmén's disillusion with the materialistic and prosperous Finland of the 1980s. In neither book was Salmén willing or able to embrace a single party's standpoint (he had long since left the Communist Party); the winter monologue has a subtitle identical with its predecessor's but an even darker tone: "It occurs that I am struck by a deep pessimism and sometimes feel sharp pangs of what probably is existential loneliness." The earnestness (and taking-himself-seriously) that prevails in so much of Salmén's work possibly has its basis in his sense of no longer belonging to a cause; in a well-known poem, included in *Dans och tystnad,* he wrote, "I lack a compass for my language / to wean myself from the words is a full-time job," and in *Ikon,* "I am here, I am listening, I can see— / that is all I have left." (The former poem is dated December 1979, the month of the Soviet invasion of Afghanistan.) The pieces of exact short prose in *Livet i förorten* (1992; Life in the suburb) tell about Salmén's ever more jaundiced view of Finland and the world: "In the evening's TV program all the facts, those constant tin soldiers, take up their prescribed positions."

One of the pleasant surprises accessory to the poetic outburst of the 1970s is that the release from social or political concern created a climate in which the love poem thrived. In *Det är redan en annan dag* (1975; It is already another day) Agneta Ara (1945–) offers plenty of leftovers from the upheavals of the immediate past, including a would-be capitalist's prayer in English: "O Lord, won't you give me / a Mercedes Benz"; but she found her own tone of childhood fantasy ("The Cat and the Hedgehog") and horrible childhood shock ("The Only Wars") in *Det är som i dikter* (1977; It's as it is in poems) and particularly softhearted poems of affection in *Hästens hjärta* (1979; The horse's heart): "I am the earth between your fingers / I am the kissing light / which washes over you." Especially in *Omfamningen* (1982; The embrace), she turns to Helsingfors itself. Even the city's bad climate moves her; in "Helsingfors My Beloved" she remembers the constant rain: "The trees blew their crowns toward the sky. / It felt safe to walk there / amidst the gravestones. / And the leaves that fell and fell / loved the earth," is her picture of the Old Burial Ground on the Boulevard.

The tenderness and vulnerability of Ara's work, continued in *Korta stund* (1983; Brief moment) and, wounded, in *Glömska, eld* (1986; Forgetting, fire), was also apparent in the poetry of Brigitta Hjelt (1948–), which began, in *Ur sömnens ask* (1975; From the box of slumber), with a lush, dreamy, but uneasy romanticism ("were those parks real at all? / Were those evenings only pages in / picturebooks, come apart and carelessly put together, so that the pages got out / of order?"). This changed, in *Dikter* (1981; Poems), to an ecstatic Christianity, in which God and the Virgin Mary become one ("God!! / The Woman, Her countenance, and the words of splendor / like a precious / cloak, dress embroidered with bronze . . . / Eyes of living amber!!!"). Clearly programmatic feminist poetry filled the second, lyric section of Nyström's and Boucht's *Denna värld är vår*, often militant—not unexpectedly, considering the purpose of the book—but also diaristic and self-revelatory in Nyström's "In Woman's Memory" (see "The First Menstruation" and the love song, "your honey-hair your soft lips / the tongue's thicket of small mushrooms") and more prosaically in Boucht's "Talk about What You Know," which includes a grocery list in its chronicle of woman's subjugation. Solidarity is the order of the day, in Nyström's "Songs for Sisters" and in Boucht's suite "The One Who Knows the Direction Knows the Way," which includes a drinking song for women, demanding "REVOLUTION" as "a word that awaits its meaning." Women will seize this "empty vat" and "fill it with their own wine."

Birgitta Holma (1933–) published her first collection in 1975, simultaneously with the debuts of Ara, Boucht, Hjelt, and Nyström, and gave it a title intimate and self-deprecatory, *Detta warma rum—en tillfällighet* (This warm room — A chance occurrence). It contained a promise that she would try to go with the times:

> Poets ought to write about community
> about community and song on the squares
> about people who sit in a ring in the grass
> and hold each other's hands.

But for the most part, these were things she would do "that day when I become / happy and strong"; in the meantime she was overwhelmed by guilt toward

> the man
> the society
> the home
> the child
> my neighbor
> myself . . .
> I acknowledge my debt
> My debt is enormous.

In *Tankar av regn* (1981; Thoughts, [made] of rain) the poetic apogee of guilt/debt is reached on a trip to see a dying father in Ostrobothnia — she comes too late. Making a statement for still another instrument of the new woman's literature, *Finlandssvenska kvinnor skriver* (1984; Finland-Swedish women write), edited by Tatiana Sundgren, a handbook growing out of the second Nordic Women's Seminar, held at Lillehammar in the summer of 1982, Holma claimed that her "heart was in peace-and-women's movements." Yet another sentence in the same statement gave a key to her poetry as well as, perhaps, to her silence: "I am the eternal stranger and have difficulty, despite heroic efforts, fitting myself into groups, which unavoidably demand clear-cut social roles and labels." In 1987 she returned to publication with *Vägen till eremiten* (The way to the hermit):

> She weaves her cloak of invisibility
> . . . The questions
> make her strangely disappointed
> like her replies.

Continuing the activist role she had played so successfully in the handbook on sisterhood, Birgitta Boucht quickly took up several causes, literary (Sigrid Backman and, later, the revival of Mirjam Tuominen's reputation) and nonliterary (the situation of the homeless, based in her own and her children's experiences after a divorce, described in *Öppna rum: Insyn hos en bostadslös* [1985; Open rooms: Observation of a homeless person], domestic violence, the peace movement, and so forth). Her poetic creation often followed the same activist principle; the title of *Långa vandring* (1982; Long wandering) alluded both to the Long March of Mao's Communist army and to the much longer quest of women to get their place in the sun: "We do not exactly come stamping like an army, / the ground does not shake beneath our feet," but "we were very close to one another, / hard to tell sweat from sweat / and the smell of our blood from that of others." The exhortatory rhetoric was sometimes translated into gentler terms: "Appleblossom, sunshine flame, yellow leaf, the heart's dark voices. / Teach us to endure. / Compel. Convince." Boucht's participation in the woman's peace march to Paris in 1981 was an element in a large book of poetry and prose, *Glädjezon* (1986; Pleasure zone), which protested mainly against "neobrutalism" (the Chernobyl catastrophe, the murder of Olof Palme, the U.S. bombing raid on Libya, the massacres in the refugee camps of the Middle East, famines in Africa, the United States's policies in Latin America).

Two years later, however, she turned to a purely lyric form and spirit in *De fyrtionio dagar* (1988; The forty-nine days), a title taken from the Tibetan Book of the Dead, designating the time that passes between death and rebirth, a shift away from argumentative verse to thoughts on personal loss, employing homely images and humor to express pain: "I will adorn your grave with Jansson's Temptation [a Swedish potato-based dish], seven kinds of cake, lighted candles," a mingling of the ordinary with the solemn which approaches the tone found by Märta Tikkanen in the same decade (and calls to mind the possibility that Edith Södergran may have gotten the practice going with her "I mean to bake cathedrals"). Boucht mocks her own failure to belong to a distinct, highfalutin literary mode:

> Shall life be taken in deadly earnest?
> Would I were a surrealist, dadaist, symbolist
> postmodernist or G[unnar]
> Ekelöf!"

The mixture of styles in *Inringningen,* (1991; The encirclement) — long anaphoric poems, a dialogue between a polylingual would-be seducer and a woman more than his match, sweet verses on childhood memories — indicates that a search for a *vox propria* is not among Boucht's major concerns. The book's finale demonstrates that, for Boucht, existence itself suffices:

> The dead are finally dead
> the living eat and drink
> For another twenty minutes it's love
> then come July, August,
> September, October
> It doesn't matter.
> It's breathing.

Boucht's cheerful acceptance has a more complicated parallel in the work of Bodil Lindfors (1951–), whose *Trädgård i förvandling* (1976; Garden in transformation) was full of affirmation ("Build yourself no bridges. / Bridges break. Depend on the living water / which bears," and "You shall not be afraid. / Sun exists and birds, / smoke and water. / Desire no more"), coupled with a disingenuous fear of a normative-punitive society ("Tell me: is it true / that in this country they put out the eyes / of all who have not been born blind"). These elements were still present but much dressed up (with references to William Blake, Björling, Tolkien, the *I ching*) in the prizewinning *Anteckningar från ett hus vid floden* (1978; Notes from a house by the river) — the river is the Aura in Åbo. In her essay on Finland-Swedish women's books in the Swedish publication *Kvinnornas litteraturhistoria 2* (1983; The women's literary history 2) Birgitta Boucht named Lindfors, with Agneta Ara and Inga Britt Wik, as lyricists who have contributed much to "the mapping of a living Finland-Swedish reality," and many of Lindfors's poems do just that, for example, in the descriptions of what can be seen from the balcony of her Åbo apartment. Also, Lindfors had an expansive sensual imagination to which she gave full rein in "The Song about Those Who Were Sucked Out by the Sea" and the many poems in the Åbo book transforming a humdrum place into an almost mythic entity; in *New York nätter och dagar* (1982; New York nights and days) a sticky summertime Manhattan is reproduced with anatomical and zoological metaphors:

> Great stomach in whose labyrinths
> we swim
> with our snout lifted, to split the muddy water
> like otters
> or, cowed, floating with the stream
> like unborn protoplasma.

Lindfors can even make a bath in rusty water seem an exotic adventure, as in a poem in *Om glädjens alkemi* (1986; Concerning happiness's alchemy), and she can illustrate the decline of a marriage in *Den förnekade bilden* (1986; The denied image) by adducing a remarkable menagerie — she never rejects images, despite the title's claim:

> I am left
> Behind this lamentable disguise
> Frog-knees, lizard-feet, snake-cunt,
> the nettle shirt. . . .

Cities remain a favorite object of Lindfors's attention, Barcelona, New York again, Venice, and in her prose travel book, *Equinox* (1986), Lima as well as smaller and less attractive South American places. A poem in the collection of 1986, named "Århus," is in fact a long description of a monkey caged behind a Kentucky Fried Chicken outlet in that Danish provincial capital; her fascination with living creatures great and small led, it would seem, to the metamorphoses of *Insektliv* (1989; Insect life). Lindfors's eye ("It will never be a camera . . . it sits / too deeply bedded in a chain of events and vacuums") nonetheless records almost everything it sees, from a fat middle-aged woman on a train to a caterpillar on the poet's arm. No one could charge Lindfors's lyric with a lack of richness of subjects, or the words to describe them; but as Michel Ekman tartly observed, a "difficulty in achieving closure" is apparent throughout her career ("Finlandssvensk skönlitteratur 1989," 104).

Among the debutants of the 1970s, Tua Forsström (1947–) has maintained a consistently high level of achievement in her sparse production. She opened with *En dikt om kärlek och annat* (1972; A poem about love and other things): scenes from Helsingfors life (political demonstrations, the bustling cosmetic department of the city's great department store) are mingled with a lament about loneliness; "the poet's beloved sits freezing," and "freezing," "being cold," is a leitmotif of the whole: "I am tired and heavy and freeze as when / one has awakened." The second of her extra-long poems, or symphonies without pause, *Där anteckningarna slutar* (1974; Where the notations end), was a variant of impure poetry; the rules for inmates in Finland's prisons were provided with a lyric gloss in which the impotence, apathy, and ultimate desperation of the prisoner of everyday life, outside the walls, were expressed. Forsström had a gift, probably encouraged by her mentor Claes Andersson, for snatching up snippets of trite middle-class conversation and employing them to explore emotional, intellectual, or moral vacuity; the title of *Egentligen är vi mycket lyckliga* (1976; Actually, we are very happy) is an example of this ironic art, used repeatedly to underscore the meaninglessness of a not uncomfortable existence:

> For there is nothing but cement here, these blind high-rise buildings
> and always the sirens in the background . . .
> Actually we are very happy.
> After all, we have everything we haven't wished for.

Tallört (1979; Yellow bird's nest) and *September* (1983) mark a second phase in Forsström's work, an outpouring of affection for a sometimes diffident but devoted poet-lover and a child. The critic Kaj Hedman has observed that, despite Forsström's claim that the speaker, the "I" of these poems, is not to be identified with herself, a strong personal voice is the driving force of all her poetry: "How I loved you! With a donkey's melancholy / persistence, like a comical tourist who's forgotten his destination." Further, Forsström constantly admonishes or coaxes a personal listener: "Don't laugh! I believe in / the language as a possibility of change / I believe in the clumsy part, the confused part, the unsureness." Language fulfills its noble purpose in poetry:

> There remains [a] language of strange
> signs, images piled in layer
> on layer. They must be consolation and
> reflection of our dreams.

This short poem of hers on language, worthy of a Rilke, is in penultimate position in *September,* a collection in which the expression of personal love is intensified:

> that summer I remember for all that
> was love
> . . . Today I saw a brimstone butterfly, then one knows for sure
> that it is early summer or autumn.

The quiet yet confident *tremulando* of her diction, and its physical feeling ("physical" is one of her favorite words), won much praise for *Snöleopard* (1987; Eng. tr. *Snow Leopard,* 1990) and, as well, a broad complement of readers, who could identify her perceptions as their own and understand what she meant by them: "Bedrooms smell differently in summer" and

> There is something about
> the taxi-driver's childish
> cheek which means:
> that there's existence.
> That there's really existence.
> That there streams a nocturnal
> music along the icecold road.

Simple smell and sight are the great poetic instruments of Forsström, as is her unashamedness — see the oratorio *Marinergraven* (1990; The Marian channel): "I miss you. / You are in the water's circulation." Her senses are open, both to chance beauty ("A window stands barely ajar in the morning light, / Someone rakes gravel, singing *Die Forelle*") and to stench, rot, chilly discomfort: in *Parkerna* (1994; The parks) a circus director, wishing he were far away from "this muddy marketplace in Ekenäs," yearns for countries "where it is never / October with snow-mixed rain."

Tomas Mikael Bäck (1946–), whose intellectualism is as strong as Forsström's physicality, appeared on the lyric scene the same year as Forsström and got overawed approval for his precocious maturity and "advanced techniques." *Andhämtning* (1972; Catching breath) contained a poem sure to adorn anthologies in years to come, "Homage," a salute by means of brief quotation or allusion, to modernism's great names (e.g., Södergran, Björling, Diktonius, Enckell), and simultaneously a farewell, neither helpful nor harmful to Bäck's search for new ways in poetry:

> Realize
> with sadness
> that most everything
> is adiaphora.

Like Forsström, Bäck has an astonishing faith in language: "Master your sadness. / As long as the language, the language lives, / the interpersonal lives too." His earlier collections, whose poems are mostly models of brevity, still have a relative translucence, all the more because the obvious care Bäck takes with each text wins the reader's immediate confidence if not an immediate comprehension. Some of the characteristics of *Och hastigt förstå* (1975; And quickly understand) are the beginning of a poem in medias res, as if an observation had suddenly come to the mind's surface; a love of unusual words ("Chironomid-light," "tenebral"); and a desire to ponder the nature of poetry:

> In the wet moss
> the veined woodpiece lies
> and rots.
> A stone (poemlike), a mightily congealed piece of sky,
> (a caress-free dissonance without association)
> remains.

Such poetological statements are common in *Början av ett år* (1977; Beginning of a year), "The simplest thing is not to be sound," and "I shall not desire simplicity"; the same collection, much of which is addressed to another being ("You still will live under bright skies, with a blond softness over your forehead"), appears to be a well-disguised set of love poems.

A resemblance to the development of the young Bo Carpelan is detectable; isolation is frequently mentioned, and evidence turns up of a quest for a way out of this lack of contact. In *Tills vi äger våra liv* (1980; Until we own our lives) the question is put with some plainness: "With what eyes shall I look at what landscapes / [I am] tired as trash"; in *Denna dag* (1982; This day) a poem tells about playing the accordion: "It's all right as company, / it's rare one has such a responsive partner, / A little activity of its own from the instrument is what I miss." Frequently, a poem can be read on several levels, including that of sly humor; in *Regnljus och snö* (1984; Rainlight and snow) the poem's speaker goes out into the rain "to meet nobody, / as foolishly credulous / as a dog in his smell-sense." The subtitle of *Språngmarsch på stället: Blad rivna ur en dagbok* (1985; Double time in place: Sheets torn from a diary) is intentionally misleading; its parts are carefully laid out prose aphorisms ("When I listen to a Mahler symphony, I am astonished every time by how frenetically this music struggles to become what it is," and the reduction of the modern German lyric to two words and two names, "Traumgekrönt—hinausgespien [Dream-crowned—spat out], Rilke and Celan"), short narrative interludes, and then (as Bäck announces in an English-language title) "The Real Theme," a search for life's meaning amid the surreal piles of words ("Among thirsting eagles, is / the chalice of life overflowing cactus?"), and an "Epitaph" with still another self-instruction for the poet:

> Walk, walk among words
> like boils, wander gently:
> no values are given to
> be wasted—The earth: yours.

Bäck *does* walk carefully among words, choosing from an enormous palette but constructing a private language. The jokes of *Flytande avsatser* (1986; Floating landings) led a reviewer to say that his verse "flows out into a labyrinthine no-man's land, where the reader feels abandoned"; with the poems and aphorisms of *Frågare* (1988; Questioner), a retort to his critics, Bäck delivered an attack against the view that seeks to reduce a poem simply to a meaning: "One-meaning-poem, ex-meaning-poetry."

Bäck's work provides a measure of how far the lyric has come since the clear-cut accusations and ironies of a Claes Andersson; maybe stimulated at the outset by the language awareness of his fellow Ostrobothnian Huldén (and certainly, then, by the love of paradox of Gösta Ågren, to whose *festskrift* of 1986 Bäck contributed impenetrable sayings), Bäck has moved into a realm of wordplay (see *Spånkorg* [1990; Chip basket]) in which the reader clutches thankfully at the occasional obviosities: "You are already, which makes no difference at all." Logodaedalia has become the purpose here; Bäck's later books defy translation—puns, alliterations, homonyms, associations are everywhere. In *Frågare* Bäck stated his metaphoric purpose: "Poetry's lightly flying offshoots and playful lightning-likenesses move on a mostly inaccessible plane, strangely removed from the preserve of meaning itself. From such dark spiritual depths does there not surely stem the liberating sense of discovery poetry momentarily imparts?"

Jan-Christer Wahlbeck (1948–) has played a poetic game as well, but not as sophisticatedly or tryingly. The short poems of *Steg på hållplatsen* (1977; Steps at the bus stop) are paradoxical, like Ågren's or Bäck's ("The best poems / are written with chalk / on asphalt / that has dried in the sun") but not cryptic; an undemonstrative homeliness hangs over the whole ("You're sweating out your fever / with a bathrobe over pajamas / and I fetch potatoes from the market hall's stone floor / phone acquaintances and buy / fresh tulips / straight from a truck"). *Bussen stannar bakom hörnet* (1979; The bus stops around the corner) and *Mognadens opera* (1981; Opera of maturity) have the same tone, often with a splash of the mildly absurd (or, less often, the surreal), which was now—again thanks, one might suspect, to the popular success of Lars Huldén—becoming fashionable: "Beside the seabank's grass or the improbable clouds / a secret sand path lies cleansed after the poet's anger / ... / like will-o'-the-wisps and evening peace in this opera of maturity," a happy idyll attained, treasured, and possibly laughed at. Wahlbeck's autobiographical novel, *Näckrosen och bränt vatten* (1983; Water lily and burnt water) was not, however, despite the title's hint, a work of absurdist prose, but rather a standard description of the process of maturing; the odd mixture of the religious and the sexual-burlesque once favored by Peter von Martens was gracefully outdone in the finale's erotic-instructional scenes.

Wahlbeck's career took a turn toward originality (or a refurbishing of a method used effectively by Claes Andersson almost a generation before) in *Katastrof efter katastrof* (1984; Catastrophe upon catastrophe); the poems are long (about forty lines each) and each depicts a dreadful or ridiculous scene, the pediatric ward of a hospital ("[The children] cry out so that their shrieks / gallop like wild horses / along white ceilings and walls / they confuse the possessors / of jobs and labor contracts"), the nation's rulers ("The Diet could be a barn," where the Speaker digs in the manure of repetition, "The government could be a marketplace, / the prime minister would weigh potatoes / by balancing between extremes," "The president could be a statue, / resting unshakable on the constitution"). The extravagances and oddities of a world too well off get their due in *Bilen och lidelserna* (1991; The car and the passions), a series of forty mock "eulogies" (like those in *Katastrof efter katastrof*), of equal length and with lines of a discernible trochaic pentameter or hexameter meter: regular rhythm has staged a come-back. They bear such titles as "Praise of the Filling Station's Indifference and Depression," "Praise of the Wrecked Car's Place at the Junkyard," "Praise of the Hot Kisses and Hugs in the Car." (Car literature has become a subgenre of Finland-Swedish letters: compare Påwals's salad-green mistress and Robert Alftan's "My Car as a Whore, I Its Pimp," Henrik Tikkanen's several eulogies, the nondriver Christer Kihlman's saga of his romantic ride in a junkheap through South America in *Livsdrömmen rena*.)

The Rock Generation
Like Tomas Mikael Bäck, Thomas Wulff (1953–) was impelled to bid modernism hail and farewell. His poem "We Come Laughing across the Emptinesses' Starstrewn Horde," in *Månsten* (1973; Moonstone), suggests "Creator Figures" of Edith Södergran's *Framtidens skugga*, "Rocking in loose saddles we come / unknown, lightminded, strong," and the adjective "starstrewn" is present elsewhere in the same Södergran volume: "Where is my homeland? Is it distant Finland, starstrewn?" Wulff's riders are not Södergran's heroes and heroines, but "the necktieless dregs / the cancer boil in society's body, / who neither wear a suit / nor the short hair of submission," ragtag leftovers from the days of student revolt. A sense of vast inanity leads to the grim aubade, "Dawn Lament (A Song for Rotten Ruth)": "Oh plastic doll so painted and lifeless / let me kiss you / and your hollow love balloons," and to the catalog of

> our generation
> priests or drug addicts, drunks or robots
> whores or dolls
> the war's grandchildren
> clouds' children, in eternal pursuit of cosmos flight or drunkenness
> diverse ways to forget.

Thus having made himself the scolding but participant voice of a new lost generation, Wulff became an editor of the little magazine *Fågel Fenix* (The bird phoenix), which came out in six issues between 1975 and 1977. Abandoning political and social agitation for a vaguely defined permissiveness, with "FREEDOM" at its masthead, the magazine regarded itself as a "cultural organ for a small minority awaiting the culture's expansion" and for "the category of people who attempt to create an alternative existence outside conventional society, or attempt to change society proceeding from the demands of this alternative existence."

The reaction from the established Left was punitive — and conservative: Leif Salmén called the short-lived journal "nothing but a drugged-out kite." *Fågel Fenix* and its group saw its *locus amoenus* in the dropout community of Copenhagen's Christiania and its musical idols in Patti Smith, Frank Zappa, and Jimi Hendrix; William Burroughs and Lenny Bruce were introduced in its pages. Yet the very slovenliness of its layout and the fact that it offered a fuzzy target (it was characterized as a specimen of "romantic absurdism") kept it from attracting as much attention as papers of the past, *Ultra* and *Quosego, Arena* and FBT. In another little magazine that tried to carry on its predecessor's work for a while, *Otid* (1979–82; Untime, seven numbers), Thomas Wulff complained that *Fågel Fenix* had been "silenced to death." But *Fågel Fenix* had several contributors who, in the formulation of Henrik Jansson (1953–), constituted an underground culture, "a reserve capital for [the] overground culture" to come. Wulff, Marianne Backlén, Martin Enckell, Joakim Groth, and Kjell Lindbad (see below) all became important figures of the 1980s.

In his production Wulff exploited aimlessness, which he sometimes richly enjoyed. *Nattens fabler* (1974; The night's fables) was described as "an obstacle course of 166 pages" about youth devoted to rock and hash: "A shudder's songwhining through bodyfleshskinsoul and his hands jerk spasmodic as an old drug addict's morningsupports jumpingtickling ants through the legsSpeedKills!" and "A first-careful sunbeam glides slowly easily&gently through stagnant stinkair the dustparticles' goldendance alcoholtobaccosweat badbreaths hash&incense." The centerpiece of the novel, called "The Morning after the Party," is a lengthy conversation between "Uncle Wolf" and "Little Red Riding Hood"; the lustful wolf, hankering for love, delivers one of the home truths lying at the core of this late mutation of *Scènes de la vie de Bohème*, in which the hedonists are infinitely degraded: "Finally everything loses its meaning. The smell of shit and degradation impregnated in you in your body. The brain loses its keenness. Becomes a blacksucking maelstrom filled with the surrounding's monsters and monstrosities."

Hjärtats stråtrövare: Pusselpoesi 1973–1975 (1976; The heart's highwaymen: Puzzle poetry 1973–1975) is a book of mostly long poems or suites of poems couched in a language that keeps sliding in and out of focus; as in

Wulff's prose, images momentarily capture a sight, a mood, or an insight, only to float away once again. The eighth(!) section from the so-called seven variations of the concluding (and title) suite gives a sample of the technique:

> Shewho casts weeping [ ] on the backstreets a handful
> at a time seizes [ ] the moment and holds it
> coldly. The strangeness that still ishere
> flees, remaining [ ] concealed
> intermittently but neverwholly [ ] dead.

The run-together words, the intralinear spaces, and the puns provide an air of hallucination (or too much reading of Joyce); the variations in question seem to be about Odysseus, also called "Oduzeuss," and "the stake is sunk deeply into all the Poly*fem*eyes"—*fem* in Swedish means "five." In *Trance dance: Sekvenser* (1980; Trance dance: Sequences) the "explanatory words" of the introduction reveal that it is a vision of the future, "of an incredibly repressive, police-guarded, strongly class-divided society."

Neither the opacity of *Trance dance* nor the fey humor of the phantasmagoria *Sumpråttans resa* (1980; The Swamp Rat's journey) helped increase the popularity of Finland's "best-known unread author." This "Adventure Story in a Lot of Parts"—plainly inspired by Kenneth Grahame's *Wind in the Willows* and by the Finnish children's classic, Kirsi Kunnas's *Tiitiäisen satupuu*—tells of the idealistic Rat, "the born gentleman," with his "(unhappy) mustaches," pestered by the ever contemptuous Squirrel—who "spat angrily out over the bog in a completely sovereign (the Squirrel had practiced for a long time) bow"—and tried by the indolence of the Lizard: "She limited herself (voluntarily, it may be noted, precisely) only to sleep (possibly) to regenerate." As in Grahame, there is a dangerously active Toad—"(?toads with teeth?) Possibly (certainly) an (early) mistake in copying." The verbal and punctuative wit is variously charming or annoying, and the conclusion of the Swamp Rat's journey is dark: "the Snakes devour"—among others—"the Swamp Rat (fatty) and the Toad (tough)." A third publication from the same annus mirabilis, *Snap-Shots: Mumlade mytologier* (1980; Snap-shots: Mumbled mythologies), was similarly baffling; the melange included poetry, some in English, and a sampler of prose, science fiction, exotic tales, imaginary conversations, and "anecdotes from Eugen Schaumann's life." (The historical Schauman [1873–1904], spelled with one *n*, had a place of honor in the Finland-Swedish pantheon as the assassin of the Russian governor-general Bobrikoff. Wulff's Schaumann, who "constantly bore a copy of *The Tales of Ensign Stål* by Topelius [*sic*] in his pocket," is an awkward specimen of the "un-Finland-Swedish activity" that had flourished in letters for some two decades.)

The lack of an audience may have had a sobering effect on Wulff; subsequent books have been easier going and repeat material from his long enfance terrible in a simpler and more digestible form. *Utspelad i Ulan-Bator* (1983; Out of the game in Ulan-Bator) has elements of the spy thriller, again played out in a repressive society (a girl is found dead in her jail cell, the report of her death can be read only in the unnamed country's sole legal newspaper); the main figure is the mysterious Travis (after B. Traven or John R. MacDonald's fictional supersleuth, Travis MacGee?), who is introduced to the activities of a police (and/or terrorist) group in a country that resembles the Chile of the Pinochet dictatorship. Switching into a split between genres, Wulff produced *Kirurgens park: Kineserier* (1985; The surgery's park: Chinoiseries), in which much of the poetry (including "Black Sun" and the English-language "In the Presence of the Monster") is grim in tone; the prose—the fairy tales—could well be illustrated by Edward Gorey: "Only to the Teddybear therefore did Bertrand confide his plan, long worked out, of murdering all the rest of his family." Attracted to the possibilities of American violence, Wulff next wrote a study of gangster fiction and film (including *The Untouchables* series from television) in *Det ondas tjusning: Anteckningar om gangstermytologi och verklighet* (1987; The charm of evil: Notes about gangster mythology and reality); he saw the gangster as a semidivinity (a Loki, the ambiguous god of Nordic mythology), fulfilling a modern need of myth, however bogus, in a world where, once again, "everything loses its meaning."

But his true home is Helsingfors, not Capone's Chicago, and in *Helsinki-Romanka* (1990) Wulff went back to the site of *Nattens fabler* and, as well, to the deflating humor that made some parts of the *Mumlade mytologier* into a Finland-Swedish equivalent of Jules Laforgue's *Moralités légendaires* (1887). The second title segment in the book of 1990 is a Russified version of *roman*, "novel," and this most readable piece of Wulff's narrative prose—opening, in a traditional style, with "One of those hopelessly rainy and raw November nights that are a Helsingfors specialty"—takes place among the leftovers of the drugged 1970s, quieted down but still belonging to a halfway Bohemia, dependent on part-time jobs and, even now, parental support. Among the several strands of narration, the principal one belongs to the free-lance translator Bison, who may be a new version of the much-put-upon swamp rat of Wulff's fable. (A book about Travis also turns up in the library of Ruben, a member of Bison's extensive coterie.) Further, a detective novel, *Hot in Helsingfors,* is enclosed within the main text, one of several tales taking place "simultaneously," as paragraph openings constantly remind the reader, one of Wulff's efforts (there are sometimes flashes of reader-friendliness amid the obstacles to understanding) to guide his audience through the comic maze. But as always, Wulff speaks principally to his aficionados: "The Message" in *Kirurgens park* says, "There is a language / that only those affected can understand."

A colleague of Wulff at *Fågel Fenix,* a grandson of Olof Enckell, Martin Enckell (1954–), to whom Wulff dedicated a "Mantra mass (Reggae)" in *Kirurgens park,* has been less productive but has received the accolade from Trygve Söderling, the "court critic" of the group, that he is its truly talented member ("Nightdrivers in Moomin Valley," 74). Taken aback by such causeless rebels, Claes Andersson employed a word made popular in the days of Allan Ginsberg, calling Enckell "the guru of the new generation." Enckell struck his tone of disgust early, in twenty-five poems (beginning "Let my sickness / spurt out / in a cascade / of repugnance, / out of the primary mouth, / the anus / the taste glands of madness") in Schildts's anthology, *Ny lyrik 1974* (New lyric 1974). He did not grow any nicer in the double volume of 1978, composed of Johan Donner's *Sinnenas realismer* (The senses' realisms) and his own *Ingen & den knottriga damen* (No one & the knotty lady): like Wulff and others of the *Fågel Fenix* circle, Enckell had a fondness for the ampersand. (Johan Donner is the son of Jörn Donner and Inga-Britt Wik; this was his only venture into belles lettres.) The poems of *Ingen & den knottriga damen* have the air of shocking song texts about them; in "forskarens facit" ("the researcher's conclusion" — sometimes Enckell avoids capital letters, on other occasions he uses them exclusively) a naked Boy Scout ponders suicide in his stuffy bedroom, his little sister practices ballet steps, "his mother hides her aging in a henna-red bathroom," and his father sits "sewed into his stomach ulcers & informs everyone / how happy they will be / the day he dies." Enckell is careful, as Wulff was, to distribute his lines eye-catchingly over the page, an extreme version of Charles Olson's projective verse, a form much favored by subsequent poets, for example, Henrika Ringbom and Agneta Enckell:

& the scout makes loops
in his Christmas ties and fantasizes
about blackening tongues
& spotted thirst

Sortie (1979; Sally) was Enckell's first independent venture, published at a new alternative house called Kain, which in turn took its name from a rock band, The Kain Boys, whose members read their poems aloud to musical accompaniment. (The rock element is supposedly echoed in the "heavily rhythmic and paradoxically melodic texts" of Enckell.) The studied pose of the *poète-musicien maudit,* an essential in the world of rock, is the stuff of one of *Sortie*'s shorter poems:

> but even when dead
> I shall lie
> with welder's flames
> under my eyelids.

Enckell and his contemporaries liked to call themselves members of the "freak generation," putting one of their many loanwords from American-English slang to demonstrative use; he also came up with another and equally quotable coinage:

> I am a bloodhound sniffing at my delayed
> puberty & a lost rear-view mirror from an
> ambulance & a man transformed from *day waster* to *night driver.*
> (Italics added)

The first element in the play on words, Swedish *dagdrivare,* is the term for the blasé generation of Runar Schildt and Torsten Helsingius; the second is Enckell's own quasi-American coinage. (From a literary-historical point of view the yoking makes sense: the *dagdrivare* and the "night drivers" have an attitude of self-romanticizing tiredness in common; but the impotent despair of the former was quickly dispelled by independence from Russia and the Civil War; the latter had only a consumer society to lament and enjoy.)

The mysterious Russian-English title of Enckell's *Pravda — Love* (1983), a language mixture preceding Wulff's macaronic *Helsinki-Romanka,* may have been an echo of the most famous of the James Bond novels and films, *From Russia with Love;* the narrator, Martin, comes off far less well in his confrontations with international villains than Ian Fleming's Bond does but is much more literarily inclined; the book comprises Martin's tale of adventure and a coda made up of his poems. In her study of Finland-Swedish novels (*Det trånga rummet,* 210–11) Merete Mazzarella quoted the hyperbolic praise the book received: "a Nordic *Fleurs du mal,* a literary corkscrew toward a new cultural epoch" (Thomas Wallgren), with "fearfully compressed, tightened, laconically beautiful language" (Trygve Söderling); Söderling further implied he had read *Pravda — Love* three hundred times. Historically aware, Mazzarella pointed out that, like Tavaststjerna's *Barndomsvänner, Pravda — Love* was "an autobiographical developmental novel that just as well could be called a novel of coming apart." (Tavaststjerna himself used the division between narration and the protagonist's appended poetry in his verse epic *Laureatus*.) Television has been the "best brother" of Martin as a child; he has learned to know violence while glued to the big living-room screen. Grown, he falls into a lifestyle like that repeatedly depicted in Wulff's Helsingfors novels, odd jobs, drink, drugs, and endlessly repeated fornications. Going to Guatemala as a drug courier, he meets and falls in love with Carlita, a member of a guerrilla family, and becomes involved with her cause but later is "taken in by the opposite side," that of the general. ("It doesn't matter that it was in other countries. In Bolivia [I was] bought for money's sake.") Discovering that Carlita has been murdered by government forces, Martin goes on with his meaningless existence, as little moved by the sight of Carlita's decaying corpse as he had been by the suicide of a childhood friend, Hannele, whose death had caused him (to the extent that causation exists in Martin's case) to set out on his South American journey. One of the poems in the lyric appendix is called "ich über alles" and begins:

> clinically free
> from feelings; a wish; a demand; I demand I can't deal with it; I am not interested in feelings; I am
> feeling . . .

Mazzarella noted that *Pravda — Love* was actually a moralizing book, a "raging protest against emptiness."

Hibakusha Go-Go (1987) is a repetition of *Pravda — Love;* the narrator (who has "cremated, cremated all [his] feelings") travels around the world as a merchant seaman and occasional tourist; the structural pattern here is the tale of a sailor's experiences, a reemergence of the one-time best seller, *Havets bröd* (1954; The sea's bread), of Håkan Mörne (1900–61). The title comes from a discotheque in Berlin, "whose moods were more than welcomely ego-erasing." Amid the frenetic traveling (a common feature of many of the narrations of the time) and the equally frenetic consumption of drugs and sex, Enckell's sequel to *Pravda — Love* makes even more extensive use of foreign languages, with passages in some two dozen, American English foremost among them. Subsequently, Enckell discovered an exotic refuge in the poetic suite *Gud All-en* (1989; dedicated to the Sufi mystic Mansur al-Hallaj):

> [I] adorned
> my hatred with sovereign loneliness

> decorated my loneliness with the loneliness of others
> loved a dark woman,
> loved a blond one
> other wars did not touch me until al-Hallaj pressed
> into my dreams, forced me
> to awaken into his, forced me
> to write *loneliness* and to live [*sic*] riddance to the wars.

It may be assumed, incidentally, that the dark and light women are the would-be female saviors of *Pravda — Love,* representatives of a "life-feeling" that Martin failed to value — one more indication of Enckell's essential romanticism.

The novel of degeneration is practiced by Joakim Groth (1953–) as well, another member of the *Fågel Fenix* group. Groth's "epic poem cycle," *Blindfönster vidare* (1979; Blind windows onward), enters the thoughts of Johan K., "closed inside his bell glass / grown into the mirror, satisfied with his refuge / in the midst of the war which is the city's being." The scene of his isolation is Helsingfors (not Joseph K's Prague), but it could as well be any metropolis:

> over the city's market face
> the queues of cars sing their voice in the furrows
> like vassals in armor
> while the bodies climb forth from the pores.

The poet either observes Johan K., "twenty three years old," at a distance,

> hesitatingly freezing forth from the traffic snarl
> a lonely swirl of ice in the bodies' stream,
> a cold flame
> a rhythmic silence

or becomes united with him. Infinitely more complex than Ture Janson's *Mitt Helsingfors,* Groth's debut still maintains the peripatetic structure and flaneur attitude of Janson's little cycle of 1913:

> But it was when he stopped
> in front of a dark display window
> and for the second time met the face
> which was his share of the city.
> Then it was: a caricature
> where he met his own pessimism.

Enckell was aware of his *dagdrivare* heritage; aware or not, Groth also repeats their melodramatic hopelessness: "Yes. The face sprawled toward him / from long black tunnel: blind window." Johan, at least by name, reappears in Groth's autobiographical novel *Anteckningar från en stad* (1981; Notes from a city), a youth's melancholy progress from a small town to the capital, his slow adjustment, and his travels; in 1986 Groth retold the story, with another protagonist, in *Världen enligt Edi* (The world according to Edi). Here the prose abandoned the normal procedures of its predecessor and became the single paragraphless flow (more than three hundred pages) of Edi's experiences and thoughts, the latter usually indicated by italics. In his aboulia, his lack of will, Edi is a gentle brother of the types presented by Wulff (the aimless joker) and Enckell (the aimless adventurer); attempting to characterize Edi (or his predecessors Johan K. and Johan), Trygve Söderling wrote that he was a character who would be "equally happy to read yesterday's newspaper, day after day, if someone else at the breakfast table wants to read today's" ("Nightdrivers in Moomin Valley," 78).

Unlike Joakim Groth's dreamers, the young and slowly aging men depicted by Henrik Jansson (1955–) are rock musicians, whose world Jansson knows from the inside. (The author of a doctoral dissertation on the Swedish documentary novelist Per Olof Enquist, Jansson also wrote a cogent account of *Fågel Fenix*.) In the stories of *Lit de parade* (1981) Jansson introduced his main figure, the guitarist Simon and his friends, including the gifted Spider, on whom Simon has a semihomosexual fixation, the steadier Robbe, and their girlfriends. The ingredients of Jansson's later novels are already present: the strangely erotic-mechanical thrills of rock performance, the drug dependencies and drug deaths, the constant quotations from the musical literature (and American vocabulary) of rock, and the shifting scenes of the so-called concerts, Åbo, Helsingfors, Stockholm, Copenhagen, Tallinn. In the short novel *Gruppen hette No C:o* (1984; The group was called the No Co.) the kaleidoscope was larger; the underlying tone of condemnation (related to Enckell's implicit moralizing) comes to the surface in a denunciation by Robbe: "You and Spider, you've really swallowed the rock myth one hundred percent. . . . You wave with your guitar-and-bass necks just the way all the rock stars before you have done. As if the instruments were long penises. And so you drag in the girls, don't you, and that's a part of the show too."

Simon's flummoxed father and a rival brother make their appearance, just as the subtitle promises, in *Encore: En familjeroman* (1986; Encore: A family novel); but the erotic problems of Simon remain at stage center: he experiences the first symptoms of the impotence that will make his life still more miserable in *Isbergens tid* (1988; Time of the icebergs), a title taken from one of the stories in *Lit de parade*. In this third novel Simon, grown older and sadder but not wiser, shares the spotlight with the sometime guitarist, present academician, and novelist Mats Ahlman; yet save for Mats's university affiliation (Ralf Nordgren likewise split his hero between a university teacher and a would-be free spirit in *Det kluvna äpplet* from the same year), little difference exists between Mats and his old friend and colleague: both suffer from substance dependencies, sexual collapse, and gnawing malaise. However repetitious the events of these rock novels become, Jansson provides textbook examples of the rock generation's tenor of discourse: numberless American and hybrid Swedish-American words, numberless obscenities and scatological expletives. Beneath the bravado lies the despair Wulff held off with insouciance; Enckell with adventure, roamings, and (eventual) Eastern mysticism; Groth with languor; and Kim Weckström (1952–) with his objectivity in *Trägrottan* (1984; The tree cave), a detailed report on Helsingfors youth (drugs, rock, frenetic sex), blended into a detective novel based on authentic documents about narcotics smuggling. Yet, more cruelly than any of his counterparts in the instances just listed, Jansson's Simon is assailed by time itself: "Why should he remember? All the months that after his thirty-second birthday were compressed into nameless fragments of where, when or why — why should he remember?" His birthday present to himself, a pathetic and comical gesture, is a visit to the barber, to get "a haircut so short that even a little of his ears peeked out." (It will be remembered that the archetypical decadent of a century before, Des Esseintes in J. K. Huysmans's *A rebours* [1884; Eng. tr. *Against the Grain*, 1922; *Against Nature*, 1959], likewise thirtyish and impotent, keeps a specially lettered copy of Baudelaire's poem on time, "L'ennemi," on a prie-dieu in his bedchamber.)

Kjell Lindblad (1951–) came from the same rock music background as Jansson; a drummer, he was a member of the Kain band and had been attached to *Fågel Fenix, Otid*, and the alternative publishing house Boklaget, at which works by Tomas Mikael Bäck, Wulff, Jansson, and Groth had appeared. His own book-length publications, appealing to a less specific public, found a home at Schildt's; he chose the familiar form of the short story, was able to function without obvious autobiographical references, and wrote a language relatively uncluttered by slang and Americanisms. (Following the practice growing ever more common in Finland-Swedish prose, he inserted conversational passages in Finnish.) In addition, Lindblad often wrote not about extended adolescence and midlife crises but about childhood, the time of life frequently favored by Finland-Swedish prosaists in the past. Nevertheless, his tales of children are surely not readings for them, and his adult characters are similarly tormented by uneasiness or sheer terror. In *Före sömnen* (1984; Before the slumber) hospital workers take an unruly corpse to the morgue; after an atomic explosion a child writes shorter and shorter letters to his father; all the dogs disappear from a city and a country; a pig, keeping a diary, looks forward to the Christmas slaughter; a man slowly divests himself of wife, position, possessions; the concluding, title story is a child's nightmare of losing his father in an icy park and freezing to death. These *contes cruels* — has Lindblad read Villiers, Saki, Meyrink? — were followed by *Regnmannens berättelser* (1988; The rainman's stories); the rainman is a bogey born of a child's anxiety, and Lindblad's adults are no better off, confronted by situations or milieus, real or imagined, they can neither understand nor control.

Aftonbarn (1991; Evening children), a short novel, formed a complement to the numerous stories about the very young; children in an apartment house — one of them lame, confined to a wheelchair — grow increasingly aware of the uncanniness of existence, an awareness variously numbed or heightened by their main amusement, the television set. Lindblad, who has ties to media theater, has created a popular and easily digestible version of the literature of estrangement so often provided in a more difficult form by his generational fellows; without the noise of rock and without the swirl of swiftly passing and highly vocal characters, his understated tales, reduced to the construction or reproduction of extreme emotional states, have little local color about them (just as his characters are mostly nameless), and the travel frenzy that marks the work of his contemporaries is missing. The destination of a young woman trying to get away from it all in "Fasting Time" is an empty island in early autumn, where this temporary Crusoe is forgotten by the old man supposed to pick her up after a two-week stay. The island's name is Karon.

Otherwise, travel is a dominant motif of the fiction of the 1980s. Martin in *Pravda — Love* recites its litany: "Mannerheim Road in Helsingfors. Ways, streets, alleys. Alleys in Bangkok. Climbing labyrinths on the slopes of Rio de Janeiro.... A street in Lagos. Nigerian eyes run through my flesh. Future trips. Superhighways out of cities through countries, through my brain, through me." Jörn Donner's globetrotting of the 1950s and afterward has become commonplace, but with a difference: whereas Donner traveled as a gatherer of facts on which he could pass judgment, the new-age travelers are of a different sort, looking for places that offer release from themselves. The South American junkets of Christer Kihlman, ostensibly undertaken to find material for a continuation of *Dyre prins,* prefigure the trips of Enckell and company, in that Kihlman's experiences on the road culminate in blissful release. To be sure, Kihlman was still very much the middle-class traveler (like Tikkanen, car-borne and newspaper-financed), living in excellent hotel rooms; when he misses "bath and shower and breakfast in the room," he momentarily has a sense of true adventure, feeling "proud" and "happy as a lark." For younger literary travelers, low- or no-budget travel is the norm; the chance encounter is more readily achieved while living out of a backpack.

Like Martin Enckell, Marianne Backlén entered literature in *Ny lyrik 1974,* with sixteen poems, "The Band of Siblings"; among them were tributes to the imaginary pop star Gary Glitter and to the real David Bowie, Leo Sayer, Alice Cooper, and Marc Bolan. As "the Girl" in *Minnet av Michael* (1975; The memory of Michael), Backlén moves through the discos and bars of Helsingfors with a circle of friends devoted more to soul music and hash than to studies; many are from abroad: Hassin, "the Sunshine Boy from Nazareth"; the Danish-American Tom, "Bob Dylan's little brother"; Diana, a spaced-out Finnish-American. The attitude toward American and Americans is of the essence; the title figure is the boy of the Girl's memories and dreams, Michael, at home "mostly somewhere in California, in the Bahamas, in Mexico, in Panama—but seldom in New Jersey." The Girl's cultural references (like those of her friends) belong almost entirely to American pop culture—Stevie Wonder, Jimi Hendrix, and Ken Kesey; yet the America she has seen as an exchange student (described in her lengthy "Fairy Tale of America's Daughter," told by the Girl about her experiences abroad) is a monstrous society, riddled with fear and hatred. Backlén presents a major attitudinal dichotomy, the love-hate relationship with America endemic in writers (and others) of her generation.

Den osynliga draken (1980; The invisible dragon) undertakes journeys not only in geography (America once again, Paris, Moscow, with concomitant loves) but in time; the "dragon girl's" life passes from her Helsingfors childhood of the 1950s to the year 2036, a stretch reflected both in the novel's "real" events and in the magical flights on which her extraordinary ability for daydreaming takes her. She is a communicant of the invisible dragon: "The dragon ruled in the air and in space, the dragon flew higher than any bird or insect.... At the sight of a dragon, the other animals gave a friendly smile and nodded in recognition. All save the children of men: they no longer believed in dragons." The vague Orientalism as well as the fairy-tale tone are reminiscent of Hagar Olsson, and Edith Södergran is among the "dragon girl's" cultural icons, together with Jack Kerouac of *On the*

Road and Sylvia Plath. The book's whimsy is combined, just the same, with the girl's clinical descriptions of her many lovers. Backlén's novels of magic realism went on in *Den sista sommaren* (1982; The final summer); "Tibet's great yogi," Milarepa, appears in Helsingfors, transformed into a young divorcée, Mila Repo (née Grönqvist), and Milarepa's venerable teacher in Tibetan lore, Marpa the Translator, becomes Mika's rickety landlady in an apartment on picturesque Skatudden, a sometime professional translator named Martta Laamanen (the allusion to "lama" will escape no one); the yogi's little sister becomes Mila's little sister Petra Grönkvist. (Like Mila, Petra is charmingly mythomanic; she claims that three wind gods live near Skatudden, "the Indian Indra, the Iranian Vayu, and the Finnish Ilmarinen." Both sisters are devoted readers of Tove Jansson's Mumin books.) During the last chapter the drums of the Helsingfors watch parade mingle with those of Buddhist monks; in a verse epilogue Mila says she wishes to cast a golden patina over Finland's capital—she will no longer collect clothes in her wardrobe nor will she swallow contraceptives every day: "In the refreshing festival drink of nettles and berries / there is an elixir pleasing unto the gods." Backlén's variety of Helsingfors romanticism stands in contrast to that of Wulff, Enckell, Groth, and Jansson, who are less willing to cast a golden patina over their seedy hangouts; but a yearning for ecstasy, attained by whatever means, is common to all.

The mechanized and expanding capital and its uniform suburbs (unlike turn-of-the-century, many-gabled Skatudden) are the background of the adventures of Kati, the would-be Finnish Hindu in the title story of Backlén's *Östra centrum: ändstation* (1984; Eastern center: Last stop): other stories take place in Kansas City during the swing-band era and flash back, via letters, to New Orleans in the 1880s or go ahead in time to a science-fiction world in "After the Great Cosmic War." (Backlén's Finland scenes and reactions are always her most convincing, not least in her occasional thoughts on relations between Finnish and Swedish speakers; one of Kati's several lovers is a married and perverse Finland-Swede, who lives up to her up-country parents' prejudices against the minority's members.) Throughout her literary career Backlén has engaged in a sometimes ostentatious, sometimes entertaining multiculturalism, and in *Skuggan av Ninja* (1987; The shadow of ninja) she moved her location to New York, like Bodil Lindfors in *New York nätter och dagar*. Already broached in *Den sista sommaren,* the notion of a gynecocracy returns; the foreground figures are women of an artistic stripe: a Finland-Swedish novelist named Backman; an Estonian, Mira, in flight from American suburbia; a folksinger from Iowa; a wise and orderly Japanese. The men are weaker or less dependable, all save the marvelous boy Michi, the son of the Japanese and a blind, black bass player; Michi's tale of the samurai and the ninja (in which the samurai represents power, the ninja the bold outsider) provides the title of the book. Outsiders are the truly creative spirits; the child of two races has special visionary qualities, even more than the would-be Orientals, the dragon girl and Kati, who pretends to be the goddess Vishakya Govinda, "the sisterly friend of Radha, shimmering in gold." The hodgepodge structures and the dream of a utopian society, plus the spiritual search, continue in Backlén's work; in *Hundarna i Kingston* (1993; The dogs in Kingston) she reached Jamaica in her worldwide journey.

Prose of the 1980s: An Embarrassment of Riches
The search based directly on Christian tradition — cultivated, once upon a time, by Jarl Hemmer in *En man och hans samvete* and then by Tito Colliander and Göran Stenius in book after book — makes a strong reappearance in the work of Paul von Martens (1930–), the son of the "night missionary" (a pastor of the derelict and homeless) Arvid von Martens. Himself a Lutheran clergyman, Paul von Martens was active in church, radio, and television, delaying his literary debut, which came with the short novel *Mannen som byggde en båt* (1977; The man who built a boat); the amateur boat builder is the first of von Martens's several protagonists to undergo a midlife crisis. The nonfictional *Glädjen* (1979; Happiness) is the genuinely touching account of the author's motorcycle trip with a daughter who has Down's syndrome — the book was a predecessor to Märta Tikkanen's *Sofias egen bok*. Henrik, the country pastor in *Herdarnas natt* (1981; The shepherds' night), finds himself in a blind alley, able to maintain contact neither with his congregation nor with the God he once thought he knew; the novel begins with a quotation from *Der cherubinische Wandersmann* (1657/1675) of the Silesian mystic Angelus Silesius, "Mein Gott, wie kalt bin ich" (My God, how cold I am). The tormented pastor, having beheld a vision of the shepherds watching in the fields on Christmas Eve, understands at last that he may not turn away from the source of his suffering and his strength.

In *Fadershuset* (1983; The father's house) the religious plane is apparently left for power struggles in the business world; but the action quickly veers once again toward matters of salvation. An executive, forced out of his firm, meets an old friend after long separation and watches with some envy the friend's apparent triumph over adversity; he builds a great house into which he hopes to gather the children of his several marriages — the house also has a chapel. Yet when George, the builder of the patriarchal house, is thwarted in his plans, he is finally seen through by Stig, the man of seemingly smaller spiritual gifts: "I feel sorry for him, but I'm not worried. When . . . his house collapses, he will simply take a step to one side and look at the collapse with the pleasure an explosives expert knows when he sees the great factory smokestack fall just as he had predicted. . . . He'll stand there, relaxed, one hand in his pocket, the right one that's always ready, quick as a wink, to seize the heavenly hand when — in rescue — it is stretched toward him through the dust and smoke." In his piety and his praiseworthy desire to provide a nest for his neglected offspring, George has performed an act of false humility, based on an extreme self-love. What von Martens attempts, in novel after novel, is a series of spiritual experiments, in which the subtleties and pitfalls of faith are charted. A reader of Mauriac and Graham Greene as a young man, he dissects more serious ills of the soul than George's spiritual self-satisfaction in *Visa mig stjärnan* (1985; Show me the star); the quest takes Thomas, a journalist specializing in foreign news and a doubter, to the Greek cloister of Athos, where he becomes aware not of the presence of grace but of the devil. A prophetic monk, straight from the Valamo chapter in Hagar Olsson's *Träsnidaren och döden,* says to him: "We move toward bad times. Dark powers are gathering on the earth." The narrator follows the thread of evil (in spy-novel scenes) back to Helsingfors and believes he has found its source in a blind former officer, a sadist and the president of a security systems company; but in his pursuit Thomas himself may have been changed into evil's calculating servant.

Ömt älskade (1987; Dearly beloved) has double antiheroes: a charming but irresponsible workman who, in the early twentieth century, deserts wife and children to go to America, never to return, and a contemporary author who, riddled by disease, goes back to Finland to pass his last days by finishing a novel based on the papers and photographs of the long-ago runaway. The emigrant made a careless departure from his devoted daughter; the author is reunited with his own daughter on his deathbed. The question of the betrayal or mutilation of relationships, particularly within the family, which already occupied von Martens in *Mannen som byggde en båt,* is given a strong erotic charge in *Hagar* (1989). A childless couple — successful in their callings, he as a responsible maker of industrial and scientific policy, she as a specialist in the history of the Eastern Church — offers shelter to a girl who has a daughter's function in their home before she begins an affair with the conscientious and guilt-ridden husband. The drama has an uplifting end; almost simultaneously, the girl, to whom an angel has spoken (as to Hagar in Scripture), and the wife (suddenly grown fertile, like Sarah) will bear the children of Waldemar, a modern Abraham.

The wife, Laura, whose research has concentrated on the Greek theologian Gregorius Palamas (1296–1359), shows her husband her translation of Gregorius's words about Saint Stephen: "He had received no assistance from the angels, but nonetheless he had seen God's glory!" Zvonimir, a visiting Serbian writer, speaks of "an eighth day, when all is fulfilled, but yet nothing is finished," and the nubile Anna (like Hagar in Genesis 16:13, quoted in the novel's epigraph) thinks, "Have I also here looked after Him that seeth me?" and tells Waldemar, who has styled himself "an old, dried-up tree," that instead "a great richness has indeed come upon you.... You are like a great tree!"

Elsewhere, von Martens has written an essay about the author's responsibility in "the time of the change of values"; his creative work shows how earnestly he takes the tasks of proclaiming moral responsibility, of discerning the pitfalls of Christian practice, and of describing the fleeting vision of the godhead. The *Deus absconditus*, the hidden God, reveals himself to unlikely candidates, as in the case of Chorell's religious novels; Roger Holmström ("Vardag och vision") has noticed how von Martens's novels challenge his readers, daring them to strive for self-recognition.

Other authors also provided counterweights to the several kinds of permissiveness and self-disgust flourishing in the literature of the rock generation. Kristina Björklund (1941–) was at work on a doctoral dissertation (which appeared in 1982) about the novels of childhood reminiscence of her mentor, Oscar Parland, when she published two books of stories, *De andras röster* (1975; The others' voices) and *Festen* (1980; The party); she has characterized them as tales about "lonely women and odd existences"— the superficial contacts of writers' workshops; imaginary or evanescent lovers; parties ending in disappointment, humiliation, and sadness; the lives of the emotionally and physically handicapped. Then, inspired by Parland's example, Björklund began a series of books about a child named Mitra, of which three have thus far appeared, starting with *Månens tid* (1985; The moon's time). The fascination of Finland-Swedish literature with the family, and with childhood, is apparently endless, perhaps to be explained in part by the importance of the familial bond in the preservation of a minority. In addition, early childhood—the books of Österberg touched on this neglected aspect of the linguistic problem—is a time of language innocence, before the sense of belonging to a minority has wholly dawned. Björklund goes back very far in Mitra's life, to her second year: the little girl has devoted parents and grandparents from the lost paradise of Viborg, as well as an assortment of other relatives, some of whom she meets during summers at a family farm in what remains of Karelia.

In the tales of her grandfather and her father Mitra vividly experiences Karelia's old capital; but the death of the grandfather—whose wonderful golden watch told both real time and "the moon's time" of his stories—causes the first great upset for the little girl, followed by her father's move to Lapland (joined later by wife and daughter), thus adding another picturesque locale before Mitra begins school in the capital. *Månens tid* ends with the onslaught of a disease that makes Mitra lame; in *Barnen i spegeln* (1988; The children in the mirror) her isolation grows: she is puzzled by her father's account of the destruction of wonderful Viborg during the Winter War just as she is by the deterioration of her parents' marriage. By the Olympic summer of 1952 the collapse of childhood dreams is complete. Before going home after a stroll with her beloved father, Mitra "stretched up on her toes and kissed Pappa, who bent down over her. Then she let go his hand and walked across the square." The adagio of the Mitra books perfectly suits Björklund's material, a childhood in comfortable circumstances but blighted by a physical handicap. A third part, *Huset med himmelsbalkongen* (1993; The house with the sky balcony), brings Mitra to the brink of puberty.

The parental relationship has also been a main factor in the oeuvre of Merete Mazzarella (1945–). The daughter of a member of Finland's diplomatic corps, Mazzarella spent much of her early life abroad, in Switzerland, China, and England, giving her the advantage of a special point of view, the outsider-insider. As in Björklund's case, she became a literary scholar, completing a doctoral dissertation on the Swedish novelist Eyvind Johnson in 1981; since then she has been a leading critic of the minority's literature, with studies on Finland-Swedish women writers (1985), on the "narrow room" of the novel (1989), and on memoir literature (1993). Her earlier books of creative prose—*Först sålde de pianot* (1979; First they sold the piano) and its continuation *Att spela sitt liv* (1981; To play one's life)—do not take refuge under the generic subtitle of novel; frankly autobiographical, although far more tasteful than the scurrilous exposés by Henrik Tikkanen, they created a small storm because of their murderously amusing or wry portrayal of persons and experiences. She impales her several teachers around the world (at Bangatan's elementary school in Helsingfors, also attended by Björklund's little Mitra, at the school of the Sacred Heart in Peking, at Wispers School in Sussex) and tells of her marriage to a half-Italian, half-English academician and cricket lover, her summers in a cat-terrorized manor in Canterbury, her son's birth in a British obstetrics ward, her job as a lecturer to a band of conspicuous consumers on a cruise ship, her divorce. One episode in *Att spela sitt liv* pays a visit to a commune of sorts in Copenhagen, the closest Mazzarella came to what then was called hippiedom; otherwise, her recorded behavior, as a well-brought-up child, as a *mademoiselle diplomatique,* and as a dangerously observant grownup, was fairly conservative.

In *Påsk* (1983; Easter) Mazzarella tried the novel, and her tone became serious throughout; a teacher in early middle age spends the Easter weekend alone at her family's summer villa, remembering the past and contemplating her present lot, an earnest and cultivated woman faintly disappointed by life. Almost estranged from her husband, a successful business-technocrat, she knows what shaped him — a magnetic father he deeply loved, an impossibly snobbish and dim-witted mother. Mazzarella is expert at composing a Finland-Swedish *sinfonia domestica* for chamber orchestra; Birgitta recalls her childhood as she cleans the villa's playhouse and tells herself the story of her beloved father's slow death, which leads to her realization that her own existential anxiety comes from him. Another novel, *Den okända sällskapsresenären* (1987; The unknown group traveler), takes place, like its predecessor, during a brief and clearly defined time, five days in the lives of five travelers, thrown together in Rome by the luck of travel arrangements, a graver extension (with elements of the mystery novel) of the travel and familial themes treated with so much painful humor in her autobiographical books.

Possessing an extremely keen sense of social and national nuance, she applied this awareness in a book unburdened by a fictional frame: *Samtal* (1990; Conversations) is an elegantly meandering book meant to elucidate what conversation (and storytelling and gossip) are good for. Sticking close to home (but also jabbing at American cocktail party and beauty parlor practices), she pays attention to her minority's peculiarities, its hesitation to talk about "love" and "death" (even though its creative literature has much to say about both), its genius for not losing track of its members, its fanatic memory for *petite histoire.* Desultorily functioning as a literary critic in the course of her king-sized essay, she complains about the debasement of gossip in the address books of Henrik Tikkanen but has a good word for the old-fashioned simplicity of Topelius, for the once popular historian Bernd Estlander, and for Anni Blomqvist. Her diaristic work about her mother's death, *Hem från festen* (1992; Home from the party), added a document of dignified grief to a literature in which revelations have recently been more about sexual practices or substance abuse than loss.

The reflective nonfictional book has flourished in other hands as well, a product to be expected of an old culture. Several works of the architectural historian Nils-Erik Wickberg (1909–) are examples: *Tonfall* (1976; Intonation), *Ett tänkande rö* (1985; A thinking reed), and *Aftonläsning* (1987;

Evening reading). Like Mazzarella in *Samtal,* Wickberg ponders the nature of Finland-Swedishness, among much else, and laments, with considerable irony, the vast ignorance that pertains among Swedes in Sweden concerning "their nearest relatives." (With a gently humorous double novel, *Semikolon 1-2,* [1978-79; Semicolon], Wickberg also had his try at depicting his home city, Helsingfors, between the wars.) A different kind of reflective literature has come from Jutta Zilliacus (1925–), for many years a member of the Finnish Parliament, whose books, *Rökringar* (1975; Smoke rings), *Innan du vet ordet av* (1975; Before you know what happened), *En bit av det stora äpplet* (1978; A piece of the big apple), and *Vändpunkt* (1987; Turning point), deal principally with political events but on a high level of intelligence and with a wealth of cultural reference; in the book of 1975 she was tempted to go over, ever so discreetly, into the confessional mode of the time and into autobiography.

More and more in the 1980s a pull in opposed directions, centrifugal (foreign milieus and characters, travel as an essential part of the plot) and centripetal (family, tradition, minority awareness), characterized Finland-Swedish creative literature, sometimes within the oeuvre of the same author. The 1980s were called a "boom time" of narrative prose, for once as vigorous, interesting, and original as the lyric; authors with fairly long careers behind them suddenly produced fiction of great solidity and worth. Ulla-Lena Lundberg (1947–), a pastor's daughter from Åland, started out with the snippy poem to the "old ladies" who believed in "a reasonable and nice little U-L" (in *Utgångspunkt* [1962; Point of departure]). She studied in America (1964–65) and in Japan (1968–69); *Strövtåg* (1966; Excursions) was a book of opinions and impressions mostly from the United States (like the Norwegian neoromantic, Sigbjørn Obstfelder, Lundberg was not entranced by Milwaukee), followed by the fiction, using the same experiences and backgrounds, of *En berättelse om gränser* (1968; A story about boundaries), a book distinguished by its unimpassioned and factual tone as it takes up reactions to the Vietnam War on U.S. college campuses. An equally factual (yet personal) travel book followed, *Gaijin: Utlänning i Japan* (1970; Gaijin: foreigner in Japan). Lundberg made informative and involved reportage a specialty; *Kökar* (1976) was a study of her home in the Åland Islands; *Öar i Afrikas inre* (1981; Islands in Africa's interior), the result of her repeated visits to that continent; *Franciskus i Kökar: Det lilla samhället möter den stora traditionen* (1985; Saint Francis on Kökar: The little society meets the great tradition) was another specimen of her historically well informed reporting — at some remove from Valdemar Nyman's treatment of similar Åland topics.

Parallel to her reasonable and personal journalism, there ran a considerable creative current; it was a tribute to the quality of her work that Lundberg was able to publish *När barometern stod på Karl Öberg och andra hörspel* (1974; When the barometer stood at Karl Öberg and other radio plays), in which the title play starts in Åland in 1952 but goes back to the great days of the Åland merchant skippers; the longest, *Harald Grönberg 1941*, has as its hero a peace-loving tubercular painter from the Nyland countryside, deferred from military service. *Tre afrikanska berättelser* (1977; Three African tales) used travel experience for fiction; the two with contemporary settings did not glorify the newly established African states and, in their irony, could have been written by a Joyce Cary. *Kungens Anna* (1982; The king's Anna) and *Ingens Anna* (1984; Nobody's Anna) together constituted an unsentimental story in which an Åland girl—a descendant in spirit but not in behavior of Salminen's *Katrina*—manages to lead an independent life despite poverty and confrontations with places (Stockholm, the Finnish mainland) and men (a Swedish artist, an Åbo teacher) more sophisticated than her own home island and herself. Local patriotism enters a union with moderate feminism. *Sand* (1986; Sand) returned to Africa: a female Swedish anthropologist and her male American colleague become the hostages of a frightened and trigger-happy member of the South African Security Forces in the Kalahari Desert, a narration whose suspense and perceptive psychology could make it the basis for a film: the members of three related cultures, almost of the same age, cannot understand one another.

The last of the stories in *Tre afrikanska berättelser* had described the illness and death, in a Moroccan port, of the commander of a merchant ship from Åland in 1928; this sad account, called "A Man Too Short," and the radio play about Åland merchantmen were Lundberg's first steps toward the triple novel that would be her masterpiece thus far: *Leo* (1989) is an epic of Åland seafaring life from the eve of the Bomarsund War (the local name for the Crimean War, the location of the great Russian fortress destroyed by combined British and French fleets during the conflict) until the turn of the century; *Stora världen* (1991; The great world) takes the prosperous captains up to the "grain races" from Australia to Europe between the two world wars and the end of the Åland sailing fleet. Chronicles of Finland-Swedish industrial families had been done by other hands; Lundberg chose to follow the rise and fall of an Åland phenomenon, peasant families that achieved wealth and prestige by following the sea. Near the end of *Leo*, after his beloved wife's passing, the great captain Carl Gustaf perishes horribly of gangrene, leaving five sons behind; their fates (including the unfortunate ship's officer who dies in Africa) and those of the men and women around them are told in brisk and succinct detail in the sequel. The main figure in the enormous cast, however, is Carl Gustaf's nephew, Josef, "the handsomest fellow in the whole Åland merchant fleet," who comes to grief in the race of 1936, running the mighty *Herzogin* aground near Eddystone Light on the Devon coast.

Lundberg squeezes much into her slender texts (which need genealogical charts to be fully enjoyed), figures, facts, events; yet like the anonymous authors of the Icelandic family sagas, she gives her books an air of being well populated but not crowded, and the tempo—despite the many grand set pieces at sea and ashore—is remarkably swift, a triumph of polyphonous storytelling. The narrator of *Leo* is a simple stay-at-home, outside the struggle for maritime and economic greatness and social respect; in *Stora världen,* as in Lundberg's radio plays, the narrative voices multiply, although only one—no doubt significantly for the message contained in the epic— belongs to a determined achiever, the emotionally stunted captain whose beloved twin died in Morocco long ago. Instead, two of the storytellers are the least successful of Carl Gustaf's sons, a rootless dreamer and a conscientious but bumbling pastor, while a third is a steward of modest intelligence, unenthusiastic about going to sea, the grandson of a sailor accidentally killed in Copenhagen during *Leo*'s maiden voyage. The books may be taken as an implicitly anticapitalistic morality tale, in that pride, and the desire for individual material success, go before a fall; yet they also evince enormous respect for the men who took risks for glory and profit and the sometimes unrequited women who supported them: the last speaker is the ever beautiful Elise, Josef's mother, the wife of Carl Gustaf's miserly brother-in-law. In 1996 Lundberg finished the trilogy with *Allt man kan önska sig* (Everything you can ask for), in which the present-day narrator, an anthropologist, is a descendant of the captains of old.

Another tale about economics and competition was told in 1988 by Fredrik Lång (1947–), a novelist and social philosopher whose learned works, *När Thales myntade uttryck: En bok om det sakliga tänkandets uppkomst* (1982; When Thales coined expressions: A book concerning the genesis of objective thought) and *Det industrialiserade medvetandet: Arbete och rationalitet från Platon till Nietzsche* (1986; The industrialized consciousness: Labor and rationality from Plato to Nietzsche), lie outside the perimeters of literary history. Like Lundberg, Lång has tried many modes of literary expression, although without the critical success Lundberg enjoyed almost from the start of her career. *Ockupationen* (1973; The occupation) has its origin in the brief seizure of the Old Student Union at Helsingfors University on 25 November 1968, on the eve of the centennial of the student body's establishment as a formal entity. Schematically, Lång analyzed what he saw as a crisis of humanistic education by applying a time-honored device: two friends from different backgrounds, the middle class and the working class, view the (actually very tame) "revolution" from their respective standpoints. The tractate novel's seemingly endless discussions cause even the narrator, the bourgeois youth, to nod: "Once again I must confess that I lost the thread, that I actually was on the verge of falling asleep."

Lång's sense of humor got freer play in his *jeu d'esprit* about marriage, feminism, and loyalty, *Sommaren med Sue: En komedi tillägnad Tant Svea* (1984; The summer with Sue: A comedy dedicated to Aunt Svea), jam-packed with witty jabs by the husband-narrator at his phrase-filled wife: "all Sue's friends were simply called Gita or Pia and Mia or Fia; you never found out what their last names were, last names were a patriarchal vestige which it was indecent to take into your mouth"). Nevertheless, the book, whose title refers to a Swedish novel by Per Anders Fogelström, *Sommaren med Monika* (1951; The summer with Monika), made into a film by Ingmar Bergman (1952), has a somewhat syrupy happy ending, unlike its Swedish model. Much more cruelly, Lång would return to the theme of marital upset in the three novellas, erotic or antierotic, of *Kärlek utan nåd: Tre variationer på ett tema* (1992; Love without mercy: Three variations on a theme).

The imbalance between genuine narrative and theoretical exposition, evident in *Ockupationen,* was avoided when Lång divided his treatment of the moral implications of the development of atomic power into two books, a thriller about the mysterious death of a Finnish scientist, *Sabotaget* (1983; The sabotage), and *Återblick—Nu* (1986; Backward glance— Now), comprising a set of poems from 1975 (rather Björling-like: "is this not morning, say? / and white lanterns blind the western sky's late stars") and epigrams from 1985, written "after having wandered for ten years in the borderland between analysis and experience," concerning both abstractions ("cosmologies and utopias," "the exact numerical definition of existence") and such mundane matters as "crows" and "what a bog is good for"—a further example of Lång's binary mode of thought and work. Lång's needling of academic pomposity and shiftiness is on a level with David Lodge's in a novel on an art historian's frustrating research trip, *Bagges italienska resa* (1991; Bagge's Italian journey), but the entertainment is repeatedly interrupted by long and earnest disquisitions about obscure aspects of Leonardo da Vinci, the object of Vilhelm Bagge's research.

One of the troubles of Kai Wilhelms in *Sommaren med Sue* arises from his wish to write "a novel with footnotes"; the skepticism with which publishers have regarded Lång's public appeal may be reflected in his erratic course between various houses; like *Sommaren med Sue,* the short novel *Porträttet av direktör Rask: En tragedi* (1988; The portrait of Director Rask: A tragedy), Lång's most successful work, appeared at the small publisher Draken (The Dragon) before its serialization in Finland's Swedish radio service. Stig-Evert Rask is the son of an impractical man who went to America before the First World War, seeking a nest egg to support his family in Yttermark, "Ostrobothnia's Ostrobothnia," and returned broken in health. Lacking elementary social skills, clumsy with women (as Lång's shy heroes are wont to be), a hard worker, the younger Rask rapidly makes his way up the local economic ladder and becomes the director of a timber-export firm, proclaiming—in response to the rumor that his father was a Communist—that "in Helsingfors the professors believe . . . it is the ideas and politics and institutions that build up a vital society." But in Ostrobothnia people have known better for two hundred years: "the only thing that can create true freedom is commercial life. Freedom is the right to produce and trade." The Russian wars of 1939–40 and 1941–44 help Rask enlarge his firm; an essential civilian worker, he is never called up for service.

Finally, the little empire of Rask, "the region's most forward-looking businessman," declines and collapses under pressure from strikes, changed economic conditions, and the competition of larger and much more powerful concerns; Rask is left with a wife who has become "a little strange," uncomprehending children, a ruined reputation, and a portrait of himself (intended to be hung in his firm's boardroom on his fiftieth birthday) — should he want to buy it. Lång's tale of Rask's fortune and fall, an Ostrobothnian César Birotteau, is told with considerable sympathy for the little capitalist destroyed by forces he cannot understand. Yet Lång's heart lies, as is made clear in a *coup de théâtre,* with the honest working men Rask has unwittingly exploited on his way to prosperity; one of Rask's sons is saved from drowning by a union activist whom Rask has fired. During an embarrassed meeting between the two men, Rask clings stubbornly to his capitalist faith: "With private capitalism it's this way, things go well for one person and poorly for another. But with socialism things go poorly for everyone."

Almost simultaneously with Lundberg's Åland epic and Lång's Ostrobothnian tragedy, a third and still more ironic tale of independent enterprise was told by Lars Sund (1953–). Sund had started as a poet, very much of his time; *Stadens ljus* (1974; The city's lights) has a poem in which a child directs pointed questions to General Franco, as well as tributes to Mayakovsky, the unavoidable Neruda, "Marilyn Monroe, if I ever met her" (in *Snöleopard* Tua Forsström would also console the actress's shade), to Åbo Academy (mockingly), and to Ostrobothnia (devotedly); its conclusion salutes "Music Row," "janis joplin, brian jones, jimi hendrix, blind lemon jefferson, and w c handy" (all without capitals). In 1975 Sund turned to prose, with *Natten är ännu ung* (The night is still young), on teenagers in Jakobstad, an Ostrobothnian equivalent to the Texas town in Peter Bogdanovich's film *The Last Picture Show* (1971), a novel full of cars, alcohol, and slang. Sometimes Sund's Eki Bergman sounds like a less sophisticated Holden Caulfield: "I live in Jakobstad, which is a damned rathole. I go to Jakobstad's lyceum, an even worse rathole, and I still don't understand what I'm supposed to be doing there."

The next stage on life's way was the academic novel *Vinterhamn* (1983; Winter harbor): Harry, a young man from Jakobstad, experiences Åbo Academy as he works on a dissertation about Anders Chydenius; his immediate circle is composed of a radical student, Skrifvars (the constellation is like that in Lång's *Ockupationen*), involved with Harry's sister, and Martina Höchst, the object of Harry's affections. The erotic exercises of Sund's characters are reproduced much more specifically than in Kurt Sanmark's Åbo novel, *Insyn,* of a quarter-century before; the political exercises come to a climax with Skrifvars's turn away from his cherished and one-sided leftism: "It was standard answers we had all the time. Take the peace question for example. Why is the USA's arming a threat to peace, while on the other hand a strong Soviet defense force serves peace?" and "The problem, Harry, is that I discovered a split between what I thought and said and reality. But I refused to acknowledge it. I carefully collected arguments for the socialist states. . . . And certain things I totally repressed. . . . Such as Poland, for example. That workers in Poland were shot in 1970 and 1976 when they protested against the regime." Lowering their revolutionary sights, Harry and Skrifvars make a vain gesture to preserve the Åbo past, by trying to prevent the razing of a landmark restaurant. When Skrifvars sets out for more useful kinds of protest, "against the destruction of milieus and natural resources. And against the armament race and atomic weapons," Harry doubts that these efforts will have a result; in a final vignette a seagull rejoices in the simple sensation of living.

A second long hiatus in Sund's production ensued; then *Colorado Avenue* (1991) appeared, a novel that, unlike some Finland-Swedish fiction, avoided the autobiographical element and gave much evidence of careful planning and careful writing. Sund enjoys both the act of narration and the riches of his native language, including dialect. (Lundberg, Lång, and Sund all come from parts of Finland more unashamedly and uncomplicatedly "Swedish" than the capital.) *Colorado Avenue* — is its street title a sly dig at the street-address revelations by Henrik Tikkanen, about the decadence of establishment families in Helsingfors? — recounts a fairly simple set of events. Another of the several brave and independent fictional women from the islands off Finland's coast, Hanna migrates to America and, after employment by a daffy society dame in Manhattan, makes her way to Telluride, Colorado (called "To Hell You Ride" by those who labor in its mines), takes over a boardinghouse, marries labor organizer Ed Ness (like her an Ostrobothnian), and, following his death in the miners' strike of 1903, returns to her home province, a prosperous "Dollar Hanna," with her son Otto. Grown up, Otto — another of the believers in free enterprise who populate the Finland-Swedish novel of the later 1980s — becomes a gallant bootlegger, the "Canister King," during Finland's Prohibition; in 1928 he is apprehended by the detective who plays Chauvelin to Otto's Pimpernel, but escapes — *Lanthandlerskans son* (1997; The country storekeeper's son) provides a sequel.

The novel, which recounts much recent Finnish history seen from an Ostrobothnian perspective, could have turned out to be a plodding cavalcade (like the migration to America, the Civil War of 1918 has become worn from overuse in Finland-Swedish fiction); yet, thanks to a nimble narrative technique, Sund has created — if not that fata morgana, the "great Finland-Swedish novel" — a superior piece of narrative prose, surely worthy of rank with its counterparts on the Finnish side of the language line, the novels of Sund's fellow Ostrobothnian Antti Tuuri. The American sections of the novel occasionally resemble the documentary style of John Dos Passos; the whole tale is told by a serenely cheerful narrator.

The bloom of the novel (with regional settings) at the end of the 1980s was enhanced by substantial works from other writers who dealt with Helsingfors or an international milieu. Agneta Ara, known for her poetry, tried out with *Antonio Gades kommer inte* (1990; Antonio Gades is not coming); it has aspects of the thriller, as practiced by Bargum and Lång, among others, and of the motion picture: Ara's title, and some of her action, have to do with the choreographer-star of Carlos Saura's flamenco film, *Carmen,* of 1983. Beyond these extensive and glittering trappings and the intense eroticism (which has become commonplace), the novel contains the female lead's memories of parents and siblings, images from happier and simpler times: "All the lamps are burning in the doll's house. Mama sits knitting in front of the fire. Pappa comes whistling down the stairs with a newspaper in his hand. He sits beside Mama and gives her a kiss. 'Look out for my knitting," she laughs." Very effectively, Ara follows the fashion of the 1980s in her nostalgia for parents and childhood (see Bargum's *Pappas flicka* and *Sommarpojken,* Groth's Edi, Kjell Lindblad's timorous children, Merete Mazzarella's tributes to her father and mother).

The same year as Ara's book, another large novel with motifs from dance, eroticism, and childhood appeared, *Byte* (1989; an ambiguous title meaning either "Exchange" or "Prey"), by Pirkko Lindberg (1942–). The protracted and painfully comic *tango formidable* between a case-hardened woman artist and an actor of less than Olivieran gifts may be summed up in the concluding words of the artist's cynical friend: "A good many loving couples let themselves be broken on the wheel, turn after turn. . . . But others topple off the wheel. And then they pick up their odds and ends and go off to let themselves be fastened to new wheels with completely new people." Like Ara, Lindberg is concerned to bring some subtlety and variety into the tedious love-play rampant in Finland's recent novel; but the essence of the book lies (once more) in the bond between the artist and her late mother, who disappeared when swimming one day in a lake with the symbolic name Totuudenjärvi (Truth's Lake), somewhere in the Karelian paradise. (That province, partially lost in 1944, seems destined for a dreamlike immortality in Finland-Swedish letters, from Jac. Ahrenberg to Kristina Björklund; shortly after Lindberg's novel came out, the veteran journalist and man of the theater Benedikt Zilliacus [1921–], the son of Emil Zilliacus, gave the public his memories of Karelian boyhood summers in *Båten i vassen: En berättelse om en förlorad ö* [1991; The boat in the reeds: A tale about a lost island].)

The daughter's nostalgia for her mother's (and maternal grandmother's) summertime language, Finnish, should not be overlooked: "Finnish was my first language," the artist Inna says, "and it was actually only when Mama died that Swedish got the upper hand." The relationship of the actor Sten Zhurikoff (from a Lutheran pastor's family, despite the Russian surname) to Finland's majority language is much more strained; taking up a crux not often discussed in Finland-Swedish literature, Lindberg lets her two main characters represent two Finland-Swedish standpoints in the language question: the notion of Finnish as the truer, deeper (and more maternal) language of Finland, which inspired so many Swedish-speaking Fennomanes of the nineteenth century to struggle with it and surrender to it, and the conception of Swedish as the comfortable, reasonable tongue, with Finnish remaining forever a barrier. Zhurikoff's mother remembers that Finnish had always given her a headache in school, and her son is highly skeptical of Inna's claim that "some words have a power and patina in Finnish they can never acquire in Swedish."

How long will the flowering of the Finland-Swedish novel continue? It might be a sign of a flagging urge that Lundberg returned to the personal travel book with *Sibirien: Ett självporträtt med vingar* (1993; Siberia: A self-portrait with wings) and that Lindberg made a trip around the world, described in *Tramp* (1993), followed by the *Candide* pastiche *Candida* (1996). Conversely, Kjell Westö (1961–), in his first book of eight stories, *Utslag* (1989; Rash, but the word may also mean, i.a., "Outcrop"), meets Helsingfors life of the 1980s as directly and memorably as Runar Schildt did some seventy years before. The capital as Westö knows it is no longer a place where Swedish-speakers can lead their lives separate from the linguistic majority. Westö's "Kabana" is the story of a middle-class, almost bilingual young Finland-Swede among tough Finnish workers; "Brief Solos for Guitar" is once again in the world of rock music; the long title story is about journalism and its ethical demands; but "Bruno" and "Aunt Elsie" are back in the well-known narrow room of the Finland-Swedish family; "He Came In through the Bathroom Window" (a Beatles title) and "Triangle" are about shifting erotic arrangements; "When Night Falls" moves a small town into the twilight zone, a further example of the lure the supernatural had suddenly acquired.

In the three short novels, or novellas, put together in *Fallet Bruce* (1992; The Bruce case) Westö found his skillful way—in the story "Melba, Mallinen and I"—into the gangs of childhood and adolescence and into the often ignored possibility that young members of the minority, wanting desperately to belong, become the target of bullying. The title calls to mind a Swedish boyhood classic, Fritiof Nilsson-Piraten's *Bombi Bitt och jag* (1931; Bombi Bitt and I), but Westö's narrator is far less confident than Nilsson-Piraten's Eli and Bombi Bitt in their monolingual Scanian world. (Westö expanded the story into a novel, *Drakarna över Helsingfors* [1996; Kites over Helsingfors].) Instead, he is out of place both in his home city of Helsingfors—or, with Westö's admirable precision, in a suburban development quaintly named Marracott Hill, where there reside "workers, lower-middle-class, and Middle Class Which Certainly Wants to Move Up Quickly," and then in the decidedly upscale Marracott Beach—and in Stockholm, where he lives for sixteen months and feels odd because of his Finland-Swedish accent: "I was accustomed to being in the wrong place at the wrong time." "Iiro and the Boy" combines the burdens of middle age's approach with those of uncomfortable fatherhood; the rock musician Iiro attends a Christmas party at his son's school, clad "in black jeans, boots, and a college sweater with the [English] slogan, 'So What?' under a picture of a drunken pig." The title story plays with writers and artists, with Finland's cultural tradition, and with "the little Swedish Helsingfors, a nest of gossip through and through." Minimally gifted, the narrator "pokes around a little in Runeberg" and then undertakes a Jungian reading of Mikael Lybeck; during a winter of Sibelius enthusiasm he concludes that the master was "a hitmaker of his time," and in a modern day, "Finlandia" would have come out as "Don't Cry for Me, Finlandia," like the song from Andrew Lloyd Webber's *Evita*. This envious friend tries to write a research report about Bruce, by general opinion a genius: "Against my better knowledge, I became involved more and more in Bruce's chaotic brain."

Westö had thorough knowledge of the Helsingfors *vie littéraire*, as well as of the several other contemporary milieus he describes; he was a member of the editorial staff of the little magazine KLO (another undeciphered acronym) during its short life, from 1985 to 1987. As described by Michel Ekman ("Varken förklara," 8), KLO was the organ of a new generation of authors, "for whom neither Communism nor the post-Communistic hangover had been much of a problem." (He alludes to *Fågel Fenix*, that "distinctly defensive and rather melancholy journal," and *Otid*, "dominated by young sometime Communists who confessed.") Nevertheless, Ekman saw a community of interest between *Fågel Fenix* and KLO, born a decade apart, in their reaction against the strongly politicized climate of Finland, and in the decision that their most important task, in both cases, was "to do battle in support of artistic freedom and integrity," instead of letting literature be reduced to mere propaganda. Westö saw that "a chasm" separated him from the 1960s and FBT (which had begun to appear when he was a four-year-old): "We don't have the same goal. Quite simply, I don't think in systems." KLO also had only a limited interest in literary theory, that great academic fad of the 1980s, and in contemporary philosophy; instead, it went about the business of presenting new writers, concerned with "existentialist-inspired questions about the responsibility of the individual for his own life." This sense of moral obligation was developed in opposition to quite specific foes, an "individually unconcerned expansion of consumption" in a Finland grown ever more prosperous, and "a postmodern" attitude toward life which plumped for the "direct, individual satisfaction of personal needs and declared that absolute ethical values were out of the question." (At the same time, older authors, Bo Carpelan and Johannes Salminen, Mikael Enckell and Paul von Martens, gave expression in several genres to a similar dislike of contemporary selfishness.)

Apart from Westö, it has been argued that the prose writer who best represents the search for a "sense of responsibility for one's own actions and thoughts" by means of deterrent examples is another sometime member of the KLO group, Monika Fagerholm (1961–). In the stories by Westö the protagonists are male (albeit sometimes much under the influence of women); Fagerholm's world has been called "unmasculinized," with men as mere extras or objects of feminine ego projection. In her books of tales, *Sham* (1987) and *Patricia* (1990), girls and women may well seem to be "unlikable, empty, tiresome — they concern themselves with extremely trivial matters and drift through life, apparently without achieving anything" (Sandin, 4). Her protagonists are an appalling bunch: obese Katrin who cannot resist Big Macs, Nathalie and Felicity who perform group sex with two Lebanese (the girls "laugh at the evening's events, they know that everything would be repeated"), the treacherous Lesbian in the title story of *Sham,* the unpleasant roommates in "Veronica Granit," the opportunist "Patricia Rabbit," and the nameless woman in "The Call of the Blood," *Patricia*'s concluding story, who gives up her job, finds a love of sorts, gives birth to a child (who becomes a famous tenor), and ends, in this brief curriculum vitae, as an enormous and loathsome barfly in a hot and equally nameless port — a descendant of Gargantua in the anomalous tale by Hagar Olsson. Are these lives intended to instruct by arousing disgust (as the woman "with a bass voice and an accent" waddles off through the "afternoon's humidity and heat ... a large wet spot spreads out on the back of her dress"), or are they meant, by the very flamboyance of their sordidness, to demonstrate women's freedom? Fagerholm has announced that she is a reader of Colette, Julia Kristeva, and Hélène Cixous; a critic advances the thought that she contributes "towards the demolition of the whoremadonna dichotomy found in so much writing, even today" (Dickens, "Monika Fagerholm"). Recently, Fagerholm's novel *Underbara kvinnor vid vatten — en roman om syskon* (1994; Wonderful women by the water — A novel about siblings) has turned to the traditional Finland-Swedish milieu, the summer home in the skerries, and to the traditional Finland-Swedish structure, the family, for a much-praised picture of the prefeminist — or protofeminist? — 1960s.

Lyric of the 1980s: A Similar Abundance

The main literary product, otherwise, to come out of the KLO circle was the lyric, quite in accordance with the ancient Finland-Swedish pattern. The poetry of Bruce in Westö's story, as quoted by the genius's biographer, is a subversive reflection of Westö's own poetry; Westö began as a lyricist with

Tango orange (1987), so generous with words and with depictions of Helsingfors figures that Pekka Tarkka dared almost "to place him in the tradition of Walt Whitman" (p. 68); but Westö was the Whitman of a generation that had lost its way in the midst of prosperity, when Finland liked to think of itself as the "Japan of the North." Westö picks out a good many contemporary and lamentable faces from the city's crowd, a woman derelict ("The winter stuck like pins in her eyes"), a drink-sodden veteran outside the state alcohol store at Christmastime, the guests and hangers-on at Hotel Intet ("Hotel Nothing," but the name is a play on Helsingfors's Hotel International), Carita ("beautiful as a tarantula in [her] black decolletage"), Fat Molly, who buys lovers at the bar and is found mutilated and murdered.

In *Epitaf över Mr. Nacht* (1988; Epitaph concerning Mr. Nacht) Westö's linguistic exuberance, his composition of rock quasi-ballads, and his undeniable weakness for melodrama perhaps wore a little thin; just the same, by means of his vigor, contrasting so strangely with his pictures of degradation and emptiness, he turned out memorable images from pop music ("Look at that man! Doesn't he resemble a chattering / saxophone solo, performed with brilliant technique / and great routine?"), science-fiction poems ("The Time Machine" and "War Games"), feigned biographies and autobiographies. With *Avig-bön* (1989; Backward prayer) Westö — writing under the pseudonym Anders Hed — strikes out in the direction of even wilder but still cogent imagery, describing his city in "Helsingfors Refrain" as

> fragility bird, babushka crone,
> quick to act big
> ....
> within your stomach the child may cough;
> first rustspot in silvery flute
> back's bent vertebra, human shards have built you
> remember the skinny wretch you were
> ....
> you may have suffered,
> that is true
> today you swell like a mutant rat
> you squat over fief-towns, greedy Saturn
> all you; city bacchanal and cannibal.

The expansion of language, sometimes brilliantly successful, sometimes falling flat, almost always defying translation because of neologisms, onomatopoeia, wordplays, interior rhymes, jumbled syntax, is palpable everywhere: who else would have thought to say of Helsingfors: "in your throat the old man may cough: / a concerto for corroded trombone"?

As Bruce and Anders Hed bear witness, Westö also enjoys role-playing:

prayer in reverse
is mockery and role-play
looks to be what it is not
prayer in reverse is foolery and funning
giving out a ware it perhaps is.

Nevertheless, beyond the fireworks, there is a sobering message; "The Repentant," in *Epitaf över Mr. Nacht,* says, "We who plan, we who build, we who demolish, / we all have a plan, it lets us forget existence." In the little magazine *Ai-ai* he published a prose suite, "Suburb of the 1960s. Renovated," about a suburb on its way from emptiness to glamorous falsification. The first part begins: "The churches in brick, small and compact. There was no need to overemphasize the metaphysical question. The shopping centers resembled fortresses. People moved in, all strangers. Like fortresses boredom and paleness bored into the people hurrying home. The statistics ate their way like termites through the house." In the third part: "He returns to the same place twenty-five years later. It's called Galleria now, has bay windows and irregular forms suggesting caprice and a happy marketplace. Now he's a suburban father, and surprised; did this actually remain, did I become here?"

Other poets associated directly with KLO were its chief editor, Merja-Riitta Steenroos (1963–), and Henrika Ringbom (1962–), both of whom published subsequently in *Ai-ai*. This journal, which lasted from 1988 to 1991, was edited by Peter Mickwitz (1964–) and Mårten Westö (1967–); fostering a number of new poets, it proceeded from the conviction that it should avoid "the trivial and dangerously simple notion of how one can understand and comment on society"; according to its announcement, it was a "journal for the time," with a "pronounced air of contemporary commentary" about it. During her editorship Steenroos had a bright and enthusiastic correspondence with an avuncular Claes Andersson in the epistolary dialogue by various hands, *Rockad: Ett brevbok* (1986; Castled: a book of letters). (The other pairs of correspondents were the critic Trygve Söderling and Jörn Donner; Tapani Ritamäki, literary and rock critic, and Merete Mazzarella; Kjell Westö and columnist Johan von Bonsdorff.) The letter volume, which, among other things, looked back to the sixties and compared them with the eighties while promising a glance into the nineties, was published by Boklaget, which from 1983 on had concentrated its efforts on such multiauthor undertakings, bringing out still another little magazine, or rather annual, BLÅ, *Boklagets Litterära Årsmagasin,* from 1983 to 1986. The joke lay in the fact that the acronym also meant "Blue"; Steenroos was an editor of its 1985 number, along with Monika Fagerholm.

Steenroos's poems in *Guldgrävarens tårar* (1981; The gold digger's tears) were marked by naive youthfulness, chattiness, and a dash of despair ("we gold diggers, / we lonely wanderers and self-assured statues, / renovators who continue the destruction, / . . . the city is out of joint, we with it"), together with old-fashioned sentiment ("I think of your face / as of the glass of wine before the night"). In *Fri marknad* (1983; Free market) Södergranian echoes become even plainer ("He taught me disappointment's sweet smell: / the city's fingermarks, fragments, the child's / birth and death and what there is in between"); like many of her contemporaries, Steenroos feels obliged to say why and how she writes poetry ("The poem ought to be like the hillswallow's flight, self-understood / no one gives the swallow orders to fly and / no one moves barriers out of its way"). The letters to Claes Andersson (who had been a friendly reviewer of her debut collection, calling it both "intimate and objective") told how she had undergone a poetic renewal after reading Westö's *Tango orange* and Andersson's critical praise of it; the language of her *Kanariefågel blues* (1985; Canarybird blues) is much more florid and imaginative, ranging from the bird epicedium of the misleadingly simple title poem to a drug lyric, "The White Alligator" (who "bears no jewels her tongue / is covered by thick pearls, her hand / is your secret sin"), and the fantasy on fragments of Old Irish texts (translated by the poet), which continues — as other poems in the book do — the alligator theme.

Henrika Ringbom is more stringent, if more cryptic, in her language than her sometime colleagues Westö and Steenroos. *Båge* (1988; Bow) is a mixture of prose fragments, small stories, city scenes, portraits ("Tina, Eighteen": "I walk on sidewalk. I bear emptiness with me"), interiors (a messy bathroom), childhood memories ("In that landscape a little girl's laughter comes trickling down like the pearls from a necklace whose thread has snapped, the laughter she laughs when her pappa lifts her over his head and she's an airplane"), and comments on the writing of poetry ("I do not want / symbols, I want that / which has effect. / If it's images, sounds / I want them"). Ringbom's fascination with dreams (and her background in literary history) is illustrated by her verse commentary on a passage from Almqvist's dialogue novel *Amorina* (1822, 1839); as in Steenroos's case there is a display of learned intertextuality. Sentence fragments, heard as if in sleep, get the upper hand in *Det jag har* (1990; What I have):

> What I have
> I leave
> at a place
> when I go
> to another and do not go to another.

Ringbom borrows her epigraph from the dancer Merce Cunningham ("No, just go ahead and *do* it / Do it till you find out what it is"). Word fragments, broken words ("Beige and white sur / face"), mixtures of Swedish and English all stand in the way of understanding; Michel Ekman remarks that Ringbom, following deconstructionist theory, emphasizes the "meaningless character" of the text, which "gets its meaning only in confrontation with the reader" ("Varken förklara," 17). The reader may or may not be able to deal with such poems (quoted in their entirety) as: "I am powerfully dressed in red," and "I neither can nor try / to blow the rings of smoke / which uniform lift, dissolve," or "Playing," with its incomplete punctuation and conjunctions that lead nowhere:

> Now I shall really just
> Therefore semantic empty)
> In a hermetic structure
> With somebody else (and.

Other poets do not administer such tests to their audience. Gungerd Wikholm (1954–) moves in more familiar territory, building up atmospheres, as she does in the "Summer with Men" of *Torplandet* (1982; The sharecropper's land): "rain again, like dying dandelion fall / with insectlegs creeping over the window, / here inside the conversations about the war are repeated." Wikholm's emotional intensity resembles Tua Forsström's ("how can you be anything other / than sorrel with strange movements / constant longing for light"), and her directness is extended into *Aria* (1987); the immediacy of her impressions and feelings, transmitted without verbal play, can be seen in the numerous poems about old people, old times in Ostrobothnia, even old smells ("When a person dies, he takes the odor in his rooms with him"). Just so, in *Anhalter, svarta och röda* (1990; Way stations, black and red), the memories arising from old pictures are unsentimentally celebrated:

> Time frozen into a mirror,
> a real aroma of wild strawberries
> Turning one's pages backward:
> the lover with a strong smell of shaving lotion
> on the path in the evening light, wild grass.

Wikholm makes no attempt to develop a new linguistic style; her undeniable resemblance to the lyric of the 1960s comes not from any political agenda but from her inherent sympathy for her mostly rural subjects, with whom she feels a complete unity: "Cut me and soil shall run out, dry and gray / or dark and heavy after long rain. / In childhood it rained more than memory knows." If Ringbom's poetry defies translation, Wikholm's cries out for it.

Diana Bredenberg (1963–) deals in emotions and loyalties, like Wikholm; but unlike Wikholm (who seldom forgets the south Finnish countryside from which she comes), Bredenberg persistently gazes into herself. The introverted quality of her verse, often almost masochistic in its sense of abandonment, has been apparent from *Barndomskriget* (1984; The childhood war) on and has not undergone any sweeping change. *Hundra dikter* (1986; Hundred poems) continues to make the plain pronouncements of unhappiness, as in number 69 (in its entirety): "Sleep's mercifulness / like padding through the body. / The sharp awakening"; number 88 is a statement of her simple poetics:

> The poem must not be large.
> The poem must not be long.
> The poem must live
> like blood rushing through the body.

Rast (1988; Rest) is made up of short cycles; the main one provides the title for the collection and has an appropriate epigraph from the Swedish author Stig Dagerman (1923–54), with whom Bredenberg's affinity is great: "Our need of consolation is immeasurable." Bredenberg's poems are heartrending in their personal hopelessness; see *Hinna* (1989; Membrane): "It is cold at all the stations. / The leaves feel no pain in their leaf-graves," and

> Filled plastic bags with staggering forms
> on the way toward the closed rooms.
> Children's giant cries across the courtyard: Mamma Mamma Look
>   Look
> The weeping of small animals, their homelessness's owners.

But Bredenberg's melancholy does not remain entirely existential; it also results from dismay at the forever expanding urban sprawl and at nature's destruction. The opening of *Sekvens* (1991; Sequence) desperately lists: "The trucks, the rumbling sounds / of backhoes beyond the forest. / Filled loads, freshly baked asphalt."

Wikholm and Bredenberg follow a time-honored Finland-Swedish tradition (see Runeberg's often cited praise of that which is "clear, unaffected, and artless"); their lucidity has to be contrasted with the difficulties erected by Eva-Stina Byggmästar (1967–). *I glasskärvornas rike* (1986; In the realm of the glass shards), with illustrations by the poet, offered no problems of interpretation to anyone well read in Södergran; the very title echoed a famous poem in *Dikter*, and such lines as "Far away from the land of Reality / there is another land, / the land Nowhere," and "You gave me a dream, / it warmed / it did not burn" could scarcely deny their ancestry. The same Södergranian quality can also be found in *Amuletten* (1987; The amulet), again self-illustrated. But in their striking expressions of her loyalty to the women's movement, some of Byggmästar's images seem fetched from the world of adventure fiction:

> They carry the priestess away.
> They lead me after her.
> I hold her given amulet
> concealed beneath my bloodsoaked vestment,
> our common fate
> between my breasts.

Spiralens form (1988; The spiral's form) is a single long poem, describing a journey—as in Lindén's *Maras ö*—through a mythic landscape; womanhood possesses an intimate relationship with nature not vouchsafed men, the argument also lying at the base of *Drivkrafter* (1990; Driving forces). Now the language has exploded, and an address to "Shakti" turns into simple sibilants ("sss ssss"). (Like Fagerholm in *Patricia* and Steenroos in *Kanariefågel blues,* Byggmästar provides footnotes explaining her gynolatric references: Shakti is "The God-mother. Everything's origin"; Amaterasu is "the highest divinity," the sun goddess of Japanese Shintoism; Hathor is the Egyptian goddess who "could assume the form of various animals.")

För upp en svan (1992; Lead up a swan) moves into nonsense poetry, amusing in its word-inventiveness ("oppositionalmindedcarrot," "elevatorhappiness," "ciphersnow over the cathouse's roof"), even as her poems tear themselves to pieces on the printed page, spreading out their component parts; some items open with repetitive nasals ("n/nnnnnnn" and so forth) or burst into lines of affirmation ("O yes o, yes o, yes o, yes o, yes"); the sketches accompanying the earlier volumes are now replaced by abstract typographical patterns. A characteristic of Byggmästar's intensely productive career has been her search for her own style, leading her to employ the "meaninglessness" of the text also embraced by Bäck and Ringbom; Byggmästar succeeded to the extent that she was designated by a critic as the "most important" of the numerous women poets in the stable of Författarnas andelslag, where her first four books appeared before she transferred to Söderström & Co. in 1992. The ever helpful Michel Ekman has described *För upp en svan* as "rollicking . . . she lifts out the words and shows them in all their inherent nonsense" ("Varken förklara," 22). She may have found her niche as an Ostrobothnian Lewis Carroll:

> sadness after small jackrabbit, most resembles doorpost
> or stonepile. Kisses chicken goodnight under wing, with
> big white teeth.
> Horse which laughs.

She has ancestors, of course, in the extravagance of Björling in his dadaist period and the rather tame nonsense poetry of Mauritz Nylund.

The figure among younger lyricists who, after Westö, has attracted the most critical attention is Agneta Enckell (1957–). Not a member of the KLO circle, she nonetheless was ready to admit to a similarity of aims — a renewal of poetic language through experimentation, and an avoidance of political stance. Her *Förvandlingar mot morgonen* (1983; Transformations toward the morning) was one of those fairly numerous works dealing with institutional life (e.g., Donner's book about his hospital service, Claes Andersson's asylums, Wikman's old people's homes, Siv Alander's hospitals); a section of it is called "Open Ward," a report on the apparent freedom of both inmates and attendants at a mental institution:

> We
> are free
> to go wherewewill
> wherewewill
> and we constantly return.

Yet the mental institution is not the only enclosed space; the Stockholm subway is another such location ("the workdays' end and beneath / Stockholm's streets / through black tunnels . . . threatening"). Further, the suburban environment, so often assailed in the literature of the 1980s, is a dead space of its own: "Look at the houses: mute / Rollingstones whispering / in the twilight," and

> on a sunny morning a runaway dog
> lured me out among
> the colossi
> the concrete labyrinths the asphalt's
> melting tones
> in bathrobe and wooden shoes.

Finland-Swedish Literature

The claustrophobic-agoraphobic pressures increased in *rum: berättelser* (1987; room[s]: narratives), whose first part, "In the Blind Woman's Café," is filled with "collecting eyes" and "the blind woman's intensive eyes." The second part is called "mellan jag å jag" ("between I and I"); conscious of the poem's sound effect, as she is of its typographical arrangement, Enckell uses the comic-strip "å" instead of the standard "och" (compare Thomas Wulff's ampersand). The site is once again an underground transportation system or, worse, the realm of the dead: "she betook herself through subwaytunnels, through symbolic places where there were creatures out together half and doubly, they waited by the tunnels' walls, where dampness smelling dripped mustily," a prose passage inserted into the long, dreamlike narrative of the flight of a girl named Pipa ("singing, endlessly climbing"). A resolution comes with a quotation, duly identified in a footnote, "you shall love God although you do not know His existence, you shall love —," from Simone Weil (1909–43), a paradoxical thinker likewise admired by Enckell's Finnish-language counterpart, Kirsti Simonsuuri (see chapter 5).

Eurydice, vanishing into the Underworld for the sake of love, appears in passing in *rum: berättelser;* she returns in *Falla (Eurydike)* (1991; To fall [Eurydice]), which is again cyclical in construction and located, as before, in an underworld, either the passages of a high-rise apartment complex or Hades itself. Yet Hades is the woman's sexuality, and as has been repeatedly noted by reviewers (it may have helped *Falla [Eurydike]* to a second edition, an unusual accolade for a book of Finland-Swedish lyrics), Enckell's constant concern with the woman's body is the overriding theme, an expression of "woman's visibility and her right to her own language." A murderer, "man," hides in the underground tunnels, and his victim is the woman; Enckell plays on the double meaning of "man" in Swedish, both "you/one" and a male being: "Man murders because skin is soft, because SKIN HAS HOLES." (Like her cousin Martin Enckell, Agneta Enckell likes to use capitals to reinforce messages.) At the same time, *Falla (Eurydike)* is about the writing of poetry and poetic language itself; Enckell shares the metapoetic concerns of so many of her contemporaries:

the
language falls, absent
signs through the tremblings
as words impenetrable
meanings rushing
between us.

The argument for an evanescent, fleeing, falling poetic language contrasts with the concrete sites through which her feminine persona moves; her lyric cadenzas contrast with the narrative urge carried over from her earlier books. *Falla (Eurydike)* can be seen as an *ars poetica,* for women, and simultaneously a sexual thriller, its effect heightened by an obsessive nastiness ("disgusting holes ugly holes, one doesn't know what's in them, no"); disingenuously, Enckell has said herself that she regards her work as "an invisible provocation against everything that is supposed to be efficient and clear and unambiguous and easily understood . . . this is what makes people so annoyed."

At the end of *rum: berättelser* there is a surprising reference, in a prose coda, to "the mirror, the picture where Oscar Wilde [is] absorbed with himself," and Enckell has likewise managed to create (thanks not least to a remarkable photogenic quality) a highly dramatic public image. It cannot have escaped notice that she is to the poetic manor born: the daughter of the essayist Mikael Enckell, and thus the granddaughter of Rabbe Enckell and the legendary beauty Heidi Runeberg-Enckell-Parland, who in her turn had been the granddaughter of Finland's great nineteenth-century sculptor Walter Runeberg and the great-granddaughter of Runeberg himself. (Again, how much of Finland-Swedish literary and cultural history is a genealogy!) To be sure, it may be wondered what Runeberg, the determinedly masculine poet, would have thought of his descendant's verse. He was also proud of his eroticism.

Finally, another Finland-Swedish literary tradition has come to the surface again on the threshold of the 1990s, the academician who is also a creative writer. The pattern was set by the professor-poets of Åbo Academy (Achrelius, Rudeen) and continued by Frans Mikael Franzén before his removal to Sweden; in the nineteenth century Runeberg was docent of Latin language and literature at the university and then a schoolmaster; Topelius became professor of history; Arvid Mörne was docent in Finland's literature for some thirty years; Emil Zilliacus, docent of literary history and professor extraordinary of classical literature; Lars Huldén brilliantly represented the blend, his philological knowledge feeding his poetry. (For decades, much creative criticism was in academic hands: see C. G. Estlander, Yrjö Hirn, Werner Söderhjelm, Olaf Homén; Olof Enckell abandoned newspaper criticism and literary creation for the academy; Merete Mazzarella continues the line.) On the Finnish side August Ahlqvist as "A. Oksanen," Julius Krohn as "Suonio," Otto Manninen, V. A. Koskenniemi, the university librarian Volter Kilpi, and, of late, Markku Envall and Kirsti Simonsuuri have had similar double interests.

Torsten Pettersson (1954–), sometimes docent in English literature and literary theory at Åbo Academy, associate professor of general literature and aesthetics at Helsingfors, and at present professor of literature at Uppsala, continues the practice, with lyrics—*Besvärjelse* (1985; Conjuration), *Solen är en tunnel* (1989; The sun is a tunnel), *Ser du dem inte?* (1987; Don't you see them?)—and the stories of *Vargskallen* (1991; The wolf skull). Perhaps because of his very expertness in literary theory and interpretation, he resists the temptation to enter the wilder realms of experimentation, maintaining a compactness and clarity that is a perfect and suggestively contrastive medium for the anxiety, fear, and mystery permeating his work. (He has not been an interpreter of Joseph Conrad for nothing.) A stroller on a beach sees a flock of resting geese; grown tired of watching them, he continues his walk, yet looks around:

> —they are gone
> they have vanished silently and without a trace
> as though displaced by a marginally
> different universe.
>
> Nine geese see a human being from behind
> suddenly he is gone.

Or:

> you have tracked down
> the figure from a detective story who robbed you
> during the mugging he mumbles,
> almost smiling:
> you can do nothing to me
> that hasn't been done before.

Or:

> on the way to work
> I meet a loathsome beast
> it is hard to catch sight of: grayback perhaps hairy,
> hops in through my eyes in order to destroy me.

Among his stories (which add to the literature of the uncanny, recently flourishing in Bargum, Lindblad, Westö), the diary of a ship's doctor, sailing to an unknown island off Greenland's coast, is central: "We felt no haste to return."

The uncanny, for the rest, may at present be a necessary spice for authors so long confronted (and stimulated) by the external and internal perils of a country that now appears fully to partake of a general Nordic security. Since the 1950s Finland has moved off the front pages of the foreign press, certainly to its own advantage and comfort. (In his letters from the 1930s Elmer Diktonius told how literary visitors from placid Sweden were curiously envious of the whiff of danger in the Finnish air.)

The fragile minority has remained similarly unthreatened in this less visibly troubled age, thanks to Finland's constitution, the nation's common sense, the prevalence of bilingualism among the minority's members, and, truth to tell, their small numbers — they could scarcely assert themselves as a group, even if they wanted to do so. What is startling about "Swedish Finland's" cultural fate is the vigor of its literature, during a time when the proportional representation of Swedish-speakers in Finland's populace has steadily decreased and when the minority, as it were, has become ever more invisible in life at large — but scarcely in the realm of letters.

Children's Literature in Finland

Children's Literature

Maija Lehtonen
Translated by Donna Palomäki

11

Early Didactic and Moralizing Literature
One may begin a history of Finnish children's literature with Mikael Agricola, the founder of the Finnish literary language, and his primer (*ABC kiria*, 1543). The primer was intended not only for children but also for the peasantry, two groups that were often set side by side even in later publications.

The phrase "children's literature" calls to mind the Enlightenment ideal of the 1700s, which was influenced by a new, Rousseau-inspired conception of children and a new pedagogy. Before that time works designed for children were not only primers and lesson books but also religious literature and guides to good behavior. Between 1593 and 1850 only 101 printed items intended for children appeared in Finland. Of these, 26 works were originally written in Finnish, 17 in Swedish; the others were translations from Swedish or German into Finnish.

Didacticism and moralizing still occupied a central position in the children's literature of the Enlightenment, but at the same time writers attempted to find a childlike manner of presentation and to combine pleasure with utility. In Finland at the end of the 1700s Jacob Tengström, bishop, professor, and a member of Porthan's circle, published two books inspired by the spirit of the Enlightenment, *Läse-öfning för mina barn* (1795; Reading practice for my children) and *Tidsfördrif för mina barn* (1799; Entertainment for my children). They were modeled on the publications of German humanitarians. In the early nineteenth century, too, the most prominent representatives of the intelligentsia were much concerned with the development of children's literature in Finland.

The true beginning of the growth of children's literature, however, occurred at the middle of the century, even as it did elsewhere in Europe and in America as well. But a special feature of Finnish children's literature is that it does not follow the usual path. According to Zohar Shavit (p. 3), "children's literature began to develop only after adult literature had become a well-established institution"; in Finland, children's literature was born simultaneously with literature in the Finnish language, which suffered at the start from the lack of a usable literary language.

Topelius and the Fennomane Movement
The first noticeable phase in the development of Finnish children's literature was associated with romanticism and the Finnish national awakening. A new concept of childhood favored by the romantics created a basis for a new kind of children's literature, one that gave primacy not to reason and usefulness but rather to feeling and imagination.

Zachris Topelius (1818–98) best represents the ideals of romantic children's literature in Finland; in his own time he was enormously popular both at home and in the rest of the North, and his tales were translated, as well, into English and other languages. Yet although his works became classics of children's literature, Topelius was also a many-sided writer and exerted an almost immeasurable influence on Finland's culture (see chapter 7): his historical narratives were at first thought to be adult literature but in later days were considered to be closer to books for young people.

Topelius began writing for children in the 1840s, at about the same time as he began his work as a newspaperman, and most of his fairy tales first appeared in children's periodicals. In them he spoke to an audience he knew well, a circumstance that is undoubtedly responsible for their familiar tone. Gathered into book form, his fairy tales appeared in eight collections called *Läsning för barn* (1865–96; Reading for children; in Finnish, *Lukemisia lapsille*).

He presented his ideas about children's literature in a few articles that he published in his paper, *Helsingfors Tidningar*, for 1855, numbers 88–90 ("Om läsning för barn 1–4" [About reading for children]). Here he developed some typical ideas of romanticism: he opposes excessive intellectuality in upbringing (which he satirizes in a few of his fairy tales), and imagination and feeling must also be allowed their rights; the human will is to be cultivated as well. The child represents the original unity and harmony of human nature, which must not be sundered by reflection too early in life. Sometimes Topelius concentrates on the significance of physical education; he is one of the first writers for children who depicted the pleasures of winter sports. He also supported the emancipation of girls in a moderate way.

According to Topelius, children's literature should contain a moral, but it should be naturally embedded within the story. He was not always able to follow his own dictum, however: the moralizing outlook of the Enlightenment still influenced his production. Nonetheless, the lessons Topelius chose to teach were simple and practical, emphasizing honesty and unselfishness. For Topelius, the idealization of childhood did not mean an infantile fixation on that happy age. Childhood has its special worth, but a child must "grow" to complete his tasks in the world: "to grow" is one of Topelius's favorite verbs. In general, the same values and ideals are emphasized in his fairy tales as in his other works: Christianity, patriotism, social compassion, love of one's fellow man, and love of nature. *Läsning för barn* contains not only fairy tales and stories but poems and plays. The tone of the contents of the eight volumes is quite varied, and the "readings" are intended for children of different ages.

Topelius was influenced by folktales, by German romanticism, and by Hans Christian Andersen. He is most often compared with Andersen: one may justifiably maintain that he is able to assimilate a child's world view more easily than the famous Dane. On the other hand, his fairy tales rarely have the complexity and psychological depth that come naturally to Andersen. Nevertheless, Topelius's world view is not simplistic: in his works one occasionally meets reflections and symbols whose meanings only an adult reader will understand.

As with Andersen, many of Topelius's stories are set entirely in everyday reality. He portrays an idealized middle-class family life of the nineteenth century with many concrete, realistic, individual details. Topelius knew children well and brought to children's literature lively, active, unsentimentally portrayed boys and girls, even young rascals ("Walters äventyr" [Walter's adventures], "Bullerbasius").

In many tales fantastic topics are joined to a portrait of reality. Few of them take place in a purely imaginary, timeless fairy-tale world. Often the milieu of the tale is the Finnish forest, at other times the seashore. The scene of some of the fairy tales is mysterious Lapland. "Sampo Lappelill" (1860; Eng. tr. 1896, 1907), with its grand and gloomy assembly of trolls, goblins, and Arctic animals around the King of the Fells, is one of the most imposing and uncanny of Topelius's tales, and "Stjärnöga" (1873; Eng. tr. "Star-Eye," 1984) — the nickname belongs to a delicate Lapp child, with supernatural powers, hated by her "settler" foster-mother — is a tale of cultural intolerance and of loss. (Lapland and its magic have exerted a long fascination on Nordic writers, even those resident in faraway Denmark, from H. C. Andersen and his "Snow Queen" [1844] to Karen Blixen in "The Sailor Boy's Tale" [1942] and "The Bear and The Kiss" [1958].)

Nature is a central actor in Topelius's fairy tales. Sometimes a personified nature offers a portrait of human life, and in this case the tone may be ironic, somewhat in the style of Andersen. More often, however, plants, animals, and insects function on their own. The powers of nature may also appear in the forms of the traditional figures of fantasy. Topelius enjoys giving childlike features to nature or to figures representing nature — in these tales there is even a trace of infantile eroticism. The romantic conception of nature is the basis of his imaginary world. For Topelius, beings and things constitute a great, living organism. Now and then this idea appears in a way that may seem to be pantheistic, but Topelius easily unites his conception of nature with his Lutheran Christianity.

Topelius freely introduces variations into the subject matter of traditional fairy tales. In some of his fairy-tale plays — *Fågel Blå* (1859; Blue Bird), *Prinsessan Törnrosa* (1870; Sleeping Beauty) — he perhaps follows his sources more faithfully than in his tales but adds comic material to them. At times his tales of the marvelous have a historical basis. This is the case with one of his most famous stories, "Björken och stjärnan" (1852; Eng. tr. "The Birch Tree and the Star," 1899, 1907), which symbolized love of one's homeland for many generations of Finns. Told in the style of a legend and with biblical cadences, it is the story of a little boy of five and his four-year-old sister, who are carried off to "foreign lands" during a terrible invasion of Finland. (Although the time is set at "about two hundred years ago," readers may well have thought of the somewhat more recent Great Wrath of 1713–21 [see chapters 2 and 6], concluding that the children fell into "friendly hands" in Russia.) Ten years later the siblings decide that they must go home, despite the warnings of their kindly hosts, and miraculously they make their way "northwest" over the many miles to their parents' farm, guided by their memory of the birch that stood in the yard and the star that shone through its branches at eventide. Topelius also likes to include the dimension of time in his stories, and often there is a question of relation among the past, present, and future. The fragility of human life is depicted with a gentle melancholy.

Topelius's *Läsning för barn* is an important part of his production; in an artistic sense it is of the same quality as his other works, and in his tales Topelius must be regarded as the originator of Finnish children's literature. To be sure, the artistic and social prestige of children's literature increased greatly because Topelius was also an extremely well known "adult" writer and, in general, one of the country's most esteemed citizens.

Topelius was a representative of Finnish nationalism for the country's liberals, and his tales became the property of children in both language groups. Children's literature in Finland became associated with the intellectual ideals of the time on other fronts as well: the relationships of the Fennomane movement to children's literature is especially interesting. When, in the spirit of Snellman's program, it became desirable to cultivate a Finnish-speaking intelligentsia, Finnish-language reading material also became a necessity. Snellman himself gave this matter some attention, and in his monthly, *Litteraturblad för allmän medborgerlig bildning* (1847–63; Literary paper for general civic culture), he favorably evaluated the first modest productions of Finnish-language children's literature. The translation of suitable books was also considered important, and by the end of the century a relatively large number of works of foreign children's literature had appeared in Finnish. Most of the translations were of weak, sentimental German stories, but Finnish versions of such English classics as *Robinson Crusoe* and *Gulliver's Travels* also appeared, as well as the works of Captain Marryat, Louisa May Alcott, and Mark Twain.

Some of the figures in the very forefront of cultural life were active as translators, critics, or producers of children's literature: Elias Lönnrot, August Ahlqvist, Yrjö Sakari Yrjö-Koskinen, Julius Krohn, and, at the turn of the century, Juhani Aho. Many of the elders of the Fennomane movement abandoned their Swedish mother tongue and began to speak Finnish with their children: sometimes these fathers and mothers wrote Finnish-language texts for their offspring to read or edited children's magazines. The poet and academician Julius Krohn (1835–88) is a special case, as he was of Baltic German origin but began to write both creative literature and academic studies in Finnish (see chapter 3). He became the nineteenth century's most prominent author of Finnish-language children's poetry, and his joyful, rhythmic poems portraying small, everyday events have stayed alive through several generations.

In Finland as elsewhere the idea of national identity was linked to the study of folklore. The significance of the *Kalevala* and other folk poetry for Finland's literature is well known and is discernible in literature to this very day, not least in the *Kalevala* editions published for children. Along the same folkloristic line, Eero Salmelainen (the pseudonym of Erik Rudbeck, 1830–67) became a cornerstone of Finnish-language children's literature with the publication of his folktale collection, *Suomen kansan satuja ja tarinoita* (1852–66; Fairy tales and stories of the Finnish people), which was originally intended to be a scholarly work but quickly found its way, at least in part, into the hands of young readers. Later many collections of folktales and folk songs for children were published, and authors have received powerful impressions from this source. Even today writers of children's poetry in Finnish gladly turn to the wellspring of folk poetry.

In its early phases Finnish children's literature was particularly aimed at the children of the educated classes. The circle of readers broadened to some extent at the end of the century, when the primary school statute came into effect. At that time many teachers also began to write texts for their charges. Simultaneously, Finnish-speaking and Swedish-speaking suffragettes became interested in children's literature. As the century moved toward its end, a considerable amount of children's literature appeared in Finland. The quality, however, was not high. For the most part, the authors were pale epigones of Topelius who taught children patriotism, religious values, charity, ideals of temperance, and love of nature.

Differentiation and New Genres, 1900–1945

The postromantic, idealistic, and nationalistic tradition of the previous century was long preserved in children's literature. This literature had consolidated its position in both the Finnish- and Swedish-speaking sectors of the population, and publishers began to issue special series for children and adolescents.

Children's literature written originally in Finnish gained its first classics at the beginning of the twentieth century, written by Anni Swan (1875–1958), who worked for decades as an author and editor of a children's periodical. She raised Finnish-language children's literature to an international level, with fairy tales, short children's plays, and more than ten narratives for adolescents, almost entirely "girls' books."

Anni Swan's background was typical of the time: her father was a Swedish-speaking Fennomane who founded a Finnish-speaking family. Long employed as a primary school teacher, Swan simultaneously moved in Helsinki literary circles, and married the poet Otto Manninen; the dramatist Gustaf von Numers was her cousin. Her fairy tales reached their highest level of artistic achievement in the early years of the new century. The influence of symbolism, which was dominant at the time, is noticeable in them. A narrative line easily understood by children unites symbolic imagery with individual problems: an enchanted flower castle, an island of happiness with its swans, a world under the sea are images for the landscape of soul. Themes of adventure portray the young maiden's longing for love and her fear of it. On the other hand, the landscapes and thematic points of departure for Swan's fairy tales are often the Finnish forest with its animal and fairy-tale creatures; her characters are the timeless children of country villages, and the point of view is theirs. Her favorite fairy-tale creature, especially in her later collections, is a friendly forest elf.

In an original way Swan's tales introduce variations on folklore themes and structures (the number three, wonderful animal helpers, transformations). The composition of the tales is solid, the plot is straightforward, the style is clear and concrete with a simple elegance. A restrained humor contributes to the charm of the tales. Later, beginning in the 1920s, the romantic, colorful fairy-tale world begins to recede into the background, and marvels are relegated to the nursery. In Swan's tales pedagogical material does not have the same significance as it does in Topelius's work; the conception of children's literature has changed. The author's humane, openly Christian world view is the foundation for her entire production, but it is not excessively displayed. Until the 1930s, and in some notable cases even beyond, the triple influence of folklore, Topelius, and Swan dominated Finnish-language fantasy literature. The most common types of tales were romantic wonder-and-adventure tales and animal tales built on a folkloristic base; they began, bit by bit, to incorporate new satiric tones when material from modern life was placed in an animal world.

An uncommonly popular poet was the bilingual Arvid Lydecken (1884–1960), a many-sided children's writer and influential figure: the owner from 1916 until his death of the important Helsinki art salon, Strindberg's; editor of a series of books for the young and a children's periodical; and Finland's first real critic of children's books. His cozy, naively humorous poems and songs for small children have attained the status of classics; one of his early successes — during his long life he wrote a great deal — was *Ihmeellinen kalaretki* (1912; The remarkable fishing trip), which appeared simultaneously in Swedish as *Sagoresan* (The fairy-tale trip). Both versions were provided with pictures and music, for their verses, by Väinö Hämäläinen (1876–1940). Lydecken was able to write for children of quite disparate ages; in 1928, for example, he brought out the picturebooks *Matin makeiset* (Matti's candy) and *Nallen seikkailut* (The adventures of Teddy Bear) for little folks and, for boys with a taste for historical adventure, *Suomenlahden risteilijä* (The cruiser of the Gulf of Finland) — as well as a primer, about learning to count, in Finnish and Swedish.

A pinch of Eastern exoticism, which may have been related to the interest in the East expressed by the Torch Bearers (Tulenkantajat; see chapter 4), is found in the colorful, satiric tales of Raul Roine (1907–60), as productive an author as Lydecken. Roine's enormous oeuvre, beginning with *Satuposetiivi* (1935; The fairy-tale hurdy-gurdy) and *Porsliiniprinsessa* (1936; The china princess), illustrated by Rudolf Koivu (see below), included many books, from 1939 to 1956, about a doughty rustic youth named Antti Puuhaara (i.e., Tree Branch); on his final outing Antti visits the land of giants. Earlier, among other things, he has been a master tailor, a smith, and a bear tamer. A lasting contribution to Finnish children's literature from Roine's indefatigable hand was the collection of Finnish tales plucked from the folklore archives of the Finnish Literary Society and retold for children, *Suomen kansan suuri satukirja* (1946; The Finnish people's great fairy-tale book).

On the Finland-Swedish front development had also continued toward a less didactic children's literature. The most prominent Swedish-language writer of tales at the turn of the century was Nanny Hammarström (1870–1953), a biology teacher who published quite influential animal stories: her masterpiece, *Två myrors äventyr* (1907; Eng. tr. *The Adventures of Two Ants*, 1910), has been translated into several languages. Underlying these animal tales is a sure expertise in natural history, but Hammarström also has the imagination of a genuine storyteller with which to enliven them. Animals are not simply depictions of humanity; certainly they feel, think, and speak in a somewhat "human" way, but they retain their own identities, and as biological creatures, they behave appropriately for their species. The world is seen from the perspective of an ant, a frog, or a swallow. The struggle that rules life in nature is not disguised, although the basic tone of the books is a happy one.

From the century's start Finland-Swedish fairy-tale literature was more open to international influence than literature in Finnish, and as early as the 1920s, nonsense items and a characteristic combination of everyday reality with imaginary worlds revealed the influence of the modernist movement. Without a doubt, Swedish-speaking authors also felt themselves closer to the Anglo-Saxon storytelling tradition, which already contained these elements. In any event, it is interesting that some Finland-Swedish poets writing for a "mature" audience also wrote for children. Among those worthy of mention is Viola Renvall (see chapter 9), who created her own lyrical version of the "forest tale" and wrote tales, as well, that mix everyday life with fantasy. Renvall's *Skogsfolket* (1932; The forest folk) and *Den borttappade hallonmasken och andra sagor ur skogsfolkets värld* (1935; The lost raspberry worm and other tales from the forest folk's world) became favorites among the minority's young readers; they were subsumed, in 1973, as *Tio sagor om Skogsfolket* (Ten tales about the forest folk) in a series of Finland-Swedish minor classics. Renvall also wrote books aimed at "young" (i.e., adolescent) readers, such as *Ingegärd på Rönninge* (1938; Ingegard on Rönninge) and *Den olydiga stjärnan* (1940; The disobedient star).

The "novel for young people" experienced a great boom in Europe and America toward the end of the nineteenth century and was clearly differentiated from books "for girls and boys." In Finland the first attempts at the genre appeared in the 1800s: the best of these early works was written by Toini Topelius (1854–1910), the daughter of Zachris Topelius: *I utvecklingstid* (1889; In times of development), a slightly emancipatory portrayal of schoolgirls. (Later she followed in her father's footsteps with two volumes of "fairy tales and stories," *Sommarsjö och vintersnö 1–2* [1897, 1900; Summer sea and winter snow].) A true pioneer in this area was Anni Swan, whose first story for young people appeared in 1914. In a few of her stories a boy is the protagonist and the plot is more exciting than usual, but for the most part she tells stories about girls, just as girls have been her primary readers. Her books are usually set in the present moment or sometimes during the author's own childhood. Her artistically accomplished stories, *Pikkupappilassa* (1922; In the little parsonage) and its sequel, *Ulla ja Mark* (1924; Ulla and Mark), offer a lively portrait of life at end of the 1800s.

The novels Swan wrote for young people chiefly belong to the Anglo-Saxon girls' book tradition, but she portrayed the circles and the types of people that she herself knew well: refined homes and schoolchildren in Helsinki, in Finland's small towns, and in the country. Thus she gave her own, Finnish coloring to the international Cinderella theme, which then became very popular in Finland, thanks to her *Iris rukka* (1916; Poor Iris). Cinderella's "reward" is not based on finding the prince — themes of love do not appear in Swan's books — nor is it the result of external events, but rather demands the growth of the heroine's character. Swan does not moralize in her stories, although she stresses certain values such as friendliness, tolerance, and love of nature.

In many of Swan's novels for young people a subject common in much juvenile literature appears — that is, the relationship between the rich and the poor, which she handles in a conciliatory fashion. Her romantic turns of plot, such as kidnapping or disappearances, indicate membership in the tradition of the adventure story. Essential to her stories, however, are warm and deft character sketches, particularly the portraits of young girls, a cozy atmosphere, and intelligent, fresh humor, which sometimes can attain an ironic pungency.

The creator of a different type of girls' book was the English-oriented and bilingual Kersti Bergroth (1886–1975), an essayist, aphorist, and the editor of a cultural journal who also wrote novels, plays, and memoirs, the two last about her Viipuri girlhood and her long residence abroad, particularly in Rome. (Her "Karelian idyll," *Anu ja Mikko* [1932; Anu and Mikko], was a crowd pleaser on the Finnish stage for years.) As the author of children's books, she used the pen name Mary Marck and wrote her books in both Swedish and Finnish. Beginning at the same time as Anni Swan, "Mary Marck" introduced the school novel to Finnish literature; it came to mean primarily girls' literature, although coeducational schools were usually depicted in it. The genre was especially popular in the 1920s and 1930s. The novels of Mary Marck, about a dozen altogether, bore a strong resemblance to one another. The most popular and perhaps the best are *Evas klass/Eevan luokka* (1917; Eva's class) and its sequels. In these books the plot is thin and stereotyped, and the school experience in and of itself is not the central theme. Most important are the personal portraits: the protagonist is a cheerful, lively, sociable, and popular girl who appears surrounded by girl friends and a few boys. The other members of the class form a backdrop and sounding board for them. The scene is most often Helsinki and its refined middle-class homes at the beginning of the century. A telling portrait of the time is conveyed in amusing glimpses: Mary Marck's schoolchildren live in a particularly sheltered world. Structurally, the most important element in these books is the dialogue, in which the characters clarify their relationships, talk about their dreams for the future, and philosophize about the great questions of life in a naive way. The humor of the books at times grows out of the clever wordplay of the characters, at times out of a gentle irony toward them displayed by the witty narrator.

Mary Marck's books set the pattern for other modern Finnish and Finland-Swedish girls' books during the 1920s and 1930s, placed in a realistic urban environment. They reflect the new ideal of the independent woman, who appeared after the First World War in women's popular literature. These books are brisk and unsentimental; the heroines are spirited tomboys or mischief makers. Love enters into the picture and usually tames the troublesome hoyden at the end. At first this trend was an innovation, but by the 1930s it had degenerated into formula fiction.

Since the beginning of the century the boys' book has been an important type of Finnish-language juvenile literature; for whatever reason, it does not play as great a part in Finland-Swedish literature. Many stories of adventure in the wilderness have been written — this topic has always been popular, from Aleksis Kivi's *Seitsemän veljestä* (1870) on. Perhaps influences also came from the books of the English-born American, Ernest Thompson Seton (1860–1946), a naturalist and the author of *Wild Animals I Have Known* (1898) and *The Biography of a Grizzly* (1900). Alfred Emil Ingman (1860–1917) gave the genre its start with *Rimpisuon usvapatsas* (1915; The fog statue of Rimpi Bog) and *Latvasaaren kuninkaan hovilinna* (1916; The court palace of the king of Treetop Island). The latter also contains a trace of science fiction. In Ingman's books there is a great deal of information about nature, wilderness life, and the means of survival under difficult circumstances in the wilds, all disguised in the form of an exciting story, filled with adventure. Out of the Finnish backwoods came a sort of home-grown equivalent of the Wild West story. One may also speak of Finnish "Robinsonades." The pedagogical idea is the young boy's growth into adulthood through his struggle with nature. Jalmari Sauli (1889–1957), among others, was a distinguished and prolific writer of boys' hunting and fishing adventures during the 1920s, as well as patriotic tales with a background in Finnish history, such as *Amiraali Spoofin rumpalipoika* (1927; Admiral Spoof's drummer boy); "Admiral" Carl Spoof was in fact a sergeant, a partisan fighter in the Swedo-Russian war of 1808–9.

One variant on the boys' book, which blossomed in the period between the 1920s and the 1950s, was the humorous portrayal of boys, rather along the lines of *Tom Sawyer*. Its little hero lives in a country or small town environment, viewed somewhat nostalgically. His adventures remain within the limits of everyday life, but psychologically speaking, the figure is one-dimensional. He does not develop. The best known of such books were about the lovable rascals Pertsa and Kilu (1952, 1953, 1955, 1957) by Väinö Riikilä (1906–69).

In the 1920s, the early days of the independent Finnish Republic, both educators and publishers greatly stressed literature for young readers: it was intended to awaken the desire to study and to educate the members of its public to be good citizens. The domestic production of children's books increased dramatically, and criticism showed a greater interest in the field as well. As in the previous century, there now appeared a conscious effort both to strengthen the national identity of children and to offer them positive role models and examples. This tendency appears most clearly in the long and popular series of adventure books called "Poikien seikkailukirjasto" (Boys' adventure library), which Arvid Lydecken edited at Otava and whose first volume was by Jalmari Sauli, *Ajojahti* (1925; Hue and cry), a "tale of adventure from the time of the Great Wrath," the Russian occupation of Finland in 1713–21. (Sauli's *Siniristi ja punatähti* [1934; Blue cross and red star], volume 49 in Otava's series, demonstrated how aware publishers were of the public atmosphere in the 1930s, when memories of the Civil War still were vivid and fears of Stalin's Russia grew ever stronger.) Of course, the series contained stories of boys on the track of criminals and spies, but historical stories were most typical of these books. The plot often involved a Finnish soldier or guerrilla single-handedly overcoming a dangerous situation in the wilderness. These stories took advantage of the opportunity to strengthen the self-awareness of the young nation. They were later criticized for ideological reasons, but looking at them in the context of the time, one notices that the young reader was expected to identify with an independently functioning individual, not with a mass movement or with a representative of an idea.

In the 1930s, however, the general interest in children's literature fell off and the level of performance declined; authors chiefly wrote according to the formulas created in the past.

The Modern Fairy Tale, 1945–1990

After the Second World War various steps were taken to improve children's literature. Criticism again began to make greater demands on it, and publishers invested more in it than they had before. The postwar years, particularly the 1950s, marked a turning point in the development of Finnish children's literature, as they did in other types of Finnish literature. The recent decades have been a time of great expansion and differentiation.

In the fantasy genre a new line of nature tales began during wartime with the appearance of the influential *Pessi ja Illusia* (1944; Pessi and Illusia) by the veterinarian Yrjö Kokko (1903–77), which had possibly been influenced in turn by such English stories as the works of Kenneth Grahame (1859–1932). In Kokko's book there is a lyrical feeling for nature and nature's symbolism. It became a prototype for the most sophisticated nature tales of the 1950s. (Kokko—who was a pioneer in nature photography—later became equally well known for his writings about Lapland and his photographs of that far northern world, especially in *Neljän tuulen tie* [1947; Eng. tr. *The Way of the Four Winds*, 1954] and *Laulujoutsen: Ultima Thulen lintu* [1950; The song swan: The bird of Ultima Thule].) One of the most original of the later creators of animal tales is Jukka Parkkinen (1948–); see *Korppi ja kumppanit* (1978; Raven and friends) and its sequels, *Korppi ja korven veikot* (1979; Raven and the brothers of the backwoods) and *Korppi ja Korpin poika* (1980; Raven and Raven's boy). Parkkinen's animal world has its roots in folklore, but it also has a modern and personal stamp. A delicious absurd humor and wordplay mark his novels.

Fantasy experienced a true renaissance in the 1950s. Many writers for adults (for example, Aila Meriluoto, Iris Kähäri) began to write for children, and important influences came from English fairy-tale and fantasy literature. (Although Lewis Carroll's works had been translated earlier, such literature found its way into the Finnish language much later than into

Swedish: the first Swedish translation of *Alice's Adventures in Wonderland* appeared in Stockholm in 1870, whereas Anni Swan's pioneer Finnish version came out in 1906. By way of oddity, it can be added that J. L. Runeberg's grandson, Nino Runeberg [1874–1934], made a "free translation" of the classic in 1921.) Now, too, interest was aroused in the nonsense features of Finnish folklore.

A new kind of tale and a new kind of children's poetry, based on dreamlike visions and associations and using the resources of the language effectively, was possibly linked with the contemporary change — that is, the rise of modernism — in Finnish-language poetry. The scope of the modernistic fairy tale expanded to include a type of fantasy that unites a mystic vision of everyday reality with fairy-tale elements, as in the books of Aila Nissinen (1916–73) and Marjatta Kurenniemi (1918–). These tales were free from didacticism, and their creators managed to empathize with a child's psyche. The language of children and an everyday vocabulary were also used to good effect. The modernist conception of the subjective and irrational nature of reality acted as a foundation for the world of tales. Both these authors favored motifs from nature and introduced animals with altogether human traits. The critic of children's literature Minna Vuorinen (p. 59) has proposed that Nissinen learned from Kenneth Grahame's *The Wind in the Willows* (1908), as might easily be deduced from the text of "one of the first Finnish-language fairy-tale novels," Nissinen's *Myyrä Matikaisen malliauto* (1955; The mole Matikainen's model car). In the 1960s, like so many other children's writers, Nissinen lamented the ills of contemporary society, the housing shortage in *Talitintin tornitalo* (1966; The titmouse's tower house) and the ravaging of the milieu (by a superhighway) in *Terva-apila* (1968; The tar clover), subtitled a "magic tale." Prodigiously active as a translator of books for children (ranging from Walt Disney cartoon spinoffs to Richard Scarry), Kurenniemi, as an original writer, produced what has been called a classic among Finnish children's books, *Oli ennen Onnimanni* (1953; Once there was Onnimanni).

In the 1960s the fairy tale and the imagination itself fell into disfavor. Psychologists began to regard the fairy tale suspiciously; the cruelty of folktales was considered particularly dangerous for children. In literature a socially critical realism was held in high regard. "Relevance" was also demanded of children's literature, which was now expected to deal with social problems. The kind of literature that resulted was heavily didactic, although the subjects and stances that it taught children were new. By the end of the 1970s the tide turned again. Everyday realism had shown itself to be banal, and imagination again received its due. The search for "roots" brought forth a wave of new publications of folklore in the Finnish language. People also began to favor books that presented Finland's recent history in fictional form.

The characteristic form of Finnish- and Swedish-language fantasy literature in recent decades is the long, continuous story, which has been called the "fantasy novel." It usually has an exciting plot, but above all it reveals its author's philosophy of life. (Sometimes the writer creates an entire imaginary world that stretches from book to book, as in Tove Jansson's Moomin books.) Hannu Mäkelä, who has also written books for adults (see chapter 5), belongs to the humorists in the crowd of Finnish-language fantasy writers. The most important of his fantasy books are *Herra Huu* (1973–75; Mr. Boo) and its sequels. With their several episodes these represent the modern type of tale, in which older patterns are turned upside-down. For example, a small, helpless wizard tries in vain to frighten children and makes friends with them instead. Amusing adventures, warmly absurd nonsense elements, and clever language usage all occur in the Mr. Boo books. Artistically speaking, however, the best Finnish-language fantasy writer of the 1970s and the 1980s is Kaarina Helakisa (1946–98). She writes fantasy novels about the search for individual identity and about the borders between dream and reality, time and death, love and friendship. A sure sense of form, generous amounts of effervescent imagination, and a unique humor stamp Helakisa's works. Her language is poetic but at the same time concrete. Helakisa's tales have points of contact with tradition, particularly folktales. But they have more than one base, and they speak to readers of all ages. One of her finer works is *Olena ja Vassuska* (1979; Olena and Vassuska). A colorful, luminous tale about faithful love, it follows folktale patterns and is set in a fantasy Russia. A completely different kind of fantasy novel is *Ainakin miljoona sinistä kissaa* (1978; At least a million blue cats), which sets the world of children and the world of adults against each other. The book portrays loneliness and the need of a compensation for it. The child represents the victory of creative imagination over matter and materialism.

In the tales for children by Marja-Leena Mikkola (she is perhaps still better known as a writer for adults: see chapter 5), nature is among the central themes, and she manages to integrate popular conservation ideas seamlessly into her fantastic narratives. With motifs taken from Finno-Ugric folktales she captured the public imagination with *Amalia, karhu* (1975; Amalia the bear), a "fairy tale for children and contemporaries," in which the bear of the title descends from the skies, lands in the middle of Helsinki, befriends a little boy named Posse, and succeeds in saving the fairy-tale world and its mythological figures from the threats of modern society. Her

Anni Manninen (1977; the title of the Swedish translation by Marita Lindquist, *Sagan om Anni, djuren, och Gröna sjön* [1979; The fairy tale of Anni, the animals, and Green Lake], is more descriptive), followed hot on the bear story's heels. As its eponymous heroine it has a little girl with red hair, green eyes, and the ambition to be a good witch, who goes forth to find Mother Nature and, again, save the world from environmental destruction.

The colorful, fanciful novel of Asko Martinheimo (1934–) depicting the life of ancient people, *Tuhkanaama ja taivaantakoja* (1987; Cinderface and the hearths of heaven), chiefly resembles Tolkien's imaginary world. Earlier, though, Martinheimo had devoted much energy to books about children unable to cope with their oppressive surroundings. A handicapped pupil is subjected to bullying in *Pääkallokiitäjä* (1971; The death's head butterfly), and a dreamy girl is out of place in her home in *Saari taivaanrannassa* (1979; The island on the horizon).

The best-known names in modern Finland-Swedish fantasy literature belong to Tove Jansson (1914–) and Irmelin Sandman Lilius (1936–). The works of both have been translated into several languages, and Tove Jansson's Moomin books (1945–70) have attained a worldwide reputation (see also chapter 9). Her Moominland has its own place in the universe of fantasy, on a level with Tolkien's Middle Earth or C. S. Lewis's Narnia. Moominvalley, however, is not a mythical world. It is close to current reality; furthermore, it clearly depicts the character of Finland's skerries. Tove Jansson and Irmelin Sandman Lilius have both written "books for adults," but the unquestionable emphasis is on the fantasy tales; both adults and children read their stories. Although in Tove Jansson's case there is no reason to speak (as is sometimes done) of any "development" from writing for children to writing for adults, in the Moomin books one may perceive a clear progression toward greater psychological depth and a more sophisticated control of literary devices.

The predominant theme of the Moomin books is the tension between order and chaos, the idyll and the threat of ruin. A clear-cut opposition between good and evil is not the question, however. The idyll may start to feel too narrow or confining; the proximity of danger and general upheaval stimulates the Moomins and opens their perspectives. The books give voice to a particular "Moomin philosophy," which is characterized by such ideals as freedom, tolerance, and individualism. At times the Moomins are able to enjoy a bourgeois home idyll; at times they are independent of material values and adjust rapidly to new situations. The characters of the Moomin books are partially individuals, partially types. Moominmamma represents basic security, warmth, and practicality; Moominpappa, the masculine longing for adventure and heroic deeds; the young Moomintroll develops from childhood to adulthood. Many figures are amusing, some sorrowful, like Mårran, the symbol of loneliness. Each must dare to fulfill itself, but none can live without the others.

An essential feature of the Moomin world is the sea; Tove Jansson has written some of the finest descriptions of a stormy sea in Finnish literature, and the sea has itself become a symbol of the irrational forces of unpredictable life. In *Moominland Midwinter* (1958) wintry nature assumes mythic proportions. Nature in the Moomin books is not merely good and friendly; adapting to its rhythms, however, reveals one secret of the art of living. The serious and even tragic sides of life emerge in the Moomin books; at bottom, nonetheless, there is an invincible optimism toward life. The most lovable feature of the Moomin books is their humor, which grows not only out of situations and the personalities of the characters and their speeches but out of literary allusions as well.

The elements that the Moomin books have in common with English-language fantasy literature have perhaps been overemphasized. In her dissertation on the Moomins (*Familjen i dalen* [1988; The family in the valley]) Boel Westin has shown that the books exhibit extensive intertextuality; allusions to classical literature are a part of this aspect. Above all, Jansson applies the poetics of naiveté to great effect. She also uses different literary genres: fairy tale, fantasy, adventure story, drama, memoir. This variety accounts to a great extent for the gentle irony and parodylike effects of her books.

In the 1960s the career of Irmelin Sandman Lilius was given over to books for and about small children, specifically her daughter Muddle and the daughter's friend Rufa, but then she constructed a whole imaginary realm of her own. The principal scene of action is the fictional small town of Tulavall, somewhere on the south coast of Finland, a place not altogether unlike the port and summer resort of Hanko (Hangö), where Sandman Lilius lives with her husband, the author and artist Carl Gustaf Lilius (see chapter 10). (Tulavall also recalls other coastal towns of greater antiquity, however, such as Porvoo [Borgå], Ekenäs [Tammisaari], and Topelius's birthplace, Nykarleby [Uusikaarlepyy]; Sandman Lilius is a devoted Topelian.) *Kung Tulle* (1972; Eng. tr. *King Tulle*, 1979) and *Tulles resa sunnantill* (1975; Tulle's trip southward) tell the story of the founder of Tulavall, who lives in a mythical Nordic antiquity: both books clearly show the influence of the Icelandic saga tradition. Although brave and forthright, Tulle is not a warlike hero; he attempts to maintain harmony, when possible, with man and nature. The third son of King Sigulf but envied by his elder siblings Steinulf and Bork, Tulle finds a bride, Libite, who can change herself into a fox; in his fights against trolls he is aided by the mysterious Half Person, perhaps a troll himself. Tulle's brothers covet his realm, but the treacherous Bork freezes to death in a terrifying scene; generously, Tulle aids Steinulf against the wild Kiralians, who attack the latter's castle. Falling ill, Tulle is sent home by the ungrateful Steinulf, despite the possibility that Tulle's little band might be ambushed by marauding Kiralians. Nonetheless, he succeeds in returning to the fields of Tuntula, where Libite awaits him. In the sequel Tulle meets further adventures while looking for his mother, who disappeared after his birth.

At their core the "historical" tales of Tulle contain a good helping of resigned worldly wisdom; the centerpiece of the actual Tulavall series, comprising the trilogy with the collective name *Fru Sola* (1969–71; Mistress Sola) — *Gullkronas gränd* (Eng. tr. *Gold Crown Lane*, 1980), *Gripanderska gården* (Eng. tr. *The Goldmaker's House*, 1980), and *Gångande Grå* (Eng. tr. *Horses of the Night*, 1980) — is somehow more childlike and brighter in spirit. The trilogy obviously belongs to the Anglo-Saxon fantasy tradition but also foreshadows the new wave of that fantasy, represented in Finnish-language literature by the novels of Kaarina Helakisa, Marja-Leena Mikkola, and Tiina Kaila (see chapter 5). The events of the Mistress Sola books take place at the end of the nineteenth century; the color of the time is quite authentic as to detail, although the historic background is not very carefully delineated. Along with everyday reality, however, there is also an invisible reality, which only those people equipped with visionary ability can see. Time also exists on more than one level: the past and present are simultaneous. The course of time is cyclical and everything is repeated. The mythical queen, Mistress Sola, who lived long ago, intervenes in the life of the city and in the fates of the people of the present day. These "contemporary" figures are numerous and portrayed with much care. Sanna, Silja, and Sissela, the three daughters of Adam Haller, a sailor injured in an accident at sea and a little "strange in the head," are still entertained by his tales, while their unimaginative brother seems destined to become a ne'er-do-well; their overworked mother eventually falls ill, leaves home, and is cared for by the herb woman Fia. The girls' best friend is the orphan Bonadea, first encountered in the book of the same name (1967), which is a prelude to the trilogy; she eventually becomes the servant of the dabbler in alchemy, Master Turiam. Together with his secrets, the improvident Turiam falls into the clutches of the powerful Councillor Klingkors, who wants to build a gunpowder factory in Tulavall. In the third volume Klingkors's plans are crossed by the rebellious boy Krullasse—who has fled from Tulavall in volume 1—aided by Silja and Fia.

A set of paralipomena to the sagas of Tulle and the trilogy is provided in the tales, many told by Adam Haller or remembered by Silja, found in *Skeppet Flygande Gedda* (1976; The ship *Flying Pike*), *Svanarna* (1977; The swans), and *Storsjöhamnen* (1978; The great sea harbor). In still other books, *Kapten Grunnstedt* (1974; Captain Grunnstedt) and *Mattan från Kars* (1989; The rug from Kars), the realm of reality lies in Tulava, the realm of fantasy in the Caucasus, where Captain Grunnstedt had been stationed as an officer in Russian service during the 1850s. It is typical of the care with which Sandman Lilius works that—like another great writer of adventure books for the young, John Buchan (1875–1940) in *Prester John* (1910)— she provides maps for her readers, both of Tulavall and of the scene of Grunnstedt's Caucasian adventures.

The themes of the Mistress Sola books include the opposition of masculine and feminine principles. Fire symbolizes masculine intellect, the search for knowledge, and destructiveness; water symbolizes the feminine life force and motherhood. The alchemist represents the former, the ageless wise old woman the latter. Folklore, folktales, and games are woven together in the colorful fabric of the tale. The basis of Sandman Lilius's mythical world view is a conception of nature as a great unity, one to which the human being belongs in both his physical and his spiritual being. In her authorial voice Irmelin Sandman Lilius is highly original. Her language is rich and poetic, full of metaphors and symbols; adding to its distinct quality, at times there are elements of Finland-Swedish dialect.

Interviewed by the Swedish journal BLM in 1980 (p. 221), Sandman Lilius said: "I do not write for children.... When a story has been written, when it has been published as a book, when it has been read—then I find out which [readers] I have written for." Her books can be read at many levels, as has been demonstrated by her popularity among devoted young readers on the one hand and serious scholars on the other. In a trilogy from the 1980s she seems to have aimed at a somewhat more grownup audience than before; in *Främlingsstjärnan* (1980; The stranger's star) she describes the budding love between the fifteen-year-old painter, Ellen Skrävmark, visiting relatives in Tulavall, and the town's outsider and poet, Rudolf, considerably older than the girl and bearing a name surely taken from *La Bohème*. In *Främlingsvägen* (1982; The stranger's way) travels in Karelia, Rome, and Paris lead the two apart, but in *Främlingsstaden* (1985; The stranger's city) the two are together again, walking through a city that, thanks to magic realism, combines the fin de siècle with the contemporary Paris of jeans, television, and African immigrants.

Marita Lindquist (1918–) began by intermingling fanciful stories, such as *Lilla Barbro Björkelöv* (1948; Little Barbro Birchleaf) and *Anderssons klocka i fara* (1957; Andersson's bell in danger), the tale of a family of miniature folk that lives in a treetop, with more realistic matter, a book about two little girls in contemporary Helsinki, *Stina och jag* (1955; Stina and I). But her major contribution to children's literature has been the Malena series (1964–75), which follows its quiet, shy heroine from preschool years on, *Malenas nya bror* (1964; Malena's new brother), *Malena börjar skolan* (1966; Malena begins school), *Malenas finaste sommar* (1967; Malena's finest summer), *Malena och glädjen* (1969; Malena and happiness), and *Malena 11 år* (1975; Malena at eleven). As Marita Rajalin has pointed out ("Finlandssvenska realistiska berättelser," 108), the books have a traditional backdrop: a father who is a teacher, a mother in the home, a helpful grandmother, a single-family house. In Lindquist's Kotten series (1972–78), however, Kotten suffers from dyslexia, lives with her father, a television director whose wife has left him, finds a happy modus vivendi when the father's girlfriend moves in, and, rather glamorously, goes on a trip to Swedish Lapland, where her father is making a documentary. Elsewhere, Marita Lindquist has devoted three books (1976–79) to her grandchildren, Toffe and Andrea, and in the Robban books (1979–81) has addressed the troubles of a little boy who lacks self-confidence.

The poet Bo Carpelan has also written stories for children (see chapter 9). Carpelan's diction is restrained, but his expressive style gives significance and beauty even to trivial matters and places the everyday world in a cosmic perspective. Carpelan has also published a collection of children's poems: *Måla himlen* (1988; To paint the sky). At times the poems express a spontaneous feeling for nature, at times a child's search for identity, and a wonder at the opening of life. The language is concrete, sometimes with a trace of humor or nonsense.

In recent decades the production of Finland-Swedish children's poetry has been quite sparse, but a good amount has been published in Finnish. Some modernist poets wrote or translated children's poetry. Kirsi Kunnas (1924–), who had already become known as a prominent representative of the modernist poets of the 1950s, began all over again as a writer for children. She translated *Mother Goose's Nursery Rhymes* into Finnish as *Hanhiemon iloinen lipas* (1954; Mother Goose's happy cupboard) and a little later published her own collection of nonsense poems, *Tiitiäisen satupuu* (1956; Tumpkin's fairy-tale tree), which came to have a distinct influence on the development of Finnish children's literature. In this instance, an original poetic imagination has found an adequate expression in children's poetry. Kunnas's poetry contains humor, a lyrical mood, and a compelling rhythm; her poems play with language and surprising associations; and repetition, hyperbole, and phonetic effects exercise a large role (see chapter 4).

The Illustrated Book

The history of the Finnish picturebook began in the 1880s. Just as many important cultural trendsetters concerned themselves with Finnish children's literature in its early stages, so many famous artists appeared as illustrators of early Finnish- and Swedish-language picture books, from Albert Edelfelt (1854–1905) to Venny Soldan-Brofeldt (1863–1945). Rudolf Koivu (1890–1946), originally a painter of well-received impressionistic landscapes, is surely worth mentioning as a major illustrator of children's books, in a style that could remind American or English readers of the immortal Arthur Rackham (1867–1939) or sometimes N. C. Wyeth (1882–1945). His decorative illustrations are stamped with a trace of the exotic *Jugend* style, then with expressionism, depending on the time and the text: the Brothers Grimm, H. C. Andersen, Topelius, Anni Swan. Many of the products of his decades-long collaboration with Raul Roine (see above) were posthumously gathered in what has become a standard volume, *Suomalaisia satuja* (1975; Finnish fairy tales). When the fairy tale experienced a renaissance in the 1950s, a great crowd of illustrators and creators of picturebooks also appeared, reviving the genre. The style became more modern and more concentrated and approached abstract art.

Beginning in the 1970s a new interest in folklore and history appears in picturebooks such as the *Suomalainen tonttukirja* (1979; Finnish goblin book), written and illustrated by Mauri Kunnas (1950–). A poetic imagination marks the illustrations of Kaarina Kaila (1941–), who provided the pictures for Marja-Leena Mikkola's *Anni Manninen* and Mikkola's much-admired *Lumijoutsen* (1978; The snow swan), as well as for the Grimms and Andersen. On the Finland-Swedish side Irmelin Sandman Lilius has published picturebooks for which she herself has written the text, as did Tove Jansson. Camilla Mickwitz (1937–89) also composed both words and pictures for her books but said she regarded herself primarily as an illustrator. Her style of illustration is both vivid and grotesque. Her popular series (1975–78) about a little boy named Jason has a strong air of contemporary reality about it: Jason's mother, Kaarina, is a single parent, working in a cannery by day and as an artist's model in the evenings; they dwell in a crowded apartment house near a comically terrifying old woman who appears as a central figure in *Jason ja vihainen Viivi* (1977; Jason and vicious Viivi). At the conclusion of the series, *Jason muuttaa maasta* (1978; Jason changes country), the cannery closes; mother and son move to Sweden, a country whose language they do not speak. The next Mickwitz series — about a clever little girl named Emilia, who lives with her father, Oskar — has a brighter and more fairy tale–like atmosphere: see, for example, *Emilia ja kuningas Oskari* (1980; Emilia and King Oskar), *Emilia ja Oskarin nukke* (1980; Emilia and Oskar's doll), *Emilia ja kaksoset* (1981; Emilia and the twins). (From a technical standpoint, Mickwitz's work offers signs of the times; both Jason and Emilia have appeared as cartoon figures on television, and Mickwitz, whose mother tongue is Swedish, translates the texts into Finnish herself, the language in which her books first appear.)

The Young Adult Novel
When the books "for boys and girls" of the past had fossilized into stereotypic forms, a new genre was born: the "teiniromaani," or young adult novel. J. D. Salinger's *Catcher in the Rye* (1951) gave the psychological and stylistic impetus for the development in Finland, as in other countries: here it was born around 1960. At present it is a well-established genre but appears almost exclusively in Finnish-language literature. These novels attempt to give a realistic portrait of modern teenage life. The development of the "adult" Finnish novel, with the generous use of dialect and slang, has also influenced the genre. Writers have been freed from certain old patterns, but the pedagogical tendency still exists, although more discreetly.

The central theme of the young adult novel is, naturally enough, the initiation into adult life, an initiation that may include crises and disappointments. Subject matter may cover relationships with parents or erotic experiences. The protagonist seeks his identity, and in discovering himself he is forced to come into an understanding of the lives of other people and must learn to accept the facts of human life.

Finnish teenage fiction at first portrayed the middle class more often than Finnish literature in general does. Starting in the 1970s, however, the children of working-class homes entered the picture more often. In the majority of cases the setting is the city, although Anna-Liisa Haakana (1937–) provides an interesting exception by depicting village life in Lapland she is a native of Rovaniemi — without romanticizing the milieu. In *Ykä yksinäinen* (1980; Ykä all alone) a boy on an isolated north Finnish farm, beset by the miseries of puberty, finds friendship with an invalid, only to lose him to leukemia. *Ykköstyttö* (1981; Fun girl) confronts themes that would have been unthinkable for "Mary Marck" and her contemporaries, teenage pregnancy and abortion. (Both books appeared in the "17-sarja" [17 series] published by WSOY.)

A comparison with the earlier youth novel shows that the writers of the young adult novel have created some new types of characters. One is the intellectual, "soft," and sensitive male adolescent with psychological problems, an individualist and antihero, a type introduced into Finnish teenage fiction by Uolevi Nojonen (1939–) in the 1960s. A variant is the boy who has toughness imposed on him by his surroundings but who is actually insecure and depressed. Initially, Nojonen saw happy solutions: in *Sigmund Freudin kaamea flunssa* (1968; Sigmund Freud's terrible flu) the teenaged narrator, Jonni, intelligent, sensitive, and shy, has to learn how to help others in order to escape his isolation; in *Tinatähti ja Anselmin aarre* (1974; The tin star and Anselm's treasure) a boy, small for his years and often bullied, eventually learns that a toy sheriff's star and a starter's pistol will not enhance his status, though his intellectual accomplishments will; in *Matalat aidat* (1978; Low hurdles) an overstressed father gets aid from his seventeen-year-old son as they spend time together on an island. But subsequently, Nojonen's view turned darker, in his portrayal of incipient youthful criminality, *Luumujengi* (1980; The plum gang). In extreme circumstances the boy may even become a criminal, as in the books by Arvi Arjatsalo (1927–), such as *Kovikset* (1976; The tough guys) and *Mä oon Maukka* (1981; I'm Maukka), advancing the argument that bad conditions at home lead to disruptive or brutal behavior at school, against which overworked teachers can do but little — observations that could easily apply in the United States.

The familiar figure of the active, sensitive heroine, often artistically gifted, was modernized and became the object of intensive psychological investigation, especially in the books of Merja Otava (1935–) of the 1960s, written in an impressionistic, artistic style. Since the 1960s the girls in the novels have become less romantic. They sometimes possess neurotic characteristics that may be related to conflicts in their families. Love and sex are, of course, important themes, and in the depiction of sex many taboos have disappeared. Yet the attitudes of the authors themselves are rather conservative. Current feminist debates, which have been immediately reflected in the teenage fiction of Sweden, have rarely appeared in the Finnish young adult novels. In general, the Finnish genre has not followed ideological fashions very enthusiastically, a restraint that has saved it at times from too journalistic an attitude in both style and content. The pedagogical intention of the authors reveals itself in their eagerness to deal with various topics that are supposed to trouble young people: anguish, alcoholism, anorexia, and divorce within the family. The writers attach special importance to such values as tolerance, solidarity, human warmth, and togetherness.

The popularity of historical material is one of the newer trends in the Finnish young adult novel. The narrative is often set in the time of the author's childhood, but it may also be in the recent or more distant past. After his social-problem books of the 1970s Arjatsalo has taken up the Civil War in his *Varastettu enkeli* (1980; Stolen angel) and has written a biographical novel on the early years of Lönnrot, *Sammatin Elias* (1982; Elias of Sammatti). Similarly, after having dealt with the often unrealizable dreams of adolescence in such books as *Kuningashitti* (1974; Top hit) and *Kameran silmissä siniset unet* (1976; Blue dreams in the camera's eye), about the realities of photo modeling, Lasse Raustela (1932–) has attempted to portray the Finland of the Second World War and its immediate aftermath in an extended series of the novels (1979–89) about the fate of a Turku family.

The narrative techniques of these writers tend to avoid exciting plots, closure, and happy endings. Their aim is to bring their characters as close as possible to the readers. Thus the old convention of the impersonal, authoritative narrator has been abandoned. Quite often, especially in the more interesting books, they use the first-person narrator. This form is probably well suited for reflecting the egocentric world view of the teenager. Even when the narrative voice is not that of the teenager, the point of view is his or hers. Dialogue is a key structural element. For the most part, the boys and girls express themselves in teenage slang; dialect is used occasionally, as in recent Finnish literature in general. The language of these books is growing more and more naturalistic and even crude; in this respect the boundaries between teenage fiction and adult literature have become blurred.

Finnish / Swedish Glossary of Place-Names

FINNISH	SWEDISH
Ääninen, Äänisjoki, Äänisjärvi	Onega
Ahvenanmaa	Åland
Eläintarha	Djurgården
Espoo	Esbo
Hamina	Fredrikshamn
Häme	Tavastland
Hämeenlinna	Tavastehus
Hanko	Hangö
Helsinki	Helsingfors
Iisalmi	Idensalmi
Inkeri	Ingermanland (Ingria)
Itä-Karjala	Östkarelen
Kaisaniemi	Kajsaniemi
Käksisalmi	Kexholm
Kaivopuisto	Brunnsparken
Kajaani	Kajana
Karjala	Karelen (Karelia)
Karjalan kannas	Karelska näset (Karelian isthmus)
Katajanokka	Skatudden
Kauniainen	Grankulla
Keski-Suomi	Mellersta Finland
Kokkola	Karleby (Gamlakarleby)
Kristiinankaupunki	Kristinestad

Kruununhaka	Kronohagen
Kulosaari	Brändö
Laatokka	Ladoga
Länsi-Pohja	Västerbotten
Lahti	Lahtis
Lappeenranta	Villmanstrand
Lapua	Lappo
Lappi	Lapland
Lauttasaari	Drumsö
Loviisa	Lovisa
Mikkeli	Sankt Michel
Oulu	Uleåborg
Parainen	Pargas
Pietarsaari	Jakobstad
Pohjanmaa	Österbotten (Ostrobothnia)
Pohjois-Karjala	Norra Karelen
Pori	Björneborg
Porkkala	Porkala
Porvoo	Borgå
Raahe	Brahestad
Rauma	Raumo
Savo	Savolax
Savonlinna	Nyslott
Sörnäinen	Sörnäs
Sortavala	Sordavala
Suomenlinna (until 1918 Viapori)	Sveaborg
Tammisaari	Ekenäs
Tampere	Tammerfors
Töölö	Tölö
Turku	Åbo
Uusikaarlepyy	Nykarleby
Uusikaupunki	Nystad
Uusimaa	Nyland
Vaasa	Vasa
Varsinais-Suomi	Egentliga Finland
Viipuri (Russian: Vyborg)	Viborg

Bibliography

ABBREVIATIONS

ASR	*American-Scandinavian Review,* after 1975 *Scandinavian Review* (SR)
BA	*Books Abroad,* after 1977 *World Literature Today* (WLT)
BFF	*Books from Finland*
BLM	*Bonniers Litterära Magasin*
EFO	*Études Finno-Ougriennes*
FG	*Finländska gestalter*
FOU	*Förhandlingar och uppsatser* (subseries in SSLF, 1885–1923)
FT	*Finsk Tidskrift*
FVSÅ	*Finska vetenskaps-societetens årsbok*
HLS	*Historiska och litteraturhistoriska studier* (subseries in SSLF)
HYKJ	*Helsingin yliopiston kirjaston julkaisuja*
HTF	*Historisk Tidskrift för Finland*
JFF-DL	*Jahrbuch für finnisch-deutsche Literaturbeziehungen*
JFS	*Journal of Finnish Studies*
KTSV	*Kirjallisuudentutkijain Seuran vuosikirja*
NA	*Nya Argus*
NT	*Nordisk Tidskrift*
OOB	*Ord och Bild*
SBR	*Swedish Book Review*
SCAN	*Scandinavica*
SKHST	*Suomen Kirkkohistoriallisen Seuran toimituksia*
SKS	*Suomalaisen Kirjallisuuden Seura*
SLF	Svenska Litteratursällskapet i Finland
SLT	*Svensk Litteraturtidskrift*
SMS	*Suomen Musiikkitieteellinen Seura*
SNF	*Studier i Nordisk Filologi* (subseries in SSLF, 1910–)

SR   Scandinavian Review, until 1975 American-Scandinavian Review
        (ASR)
SS   Scandinavian Studies
SSF   Societas Scientiarum Fennica
SSLF   Skrifter utgivna av Svenska Litteratursällskapet i Finland
SUS   Suomalais-Ugrilainen Seuta
TFL   Tidskrift för litteraturvetenskap
UAJ   Ural-Altaische Jahrbücher/Ural-Altaic Yearbook
WLT   World Literature Today, until 1977 Books Abroad (BA)
WSOY   Werner Söderström Oy

General References

BIBLIOGRAPHIES AND HANDBOOKS

Elmgren, Sven Gabriel. *Öfversigt af Finlands litteratur ifrån år 1542 till 1770.* Helsingfors: J. C. Frenckell & Son, 1861.

Grönroos, Henrik. *Finlands bibliografiska litteratur: Kommenterad förteckning.* Ekenäs: Ekenäs Tryckeri Aktiebolag, 1975.

———. *Suomen bibliografisen kirjallisuuden opas.* Helsinki: SKS, 1965.

Haanpää, Eera-Liisa, and Marja-Leena Rautalin, eds. *Suomalaisen kirjallisuuden käänösbibliografia, 1976–1993.* Helsinki: SKS, 1996. Continuation of Haltsonen and Puranen below.

Haltsonen, Sulo. *Luettelo suomalaisista kirjallisuudentutkimuksista, 1901–1925.* KTSV 11 (1954).

———. *Luettelo suomalaisista kirjallisuudentutkimuksista, 1938–1950.* KTSV 17 (1959).

———. *Luettelo suomalaisista kirjallisuudentutkimuksista, 1951–1960.* KTSV 19 (1963).

Haltsonen, Sulo, Kaarlo Lohikoski, and Vihtori Laurila. *Luettelo suomalaisista kirjallisuudentutkimuksista, 1926–1933.* KTSV 4 (1936), 309–98.

Haltsonen, Sulo, and Eino Nivanka. *Luettelo suomalaisista kirjallisuudentutkimuksista, 1934–1937.* KTSV 5 (1939), 331–401.

Haltsonen, Sulo, and Rauni Puranen. *Kaunokirjallisuutemme käännöksiä.* Helsinki: SKS, 1979, 10–14. Translations of Finnish-language belles-lettres into English.

Hirvonen, Maija, Hannu Launonen, Anna Nybondas, and Inger Bäcksbacka, eds. *Suomen kirjailijat, 1945–1980.* Helsinki: SKS, 1985.

———. *Suomen kirjailijat, 1809–1916.* Helsinki: SKS, 1993.

Karttunen, Päivi, and Lasse Koskela. *Luettelo suomalaisista kirjallisuudentutkimuksista, 1971–1980.* KTSV 36 (1984).

———. *Luettelo suomalaisista kirjallisuudentutkimuksista, 1981–1985.* KTSV 39 (1986).

Launonen, Hannu, Anna Makkonen, Maija Hirvonen, Anna Nybondas, and Inger Bäcksbacka, eds. *Suomen kirjailijat, 1917–1944.* Helsinki: SKS, 1981.

Launonen, Hannu, Satu Apo, Tuulikki Hannelius, Irma-Riitta Järvinen, and Holger Lillquist, eds. *Suomen kirjailijat, 1945–1970.* Helsinki: SKS, 1977.

Rantala, Risto. *Suomalaisia kirjailijoita 1500-luvulta nykypäivään.* Helsinki: Otava, 1994.
Screen, J. E. G. *Finland (World Bibliographical Series,* 31). Oxford: Clio, 1981.
Steinby, Gunnel. *Journalister och publicister i svensk press i Finland under tvåhundra år: En matrikel.* Åbo: Åbo Akademi, 1981.
Tarkka, Pekka. *Författare i Finland.* Helsingfors: Söderström & Co., 1990.
———. *Suomalaisia nykykirjailijoita.* Helsinki: Tammi, 1980.
———. *Suomalaisia nykykirjailijoita.* Helsinki: Tammi, 1989.
Tarkka, Pekka, Kai Laitinen, and Sven Willner, eds. *Författare i Finland.* Helsingfors: Söderström & Co., 1983.
Tiitinen, Ilpo. *Luettelo suomalaisista kirjallisuudentutkimuksista, 1961-1970.* KTSV 29 (1975), 7-175.
Zuck, Virpi, with Niels Ingwersen and Harald S. Naess, eds. *Dictionary of Scandinavian Literature.* Westport CT: Greenwood, 1990.

HISTORY OF FINLAND'S LITERARY CRITICISM

Varpio, Yrjö. *The History of Finnish Literary Criticism, 1828-1918.* Tampere: Societas Scientiarum Fennica, 1990.
———. *Suomalaisen kirjallisuudentutkimuksen historia.* Porvoo: WSOY, 1986.

INSTITUTIONS AND ORGANIZATIONS

Hautala, Jouko, Eino Nivanka, and Toivo Vuorela. *Activities of the Finnish Literary Society, 1831-1956.* Helsinki: SKS, 1957.
Klinge, Matti. *Studenter och idéer: Studentkåren vid Helsingfors universitet, 1828-1960.* Trans. Bertel Kihlman. Helsingfors: Studentkåren, 1969-79.
———. *Ylioppilaskunnan historia 1-4.* Helsinki: WSOY, 1966-67, 1978.

HISTORY OF THE PRESS

Rytkönen, Alli. *Päivälehden historia 1-3.* Helsinki: Päivälehti, 1940-49.
Steinby, Torsten. *Finlands tidningspress.* Stockholm: Sveriges Finlandsföreningars Riksförbund: Fadderortsrörelsen, 1964.
———. *In Quest of Freedom: Finland's Press, 1771-1971.* Helsinki: Government Printing Center, 1971.
Zilliacus, Clas, and Henrik Knif. *Opinionens tryck: En studie över pressens bildningsskede i Finland.* Helsingfors: SLF, 1985.

PUBLISHERS AND PUBLISHING HOUSES

Gedin, Per. "Family Business: Otava, 1890-1990." BFF (1990), 154-59.
Koskenniemi, V. A. *Werner Söderström.* Porvoo: WSOY, 1950.
Koskimies, Rafael. *Otavan historia 1.* Helsinki: Otava, 1946.
Lassila, Pertti. *Otavan historia 3: 1941-1975.* Helsinki: Otava, 1990.

Manninen, Kerttu, ed. *Tammen kirjallisuutta*. Helsinki: Tammi, 1973.
Mustelin, Olof. *En förläggare och några av hans författare: Kring Holger Schildts förläggardebut, 1913-1917*. Helsingfors: Schildts/Svenska folkskolans vänner, 1983.
Slotte, Ulf-Erik. "Swedish-Language Publishing in Finland." BFF (1985), 173-77.
Stjernschantz, Göran. *Ett förlag och dess författare: Söderström & Co. Förlags Ab, 1891-1991*. Helsingfors: Söderström & Co., 1991.
Tarkka, Pekka. *Otavan historia 2: 1918-1940*. Helsinki: Otava, 1980.
———. "Profile: Werner Söderström Publishers." BFF (1978), 140-45.
Wiio, Osmo Antero. *Oy Weilin & Göös Ab, 1872-1972*. Helsinki: Weilin & Göös, 1972.
Wikström-Hollander, Erica. *Förlaget BRO och folksmaken*. Åbo: Åbo Akademi, Litteraturvetenskapliga institutionen, 1984.

HISTORY AND CULTURAL HISTORY

Christiansen, Eric. *The Northern Crusades: The Baltic and the Catholic Frontier, 1100-1525*. Minneapolis: University of Minnesota Press, 1980, 109-17, 178-80, 193-96, 208-10.
Edgren, Torsten, and Lena Törnblom. *Finlands historia 1*. Helsingfors: Schildts, 1993.
Estlander, Bernhard. *Elva årtionden ur Finlands historia 1-4*. Helsingfors: Söderström & Co., 1929.
Fagerlund, Rainer, Kurt Jern, and Nils Erik Villstrand. *Finlands historia 2*. Helsingfors: Schildts, 1993.
Hämäläinen, Pekka Kalevi. *In Time of Storm: Revolution, Civil War, and the Ethnolinguistic Issue in Finland*. Albany: State University of New York Press, 1979.
———. *Nationalitetskampen och språkstriden i Finland, 1917-1939*. Trans. Thomas Warburton. Helsingfors: Schildts, 1969.
Jutikkala, Eino, and Kauko Pirinen. *A History of Finland*. New York: Praeger, 1974.
———. *Suomen historia*. Helsinki: Weilin & Göös, 1966.
Juva, Einar W., and Mikko Juva. *Suomen kansan historia 1-5*. Helsinki: Otava, 1964-67.
Kallio, Veikko. *Finland: A Cultural History*. Trans. Peter Herring. Helsinki: WSOY, 1994.
———. *Finland: Cultural Perspectives*. Trans. Peter Herring. Helsinki: WSOY, 1989.
Kirby, D. G. *Finland in the Twentieth Century: A History and an Interpretation*. Minneapolis: University of Minnesota Press, 1979.
Kivikoski, Ella. *Finland (Ancient Peoples and Places)*. New York: Praeger, 1967.
Klinge, Matti. *A Brief History of Finland*. Helsinki: Otava, 1981.
———. *Finlands historia 3: Kejsartiden*. Helsingfors: Schildts, 1996.
Mead, William Richard. *Finland*. London: Benn, 1968.
———. "Uppfattningar om Finland." HTF (1987), 333-50.
Mead, William Richard, and S. H. Jaatinen. *The Åland Islands*. Newton Abbot U.K.: David & Charles, 1975.

Mead, William Richard, and Helmer Smeds. *Winter in Finland*. London: Evelyn, 1967.
Nickels, Sylvie, Hillar Kallas, and Philippa Friedman. *Finland: An Introduction*. New York: Praeger, 1973.
Norrback, Märtha, gen. ed. *Finlands historia 1–(4)*. Helsingfors: Schildts, 1993–96.
Paasivirta, Juhani. *Finland and Europe: The Period of Autonomy and the International Crises, 1808–1914*. Minneapolis: University of Minnesota Press, 1981.
Puntila, L. A. *Finlands politiska historia, 1809–1955*. Trans. J. O. Tallqvist. Helsingfors: Schildts, 1964.
———. *Political History of Finland, 1809–1966*. Trans. David Miller. London: Heinemann, 1975.
———. *Suomen poliittinen historia, 1809–1955*. Helsinki: Otava, 1963.
Schoolfield, George C. *Helsinki of the Czars: Finland's Capital, 1808–1918*. Columbia SC: Camden House, 1996.
Sihvo, Hannes. "Karelen i Finlands historia—vädjobana, bro, myt." HTF (1987), 412–35.
Singleton, Fred. *A Short History of Finland*. Cambridge: Cambridge University Press, 1989.
Suolahti, Gunnar, Esko Aaltonen, Eino Jutikkala, Lauri Kuusanmäki, Pentti Renvall, and Heikki Waris, eds. *Suomen kulttuurihistoria 1–4*. Jyväskylä: Gummerus, 1933–36.
Tommila, Päiviö. *Suomen kulttuurihistoria 1–3*. Helsinki: WSOY, 1979–81.
Upton, Anthony F. *The Finnish Revolution, 1917–1918*. Minneapolis: University of Minnesota Press, 1980.
Ylikangas, Heikki. "Österbotten i Finlands historia." HTF (1987), 397–411.

Finnish-Language Literature

ANTHOLOGIES

Jäntti, Yrjö, Kristiina Kivivuori, and Pekka Saloranta, eds. *Suomen sana 1–24*. Helsinki: WSOY, 1963–67.
Kankaanpää, Hannu, Satu Marttila, and Mirjam Polkunen, eds. *Suomen runotar 1–2*. 6th ed. Helsinki: Kirjayhtymä, 1990.
Laitinen, Kai, Matti Suurpää, and Hannu Mäkelä (7–8), eds. *Suomen kirjallisuuden antologia 1–8*. Helsinki: Otava, 1963–75.
Setälä, Emil Nestor, Viljo Tarkiainen, and Vihtori Laurila, eds. *Suomen kansalliskirjallisuus 1–15*. Helsinki: Otava, 1930–43.

ANTHOLOGIES IN TRANSLATION

Allwood, Martin, gen. ed. *Modern Scandinavian Poetry*. New York: New Directions, 1982, 331–90.

Armstrong, Robert. *Finnish Odyssey: Poetry and Folk Songs of Finland in Translation.* London: Research Publishing Co., 1975.

Bosley, Keith. *Skating on the Sea.* Newcastle-upon-Tyne: Bloodaxe, 1996.

Carpelan, Bo, Veijo Meri, and Matti Suurpää, eds. *A Way to Measure Time: Contemporary Finnish Literature.* Helsinki: Finnish Literature Society, 1992.

Dauenhauer, Richard, and Philip Binham, eds. *Snow in May: An Anthology of Finnish Writing, 1945–1972.* Teaneck NJ: Fairleigh Dickinson University Press; London: Associated University Presses, 1978.

Fried, Anne, ed. and trans. *Thank You for These Illusions: Poems by Finnish Women Writers.* Helsinki: WSOY, 1981.

Hawkins, Hildi, and Soila Lehtonen, eds. *On the Border: New Writing from Finland.* Manchester: Carcanet, 1995.

Henderson, Helen, ed. and trans. *The Maiden Who Rose from the Sea and Other Finnish Folktales.* Enfield Lock, Middlesex: Hisarlik, 1992.

Jarvenpa, Aili, ed. and trans. *Salt of Pleasure: Twentieth-Century Finnish Poetry.* Introduction by K. Börje Vähämäki. St. Paul MN: New Rivers Press, 1983.

Jarvenpa, Aili, and Michael G. Karni, eds. *Sampo: The Magic Mill.* St. Paul MN: New Rivers Press, 1989.

Krook, Anna, ed. and trans. *Finnish Songs: A Collection of Poems.* Helsinki: G. W. Edlund, 1904; revised and enlarged as *Songs of the North: A Collection of Poems.* Helsinki: Söderström & Co., 1926.

Laitinen, Kai, ed. *Modern Nordic Plays: Finland.* New York: Twayne, 1973. Introduction, 7–16; Paavo Haavikko, *The Superintendent,* trans. Philip Binham, 17–49; V. V. Järner, *Eva Maria,* trans. Dympna Connolly, 49–90; Eeva-Liisa Manner, *Snow in May,* trans. Philip Binham, 91–170; Veijo Meri, *Private Jokinen's Marriage Leave,* trans. J. R. Pitkin, 171–304.

Leander, Kajsa, and Ernst Malmsten, eds. *The Nordic Poetry Festival Anthology.* New York: Nordic Poetry Festival, 1993.

Lomas, Herbert, ed. and trans. *Contemporary Finnish Poetry.* Newcastle-upon-Tyne: Bloodaxe, 1991.

———. *Territorial Song: Contemporary Writing from Finland.* London: London Magazine Editions, 1981.

Moseley, Christopher, ed. and trans. *From Baltic Shores.* Norwich: Norvik Press, 1994.

Schoolfield, George C., ed. "Finland's Literature." In *Dimension: Special Issue: Contemporary Nordic Literature,* gen. ed. John Weinstock (1994), 60–363.

Schoolfield, George C., ed. and trans. "Finland." In *The Nordic Mind: Current Trends in Scandinavian Literary Criticism,* ed. Frank Egholm Andersen and John Weinstock. Lanham MD: University Press of America, 1986, 111–64.

Simonsuuri, Kirsti, ed. and trans. *Enchanting Beasts: An Anthology of Modern Women Poets in Finland.* London: Forest Books, 1990.

Tompuri, Elli, ed. *Voices from Finland: An Anthology of Finland's Verse and Prose in English, Finnish, and Swedish.* Helsinki: Sanoma, 1947.

Väänänen-Jensen, Inkeri, and K. Börje Vähämäki, trans. *Finnish Short Stories*. St. Paul MN: Nordic Translators, 1982; Iowa City IA: Penfield Press, 1991.

Wilmer, S. E., ed. *Portraits of Courage: Plays by Finnish Women*. Helsinki: University of Helsinki Press, 1997. Minna Canth, *Anna-Liisa*, trans. Aili and Austin Flint, 4–107; Maria Jotuni, *The Golden Calf,* trans. Ritva Poom, 168–217; Hella Wuolijoki, *Law and Order,* trans. S. E. and Maria Wilmer, 218–97.

LITERARY HISTORY

Ahokas, Jaakko A. *A History of Finnish Literature*. Bloomington: Indiana University (for the American-Scandinavian Foundation), 1973.

Hormia, Osmo. *Den finska litteraturens historia fram till 1917*. Jyväskylä: Akademilitteratur, 1982.

Koskimies, Rafael. *Elävä kansalliskirjallisuus 1–3*. Helsinki: Otava, 1944–49.

Krohn, Julius. *Suomalaisen kirjallisuuden vaiheet*. Helsinki: SKS, 1897.

Kuusi, Matti, gen. ed. *Suomen kirjallisuus 1–8*. Helsinki: Otava, 1963–70.

Laitinen, Kai. *Finlands litteratur*. Trans. Kerstin Lindqvist and Thomas Warburton. Helsingfors: Söderström & Co., 1988.

———. *Finlands moderna litteratur: Konturer, huvudlinjer, resultat, 1917–1967*. Trans. Thomas Warburton. Helsingfors: Schildts, 1968.

———. *Literature of Finland: An Outline*. Trans. Philip and Timothy Binham. Helsinki: Otava, 1985, 1994.

———. *Suomen kirjallisuus, 1917–1967: Ääriviivoja, päälinjoja, saavutuksia*. Helsinki: Otava, 1967.

Laitinen, Kai, with Satu Apo and Gun Herranen. *Suomen kirjallisuuden historia*. Helsinki: Otava, 1981.

Laitinen, Kai, Juhani Niemi, Ingmar Svedberg. *Finlands litteratur efter år 1965*. Helsingfors: Suomen kirjastoseura/Finlands biblioteksförening, 1975.

Leino, Eino. *Suomalaisen kirjallisuuden historia*. Helsinki: Weilin, 1910.

———. *Suomalaisia kirjailijoita: Pikakuvia*. Helsinki: Otava, 1909.

Lönnbeck, Albin. *Studier i finska vitterheten efter 1830*. Helsingfors: P. H. Beijer, 1883.

Nevala, Maria-Liisa, ed. *"Sain roolin johon en mahdu": Suomalaisen naiskirjallisuuden linjoja*. Helsinki: Otava, 1989.

———. "Women in the Finnish Literary Establishment." In *The Lady with the Bow: The Story of Finnish Women*, ed. Merja Minninen and Päivi Setälä. Helsinki: Otava, 1990, 91–108.

Tarkiainen, Viljo. *Finsk litteraturhistoria*. Trans. E. N. Tigerstedt. Stockholm: Gebers, 1950.

———. *Suomalaisen kirjallisuuden historia*. Helsinki: Otava, 1934; 4th ed., with Eino Kauppinen, 1967.

THEATRICAL HISTORY

Aspelin-Haapkylä, Eliel. *Suomalaisen teatterin historia 1–4*. Helsinki: SKS, 1906–10.

Binham, Philip. "New Finnish Drama: The Fifties and After." In *Snow in May: An*

Anthology of Finnish Writing, 1945–1972, ed. Richard Dauenhauer and Philip Binham. Teaneck NJ: Fairleigh Dickinson University Press; London: Associated University Presses, 1978, 48–52.

———. "Protest and After in the Finnish Theatre." *WLT* (1980), 58–61.

Heikkilä, Ritva, ed. *Suomen Kansallisteatteri: The Finnish National Theatre.* Porvoo: WSOY, 1962.

Koskimies, Rafael. *Suomen Kansallisteatteri, 1902–1950. 1: 1902–1917; 2: 1917–1950.* Helsinki: Otava, 1953–72.

Schoolfield, George C. "Finland's Drama." In *McGraw-Hill Encyclopedia of World Drama,* ed. Stanley Hochman. New York: McGraw-Hill, 1984, 2:159–71.

Tiusanen, Timo. *Teatterimme hahmottuu.* Helsinki: Kirjayhtymä, 1969.

Finland-Swedish Literature

ANTHOLOGIES

Andersson, Claes, and Bo Carpelan. *Modern finlandssvensk lyrik.* Helsingfors: Söderström & Co., 1986.

Carpelan, Bo, ed. *Finlandssvenska lyrikboken: En antologi.* Helsingfors: Söderström & Co., 1967.

Ekman, Michel. *11 finlandssvenska poeter.* Helsingfors: ai-ai, 1992.

Enckell, Olof, ed. *Modern finlandssvensk prosa i urval.* Tammerfors: Söderström & Co., 1938.

Enckell, Rabbe, ed. *Modärn finlandssvensk lyrik: I urval och med en inledning.* Helsingfors: Söderström & Co., 1934.

Hulden, Lars, ed. *Österbottnisk läsebok.* Helsingfors: Söderström & Co., 1976.

Kihlman, Erik, ed. *Ur Finlands svenska lyrik. 1: Intill 1900-talets början; 2: Nittonhundratalet.* Ed. Thomas Warburton. Lund: C.W.K. Gleerups Förlag, 1949.

Mazzarella, Merete, and Helena Solstrand, eds. *Finlandssvenska noveller.* Helsingfors: Söderström & Co., 1975.

Sundgren, Tatiana. *Finlandssvenska kvinnor skriver.* Helsingfors: Schildts, 1984.

Warburton, Thomas, ed. *Facklor över jorden: Lyrik, 1916–1959.* Helsingfors: Schildts, 1960.

———. *Från Södergran till Carpelan: Tretton finlandssvenska modernister i urval.* Stockholm: Wahlström & Widstrand, 1965.

ANTHOLOGIES IN TRANSLATION

Bruce, Lennart, and Sonia Bruce, eds. and trans. *Speak to Me.* New York: The Spirit That Moves Us Press, 1989.

Korsström, Tuva, ed. *New Finland-Swedish Writing.* SBR, supplement (1992).

McDuff, David, ed. and trans. *Ice around Our Lips: Finland-Swedish Poetry.* Newcastle-upon-Tyne: Bloodaxe, 1989.

Schoolfield, George C., ed. *Finland-Swedish Issue*. SBR 1 (1989).
——, ed. and trans. *Swedo-Finnish Short Stories*. New York: Twayne and American-Scandinavian Foundation, 1974.

LITERARY HISTORY

Ekelund, Erik. *Finlands svenska litteratur 2: Från Åbo brand till sekelskiftet*. Helsingfors: Söderström & Co., 1969.
Hedvall, Ruth. *Finlands svenska litteratur*. Borgå: Schildts, 1917.
Huldén, Lars, Jarl Gallén, Olof Enckell, and Erik Ekelund. *Finlands svenska litteratur 1: Från medeltiden till Åboromantiken*. Helsingfors: Söderström & Co., 1968.
Lagus, Gabriel. *Den finsk-svenska litteraturens utveckling 1–2*. Borgå: G. L. Söderström, 1866; Åbo: G. W. Wilén, 1867.
Lindström, Hans. *Finlandssvensk nittonhundratalslitteratur*. Stockholm: Sveriges Finlandsföreningars Riksförbund/Fadderortsrörelsen; Helsingfors: Schildts, 1966.
Linnér, Sven, ed. *Från dagdrivare till feminister: Studier i finlandssvensk 1900-talslitteratur*. Helsingfors: SLF, 1986.
Mazzarella, Merete. *Att skriva sin värld: Om den finlandssvenska memoartraditionen*. Helsingfors: Söderström & Co., 1993.
——. "Den finlandssvenska memoartraditionen—Några tolkningsmöjligheter." HLS 67 (1992), 7–16.
——. *Från Fredrika Runeberg till Märta Tikkanen: Frihet och beroende i finlandssvensk kvinnolitteratur*. Helsingfors: Söderström & Co., 1985.
——. *Det trånga rummet: En finlandssvensk romantradition*. Helsingfors: Söderström & Co., 1989.
Mazzarella, Merete, Johannes Salminen, Ingmar Svedberg, and Sven Willner. *Författare om författare: 24 finlandssvenska författarporträtt*. Helsingfors: Söderström & Co., 1980.
Schoolfield, George C. "The August Light of Abiding Memories: Finland-Swedish Memoir Literature." WLT (1980), 15–20.
——. "The History of the Literary Essay in Finland." In *The Nordic Mind: Current Trends in Scandinavian Literary Criticism*, ed. Frank Egholm Andersen and John Weinstock. Lanham MD: University Press of America, 1986, 103–10.
Sievänen-Allen, Ritva. "Everyday Song." BFF (1971), 3:2–8.
Steenwall, Åsa. *Hur flickor blir kloka: Om flickuppväxt i nyare finlandssvensk litteratur*. Helsingfors: Schildts, 1987.
Warburton, Thomas. *Åttio år finlandssvensk litteratur*. Helsingfors: Schildts, 1984.
——. *Finlandssvensk litteratur, 1898–1948*. Stockholm: Forum, 1951.
Willner, Sven. "Den finlandssvenska essätraditionen lever vidare." *Horisont* 38 (1991), 3:60–67.
——. "Författarna och deras sociala bakgrund." In Willner, *Söner av nederlaget*. Ekenäs: Ekenäs Tryckeri, 1979, 113–52.
——. "De tre storhetstiderna." In Willner, *Söner av nederlaget*. Ekenäs: Ekenäs Tryckeri, 1979, 7–50.

CULTURAL ORGANIZATIONS

Andersson, Otto. "Föreningen Brage." In Andersson, *Finländsk folklore*. Stockholm: Svenskt Visarkiv, 1967, 228–71.

Cavonius, Gösta. *Tanke och gärning*. Helsingfors: Svenska folksskolans vänner, 1982.

Jernström, Frank. *Svenska kulturfondens 75-års-historik*. Helsingfors: Svenska kulturfonden: Schildts, 1985.

Steinby, Torsten. *Svenska litteratursällskapet i Finland, 1885–1985. 1: Det första halvseklet*. Mustelin, Olof. *2: Det andra halvseklet*. Pettersson, Magnus. *3: Register*. Helsingfors: SLF, 1985, 1986, 1989.

THEATRICAL HISTORY

Colliander, Erland. *Svenska inhemska teatern, 1894–1919*. Helsingfors: Söderström & Co., 1920.

Frenckell, Ester-Margaret von. *ABC för teaterpubliken*. Helsingfors: Söderström & Co., 1971.

Lüchou, Marianne, ed. *Svenska Teatern i Helsingfors: Repertoar, 1860–1975*. Helsingfors: Stiftelsen för Svenska Teatern, 1977.

Qvarnström, Ingrid. *Svensk teater i Finland 1–2*. Helsingfors: Schildts, 1946–47.

Viljo, Eeva Maija, Lena Nyman, and Clas Zilliacus. *Åbo teaterhus 150 år*. Åbo: Åbo Akademi, 1989.

FINLAND-SWEDES AND FINLAND-SWEDISH

Ahlbäck, Olav. *Svenskan i Finland*. Stockholm: Läromedelsförlagen, 1971.

Allardt, Erik, and Christian Starck. *Språkgränser och samhällsstruktur: Finlandssvenskarna i ett jämförande perspektiv*. Stockholm: Almqvist & Wiksell/Gebers, 1981.

Allardt Ekelund, Karin. "Modersspråket." In Allardt Ekelund, *Traneplogar*. Helsingfors: Söderström & Co., 1977, 14–20.

Bergroth, Hugo. *Finlandssvenska: Handledning till undvikande av provinsialismer i tal och skrift*. Helsingfors: Schildts, 1917.

Dahl, Hjalmar. *Finlandssvenskar*. Stockholm: Natur & Kultur, 1957.

Engman, Max. "Kejsarens balter, böhmare och finnar: Finlandssvenskarna i ett jämförande historiskt perspektiv." HLS 66 (1991), 267–82.

Engman, Max, and Henrik Stenius, eds. *Svenskt i Finland: Studier i språk och nationalitet efter 1860 1–2*. Helsingfors: SLF, 1983–84.

Finnäs, Fjalar. *Den finlandssvenska befolkningsutvecklingen, 1950–1980: En analys av en språkgrupps demografiska utveckling och effekten av blandäktenskap*. Helsingfors: SLF, 1986.

Freudenthal, A. O., ed. "Skiljaktigheter mellan finländska svenskan och rikssvenskan upptecknade å Helsingfors landsmålsföreningens sammanträden, 1893–1899." FOU 15 (1901), 35–115.

Hultman, O. F. "Om uppkomsten av den bildade talsvenskan i Finland." *FOU* 28 (1914), 231–52.
Laurén, Christer, ed. *Finlandssvenskan — Fakta och debatt.* Helsingfors: Söderström & Co., 1978.
———. *Normer för finlandssvenskan: Från Freudenthal till 1970-tal.* Helsingfors: Schildts, 1984.
Lönnqvist, Bo. *Suomenruotsalaiset: Kansatieteellinen tutkielma kieliryhmästä.* Jyväskylä: Gummerus, 1981.
Loman, Bengt. "Högspråk och lågsspråk i finlandssvensk prosadiktning." In *Språken i vårt språk,* ed. Inge Jonsson. Stockholm: Pan/Norstedt, 1980, 119–39.
Mustelin, Olof. "'Finländsk' och 'finländare': Om ett ordpar och dess historia." *HLS* 37 (1962), 65–100.
Nikander, Gabriel, gen. ed. *Det svenska Finland 1–3.* Helsingfors: Schildts; Stockholm: Fröléen, 1919–21.
Nordenstreng, Rolf. "Finländsk svenska på 1700-talet." *FOU* 16 (1902), 20–84.
———. "Till frågan om vår finländska svenska." *FT* (1900), 184–200.
Puntila, L. A. *Suomen ruotsalaisuuden liikkeen synty.* Helsinki: Otava, 1944.
Reuter, Mikael. "Svenskan i Finland." *Språk i Norden* (1983), 65–78.
———. "Vad år finlandssvenska?" *Språkbruk* (1987), 1:3–10.
Saxén, Rolf. "Finländsk svenska." *FT* (1904), 299–314.
Törnudd, Klaus. "The Language Situation in Finland." *ASR* 51 (1963), 27–32.
———. *Svenska språkets ställning i Finland.* Helsingfors: Schildts, 1978.

Chapter Bibliographies

CHAPTER 1: FINNISH ORAL POETRY, *KALEVALA,* AND *KANTELETAR*

TRANSLATIONS

The Kalevala: The Epic Poem of Finland. Trans. John Martin Crawford. New York: J. B. Alden, 1889.
The Kalevala or Poems of the Kaleva District Compiled by Elias Lönnrot. Prose translation with foreword and appendices by Francis Peabody Magoun Jr. Cambridge: Harvard University Press, 1963.
The Old Kalevala and Certain Antecedents Compiled by Elias Lönnrot. Prose translations with foreword and appendices by Francis Peabody Magoun Jr. Cambridge: Harvard University Press, 1969.
Kalevala. The Land of the Heroes. Trans. W. F. Kirby. Preface and introduction by M. A. Branch. London: Athlone, 1985; Helsinki: SKS, 1985.
The Kalevala: An Epic Poem after Oral Tradition by Elias Lönnrot. Translated from the Finnish with introduction and notes by Keith Bosley. Foreword by Albert B. Lord. Oxford: Oxford University Press, 1989.

The Kalevala: Epic of the Finnish People. Trans. Eino Friberg. Ed. George C. Schoolfield. Helsinki: Otava, 1988.
La Kantélétar. Trans. Jean-Luc Moreau. Paris: Pierre Jean Oswald, 1972.
Kanteletar: [62] Alte Volkslieder und Balladen aus Finnland. Trans. Erich Kunze. Helsinki: Otava, 1976.
The Kanteletar: Lyrics and Ballads after Oral Tradition by Elias Lönnrot. Trans. and ed. Keith Bosley. Oxford: Oxford University Press, 1992.

SECONDARY LITERATURE

Austerlitz, Robert. "The Poetics of the Kalevala." In *Kalevala, 1835–1985: The National Epic of Finland*. Helsinki: Helsinki University Library, 1985, 44–47.
Branch, Michael. *A. J. Sjögren: Studies of the North*. Helsinki: SUS, 1973.
———. "The Invention of a National Epic." In *The Uses of Tradition: A Comparative Enquiry into the Nature, Uses, and Functions of Oral Poetry in the Balkans, the Baltic, and Africa*, ed. Michael Branch and Celia Hawkesworth. London: University of London School of Slavonic and East European Studies; Helsinki: SKS, 1994, 195–211.
———. "Kalevala: From Myth to Symbol." In *Kalevala, 1835–1985: The National Epic of Finland*. Helsinki: Helsinki University Library, 1985, 1–8.
DuBois, Thomas. "From Maria to Marjatta: The Transformation of an Oral Poem in Elias Lönnrot's *Kalevala*." *Oral Tradition* 8 (1993), 247–288.
Fromm, Hans. *Kalevala: Das finnische Epos des Elias Lönnrot. 2: Kommentar.* München: Hanser, 1967.
Haavio, Martti. *Väinämöinen, Eternal Sage*. Trans. Helen Goldthwait-Väänänen. Helsinki: SSF, 1952.
Hautala, Jouko. *Finnish Folklore Research, 1828–1918*. Helsinki: SSF, 1969.
Honko, Lauri. "The *Kalevala*: Problems of Interpretation and Identity." In *Religion, Myth, and Folklore in the World's Epics: The Kalevala and Its Predecessors*, ed. Lauri Honko. Berlin: Mouton/de Gruyter, 1990, 555–75.
———. "The *Kalevala*: The Processual View." In *Religion, Myth, and Folklore in the World's Epics*, ed. Honko, 181–229.
———. "The *Kalevala* and the World's Epics: An Introduction." In *Religion, Myth, and Folklore in the World's Epics*, ed. Honko, 1–26.
———. "The *Kalevala* Process." In *Kalevala, 1835–1985: The National Epic of Finland*. Helsinki: Helsinki University Library, 1985, 16–23.
Honko, Lauri, Senni Timonen, and Michael Branch, eds. *The Great Bear: A Thematic Anthology of Oral Poetry in the Finno-Ugrian Languages*, with translations by Keith Bosley. Helsinki: SKS, 1993.
Hroch, Miroslav. *Social Preconditions of National Revival in Europe*. Cambridge: Cambridge University Press, 1985.
Karkama, Pertti. "Lönnrotin eeppinen idea." *Tiede ja Edistys* 2 (1985), 96–107.
Kaukonen, Väinö. *Elias Lönnrotin Kalevalan toinen painos*. Helsinki: SKS, 1956.
———. *Elias Lönnrotin Kanteletar*. Helsinki: SKS, 1984.

———. "The Kalevala as Epic." In *Religion, Myth, and Folklore in the World's Epics: The Kalevala and Its Predecessors,* ed. Lauri Honko. Berlin: Mouton/de Gruyter, 1990, 157-79.

———. *Lönnrot ja Kalevala.* Helsinki: SKS, 1979.

Kiparsky, Paul. "Oral Poetry: Some Linguistic and Typological Considerations." In *Oral Literature and the Formula,* ed. Benjamin A. Stolz and Richard S. Shannon. Ann Arbor: Center for the Coordination of Ancient and Modern Studies, University of Michigan, 1976, 73-106.

Kolehmainen, John I. *Epic of the North: The Story of Finland's Kalevala.* New York Mills MN: Northwestern, 1973.

Kuusi, Matti. "Epic Cycles as the Basis for the *Kalevala.*" In *Religion, Myth, and Folklore in the World's Epics: The Kalevala and Its Predecessors,* ed. Lauri Honko. Berlin: Mouton/de Gruyter, 1990, 133-55.

Kuusi, Matti, Keith Bosley, and Michael Branch. *Finnish Folk Poetry: Epic: An Anthology in Finnish and English.* Helsinki: SKS; London: Zurst; Montreal: McGill-Queen's University Press, 1977.

Laaksonen, Pekka, ed. *Lönnrotin aika.* Helsinki: SKS, 1984.

Nummi, Jyrki. "*Kalevala* and the Epics of the World." *UAJ* 61 (1989), 140-43.

Pentikäinen, Juha Y. *Kalevala Mythology.* Ed. and trans. Ritva Poom. Bloomington: Indiana University Press, 1989.

Sarajas, Annamari. "Suomen kansanrunouden tuntemus 1500-1700-lukujen kirjallisuudessa." Ph.D. dissertation, Helsinki University, 1956. Translated by Bertel Kihlman under the title *Studiet av folkdiktningen i Finland intill slutet av 1700-talet* (Stockholm: Kungliga Vitterhets Historie och Antikvitets Akademien, 1982).

Siikala, Anna-Leena, and Sinikka Vakimo, eds. *Songs beyond the Kalevala: Transformations of Oral Poetry.* Helsinki: SKS, 1994.

Smith, Anthony D. *The Ethnic Origins of Nations.* Oxford: Oxford University Press, 1986.

———. *National Identity.* Reno: University of Nevada Press, 1991.

Timonen, Senni. "Lönnrot and His Singers." In *Kalevala, 1835-1985: The National Epic of Finland.* Helsinki: Helsinki University Library, 1985, 24-29.

Wilson, William A. *Folklore and Nationalism in Modern Finland.* Bloomington: Indiana University Press, 1976.

CHAPTER 2: NEW BEGINNINGS, LATIN AND FINNISH

INTELLECTUAL AND LITERARY HISTORY

Castrén, Gunnar. "Sällskapet Aurora." *FOU* 14 (1900), 144-95.

Häkli, Esko, ed. *Gelehrte Kontakte zwischen Finnland und Göttingen zur Zeit der Aufklärung: Ausstellung aus Anlaß des 500 jährigen Jubiläums des finnischen Buches.* Göttingen: Vandenhoeck & Ruprecht, 1988.

Klinge, Matti. "International Relations: Finland and Europe before 1809." *BFF* (1988), 12-17.

———. *Professoreita.* Helsinki: Otava, 1984.

Laitinen, Kai. "The Birth of a Literature." *BFF* (1988), 2–8.
Schoolfield, George C. "Does Finland Have a Baroque Literature?" In *Cultura Baltica: Literary Culture around the Baltic, 1600–1700,* ed. Bo Andersson and Richard Schade. Stockholm: Almqvist & Wiksell, 1996, 111–42. Acta Universitatis Upsaliensis: Studia Germanistica Upsaliensia, 35.

THE FINNISH BIBLE

Puukko, Antti Filemon. *Raamatunsuomennokset: Vanhat suomalaiset Raamattumme ja uusi Vahan testamentin suomennos.* Porvoo: WSOY, 1933.

———. *Suomalainen Raamattumme Mikael Agricolasta uuteen kirkkoraamattuun.* Helsinki: Otava, 1946.

MONOGRAPHS AND ARTICLES

Achrenius, Abraham

Ruuth, Martti. *Abraham Achrenius 1–2.* Viipuri, 1907; Porvoo: WSOY, 1921. Reprinted in *SKHST* 17 (1922).

Achrenius, Anders (Antti)

Sainio, Matti. "Antti Achrenius ja 'Halullisten sieluin hengelliset laulut.'" *SKSV* 1947–48 (1949), 27–39.

Suurkari, Vilho. "Antti Achrenius." In *Mikael Agricolasta E. W. Pakkalaan: Suomen kirkon paimenien elämäkerrasto,* ed. Jaakko Haavio. Porvoo: WSOY, 1947, 226–34.

Achrenius, Henrik

Anttila, Veikko. "Henrik ja Simo Achrenius runoilijoina." *KTSV* 13 (1954), 154–72.

Leino, Pentti. "Kieli ja kaava—Henrik Achreniuksen runot." *Virittäjä* 73 (1969), 247–64.

Achrenius, Simo

Anttila, Veikko. "Henrik ja Simo Achrenius runoilijoina." *KTSV* 13 (1954), 154–72.

Tarkiainen, Viljo. "Simo Achrenius: Suomalainen runoilija 17-luvun jälkipuoliskolla." *Historiallinen Arkisto* 47 (1940), 71–88.

Aejmelaeus, Nils

Jokipii, Mauno. *Nils Aejmelaeus: Piirteitä suomalaisen novellin uranuurtajasta.* Helsinki: SKS, 1971.

Agricola, Mikael

Harviainen, Tapani, Simo Heininen, and Aare Huhtala. *Opi nyt vanha ja nuori: Mikael Agricola tänään.* Helsinki: Otava, 1990.

Tarkiainen, Viljo, and Kari Tarkiainen. *Mikael Agricola: Suomen uskonpuhdistaja.* Helsinki: Otava, 1985.

Bång, Petrus

Kajanto, Iiro. *Humanism in a Christian Society. 1: The Attitude to Classical Mythology and Religion in Finland, 1640–1713.* Helsinki: Suomalainen Tiedeakatemia, 1989, 81–83.

Simolin, Johan Albin. *Petrus Bång: En biografisk studie.* Helsingfors: Finska kyrkohistoriska samfundet, 1912.

Bergh, Samuel Gustav (Kallio)
Mäkelä, Hannu. "Samuli Kustaa Berg." In *Suomalaisia kirjailijoita*, ed. Mirjam Polkunen and Auli Viikari. Helsinki: Tammi, 1982, 57–84.
———. *Samuli Kustaa Berg.* Helsinki: Hannu Mäkelä, 1982.
Tarkiainen, Viljo. "Samuli Kustaa Kallio ja hänen runonsa 'Oma maa.'" In Tarkiainen, *Piirteitä suomalaisesta kirjallisuudesta.* Porvoo: WSOY, 1922, 121–36.

Cajanus, Johan (Juhana)
Forsman (Koskimies), Rafael. "Juhana Cajanus, kuoleman runoilija." *Aika* (1920), 340–52.
Rapola, Martti. "Reunamerkintöjä Juhana Cajanuksen virren julkaisuasuihin." In Rapola, *Kielen kuvastimessa: Sana- ja tyylihistoriallisia tutkielmia kirjasuomen aiheista.* Helsinki: WSOY, 1962, 193–206.
Tarkiainen, Viljo. "Juhana Cajanuksen virsi." In Tarkiainen, *Piirteitä suomalaisesta kirjallisuudesta.* Porvoo: WSOY, 1922, 78–95.

Calamnius, Joseph
Virrankoski, Pentti. "'Kuka oli Narvan ilolaulun sepittäjä IGHS?" *Sananjalka* 10 (1968), 37–54.

Castrén, Mathias Alexander
Estlander, Bernard. *Mathias Alexander Castrén: Hans resor och forskningar.* Tampere: Söderström & Co., 1928. Translated under the title *Mathias Alexander Castrén: Hänen matkansa ja tutkimuksensa* (Helsinki: Otava, 1929).

Collan, Fabian
Vasenius, Valfrid. *Fabian Collan: Valda skrifter, med biografi.* Helsingfors: G. W. Edlund, 1872.

Ericus Erici (Sorolainen)
Holmström, Rafael. *Eerikki Eerikinpoika Sorolainen, piispa ja teologi, kansanopettaja ja saarnaaja.* Helsinki: SKHS, 1937 (*SKHST* 39).

Europaeus, D.E.D.
Haltsonen, Sulo. "Pieni Runon-seppä: Tilkkeitä D.E.D. Europaeuksen kirjailijakuvaan." In *Eino Kauppisen juhlakirja.* Tampere: Acta Universitatis Tamperensis A:36 (1970), 23–27.
Kuusi, Matti, Pekka Laaksonen, and Senni Timonen, eds. *D.E.D. Europaeus — Suurmies vai kummajainen.* Helsinki: SKS, 1988.

Finno, Jacobus (Suomalainen)
Juva, Mikko. "Jaakko Finno Rukouskirjansa valossa." *SKHST* 52 (1952), 72–109.

Florinus, Henrik
Kuusi, Matti. "Erasmus Aboensis 1670." *JFF-DL* 22 (1990), 70–73.

Ganander, Christfrid
Hormia, Osmo. *Gananderin sanakirjan lähteet*. Helsinki: SKS, 1961.

Gezelius the Elder, Johannes
Laasonen, Pertti. *Johannes Gezelius vanhempi ja suomalainen täysortodoksia*. Helsinki: SKHS, 1977 (SKHST 103).
Tengström, Johan Jakob. *Biskopen i Åbo stift Johan Gezelii den äldres minne*. Helsingfors: G. O. Wasenius, 1825.

Gezelius the Younger, Johannes
Hyötyniemi, J. E. "Juhana Gezelius nuorempi." In *Mikael Agricolasta E. W. Pakkalaan: Suomen kirkon paimenien elämäkerrasto*, ed. Jaakko Haavio. Porvoo: WSOY, 1947, 115–29.
Tengström, Johan Jakob. *Gezelii den yngres minne*. Helsingfors: G. O. Wasenius, 1833.

Gottlund, Carl Axel
Heikinheimo, Ilmari. *Kaarle Aksel Gottlund: Elämä ja toiminta 1*. Porvoo: WSOY, 1933.
Järv, Harry. "Esipuhe/Efterskrift." In C. A. Gottlund, *Pieniä Runoja Suomen Pojille Ratoxi*. Näköispainos/Faksimilutgåva. Helsinki: Suomalais-Ruotsalainen Kulttuurirahasto/Kulturfonden för Sverige och Finland, 1985, 5–17 (esipuhe), 79–91 (efterskrift).

Granlund, Johan (Juhana) Fredrik
Kohtamäki, Ilmari. "Juhana Fredrik Granlund: Elämä ja kirjalliset sepitelmät." KTSV 4 (1936), 108–211.

Hannikainen, Pietari
Kohtamäki, Ilmari. *Pietari Hannikaisen "Kanava": Uudenaikaisen lehdistömme ladunavaaja*. Helsinki: SKS, 1959.

Hemminki, Maskun
Utrio, Kaari. "A.D. 1616: Kirjailija Suomessa. Maskun Hemminki ja virsikirja." In *Suomalaisia kirjailijoita: Kirjailijat kirjailijoista*, ed. Mirjam Polkunen and Auli Viikari. Helsinki: Tammi, 1982, 18–32.

Juslenius, Daniel
Pietilä, Antti J. *Daniel Juslenius: Hänen elämänsä ja vaikutuksensa 1–2*. Tampere: n.p., 1907; Porvoo: WSOY, 1910.

Juteini, Jaakko (Jakob Judén)
Kähäri, Iris. "Kynäys Maallisen Wiisauden Tohtorin Jaakko Juteinin Muistokirjaan." In *Suomalaisia kirjailijoita: Kirjailijat kirjailijoista*, ed. Mirjam Polkunen and Auli Viikari. Helsinki: Tammi, 1982, 33–56.
Talvi-Oja, Kunno A. *Jaakko Juteini ja hänen kirjallinen toimintansa 1*. Heinola: n.p., 1915.

Tarkiainen, Viljo. "Jaakko Juteinin 'Arvon mekin ansaitsemme.'" In Tarkiainen, *Piirteitä suomalaisesta kirjallisuudesta*. Porvoo: WSOY, 1922, 109–20.

Juusten, Paul
Schmidt, W. A. "Paavali Juusten." In *Mikael Agricolasta E. W. Pakkalaan: Suomen kirkon paimenien elämäkerrasto*, ed. Jaakko Haavio. Porvoo: WSOY, 1947, 13–23.
Simolin, Johan Albin. *Wiborgs stifts historia*. Helsingfors: Aktiebolaget Lilius & Hertzberg, 1909.

Keckman, Carl Niklas
Aßman, Dietrich. "Schweizerisch-finnische Literaturbeziehungen im 19. Jahrhundert." In *Bausteine: Die Schweiz und Finnland im Spiegel ihrer Begegnungen*, ed. Ingrid Schellbach-Kopra and Marianne von Grüningen. Zürich: Neue Züricher Zeitung, 1991, 222–32.

Kellgren, Herman
Castrén, Gunnar. *Herman Kellgren: Ett bidrag till 1840-och 1850 talens kulturliv*. Helsingfors: SLF, 1945.

Korhonen, Paavo
Haavio, Martti. "Paavo Korhosesta, rautalammelaisesta kansanrunoilijasta." *Suomi* 5:2 (1923), 65–119.

Kothen, Casimir von
Lagerborg, Rolf. *Sanningen om Casimir von Kothen*. Helsingfors: Söderström & Co., 1953.

Lagervall, Jakob (Jaakko) Fredrik
Suomalainen, Lauri. *Jaakko Fredrik Lagervall*. Helsinki: SKS, 1903.

Lizelius, Anders (Antti)
Otava, T. K. *Antti Lizelius ja hänen "Suomenkieliset tietosanomansa."* Tampere: SKS, 1931.

Lönnrot, Elias (see also chapter 1)
Anttila, Arne. *Elias Lönnrot: Elämä ja toiminta 1–2*. Helsinki: SKS, 1931–35, 1985.

Missale Aboense
Häkli, Esko. "Books and Bookmakers." BFF (1988), 22–30.
———. "Missale Aboense." BFF (1978), 70–73.
Häkli, Esko, and Friedhilde Krause, eds. *Bibliophilie und Buchgeschichte anlässlich des 500: Jubiläums des Missale Aboense*. Berlin: Deutsche Staatsbibliothek; Helsinki: Universitätsbibliothek, 1988.

Peasant poetry
Kukkonen, Jukka, and Hannes Sihvo, eds. *Wäinämöisen weljenpojat: Tutkielmia talonpoikaisrunoudesta. Kalevalaseuran vuosikirja* 55 (1975).

Piae Cantiones
Lagerborg, Rolf. "Vår äldsta konstdiktning." *FOU* 26 (1906), 57–111.
Norlind, Tobias. *Latinska skolsånger i Sverige och Finland: Lunds universitets årsskrift*, n.s., sec. 1, vol. 5:2 (1909).

Petraeus, Eskil
Perälä, Väinö. *Eskil Petraeus: Turun yliopiston professori ja hiippakunnan piispa, 1593–1657*. Turku: SKHS, 1928 (*SKHST* 25).

Poppius, Abraham
Laurila, Vihtori. "Varhaisin lyyrinen romantikkomme." In Laurila, *Laulu ja rapiat*. Oulu: Pohjoinen, 1968, 106–22.

Porthan, Henrik Gabriel
Kajanto, Iiro. *Porthan and Classical Scholarship: A Study of Classical Influences in Eighteenth-Century Finland*. Helsinki: Suomalainen Tiedeakatemia, 1984.
Klinge, Matti. *Mikä mies Porthan oli?* Helsinki: SKS, 1989.
Koskimies, Rafael. *Porthanin aika*. Helsinki: Otava, 1956.
Schybergson, M. G. *Henrik Gabriel Porthan: En levnadsteckning, 1–2*. Helsingfors: SLF, 1908–11.
Tarkiainen, Viljo. *Henrik Gabriel Porthan*. Helsinki: SKS, 1948.

Salamnius, Mattias
Luojola, Yrjö. "Kristuksen ihmiseksitulo ja pelastusmerkitys Matthias Salamniuksen messiadissa." In Luojola, *Kristus ja ihminen*. Porvoo: WSOY, 1967, 13–20.
Tarkiainen, Viljo. "Suomalainen messiadi." In Tarkiainen, *Piirteitä suomalaisesta kirjallisuudesta*. Porvoo: WSOY, 1922, 60–77.

Schröter, Hans Rudolph von
Kunze, Erich. "Ludwig Uhlands Abhandlung über das deutsche Volkslied und ihr finnisches Vergleichsmaterial." In Kunze, *Deutsch-Finnische Literaturbeziehungen: Beiträge zur Literatur- und Geistesgeschichte*. Helsinki: Universitätsbibliothek Helsinki, 1986, 116–23.

Sjögren, A. J.
Branch, Michael. *A. J. Sjögren: Studies of the North*. Helsinki: SUS, 1973.

Snellman, Johan Vilhelm (see also chapter 7)
Rein, Thiodolf. *Johan Vilhelm Snellman 1–2*. 2d illus. and rev. ed. Helsingfors: Otava, 1904. Translated under the title *Juhana Vilhelm Snellmanin elämä* (Helsinki: Otava, 1904–5). First published 1895–1900; fourth Finnish edition, 1981.
Vest, Eliel. *Johan Vilhelm Snellman: En biografisk studie 1–2*. Helsingfors: G. W. Edlund, 1904–5. Translated under the title *Juhana Vilhelm Snellman: Elämäkerrallinen tutkielma* (Helsinki: G. W. Edlund, 1906).

Tammelinus, Gabriel
Kuusi, Matti. "Erasmus Aboensis 1670." *JFF-DL* 22 (1990), 70–73.

Tengström, Jakob
Anthoni, Eric. *Jakob Tengström och stiftstyrelsen i Åbo stift 1808–1832 1–2*. Helsingfors: Finska kyrkohistoriska samfundet, 1923–28.
Nikander, Gabriel. *Jacob Tengström som akademisk lärare och biskop intill 1808*. Helsingfors: n.p., 1913.
Schybergson, M. G. *Finlands svenska vitterhet. 1: Jakob Tengströms vittra skrifter i urval med en lefnadsteckning*. Helsingfors: SLF, 1899.

Tengström, Robert
Castrén, Gunnar. "Robert Tengström." *FOU* 17 (1903), 22–90.

Tikkanen, Paavo
Hytönen, Viljo. "Paavo Tikkanen." *Suomalaisuuden merkkimiehiä* 2 (1917), 3–55.

Topelius the Edler, Zachris
Hautala, Jouko. *Finnish Folklore Research, 1828–1918*. Helsinki: SSF, 1969.

Warelius, Antero
Ikola, Niilo. "Antero Warelius ja Lönnrotin sanakirjatyö." *Virittäjä* (1929), 7–23.
Kuuliala, Wiljo-Kustaa. "Antero Warelius." In *Mikael Agricolasta E. W. Pakkalaan: Suomen kirkon paimenien elämäkerrasto*, ed. Jaakko Haavio. Porvoo: WSOY, 1947, 443–54.

Wegelius, Johannes
Kansanaho, Erkki. "Johannes Wegelius och hans postilla." *Från bygd och vildmark: Luleå stifts julbok* 49. Luleå: Luleå stift, 1962, 83–89.

CHAPTER 3: THE RISE OF FINNISH-LANGUAGE LITERATURE, 1860–1916

LITERARY HISTORY

Ervasti, Esko. *Suomalainen kirjallisuus ja Nietzsche. 1. 1900-luvun vaihde ja siihen välittömästi liittyvät ilmiöt*. Turku: Turun yliopisto, 1960.
Huhtala, Liisi. *Kuu torpparin aurinko: Torppari-aihe suomalaisessa kaunokirjallisuudessa, 1808–1918*. Helsinki: SKS, 1981.
Koskimies, Rafael. "Dekadenssityyli Suomen kirjallisuudessa." In *Kauko Kyyrön juhlakirja*. Tampere: Acta Universitatis Tamperensis A:18 (1967), 1–21.
Kupiainen, Unto. *"Pienoishuumorin" vuosikymmen suomalaisessa kirjallisuudessa: Humoristinen kirjallisuus Aleksis Kiven ja 1880-luvun realismin välisenä aikana*. Helsinki: SKS, 1939.
Nokkala, Armo. *Tolstoilaisuus Suomessa*. Helsinki: Kirkkohistoriallinen Seura, 1958.
Rantavaara, Irma. "A Nation in Search of Identity: Finnish Literature, 1830–1917." In *Literature and Western Civilization 5: The Modern World. 2: Realities*, ed. David Daiches and Anthony Thorlby. London: Aldus, 1972, 329–61.
Sarajas, Annamari. *Elämän meri: Tutkielmia uusromantiikan kirjallisista aatteista*. Porvoo: WSOY, 1961.
———. *Tunnuskuvia, Suomen ja Venäjän kirjallisen realismin kosketuskohtia*. Porvoo: WSOY, 1968.

———. *Viimeiset romantikot: Kirjallisuuden aatteiden vaihtelua 1880-luvun jälkeen.* Porvoo: WSOY, 1962.

Tarkiainen, Viljo. *Suomalaisen kirjallisuuden historia.* Helsinki: Otava, 1934.

KALEVALA ROMANTICISM AND KARELIANISM

Hirn, Yrjö. "Kalevalaromantiken och Axel Gallen-Kallela jämte några betraktelser över Carelianismen i Finlands kulturliv." In Hirn, *Lärt folk och landstrykare i det finska Finlands kulturliv.* Stockholm: Wahlström & Widstrand, 1939, 189–225.

Sihvo, Hannes. *Karjalan kuva: Karelianismin taustaa ja vaiheita autonomian aikana.* Heksinki: SKS, 1973.

———. *Karjalan löytäjät.* Helsinki: Kirjayhtymä, 1969.

Tanner, Kerttu. *Kalevalainen romantiikka suomalaisessa kirjallisuudessa vuosina, 1890–1910.* Turku: Turun yliopisto, 1960.

SOCIALIST AND WORKERS' LITERATURE

Kalemaa, Kalevi, ed. *Taisteleva kritiikki: Valikoima suomalaista sosialistista kirjallisuuskritiikkiä.* Helsinki: Tammi, 1979.

Karkama, Pertti. *Sosiaalinen konfliktiromaani: Rakennetutkimus suomalaisen yhteiskunnallisen realismen pohjalta.* Helsinki: Tammi, 1971.

Palmgren, Raoul. *Joukkosydän: Vanhan työväenliikkeemme kaunokirjallisuus 1–2.* Porvoo: WSOY, 1966.

———. *Työläiskirjallisuus (proletaarikirjallisuus): Kirjallisuus-ja aatehistoriallinen käsiteselvittely.* Porvoo: WSOY, 1965.

MONOGRAPHS AND ARTICLES

Aho, Juhani (Johannes Brofeldt)

Squire Hellmann and Other Stories. Trans. R. Nisbet Bain. London: T. Fisher Unwin, 1893.

Aho, Antti J. *Juhani Aho: Elämä ja teokset 1–2.* Porvoo: WSOY, 1951.

Castrén, Gunnar. *Juhani Aho 1–2.* Helsingfors: Schildts, 1922.

Alkio, Santeri

Alanen, Aulis J. *Santeri Alkio.* Porvoo: WSOY, 1976.

Asp, Isa

Tuulio, Tyyni. "Isa Asp." In Tuulio, *Fredrikan Suomi: Esseitä viime vuosisadan naisasta.* Porvoo: WSOY, 1979, 179–215.

Canth, Minna

Sanoi Minna Canth: Otteita Minna Canthin teoksista ja kirjeitsä. Pioneer Reformer: Extracts from Minna Canth's Works and Letters. Ed. Ritva Heikkilä, trans. Paul Sjöblom. Porvoo: WSOY, 1987.

Frenckell-Thesleff, Greta von. *Minna Canth och "Det unga Finland."* Helsingfors: Schildts, 1942.

Hagman, Lucina. *Minna Canthin elämäkerta 1–2.* Helsinki: Otava, 1906–11.

Schoolfield, George C. "Minna Canth." In *McGraw-Hill Encyclopedia of World Drama,* ed. Stanley Hochman. New York: McGraw-Hill, 1984, 1:461–63.

Erkko, J. H.
Jukola, Martti. *Juhana Heikki Erkko: Elämä, runoilijatoiminta ja teokset 1–2.* Helsinki: Otava, 1930–39.

Haapasalo, Kreeta
Tuulio, Tyyni. "Kreeta Jaakontytär Haapasalo." In Tuulio, *Fredrikan Suomi: Esseitä viime vuosisadan naisista.* Porvoo: WSOY, 1979, 149–78.

Ivalo, Santeri
Laitinen, Kai. "Santeri Ivalo." In Santeri Ivalo, *Valitut teokset.* Porvoo: WSOY, 1953, v–xviii.
Tarkiainen, Viljo. "Santeri Ivalon *Juho Vesainen.*" In Tarkiainen, *Piirteitä suomalaisesta kirjallisuudesta.* Porvoo: WSOY, 1922, 252–68.

Jännes, Arvi (Arvid Genetz)
Harmaja, Leo, ed. *Arvid Genetz — Arvi Jännes: Elämänvaiheet ja elämäntyö.* Porvoo: WSOY, 1949.

Järnefelt, Arvid
Häkli, Pekka. *Arvid Järnefelt ja hänen lähimaailmansa.* Porvoo: WSOY, 1955.
Kolehmainen, John I. "When Finland's Tolstoy Met His Russian Master." *American Slavic and East European Review* 16 (1957), 534–41.
Kopponen, Tapio. "Arvid Järnefelt 16.11.1861–24.12.1932." In *Arvid Järnefelt 1. Kodin suuret klassikot.* Espoo: Weilin & Göös, 1986, 5–95.
Laitinen, Kai. "A Writer and His Conscience." BFF (1993), 11–13.
Salminen, Johannes. "I Tolstojs fotspår." In Salminen, *Gränsland.* Helsingfors: Söderström & Co., 1984, 35–48.
Sarajas, Annamari. "Arvid Järnefeltin tie kirjailijaksi." In Sarajas, *Orfeus nukkuu: Tutkielmia kirjallisuudesta.* Porvoo: WSOY, 1980, 280–90.

Jalkanen, Huugo
Laitinen, Kai. "Vapaarytmisen runon vaiheita." In Laitinen, *Metsästä kaupunkiin.* Helsinki: Otava, 1984, 289–309.
Viikari, Auli. *Ääneen kirjoitettu: Vapautuvien mittojen varhaisvaiheet suomenkielisessä lyriikassa.* Helsinki: SKS, 1987.

Jotuni, Maria
Niemi, Irmeli. "Dreams of Freedom." BFF (1992), 222–24.
———. "Maria Jotuni: Money, Morals, and Love." BFF (1980), 20–26.
———. *Maria Jotunin näytelmät.* Helsinki: Otava, 1964.
———. "Maria Jotunin pienproosan ääriviivoja." In *Maria Jotuni, Novelleja ja muuta proosaa 1,* ed. Irmeli Niemi. Helsinki: Otava, 1980, 5–14.
Sarajas, Annamari. "*Huojuva talo* — Nykyajan moraliteetti." In Sarajas, *Orfeus nukkuu: Tutkielmia kirjallisuudesta.* Porvoo: WSOY, 1980, 210–19.
———. "Vuosisadan alku Maria Jotunin tuotannossa." In Sarajas, *Orfeus nukkuu,* 280–90.

Schoolfield, George C. "Maria Jotuni." In *McGraw-Hill Encyclopedia of World Drama*, ed. Stanley Hochman. New York: McGraw-Hill, 1984, 3:113-14.

Kallas, Aino
Laitinen, Kai. "Aino Kallas: Ambassador Extraordinary." BFF (1978), 159-63.
——. *Aino Kallas, 1897-1921: Tutkimus hänen tuotantonsa päälinjoista ja taustasta.* Helsinki: Otava, 1973.
——. *Aino Kallaksen maailma: Kuusi tutkielmaa Aino Kallaksen vaiheilta*. Helsinki: Otava, 1978.
Viljanen, Lauri. "Aino Kallaksen Eeden-myytti." In Viljanen, *Ajan ulottuvuudet: Kotimaisen ja yleisen kirjallisuuden tutkielmia*. Porvoo: WSOY, 1974, 44-60.

Kauppis-Heikki (Heikki Kauppinen)
Havu, Ilmari. *Kauppis-Heikki: Elämäkerrallis-kirjallinen tutkimus*. Porvoo: WSOY, 1925.

Kianto, Ilmari
DuBois, Thomas. "A Farmwife's Lot: The Politics of Portrayal in Ilmari Kianto's *Punainen viiva* and *Ryysyrannan Jooseppi*." SS (1993), 521-38.
Kupiainen, Unto. "*Kiannon Punainen viiva* ja *Ryysyrannan Jooseppi* humoristisina teoksina." KTSV 8 (1945), 196-211.
Laurila, Vihtori. *Ilmari Kianto: Kirjailijakuvan piirteitä*. Helsinki: Otava, 1944.
Nevala, Maria-Liisa. *Ilmari Kianto: Anarkisti ja ihmisyyden puolustaja*. Helsinki: SKS, 1986.
Niemi, Juhani. "Kansanrakastaja vai kansanvihollinen: Näkökulmia Ilmari Kiannon Punaiseen viivaan." KTSV 30 (1977), 111-23.

Kiljander, Robert
Lilja, Pekka. "Robert Kiljander—Pikkukaupunkinäytelmän klassikko." In *Robert Kiljander, 1848-1924*, ed. Ritva Loimio and Leena Väisänen. Jyväskylä: Jyväskylän yliopiston kirjaston julkaisuja, 1987, 7-17.
Suomela, Leo. *Dialogens förnyare: En kvantitativ analys av stil och variation hos dramatikerna Minna Canth, Robert Kiljander och Matti Kurikka under 1880-talets finska realism*. Stockholm: Stockholms universitet, 1984.

Kilpi, Volter (see also chapter 4)
Kalliokoski, Jyrki. "Tupa ja sali, pöytä ja ikkuna: Silmäys Ylistalon tupaan." KTSV 38 (1985), 127-37.
Laitinen, Kai. "Volter Kilpis senare produktion." *Horisont* 13 (1966), 1:7-14.
——. "Volter Kilven myöhäistuotanto." In Laitinen, *Metsästä kaupunkiin*. Helsinki: Otava, 1984, 97-123.
Lyytikäinen, Pirjo. *Mielen meri, elämän pidot: Volter Kilven Alastalon salissa*. Helsinki: SKS, 1992.
Suomi, Vilho. "Nuori Volter Kilpi: Vuosisadanvaihteen romantiikko." Ph.D. dissertation, Helsinki University, 1952.
——. "Volter Kilpi." In Kilpi, *Valitut teokset*. Helsinki: Otava, 1954, 6-14.

Tarkka, Pekka. "Volter Kilpi och Elmer Diktonius." NA (1990), 166–70.
Viljanen, Lauri. "Volter Kilpi." OOB 57 (1948), 460–64.

Kivi, Aleksis (Alexis Stenvall)
Heath Cobblers: A Comedy in Five Acts; Kullervo: A Tragedy in Five Acts. Trans. Douglas Robinson. St. Cloud MN: North Star, 1993.
Odes. Trans. Keith Bosley. Helsinki: SKS, 1994.
Seven Brothers. Trans. Alex Matson. Preface by Aino Kallas. London: Faber & Faber; New York: Coward-McCann, 1929.
Seven Brothers: A Novel. Trans. Alex Matson. Helsinki: Tammi, 1959; New York: American-Scandinavian Foundation, 1962.
Seven Brothers: A Novel. Trans. Alex Matson, rev. Irma Rantavaara. Helsinki: Tammi, 1973.
Seven Brothers: A Novel. Trans. Richard A. Impola. New Paltz NY: Finnish American Translators' Association, 1991.
Achté, Kalle, and Rath, F. "Aleksis Kivi: Eine pathographische Studie." Psychiatria Fennica (1975), 39–46.
Barrett, David. "Kullervo: On Not Translating a Tragedy." BFF (1989), 35–38.
Ege, Friedrich. "Das Epos vom finnischen Menschen: Aleksis Kivis Sieben Brüder." In Ege, Kinder der finnischen Oedemark: Zwei literatursoziologische Essays. Karlsruhe: Der Karlsruher Bote, 1972, 7–50.
Ekelund, Erik. Aleksis Kivi. Stockholm: Natur & Kultur, 1960.
Hein, Manfred Peter. Die Kanonisierung eines Romans: Alexis Kivis "Sieben Brüder," 1970–1980. Helsinki: Otava; Stuttgart: Klett-Cotta, 1984.
Kinnunen, Aarne. Aleksis Kiven näytelmä. Porvoo: WSOY, 1967.
Lounela, Pekka. "The Stages of Aleksis Kivi." BFF (1984), 107–12.
Meri, Veijo. "Aleksis Kivi." Excerpt translated in The Nordic Mind: Current Trends in Scandinavian Literary Criticism, ed. Frank Egholm Andersen and John Weinstock. Lanham MD: University Press of America, 1986, 131–42.
———. Aleksis Stenvallin elämä. Helsinki: Otava, 1975.
Mörne, Arvid. Aleksis Kivi och hans roman Seitsemän veljestä. Helsingfors: Ateneum, 1911.
Paddon, Seija. "Aleksis Kivi and the Finnish Georgics." Scandinavian-Canadian Studies (1992), 65–79.
Schoolfield, George C. "Aleksis Kivi." In McGraw-Hill Encyclopedia of World Drama, ed. Stanley Hochman. New York: McGraw-Hill, 1984, 3:158–61.
———. "Aleksis Kivi/Alexis Stenvall." Critical Survey of Drama: Foreign Language Series. Pasadena: Salem Press, 1986, 1058–70.
Tarkiainen, Viljo. Aleksis Kivi: Elämä ja teokset. Porvoo: WSOY, 1915. Often reprinted.
Vähämäki, Börje. "Aleksis Kivi's Kullervo: A Historical Drama of Ideas." SS (1978), 268–91.
Viljanen, Lauri. Aleksis Kiven runomaailma. Porvoo: WSOY, 1953.

Kramsu, Kaarlo
Leino, Pentti. "Kaarlo Kramsun metriikka." KTSV 32 (1980), 7–90.
Niinistö, Maunu. *Kaarlo Kramsu.* Helsinki: SKS, 1971.

Krohn, Julius
Krohn, Helmi. *Isäni Julius Krohn ja hänen sukunsa.* Helsinki: Otava, 1942.
Sarlin, A. J. *Julius Leopold Fredrik Krohn, hänen elämänsä ja toimintansa.* Helsinki: Otava, 1926.

Kuusinen, Otto Wille
Henrikson, Thomas. *Romantik och marxism: Estetik och politik hos Otto Wille Kuusinen och Diktonius till och med 1921.* Helsingfors: Söderström & Co., 1971.
——. "Torpedon och solen: Två revolutionssymboler hos O. W. Kuusinen." In *Festskrift till Olof Enckell 12.3.1970,* ed. P. O. Barck, Johan Wrede, and Ingmar Svedberg. Helsingfors: SLF, 1970, 166–86.

Larin-Kyösti (Kaarlo Kyösti Larsson)
Northern Lights: A Collection of Short Stories. Trans. Alex Matson and Valfrid Hedman. Helsinki: Suomalainen Kirjapaino Osakeyhtiö, 1937.
The Kantele: A Selection of [Larin-Kyösti's] Poems. Trans. E. Howard Harris and Aulis Nopsanen. London: Fortune Press, 1941.
Salokas, Eino. "Larin Kyösti hämäläiskylän runoilijana." KTSV 7 (1943), 231–46.

Lassila, Maiju (Algot Untola)
Huhtula, Liisi. "Maiju Lassila 28.11.1868-21.5.1918." In *Maiju Lassila. Kodin suuret klassikot.* Espoo: Weilin & Göös, 1987, 5–72.
Lindsten, Leo. *Maiju Lassila: Legenda jo eläessään.* Porvoo: WSOY, 1977.
Meri, Veijo. "Ihmeellinen Maiju Lassila." In Meri, *Goethen tammi.* Helsinki: Otava, 1978, 111–16.
Salminen, Johannes. "Maiju Lassila och den röda våren." In Salminen, *Gränsland.* Helsingfors: Söderström & Co., 1984, 49–55.

Lehtonen, Joel
Aalberg, Veikko. "The Suicide of a Finnish Writer: A Psychodynamic Study." *Psychiatria Fennica* (1972), 347–50.
Ege, Friedrich. "Zu Joel Lehtonens Roman *Putkinotko:* Eine literarische Quelle zu den Ursachen des finnischen Bürgerkrieges 1918." In Ege, *Kinder der finnischen Oedemark: Zwei literatursoziologische Studien.* Karlsruhe: Der Karlsruher Bote, 1972, 51–122.
Kivimaa, Arvi. "Joel Lehtonen och Finlands natur i hans skildring." NT, n.s. 13 (1937), 358–66.
Kunnas, Tarmo. "Der Nietzsche-Einfluss bei Joel Lehtonen." *Nerthus* 4 (1979), 87–92.
Meri, Veijo. "Joel Lehtosen rouva Bovary: Joel Lehtosen, Putkinotkon herra, Otava 1969." In Meri, *Kuviteltu kuolema.* Helsinki: Otava, 1974, 105–16.
Suomi, Vilho. "Joel Lehtonen (1881–1934)." OOB 68 (1959), 361–67.

Tarkka, Pekka. "Joel Lehtonen and His Alter Ego." BFF (1981), 140–41.
———. "Joel Lehtonen and Putkinotko." BFF (1977), 239–45.
———. "Joel Lehtonen 27.11.1881-20.11.1934." In *Joel Lehtonen 1*. Kodin suuret klassikot. Espoo: Weilin & Göös, 1986, 5–88.
———. *Putkinotkon tausta: Joel Lehtosen henkilöt, 1901–1923*. Helsinki: Otava, 1977.

Leino, Eino (Eino Lönnbohm)
Moment Musical. Trans. Anna Swan Cutler. Helsinki: Fazer, 1978.
Whitsongs 1. Trans. Keith Bosley. Intro. Michael Branch. London: Menard Press, 1978.
Kunnas [Nevala], Maria-Liisa. *Mielikuvien taistelu: Psykologinen aatetausta Eino Leinon tuotannossa*. Helsinki: SKS, 1972.
Nuorto, Olli. *Eino Leino: Lyhyt johdatus runoilijan elämään ja tuotantoon*. Helsinki: Otava, 1938.
Riikonen, Hannu. "Eino Leino, *Hauptzüge der finnischen Literatur.*" JFF-DL 14 (1980), 136–45.
Sarajas, Annamari. "Eino Leino, 1878–1926." BFF (1978), 40–46.
Tarkiainen, Viljo. *Eino Leinon runoudesta*. Helsinki: Otava, 1954.

Leino, Kasimir (Kasimir Lönnbohm)
Kaukonen, Väinö. *Kasimir Leino runoilijana*. Helsinki: Otava, 1966.

Linnankoski, Johannes (Vihtori Peltonen)
Mäittälä, Leevi. *Elämän tulipunakukka: Vihtori Peltonen—Johannes Linnakoski*. Porvoo: WSOY, 1979.
Söderhjelm, Werner. *Johannes Linnakoski: En finsk diktarprofil*. Helsingfors: Schildts, 1918.

Manninen, Otto
Fromm, Hans. *Otto Manninen: Ein finnischer Dichter*. Baden-Baden: Verlag für Kunst und Wissenschaft, 1952.
Tarkiainen, Viljo. *Otto Manninen runoilijana*. Porvoo: WSOY, 1933.

Oksanen, A. (August Ahlqvist)
Kohtamäki, Ilmari. *Ankara puutarhuri: August Ahlqvist, suomen kielen ja kirjallisuuden arvostelijana*. Helsinki: SKS, 1956.

Onerva, L. (Onerva Lehtinen)
Nevala, Maria-Liisa. "A Life of One's Own: L. Onerva, an Early Feminist Writer." BFF (1984), 32–34.
Nieminen, Reetta. *Elämän punainen paivä: L. Onerva, 1882–1926*. Helsinki: SKS, 1982.

Päivärinta, Pietari
Havu, Ilmari. *Pietari Päivärinta: Kirjallishistoriallinen tutkimus*. Porvoo: WSOY, 1921.

Pakkala, Teuvo
Karkama, Pertti. *Teuvo Pakkalan romaanit: Yhteiskunnallisideologinen tausta ja rakenne.* Oulu: Pohjoinen, 1975.

Pohjanpää, Lauri
Saarenheimo, Kerttu. "Lauri Pohjanpää." *Valvoja* 82 (1962), 272-75.

Salmelainen, Eero
Haltsonen, Sulo. *Eero Salmelainen: Elämäkerrallisia piirteitä.* Tampere: SKS, 1931.

Siljo, Juhani
Kunnas (Nevala), Maria-Liisa. "Juhani Siljon kirjallisuus-ja taidekäsitys." KTSV 28 (1974), 99-134.
Kunnas, Tarmo. "Juhani Siljo et Nietzsche." EFO 15 (1978-79), 217-26.
Kupiainen, Unto. "Juhani Siljon lyriikka." In Juhani Siljo, *Runot.* Porvoo: WSOY, 1947, 5-35.

Soini, Wilho
Alhoniemi, Pirkko. *Idylli särkyy: Kansallisromanttisten ideaalien mureneminen jälkiromantiikan ja realismin kauden kirjallisuudessamme.* Helsinki: SKS, 1972.
Kupiainen, Unto. *"Pienoishuumorin" vuosikymmen suomalaisessa kirjallisuudessa.* Helsinki: SKS, 1939.

Talvio, Maila
Koskenniemi, V. A. *Maila Talvio: Kirjailijakuvan ääriviivoja.* Porvoo: WSOY, 1946.
Suolahti, Eino E. "Maila Talvion helsinkiläisromaanien todellisuustausta." In Suolahti, *Esseitä,* ed. Matti Klinge and Anto Leikola. Porvoo: WSOY, 1981, 145-57.
Tuulio, Tyyni. *Maila Talvion vuosikymmenet. 1: 1871-1911. 2: 1912-1951.* Porvoo: WSOY, 1963, 1965.

Wilkuna, Kyösti
Railo, Eino. *Kyösti Wilkuna ihmisenä, kirjailijana, itsenäisyysmiehenä 1-2.* Helsinki: Kirja, 1930.

CHAPTER 4: THE PERIOD OF INDEPENDENCE I, 1917-1960

LITERARY HISTORY

Kunnas (Nevala), Maria-Liisa. *Kansalaissodan kirjalliset rintamat eli kirjallista keskustelua vuonna 1918.* Helsinki: SKS, 1976.
Kupiainen, Unto. *Suomen lyriikka Juhani Siljosta Kaarlo Sarkiaan.* Porvoo: WSOY, 1948.
Laitinen, Kai. "The Finnish War Novel." WLT (1984), 31-35.
Laitinen, Kai, with Satu Apo and Gun Herranen. *Suomen kirjallisuuden historia.* Helsinki: Otava, 1981.
Lassila, Pertti. *Uuden aikakauden runous: Ekspressionistinen tematiikka 1910- ja 1920-luvun suomenkielisessä lyriikassa.* Helsinki: Otava, 1987.

Nevala, Maria-Liisa. *Muodon vallankumous: Modernismin tulo suomenkieliseen lyriikkaan, 1945–1959*. Helsinki: SKS, 1981.
Niemi, Juhani. *Viime sotien kirjat*. Helsinki: SKS, 1988.
Palmgren, Raoul. *Kapinalliset kynät: Itsenäisyysajan työväenliikkeen kaunokirjallisuus. 1: Kaksi puoluekirjallisuutta ja muotovallankumous (1918–1930). 2: Pulan, fasismin ja sodan varjossa (1930–1944). 3: Rauhan ja edistyksen optimismista kylmään sotaan (1944–1951)*. Porvoo: WSOY, 1983–84.
———. *Kaupunki ja tekniikka Suomen kirjallisuudessa*. Helsinki: SKS, 1989.
Salokannel, Juhani. *Linnasta Saarikoskeen*. Helsinki: WSOY, 1993.
Tarkka, Pekka. "The Roots of the Finnish War Novel." Translated in *The Nordic Mind: Current Trends in Scandinavian Literary Criticism,* ed. Frank Egholm Andersen and John Weinstock. Lanham MD: University Press of America, 1986, 143–52.
———. *Suomalaisia nykykirjailijoita*. Helsinki: Tammi, 1980.
———. *Suomalaisia nykykirjailijoita*. Helsinki: Tammi, 1989.
Viikari, Auli. *Ääneen kirjoitettu: Vapautuvien mittojen varhaisvaiheet suomenkielisessä lyriikassa*. Helsinki: SKS, 1987.
Vuotila, Leo. *Kirjailija ja omatunto: Pekkanen, Linna, Siipainen ja Viita eettisinä kirjailijoina*. Porvoo: WSOY, 1967.
Wrede, Johan. "Om relationer mellan idéer, ideologier och litteratur i repliken Finland." In *Ideas and Ideologies in Scandinavian Literature since the First World War,* ed. Sveinn Skorri Höskuldsson. Reykjavík: University of Iceland Institute of Literary Research, 1975, 19–37.

THE TORCH BEARERS
Marjanen, Kaarlo. *Näkökulma: Tutkistéluja, esseitä, arvosteluja*. Porvoo: WSOY, 1958.
Saarenheimo, Kerttu. *Tulenkantajat: Ryhmän vaiheita ja kirjallisia teemoja 1920–luvulla*. Porvoo: WSOY, 1966.

MONOGRAPHS AND ARTICLES
Anhava, Tuomas
In the Dark Move Slowly: Poems. Trans. Anselm Hollo. London: Cape Goliard, 1969.
Liukkonen, Tero. *Kuultu hiljaisuus: Tuomas Anhavan runoudesta*. Helsinki: SKS, 1993.
Lomas, Herbert. "Tuomas Anhava: Landscapes of the Mind." BFF (1986), 85–89.
Niemi, Juhani. "Tuomas Anhava, kirjailijaprofessori." In Niemi, *Kirjailijoita ja epäkirjailijoita*. Helsinki: SKS, 1983, 57–64.

Haanpää, Pentti
Karonen, Vesa. *Haanpään elämä*. Helsinki: SKS, 1985.
Kinnunen, Aarne. "The Bad and the Ugly in the Writings of Pentti Haanpää." BFF (1984), 174–75.
———. *Haanpään pitkät varjot: Pentti Haanpään kertomataiteesta*. Helsinki: Otava, 1982.

Haavikko, Paavo
Selected Poems. Ed. and trans. Anselm Hollo. London: Cape Goliard, 1968.
Selected Poems. Trans. Anselm Hollo. London: Penguin Books, 1974.
Selected Poems (1959–1988). Trans. Anselm Hollo. Manchester: Carcanet, 1991.
Anhava, Tuomas. "Haavikko ja kritiikki." *Parnasso* (1973), 413–22.
———. "Paavo Haavikko: *Yksityisiä asioita.*" In *Romaani ja tulkinta,* ed. Mirjam Polkunen. Helsinki: Otava, 1973, 1979, 73–93.
Ivask, Ivar, ed. "Homage to Paavo Haavikko." *WLT* (1984), 493–674. Entire issue, with essays, tributes, and translations, devoted to Haavikko and his work.
Kinnunen, Aarne. *Syvä nauru: Tutkimus Paavo Haavikon dramatiikasta.* Helsinki: SKS, 1977.
Paddon, Seija. "John Ashbery and Paavo Haavikko, Architects of the Postmodern Space in Mind and Language." *Canadian Review of Comparative Literature/Revue Canadienne de Littérature Comparée* 20 (1993), 409–16.
Rajala, Panu. "Rauta-aika." *Parnasso* (1982), 233–36.
Salminen, Johannes. "Haavikko och Bysans." In Salminen, *Minnet av Alexandria.* Helsingfors: Söderström & Co., 1988, 128–43.
Schoolfield, George C. "Paavo Haavikko." In *McGraw-Hill Encyclopedia of World Drama,* ed. Stanley Hochman. New York: McGraw-Hill, 1984, 2:439–40.
Tammi, Pekka. "Haavikon tekstit ja subtekstit." *KTSV* 33 (1980), 145–99.

Hämäläinen, Helvi
Haavikko, Ritva, and Helvi Hämäläinen. *Ketunkivellä: Helvi Hämäläisen elämä, 1907–1954.* Helsinki: WSOY, 1993.
Lehtonen, Soila. "Love and War." *BFF* (1993), 244–50.
Siltala, Pirkko. "Naisen luovuus elämänprosessissa." In *Luovuuden ulottuvuudet,* ed. Ritva Haavikko and Jan-Erik Ruth. Espoo: Weilin & Göös, 1984, 61–87.
Valkonen, Kaija. "Helvi Hämäläinen: Poet of the Senses." *BFF* (1988), 81–83.

Harmaja, Saima
Helakisa, Kaarina. *Saima Harmaja: Legenda jo eläessään.* Porvoo: WSOY, 1977.
Lehtonen, Maija. "Saima Harmaja—Nuoruuden runoilija." *Parnasso* (1959), 4–11.

Heikkilä, Lasse
Hamberg, Lars. "Två franska finnar." *FT* (1957), 303–8.
Tarkka, Pekka. "Lasse Heikkilä." In Tarkka, *Suomalaisia nykykirjailijoita,* 2d ed. Helsinki: Tammi, 1967, 35–37.

Hellaakoski, Aaro
Kantola, Kaisa. *Olen, enkä ole: Minuus ja oleminen Aaro Hellaakosken runoudessa.* Porvoo: WSOY, 1972.
Kupiainen, Unto. *Aaro Hellaakoski: Ihminen ja runoilija.* Porvoo: WSOY, 1953.
Laitinen, Kai. "Nature and Love—The Poems of Aaro Hellaakoski." *BFF* (1986), 68–69.

Holappa, Pentti
Niemi, Juhani. "Pentti Holappa, kirjallinen sabotööri." In Niemi, *Kirjailijoita ja epäkirjailijoita*. Helsinki: SKS, 1983, 30–38.

Huovinen, Veikko
Tale of the Forest Folk. Trans. Tim Steffa. Helsinki: Otava, 1994.
Karonen, Vesa. "Veikko Huovinen: Satirist of the Forest." BFF (1987), 154–56.
Niemi, Juhani. "Veikko Huovinen, naurulintu." In Niemi, *Kirjailijoita ja epäkirjailijoita*. Helsinki: SKS, 1983, 21–29.

Hyry, Antti
Mäkelä, Matti. "Antti Hyry—Lestadiolainen modernisti." *Parnasso* (1979), 167–69.
Salokannel, Juhani. "Kertoja Antti Hyryn teoksissa." KSV 27 (1973), 131–43.
Tyyri, Jouko. "Antti Hyry: *Kotona.*" In *Romaani ja tulkinta*, ed. Mirjam Polkunen. Helsinki: Otava, 1973, 1979, 94–101.
Viikari, Auli. "Hyryä lukiessa 1–2." *Parnasso* (1976), 265–74, 473–85.
Viksten, Vilho. "Antti Hyry: *Maantieltä hän lähti.*" In *Novelli ja tulkinta*, ed. Mirjam Polkunen and Pekka Tarkka. Helsinki: Weilin & Göös, 1969, 248–54.

Joenpelto, Eeva
Koskimies, Rafael. "Eeva Joenpelto." BFF (1977), 3:176–84.
Laitinen, Kai. "Eeva Joenpelto and Her Lohja Trilogy." WLT (1980), 33–37.
———. "Elämän saumakohdassa: Eeva Joenpellon Lohja-sarja." In Laitinen, *Metsästä kaupunkiin: Esseitä ja tutkielmia kirjallisuudesta*. Helsinki: Otava, 1984, 229–42.
Lehtola, Erkka. "Eeva Joenpelto: Portraits of Change." BFF (1987), 1:25–28.
Niiniluoto, Marja. "A Literary Portrait: Eeva Joenpelto." BFF (1969), 2:8–9.

Juvonen, Helvi
Kilpi, Mikko. "Helvi Juvonen, uudistuvan lyriikkamme klassikko." In Helvi Juvonen, *Kootut runot*. Porvoo: WSOY, 1960, v–xiv.
Lehtonen, Soila. "Images of Isolation." BFF (1992), 17–23.
Luojola, Yrjö. "Helvi Juvonen kärsimyksen runoilijana." In Luojola, *Kristus ja ihminen*. Porvoo: WSOY, 1967, 70–81.

Jylhä, Yrjö
Kare, Kauko. *Yrjö Jylhä: Runoilijan- ja soturinkohtalo*. Helsinki: Otava, 1957.
Viljanen, Lauri. "Yrjö Jylhän daimoni." In Viljanen, *Lyyrillinen minä ja muita kirjallisuustutkielmia*. Porvoo: WSOY, 1959, 103–13.

Kailas, Uuno
Lounela, Pekka. "Uuno Kailas: Runoilijan tahto." In *Suomalaisia kirjailijoita: Kirjailijat kirjailijoista*, ed. Mirjam Polkunen and Auli Viikari. Helsinki: Tammi, 1982, 227–44.
Niinistö, Maunu. *Uuno Kailas: Hänen elämänsä ja hänen runoutensa*. Porvoo: WSOY, 1956.

Viljanen, Lauri. "Uuno Kailas, eurooppalainen runoilija." In Viljanen, *Ajan ulottuvuudet: Kotimaisen ja yleisen kirjallisuuden tutkielmia.* Porvoo: WSOY, 1974, 9–16.

Kajava, Viljo
Kankaanpää, Hannu. "Viljo Kajavas diktning genom fem decennier." NA (1981), 179–82.
Laitinen, Kai. "Viljo Kajavan runouden murros." In Laitinen, *Metsästä kaupunkiin: Esseitä ja tutkielmia kirjallisuudesta.* Helsinki: Otava, 1984, 183–206. Previously published in *Rivien takaa: Nykykirjallisuuden tutkimusta kirjailijahaastattelujen pohjalta,* ed. Ritva Haavikko (Vaasa: SKS, 1976), 69–92.
Nummi, Lassi. "Literary Portrait: Viljo Kajava." BFF (1969), 4:8–10.

Kianto, Ilmari (see also chapter 3)
Nevala, Maria-Liisa. *Ilmari Kianto: Anarkisti ja ihmisyyden puolustaja.* Helsinki: SKS, 1986.

Kilpi, Volter (see also chapter 3)
Hellaakoski, Aaro. "Eräs kirjallisuutemme monumentaaliteos." *Suomalainen Suomi* 1937, 19–26. Reprinted in Hellaakoski, *Kuuntelua: Esseitä teoksista ja tekijöistä.* Porvoo: WSOY, 1950.

Kivikkaho, Eila
Polkunen, Mirjam. "Jälkilause." In Eila Kivikkaho, *Kootut runot.* Helsinki: WSOY, 1975, 387–430.

Korpela, Jorma
Laitinen, Kai. "Merkintöjä Jorma Korpelan henkilötyypeistä ja eräistä peruskuvioista." In Laitinen, *Metsästä kaupunkiin: Esseitä ja tutkielmia kirjallisuudesta.* Helsinki: Otava, 1984, 217–28.
Sarajas, Annamari. "Ivan vai Aljoša? Jorma Korpelan romaaneista." In Sarajas, *Orfeus nukkuu: Tutkielmia kirjallisuudesta.* Porvoo: WSOY, 1980, 57–77.
Vainio, Matti. "Jorma Korpela: Tohtori Finckelman." In *Romaani ja tulkinta,* ed. Mirjam Polkunen. Helsinki: Otava, 1973, 1979, 31–43.

Koskenniemi, V. A.
Krohn, Eino. "V. A. Koskenniemen aforismien maailmankuvaa." In Krohn, *Kaksi lukittua lipasta: Tutkielmia kirjallisuuden ja estetiikan alueilta.* Helsinki: WSOY, 1961, 22–27.
Luojola, Yrjö. *V. A. Koskenniemen totuudenetsijä-motiivi.* Porvoo: WSOY, 1962.
Mattila, Pekka. "Aforismi V. A. Koskenniemen modernina ilmaisulajina." KTSV 18 (1960), 221–34.
———. *V. A. Koskenniemi lyyrillisenä taiteilijana: Tutkimus hänen symbooleistaan, kielestään ja rytmistään.* Porvoo: WSOY, 1954.
Salminen, Johannes. "Stålets kalla doft." In Salminen, *Gränsland.* Helsingfors: Söderström & Co., 1984, 121–37.

Siltala, Touko, ed. *Kurkiauran varjo: Esseitä V. A. Koskenniemestä*. Helsinki: WSOY, 1985.

Linna, Väinö

Boström, Tage. *Okänd soldat och kända soldater: Beteenden, attityder och struktur in Väinö Linnas krigsroman*. Umeå: Umeå Studies in the Humanities 52 (1983).
Klinge, Matti. "Suomen kansallisromaani." In Klinge, *Suomen sinivalkoiset värit*. Helsinki: Otava, 1981, 280–89.
Laitinen, Kai. "Väinö Linna and Veijo Meri: Two Aspects of War." BA (WLT) (1962), 365–67.
Matson, Alex. "Väinö Linna: *Täällä Pohjantähden alla*." In *Romaani ja tulkinta*, ed. Mirjam Polkunen. Helsinki: Otava, 1973, 1979, 58–69.
Niemi, Juhani. "Many Unknown Soldiers." *Film in Finland* (1985), 36–39.
Nummi, Jyrki. *Jalon kansan parhaat voimat: kansalliset kuvat ja Väinö Linnan romaanit Tuntematon sotilas ja Täällä Pohjantähden alla*. Porvoo: WSOY, 1993.
——. "What Do the People Sing? Singing in Väinö Linna's Novel, *The Unknown Soldier.*" In *FU SAC '88: Proceedings of the Sixth Annual Meeting of the Finno-Ugric Studies Association of Canada*, ed. Joel Navis. Lanham MD: University Press of America, 1989, 9–22.
Stormbom, N.-B. *Väinö Linna*. Helsingfors: Schildts, 1964.
Varpio, Yrjö. *Pentinkulma ja maailma: Tutkimus Väinö Linnan teosten kääntämisestä, julkaisemisesta ja vastaanotosta ulkomailla*. Porvoo: WSOY, 1979.

Manner, Eeva-Liisa

Fog Horses. Trans. Ritva Poom. Merrick NY: Cross-Cultural Communications, 1986.
Selected Poems. Trans. Herbert Lomas. Guildford U.K.: Making Waves, 1996.
Aaltonen, Anja. "Hamletin uudet hahmot." KTSV 42 (1988), 89–140. On *Hamlet* translations by Lauri Sipari, Manner, and Veijo Meri.
Ahokas, Jaakko. "Eeva Liisa Manner: Dropping from Reality into Life." BA (WLT) (1973), 60–65.
Elovaara, Raili. "Spinoza and Finnish Literature." *Studia Spinoziana* 5 (1989), 59–79.
Hökkä, Tuula. "Silence and the Void." BFF (1992), 135–38.
Tuohimaa, Sinikka. "Language of Silence: A Feminist Analysis of Eeva-Liisa Manner's Play, *Burnt Orange.*" In *Center and Periphery in Representations and Institutions*, ed. Eero Tarasti, Paul Torsell, and Richard Littlefield. Imatra: International Semiotics Institute, 1992, 323–31.
——. "The Poetry of Eeva-Liisa Manner—Unveiling Reflections of Life." WLT (1987), 37–40.
Tuurna, Marju. "Kiinalainen Manner." KTSV 21 (1965), 92–105.

Mannerkorpi, Juha

Kinnunen, Aarne. "Juha Mannerkorpi and the Metamorphosis of the Self: An Extract from *Sudenkorento* translated by Aili and Austin Flint." BFF (1982), 58–65.

Makkonen, Anna. "Avaimia Juha Mannerkorven *Avaimeen:* Raamatusta, intertekstuaalisuudesta, tulkinnasta." KTSV 40 (1986), 63–82.
———. "Babel and Gethsemane: Biblical Myths in 'The Key' by Juha Mannerkorpi." SS (1986), 37–47.
Mikkola, Marja-Leena. "Juha Mannerkorpi ja novelli." In *Suomalaisia kirjailijoita: Kirjailijat kirjailijoista,* ed. Mirjam Polkunen and Auli Viikari. Helsinki: Tammi, 1982, 297–306.
Pennanen, Eila. "Juha Mannerkorpi: *Jälkikuva.*" In *Romaani ja tulkinta,* ed. Mirjam Polkunen. Helsinki: Otava, 1973, 1979, 139–48.

Meri, Veijo
Alhoniemi, Pirkko. "Veijo Meren *Peiliin piirretty nainen.*" *Sanajalka* 9 (1967), 188–97. With German summary.
Envall, Markku. "Veijo Meri: Alamaisen tajunnanvirtaa." In Envall, *Kirjailijoiden kentät ja kasarmit: Varusmieselämän kuvaukset Suomen kirjallisuudessa.* Helsinki: SKS, 1984, 73–76.
Flint, Austin. "Death of a Poet." BFF (1989), 212–26.
Hallikainen, Pertti. "Sankari karannut—Vilauksia Veijo Meren henkilöistä." KTSV 24 (1969), 178–98.
Karonen, Vesa. "Veijo Meren karkurit." KTSV 27 (1973), 20–30.
———. "Veijo Meri: *Manillaköysi.*" In *Romaani ja tulkinta,* ed. Mirjam Polkunen. Helsinki: Otava, 1973, 1979, 44–57.
———. "Veijo Meri: *Tappaja.*" In *Novelli ja tulkinta,* ed. Mirjam Polkunen and Pekka Tarkka. Helsinki: Weilin & Göös, 1969, 223–41.
Schoolfield, George C. "Veijo Meri." In *McGraw-Hill Encyclopedia of World Drama,* ed. Stanley Hochman. New York: McGraw-Hill, 1984, 3:373–74.
Stormbom, N.-B. "Veijo Meri and the New Finnish Novel." SR (ASR) 55 (1967), 264–69.

Meriluoto, Aila
Statues of Fire: The Collected Early Poetry. Trans. Leo Vuosela and Steve Stone. New Paltz NY: Marathon Press and Finnish-American Translators' Association, 1993.
Laitinen, Kai. "Aila Meriluoto: A Poet's Perspective." BFF (1986), 217–18.
Toivonen, Pirjo-Maija. *Aila Meriluodon varhaislyriikan modernismi ja sen tausta.* Jyväskylä: Jyväskylän yliopisto, 1986.

Mustapää, P. (Martti Haavio)
Ahokas, Jaakko A. "No Serious Songs: P. Mustapää, Poet and Professor." WLT 54 (1980), 38–40.
Laitinen, Kai. "P. Mustapään lyriikasta." In P. Mustapää, *Kootut runot.* Helsinki: WSOY, 1948, 5–51.
Larmola, Maija. "Läkkiseppä Lindblad, oppinut herra ja P. Mustapää." In *Rivien takaa: Nykykirjallisuuden tutkimusta kirjailijahaastattelujen pohjalta,* ed. Ritva Haavikko. Vaasa: SKS, 1976, 93–119.

Nieminen, Pertti
Launonen, Hannu. "Sävelet suussa, silmissä maailman maisemat: Pertti Niemisen lyriikasta." *Parnasso* (1979), 218–24.

Nummi, Lassi
Alanko, Anna-Liisa. "Minä ja maisema: Lassi Nummen runoudesta." *Virke* (1985), 6, 5–11.
Kinnunen, Aarne. "Nummen maisema." *Parnasso* (1981), 8:517–19.
Tyyri, Jouko. "Lassi Nummi." BFF (1979), 8–11.

Olli (Väinö Nuorteva)
Kivimaa, Arvi. "Suomen vaatimattomin nero." In Kivimaa, *Kasvoja valohämystä*. Helsinki: Otava, 1974, 101–4.

Paavolainen, Olavi
Kurjensaari, Matti. *Loistava Olavi Paavolainen*. Helsinki: Tammi, 1975.
Laitinen, Kai. "Olavi Paavolainen." In Paavolainen, *Valitut teokset 1*. Helsinki: Otava, 1961.
Paavolainen, Jaakko. *Olavi Paavolainen: keulakuva*. Helsinki: Tammi, 1991.
Salminen, Johannes. "Den kluvne Olavi Paavolainen." In Salminen, *Gränsland*. Helsingfors: Söderström & Co., 1984, 109–20.

Pekkanen, Toivo
Ahti, Keijo. *Toivo Pekkasen kirjailijantie. 1: Kehitys vuoteen 1941*. Porvoo: WSOY, 1968.
Kupiainen, Unto. *Toivo Pekkanen runoilijana*. Helsinki: Pellervo-Seura, 1955.
Warburton, Thomas. "Introduction." In Toivo Pekkanen, *My Childhood*. Madison: University of Wisconsin Press, 1966, vii–xvii.

Pennanen, Eila
Niemi, Juhani. "Eila Pennanen: *Mutta*." In *Romaani ja tulkinta*, ed. Mirjam Polkunen. Helsinki: Otava, 1973, 1979, 102–11.
Tarkka, Pekka. "Eila Pennanen — Reality versus Morality." BFF (1982), 94–97.

Rekola, Mirkka
Envall, Markku. *Suomalainen aforismi*. Helsinki: SKS, 1987.

Rintala, Paavo
Kytöhonka, Arto. "Paavo Rintala: *Sotilaiden äänet*." In *Romaani ja tulkinta*, ed. Mirjam Polkunen. Helsinki: Otava, 1973, 1979, 149–64.
Tarkka, Pekka. *Paavo Rintalan saarna ja seurakunta*. Helsinki: Otava, 1966. Translated under the title *En roman [Sissiluutnantti] och dess publik* (Stockholm: Bonniers, 1970).

Saastamoinen, Tyyne
Hamberg, Lars. "Två franska finnar." FT (1957), 303–8.
Tarkka, Pekka. "Tyyne Saastamoinen." In Tarkka, *Suomalaisia nykykirjailijoita*, 2d ed. Helsinki: Tammi, 1967, 132–33.

Sarkia, Kaarlo
Hiisku, Aune. *Kaarlo Sarkia, uneksija — kilvoittelija.* Porvoo: WSOY, 1972.
Viljanen, Lauri. "Kaarlo Sarkia lapsuuden runoilijana." *Parnasso* (1952), 96–103. Reprinted in Viljanen, *Lyyrillinen minä,* Porvoo: WSOY, 1959, 114–25.

Sillanpää, F. E.
Kinneavy, Gerald. "Sillanpää." SCAN (1981), 205–12.
Laitinen, Kai. "F. E. Sillanpää: Life and Sun, the Writer and His Time." BFF (1988), 102–7.
——. "The Legacy of Sillanpää." JFS (1997), 25–33.
Orton, Gavin. "F. E. Sillanpää's *Människor i sommarnatten:* A Musical Suite." *Edda* 92 (1992), 147–58.
Paddon, Seija. "The De-centred Subject in F. E. Sillanpää's Short Fiction." SCAN (1990), 207–13.
Rajala, Panu. *F. E. Sillanpää vuosina 1888–1923.* Helsinki: SKS, 1983.
——. *Siljan synty: F. E. Sillanpää vuosina 1923–1931.* Helsinki: SKS, 1988.
——. *Korkea päivä ja ehtoo: F. E. Sillanpää vuosina 1931–1964.* Helsinki: SKS, 1993.
Tarkka, Pekka. "The Nobel Pursuit." BFF (1988), 108–10.
Vaaskivi, Tatu. *F. E. Sillanpää, elämä ja teokset.* Helsinki: Otava, 1937.
Warburton, Thomas. "Introduction." In F. E. Sillanpää, *People in the Summer Night.* Madison: University of Wisconsin Press, 1966, vii–xiii.

Tapio, Marko
Fried, Ann. *Marko Tapio.* Porvoo: WSOY, 1975.
Makkonen, Anna. "Romaani alkaa siitä: Marko Tapiosta." *Parnasso* (1985), 83–92.
——. *Romaani katsoo peiliin: Mise en abyme-rakenteet ja tekstienvälisyys Marko Tapion Aapo Heikasen viikatetanssissi.* Helsinki: SKS, 1991.
Sarajas, Annamari. "Itkevä Klovni. Marko Tapion romaani." In Sarajas, *Orfeus nukkuu: Tutkielmia kirjallisuudesta.* Porvoo: WSOY, 1980, 121–29.

Turtiainen, Arvo
Karonen, Vesa. "Arvo Turtiaisen tie 30-luvun pilven alta." In *Rivien takaa: Nykykirjallisuuden tutkimusta kirjailijahaastattelujen pohjalta,* ed. Ritva Haavikko. Vaasa: SKS, 1976, 164–80.

Tynni, Aale
Alhoniemi, Alho. "Aale Tynni." *Suomen kirjallisuus* 6 (1967), 417–21.
Oinonen, Yrjö. "Aale Tynni: Runoilijakuva." KTSV (1946), 118–37.
Rainio, Ritva (Haavikko, Ritva), ed. *Miten kirjani ovat syntyneet.* Helsinki: WSOY, 1969, 23–32.
Sala, Kaarina. "Maan sydän — Aale Tynnin runouden tavoitteista ja ilmaisukeinoista." In *Rivien takaa: Nykykirjallisuuden tutkimusta kirjailijahaastattelujen pohjalta,* ed. Ritva Haavikko. Vaasa: SKS, 1976, 209–27.

Uurto, Iris
Laurila, Aarne. "Iris Uurto." *Suomen kirjallisuus* 5 (1965), 535–41.

Vaara, Elina
Viljanen, Lauri. "Elina Vaara eli uni ja todellisuus." In Viljanen, *Lyyrillinen minä ja muita kirjallisuustutkielmia*. Porvoo: WSOY, 1959, 77–89.

Vaaskivi, T.
Barck, P. O. "Ett ungt geni." In Barck, *Ansikten och möten*. Helsingfors: Söderström & Co., 1972, 214–21.
Lybäck, Holger. *T. Vaaskivi, ihminen ja kirjailija*. Porvoo: WSOY, 1950.
Salminen, Johannes. "Cairo-Capri-Istanbul." In Salminen, *Gränsland*. Helsingfors: Söderström & Co., 1984, 93–107.

Vala, Katri
Paavolainen, Olavi, ed. *Katri Vala — Tulipatsas*. Porvoo: WSOY, 1946.
Saarenheimo, Kerttu. *Katri Vala: Aikansa kapinallinen*. Porvoo: WSOY, 1984.
———. "Katri Valan lyriikan kolme maisemallista kiinnekohtaa." In *Rivien takaa: Nykykirjallisuuden tutkimusta kirjailijahaastattelujen pohjalta*, ed. Ritva Haavikko. Vaasa: SKS, 1976, 120–29.

Vartio, Marja-Liisa
Alhoniemi, Pirkko. "Marja-Liisa Vartio: Concrete Dreams." BFF (1986), 136–38.
———. "Marja-Liisa Vartio: *Hänen olivat linnut*." In *Romaani ja tulkinta*, ed. Mirjam Polkunen. Helsinki: Otava, 1973, 1979, 165–79.
———. "Marja-Liisa Vartion *Kaikki naiset näkevät unia* ja Paavo Haavikon *Toinen taivas ja maa rinnakkain*." KTSV 26 (1972), 9–23.
Särkilahti, Sirkka-Liisa. *Marja-Liisa Vartion kertomataide*. Tampere: Acta Universitatis Tamperensis Ser. A, 48 (1973).

Viita, Lauri
Kaasalainen, Marjukka. "Lauri Viita runoilijana." In Lauri Viita, *Kootut runot*. Helsinki: WSOY, 1966, vii–xliv.
Laitinen, Kai. "Lauri Viita: *Moreeni*." In *Romaani ja tulkinta*, ed. Mirjam Polkunen. Helsinki: Otava, 1973, 1979, 18–30.
———. "Lauri Viita, Builder of Words." BFF (1988), 208–10.
Meriluoto, Aila. "Lauri Viita: A Big Man from a Small Village." BFF (1988), 219–23.
Varpio, Yrjö. *Lauri Viita: Kirjailija ja hänen maailmansa*. Porvoo: WSOY, 1973.

Viljanen, Lauri
Viljanen, Aulimaija. "Maisema sieluntilana — Lauri Viljanen runouden näkymiä." In *Rivien takaa: Nykykirjallisuuden tutkimusta kirjailijahaastattelujen pohjalta*, ed. Ritva Haavikko. Vaasa: SKS, 1976, 130–47.

Vuorela, Einar
Erho, Elsa. "Einar Vuorela." In *Suomen kirjallisuus* 6 (1967), 138–46.

Waltari, Mika
Envall, Markku. *Suuri illusionisti: Mika Waltarin romaanit*. Porvoo: WSOY, 1994.
Haavikko, Ritva, ed. *Mika Waltari — Mielikuvituksen jättiläinen*. Porvoo: WSOY, 1982.

Vallinkoski, Jorma, and A. Juurinen. *Mika Waltari ulkomailla/Mika Waltari Abroad: Käännösten bibliografia.* HYKJ 40 (1978).

Wuolijoki, Hella

Ammondt, Jukka. *Niskavuoren talosta Juurakon torppaan.* Jyväskylä: Jyväskylä Studies in the Arts, 1980.

Deschner, Margareta Neovius. "Wuolijoki's and Brecht's Politicization of the Volksstück." In *Bertolt Brecht: Political Theory and Literary Practice,* ed. S. N. Weber and Hubert Heinen. Athens: University of Georgia Press, 1980, 115-28.

Lounela, Pekka. *Hella Wuolijoki: Legenda jo eläessään.* Porvoo: WSOY, 1979.

———. "Hella Wuolijoki (1886-1954): A Woman of Contrasts." BFF (1979), 120-29.

Schoolfield, George C. "Hella Wuolijoki." In *McGraw-Hill Encyclopedia of World Drama,* ed. Stanley Hochman. New York: McGraw-Hill, 1984, 5:173-74.

CHAPTER 5: THE PERIOD OF INDEPENDENCE 2, 1960-1990

LITERARY HISTORY

Andersson, Claes. "Disillusions: The Problems of Evil in New Finnish Writing." BFF (1987), 80-83.

Envall, Markku. "The Aphorism Reborn: Mirkka Rekola, Samuli Paronen, Paavo Haavikko, Erno Paasilinna." BFF (1986), 229-34.

Laitinen, Kai, with Satu Apo and Gun Herranen. *Suomen kirjallisuuden historia.* Helsinki: Otava, 1981.

Lassila, Pertti. "Zwischen globalem Bewusstsein und regionalem Idyll: Zur finnischen Literatur der siebziger Jahre." In *Der nahe Norden: Otto Oberholzer zum 65. Geburtstag,* ed. Wolfgang Butt and Bernhard Glienke. Frankfurt am Main: Peter Lang, 1985, 307-22.

Launonen, Hannu. *Suomalaisen runon struktuurianalyysia.* Helsinki: SKS, 1984.

Mäkelä, Matti. "The Great Move in Finnish Literature in the 1960s and 1970s." BFF (1987), 36-38.

———. *Suuri muutto: 1960-1970-lukujen suomalaisen proosan kuvaamana.* Helsinki: Otava, 1986.

Simonsuuri, Kirsti. "From Orality to Modernity: Aspects of Finnish Poetry in the Twentieth Century." WLT (1989), 52-54.

Tarkka, Pekka. *Suomalaisia nykykirjailijoita.* Helsinki: Tammi, 1980.

———. *Suomalaisia nykykirjailijoita.* Helsinki: Tammi, 1989.

MONOGRAPHS AND ARTICLES

Ahti, Risto

Narcissus in Winter. Trans. Herbert Lomas. Guildford U.K.: Making Waves, 1994.

Poems. Trans. Herbert Lomas. London: Ambit, 1994.

Tarkka, Pekka. "Ahti lähteellä (Risto Ahti: *Narkissos talvella*)." In Tarkka, *Sanat sanoista: Arvosteluja ja kirjoituksia, 1957-1984.* Helsinki: Otava, 1984, 274-76.

Anhava, Helena
Rekunen, Eilo. "Aforismin kolme tunnusmerkkiä." *Kanava* (1977), 182–84.

Envall, Markku
Lehtola, Erkka. "Mirrors of Madness." BFF (1990), 3–5.
Schellbach-Kopra, Ingrid. "Markku Envall und sein preisgekröntes Werk." JFF-DL 22 (1990), 25–26.

Idström, Annika
Ahola, Suvi. "Real Lives." BFF (1990), 20–22.
Korsström, Tuva. "Annika Idström." In Korsström, *Berättelsernas återkomst*. Helsingfors: Söderström & Co., 1994, 73–96.

Jäntti, Mariaana
Malmio, Kristina. "Amorfiaana — ett kalajdoskop: Kropp / språk / kropp / text / kropp / kvinna / kanon." *Horisont* 39 (1992), 5:51–60.

Jalonen, Olli
Huotari, Markku. "Olli Jalonen, Chilly Climates: An Interview." BFF (1984), 75–77.
Korsström, Tuva. "Olli Jalonen." In Korsström, *Berättelsernas återkomst*. Helsingfors: Söderström & Co., 1994, 259–74.

Joenpolvi, Martti
Lomas, Matti. "Martti Joenpolvi: Lucky to Die Unborn." BFF (1979), 152–56.
Seppälä, Arto. "Martti Joenpolvi: Life and the Short Story Writer." BFF (1986), 77–78.
Tarkka, Pekka. "Novellin mestaruutta (Martti Joenpolvi, *Kauan kukkineet omenapuut*)." In Tarkka, *Sanat sanoista*. Helsinki: Otava, 1984, 271–73.

Kaila, Tiina
Korsström, Tuva. "The Living and the Dead." BFF (1995), 12–17.

Kaipainen, Anu
Polkunen, Mirjam. "Anu Kaipainen: *Magdaleena ja maailman lapset.*" In *Romaani ja tulkinta*, ed. Mirjam Polkunen. Helsinki: Otava, 1973, 1979, 180–88.

Katz, Daniel
Korsström, Tuva. "Full Circle." BFF (1993), 122–23.
Tarkka, Pekka. "Daniel Katz." BFF (1980), 146–47.

Kauranen, Anja
Ahola, Suvi. "The Personal IS Real." BFF (1994), 55–56.

Kilpi, Eeva
Dana, Kathleen Osgood. "Eeva Kilpi: Writer, Woman, Karelian, Finn." WLT (1985), 354–57.
Deschner, Margareta Neovius. "Eeva Kilpi: Home and Solitude." BFF (1984), 118–19.

Kirstinä, Väinö
Niemi, Juhani. "Väinö Kirstinä: Kielipelien runoilija." In Niemi, *Kirjailijoita ja epäkirjailijoita*. Helsinki: SKS, 1983, 73–80.

Krohn, Leena
The Eyes of the Fingertips Are Opening. Trans. Herbert Lomas. Helsinki: Musta taide, 1993.
Lehtonen, Soila. "Contradictory Logic." BFF (1991), 138–40.
——. "Leena Krohn: Strange and Familiar." BFF (1986), 23–24.

Kylätasku, Jussi
Mary Bloom. Trans. Tim Steffa. In *Drama Contemporary: Scandinavia*, ed. Per Brask. New York: PAJ, 1989, 175–213.
Rajala, Panu. "Jussi Kylätasku, näytelmäkirjailija." *Parnasso* (1981), 104–7.
Rønning, Helge. "Kylätasku — En finsk dramatiker." *Samtiden* (1981), 5, 38–40.
Vainio, Väinö. "Mary Bloom — A Modern Mystery Play." BFF (1983), 134–36.

Lahtela, Markku
Salokannel, Juhani. "Unusual Men — Three Masters of Contemporary Finnish Prose." WLT (1980), 24–27.

Laine, Jarkko
Niemi, Juhani. "Jarkko Laine, sukupolvensa tulkki." In Niemi, *Kirjailijoita ja epäkirjailijoita*. Helsinki: SKS, 1983, 132–39.
Nikula, Karl Henrik. "Åbos Buffalo Bill." *Horisont* (1971), 1, 50–52.

Liehu, Rakel
Cubisms. Trans. Seija Paddon. Toronto: Exile, 1994.
Krogerus, Tellervo. "Rakel Liehu." In *Suomalaisia kirjailijakuvia*, ed. Liisa Enwald. Helsinki: Kirjaryhtymä, 1987, 181–84.

Liksom, Rosa (Anni Ylävaara)
One Night Stands. Trans. Anselm Hollo. London: Serpent's Tail, 1993.
Salmela, Pia. "Bild och berättelse: Rosa Liksoms noveller." FT (1988), 128–34.
Tarkka, Pekka. "Rosa Liksom: Too Much or Too Little Love." BFF (1987), 10–11.

Linkola, Pertti
Virkkula, Simopekka. "One Man's War." BFF (1990), 45–47.

Mäkelä, Hannu
Kirstinä, Leena. "Hannu Mäkelä: Journeys to Friendship." BFF (1983), 143–45.

Melleri, Arto
Tarkka, Pekka. "Poems: Introduction." BFF (1981), 14–15.

Mikkola, Marja-Leena
Stenius, Yrsa. "Kvinnors sökan — Om Marja-Leena Mikkolas författarskap." *Horisont* (1970), 1:43–46.

Mukka, Timo K.
Paasilinna, Erno. *Timo K. Mukka: Legenda jo eläessään.* Porvoo: WSOY, 1974.
Rajala, Panu. "Timo K. Mukka: *Maa on syntinen laulu.*" In *Romaani ja tulkinta,* ed. Mirjam Polkunen. Helsinki: Otava, 1973, 1979, 127–38.

Oksanen, Aulikki
Ahola, Suvi. "Lady into Bird." BFF (1991), 11–13.

Origo (Jouni Lompolo)
Taanila, Hannu. "Pakina." In *Suomen kirjallisuus 8,* gen. ed. Matti Kuusi. Helsinki: Otava, 1963–70, 266–98.

Paasilinna, Erno
Brotherus, Heikki. "Erno Paasilinna: In the World's Clutches." BFF (1984), 178–87.
Niemi, Juhani. "Erno Paasilinna, arktinen satiirikko." In Niemi, *Kirjailijoita ja epäkirjailijoita.* Helsinki: SKS, 1983, 123–31.

Päätalo, Kalle
Pennanen, Eila. "Muistelija ja hänen isänsä." In Pennanen, *Kirjailijatar ja hänen miehensä sekä muita esseitä.* Porvoo: WSOY, 1982, 37–51.
Rajala, Panu. "Kalle Päätalo — Work Hero of Finnish Literature." BFF (1987), 217–20.

Paronen, Samuel
Hosiaisluoma, Yrjö. *Järjestyksen kourista vapauden valtakuntaan: Samuli Parosen elämä, tuotanto ja yhteiskuntakritiikki.* Helsinki: SKS, 1990.
Raento, Esko. "Johdanto, ja sivulauseita Samuli Parosen tuotantoon." In *Suomalaisia kirjailijoita: Kirjailijat kirjailijoista,* ed. Mirjam Polkunen and Auli Viikari. Helsinki: Tammi, 1982, 317–38.

Parras, Tytti
Tarkka, Pekka. "All at Sea." BFF (1993), 149–50.

Pellinen, Jyrki
Launonen, Hannu. "Kauas, lähelle, silmänkantamattomiin." *Parnasso* (1977), 113–21.

Pimenoff, Veronica
Tarkka, Pekka. "Vapauden labyrintit (Veronica Pimenoff: *Pohjoiset pelit*)." In Tarkka, *Sanat sanoista: Arvosteluja ja kirjoituksia.* Helsinki: Otava, 1984, 135–40.

Pulkkinen, Matti
Makkonen, Anna. "Trick or Treat? Matti Pulkkinen and His Controversial Novel [*Romaanihenkilön kuolema*]." BFF (1986), 35–38.
Salokannel, Juhani. "Unusual Men: Three Masters of Contemporary Finnish Prose." WLT (1980), 24–27.

Rauhala, Niilo
Pohjanen, Bengt. "Som springande hästar i vinterkylan: Om Niilo Rauhalas diktning." *Vår lösen* (1981), 2, 102-5.
Rekola, Juhani. "Onnittelen teitä, lapset." In Rekola, *Kadotetun paratiisin portilla*. Helsinki: Kirjapaja, 1982, 99-103.

Ruuth, Alpo
Toivonen, Timo. "Alpo Ruuth: *Kämppä*." In *Romaani ja tulkinta*, ed. Mirjam Polkunen. Helsinki: Otava, 1973, 1979, 202-13.

Saarikoski, Pentti
Dances of the Obscure. Trans. Michael Cole and Karen Kimball. Durango CO: Logbridge-Rhodes, 1987.
Helsinki: Selected Poems. Trans. Anselm Hollo. London: Rapp & Carroll, 1967.
Poems, 1958-1980. Trans. Anselm Hollo. West Branch IA: Toothpaste Press, 1983.
Kolu, Kaarina. "Runoksi purkautuu liike." *Parnasso* (1981), 27-36.
Leitch, Vincent B. "The Postmodern Poetry and Poetics of Pentti Saarikoski." SR (1982), 4, 61-68.
Riikonen, H. K. "Travels in Language." BFF (1994), 23-25.
Simonsuuri, Kirsti. "The Futurist Experience: Notes on the Poetry of Pentti Saarikoski." BFF (1985), 194-99.
———. "Myth and Material in the Poetry of Pentti Saarikoski since 1958." WLT (1980), 41-46.
Tarkka, Pekka. "The Death of a Poet." BFF (1983), 129-32.

Saaritsa, Pentti
Gathering Fragments. Trans. Seija Paddon. Waterloo ON: Penumbra, 1991.

Säisä, Eino
Baschmakoff, Natalia, and Mohammed Dib. "Eino Säisä, Grande chronique des neiges et des hommes." BFF (1983), 1, 7-9.

Saisio, Pirkko
Pekkarinen, Immo. "Suojattomat — Pirkko Saision Hävinneiden legenda-näytelmän tematiikasta." *Kulttuurivihkot* (1985), 5, 20-23.

Salama, Hannu
Tarkka, Pekka. *Hannu Salama*. Helsinki: Otava, 1973.
———. *Hannu Salama*. Trans. Tuuli Forsgren. Stockholm: Rabén & Sjögren, 1976.
———. "Hannu Salama: Writer between the Social Classes." WLT (1980), 26-32.
———. "The Name in Vain? Hannu Salama and His *Finlandia.*" BFF (1986), 32-25.

Salo, Arvo
Niemi, Irmeli. "The Lapua Opera." In *Twentieth-Century Drama in Scandinavia*, ed. Johan Wrede, Ulla Terling Hasan, Irmeli Niemi, and Clas Zilliacus. Helsinki: University of Helsinki, Department of Swedish Literature, 1979, 177-86.

Niemi, Juhani. "Kirjallisuus ajankohtansa heijastajana: Arvo Salon Lapualaisoopperan tarkastelua." *KTSV* 27 (1973), 87–100.

Sariola, Esa
Mäkelä, Matti. "Moraalinen ongelma." *Parnasso* (1987), 2:126–27.

Siekkinen, Raija
Bargum, Marianne. "Raija Siekkinen: Soulscapes." *BFF* (1987), 97–98.

Simonsuuri, Kirsti
Flint, Austin. "Kirsti Simonsuuri: Encounter with the Real." *BFF* (1987), 166–67.

Skiftesvik, Joni
Jama, Olavi. "Joni Skiftesvik: Arctic Storyteller." *BFF* (1984), 166–68.
Tarkka, Pekka. "Vaihtuvien todellisuuksien taikuri (Joni Skiftesvik: *Puhalluskukkapoika ja taivaan-korjaaja*)." In Tarkka, *Sanat sanoista: Arvosteluja ja kirjoituksia, 1957–1984*. Helsinki: Otava, 1984, 277–80.

Stenberg, Eira
Wings of Hope and Daring: Selected Poems. Trans. Herbert Lomas. Newcastle-upon-Tyne: Bloodaxe, 1992.

Suosalmi, Kerttu-Kaarina
Haavikko, Ritva, ed. *Miten kirjani ovat syntyneet 2*. Porvoo: WSOY, 1980, 168–87.
Niemi, Juhani. "Kerttu-Kaarina Suosalmi, maakylän Shakespeare." In Niemi, *Kirjailijoita ja epäkirjailijoita*. Helsinki: SKS, 1983, 49–56.
Nupponen, Terttu. "Kerttu-Kaarina Suosalmi: *Hyvin toimeentulevat ihmiset.*" In *Romaani ja tulkinta,* ed. Mirjam Polkunen. Helsinki: Otava, 1973, 1979, 189–201.
Viikari, Auli. "The Search for Spontaneity: Conversation with Kerttu-Kaarina Suosalmi." *BFF* (1980), 52–61.

Tiihonen, Ilpo
Black and Red. Trans. Herbert Lomas. Guildford U.K.: Making Waves, 1993.
Rossi, Matti. "Soitto ja sanoma: Ilpo Tiihosen runouden arviointia." In Rossi, *Sarvikuonon muistiinpanoja*. Helsinki: Tammi, 1981, 230–35.

Turkka, Jouko
Lehtonen, Soila. "Jouko Turkka's Factory of Ideas." *BFF* (1986), 165–67.
Paavolainen, Pentti. *Turkan pitkä juoksu: Jouko Turkan ohjaukset*. Helsinki: Gaudeamus, 1987.

Turkka, Sirkka
Not You, Not the Rain: Poems. Trans. Seija Paddon. Waterloo ON: Penumbra, 1991.
Kytöhonka, Arto. "Sirkka Turkka: Introduction." *BFF* (1982), 53–54.

Turunen, Heikki
Enwald, Liisa. "Heikki Turunen." In *Suomalaisia kirjailijakuvia,* ed. Liisa Enwald. Helsinki: Kirjayhtymä, 1987, 317–29.
Mäkelä, Matti. "Simpauttaja: Myytti kuolee?" *Parnasso* (1974), 370–73.

Tuuri, Antti
Niemi, Juhani. "Antti Tuuri, vaihtoehtojen kirjailija." In Niemi, *Kirjailijoita ja epäkirjailijoita*. Helsinki: SKS, 1983, 140–48.
Salokannel, Juhani. "Unusual Men: Three Masters of Contemporary Finnish Prose." WLT (1980), 24–27.
Tarkka, Pekka. "Antti Tuuri: 'The Engineer's Story.'" BFF (1981), 46–48.

Utrio, Kaari
Mäkinen, Erkki. "Kaari Utrio." In *Suomalaisia kirjailijakuvia*, ed. Liisa Enwald. Helsinki: Kirjayhtymä, 1987, 351–60.
Malmio, Kristina. *Lilja av stål: Kaari Utrio och den romantiska genrens normer*. Åbo: Åbo Akademi, Litteraturvetenskapliga institutionen, 1992.
Tarkka, Pekka. "Kansallinen taistelu ja naisten taistelu (Kaari Utrio, *Aatelisneito, porvaristyttö*)." In Tarkka, *Sanat sanoista: Arvosteluja ja kirjoituksia, 1957–1984*. Helsinki: Otava, 1984, 184–87.

Westerberg, Caj
Enwald, Liisa. "Kivusta, kirkkaudesta." *Parnasso* (1986), 1:43–44.
Talvila, Ensio. "Maailma." *Parnasso* (1969), 5:314–16.

CHAPTER 6: A PART OF SWEDEN

LITERARY HISTORY

Fehrman, Carl. "Karolinsk barock och klassicism." In *Ny illustrerad svensk litteraturhistoria 2*, gen. ed. E. N. Tigerstedt. Stockholm: Natur & Kultur, 1967, 3–85.
Huldén, Lars, Jarl Gallén, Olof Enckell, and Erik Ekelund. *Finlands svenska litteratur 1: Från medeltiden till Åboromantiken*. Helsingfors: Söderström & Co., 1968.
Hultin, Arvid. *Det ekonomiska tidevarvet i Finlands litteraturhistoria: Ur odlingens hävder under frihetstidens senare del*. Helsingfors: SLF, 1910.
———. *Finlands svenska vitterhet 4: Den svenska vitterheten i Finland under stormaktstiden, 1640–1720*. Helsingfors: SLF, 1904.
Kajanto, Iiro. *Humanism in a Christian Society. 1: The Attitude to Classical Mythology and Religion in Finland, 1640–1713*. Helsinki: Suomalainen tiedeakatemia, 1989.
Klinge, Matti. *Professorer*. Helsingfors: Söderström & Co., 1989.
Schoolfield, George C. "Does Finland have a Baroque Literature?" In *Cultura Baltica: Literary Culture around the Baltic, 1600–1700*, ed. Bo Andersson and Richard Schade. Stockholm: Almqvist & Wiksell, 1996, 111–42. Acta Universitatis Upsaliensis: Studia Germanistica Upsaliensa, 35.

MONOGRAPHS AND ARTICLES

Achrelius, David
Hultin, Arvid. "Daniel Achrelius: En finsk vitterlekare i slutet af 17:de seklet." FOU 9 (1894–95), 257–309.
———. "Ett prässåtal i Åbo i slutet af 17:de seklet." FOU 7 (1892–93), 83–88.

Birchenbaum, Christina Regina von
Schück, Henrik. *Lars Wivallius: Hans lif och dikter 2*. Uppsala: Edvard Berling, 1895, 39–40.

Budde, Jöns
Ahlbäck, Olav. "Jöns Buddes språk och landsmansskap." *Studier i nordisk filologi* 40–41 (1952), 2–148.
Klockars, Birgit. *I Nådens dal: Klosterfolk och andra c. 1440–1590*. Helsingfors: SLS, 1979.
Laurén, Christer. "En fattig munk från Nådendal." *Horisont* (1970), 2:2–9.
Pipping, Rolf. "Jöns Budde: Föredrag hållet vid Finska Vetenskaps-Societetens sammanträde den 18 september 1944." *SSF: Årsbok-Vuosikirja* 23B no. 1 (1944), 3–24.

Choraeus, Mikael
Lagus, Ernst. *Finlands svenska vitterhet 2: Mikael Choraei valda dikter med en lefnadsteckning*. Helsingfors: SLF, 1901.
Snoilsky, Carl. "Michael Choraeus." In Snoilsky, *Minnesteckningar och andra uppsatser*. Stockholm: Gebers, 1904, 203–72.

Chronander, Jakob
Cygnaeus, Gustaf. "Drag ur Finlands teaterhistoria under sextonhundratalet." *FOU* 10 (1895–97), 1–28.

Chydenius, Anders
Krook, Tor. "Anders Chydenius, samhällsreformator och församlingsherde." *Arkiv för Svenska Österbotten: Österbottnisk årsbok* (1951–52), 7–8.
Schauman, Georg. *Biografiska anteckningar om Anders Chydenius*. Helsingfors: SLF, 1908.
Virrankoski, Pentti. *Anders Chydenius: Demokraattinen poliitikko valistuksen vuosisadalta*. Helsinki: WSOY, 1986.
Willner, Sven. "Anders Chydenius." In Willner, *Mellan hammaren och städet*. Helsingfors: Söderström & Co., 1974, 9–35.

"Eskolagubbens visor"
Hultin, Arvid. "Tillfällighetspoesin under frihetstiden: Eskolagubbens visor och deras författare." *FOU* (1903), 137–62.

Forsius, Sigfrid Aronus
Ahnlund, Nils. "Daniel Hjort." In Ahnlund, *Svensk sägen och hävd: Kulturbilder*. Stockholm: Gebers, 1928, 203–38.
Belfrage, Sixten. "Översättningen av Reyncke Fosz 1621." *Nysvenska studier* 4 (1924), 172–207.
Dymling, Carl Anders. "Reyncke Fosz och Forsius." *Nysvenska studier* 4 (1924), 213–29.
Fehrman, Carl. "1600-talets ålderstavlor." In Fehrman, *Diktaren och döden: Dödsbild och förgängelsetanke i litteraturen från antiken till 1700-talet*. Stockholm: Bonniers, 1952, 278–85.

Liedgren, Emil. *Svensk psalm och andlig visa*. Stockholm: Svenska kyrkans diakonisstyrelses bokförlag, 1926.

Lindroth, Sten. *Paracelsismen i Sverige till 1600-talets mitt*. Uppsala: Almqvist & Wiksell, 1943, 391–419.

Paludan, Julius. "Til Oplysning om et Par ældre svenske Digte." *Samlaren* 18 (1897), 91–101.

Franzén, Frans Michael

Castrén, Gunnar. *Frans Michael Franzén i Finland*. Helsingfors: SLF, 1902.

Ek, Sverker. *Franzéns Åbodiktning: Ett bidrag till Finlands svenska litteraturhistoria*. Stockholm: Svanbäck, 1916.

Frese, Jacob

Enckell, Rabbe. "Frese och Stenbäck." In Enckell, *Relation i det personliga*. Stockholm: Wahlström & Widstrand, 1950, 19–34. First published in NA (1926), 178–82.

Fehrman, Carl. "Karolinska tiden: Karolinsk barock och klassicism." In *Ny illustrerad svensk litteraturhistoria, Andra delen*, gen. ed. E. N. Tigerstedt. Stockholm: Natur & Kultur, 1967, 3–85, esp. 66–69.

Hultin, Arvid. *Finlands svenska vitterhet. 3: Valda skrifter af Jakob Frese med en teckning af hans lefnad och skaldskap*. Helsingfors: SLF, 1902.

Swahn, Sven Christer. *Jacob Frese: Från en finlandssvensk 1700-talsförfattares liv och dikt*. Stockholm: Läromedelsförlagen, 1971.

Gadd, Per Adrian

Hultin, Arvid. "Per Adrian Gadd: Till tvåhundraårsminnet av hans födelse." FT 112 (1927), 366–79.

Gestrinius, Ernst

Hultin, Arvid. "Ernst Gestrinius: En finsk vitterlekare från stora ofredens tid." FOU 13 (1900), 22–29.

Löfving, Stefan

Schoolfield, George C. "Stefan Löfving—A Finnish Simplex?" In *"Der Buchstab tödt—Der Geist macht lebendig": Festschrift zum 60. Geburtstag von Hans-Gert Roloff*, ed. James Hardin and Jörg Jungmayr. Bern: Peter Lang, 1992, 1:337–61.

Renner, Michael

Hultin, Arvid. "Michael Renner och den religiösa dikten i slutet af 17:de seklet." FOU 7 (1892–93), 89–100.

Rudeen, Torsten

Hultin, Arvid. *Torsten Rudeen: Ett bidrag till karolinska tidens litteratur och lärdomshistoria*. Helsingfors: SLF, 1902.

Svenonius, Enevaldus

Salminen, Seppo J. *Enevaldus Svenonius 1–2*. Helsinki: SKHST 106 (1978), SKHST 134 (1985).

Tuderus, Gabriel
Itkonen, Tuomo. "Gabriel Tuderus." In *Mikael Agricolasta E. W. Pakkalaan*, ed. Jaakko Haavio. Porvoo: WSOY, 1947, 101-14.
Tudeer, Lauri O. "Gabriel Tuderuksen 'Weisu talonpoille cunniaxi.'" *Miscellanea bibliographica* 5 (1947), 12-18.

CHAPTER 7: NATIONAL ROMANTICISM — A GOLDEN AGE?
LITERARY HISTORY
Castrén, Gunnar. "Sällskapet Aurora." *FOU* 14 (1900), 143-95.
Ekelund, Erik. *Finlands svenska litteratur 2: Från Åbo brand till sekelskiftet*. Helsingfors: Söderström & Co., 1969.
Manninen, Juha. "Hegelianismen i Finland på 1800-talet." *Lychnos 1977-1978* (1979), 87-114.
Öller, Ragnar. *Ett kvarts sekel av vårt litterära liv 1828-1853. 1: Poesin*. Helsingfors: Söderström & Co., 1920.
Söderhjelm, Werner. *Åboromantiken och dess samband med utländska idéströmningar*. Borgå: Schildts, 1915.
Tideström, Gunnar. "Runeberg och den finlandssvenska litteraturen." In *Ny illustrerad svensk litteraturhistoria*, gen. ed. E. N. Tigerstedt. Stockholm: Natur & Kultur, 1967, 441-97.

MONOGRAPHS AND ARTICLES
Arnell, Lars
Dahlström, Svante. *Lars Arnell: Bidrag till hans biografi*. Åbo: Åbo Akademi, 1948.

Arwidsson, Adolf Ivar
Castrén, Liisa. "Adolf Ivar Arwidsson: Nuori Arwidsson ja hänen ympäristönsä." Ph.D. dissertation, Helsinki University, 1944.
Estlander, Carl Gustaf. "Adolf Arwidsson som vitter författare: Akademisk inbjudningsskrift, 1893." In Estlander, *Skrifter II, 3, 1: Litteratur och konst samt allmänna ämnen. 3: Åren 1893-1910*. Helsingfors: SLF, 1921, 29-94.
Jokipii, Mauno, ed. *Adolf Ivar Arwidsson: Näkijä ja tekijä*. Jyväskylä: Atena, 1992.
Junnila, Olavi. *Ruotsiin muuttanut Adolf Ivar Arwidsson ja Suomi (1823-1858)*. Helsinki: Suomen Historiallinen Seura, 1972.

Berndtson, Fredrik
Björkstén, Carita. "Fredrik Berndtson." In *Nyländska öden 2*. Ekenäs: Ekenäs Tryckeri, 1966, 47-106.

Cygnaeus, Fredrik
Forsman (Koskimies), Rafael. *Fredrik Cygnaeus kirjailijana ja ajanilmiönä 1-2*. Porvoo: WSOY, 1923-25.
Hultin, Arvid. "Fredrik Cygnaeus som litterär kritiker: Till hundraårsminnet den 1 april 1907." *FT* 62 (1907), 255-94.

Kihlman, Erik. "Fredrik Cygnaeus: Kritikern." NA (1923), 77–81.
——. "Fredrik Cygnaeus: Poeten." NA (1923), 58–61.
Tarkiainen, Viljo. *Fredrik Cygnaeus runoilijana*. Porvoo: Werner Söderström, 1911.

Ehrnrooth, Adelaïde
Tuulio, Tyyni. "Adelaïde Ehrnrooth." In Tuulio, *Fredrikan Suomi: Esseitä viime vuosisadan naisista*. Porvoo: WSOY, 1979, 62–87.
Westermarck, Helena. *Adelaïde Ehrnrooth: Kvinnospår i finländskt kulturliv*. Lovisa: Söderström & Co., 1928.

Estlander, Carl Gustaf
Mustelin, Olof. "Carl Gustaf Estlander." FG 2 (1962), 55–79.
Schyberson, M. G. *Carl Gustaf Estlander: En levnadsteckning*. Helsingfors: SLF, 1916.

Idestam, Gustaf
Heinricius, G. "En glömd diktare: Gustaf Idestam." FT (1908), 113–24.

Ingelius, Axel Gabriel
Hirn, Yrjö. "Heinolablomman: En roman om inhemsk teater." In *Teatrar och teaterstrider*. Helsingfors: Schildts, 1949, 39–82.
Öller, Ragnar. "En finländsk romanskrivare från 1850-talet: Några blad om romanskriveriet i vårt land och om en av dess första idkare." FOU 33 (1920), 6–187.

Lagus, Gabriel
Homén, Olaf. *Gabriel Lagus: En minnesteckning 1*. Helsingfors: Schildts, 1919. Volume 2 did not appear.
Tigerstedt, E. N. "Den första finlandssvenska litteraturhistorien." HLS 20 (1944), 37–57.

Linder, Marie (Stella)
Lehto, Katri. *Kytäjän kreivitär: Marie Linderin elämä*. Helsinki: Otava, 1985.
Tuulio, Tyyni. "'Eräs aikamme nainen.'" In Tuulio, *Fredrikan Suomi: Esseitä viime vuosisadan naisista*. Porvoo: WSOY, 1979, 105–24.

Nervander, Johan Jakob
Hultin, Arvid. "Johan Jakob Nervander: Till hundraårsminnet av hans födelse." FOU 19 (1906), 91–186.
Steinby, Torsten. *Johan Jakob Nervander (1805–1848)*. Helsingfors: Föreningen Konstsamfund, 1991.

Nordström, Wilhelmina
Tuulio, Tyyni. "Wilhelmina Nordström." In Tuulio, *Fredrikan Suomi: Esseitä viime vuosisadan naisista*. Porvoo: WSOY, 1979, 125–38.

Qvanten, Emil von
Hultin, Arvid. "Emil von Qvanten: Till hundraårsminnet av hans födelse." FT 113 (1927), 30–55.

Mörne, Arvid. "Emil von Qvantens lyrik." In *Festkrift tillägnad Yrjö Hirn*, ed. Gunnar Castrén, K. S. Laurila, and Hans Ruin. Helsingfors: Schildts, 1930, 313–34.
———. "Kring Emil von Qvantens 'Fennomani och skandinavism.'" *HLS* 8 (1932), 1–85.

Runeberg, Fredrika
Ekelund, Karin Allardt. *Fredrika Runeberg: En biografisk och litteraturhistorisk studie*. Helsingfors: SLF, 1942.
Mazzarella, Merete. *Från Frederika Runeberg till Märta Tikkanen: Frihet och beroende i finlandssvensk kvinnolitteratur*. Helsingfors: Söderström & Co., 1985.
Stenwall, Åsa. *Den frivilligt ödmjuka kvinnan: En bok om Fredrika Runebergs verklighet och diktning*. Stockholm: Natur & Kultur, 1979.
Tuulio, Tyyni. "Fredrickeja Runeberg." In *Fredrikan Suomi: Esseitä viime vuosisadan naisista*. Porvoo: WSOY, 1979, 7–61.

Runeberg, Johan Ludvig
King Fjalar: A Poem in Five Songs. Trans. Anna Bohnhof. Intro. Bernhard Estlander. Helsingfors: Helios, 1904.
King Fialar: A Poem in Five Songs. Trans. Eirik Magnússon. London: Dent, 1912.
Book 1. Voices of the North: King Fjalar. Trans. George Handley Knibbs. London: Alston Rivers, 1913.
Runeberg's Lyrical Songs, Idylls, and Epigrams. Trans. Eirik Magnússon and E. H. Palmer. London: Kegan Paul, 1878.
A Selection from the Series of Poems Entitled Ensign Stål's Songs. Trans. Isabel Donner. Helsingfors: C. W. Edlund, 1907.
The Songs of Ensign Stål. Trans. Clement Burbank Shaw. New York: G. E. Stechert, 1925.
The Tales of Ensign Stål. Trans. Charles Wharton Stork. Intro. Yrjö Hirn. Princeton: Princeton University Press; New York: American-Scandinavian Foundation; London: H. Milford, Oxford University Press, 1938, 1960. Thirteen of the eighteen poems in part 1, thirteen of the seventeen poems in part 2.
Bengtsson, Frans G. "Myter och sagor." *OOB* 36 (1927), 561–70. Reprinted in *Litteratörer och militärer*. Stockholm: Bonniers, 1929, 239–58.
Castrén, Gunnar. *Johan Ludvig Runeberg*. Stockholm: Natur & Kultur, 1950.
Enckell, Rabbe. "'Det absoluta mästerverket.'" In Enckell, *Relation i det personliga*. Stockholm: Wahlström & Widstrand, 1950, 142–47. First published in *Nya Argus*, 1949.
Gosse, Edmund. *Northern Studies*. London: Walter Scott, 1890, 134–73. First published in *Studies in the Literature of Northern Europe*, 1879.
Hagberg, Knut. "Runebergs moral." In Hagberg, *Bygd och hävd*. Stockholm: Natur & Kultur, 1934, 164–73.
Hirn, Yrjö. *Runebergskulten*. Helsingfors: SLF, 1935.
Klinge, Matti. "Runeberg's Two Homelands." Translated in *The Nordic Mind: Current Trends in Scandinavian Literary Criticism*, ed. Frank Egholm Andersen and John Weinstock. Lanham MD: University Press of America, 1986, 117–30.

Nilsson, Kim. "J. L. Runeberg as a Modern Writer: The Evidence of *Julqvällen.*" ss 58 (1986), 1–9.

Schoolfield, George C. "Johannes Ludovicus Tyrannus." In *Studies in Finnish Language and Culture: Proceedings of the Third Conference of Finnish Studies in North America*, ed. Royal Skousen. Helsinki: Ministry of Education, 1986, 101–19.

———. "Poetry and Patriotism: Johan Ludvig Runeberg." BFF 19 (1985), 240–48.

———. "Transfigured Moments: Johan Ludvig Runeberg." SR (1987), 70–86.

Söderhjelm, Werner. *Johan Ludvig Runeberg 1–2.* Helsingfors: SLF, 1904–6, rev. 1929.

Tideström, Gunnar. *Runeberg som estetiker.* Helsingfors: SLF, 1941.

Viljanen, Lauri. *Runeberg ja hänen runoutensa, 1804–1837.* Porvoo: WSOY, 1944. Translated by Kai Lindgren under the title *Runeberg och hans diktning, 1804–1837* (Helsingfors: Schildts, 1947).

———. *Runeberg ja hänen runoutensa, 1837–1877.* Porvoo: WSOY, 1948. Swedish translation: *Runeberg och hans diktning, 1837–1877.* Trans. Eva Stenius. Lund: Gleerup; Helsingfors: Schildts, 1969.

Wrede, Johan. *"Jag såg ett folk . . .": Runeberg, Fänrik Stål och nationen.* Helsingfors: Söderström & Co., 1988.

———. "Runeberg's *Fänrik Ståls sägner:* On the Life and Significance of a Patriotic Work." In *Studies in German and Scandinavian Literature after 1500: Festschrift for George C. Schoolfield*, ed. James A. Parente Jr. and Richard Erich Schade. Columbia SC: Camden House, 1993, 155–65.

Wretö, Tore. *J. L. Runeberg.* Boston: Twayne, 1980.

Saturday Society

Havu, Ilmari. *Lauantaiseura ja sen miehet.* Helsinki: Otava, 1945.

Palmgren, Raoul. "Lauantaiseura ja J. J. Nervander." In Palmgren, *Suuri linja.* Helsinki: Kansankulttuuri, 1948, 1976, 55–65.

Sjöström, Axel Gabriel

Söderhjelm, Werner. "Axel Gabriel Sjöström och hans vittra verksamhet." FOU 9 (1894–95), 55–180.

Snellman, Johan Vilhelm (see also chapter 2)

Salminen, Johannes: "Är Snellman passé?" In Salminen, *Pelare av eld.* Helsingfors: Söderström & Co., 1967, 22–31.

———. "Snellman och Finlands ideologiska profil." In Salminen, *Gränsland.* Helsingfors: Söderström & Co., 1984, 79–81.

———. "Snellman på gott och ont." In Salminen, *Snellman i urval.* Helsingfors: Söderström & Co., 1981, 7–30.

Stenbäck, Lars

Castrén, Gunnar. "Studier i Lars Stenbäcks lyrik." FOU 26 (1913), 63–94.

Salminen, Johannes. "Lars Stenbäck." In Salminen, *Lars Stenbäck: Dikter och prosa.* Helsingfors: SLF, 1974, 7–49.

Topelius, Zachris (see also chapter 11)

Enckell, Olof. "Topelius' dikt 'Kommunismens vagga.'" HLS 45 (1970), 5–27.

Granér, Martin. *Zachris Topelius' kärlekslyrik*. Helsingfors: Mercators tryckeri, 1946.

Hornborg, Eirik. "Fältskärns berättelser." SLT (1943), 1–8.

Hultin, Arvid. "Fältskärns Regina: Dramatisk omklädnad." In *Zachris Topelius: Hundraårsminne: Festskrift den 14 januari 1918*. Helsingfors: SLF (1918), 148–91.

Lehtonen, Maija. "Intertextualitet i Topelius' berättelser." HLS 65 (1990), 49–79.

Nyberg, Paul. *Zachris Topelius: En biografisk skildring*. Helsingfors: Söderström & Co., 1949.

Schoolfield, George C. "Zacharias Topelius." In *McGraw-Hill Encyclopedia of World Drama*, ed. Stanley Hochman. New York: McGraw-Hill, 1984, 5:36.

Söderhjelm, Werner. "Topelius' tidigaste lyriska diktning." HLS 7 (1931), 1–82.

Vasenius, Valfrid. *Zacharias Topelius: Hans liv och skaldegärning 1–6*. Stockholm: Bonniers, 1912–30.

Wacklin, Sara

Nordmann, Petrus. "Sara Elisabet Wacklin." FOU 27 (1914), 190–222.

Snellman, Kaj. "Sara Wacklin." FG 10 (1974), 55–90.

Wallin, Georg August

Mead, William Richard. *G. A. Wallin and the Royal Geographic Society*. Helsinki: Suomen Itämainen Seura, 1958.

Salminen, Johannes. "Georg August Wallins orient." In Salminen, *Minnet av Alexandria*. Helsingfors: Söderström & Co., 1988, 103–15.

Schildt, Göran. "Förord." In Georg August Wallin, *Källan i fjärran öknen*. Stockholm: Rabén & Sjögren, 1976, 7–12.

Tallqvist, Knut. "Lefnadsteckning." In *Bref och dagboksanteckningar af Georg August Wallin*. Helsingfors: SLF, 1905, i–cxxxiv.

Widén, Gustaf. "Den oppositionelle muslimen från Sund." NA (1984), 217–22.

Wecksell, Josef Julius

Enckell, Mikael. "Josef Julius Wecksell." In Enckell, *Över stumhetens gräns*. Helsingfors: Söderström & Co., 1972, 76–159.

Hird, Gladys. "*Daniel Hjort*: Classic or Outdated Nationalist Drama?" SS (1982), 123–36.

Mörne, Arvid. *Josef Julius Wecksell: En studie*. Helsingfors: SLF, 1909.

——. *Wecksell-studier*. Helsingfors: SLF, 1920.

Salminen, Johannes. "Livets ljuvt violblå färg." In Salminen, *Pelare av eld*. Helsingfors: Söderström & Co., 1967, 44–59.

Schoolfield, George C. "Josef Julius Wecksell." In *McGraw-Hill Encyclopedia of World Drama*, ed. Stanley Hochman. New York: McGraw-Hill, 1984, 5:126.

——. "Josef Julius Wecksell and Finland's Swedish Lyric." SS (1964), 1–33.

CHAPTER 8: A SENSE OF MINORITY

LITERARY HISTORY

Beyer, Harald. "Fra hundreårsskiftet til 'modernismens' tid i finlandssvensk litteratur." In Beyer, *Nietzsche og Norden 2*. Bergen: Universitetet i Bergen Årbok, 1959, 288–319.

Bondestam, Anna. *Arbetet: En tidning i Åbo på 1910-talet och människorna kring den*. Helsingfors: SLF, 1968.

Castrén, Gunnar. "Finlandssvensk litteratur 1880–1914." In *Ny illustrerad svensk litteraturhistoria 4*, gen. ed. E. N. Tigerstedt. Stockholm: Natur & Kultur, 1967, 349–409.

———. "Sekelskiftets finlandssvenska skalder." *OOB* (1925), 577–88.

Holmqvist, Bengt. *Modern finlandssvensk litteratur*. Stockholm: Natur & Kultur, 1951.

Holmström, Roger. "Traditionalister och modernister — Linjer i finlandssvensk litteraturkritik på tio- och tjugotalet." In *Från dagdrivare till feminister*, ed. Sven Linnér. Helsingfors: SLF, 1986, 119–68.

Homén, Olaf. *De nya författarna*. Borgå: Schildts, 1915.

Landquist, John. *Modern svensk litteratur i Finland*. Stockholm: Natur & Kultur, 1929.

Linder, Erik Hjalmar. "'Dagdrivarprosa' och lyrisk humanism i svenska Finland." In Linder, *Fem decennier av nittonhundratalet*. Stockholm: Natur & Kultur, 1965, 233–45.

Mustelin, Olof. "Ateneum, 1898–1903: Några anteckningar om finlandssvenska kulturtidskrifter kring sekelskiftet 1900." *HTF* 47 (1962), 1–24.

———. *Euterpe: Tidskriften och kretsen kring den*. Helsingfors: SLF, 1963.

Nordenson, Eva, ed. *Finskt sekelskifte: En konstbok från Nationalmuseum*. Stockholm: Rabén & Sjögren, 1971.

Pettersson, Torsten. "Nio decennier finlandssvensk litteratur." *Horisont* 37 (1990), 6, 37–49.

———. "Det svårgripbara livet: Ett förbisett tema i dagdrivarlitteraturen." In *Från dagdrivare till feminister*, ed. Sven Linnér. Helsingfors: SLF, 1986, 9–40.

Söderhjelm, Henning. "Utvecklingen inom Finlands moderna svenska litteratur." *OOB* (1928), 57–63.

Tigerstedt, E. N. *Det religiösa problemet i modern finlandssvensk litteratur*. Helsingfors: SLF, 1939.

Törnudd, Klaus. *Svenska språkets ställning i Finland*. Helsingfors: Schildts, 1978.

Warburton, Thomas. *Åttio år finlandssvensk litteratur*. Helsingfors: Schildts, 1984.

Willner, Sven. "Söner av nederlaget." In Willner, *Söner av nederlaget*. Ekenäs: Ekenäs Tryckeri, 1979, 51–112. On the *dagdrivare*.

Wrede, Johan. "*Den hemliga glöden*: An Episode in the History of the Reception of Finland-Swedish Modernism." In *Facets of European Modernism: Essays in Honour of James McFarland*, ed. Janet Garton. Norwich: University of East Anglia, 1985, 257–74.

MONOGRAPHS AND ARTICLES

Ahrenberg, Jac.
Ekelund, Erik. *Jac. Ahrenberg och östra Finland.* Helsingfors: SLF, 1943.
Loman, Bengt. "Jac. Ahrenbergs *Samlade berättelser.*" In *Festskrift till Carl-Eric Thors 8.6.1980.* SNF 62 (1980), 177–92.

Allardt, Anders
Mörne, Arvid. "Anders Allardts och Oscar Behms nyländska noveller från 1880- och 1890-talet." *FOU*, n.s. (1928–29), 111–26.

Alm, Gustav (Richard Malmberg)
Bruhn, Karl. *Richard Malmberg: Novellist och pedagog.* Helsingfors: SLF, 1957.
Kihlman, Erik. "Gustav Alm." In Kihlman, *Svensk nutidsdikt in Finland.* Helsingfors: Söderström & Co., 1928, 65–95.

Backman, Sigrid
Carpelan, Bo. "Sigrid Backman — En skiss." In *Författare om författare: 24 finlandssvenska författarporträtt*, ed. Merete Mazzarella, Johannes Salminen, Ingmar Svedberg, and Sven Willner. Helsingfors: Söderström & Co., 1980, 112–19.
Langenskjöld, Agnes. "'Överflödiga människor.'" *FT* (1933), 1, 63–64.
Mazzarella, Merete. "Sigrid Backman — 'Oavhängig kvinna och människa?'" In Mazzarella, *Från Fredrika Runeberg till Märta Tikkanen: Frihet och beroende i finlandssvensk kvinnolitteratur.* Helsingfors: Söderström & Co., 1985, 74–91.

Behm, Oscar
Barck, P. O. "Inledning." In Oscar Behm, *Berättelser i urval.* Helsingfors: Söderström & Co., 1936, 7–34.
Mörne, Arvid. "Anders Allardts och Oscar Behms nyländska noveller från 1880- och 1890-talet." *FOU*, n.s. (1928–29), 111–26.

Bengts, Josefina
Granit, Karin. "Josefina Bengts." *HLS* 13 (1937), 191–294.

Castrén, Gunnar
Tallqvist, J. O. "Gunnar Castrén." *FG* 4 (1964), 125–44.

Ekelund, Ragnar
Cronström, Nils-Gustav. "Tolkning och verklighet: Om Ragner Ekelunds poetiska självuppgörelse 1922." *FT* (1975), 410–21.
Ruin, Hans. "Målare och poet." In Ruin, *Världen i min fickspegel.* Stockholm: Wahlström & Widstrand, 1969, 77–96.
Salminen, Johannes. "Poeten Ragnar Ekelund." In Salminen, *Levande och död tradition.* Helsingfors: Söderström & Co., 1963, 101–8.

Ekhammar, Hugo
Ruin, Hans. "Målare och poet." In Ruin, *Världen i min fickspegel.* Stockholm: Wahlström & Widstrand, 1969, 77–80.

Stormbom, N.-B. "Under torparsol och i norrfånget land." In Stormbom, *Pejlingar: Essäer.* Borgå: Söderström & Co., 1973, 96–101.

Fahler, Alfred
Ruin, Hans. "I förbund med döden." In Ruin, *Det finns ett leende.* Helsingfors: Schildts, 1943, 227–29.

Freudenthal, Axel Olof
Mjöberg, Jöran. "Vikingaidealiteten i Finland." In Mjöberg, *Drömmen om sagatiden* 2. Stockholm: Natur & Kultur, 1968, 96–120.
Mörne, Arvid. *Axel Olof Freudenthal: Liv och gärning.* Helsingfors: Frenckell, 1936.
Puntila, L. A. *Suomen ruotsalaisuuden liikkeen synty.* Helsinki: Otava, 1944, 61–78.

Gripenberg, Alexandra
Loman, Bengt. "'Aarne' och språkstriden." *Folkmålsstudier* 32 (1989), 97–110.
Mörne, Arvid, "Från det glömda åttitalet: Alexandra Gripenberg." In Mörne, *Lyriker och berättare: Finlandssvenska studier.* Helsingfors: SLF, 1939, 163–86.
Tuulio, Tyyni. *Aleksandra Gripenberg: Kirjailija, taistelija ja ihminen.* Porvoo: WSOY, 1959.

Gripenberg, Bertel
Mazzarella, Merete. "'Nu nalkas Teodora'—Tankar kring Bertel Gripenbergs erotiska diktning." *HLS* 68 (1993), 177–88.
Salminen, Johannes. "Varianter av utposttanken." In Salminen, *Levande och död tradition.* Borgå: Söderström & Co., 1963, 39–47.
Willner, Sven. "Bertel Gripenberg." *FG* 7 (1968), 67–86.
———. "Från *Euterpe* till Lapporörelsen." In Willner, *Dikt och politik.* Helsingfors: Söderström & Co., 1968, 124–52.

Grotenfelt, Erik
Hemmer, Jarl. "Förord." In Erik Grotenfelt, *Valda dikter.* Helsingfors: Schildts, 1919, 5–14.
Ruin, Hans. "I förbund med döden." In Ruin, *Det finns ett leende.* Helsingfors: Schildts, 1943, 169–240.
Waltå, Göran Olson. "Erik Grotenfelt och den förtärande elden." *Horisont* 38 (1991), 43–48.
Willner, Sven. "Myten Erik Grotenfelt." In Willner, *Dikt och politik.* Helsingfors: Söderström & Co., 1968, 153–65.

Hedberg, John
Mörne, Arvid. "John Hedberg." In Mörne, *Lyriker och berättare: Finlandssvenska studier.* Helsingfors: SLF, 1939, 225–54.

Hemmer, Jarl
Nordman, Marianne. "Jarl Hemmers En man och hans samvete—Om kritikerna och romanen." *HLS* 58 (1983), 317–26.

Ruin, Hans. "En minnesteckning." In Jarl Hemmer, *Skrifter i minnesupplaga 1*. Stockholm: Bonniers, 1945, 7–50.

——. "Sliten mellan mörker och ljus." In Ruin, *Världen i min fickspegel*. Stockholm: Wahlström & Widstrand, 1969, 23–62.

Salminen, Johannes. *Jarl Hemmer: En studie i liv och diktning, 1893–1931*. Helsingfors: SLF, 1955.

Hirn, Yrjö

Rantavaara, Irma. *Yrjö Hirn: Humanisti ja tutkija 1–2*. Helsinki: Otava, 1977, 1979.

Ruin, Hans. "Yrjö Hirn: Estetikern och människan." OOB (1930), 571–80.

Homén, Olaf

Huldén, J. J. "Olaf Homén." SLT (1950), 145–58.

Janson, Ture

Barck, P. O. *Ture Janson: Författaren och journalisten*. Helsingfors: SLF, 1962.

Kihlman, Erik. "Hr. X i genomskärning." In Kihlman, *Svensk nutidsdikt i Finland: Essayer*. Helsingfors: Söderström & Co., 1928, 99–121.

Stormbom, N.-B. "De ensamma svenskarna." In Stormbom, *Pejlingar: Essäer*. Borgå: Söderström & Co., 87–95.

Kihlman, Erik

Willner, Sven. "Erik Kihlman." In Willner, *Mellan hammaren och städet*. Helsingfors: Söderström & Co., 1974, 98–134.

Lange, Ina (Daniel Sten)

Mörne, Arvid. "Ina Lange." In Mörne, *Lyriker och berättare: Finlandssvenska studier*. Helsingfors: SLF, 1939, 198–224.

Nevala, Maria-Liisa. "Kuka oli Daniel Sten?" In *"Sain roolin johon en mahdu": Suomalaisen naiskirjallisuuden linjoja*, ed. Maria-Liisa Nevala. Helsinki: Otava, 1989, 200–212.

Lindh, Theodor

Mörne, Arvid. "Theodor Lindh." In Mörne, *Lyriker och berättare: Finlandssvenska studier*. Helsingfors: SLF, 1939, 1–24.

Londén, Lilly

Törnudd, Alvar. "Lilly Londén: En glömd och gömd skriftställarinna." NA (1938), 20–21.

Lybeck, Mikael

Gulin, Åke. "Mikael Lybeck och den norska litteraturen." HLS 7 (1931), 161–203.

Kihlman, Erik. *Mikael Lybeck: Liv och diktning*. Helsingfors: SLF, 1932.

Salminen, Johannes. "Aspekter på inbördeskriget och finlandssvenskarna." In Salminen, *Levande och död tradition*. Borgå: Söderström & Co., 1963, 61–98.

——. "Mikael Lybeck, moralisten." In Salminen, *Pelare av eld*. Helsingfors: Söderström & Co. 1967, 70–79.

Mattsson, Guss
Hjelt, Edvard. *Gustaf Mattsson: Levnadsteckning.* Helsingfors: Schildts, 1920.
Kurtén, Björn. "Gustaf Mattsson och populärvetenskapen." In *Författare om författare: 24 finlandssvenska författarporträtt,* ed. Merete Mazzarella, Johannes Salminen, Ingmar Svedberg, and Sven Willner. Borgå: Söderström & Co., 1980, 60–63.
Steinby, Gunnel. *Apropos Guss Mattsson: Till 28 års ålder.* Helsingfors: Söderström & Co., 1975.
——. *Oss väl och ingen illa: Guss Mattsson publicisten och kemisten, 1902–1914.* Helsingfors: Söderström & Co., 1976.

Mickwitz, Gerda von
Mörne, Arvid. "Från det glömda åttitalet: En roman av Gerda von Mickwitz." In Mörne, *Lyriker och berättare: Finlandssvenska studier.* Helsingfors: SLF, 1939, 187–97.

Mörne, Arvid
Barck, P. O. *Arvid Mörne och sekelskiftets Finland.* Helsingfors: SLF, 1953.
Hedlund, Tom. *Poeten Arvid Mörne: Idéer, teorier och metoder i Mörnes poesi, 1924–1946.* Helsingfors: SLF, 1974.
Ruin, Hans. *Arvid Mörne: Liv och diktning.* Stockholm: Wahlström & Widstrand, 1946.
——. "Arvid Mörne och Finland." *SLT* (1944), 49–76.
Wrede, Johan. "Arvid Mörne—Med och utanför." In *Fem par: Finlandssvenska författare konfronteras,* ed. Roger Holmström. Helsingfors: SLF, 1995, 11–22.
——. *Arvid Mörnes lyrik från och med den poetiska förnyelsen omkring 1920.* Helsingfors: SLF, 1968.

Neiglick, Hjalmar
Mustelin, Olof. *Hjalmar Neiglick.* Helsingfors: SLF, 1986.

Numers, Gustav von
Schoolfield, George C. "Gustav von Numers." In *McGraw-Hill Encyclopedia of World Drama,* ed. Stanley Hochman. New York: McGraw-Hill, 1984, 3:558.
Tarkiainen, Viljo. *Gustaf von Numers: Elämä ja teokset: Kirjallisuushistoriallinen tutkielma.* Helsinki: Otava, 1922.

Nygren, Anders Johan
Sahlström, Anna-Lisa. "Nordan är ju kall—Liik vadan an blååsär: Anders Johan Nygren." In *Författare om författare: 24 finlandssvenska författarporträtt,* ed. Merete Mazzarella, Johannes Salminen, Ingmar Svedberg, and Sven Willner. Borgå: Söderström & Co., 1980, 47–59.

Österblom, Frans
Andersson, Otto. "Frans Österblom och hans kritiker." *FT* (1952), 115–26.

Paul, Adolf
Shelley, Henry C. "Introduction." In Adolf Paul, *The Language of the Birds,* trans. Arthur Travers-Borgstroem. London: Alfred Montgomery, 1922, pp. 3-10.

Procopé, Hjalmar
Willner, Sven. "Hjalmar Procopé." FG 4 (1964), 43-61.

Reuter, Ernst Odert
Ingman, Doris. "Ernst Odert Reuter: En författarpräst på 1800-talet." In *Nyländska öden 1.* Ekenäs: Ekenäs Tryckeri, 1965, 9-48.

Reuter, Jonatan
Cederlöf, Henrik. *Jonatan Reuter och hans skärgårdsberättelser (Nyländska öden 3).* Ekenäs: Ekenäs Tryckeri, 1972.

Ruin, Hans
Mazzarella, Merete. "Om att återvända till utgångspunkten: Tid och minne i Hans Ruins memoarverk." HLS 66 (1991), 169-82.
Ruin, Olof. "Beundra, fördöma och förlåta: En nordisk humanists syn på Tyskland under 1900-talets första hälft." NA (1991), 1:5-9.
———. *Spänningar: Finland speglat i en familj.* Stockholm: Alba, 1987.

Schildt, Runar
Castrén, Gunnar. *Runar Schildt.* Helsingfors: Schildts, 1927.
Cederlöf, Henrik. *Stilstudier i Runar Schildts novellistik.* Helsingfors: SLF, 1967.
Forsell, Pia, ed. *Runar Schildts roller.* Helsingfors: SLF, 1989. Johannes Salminen, "Främling under kristallkronorna," 9-22; Christoffer Schildt, "Släkt och tradition," 23-40; Göran Schildt, "Runar Schildt som boksamlare," 41-56; George C. Schoolfield, "Runar Schildt in His European Context," 57-80; Auli Viikari, "Runar Schildt som dramatiker," 81-84; Virpi Zuck, "Film Adaptations of Runar Schildt's Works," 95-112.
Holmström, Roger. "Distansen till det pulserande livet: Om Runar Schildt och några av hans kritiker." *Horisont* (1989), 2, 40-51.
Huldén, Lars. "Runar Schildt och namnen: Några iakttagelser." In *Studies in German and Scandinavian Literature after 1500: Festschrift for George C. Schoolfield,* ed. James A. Parente Jr. and Richard Erich Schade. Columbia SC: Camden House, 1993, 249-58.
Londén, Anne-Marie. *Litterärt talspråk: Studier i Runar Schildts berättarteknik med särskild hänsyn till dialogen.* Helsingfors: SLF, 1989.
Mazzarella, Merete. "Den segrande Eros: En själarnas komedi." HLS 63 (1988), 191-207.
Ruin, Hans. "Nattlig vandring med Runar Schildt." In Ruin, *Världen i min fickspegel.* Stockholm: Wahlström & Widstrand, 1969, 13-22.
Schoolfield, George C. "Runar Schildt." In *McGraw-Hill Encyclopedia of World Drama,* ed. Stanley Hochman. New York: McGraw-Hill, 1984, 4:331-32.
———. "Runar Schildt: Life as an Outsider." BFF (1988), 155-62.

———. "Runar Schildt and Swedish Finland." ss (1960), 7–17.
Söderhjelm, Alma. "Werner Söderhjelm—Gustaf Mattsson—Runar Schildt." SLT (1944), 88–96.
Zuck, Virpi. *Runar Schildt and His Tradition: An Approach through Genre*. Helsingfors: Meddelanden från avdelningen för svensk litteratur, Nordica, Helsingfors universitet, 3 (1983).

Söderhjelm, Alma
Engman, Marja. *Det främmande ögat: Alma Söderhjelm*. Helsingfors: SLF, 1996.

Söderhjelm, Werner
Söderhjelm, Henning. *Werner Söderhjelm*. Helsingfors: Schildts, 1960.

Sund, Viktor
Djupsund, Bodil. "'Där björkarna susa . . .': En missförstådd dikt." In *Pegas och snöbollskrig: Litteraturvetenskapliga studier tillägnade Sven Linnér*, ed. Roger Holmström, Krister Segerberg, and Clas Zilliacus. Åbo: Åbo Akademi, 1979, 69–78.

Tavaststjerna, Karl August
Ekelund, Erik. *Tavaststjerna och hans diktning*. Helsingfors: SLF, 1950.
Hennings, Lennart. "Språkliga iakttagelser i K. A. Tavaststjernas diktning." FT (1899), 185–207. With a reply by R. F. von Willebrand, 207–11.
Kihlman, Erik. *Karl August Tavaststjernas diktning*. Helsingfors: SLF, 1926.
Söderhjelm, Werner. *Karl August Tavaststjerna*. Helsingfors: SLF, 1900.
Tigerstedt, E. N. "Kristus-neurosen hos Tavaststjerna: Ett bidrag till tolkningen av *Laureatus*." In *Festskrift tillägnad Gunnar Castrén den 27 december 1938*, ed. Emil Hasselblatt, Yrjö Hirn, Holger Nohrström, Hans Ruin, and Emil Zilliacus. Helsingfors: SLF, 1938, 394–408.

Tegengren, Jacob
Rydsjö, Daniel. "Jacob Tegengren." SLT (1940), 26–37.
Willner, Sven. "Jacob Tegengren." FG 2 (1962), 81–98.

Wallenius, Allan
Mustelin, Olof. "Allan Wallenius—Biblioteksman, publicist och revolutionär i 1900-talets Finland." HLS 59 (1984), 269–389.
Willner, Sven. "Idealist och revolutionär." In Willner, *Dikt och politik*. Helsingfors: Söderström & Co., 1968, pp. 47–77.

Weman, Adèle (Parus Ater)
Huldén, Johan Jakob. *Kring Sagalund: Två banbrytares levnad*. Helsingfors: Mercator, 1941. (Oskar Jansson-Vretdal and Adèle Weman.)

Westermarck, Helena
Mazzarella, Merete. "Helena Westermarck—Att vidga hemmets gränser." In Mazzarella, *Från Fredrika Runeberg till Märta Tikkanen: Frihet och beroende i finlandssvensk kvinnolitteratur*. Helsingfors: Söderström & Co., 1985, 49–73.
———. "Kvinnofrigörelse i Helena Westermarcks romaner." HLS 59 (1984), 221–40.

Zilliacus, Emil
Landquist, John. "Emil Zilliacus." *Svensk Litteraturtidskrift* 4 (1962), 145-59.
Salminen Johannes. "Emil Zilliacus och drömmen om Hellas." In Salminen, *Pelare av eld*. Helsingfors: Söderström & Co., 1967, 80-89.
Stenius, Göran. "Itaka och Karelen: Emil Zilliacus och hans hembygd." NT (1962), 449-57.

CHAPTER 9: THE AGE OF MODERNISM, 1916-1960

LITERARY HISTORY
Donner, Jörn. "Den finlandssvenska skepnadens riddare." BLM 29 (1960), 122-39.
Enckell, Olof. "Vägen till Quosego." In *Quosego: Tidskrift för ny generation*, ed. Olof Enckell. Reprint. Borgå: Söderström & Co., 1971, v-xli.
Enckell, Rabbe. "Inledning." In *Modärn finlandssvensk lyrik*, ed. Rabbe Enckell. Helsingfors: Söderström & Co., 1934, 3-117.
Hellman, Ben. "'Det hemliga vapnet': En studie i den finländska vinterkrigsdiktningen." In *Från dagdrivare till feminister*, ed. Sven Linnér. Helsingfors: SLF, 1986, 195-234.
———, ed. *Dikt i krig: Fem studier i finlandssvensk lyrik, 1939-1945*. Helsingfors universitet: Avdelningen för svensk litteratur, 1985.
Henrikson, Thomas. "*Arena.*" *Tidskrift för litteraturvetenskap* (1973-74), 97-109.
Holmqvist, Bengt. *Modern finlandssvensk litteratur*. Stockholm: Natur & Kultur, 1951.
Holmström, Roger. *Karakteristik och värdering: Studier i finlandssvensk litteraturkritik, 1916-1929*. Åbo: Åbo Akademi, 1988.
Jansén, John-Erik. "Ingen tid för trosvissa fanfarer: *Arena*, 1951-1953." In *Från dagdrivare till feminister*, ed. Sven Linnér. Helsingfors: SLF, 1986, 237-56.
Korsström, Tuva. "The Modernists Live On." SBR (1992): Supplement, 99-105.
Linder, Erik Hjalmar. "Modernism i Finland: Edith Södergran, Elmer Diktonius." In Linder, *Fem decennier av nittonhundratalet*. Stockholm: Natur & Kultur, 1965, 666-721.
Mazzarella, Merete. *Det trånga rummet: En finlandssvensk romantradition*. Helsingfors: Söderström & Co., 1989.
Petherick, Karin. "Four Finland-Swedish Prose Modernists: Aspects of the Work of Hagar Olsson, Henry Parland, Elmer Diktonius, and Rabbe Enckell." SCAN (1976), 45-62.
Pettersson, Torsten. "Tre mogna lyriker: Solveig von Schoultz, Ole Torvalds och Peter Sandelin." FT (1987), 67-76.
Ruin, Hans. "Finlandssvensk modernism." SLT (1947), 49-66.
Salminen, Johannes. "Så har jag åter fot mot jord." In Salminen, *Levande och död tradition*. Helsingfors: Söderström & Co., 1963, 118-34.
Schoolfield, George C. "The Postwar Novel of Swedish Finland." SS (1962), 85-110.

Stormbom, N.-B. "Två årtionden finlandssvensk lyrik [1929–1949]." HLS 51 (1976), 17–54.
Warburton, Thomas. *Åttio år finlandssvensk litteratur.* Helsingfors: Schildts, 1984.
Willner, Sven. "Det anonyma 50-talet." In Willner, *Det anonyma 50-talet.* Helsingfors: Söderström & Co., 1988, 9–57.
——. "*Nya Argus* tjugotal." In Willner, *Mellan tvång och frihet.* Helsingfors: Boklaget, 1989, 91–100.
Wrede, Johan. "The Birth of Finland-Swedish Modernism: A Study in the Social Dynamics of Ideas." SCAN (1976), 73–103.
——. "Den finlandssvenska modernismens genombrott: En studie i idéernas social dynamik." In *Från dagdrivare till feminister,* ed. Sven Linnér. Helsingfors: SLF, 1986, 41–70.
——. "*Den hemliga glöden:* An Episode in the History of the Reception of Finland-Swedish Modernism." In *Facets of European Modernism: Essays in Honour of James McFarland,* ed. Janet Garton. Norwich: University of East Anglia, 1985, 257–74.
——. "Om politiska idéer och litteratur i Finland, 1917–1948." In *Från dagdrivare till feminister,* ed. Sven Linnér. Helsingfors: SLF, 1986, 169–94.
——. "Tidskriften *Ultra.*" In *Festskrift till Olof Enckell 12.3.1970,* ed. P. O. Barck, Johan Wrede, and Ingmar Svedberg. Helsingfors: SLF, 1970, 145–65.
Zilliacus, Clas. "'Erhållit Europa/vilket härmed erkännes': Modernism i finlandssvensk och östeuropeisk 20-talslyrik." In *Från dagdrivare till feminister,* ed. Sven Linnér. Helsingfors: SLF, 1986, 71–118.

MONOGRAPHS AND ARTICLES
Ågren, Leo
Ågren, Gösta. *En man gick genom stormen: Leo Ågrens liv och diktning.* Vasa: Maxicopy, 1983.
Willner, Sven. "Det anonyma 50-talet." In Willner, *Det anonyma 50-talet.* Helsingfors: Söderström & Co., 1988, 41–46.

Björling, Gunnar
Borum, Poul. "Björling — Upplevaren och upptäckaren." In Gunnar Björling, *Valda dikter.* Höganäs: Bra Lyrik, 1989, 2:191–99.
Carpelan, Bo. "Gunnar Björling: The Universal Eye." BFF (1985), 118–19.
——. *Studier i Gunnar Björlings diktning, 1922–1933.* Helsingfors: SLF, 1960.
Dickson, Walter. *En livslivets diktare: Studier i Gunnar Björlingtext.* Stockholm: Wahlström & Widstrand, 1956.
Enckell, Mikael. "Gunnar Björling." In Mikael Enckell, *Över stumhetens gräns.* Tammerfors: Söderström & Co., 1972, 5–75.
——. "Poeten som profet: Björling." In Mikael Enckell, *Till saknadens lov.* Ekenäs: Söderström & Co., 1988, 56–84.
Enckell, Rabbe. "Gunnar Björling." In Rabbe Enckell, *Essay om livets framfart.* Stockholm: Wahlström & Widstrand, 1961, 135–38.
Engdahl, Horace. "Björling's Words Made the Birds Hold Their Breath." SBR (1992): Supplement, 109–12.

Nilsson, Kim. "Björling, Gunnar." In *Dictionary of Scandinavian Literature*, ed. Virpi Zuck. Westport CT: Greenwood, 1990, 61–63.

———. "Semantic Devices in Björling's Poetry." *Michigan German Studies* 3 (1977), 54–73.

Sandelin, Peter. "Det fräcka med Björling." In *Författare om författare: 24 finlandssvenska författarporträtt*, ed. Merete Mazzarella, Johannes Salminen, Ingmar Svedberg, and Sven Willner. Borgå: Söderström & Co., 1980, 188–94.

Thölix, Birger. "God and the Incomplete." BFF (1993), 143–45.

Zilliacus, Clas, and Michel Ekman, eds. *Björlingstudier: Föredrag vid Gunnar Björling-symposiet den 18–19 maj 1992*. Helsingfors: SLF, 1993.

Carpelan, Bo

Homecoming: Selected Poems. Trans. David McDuff. Manchester: Carcanet, 1992. Includes *The Cool Day, The Courtyard, Years Like Leaves*.

Room without Walls: Selected Poems. Trans. Anne Born. London: Forest Books, 1987.

Envall, Markku. *Toinen minä: Tutkielmia kaksoisolennon aiheesta kirjallisuudessa*. Porvoo: WSOY, 1988, 198–203.

Laitinen, Kai. "Bo Carpelan: The Nordic Council Literary Prize 1977." BFF (1977), 189–91.

Maehle, Leif. "Diktaren som språkets miljövårdare." *Hufvudstadsbladet*, 3 April 1977; also in *Nordisk Tidskrift* (1977).

Schoolfield, George C. "Introduction." In *Voices at the Late Hour*, trans. Irma Margareta Martin. Athens: University of Georgia Press, 1988, v–xxxii.

Tuomolin, Kerstin. *Linjer i Bo Carpelans sextiotalslyrik: En studie i bildspråk och metoder*. Åbo: Åbo Akademi, Litteraturvetenskapliga institutionen, 1985.

Willner, Sven. "Bo Carpelan som kritiker." In Willner, *Det anonyma 50-talet*. Helsingfors: Söderström & Co., 1988, 58–85.

Chorell, Walentin

The Sisters. Trans. Tina Morduch. Intro. George C. Schoolfield. In *Five Modern Scandinavian Plays*, ed. Henry W. Wells. New York: Twayne/American-Scandinavian Foundation, 1971, 101–88.

Björklöf, Eva. "Walentin Chorell som prosaist." FT (1968), 135–37.

Hamberg, Lars. "Walentin Chorells väg till *Guldkusten*." *Horisont* 36 (1989), 6:5–14.

Jones, W. Glyn. "Ethics and the Individual: The Drama of Walentin Chorell." BFF (1984), 24–27.

Salminen, Johannes. "I strandlinjen." In Salminen, *Levande och död tradition*. Helsingfors: Söderström & Co., 1963, 147–52.

———. "Walentin Chorell: An Appreciation." SR (ASR) (1968), 136–39.

Schoolfield, George C. "Walentin Chorell." In *McGraw-Hill Encyclopedia of World Drama*, ed. Stanley Hochman. New York: McGraw-Hill, 1984, 1:516–17.

Colliander, Tito

Jones, W. Glyn. "Tito Colliander: Glimpses into the Past and Present." BFF (1979), 23–28.

Pettersson, Torsten. "'Att han ingenting förstod': Psyket och yttervärlden i Tito Collianders romaner." In *Tio finlandssvenska författare*, ed. Ben Hellman and Clas Zilliacus. Helsingfors: SLF, 1986, 9–20.

Salminen, Johannes. "Vägen till Petjorij." In Salminen, *Gränsland*. Helsingfors: Söderström & Co., 1984, 56–64.

Diktonius, Elmer

Enckell, Olof. *Den unge Diktonius*. Helsingfors: Schildts, 1946.

Romefors, Bill. *Expressionisten Elmer Diktonius*. Helsingfors: SLF, 1978.

Salminen, Johannes. "Once upon a Time There Was a Jaguar: Diktonius's Political Views." Translated in *The Nordic Mind: Current Trends in Scandinavian Literary Criticism*, ed. Frank Egholm Andersen and John Weinstock. Lanham MD: University Press of America, 1986, 153–64.

Schoolfield, George C. *Elmer Diktonius: Poetry and Politics in Finland*. Westport CT: Greenwood, 1985.

———. "Elmer Diktonius and Edgar Lee Masters." In *Studies in Scandinavian-American Relationships, Dedicated to Einar Haugen*, ed. Sigmund Skard and Harald Naess. Oslo: Universitetsforlaget, 1971, 307–27.

———. "Elmer Diktonius and the Art of Orchestration." *SS* (1981), 183–209.

———. "Elmer Diktonius as a Music Critic." *SCAN* (1976), 29–44.

———. "Schubert-Stolberg-Diktonius." In *Aufnahme und Weitergabe, Literarische Impulse um Lessing und Goethe: Festschrift für Heinz Moenkemeyer zum 68. Geburtstag*, ed. Albert Kipa and John McCarthy. Hamburg: Helmut Buske, 1982, 262–68.

———. "Strindberg and Diktonius: A Second Chapter." In *Structures of Influence: A Comparative Approach to August Strindberg*, ed. Marilyn J. Blackwell. Chapel Hill: University of North Carolina Press, 1981, 183–99.

Vainio, Matti. *Diktonius: Modernisti ja säveltäjä*. Helsinki: SMS, 1976. With Swedish summary.

Eklund, R. R.

Pettersson, Torsten. "Att vara seende: En studie i R. R. Eklunds författarskap." *HLS* 66 (1991), 183–220.

Ruin, Hans. "Den store tigaren." In Ruin, *Världen i min fickspegel*. Stockholm: Wahlström & Widstrand, 1969, 63–76.

Schoolfield, George C. "Five Poems of R. R. Eklund." *SS* (1966), 177–203.

Tuominen, Mirjam. "R. R. Eklund och det österbottniska landskapet." In Tuominen, *Studier*. Helsingfors: Söderström & Co., 1947, 131–42.

Enckell, Olof

Ekelund, Erik. "Karelsk exotism." In Ekelund, *Synvinklar*. Helsingfors: Söderström & Co., 1956, 80–98.

Wrede, Johannes. "Olof Enckell: Minnestal." *Sphinx: SSF, Årsbok-Vuosikirja*, ser. B (1990), 99–103.

Enckell, Rabbe
Ekelund, Louise. *Rabbe Enckell: Modernism och klassicism under tjugotal och trettital.* Helsingfors: SLF, 1974.
——. *Rabbe Enckell: Lyriker av den svåra skolan. Studier i diktningen, 1935–1946.* Helsingfors: SLF, 1982.
Enckell, Mikael. *Under beständighetens stjärna: En biografisk studie över Rabbe Enckell, 1903–1937.* Helsingfors: Söderström & Co., 1986.
——. *'—dess ljus lyse!'—En biografisk studie över Rabbe Enckell, 1937–1950.* Helsingfors: Söderström & Co., 1991.
Enckell, Olof. *Rabbe Enckell i Borgå: En kommentar till hans sena diktning.* Helsingfors: Schildts, 1978.
Lindelöf, Lisbet. "På tværs af alle genrer: En analyse af Rabbe Enckells *Landskapet med den dubbla skuggan.*" HLS 50 (1975), 261–346.
Schoolfield, George C. "Rabbe Enckell's 'Mot Itaka.'" *Germanic Notes* 7 (1976), 2:17–22 and 3:36–39.

Enehjelm, Helen af
Enckell, Barbro. "Helen af Enehjelm och hennes hemlängtan." *Horisont* 38 (1991), 5–6:81–83.
Myllyniemi, Kaija. "Helen af Enehjelms litterära verksamhet." HYKJ 32 (1965), 39–80.

Jansson, Tove (see also chapter 11)
Ahola, Suvi. "Towards the Empty Page." BFF (1991), 131–37.
Fleisher, Frederic, and Boel Fleisher. "Tove Jansson and the Moomin Family." SR (ASR) (1963), 47–54.
Jones, W. Glyn. *Tove Jansson.* Boston: Twayne, 1984.
Lurie, Alison. "Undiscovered Country." *New York Review of Books,* 17 December 1992, 16–20.
Ranheim, Kirsten. "Utviklingen i Tove Janssons Muminforfatterskap." *Norsk Litterær Årbok* (1976–77), 54–72.
Westin, Boel. *Familjen i dalen: Tove Janssons muminvärld.* Stockholm: Bonniers, 1988.

Lind, Christer
Lillius, Carl-Gustaf. "'Offrad åt de eviga vindarna': Christer Lind 14.11.1912–13.8.1942." In *Författare om författare: 24 finlandssvenska författarporträtt,* ed. Merete Mazzarella, Johannes Salminen, Ingmar Svedberg, and Sven Willner. Helsingfors: Söderström & Co., 1980, 217–40.

Mörne, Barbro
Pettersson, Torsten. "Från det transcendenta mot det immanenta. En studie i Barbro Mörnes författarskap." TFL 19 (1990), 2:25–45.

Mörne, Håkan
Zilliacus, Clas. "Håkan Mörne, vagabond: Spår i finlandssvensk reselitteratur." In *Fem par: Finlandssvenska författare konfronteras,* ed. Roger Holmström. Helsingfors: SLF, 1995, 59–70.

Niininen, Margit
Mazzarella, Merete. "Margit Niininen, Tora Markman och den förträngda irrationaliteten." HLS 69 (1994), 129–46.

Nyman, Valdemar
Salminen, Johannes. "Valdemar Nyman." In Salminen, *Levande och död tradition*. Helsingfors: Söderström & Co., 1963, 140–46.
Stormbom, N.-B. "Inledning." In Valdemar Nyman, *Margareta Jönsdotter till Bastö*. Helsingfors: Schildts, 1960, 5–9.

Olin, Ulla
Barck, Ghita. "Dikt som bevarar verkligheten: Ulla Olins lyrik." FT (1988) 98–105.

Olsson, Hagar
Ekelund, Erik. "Resa till det förflutna." In Ekelund, *Synvinklar*. Helsingfors: Söderström & Co., 1956, 160–76.
Enckell, Olof. *Den unga Hagar Olsson*. Helsingfors: SLF, 1949.
Fridell, Lena. *Hagar Olsson och den nya teatern*. Göteborg: Göteborgs universitet, 1973.
Holmström, Roger. *Hagar Olsson och den öppna horisonten. Liv och diktning 1: 1920–1944*. Helsingfors: Schildts, 1993.
———. *Hagar Olsson och den växande melankolin: Liv och diktning, 1945–1978*. Helsingfors: Schildts, 1995.
Petherick, Karin. "Four Finland-Swedish Prose Modernists." SCAN (1976): Supplement, 45–62.
Schoolfield, George C. "Hagar Olsson." In *McGraw-Hill Encyclopedia of World Drama*, ed. Stanley Hochman. New York: McGraw-Hill, 1984, 4:20–21.
———. "Hagar Olsson's *Chitambo*: Anniversary Thoughts on Names and Structure." SS (1973), 223–62.
———. "Introduction." In Hagar Olsson, *The Woodcarver and Death*. Madison: University of Wisconsin Press, 1965, ix–xxxix.
Schoolfield, George C., and Laurie Thompson, eds., with Michael Schmelzle. *Two Women Writers from Finland: Edith Södergran and Hagar Olsson*. Edinburgh: Lockharton Press, 1995. Sixteen essays, including five on Olsson, two on Södergran and Olsson.
Stormbom, N.-B. "Inward Journey: The Works of Hagar Olsson." SR (ASR) 52 (1964), 261–66.
Törnquist, Egil. "Hagar Olsson's First Play." SCAN (1976), 63–72.
Zilliacus, Clas. "Snöbollskrig som frös bort: Hagar Olsson och dramatiken år 1939." In *Pegas och snöbollskrig: Litteraturvetenskapliga studier tillägnade Sven Linnér*, ed. Roger Holmström, Krister Segerberg, and Clas Zilliacus. Åbo: Åbo Akademi, 1979, 171–85.
Zuck, Virpi. "In Defence of Human Dignity: Hagar Olsson and *Tidevarvet*." In *Studies in German and Scandinavian Literature after 1500: Festschrift for George C. Schoolfield*, ed. James A. Parente Jr. and Richard Erich Schade. Columbia SC: Camden House, 1993, 259–70.

Parland, Henry
Barck, Ghita. "Henry Parland." HLS 27-28 (1952), 137-218.
Butt, Wolfgang. "Nachwort." In Henry Parland, *Z.B. schreiben wie gerade jetzt: Gedichte.* Helsinki: Otava, 1984, 159-74.
Nilsson, Kim. "Henry Parland." In *Dictionary of Scandinavian Literature,* ed. Virpi Zuck with Niels Ingwersen and Harald Næss. Westport CT: Greenwood, 1990, 473.
Robbins, Betsy, and Stefan Malmberg. *Studier i Henry Parland.* Åbo: Åbo Akademi, Litteraturvetenskapliga institutionen, 1985.
Stenmark, Erik. "Två ledmotiv i Henry Parlands *Sönder.*" FT (1968), 436-54.

Parland, Oscar
Björklund, Kristina. *Riki och den fortrollade vägen: Studier i Oscar Parlands berättarkonst.* Helsingfors: SLF, 1982.

Parland, Ralf
Fallberg, Sören. "Hem till sitt hav: Livskänslan hos Ralf Parland." OOB 73 (1964), 342-50.

Pettersson, Joel
Holm, Nils G. "Joel Pettersson och religionen." *Horisont* 35 (1988), 4:31-38.

Quosego
Enckell, Olof. "Vägen till *Quosego.*" In *Quosego: Tidskrift för ny generation,* ed. Olof Enckell. Reprint. Borgå: Söderström & Co., 1971, v-xli.

Salminen, Sally
Bäckman, Ann-Lisa. "Upptäcktsresan: Om Sally Salminen." In *Kvinnornas litteraturhistoria,* ed. Marie Louise Ramnefalk and Anna Westberg. Stockholm: Författarförlaget, 1981, 440-460.
Bukdahl, Jørgen. "Sally Salminen." In Bukdahl, *Mellemkrigstid.* Copenhagen: Aschehoug Dansk Forlag, 1945, 124-33.
Mazzarella, Merete. *Att skriva sin värld: Om den finlandssvenska memoartraditionen.* Helsingfors: Söderström & Co., 1993, 34, 43.
Stenwall-Albjerg, Åsa. "Utanförskapet hos Sally Salminen." In *Fem par: Finlandssvenska författare konfronteras,* ed. Roger Holmström. Helsingfors: SLF, 1995, 85-96.

Sandelin, Peter
Borum, Poul. Review of Sandelin. *Vindrosen* (1968), 1, 71.
Ekman, Michel. "Försjunkande och elevation: Två centrala teman i Peter Sandelins tidiga författarskap." HLS 68 (1993), 189-218.
Hedlund, Tom. "Bland de små universella frågorna—Synpunkter på Peter Sandelins poesi (1972-1977)." In Hedlund, *Dikten som liv.* Stockholm: Liber, 1980, 150-65.
Holmström, Roger. "Rymdperspektivet i Peter Sandelins diktning." FT (1978), 251-59.

Wängsö, Thomas. "'Gräset sträcker sig mot rymden': En översiktlig presentation av lyrikern Peter Sandelin, 1951–1986." *Horisont* 35 (1988), 2:50–63.
Willner, Sven. "Peter Sandelin." In Willner, *Vägar till poesin*. Helsingfors: Söderström & Co., 1985, 134–47.

Södergran, Edith
Collected Poems. Trans. Martin Allwood, with Cate Ewing and Robert Lyng. Mullsjö: Anglo-American Center, 1980.
Complete Poems. Trans. David Mcduff. Newcastle-upon-Tyne: Bloodaxe, 1984, rev. ed. 1992.
Love and Solitude: Selected Poems, 1916–1923. Trans. Stina Katchadourian. Seattle: Fjord Press, 1981, rev. 1985, 1992.
Poems. Trans. Gounil Brown. Gwynedd: Zean, 1990; rev. ed. Eastbourne: Icon Press, 1994.
Violet Twilights. Trans. Daisy Aldan and Leif Sjöberg. Merrick NY: Cross-Cultural Communications, 1993.
Broomans, Petra, Adriaan van der Hoeven, and Jytte Kronig, eds. *Edith Södergran: A Changing Image on the Work of a Finnish Avant-Garde Poet*. Groningen: R.U.G. Werkgroep Vrouwenstudies Letteren, 1993.
Jones, W. Glyn, and M. A. Branch, eds. *Edith Södergran: Nine Essays on Her Life and Work*. London: School of Slavonic and East European Studies; Helsinki: SKS, 1992.
Pettersson, Torsten. "Den dubbla blicken hos Edith Södergran." In *Fem par: Finlandssvenska författare konfronteras*, ed. Roger Holmström. Helsingfors: SLF, 1995, 35–46.
Schoolfield, George C. *Edith Södergran: Modernist Poet in Finland*. Westport CT: Greenwood, 1984.
——. "No End of Edith." *SBR* (1992): Supplement, 5–17.
Schoolfield, George C., and Laurie Thompson, eds., with Michael Schmelzle. *Two Women Writers from Finland: Edith Södergran and Hagar Olsson*. Edinburgh: Lockharton Press, 1995. Sixteen essays, including nine on Södergran, two on Södergran and Olsson.
Tideström, Gunnar. *Edith Södergran*. Stockholm: Wahlström & Widstrand, 1949, 1960.

Söderholm, Kerstin
"Diary (Excerpts)." Intro. and trans. George C. Schoolfield. In *Scandinavian Women Writers: An Anthology from the 1880s to the 1980s*, ed. Ingrid Claréus. New York, Westport CT: Greenwood, 1989, 113–28.
Allardt Ekelund, Karin. "'Ej nöd så länge själen har vingar': Kring Kerstin Söderholms livsväg." *HLS* 60 (1985), 183–220.
——. "Kerstin Söderholm." In Kerstin Söderholm, *Endast med mig själv*. Helsingfors: Söderström & Co., 1947, 5–54.
——. "Kerstin Söderholms diktning." In Allardt Ekelund, *Traneplogar*. Helsingfors: Söderström & Co., 1977, 97–105.

Pettersson, Torsten. "Den svåra gemenskapen: En studie i Kerstin Söderholms författarskap." *Horisont* 37 (1990), 2-3:68-81.
Piekkala, Jussi. "Kvinnorna och kriget." In *Dikt i krig: Fem studier i finlandssvensk lyrik, 1939-1945*, ed. Ben Hellman. Helsingfors universitet: Avdelningen för svensk litteratur, 1985, 57-72.

Stenius, Göran
Ekelund, Erik. "Karelsk exotism." In Ekelund, *Synvinklar*. Helsingfors: Söderström & Co., 1956, 80-98.
Jones, W. Glyn. "For Keller Read Stenius." *SS* 53 (1981), 391-96.
———. "Göran Stenius' Philosophical Novels." *SCAN* 17 (1977), 93-108.
Salminen, Johannes. "Göran Stenius: Karelare och katolik." In *Tio finlandssvenska författare*, ed. Ben Hellman and Clas Zilliacus. Helsingfors: SLF, 1986, 21-37.

Tigerstedt, Örnulf
Barck, P. O. "Svart harnesk." In Barck, *Dikt och förkunnelse*. Stockholm: Natur & Kultur, 1936, 185-220.
Ekelund, Erik. "Poet i harnesk och tagelskjorta." In Ekelund, *Synvinklar*. Helsingfors: Söderström & Co., 1956, 144-59.
Enckell, Olof. "Inledning." In Örnulf Tigerstedt, *Valv och båge: Valda dikter*. Strängnäs: Fahlcrantz & Gumælius, 1951, 7-35.
Waltå, Göran Olson. *Poet under Black Banners: The Case of Örnulf Tigerstedt and Extreme Right-Wing Swedish Literature in Finland, 1918-1944*. Uppsala: Litteraturvetenskapliga institutionen, 1993.

Torvalds, Ole
Storå, Siv. "Ole Torvalds lyrik: Tolk för ett klarnande jag." *FT* (1976), 499-511.
Stormbom, N.-B. "Två årtionden finlandssvensk lyrik [1929-1949]." *HLS* 51 (1976), 17-54.

Tuominen, Mirjam
Selected Writings. Intro. Tuva Korsström. Trans. David McDuff. Newcastle-upon-Tyne: Bloodaxe, 1994.
Barck, Ghita. *Mirjam Irene Tuominen i liv och dikt*. Helsingfors: SLF, 1983.
Korsström, Tuva. "Dark Gods." *BFF* (1991), 195-206.
Linnér, Sven. "Mirjam Tuominen som kritiker." In *Från vän till vän: Festskrift till Olof Mustelin — historiker och bibliotekarie — på hans 60-årsdag*, ed. Torbjörn Söderholm. Åbo: Åbo Akademis bibliotek, 1984, 219-35.

Ultra
Warburton, Thomas. "Tidskriften *Ultra*." *BLM* (1945), 51-52.

von Schoultz, Solveig
Heartwork: Short Stories. Trans. Marlaine Delargy and Joan Tate. London: Forest Books, 1989.
"A Little Consideration." Intro. and trans. Margareta N. Deschner. In *Scandinavian*

Women Writers: An Anthology from the 1880s to the 1980s, ed. Ingrid Claréus. Westport CT: Greenwood, 1989, 169–80.
Poems, 1940–1980. Trans. Jeremy Parsons. London: Limited edition, 1982.
Snow and Summers (Poems, 1940–1989). Trans. Anne Born. London: Forest Books, 1989.
Schoolfield, George C. "The Narrative of Solveig von Schoultz." SBR (1989), 19–26.
Wrede, Petra. "En barnskildring av Solveig von Schoultz." In *Pegas och snöbollskrig: Litteraturvetenskapliga studier tillägnade Sven Linnér,* ed. Roger Holmström, Krister Segerberg, and Clas Zilliacus. Åbo: Åbo Akademi, 1979, 155–70.

Warburton, Thomas
Willner, Sven. "Lärodiktaren Th. Warburton." In Willner, *Vägar till poesin.* Helsingfors: Söderström & Co., 1985, 109–16.

Wichman, Eva
Bonsdorff, Monica von. *Eva Wichman och politiken.* Helsingfors: Bildningsförbund, 1983.
Salminen, Johannes. "Eva Wichman." In Salminen, *Levande och död tradition.* Helsingfors: Söderström & Co., 1983, 135–39.
Wik, Inga-Britt. "'Sökande efter eget': Från Mania till Marina i Eva Wichmans prosa." In *Författare om författare: 24 finlandssvenska författarporträtt,* ed. Merete Mazzarella, Johannes Salminen, Ingmar Svedberg, and Sven Willner. Helsingfors: Söderström & Co., 1980, 204–16.
Willner, Sven. "Lyrikern Eva Wichman." In Willner, *Vägar till poesin.* Helsingfors: Söderström & Co., 1985, 85–108.

CHAPTER 10: A STARTLING GROWTH, 1960–1990

LITERARY HISTORY

Boucht, Birgitta. "När litteratur blir kropp: Om finlandssvenska kvinnors böcker." In *Kvinnornas litteraturhistoria. 2: 1900-talet,* ed. Ingrid Holmqvist and Ebba Witt-Brattström. Malmö: Författarförlaget, 1983, 461–78.
Ekman, Michel. "Finlandssvensk skönlitteratur 1988." FT (1989), 77–90.
———. "A Literature Written by Poets." SBR (1992): Supplement, 26–31. Lyricists of the 1980s.
———. "Varken förklara eller låta sig anrättas — Om de senaste decenniernas unga finlandssvenska poesi." In *11 finlandssvenska poeter,* ed. Michel Ekman. Helsingfors: ai–ai, 1992, 5–25.
Hellman, Ben, and Clas Zilliacus, eds. *Tio finlandssvenska författare.* Helsingfors: SLF, 1986. Gösta Ågren, Claes Andersson, Tito Colliander, Hans Fors, Christer Kihlman, Ulla-Lena Lundberg, Paul von Martens, Irmelin Sandman Lilius, Göran Stenius, Henrik Tikkanen.

Huldén, Lars. "Swedish Poetry in Finland on the Threshold of the Eighties." *WLT* (1980), 47–50.

Ingström, Pia. "Bloom Time for the Finland-Swedish Novel." *SBR* (1992): Supplement, 48–53. Novelists of the 1980s.

Jansson, Henrik. "Ur askan: Om *Fågel Fenix*." In *Från dagdrivare till feminister,* ed. Sven Linnér. Helsingfors: SLF, 1986, 293–316.

Kihlman, Christer. "The Shadow Cast by Swedishness." In *The Nordic Mind: Current Trends in Scandinavian Literary Criticism,* ed. Frank Andersen and John Weinstock. Lanham MD: University Press of America, 1986, 111–15.

Långbacka, Lena, and Benita Alanne. *Finlandssvenskt författarskap: Kåren och villkoren: Två undersökningar.* Åbo: Åbo Akademi, 1993.

Mazzarella, Merete. "Den kvinnomedvetna prosan efter 1970." In *Från dagdrivare till feminister,* ed. Sven Linnér. Helsingfors: SLF, 1986, 317–44.

———. *Det trånga rummet: En finlandssvensk romantradition.* Helsingfors: Söderström & Co., 1989.

Pettersson, Torsten. "Nio decennier finlandssvensk litteratur." *Horisont* 37 (1990), 6, 37–49.

Rönnholm, Bror. "*FBT*—Tidskrift i tiden." In *Från dagdrivare till feminister,* ed. Sven Linnér. Helsingfors: SLF, 1986, 257–92.

Söderling, Trygve. "Liv & tvång; sortie; encore—'Våra litterära hemmaexpressionister.'" *FT* (1987), 32–48.

———. "Nightdrivers in Moomin Valley: Seven Radar Scans over Finland-Swedish Prose-Writing, 1987." *SBR* (1992): Supplement, 71–80. Originally published as "Nightdrivers i Mumindalen: 7 radarsvep över ung finlandssvensk prosa," *Horisont* (1987), 1, 21–33.

Stürmer, Wava. "Författaraktivitet i Österbotten: Ett tjuguårigt perspektiv." *FT* (1978), 357–65.

Willner, Sven. "70-talet i finlandssvensk litteratur." In *Författare i Finland,* ed. Kai Laitinen and Sven Willner. Helsingfors: Söderström & Co., 1983, 24–41.

MONOGRAPHS AND ARTICLES
Ågren, Gösta

A Valley in the Midst of Violence: Selected Poems. Trans. David McDuff. Newcastle-upon-Tyne: Bloodaxe, 1993.

Benrós, Jette Eriksen. "Där du går finns det du söker: En läsning av Gösta Ågrens poesi." *Horisont* 38 (1991), 5–6:16–23.

Huldén, Lars. "Det paradoxala i Gösta Ågrens lyrik." In *Tio finlandssvenska författare,* ed. Ben Hellman and Clas Zilliacus. Helsingfors: SLF, 1986, 124–48.

Willner, Sven. "Gösta Ågren" In Willner, *Det anonyma 50-talet.* Helsingfors: Söderström & Co., 1988, 204–19.

Alander, Siw
von Wright, Marianne. "Svag och utsatt i ekorrhjulet—Siw Alanders kvinnovärld." *FT* (1983), 119–23.

Alopaeus, Marianne
Mazzarella, Merete. "Marianne Alopaeus—Kvinna eller mänska?" In Mazzarella, *Från Fredrika Runeberg till Märta Tikkanen: Frihet och beroende i finlandssvensk kvinnolitteratur.* Helsingfors: Söderström & Co., 1985, 155–70.

Andersson, Claes
Poems in Our Absence. Trans. Lennart Bruce and Sonia Bruce. Cleveland: Bonne Chance Press, 1994.
Selected Poems. Trans. Rika Lesser. Los Angeles: Sun & Moon, 1996.
Warburton, Thomas. "Claes Andersson: The Poet as Progressive." BFF (1979), 94–96.
Zilliacus, Clas. "'Att dikta är att förändra ljuset': Utvecklingslinjer i Claes Anderssons lyrik." In *Tio finlandssvenska författare,* ed. Ben Hellman and Clas Zilliacus. Helsingfors: SLF, 1986, 149–68.

Bäck, Tomas Mikael
Ekman, Michel. "Det drunknande jaget eller vad menar Tomas Mikael Bäck?" FT (1991), 160–67.

Bergman, Karl-Erik
Storå, Siv. "Kontrasten—Ett riktmärke i Karl-Erik Bergmans lyriska självsyn." FT (1979), 54–66.

Björklund, Kristina
Rajalin, Marita. "Riki och Mitra: Kristina Björklund som barndomsskildrare." FT (1986), 78–86.
Stenwall, Åsa. "'I dockskåpet hade pappadockan försvunnit': Kristina Björklunds *Månens tid.*" In Stenwall, *Hur flickor blir kloka: Om flickuppväxt i nyare finlandssvensk litteratur.* Helsingfors: Schildts, 1987, 135–65.

Blomqvist, Anni
Steinby, Ann-Gerd, and Ann Christin Waller. *Anni Blomqvist: Stormskärs-Majas skapare.* Helsingfors: Söderström & Co., 1993.

Byggmästar, Eva-Stina
Ekman, Michel. "Kroppslighet och utopi i Eva-Stina Byggmästars poesi." In *Fem par: Finlandssvenska författare konfronteras,* ed. Roger Holmström. Helsingfors: SLF, 1995, 47–56.

Cleve, Anders
Gustafsson, Lars. "Finlands nya väg." BLM (1962), 849–52.
Storå, Siv. "Anders Cleve—Sökare i labyrint." In *Fem par: Finlandssvenska författare konfronteras,* ed. Roger Holmström. Helsingfors: SLF, 1995, 117–32.
———. "Anders Cleves författarskap under tjugo år." FT (1975), 140–53.
Willner, Sven. "Anders Cleve." In *Författare i Finland,* ed. Pekka Tarkka, Kai Laitinen, and Sven Willner. Helsingfors: Söderström & Co., 1983, 67–69.
———. "Anders Cleve." In Willner, *Det anonyma 50-talet.* Helsingfors: Söderström & Co., 1988, 158–77.

Donner, Jörn
Cowie, Peter. "The Finno-Swedish World of Jörn Donner." *SR* (1985), 88–95.
Holmström, Roger. "Jakob och den ogripbara friheten: Ett tema i Jörn Donners romankonst." *FT* (1979), 41–49.
Lehtola, Erkka. "Jörn Donner: Action Man." *BFF* (1986), 10–13.

Emtö, Solveig
Ekman, Michel. "Finlandssvensk skönlitteratur 1988." *FT* (1989), 77–90.
Högnäs-Sahlgren, Brita. "Solveig Emtö—Viktig och stor." *FT* (1982), 35–39.

Enckell, Agneta
Ekman, Michel. "Reclaiming the Body." *BFF* (1992), 145–47.
——. "Rummet och fallet: Tematiska anteckningar om Agneta Enckells poesi." *Kontur* (1993), 3–4:11–14.
Ingström, Pia. "I samtal med Agneta Enckell." *Kontur* (1993), 3–4:2–5.

Enckell, Martin
Mazzarella, Merete. "Martin Enckell." In Mazzarella, *Det trånga rummet: En finlandssvensk romantradition*. Helsingfors: Söderström & Co., 1989, 210–22.

Enckell, Michael
Mazzarella, Merete. *Samtal*. Helsingfors: Söderström & Co., 1990, 130–36.

Fagerholm, Monika
Dickens, Eric. "Monika Fagerholm." *SBR* (1992): Supplement, 86.
Sandin, Maria. "Det ofärdiga jagets förvandlingar: Samtal med Monika Fagerholm." *Horisont* 38 (1991), 5–6:2–10.

Fors, Hans
Hellman, Ben. "Österbottningen Hans Fors." In *Tio finlandssvenska författare*, ed. Ben Hellman and Clas Zilliacus. Helsingfors: SLF, 1986, 93–107.

Forsström, Tua
Andersson, Claes. "Between Eros and Thanatos." *BFF* (1989), 151–53.
Hedman, Kaj. "Tua Forsström på två plan." *Horisont* (1989), 2:20–23.

Högnäs, Kurt
Torvalds, Ole. "Vindbudskap lövledes: Om prosalyrikern Kurt Högnäs." *FT* (1988), 91–97.

Högnäs-Sahlgren, Brita
Stenwall-Albjerg, Åsa. "Den otillfredsställda kvinnan—En gestalt i Brita Högnäs-Sahlgrens författarskap." *FT* (1989), 91–101.

Huldén, Lars
The Chain Dunce: Selected Poems. Trans. George C. Schoolfield. Columbia SC: Camden House, 1991.
Mazzarella, Merete, and Lars Huldén. "Samtal kring en dikt ['Kom och var du mitt täcke']." *HLS* 65 (1990), 165–74.

Storå, Siv. "Gycklet skall hjälpa sanningens ord: Lek och allvar i Lars Huldéns lyrik." FT (1976), 7–24.
Willner, Sven. "Lars Huldén, tillfällighetsdiktare." In Willner, *Vägar till poesin.* Helsingfors: Söderström & Co., 1985, 148–65.

Kihlman, Christer
Nordgren, Elisabeth. "Värderevolten hos Christer Kihlman." In *Tio finlandssvenska författare,* ed. Ben Hellman and Clas Zilliacus. Helsingfors: SLF, 1986, 61–75.
Schoolfield, George C. "Afterword." In *The Blue Mother,* trans. Joan Tate. Lincoln: University of Nebraska Press, 1990, 289–308.
Svedberg, Ingmar. "Extending the Bounds of Reality: An Approach to the Work of Christer Kihlman." BFF (1976), 7–10.

Kurtén, Björn
Hård, Gunnar. "Björn Kurtén." *Horisont* 31 (1984), 5:36–39.
Leikola, Anto. "The Palaeo-Fiction of Björn Kurtén." BFF (1983), 18–22.

Lång, Fredrik
Högnäs, Gunnar. "Den långa marschen från Gamla Studenthuset till Yttermark." FT (1989), 102–14.

Lindberg, Pirkko
Antas, Maria. "En vagabond flyger aldrig: Pirkko Lindbergs *Tramp* och den ekologiska reserapporten." In *Fem par: Finlandssvenska författare konfronteras,* ed. Roger Holmström. Helsingfors: SLF, 1995, 71–84.

Lindén, Gurli
Lund, Solveig. "Gurli Lindén, vetgirig visionär." FT (1985), 95–105.
Stenwall, Åsa. "Att följa älven: Gurli Lindén, *Första damernas.*" In Stenwall, *Hur flickor blir kloka: Om flickuppväxt i nyare finlandssvensk litteratur.* Helsingfors: Schildts, 1987, 67–88.

Lindfors, Bodil
Abrahamsson, Birgitta. "Bodil Lindfors — Lyriker i förvandling." FT (1987), 49–58.
Ekman, Michel. "Finlandssvensk skönlitteratur 1989." FT (1990), 100–111.

Lundberg, Ulla-Lena
Lindfors, Mette. "Anna Petterssons val: Den fiktiva romanpersonens livscykel i Ulla-Lena Lundbergs roman om Anna." In *Fem par: Finlandssvenska författare konfronteras,* ed. Roger Holmström. Helsingfors: SLF, 1995, 97–116.
Snickars, Ann-Christine. "Ulla-Lena Lundberg: Det personliga och det antropologiska perspektivet." In *Tio finlandssvenska författare,* ed. Ben Hellman and Clas Zilliacus. Helsingfors: SLF, 1986, 169–83.
Stenwall, Åsa. "I förlustens landskap: Ulla-Lena Lundberg: *Kungens Anna.*" In Stenwall, *Hur flickor blir kloka: Om flickuppväxt i nyare finlandssvensk litteratur.* Helsingfors: Schildts, 1987, 13–66.
Waller, Ann-Christian. "Att stilla smärtan i en sökande själ: En fas i Ulla-Lena Lundbergs författarskap." FT (1978), 224–33.

Martens, Paul von
Holmström, Roger. "Vardag och vision i Paul von Martens' prosa." In *Tio finlandssvenska författare*, ed. Ben Hellman and Clas Zilliacus. Helsingfors: SLF, 1986, 77–93.
Johansson, Eva. "Romanen som förmedlare av en religiös erfarenhet — Ett studium i Paul von Martens författarskap." *Horisont* 35 (1988), 4:39–43.

Nordgren, Ralf
Jones, W. Glyn. "The Elusive Reality of Ralf Nordgren." BFF (1982), 4–6.
Sundholm, John. "Vem är jag? Jag förstås! Ralf Nordgrens roman *med* och det moderna jagets sociologi." In *Fem par: Finlandssvenska författare konfronteras*, ed. Roger Holmström. Helsingfors: SLF, 1995, 23–34.

Österberg, Anna-Lisa
Stenwall, Åsa. "'På en smal bräda genom tillvaron': Anna-Lisa Österberg: *Kvinnoträdet* och *Flickan*." In Stenwall, *Hur flickor blir kloka: Om flickuppväxt i nyare finlandssvensk litteratur*. Helsingfors: Schildts, 1987, 117–34.
Stenwall-Albjerg, Åsa. "Anna-Lisa Österberg — En viktig röst." FT (1984), 114–21.

Påwals, Per-Hakon
Willner, Sven. "Per-Hakon Påwals." In Willner, *Det anonyma 50-talet*. Helsingfors: Söderström & Co., 1988, 220–41.

Salmén, Leif
Willner, Sven. "Leif Salmén: The Poet and the Politician." BFF (1987), 198–200.

Salminen, Johannes
Mazzarella, Merete. *Samtal*. Helsingfors: Söderström & Co., 1990, 130–36.

Sandell, Tom
Willner, Sven. "Tom Sandell." In Willner, *Det anonyma 50-talet*. Helsingfors: Söderström & Co., 1988, 242–64.

Schildt, Göran
Scobbie, Irene. "Göran Schildt." SBR (1994): Supplement, 53–54.
Zilliacus, Benedict. "Göran Schildt: Sailing the Southern Seas." BFF (1988), 115–17.

Tikkanen, Henrik
Schoolfield, George C. "Afterword." In *The Thirty Years' War*, trans. George Blecher and Lone Tygesen Blecher. Lincoln: University of Nebraska Press, 1987, 123–58.
Wrede, Johan. "Henrik Tikkanen: Psykologiska utgångspunkter för ett författarskap." In *Tio finlandssvenska författare*, ed. Ben Hellman and Clas Zilliacus. Helsingfors: SLF, 1986, 37–60.

Tikkanen, Märta
Mazzarella, Merete. "Märta Tikkanen — Passion eller jämlikhet?" In Mazzarella, *Från Fredrika Runeberg till Märta Tikkanen: Frihet och beroende i finlandssvensk kvinnolitteratur*. Helsingfors: Söderström & Co., 1985, 171–87.

Valtiala, Nalle
Ekman, Michel. "Finlandssvensk skönlitteratur 1988." FT (1989), 77–90.

Westö, Kjell
Dickens, Eric. "Kjell Westö." SBR (1992): Supplement, 90.
Rönnholm, Bror. "Den ihåliga identiteten—Ett tema hos Kjell Westö." In *Fem par: Finlandssvenska författare konfronteras,* ed. Roger Holmström. Helsingfors: SLF, 1995, 133–46.
Tarkka, Pekka. "How to Survive in the Fast Lane." BFF (1991), 67–68.

Wik, Inga-Britt
Nyström, Carita. "'Att finna varandra—Levande': Tankar kring Inga-Britt Wiks *Ingen lycklig kärlek.*" FT (1989), 115–22.
Willner, Sven. "Inga-Britt Wik." In Willner, *Det anonyma 50-talet.* Helsingfors: Söderström & Co., 1988, 121–39.

Wright, Georg Henrik von
Schilpp, P. A., ed. *The Philosophy of Georg Henrik von Wright.* Kinderhook: E. J. Brill, 1985.
Schoolfield, George C. "Georg Henrik von Wright, *Vetenskapen och förnuftet.*" SR (1988), 113–17.

Wulff, Thomas
Jansson, Henrik. "Thomas Wulff—Experimentator och revoltör." FT (1982), 14–28.

CHAPTER 11: CHILDREN'S LITERATURE

LITERARY HISTORY

Ahola, Suvi. "Fantasy and Exploitation: Contemporary Finnish Children's Literature." BFF (1985), 164–71.
Dixon, Roderick. "The Whole Place Is Swarming with Blue Cats." *Look at Finland* (1979), 3, 40–45.
Helakisa, Kaarina. "Stories for the Young at Heart." BFF (1979), 56–63.
Kuivasmäki, Riitta. *Siiwollisuuden tuntoa ja ylewätä kauneuden mieltä: Suomenkielinen nuorisokirjallisuus, 1851–1899.* Jyväskylä: Jyväskylän yliopisto, 1990.
Kurki-Suonio, Sirkka. "Nuortenkirjallisuus." *Suomen kirjallisuus 8.* Helsinki: Otava, 1970, 322–70.
Lappalainen, Irja. *Suomalainen lasten- ja nuortenkirjallisuus.* Tapiola: Weilin & Göös, 1976.
———, ed. *Ungdomsboken i Finland förr och nu.* Helsinki: Otava, 1970.
Lehtonen, Maija. "Huomiota suomalaisesta teiniromaanista." In *Sininen lamppu: Näkökulmia lasten- ja nuortenkirjallisuuteen ja sen tutkimukseen,* ed. Riitta Kuivasmäki, Inka Makkonen, Hannele Suomi, and Tuula Koralainen. Tampere: Suomen Nuorisokirjallisuuden Instituutin julkaisuja 3 (1983), 77–90. With English summary.

———. "Teenage Fiction in Finland." BFF (1982), 12–15.
Lehtonen, Maija, and Marita Rajalin, eds. *Barnboken i Finland förr och nu*. Stockholm: Rabén & Sjögren, 1984.
Lehtonen, Ulla. *Lastenkirjallisuus Suomessa, 1543–1850: Kirjahistoriallinen tutkimus*. Tampere: Suomen Nuorisokirjallisuuden Instituutin julkaisuja 1 (1981).
Manninen, Kerttu. "Suomenkielisen nuorisokirjallisuuden vaiheita." In *Lue lapsille!* ed. Tuula Ikonen, Satu Marttila, and Kari Vaijärvi. Helsinki: Weilin & Göös, 1981, 87–103.
Rajalin, Marita. "Flickan och omvärlden i den finlandssvenska flickboken." In *Sininen lamppu: Näkökulmia lasten- ja nuortenkirjallisuuteen ja sen tutkimukseen*, ed. Riitta Kuivasmäki et al. Tampere: Suomen Nuorisokirjallisuuden Instituutin julkaisuja 3 (1983), 63–76. With English summary.
Rosenqvist, Kerstin. *Finlandssvensk barnlitteratur fram till år 1900*. Projektet Barn- och ungdomslitteratur i Sverige, no. 2. Uppsala: Avdelning för litteratursociologi vid Litteraturvetenskapliga institutionen i Uppsala, 1974.
Shavit, Zohar. *Poetics of Children's Literature*. Athens: University of Georgia Press, 1986.
Suhonen, Pekka. "The Illustrated Fairy Tale." BFF (1979), 53–55.

MONOGRAPHS AND ARTICLES
Hammarström, Nanny
Åström, Margit. "Sagoförfattaren Nanny Hammarström och livsbejakelse." FG 11 (1976), 125–62.

Jansson, Tove (see also chapter 9)
Kurhela, Virpi, ed. *Muumien taikaa: Tutkiretki Tove Janssonin maailman*. Helsinki: Kirjastopalvelu, Suomen Nuorisokirjallisuuden Instituutti, 1996.

Lindquist, Marita
Rajalin, Markita. "Finlandssvenska realistiska berättelser för små barn och barn i slukaråldern." In *Barnboken i Finland*, ed. Maija Lehtonen and Marita Rajalin. Stockholm: Rabén & Sjögren, 1984, 106–14.

Mäkelä, Hannu
Mäkelä, Hannu. "How I Came upon Mr. Huu." BFF (1976), 15–18.

Mickwitz, Camilla
Alapuro, Kristina. "Exploring the Child's World with Anna Tauriala and Camilla Mickwitz." BFF (1979), 48–54.

Nissinen, Aila
Vuorinen, Minna. "Finskspråkig sago- och fantasilitteraturen, dikter." In *Barnboken i Finland*, ed. Maija Lehtonen and Marita Rajalin. Stockholm: Rabén & Sjögren, 1984, 57–76.

Sandman Lilius, Irmelin
Korsström, Tuva. "On a Magic Carpet: Irmelin Sandman Lilius." BFF (1990), 135–37.

Nettervik, Ingrid. "Med Irmelin Sandman Lilius på främlingsvägar genom verkligheten." SLT (1982), 38–44.
Sandman Lilius, Irmelin. "Bakom skärmen." BLM (1980), 219–21.
Schottenius, Maria. "En Tulavärld i våra hjärtan." BLM (1980), 398–400.
Warburton, Thomas. "Irmelin Sandman Lilius: Mistress of Tulavall." BFF (1977), 91–94.
Wrede, Petra. "*Fru Sola*-trilogin: En undersökning av struktur, symboler och motiv hos Irmelin Sandman Lilius." In *Tio finlandssvenska författare*, ed. Ben Hellman and Clas Zilliacus. Helsingfors: SLF, 1986, 107–24.
———. "Irmelin Sandman Lilius' sagovärld—En hamn med många inlopp." FT (1979), 30–40.
———. "Tulavall och Ugglesalien: Irmelin Sandman Lilius på nya vägar." FT (1983), 107–18.

Swan, Anni
Lehtonen, Maija. *Anni Swan*. Porvoo: WSOY, 1958.

Topelius, Zachris (see also chapter 7)
The Birch and the Star and Other Stories. Trans. G. Thorne-Thomsen. Chicago: Row, Peterson, 1915.
Canute Whistlewinks and Other Stories. Trans. C. W. Foss. London: Longmans, 1927.
Northern Lights: Stories from Swedish and Finnish Authors. Trans. Selma Borg and Maria A. Brown. Philadelphia: Porter & Coates, 1873. Contains six children's stories by Topelius.
The Seaking's Gift and Other Tales from Finland. Trans. Irma Kaplan. London: F. Muller, 1973.
Stories for Children. Trans. C. W. Foss. Rock Island IL: Augustana, 1902–11.
Apo, Satu. "The Two Worlds of the Finnish Fairytale: Observations on the Folk and Literary Fairytale Tradition of the Nineteenth Century." *Arv: Scandinavian Yearbook of Folklore* 44 (1988), 27–48.
Laurent, Kaarina. *Topelius saturunoilijana*. Helsinki: WSOY, 1947.
Schoolfield, George C. "Fairy Tales of a Journalist." BFF (1984), 8–12.
Suhonen, Pekka. "The Pit of Star-Eye." BFF (1984), 20–22. Preceded by W. Glyn Jones, trans., "Star-Eye," 13–19.

The Contributors and Translators

Michael Branch is director of the School of Slavonic and East European Studies (London) and professor of Finnish. His research has focused on Finnish-Karelian oral tradition, Finnish literature, and the uses of language, literature, and oral tradition in shaping a Finnish cultural identity. His publications include studies of the Finnish historian A. J. Sjögren and the writers Eino Leino and F. E. Sillanpää, the 1985 edition of the Everyman *Kalevala,* and the collaborative works *Finnish Folk Poetry: Epic* (1977) and *The Great Bear* (1993, 1994). His recent edited volumes are *The Uses of Tradition* (1994, with Celia Hawkesworth) and *Finland and Poland in the Russian Empire* (1995, with Janet Hartley and Antoni Maczak). He was an editor of *Books from Finland* from 1976 to 1980. In 1980 he was made a commander of the Order of the Finnish Lion and in 1983 received an honorary doctorate from the University of Oulu.

Markku Envall has been docent in Finnish literature at the University of Helsinki and in 1996 began holding a three-year writer's grant from the Finnish state. His career as a creative writer, particularly as an aphorist, is described in the present volume (chapter 10); his scholarly production includes theme studies, *Kirjailijoiden kentät ja kasarmit* (1984) and *Nasaretin miehen pitkä marssi* (1985); the exhaustive genre study *Suomalainen aforismi* (1987); the study of the alter ego in literature, *Toinen minä* (1988); and *Suuri illusionisti,* a life-and-works volume on Mika Waltari (1994), as well as the essays of *Onni tieto tuska* (1990), *Käsioraakkeli ja muita esseitä* (1996), and *Asumaton huone ja muita esseitä* (1997).

Kai Laitinen is professor emeritus of Finnish literature at the University of Helsinki. He has been a literary critic for *Helsingin Sanomat;* editor-in-chief of the journal *Parnasso,* of *Books from Finland,* and of the major anthology *Suomen kirjallisuuden antologia;* chairman of the *Suomalaisen kirjallisuuden seura,* and *Kirjallisuudentutkijain seura*; and member of major Finnish and Scandinavian prize committees and the Neustadt Literary Prize committee. Among his publications are the essay collections *Puolitiessä* (1958) and *Metsästä kaupunkiin* (1984); the volumes of literary history *Suomen kirjallisuus 5* (1965, with Annamari Sarajas and Thomas Warburton), *Suomen kirjallisuus, 1917–1967* (1967), and *Suomen kirjallisuuden historia* (1981); the doctoral dissertation *Aino Kallas, 1897–1921* (1973); and the studies in *Aino Kallaksen maailmaa* (1978) and *Aino Kallaksen mestarivuodet* (1995). *Suomen kirjallisuus 1917–1967* and *Suomen kirjallisuuden historia* have also appeared in Swedish, the former also in German, and the latter also in Hungarian and in Estonian.

Maija Lehtonen has been assistant and docent in aesthetics and modern literature at the University of Helsinki, professor of French literature at Uppsala University, and professor of general literature and aesthetics at the University of Helsinki, from which she is now retired. Among her works are *Anni Swan* (1958), *L'expression imagée dans l'oeuvre de Chateaubriand* (1964), *Essai sur Dominique de Fromentin* (1972), *Essai sur la Confession d'un enfant du siècle* (1982), and *Essais sur le romantisme français* (1995); she has edited and contributed to *Barnboken i Finland förr och nu* (1984). She has also been a translator of French authors — Balzac, Mauriac, Weil, and Camus — and has written articles and reviews for Finnish periodicals, especially *Kanava* (1951–).

George C. Schoolfield is professor emeritus of German and Scandinavian literature at Yale University. Among his publications on the German (and neo-Latin) side are *The Figure of the Musician in German Literature* (1956), *The German Lyric of the Baroque* (1961), *Rilke's Last Year* (1969), and *Janus Secundus* (1980); with Donald Crosby, he edited and participated in *Studies in the German Drama* (1974), and with Thomas Kerth, in *Life's Golden Tree: Essays in German Literature from the Renaissance to Rilke* (1996). His books about Nordic topics are *Edith Södergran* (1984), *Elmer Diktonius* (1985), and *Helsinki of the Czars* (1996); with Laurie Thompson, he edited and participated in *Two Women Writers from Finland* (1995). He has translated works by Hagar Olsson, Fredrik Böök (on H. C. Andersen), and Henning Fenger (on Kierkegaard) and the poetry of Lars Huldén, as well as editing and translating *Swedo-Finnish Short Stories* (1974) and editing and (partially) translating the Finland section of the special Nordic issue of *Dimension* (1994). In 1976 he was made a knight of the Order of the White Rose, First Class; in 1989, a commander of the Order of the Finnish Lion; he received an honorary doctorate from the University of Helsinki in 1990, was awarded the Edith Södergran Prize in 1992, and received the Hagfors Medal of Svenska folkskolans vänner in 1996.

Philip Binham, a native of Britain and holder of an M.A. from Oxford, has resided in Finland for many years and is a lecturer at the Helsinki School of Economics. Among his numerous translations of Finnish belles-lettres into English are Paavo Haavikko's libretto for Aulis Sallinen's opera, *Ratsumies* (1974; *The Horseman*),

Haavikko's play *Ylilääkäri* (1973; *The Superintendent*), Eeva-Liisa Manner's *Toukokuun lumi* (1973; *Snow in May*), and Eeva Kilpi's *Tamara* (1978). With Richard Dauenhauer, he was editor and partial translator of *Snow in May: An Anthology of Finnish Writing* (1978); with his son Timothy Binham, he has translated Kai Laitinen's *Literature of Finland: An Outline* (1985, 1994). As well, he has written a number of texts for the study of English as a foreign language, for example, *Executive English* (1968), *Speak Up: A Guide to International Communication in English* (1975), and *Hotel English* (1988). He has been a regular contributor to *World Literature Today* for many years. He was awarded the Order of the Finnish Lion in 1973 and the Finnish State Prize for Foreign Translations in 1990.

Donna J. Palomäki holds a doctorate in Scandinavian and Finnish Studies from the University of Wisconsin at Madison, with the dissertation *Sage and Artist: A Shamanic Subcurrent in Finnish Literature*. She taught Finnish at the University of Minnesota in Minneapolis before becoming head of the Finnish-American Heritage Center at Suomi College in Hancock, Michigan. She has been active as a translator and lecturer, particularly on Saami language, folklore, and culture.

Ritva Poom is a widely published translator of Finnish and Estonian literature. Among the authors she has translated are Paavo Haavikko and Ilpo Tuomarila (Finnish), and Mati Unt and Paul-Eerik Rummo (Estonian). *Fog Horses*, a selection from Eeva-Liisa Manner's poetry, was awarded the Columbia University Translation Prize. She is the editor and translator of Juha Y. Pentikäinen's *Kalevala Mythology* (Indiana University Press, 1989, augmented edition 1998) and the recipient of fellowships from the National Endowment for the Humanities and the National Endowment for the Arts. In 1993 she won the American-Scandinavian Foundation Translation Prize for her translations of Raija Siekkinen's prose. Her translation of *Estonian Short Stories* was published by Northwestern University Press in 1996. Her translations of Hella Wuolijoki's play *Juurakon Hulda* (*Hulda Juurakko*) in *Modern Drama by Women, 1880s–1930s*, edited by Katherine E. Kelly (1996), and Maria Jotuni's *Kultainen vasikka* (*The Golden Calf*) in an anthology of women dramatists from Finland, *Portraits of Courage* (1997), are among the latest products of her translating activity.

Tuula Starck is a professional translator from Finnish, resident in California.

Index

For reasons of space, the range of the index has been severely limited; thus, for example, foreign authors and works do not appear. However, since the volume belongs to a series devoted to Scandinavian letters, major figures from the other Nordic countries are included. Principally, the index lists authors, titles, movements, scholars and critics, and other pertinent phenomena from Finland's literature, as well as historical and political figures and events of central importance. In alphabetizing entries, the character å precedes a; ä and ö (ø) and other special characters are alphabetized as if the diacritical mark did not appear.

Åbo Academy (Turku Academy), 19, 21–22, 38, 40, 42, 46, 52–54, 57, 278, 284, 287–89, 291, 296–97, 300, 306, 415, 474, 520, 532, 546, 651, 653, 710, 724–25
Åbo Morgonblad, 53, 298
Åbo Nya Tidningar, 298
Åbo Tidning (1800–9), 294, 298
Åbo Tidningar (1791–99), 50, 298
Åbo Underrättelser, 51, 347
Ådror av sten, 548
Ågren, 647
Ågren, Erik, 674, 676
Ågren, Gösta, 546, 549, 647–51, 673–74, 686
Ågren, Leo, xxviii, 544–45

Åhlström, Axel, 459
Åhlström, Olof, 297
Åland Islands, xxiv, 365, 393, 396, 409, 414, 448–49, 461, 465, 499, 530–32, 534–36, 537, 539, 541–42, 546, 550, 558, 613, 633, 637, 671–73, 705–6, 709
Ålandsjungfrun, 449, 538
Ålandskungen, 633
Åland vintern 1918, 542
Året ingenting hände, 620
Århundradets kärlekssaga (*The Love Story of the Century*), 657
År och öden, 428
År som löv (*Years Like Leaves*), 587
Åström, Emma Irene, 343
Återblick-Nu, 708
Återsken, 482, 484
Åtta noveller, 610
Åttio år finlandssvensk litteratur, xviii, 478, 505, 531
Åttonde dag, 612
Ääneen, 216
Aapo Heiskasen viikatetanssi, 202
Abals död, 639
ABC kiria, 35–36, 729
Abel y Aifurs sånger, 527
Abou vetus et nova, 9, 45
Aboicus, Laurentius Petri, 40
Achrelius, Daniel, 284–86, 724
Achrenius, Abraham, 49
Achrenius, Antti (Anders), 49

Achrenius, Henrik, 49, 56
Achrenius, Simo (Simon), 49
Ad astra, 121
Aejmelaeus, Nils (Niilo), 63
Aenigmata fennica, 48
Affärer, 362
Afrikan tähti, 233
Aftnar i Tavastland, 419
Aftonbarn, 697
En afton i Kajsaniemi, 388
Aftonläsning, 704
Agamemnon, 478
"Äger finska folket en historie?" 337
Ägg och nejlika, 643
Äggskalet, 569
Agneta och lumpsamlaren, 569
Agricola, Mikael, 9, 34–37, 41, 43, 141, 729
Ahlqvist, August (pseud. A. Oksanen), 53, 55, 60, 62, 66–71, 77–79, 81–82, 112, 162, 240, 724, 733
Ahlstubbe, Henriette, 309
Ahmala, Kössi, 110
Aho, Juhani, xxi, xxiii, 83–86, 88–95, 97–99, 101–5, 107–8, 113, 122, 129–30, 141, 144, 148, 360, 363, 366, 377, 400, 434, 523, 667, 733
Ahrenberg, Jac. (Johan Jakob), 369–76, 378, 381, 394, 396, 398, 403, 436, 438, 467, 520, 712
Ahti, Risto, 218, 220
Ahti, Seppo (pseud. Bisquit), 241–42
Ai-ai, 717
Aiheita, 267
Aikansa lapsipuoli, 98
Aika saaressa, 233
Ainakin miljoona sinistä kissaa, 742
Aino, 82
Aivan kuin joku itkisi, 250
Ajax, 316
Ajojahti, 739
Akvareller, 428
Alakoulu, 207
Alander, Rainer, 637
Alander, Siw, 670–71, 722
Älä pelkää!, 192
Alastalon salissa 1–2, 152
Aleksis Stenvallin elämä, 206

Alexander I (czar of Russia), xx, 50, 57, 61, 315, 357, 480, 521, 591
Alexander II (czar of Russia), xviii, xx, 56–57, 65, 113, 331, 336, 357–58
Alexander III (czar of Russia), 101, 357, 372
Alftan, Robert, 621–22, 627, 638, 653, 687
Alkio, Santeri, 98
Alkman, 478
Alla mina söner (*All My Sons*), 593
Allardt, Anders, 394–96, 444
Alla träd väntar fåglar, 505–6
Alm, Gustav. *See* Malmberg, Richard
Alma, 75
Almqvist, C. J. L., 76, 306, 315, 318, 335, 348, 350, 465, 718
Alopaeus, Marianne, 562, 565, 574, 593, 596
Den älskades anlete, 564
Alue, 216
Alumiinipaita, 237
Amalia, karhu, 742
Amalia, ystävämme, 80
Amaryllis, 538
Ameriikan raitti, 256
Amerika: En handbok för menige man, 380
Amerikas Förenta Stater, 380
Amiraali Spoofin rumpalipoika, 739
Amorfiaana, 262
Amorina, 718
Amor och Apocalypsis, 641
Amuletten, 721
Ända hit de avlägsna vattnen, 670
Andedräkt av koppar, 479
Andelige psalmer och wijsor, 276
Andersen, Hans Christian, xxiii, 69, 253, 318, 323, 485, 507, 572–73, 585, 644, 731–32, 748
Anders i stan, 583
Anders på ön, 583
Andersson, Claes, 262, 505, 549, 558, 600, 609, 614–17, 618–20, 622–23, 628, 633, 643–46, 682, 685–86, 691, 717–18, 722
Andersson, Otto, 428, 546
Anderssons klocka i fara, 747
Andhämtning, 684
Den andra guden, 649
De andras röster, 702
Den andra tonen, 508

Index   834

Andrén, Erik, 675–76
Angela och kärleken, 597
Angelas krig, 597
Anhalter, svarta och röda, 719
Anhava, Helena, 244–45
Anhava, Tuomas, 179, 184, 187–90, 210, 212, 246, 614
Animalia, 231
Anna Liisa, 91
Anna-Magdalena, 669
Anna minä kumoan vielä tämän maljan, 250
Anni Manninen, 748
Annorlunda, 464
Det anonyma 50-talet, 632
Anor, 372, 375
Ansa och samvetet, 503
Ansiktet, 637
Anteckningar af tankar uti varianta ämnen, 55
Anteckningar, drömmar, 652
Anteckningar från det Helsingfors som gått, 344
Anteckningar från en stad, 695
Anteckningar från ett hus vid floden, 681
Anteckningar under en ekonomisk resa från Finland öfver nordvestra Tyskland samt Nederländerna till Paris 1700–1800, 293
Anteckningar under en resa till Ostindien 1782–1786, 293
Anteckningar under min vistelse i Lappmarken, 493
Antinous, 132
Antonio Gades kommer inte, 711
Ants Raudjalg, 124
Antti Keplerin lait, 261
Anttonius Putronius eli Antti Puuronen, 62
Anu ja Mikko, 737, 738
En apa for till himmelen, 529
Aperitiff–avoin kaupunki, 251
Ara, Agneta, 678, 681, 711–12
Arbetarbladet, 459, 461, 499
Arbetare i natten, 465
Arbetet, 442, 542
Arbetslust, 674
Arena, 591, 688
Det är ett helvete att måla himlar, 659
Argus, 402, 423

Det är inte lätt att vara villaägare i dessa tider, 616
Arjatsalo, Arvi, 750–51
Arkielämää, xxi, 136
Arkkienkeli Oulussa, 230
Arktinen hysteria, 203, 646
Den ärliga bedragaren, 574
Armas Fager, 438
Arnaía kastad i havet, 658
Arnell, Lars, 322
Aronpuro, Kari, xxx, 251, 268, 277
Det är redan en annan dag, 678
Arvet, 534
Arvo: Vanhaäiti puhuu runonsa, 195
Arwidsson, Adolf Ivar, 50–54, 299–300
Asmodeus och de tretton själarna, 436
Asp, Hilda, 383
Ateneum, 400–401
Atlantisk bränning, 410–11
Att i sitt öga, 472–73
Att resa sig, 665
Att skriva sin värld, 537
Att spela sitt liv, 703
Att varje dag, 676
Aura, 51, 298, 300
Auringonlaskun torni, 268
Auringontytär, 193
Aurora Society, 46, 50, 298
Austerlitz, Robert, 7
Avain, 191
Ave Maria, 514
Även dina kameler, 503
Äventyret, 610
Avig-bön, 716
Av samma blod, 559
Avsked i augusti, 562
Avstånd, 527
Axel (Carpelan; 1986), 241, 588
Axel (Tegnér; 1822), 328

Bäck, Tomas Mikael, 684–87, 696, 721
Backlén, Marianne, 688, 698–700
Bäckman, Anna-Lisa, 536
Båge, 718
Bågen (Bow Island), 584
Bång, Petrus, 9, 40–41, 45
Båten i vassen: En berättelse om en förlorad ö, 712

Backman, Sigrid, 448–51, 460, 467, 507, 538, 543, 573–74, 607, 663, 679
Bagges italienska resa, 708
Bakom bilderna, 618
Bakom gallret, 566
Bakom Kuopio, 389
Ballad, 545
Balladeja ja romansseja, 180
Balladen om Siimas-Fii och Sjunga-Matt, 664
Bandet: En kvinnas ofrid, 670
Bang, Herman, 100, 361, 381, 417, 567
Det bara ansiktet, 602
Barbara von Tisenhusen (Eros the Slayer), 125–26, 538
Bargum, Johan, 599–602, 611, 657, 711–12, 725
Bargum, Marianne, 264–65
Barlast, 637
De barmhärtiga, 569
Barndomens land, 536
Barndomskriget, 720
Barndomsvänner, 316, 359–60, 411, 500, 692
Barnen i spegeln, 703
Barnen står på rymdens strand, 577
Barnlek, 422
Bässpojken, 673
Basturesan, 533
Bathseba, 131–32
Bathseba Saarenmaalla, 127
Bättre tider måste komma, 620
Bävervägen 11 Hertonäs Tel. 78035, 655
von Becker, Reinhold, 21, 51–52, 54
Bedröfvade Finnars under-dåniga Sorge-Quäde och sörjande Norrlänningars bedrövliga Klage-Wijsa, 288
Begäret, 676
Behm, Oscar, 394–95, 397, 427, 539
Belägringen, 315
Bele Snack, 279
Bellman, Carl Michael, 49, 53, 56, 306, 565, 622
Belsazars gästabud, 412–13
Bengts, Josefina, 431–32, 451, 500, 672
Bengt Walters lycka, 440–41
Berättelser från Finland, 387
Berättelser och bilder, 397
Berättelser om hav och människor, 672

Berättelser om levande och döda, 392
Berättelser om mig själv och andra, 625
Berättelser ur mitt förflutna liv, 625
Bergbom, Emilie, 79, 389
Bergbom, Kaarlo (Karl Johan), 75, 78–79, 84, 89–90, 102, 240, 389–90
Berger, Henning, 433
Bergh, Samuel Gustav (pseud. Kallio), 54, 56, 61
Bergman, Karl Erik, 672–73
Bergroth, Hugo, 361, 435
Bergroth, Kersti (pseud. Mary Marck), 737, 749
Bergsväg, 647
Bergtagen, 543
Berndtson, Fredrik, 328–30, 366
Besk brygd, 512
De besmittade, 675
Besvärjelse, 725
Betonimylläri, 182
Betoniyö, 258
Betraktelser kring en gräns, 563
Bevarat, 519, 526
Bevingad vardag, 659
De bildande konsternas historia från slutet af adertonde århundradet till våra dagar, 351
Bilder ur familjkretsarne i Finland: Familjen Wärnsköld, 332
Bilder ur Skatuddslifvet i forna dagar, 388
Bildhuggarens dotter (The Sculptor's Daughter), 571, 573
Bilen och lidelserna, 687
von Birchenbaum, Christina Regina, 278
Biskop Thomas, 428
Bispen, 428
Bisquit (Seppo Ahti), 241–42
Bitar av livet, belysta, 511
En bit av det stora äpplet, 705
Björklund, Kristina, 702–3, 712
Björling, Gunnar, xxiii, xxvii, 187–88, 327, 444, 454, 460, 469–74, 477, 481, 483, 487, 489–91, 495, 500, 505, 511, 513, 530–31, 552, 575, 580–81, 591, 617, 634, 639, 652, 681, 684, 708, 722
Björnen från Drakhålan (The Cave Bear's Story), 635
Bjørnson, Bjørnstjerne, xxi, 85, 91, 118, 359, 382–83, 389–91, 625

De blå bergen, 664
Blå duvan, 670
Blå infart, 605
Den blå modern (*The Blue Mother*), 592–93, 610
Det blåser upp till storm, 467
Den blå stenen, 633
Blått och frontgrått, 607
Det blå undret, 468
Bladh, Peter Johan, 293
Bland annat om Jeder, 561
Bland cypresser, 441
Bland fattiga och rika, 332–34
Bland noider och nomader, 493
Bland ödebygder och skär: Berättelser från Finland, 386
Bländverket, 529
Blindfönster vidare, 694
Blindtrappan, 568
Bli till, 666
Bli, tillsammans, 616
Bliva ingen, 512–13
Bliv till, 518
Block och öde, 497, 499
Blomqvist, Anni, 671–72, 676, 704
Den blomstertid, 503
Blott du, 651
Bobrikov, Nikolaj Ivanovich, 101, 108, 399, 408, 418
Bojorna, 517
Boken om Helsingfors, 434
Boken om vårt land, 342, 345, 596
Boklaget, 696, 718
Boklagets Litterära Årsmagasin, 718
En bok om en människa I–III, 378–79
Bondestam, Anna, 419, 542–44, 560, 675
von Bonsdorff, Jakob, 319
von Bonsdorff, Johan, 319
Bordet, 595
Borgå barn och borgare, 376
Borgå Tidning, 327
Början, 519
Början av ett år, 684
Borta bra, 547
Bortom gryningen, 599
Den borttappade hallonmasken och andra sagor ur skogsfolkets värld, 736

Den bortvända glädjen, 502
Borum, Poul, 474, 576
Bosley, Keith, 29, 114
Bostadsbolaget Sjuan i Lergränden, 450
Boucht, Birgitta, 515, 663, 665, 678–81
Brahe, Per (the Younger), 278, 352
Branch, Michael, xxiii, 24, 32, 43
Brandes, Georg, xxi, 85, 91, 99–100, 109, 368–69, 377–78, 386, 401, 543
Brändövägen 8 Brändö Tel. 35 (*A Winter's Day; Snob's Island*), 655
Brännmärken, 666
Bredenberg, Diana, 720
Brev, 595
Breven till Cecilia, 406
Ett brev från Helsingfors, 647
Brev från Klara, 571, 574
Brev till vänner, 447–48
Brinn eld, 541
Brita Skrifvars, 341
Bro, Förlaget, 546–47
Bröd av lera, 554
Broder Kilian, 530–31
Brödet och elden, 460
Brödet och stenarna, 520
Brokiga iakttagelser, 456
Bronspojken från Ostia, 522
Bror och syster, 405, 425, 585
Bruno, 268
Brytningstid, 675
Brytningstider: En historia från Finland, 376
Budde, Jöns, 34, 275
Budskap, 447
Bukdahl, Jørgen, 535
Bunden och fri, 598
Burgundiska sviten, 642
Bussen stannar bakom hörnet, 686
Byberättelser, 394
Byggmästar, Eva-Stina, 721
Byn, 675
Byte, 712
Byyrallor, 396

Cajander, Paavo, 81–82, 181
Cajanus, Erik, 42
Cajanus, Johan (the Younger), 42–43, 49
Calamnius, Gabriel, 44

Index   837

Calamnius, Ilmari. *See* Kianto, Ilmari
Calamnius, Joseph Gabriel, 43, 44
Calibans dag, 568
Candida, 713
Canth, Minna (née Johnsson), xxviii, 79, 84–92, 94–95, 98, 120–21, 268, 389, 397, 658, 664
Canzio, 72
Carling, Finn, 675
Caroline, 609
Carpelan, Bo, 187, 241, 252, 416, 450, 471, 474, 505, 541, 549, 575, 577, 580–89, 600, 614, 622, 625, 638, 660, 676, 685, 714, 747
Castrén, Gunnar, xviii, xxiii, 307, 401–2, 415–16, 421, 454, 534
Castrén, Mathias Alexander, 53, 60–61, 323, 334–35, 346
Cellens dagrar, 648
Charles IX (king of Sweden), 37, 276, 349–50
Charles XI (king of Sweden), 39, 284, 286, 288, 340
Charles XII (king of Sweden), 39, 44, 282–83, 287–91, 313, 338, 541
Chitambo, 465, 467, 469, 523, 574, 590
Choraeus, Michael, 293, 295–97, 301, 303
Chorell, Walentin, 567–71, 608, 702
Christus nascens, patiens et triumphans, eller Den Nyfödde, Korszfeste, och Opståndne Christus, 283
Chronander, Jacobus, 279–81
Chronicon episcoporum Finlandensium, 36–37
Chydenius, Anders, 292–93, 647, 710
Chydenius, Kaj, 239–40
Civil War (1918), xx, 104, 109–11, 138, 142, 144–45, 148, 150, 156, 159, 170, 173, 210, 228, 240, 266, 290, 311, 331, 341, 380, 407, 409, 413, 419, 437–41, 442–43, 445, 447, 449, 454, 459, 461, 467, 470, 534, 542–43, 545, 555, 586, 588, 606–7, 674, 692, 711, 739, 751
Cleve, Anders, 277, 361, 599, 602–4, 606–7, 609, 650
Club War, 37, 82, 275, 325, 338, 349
Collan, Fabian, 59
Colliander, Tito, xx, 467, 515–19, 521, 523, 526, 530, 536, 551, 565, 571, 603, 654, 666, 669–70, 700
Colorado Avenue, 710–11
Continuation War (1941–44), xx, 146, 170, 176, 199, 205, 213, 227, 260, 315, 340, 494, 499, 501, 533, 546, 553–54, 592, 595, 607, 615, 618, 627, 638, 653
Creutz, Gustaf Philip, 293, 295
Crimean War, 328, 336, 368, 396, 437, 521
Cronstedt, Carl Olof, 313
Cygnaeus, Fredrik, xxi, 54, 71, 75, 78, 240, 302, 306, 317–19, 325, 327, 336, 347, 349–51
Cypresstunneln, 564

Dagbok, 652
Dagdrivare, 432–33
Dagen, 602
Dagen är, 518, 521
Dagens Press/Svenska Pressen, 465, 486
Dagens Tidning, 422–23
Dagen vänder, 587
Dagmar: En hvardagshistoria, 333
Dagövning, 557
Dahl, Lars Hjalmarsson, 560
En dal i våldet (A Valley in the Midst of Violence), 648–49
Daniel Hjort, 37, 276, 347, 349
Dansande bin, 551
Dansens yta, 640
Dans och tystnad, 676–77
Daphne, 636
Daphne och Apollon, 636
Där anteckningarna slutar, 682
Därför, 664
Därför att ljuset, 659
Där jag vet att du, 473
Där står du, 503
Där vi går, 509
Dauidin Psalttari, 36
December, 503
En del av världsrymden, 628
Delfiini, 252
Denna dag, 685
Denna natt är ett prov, 551
Denna värld är vår: Handbok i systerskap, 663, 678

Det jag har, 718
Detta warma rum-en tillfällighet, 678
De vita hominis, 277
Dianas ö, 636
Dikt (Rabbe Enckell), 478
Diktarhemmet, 412, 414, 418, 422, 445, 480, 617, 622
Dikter (Barbro Mörne), 491
Dikter (Rabbe Enckell), 474
Dikter (Gripenberg), 417
Dikter (Grotenfelt), 440
Dikter (Hjelt), 678
Dikter (Lagus), 350
Dikter (Procopé), 412-13
Dikter (Reuter, O. M.), 393
Dikter (Runeberg), 302-3
Dikter (Sandell), 644
Dikter (Södergran), 413, 442, 455-56, 458, 491-93, 500, 667, 721
Dikter (Tavaststjerna), 367
Dikter (Tegengren), 414
Dikter: Andra häftet (Runeberg), 304
Dikter: Tredje häftet (Runeberg), 304
Dikter för medelålders, 645-46
Dikter från Bohuslän, 639
Dikter från Lofoten, 638
Dikter från trettio år, 587
Dikter i fosterländska ämnen, 623
Dikter i svartvitt, 648
Dikter i väntan, 362
Dikter med varandra, 577, 676
Dikter mellan vinter och vinter, 578
Dikter 1960 (Wichman), 508-9
Dikter nu, 510
Dikter om jorden, 548
Dikter III (Lybeck, M.), 404
Dikter III (Tuominen), 514-15
Dikter vid särskilda tillfällen, 624
Dikt i dag, 508
Dikt och drapa, 355
Dikt och politik, 632
En dikt om kärlek och annat, 682
Diktonius, Elmer, xxii, xxvii, 110, 170, 225, 336, 345, 361, 420, 443, 445, 454, 457-65, 471, 474, 476, 483, 485, 489-90, 492, 495, 499-501, 505, 507, 510-11, 514,

526-28, 532, 534, 552, 590, 602-3, 612, 617, 621, 630, 676, 684, 726
Din gestalt bakom dörren, 585
Din vredes dag, 599
Disputatio de Väinämöine priscorum Fennorum numine, 51
Disticha, 444
Djävulens ansikte (The Films of Ingmar Bergman), 596
Djungel, 560
Dockorna, 570
Dockskåpet, 573
Döda år, 408-9
Döda drömmar, 441
Dödens Venedig, 653
Dödsfången, 407
Dolda makter: Bilder och hägringar, 385
Det dolda motivet, 634
Domprosten Bomander, 405
Donna Quijote ja muita kaupunkilaisia (Donna Quixote and The Gold of Ophir), 253
Donner, Jörn, 374, 460, 462, 466, 565, 574, 590-91, 595-601, 603, 607, 614, 629, 632, 647, 653, 657, 691, 697, 717, 722
Dråtte-Skald, 288
Drabbad av Sverige, 563, 596
Drakarna över Helsingfors, 713
Dräpa näcken, 622
Drivkrafter, 721
Drivsnö, 418
Drömlandet, 433
Drömmar, 468
Dröm utan slut, 562
Drottning liv, 433
Du, 645
Den du är, 492
Du går de ord, 472
Du jord du dag, 473
Du, människa, 554
Du mörka överlevande, 541, 580-81
Dusch, 527
Du skall icke hava lust, 664
Du stallbror med gud, 487-88
Du vet inte att du ler, 628
Dynastien Peterberg, 404
Dyre prins (Sweet Prince), 593, 594, 598, 698

Ebonit, 527
Eddan och dess ödestragik, 493
Edelfelt, Albert, 99, 101, 378, 399, 748
Eden, 637
Een skön och lustigh Wijsa om Bondeståndet och thes Embete, 284
Eerikki Puke, 389
Efter femtio år, 340
Efter hjältedöden, 654
Efter striden, 419
Efterwärme, 556
Egentligen är vi mycket lyckliga, 682
Ehrnrooth, Adelaïde (pseud. A-ï-a), 332–34, 384
Ei-Kaj Plumps: Hyppyjä Helsinkiin, 249
Ei koskaan huomispäivää! (Never a Tomorrow), 164
Ekelund, Erik, xviii, 336, 369, 375, 469, 521, 523
Ekelund, Ragnar, 443–44, 456, 474, 488, 490
Ekelund, Vilhelm, 416, 430–31, 465, 485, 490–91, 514
Ekhammar, Hugo (Ekholm, Hugo), 435, 451, 498, 547, 650
Eklund, Artur, 420, 486, 501
Eklund, R. R. (Ragnar Robert), 469, 484–89, 500, 526, 550
Ekman, Michel, 610, 662, 682, 714, 719, 722
Eko och återsken, 635
Elämä edestakaisin, 231
Elämä ja aurinko, 150
Elämän evakkona, 231
Elämän havainnoita, 81
Elämän helle, 143
Elämän herrat, 258
Elämäni, 81
Elämän kasvot, 123
Elämän keskipiste, 264
Elämän koreus, 115
Elämänmeno, 257
Elämän meri, 105
Elämän puu, 223
Elämän rouva, rouva Glad (The Bride of Life), 202
Elävien kirjoissa, 250
Eldtände, 540
Eldvagnarna, 662

Elgskyttarne, 22, 135, 304, 319
Elinan surma, 11, 389
Elokuu, 150
Elsa, 95
Emigrantöden, 547–48
Emilia ja kaksoset, 749
Emilia ja kuningas Oskari, 749
Emilia ja Oskarin nukke, 749
Emtö, Solveig, 662–64, 670
En bland dessa, 675
En dag tittade jag på dig genom en förstoringsglas, 627
Enckell, Agneta, 691, 722–24
Enckell, Martin, 688, 691–96, 698–99, 723
Enckell, Mikael, 349, 470, 474, 476, 478, 634–35, 714, 724
Enckell, Olof, xviii, 285, 454, 464–65, 467–68, 474, 476–77, 479–80, 484, 486, 490, 499–500, 519, 522–25, 560, 691, 724
Enckell, Rabbe, xxiii, 290, 310, 416, 454, 465, 469, 474–80, 482, 484, 487–89, 490, 492, 496, 499–502, 505–6, 522, 526, 549, 558–59, 564, 575, 581, 591, 611, 617–18, 634, 636, 640, 684, 724
Encore: En familjenroman, 695
Encyclopedia synoptica, 40
Enda sonen, 449
Endast med mig själv, 494
af Enehjelm, Helen (née Moller; pseud. Helena Ensam, Helen California), 563–65
Enkelten pysäkki, 269
Ennen kuolemaa, 231
Ennen sotaa oli nuoruus, 198
Enrönnen, 623
Ensam herre, 560
Ensamma ansikten, 566–67
De ensamma svenskarna, 434
Ensam sökan, 571
Ensimmäinen purjehtia, 63
Enskilt område, 543
En soisi sen päättyvän, 216
Entäs sitten, Leevi, 183
Entiset vyötäröt, 237
Envall, Markku, xxx, 270–71, 585, 724
Eolita, 529
Epitaf över Mr. Nacht, 716–17

Index 840

Equinox, 682
Erään opportunistin iltapäivä, 186
Erik Falander, 429
Erik Puke, 389
Erikson, Åke. *See* Gripenberg, Bertel
Erinnyerna, 642
Erkko, Juhana Henrik, 81–82, 98, 112, 155
Eros och elektronerna, 529
Eros och Logos, 641
Eskola gubbens visor, 292
Essay om livets framfart, 479
Estlander, Carl Gustaf, 299, 325, 345, 351–54, 356–57, 364, 367, 384, 402, 724
Eteisiin ja kynnykselle, 202
Että olisit läsnä, 196
Ettei maa viheriöisi, 205
Etyder, 575
Euroopan ryöstö, 269
Europaeus, D. E. D., 60
Euterpe: Veckoskrift för musik, teater och skönlitteratur, 109, 377, 400–402, 414–15, 417, 453
Evakko, 176
Eva Maria, 608
Evangelium för barn, 342
Evas klass/Eevan luokka, 738
Everstin autonkuljettaja, 206
Exekutionen, 608
Exercitia, 497
Exil, 639
Existens, 579–80

Fågel badar snart i vatten, 471–72
Fågel Blå, 732
Fågel Fenix, 687–88, 691, 694–96, 714
Fågeln flyger långt, 429
Fågeln i stenmuren: Dagboksblad, 576–77
Fågel över sju floder, 638
Fågelvind, 660
Fångstmän, 425–26
De fåvitska trollen, 450, 573–74
Fabeln om den hårlösa kön, 638
Fabian öppnar portarna, 570
Fackeltåget, 608
Facklor över jorden, 549
Fäderna, 431, 451
Fädernearvet, 410

Fadershuset, 700
Fädrens blod, 545
Fagerholm, Monika, 267, 715, 718, 721
Den fagraste vår, 618, 644
Fahler, Alfred, 441–42
Fahrenheit 121, 189
Falander, Axel. *See* Tigerstedt, Örnulf
Falla (Eurydike), 723–24
Fällas eller falla, 555
Fallet Bruce, 713
Fältskärns berättelser (*The King's Ring*), 63, 291, 338, 340, 342, 346, 532
Familjen Brinks öden, 449
Familjen i dalen, 744
Familjen på Haapakoski, 373, 375
Fänrik Ståls sägner (*The Songs of Ensign Stål; The Tales of Ensign Stål*), 82, 176, 230, 269, 303, 311, 316–17, 329–30, 332, 340, 364, 399, 442, 496, 598
Färdas, 631
Färd genom verkligheter, 640
Färgernas strand, 509
Farlig midsommar (*Midsummer Madness*), 573
Far och son, 597–98
Farväl Daphne, 636
Farväl Julie, 598
Fästningen, 520, 534
Fattiggubbens brud, 447
FBT, 605, 614, 617–19, 621–22, 632–33, 640, 645, 688, 714
February Manifesto, 101, 107, 113, 121, 357, 399, 404, 422
Feliks onnellinen (*The Tongue of Fire*), 165
Fellman, Jakob, 493
Fem spel, 571
Femte advent, 600
Fennomani och skandinavism, 328
Ferlin, Nils, 554
Festen, 702
Fine van Brooklyn, 164
Finland i 19de seklet, 345, 351
Finland i ord och bild, 393
Finlands Allmänna Tidning, 329
Finländsk bokföring: Dagbok från tredje republiken, 677
Finlandssvenska: Handledning till undvikande av provinsialismer i tal och skrift, 361

Finlandssvenska kvinnor skriver, 679
Finlandssvensk lyrik (Wahlund), 549
Finne, Jalmari, 102
Finnish Literary Society (Suomalaisen Kirjallisuuden Seura, SKS), xx, 7, 20, 22, 28, 52, 58–59, 62, 71, 78, 306, 321, 347, 736
Finnish Theater (National Theater), 75, 79, 89, 99, 102, 110, 249, 356, 389
Finno, Jacobus (Jaakko Suomalainen), 37
Finns det tigrar i Congo?, 601
Det finns ett leende, 451
Finska förhållanden, 328
Finska Helicons underdånige Fägne-Sånger, 286
Finska Nationens Underdånige Lyck-Önskan och Glädie-Sång, efter mycken Sorg och Tvång, 288
Finsk anthologi, 59
Finska vikens hemlighet, 366
Finsk rulett, 600
Den finsk-svenska litteraturens utveckling, xviii, 346
Finsk Tidskrift, 351, 353, 360, 384, 395, 402
Fiskens tecken, 521
Fjäriln, 655
Fjärilsörat, 612–13
En flanör, 432
Flickan, 663
Flöjtblåsarlycka, 475
Florinus, Henrik, 9, 39–40, 46
Flyende spegel, 479
Flytande avsatser, 685
Folk i skären, 537
Folk klättrar omkring, 611
Folkliv, 394
Folkvargarna, 647
Fönstret (Colliander), 518
Fönstret (Wik), 629
Förbarma dig, 517–19, 526
Före hanegället, 550
Före sömnen, 697
Författarnas andelslag, 651, 659, 662, 665, 674
De förlorade, 595, 597
Det förlorade landet, 411
För morgonbris, 359
Den förnekade bilden, 682

Det forntida Östersverige och svenskdomen, 431
Fors, Hans, 599, 605–9, 665, 676
Forseen, Samuel, 40
Forsius, Sigfrid Aronus, 251, 276–78, 325, 336, 338, 549, 604
Förskjutningar, 651
Förslag till svensk psalmbok för de evangelisklutherska församlingarne i storfurstendömet Finland, 313
Forsskål, Petter, 292
Forsström, Tua, 250, 617, 619, 682–84, 710, 719
Första damernas, 666–67
Första varningen, 364
Forstén, Ina. *See* Lange, Ina
Först sålde de pianot, 703
Den förtrollade vägen (*The Enchanted Way*), 525–27
För upp en svan, 721–22
Förvandlingar, 525–26, 560
Förvandlingar mot morgonen, 722
Fosterländskt album, 58
Frågare, 685, 686
Från Ålands skär, 396
Från barnaår till silfverhår, 375
Från fjärdarna, 411
Från Rom till Rom, 521
Från sex årtionden i Finland, 376
Från skog och sjö, 396
Från stigar och hult, 396
Från vargtider och vallpojksår, 431
Framåt, 384
Främlingen, 568
Främlingsstaden, 746
Främlingsstjärnan, 746
Främlingsvägen, 746
Framtid, 668
Framtidens skugga, 456, 458, 687
Franciskus i Kökar: Det lilla samhället möter den stora traditionen, 705
Franzén, Frans Michael, 48–50, 60, 293–98, 300–303, 306, 321–22, 326, 334–36, 484, 724
Fredenheim, Carl Frederik, 46–47
Frese, Jacob, 289–90, 297, 376, 476
Freudenthal, Axel Olof, xxvi, 109, 354–56, 392, 395, 408, 650

Friaren från Åbo, 329
Friaren från landet, 315
Fridegård, Jan, 177, 536, 545
Frifågel, 540
Frihetens fångar, 597–98
Fri marknad, 718
Fröding, Gustaf, 121, 132–33, 249, 367, 413
Frögde-Qwäde, 289
Fröken Elna Johansson, 543
Fröken Ur ville inte komma, 620
Frosterus, Johan, 41–42
Fru Blubes hus, 608
Fru Catharina Boije och hennes döttrar, 291, 324
Fru Sola, 745
De fyra flöjtspelarna, 505–6
De fyrtionio dagar, 680
Fyrtio vintrars snö, 599

Gåas Kong: En lustig och kortwilig dicht om Mårtens Gåås, 276–77
Gångande Grå (Horses of the Night), 745
Gånge Rolf (V. K. E. Wichmann), 355–56, 374
Det går an: En tavla ur livet, 318
Gården (The Courtyard), 584–85, 588, 625, 676
Den gåtfulla gästen, 486
Gabriels dag, 597
Gadd, Pehr Adrian, 292
Gaijin: Utlänning i Japan, 705
En galen tebjudning, 611
Galgmannen: En midvintersaga (The Gallows Man: A Midwinter Tale), 439
Gallen-Kallela, Akseli, xxvii, 100–101, 261, 399, 467, 520
Gallergrinden, 418
Galleria, 251
Gamla baron på Rautakylä, 340
Den gamla spinnrocken, 450
Den gamle polisgevaldigerns berättelser: Bilder ur Helsingforslifvet, 388
Den gamles minnen, Bilder från finska skogsbygden, 328–29
Den gamle trädgårdsmästarens brev, 103, 305
En gammal mans dag, 585
Ganander, Christfrid, 10, 19, 47–48, 51

Ganander, Henrik, 49
Garborg, Arne, xxi, 85, 105, 141, 365, 382
Gatans dikter, 444
Gatstenar, 361, 602–3, 607
Genesis aetherea eller Jesu Christi födelse, 280, 284
Genetz, Arvid (pseud. Arvi Jännes), 81
Genom sekler, 376
Genom sprickorna i vårt ansikte, 616
Georgsgatan, 655
Gerdt Bladhs undergång (The Downfall of Gerdt Bladh), 594, 598, 601
Gestrinius, Ernst, 288–89
Gezelius, Johannes (the Elder; 1615–90), 39–40, 42–43, 46
Gezelius, Johannes (the Younger; 1647–1718), 38
Ett giftermål, 381
Gissel och möjor, 487–89
Givet, 519
Glädjen, 700
Glädjezon, 680
Glas emellan, 627
Glashus, 631
Glidande bilder, 493
Glimtar från Tyskland, 516
Glömska, eld, 678
Glorias gåva, 537–38
Go Moskova Go, 266
Gottlund, Carl Axel, 21, 52–54, 56, 60, 238, 299
Goubitsky och jag, 608
Gråsparven, 332
Grått och gyllne, 485–86
Grammatica Fennica, 44
Granholm, Olof, 665, 673–74, 676, 713
Granlund, Johan Fredrik, 56, 200
Gränsland, 633
Gräset, 570
Gräs och granit, 463
Great Northern War, xx, 45, 141, 282, 339, 531, 545
Great Wrath (1710–21), xx, 44, 46, 324–25, 287, 290, 732, 739
Greeta ja hänen Herransa, 106
Gripanderska gården (The Goldmaker's House), 745

Gripen, 519
Gripenberg, Alexandra (pseud. Aarne), 334, 382–83, 417
Gripenberg, Bertel (pseud. Åke Erikson), xxi–xxiii, 327, 356, 401–2, 410, 416–21, 426, 428, 440, 442, 445–46, 448, 453, 459, 470, 496, 498, 500, 552, 559, 607, 662
Grodan, 569
Grotenfelt, Erik, 440–41, 443, 456, 484
Groth, Joakim, 267, 688, 694–96, 699, 712
Grottan, 518
Grundtvig, N. F. S., 82
Gruppen hette No C:o, 695
Gud All-en, 693
Gud är närvarande, 514
Guds barn, 448
Gud, verlden och menniskan, 53
Det gula slottet, 662
Guldgrävarens tårar, 718
Guldkedjan, 523
Guldkust, 570
Gulin, Åke, 403, 557–58
Gullkronas gränd (Gold Crown Lane), 745
Gummerus, E. R., 534, 556, 593
Gunnar, 637
Gustav II Adolf (king of Sweden), xxv, 9, 276, 341–42, 338–39, 346
Gustav III (king of Sweden), 39, 49, 175, 291, 302, 315, 337–38, 340, 374, 622
Gustav IV Adolf (king of Sweden), 39, 312
Gycklare och apostlar, 451
Det gyllene spöket, 337
Gyllensten, Lars, 195

Hårda sånger, 460, 489
Hårda tider, 358, 362, 366
Hård höst, 513
Hård kust, 675
Hårt ljus, 528, 529
Haakana, Anna-Liisa, 749
Haaksirikko, suomalainen perustuskielinen taru, 63
Haanpää, Pentti, xxiii, 129, 163, 165–66, 176–77, 238, 265, 267, 560
Haapoja, 241
Haarla, Lauri, 489

von Haartman, Lars, 558–59, 593
Haastemies, 239
Haavikko, Paavo, xx, xxiii, 179, 184–88, 210–11, 213–15, 218, 229, 231, 246, 270, 573, 586, 633
Haavio, Martti. *See* Mustapää, P.
Hacks, Alexander, 291–92
Hagar, 701
Hagberg, Knut, 310
Hagelstam, Wentzel, xxi, 400–401
Hagfors, Johan Fridolf, 356–57
Hahl, Nils-Gustaf, 490
Häikäisy, 264
Halfdan skald, 427
Halla, 114
Hälleberget och Kavaljeren, 448
Hälli, Matti, 177
Hallitsija, 235
Hallonskogen, 540
af Hällström, Raoul, 489
Halmstacken, 523
Halonen, Pekka, 101
Hälsningar från San Francisco, 637
Halullisten sieluin hengelliset laulut, 49
Halusit tai et, 202
Ett halvår i Nya världen (A Half Year in the New World), 383
Hämäläinen, Helvi, 171–72, 179
Hämäläinen, Väinö, 735
Hämärän tanssit (Dancers of the Obscure), 216
Hamlet sade det vackrare, 482
Hammarström, Nanny, 736
Hamsun, Knut, xxiii, 97, 101, 133, 364, 400–401, 406, 418, 434, 585
Ett handelshus i Wiborg 1–2, 498
En handfull ljus, 631
Hänen olivat linnut, 204
Hanhiemon iloinen lipas, 747
Han kommer, han kommer, 647
Hanna, 88, 305, 307
Hannikainen, Pietari, 61–63
Han sa, hon sa, 626
Hansen, Martin A., 532, 536
Häpeä, 268
Harald Grönberg 1941, 706
Det har aldrig hänt, 613

Häräntappoase, 262
Här är allt som förut, 507, 573
Härfärd till Turkiet, 599
Harhaileva aamupäivä, 235
Harhama, 139, 140
Härkönen, Anne-Leena, 262
Harmaja, Saima, 158, 167–68, 182
Hasselblatt, Emil, 401
Hästens hjärta, 678
Hästhandlarens son, 674
Hautaviita, 669
Havet finns inte mer, 672
Havets bröd, 693
ett hav, ett vatten, 631
Havsfärd, 556
Havslyktan, 553
Havukka-ahon ajattelija, 201
Häxskogen, 438
Hed, Anders (Kjell Westö), 713–18, 725
Hedberg, John, 396–97
Hedman, Kaj, 683
Hedvall, Ruth, xviii, 513
Hedvig och Desirée, 598
von Heidenstam, Verner, 345, 367–69, 416, 497
Heikkilä, Kauko, xviii
Heikkilä, Lasse, xxix, 179, 181, 195–96
Heim/Hem, 624, 626
Heinolablomman, 330
Hekuba, 478–79
Helakisa, Kaarina, 742, 745
Helg, 446
Det heliga skrinet (The Sacred Shrine), 421
De heliga vägarna, 497
Helkavirsiä (Whitsongs), xxii, 115–17, 121, 144, 555
Hellaakoski, Aaro, 144, 152, 154–55, 157, 161–62, 168, 176–77, 179, 191
Hellberg, Helle, 537–39, 541
Helmivyö, 65
Helsingfors Dagblad, 325, 330, 357
Helsingfors-Monaco, 388
Helsingfors Morgonblad, 59, 302, 305–6, 313, 315, 322, 326, 329
Helsingfors Tidningar, 337–38, 344–45, 730
Helsingfors University. *See* Helsinki University

Helsingin Sanomat, 84, 142, 270, 653–54
Helsingius, Torsten, 432–34, 692
Helsinkiin, 92–93
Helsinki-Romanka, 690, 692
Helsinki University (Helsingfors University), 31, 52, 57, 62, 65–66, 70, 112, 117, 296, 370, 377, 408, 424, 501, 520, 523, 558, 613, 622, 653, 707–8
Helvetets himmelsfärd, 443
Hem från festen, 704
Hemgården och byn, 547–48
Hemkomst: Tre berättelser (Hagar Olsson), 468
Hemkomsten (Runar Schildt), 437
Hemlängtan, 564
Den hemliga glöden, 420
De hemliga rummen, 533
Hemligt medansvar, 553
Hemma, 370
Hemma i universum, 576
Hemmer, Jarl, xxiii, 410, 441–48, 453–54, 456, 459, 475, 488, 495, 500, 515, 534, 550, 633, 700
Hem till sitt hav, 529
Hem till sommaren, 452, 632
Henkien taistelu, 154
Henkivartija, 237
Hennerson, 406
Henrici, Hemmingius, 35, 37
Henrik Ibsen: Ett skaldeporträtt, 376
Henriksgatan, 655
Henrik tiger inte, 654
Henry, Saint, 9, 34–35, 236
Hentomielinen Hilarius, 241
Herääminen, 105
Heränneitä, 103, 141
Herdarnas natt, 700
Herdedikter, 623, 676
Herman, min Herman, 669
Herr Agaton Vidbäck och hans vänner, 424–25
Herra Huu, 742
Herrar till natt och dag, 477
En herre for till Zanzibar, 422
Herr Puntila und sein Knecht Matti, 173
Herr Varg!, 623
Hertiginnan af Finland, 337–38
Hertzberg, Rafael (pseud. Sphinx, Jung Junior), 388–89

Heyman, Nils (pseud. Osvald Alving), 401
Hibakusha Go-Go, 693
Hid, 649
Hietamies, Laila, 244
Hihuliter, 371, 375
Hildén, Henrik, 433–34
Hiljaa, hyvin hiljaa teen päivistäni kirjaa, 194
Himlens stenar, 529
Det himmelska ljuset, 643
Himmelstimran, 486
Himmun rakkaudet, 198
Hinna, 720
Hirn, Yrjö, 100, 252, 398, 421–22, 451, 524, 551, 564, 724
Hitaat auringot, 211
Hjältarna är döda, 561, 654
Hjärtats pantomim, 468
Hjärtats stråtrövare: Pusselpoesi 1973–1975, 688
Hjärtfäste och hungertorn, 487
Hjelt, Brigitta, 678
Hjort, Daniel, 276, 325
Högholm, Gunnel, 661–64
Högnäs, Sven-Olof, 546–47, 668
Högnäs-Sahlgren, Brita, 668–70
Holappa, Pentti, 179, 184, 190–92
Holberg, Ludvig, xxi, 62, 71, 74, 79, 477
Hölderlin, 634
Holländsk himmel, 564
Hollmerus, Viveca, 599
Hollo, Anselm, 185, 216, 266
Holma, Birgitta, 678
Holmqvist, Bengt, xviii, 414, 470, 487, 556
Holmström, Roger, 453, 575, 702
Homén, Olaf, 402, 405, 414, 421, 448–49, 724
Honko, Lauri, 20, 23, 25, 27
Horisont, 547, 651
Horn, Arvid, 39, 283, 338–39
Hornborg, Harald, 532, 560
Hornstedt, Klas Fredrik, 293
Hörnstenar, 391
Horologium eternae sapientiae, 642–43
Höståker, 557
Höstdagar: En Helsingforshistoria, 423–25, 433
Höstispiggarne, 317
Höstlig bastu, 463

Höstlig dikt, 409
Hotelli eläville, 259
Hot in Helsingfors, 690
Hroch, Miroslav, 28
Huden där den är som tunnast, 619
Hufvudstadsbladet, 376, 454–56, 476, 524, 582, 653, 656
Huhtala, Liisi, 139
Huldén, Evert, 547–48
Huldén, J. J. (Johan Jakob), 392, 547
Huldén, Lars, xviii, 240, 276, 285, 426, 548, 557, 621–26, 628, 630–31, 638, 660, 672, 676, 685–86, 724
Humanismen som livshållning och andra essayer, 636
Hundarna i Kingston, 700
En hundpredikan, 529
Hundrade minnen från Österbotten, 322, 334
Hundra dikter, 720
Hund skenar glad, 473
Hungergropen, 520
Hunger i skördetid, 544
Huojuva talo, 137, 154
Huone puutalossa, 226
Huovinen, Veikko, 197–98, 201, 213, 266
Hupeli, 257
Hur man fryser en mammut (*How to Deep Freeze a Mammoth*), 635
Hurrarna, 650–51, 674
Hurskas kurjuus (*Meek Heritage*), 146, 150
Hus, 625
Husdjur, 601
Huset där det dracks, 516
Huset med den gröna gardinen, 566
Huset med himmelsbalkongen, 703
Ett hutlöst pris, 668
Huulilla kylmä tuuli, 218
Huutomerkki, 213
Hvardagslifvets skuggor och dagrar, 333
Hymner från Santsche-Pi, 528
Hyödyllinen huwitus luomisen töistä, 41
Hyötysuhde, 232
Hypnoosi, 267
Hyry, Antti, 197–98, 206–7, 222, 560
Hyvästijättö Lintukodolle, 154
Hyvin toimeentulevat ihmiset, 229

I åratal, 518
Ibsen, Henrik, xxi, xxiii, 79, 85, 91, 96, 100, 118, 121, 133, 138, 143, 301, 316–17, 342, 349, 351–52, 359, 365–66, 369, 376, 378, 381, 383, 389–91, 403–5, 427, 432, 585, 586
I dagens intressanta samhällsfrågor, röst från en icke röstberättigad, 334
I Danmark, 537
Idealrealisation, 481–82
I de mörka rummen, i de ljusa, 586–87, 676
Idestam (Idman), Gustaf, 300–301, 328
Idrottens filosofi, 421
Idström, Annika, 262–64
Idyll och epigram, 134, 587, 612
Idyll och program, 612
Idyll under åskmoln, 591
I egna ögon — och andras: En bok om att känna sig själv, 422
I: En roman om förhävdelsen, 528
I fängelse och fångläger, 442
I förbindelser, 362
I förbund med döden, 364–65
I Fru Ulrikas hem, 384
IGHS (Iosephus Gabrielis Haapajärviensis Sacellanus; Joseph Gabriel Calamnius), 43, 44
I glasskärvornas rike, 721
Ihana on Altyn-Köl, 229
Ihmeellinen kalaretki, 735
Ihminen n:o 503/42, 170
Ihmiselon ihanuus ja kurjuus, 150
Ihmisen ääni, 214, 231
Ihmisen ja isänmaan puolesta, 271
Ihmisen vaatteissa, 253
Ihmisestä ja elämästä, 132
Ihmiset suviyössä (People in the Summer Night), 150
Ihmiskohtaloja, 105
Ihmiskunnan viholliset (The Roman), 165
Ihmisten puheet, 201
I järnhälens tid: Kampdikter, 443
I kamp med havet, 671
Ikon, 677
Ikuinen taistelu, 130
Ilmaa: Kaikuu, 195
Ilmalaiva "Italia", 250

Ilo ja häpeä, 259
Ilo-Laulu Jesuxesta, 43
Ilvolan juttuja, 134
I Mark Twains hjulspår, 610
I måsens vingar bor en frihet, 672
I minnet lyser vägen ljus, 661
Improvisationer, 444
Inblandningar, utmaningar, 593
Indiankriget: Amerikanska gränsmarkshistorier, 380
Indiansommar, 433
En inföding, 361
Inför Dionysos anlete, 493
Inför havets anlete, 411
Inga medmänniskor: Fragmentarisk berättelse, 434
Ingegärd på Rönninge, 736
Ingelius, Axel Gabriel, 329–30
Ingen & den knottriga damen, 691
Ingen dag förgäves, 503
Ingen lycklig kärlek, 629
Ingenmansland, 656
Ingens Anna, 706
Ingenting, 454, 489
Ingenting och andra novellistiska skisser, 461–62
Ingenting ovanligt, 503, 562
Ingman, Alfred Emil, 738
In memoriam, 559
Innan dagen börjar, 541
Innan du vet ordet av, 705
I nöd och lust, 672
Inringningen, 680
Insektliv, 682
Inspektorn på Siltala, 414
Insyn, 651–52, 710
Inte från aporna (Not from the Apes), 635
Intim journal, 568
Invita Minerva, 422
I nyländska stugor, 431
Iokasta, 478
Irene: "Silke-Saras" minnen, 566
Iris rukka, 737
Irralliset, 205, 586
Isä ja poika, 207
Isäksi ja tyttäreksi, 259
I sanden, 413

Isäni rakkaani, 263
Isäni, sankari, 265
Isänmaa, 105
Isästä poikaan, 163
Isbergens tid, 696
Island i december, 623
I societeten; En Helsingfors-berättelse, 381
Iso-heikkilän isäntä ja hänen renkinsä Matti, 173
Isoisää etsimässä, 260
Isoisko ja pikkuveli, 237
Isolde pakolainen, 250
Isristning, 643
Istiden (The Ice Age), 635
I stoftet, 492
I stormens spår, 671
Italiensk svit, 631
Itämeren tytär, 123
I tätnande led, 382
I tunga hängen mognar bären, 514
I utvecklingstid, 737
Ivalo, Santeri, 98, 141
I väntan på krevaden, 591

Jääkiekkoilijan kesä, 206
Jääkynttilät, 317
Jaana Rönty, 117
Jääpeili, 155, 157
Jack's Café, 630
Jacobsen, J. P., xxii, 351, 365–66, 374, 381, 384, 441, 476, 530
Jag, Erik Anders, 595
Jag, Jörn Johan Donner, 596–97
Jag bands av årets tider, 492
Jag blir gammal, kära du, 624
Jag har ju sett, 540
Jag kan inte säga för mycket, 612
Jag lever, 468
Jag minns att jag drömde, 586, 588
Jag såg all möda, 675
Jag sjunger för Bertrand Russell, 628
Jakob och friheten, 597
Ja korjaa meri, 214, 255
Jalkanen, Huugo, 143–44, 158
Jälkikuva, 191
Jalmarin kirja, 241
Jalonen, Olli, 252–53, 259

Jäniksen vuosi (The Year of the Hare), 260
Janne Kubik: Ett träsnitt i ord, 454, 462, 532, 590, 603
Janne Kuutio, 462
Jännes, Arvi (Arvid Genetz), 81
Janson, Ture, 392, 434–35, 438, 442, 449, 460, 501, 504, 552, 694
Jansson, Henrik, 267, 688, 695–96
Jansson, Tove, xxvii, xxviii, 197, 567, 571–74, 699, 742–44, 748
Jäntti, Marianna, 262
Ja pesäpuu itki, 258
Ja poika vaikenee, 255
Järnefelt, Alexander, 59, 86, 106, 399, 417
Järnefelt, Armas, 86
Järnefelt, Arvid, xx, xxi, 59, 86, 104–7, 123, 148
Järnefelt, Eero, 70, 86–87, 91, 101, 109, 138, 489
Järnefelt, Elisabet, 86, 106–7
Järnefelt, Kasper, 86, 107
Järner, V. V. (Väinö Vilhelm), 607–9
Järnsängen, 609
Jaska och hans tös, 565
Jason ja vihainen Viivi, 749
Jason muuttaa maasta, 749
Jätten, 637
Jeesuksen kylä, 195
Jeesuksen pieni soturi, 229
Jeftan tytär, 131
Jephtas bok: En minnes-sång i Israel, 318–19
Jesus Christus lyra, 514
J. L. Runeberg och hans vänner, 624, 676
Joenpelto, Eeva, 197–98, 201–2, 213, 233, 560, 658
Joenpolvi, Martti, 215, 238–39,
Joensuun Elli, 257
Joe-setä, 201
Johan ja Johan, 259
Johanneksen leipäpuu, 239
Johannes Angelos (The Dark Angel), 164
Johdatus 1990-luvun ajatteluun, 271
Johnny B. Goethe, 250
Johnson, Eyvind, 421, 463, 536, 615, 703
Jojo, 237
Joki sepittää minulle, 248
Joki virtaa läpi kaupungin, 256

Jones, W. Glyn, 521-22, 572-73
Jordaltaret, 484-85
Jorden har alltid sitt ljus, 638
Jordisk ömhet, 463-64
Jordlös bonde, 647
Jordnära, 544
Jord och drömmar, 547
Jordstjärna, 493
Jörgen Hemmelinks stora augusti, 568
Jørgensen, Johannes, 100
Josef från Arimatea, 606
Jotuni, Maria, xxi, 92, 122, 129, 131, 135-38, 141-42, 144, 154, 204, 266, 658, 668
Joukahainen, 58
Journalisten Bergman, 435
Judas Iskariot Samfundets Årsbok 1987, 624
Judén, Jacob (Jaakko Juteini), 54-56, 61-62
Juha, 103-4, 523
Juhannustanssit, 55, 178, 212, 224
Juho Vesainen, 98
Julius Blom: Ett huvud för sig, 588
Julma prinsessa ja kosijat, 206
Julqvällen, 307-9, 314, 333
Jumalan myllyt, 167
Jumala on kauneus, 204
Jumala pullossa, 234
Junamatkan kuvaus, 207
Juslén, Per, 46-47, 298
Juslenius, Daniel, 9, 45-46, 48
Just det, dvs livet, 645
Juteini, Jaakko (Jacob Judén), 54-56, 61-62
Juurakon Hulda (Hulda Juurakko), 173
Juusten, Paul, 36, 48
Juvonen, Helvi, 179-80, 183, 188, 193
Jylhä, Yrjö, 159, 161-62, 176
Jyrsijät, 191

Kåhre, Georg (pseud. Stefan Sylvander), 550
Käännekohta, 218
Kaarina Maununtytär, 164
Kaarle herttua, 9, 11
Kaatra, Kössi, xxix, 110
Kadonnut armeija, 242
Kadonnut aurinko, 258
Kähäri, Iris, 740
Kahdeksan kuukautta Shpalernajassa, 141-42

Kahdeksantoista runoniekkaa, 57
Kaikki alennuksella, 239
Kaiku, 83
Kaila, Tiina, xxx, 268, 745
Kailas, Uuno, 158-62, 167-68, 179-80, 183, 490
Kainin tytär, 258
Kainuism, 213
Kaipainen, Anu, 224, 228-31
Kaipaus, 259
Kaivos, 226
Kajanto, Iiro, 286
Kajanus, Robert, 101, 399
Kajava, Viljo, 154, 158, 161, 167, 169-70, 177, 185, 210
Kajornas kyrka, 564
Kakku, 227
Kaksoiskuva, 185
Kala on meren kuva, 268
Kalastaja Merlin, 250
Kalervo, Leo, 224, 232-33
Kalevala (Kalewala, taikka Wanhoja Karjalan Runoja Suomen Kansan Muinosista Ajoista), xxiii, xxvii, 3-29, 31-33, 51-52, 58-60, 63, 66, 68, 70-72, 76, 82, 84, 100, 113, 115, 116, 118, 121, 186, 229, 261, 317, 323, 335, 346, 352, 355, 461, 488, 519, 546, 625, 733
Källan, 586, 676
Kallas, Aino (née Krohn; pseud. Aino Suonio), 70, 122, 124-27, 129, 137-38, 144, 148, 538, 658
Kallio, 54, 56, 61
Källorna sorlar i väster: Färder i Sverige, 498
Kalm, Pehr, 292, 383
Kalpea aavistus verenkierrosta, 251
Kameran silmissä siniset unet, 751
Kämppä, 226
Kanariefågel blues, 718, 721
Kanava, 61
Kan ej: Familjemålning i 2 akter, 315-16
Kanervala, 78
Kani Kaniinin kuperkeikat, 197
Kanon, 525
Kansakunnan synty, 186
Kansalaisvapaudesta, 186
Kansallista itsetutkistelua, 133

Kansan Uutiset, 194
Kantaja, 263
Kanteletar (Kanteletar taikka Suomen Kansan Wanhoja Lauluja ja Wirsiä), 3–6, 23–33, 58, 63, 156, 305, 328, 346, 389, 546, 555
Kantola, Kaisa, 155
Kaos och kristall, 499
Kapakoiden maa, 198
Käpphelvetet, 598
Käppyräinen, 182
Kaptener och kaptenskor, 392
Kapten Grunnstedt, 746
Kapten Tärnberg och andra berättelser, 365
Kära Alexander, 664
Kära gamla värld, 630
Karelia, xix, 6–9, 12, 14, 18–20, 22, 24, 27, 29, 53, 62, 68, 100, 102, 110–11, 138, 142, 181, 213, 244, 252, 257, 277–78, 290, 293, 351, 372–73, 380, 389, 396–97, 447, 465, 467, 500, 519–23, 530, 563, 653, 702–3, 746
Karelianism, 99–100, 104, 109, 129, 153, 467, 519, 520
Karin Månsdotter, 379
Karkama, Pertti, 31–32
Karkurit, 72, 79
Karlebybor: Historier från allmoge och småstadsliv, 427
Kärleken: En utvecklingshistoria i episoder, 382
Kärlekens död, 469
Kärlek utan nåd: Tre variationer på ett tema, 708
Karlfeldt, Erik Axel, 367, 413, 431
Kärnor av ögonblick, 479
Kärsimys, 128
Karu laidunrinne, 185
Katajainen kansani, 102
Katastrof efter katastrof, 686–87
Katedralen, 498
Katinka Rabe, 125
Katrina, 534–37, 672, 706
Katsokaa silmiänne, 192
Kattorna (The Cats), 570
Katuojan vettä, 171
Katz, Daniel, xxx, 260–61
Kauan kukkineet omenapuut, 239
Kaukana maailmasta, 242

Kaukonen, Väinö, 25, 27, 31
Kaunis hallayö, 197
Kauppa-Lopo, 89, 98
Kauppila, Impi, 179
Kauppinen, Heikki (Kauppis-Heikki), 86, 98, 107
Kaupunki ja villivaahtera, 196
Kauranen, Anja, 262
Keckman, Carl Niklas, 62
Keinuva maa, 247
Kejsarstaden, 599
Kekkonen, Urho, 205, 208, 240, 598, 609, 613, 625, 648, 655
Kellgren, Herman, 58–60
Kellgren, Johan Henrik, 293–94, 298, 302
Kellomorsian, 230
Kemppinen, Jukka, xxx, 269
Kenttä ja kasarmi, 166
Kenttävartio, 201
Kerran kesällä, 153
Keskipäivä, delta, 184
Keskitie, 190
Keskiviikko, syyskuu, syksy, 627
Keskustelu hämärässä, 268
Kettil Rödes saga, 493
Kevään ajoilta, 80
Kevään kuusi päivää, 238
Kevät, 143
Kevät ja takatalvi, 102–3
Kevättä ja syksyä, 207
Kevättä kohti, 233
Kianto (Calamnius), Ilmari, xx, xxii, 122–23, 127–29, 131, 141–42, 144, 151, 524
Kielland, Alexander, xxi, 96, 360, 362, 371–72, 374, 381–82, 387, 405
Kierkegaard, Søren, xxiii, 132, 228, 405, 485, 536
Kiertävä kivi on kuollut, 269
Kihlaus (Eva), 72
Kihlman, Bertel, 590
Kihlman, Christer, 214, 255, 477, 487, 565, 590–95, 598–600, 602–3, 607, 609–11, 619, 623, 651, 656, 668, 687, 697–98
Kihlman, Erik, 360, 404, 425, 435, 445, 454, 590, 632, 637, 646, 650, 653, 657
Kiila, 167–70, 178–79
Kiinan ja Rääkkylän runot, 251

Index 850

Kiinan runoutta 1-4, 190
Kiinnitys menneesyyteen, 232
Kiirastuli, 162, 176
Kiljander, Robert, 80, 84, 87
Kilpi, Eeva, 223-24, 228, 231, 244, 658, 675
Kilpi, Volter, 122-23, 129-33, 141, 144, 148, 151-52, 199, 400, 724
Kinesisk utflykt, 468-69
Kinnunen, Aarne, 166, 186
Kiparsky, Paul, 14
Kiri-ra!, 471
Kirjailijatar ja hänen miehensä, 199
Kirjailijoiden kentät ja kasarmit, 270
Kirjaimet tulevat, 251
Kirjalinnen kaukauslehti, 65, 78
Kirjallisuuslehti, 169
Kirjavia kuvia pölkkyjen historiasta, 81
Kirjeitä Trinidadiin, 263
Kirjoja ja kirjailijoita, 149
Kirkas nimetön yö, 223
Kirkolle, 152
Kirsti Fleming, 389
Kirstinä, Väinö, 211-12, 217, 244, 622
Kirurgens park: Kineserier, 690-91
Kissansilmät: Unia, ufoja, kissoja, 193
Kiusaaja, 263
Kivenpyörittäjän kylä, 257
Kivi, Aleksis, xxi, xxii, xxiii, xxix, 45, 47, 56-57, 62-63, 68, 70-74, 75-79, 81-84, 91-93, 111, 113, 129, 132, 149, 199, 206, 214, 240, 260, 268, 347, 409, 463, 468, 738
Kivikausi, 189
Kivikkaho, Eila, 178-81, 183, 188, 193
Kivimaa, Arvi, 159
De klagande vindarnas ö, 479
Klagelig röst i en troiinnerlig bön om hielp uti nöden till frelsaren Jesum, 288
Klas-Kristians julnatt, 411
Klas Kurck och liten Elin, 389
Klassiliset tunteet, 195
Klaus, Louhikon herra, 137
Klinge, Matti, 45, 48, 284
KLO, 714-15, 717, 722
Klockan 5 och klockan ingenting vid havet, 579
Klockan i havet, 446
Klockorna i Rom (The Bells in Rome), 521

Ett klosteräventyr, 523
Det kluvna äpplet, 613, 696
Klyftan, 543-44, 560
Klyftan och stjärnan, 535
Knape, Ernst V., 428-30
Knappen, 569
Knock me down: Helsingfors noveller, 435
Kobaggen, 674
Koillismaa (Our Daily Bread), 243
Koiranheisipuu ja neljä muuta pienoisromaania, 164
Koiran kuolema, 234
Koivisto, Mauno, 208, 655, 677
Koivu, Rudolf, 735, 748
Kojo, Viljo, 144, 158, 490
Kökar, 705
Kokko, Yrjö, 740
Kokkonen, Jonas, 241
Kokkonen, Lauri, 240
Kollanius, Abraham, 40
Kolmannen valtakunnan vieraana, 174, 517
Kolme naista, kolme kohtaloa, 127
Kolmen hevosen mies, 257
Kolmodin, Ericus, 280, 284
Kolteckning, ofullbordad, 504
Kometen kommer (Comet in Moominland), 572
Kometjakten, 572
Kontrakurs, 636
Kootut runot (Juvonen), 184
Kootut runot (Kivikkaho), 182
Kootut runot (Koskenniemi), 149
Kootut runot (Suhonen), 252
Koreuden tähden, 198
Korhonen, Paavo, 57
Korpela, Jorma, 177, 197-98, 200-201, 203
Korpi ja puutarha, 153
Korpinäkyjä, 121
Korpisota, 176
Korppi ja Korpin poika, 740
Korppi ja korven veikot, 740
Korppi ja kumppanit, 740
Korpraali Julin, 226
Korset och löftet, 471
Korsholm, 606
Korståget, 517-19
Korta brev från en lång bröllopsresa, 364

Index 851

Korta brev från hemmets lugna härd, 364
Korta stund, 678
Kort parlör, 555
Kortteeri, 226
Koskenniemi, V. A., 75, 120, 123, 142, 144, 147–50, 154, 158, 160–62, 176, 180, 498, 724
Koskinen, Yrjö Sakari (Georg Forsman), 63, 65, 82, 240, 349, 733
Kosola, Vihtori, 240
von Kothen, Casimir, 61, 593
Kotimaa, 227
Kotona, 207
Kouta, Aarni, 121
Kovan onnen lapsia, 88–89
Kovikset, 750
Köyhää kansaa, 88, 91–92
Köyhyyden trilogia, 216
Kråkdikter, 629
Kråkögat, 665
Kråkslottet, 609
Kråkvals, 665
von Kraemer, Alexis, 401
Kraft och tanke, 647
Kramsu, Kaarlo, 81–82
Krigaren och bonden, 522
Krigsbarn 13408, 662
Krigshistoria, 545–46
Kristina (queen of Sweden), 57, 276, 342–43
Kristina Bjur, 411
Krohn, Julius (pseud. Suonio), xvii, 65–66, 69–71, 77, 79, 81–82, 124, 162, 724, 733
Krohn, Leena, 252–54
Krokfors, Hjalmar, 550, 553–54, 557
Krokushuset, 662
Kronofogdens pengar, 374
Kuikka, 201
Kuinka voitte?, 193
Kuin kekäle kädessä, 202
Kukkivat roudan maat 1–6, 214, 233
Kukunor, 182
Kuljen missä kuljen, 216
Kullervo, 62–63, 71–72, 82
Kullervon tarina (Kullervo's Story), 186
Kultainen vasikka (The Golden Calf), 137
Kultala, 62

Kungarne på Salamis, 316, 347, 478
Kung Carls jagt, 340
Kungen, 637
Kungens Anna, 706
Kung Fjalar: En dikt i fem sånger (King Fjalar), 299, 310–11, 315, 369
Kung Kristian den Andre, 379, 404
Kungörelser, 647
Kungsådern, 545
Kung Tulle (King Tulle), 744
Kuningashitti, 751
Kun isoisä Suomeen hiihti, 260
Kun kaikki kellot sydämessä soivat, 250
Kun kansa nousee, 142
Kun lesket lempivät, 140
Kunnas, Kirsi, xxx, 196–97, 689, 747–48
Kunnas, Mauri, 748
Kun on tunteet, 135
Kun ruusut kukkivat, 140
Kunskap och inlevelse: Essäer och minnen, 525
Kuolema, 105, 111
Kuolismaantie, 226
Kuolleet omenapuut, 153
Kuolleet vedet, 189
Kuolleiden evankeliumi, 204
Kuolleista herännyt, 140, 144
Kuopion takana, 389
Kuparirahaa, 239
Kupiainen, Unto, 80, 159, 162
Kurenniemi, Marjatta, 741
Kurjensaari, Matti, 172, 174–75, 210
Kurtén, Björn, 635
Kustbor, 675
Kustland, 550
Kutter, Hans, 490
Kuudes kirja, 188
Kuun kuva meissä, 197
Kuun maisema, 164
Kuun puutarhat, 264
Kuun tarinoita, 69
Kuuntelua, 152, 155
Kuusi, Matti, xviii, 9–11, 14–15, 17, 30
Kuusinen, Otto Ville, 110, 225, 442, 459
Kuvat kertovat, 233
Kvällar, 629
Kvarteret barmhärtighet, 570
Det kvidande och muntrade Sverige, 288

Kvinnan, 568
Kvinnan och nåden, 466, 484, 667
Kvinnomorgon, 661
Kvinnoregemente, 366, 368
Kvinnoträdet, 663
Kylätasku, Jussi, 241
Kylliksi: Tai liikaa, 238
Kylmät hypyt, 242–43
Kylväjä lähti kylvämään, 191
Kysy hiljaisuudelta itseäsi, 245
Kyyhky ja unikko, 234

Lågor under vattnet, 643
Lågt i tak, 543
Lånade vingar: Ungdomsminnen, 636
Lång, Fredrik, 707–11
Långa längtan, 630
Långa vandring, 680
Den långa våren (Marianna), 535–36
Labyrint, 604
Laestadianism, 204, 207, 220–22, 234, 248, 305
Lagerborg, Rolf, 382, 401, 422, 491, 494
Lagerkvist, Pär, 465–66, 489, 553
Lagerlöf, Selma, xxiii, 121, 123, 345, 358–59, 361, 385, 535–37
Lagervall, Jacob Fredrik, 62
Lagus, Gabriel, xviii, 283, 297, 346, 349–50, 376
Lahtela, Markku, 224, 234–35
Lähtevien laivojen kaupunki, 125
Laine, Jarkko, 218, 220–21
Laitinen, Kai, xviii, xix, xxiii, 147, 165, 177, 192, 194, 204, 608, 622
Laiva, 226
Lakeuden kutsu, 256
Lakeus, 211
Laki ja järjestys 1918 (Law and Order), 173
Lampi, Vilho, 204
Landet Marita och andra noveller, 610
Landet som icke är, 457, 493
Ett land i kamp, 445, 448
Landskapet med den dubbla skuggan, 477
Landskapets förvandlingar, 582
Landskap i öster, 633
Lange, Ina (née Forstén; pseud. Daniel Sten), 386–87, 398, 403, 449

Längs vattenbrynet, 502
Lans och lyra, 416
Lanthandlerskans son, 711
Lapland War (1944–45), xx, 146, 236
Lapplandsresan, 493
Lapsia, 96, 369
Lapsuuteni (My Childhood), 166–67
Lapsuuteni muistoja, 95
Lapualaisooppera, 239
Larin-Kyösti (Kyösti Larson), 120–21, 154
Lärkan, 327–28
Lärospån, 435
Lars Laurila, 535
Larsson, Jukka (Pirkko Saisio), 252–53, 257–58, 263
Lars Thorman och döden, 466
Läse-öfning för mina barn, 729
Lasi Claudius Civiliksen salaliittolaisten pöydällä, 186
Lasimaalauksen läpi, 182
Lasimaalaus, 182
Lasinen pyykkilauta, 202
Läsning för vandrare, 623
Lassila, Maiju (Algoth Tietäväinen, later Algoth Untola; pseud. Irmari Rantamala, J. I. Vatanen), xxix, 122–23, 129, 135, 138–44, 148, 261
Lassila, Pertti, 159
Lastmärket, 637
Lastuja, 93
Latuja lumessa, 162
Laturi, 261
Latvasaaren kuninkaan hovilinna, 738
Laulujoutsen: Ultima Thulen lintu, 740
Laulu laululta pois, 216
Laulu rakkaudesta, 231
Laulu Sipirjan lapsista, 234
Laulu tulipunaisesta kukasta (The Song of the Blood-Red Flower), 130–31
Laureatus, 348, 368, 693
Laurén, Per Åke, xxii
Laus manus, 284
Lausui alustaja, joka korosti, 243
Lea, 74–75, 79
Leendets magma, 670–71
Lehdet lehtiä, 211
Lehmusten kaupunki, 244

Lehtimäki, Konrad, xxix, 110–11
Lehtinen, Onerva (pseud. L. Onerva), 120, 142, 490
Lehtonen, Joel, xxii, xxiii, 122–23, 129–31, 133–35, 137–41, 144, 148, 151, 153–54, 489, 555
Lehtonen, Soila, 254, 267
Leijan ilma vihreää, 196
Leikkejä kahdelle, 218
Leino, Eino, xvii, xxii, xxiii, 56, 82, 99, 101–2, 106, 108–13, 114–21, 127, 134, 142–44, 148, 154–55, 158, 238, 377, 400, 464, 490, 555
Leino, Kasimir, 98–99, 112
Leistenius, Jakob Gabriel, 327, 350
Lekhagen, 570
Lektion för döden, 568
Lencquist, Erik, 47
Leningradin kohtalonsinfonia, 205
Leo, 706–7
Leo ja Liina, 74
De levande, 508
Levande och död tradition, 633
De levandes mod, 557
Leve generalkonsuln!, 608
Leve revisionismerna, 555
Levertin, Oscar, 377, 401–2, 413–14
Lexicon Latino-Scondicum, 40
Libellus aureus de civilitate morum puerilium, 39
Lie, Jonas, xxi, 85, 359, 373, 383–84
Liehu, Rakel, 245, 248
Lihaa ja rakkautta, 267
Liika viisas, 140
Likinäköinen adjutantti, 266
Liksom, Rosa (Anni Ylävaara), xxx, 250, 266–67
Lilius, Carl Gustaf, 551, 642–43, 744
Lilius, Henrik, 44
Lilius, Irmelin Sandman, xxx, 549, 642, 743–44, 746–48
Lilla Barbro Björkelöv, 747
Lilla Guldmärket, 661
Lille, Axel, 355, 615, 650
Lille, Bengt Olof, 321
Lille Karl, 358, 369, 526
Lind, Christer, 525, 551–52

Lindberg, Pirkko, 712
Lindblad, Kjell, 688, 696–97, 712, 725
Lindegren, Erik, 195, 546, 556, 581, 646
Lindén, Gurli, 250, 665–66, 668, 670, 721
Linder, Marie (pseud. Stella), 330–32
Lindfors, Bodil, 681–82, 699
Lindgren, Sören G., 639–40
Lindh, Theodor, 349–50
Lindquist, Marita, 747
Linguae Finnicae brevis institutio, 9, 38
Linkola, Pentti, 271, 272
Linna, Väinö, xxiii, 56, 129, 165, 176, 178, 197–200, 203, 210–11, 213–14, 223, 541–42, 560, 602
Linnankoski, Johannes, xxi, xxiii, 122–23, 129–31, 139, 141
Linnoituksen iloiset rouvat, 123
Linnusta länteen, 269
Linsén, Johan Gabriel, 52, 300
Lintukoto, 154
Lit de parade, 695–96
Liten drömmarpilt, 486
Liten stad vid havet, 638
Lithovius, Zacharias, 288
Litteraturblad för allmän medborgerlig bildning, 48, 59, 323, 733
Little Wrath (1741–43), xx, 46, 288, 303, 315, 739
Ett liv, 411
Livet det är viktigt, 538
Livet i förorten, 677
Livets bryggor: En berättelse om Österbotten, 606
Livsdrömmen rena: Bok om maktlöshet, 594, 687
Livsstycket, 569
Livsvilja, 550
Lizelius, Anders (Antti), 47
Ljud i natten, 384
Ljung, 336
Ljungars saga, 344
Ljungblommor, 335
Ljusdunkel, 477
Ljuset, 517
Ljuset i rummet, 643
Ljust i mörkt, 444
Locknät, 604–5

Löfving, Stefan, 141, 289–91, 298, 324
Loggbok på landbacken, 486
Loistava Armfelt, 175
Loistava Helena, 254
Loistava Olavi Paavolainen, 175
Lokomonyliopisto, 251
Lomapäivä, 225
Lompolo, Jouni (pseud. Origo), 241–42
Londén, Lilly, 332, 397–98, 400, 523
Lönnrot, Elias, xxi, 3–5, 14, 17, 19–25, 27–33, 41–42, 45, 48, 51, 53–54, 57–60, 62–63, 65, 68–71, 103, 121, 156, 305–6, 335, 556, 733, 751
Lotsarnas kamp, 411
Lotus: En berättelse om kärlek, 610
Lovart och lä, 392
Luba: En studie, 387–88
Lucidarius, 275
Lucidor, Lasse (Lars Johansson), 42, 282, 623
Luen muutosten kirjaa, 189
Luettua, läheistä, 199
Lukemisia lapsille, 730
Lumi, 196
Lumijoutsen, 748
Lumipalloja, 155
Lumisota, 468
Lundahl, Augusta, 326–27
Lundberg, Ulla-Lena, 705–7, 709–10, 713
Luonnollinen tanssi, 211–12, 217
Luonnon lapsia, 140
Lutad över brunnen, 479
Luumujengi, 750
Lybeck, Mikael, 398, 400, 402–5, 407, 425–26, 428, 436, 446, 500, 524, 585, 632, 638, 714
Lybeck, Paul Werner, 406, 426, 500
Lybeck, Sebastian, 638–40
Lyckoriddaren, 439
Lydecken, Arvid, 735, 739
Lyrik i Finland nu/Suomen lyriikkaa tänään, 621
Lyrik 1912–1926 (Ragnar Ekelund), 444
De lysande och de döda, 575
Lysaren, 676
Lyssnerskan, 573
Lyyli, 110

Måla himlen, 747
Målare, 558
Måltid, 519
Månen är en säl, 533
Månens tid, 702–3
Många är livets drömmar, 628
Månsten, 687
Maaemon lapsia, 106
Maailman kourissa, 242
Maailman murjoma, 92
Maailman myötä ja vastaan, 254
Maailmanteatteri, 180
Maailman virrassa, 227
Maailma on sana, 226
Maailmasta, 211, 215
Maa kallis isien, 228
Maa kuuluu kaikille!, 106
Maa kuuntelee sinua, 232
Maaliskuun lauluja, 112
Maamiehen Ystävä, 59
Maan avaruus, 256
Maan puoleen, 142
Maantieltä hän lähti, 207
Maan veri, 257
Maa on syntinen laulu, 234
Maaria Blomma (Mary Bloom), 241
Maata näkyvissä, 177
Madame, 570
Madeleine, 592–93
Madetoja, Leevi, 104
Magdaleena ja maailman lapset, 230
Magnus principatus Finlandia, 45, 282, 300
Magoun, Francis Peabody, 23–24
Maja, 671
Mäkelä, Hannu, 238, 742
Makten och härligheten: Skådespel från 1600-talets Österbotten, 606
Malena börjar skolan, 747
Malena 11 år, 747
Malena och glädjen, 747
Malenas finaste sommar, 747
Malenas nya bror, 747
Malinen, Ontrei, 25
Malmberg, Richard (pseud. Gustav Alm), 423–25, 428–29, 433, 500, 585
Malmström, Karl Robert, 349–51
Malmström, Nicken, 490, 492–93

Malttamaton nuoruus, 232
Mammutens rådare (Singletusk: A Novel of the Ice Age), 635
Mandariini kainalossa, 190
Mandelstam, Karin, 551, 557
En man går över torget, 561
En man gick genom stormen, 546
Mania, 507
Manillaköysi (The Manila Rope), 205, 560
Män kan inte våldtas (Manrape), 657
Mannen som byggde en båt, 700–701
Mannen som försökte smita, 531
Mannen som uppfann vädret: En rötmånadssaga, 522
Manner, Eeva-Liisa, 179, 184, 187–89, 197, 527, 658
Mannerheim, Carl Gustav, 205–6, 214, 236, 240, 266, 353, 357, 407, 442, 447, 545, 593, 616, 654
Mannerkorpi, Juha, 177, 179, 184, 190–91, 560
Manninen, Anni, 743
Manninen, Otto, 109, 117–19, 142, 144, 148, 154, 179, 180–81, 183, 402, 413, 724, 734
Människans anlete, 651
Människan som skalv: En bok om det oväsentliga, 214, 593, 619, 651, 657
Människor jag känt, 375
En man och hans samvete (A Fool of Faith), 447, 534, 700
En mänska börjar likna sin själ, 618
Mänskliga människor, 630
Manuale seu exequiale Aboense, 35
Mä oon Maukka, 750
Maras ö, 667, 670, 721
Marck, Mary (Kersti Bergroth), 737, 749
Margareta, 75
Margareta Jönsdotter till Bastö, 530
Marginalia till grekisk och romersk diktning, 587
Mariegatan 26, Kronohagen, 655
Marina Maria, 597
Marinergraven, 684
Marin och genre, 362
Marjamiesnaisen muistiinpanoja, 195
Marjanen, Kaarlo, 150, 157

Markkinoilta, 134
Marmorilaiva, 271
Marmoriuni, 239
von Martens, Paul, 262, 700–702, 714
von Martens, Peter, 609, 686
Martinheimo, Asko, 743
Martinius, Mathias, 38, 44
Martinmaa, mieshenkilö, 200
Martinson, Harry, 490, 528
Martva, 139–40
Maskinmänniskan, 435
Maskun Hemminki (Hemmingius Henrici), 35, 37
Massmöte på jorden, 648
Matalat aidat, 750
Mataleena, 133–34
Mathilda, 328
Matias Tallgrenin yksityiselämä, 234
Matikanopettaja, 201
Matin makeiset, 735
Matkalippuja kaikkiin juniin, 191
Matkalla niityn yli, 185
Matkamies, 119
Matkoilla kaiken aikaa, 238
Mattan från Kars, 746
Matti Väkevä, 241
Mattsson, Gunnar, 637, 646, 657
Mattsson, Gustaf (Guss; pseud. Ung Hans), 402, 408, 422–23, 439, 500, 634–35, 654
Mau-Mau, 250
Mazzarella, Merete, 385, 534, 537, 562, 571, 611, 635, 662, 667, 670, 692–93, 703–5, 712, 717, 724
Mechelin, Leo, 353, 357
Med, 612–13
Medaljongen, 414
Medborgare i republiken Finland, 462, 603
Medborgare II, 462, 526
Med det falska och det ärliga ögat, 378–79
Med havet som granne, 671
Meditationes sacrae, 39
Med öppna händer, 518
Med styrkans rätt, 374
Mehiläinen, 57, 59
Meille jäi kiireetön ilta/Kvällen gör sig ingen brådska, 216
Mein Lebenslauf, 391

Meitä kohti, 235
Mellan hammaren och städet, 632
Mellan is och eld, 554
Mellan jul och ragnarök, 624
Mellan två skymningar, 672
Melleri, Arto, xxx, 245, 250–51
Men blåser violer på havet, 474
Men den skrattade bara/Mutta se nauroi vain, 626
Mennander, Carl Fredrik, 46, 298
Menshikov, Aleksander Sergeyevich, 59, 64
Mera du, 620
Mer än älska, 598
Meren takaa, 124
Meri, Veijo, xxiii, 191, 197–98, 204–6, 210–11, 213–14, 225, 261, 267, 542, 560, 586, 616
Meri, ei mikään maa, 269
Merikanto, Aarre, 104
Merikanto, Oskar, 98, 617, 677
Meriluoto, Aila, 179–80, 182, 740
Merkillistä menoa, 251
Metallin maku, 265
Metsäherran herjaaja, 128
Metsän satuja, 143
Metsän seinä on vain vihreä ovi, 244
Metsytiska boken, 643
Mickwitz, Camilla, 748–49
von Mickwitz, Gerda, 332, 381–82, 398
Mickwitz, Johan, 620–22
Middagsdemonerna, 633
Miehen kylkiluu, 137
Miehen tie, 150
Miekkalintu, 195
Mies ja punapartaiset herrat, 167
Mikael Hakim (*The Sultan's Renegade*), 164
Mikael Karvajalka (*Michael the Finn*), 164
Mikkola, Marja-Leena, 223, 227–28, 742, 745, 748
Mikko Papirossin taivaallinen niskalenkki, 261
Mimmi Paavaliina, 141
Mina bästa dagar, 619
Mina huudan, 255
Minä, maani, maailmassa, 235
Min amerikanska saga, 537
Minä, Olli ja Orvokki, 224
Minä se olen, 247
Minä viihtyy, 251
Min dikt, 460
Miniatyrer, 414
Min lyra, 454
Minnesaltaret, 416
Minnet är en vinge, 627
Minnet av Alexandria, 633
Minnet av Michael, 698
Min pennas saga, 322
Min salladsgröna älskarinna, 628
Min timme, 505, 580
Minus sju, 582, 586
Minuter på jorden, 576
Min värld, 520
Mirdja, 120
Mirjam, 568
"De miseriis Fennorum," 46
Missale Aboense, 35
En misstanke, 397–98, 523
Mitä tapahtuu todella?, 211–12, 215, 217, 614
Miten kirjani ovat syntyneet, 180
Mitt Helsingfors, 434, 552, 653, 694
Mitt i den nordiska idyllen, 639
Mitt kära krig, 560
Mnemosyne, 51, 53, 298, 300
Moberg, Vilhelm, 545, 650, 675
Modärn finlandssvensk lyrik (1934), 476, 496, 500
Modellfilaren, 674
Modern finlandssvensk lyrik (1986), 549
Modern finlandssvensk prosa, 500
modernism, xviii, 157, 177, 181, 186, 190, 195, 213–14, 453, 455, 471, 476, 485, 489, 495, 500–501, 558, 567, 618, 640, 687, 741
Mognadens opera, 686
Möjligheter, 632
Moln, som slits sönder, 640
Molnet såg mig, 507
Molnsommar, 648
Mona-Lisa, rakkaudella, 241
Monochord, 514
Monologit, 195
Moonscape and Other Stories, 164
Moralia eller Några Korta Regler, 284–85
Mordet på Kiron, 478
Moreeni, 178, 183

Morgonen, 443
Morgongåvan, 448
Morgonstjärnan, 410
Mörka gudar, 512, 541
Mörk längtan, 541
Mörk ligger jorden, 541, 556
Mörkret och människan, 496
Mörkrets kärna, 562–63, 565, 593
Mörkret som ger glädjen djup, 348, 657
Mörkrum, 600, 657
Mörne, Arvid, xxiii, 348–49, 354–56, 374, 387, 400, 402, 407–12, 414, 426, 428, 431, 434, 443, 453–54, 463, 465, 485, 490–92, 500, 556, 650, 724
Mörne, Barbro, 490–92
Mörne, Gudrun, 491
Mörne, Håkan, 491, 693
Morsiamen kuolema, 9
Moskovalainen huivi, 252
Moskovan ikävä, 251
Mötesplats, 557
Mot fullbordan, 527
Mot fyren, 395
Motiv, 519
Mot ljuset på bergen, 495
Motlut, 557
Mot morgondag, 528
Mot öknen, 412
Motsols, 545
Mr. Gogo kommer till Europa, 653
Mr. Jeremias söker en illusion, 466
Muistatko—?, 104
Muistista, 195
Muistojen tie, 119
Mukka, Timo K., 224, 233–34
Mull och moln, 463
Muminpappas bravader (*The Exploits of Moominpappa*), 572
Muminpappas memoarer, 572
Mummoni ja Mannerheim, 205
Münchhausen/Nuket, 186
Munkmonolog, 591
En mun vid hand, 473
Muodonmuutoksia, 192
Muovinen Buddha, 220
Murar, 511
Murattikaide, 269
Murheellisen kuullen on puhuttava hiljaa, 245
Murtovarkaus, 87, 268
Murtoviivoja, 120
Musta hurmio, 167
Mustan perhosen aika, 196
Mustapää, P. (Martti Haavio), 154, 158–59, 161–62, 177, 179–80, 249
Musta rakkaus, 199, 541
Mustarinnan lapset, 257
Mutta, 198
Mutta minulla ei olisi rakkautta, 236
Muuttopäivät, 196
Myöhäinen kevät, varhainen syksy, 196
Myrsky Koillismaassa (*Storm over the Land*), 243
Myrtti ja alppiruusu, 134
Mythologia Fennica, 10, 48
Myyrä Matikaisen malliauto, 741

Några ord om nejderne, folklynnet och lefnadssättet i Saarijärvi Socken, 303–4
Några Poetiske Samblingar, 289
Naamioita, 116
Näckrosen och bränt vatten, 686
Nadeschda: Nio sånger, xx, 309–10
Nahkapeitturien linjalla 1–2, 205
Naimisiin, 226
Naisen kunnia, 198
Naisen päiväkirja, 232
Naisen torso, 261
Naisia, 227
Naistentanssit, 230
Näkki, 254
De nakna och de saliga, 594, 656
Näkyväistä maailmaa, 186
Nallen seikkailut, 735
Napapiirin äänet, 205
Nära, 519
När barometern stod på Karl Öberg och andra hörspel, 706
När gudarna dör, 545
Narkissos, 610
Närmare någon, 503
Narratio de legatione sua Russica, 37
När Thales myntade uttryck: En bok om det sakliga tänkandets uppkomst, 707
Nasaretin miehen pitkä marssi, 270

Nästa dag, 504
Nätet, 505
Den nationella vinsten (*The National Gain*), 292
Nationens hjälte, 610
Natten är ännu ung, 710
Nattens fabler, 688, 690
Nattens rötter, 605
Nattlig äng, 505, 506
Nattvinge, 620
Naturens bok, 342
Näytelmän henkilöt, 218
Näytelmistö, 79
Neckermans, 538
Nedoviggen, 674
Neiglick, Hjalmar, 359–62, 377–78
Neito kulkee vetten päällä (*The Maiden Walks upon the Water*), 202
Neitsyt, 228
Neljän tuulen tie (*The Way of the Four Winds*), 740
Nenän pakinoita, 217
Nervander, Emil, 75, 240
Nervander, Johan Jakob, 302, 306, 309, 318–19, 334
Nevala, Maria-Liisa, 127, 151, 249
New Theater. *See* Swedish Theater
New York nätter och dagar, 681, 699
Nicholas I (czar of Russia), 61, 64, 303, 309, 336, 387
Nicholas II (czar of Russia), 101, 357, 372, 408, 481
Nick Naantali itäisillä mailla, 221
Nieminen, Kai, 245–47
Nieminen, Pertti, 180, 187, 189–90, 212, 246
Nietzscheanism, 91, 100, 109, 120, 368, 382, 418, 456, 470, 490
Niininen, Margit, 566–67
Niinkuin minä näin, 155
Niityltä pois, 179, 181
Nilsson, Kim, 308, 473, 480
Nimipäivä, 55
Niniven lapset, 123
Niskavuoren tarina, 173
Nissinen, Aila, 741
N.N., 645
Nödlijdande flychtingars klagan öfver sitt långsamma kårss och elände, 288

Noidanlukko, 231
Noitaympyrä, 166
Nojonen, Uolevi, 750
Nomenclatura, 46
Nordan, 446
Nordgren, Aili, 541–42, 546, 558, 611–14, 616, 622, 696
Nordmann, Petrus, 376, 395
Nordström, Vilhelmina, 326–27
Nörråkers: Berättelsen om en släktgård, 547
Det norrfångna landet, 430, 547
Notvarp i Saragassohavet, 610
Nousukausi, 227
Novelleja (Samuli S.), 80
Noveller (Tigerstedt), 497
Novellit (Salama), 225
Novembervår, 464
Nubb, 669
Nuijasota, 349
Nu imorron, 656
Nukun silmät auki, 249
Nu måste du, 597
von Numers, Gustaf, 389–90, 734
von Numers, Lorenz, 532–33, 552, 556–57, 560, 565
Nummi, Lassi, 180, 184–85, 193
Nummisuutarit (*The Heath Cobblers*), 71, 73–74, 347
Nu och förr, 376
Nuorena nukkunut (*The Maid Silja*), 150
Nuori mylläri, 140–41
Nuori Suomi, 84, 101
Nuoruuden päiväkirjat, 217
Nuoruuden trilogia, 177
Nuoruus, 134
Nu sjunger fåglarna igen, 609
Nyårsafton, 675
Nya Argus, 402, 415, 423, 454, 528, 590–91
Nya blad, 336
Nya boken om vårt land, 596
Nya dikter (Tegengren), 414
De nya författarna, 448
Det nya fosterlandet, 440
Nya land, 535
Nya noveller (Hellberg), 538
Nya Pressen, 355, 357, 402, 456, 639
Nya vers (Tavaststjerna), 359

Nya Wecksell-studier, 348
Ny dag, 566
Ny dag börjar, 486
Ny generation, 157, 465
Nygren, Anders John, 396, 426
Nygren, Gun, 667
Nygrén, Maria, 302
Nykvist, Ingmar, 544
Nykyaika, 112
Nykyaikaa etsimässä, 157, 174
Nykypäivä, 174
Nylund, Mauritz, 621-22, 625-27, 645, 722
Ny lyrik 1974, 691, 698
Nyman, Valdemar, 530-31, 539, 705
Nyström, Carita, 663, 665, 678
Ny tid (Chicago), 442
Ny tid (Helsingfors), 499
Ny tid (Arvid Mörne), 408
Nytt Finskt Lexikon, 48

Öar i Afrikas inre, 705
Obelyst kust, 550
Obeväpnad till tänderna, 645, 647
Objekt för ord, 582
Obstfelder, Sigbjørn, 358, 401, 485, 705
Obundna texter, 652
Och dagen kom, 598
Och hastigt förstå, 684
Och leker med skuggorna i sanden, 473
Och ryktet går, 547
Och sanning?, 479
Ockupationen, 707-8, 710
Ödemark, 429
Ödlan, 404
Ödlorna, 561, 654
Den odöpta hästen: Eskapad i tre akter, 626
Offereld, 415
Offer och segrar, 409
Ofinlandssvensk verksamhet, 626
Oheisia, 200
Ohjälpligheten, 472
Ohörbart vattenfall, 507
Ohördas rop, 605
Ointagligt land, 553
Ojaharju, Jorma, 213, 223, 227-28
Det okända helgonets kloster, 521
Den okända sällskapsresenären, 704

Oksanen, A. *See* Ahlqvist, August
Oksanen, Aulikki, xxx, 236-37, 249
Old Finnish Party, 63, 138, 377, 383, 418
The Old Kalevela, 3
Olena ja Vassuska, 742
Olen lähtenyt kauas, 194
Oli ennen Onnimanni, 741
Olin, Ulla, 194, 541, 556-57
Olli (Väinö Nuorteva), 172-74, 241-42
Olli Suurpää, 117
Olsson, Hagar, 131, 144, 151, 157, 420, 456-58, 460, 464-69, 471, 476, 484, 486, 489-91, 494, 500, 503, 507-8, 511-13, 516, 521, 523, 551, 573-74, 590, 658, 667, 698, 701, 715
Olviretki Schleusingenissä, 74
Den olydiga stjärnan, 736
Om de fordna Finnars sällskaps-nöjen och tidsfördrif, 50
Omfamningen, 678
Om Finnarnes magiska medicin, 52
Om finska landthushållningen och medlen till dess upphjelpande, 293
Om glädjens alkemi, 681
Om mörkret är allt, 626
Det omöjliga möjligt, 390
Ömt älskade, 701
Det omvända anletet, 634
Om vintern och om våren, 627
Det ondas tjusning: Anteckningar om gangstermytologi och verklighet, 690
Onerva, L. (Onerva Lehtinen), 120, 142, 490
On neidolla punapaula, 230
Onnela: Finsk idyll, 461
Onnellinen mies, 260
Onnen aika, 216
Onnen metsämies, 229
Onnen poika, 153
Onni, 183
Onni Kokko, 447
Önskeleken, 502
Ön som förtärdes av havet, 636
Oofirin kultaa (Donna Quixote and The Gold of Ophir), 253
Operaatio Finlandia, 260
Öppna rum: Insyn hos en bostadslös, 680

Opus 12: Musik, 462
Ord, 443
Ord i natten, 495
Orfeus och Eurydike, 478
Orientering, 510
Origins of Art: A Psychological Study, 421
Origo (Jouni Lompolo), 241–42
Orjan oppi, 105
Ormöga, 508
Örn, W. A., 414
Ornament, 639
Orvar Kleinin kuolema, 261
Osamse strängar, 413
Oskyldigt ingenting, 53
Osmund Kåresunds ungdom, 531
Osmund och aftonstjärnan, 531
Österberg, Anna-Lisa, 663, 668, 702
Österblom, Frans, 275, 395–96, 537
Österbottningar, 428
Österut, 371
Ostindisk resa 1770–1771, 293
Östra centrum: ändstation, 699
Östra Nyland, 431
Ostrobothnia, xxiv, 38–39, 42, 46, 50–51, 59, 98, 103, 252, 256, 275, 296, 301, 319, 321, 341, 351, 355, 390, 393, 396, 411, 414–15, 424, 426–28, 430, 446, 486–87, 513, 530, 535, 542, 545–46, 605–6, 612, 624, 629–31, 647–48, 651, 658–59, 661, 664, 669, 673–75, 679, 709–10, 713, 719
Osv, 652
Den osynliga draken, 698
Otava, 109, 194, 196, 214, 244, 246, 389, 621, 739
Otava, 56
Otava, Merja, 750
Otava eli Suomalaisia huvituksia, 52–53
Otid, 688, 696, 714
Oting, 533
Ottopoika, 225
Oulua soutamassa, 95, 98
Oulun Wiikko-Sanomat, 61
Oväder, 413
Ovala rutor, 628
Över dunklet, 445–46
Övergång, 561
Det övergivna samvetet, 411

Över havet brann Mars, 410
Överskridningar, 631
Över stumhetens gräns, 634
Oxbollen, 673

På åländska vägar till lands och till sjöss, 532
På drift i förlustens landskap, 594
På ett sjukhus, 596
På färder i Israel, 537
På finländsk grund, 411
På flykt från världsåskådningar, 632
På främmande botten, 370
På fri fot, 611
På Kanaanexpressen, 466
På Karlssons himmel, 609
Påläggskalven, 674
På lös sand, 535
Påminnaren, 605
Påsk, 704
Påskägget, 604
På stranden, 564
På tallriksflatan, 638
På Vikarsvallen, 429
Påwals, Per-Hakon, 627–28, 687
Pääkallokiitäjä, 743
Päämäärä, 199
Paasilinna, Arto, xxx, 259–60, 266
Paasilinna, Erno, 214–15, 234, 242–43, 259, 266
Päätalo, Kalle, 243–44
Paatos ja lyyra, 195
Paavo Korhosen viisikymmentä runoa ja kuusi laulua, 57
Paavolainen, Olavi, 157, 159, 162, 172, 174, 178, 517
Pacius, Fredrik, 312, 328, 340–41
Pahat unet, 179, 182
Pahojen henkien historia, 270
Paholaisen viulu, 133
Paholaispoika (Boy Devil), 268
Painuva päivä, 115
Päivä Helsingissä, 116
Päivälehti, 84, 100–101, 112
Päivänsinet, 191
Päivärinta, Pietari, 80–81, 84
Päiviä, sateita, 196
Pakkala, Teuvo, 88, 95–98, 369

Index 861

Pakolaiset, 130–31
Palava omaisuus, 252
Palm, Göran, 576, 640
Palmgren, Raoul, 168
Paloheimo, Oiva, 177
Panik i Rölleby, 543
Panu, 102–3
Papin perhe, 89–90
Papin rouva, 89, 93–94, 99, 104
Papin tytär, 89, 93, 667
Pappan och havet (*Moominpappa at Sea*), 572
Pappas flicka, 600, 712
Paracelsus Baselissa, 164
Paradiset (*Dolphins in the City*), 584
Paradisplantan, 547, 668
Paraske, Larin, 230
Paratiisin valloitus, 179
Paratiisin vangit, 264
Paratiisisaaren vangit, 260
Paremmassa maailmassa, 228
Parkerna, 684
Parkkinen, Jukka, 740
Parland, Henry, 480–81, 483–84, 490, 500, 526, 532, 549, 558
Parland, Oscar, 482, 484, 519, 525–27, 531, 560, 578, 702
Parland, Ralf, 527–29, 643
Parnasso, 177
Paronen, Samuli, 215, 223, 225–26
Parras, Tytti, xxx, 237–38
Parsifal, 132
Parus Ater (Adèle Weman), 395, 537
Passions-Tankar, 289–90
Pastor Jussilainen, 390
Pastorsvalet i Aulango, 337
Patent 711 Krumelur, 639
Patricia, 715, 721
En patriot utan fosterland, 348, 368
Paul, Adolf, 364, 378–80, 387–88, 398, 400, 404
Paulinus, Johan (Count Lillienstedt), 45, 282–84, 298, 300
Pavlovs hundar, 646
peasant poets (*talonpoikaisrunoilijat*), 56–57
Peikkokuninkaat, 192
Peiliin piirretty nainen, 205

Pekka Malm. *See* Söderhjelm, Werner
Pekkanen, Toivo, 129, 163–67, 177, 223, 238, 466, 560
Pelare av eld, 633–34
Pelaren, 445
Pelivara, 232
Pellinen, Jyrki, 218
Peltisepän päivällinen, 261
Peltiset enkelit, 251
Peltonen, Vihtori. *See* Linnankoski, Johannes
Pennanen, Eila, 177, 191, 193, 197–99, 210, 213, 244
Perdita, 437
Perhe-kunda, 55
Perhosen siivissä keltainen tuuli, 194
Perillisen ominaisuudet, 192
Perm, 133
Personerna, 637
Personer och minnen, 400
Pessi ja Illusia, 740
Pete Q, 250,
Petraeus, Eskil, 9, 38, 44
Petra och silverapan, 502
Petrei, Joseph, 292
Pettersson, Joel, 532, 539–41
Pettersson, Torsten, 367, 440, 487–88, 494, 651, 667, 725
Pettersson, Viktor, 388
Physica Eller Naturlighe Things Qualiteters och Egendomars beskrijfuelse, 251, 277, 604
Piae cantiones, 35, 37
Pianobärarna, 613
Pieniä runoja, Suomen pojillen ratoxi, 52
Pieni elämäntarina, 97, 98
Pieni hyvinkasvatettu tyttö, 237
Pieni valhe, 264
Pienoisromaanit, 164
Pietà, 564
Pihlamäkeläiset, 232
Pikakuvia 1867 katovuodesta, 81
Pikku ihmisiä, 96
Pikkupappilassa, 737
Pikku paratiisi, 252
Pila pahoista hengistä, 55
Pillastunut runohepo, 110
Pimeän pihan piilot, 254

Pimeänpirtin hävitys, 123
Pimenoff, Veronica, 252–54
Pingoud, Ernst, 483, 489, 528
Pirttipohjalaiset, 140
Pirunnyrkki, 191
Pisaroita iholla, 193
Pitäjän pienempiä, 152
Pitkän tähtäyksen LSD–suunnitelma, 217
Pitkän tien kulkijat, 192
Pizzamordet, 570
Planeternas skyddslingar, 342
Poesiens mystik, 451
De poesi fennica, 10, 47–49
Pohjanmaa, 256
Pohjanpää, Lauri, 143, 154
Pohjan-piltti, 63
Pohjoinen yökirja, 268
Pohjoiset pelit, 254
Pohjolan häät, 82
Poimisin heliät hiekat, 230
Pojat, 204
Pojken, 327
Pojken och den gråa byn, 539
Politiska dikter, 640
Pombal och jesuiterna, 389
Poppius, Abraham, 52–53, 55, 63, 299
Porsliiniprinsessa, 735
Porten, 495
Porthan, Henrik Gabriel, xx, 10, 19, 20, 37, 39, 41, 45–48, 50–51, 54, 57, 287, 294, 298, 302, 320, 729
Ett porträtt, 477
Porträtt av Hanna, 502
Porträttet av direktör Rask: En tragedi, 709
Porträtt med blomma, 552
Porvoo (Borgå), 35, 46, 50, 58, 79, 306–7, 309, 312, 322, 326, 356, 394, 412–13, 418, 422, 439, 445, 480, 502, 516, 591, 607–9, 617, 622, 652, 744
Postikonttorissa, 80
De praecipuis dialectis linguae fennicae, 47
Pravda-Love, 692–93, 697
Presidenten, 598
Presidentspelet, 561
Prinsessan (*The Princess*), 637
Prins Efflam (*The Prince from the Sea*), 536
Prinsen, 637

Prinsessan af Cypern: Sagospel efter motiver ur Kalevela, 341
Prinsessan Törnrosa, 732
Priscorum Sveogothorum ecclesia, seu historia ecclesiastica de priscis Sveogothicae terrae colonis, 40
Den privata detektiven, 600–601
Procopé, Hjalmar, 348, 412–14, 495, 623
Professoreita, 45
Promenad med favoriter, 564
Pronssikausi, 239
Psalmer för trolösa kristna, 624
Puhalluskukkapoika ja taivaankorjaaja, 265
Puhe on Suomesta, 634
Puhetta, 211, 217
Puhua, vastata, opettaa, 246
Pulkkinen, Matti, 252–53, 258
Punahongan hehku, 257
Punainen mylly, 134
Punainen ruukku, 248
Punainen viiva, xxii, 128–29, 151, 524
Punaista, 234
Puolikuun alla, 134
Putkinotko, xxii, 135, 151, 153
Putkinotkon tausta, 153
Puukkojunkkarit, 98
Puupuu ja Käpypoika, 197
Puut, kaikki heidän vihreytensä, 185
Pyhä Birgitta, 198
Pyhä Henrik, 9, 11
Pyhä kevät, 176
Pyhän Joen kosto, 126
Pyhä rakkaus, 128
Pyhä viha, 128
Pylkkänen, Tauno, 127
Pylkkönen, Maila, xxix, 194–95
Pyörille rakennettu, 232
Pystyyn haudattu, 265

von Quanten, Emil, 327–28
Quosego, 471, 481, 489–90, 688
En qvinna af vår tid: Karaktärsteckning, 331
Qvinnans skapelse, 328

Rågens rike (*The Realm of Rye*), 446
Råttansiktet, 639
Rajala, Panu, 150

Index 863

Rakkaat, 237
Rakastan sinua, musta tuuli, 235
Rakastavat ne miehetkin, 627
Rakastunut rampa, 154
Rakeita, 270
Rakkaita muistoja, 134
Rakkausuhri, 143
Rakkautta, xxi, 135–36, 138, 266, 668
Ramsey, Anders Edvard, 375
Rantamala, Irmari. *See* Lassila, Maiju
Rapina, 254
Rapport från Berlin (*Report from Berlin*), 595
Rapport från Donau, 595
Rapport från Europa, 597–98
Rapport från ödemarken, 522
Rasa, Risto, 244
Rast, 720
Räty, Antti, 60
Rauhala, Niilo, 218, 220–22, 248
Rauhan erakko, 104, 144
Rauhanpiipuu, 201
Raustela, Lasse, 751
Rauta-aika, 186
Rautaportista tulevat etelätuuli ja pohjoistuuli ja vihassa kaikki tuulet, 190
Rautatie, 84, 86, 92–93, 129, 141
Rävsaxen, 570
Rävspel, 626
Regina von Emmeritz, 341
Regnbågen, 437
Regnbågens död, 529
Regnljus och snö, 685
Regnmannens berättelser, 697
Reigin pappi (*Eros the Slayer*), 125–26
Rein, Carolus, 640–42
Rekola, Mirkka, 180, 184, 187–88, 190, 193, 215
Relation i det personliga, 476
Relief, 528
Renault mon amour: En autobiografi, 655
Renner, Michael, 285–86
Rent spel, 574
Renvall, Gustaf, 48, 53
Renvall-Krokfors, Viola, 549–50, 553, 557, 736
Resa med lätt bagage, 574
Resan till Raivola, 625

En Resa till Norra Amerika (*Travels into North America*), 292
Reseskildring, 558
Resonören med fågelfoten, 480
Resor, 601
Res västerut, unge man, 610
Reuter, Jonatan, 359, 392, 428
Reuter, Odo Morannal, 393–95
Reuter, Ossian, 431
Revari, 241
Reviirilaulu, 223
Reyncke Fosz. Thet är: En skön och nyttigh Dicht full medh Wijsshet, godh Läro, och lustige Exempel, 277
Ridturen och andra berättelser, 468
Riikilä, Väinö, 739
Riitamaa, 269
Rikas ja köyhä, 204
Rimpisuon usvapatsas, 738
Ringar i stubben, 460
Ringbom, Henrika, 691, 717–21
Rintala, Paavo, 197–98, 204–5, 212–13, 222, 236
The Ripper (*Uppskäraren*), 378
Rockad: Ett brevbok, 717
Den röda frun, 433–34
Röda skyar, 412
Det röda strecket, 525
Det röda vinets barn, 440
Rödbränd mark, 541, 613
Den röde André, 404
Rödgula vägar, 495
Rödluvan, 658, 670
Roine, Raul, 735–36, 748
Roinilan talossa, 87
Rojalister och patrioter: En sommarsaga från 1788, 374
Rökringar, 705
Romaanihenkilön kuolema, 258
Romanser (Lagus), 350
Rönnbär och flanell, 662
Rönnberg, Hanna, 396
Rönnbruden och Prövningens dag, 437, 449, 538
Ro, ro till dödmansskär, 659
Rosen, 669–70
Rosenaltaret, 456, 458, 484–85, 495

Index 864

Rosenstaden, 418
Rossi, Matti, 212, 218–19, 236
Röster, händer utsträckta, 606
Rösterna, 445
Rösterna i den sena timmen (*Voices at the Late Hour*), 585
Röster över vattnet, 564
Röster ur tingen, 495
Rothovius, Isak, 38
Rotlösa, 661
Rövaren och jungfrun, 469
Rucous Bibliasta, 36
Rucouskiria, 9
Rudbeck, Erik (pseud. Eero Salmelainen), 65, 733
Rudbeck, Olaus (Olof), 41, 45
Rudeen, Torsten, 286–87, 289, 623, 724
Ruin, Hans, 408, 431, 436, 441–42, 444–47, 451–52, 456, 485, 487, 494, 556, 632, 636
rum: berättelser, 723–24
Rummen vid havet, 591
Rummet fullt med svalor, 558
Rummet med de fyra fönstren, 452
Rummet och regnbågen, 561
Rumskamrater, 616, 617
Runar ja Kyllikki, 241
Rundt, Joel, 429
Runeberg, Fredrika (née Tengström), 290, 301, 316, 318, 322–27, 346–47, 349, 384, 656
Runeberg, Johan Ludvig, xvii, xx, xxiii, xxvi–xxvii, 20–22, 47–48, 54, 56, 58–61, 66, 68–69, 71, 75–77, 81–82, 84, 103, 109–10, 112–13, 117–18, 121, 129, 134–35, 176, 230, 240, 269, 276, 282–83, 294, 296–97, 299–317, 319–29, 333–35, 339, 345–48, 350–54, 356, 358, 360, 366, 369, 371, 376, 396, 407, 414–15, 421, 428, 442, 444, 454, 458, 464, 478, 480, 496, 502, 513, 539, 550, 555, 583, 587, 591, 609, 612, 621, 624–25, 653, 656, 714, 720, 724, 741
Runeberg, Walter, 357, 724
Runoelmia (Kramsu), 82
Runoelmia (Suonio), 69
Runoilijan kuolema, 206
Runoja (Tuomas Anhava), 187

Runoja (Kailas), 159–60
Runoja (Koskenniemi), 149
Runoja *1956–1977* (Manner; *Fog Horses*), 189
Runoja (Siljo), 142
Runoja *1958–1977* (Kirstinä), 217
Runola, 53
Runon historiaa, 155
Runon portilla, 254
Runot (Sarkia), 167
Runot (Selja), 193
Runot (Vuorela), 156
Runot ja Hipponaksin runot, 215
Runot *1945–1954* (Mannerkorpi), 191
Runot *1951–1966* (Tuomas Anhava; *In the Dark Move Slowly*), 187
Runot *1971–1990* (Helena Anhava), 246
Ruotsalainen, Paavo, 103, 240, 305
Russo-Swedish War (1808–9), 34, 49, 230, 302, 414
Ruumiin viisaus, 171
Ruunulinna, 62
Ruusuja Rosa Luxemburgille, 250
Ruusuköynnös, 198
Ruuth, Alpo, 223, 226–27
Ruuth (Ruuta), Theodoricus Petri, 35
Rydberg, Viktor, 121, 542, 630
Rymdbruden, 504
Rymd och människa, 486, 487
Rytm och rim, 409
Ryysyrannan Jooseppi, xxii, 129, 151

Så fjärran skäller, 473
Så länge vi minns, 660
Sången om Taimi och Sonja, 664
Sånger för sena älskande, 630
Sånger och hymner, 415
Sånger och syner, 427
Sårad: En roman från fortsättningskriget, 674
Säädyllinen murhenäytelmä, 171
Säännöstelty eutanasia, 217
Saari, 264
Saari joka nousi merestä, 268
Saarikoski, Pentti, xxiii, 216–17, 180, 211, 215, 244, 602, 614, 677
Saari taivaanrannassa, 743
Saaritsa, Pentti, 212, 218–19
Saastamoinen, Tyyne, xxix, 194

Saavalainen, Teuvo, 214, 252–53, 255
Sabotaget, 708
En saga från ödemarken, 379
Sagan om Anni, djuren, och Gröna sjön, 743
Säg farväl åt natten, 647
Sägner i dimman, 337
Sagoresan, 735
Sagor och minnen, 322
Saima, 59, 61
Säisä, Eino, 213–14, 224, 233
Saisio, Pirkko (pseud. Jukka Larsson), 252–53, 257–58, 263
Säjinteannat, 482
Säkeitä (Manninen), 119
Säkeniä, 67
Saksalainen sikakoira, 261
Salama, Hannu, 55, 178, 212–14, 223–26
Salamnius, Matthias, 42, 43
Salava, L. A., 489–90
Salmén, Leif, 676–77, 688
Salminen, Johannes, xix–xx, 318–19, 350, 407, 416, 421, 444, 501, 571, 573, 633–35, 714
Salminen, Runar, 558
Salminen, Sally, 534–37, 539, 541–42, 546, 558, 611, 672, 706
Salo, Arvo, xxx, 212, 239–40, 267
Saltkaret, 569
Samhället vi dör i, 615, 646
Samhället vi lever i, 615
Samhällsuppfostran, 390
Samlade arbeten (Lybeck), 403
Samlade dikter (Wecksell), 348
Sammatin Elias, 751
Sampo, 53
"Sämre folk," 386, 388
Samtal, 534, 635, 704–5
Samtal med Lackau, 407
Samtal med smärtan, 518
Samurai nukkuu, 270
Sanan Saattaja Viipurista, 55, 61
De sancto Henrico, episcopo et martyre, 34
Sand, 706
Sandelin, Carl Fredrik, 575, 599, 561
Sandelin, Peter, 575–79, 586, 622, 625, 638, 676
Sandell, Tom, 643–47

Sandin, Maria, 715
Sandkornet, 637
Sand lyser, 548
Sandqvist, Kurt, 560
Sandsten, 620
Sanmark, Kurt, 651–52, 710
Sarajas, Annamari, xx, 10, 86, 87, 100, 121
Sariola, Esa, 262, 265
Sariola, Mauri, 600
Sarjoja, 155
Sarkia, Kaarlo, 158, 167–68, 180, 191
Sarkunmäen palo, 248
Sataa suolaista vettä, 202
Satakunta, 138
Satama lyö leiman, 255
Satavuotias muna, 261
Ett sätt att räkna tiden, 505–6
Satuposetiivi, 735
Saturday Society (Lördagssällskap), 51, 58, 306, 310, 312, 317–18, 320–22, 334
Sauli, Jalmari, 739
Sävens krona, 548
von Schantz, Eric, 565–66
von Schantz, Filip, 341
Schauman, August, 300, 329, 346, 357, 376
Schauman, Eugen, 108, 418, 689
Schauman, Georg, 634
Schauman, Sigrid, 556
Schildt, Göran, 319, 501–2, 635–36, 646
Schildt, Holger, 360, 439, 455
Schildt, Runar, xxiii, 372, 406, 431, 435–40, 449, 459, 500–501, 537–38, 601, 627, 635, 692, 713
Schjerfbeck, Helene, 514
Schlaageriseppeli, 250
Schoderus, Ericus, 40
Schopenhauer, 405
von Schoultz, Solveig (née Segerstråle), 502–6, 511–12, 516, 526, 557, 560, 562, 564, 570, 573, 577, 580, 605, 622, 629, 658
Schreck, Jyri, xxix, 195–96
von Schröter, Hans Rudolph, 52
Se, 234–35
Se, drömmaren kommer där, 567
Seende, 641
Den segrande Eros, 372, 436

Seitsemän veljestä (Seven Brothers), xxi, xxii,
   45, 75, 77–78, 84, 129, 199, 240, 268,
   409, 463, 738
Sekasointuja, 120
Sekvens, 720
Selja, Sirkka, xxix, 179, 192–94
Selman juonet, 75
Selvää jälkeä: Runoja, 251
Selvään veteen, 142
Selvitys oikeuskanslerille, 267
Semikolon 1–2, 705
Sensommar, 601
Sent i november (Moominvalley in November),
   571
Se on sitten kevät, 203
Seppänen, Unto, 176
September, 683
Septemberlyran, 456, 458
Se pyhä ewangeliumillinen walkeus, 41
Ser du dem inte?, 725
Serlachius, Karl, 287–88
Serviska folksånger, 21
Se tavallinen tarina, 224
Seth Mattsonin tarina, 248
Sett och återbördat, 479
Se upp Salige!, 591–92
73 dikter, 577, 584
Sfinxen och pyramiden, 410
Sham, 715
Sibelius, Jean, xxvii, 67, 86, 100–101, 105,
   107, 112, 241, 261, 303–5, 347, 378–79,
   388, 399, 404, 412, 454, 463, 467, 504,
   520, 588, 594, 677, 714
Sibirien: Ett självporträtt med vingar, 713
Siekkinen, Raija, 264–66
Sigfridi, Johannes, 277
Sigmund Freudin kaamea flunssa, 750
Sigrid Liljeholm, 325
Siinä näkijä missä tekijä, 213, 224–25
Siippainen, Olavi, 177, 223
Siljo, Juhani, 142–43, 148, 159, 180, 202
Sillanpää, Frans Eemil, 87, 106, 126, 137,
   144, 146, 148–51, 175, 252
Silmän-kääntäjä, 62
Silmä yössä, 123
Silta liikkuu, 207
Simberg, Hugo, 510, 587

Simon matkat Peilikaupunkiin, 268
Simonsuuri, Kirsti, xxx, 268–69, 723–24
Simpauttaja, 257
Simson ja Delila, 131
Sin egen verklighet, 567
Sinervo, Elvi, 178, 618
Sininen Lasarus, 248
Siniristi ja punatähti, 739
Sinisen taivaan, harmaan jään, 238
Sinitaivas, 263
Sinkkonen, Lassi, xxx, 235–37, 569
Sinne-afvel, 281–82
Sinnenas realismer, 691
Sinuhe, egyptiläinen (Sinuhe the Egyptian),
   164
Sinusta huomiseen, 235
Siriuksen vieraat, 251
Sirkkelisirkus: Balladi, 236
Sirkus, 235
Sisarukset, 258
Sissiluutnantti (The Long Distance Patrol),
   205, 212
Sista etappen, 496–97
Sista leken, 569
Sista milstolpen, 415
Sista ronden, 420
Den sista sommaren, 597, 699
Sitten tulivat laivat, 255
Sivusta, 245–46
Siwertz, Sigfrid, 432–33
Själarnas ansikten, 466
Sjöblom, Jarl, 637–38
Sjögren, Anders Johan, 20–21, 52, 299
Sjöstrand, Levi, 544, 675–76
Sjöström, Axel Gabriel, 300, 302
De sju dagarna, 502–3
Sjunger näktergalen än i Dorpat?, 634
*En skæbne: Fortælling fra vore Bedsteforældres
   Tid*, 387
Skaldestycken (Franzén), 296
Den skapande handen, 499
Skärgårdens vår, 409
Skärseld: Dikter och dokument, 445–46
Skeppet "Flygande Gedda," 746
Det sker med ens, 510
Skiftesvik, Joni, 265–66
Skimskäla, 672

Skogsfolket, 736
Skogsstämning, 396
Sko, sko, hästen, 530
Skott i överkant, 498
Skruven, 669
Skuggan av Ninja, 699
Skuggboxaren, 646
Skuggspel, 419
De skuldlösa mördarna (The Innocent Assassins), 635
Skyddsrummet, 608
De skymda ljusen, 447
Skymmande land, 420
Skymningens barn, 538, 541
Skymningsrummet, 491
Skytte, Martin, 35
Slå dej inte till ro, 595
Slå tillsamman, 659
Slagruta, 554-55
Slagsidor, 621
Slavar kastar ingen skugga, 633
Slotte, Alexander, 426-29, 438
Slyngeln Måhrberg, 565
Små bönders, 547
Småstad, 516
Småtrollen och den stora översvämningen, 571
Små världar, 535
Smärre berättelser, 313
Smith, Anthony D., 19-21, 31
Smugglarkungen, 625
Snap-Shots: Mumlade mytologier, 689-90
Snellman, Johan Vilhelm, xxii, 20, 31, 48, 54, 56, 58-61, 65, 103, 109, 192, 240, 302, 306, 317-18, 320-21, 323, 325, 328, 334, 500, 546, 633, 733
Snoilsky, Carl, 297, 359, 362
Snöleopard (Snow Leopard), 683, 710
Snuviga gatlyktor, 627
Sodan ja rauhan äänet, 205
Söderberg, Hjalmar, 401, 432
Södergran, Edith, xx, xxiii, xxvi-xxvii, 144, 158, 179, 193, 290, 410, 413, 454-55, 457-58, 461, 465-67, 469, 471, 480, 484-85, 489-93, 495, 500, 505-6, 508, 510, 512, 515-16, 520, 526, 529, 548-51, 618, 625, 631, 638, 645, 658, 667, 680, 684, 687, 698, 721

Söderhjelm, Alma, 439, 520
Söderhjelm, Henning, 435-36
Söderhjelm, Torsten, 401-2
Söderhjelm, Werner (pseud. Pekka Malm), xxiii, 335, 368, 376-77, 400-402, 421, 435, 520, 724
Söderholm, Kerstin, 490, 494-96, 502, 551
Söderling, Trygve, 691-92, 695, 717
Söderström & Co., 356, 389, 469, 490, 499, 514, 633, 640, 660, 662, 722
Sofias egen bok, 657, 700
Soini, Wilho, 81
Sökare och syndare, 566
Solbåten, 636
Solbärgning, 410
Solblåst, 660
Soldan-Brofeldt, Venny, 748
Solen är en tunnel, 725
Solen på Mallorca, 610
Solglöd och andra skizzer, 381
Solgrönt, 471
Solnedgång, 524, 560
Solskensfolk, 427
Solstaden (Sun City), 574
Solvarm stig, 661
Solveigin laulu, 235
Solveig ja Jussi, 236, 569
Det som alltid är, 648
Det som blev ord i mig: Dikter 1962-1987, 619
Som en dunkel värme, 541, 580
Somliga mornar, 504, 570
Som lyser mellan gallren, 619
Sommar av kärlek och sorg, 596
Sommarboken (The Summer Book), 574
Sommaren med Sue: En komedi tillägnad Tant Svea, 708-9
En sommarfärd till de lyckliga öarna, 422
Sommarflanör i Amerika, 560
Sommarnatten, 409
Sommarpojken, 600, 712
Sommarsjö och vintersnö, 737
Som om ingenting hänt, 614, 617
Som tusen liljor, 530
Sonat för fallskärm och kalebass, 529
Sönder, 482-83, 532
Söner av nederlaget, 632
Sönerna, 534

Sonja O. kävi täällä, 262
Sopimus Mr. Evergreenin kanssa, 250
Sorolainen, Ericus Erici, 37–39
Sortie, 691–92
En sorts frihet, 637
S. O. S., 468
Sotahevonen, 260
Sotilaiden äänet, 205
Spånkorg, 686
Spånskottaren, 674
Spartacus, 111
Speculum vitae humanae: Om menniskionnes Leffuerne, 277
Spegelmakaren och aftonstjärnan, 538
Spegelskrift, 635
Spegling, 567
Speletuss, 622
Spelmannen (Ingelius), 330
Spelmännen (Hellberg), 537–38
Spiken, 668
Spillror, 419
Spiralens form, 721
Splitter, 621
Den splittrade båten, 668
Spöfågel, 622
Språngmarsch på stället: Blad rivna ur en dagbok, 685
Squire Hellman and Other Stories, 85
Ståhlberg, Ester, 567
Stålets sång, 565
Staden, 629
Staden heter Helsingfors, 614
Stadens bröd, 544
Stadens ljus, 709
Stadens ofullmäktige, 659
Stadier, 513
En stad i förvandling, 542
Stad i uppror, 599
Städren, 649
Stalinkanalen: Hur bolsjevikerna skapa mänskor och frihet, 443
Den starkare, 403–4, 406
Stark men mörk, 461
Statspolisen slår till, 498
Statsrådet, 388
Steenroos, Merja-Riitta, 717–18, 721
Steg på hållplatsen, 686

Sten i glashus, 632
Sten, Daniel. *See* Lange, Ina
Stenåkern, 574
Stenbäck, Lars, 103, 305, 319–21, 351, 414, 633
Stenberg, Eira, 262, 264
Stenius, Göran (pseud. Georg Keller), 467, 519–23, 536, 593, 700
Stenkol, 460–61
Stensamling, 612
Stenslottet, 599
Stenvall, Alexis. *See* Kivi, Aleksis
Stiernhielm, Georg, 281, 292, 622
Stigar mellan Elysion och Hades, 641
Stigen och regnbågen, 551
Stina och jag, 747
Stjäl dig ett liv, 613
Stjärnornas kungabarn, 342, 465, 532
Stockjunkarn, 371, 375
Stoft och öde, 499
Stölden, 569
Den stora dagenefter, 482
Den stora flykten, 531
Den stora islossningen, 427
Den stora rollen, 439
Den stora tiden, 419
Stora världen, 706
Storfångaren, 658
Stormbom, N.-B., xxii, 240, 531, 554, 602
Storön: En bok om havet och kärleken, 433
Storsjöhamnen, 746
St. Petersburg, xx, 24, 42, 59, 66, 80, 86, 106, 127, 138, 139, 141, 288, 309, 357, 373–74, 398, 417, 455–57, 481, 516–17, 546
Strån, 382
Strandbyggaröden, 411
Strängar av aska, 554
Sträv gryning, 568
Striden vid Tuukkala, 389
Strindberg, August, xxii–xxiii, 86, 91, 100, 121, 133, 138, 151, 154, 267–68, 344, 349, 352, 364, 379–80, 385–86, 403, 426, 468, 500, 510, 513, 537, 592, 651, 735
Strofer i grått, 444
Strömborg, Johan Elias, 307, 316
Strövtåg, 705
Stunder av ljus, 575

Stürmer, Wava, 659–61, 666–67, 670
Sudenkorento, 191
Sudenmorsian (*The Wolf's Bride*), 125–27
Suhonen, Pekka, xxx, 251–52
Suhteita, 135
Sujut, 206, 560
Sukupolveni unta, 172
Sumpråttans resa, 689
Sumuruisku, 235
Sund, Lars, 709–11
Sund, Viktor, 427
Sundgren, Tatjana, 679
Suolamänty, 265
Suomalainen, 60
Suomalainen, Jaakko (Jacobus Finno), 37
Suomalainen, K. G. S. (pseud. Samuli S.), 80
Suomalainen aforismi, 270
Suomalainen runousoppi, 67
Suomalainen Sana-Kirja; Lexicon Linguae Fennicae 1–2, 48
Suomalainen tonttukirja, 748
Suomalaisen Kirjallisuuden Seura. *See* Finnish Literary Society
Suomalaisen Sana-Lugun Coetus, 46
Suomalaisia sankareita, 141
Suomalaisia satuja, 748
Suomen kansan arvoituksia, 63
Suomen kansan historia, 65
Suomen kansan satuja ja tarinoita, 65, 733
Suomen kansan suuri satukirja, 736
Suomen kansan vanhat runot, 7
Suomen Kansan Wanhoja Runoja ynnä myös Nykyisempiä Lauluja, 22, 54
Suomen kirjallisuuden historia (Krohn), 70
Suomen marsalkka, C. G. Mannerheim, 206
Suomenkielinen runollisuus Ruotsinvallan aikana, 65
Suomenkieliset Tieto-Sanomat, 47
Suomenlahden risteilijä, 735
Suometar, 60–61, 66, 653
Suomettaren kosiat, 30
Suomi, 60
Suomi, Vilho, 132
Suonio. *See* Krohn, Julius
Suosalmi, Kerttu-Kaarina, 223, 228–29
De superstitione et veterum Fennorum theoretica et practica, 47

Surge eller Flijt-och oflijtighetz Skode Spegel, 279, 281
Surupukuinen nainen, 230
Suru-runot suomalaiset, 44
Suuntana läntinen, 177
Suuri illusioni, 163
Suursiivous, 157, 174
Suutarikin suuri viisas, 182–83
Den svåra vägen, 415
Svår glädje, 553
En svag stackare, 427
Den svala dagen, 583–84
Svanarna, 746
Den svarta portföljen, 601
Svarta segel, 559
Svarta sonetter, 418
Den svarta tigern (*Dance of the Tiger*), 635
Svart harnesk, 552
Svartvitt, 599
Svenonius, Enevald, 281, 284
Den svenska jorden, 411
Svenska Österbottens litteraturförening, 546
Svenska vyer, 297
Svenskt i Finland: Ställning och strävanden, 421
Sverigeboken, 596
Swan, Anni, 117, 734–35, 737–38, 741, 748
Swedish Literary Society in Finland (Svenska Litteratursällskapet i Finland), 352, 454, 469
Swedish (People's) Party, 108, 356, 357, 596
Swedish Theater (New Theater), 90, 102, 315–16, 329, 341, 347, 356, 379, 381, 386, 389–90, 405, 412, 414, 427, 439, 491, 664
Swedo-Russian War (1788–90), 302, 374
Sylvander, Stefan (Georg Kåhre), 550
Sylvi, 90–91
Synkkä yksinpuhelu, 174, 178
Synkkyys, pohjaton, niin myös iloni, onneni, 238
Synti, 228
Syömäköyhä, 232
Syskon till ingen, 640
Systrarna (*The Sisters*), 570
Systrar och vänner, 564–65
Syvä nauru, 186

Tårar wedh Frelsarmansens Jesu Kristi korss, 285

Täällä Pohjantähden alla, 199, 203, 210, 213
Täältä jostakin, 234
Taarnet, 100
Tabermann, Tommy, xxx, 245, 250
Tabu, 234
Ta fast malen, 608
Taggiga lågor, 460, 507
Tähtirinta, 238
Taina, 516
Tainaron, 253
Taisteleva humanismi, 162
Taistelija, 111
Taistelu huomispäivästä, 174–75
Takanen, Johannes, 375
Tala, o sång, 429
Talitintin tornitalo, 741
Tallört, 683
Tallqvist, Allan, 565–66
Tallqvist, Cid Erik, 471, 490
Tallqvist, J. O., 486
Tallqvist, Knut, 319
Talo maalla, 217, 244
Talo nimeltä villiruusu, 193
Talven talossa, 268
Talven tulo, 264
Talvi, Jussi, 176–77
Talvio, Maila, xxi, 122–24, 129, 149, 658
Talvipalatsi, 185
Talvisodan aika, 232
Talvisota, 256
Talvi-yö, 114
Tämä matka, 179, 189
Taman lauluja, 179, 192
Tamara, 231, 675
Tammelinus, Gabriel, 39
Tampereen runot, 169
Tandefelt, Otto (Otto Tarvanen), 63
Tango orange, 716, 718
Ett tänkande rö, 704
Tankar av regn, 679
Tankar om den medborgerliga friheten, 292
Tanke och förkunnelse, 636
Tän pojan kevätrallatuksia, 121
Tanssi yli hautojen, 164
Tanttu, Kasper, 110
Tapetdörren, 480
Tapio, Marko, 197–98, 202–3, 213, 646

Tarinain lähde, 180
Tarkiainen, Viljo, xvii–xviii, 85, 137
Tarkka, Pekka, 134–35, 153, 182, 192, 203, 205–6, 212, 218–21, 224, 228, 236, 238, 247–49, 263, 716
Tarulinna, 134
Tarvanen, Otto (Otto Tandefelt), 63
Taskspelaren, 560
Tätä mieltä, 206
Tavaststjerna, Karl August, 98, 109, 316, 329–30, 348, 352, 354, 358–69, 376–78, 388, 392, 398, 400, 411–12, 446, 500, 526, 692–93
Tecken och minnesskrift från 1800-talet, 384
Tecken och spår, 632
Teckningar och drömmar, 323–24
Tegengren, Jacob, 400, 412, 414–15, 429
Tegnér, Esaias, 21, 56, 302, 306, 310, 328, 355, 416
Tehtaan varjossa, 166
Tema med variationer, 513, 515
Tengström, Fredrika, 302–3, 322
Tengström, Jacob, 38, 50, 51, 52, 302, 653, 729
Tengström, Johan Jacob, 51–52, 58, 60, 283, 653
Tengström, Robert, 31, 58–59
Teokset (Pekkanen), 165
Terrassen, 505, 577
Terra Mariana, 196
Terserus, Johannes, 281
Terva-apila, 741
Terveessä ruumiissa, 239
Terveisin, 231
Terveydeksi, 251
Therman, Erik, 490–91, 493, 551–52
Therman, Tor, 491
30-åriga kriget (*The Thirty Years' War*), 654
Thirty Years' War, xxv, 38, 278, 328, 338–39, 341–43, 411, 604, 654, 675
Tiainen, Arja, xxx, 245, 249
Ticklén, Eerikki, 54, 61
Ticklén, Pietari, 61
Tiden går och vi med den, 333
Tidens makt, 333
Tidig tvekan, 511
Tidningar utgivne af et sällskap i Åbo, 47, 298

Index 871

Tidsfördriffor mina barn, 729
Tietäväinen, Algoth. *See* Lassila, Maiju
Tigerstedt, Örnulf (pseud. Axel Falander), 465, 490–91, 496–501, 556, 559, 607
Tihlä, Hilda, 110
Tiihonen, Ilpo, 245, 248–49
Tiitiäisen satupuu, 196, 689, 747
Tiitiäisen tarinoita, 197
Tikkanen, Henrik, 60, 214, 250, 255, 266, 477, 560, 565, 594, 625, 637, 639, 646, 650, 653–57, 687, 698, 703–4, 711
Tikkanen, Johan Jacob, 60, 653
Tikkanen, Märta (née Cavonius), 250, 348, 656–58, 670, 680, 700
Tikkanen, Paul (Paavo), 60, 653
Tilaisuus, 218
Tilapää, 198
Tillbaka, 632
Tillblivelse, 477
Tillblivelsedag, 556
Tillkortakommanden, 618
Till saknadens lov, 635
Tills vi äger våra liv, 685
Tinaa, 192
Tinatähti ja Anselmin aarre, 750
Tio sagor om Skogsfolket, 736
Titus, 105
Tjurens år (*The Year of the Bull*), 525–26
Tohtori Finckelman, 200, 203
Tohvelisankarin rouva, 135, 137
Toinen minä, 270
Toinen taivas ja maa, 185
Toisinajattelijan päiväkirjasta, 271
De tolv, 639
Tomas Indal: En början och ett slut, 402, 405–6, 425, 585
Tonbrädet, 475
Toner från stugor och stigar, 428
Tonfall, 704
Topelius, Toini, 737
Topelius, Zachris (Zacharias), xvii, xxiii, xxvii–xxviii, 22, 59, 63–64, 66, 69, 109, 117, 121, 252, 276–77, 282, 291, 297, 321, 323–24, 327, 330–32, 335–48, 350–52, 356, 358, 360, 366, 369, 375–76, 398, 400, 403, 414, 421, 465, 477, 507, 526, 540, 572, 596, 616, 623, 689, 704, 724, 731–32, 734–35, 737, 744, 748

Topelius, Zachris (Zacharias; the Elder), 54, 334
Topi från Sörnäs, 565
Toppelius, Mikael, 334
Toppelius, Oscar, 62
Tora Markman och hennes syster, 566
Torch Bearers, 148, 156–59, 161–63, 167–69, 735
Torget, 607
Törnegren, C. W., 346, 350
Törnudd, Margit (née Niininen), 566–67
Torplandet, 719
Torvalds, Ole, 553–54, 557
Toukokuu, ikuinen, 186
Det trånga rummet, 571, 692
Trädens sånger, 618
Trädet, 646, 647
Trädgård i förvandling, 681
Trädmammans famn, 667
Träd står i sina rader, 473
Trägrottan, 696
Traktat, 479
Tramp, 713
Trance dance: Sekvenser, 689
Träsnidaren och döden (*The Woodcarver and Death*), 467–68, 501, 508, 516, 573, 701
Tre afrikanska berättelser, 706
Tre dagar i augusti, 561
Tre friare, 347
Tre (3) månader à dato: Idyll i funkis, 524
Tre pjäser (Järner), 608
Tre skådespel (Bargum), 601
Tre skådespel (Järner), 608
Tre två ett, 600
Trollfiolen, 443
Trollvinter (*Moominland Midwinter*), 572
TTT, 654
Tuderus, Gabriel, 43, 284, 493
Tuhat laulujen vuotta, 181
Tuhkanaama ja taivaanntakoja, 743
Tukhimo ja Mefisto, 250
Tukkijoella, 98
Tulenkantajat, 169
Tule takaisin, pikku Sheba, 247
Tulevaisuuden edessä, 133
Tulia yön puutarhassa, 252
Tulijoutsen, 121

Tuliteema, 170
Tulitikkuja lainaamassa, 139–40, 261
Tulitikkutehtaantyttö, 267
Tulles resa sunnantill, 744
Tummat, 233
Tunneln, 670–71
Tunnuskuvia, 87
Tunnustelua, 199
Tunnustus, 201
Tuntematon sotilas (*The Unknown Soldier*), 176, 178, 199, 602
Tuntematon tekijä, 269
Tuntosarvilla, 192
Tuomas Vitikka, 117
Tuominen, Mirjam, 264, 489, 511–15, 526, 541, 551, 565, 574, 679
Tuomio, 108
Tuomiopäivän sävärit, 250
Tuomitut, 264
Tupakkakauppiaan moraali, 239
Tuppisuu suomalainen, 232
Turkka, Jouko, xxx, 267–68
Turkka, Sirkka, 245, 247–48, 586
Turkkilainen satula, 237
Turms, kuolematon (*The Etruscan*), 164
Turtiainen, Arvo, 161, 167, 169–71, 235, 249, 655
Turunen, Heikki, 213, 252, 255, 257
Turun Lehti, 357
Turun Wiikko-Sanomat, 51, 298
Tuukkalan tappelu, 389
Tuulenpesä, 266
Tuulen poika, 265
Tuuli nousee, 196
Tuuri, Antti, 115, 214–15, 252, 255–56, 599, 711
Två finskors lustvandringar i Europa och Afrika åren 1876–77 och 1884, 334
Två myrors äventyr (*The Adventures of Two Ants*), 736
20 år ung dikt, 490, 492
Tyhjän tien paratiisit, 266
Tykkimiehen syli, 237
Tynni, Aale, 177, 180–82
Työmiehen vaimo, 87–88, 397
Työmies, 138
Tyskland, skildringar och omdömen från en resa 1840–41, 318

Tystnadens spår, 491
Tyst stiger havet, 577, 579, 676
Tyttö kuin kitara, 227
Tyttö, poika ja voileivät, 232
Tyttö ruusutarhassa, 137

Uivat saaret, 196
Ulla ja Mark, 737
Ultra, 457, 460, 485, 489–90, 591, 688
Umbra, 254
Under, 619
Underbara kvinnor vid vatten-en roman om syskon, 715
Under fanan, 419
Under Häxböles sol, 451
Under höga träd, 606
Under jorden sjönk, 513
Den undermedvetna staden, 578, 580
Under rasten, 395
Under solen, 492
Under stjärnorna, 413
Under torparsolen, 430, 451
Unelma onnesta numero 5, 238
Unelmat paremmasta maailmasta, 271
Unet ja Medeia, 195
Unga år, 364
Det unga ögat, 487
Ungdom, 372
Ungdomsdrömmar, 338
Ung Hans kärleksbrev, 379
Ungt hav, 460
Uni palaa rikospaikalle, 271
Unohdettu sotilas, 654
Unohdettu vartti, 266
Untola, Algoth. *See* Lassila, Maiju
Uppbrott, 550, 562
Uppgörelse, 620
Upptäcktsresan, 537
Uramo torp, 363
Ur clownens garderob, 644
Ur lifvets strid, 329
Ur sömnens ask, 678
Ur svalens loggbok, 575
Urvind, 588–89
Uskela, Kaarlo, 110
Utåt ljungen, 548
Utanför, 562

Utan örnar, 498
Utblick mot framtiden, 547
Utgångspunkt, 705
Utlämnad, 675
Utrio, Kaari, 243-44
Utslag, 713
Utspelat i Ulan-Bator, 690
Utvandrare, 380
Utveckling, 432
Uudet hengelliset runot läsnä olewaisista ja tulewaisista tiloista, 49
Uuni, 241
Uurto, Iris, 171
Uusi Jerusalem, 256
Uusi Suometar, 60, 66, 389
Uusi Suomi, 60, 172

Vågbrytningar, 641
Vågmärken: Skärgårdsdikt 1937-1987 (Torvalds), 553
Vågor, 497
Våld, 391
Våra filmproblem, 595
Våra gossar på Cypern, 621
Vår dag, 660
Vårens cistern, 475
Vårfrudag, 549
Vår historia: En krönika om det finlandssvenska folkets öden, en analys av vårt lands historia, 650, 674
Vår korta stund tillsammans, 676
"Vår landsman," 373-74
Vårarna, 630
Vår soliga vardag, 564
Vårsvart, 641
Vårt hjärta, 523
"Vårt land," 68, 77, 312, 328, 335
Vääpeli Sadon tapaus, 166
Vaara, Elina, 159, 163, 176
Vaaralla, 95
Väärällä uralla, 127
Vaaskivi, T(atu), xxix, 175
Väderilar, 550
Vaeltanut, 196
Vägarna, 444
Vägar till poesin, 632
Vägen från Stormskäret, 671

Vägen till eremiten, 679
Vägen till Hangö, 638
Vägen till himlen stängd, 611
Vägen till staden, 544
Vägen till Stormskäret, 671
Vägen till verkligheten, 547
Vägen upphör men jag fortsätter, 578
Vähäfysiikka, 251, 277
Vaikea tie, 141
Vaikka aamuun on vielä aikaa, 190
De Väinämöine, priscorum fennorum numine, 21
Vaka, 519
Vakt i Öster: Vandringar i Gränskarelen, 522
Vala, Katri, 158-61, 169, 179, 193, 263, 490
Valaan vatsassa, 247
Valamon yksinäinen, 244
Valbäck, F. J. (Frans Johan), 388
Valda ungdomsdikter (Wecksell), 347, 349
Valehtelijan muistelmat, 205
Väliasema Gagarin, 266
Valikoima runoja (Kunnas), 196
Välirauha, ikävöinnin aika, 232
Valitut teokset (Kurjensaari), 174
Väljät vaattet, 235
Väljer du stormen, 542
Valkoinen huvimaja, 239
Valkoinen kaupunki, 228
Vallan Casanovat, 249
Vallan miehet, 240
Vallilan rapsodia, 169
Valoa kaikki kätketty, 197
Valon lapset, 198
Valon nälkä, 268
Välsignade liv!, 595
Valta, 195
Valtakunnan salaisuus (The Secret of the Kingdom), 165
Valtiala, Nalle, 610-11
Valvet, 478
Valv och båge, 499
Valvoja, 84, 133, 142
Vammelvuo, Anja, xxix, 179, 193
Vampyyri, 221
Vändpunkt, 705
Vandrande skugga, 585, 600
Vandrare, 384-85

Vandring, 416
Vandringen och vägen, 409
Vandringsman, 570
Vanhain Suomen maan pijspain ja kircon
 esimiesten latinan kielised laulud, 35
Vanhempieni romaani, 59, 106–7
En vanlig solig dag, 576
Vänskapsbyn, 435
Väntan, 445
Väntansväg, 660, 666–67, 670
Väntrum, 664
Vapaita aatteita, 89
Det var, 432
Var är din bror?, 675
Varastettu enkeli, 751
Var det du?, 577, 676
Det var de tiderna, 417
Vargskallen, 725
Variationer, 580–81
Det var icke verklighet, 495
Var inte rädd, 648
Världen är endast du, 641
Världen enligt Edi, 695
Världen öppnar sig, 537
Världens ända, 561
Värld från veranda, 487, 501
Världsboken, 595
Varning för människan, 610
Varokaa, voittajat, 188
Varsel, 463, 527
Vartio, Marja-Liisa, 191, 197–98, 202–4, 560, 658
Vartiossa, 162
Vasenius, Valfrid, 85, 376
Vassvinter, 620
Vatikanen, 521
Väven, 651, 652
Veitikka, 201
Velipoika löi kerran, 255
Veljekset, 105
Veljeni Sebastian (My Brother Sebastian), 263
Vem bryr sej om Doris Mihailov?, 657
Vendela, 244
Veneh'ojalaiset, 106
Vene lähdössä, 191
Vennberg, Karl, 195, 348, 556, 581
Ventil, 614

Verkligheten, 435
Verklighetens idyller, 556
Vers och visa (Procopé), 413
Vetää kaikista ovista, 202
Vetenskapen och förnuftet: Ett försök till orientering, 636
Vetsikko, 238
Vhaël, Bartholdus, 44
Vida gavlar, 621
Vidare, 519, 526
Vida vägar, 417
Vid gaitans, 514
Vid gränsen (1928; Tigerstedt), 496–97
Vid gränsen (1930; Gripenberg), 420
Vid havet, 536
Vierailulla ketun talossa, 193
Vieras, 238
Vieras maa, 194
Vieras veri, 125
Viettelijä, 263
Viiden pennin Hamlet, 220
Viimeinen Kleopatra, 194
Viimeinen kesävieras, 253
Viimeiset kiusaukset, 240
Viimeiset romantikot, 121
Viipuri (Viborg), xix, 35–36, 41, 46, 54, 61, 66, 81, 138, 236, 244, 277, 287–90, 299, 369–72, 376, 416, 465, 480–81, 520–23, 538, 702, 703, 737
Viita, Lauri, 177–80, 182–83, 213, 560, 570
Vikingen, 355
Vilande dag, 469, 489
Viljami Vaihdokas, 178
Viljanen, Lauri, 124, 158–59, 161–63
Villi, 133
Villiomenapuu, 196
Villiomenoita, 110
Vincent Vågbrytaren, 337
Vindarnas bröllop, 551–52
Vind av stoft, 651
Vindiciae fennorum, 45
Vindspel, 448
Vinet och lägeln, 567
Vinterhamn, 710
Vinterljus, 559
Vinterqvällar, 337
Vintertid, 561

Index

Vintertvätt, 556
Vi resa söderut, 498
Virrantyven, 119
Visa en väg, 541
Visa mig stjärnan, 701
Vi ser på Helsingfors, 653
Vi sjunger inte för dem, 553
Vi ska slå upp portarna!, 639
Vi som är kvar, 518
Visshet, 512
Den vita natten, 674
Den vita orten, 578
Vit eld, 277, 603
Voiman ääni, 247
Vuoden 1918 tapahtumat, 205–6, 210, 542
Vuodet, 185
Vuonna 1932, 232
Vuorela, Einari, 154–56, 158
Vuorosanoja, 245
Vuosi elämästäni, 214

Wacklin, Sara, 230, 321–23, 326, 334
Wähäinen cocous suomalaisista runoista, 44
Wahlbeck, Jan-Christer, 686
von Wahlberg, Ferdinand, 390–91, 599
Wahlund, Per Erik, 487, 549
Waikia walitus-runo, 44
Wallenius, Allan (pseud. Don Q, Dr. Per Nelsson), 442–43
Wallin, Georg August, 319, 321, 383
Wall Streets imperialistiska intriger, 442
Waltari, Mika, xxiii, 126, 159, 163–65, 177, 210, 270, 345, 531
Wanhain Suomalaisten Tawaliset ja Suloiset Sananlaskut, 40
Warburton, Thomas, xviii, xxii, 440, 478, 490, 505, 531, 549, 554–55, 557, 572, 611
Warelius, Anders (Antero), 60
Wecksell, Josef Julius, 37, 62, 66, 83, 276, 301, 346–50, 354, 426, 634
Weckström, Kim, 696
Wegelius, Johan (the Younger), 41
Weman, Adèle (pseud. Parus Ater), 395, 537
Westerberg, Caj, 218, 220, 222–23
Westerholm, Victor, 396, 540
Westermarck, Edvard, 421–22, 470
Westermarck, Helena, 334, 383–85

Westö, Kjell (pseud. Anders Hed), 713–18, 725
Wetterhoff, Onni, 396
Wexionius, Michael (Baron Gyldenstolpe), 278, 281, 284
Wexionius, Olof, 281
Wexionius, Olof (the Younger), 281–82
Wichman, Eva, 193, 505–11, 516, 543, 549, 573, 602–3, 612
Wichmann, V. K. E. (pseud. Gånge Rolf), 355–56, 374
Wickberg, Nils-Erik, 704–5
Wik, Inga-Britt, 250, 511, 629, 631, 681, 691
Wikholm, Gungerd, 719–20
Wikman, Anita, 664–65, 670, 722
Wilkuna, Kyösti, xxix, 123, 141
von Willebrand-Hollmerus, Margit, 532, 598–99, 671
Willman, Elvira, 110
Willner, Sven, 412, 419, 443, 508–10, 545, 555, 576, 582, 605, 629, 632–33
Winckelmann, Barbara, 244, 598–99
Wintermonolog, 677
Wintermusik, 564
Winter War (1939–40), xviii, xx, 145–46, 148, 162, 170, 172, 176, 205, 269, 315, 463, 467, 501–2, 519, 522, 541, 546, 553, 561, 563, 599, 606–7, 650, 703
Wirtanen, Atos, 490, 499–500, 632
Wrede, Johan, 410, 420, 453, 470–71
von Wright, Georg Henrik, 636
von Wright, Magnus, 370
WSOY (Werner Söderström), 79, 214, 356, 750
Wulff, Thomas, 267, 687–93, 695–96, 699, 723
Wuolijoki, Hella, 92, 172–73, 463

Yhdeksän miehen saappaat, 176
Yhden yön pysäkki, 266
Yhden yön tarinat, 205
Ykä yksinäinen, 749
Ykköstyttö, 749
Yksilön ylösnousemus, 255
Yksin, 92–93, 99, 107
Yksinäinen mies, 235

Yksinäisyys, 239
Yksinvaltias, 175
Yksityisiä asioita, 185, 210
Yks perkele, yks enkeli, 240
Ylävaara, Anni (Rosa Liksom), xxx, 250, 266–67
Ylistys, 269
Ylös helvetistä, 111
Ynglingen, 327
Yö aukeaa kuin vilja, 247
Yö ja päivä, 74
Yö jona jäät vahvistuivat, 239
Yön sarvet, 194
Yöstä tullut, 233
Yöta, päivää, 217
Young Finns, 84, 90, 100, 108, 374
Yrjö-Koskinen. *See* Koskinen, Yrjö Sakari

Ystävia ja vihollisia (*Friends and Enemies*), 176
Yxi Caunis Suomen-Kielinen Weisu, Talonpoille Cunniaxi ja Ylistöxexi, 284
Yxi Wähä Rucous Kirja, 37
Yxi Wähä Suomenkielinen Wirsikiria, 37

Zilliacus, Benedikt, 653, 712
Zilliacus, Clas, 614–15
Zilliacus, Emil, 398, 400, 402, 412, 415–16, 421, 444, 478, 614–16, 712, 724
Zilliacus, Jutta, 705
Zilliacus, Konni (Konrad), 380–81, 383
Zionin juhlavirret, halullisten sieluin ylöskehoituxexi, 49
Zoo, 250
Zuck, Virpi, xxvi, 440

In the *Histories of Scandinavian Literature* series

Volume 1
A History of Danish Literature
Edited by Sven H. Rossel

Volume 2
A History of Norwegian Literature
Edited by Harald S. Naess

Volume 3
A History of Swedish Literature
Edited by Lars G. Warme

Volume 4
A History of Finland's Literature
Edited by George C. Schoolfield